8A-6 *a* Year 4 index, 125%; *b* Inventory at end of Year 4, $81,600

8A-7 A: decrease in income, $49,000; B: inventory end of Year 5, $255,000

8B-1 *a* Inventory, $109,500; *b* Gross profit, $166,200

8B-2 *a* Inventory March 31: (1) $72,000; (2) $42,000

8B-3 *a* Inventory at March 31: (1) $7,000; (2) $6,600; (3) $6,848. *b* Inventory at March 31: (2) $5,600; (3) $6,356

8B-4 *a* Inventory at end of Year 5, $91,000

8B-5 *a* Inventory: (1) $8,817; (2) $8,976; (3) $8,992

8B-6 Part A: *b* $42,160

8B-7 *a* Inventory at cost, $80,635; *b* Net income, $62,660; *c* Total assets, $419,500

9A-1 *a* Ending inventory, $23,800

9A-2 A Ending inventory, $44,400; B 3d quarter net income, $63,360

9A-3 Ending inventory: *a* $44,250; *b* $45,500; *c* $38,640

9A-4 Fire loss, $116,880

9A-5 Loss before income taxes, $110,000

9A-6 *a* Income: (1) $145,000; (2) $208,500; *b* (2) Costs in excess of billings, $116,750

9B-1 Ending inventory; *a* $64,384; *b* $60,620

9B-2 A Fire loss, $178,160; B Ending inventory, $45,500; C Gross profit Year 3, $25,800

9B-3 Ending inventory: *a* $87,000; *b* $81,114

9B-4 Fire loss, $51,400; cost percentage, 58%

9B-5 *a* Gross profit: (1) $2,000; (2) $113,375; *b* (1) $40,000; (2) $82,000; *c* (1) $151,375; (2) $82,000

9B-6 *b* Total gross profit earned, $47,900; *c* Deferred income tax liability, $5,280

10A-1 *a* Cost of machine, $18,775; *c* Note payable (net), $14,164

10A-3 Current liabilities, $314,900

10A-4 Bonus: *b* $45,000; *c* $23,571

10A-5 *b* (4) Promotional expense, $4,400

10A-6 *a* Recoverable unearned royalties at end of year, $4,000

10A-7 *a* Estimated liability at June 30, $455,000

10B-1 *a* Cost of machine, $19,223; *c* Note payable (net), $14,545

10B-3 Interest on note through Dec. 31, $588

10B-4 *a* Federal tax, $150,000; state tax, $25,000

10B-5 *b* Estimated liability for coupons outstanding, $45,900; promotional expense, $68,200

10B-6 *a* (1) Income tax expense, $7,252; (3) Sales net of sales tax, $300,000

10B-7 Current assets, $189,050; total assets, $392,150; retained earnings, $180,075

11A-1 *a* Balance, $3,050,00... $309,000 ...

11A-2 *a* Realize... unrealized loss in Year 2, $27,000

11A-3 *a* Imputed goodwill, $120,000

11A-4 *a* Amount paid for bonds, $466,025

11A-5 *a* (3) 11.5%; *b* (3) Market and carrying value, $1,269,375

11A-6 *a* Fund balance end of Year 3, $120,767

11A-7 *a* Investment in V Co., $1,494,000; *d* Investments (after allowance of $37,500), $2,016,100

11B-1 *a* Investment balance 12/31, $266,560; gain on sale of rights, $1,050

11B-2 Cost of preferred stock, $38,750; amortization on 12/31, $160

11B-3 *a* Imputed goodwill, $950,000; *d* Loss from revaluation, $182,875

11B-4 *a* Amount paid for bonds, $423,304

11B-5 *a* Gain on sale of rights: (1) $565; (3) $525; *b* Total cost of shares, $135,185

11B-6 *a* Interest revenue under Plan 1, $9,513

11B-7 *b* Total investments, $624,775

12A-1 (1) Recoverable on Policy A, $288,000; Policy B, $74,667

12A-2 (1) Debit discount on bonds payable, $1,110; (3) Loss on exchange, $850

12A-3 *a* Cost of machine, $517,500; *b* Incremental cost, $339,000

12A-4 *a* Discount on note payable, $14,510; *b* Interest expense, $6,775

12A-5 *a* Gain, $72,905; *c* Cost of building, $70,445

12A-6 *a* Fire loss, $57,600; *b* Total claims, $55,800

12B-1 (1) Amount recoverable, $45,000; (3) Cost of equipment, $13,860; (5) Depreciation, $1,500

12B-2 Loss on sale of machine, $1,520

12B-3 *a* Land, $354,400; building, $535,700

12B-5 *a* Land, $87,378; building, $203,882; *c* Cost of land, $93,450

12B-6 *a* Inventory lost in fire, $66,000; *b* Total to be recovered, $111,500; *c* Net gain, $12,500

13A-1 *a* Cost of machine, $64,600

13A-2 Balance in accum. depr.: *a* $17,150; *c* $40,950

13A-3 *a* Depreciation for Year 5, $9,370; *b* Loss on sale of machine, $3,630

13A-4 *b* $747,500; *e* $85,400; *m* $30,600

13A-5 *a* Balance in accum. depr. at end of Year 5, $10,200

13B-1 *a* Cost of land, $24,000; *b* Depr. for Year 3: (2) $6,993; (3) $7,300

13B-2 Depreciation for Year 5: *d* $900; *e* $1,297

13B-3 *a* Depreciation for Year 18, $27,550; *b* Loss on sale of machinery, $4,750

13B-4 *a* Net income, $1,040,000; *b* Total variable costs, $2,150,000

(continued on back cover)

INTERMEDIATE ACCOUNTING

INTERMEDIATE ACCOUNTING

FOURTH EDITION

WALTER B. MEIGS, Ph.D., C.P.A.
Professor of Accounting
University of Southern California

A. N. MOSICH, Ph.D., C.P.A.
William C. Hallett Professor of Accounting and
Chairman, Department of Accounting
University of Southern California

CHARLES E. JOHNSON, Ph.D., C.P.A.
Late Professor of Accounting
University of Oregon

McGRAW-HILL BOOK COMPANY

New York St. Louis San Francisco Auckland Bogotá Düsseldorf
Johannesburg London Madrid Mexico Montreal New Delhi
Panama Paris São Paulo Singapore Sydney Tokyo Toronto

**INTERMEDIATE
ACCOUNTING**

Copyright © 1978, 1974, 1968, 1963 by McGraw-Hill, Inc.
All rights reserved. Printed in the United States of America.
No part of this publication may be reproduced, stored in a
retrieval system, or transmitted, in any form or by any means,
electronic, mechanical, photocopying, recording, or otherwise,
without the prior written permission of the publisher.

1 2 3 4 5 6 7 8 9 0   DODO   7 8 3 2 1 0 9 8 7

This book was set in Vega by Progressive Typographers.
The editors were Donald E. Chatham, Jr., Marjorie Singer,
and Edwin Hanson;
the cover was designed by Jo Jones;
the production supervisor was Dennis J. Conroy.
The drawings were done by J & R Services, Inc.
R. R. Donnelley & Sons Company was printer and binder.

Cover photograph of an abstract abacus is by Zvonko Glyck.

Library of Congress Cataloging in Publication Data

Meigs, Walter B
    Intermediate accounting.

    Includes index.
      1. Accounting. I. Mosich, A. N., joint author.
II. Johnson, Charles E., joint author. III. Title.
HF5635.M493 1978   657'.044   77-11631
ISBN 0-07-041255-3

CONTENTS

Unidentifiable Intangible Assets: Goodwill

The nature of goodwill. Negative goodwill. Recognition of goodwill (excess of cost over net assets acquired). Estimating the amount of goodwill. Non-compete agreement or goodwill? Controversy over amortization of goodwill

Accounting for Research and Development Costs

FASB Statement No. 2, "Accounting for Research and Development Costs". Evaluation of FASB Statement No. 2. Deferred charges. Accounting for development-stage companies. Plant assets and intangibles in the balance sheet.

Types of bonds issued by corporations. Financial management considerations. Issuance of bonds. Bond interest expense. Interest method of amortization. Straight-line method of amortization. Presentation of discount and premium in the balance sheet. Bond issue costs. Bonds issued between interest dates. Early extinguishment of debt. Serial bonds. Refunding a bond issue. Convertible bonds. Bonds issued with warrants attached. Bond sinking fund and appropriation of retained earnings. Notes and mortgages payable. Distinguishing between liabilities and stockholders' equity. Accounting for restructured debt. Long-term debt in the balance sheet.

Leases

Terminology. Accounting by lessees. Accounting by lessors. Accounting for a capital lease illustrated. Accounting for a sales-type lease illustrated. Illustration of accounting for a direct financing lease with initial direct costs. Sale-leaseback transactions. Leveraged leases. Effective dates of FASB Statement No. 13. Disclosure in financial statements.

Pension Plans

Funded and unfunded pension plans. General accounting guidelines for pension plans. Minimum-maximum range for pension expense. Actuarial cost methods. Actuarial gains and losses. Accounting for the cost of a pension plan illustrated. Deferred compensation contracts. The Employee Retirement Income Security Act of 1974 (ERISA). Presentation of pension plans in financial statements.

Structure of the corporation. Elements of corporate capital. Components of stockholders' equity. Rights associated with stock ownership. Common stock and preferred stock. Class A and Class B stock. Characteristics of preferred stock. Par value and no-par value stock. Stated (or legal) capital. Accounting for capital stock transactions. Ledger accounts for paid-in capital. Discount on capital stock. Assessments on capital stock.

Issuance price and subsequent market price of stock. Subscriptions for capital stock. Defaults by subscribers to capital stock. Stockholders' ledger and stock certificate book. Issuance of two types of securities as a unit. Capital stock issued for property or services. Watered stock and secret reserves.

Incorporation of a Partnership

Establishing accounting records for the new corporate entity. Tax aspects concerning incorporation of a partnership.

Stock Rights and Warrants

Rights granted to existing stockholders. Rights to purchase convertible bonds. Warrants issued in combination with bonds or preferred stock.

Stock Option Contracts

Impact of income tax requirements. Theoretical issues. APB Opinion No. 25, "Accounting for Stock Issued to Employees". Accounting for employee stock ownership plans (ESOP). Disclosure requirements for stock option plans.

Convertible Securities

Characteristics of convertible preferred stock. Definitions applicable to convertible preferred stock. Conversion of preferred stock into common stock. Conversion of bonds into common stock. APB Opinions and convertible bonds. Protection against dilution of conversion rights. Presentation of stockholders' equity in the balance sheet. Pro forma financial statements.

Retained Earnings

Distinguishing between paid-in capital and earned capital. Classifying corporate capital by source. Currently accepted terms for the stockholders' equity section. The Retained Earnings account.

Dividends

Cash dividends. Dividends paid in form of nonmonetary assets (property dividends). Dividends in scrip (liability dividends). Liquidating dividends. Earnings and dividends. Stock splits. Stock dividends. Large stock dividends and stock splits. Dividing line between "large" and "small" stock dividends. Fractional shares. Business combinations—purchase versus pooling of interests.

Statements of Retained Earnings and Stockholders' Equity

Statement of retained earnings. Reporting changes in paid-in capital or stockholders' equity.

Appropriations of Retained Earnings and Reserves

Restrictions on retained earnings. Reserves as a separate category in the balance sheet.

Quasi-Reorganizations

Typical steps in a quasi-reorganization. Illustration of a quasi-reorganization.

PREFACE

This fourth edition of *Intermediate Accounting* is the second volume in a coordinated accounting *series.* This book is designed for use in an intermediate-level accounting course following the introductory course in accounting. The emphasis throughout is on accounting theory and concepts and on analysis of the problems that arise in applying these underlying concepts to financial accounting. As in the introductory volume of the series, attention is focused on the use of accounting information as a basis for decision making by management, stockholders, creditors, and other users of financial statements and accounting reports.

The fourth edition reflects the dramatic changes which have been occurring in the development and application of accounting concepts, with special attention to the official pronouncements and the exposure drafts of the Financial Accounting Standards Board and the Securities and Exchange Commission. Chapter 1 serves to place in perspective for the student the development and application of accounting concepts. Increased emphasis is given to the objectives of financial statements and to the influence of the FASB. The increasingly active role of the SEC in stressing disclosure and in protecting investors also receives attention.

A brief and rapid review of basic data-collecting processes in Chapter 2 reinforces the student's understanding of fundamental recording, classifying, and summarizing procedures. This background leads naturally to a consideration, in Chapters 3 and 4, of the assumptions and basic principles on which the accountant's determination of periodic income and periodic reports of financial position are based. The discussion in these chapters (and throughout the remainder of the book) is not limited to a description of acceptable practices. We believe it is important at this stage in accounting education to encourage students to participate in a critical evaluation of accounting concepts and to make students aware of the conflicts and shortcomings that exist within the traditional structure of accounting theory. At the same time it is important to provide students with an analytical basis for making this evaluation, to help them see that most of the controversial areas of accounting ultimately center on underlying issues and questions to which there are no neat and simple answers. To this end, the critical evaluation of accounting concepts is correlated with the **Statements** of the Financial Accounting Standards Board, the **Opinions** and **Statements** of its predecessor the Accounting Principles Board, and with the **Accounting Series Releases** of the SEC.

The first four chapters of the book constitute an overview of the entire accounting process and are designed to provide a gradual transition from the introductory course in accounting to the more rigorous professional level of analysis in the following chapters.

Chapter 5 is a new chapter devoted to the concepts of present value. The early introduction of this topic paves the way to using present value and future value concepts for certain receivables and liabilities, for amortization of discounts and premiums, and for leases, pension plans, and fund accumulations.

Chapters 6 through 10 deal with the problems that arise in accounting for and controlling cash, marketable securities, receivables, and current liabilities. Chapter 11, "Long-Term Investments," emphasizes the equity method of accounting for long-term investments in corporate securities and analyzes the impact of the most recent FASB views on valuation of securities.

In Chapters 12 through 14, attention is centered on the problems of accounting for and reporting on a firm's investment in plant and equipment and intangible assets.

Chapters 15 through 21 are concerned with special accounting problems peculiar to corporate organizations. These problems are focused largely on the stockholders' equity and long-term debt sections of the balance sheet, but their implications are often considerably broader. Such contemporary and controversial topics as the reporting of leases in financial statements and accounting for pension plans (Chapter 16), stock options (Chapter 18), earnings per share (Chapter 20), and income tax allocation (Chapter 21) are explored in depth.

Chapter 22, "Accounting and Inflation," recognizes the increasing impact on accounting of changes in the purchasing power of the dollar and the economic value of assets. Included in this chapter is a thorough discussion and analysis of the disclosure of replacement cost information as required by recent actions of the SEC.

Chapter 23 explains the standards of disclosure required when corporations make significant accounting changes. It also deals with the effect of errors on financial statements and the process of constructing financial statements from incomplete records.

The newest of the basic financial statements, the Statement of Changes in Financial Position, is presented in Chapter 24 along with evaluation of the significance of cash flow and other fund flow informtion. The final chapter, 25, is devoted to the important issues that make the analysis of financial statements both a demanding and interesting process.

New features and features carried forward from prior editions

One of the new features of this edition is an *Examination Question Manual* with test material arranged chapter by chapter for the entire text. This examination manual contains objective questions in a variety of formats and also numerous short exercises for each chapter. It should be a most useful source for instructors who prefer to assemble their own examinations and to emphasize certain chapters or topics.

An especially useful supplement carried forward from the prior edition is a *Study Guide* prepared by the authors and designed to help students measure their progress by immediate feedback. The *Study Guide* contains for each chapter an outline of the most important points in the textbook plus a variety of objective questions and short exercises. Answers to the questions and exercises appear in the back of the *Study Guide* to help students in prompt self-evaluation of their understanding of each chapter.

This edition like the preceding one contains two groups of problems, Group A and Group B. This arrangement allows individual instructors to vary their problem assignments in different sections of the course, or from year to year. The problems in the two groups are of similar difficulty and require about the same solution time. Either the A Group or B Group of problems provides more than enough material for assignments throughout an offering of the course.

Questions, exercises, cases, and problems

An abundance of question and problem material is provided at the end of each chapter. This material is divided into four groups: questions, exercises, short cases for analysis and decision, and problems.

The questions are intended for use by students as a self-testing and review device to measure their comprehension of key points in each chapter. Many of the questions are also of a provocative nature, which makes them suitable for written assignments and engenders lively class discussion. Short exercises appear at the end of each chapter. Typically, an exercise covers a specific important point or topic and does not require extensive computations. Many instructors will wish to use the exercises to supplement problem assignments, for class discussion, and for examination purposes.

The short cases for analysis and decision are essentially problems that require analytical reasoning but involve little or no quantitative data. In this category of problem material students are called upon to analyze business situations, to apply accounting principles, and to propose a course of action. They are not required, however, to prepare lengthy schedules or otherwise to manipulate accounting data on an extensive scale. These short cases have all been class-tested and have proved their worth as a means of encouraging students to take clear-cut positions in the argument of controversial accounting issues. In all but the early chapters of the book, a number of the short cases for analysis have been adapted from CPA examination material. The cases (and selected questions) are especially recommended if the instructor wishes to develop in students skill in communicating accounting concepts and in weighing the merits of opposing arguments.

Problem material has been extensively revised. Many of the problems are new, and those carried over from the preceding edition have been throughly revised. Special attention has been given to the inclusion of an adequate number of shorter problems in each chapter. The problems range in difficulty from simple to complex. Most of the problems in the Accounting Theory and Accounting Practice sections of recent Uniform CPA Examinations which are appropriate to intermediate accounting are included, although many have been considerably modified. In addition, several problems have been designed especially to demonstrate the concepts presented in the theoretical discussion. Probably no more than a fourth of the total case and problem material would be used in a given course; consequently ample opportunity exists to vary problem assignments from year to year.

Aiding the student to achieve proficiency in handling professional-level problems

A feature of this fourth edition is the inclusion of a greater number of short problems closely correlated with the text material. No CPA problems are used in the early chapters of the book. The gradation of problems in difficulty is carefully tailored to aid the student in a smooth progression from introductory accounting to a professional level of achievement.

A checklist of key figures is provided for most problems. The purpose of the checklist is to aid students in verifying their problem solutions and in discovering their problem solutions and their own errors. The checklist appears on the inside front and back covers of the text.

Two sets of partially filled-in working papers are published separately from the textbook. One set is designed for Group A problems and one set for Group B problems. Partially filled-in working papers are thus provided for *all* problems. On these work sheets, the company names, problem numbers, numerous headings, and some preliminary data (such as trial balances) have been entered to save student time and to facilitate rapid review by the instructor. Abundant material is included in either set of problems for a comprehensive course, hence the acquisition of a single set of partially filled-in working papers will meet a student's needs for the course.

Transparencies of problem solutions

These transparencies prepared by the publisher are available for the instructor, who wishes to display in a classroom complete solutions to most problems. For longer more complex problems, the transparencies are considered by many instructors to be a highly effective means of showing desired organization and format of solutions.

Contributions by others

The many instructors and students who used the earlier editions of this book have contributed immeasurably to the improvements in this edition. Their suggestions for modification of certain problems and expansion or contraction of certain sections of the text material have been most useful and constructive. Especially helpful was the advice received from Professors Charlene Abendroth, California State University, Hayward; Leonard A. Bacon, West Texas State University; Brian J. Briggs, Rochester Institute of Technology; Andrew Butula, Middlesex Community College; Robert K. Eskew, Purdue University; Kenneth L. Fox, Kansas State University; Lou Gilles, University of South Carolina–Coastal Carolina; Robert W. Hill, California Polytechnic University at San Luis Obispo; Edgar A. Houston, Rider College; Carol Inberg, California State University, Hayward; Richard Kochanek, University of Connecticut, Storrs; John Lacey, University of California, Los Angeles; George F. Malecek, St. Mary's University of San Antonio; Robert F. Meigs, California State University, San Diego; Cornelius Russell, Marist College; W. F. Rylander, Texas A&I University, Corpus Christi; Thomas G. Secoy, Illinois State University; Jane Stockard, Kansas State University; A. M. Tchobanian, San Francisco State University; Richard L. Townsend, University of Tennessee, Knoxville; Richard J. Vargo, University of Texas, Arlington; DuWayne Wacker, University of North Dakota; Jerold M. Weiss, Hunter College; Gerald F. Wiles, State University of New York Agricultural and Technical College, Alfred; and Lance G. Collins, Douglas Hester, Robert R. Smith, and Miklos A. Vasarhelyi of the University of Southern California.

We are especially indebted to Professor Joseph F. Guy of Georgia State University and Professor Walter A. Parker of Central Connecticut State College for their thorough review of end-of-chapter problem material for accuracy and clarity.

Our appreciation goes also to the following students at the University of Southern California: James Costello, Ann Haggard, Jane Iizuka, Daryl Jamison, David Loeser, Steven Robinson, Rose Sadowski, and John Stanek.

We acknowledge with appreciation permission from the American Institute of Certified Public Accountants to quote from many of its pronouncements and to utilize materials adapted from the Uniform CPA Examinations. All quotations and material from the Uniform CPA Examinations are copyright by the American Institute of Certified Public Accountants.

We also are grateful to the Financial Accounting Standards Board which granted us permission to quote from FASB Statements, Discussion Memoranda, Interpretations, and Exposure Drafts. All quotations used are copyrighted © by the Financial Accounting Standards Board, High Ridge Park, Stamford, Connecticut 06905, U.S.A., and are reprinted with permission. Copies of the complete documents are available from the FASB.

Walter B. Meigs
A. N. Mosich

CHAPTER 1

THE DEVELOPMENT OF ACCOUNTING THEORY AND PRACTICE

Today's challenges to the accounting profession

Fair presentation of financial affairs is the essence of accounting theory and practice. With the increasing size and complexity of American business organizations and the increasing economic role of government, the responsibility placed on accountants for presenting fairly the results of business operations is greater today than ever before. If accountants are to meet this challenge fully, they must have a logical and consistent body of accounting theory to guide them. This theoretical structure must be realistic in terms of the economic environment and designed to meet the needs of the major users of financial statements.

Financial statements and other reports prepared by accountants are vital to the successful working of our society. Economists, investors, business executives, labor leaders, bankers, and government officials all rely upon these reports as fair and meaningful summaries of the multitude of financial transactions which comprise day-to-day economic history. In addition, these groups are making increasing use of accounting information as a basis for forecasting future economic trends. The accountant is being challenged to go beyond the timely reporting and interpretation of past events and to aid in the creation of useful forecasts of future operations. Accountants and the theoretical principles they use, therefore, stand at the very center of our financial and economic activities.

Internal and external users of accounting information

The basic assumptions which underlie current accounting practice have evolved over the years in response to the needs of various users of financial reports. The users of accounting information may conveniently be divided into two broad groups: the *internal users* and the *external users.*

The internal users include all the management personnel of an organization who use accounting information either for planning and controlling current operations or for formulating long-range plans and making major decisions. The term *managerial accounting* relates to internal reporting; it includes the development of detailed current information helpful to all levels of management in decision making designed to achieve the organization's goals.

The external users of accounting information include stockholders, bondholders, potential investors, bankers and other creditors, financial analysts, economists, labor unions, and numerous government agencies. The field of *financial accounting* is directly related to external reporting, that is, providing investors and other outsiders with the information they need for decision making.

In this book we are primarily concerned with financial accounting, and we shall therefore concentrate upon the accounting principles and reporting standards that produce timely and informative financial statements. The increasing importance of financial accounting rests upon the premise that the public has a right to know whether large business organizations are functioning efficiently and in harmony with the broader goals of society.

Objectives of financial statements

The objectives of financial statements are derived from the needs of the external users of accounting information. Financial statements intended to serve all external users are often called *general-purpose financial statements.* Stating the objectives would be simpler if all external users had the same needs and interests, but they do not. For example, the banker considering the granting of a 90-day loan is primarily interested in the short-run debt-paying ability of the reporting entity, whereas the long-term investor in common stocks is more concerned with earning capacity, potential growth in earnings per share, and the ability of the reporting entity to survive as a going concern.

Because general-purpose financial statements serve a variety of users, the needs of some users receive more emphasis than the needs of others. In present-day practice the needs of the potential investor or creditor are subordinated to those who have already committed resources to the company. This emphasis leads management to stress the use which has been made of the resources entrusted to it. A deep concern over reporting on management's role as custodian of resources may be one reason for the adherence to historical cost despite substantial changes in the general price level in recent years. This tradition may also explain, in part, the omission from the financial statements of *social costs,* which may be increasingly important to a society becoming more aware of the need for preserving the quality of its environment.

In recent years the environment in which business enterprises operate has been changing at a rapid pace. Changes in the economic, political, and social structure of society cause changes in the informational needs of users of financial statements. Higher standards of measurement and reporting, along with a significant expansion of the amount of information disclosed, have been foremost among the new needs of users of financial statements. The accounting profession has responded to these changing expectations of users by developing new accounting principles and disclosure requirements and by giving attention to the overall objectives of financial statements.

Stated concisely, the objective of financial statements is "to provide quantitative financial information about a business enterprise that is useful to statement users, particularly owners and creditors, in making economic decisions."[1] The Study Group on the Objectives of Financial Statements identified twelve objectives. The first six are:

1 To provide information useful for making economic decisions.
2 To serve primarily those users who have limited authority, ability, or resources to obtain information and who rely on financial statements as their principal source of information about an enterprise's economic activities.
3 To provide information useful to investors and creditors for predicting, comparing, and evaluating potential cash flows to them in terms of amount, timing, and related uncertainty.
4 To provide users with information for predicting, comparing, and evaluating enterprise earning power.
5 To supply information useful in judging management's ability to utilize enterprise resources effectively in achieving the primary enterprise goal.
6 To provide factual and interpretive information about transactions and other events which is useful for predicting, comparing, and evaluating enterprise earning power. Basic underlying assumptions with respect to matters subject to interpretation, evaluation, prediction, or estimation should be disclosed.[2]

The next three objectives related to those financial statements which emphasize transactions and events having a significant effect on enterprise earning power. Such information should include actual and prospective cash impact, facts and interpretations of transactions, and the amount and timing of cash flows. The Study Group recommended the

---

[1] *APB Statement No. 4,* "Basic Concepts and Accounting Principles Underlying Financial Statements of Business Enterprises," AICPA (New York: 1970), p. 32.
[2] *Report of the Study Group on the Objectives of Financial Statements,* AICPA (New York: 1973), pp. 61–66.

following financial statements: the statement of financial position (balance sheet); the statement of earnings (income statement); and a statement of financial activities (statement of changes in financial position). The last three objectives called for disclosure of predictive information (including financial forecasts), activities of the enterprise affecting society, and information useful for evaluating the management of resources in achieving the goals of governmental and not-for-profit organizations.

The Study Group also identified seven **qualitative characteristics** of the information contained in financial statements: relevance and materiality, form and substance, reliability, freedom from bias, comparability, consistency, and understandability. The Study Group summarized these qualitative characteristics as follows:

> The qualitative characteristics of financial statements, like objectives, should be based largely upon the needs of users of the statements. Information is useless unless it is relevant and material to a user's decision. Information should be as free as possible from any biases of the preparer. In making decisions, users should not only understand the information presented, but also should be able to assess its reliability and compare it with information about alternative opportunities and previous experience. In all cases, information is more useful if it stresses economic substance rather than technical form.[3]

The report of the Study Group was submitted to the Financial Accounting Standards Board (FASB) and its key provisions were included in an **FASB Discussion Memorandum.**[4]

Conceptual framework for financial accounting and reporting

One of the initial projects of the FASB was a study designed to identify the "broad qualitative standards for financial reporting." After extensive work on the project, the Board decided to expand the scope of the project to include the entire conceptual framework of financial accounting and reporting, including objectives, qualitative characteristics, and the information needs of users of accounting information. The Board offered the diagram on page 5 depicting the elements of a conceptual framework for financial accounting and reporting.[5]

The **fundamentals** of accounting and reporting are the basic concepts underlying the measurement and disclosure of transactions and events. For example, fundamentals might include the definitions of an accounting entity, assets, liabilities, net income, revenue, expenses, realization. **Accounting and reporting standards** represent general solutions to financial accounting problems and **interpretations** clarify or elaborate upon the accounting and reporting standards as an aid to their application in

---

[3] Ibid., p. 60.
[4] *FASB Discussion Memorandum,* "Conceptual Framework for Accounting and Reporting: Consideration of the Report of the Study Group on the Objectives of Financial Statements," FASB (Stamford: 1974).
[5] Ibid., p. 15.

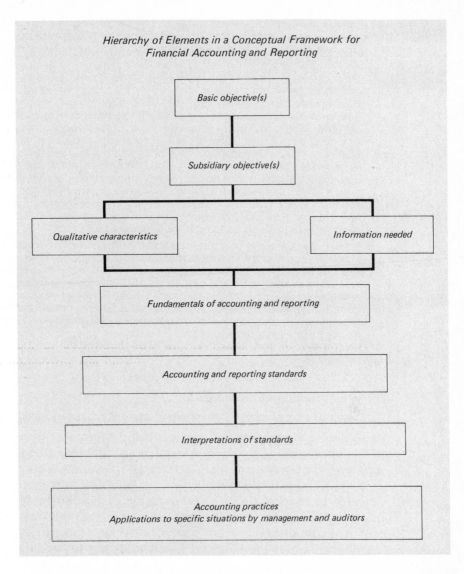

Hierarchy of Elements in a Conceptual Framework for Financial Accounting and Reporting

accounting practices. **Accounting practices** are the means used by managements and independent auditors to achieve the objectives of financial statements.

The expanded conceptual framework project undertaken by the FASB resulted in the publication of a three-part **Discussion Memorandum** in which the Board developed the following tentative conclusions about the objectives of financial statements:

1 Financial statements of business enterprises should provide information, within the limits of financial accounting, that is useful to present and potential investors and creditors in making rational investment and credit de-

cisions. Financial statements should be comprehensible to investors and creditors who have a reasonable understanding of business and economic activities and financial accounting and who are willing to spend the time and effort needed to study financial statements.

2 Financial statements of business enterprises should provide information that helps investors and creditors assess the prospects of receiving cash from dividends or interest and from the proceeds from the sale, redemption, or maturity of securities or loans. Those prospects are affected (1) by an enterprise's ability to obtain enough cash through its earning and financing activities to meet its obligations when due and its other cash operating needs, to reinvest in earning resources and activities, and to pay cash dividends and interest and (2) by perceptions of investors and creditors generally about that ability, which affect market prices of the enterprise's securities relative to those of other enterprises. Thus, financial accounting and financial statements should provide information that helps investors and creditors assess the enterprise's prospects of obtaining net cash inflows through its earning and financing activities.

3 Financial statements of a business enterprise should provide information about the economic resources of an enterprise, which are sources of prospective cash inflows to the enterprise; its obligations to transfer economic resources to others, which are causes of prospective cash outflows from the enterprise; and its earnings, which are the financial results of its operations and other events and conditions that affect the enterprise. Since that information is useful to investors and creditors in assessing an enterprise's ability to pay cash dividends and interest and to settle obligations when they mature, it should be the focus of financial accounting and financial statements.[6]

The attest function and the CPA

A conflict of interest may exist between a business preparing financial statements and some of the persons using those statements. For example, a company applying for a loan from a bank may tend to be overly optimistic in portraying its financial strength. Similarly, a corporation attempting to raise funds by selling its capital stock to the public has an incentive to exaggerate its earnings capacity. To protect the users of financial statements against a natural bias or outright misrepresentation, it is important to have independent professional accountants (auditors) examine the financial statements (and supporting evidence) prepared by the internal accounting staff of a company. The auditors then have a basis for expressing their professional opinion on the fairness of the financial statements. This **attest function** is the primary role of **certified public accountants.** To attest to financial statements means to vouch for their fairness and validity, thus avoiding a "credibility gap." Performance of the attest function requires the existence not only of an independent public accounting profession, but also of a body of generally accepted accounting principles to serve as guidelines for both

[6] *FASB Discussion Memorandum,* "Conceptual Framework for Financial Accounting and Reporting: Elements of Financial Statements and Their Measurement," FASB (Stamford: 1976), pp. 10–11.

the preparation and the audit of financial statements. Adherence to generally accepted accounting principles provides assurance that financial statements are reasonably comparable. If financial statements are comparable, then investors are better able to form an opinion as to the relative merits of supplying capital to various business enterprises.

Because of the public interest in **audited financial statements,** each state recognizes public accountancy as a profession and issues the certificate of Certified Public Accountant to those who demonstrate through written examinations and the satisfaction of educational and experience requirements their competence to enter the public accounting profession.

Organizations and institutions affecting financial accounting

Certain professional organizations, governmental agencies, and legislative acts have been extremely influential in shaping the development of the existing body of accounting theory. Among the most important of these institutional forces have been the American Institute of Certified Public Accountants, the Financial Accounting Standards Board, the American Accounting Association, the Securities and Exchange Commission, and the Internal Revenue Code. Of course many other organizations have exerted significant influence on the development of accounting principles. Among these might be mentioned the New York Stock Exchange, the National Association of Accountants, the Financial Executives Institute, the Cost Accounting Standards Board, the Institute of Internal Auditors, the Federal Government Accountants Association, and the whole complex of federal, state, and local tax regulations.

Awareness of the roles of these institutional forces is helpful in gaining an understanding of current accounting practice. Efforts to improve existing principles of accounting will have a better chance of success if they are made with full recognition of the needs and special problems of the business executives, financial analysts, investors, government agencies, and others who use accounting data in performing their respective functions.

American Institute of Certified Public Accountants (AICPA) The American Institute of Certified Public Accountants is the professional organization of the practicing certified public accountant. As a professional organization, the Institute has been vitally concerned with developing standards of practice, both ethical and professional, of its members. The AICPA publishes **The Journal of Accountancy** monthly as a forum for the practitioner. Beginning in the early 1930s the Institute, in concert with the newly created Securities and Exchange Commission, began to develop standards of financial reporting. From 1939 to 1959, the Institute published a series of **Accounting Research Bulletins** dealing with a wide variety of accounting and reporting problems.

Accounting Principles Board (APB) In 1959 the AICPA took the formal step of committing itself to a more comprehensive program of research into the problems of financial reporting. The Accounting Principles Board was formed with the responsibility of formulating accounting principles related to financial reporting based on underlying research.

The APB issued two separate series of publications. The more influential series consisted of the *Opinions of the Accounting Principles Board,* 31 separate Opinions published between 1959 and 1973. Prior to 1964, pronouncements by the AICPA were not binding upon practicing CPAs but merely dependent upon their persuasiveness for acceptance. In October 1964, however, the Institute began requiring that departures from *APB Opinions* be disclosed either in notes to financial statements or in the audit reports of members in their capacity as independent auditors. Stated bluntly, this pronouncement meant that CPAs could not give their approval to financial statements which deviated from *APB Opinions* unless they wanted to assume the considerable personal risk and burden of proof of defending the "unauthorized practices." Since few companies or auditors were anxious to assume in public the burden of defending financial statements which differed from *APB Opinions,* this action gave a new strength and authority to Opinions of the APB. In brief, *APB Opinions* achieved the status of constituting substantial authoritative support for generally accepted accounting principles.

A second series of APB publications consisted of *Statements,* which did not carry the official force of Opinions but which constituted recommendations which hopefully would lead the way in the development of improved accounting principles and practices. Especially important was *Statement No. 4,* "Basic Concepts and Accounting Principles Underlying Financial Statements of Business Enterprises." *Statement No. 4* was intended to advance the written expression of financial accounting principles for the purpose of increasing the usefulness of financial statements.

In addition to the two series of publications described above, 15 *Accounting Research Studies* were published by the Director of Accounting Research of the AICPA with the intent of providing the APB with background material that would aid in establishing accounting principles.

Financial Accounting Foundation The Financial Accounting Foundation was established in 1972 with the principal purpose of appointing members of the Financial Accounting Standards Board and raising funds for its operation. The Foundation has nine trustees, of whom four must be CPAs engaged in the public practice of accounting. The other five trustees are chosen from the ranks of financial executives, financial analysts, and accounting educators, thus assuring a broader perspective than if the Foundation represented only the public accounting profession.

Financial Accounting Standards Board (FASB) The Financial Accounting Standards Board was established in 1972 for the purpose of developing and issuing financial accounting standards for business entities and not-for-profit organizations. This new independent body, in contrast to the former Accounting Principles Board, is limited to seven full-time, well-paid members, whereas the APB consisted of 21 part-time individuals serving without pay.

Lending support and counsel to the FASB are the Financial Accounting Standards Advisory Council, a Screening Committee on Emerging Problems, and numerous Task Forces consisting of financial executives, accounting educators, lawyers, and certified public accountants.

Certified public accountants are not the only persons deeply concerned with financial reporting. Consequently, the articles of incorporation creating the Financial Accounting Standards Board require that only four members shall be CPAs drawn from public practice; the other three members must be highly qualified in the field of financial reporting but need not be certified public accountants. An individual appointed to the FASB must sever all economic connections with other organizations in order to avoid any suggestion of conflict of interest. Briefly stated, the public accounting profession is now engaged in a strenuous effort to improve the quality of financial reporting through an independent rule-making body which includes representatives from outside the field of public accounting.

The FASB is authorized to issue *Statements of Financial Accounting Standards* as well as *Interpretations* to guide persons and organizations in preparing and auditing financial statements. Before a formal statement is drafted, the FASB frequently issues a *Discussion Memorandum* which identifies and analyzes the issues to be considered. An Exposure Draft of the proposed Statement is circulated in order to secure written comments from interested parties. Public hearings are then held on the Exposure Draft. These steps are designed to encourage the widest participation possible by all interested parties before a new financial accounting standard is issued. As of the middle of 1977, the FASB had issued 16 Statements. Those Statements dealing with the subject matter of Intermediate Accounting have been incorporated in this book to the maximum extent possible.

American Accounting Association (AAA) The American Accounting Association, an organization of college professors and of practicing accountants, has had an important part to play in the development of accounting principles. The activities of this group have emphasized the development of a logical and theoretical basis of accounting rather than the application of the theory to practical situations. The AAA encourages accounting research and continuous appraisal of accounting concepts through the quarterly publication of *The Accounting Review* and the work of its members in committees.

Securities and Exchange Commission (SEC) The Securities and Exchange Commission was established in 1934 by an act of Congress for the purpose of regulating the sale of securities to the general public, including the securities listed on stock exchanges. This mandate from Congress gave the SEC broad authority to prescribe accounting principles, forms to be filed, and information to be disclosed by companies falling under the regulatory control of the Commission. Although the Commission has the legal authority to prescribe accounting principles, it generally has relied on the accounting profession to perform this function. However, the Commission has exerted great influence on the development of accounting principles and reporting practices. SEC actions have included: (1) continual review (and occasional rejection) of financial statements; (2) issuance of *Regulation S-X* which prescribes detailed accounting and financial reporting requirements; (3) publication of more than 200 *Accounting Series Releases* (ASRs) and numerous *Staff Accounting Bulletins;* and (4) prodding the private sector (FASB and registrants) to develop or revise certain accounting and reporting practices.

A company which intends to issue securities to the public must prepare a *prospectus* and have it approved by the Commission. This prospectus contains detailed information about the company's products, competition, management, and audited financial statements. Companies which are under the jurisdiction of the SEC must file voluminous documents, including an annual report (Form 10-K) which includes considerably more information than does the annual report to shareholders, and a quarterly report (Form 10-Q). The financial statements included in the annual report filed with the Commission must be audited by independent CPAs; the financial information included in the quarterly reports need not be audited but must be reviewed by independent CPAs.

Stated briefly, the primary concern of the SEC is *disclosure* of all relevant and material facts about the financial affairs of publicly owned companies. In recent years, the Commission has become increasingly more active in its role as the watchdog for investors. The chief accountants of the SEC have pushed to expand the quality as well as the quantity of information disclosed to the public. The Commission has been primarily responsible for expansion of disclosure into such areas as inventory profits caused by inflation, replacement costs of inventories and plant assets, unusual risks and uncertainties, and change of independent auditors. Particular emphasis has been placed by the SEC on the concept of *continuous disclosure* of *relevant* information on a *timely basis* so that the information will be of maximum value to investors. Accordingly, the Commission has urged independent auditors to review the quarterly financial reports and also has urged companies to issue financial forecasts. As further evidence of its deep concern with disclosure, the Commission in 1976 appointed an Advisory Committee on Corporate Disclosure to prepare a study which would offer recommendations for the complete overhaul of the corporate disclosure system in the United States.

Cost Accounting Standards Board (CASB) Although our interest in this book is focused on financial accounting rather than managerial or cost accounting, our listing of organizations which are contributing importantly to improved accounting practices must include the federal Cost Accounting Standards Board. The primary goal of the CASB is to issue standards that achieve more uniformity in accounting practices among companies holding government contracts and more consistency in the accounting treatment of various types of costs incurred by these contractors. Because almost every large industrial business holds government contracts, the issuance of standards by the CASB will inevitably have considerable impact upon financial statements as well as the measurement of contract costs. The Board has issued numerous standards ranging in scope from home-office expense allocation to the composition and measurement of pension and deferred compensation costs.

The Income Tax Law The enactment of the federal income tax law in 1913 and the subsequent amendments and legal interpretations comprising the present tax law have been perhaps the most important forces on the development of applied accounting procedures, as distinguished from accounting theory. As the rate of taxation has increased, business managers have attempted to lessen the impact of the tax on their firms. The result has been the adoption of accounting procedures which purportedly conform to the basic principles of accounting and which minimize taxable income.

The Internal Revenue Code has developed with the interests of the government as its focal point, which means that Congress has been more concerned with public policy objectives than with the development of accounting theory. The acceptance of certain tax regulations as the basis for accounting has resulted in the adoption of procedures which have as their primary rationale the fact that they result in accelerating the recognition of expenses or postponing the recognition of revenue. In Chapter 21 we shall consider some of the reporting problems created by these differences, and throughout the book reference will be made to income tax regulations and their specific impact on accounting practice. We must keep in mind, however, that this book is concerned with the principles and procedures of accounting, not of income taxation, and the issues of accounting will be evaluated in this light.

Generally accepted accounting principles (or standards)

The term *generally accepted accounting principles* has long been used in the standard form of audit report and in accounting literature generally.

This term is used by CPAs in their audit reports to indicate whether the company being audited has prepared its financial statements in an acceptable manner, so that they may fairly be compared with the prior year's statements and with the financial statements of other companies.

Alternative terms for *accounting principles* have included standards, practices, postulates, assumptions, basic concepts, axioms, and conventions. The variety of terms employed indicates the many efforts that have been made to formulate a satisfactory conceptual framework for accounting and reporting. These efforts are still in process, and the goal of a concise and consistent statement of accounting principles has not yet been achieved. The principles of accounting are not rooted in the laws of nature as are the physical sciences. Therefore, *accounting principles or standards must be developed in relation to what we consider to be the key objectives of financial statements.* Reaching agreement on the objectives of financial statements has not been an easy task. However, these difficulties in devising a satisfactory conceptual framework for accounting and reporting have not prevented great improvements in the quality of financial statements and reporting in recent years, and further improvements are being developed by the FASB and the SEC with the cooperation and support of the business community.

Sources of generally accepted accounting principles

Although a body of generally accepted accounting principles has long been recognized by business executives, courts, and governmental agencies, as well as by professional accountants, no complete official list of such accounting principles exists. The most authoritative sources of generally accepted accounting principles in recent years have been the **Statements** issued by the FASB, the **Opinions** issued by the APB, the **Accounting Research Bulletins** issued by the AICPA Committee on Accounting Procedure, and **Accounting Series Releases** issued by the SEC.

Accounting textbooks represent another source of detailed accounting principles in areas not specifically covered by official pronouncements. Although no one textbook by itself establishes accounting principles, a consensus of opinion by numerous writers indicates the existence of detailed principles in addition to those set forth above. The important influence on accounting theory of publications by the American Accounting Association has already been noted. In summary, we may say that the sources of generally accepted accounting principles include accounting literature as a whole, but that the official pronouncements of the FASB, APB, and SEC represent the most authoritative sources with the greatest impact upon current practice.

In the remainder of this chapter we shall discuss a number of fundamental accounting principles and concepts. These principles and concepts are broad in nature and have been developed by the accounting profession in an effort to meet the needs of the users of financial statements. In later chapters we shall consider the more detailed application of these broad principles and concepts to specific accounting and reporting issues.

The business entity principle

Since economic activity is carried on by various legal and economic entities, accounting results are summarized in terms of these entities. Accountants deal primarily with three general kinds of business entities: the individual proprietorship, the partnership, and the corporation. Regardless of the form of organization, however, the business is considered an entity and its affairs are distinguished from those of its owners. We see the effect of this principle when accounting income is measured as it accrues to the entity in the form of realized increases in net assets, not when it is distributed to owners. Similarly an obligation of the entity to owners is treated as a liability in the balance sheet, despite the fact that in a sense the owners owe a portion of the debt to themselves.

The accountant sometimes finds it useful to prepare financial statements for economic entities that do not coincide with legal entities. For example, *consolidated financial statements* are often prepared for an economic entity which includes several corporate entities operating under common control exercised through stock ownership. On the other hand, separate financial statements may be prepared for divisions of a single corporation, when such divisions are operated as distinct profit centers.

The continuity or going-concern principle

Briefly stated, the continuity principle means that the accountant assumes that the business entity will continue indefinitely. In deciding how to report various items in financial statements, the accountant is often faced with this issue: "Shall I assume that the business will continue to operate, or shall I assume that the business will be terminated in the near future?" The most probable situation for businesses in general is that they will continue to operate for an indefinite period of time, and this general assumption, commonly known as the *continuity* or *going-concern* principle, is one of the basic assumptions of accounting.

To illustrate the significance of the continuity principle, consider the possibility that if a business ceased operations certain liabilities would mature immediately and require a payment in excess of their carrying value. Productive assets such as machinery might be salable only at a substantial loss. The assumption of continued existence, on the other hand, provides the logical basis for recording probable future economic benefits as assets and probable future outlays as liabilities.

The continuity principle implies not permanence of existence but simply that the business will continue in existence long enough to carry out present plans and meet contractual commitments. This principle affects the classification of assets and liabilities in the balance sheet. Because it is assumed that assets will be used and obligations paid in the normal course of operation, no attempt is made to classify assets and liabilities in terms of their ultimate disposition or legal priority in case of liquidation.

There are times when the going-concern principle gives way to evidence that a business entity has a limited life or intends to terminate operations. The accountant is sometimes called upon to prepare a balance sheet for a firm contemplating liquidation.

The monetary principle

The monetary principle means that accountants assume money to be a useful standard measuring unit for reporting the effect of business transactions. Money is thus the common denominator throughout the accounting process. Some of the information necessary to give a comprehensive picture of a business entity is difficult or impossible to quantify and express in money or other units of measurement. Examples are the competence, health, and morale of management and employees, and the effect of the operations of the entity upon the natural environment. If information is to be included in the body of financial statements, however, it must be expressed in monetary terms. If such measurement is not practicable, a possible alternative method of communication is to use explanatory notes which accompany the financial statements.

In the United States the monetary unit is the dollar. To meet the test of being a *useful standard measuring unit,* the dollar should ideally be of unchanging value. Prior to World War II the rate of price-level change in the United States was not considered to be great enough to cast any serious doubts on the usefulness of the dollar as a stable measuring unit. In more recent years, however, the continuing and relatively rapid inflation has significantly reduced the "size of a dollar" and has made the monetary principle one of the most controversial elements of generally accepted accounting principles. By the "size of a dollar" we usually mean the quantity of "real" goods and services that this monetary unit will command. What kind of common denominator will enable us to measure the physical quantities of all the diverse goods and services that money will buy?

The statistical solution to this question is the familiar *price index.* An index number is a somewhat imperfect device for measuring changes in the weighted-average price of a representative collection of goods and services between two points in time. Despite all their shortcomings, price indices covering broad categories of goods and services are useful, if rough, tools for measuring changes in the value of money, that is, the size of the dollar.

When inflation causes a substantial rise in the price of goods and services, the value of the dollar goes down and the monetary principle becomes the weakest link in the chain of accounting principles. The accounting profession and the SEC have considered several possible alternatives to the stable-price-level assumption and have implemented some steps to make financial statements more meaningful in an inflationary environment. For example, the SEC currently requires the disclosure of "inventory profits" caused by inflation as well as the replacement cost of inventories and plant assets. In **APB Statement No. 3,** "Financial Statements Restated for General Price-Level Changes," the APB recommended that price-level-adjusted financial statements be presented as supplements to conventional financial statements. The FASB issued a Discussion Memorandum and an Exposure Draft of a Statement relating to price-level adjustments, but later withdrew them. These and other possible solutions to the impact of inflation on financial statements are considered in detail in Chapter 22.

The revenue realization principle

Revenue may be defined as the value of goods and services which a business entity transfers to its customers. Thus, revenue is the factor responsible for all increases in the net assets of a business, apart from investments by owners. For a given time period, revenue is equal to the inflow of cash and receivables from sales made during that period. For a single transaction, revenue is equal to the values of assets received from the customer.

Any definition of revenue immediately raises questions as to timing—the concept of **realization** of revenue. At what point or points during the creation of marketable products or services should revenue be recognized? What is the **critical event** which indicates revenue has been realized and which justifies recording a change in net assets by replacing the carrying value (cost) of assets such as inventories with a higher valuation representing their market value? Ideally, since each step in the process of producing and distributing goods is essential to earning revenue, the accounting recognition of revenue should be continuous rather than being linked to a single critical event. However, as a practical matter, objective evidence is needed to support the recognition of revenue, and for most businesses that evidence lies in an arm's-length transaction in which title to goods passes to the customer. Thus, the revenue realization principle dictates that assets be carried **at cost** until appreciation in value is realized through sale. The reasoning underlying this practice of recognizing revenue at the point of sale will be expanded in Chapter 3.

The cost principle

The cost principle is a pervasive concept that affects most aspects of financial accounting. *Cost* (or *historical cost*) is assumed to be the proper basis of accounting for assets acquired, for services received, and for the interests of creditors and owners of a business entity. Completed transactions are the events to be recognized and made part of the accounting records under the cost principle. At the time of a transaction, the exchange price usually represents the current fair value of the goods or services exchanged, as evidenced by the agreement of an informed buyer and seller. With the passage of time, the current fair value of an asset such as land or a building may change greatly, particularly in periods of inflation. However, the cost principle requires that historical cost, rather than a later "current fair value," continue to serve as the basis for values in the accounts and in the financial statements.

How should cost be measured when assets or services are acquired in noncash transactions? For example, land and buildings may be acquired in exchange for a corporation's own shares of capital stock. Cost is then defined as the cash equivalent or current fair value of the assets acquired, or the cash equivalent (current fair value) of the capital stock issued, whichever is more clearly evident. If the capital stock is listed on a stock exchange and widely traded, the existing market price of the shares will be stronger, more objective evidence of the cost of the land and buildings being acquired than an appraisal of the property.

The cost principle applies to the measurement of liabilities as well as of assets. The dollar valuation assigned to a liability should be its cash equivalent. For example, if a business borrows $100,000 and signs a note promising to repay $106,000 a year later, the cash equivalent value of the liability is $100,000, and this is the net amount at which the liability should be shown in a balance sheet prepared immediately after obtaining the loan. Thus, the cost principle is consistently applied to all types of business transactions.

The implications of the cost principle will be considered in more detail in our study of income determination in Chapter 3 and in later chapters of this book.

The matching principle

The *matching principle* means that after the revenue for an accounting period has been determined, the costs associated with that revenue must be deducted in order to measure net income. The term *matching* refers to the close relationship that exists between certain costs and the revenue realized as a result of incurring those costs. Thus, the use of matching as a pervasive principle in income measurement offers another practical reason for the widespread use of the cost principle.

Expenditures for advertising attract customers and generate sales. The outlay for the advertising is one of the costs to be deducted from the revenue of the period. The recognition of doubtful accounts expense illustrates the importance of the time period in the matching of costs and revenue. Doubtful accounts expense is caused by selling goods on credit to customers who fail to pay their bills. To match this expense with the related revenue, the expense must be recorded and deducted from revenue in the year the sales are made, even though the receivables are not determined to be uncollectible until the following year. The use of estimates is necessary in this and in many other cases in order to carry out the matching principle.

The objectivity principle

To the maximum degree possible, accounting should be based on objective evidence. Supporting documents showing the details of "arm's-length" completed transactions provide clear strong evidence that can be verified. To *verify* means to prove something to be true by examination of evidence or underlying facts. As suggested in our earlier discussion of the qualitative characteristics of the information contained in financial statements (page 4), if accounting information is free from bias on the part of the preparer, the same conclusions would be reached by different accountants working independently and following the same measurement standards. In most cases, actual costs provide the most objective data capable of being independently verified.

Of course financial statements are not completely factual; estimates on such matters as the economic life of depreciable assets, the realizable value of inventory, and the collectibility of accounts receivable are inherent in the accounting process. However, the objectivity principle calls for accountants to adhere as closely as possible to objective evidence. The alternative approach would be to establish accounting values through unrestricted use of appraisal reports, estimates of future events, and expressions of opinion. Such an approach to accounting, although often helpful in providing more relevant data to users of financial statements, makes it more difficult for the CPA to perform an independent verification of financial statements. However, accountants have come to recognize that a trade-off exists between relevance and objectivity of data used in the preparation of financial statements. In recent years, the SEC consistently has favored relevance as the more useful criterion. For example, the SEC has encouraged the issuance of financial forecasts and has required the disclosure of replacement cost data (both based on estimates), on the grounds that such information would be useful to investors.

The consistency principle

Comparability of the financial statements of a business from one period to the next is essential if favorable and unfavorable trends in the business are to be identified. If the financial statements for the current period show higher earnings than for the preceding period, the user is entitled to assume that operations have been more profitable. However, if a material change in an accounting principle has occurred, the reported increase in earnings *could* have been caused solely by this accounting change, rather than by any improvement in the underlying business activity. Consistent application of accounting principles for a business entity from one period to the next is therefore needed so that the financial statements of successive periods will be comparable.

An important part of the opinion issued by certified public accountants in reporting on their audit of a company's financial statements deals with consistency. This part of the standard audit report is worded as follows:

> In our opinion the aforementioned financial statements present fairly the financial position of X Company at December 31, 19___, and the results of its operations and the changes in its financial position for the year then ended, in conformity with generally accepted accounting principles applied on a basis *consistent with that of the preceding year.*[7]

The consistency principle does not mean that a particular method of accounting once adopted can never be changed. Accounting principles and methods change in response to changes in the environment of accounting. When an accounting change is desirable, it should be made, *together with appropriate disclosure* of the change and its effect in dollar amounts on the reported income of the year in which the change is made. *APB Opinion No. 20,* "Accounting Changes," stated that:

> The presumption that an entity should not change an accounting principle may be overcome only if the enterprise justifies the use of an alternative acceptable accounting principle on the basis that it is preferable. . . .
> The nature of and justification for a change in accounting principle and its effect on income should be disclosed. . . . The justification for the change should explain why the newly adopted accounting principle is preferable.[8]

Effective in 1976, the SEC adopted a requirement that whenever a company changed from one accounting principle to another, the independent auditors for the company must state in writing whether in their judgment the principle adopted was, under the circumstances, preferable to the principle formerly used.[9]

---

[7] *Statement on Auditing Standards No. 1,* "Codification of Auditing Standards and Procedures," AICPA (New York: 1973), p. 81.
[8] *APB Opinion No. 20,* "Accounting Changes," AICPA (New York: 1971), p. 391.
[9] *Accounting Series Release No. 177,* SEC (Washington: 1976).

The disclosure principle

The disclosure principle requires that financial statements be complete in the sense of including all information necessary to a fair presentation. If the omission of certain information would cause the financial statements to be misleading, then disclosure of such information is essential.

Published accounting reports include not only the financial statements themselves but also the attached explanatory notes, which are considered to be an integral part of the statements. Disclosures made in the attached notes should *supplement* the information in the body of the statements, however, and should not be used to correct improper presentation of information in the body of the financial statements.

Typical examples of information often disclosed in notes attached to financial statements include the following: a summary of significant accounting policies, descriptions of stock option plans and pension plans, status of litigation in which the company is a party, amount and nature of contingent liabilities and commitments, terms and status of proposed mergers or acquisitions, unusual risks and uncertainties, and replacement costs of inventories and plant assets. The first item listed above (a summary of significant accounting policies) is prescribed by *APB Opinion No. 22,* "Disclosure of Accounting Policies" as essential. Among the policies to be described in this particular note to financial statements are changes in accounting principles and justification therefor, depreciation methods, inventory pricing methods, and translation of foreign currencies.[10]

If the accounting principles used in audited financial statements represent departures from official positions set forth by the FASB and the APB, it is essential that the departures be disclosed either in notes accompanying the financial statements or in the report of the independent auditor.

The concept of disclosure applies not only to transactions and events that have occurred during the period covered by the financial statements, but also to material *subsequent events* that occur after the balance sheet date but before published financial statements are released. For example, the sale or destruction of a major segment of the business, a significant decline in the market price of raw materials, the institution or settlement of important legal proceedings are all events likely to have a substantial influence on the earnings and financial position of a company, and they should therefore be disclosed in financial statements.

The examples cited indicate that disclosure by notes to financial statements may be rather lengthy and involved. However, these notes, as well as the financial statements themselves, should be as concise as

[10] *APB Opinion No. 22,* "Disclosures of Accounting Policies," AICPA (New York: 1972), p. 436.

possible in order to keep financial reporting understandable and not excessively detailed.

Disclosure should *not* be made of events that are merely interesting, rather than essential to a fair presentation. Neither should there be disclosure of ordinary risks or uncertainties which apply to most business entities, such as the threat of war, a business depression, or the probable appearance of new competitors.

Materiality

Materiality is an accounting concept closely related to the disclosure principle. Disclosure is necessary in financial statements only for *material* matters. The meaning of materiality in an accounting context is a state of *relative importance.* Items that are trifling in amount need not ordinarily be treated in strict accordance with accounting theory but rather should be handled in the most economical and convenient manner.

For example, most companies establish a minimum dollar amount in considering whether an expenditure should be recorded as a depreciable asset. In theory the cost of a new pencil sharpener or wastebasket should be capitalized and depreciated over its useful life. As a practical matter, however, the expense of making such allocations of cost would exceed the cost of the item and would represent an unjustifiably wasteful accounting policy. Even though more than one accounting period will benefit from the use of a pencil sharpener, the concept of materiality indicates that the cost of such an item should be recorded as an expense. However, such exceptions to accounting standards should be carefully controlled by clearly stated written policies; otherwise, the argument that convenience should outweigh good accounting practices may be applied to more and larger transactions, with the end result of defeating the basic objectives of financial accounting.

That which is material for one business may not be for another. In a small company an uninsured loss, say $50,000, might be considered as material; in a large company it would not be a significant event. In deciding upon the materiality of an item in terms of financial statement disclosure, it is helpful to consider whether knowledge of the item would be likely to influence the decisions of persons using the financial statements as a basis for economic decisions.

Qualitative standards should be considered in judging the materiality of an item as well as its dollar amount. For example, a transaction between a company and its president is not at arm's length and suggests a possible *conflict of interests.* Disclosure of the transaction may therefore be appropriate, even though disclosure of a similar transaction between parties dealing at arm's length would not be warranted.

In this discussion of materiality, we have described it as an accounting *concept* rather than as an accounting *principle.* One reason for the distinction is that the concept of materiality tells us that we may under carefully designed policies disregard certain accounting principles in favor of expediency in the treatment of insignificant details.

The accounting profession has been attempting for many years to develop definitive standards for materiality. One of the initial projects undertaken by the FASB in 1973 was a study which would identify the criteria for determining materiality. An **FASB Discussion Memorandum**[11] was published in 1975, but an exposure draft of a **Statement** had not been issued as of late 1977.

Conservatism *Concept*

Many decisions by the accountant in the areas of asset valuation and income determination involve the making of estimates and the exercise of judgment. In other words, many accounting determinations do not have a single "correct answer"; a choice must be made among alternative assumptions under conditions of uncertainty. The concept of conservatism holds that when reasonable support exists for alternative methods and for different measurements, the accountant should select the accounting option with the least favorable effect on net income and financial position in the current period.

Conservatism is usually regarded not as an accounting principle, but as a powerful influence stressing caution against the danger of overstating earnings or financial position. However, many companies are definitely not in favor of conservative accounting policies. Companies trying to raise capital by selling capital stock to the public naturally try to project an image of superior management and rising profits. A business that reports higher earnings year after year gains the reputation of being a "growth company"; financial analysts refer to its capital stock as a "glamor issue"; and the market price of its stock often rises to a high multiple of earnings per share. Once such a reputation is established, a company finds it easier to raise more capital through the issuance of additional securities or through bank loans. Attracting able ambitious employees is also easier. Executive compensation tends to rise, both in salaries and through stock option and pension plans. All these pleasant consequences of a reputation for rising earnings give corporate management a powerful incentive to choose accounting methods that *maximize* current income.

On the other hand, companies must be alert to the possible consequences of following unconservative accounting policies. The issue we are raising relates to the *quality* of *reported earnings.* The earnings of a company using unconservative accounting policies are viewed as being of lower quality and its common stock will tend to sell at a low price-

---

[11] *FASB Discussion Memorandum,* "Criteria for Determining Materiality," FASB (Stamford: 1975).

earnings ratio. Small businesses that do not seek capital from the public and do not report their earnings to anyone other than income tax authorities have an incentive to choose accounting alternatives that hold income to the lowest level that can be justified.

All companies with capital stock widely held by the public must be audited each year by certified public accountants. Many small businesses are not audited at all. The professional auditing firm thus has many clients with reasons to choose accounting practices that tend to overstate rather than to understate net income. Certified public accountants have often been named as defendants in lawsuits by investors who claim that audited financial statements on which they relied in making investments actually overstated the net income and financial position of the companies. Almost never is a CPA firm sued on the grounds that audited financial statements were too conservative and understated net earnings and stockholders' equity. Consequently, CPAs, although trying to be objective and impartial in their role as *independent* auditors, have reason to favor a conservative resolution of doubtful accounting issues. Conflicting views between the client company and the CPA firm on such matters have sometimes led to the replacement of the auditors with another CPA firm.

Ideally, accountants should make estimates and select accounting methods which neither overstate nor understate the current income and financial position of a business. The concept of conservatism should not be distorted to the point of deliberate understatement; however, the judicious use of conservatism in accounting may help to prevent the catastrophes which have befallen many investors and many employees when companies with excessively optimistic accounting policies suddenly reached the limit of credibility and collapsed.

Among the familiar examples of the influence of conservatism on accounting practices are the valuation of inventories at the lower of cost or market, the use of an accelerated method of depreciation, the prompt write-off of assets when doubt arises as to their value, and the refusal to recognize appreciation in the value of assets until confirmed by a completed sales transaction.

A new business which adopts the conservative practice of valuing inventories at the lower of cost or market will probably have a more conservative income statement and balance sheet at the end of the first year, but not necessarily for the following year. Inventory written down below cost at the end of the first year of operations and sold in the second year will show a larger profit in the second year than if the write-down had not occurred.

In a growing enterprise which is adding new units of plant and equipment more rapidly than old, fully depreciated units are being retired, the use of an accelerated method of depreciation may cause the financial statements to be increasingly conservative as long as the growth of plant and equipment continues.

Cash flows and income measurement

Accountants assume that a business entity has continuous existence. Therefore, they record the prospect of future cash inflows as an increase in assets and as revenue whenever they have objective evidence of the amount of the future cash receipt. Cash inflows often occur before a business has performed its part of the bargained contract. In this latter case, an increase in assets is recorded but a liability is recognized instead of revenue. The liability indicates an obligation on the part of the enterprise to perform in accordance with the contract. When performance is completed, the revenue will be earned and recognized. We can readily see that cash inflows are closely related to revenue recognition; however, the assumptions lying behind the timing of revenue recognition do not always permit cash inflows and revenue to be recorded in the same accounting period.

Similarly, cash outflows are closely related to business expenses; however, the cash outflow and the expense may not be recorded in the same period. For example, businesses frequently acquire for cash in one period property which will be productive over several future periods, and property which is productive only during the current period is often acquired in exchange for a promise to pay cash in a future period.

Information concerning cash flows during any period is extremely valuable in judging the ability of the firm to pay its debts, to maintain regular dividend payments, to finance replacements of productive assets, and to expand the scope of the business operations. However, the net increase or decrease in cash during a given period is not very useful in evaluating a company's operating performance because cash receipts and payments are not representative of the economic activities carried on in specific periods.

Accrual basis versus cash basis of accounting

The *accrual basis of accounting* is assumed throughout this book. Revenue is recognized when it is realized and expenses are recognized when incurred, without regard to the time of receipt or payment. The focus of accrual accounting is on the realization of revenue, the incurrence of costs, and the matching of revenue realized and the costs expired. Adopting the assumption that revenue is recognized when realization occurs and the corollary assumption that costs contributing to the earning of this revenue can be traced through the earning process requires the use of an accrual-deferral system of accounting.

The need for frequent measurement of the past performance of the enterprise as the basis for decisions about the future by management and investors alike has forced accountants to adopt the accrual basis of accounting. Under the accrual system, the accounts are adjusted periodically to make the data which have been recorded consistent with the basic assumptions of the system.

Under the *cash basis of accounting,* revenue is recognized only when cash is received; expenses are recorded when they are paid in cash. The determination of income thus rests upon the *collection* of revenue and the *payment* of expenses, rather than upon the *earning* of *revenue* and the *incurring* of expenses. A business using the cash basis of accounting is not following the *matching principle* described earlier in this chapter. Consequently, financial statements prepared on the basis of cash receipts and cash payments do not present the financial position or operating results of a business in conformity with generally accepted accounting principles.

A strict cash basis of accounting is seldom found in practice, but a *modified cash basis* (really a mixed cash-accrual basis) is allowed for income tax purposes. Under the modified cash basis accounting, taxpayers who buy property having an economic life of more than one year cannot deduct the entire cost in the year of purchase. They must treat the cost as an asset to be depreciated over its economic life. Expenses such as rent or advertising paid in advance are also regarded as assets and are deductible only in the period to which they apply. Expenses paid *after* the year in which incurred are deductible only in the year paid. Revenue is reported for tax purposes in the year received. However, in any business in which the purchase, production, or sale of merchandise is a significant factor, these transactions must be reported on an accrual basis. For example, when merchandise is sold on credit, the revenue must be recognized immediately. The cost of goods sold must reflect purchases on credit and inventories on hand whether paid for or not. In any merchandising business the revenue from sales, the cost of goods sold, and the gross profit on sales will be the *same* on either the accrual basis of accounting or the modified cash basis of accounting.

Illustration The difference between the cash and accrual basis of accounting will be illustrated for Tim McClean, a practicing CPA, who keeps his accounting records on a cash basis. During Year 10, McClean collected $150,000 from his clients and paid $80,000 for operating expenses, resulting in a cash basis net income of $70,000. Fees receivable, accrued liabilities, and short-term prepayments at January 1 and December 31, Year 10, were as follows:

	Jan. 1, Year 10	Dec. 31, Year 10
Fees receivable	$18,200	$37,000
Accrued liabilities	6,200	4,000
Short-term prepayments	3,500	2,500

A working paper showing the necessary adjustments to restate Mc-Clean's income statement from the cash basis to the accrual basis is illustrated below:

TIM McCLEAN, CPA

Restatement of Income Statement from Cash Basis to Accrual Basis of Accounting

For Year 10

	Cash collected from revenue and paid for expenses	Adjustments to convert to accrual basis of accounting		Income statement on accrual basis of accounting
		Add	Deduct	
Revenue from fees	$150,000			
Add: Fees receivable, Dec. 31, Year 10 . .		$37,000		
Less: Fees receivable, Jan. 1, Year 10 . .			$18,200	$168,800
Operating expenses	80,000			
Add: Accrued liabilities, Dec. 31, Year 10 . .		4,000		
Short-term prepayments, Jan. 1, Year 10		3,500		
Less: Accrued liabilities, Jan. 1, Year 10 . .			6,200	78,800
Short-term prepayments, Dec. 31, Year 10			2,500	
Net income on cash basis . .	$ 70,000			
Net income on accrual basis				$ 90,000

Because the revenue from fees on the cash basis does not include the fees receivable at December 31, which were earned in Year 10, this amount is added to the cash collected in the restatement of revenue from fees to the accrual basis of accounting. Because fees receivable at January 1 were earned in Year 9 and collected in Year 10, this amount is subtracted from cash collections in the restatement of revenue from fees to the accrual basis of accounting.

The adjustments to restate operating expenses from the cash to the accrual basis of accounting are briefly explained below:

Additions The amount of accrued liabilities at December 31, Year 10, represents expenses incurred in Year 10 which will be paid in Year 11, and the amount of short-term prepayments at January 1, Year 10, represents services paid for in Year 9 which were consumed in Year 10. Therefore, both amounts are added to the amount of cash paid in the restatement of operating expenses for Year 10 to the accrual basis of accounting.

Deductions The amount of accrued liabilities at January 1, Year 10, represents expenses of Year 9 paid for in Year 10, and the amount of short-term prepayments at December 31, Year 10, represents cash outlays in Year 10 for services which will be consumed in Year 11. Therefore, both amounts are subtracted from the amount of cash paid in the restatement of operating expenses for Year 10 to the accrual basis of accounting.

REVIEW QUESTIONS

1 Identify the institutional forces or organizations that have been primarily responsible for the development of present accounting principles and practices. What is the relationship between each of these forces or organizations and the practicing certified public accountant?

2 Are generally accepted accounting principles equally applicable to the fields of financial accounting and managerial accounting? Explain.

3 Define *general-purpose financial statements* and point out the limitations of such statements.

4 Briefly state the general objective of financial statements.

5 List the first six specific objectives of financial statements as identified by the Study Group on the Objectives of Financial Statements.

6 List the qualitative characteristics of the information contained in financial statements identified by the Study Group on the Objectives of Financial Statements.

7 Among the specific qualities or characteristics considered as desirable for financial statements are *freedom from bias* and *relevance.* Are these

qualities as likely to be found in an earnings forecast as in a balance sheet? Explain.

8 If the chief accounting officer of a large corporation has a CPA certificate and was formerly a successful member of a CPA firm, would there be any reason for the corporation to retain a CPA to perform an annual audit? Explain.

9 Identify the following as being governmental organizations or part of the private sector of the economy: Financial Accounting Standards Board, Cost Accounting Standards Board, Securities and Exchange Commission, New York Stock Exchange, American Accounting Association.

10 Briefly describe the steps followed by the FASB in the development of a new accounting principle.

11 The usual audit report of a CPA firm includes an opinion that the financial statements it has examined are presented in conformity with generally accepted accounting principles. In evaluating the acceptability of specific accounting principles used by the client being audited, the CPA firm must determine whether the principle has substantial authoritative support. What sources might the CPA firm consult to determine whether an accounting principle has substantial authoritative support?

12 What is meant by the *continuity* or *going-concern principle* of accounting? How does it affect the valuation of assets? When is the principle not applicable?

13 The *monetary principle* of accounting assumes that money is a useful standard measuring unit for reporting the effects of business transactions. State and explain briefly two major criticisms or limitations of this accounting principle.

14 Define the *revenue realization principle* of accounting. How is this principle related to the *cost principle* and the *matching principle?*

15 Langley Corporation acquired land and buildings in exchange for 50,000 shares of its $5 par value capital stock. How should the *cost principle* of accounting be applied in recording this transaction?

16 Define *objectivity, consistency, disclosure,* and *materiality* as these terms are used in financial accounting.

17 Describe the concept of *conservatism.* Is a growth company with its stock widely distributed among public investors and with a reputation for consistently rising earnings per share the kind of organization in which you would expect emphasis upon conservative accounting? Explain.

18 Distinguish between the *cash basis of accounting* and the *accrual basis of accounting.* Will financial statements prepared under either method present fairly the financial position and operating results of a business in conformity with generally accepted accounting principles?

EXERCISES

Ex. 1-1 Select the best answer for each of the following multiple-choice questions.

a Several organizations have been influential in the development of an accepted body of accounting principles or concepts, which are followed by most business organizations in order that their financial statements be generally accepted. Which of the following organizations is now most active in formulating this body of accounting principles?
(1) The Securities and Exchange Commission
(2) The American Institute of Certified Public Accountants
(3) The American Accounting Association
(4) The Financial Accounting Standards Board

b The attest function as applied to financial statements means:
(1) The expression of an opinion on the financial statements by an independent firm of certified public accountants
(2) Filing of a letter with the Securities and Exchange Commission signed by officers of the company issuing the financial statements and accepting responsibility for the accuracy of the statements
(3) Compliance by a listed corporation with the regulations of the New York Stock Exchange
(4) Notarization of financial statements by a notary public licensed by the state in which the company is incorporated

c The term ***relevance*** as applied to financial statements is illustrated by:
(1) Adherence to historical cost as the basis of accounting for assets
(2) The requirement that financial statements of publicly owned companies be audited by CPAs
(3) Valuation of inventories at the lower of cost or market
(4) Disclosure of current market value of investments in marketable securities

Ex. 1-2 The financial statements of Fresno Company include the items shown below, along with the related notes accompanying the financial statements.

Cash (**Note A**) . . . . $ 96,500

Accounts receivable (**Note B**) 210,300

Note A: *The amount reported as cash includes four checking accounts, two petty cash funds, and one change fund.*
Note B: *Accounts receivable include the amount of $48,400, representing the selling price of merchandise shipped on a consignment basis and held for sale by consignees acting as agents at December 31. It is anticipated that this merchandise will be sold within the near future and that none of it will have to be returned to stock.*

You are to discuss the appropriateness of **Notes A** and **B** to Fresno Company's financial statements as a means of carrying out the disclosure principle of accounting and the objectives of general-purpose financial statements.

Ex. 1-3 The general-purpose financial statements of Bombay Corporation contain the following item and a note accompanying the financial statements.

Inventories (**Note A**) $1,760,000

Note A: *Inventories are valued at the lower of cost or market. Cost is determined on the first-in, first-out basis.*

Discuss the appropriateness of **Note A** in relation to the accounting principle of disclosure.

Ex. 1-4 Identify each of the following phrases as being associated with (1) the cash basis of accounting or (2) the accrual basis of accounting:
- **a** Revenue recognized at time of collection
- **b** Individual income tax returns
- **c** Business entity in which inventories are material in amount
- **d** Minimum amount of record keeping
- **e** Generally accepted accounting principles
- **f** Postponement of recognition of revenue
- **g** Flexibility in determining timing of expenses
- **h** Emphasis upon consistency and time period in measurement of income
- **i** Sophisticated accounting system
- **j** Small service-type firm with accounting records limited to information required for income tax purposes

Ex. 1-5 Mail Order Company uses the accrual basis of accounting. It reported advertising expense for the current year of $33,440. Prepaid advertising at the end of the year amounted to $4,820, and cash paid for advertising during the year amounted to $36,680. There was no accrued advertising expense at either the beginning or end of the current year. What was the amount, if any, of prepaid advertising at the beginning of the current year? Show computations.

SHORT CASES FOR ANALYSIS AND DECISION

Case 1-1 During the first class meeting in an intermediate accounting course, Professor Collins asked three students to explain the nature of revenue and expenses as related to the preparation of financial statements for business enterprises. Ann Haggard stated that revenue and expenses reflect changes in the owners' equity of a business entity. Daryl Jamison stated politely that Ann was dead wrong and explained that revenue represents inflows of assets and expenses represent outflows of assets. Keith Capp responded confidently as follows: "Revenue and expenses are those things which determine net income." Professor Collins took the position that each student was on the right track, but that none had presented an entirely satisfactory explanation.

Instructions Briefly evaluate the responses of the three students and describe the nature of revenue and expenses as these terms are used in financial accounting.

Case 1-2 The board of directors of Modern Media Corporation is debating whether to adopt straight-line depreciation or an accelerated depreciation method. Some directors are primarily interested in reporting steadily increasing earnings; others argue that the best way to achieve a favorable "accounting image" in the financial community is to adopt conservative accounting policies.

Instructions Explain whether the conservative effect of accelerated depreciation on net income and financial position will be felt for only a few years or whether it will continue indefinitely to result in the reporting of lower earnings and a lower valuation of plant and equipment.

Case 1-3 A financial newspaper carried an advertisement of a small manufacturing company being offered for sale by its owner. The advertisement emphasized the unusual profitability of the business. Assume that you were interested in purchasing a business of this type and you therefore contacted the owner, Ron Merriman, who stated that the Merriman Company in its first year of operation had produced a net income of $55,000. You inquired whether the accrual basis of accounting had been used in determining the $55,000 of net income and Merriman replied as follows:

"We use a mixed cash-accrual basis of accounting just as so many other small concerns do. As you probably know, a strict cash basis is not satisfactory, but a modified or mixed cash-accrual basis is acceptable for income tax purposes and meets our other needs very well. For example, our purchases of merchandise are recorded only when cash payment is made. Our sales are recorded immediately, whether on a cash or credit basis. We do not guess about doubtful accounts receivable in advance, but we do not hesitate to write off any receivable that proves to be uncollectible. We took a complete physical inventory at year-end and recorded it in the accounts. We did not record any depreciation on equipment as all equipment was acquired by issuance of long-term notes. No entry will be made for these transactions until cash payments are required. We find this system gives us better results than a pure cash basis and requires less work than a full accrual basis."

Instructions Evaluate point by point the statement made by Merriman. Would you regard his system as conforming to the usual standards of a "modified cash basis" of accounting? Would the determination of net income of $55,000 during the first year be a valid measurement? Explain.

Case 1-4 Comparative balance sheets of Utah Ore, Inc., for the years 1980 and 1970 are presented below:

UTAH ORE, INC.
Comparative Balance Sheets

Assets	1980	1970
Cash	$ 990,000	$ 200,000
Accounts receivable (net of allowance)	80,000	–0–
Inventories	200,000	–0–
Unmined iron ore (unamortized part)	800,000	1,600,000
Plant assets	400,000	400,000
Less: Accumulated depreciation	(200,000)	–0–
Total assets	$2,270,000	$2,200,000

Liabilities & Stockholders' Equity		
Current liabilities	$ 70,000	$ –0–
Capital stock, no par value	2,200,000	2,200,000
Total liabilities & stockholders' equity	$2,270,000	$2,200,000

The president informs you that the company has adopted a policy of paying cash dividends in an amount equal to net income each year; in spite of this, there has been a continual increase in the cash balance, as is apparent in the above balance sheets.

Instructions Explain to the president why the cash balance has been increasing. Include in your explanation an analysis of the changes in individual balance sheet items during the 10-year interval between the two balance sheets.

PROBLEMS

Group A

1A-1 Edward Gill and Samuel Mann formed Gillmann Corporation for the purpose of operating a charter fishing boat. Each contributed $27,000 cash, for which each received 3,000 shares of $1 par value capital stock. The corporation also issued 1,200 shares of its stock to acquire a used boat. Eugene Greene, the former owner of the boat, had pledged it as collateral for a $22,500 bank loan and this $22,500 liability was assumed by Gillmann Corporation in the agreement for acquisition of the boat.

Eugene Greene's accounting records showed that the original cost of the boat when new had been $75,000 and that he had written off by straight-line depreciation a total of $45,000.

Gillmann Corporation acquired fishing equipment for $6,000 cash and supplies for $750 cash. A crew member was hired to begin work the following week at a weekly salary of $275.

Instructions
a What effect, if any, does the amount of recorded depreciation and the depreciation method used by Eugene Greene have upon the depreciation program to be used for the boat by Gillmann Corporation? State briefly the reasoning supporting your answer.
b What cost should be recorded for the boat acquired in exchange for 1,200 shares of Gillmann Corporation stock? Explain fully.
c Record the transactions completed by Gillmann Corporation in general journal form.

1A-2 Sunset Company is a successful enterprise and is expanding rapidly. On May 1 additional manufacturing facilities were acquired from the partnership of Thomas and Hester, which was terminating operations because of a dispute between the partners. The property had been advertised for sale at a price of $950,000. Thomas asserted that the land alone was worth that much and that the building was insured for $500,000, its cost of construction.

Sunset Company acquired the property by issuing to the partnership 60,000 shares of its $5 par value capital stock and agreed to assume full responsibility for a $250,000 mortgage note payable on the property which was owed to a bank. Prior to the acquisition, Sunset Company hired a firm of industrial engineers to inspect and appraise the building. The report from this firm set forth a current fair value for the building of $480,000. The stock of Sunset Company is listed on a stock exchange and was being actively traded on May 1 at a price of $11 a share.

Shortly after acquiring the property, Sunset Company received a letter from a large corporation offering to buy the property for $1,000,000 cash.

Instructions
a At what dollar amount should this transaction be recorded by Sunset Company? State the dollar amounts applicable to land and to the building.
b Identify the accounting principle or principles involved and explain the reasoning underlying your answers to part **a**.

1A-3 Capri Corporation owns several office buildings and rents space to tenants. One of these office buildings was acquired at a cost of $750,000 and has been depreciated for five years on a straight-line basis. Residual value is assumed to be zero. The carrying value, net of accumulated depreciation, will be $680,000 at the end of the current year.

At the time of acquiring the building, Capri Corporation had borrowed $750,000 from Barry Wagman, one of the founders of the company and presently a director and major stockholder. The note payable issued for the loan made no mention of interest but called for repayment of $1,000,000 five years from the date of the note. In a directors' meeting near the end of the current year, Wagman stated that because of rising price levels he considered the office building to be worth more than it had cost. Wagman offered to accept the office building in full settlement of the $1,000,000 promissory note which was about to mature.

During a discussion of the offer by the board of directors, the following opinions were expressed.

Director Keith: "If we give up this building in settlement of this $1,000,000 note payable, we would increase our earnings this year by $250,000, and we would have to correct our prior years' earnings by eliminating all depreciation on the building, because this transaction provides objective evidence that the building has not depreciated. My understanding of accounting principles is that the objectivity principle would require that our accounting treatment of the transaction utilize the objective evidence provided by Wagman's offer."

Director Loomis: "In my opinion we could accept the offer and not have to recognize any profit. The company would not be receiving cash, receivables, or any other asset so there is no gain involved. The revenue realization principle of accounting says you must have an inflow of cash or receivables in order to have revenue."

Director Magana: "The corporation received only $750,000 when it issued the note payable, and it has never paid or recorded any interest. Now we will give up an asset that cost $750,000 to discharge a recorded liability of the same amount, so this is a perfect example of the matching principle of accounting and no gain or loss is involved."

Instructions
a Evaluate the opinions expressed by each of the three directors in turn, giving special attention to the references made to an accounting principle. Use a separate paragraph or paragraphs for evaluation of each director's position and indicate what accounting principles are involved.
b Explain how the proposed transaction should be accounted for in your judgment. Indicate the accounting principle or principles you consider to be applicable. Include in your answer whether interest and depreciation should be recognized and the amount of the gain or loss, if any, which would result from acceptance of Wagman's offer.
c In the financial statements prepared immediately after carrying out the exchange with Wagman, would it be necessary to make any special disclosure of this transaction apart from the normal accounting for disposal of a building? Explain.
d Assuming that the corporation accepts Wagman's offer, draft a journal entry to record the transaction. You should assume that depreciation has been recorded for the current year but that the accounts have not been closed. No interest expense has ever been recorded on the note payable. Assume also that the entry made at the time of issuing the note payable consisted of a debit to Cash for $750,000, a debit to Discount on Notes Payable for $250,000, and a credit to Notes Payable for $1,000,000. *Suggestion:* The interest applicable to prior years may be debited to Correction of Prior Years' Income (Interest Expense). Assume that the interest expense applicable to the current year is $55,000 on a compounded basis.

1A-4 Benson Furniture Company uses the accrual basis of accounting. The company owns real estate which it rents to various tenants. The amounts of rent receivable and of unearned rental revenue at two successive balance sheet dates were as follows:

	Dec. 31, Year 4	Dec. 31, Year 5
Rents receivable	$1,800 ~	$2,450 +
Unearned rental revenue	2,200 +	820 ~

Rents collected in cash during Year 5 amounted to $54,200.

The company advertises its merchandise through local television, radio, and newspapers. Some of the advertising is paid in advance and some is paid upon receipt of invoices. The amounts of prepaid and accrued advertising expense at the beginning and at the end of Year 5 were as follows:

	Dec. 31, Year 4	Dec. 31, Year 5
Prepaid advertising expense	$2,680 ~	$3,200 +
Accrued advertising payable	3,920 +	1,450 +

Advertising expense on the accrual basis for Year 5 was $32,100.

Instructions
a Compute the amount of rental revenue which should appear in the income statement for Year 5, using the accrual basis of accounting.
b Compute the amount of cash paid for advertising during Year 5.

1A-5 The information listed below was obtained from the comparative balance sheets of Bellview Sales Company for Year 4:

	Jan. 1	Dec. 31
Accounts receivable	$ 77,500	$ 84,200
Inventory	110,000	125,000
Short-term prepayments	6,200	1,700
Accounts payable (merchandise purchases)	49,500	38,000
Accrued operating expenses payable	3,200	900
Accumulated depreciation (no retirements during the year) ..	66,000	100,000

A summary of operating results for Year 4 follows:

Cash collected from customers	$663,500
Cash paid to suppliers for merchandise	440,000
Cash paid for operating expenses	122,800

Instructions Prepare comparative income statements for Bellview Sales Company for Year 4 using (1) the accrual basis of accounting and (2) the modified cash basis of accounting whereby operating expenses (excluding depreciation) are computed on a strict cash basis. Give supporting computations and ignore income taxes.

Group B

1B-1 Meadowlark Corporation was organized by Jim Meadow and Larry Clark for the purpose of operating a hardware store. Each invested $30,000 cash and each received 1,500 shares of $1 par value common stock. Meadow also loaned $25,000 to the corporation and received a two-year, 6% promissory note. The corporation then issued 1,800 shares of its common stock in exchange for land and a building. The land alone was appraised at a value of $15,000.

A stock of merchandise costing $35,000 was acquired on open account and a salesman was employed to begin work the following week at a weekly salary of $250. The corporation plans to use the periodic inventory system. Office supplies and some used office equipment were acquired for $7,000 cash. The office supplies were valued at $800 and the used office equipment at $6,200.

Instructions
a What cost should be recorded for the land and building acquired in exchange for Meadowlark Corporation's stock? Explain the reasoning underlying your answer.
b Record the above transactions in general journal form.
c After one year of operation, Meadowlark Corporation had a strong working capital position but retained earnings amounted to only $10,000. Under these circumstances, would it be proper for the corporation to pay off the $25,000 note payable to Jim Meadow? Explain.

1B-2 In a discussion of the concept of conservatism as an influence on financial accounting and reporting, Cannon argued that conservatism was often used as a means of unjustifiably understating the income of the current period and the financial position. Mannix defended conservatism on the ground that the accountant frequently had to make choices among alternative assumptions under conditions of uncertainty and that making such choices on a conservative basis would help avoid dangerous exaggeration of earnings, which could seriously injure both investors and certified public accountants.

Cannon and Mannix considered the five following situations but were unable to reach agreement on the proper accounting treatment in any one of them.

(1) A company has expended $125,000 (which is 5% of its annual sales) for research and development in an effort to develop new commercial products. No specific products have emerged from this research as yet, but management believes that the research if continued will eventually lead to important new products. Furthermore, management believes that its existing products will lose their market appeal in a few years and that the company must have new products to survive.

Cannon favors including the $125,000 in the balance sheet as an intangible asset, Deferred Research and Development Costs. Mannix favors treating the $125,000 as expense of the current year.

(2) After occupying an old building on leased property for 17 years of a 20-year lease, the tenant company constructed a new frame building, because the old building was unsatisfactory and the owner refused to make repairs. Improvements on the land will revert to the owner at the end of the lease. There is a possibility, but no assurance, that the owner will agree to renew the lease.

Cannon favors capitalizing the cost of the building. Mannix favors writing off the cost of the building as expense of the current period.

(3) The products sold by a manufacturer are warranted for a period of one year. Cannon favors recognizing warranty expense only as claims are presented which require repair or replacement of products. Mannix favors recording warranty expense and crediting a liability of estimated amount in the period of sale.

(4) The inventory contains a large quantity of item Z for which demand has largely disappeared. Cannon wants to include item Z as an asset in the balance sheet on the grounds that the item is not subject to deterioration and

customer demand for it may revive. Mannix favors writing off the cost of this item.

(5) Credit terms are 30 days. Mannix favors writing off a large receivable six months past due from a customer who went to Europe for an extended stay and cannot be located. Cannon is opposed because the customer has been delinquent before and later paid his account in full.

Instructions For each of the above five situations, state your opinion on the proposed action and explain fully the reasoning underlying your position.

1B-3 Highly condensed balance sheet data at the end of the current year are presented below for three companies of similar size and nature of operations. All are in the same industry.

	Dean Company	Evans Company	Ferry Company
Cash	$ 30,000	$ 30,000	$ 30,000
Accounts receivable (net)	50,000	50,000	50,000
Inventories **(Note A)**	200,000	210,000	215,000
Plant and equipment (net)	200,000	200,000	200,000
Total assets	$480,000	$490,000	$495,000
Accounts payable	$ 20,000	$ 20,000	$ 20,000
Other current liabilities	65,000	65,000	65,000
Capital stock	250,000	250,000	250,000
Retained earnings	145,000	155,000	160,000
Total liabilities & stockholders' equity .	$480,000	$490,000	$495,000

Note A:

Dean Company: Three years ago, Dean Company changed its methods of pricing inventories from the cost basis to the lower-of-cost-or-market basis, which is now in use.

Evans Company: Evans Company prices its inventories at cost. Last year it used the first-in, first-out method of determining cost, but for the current year it used the last-in, first-out method.

Ferry Company: Ferry Company prices all its inventories at cost, but determines cost on the first-in, first-out method for one category of its inventories and the average-cost method for the remainder of its inventories.

The three companies had not been audited previously by independent public accountants, but this year all three companies have retained the same CPA to audit their financial statements for the current year. The president of each company is hopeful that the CPA's audit report will indicate that the financial statements were prepared "in conformity with generally accepted accounting principles applied on a basis consistent with that of the preceding year."

During an informal meeting of the three presidents, Dean expressed some fear that the differences in accounting for inventories by companies in the same industry might be regarded as a serious lack of consistency.

Instructions

a Do you believe that the accounting principle of consistency as applied to the valuation of inventories in these three companies would prevent the CPA from issuing audit reports giving full approval to the financial statements of each company and using the language quoted in the problem? Assume that the audits indicated that all other aspects of the financial statements were satisfactory. Explain fully the reasoning underlying your answer.

b Would you expect the CPA to take a different position if the three companies were in three different industries? Explain.

1B-4 Majestic Corporation issues notes payable frequently in borrowing from various sources. Some of the notes provide for payment of interest in advance; others do not. (For the purposes of this problem, you need not challenge the propriety of prepaid interest.) Majestic Company uses the accrual basis of accounting. Interest expense on the accrual basis for Year 3 was $9,800. Information relating to prepaid interest and to accrued interest payable at two successive balance sheet dates appears below:

	Dec. 31, Year 2	Dec. 31, Year 3
Prepaid interest	$400	$ 200
Accrued interest payable	850	1,100

The corporation owns several properties which it rents to tenants. Some tenants pay rent in advance; others do not. The amount of cash collected from tenants during Year 3 was $28,200. The following information relates to rents receivable and unearned rental revenue on two successive balance sheet dates:

	Dec. 31, Year 2	Dec. 31, Year 3
Rents receivable	$3,200	$2,500
Unearned rental revenue	800	1,400

Instructions
a Compute the amount of cash paid for interest during Year 3.
b Compute the amount of rental revenue for Year 3, using the accrual basis of accounting.

1B-5 A summary of operating results for Garden Supply Company for Year 2 is presented below:

Cash collected from customers	$466,000
Cash paid to merchandise creditors	268,200
Cash paid for operating expenses	82,100

The following data were taken from comparative balance sheets prepared on the accrual basis:

	Dec. 31, Year 1	Dec. 31, Year 2
Accounts receivable	$52,400	$48,600
Inventory	75,000	72,100
Short-term prepayments	4,100	9,500
Accounts payable (merchandise creditors)	32,000	37,400
Miscellaneous accrued liabilities	2,800	3,200
Accumulated depreciation (no retirements during the year) . . .	50,000	74,000

Instructions Prepare comparative income statements for Garden Supply Company for Year 2, using (1) the accrual basis of accounting and (2) the modified cash basis of accounting whereby operating expenses (other than depreciation) are computed on a strict cash basis. Give supporting computations in good form and ignore income taxes.

CHAPTER 2

THE ACCOUNTING PROCESS

Accounting has frequently been called the "language of business." This designation is applied to accounting because it is the method of communicating business information. Like other languages, it is undergoing continuous change in an attempt to discover better means of communicating.

The accounting process consists of three major parts: (1) the recording of transactions during the period, (2) the summarizing of information at the end of the period, and (3) the reporting and interpreting of the summary information.

During the accounting period the accountant records transactions as they occur, reflecting the situation as it exists at the time of the transaction. The recording phase of accounting is thus a continuing activity. At the end of each accounting period the accountant carries out the functions of summarizing and reporting. After a trial balance has been prepared to ensure that the double-entry system has maintained an equality of debits and credits, certain adjusting entries are necessary. Some adjustments must be made to the recorded data for changes that have occurred since the transactions were recorded. Other adjustments are needed for events which have not been recorded but which affect the financial position and operating results of the business. Examples of these unrecorded events are depreciation and other expiration of asset services and the accrual of expenses such as interest.

When the accounting records have been made as complete, accurate, and up-to-date as possible, the accountant prepares financial statements reflecting financial position and the results of operations. An important measure of the success of the accounting process is the responsiveness of financial reporting to the needs of the users of accounting information.

RECORDING FINANCIAL TRANSACTIONS

If the accounting process is to provide the users of accounting information with reliable, timely reports, transactions during the period must be interpreted in conformity with generally accepted accounting principles and recorded promptly and accurately. A *transaction* is an event that causes a change in the assets, liabilities, or owners' equity of a business entity. Transactions may conveniently be classified into two broad groups: (1) external transactions, or those between the business and another entity, and (2) internal transactions, such as the expiration or transfer of costs within the organization. Examples of this second group include the depreciation of assets, the recognition of obsolescence in inventory, and the transfer of production costs from goods in process to finished goods.

Supporting documents

A supporting document (sometimes called a *business paper, form,* or *voucher*) is the first record prepared for a transaction. Such papers show the date, amount, and nature of the transaction, and the persons involved. Entries in the various journals are prepared from supporting documents; for example, sales invoices support entries in the sales journal. The original copy of a sales invoice is sent to the customer, who uses it as a basis for recording the purchase; a duplicate copy is retained by the seller as evidence of the sale. Some supporting documents never leave the organization as, for example, cash register tapes, receiving reports, time cards, journal vouchers, and minutes of directors' meetings.

Any verification of financial statements or accounting records is likely to include tests in which summary figures are traced back to the underlying supporting documents. The practice of identifying each type of document with serial numbers and accounting for all numbers in the series helps prevent the omission of a transaction because of a missing document. Proper design and use of supporting documents is an important element in the system of internal control, regardless of whether the business uses a manual accounting system or has a sophisticated computer-based system.

Electronic data processing

The increasing use of computers by business, government, and other organizations has greatly modified the methods of recording, summarizing, and classifying accounting information. The computer not only processes data with incredible speed and a high degree of accuracy, but also permits the classification and summarization of data in more forms and at lower cost than has been possible with the older methods.

The input data for the computer are often on punched cards or tapes, created as a by-product when preparing business papers. The computer output, also on cards or tapes, is read by printers that can produce reports and financial statements of traditional appearance.

In business concerns using sophisticated electronic data processing systems, the recording, classifying, and summarizing steps in creating accounting information may be blended into one. With an **on-line, real-time computer system,** the recording of a transaction causes instantaneous updating of all relevant files. You have probably encountered these on-line, real-time (OLRT) systems at airline ticket offices and in savings and loan associations. At any branch of a savings and loan association, a teller can update a customer's account immediately merely by recording his deposit or withdrawal on a computer terminal. It is not difficult to envision an electronic data processing system which daily produces a set of financial statements or special reports updated to include all transactions to date and also providing the current amounts of accruals for such elements as interest, depreciation, and labor costs.

Although the traditional forms of journals and ledgers are not essential to the electronic processing of accounting information, the concepts implicit in these records are inherent in a computerized system. Furthermore, the output of the computers can be programmed to provide information in a form similar to traditional journals and ledgers.

Because our primary goal in this book is an understanding of accounting principles rather than expertise in accounting systems, we shall rely upon manual recording methods as the simplest and clearest means of illustrating the application of accounting principles to business transactions and events.

Double-entry system

The standard accounting model for accumulating data in a business entity consists of the **double-entry system** based on the fundamental accounting equation. As the name implies, the entry made for each transaction is composed of two parts: one or more debits and one or more credits. All accounting entries are made within the framework of the fundamental accounting equation (assets equal liabilities plus fects on the elements of this equation. The advantages of the double-entry system include built-in controls which automatically call attention to many types of errors and offer assurance that once assets are recorded, they will not be forgotten or simply overlooked. Management's responsibility for the custody of resources entrusted to it is thus strengthened by the internal discipline of the double-entry system. The self-balancing nature of this accounting model facilitates the preparation of a complete integrated set of financial statements as frequently as desired.

The double-entry system is in practically universal use; it takes its name from the fact that equal debit and credit entries are made for every transaction. The terms *debit* and *credit* can be related to the equation $A = L + OE$ in the following way:

Asset accounts	= *Liability + Owners' Equity accounts*
Increases are recorded by debits	*Increases are recorded by credits*
Decreases are recorded by credits	*Decreases are recorded by debits*

Assets and liabilities are the two independent variables in the above equation; the dependent variable, owners' equity, is derived from the valuation assigned to assets and liabilities. One source of change in the owners' equity is the change in the *net assets* (assets minus liabilities) as a result of operations, measured by two classes of accounts—revenue and expenses. Revenue accounts measure the inflow of assets resulting from producing and distributing goods and services to customers. Expense accounts measure the outflow of assets necessary to produce and distribute these goods and services. The change in the net assets as a result of these two flows is reflected in the owners' equity. Revenue and expense accounts are subject to the rules of debit and credit which were applied to assets, liabilities, and owners' equity accounts. The application of the rules of debit and credit for revenue and expenses may be summarized as follows:

Expenses	*Revenue*
Increases in expenses are recorded by debits	*Increases in revenue are recorded by credits*
Decreases in expenses are recorded by credits	*Decreases in revenue are recorded by debits*

As the terms *debit* and *credit* are used in accounting, they have no meaning except as a directive for recording data in ledger accounts.

Debit refers to the left side of the account and credit refers to the right side.

The accounting period

The normal accounting period is one year, beginning on any given day and ending 12 months later. A *calendar-year* accounting period ends on December 31; all other 12-month accounting periods are known as *fiscal years.* Business firms frequently adopt accounting periods that end when operations are at a low ebb in order to simplify year-end procedures and facilitate a better measurement of income and financial position. Such an accounting period is referred to as a *natural business year* because it conforms to the natural annual cycle of the enterprise.

Reports issued for shorter periods, such as one quarter of the year or one month, are called *interim reports.* These interim reports on the operating results of listed corporations are needed to assist investors in reaching decisions to buy, hold, or sell securities. Traditionally, interim reports have not been audited by certified public accountants. At present, however, there is a new awareness of the need for CPAs to review their clients' interim reports to assure consistency with the annual financial statements.[1]

The accounting cycle

The *accounting cycle* is a complete sequence of accounting procedures which are repeated in the same order during each accounting period. The cycle in a traditional manual system (and with modifications in an EDP system) includes:

1 Recording transactions in the books of original entry, the journals
2 Classifying data by posting from the journals to the ledger
3 Summarizing data from the ledger on a trial balance
4 Adjusting, correcting, and updating recorded data after due consideration of all pertinent facts
5 Summarizing adjusted data in the form of financial statements
6 Closing the accounts to summarize the activities of the period
7 Reversing certain adjusting entries to facilitate the recording process in subsequent periods[2]

When these steps are completed, the cycle begins again for the next period.

A brief explanation of journals, the ledger, and the various steps of the operating cycle is presented in the following sections.

---

[1] For a discussion of the special measurement problems relating to interim financial reports, see *APB Opinion No. 28,* "Interim Financial Reporting," AICPA (New York: 1973).
[2] This is an optional step, as explained on pp. 57–59.

The journals: books of original entry

The information shown on business papers is recorded in chronological order in the appropriate journals. Since a journal is organized chronologically by transaction, we may say that the unit of organization for a journal is the individual transaction. Although a very small business could conceivably record all transactions in a single journal, this approach is seldom used. When numerous transactions of the same nature occur (such as transactions involving the receipt of cash), a special journal can be designed as a more efficient means of entering and summarizing these transactions possessing a common characteristic. Several types of special journals are illustrated later in this chapter.

The journalizing process requires analyzing transactions in terms of debits and credits to the accounts they affect: (1) assets, (2) liabilities, (3) owners' equity, (4) revenue, and (5) expenses. In this book our interest in journal entries lies in their usefulness as a clear, concise analytical device. To portray a business transaction in a journal entry, we must identify and classify each important element of the transaction.

The ledger

We have indicated how the information on business papers is analyzed and expressed in terms of debits and credits by entry in the journals. Next is the step of transferring this information to accounts in the ledger. This transfer process is called *posting,* which means that each debit and credit amount in the journals is listed in the appropriate account in the ledger.

A ledger consists of a number of accounts. Each account represents stored information about a particular kind of asset, liability, owners' equity, revenue, or expense. As previously indicated, the transaction is the unit of organization for the journal; similarly, the account is the unit of organization for the ledger. When computers are used, accounting information may be stored on magnetic tapes rather than on the loose-leaf pages of a traditional ledger. However, the printed form of ledger page is most convenient for our illustrations and analyses and is still used by many businesses. For our purposes ledger accounts are a conceptual device for discussion of accounting principles rather than specific examples of system design.

Ledger accounts are often classified as *nominal* (temporary) and *real* (permanent) accounts. The nominal accounts are closed at the end of the period by transferring their balances to other accounts. The real accounts are the balance sheet accounts which remain open and normally show a balance after the accounting records are closed. During the accounting period, a balance sheet account or an income statement account may contain both real and nominal elements. In this situation, it is often referred to as a *mixed account.* For example, Unexpired Insurance may include both unexpired premiums and expired premiums before the end-of-period adjusting entries are made. When the time arrives for preparing financial statements, the nominal and real portions of a mixed account are separated by adjusting entries. Thus the nominal element in the Unexpired Insurance account would be transferred to Insurance Expense.

The account form shown below is illustrative of a ledger account and the information found therein.

Accounts Receivable								Account No. (7)
Date 19—		Explanation	Ref.	Amount	Date 19—		Explanation	Ref.	Amount
Jan.	1	Balance		12,682	Jan.	24		J70	150
	31		S50	42,460	Jan.	31		CR42	31,780
					Jan.	31	Balance		23,212
				55,142					55,142
Feb.	1	Balance		23,212					

In many cases greater detail is desired for a particular account included in the general ledger, and a **subsidiary** ledger is set up to contain the details supporting the main or **controlling** account. For example, the controlling account, Accounts Receivable, is adequate for general purposes; however, in order to facilitate the preparation of monthly bills, it is desirable to have each customer's purchases and payments separately classified. In such situations a subsidiary ledger is established to provide the desired information. At all times, the total of the subsidiary ledger should agree with the controlling account in the general ledger.

In addition to the use of a controlling account and subsidiary ledger for accounts receivable, other common examples of this concept include:

A Vouchers Payable controlling account supported by a voucher register (illustrated later in this chapter)

A Plant and Equipment controlling account supported by a plant and equipment subsidiary ledger

A Capital Stock controlling account supported by a stockholders' ledger

Separate sudsidiary ledgers not only provide the detailed information needed for certain purposes, but also strengthen internal control by quickly bringing to light most kinds of errors in recording transactions.

Trial balance

At the end of each period a trial balance of the general ledger is prepared to determine that the mechanics of the recording and posting operations have been carried out accurately. The trial balance consists of a listing of all accounts and their balances; it provides evidence that an equality of debits and credits exists in the ledger. The account balances are then used as a basis for preparing the financial statements. The trial balance illustrated below summarizes the account balances in the general ledger of Merchandise Mart, Inc.

MERCHANDISE MART, INC.
Trial Balance
January 31, 19___

	Debit	Credit
Cash	$ 15,450	
Accounts receivable	23,212	
Allowance for doubtful accounts		$ 850
Inventory, Jan. 31	47,860	
Unexpired insurance	200	
Land	45,000	
Building	80,000	
Accumulated depreciation: building		10,000
Equipment	16,000	
Accumulated depreciation: equipment		4,000
Vouchers payable		12,000
Notes payable		10,000
Advances from customers		500
Capital stock, $10 par		75,000
Paid-in capital in excess of par		75,000
Retained earnings		34,363
Dividends	5,000	
Net sales		55,627
Cost of goods sold	26,000	
Salaries expense	9,540	
Advertising expense	4,620	
Delivery expense	2,180	
Property taxes expense	1,220	
Interest expense	80	
Miscellaneous expenses	978	
Totals	$277,340	$277,340

Schedules of the subsidiary ledgers may also be prepared to prove that their balances agree with the balances in the related controlling accounts which are part of the general ledger. These schedules may also be used for other purposes; for example, a copy of the accounts receivable schedule (see page 46) may be sent to the credit department for use in following up collections and as a basis for setting future credit policy.

MERCHANDISE MART, INC.
Schedule of Accounts Receivable
January 31, 19__

D. A. Adams	$ 1,500
R. O. Black	3,410
(not listed here to avoid unnecessary detail)	18,302
Balance of Accounts Receivable controlling account	$23,212

The number of accounts, type of statements, and other aspects of the accounting system should be geared to meet the requirements of a particular business; the preceding examples merely suggest the type of system employed in many small and medium-sized businesses.

Use of journals

A growing enterprise is usually compelled to modify its accounting system to handle efficiently the increasing volume of transactions. One purpose of the accounting system is to facilitate the summarization of a large volume of transactions into meaningful totals for various uses. The basic accounting problems for large and small businesses are quite similar; however, the procedures adopted for accumulating and distributing accounting data are frequently quite different. When there is a large volume of data, procedures must be developed which permit the data to be handled rapidly.

Every business, regardless of its size, has certain established routines which are basic to the collection of financial data. For example, documents are used to initiate transactions or to report their occurrence. As the complexity of the business increases, methods such as the preparation of multicopies of these documents may be instituted; the use of various types of billing machines and mechanical registers may be begun; and in some cases preprinted and standard forms may be employed. In this way the time lag between the initiation of a transaction and its ultimate disposition can be shortened. Obviously, as the volume of similar transactions increases, the degree of automation possible in handling the data increases.

The great majority of financial transactions fall into one of four types, and for that reason most of the data can be handled by using four special multicolumn journals and a general journal. The four special journals are: sales journal, voucher register (or purchases journal), cash receipts journal, and a cash payments journal (or check register). The primary transaction types and the associated journals are:

Type of transaction	Journal
Sales of merchandise on credit	Sales journal
Purchases of merchandise, supplies, etc., on credit	Voucher register (or purchases journal)
Receipts of cash	Cash receipts journal
Payments of cash	Cash payments journal (or check register)
Other transactions	General journal

A set of five journals, similar to those listed, can handle the transactions of many small businesses. The general journal is necessary, regardless of the special journals involved, to record unusual and nonrepetitive transactions and also to record adjusting and closing entries at the end of the period.

The following journal forms are presented as an illustration of one possible form for each journal. The columnar headings obviously will be dictated by the circumstances of each business.

Illustration Merchandise Mart, Inc., uses special multicolumn journals to facilitate the handling of the transactions involving sales, purchases, cash collections, and disbursements. Subsidiary ledgers are used for accounts receivable and accounts payable.

The procedure for recording sales requires that all credit sales be entered at the gross amount in the sales journal and all cash sales in the cash receipts journal. There is no need for a breakdown of sales by item or department and the accounts receivable ledger is posted from the sales journal. When the individual accounts are posted, a check mark ($\sqrt{}$) is placed beside the amount in the journal. The total of the one money column is posted monthly as a debit to Accounts Receivable, account no. 7, and a credit to Sales, account no. 115. All credit sales are subject to terms 2/10, n/30.

All cash receipts are recorded in the cash receipts journal (see page 49) from a detailed list of checks received by mail, a statement by the internal auditor of daily cash sales and store collections, and a statement by the treasurer of other cash sources. If a credit customer takes the cash discount offered, it is recorded at the time cash is received. The customers' accounts are posted daily from the cash receipts journal. The sundry general ledger accounts are posted weekly from the Other Accounts columns, and the column totals are posted monthly except for the Other Accounts columns, for which totals are not posted (N/P). The treasurer is furnished with a daily statement of receipts to facilitate cash planning.

Merchandise Mart, Inc., has found that control over cash disbursements is improved with the use of the voucher system. The voucher reg-

Sales Journal				**(Page 50)**

Date 19__		Customer	Inv. no.	Ref.	Amount
Jan.	2	D. A. Adams	1001	√	600
	3	R. O. Black	1002	√	850
	5	Dan Crane	1003	√	1,020
	28	A. R. Taylor	1025	√	690
	29	Jack Urbanks	1026	√	1,215
					42,460
					(7) (115)
					Dr, A/R Cr, Sales

ister is a subsidiary ledger record of vouchers payable, as well as the book of original entry for purchases. The system of internal control requires that all checks be supported by a voucher. At the time a voucher is paid, the check number is entered in the appropriate column of the voucher register. Any vouchers entered in the register without check numbers are unpaid and constitute the liability to vendors at that time. Note in the illustrative journal on page 49 that voucher no. 1500 has not been paid and that voucher no. 1501 was paid by check no. 1001. The totals of the special columns are posted monthly and the individual accounts in the Other Accounts columns are posted at least once a month. The total liability represented by unpaid vouchers may include certain vouchers from the preceding month.

In this system the check register is designed as the book of original entry for all cash disbursements. The requirement that all disbursements be supported by a voucher means that only one column is needed in the check register. The total of this one column is posted to the Vouchers Payable account as a debit and the Cash account as a credit. Recording the payment in the subsidiary record of vouchers payable, the voucher register, is done by simply entering the check number in the voucher register. The totals of the check register are posted monthly; however, the treasurer is notified daily of the total checks written.

The general journal is used to record all transactions which do not involve accounts represented in the special journals and for adjusting, closing, and reversing entries. The vast majority of all transactions will normally be recorded in the special journals.

The posting instructions for the illustrated entries in the general journal are: Post the debits and credits to the accounts in the general

Cash Receipts Journal

Date 19__	Explanation	Sales discounts	Cash	Other accounts Name	Ref.	Amount	AR ✓	Accounts receivable Amount	Cash sales	Other accounts Name	Ref.	Amount
				Debits				**Credits**				
Jan. 2	1st Union Bank		10,000							Notes Payable	71	10,000
5	D. A. Adams	17	833				✓	850				
6	Cash sales		452						452			
8	Dan Crane	2	98	Notes Receivable	8	920	✓	1,020				
31	Cash sales		800						800			
		256	46,807			1,240		31,780	3,423			13,100
		(117)	(1)			N/P		(7)	(115)			N/P

Voucher Register

Date 19__	Payee	Explanation	Ck. no.	Vou. no.	Credit vouchers payable	Purchases	Freight-in	Accrued payroll	Other accounts Account	Ref.	Amount
						Debits					
Jan. 2	Adams Supply Co.	Merchandise		1500	8,000	8,000					
2	Bross Trucking	Freight	1001	1501	50		50				
5	1st Union Bank	Pay note and interest	1002	1502	4,040				Notes Payable	71	4,000
									Interest Expense	170	40
31	Ace Co.	Merchandise		1598	900	900					
					44,920	31,680	980	8,220			4,040
					(70)	(104)	(105)	(72)			(N/P)

		Check Register			(Page 60)
Date 19__		Payee	Vou. no.	Check no.	Amount
Jan.	5	Bross Trucking	1501	1001	50
	5	1st Union Bank	1502	1002	4,040
	31	Dart Brothers	1593	1090	570
					42,690
					(70) (1) Dr, V/P Cr, Cash

ledger indicated by the account numbers in the ledger page column. Post the $150 credit to the accounts receivable subsidiary ledger to the credit of John Dock. The check mark indicates that the posting to the subsidiary ledger has been completed.

		General Journal			(Page 43)
Date 19__		Account titles and explanations	LP	Debit	Credit
June	30	Interest Expense	170	30	
		Accrued Interest Payable	72		30
		To record interest accrued on notes payable at end of fiscal period.			
	30	Allowance for Doubtful Accounts	8	150	
		Accounts Receivable–John Dock .	7/√		150
		To write off uncollectible account. . . .			

ADJUSTING ENTRIES

Financial reporting on an annual, quarterly, or monthly basis requires the accountant to summarize the operations of the business for a specific time period. Basically, the two types of adjusting entries are those (1) to recognize *deferred* costs and revenues and (2) to record *accrued* expenses and revenues. Transactions which were recorded during the period in balance sheet or income statement accounts may affect two or more accounting periods, and an end-of-period adjustment may therefore be needed. Some financial events not recognized on a day-to-day basis must be recorded at the end of the period *to bring the accounts up*

to date. If one should choose to record depreciation daily or to accrue interest expense daily, no adjustment for depreciation or interest expense would be needed at the end of the accounting period except to correct errors.

Note that almost every adjusting entry affects both a balance sheet account and an income statement account. This characteristic of adjusting entries reflects their dual purpose of (1) proper valuation of assets and liabilities and (2) proper measurement of net income.

In illustrating the wide variety of adjusting entries, it will be helpful to classify them into the following major groups:

Apportionment of recorded costs
Apportionment of recorded revenue
Accrual of unrecorded expenses
Accrual of unrecorded revenue
Valuation of accounts receivables

Apportionment of recorded costs

Costs which will benefit more than one accounting period are frequently incurred. These costs must be apportioned between periods in a manner which approximates the usefulness derived from the goods and services in the production of revenue; this apportionment process is a necessary step in determining net income of each period.

The assignment of the periodic depreciation charge is an example of a cost-apportionment adjusting entry, as shown below:

Depreciation Expense	*12,000*	
Accumulated Depreciation: Building		*12,000*
To record depreciation expense for one year.		

The periodic depreciation expense is considered a cost of production or a period expense to be deducted from revenue, depending on the nature of the asset and the service performed. In the balance sheet, accumulated depreciation is deducted from the cost of the asset.

Cost apportionment is also involved in accounting for other prepayments. However, the adjusting entry will vary depending on the accounting procedure followed in recording the original transaction.

To illustrate, assume that office supplies are acquired during the year at a cost of $5,000. At the end of the accounting period a physical inventory reveals that supplies on hand are worth $550. At the time the supplies were acquired, the $5,000 purchase may have been debited to (1) an asset account, or (2) an expense account. The required adjusting entry for each situation is as follows:

Purchase Debited to Asset Account The adjusting entry required is to transfer the *expired* portion of the cost to an *expense* account.

	Inventory of Office Supplies		Office Supplies Expense	
Dec. 31				
Balance	5,000			
Adjusting entry		4,450	4,450	

Purchase Debited to Expense Account The adjusting entry required is to transfer the *unexpired* portion of the cost to an *asset* account as illustrated below.

	Inventory of Office Supplies		Office Supplies Expense	
Dec. 31				
Balance			5,000	
Adjusting entry	550			550

Under either original recording, the final result is the same. There is an asset valued at $550 and an expense of $4,450. In both cases the amount of the unexpired cost was determined; an adjusting entry is necessary to make the respective accounts agree with the information available to the accountant. Adjusting entries are based on recorded data in the relevant accounts and the additional information ascertained by the accountant.

Apportionment of recorded revenue

Occasionally a business will receive payment for goods and services before the goods are delivered or the service performed. A liability exists which will be satisfied when performance takes place. When cash is received, the original transaction may be recorded in either of two ways: (1) a liability account may be credited, or (2) a revenue account may be credited.

Assume that customers paid in $500,000 for magazine subscriptions during the current year; however, $75,000 represented payments for copies to be delivered in subsequent periods. The adjusting entries for each of the two methods of recording the cash receipt are:

Liability Account Credited upon Receipt of Cash The required adjusting entry to recognize the *earned* revenue for the period appears below:

	Unearned Subscriptions Revenue		Subscriptions Revenue	
Dec. 31				
Balance		500,000		
Adjusting entry	425,000			425,000

Revenue Account Credited upon Receipt of Cash The required adjusting entry is to transfer the *unearned* revenue to a liability account.

	Unearned Subscriptions Revenue		Subscriptions Revenue	
Dec. 31				
Balance				500,000
Adjusting entry		75,000	75,000	

Accrual of unrecorded expenses

The incurring of certain expenses is related to the passage of time. These expenses are usually not recorded until payment is made, unless the end of the accounting period comes before the required date of payment. Interest charges and salaries are typical of the expenses which accrue with the passage of time and which are recorded only when paid, except when the end of the accounting period occurs between the time the expense was incurred and the payment is due. In order to achieve a realistic measurement of the expenses of the period, an adjusting entry is necessary to record such an expense and the corresponding liability.

For example, interest of $18,000 on a $400,000 note payable is paid on March 1 and September 1 of each year. If the expenses and liabilities are to be reported properly at December 31, a year-end adjusting entry should be made as shown below:

Interest Expense	12,000	
Accrued Interest Payable		12,000
To record the interest owed on a 9%, $400,000 note for four		
months to Dec. 31.		

Accrual of unrecorded revenue

Revenue which has been earned but not recorded must be recognized at the end of the accounting period. For example, revenue which is earned on assets leased to others or on interest-bearing loans is seldom recorded until the cash is received, except at the end of the accounting period. In order to measure properly the results of operations and to avoid shifting income between periods, revenue should be recognized in the period earned.

To illustrate, assume that rents totaling $625 which have been earned but not collected for the month of December have not been recorded. The following year-end adjusting entry is required for a complete reporting of revenue and assets.

Rents Receivable		*625*
Rental Revenue		*625*
To record rents earned during December.		

Valuation of receivables

A policy of making sales on credit almost inevitably results in some receivables which prove wholly or partially uncollectible. To achieve a logical matching of revenue and related expenses, the estimated expense arising from sales on credit should be recognized in the period in which the sales occur. This estimate of probable expense from the granting of credit requires a year-end adjusting entry to revise the valuation originally assigned to accounts receivable. Once the estimate of the doubtful accounts is established, the following adjusting entry is made:

Doubtful Accounts Expense		*2,500*
Allowance for Doubtful Accounts		*2,500*
To record estimated doubtful accounts expense.		

The Doubtful Accounts Expense account is usually included as an operating expense on the income statement. Some accountants would prefer to deduct it directly from sales to derive a measure of net sales, since no revenue will be realized if the receivables are not collected. On the balance sheet the credit balance of the allowance account is deducted from accounts receivable to indicate the net collections expected.

CLOSING PROCEDURES

Closing revenue and expense accounts

Revenue and expense accounts are closed at the end of each accounting period by transferring the balances in each such account to a summary account, Income Summary. Revenue and expense accounts are merely extensions of the owners' equity account and are used to provide additional information about the business in each operating period. Once this information has been summarized, the accounts have served their purpose and the net increase or decrease in owners' equity is transferred to an owners' equity account. Thus the closing of the accounts keeps separate the accounting activities of each period.

If we assume that a Subscriptions Revenue account after adjustment has a credit balance of $425,000 the closing entry will be:

Subscriptions Revenue	425,000	
Income Summary		425,000
To close the Subscriptions Revenue account.		

The balance in the Subscriptions Revenue account is now zero. Temporarily, the Income Summary account will indicate a credit balance of $425,000. All other revenue accounts will be closed similarly.

To close an expense account, one must transfer its debit balance to the left side of the Income Summary account. The following journal entry to close a Salaries Expense account with a debit balance of $61,625 is illustrative of this phase of the closing process.

Income Summary	61,625	
Salaries Expense		61,625
To close the Salaries Expense account.		

The expense account now has a zero balance, and the balance in the Income Summary account is reduced by the debit for salaries expense. All other expense accounts will be closed similarly. When there are a number of expense accounts, each one can be closed individually to the Income Summary account or all of them can be closed in one journal entry, with one debit to the Income Summary account and a separate credit for each expense account.

Closing inventory and related accounts

The entry to establish the cost of goods sold for the period and the ending inventory balance may be thought of as an adjusting entry; however, since there may be little need for a ledger account for cost of goods sold, the adjusting and closing entries are frequently combined. This procedure is accomplished by closing the beginning inventory account, purchases, and all related accounts to the Income Summary. The ending inventory is then established by debiting the Inventory account and crediting the Income Summary. The balance remaining in the Income Summary account is the cost of goods sold for the period. To illustrate, let us assume the following facts: January 1 inventory, $80,000; purchases, $275,000; freight-in, $40,000; purchase returns and allowances, $2,500; December 31 inventory, including applicable freight, $60,000. The journal entries required to close the accounts and to record the ending inventory are shown below:

Purchase Returns and Allowances	2,500	
Income Summary	392,500	
Inventory, Jan. 1		80,000
Purchases		275,000
Freight-in		40,000
To close beginning inventory and cost of goods acquired for the period.		
Inventory, Dec. 31	60,000	
Income Summary		60,000
To record the ending inventory.		

The debit balance in the Income Summary account after these two entries is $332,500, the cost of goods sold for the period. Some accountants prefer to use a separate account, Cost of Goods Sold, to summarize the merchandising accounts before these costs are transferred to the Income Summary. The entry *reflecting cost of goods sold in a separate account* would be as follows:

Purchase Returns and Allowances	2,500	
Inventory, Dec. 31	60,000	
Cost of Goods Sold	332,500	
Inventory, Jan. 1		80,000
Purchases		275,000
Freight-in		40,000
To record cost of goods sold for the period.		

The entry required to close the Cost of Goods Sold account is illustrated below:

Income Summary	332,500	
Cost of Goods Sold		332,500
To close the Cost of Goods Sold account.		

Closing the Income Summary account

At this point the balance of the Income Summary account indicates the net income or loss of the business as a result of the operations of the period. A credit balance in the Income Summary account indicates a profitable year and an increase in owners' equity. A debit balance indicates a loss from operations and a decrease in owners' equity: that is, the expenses of the period exceeded the revenue. The Income Summary account is closed by transferring its balance to Retained Earnings.

REVERSING ENTRIES

After the accounts have been adjusted and closed at the end of the year, reversing entries **may be made** bearing the date of the new accounting period. The purpose of the reversing entries is to simplify the recording of routine transactions by disposing of the accrued items (assets and liabilities), which were entered in balance sheet accounts through the adjusting entries. A reversing entry, as the name implies, is the exact reverse of an adjusting entry. It consists of the same accounts and dollar amounts as the adjusting entry, but the debits and credits are reversed and the date is the beginning of the new period.

For example, assume that in Year 1 X Company borrowed $200,000 at 6% on a long-term note payable with interest of $3,000 payable every three months. The first payment of interest was made on October 31, Year 1; the next interest payment is due on January 31, Year 2. The company is on a calendar-year basis. Before the accounts are closed on December 31, Year 1, an adjusting entry must be made debiting Interest Expense and crediting Accrued Interest Payable for $2,000, the amount of interest applicable to November and December. If no reversing entry is made on January 1, Year 2, the next quarterly interest payment of $3,000 at January 31, Year 2, will be recorded by debiting Accrued Interest Payable $2,000, debiting Interest Expense $1,000, and crediting Cash $3,000. However, assume that on January 1, Year 2, the following reversing entry is made:

```
Year 2
Jan. 1  Accrued Interest Payable . . . . . . . . . . . . . . . . .  2,000
           Interest Expense  . . . . . . . . . . . . . . . . .           2,000
        To reverse the interest accrual made Dec. 31, Year 1.
```

This reversing entry has eliminated the liability account Accrued Interest Payable and has caused the Interest Expense account to start off the new year with a $2,000 credit balance. Consequently, the cash payment of three months' interest at January 31 will not need to be apportioned. The January 31 entry will consist simply of a debit to Interest Expense for $3,000 and a credit to Cash for $3,000. In other words, the interest payment at January 31 (by reason of the reversing entry) can be recorded in exactly the same manner as the three other quarterly interest payments during the year. After the January 31 interest payment has been recorded, the Interest Expense account for the new year will contain a debit for $3,000 and a credit for $2,000 which produces the correct debit balance of $1,000 representing January interest expense.

An argument for reversing entries is apparent from this example. Clerical employees with limited knowledge of accounting can be instructed to follow a standard procedure for recording all operating transactions of a given category. The reversing entries as well as the year-end adjusting entries are recorded in the general journal by an accountant who understands the issues involved.

General guidelines for reversing entries

When a *policy of using reversing entries is adopted,* the following general rules should be followed:

1 When an adjusting journal entry creates an asset or liability account which is not normally used during the accounting period, a reversing entry is required. Thus adjustments to record expense and revenue would be reversed because asset and liability accounts such as Rents Receivable and Accrued Interest Payable are not used in the normal course of accounting during the period. Similarly, if payments for insurance and supplies during the period are recorded in expense accounts or if revenues received in advance during the period are recorded in revenue accounts, the adjusting entries would have to be reversed because asset and liability accounts not used during the period would be established by the adjusting entries.

2 When an adjusting entry adjusts an asset or liability account which is normally used to record transactions during the period, no reversing entry is required. Thus, if acquisitions of supplies and other short-term prepayments are recorded during the period in asset accounts or if revenues received in advance are recorded during the period in liability accounts, the adjusting entries would merely bring *existing* asset and liability balances up to date and no reversing entry would be required. For the same reason adjusting entries for depreciation and estimated doubtful accounts are not reversed.

We have previously suggested that reversing of certain adjusting entries is an *optional procedure* designed to simplify recording of recurring transactions. Another way of stating this is that reversing entries are never required as long as adjusting entries bring all asset and liability accounts up to date. If asset and liability accounts are correct, expense and revenue accounts also will be correctly stated.

To illustrate three alternative approaches to the recording of adjusting and reversing entries, let us go back to the X Company example on page 57. Use of the three approaches described below would result in *identical balances* in the Interest Expense and Accrued Interest Payable accounts at the end of Year 2, as illustrated below:

(1) No reversing entry; first interest payment in Year 2 is apportioned	(2) Reversing entry is made; all interest payments in Year 2 are recorded in Interest Expense	(3) No reversing entry is made; all interest payments in Year 2 are recorded in Interest Expense
Interest Expense	**Interest Expense**	**Interest Expense**
(a) 10,000	(a) 12,000 Bal. 2,000	(a) 12,000
(b) 2,000	(b) 2,000	
Accrued Interest Payable	**Accrued Interest Payable**	**Accrued Interest Payable**
(a) 2,000 Bal. 2,000	(b) 2,000	Bal. 2,000
(b) 2,000		

(a) Payment of interest in Year 2; Cash account was credited.
(b) Adjusting entry at Dec. 31, Year 2.

Note that no adjusting entry was required under alternative (3) because the accrued interest payable at the end of Year 2 was the same as it was at the end of Year 1. If the accrued interest at the end of Year 2 was other than $2,000, an adjusting entry would be required to Accrued Interest Payable with a corresponding debit or credit to Interest Expense.

THE WORK SHEET

Accountants have found the work sheet to be an invaluable aid in facilitating the year-end procedures and the preparation of financial statements. The work sheet is especially useful in avoiding errors in the journal and ledger in more complex situations.

Purpose of the work sheet

A work sheet is a columnar sheet of paper designed to facilitate the organization and arrangement of the accounting data required at the end of the period. It is designed to minimize errors by automatically bringing to light many types of discrepancies which might otherwise be entered in the permanent accounting records. Accountants prepare the work sheet as an informal record strictly for their own purposes. It does not replace any record or financial statement and is never presented as the end result of the accountants' work. The work sheet is a tool which permits the adjusting and closing entries and the financial statements to be prepared informally before any part of this work is formalized.

The work sheet may be thought of as a testing ground on which the ledger accounts are adjusted, balanced, and arranged in the general form of financial statements. The satisfactory completion of the work sheet provides considerable assurance that all the details of the year-end accounting procedures have been properly brought together. The finished work sheet then serves as the source or guide for the preparation of the formal financial statements and the adjusting and closing entries which are recorded in the general journal and posted to the ledger.

Illustration of work sheet for a merchandising company

A commonly used form of work sheet with appropriate headings for Village Merchandising Co. for Year 4 is illustrated on pages 62 and 63. The work-sheet heading should contain the name of the company, the title (work sheet), and the period covered. The body of this work sheet contains six pairs of money columns, each pair consisting of a debit and credit column. The procedures required in the preparation of the work sheet are described below.

 1 Enter the ledger account titles and balances on the work sheet, using the first two money columns—the Unadjusted Trial Balance. The accountant can often save time and effort by arranging the accounts in the order in which they will appear on the financial statements. Frequently several adjustments will affect a single account; consequently, several lines should be left blank following this account to facilitate listing the adjustments.

 2 Enter the adjustments in the Adjustments columns. Adjusting entries should always be entered on the work sheet before they are journalized. One of the functions of the work sheet is to establish the correctness of the adjusting entries. The information used as the basis for the adjustments illustrated on the work sheet for Village Merchandising Co. is stated below:

 (a) The marketable securities are government bonds on which accrued interest receivable amounts to $33 at December 31.

 (b) The accounts receivable arising from sales of the current period which are expected to be uncollectible are estimated to be $\frac{1}{2}$ of 1% of gross sales.

 (c) Accounts totaling $520 are considered to be uncollectible and the credit manager has authorized the write-off of these accounts.

(d) The balances in the Short-Term Prepayments account are as follows:

	Jan. 1	Dec. 31
Unexpired insurance	$ 750	$ 450
Inventory of miscellaneous supplies	600	700
Prepaid rent	150	400
Totals	$1,500	$1,550

All cash payments for these items have been recorded in expense accounts. Village Merchandising Co. **does not reverse** any adjusting entries.

(e) The furniture and fixtures are estimated to have an economic life of 10 years, with no residual value at the end of that time.

(f) Accrued interest payable on the notes payable amounted to $40 at December 31.

(g) Salaries accrued since the last payday total $818 at December 31.

(h) The inventory on December 31 totals $28,900, and income taxes are estimated at $670.

After the adjustments **(a)** through **(g)** are entered on the work sheet, the Adjustments columns must be totaled to prove the equality of the debits and credits. Without this proof of arithmetical accuracy, errors are likely to be carried forward in the remaining work.

3 Determine the new account balances and enter these in the Adjusted Trial Balance columns. The purpose of this step is to prove the accuracy of the work of combining the adjustments and the original balances. The Adjusted Trial Balance columns are often omitted from the work sheet if adjustments are few.

4 Extend each balance from the adjusted trial balance or from the first four columns into the Income Statement, Retained Earnings, or Balance Sheet columns.

5 Enter the ending inventory in the Income Statement credit column and the Balance Sheet debit column. This procedure in effect deducts the ending inventory from the total goods available for sale to leave the costs comprising the cost of goods sold in the Income Statement columns.

6 Total the Income Statement columns. The balancing figure is the income or loss for the period before income taxes.

7 Compute the income taxes and related income tax liability at the applicable rates based on the income before taxes. Since the Adjustments columns have been balanced, this adjustment is entered in the Income Statement debit column as income taxes expense and in the Balance Sheet credit column as a liability.

8 Balance the Income Statement columns with the income taxes included. The difference between the credit and debit columns in this illustration represents the earnings of the business entity. The balancing figure is entered in the debit column of the Income Statement to achieve equality and in the credit column of the retained earnings reconciliation. The income after taxes represents an increase in the stockholders' equity as a result of operations.

9 Balance the Retained Earnings columns and enter the difference in the debit column and in the credit column of the Balance Sheet. This adjusts the retained earnings balance for changes during the period.

VILLAGE MERCHANDISING CO.
Work Sheet
For Year Ended December 31, Year 4

	Unadjusted trial balance		Adjustments		Adjusted trial balance		Income statement		Retained earnings		Balance sheet	
	Debit	Credit	Debit	Credit	Debit	Credit	Debit	Credit	Debit	Credit	Debit	Credit
Cash	8,650				8,650						8,650	
Marketable securities	2,000				2,000						2,000	
Accounts receivable	15,700			(c) 520	15,180						15,180	
Allowance for doubtful accounts		800	(c) 520	(b) 875		1,155						1,155
Inventory (periodic system)	28,000				28,000		28,000	28,900			28,900	
Short-term prepayments	1,500		(d) 50		1,550						1,550	
Furniture and fixtures	6,000				6,000						6,000	
Accumulated depreciation		1,800		(e) 600		2,400						2,400
Accounts payable		10,000				10,000						10,000
Notes payable		4,000				4,000						4,000
Capital stock		40,000				40,000						40,000
Retained earnings, Jan. 1, Year 4		3,170				3,170				3,170		
Dividends	1,500				1,500				1,500			
Sales		175,000				175,000		175,000				
Sales returns & allowances	2,500				2,500		2,500					
Sales discounts	3,150				3,150		3,150					
Purchases	128,000				128,000		128,000					
Purchase returns & allowances		3,000				3,000		3,000				

Worksheet (columns: Trial Balance Dr/Cr · Adjustments Dr/Cr · Adjusted Trial Balance Dr/Cr · Income Statement Dr/Cr · Retained Earnings / Balance Sheet Dr/Cr)

Account	TB Dr	TB Cr	Adj Dr	Adj Cr	Adj TB Dr	Adj TB Cr	IS Dr	IS Cr	Dr	Cr
Salaries expense	22,500		(g) 818		23,318		23,318			
Rent expense	5,050			(d) 250	4,800		4,800			
Advertising expense	9,000				9,000		9,000			
Janitorial expense	1,500				1,500		1,500			
Miscellaneous expenses	2,000			(d) 100	1,900		1,900			
Interest expense	120		(f) 40		160		160			
Property taxes expense	600				600		600			
Accrued interest receivable			(a) 33		33				33	
Interest revenue				(a) 33		33		33		
Doubtful accounts expense			(b) 875		875		875			
Insurance expense			(d) 300		300		300			
Depreciation expense			(e) 600		600		600			
Accrued interest payable				(f) 40		40				40
Accrued salaries payable				(g) 818		818				818
Totals	237,770	237,770	3,236	3,236	239,616	239,616	204,703	206,933		
Income before income taxes							2,230			2,230
Totals							206,933	206,933		
Income taxes expense									670	670
Net income									1,560	1,560
Totals									1,500	4,730
Retained earnings, Dec. 31, Year 4									3,230	
Totals									4,730	4,730
									62,313	62,313

63

10 Total the Balance Sheet columns. Considerable assurance of the arithmetical accuracy of the year-end procedures is provided if these two columns balance. The Balance Sheet columns prove the equation that assets are equal to the total of liabilities and stockholders' equity.

Although the work sheet proves the mathematical accuracy of what has been done, it does not prove that some important adjustments have not been omitted or that the amounts used in making the adjustments were correct.

Work Sheet and Year-End Procedures The accountant's work sheet is the source of the formal adjusting entries. Once the entries are made on the work sheet, the accountant can easily record the identical information in the general journal and the ledger. The adjusting journal entries for Village Merchandising Co. for Year 4 are illustrated below and on page 65.

Adjusting Entries

(a)	Accrued Interest Receivable	33	
	Interest Revenue		33
	To accrue interest on marketable securities owned.		
(b)	Doubtful Accounts Expense	875	
	Allowance for Doubtful Accounts		875
	To increase the allowance for doubtful accounts by ½ of 1% of gross sales.		
(c)	Allowance for Doubtful Accounts	520	
	Accounts Receivable		520
	To write off uncollectible accounts.		
(d)	Short-Term Prepayments	50	
	Insurance Expense	300	
	Rent Expense		250
	Miscellaneous Expenses		100
	To adjust short-term prepayments to year-end balance.		
(e)	Depreciation Expense	600	
	Accumulated Depreciation		600
	To record depreciation at 10% of cost.		
(f)	Interest Expense	40	
	Accrued Interest Payable		40
	To accrue interest expense on notes payable.		

(g) Salaries Expense 818
  Accrued Salaries Payable   818
  To accrue unpaid salaries.

(h) Income Taxes Expense 670
  Income Taxes Payable   670
  To record estimated income tax liability.

The closing entries can also be made by using the data in the Income Statement columns. When the work sheet is prepared, the closing process is usually summarized in a series of entries as shown below and on page 66.

Closing Entries

Income Summary 153,000
Purchase Returns and Allowances   3,000
  Purchases   128,000
  Inventory, Jan. 1, Year 4   28,000
To close beginning inventory and net purchases.

Inventory, Dec. 31, Year 4 28,900
  Income Summary   28,900
To record the ending inventory.

Sales 175,000
Interest Revenue   33
  Sales Returns and Allowances   2,500
  Sales Discounts   3,150
  Salaries Expense   23,318
  Rent Expense   4,800
  Advertising Expense   9,000
  Janitorial Expense   1,500
  Miscellaneous Expenses   1,900
  Interest Expense   160
  Property Taxes Expense   600
  Doubtful Accounts Expense   875
  Insurance Expense   300
  Depreciation Expense   600
  Income Taxes Expense   670
  Income Summary   125,660
To close revenue and expense accounts to Income Summary

Income Summary	1,560	
Retained Earnings		1,560
To close net income to retained earnings.		
Retained Earnings	1,500	
Dividends		1,500
To close Dividends account.		

Illustration of work sheet for a manufacturing company

The procedures for preparing a work sheet for a manufacturing company are similar to those used for a merchandising firm. The addition of a pair of columns to summarize the manufacturing operation is the major difference. These columns allow for one more step in the classification of the data. The adjusted trial balance, which is an optional step, is omitted from this illustration.

The following data are the basis for the adjusting entries included in the work sheet for Cole Manufacturing Company for Year 4 on pages 68 and 69.

(a) Doubtful accounts expense is estimated to be $3,000 for the current year.

(b) A three-year insurance policy was purchased 18 months ago at a cost of $1,800. The insurance expense should be divided between miscellaneous factory costs and general expense on an 80-20 basis.

(c) The wages accrued since the last pay period amount to direct labor $1,800 and indirect labor $950. The officers, office staff, and sales people are paid monthly on the last day of the month.

(d) The bonds payable bear interest at the rate of 6%, with interest payable April 1 and October 1.

(e) Depreciation for the plant assets is computed using the straight-line method on the following basis:

	Estimated economic life, years,	Estimated residual value	Cost allocation, %	
Asset			Factory	General
Building	40	$–0–	80	20
Machinery & equipment . .	10	–0–	100	–0–
Furniture & fixtures	20	2,000	10	90

(f) The light bill for December has not been received as of December 31. Based on past experience, the cost applicable to December is estimated to be $1,450. All heat, light, and power costs relate to the factory.

(g) An inventory of factory supplies on December 31 indicates that supplies costing $850 are on hand.

(**h**) The income tax rate for Cole Manufacturing Company is assumed to be 50%.

(**i**) Physical inventory counts and reasonable estimates indicate that the cost of inventories at December 31 is:

Finished goods	$41,500
Goods in process	26,350
Raw materials	12,650

Work Sheet and Year-End Procedures The entries for closing the manufacturing accounts, for adjusting the inventory balances, for closing the revenue and expense accounts, and for closing the Dividends account are illustrated below and on page 70, for Cole Manufacturing Company.

Cost of Finished Goods Manufactured	434,770	
Raw Materials, Dec. 31, Year 4	12,650	
Goods in Process, Dec. 31, Year 4	26,350	
Purchase Returns and Allowances	4,000	
Raw Materials, Jan. 1, Year 4		16,000
Goods in Process, Jan. 1, Year 4		21,000
Raw Material Purchases		125,000
Transportation-in		3,500
Direct Labor Costs		194,300
Indirect Labor Costs		73,550
Heat, Light, and Power		13,750
Miscellaneous Factory Costs		14,630
Depreciation: Building		3,000
Depreciation: Machinery and Equipment		13,000
Depreciation: Furniture and Fixtures		40

To record the ending inventory of raw materials, goods in process, and cost of goods manufactured.

Finished Goods Inventory, Dec. 31, Year 4	41,500	
Cost of Goods Sold	441,270	
Cost of Finished Goods Manufactured		434,770
Finished Goods Inventory, Jan. 1, Year 4		48,000

To record the finished goods inventory and the cost of goods sold.

COLE MANUFACTURING COMPANY
Work Sheet
For Year Ended December 31, Year 4

	Unadjusted trial balance		Adjustments		Manufacturing		Income statement		Retained earnings		Balance sheet	
	Debit	Credit	Debit	Credit	Debit	Credit	Debit	Credit	Debit	Credit	Debit	Credit
Cash	32,000										32,000	
Accounts receivable	70,000										70,000	
Allowance for doubtful accounts		1,200		(a) 3,000								4,200
Inventory, Jan. 1, Year 4:												
Finished goods	48,000						48,000	41,500			41,500	
Goods in process	21,000				21,000	26,350					26,350	
Raw materials	16,000				16,000	12,650					12,650	
Unexpired insurance	1,500			(b) 600							900	
Land	72,000										72,000	
Buildings	150,000										150,000	
Accumulated depreciation: Bldgs.		45,000		(e) 3,750								48,750
Machinery and equipment	130,000										130,000	
Accumulated depreciation: M & E		52,000		(e)13,000								65,000
Furniture and fixtures	10,000										10,000	
Accumulated depreciation: F & F		3,000		(e) 400								3,400
Accounts payable		41,300		(f) 1,450								42,750
Bonds payable		75,000										75,000
Capital stock		100,000										100,000
Paid-in capital in excess of par		100,000										100,000
Retained earnings, Jan. 1, Year 4		88,875								88,875		
Dividends	6,000								6,000			
Sales		633,600						633,600				
Sales returns & allowances	3,600						3,600					
Raw material purchases	125,000				125,000							

Account	Trial Balance Dr	Trial Balance Cr	Adjustments Dr	Adjustments Cr	Cost of Finished Goods Mfd. Dr	Cost of Finished Goods Mfd. Cr	Income Statement Dr	Income Statement Cr	Retained Earnings / Balance Sheet Dr	Retained Earnings / Balance Sheet Cr
Purchase returns & allowances		4,000				4,000				
Transportation-in	3,500				3,500					
Direct labor costs	192,500		(c) 1,800		194,300					
Indirect labor costs	72,600		(c) 950		73,550					
Heat, light, and power	12,300		(f) 1,450		13,750					
Miscellaneous factory costs	15,000		(b) 480	(g) 850	14,630					
Advertising expense	35,000						35,000			
Sales salaries expense	42,000						42,000			
Delivery expense	8,000						8,000			
Administrative salaries expense	50,000						50,000			
Office salaries expense	20,000						20,000			
Telephone & telegraph expense	1,800						1,800			
Miscellaneous general expenses	2,800		(b) 120				2,920			
Interest expense	3,375		(d) 1,125				4,500			
Doubtful accounts expense			(a) 3,000				3,000			
Accrued wages payable				(c) 2,750						2,750
Accrued interest payable				(d) 1,125						1,125
Depreciation: Bldg., factory			(e) 3,000		3,000					
general			(e) 750				750			
Depreciation: M & E, factory			(e)13,000		13,000					
Depreciation: F & F, factory			(e) 40		40					
general			(e) 360				360			
Inventory of factory supplies			(g) 850						850	
Totals	1,143,975	1,143,975	26,925	26,925	477,770	43,000				
Cost of finished goods manufactured						434,770	434,770			
Totals					477,770	477,770	654,700	675,100		
Income before income taxes							20,400			
Totals							675,100	675,100		
Income before income taxes										20,400
Income taxes expense									10,200	
Net income									10,200	
Totals									20,400	20,400
Net income										10,200
Retained earnings, Dec. 31, Year 4									93,075	6,000
Totals									99,075	99,075
Totals									546,250	546,250

Sales	633,600	
Cost of Goods Sold		441,270
Sales Returns and Allowances		3,600
Advertising Expense		35,000
Sales Salaries Expense		42,000
Delivery Expense		8,000
Administrative Salaries Expense		50,000
Office Salaries Expense		20,000
Telephone and Telegraph Expense		1,800
Miscellaneous General Expenses		2,920
Interest Expense		4,500
Doubtful Accounts Expense		3,000
Depreciation: Building		750
Depreciation: Furniture and Fixtures		360
Income Taxes Expense		10,200
Income Summary		10,200
To close revenue and expense accounts.		
Income Summary	10,200	
Retained Earnings		10,200
To close the net income to retained earnings.		
Retained Earnings	6,000	
Dividends		6,000
To close Dividends account.		

Statement of cost of finished goods manufactured

The cost of the goods completed during an accounting period is summarized in a statement of cost of finished goods manufactured. The information for such a statement, illustrated on page 71 for the Cole Manufacturing Company, is taken from the Manufacturing columns of the work sheet.

Using accounting information for business decisions

The ultimate objective of accounting is the *use* of accounting information, through analysis and interpretation as a basis for business decisions. Information derived from accounting records serves management in controlling current operations and in planning future operations. Published financial statements afford outsiders a means of analyzing and interpreting past operations of businesses in which they have an interest. These published financial statements have traditionally been for the most part reports of past events. The past is often the key to the future, however, and for this reason accounting information is highly valued by decision makers, both inside and outside the firm.

COLE MANUFACTURING COMPANY
Statement of Cost of Finished Goods Manufactured
For Year Ended December 31, Year 4

Goods in process inventory, Jan. 1, Year 4		$ 21,000
Raw materials used:		
Raw materials inventory, Jan. 1, Year 4	$ 16,000	
Raw materials purchases (net)	124,500	
Cost of raw materials available for use	$140,500	
Less: Raw materials inventory, Dec. 31, Year 4	12,650	
Cost of raw materials used	$127,850	
Direct labor costs	194,300	
Factory overhead costs (see work sheet for details) . . .	117,970	
Total manufacturing costs		440,120
Total cost of goods in process during the year		$461,120
Less: Goods in process inventory, Dec. 31, Year 4		26,350
Cost of finished goods manufactured		$434,770

Limitations of accounting data

The objective of this book is to examine the basic principles and their effectiveness as the underlying assumptions of accounting, to explore the rules and conventions, and to consider the possible uses of the data once they are accumulated. <u>One must be aware of the fact that accounting is justified only because the data so accumulated and presented are useful.</u> At the same time one must remember that the data are often limited because many factors which are not subject to measurement in terms of money have necessarily been omitted. Examples are the human resources of an organization and the political and economic environment in which the business exists. Furthermore, in recent years drastic changes in the purchasing power of the dollar have made this monetary unit an imperfect means of measurement.

REVIEW QUESTIONS

1 Describe the **accounting cycle** briefly and list the sequence of procedures.

2 State in a concise form the rules of debit and credit for the five basic types of accounts.

3 Describe briefly the function of the *journals* or books of original entry.

4 What is the function of the *ledger*?

5 Explain the advantage of using controlling accounts and subsidiary ledgers.

6 What is the purpose of the *trial balance*? Does it provide proof that there have been no errors in the recording, classifying, and summarizing of business transactions?

7 How are the temporary or nominal accounts (revenue and expense accounts) related to the equation $A = L + OE$?

8 What is the objective of utilizing special multicolumn journals?

9 With the advent of electronic computers, the cost of data-processing equipment and the complexity of operations increased many times. What economies are available to the user to offset the added costs of converting to and using this type of equipment?

10 What are *adjusting entries* and why are they necessary?

11 Why is it necessary to prepare adjusting entries to change the value of the accounts receivable when the entries of these accounts are usually made only upon objective evidence of a negotiated sales and purchase agreement?

12 Prepare the adjusting entry indicated by the following information:
a Accrued wages at June 30 total $3,000.
b The estimate of doubtful accounts is $2,000 and the allowance for doubtful accounts has a zero balance.

13 What are *closing entries*? Why are they made? What accounts are closed?

14 You are given the following information about the merchandise accounts of ABC Co. and are asked to make the necessary entries to adjust the inventory balance and close the relevant accounts to cost of goods sold.

Inventory, Jan. 1, Year 10 (ledger balance)	$ 44,000
Purchases	276,400
Purchase returns and allowances	1,700
Purchase discounts	3,800
Freight and transportation-in	4,800
Handling and storage costs	26,800
Inventory, Dec. 31, Year 10 (physical count; value at net invoice cost plus freight, handling, and storage costs)	46,200

15 What are *reversing entries* and under what circumstances are they most commonly used?

16 Which of the following adjustments might be reversed? For each entry indicate your reasons for reversing or not reversing.

a Unearned Subscriptions	10,000	
Earned Subscriptions Revenue		10,000
b Inventory of Office Supplies	5,000	
Office Supplies Expense		5,000
c Interest Expense	300	
Accrued Interest Payable		300
d Depreciation Expense	8,000	
Accumulated Depreciation		8,000

17 What is the purpose of the **work sheet** and what benefits may be derived from using it?

EXERCISES

Ex. 2-1 All but one of the accounts of Hale Shoe Store, owned by J. D. Hale, appear in the following list of balances at December 31 of the current year.

Accounts receivable	$ 7,500
Accounts payable	11,000
Accrued liabilities	300
Accumulated depreciation (plant and equipment)	10,000
Cash	5,000
Inventory	14,000
Land	6,000
Notes payable	25,000
Plant and equipment	25,000
Short-term prepayments	500

On January 1 of the current year, Hale's equity in the business amounted to $15,000. During the current year Hale withdrew $5,200 cash and made an additional investment of $3,000 in equipment which had previously been part of another business owned by Hale.

Compute the net income or net loss of Hale Shoe Store for the current year, and show in an orderly manner the data supporting your answer.

Ex. 2-2 The following events occurred during January, the first month of operations, at the Jade Paint Store.

(1) Sales on account totaled $13,000. Terms, 2/10, n/60.
(2) Cash sales amounted to $24,000.
(3) Purchases of merchandise (paint) totaled $50,000.
(4) Payments of $28,600 were made to creditors in full settlement of purchase invoices totaling $29,000.
(5) Accounts receivable in the face amount of $10,000 were collected; one-half of these collections occurred within the 10-day discount period.
(6) Jade, the owner, withdrew merchandise for personal use which had a cost

of $1,000 and had been marked for sale at $1,300. Jade also withdrew $500 in cash during the month.

(7) Inventory on hand at the end of January was determined by physical count to consist of goods which cost $23,000.

(8) Other expenses for the month totaled $8,500.

Determine the net income or net loss of Jade Paint Store for the month of January. Show supporting computations in good form.

Ex. 2-3 The accounting policies of Gina Publications, Inc., provide that subscriptions received from customers be credited to Subscriptions Revenue when received. Purchases of supplies are regularly debited to Supplies Expense at time of purchase. The post-closing trial balance at December 31, Year 5, includes the following accounts:

	Debit	Credit
Accounts receivable	$ 24,000	
Allowance for doubtful accounts		$ 2,200
Inventory of supplies	1,710	
Equipment	135,500	
Accumulated depreciation		48,000
Notes payable		20,000
Accrued interest payable		350
Accrued wages payable		1,230
Unearned subscriptions revenue		2,940

Prepare all appropriate reversing entries as of January 1, Year 6.

Ex. 2-4 The following data provide selected account balances of Lobo Company before and after the December 31 adjusting entries.

	Before adjustment	After adjustment
a Allowance for doubtful accounts	$ 2,000 credit	$ 5,500 credit
b Accumulated depreciation	14,000 credit	16,000 credit
c Sales salaries expense	24,200 debit	24,650 debit
d Income taxes payable	3,700 credit	6,250 credit
e Interest revenue	6,500 credit	6,585 credit
f Royalty revenue	5,000 credit	5,800 credit

In journal entry form, give the adjustments that were made for each account on December 31.

Ex. 2-5 Rainbow Company's records provide the following information concerning certain account balances and changes in these account balances during the current year.

a Accounts receivable: Jan. 1, balance, $15,000; Dec. 31, balance, $20,500; uncollectible accounts written off during the year, $4,100; accounts receivable collected during the year, $56,000.

b Allowance for doubtful accounts: Jan. 1, balance, $1,500; Dec. 31, balance, $2,200; adjustment entry increasing allowance at Dec. 31, $4,800.

c Inventory of office supplies; Jan. 1, balance, $1,500; Dec. 31, balance, $1,350; office supplies expense for the year, $9,500.

d Equipment: Jan. 1, balance, $20,500; Dec. 31, balance, $18,000; equipment costing $8,000 was sold during the year.

e Accounts payable: Jan. 1, balance, $9,000; Dec. 31, balance, $11,500; purchases on account for the year, $48,000.

f Interest revenue: Jan. 1, accrued, $325; Dec. 31, accrued, $475; earned for the year, $4,500.

Transaction information is missing from each of the above. Prepare the journal entry to record the missing information for each account.

Ex. 2-6 For Year 5, the gross profit on sales of Madrid Company was $96,000; the cost of finished goods manufactured was $340,000; the beginning inventories of goods in process and finished goods were $28,000 and $45,000, respectively; and the ending inventories of goods in process and finished goods were $38,000 and $52,000, respectively. Compute the amount of sales for Madrid Company for Year 5.

SHORT CASES FOR ANALYSIS AND DECISION

Case 2-1 Carmen Garcia began her working career in the accounting department of Mod Company. Although Garcia had never taken a formal course of study in accounting, she gradually developed a thorough knowledge of Mod's accounting policies and eventually she was promoted to the position of chief accountant.

While attending a regional meeting of accounting executives, Garcia was puzzled by a statement made in a group discussion. The statement was: "Reversing entries are frequently very helpful in accounting for business transactions; however they are seldom, if ever, essential to the record-keeping function." Garcia was concerned because reversing entries had regularly been used by Mod Company and she had always considered them essential.

Instructions

a Explain why reversing entries are not essential but why they may be helpful. Your answer should include an explanation as to when reversing entries are appropriate and when they should not be used.

b Using the data below, demonstrate with journal entries how reversing entries may be used or ignored. It is company policy to debit Supplies Expense for all supplies purchased. The value of supplies on hand at December 31, Year 4, was determined by count to be $1,150. The balance in the asset account, Inventory of Supplies, in the ledger was zero. The following adjusting entry was made:

Inventory of Supplies	*1,150*	
Supplies Expense		*1,150*

During Year 5, supplies were purchased at a cost of $17,500 and debited to Supplies Expense. The inventory of supplies at December 31, Year 5, was $850.

Case 2-2 On January 3, Year 5, Paul Falk established a business under the name of Falk's Nursery. His first step was to sign a three-year lease on a store building at a monthly rental of $300 and to make the first monthly payment on January 1, Year 5. Also on this date, Falk purchased store equipment for $10,000 and inventory for $16,000. The store equipment was expected to have an economic life of 10 years with no residual value. Falk made no other investment of any kind in the business.

Both Falk and his wife worked in the business; they had no employees. From time to time the Falks withdrew cash from the business to meet their personal needs. Since the Falks had no prior business experience, they chose to minimize record keeping. The only records maintained were a checkbook which was reconciled monthly with the bank statement, a file folder of unpaid purchase invoices, and a file folder of uncollected charge tickets for a few select customers.

At December 31, Year 6, Falk carried out the following procedures in an effort to see how the business stood after two years of operation.

(1) Took a physical inventory and priced the items, using invoice prices of recent purchases. This procedure indicated a total value for the inventory of $45,000.
(2) Reconciled the December 31 bank statement with the checkbook and found the cash balance to be $7,200.
(3) Added the unpaid purchase invoices in the file which showed a total liability to suppliers of $22,700.
(4) Added the uncollected charge tickets and found that the total amount receivable from customers was $4,200.
(5) Estimated that his withdrawals of cash from the business during the two-year period had amounted to $16,000.

Instructions
a Prepare a balance sheet for Falk's Nursery (a single proprietorship) at December 31, Year 6. (You are to ignore income taxes, including the fact that apparently no personal income tax return was prepared to reflect the first year of operations.)
b Explain to Falk the advantages of a double-entry accounting system as compared with his present set of accounting records. Could the same information be obtained from his present system as from a double-entry system?
c Point out to Falk what you can about the results of operations over the past two-year period.

PROBLEMS

Group A

2A-1 Kerr Steel Corporation uses a perpetual inventory system. A selected list of transactions and adjustments for the current period is given below:

(1) Sales on account totaled $46,200; the cost of the goods sold was $34,000.
(2) The corporation acquired a building and tract of land at a total cost of $310,000. One-tenth of the purchase price was paid in cash and a 9% mortgage note payable was signed for the balance. The building had an estimated current fair value of $192,000.
(3) Purchased merchandise costing $29,500. The invoice price is subject to a 2% cash discount if paid within 10 days. Kerr Steel Corporation records purchase invoices at the net amount.
(4) The corporation paid $850 for freight charges on merchandise purchased. Freight charges are recorded in a separate account.
(5) Accounts receivable of $350 were written off as uncollectible. The corporation maintains an allowance for doubtful accounts and makes provision for doubtful accounts expense at the end of each period.
(6) The invoice for the purchase of merchandise in item (3) was paid within the discount period.

(7) Collections on customers' accounts amounted to $39,880.

(8) Cash of $4,000 was received from disposal of equipment. The original cost of the equipment was $20,000 and the accumulated depreciation $17,500.

(9) Declared and paid a cash dividend of 20 cents per share on 60,000 shares of common stock.

(10) Returned defective merchandise to a supplier for full credit. The merchandise had been purchased on account for $750 (net).

(11) Kerr Steel Corporation issued 10,000 shares of its $5 par value common stock and received cash of $11 per share.

(12) A customer's check for $180, received and deposited by Kerr Steel Corporation, was returned by the bank marked "not sufficient funds."

(13) The building acquired in item (2) was used in operations for 10 months during the current period. The building has an economic life of 40 years and no residual value. Depreciation is computed by the straight-line method.

(14) Accrued property taxes at the end of the current period amounted to $280.

Instructions Record the above transactions and adjustments in general journal form. Prepare separate entries for the declaration and the payment of the dividend in item (9).

2A-2 Subsidiary ledgers and related controlling accounts for accounts receivable and accounts payable are maintained by Spring Paint Company. The following schedules summarize the two subsidiary ledgers at December 31, 1979:

Schedule of Accounts Receivable
December 31, 1979

Davis	$ 2,000
Fairly	6,000
Iverson (credit balance)	(750)
Kiley	13,500
Total	$20,750

Schedule of Accounts Payable
December 31, 1979

Edwards	$ 588
Gates (debit balance)	(570)
Loomis	8,050
Parks	2,330
Total	$10,398

Spring Paint Company offers credit terms of 2/10, n/30 to all its customers and records all sales at gross prices. Purchases of merchandise from suppliers are recorded at net prices because it is the company's policy to take all purchase discounts available.

In any transaction in which Spring Paint Company fails to take advantage of a cash discount offered by a supplier, the entry to record payment of the supplier's invoice should include a debit to Purchase Discounts Lost.

Spring Paint Company carries customers' credit balances as an offset against debit balances, and suppliers' debit balances as an offset against credit balances in the ledgers. These balances are reclassified for reporting purposes to reflect customers' credit balances as liabilities and suppliers' debit balances as assets.

Transactions for January 1980 are presented below:

(1) Received a check from Kiley for $13,230 in full settlement of his account within the discount period.
(2) Purchases from Edwards totaled $11,224.49, terms 2/10, n/30. Record at net.
(3) Payment to Loomis of $8,050 within the discount period.
(4) Sales to Iverson of $28,000, terms 2/10, n/30.
(5) Cash received from Davis, $4,500, including a $2,500 advance payment.
(6) Payment of $11,600 to Edwards in settlement of the account payable. Because of an oversight, the payment was not made until after the discount period had lapsed on the December invoice. Also made new purchase from Edwards of $13,200, terms 2/10, n/30.
(7) Cash received from Fairly, $3,940, in partial payment of his bill. The discount was allowed on this portion of the bill, since cash was received within the discount period.
(8) Paid Parks $4,330, which represented payment of the balance due within the discount period and $2,000 advance on a new order.

Instructions
a Enter the December 31, 1979, balances and the above transactions directly in the appropriate ledger accounts in both the general ledger and subsidiary ledgers for accounts receivable and accounts payable. You need not maintain a ledger account for cash. (Since this problem does not include journals or monthly totals, each transaction should be individually entered in a general ledger controlling account as well as in a subsidiary ledger account. The use of three-column, running-balance-account forms is recommended.)
b Prove the accuracy of the records by preparing schedules of the subsidiary ledgers at January 31, 1980, and by determining that the totals agree with the respective controlling accounts.
c Which accounts with customers and suppliers should be reclassified on financial statements prepared at January 31, 1980? Explain how such accounts should be presented in the balance sheet.

2A-3 The account balances listed below are taken from the ledger of Newton Company at September 30, except for the balance of retained earnings, which is the September 1 balance. The Dividends account represents the amount declared and paid during September. There are no assets or liabilities other than those listed.

Cash	$ 21,500
Accounts receivable	28,500
Inventory	48,000
Plant and equipment	120,000
Accounts payable	21,600
Accumulated depreciation	36,000
Capital stock, $10 par	120,000
Retained earnings, Sept. 1	28,000
Dividends	8,600

Instructions
a Compute the net income of Newton Company for September by arranging the information provided in a balance sheet at September 30. Include in the bal-

ance sheet the details of retained earnings: beginning balance, increase during September, decrease during September, and ending balance.

b Assume that the account receivable balance was $20,000 on September 1 and that a total of $106,000 was collected from accounts receivable and from cash sales. Compute the total sales for September.

c Assume that the inventory at September 1 was $50,000 and that purchases of merchandise during September amounted to $65,000. Compute the cost of goods sold and also the total of all other expenses for the month.

d Assume that the balance of accounts payable at September 1 was $30,000 and that the only liabilities incurred during September were for purchases of merchandise as stated in **(c)** above. Determine the total cash outlay for merchandise during September.

2A-4 The information given below for Ship Supply Company provides a basis for making all necessary adjusting entries at December 31, the end of the company's fiscal year. You may assume that all transactions were properly recorded in accordance with the company's accounting policies.

(1) On June 1, the company borrowed $60,000 by issuing a 9% mortgage note payable which called for interest to be paid quarterly.

(2) The company owns a building with an estimated economic life of 25 years and no expected residual value. Cost was $150,000. Straight-line depreciation is used.

(3) On October 1 the company paid $2,700 for three years of insurance coverage commencing on that date. The Unexpired Insurance account was debited.

(4) A nominal account was credited when $3,600 in rental revenue was received from a tenant on November 1. This amount represented six months' rent in advance.

(5) Bonds with a face value of $10,000 and an annual interest rate of 8% were purchased as an investment on May 1. Interest payment dates are April 1 and October 1.

(6) An annual city business license of $400 was paid on October 1 and recorded by debiting a nominal account.

(7) On December 31, after careful study of an aging schedule of accounts receivable, it was estimated that probable uncollectible accounts would total $3,800. The Allowance for Doubtful Accounts had a credit balance of $720.

Instructions

a Prepare the necessary adjusting entries at December 31. Include in the explanation portion of each entry any calculations you performed in developing the adjusting entry.

b Prepare the appropriate reversing entries, assuming that the company follows a policy of reversing those adjusting entries that result in a balance sheet account not used during the accounting period.

2A-5 Suburb Merchandising, Inc., maintains its accounts on the basis of a fiscal year ending October 31. The following unadjusted trial balance was prepared from the general ledger at October 31, 1980. Reversing entries had been made by Suburb Merchandising, Inc., on November 1, 1979, the first day of the current fiscal year, for the accrued interest payable and the accrued salaries and wages payable which had been recorded by adjusting entries on October 31, 1979.

	Debit	Credit
Cash	$ 52,000	
Accounts receivable	32,000	
Inventory, Oct. 31, 1979	47,000	
Land	84,000	
Building	210,000	
Accumulated depreciation: building		$ 84,000
Equipment	252,000	
Accumulated depreciation: equipment		62,700
Accounts payable		45,000
Accrued interest payable		–0–
Accrued salaries and wages payable		–0–
Bonds payable, 9%		100,000
Capital stock		200,000
Retained earnings, Nov. 1, 1979		88,800
Dividends	8,000	
Sales		820,000
Purchases	490,000	
Salaries and wages expense	56,500	
Selling expenses	122,500	
General expenses	41,000	
Interest expense	5,500	
Total	$1,400,500	$1,400,500

Additional data
(1) After a careful analysis of accounts receivable, a decision is made to establish an allowance for doubtful accounts in the amount of $2,200.
(2) Estimated economic life of the building is 40 years; residual value is zero. Estimated economic life of the equipment is 20 years with residual value of $12,000.
(3) Interest on the bonds is payable January 1 and July 1.
(4) Salaries and wages earned but unpaid on October 31 amount to $5,000.
(5) The inventory at October 31, 1980, cost $26,000.
(6) The income tax expense is estimated to be 40% of income before income taxes.

Instructions
a Prepare a 12-column work sheet to adjust the accounts and classify the balances as to income statement, retained earnings, and balance sheet. (Include a pair of columns for an adjusted trial balance.)
b Prepare closing entries in general journal form.
c Prepare reversing entries at November 1, 1980, relating to the accrued salaries and wages payable and to the interest payable.

2A-6 The unadjusted trial balance on page 81 was prepared from the ledger of Brass Manufacturing Co. at December 31, Year 4. The company used reversing entries on January 1, Year 5, to reverse accrued wages and interest payable.

	Debit	Credit
Cash	$ 15,000	
Accounts receivable	73,300	
Allowance for doubtful accounts		$ 1,335
Inventories, Jan. 1, Year 4:		
Raw materials	11,000	
Goods in process	52,000	
Finished goods	70,000	
Short-term prepayments	8,000	
Land	42,000	
Building	350,000	
Accumulated depreciation: building		55,040
Machinery and equipment	375,000	
Accumulated depreciation: machinery and equipment		100,000
Accounts payable		50,000
Accrued wages payable		–0–
Accrued interest payable		–0–
Bonds payable, 6%		200,000
Capital stock, $10 par		440,000
Retained earnings, Jan. 1, Year 4		54,000
Dividends	5,000	
Sales–net		950,000
Raw materials purchases	305,000	
Direct labor costs	281,000	
Factory overhead costs	110,000	
Selling expenses	96,000	
General and administrative expenses	47,000	
Interest expense	10,075	
Total	$1,850,375	$1,850,375

Additional data

(1) Doubtful accounts are estimated to total 5% of the Accounts Receivable balance.

(2) Short-term prepayments are as follows (insurance considered as administrative expense):

	Jan. 1	Dec. 31
Unexpired insurance	$3,500	$2,000
Factory supplies	4,500	5,400
Total	$8,000	$7,400

(3) Invoices for raw materials included in the ending inventory but not recorded total $13,000.

(4) The straight-line method of depreciation is used to allocate the cost of plant assets. Other relevant data are:

	Estimated economic life, years	Estimated residual value	Percentage allocated to	
			Factory	Administration
Building	50	$7,000	70	30
Machinery & equipment ..	10	5%	80	20

(5) Interest payments to bondholders are made semiannually on May 1 and November 1 at the annual rate of 6%.
(6) The factory power bill of $4,000 for December has not been recorded.
(7) Direct factory wages earned but not paid at December 31 total $2,100.
(8) The ending inventories at December 31 are: Raw materials, $15,000; goods in process, $49,000; and finished goods, $65,000.
(9) Income taxes are estimated to be 40% of income before income taxes.

Instructions
a Prepare a 12-column work sheet to adjust the accounts and classify the data as to manufacturing costs, income statement, retained earnings, and balance sheet. Columns for an adjusted trial balance are not to be included.
b Prepare in general journal form the entries required to adjust the inventory accounts and to record the cost of finished goods manufactured and the cost of goods sold. You are not required to prepare the entry to close the revenue, cost of goods sold, and expense accounts to the Income Summary account.
c Prepare reversing entries on January 1, Year 5, relating to the accrued wages payable and interest payable.

Group B

2B-1 Heintz Film Co. uses a periodic inventory system. Selected transactions and adjustments for Year 2 are listed below:

(1) Sales on account totaled $29,850.
(2) Building and tract of land were acquired at a cost of $260,000. The current fair value of the land was estimated at $80,000. One-fourth of the purchase price was paid in cash and an 8% mortgage note payable was signed for the balance.
(3) Merchandise costing $21,000 was purchased, subject to a cash discount of 2% if paid within 10 days. (Record invoice at net amount.)
(4) Freight charges of $405 related to merchandise acquisitions were paid.
(5) Accounts receivable of $415 were written off. Heintz Film Co. employs an allowance for doubtful accounts and makes provision for doubtful accounts at the end of each period.
(6) The invoice for the purchase in item (3) was paid within the discount period.
(7) Collections on customers' accounts totaled $27,400.
(8) Equipment which originally cost $4,800, and on which accumulated depreciation amounted to $4,000, was sold for cash of $500.
(9) A cash dividend of 15 cents per share on 100,000 shares was declared and paid. Prepare separate entries for the declaration and the payment.
(10) 20,000 shares of $10 par value common stock were sold for $16 per share.
(11) Defective merchandise, which was purchased on account for $650 (net amount), was returned for full credit.

(12) A customer's check for $80 received and deposited by Heintz Film Co. was returned by the bank marked "not sufficient funds."

(13) An expense account was debited when supplies were purchased. The Inventory of Supplies account has an unadjusted balance of $750, but the inventory of supplies at the end of Year 2 is $950.

(14) The building acquired in item (2) was used in operations for nine months during Year 2. The building has an economic life of 25 years and no residual value. Depreciation is computed by the straight-line method.

Instructions Record the above transactions and adjustments in general journal form.

2B-2 Lacey Corporation maintains subsidiary ledgers for accounts receivable and accounts payable to support the respective balances of the two controlling accounts in the general ledger. The following schedules summarize the two subsidiary ledgers at December 31, 1979:

Schedule of Accounts Receivable
December 31, 1979

Frederick	$15,500
Garr (credit balance)	(4,000)
Herman	2,500
Sothern	5,000
Total	$19,000

Schedule of Accounts Payable
December 31, 1979

Adamson	$12,250
Elwood	1,470
Farnsworth	3,530
Sumner (debit balance)	(2,270)
Total	$14,980

Lacey Corporation offers its customers a cash discount of 2% on all sales for which payment is received within 10 days from the invoice date. Sales transactions are recorded at the gross amount of the invoices. On purchases of merchandise it is the company's policy to take advantage of all cash discounts by paying within the discount period. Because of this policy the company records all purchase invoices at the net amount. Any adjustments for discounts (either because sales discounts are taken by customers or because purchase discounts are lost through failure by Lacey to pay promptly) are made at the time cash is received or disbursed.

In the preparation of financial statements, any customers' accounts which have credit balances are reclassified as liabilities, and any creditors' accounts which have debit balances are reclassified as assets. Although such accounts are reclassified in the preparation of a balance sheet, they are not removed from the subsidiary ledgers; thus a customer's account which acquires a credit balance continues to be part of the accounts receivable subsidiary ledger.

The following selected transactions occurred during January 1980:

(1) Received a check from Sothern for $4,900 representing settlement in full of his account within the discount period.
(2) Purchases from Elwood totaled $13,000, terms 2/15, n/30. (Record at net amount.)
(3) Issued to Adamson a check in the amount of $12,250.
(4) Made sales to Garr of $30,000, terms 2/10, n/30.
(5) Cash received from Herman, $3,900, including a $1,400 advance payment. Collection of the receivable existing at December 31 was after the discount period.
(6) Payment of $14,500 was made to Elwood in settlement of the account. The payment was made after expiration of the discount period. (Debit Purchase Discounts Lost.)
(7) Cash received from Frederick, $9,800, in partial payment of his bill. The regular cash discount was allowed on the portion of the receivable collected, since cash was received within the discount period.
(8) Paid Farnsworth $5,500, which represented payment of the balance due within the discount period and a $1,970 advance on a large order.
(9) Purchased merchandise from Adamson, net amount $24,500, and from Sumner, net amount $490.

Instructions

a Enter the December 31 balances in ledger accounts for both the general ledger and the subsidiary ledgers for accounts receivable and accounts payable. You need not maintain a ledger account for cash. Record each January transaction directly in both the general ledger and a subsidiary ledger. (Since this problem does not include journals or monthly totals, each January transaction should be entered in a general ledger controlling account as well as in a subsidiary ledger account. The three-column, running-balance form of account is recommended.)

b Prepare schedules of the subsidiary ledgers at January 31, 1980, and determine that the totals are in agreement with the controlling accounts.

c Determine whether any balances should be reclassified in accordance with the company's policy. If so, indicate which, and state how such balances should be presented in the balance sheet.

2B-3 Listed below are the account balances from the ledger of Madrid Yarn Company at October 31, except for retained earnings, which is the October 1 balance. There are no assets or liabilities other than those listed. The Dividends account represents the amount declared and paid during October.

Accounts payable	$ 40,000
Accounts receivable	32,000
Accumulated depreciation	64,000
Capital stock, $10 par	220,000
Cash	42,000
Dividends	8,000
Inventory	64,000
Plant and equipment	240,000
Retained earnings, Oct. 1	37,000

Instructions

a Compute the net income of Madrid Yarn Company for October by preparing a balance sheet at October 31 which includes details showing the beginning balance of retained earnings, increases and decreases, and the ending balance of retained earnings.

b What was the amount of total sales for October, assuming that the accounts receivable were $36,000 on October 1 and that $160,000 was received in collections from customers and from cash sales during October? Show computations.

c Determine the cost of goods sold for October, assuming that inventory of October 1 was $58,000 and that October purchases of merchandise totaled $110,000. What was the total of all other expenses for the month? Show computations.

d Determine the total cash outlay for merchandise during October, assuming that the beginning balance of accounts payable was $38,000 and that October purchases of merchandise (all on credit) amounted to $110,000. Show computations.

2B-4 Whitmer Corporation adjusts and closes its accounts at the end of each calendar year. The information presented below provides the basis for making the adjusting entries needed at December 31.

(1) On July 1 received $7,200 of rental revenue covering a one-year period beginning with the date of receipt. Credited a nominal (revenue) account.

(2) A balance sheet account was debited on September 1, when Whitmer paid a $5,400 premium for a three-year insurance policy effective on that date.

(3) Whitmer Corporation borrowed $90,000 on March 1 by issuing a three-year, 10% mortgage note payable with interest payable quarterly. Interest payments were made on May 31, August 31, and November 30.

(4) Bonds in the face amount of $20,000 with an interest rate of 7% were acquired as an investment on April 1. Interest payment dates are April 1 and October 1.

(5) The building occupied by Whitmer has a cost basis of $96,000. Estimated economic life is 20 years with no expected residual value. Straight-line depreciation is used.

(6) An aging analysis of the accounts receivable at December 31 indicated $4,100 to be a reasonable estimate of probable uncollectible accounts. At this date the allowance for doubtful accounts had a *debit* balance of $460.

(7) A nominal account was debited on July 1 when $1,200 was paid for office supplies. At December 31, supplies valued at $585 have not been consumed.

Instructions

a Prepare year-end adjusting entries. Include in the explanation portion of each entry any calculations used in developing the amount of the adjustment.

b Prepare the appropriate reversing entries, assuming that the company follows a policy of reversing those adjusting entries that result in a balance sheet account not used during the accounting period.

2B-5 Bell Retail Company is a merchandising business using a periodic inventory system and maintaining its accounts on a calendar-year basis. The trial balance shown on page 86 was prepared from the general ledger at December 31, 1980, and no adjusting entries have been made as yet.

Reversing entries were made by Bell Retail Company on January 1, 1980, for the accrued interest payable and the accrued salaries and wages payable which had been recorded by adjusting entries on December 31, 1979.

	Debit	Credit
Cash	$ 7,000	
Accounts receivable	40,000	
Inventory, Dec. 31, 1979	23,000	
Land	90,000	
Building	200,000	
Accumulated depreciation		$ 42,000
Equipment	240,000	
Accumulated depreciation		59,500
Accounts payable		38,000
Accrued interest payable		–0–
Accrued salaries and wages payable		–0–
Bonds payable, 6%		100,000
Capital stock		200,000
Retained earnings, Dec. 31, 1979		75,200
Dividends	15,000	
Sales		800,000
Purchases	479,500	
Salaries and wages expense	55,200	
Selling expenses	120,000	
General expenses	40,000	
Interest expense	5,000	
Total	$1,314,700	$1,314,700

Additional data
(1) The company has decided after an aging and analysis of accounts receivable to establish an allowance for doubtful accounts of $3,000.
(2) The building is being depreciated on the straight-line basis; total economic life, 40 years; residual value is zero. Estimated economic life for equipment is 15 years and estimated residual value is $15,000.
(3) Interest is payable May 1 and November 1 on the bonds payable.
(4) Salaries and wages earned by employees but unpaid at December 31 amounted to $6,000.
(5) The inventory at December 31, 1980, was determined by physical count to amount to $28,000.
(6) Income taxes are estimated to be 40% of income before income taxes.

Instructions
a Prepare a 12-column work sheet to adjust the accounts and classify the balances as to income statement, retained earnings, and balance sheet. (Include columns for an adjusted trial balance.)
b Use the work sheet as a source for preparation of closing entries in general journal form. (Adjusting entries are not to be prepared.)
c Prepare reversing entries dated January 1, 1981, with respect to the accrued salaries and wages payable and to the accrued interest payable for which adjustments were made at December 31, 1980.

2B-6 The following unadjusted trial balance was prepared from the ledger of Dalton Manufacturing Corporation at December 31, Year 10. The company used reversing entries on January 1 of each year to reverse accrued wages and interest payable.

	Debit	Credit
Cash	$ 22,050	
Accounts receivable	80,000	
Allowance for doubtful accounts		$ 200
Inventories, Jan. 1, Year 10:		
Raw materials	12,000	
Goods in process	56,000	
Finished goods	80,000	
Short-term prepayments	9,000	
Land . . . . :	50,000	
Building	457,000	
Accumulated depreciation: building		54,800
Machinery and equipment	400,000	
Accumulated depreciation: machinery and equipment		120,000
Accounts payable		70,000
Accrued wages payable		–0–
Accrued interest payable		–0–
Bonds payable, 6%		200,000
Capital stock, $10 par		400,000
Paid-in capital in excess of par		170,000
Retained earnings, Jan. 1, Year 10		56,025
Dividends	5,000	
Sales–net		980,000
Raw materials purchases	310,000	
Direct labor costs	292,900	
Factory overhead costs	120,000	
Selling expenses	95,000	
General and administrative expenses	52,000	
Interest expense	10,075	
Total	$2,051,025	$2,051,025

Additional data

(1) The allowance for doubtful accounts should be increased to make it equal to 6% of accounts receivable.
(2) Short-term prepayments are as follows (insurance considered as administrative expense) at the beginning and end of Year 10:

	Jan. 1	Dec. 31
Unexpired insurance (two years remaining Jan. 1)	$3,600	$1,800
Factory supplies	5,400	7,000
Total	$9,000	$8,800

(3) Invoices for raw materials included in the ending inventory but not recorded total $12,000.
(4) The straight-line method of depreciation is used to allocate the cost of plant assets. Other relevant data are presented at the top of page 88.

	Estimated economic life, years	Estimated residual value	Percentage allocated to	
			Factory	Administration
Building	50	$7,000	70	30
Machinery & equip-				
ment	10	5%	80	20

(5) Interest payments to bondholders are made semiannually on May 1 and November 1 at the annual rate of 6%.

(6) The factory power bill for December, $3,200, has not been recorded.

(7) Direct factory wages earned but not paid at December 31 total $1,800.

(8) The ending inventories at December 31 are: Raw materials, $18,000; goods in process, $53,000; and finished goods, $75,000.

(9) Income taxes are estimated to be 40% of income before income taxes.

Instructions

a Prepare a work sheet to adjust the accounts and classify the data as to manufacturing costs, income statement, retained earnings, and balance sheet. Do not include an adjusted trial balance.

b Prepare in general journal form the entries required to adjust the inventory accounts and to record the cost of finished goods manufactured and the cost of goods sold. You need not close any accounts to Income Summary.

c Prepare reversing entries as of January 1, Year 11, relating to the accrued wages and interest payable.

CHAPTER 3

INCOME STATEMENT AND STATEMENT OF RETAINED EARNINGS

INCOME MEASUREMENT

Arriving at an estimate of the periodic income of a business enterprise is perhaps the foremost objective of the accounting process. The word **estimate** is appropriate because income is one of the most elusive concepts in the business and economic world. The art of accounting will probably never progress to the point where periodic business income can be defined to everyone's satisfaction.

To illustrate the complexity of defining income, let us assume that newly organized Blue Hills Corporation buys a large tract of land for the purpose of developing a residential community within commuting distance of a large city. Purchase of the land required only a small down payment (and the assumption of a large mortgage), but even that small payment used up most of the corporation's cash. Some of the land is level, some rolling, and some extremely steep. A golf course, riding stables, tennis courts, and a lake are to be constructed, and a first step is to create colorful sales brochures showing how attractive the community will appear when completed. These improvements are to be financed with revenue from sale of lots, and, if possible, by borrowing.

Residential lots are immediately offered for sale to individuals at varying prices, but with a down payment of only 1% of the sales price. Assume that 100 lots are sold very quickly with an average down payment of $100 received, along with long-term sales contracts calling for monthly payments on the balance due. How much, if any, income should be recognized when the first lots are sold?

As indicated in Chapter 1, income is usually determined by measuring revenue and deducting the related costs. But how shall we measure either the revenue or the costs? Among the questions which arise are: What is the value of a long-term sales contract from a person making a small down payment on a vacant lot? How many of the 100 buyers will actually make the agreed monthly payments? What will be the costs of developing roads, sewers, the golf course, lake, and other recreational facilities which Blue Hills Corporation has promised to provide? How many lots will be sold, and at what prices and on what terms? How should the total estimated costs be allocated among the level lots, sloping lots, hillside lots, and lakefront lots?

Despite all the effort which has been devoted to developing uniform accounting standards, it is painfully clear that a wide range of answers could be given to the question of how much, if any, income is earned from the sale of the first 100 lots. We might even question whether a sale has really occurred, or whether Blue Hills Corporation is a "going concern" reasonably capable of carrying out its commitments and thus warranting application of the continuity principle.[1] Assuming that Blue Hills Corporation does carry the development project to a successful completion, the income can then be measured as the amount of revenue received from customers minus the costs of the land and the costs of developing and selling it. However, the objective of timeliness in financial reporting requires the making of decisions as to the income being earned long before the project is completed. This example of a land development company, although somewhat extreme, suggests some of the very real practical difficulties faced by accountants in measuring business income.

In this chapter we shall first consider the nature of business income and the basic assumptions made by accountants in attempting to measure it. Then we shall turn to the problem of reporting in the income statement the results of these measurement efforts.

The meaning of periodic income

In a very general sense, the objective in measuring income is to determine by how much a business has become better off during some period of time, as a result of its operations. Business income might be described as the maximum amount of resources that could be distributed to the owners over a given period of time and leave the business as

---

[1] *Accounting Series Release No. 95,* "Accounting for Real Estate Transactions Where Circumstances Indicate that Profits Were Not Earned at the Time the Transactions Were Recorded," issued by the Securities and Exchange Commission in 1962, indicates that the circumstances set forth above would make it inappropriate to recognize gross profit as realized at the time of the sale. In 1973, the AICPA took a similar position in *An AICPA Industry Accounting Guide,* "Accounting for Retail Land Sales."

well off at the end of that period as it was at the beginning. The critical words in this definition are in the phrase "as well off." Anyone who studies the concept of income will soon discover that controversies over the meaning and measurement of periodic income center on the problem of determining what the financial position of a business is at any given time, whether its position has improved or worsened, and by how much.

Let us begin with a relatively simple problem in income determination. If we were asked to measure the lifetime net income of a business at the time it was being liquidated, we could probably agree on the following computation:

Total proceeds received on liquidation of the business	$800,000
Add: Amounts withdrawn by owners during the life of the business .	300,000
Less: Amount of capital invested in the business by its owners	(600,000)
Lifetime net income of the business	$500,000

If we ignore the time value of money and assume a stable price level, lifetime net income of a business is comparatively easy to measure. The reason is that at the beginning and end of the life of any business, the value of its net assets can be established with reasonable accuracy. The original investment of the owners and the proceeds on liquidation are usually definite sums of money or their equivalent.

At any stage prior to final liquidation, however, the net assets of a business constitute a complex set of resources, whose collective value depends largely on future earning power. In theory the only direct way to determine how well off a business is at any point in time is to compute the net present value of all its future revenue and disbursements. This is sometimes called the process of *direct valuation.* Estimates of future earning power are obviously subject to a large margin of error.

Accountants readily admit an inability to determine at frequent time intervals the *direct value* of business net assets. For this they can hardly be criticized for undue caution or modesty; they are simply being realistic about their limitations. The role of an economic reporter is perhaps less glamorous than that of the economic forecaster, but it is no less useful. Thus in measuring how well off a business is at any time, in order to measure periodic income, accountants agree to reflect in their records only those changes in business position that can be substantiated by reasonably objective evidence.

The meaning of objective evidence

Facts form a basis for most intelligent decisions and forecasts of the future. Most of what is contained in accounting records purports to be factual. Like everyone else, however, the accountant often has considerable difficulty in deciding what the facts are.

Businesses are engaged in the continuing process of transforming one series of economic goods and services (inputs) into another essentially different series of goods and services (outputs), in the expectation that the aggregate output will command a higher price in the market than the cost of the input. In reporting periodic progress in this endeavor, accountants seek objective evidence to support the data they present. But what is meant by objective evidence? The important element in the objectivity of any observation or interpretation is verifiability, the agreement of competent persons as to what has been observed or experienced. The term *objective evidence,* then, means evidence that is sufficiently clear-cut that reasonable individuals will vary in their interpretation of it only within fairly narrow limits.

External Data   Purchases of asset services, hiring and paying employees, sales of goods and services, borrowing funds, selling shares of stock—all are examples of market transactions between a business and outsiders. These economic events stem from express or implied contracts and usually represent an exchange between independent parties at an arm's-length or bargained price. In other words, there is external evidence to support an accounting record of what has taken place.

At times the evidence is somewhat hazy or ambiguous. For example, if a tract of land originally acquired as a site for plant construction is exchanged directly for a smaller site with a complete operating plant and equipment, no explicit market price is established, and the accountants are forced to look for evidence of an implicit price at which to record the transaction. They try to obtain independent evidence of the current fair value of the operating plant and equipment or the current fair value of the vacant land given in exchange. Such independent evidence is needed to estimate the bargained price that would have been established had the plant and equipment been acquired and the vacant land sold for cash. A similar problem arises in the "basket purchase" situation, when two or more different assets are acquired for a single price. The problem is to divide the total price among the assets received, and the accountants must seek independent evidence to support this allocation. Despite these troublesome cases, arriving at a reasonable and acceptable basis for recording most transactions between the business and outsiders causes relatively little difficulty.

Internal Data   The second type of economic event in business leaves a much less distinct trail of evidence; consequently, it creates a far more troublesome set of problems for the accountant. The amount spent for materials, labor, and productive services can be objectively measured. The continuous process of transforming these inputs into more valuable outputs, however, is an internal, not an external, affair. In tracing the effect of this productive process and portraying it in terms of dollars, the accountant does not have the objective evidence of market transactions with outsiders as a basis for measurement.

The flow of costs

Ideally all costs should be associated with some physical product or output. If the entire resources of a business are devoted to the production and sale of a single product, this assumption might be reasonable. All costs incurred could be accumulated as inventory costs until the sale of the product provided objective evidence of gain or loss.

Even in this single-product case, however, it is apparent that some costs are more directly related to production than others. The costs of raw materials, direct labor, and some kinds of variable factory overhead, for example, can be traced to physical production because the relationship between effort and accomplishment is relatively clear. At the other extreme, such costs as sales salaries, advertising expenditures, and administrative overhead are productive, but the relationship between effort and accomplishment is far more nebulous. A sales visit today may result in a sale two years hence. The installation of a new cost accounting system may provide better control over operations and produce benefits to the business for years to come. In either case it is virtually impossible to trace these efforts to physical product with any degree of precision. When we shift this problem to the more realistic setting of a business producing not one but many different products or services, the difficulty of cost assignment increases immensely, and one can easily see that tracing costs is more an art than a science.

Confronted with this sort of vague evidence, the accountant finds it necessary to adopt a series of reasonable assumptions. It is hardly surprising that opinions as to what is "reasonable" in any given case will differ. The fact that alternative accounting principles, each of which may produce significantly different results, may be "generally accepted" stems directly from these differences of opinion.

Product and Period Costs In measuring business income certain costs, called **product costs,** are traced to physical output and are accumulated in inventory accounts until evidence of gain or loss is available. For example, the costs of direct labor and raw material used in fabricating a product can be directly identified with the cost of producing a unit of inventory.

Other costs, called **period costs,** are considered an expense of the time period in which they occur. These costs, as for example, advertising and other selling expenses, are usually not related to the flow of production and are charged against revenue immediately on the ground that the benefits expire in the same period as the expenditures are made. As pointed out in **APB Statement No. 4,** "Enterprises never acquire expenses per se; they always acquire assets. Costs may be charged to expenses in the period goods or services are acquired . . . if they only benefit the period in which they are acquired. . . ."[2]

Making a theoretical distinction between product costs and period costs may be easier than the practical application of the concept. To illustrate this problem, consider the cost of merchandise purchased by a trading concern. There are certain costs directly related to the acquisition of a given quantity of merchandise, such as the price paid to vendors and the cost of transportation-in. There are other not-so-direct costs of buying, handling, storage, and display. The salary of a purchasing agent may be one of these borderline cases. Decisions on the treatment of some costs as product costs or as period costs are likely to differ between companies and may often be resolved on the grounds of convenience. If such controversial expenditures are material in amount, different practices may lead to significantly different net income figures.

In addition to the question of product versus period costs, another issue arises when identical goods in stock have been acquired in different lots and at different prices. As these goods are sold, decisions must be made as to which of the different unit costs are to be assigned to the particular units sold. The decision to assume a first-in, first-out, a last-in, first-out, or a weighted-average flow of acquisition costs is somewhat arbitrary, but important, since different assumptions may produce materially different net income figures.

The Cost of Asset Services Certain asset services, such as buildings, equipment, or patents, are acquired in an aggregate quantity some time in advance of their use. In buying manufacturing equipment, for example, a business acquires a bundle of productive services. Some portion of the total services will be withdrawn from the bundle and used in manufacturing during the current period; other portions will not be withdrawn for several years. Accountants are faced with the problem of determining whether the cost of expired machine services is a period or a product cost. In addition, they are confronted with two even more perplexing questions: (1) How much of the total bundle of lifetime services has been used during the current period? (2) What is the cost of these used services? In the case of raw materials or merchandise, there is at least a physical flow of goods to indicate the changes that are taking place. Productive assets such as machinery, on the other hand, exhibit little or no change in their physical characteristics as they yield useful services.

The services of some productive assets expire as a function of time. If a three-year premium is paid on an insurance policy, for example, the service acquired is three years of freedom from a given amount of risk. It seems reasonable to assume that one-third of the cost of acquiring this service is used up in each of the years involved.

[2] *APB Statement No. 4,* "Basic Concepts and Accounting Principles Underlying Financial Statements of Business Enterprises," AICPA (New York: 1970), p. 85.

Suppose, however, that the asset in question is an apartment building. The services acquired are a given amount of building space which can be rented to tenants. The value of the right to occupy a new building is greater than that of an older building. It follows that the rental revenue during the early life of the building will tend to be higher than during its later years, and thus the value of the services yielded by the building will be higher in early years than in later. These facts should be considered in establishing a cost flow assumption. Objective evidence of the value of services year by year is very difficult to obtain. Furthermore, the service life of the building is indefinite. Accountants know objectively only that the investment in future building services has been X dollars, that the owners may dispose of the building at some future time, and that if they do not, the building will eventually be worthless and must be torn down. The accountants also know that the business must recover the cost of expired building services out of revenue in order to be as well off in monetary terms at the end of any period as at the time the original investment was made. In the face of these imponderables, it is likely that any solution adopted will prove to be erroneous to some degree. It is not surprising that the measurement of depreciation has always been a controversial area of accounting.

In subsequent chapters we shall consider these issues in greater detail, and examine some of the assumptions and techniques that accountants employ in dealing with internal cost data. Our purpose at this stage is to make the point that measuring costs is something far short of a precise operation. The cost factor in income determination is, at best, an intelligent estimate of the prices paid for resources used up in business operations during any accounting period.

Revenue recognition (realization)

Realization of revenue refers to the timing of its recognition in the accounts. A practical working rule is needed to signal that an increase in net assets has resulted from the activities of a business entity. Discussion of the revenue realization principle in Chapter 1 stressed that each step in producing and distributing goods and services is essential to earning revenue. Ideally, the accounting recognition of revenue should be continuous rather than occurring at a single critical point in the activities of the business.

If the plans of a business are carried out, it is clear that at some time in the productive process (in fact continuously) there is an increase in the monetary value of the resources controlled by the business entity. Since continuous direct valuation is a practical impossibility, an alternative procedure must be found to measure this increase as objectively as possible in order to reflect periodic income. The basic assumption adopted as a means of dealing with this problem is called the **revenue realization principle.**

When a business acquires asset services in exchange for money (or promises to pay money), the accountant assumes an even exchange of values; that is, that no gain or loss occurs at the time of purchase. An arm's-length exchange price is viewed as the best objective evidence of value at the time of acquisition, and a subjective judgment that the buyer has obtained something for nothing or has received the worst of the bargain is not sufficient to overcome such evidence. In tracing the flow of costs internally, the assumption of an even exchange continues to control accounting procedures. For example, in allocating raw material, direct labor, and factory overhead costs to inventories, the allocation is limited to the actual cost incurred, and the fact that there may be an increase in value beyond the costs added is ignored.

Somewhere along the line, however, objective evidence will arise that the value of the output is greater (or possibly less) than the costs of the inputs. When such evidence becomes conclusive, the accountant stops dealing solely in costs. The value of the output is measured and revenue emerges on the accounting scene. *The revenue realization principle is the set of rules adopted by accountants in deciding when a change in the value of output should be recognized in the accounting records.*

When is revenue realized?

The two primary criteria for recording in the accounts that revenue has been realized are:

1 Sufficient objective evidence exists as to the market value of the output. Usually such evidence is provided by an arm's-length sales transaction.

2 The earnings process (in essence the creation of marketable goods and services) must be substantially complete. This means that all necessary costs have been incurred or can be reasonably estimated.

Revenue Recognized at Time of Sale In applying these criteria to various practical situations, the most widely accepted evidence of revenue realization is the sale of goods. There is little question about the quality of evidence: a completed transaction with outsiders which transfers possession of, and usually title to, the product in return for money or the promise to pay money at some future date. One may question, however, why accountants choose so *late* a stage in the production process to recognize revenue and thus net income. The answer comes in two parts: (1) At any point prior to the sale, the expected sales price of non-standard products and the ability to sell them at a given price are such uncertain factors that they do not constitute good enough evidence to justify an upward revaluation of the product. (2) For most businesses, actually selling goods and services is the most important step in the earning process. Until a sale is made the future stream of revenue is in this sense "unearned." It is usually easier to make a good product than to develop adequate customer acceptance and sell the product in quantity.

Even when a sale has been made, the recognition of revenue may be delayed because of unusual terms surrounding the sales transaction. For example, in the record and printed music industry and in the book publishing industry, it is common practice to give retail stores the *right to return* products sold to them if they cannot resell these products. When customers have the right to return merchandise, the seller may continue to be exposed to the usual risks of ownership and sales revenue should not be recognized currently unless all the following conditions are met:

1 Seller's price is substantially fixed at the date of exchange.
2 The buyer either has made full payment or is indebted to the seller and payment is not deferred until the merchandise is resold.
3 Obligation to the seller is not changed because of theft or physical destruction of the merchandise.
4 Buyer must have economic substance apart from that provided by the seller; that is, the buyer is not a straw party or a conduit.
5 Seller does not have significant obligations for future performance to bring about resale of the merchandise.
6 Future returns can be predicted with reasonable accuracy.[3]

If these conditions are met and sales are recognized, provision for any costs or losses which may be expected in connection with any returns should be made at the time of sale. The sales and cost of goods sold in the income statement should exclude the portion for which returns are expected and the allowance for estimated returns should be deducted from accounts receivable in the balance sheet. Transactions for which revenue recognition is postponed should be recognized as sales when the return privilege has expired.

Although the point of sale has been widely accepted as evidence of revenue realization, the preceding discussion clearly points out that *sale* and *revenue realization* are not necessarily synonymous. Under certain circumstances, accountants are willing to record realized revenue at the three other stages in the production process discussed below.

Revenue Recognized during Production In some businesses the product consists of a few major projects which require considerable time to complete. Major construction projects such as dams or large ships are examples. For such projects, production is the major element of the earning process; the final sale is assured by a binding contract subject only to satisfactory performance by the producer. To recognize revenue

---

[3] *Statement of Position 75-1,* "Revenue Recognition When Right of Return Exists," Recommendation to FASB issued by Accounting Standards Division of AICPA (New York: 1975), pp. 4–5; *Statement of Position 76-1,* "Accounting Practices in the Record and Printed Music Industry," Recommendation to FASB issued by Accounting Standards Division of AICPA (New York: 1976), pp. 9–12.

only at the point of final sale, under these conditions, would result in a highly distorted picture of income for various accounting periods. Therefore, as progress on the project is made, portions of the construction are revalued and a percentage of the ultimate contract price is recorded as realized revenue. This procedure is discussed in Chapter 9.

Revenue Recognized when Production Is Complete When a business deals in standard goods that are sold on an organized market at prices that can be objectively determined at any time, there is a basis for valuing output as soon as it is produced. Farm products and a wide variety of commodities (such as gold and silver) sold on organized markets meet all the conditions requisite to this test of realization. In these cases it is possible to value inventories at selling prices less any marketing costs not yet incurred (sometimes called *net realizable value*), thus recognizing revenue as soon as production is completed.

Revenue Recognized when Cash Is Received The two procedures just discussed move the point of realization forward to an earlier stage in the production process, that is, prior to the point of sale. Another possibility is that the recognition of revenue should be delayed beyond the point of sale until additional evidence confirms the sales transaction. Under some conditions a transaction that purports to be a sale may be lacking in substance and therefore constitute inadequate evidence of realization. An example is found in a land sale contract in which the purchasers make only a nominal down payment, have no established credit status, and are free to cancel the agreement at any time without any penalty other than the loss of the payments they have made. In many states the seller has no legal right to take any action on such defaulted agreements other than to repossess the property sold. However, as the number of cash payments by a given customer under a sales agreement of this type accumulates, the evidence of an authentic sale and valid receivable is increased.

An extreme application of this test of revenue realization is the so-called *cash basis of accounting* described in Chapter 1. In its most unrefined state, the cash-basis procedure calls for recognizing revenue only when cash is received, and recognizing expenses at the time cash is paid out. Another practical application of the view that revenue realization coincides with the receipt of cash is a procedure known as the *installment method.* As the name suggests, this procedure is applied when the sales contract calls for payment in periodic installments. The installment method delays the recognition of revenue (and thus net income) until collections from customers are received.

Cash basis and installment methods are widely used in the computation of taxable income, because their use makes it possible for a business to *defer* the payment of income taxes. However, the acceptability of these methods for income tax purposes is not in itself any reason for their use in financial statements.[4] The income tax rules are based on the belief by government that it must collect income taxes when the taxpayer has in hand the cash arising from a business transaction, rather than upon any rational analysis of the timing of revenue recognition.

Pressures for speeding up the recognition of revenue

Many companies, in an effort to enhance their ability to attract capital from investors and bankers, are impelled to treat revenue as realized at the earliest possible moment. In the franchising field (for example, restaurants, convenience food outlets, and motels), the franchising firms have often recognized large profits at the time of signing contracts. The contracts typically called for the franchisor to guide the franchisee in locating a site, training a work staff, and commencing operations. In return, the franchisor received notes receivable but no cash. The collectibility of the notes was dependent upon the success of the proposed new business and upon a rather indefinite commitment by the franchising company to render future advisory services.

The rapidly rising earnings reported by franchising firms as they granted new franchises was often attributable to recognizing these dubious notes as assets at face amount. In part the abuse of the revenue realization principle was mitigated by issuance of *APB Opinion No. 21,* which required that notes receivable be valued not at face amount but at current fair value or (if that were not determinable) at a discounted present value computed by using an imputed interest rate consistent with the credit status of the issuer of the note.[5]

Although the discounting of receivables to their present value reduces the opportunities for the so-called "front ending" of profits on long-term agreements, it does not provide a direct answer to the question of when revenue should be recognized on the types of contracts described above.[6] Because of the current widespread use of innovative financing arrangements, accountants face a more difficult problem than ever before in determining when a "sale" is a genuine sales transaction.

Matching costs and revenue

As previously stated in Chapter 1, the interrelation of the cost and revenue realization principles is often described as a process of "matching

[4] In December 1966 the Accounting Principles Board stated that "the installment method of recognizing revenue is not acceptable" unless circumstances are such that there is no reasonable basis for estimating the collectibility of installment receivables (*APB Opinion No. 10,* p. 149).

[5] *APB Opinion No. 21,* "Interest on Receivables and Payables," AICPA (New York: 1971), par. 12–13.

[6] The problem was alleviated with the publication of *An AICPA Industry Accounting Guide,* "Accounting for Franchise Fee Revenue," AICPA (New York: 1973). This subject is covered in greater detail in Chapter 14.

costs and revenue." Accountants associate costs with output and then determine the value of output at the point of revenue realization. Any costs treated as period costs are simply related to whatever revenue has been recognized during that accounting period.

A simple illustration will make this point clear. A department store sells a dress for $60 to a charge customer. Look behind this transaction and you will find that the "product" sold in this case is a great deal more than a dress. The business has sold some portion of the service potential of the building in which the sale took place. It has also sold the services of an expert dress buyer who studied fashion trends and made one or more trips to the designers' showrooms. Freight, insurance, storage, handling, pricing, and accounting services have also been sold, as well as advertising and the services of a salesclerk. Our list is not complete, but let us assume that the cost of acquiring the dress and all services necessary to put that dress where our hypothetical customer would buy amount to $45. In exchange for this the customer gives the store a contractual promise worth $60. An ideal accounting for this transaction would show that the store had invested $45 in an asset (the "product" sold to this customer) and that this asset had been revalued from $45 to $60 (and retitled accounts receivable) at the time of sale, when evidence of value became available.

Using money as a unit of measurement

We have seen how the cost and realization assumptions affect the accounting measurement of income. Now let us look briefly at an accounting assumption that is equally fundamental—the assumption that money is a useful *standard measuring unit* for reporting the effect of business transactions.

Assume that a company invests $80 in Year 1 to produce a machine which is expected to sell for $120. The cost of producing the identical machine has risen to $130 in Year 2, and because demand is strong the company is able to sell its machine for $180 in that year. Between Year 1 and Year 2, prices in general throughout the economy have risen 10%. On these facts the income from this transaction might be computed in three different ways:

Method 1. Ordinary Accounting Mixed-Dollar Income

Revenue realized in Year 2	$180
Actual costs incurred in Year 1	80
Monetary income	$100

Method 2. Mixed-Dollar Income with Price Gain Isolated

Revenue realized in Year 2	$180
Replacement cost at the date of sale	130
Operating margin	$ 50
Add: Price gain (the difference between current replacement cost of $130	
and actual cost of $80)	50
Monetary income	$100

Method 3. Income Measured in Constant Dollars

Revenue in current (Year 2) dollars	$180
Cost of production, expressed in dollars of current (Year 2) purchasing	
power ($80 × 110%)	88
Net income measured in dollars of constant value	$ 92

Accounting income (method 1) reflects the entire difference between dollars of revenue and dollars of cost, without regard to differences in their size. Under method 2 the effect of changes in *specific* prices is isolated, and the fact that one-half of monetary income is due to a price gain is revealed.

In method 3 the unit of measurement has been changed to dollars of constant value. Both costs and revenue are expressed in Year 2 dollars. Net income in Year 2 dollars is only $92, since the firm must now recover $88 to be as well off as it was when it invested $80 in producing the machine in Year 1.

During and immediately following periods when prices in general are rising, a clear understanding of the limitations of the dollar measuring unit is invaluable in interpreting financial statements. A serious move toward measuring business income in other than mixed-dollar terms is currently under way. This topic is considered more fully in Chapter 22.

INCOME REPORTING: THE INCOME STATEMENT

We have seen that the problem of measuring income is formidable. Also important is the related problem of presenting income measurement information in a financial statement. A good income statement is something more than an itemized list of revenue and expenses. The accountant should give some thought to such issues as the system of classification, the amount of detail that is useful, the order of presentation, the relation between the elements of net income, and the titles used to describe the items appearing in an income statement.

A report of net income for the enterprise may not be as significant to management as statements showing income by products, departments, or divisions of responsibility. Managers are obviously interested in detailed accounting and statistical data that throw light on the contribution of the various segments of a business to its overall efficiency and success. Such information might also be of great interest to outsiders, but the information appearing in published income statements is usually highly condensed. More detailed income statements are often submitted to credit grantors and other persons having a special interest in the affairs of a business enterprise.

The income statements for some companies are quite complex. For example, if a change in accounting principle was made, if a major segment of business was sold, or if extraordinary items were reported, the lower section of the income statement will be significantly expanded. Finally, *earnings per share* must be presented in the income statement, and this can become quite cumbersome for companies which report *primary* as well as *fully diluted* earnings per share. In this section we shall illustrate some relatively simple income statements, to be followed by a discussion and illustrations of more complex situations.

Multiple-step versus single-step income statements

The choice between the multiple-step and single-step form of income statement is an unsettled question in income reporting. In the multiple-step form (illustrated on page 103 for Sample Corporation) various intermediate balances, such as gross profit on sales, operating income, and income before income taxes, are computed and labeled on the statement. The single-step approach (illustrated on page 104 is to group all revenue in one category, all expenses in another, and derive a single resultant net income figure. (The related financial statements for Sample Corporation are illustrated in subsequent sections of this chapter and in Chapter 4.)

Those who favor the multiple-step form argue that there are a number of significant subtotals on the road to net income. The *gross profit on sales* figure indicates the average markup on product sold which is available to cover selling and administrative expenses. The distinction between operating and financial revenue and expenses permits the showing of *income from operations* as a measure of operating results. The figure *income before income taxes* reflects pre-tax earnings and emphasizes the special nature of the income tax levy.

Proponents of the alternative single-step approach maintain that net income emerges as the overall amount by which a firm is better off after taking into account all revenue and all expenses incurred in producing that revenue. They object to the implication of the multiple-step form

SAMPLE CORPORATION
Income Statement (Multiple-Step Form)
For Year Ended December 31, Year 5
(In thousands of dollars)

Gross sales			$18,700
Less: Sales returns and allowances		$ 324	
Sales discounts		268	592
Net sales			$18,108
Cost of goods sold:			
Beginning inventories		$ 1,000	
Purchases (net of discounts)	$10,668		
Transportation-in	1,266		
Delivered cost of purchases	$11,934		
Less: Purchase returns and allowances	(366)	11,568	
Goods available for sale		$12,568	
Less: Ending inventories		580	
Cost of goods sold			11,988
Gross profit on sales			$ 6,120
Operating expenses:			
Selling expenses:			
Sales force expense		$ 1,260	
Advertising and promotion expense		880	
Product delivery expense		180	
Building occupancy expense (including depreciation of building)		240	
Other selling expenses		80	$ 2,640
General and administrative expenses:			
Administrative salaries		$ 960	
Property taxes		208	
Depreciation of equipment		80	
Other administrative expenses		372	1,620
Total operating expenses			4,260
Income from operations			$ 1,860
Other revenue and expenses:			
Investment income		$ 420	
Gain on disposal of equipment		50	
Interest expense		(230)	240
Income before income taxes			$ 2,100
Income taxes			1,043
Net income			$ 1,057
Earnings per share of common stock			$ 1.25

SAMPLE CORPORATION
Income Statement (Single-Step Form)
For Year Ended December 31, Year 5
(In thousands of dollars)

Revenue:		
Net sales		$18,108
Investment income		420
Gain on disposal of equipment		50
Total revenue		$18,578
Costs and expenses:		
Wages, salaries, and employee benefits	$ 2,320	
Merchandise and supplies	12,078	
Payments for services	1,456	
Depreciation	186	
Property taxes	208	
Interest expense	230	
Income taxes	1,043	
Total expenses		17,521
Net income		$ 1,057
Earnings per share of common stock		$ 1.25

that there is a priority of cost recovery; that is, that cost of goods sold is recovered first, then operating expenses, then financial expenses. The multiple-step form also implies relationships that do not exist. For example, showing interest revenue as a special form of income implies that interest is realized without cost; yet some administrative expenses of a business are usually incurred in producing interest revenue.

The sequence of listing of expenses and the amount of detail shown in published income statements vary considerably. The multiple-step income statement is more likely to be found in more detailed financial statements prepared for the use of management, bankers, and other creditors.

Most published income statements appear in single-step form and almost always are presented in **comparative form,** similar to the one illustrated for Texasgulf Inc., on page 105.

TEXASGULF INC. AND CONSOLIDATED SUBSIDIARIES
Consolidated Statements of Income
(Amounts in thousands)

	Year ended December 31 1975	Year ended December 31 1974
Sales	$444,645	$568,526
Royalties, interest, and other income	17,007	15,280
	461,652	583,806
Costs and expenses		
Operating, delivery and other related costs and		
expenses	246,652	260,278
Exploration	13,414	21,295
Selling, general and administrative	16,130	18,741
Interest	13,982	14,424
Income taxes	68,250	121,768
	358,428	436,506
Net income	$103,224	$147,300
Net income per share	$3.37	$4.83
Average number of shares outstanding	30,615,846	30,483,276

Comparative financial statements bring out more clearly the nature and trends of current changes and emphasize the fact that financial statements for one period are only a small part of what is essentially a continuous history of a business entity.

Classification of revenue

For most companies the major source of revenue is the production and sale of goods and services. Examples of secondary sources are dividends, royalties, interest, rents, and gains on the disposal of assets. One objective in reporting revenue on an income statement is to disclose the major sources of revenue and to separate primary from miscellaneous sources. For example, some companies report revenue from government contracts separately from revenue from nongovernment sources, which enables the reader to form some opinion of future prospects in the light of projected governmental expenditures.

Revenue offsets should be clearly distinguished from expenses and deducted from gross revenue in the income statement. Such items as sales discounts and sales returns and allowances do not represent expenses, but rather revenue that is never realized.

Classification of expenses

Expenses are classified in income statements to help the reader grasp important operating cost relationships. Classification may be according to the *nature* of the expense elements, business *functions,* areas of *responsibility,* or any other useful basis.

Natural Classification In many published income statements, expenses are reported in single-step form, classified according to the nature of the expense elements. The single-step income statement for Sample Corporation on page 104 illustrates this basis of classification, in which expenses are grouped in categories that reflect the kinds of resources used during the period.

Functional Classification The multiple-step income statement for Sample Corporation on page 103 illustrates a classification of expenses into three categories on a functional basis: (1) Cost of goods sold, (2) selling expenses, and (3) general and administrative expenses.

For internal reports, the usefulness of the functional classification system is improved by identifying many more than three functions. For example, material handling, production scheduling, assembly, packing, and crating are manufacturing subfunctions.

Expenses versus Losses Losses are nonproductive expenditures or asset expirations that have no observable relation to either current or future revenue. Thus the cost of mistakes, waste, and unusual casualties or calamities over which there can be no control may be distinguished from ordinary operating expenses on the grounds that the former are nonproductive. This distinction, although difficult to draw in many practical situations, can be quite useful for managerial purposes. For external reporting, minimum standards of disclosure require that material and unusual losses be disclosed in the income statement.

Cost offsets or savings

Cost offsets or savings should be distinguished from revenue. Revenue arises from realized increases in the value of assets. Cost offsets are expenditures that a business is able to avoid. For example, suppose that a machine can be purchased for $1,000 in cash or $1,200 on a time-payment basis. If the buying company chooses to pay $1,200, it has acquired two distinct types of asset services—the machine for $1,000 and the privilege of deferring payment for $200. If the buyer chooses to pay cash, the $200 is not a revenue but a cost saving, and the machine still costs $1,000. Similarly, cash discounts on purchases are cost savings that should not be confused with revenue.

Offsetting revenue and costs

When plant assets are sold, the price received (revenue) and the carrying value of the asset (cost) are offset and only the net gain or loss is shown in the income statement. Since the sale of such assets is not a part of ordinary operations, the net result is the significant figure.

In other cases revenue is reported as a cost reduction. For example, revenue realized through the sale of scrap or by-products is often recorded as a reduction of the cost of the main product. Because the main product and by-products usually emerge jointly from a single raw material (and joint cost allocation is a difficult problem), this procedure has merit. If carried to extremes, however, offsetting revenue against costs would detract from the significance of the gross revenue figure.

Interim report of earnings

Interim financial information may include current data on financial position, results of operations, and changes in financial position. However, interim financial reports issued to stockholders seldom include a complete set of financial statements. Although practices differ somewhat, most companies issue only highly condensed *interim reports of earnings,* such as the one illustrated on page 108 for Esmark, Inc.

Publicly owned corporations are required to issue **quarterly reports** to their shareholders, the SEC, and the stock exchanges which list their stock. Such reports are prepared in accordance with standards set forth in *APB Opinion No. 28,* "Interim Financial Reporting."[7] An audit of interim reports of earnings is not currently required. However, auditors generally perform a *limited review* of interim financial information and convey their findings in a report addressed to the company, its board of directors, or its stockholders. The auditors' report on interim financial information does not include any expressions of assurance concerning the information and each page of the interim financial information is marked as "unaudited."[8]

Income reporting to meet objectives of financial statements

Among the objectives of financial statements developed by the Study Group on Objectives listed earlier in Chapter 1 are:

1 To provide information useful to investors and creditors for predicting, com-

[7] *APB Opinion No. 28,* "Interim Financial Reporting," AICPA (New York: 1973).
[8] *Statement on Auditing Standards No. 13,* "Reports on a Limited Review of Interim Financial Information," AICPA (New York: 1976), p. 10.

ESMARK, INC.
Summary of Consolidated Revenues and Earnings
(In thousands—except per share data)

	Three months ended		Nine months ended	
	July 31, 1976	July 26, 1975	July 31, 1976	July 26, 1975
	(13 Weeks)	(13 Weeks)	(40 Weeks)	(39 Weeks)
Total revenues	$1,238,564	$1,184,123	$3,973,945	$3,428,678
Costs and expenses, including interest charges	1,221,322	1,145,519	3,876,218	3,319,836
Earnings before income taxes	$ 17,242	$ 38,604	$ 97,727	$ 108,842
Income taxes*	4,682	18,527	39,091	52,244
Net earnings	$ 12,560	$ 20,077	$ 58,636	$ 56,598
Net earnings per common share:				
Primary**	$ .68	$ 1.24	$ 3.25	$ 3.67
Fully diluted	$ .68	$ 1.16	$ 3.25	$ 3.41
Dividends per common share	$ .38	$ .28	$ 1.14	$ .84
Average common shares outstanding	17,508	15,843	17,465	15,088

Note:
  1975 share and per share data have been restated for the 5 for 4 common stock split in 1975. Primary earnings per share would have been the same as fully diluted if the preferred stock converted into common stock in 1975 had been converted at the beginning of the year.
 * The company's effective tax rate in 1976 was lower than the statutory rate of 48% and last year's as a result of increased investment tax credits and favorable tax rates relating to International Playtex' Puerto Rican operations.
** After preferred stock dividend requirements.

paring, and evaluating potential cash flows to them in terms of amount, timing, and related uncertainty.

2 To provide users with information for predicting, comparing, and evaluating enterprise earning power.[9]

The highly condensed form of income statement issued by most companies is less than adequate to achieve these two objectives. Considerable improvement in the reporting of results of operations is needed if the income statement is to be of maximum benefit to users in predicting, comparing, and evaluating the earning power of a company. For example, since the earning of income consists of *earnings cycles* which may be completed, incomplete, or prospective, it may be useful to segregate precisely measured results from estimated results. The basis of estimates might be explained so that sophisticated users could inter-

[9] *Report of the Study Group on the Objectives of Financial Statements,* AICPA (New York: 1973), pp. 62–63.

pret the reported results in line with their own judgment and experience. Also, it may be useful to report the effects of changes in values of assets and liabilities on net income and to segregate expenses between fixed and variable to help users predict prospective cash flows and the possible effects on net income of changes in volume of activity.

Financial forecasts

Another objective of financial statements is to provide information useful for the predictive process. The Study Group on Objectives urged that "*financial forecasts* should be provided when they will enhance the reliability of users' predictions."[10] The Study Group on Objectives supported its recommendation as follows:

> All economic decisions look to the future. Since economic decision-makers cannot know the future, they look to the past and the present. Financial statements that provide information about the past and the present are useful for making predictions on which to base economic decisions. In many instances, however, the past may not be a good indicator of the future. Publication of explicit forecasts of enterprise activities may well fit the objectives of financial statements. The important consideration is not the accuracy of management forecasts themselves, but rather the relative accuracy of users' predictions with and without forecasts in financial statements.[11]

The public accounting profession and the SEC have sought to find a satisfactory basis for the preparation and issuance of financial forecasts, including the results of future operations. Virtually every large business prepares forecasts of future operations as a means of defining goals and measuring performance. The problem is how to make such information available to the investing public yet avoid the danger of misleading investors through erroneous forecasts. At one time the SEC proposed to require companies making profit forecasts to meet detailed reporting standards but eventually withdrew its proposal. Although the SEC currently permits companies to file earnings forecasts with the Commission, it neither encourages nor discourages such practice.

Few companies issue financial forecasts to the public at present. However, many companies issue such forecasts to lenders, underwriters, and prospective investors in connection with obtaining debt or equity financing. In 1975, the Accounting Standards Division of the AICPA issued a **Statement of Position 75-4** "as a guide for CPAs in the preparation of financial forecasts for clients."[12] The AICPA suggested that financial forecasts generally should include at least the following information: (1) sales or gross revenue, (2) gross profit, (3) provision for income taxes, (4) net income, (5) disposal of a segment of business, (6) extraordinary items, (7) earnings per share, and (8) significant anticipated changes in financial position.

[10] Ibid., p. 65.
[11] Ibid.
[12] *Statement of Position 75-4*, "Presentation and Disclosure of Financial Forecasts," AICPA (New York: 1975).

SPECIAL PROBLEMS IN INCOME REPORTING

Income reporting in recent years has become more complicated as a result of new accounting standards relating to income tax allocation, extraordinary items, discontinued operations of a segment of a business, changes in accounting principles, and the reporting of earnings per share data. These topics are briefly discussed in the following sections.

Income tax allocation

Income taxes on corporate income constitute a major expense of doing business. *Taxable income* is a legal concept; it is related to accounting income but there are significant differences. As a result a corporation's taxable income for the year may differ substantially from its accounting income before income taxes, as reported in the income statement. Accountants have attempted to deal with this problem by *income tax allocation,* which is the subject matter of Chapter 21. At this point only the general nature of income tax allocation will be considered, with attention focused on the method of presenting clearly in the income statement the tax effect on extraordinary items, discontinued operations, and the cumulative effect of accounting changes.

Tax allocation falls into two major types: (1) interperiod tax allocation and (2) intraperiod tax allocation. *Interperiod tax allocation* means that income tax expense should be allocated between accounting periods because of *timing* differences in the recognition of income, that is, expenses or revenue appear in the income statement either before or after they appear in the tax return. By means of interperiod tax allocation, the income tax expense in the income statement is based on earnings as shown in the income statement rather than at the amount of income tax actually payable for the current period. In brief, income taxes are allocated between periods as are other expenses. *Intraperiod tax allocation* is the process of allocating income taxes to income from operations, to extraordinary items, and to other sources of income and loss which require separate presentation in the income statement. Similarly, corrections of errors made in prior periods are recorded in the Retained Earnings account net of any related income tax effect. Such allocation is a required practice, as indicated by the following statement in *APB Opinion No. 11:*

> The income tax expense attributable to income before extraordinary items is computed by determining the income tax expense related to revenue and expense transactions entering into the determination of such income, without giving effect to the tax consequences of the items excluded from the determination of income before extraordinary items. The income tax expense attributable to other items is determined by the tax consequences of transactions involving these items.[13]

[13] *APB Opinion No. 11,* "Accounting for Income Taxes," AICPA (New York: 1967), par. 52.

The important point to keep in mind is that extraordinary items and other unusual components of net income should be reported **net of income taxes in the income statement,** and prior period adjustments should be reported **net of income taxes in the statement of retained earnings.** The application of intraperiod tax allocation in the income statement, including the presentation of earnings per share, is illustrated for Complex Corporation on page 116; the reporting of a prior period adjustment is illustrated for Sample Corporation on page 119.

Extraordinary items

A troublesome problem in reporting periodic income is the proper treatment of extraordinary gains and losses. General agreement exists that unusual gains and losses, if material in amount, should be clearly disclosed in the income statement. They should be distinguished from the ordinary operating revenue and expenses of the period. However, such gains and losses should be reported as extraordinary items in the income statement only when the events or transactions giving rise to the gains and losses are **unusual in nature and infrequent in occurrence.** This standard is summarized in **APB Opinion No. 30** as follows:

> Extraordinary items are events and transactions that are distinguished by their unusual nature **and** by the infrequency of their occurrence. Thus, **both** of the following criteria should be met to classify an event or transaction as an extraordinary item:
>
> **a Unusual nature**—the underlying event or transaction should possess a high degree of abnormality and be of a type clearly unrelated to, or only incidentally related to, the ordinary and typical activities of the entity, taking into account the environment in which the entity operates.
>
> **b Infrequency of occurrence**—the underlying event or transaction should be of a type that would not reasonably be expected to recur in the foreseeable future, taking into account the environment in which the entity operates.[14]

To be considered unusual in nature, the underlying event or transaction should be abnormal and clearly unrelated to the ordinary and typical activities of the entity. The scope of operations, lines of business, operating policies, and the environment in which an entity operates should be considered in applying this criterion. The environment of an entity includes such factors as the characteristics of the industry in which it operates, the geographic location of its activities, and the degree of government regulation.

If an event or a transaction is not reasonably expected to take place in the foreseeable future, it is considered to occur infrequently. Past experience of the entity is generally a helpful guide in determining the frequency of an event or transaction. Thus only **unusual** and **infrequent** events and transactions produce extraordinary gains and losses. How-

[14] *APB Opinion No. 30,* "Reporting the Results of Operations—Reporting the Effects of Disposal of a Segment of a Business, and Extraordinary, Unusual and Infrequently Occurring Events and Transactions," AICPA (New York: 1973), pp. 564–565.

ever, these qualitative standards are difficult to apply in practice, and differences of opinion still exist in identifying extraordinary items. Listed below are some examples of how certain gains or losses should be classified for financial reporting purposes:

Extraordinary Items	Not Extraordinary Items
1 Effects of major casualties (such as earthquakes or severe hailstorms in localities where such events are extremely rare)	1 Write-down or write-off of receivables, inventories, equipment leased to others, or intangible assets
2 Effects of a prohibition under a newly enacted law or regulation	2 Gains or losses from exchange or translation of foreign currencies (including major devaluations and revaluations)
3 Loss from an expropriation of assets by a foreign country	3 Gain or losses on disposal of a segment of a business
4 Material gain or loss on extinguishment of debt	4 Other gains or losses from sale or abandonment of plant assets used in the business
5 Realization of income tax in the current period of an earlier-year operating loss carryforward	5 Effects of a strike and adjustments of accruals on long-term contracts
6 Gain or loss on sale of **only** holding of stock or land which has been owned for many years	6 Cumulative effect of a change in accounting principle

Relatively few extraordinary items are currently reported by publicly owned corporations as a result of the rigid criteria established in *APB Opinion No. 30.* The presentation of extraordinary items, including the separate per-share effect in the income statement is, illustrated below and on page 116.

Income before income taxes and extraordinary item	$500,000
Income taxes (actual income taxes payable are $80,000 as a result of the	
tax reduction from the extraordinary loss)	200,000
Income before extraordinary item	$300,000
Extraordinary loss from fire, net of income tax credit of $120,000 . . .	180,000
Net income	$120,000
Earnings per share:	
Income before extraordinary item	$ 3.00
Extraordinary item	(1.80)
Net income	$ 1.20

The effect of a material event or transaction which is considered either unusual in nature or occurs infrequently, **but not both,** should be included in determining the income before extraordinary items. The nature and effects on net income of each such event or transaction should be disclosed either in the income statement or in the notes to financial statements.

Discontinued operations of a segment of a business

A major line of business or class of customers of a company is known as a *segment of a business* for financial reporting purposes. The assets and operating results of a segment of a business should be clearly identifiable from the other assets and results of operations of the company. Users of financial statements consider the income statement to be more useful when the results from the *continuing operations* of company are reported separately from the results of material and unusual transactions or events. For this reason the operating results of a *discontinued segment* of a business (including any gain or loss on the disposal of the segment) for the current period should be reported separately in the lower section of the income statement. Such operating results and gains or losses are reported net of applicable income taxes. The purpose of such separate disclosure is to enable users of financial statements to make better predictive judgments as to the future earnings performance of the company.

Thus, the revenue and expenses included in an income statement for the year in which a segment of a business is eliminated consist only of the revenue and expenses from continuing operations. The net income or loss from the discontinued segment for the current period is reported separately, in arriving at *income before extraordinary items,* and the revenue applicable to the discontinued segment should be separately disclosed in the related notes to financial statements. Any gain or loss from disposal of a segment should be reported in conjunction with the operations of the segment and not as an extraordinary item.[15] Per-share data relating to discontinued operations "may be included on the face of the income statement or in a related note."[16] These reporting requirements are illustrated for Complex Corporation on page 116.

Accounting changes

We have stated earlier that the consistent use of accounting principles from one accounting period to another increases the usefulness of financial statements by facilitating analysis of comparative accounting data. However, management may justify a change to an alternative acceptable accounting principle on the basis that it is preferable.[17] Basi-

---

[15] Ibid., p. 557.
[16] Ibid., p. 559.
[17] *APB Opinion No. 20,* "Accounting Changes," AICPA (New York: 1971), p. 391.

cally there are two types of accounting changes: (1) change in account-ing principle and (2) change in accounting estimate.

Some changes in accounting principles (such as a change in the method of computing depreciation) are recognized by including the *cumulative effect* of changing to a new accounting principle in net income of the period of change.[18] Such changes require the restatement of assets and liabilities as of the beginning of the current period to the amounts that would have existed if the newly adopted principle had been used in prior years. The related debit or credit reflecting the *cumulative effect* of the change on earnings of prior years is reported in the current year's income statement *between* any extraordinary items and the figure for net income. The method of reporting the cumulative effect of the change is essentially the same as for extraordinary items, as illustrated for Complex Corporation on page 116.

Other changes in accounting principles (such as a change from lifo to fifo method of inventory pricing) are reported by a restatement of the financial statements of prior periods.

Another type of accounting change is a change in estimate, such as the revision of an original estimate of an 8-year economic life for aircraft to a 12-year life. The new estimate affects only the current and future years' financial statements and no correcting entry is necessary. The undepreciated cost of the aircraft at the date of the change in estimated economic life will be allocated among the remaining years of economic life.

Accounting changes are discussed and illustrated in detail in Chapter 23.

Earnings per share

The amount of earnings per share of common stock for a period is computed by dividing the net income available by the weighted-average number of shares outstanding during the period. The purpose is to show earning power on a per-share basis so that investors can relate the market price of a share of stock to the income per share. However, in situations where a company has outstanding stock options, convertible bonds or preferred stock, and other hybrid securities, we cannot compute a *single* meaningful earnings per share figure. In such cases a *dual presentation* of earnings per share is required to show *primary* and *fully diluted* earnings per share.

When extraordinary items appear in the income statement, primary and fully diluted earnings per share are presented as follows:

---

[18] Ibid., pp. 391–392.

	Year 2	Year 1
Earnings per share of common stock:		
Primary:		
Earnings before extraordinary item	$4.00	$3.35
Extraordinary item	(0.50)	1.65
Net income	$3.50	$5.00
Fully diluted:		
Income before extraordinary item	$3.55	$3.00
Extraordinary item	(0.42)	1.58
Net income	$3.13	$4.58

A more extensive example of presentation of earnings per share data appears on page 116 for Complex Corporation. This topic is covered in detail in Chapter 20.

Comprehensive illustration of income reporting

The presentation of extraordinary items, discontinued operations, cumulative effect of a change in accounting principle, and per-share data in the income statement is illustrated, along with the related notes, on pages 116–117 for Complex Corporation.

Note the extensive detail of the per-share and pro forma amounts in the lower section of the income statement for Complex Corporation, despite the fact that a dual presentation of earnings per share (primary and fully diluted) was not required.

Disclosure requirements

Companies reporting to the public are required to disclose, either in the body of the income statement or in the accompanying notes, certain information which may be helpful to users of financial statements. Although these disclosure requirements will be stressed throughout this book, some of the more important items relating directly to the income statement which call for disclosure either in reports to the SEC or in the annual report to stockholders are listed below:

1 Accounting policies, including depreciation methods, amortization of intangibles, inventory pricing, and revenue recognition procedures.
2 Management's discussion and analysis of the summary of operations, including reasons for material changes in specific items.
3 The amount of depreciation expense for the period and the amount of research and development costs charged to expense in each period for which an income statement is presented.
4 An analysis of the composition of income taxes expense, including a reconcil-

COMPLEX CORPORATION*
Income Statement
(In thousands of dollars, except per-share data)

	Year Ended Year 11	December 31, Year 10
Net sales and other revenue	$85,360	$75,750
Costs and expenses (Note 1)	65,880	60,390
Income from continuing operations before income taxes	$19,480	$15,360
Income taxes	9,350	7,370
Income from continuing operations	$10,130	$ 7,990
Discontinued operations (Note 2):		
Income from operations of discontinued Division X (less income taxes of $383 in Year 11 and $442 in Year 10)	410	470
Loss on disposal of Division X, including provision of $105 for losses during phase-out period (less income taxes of $1,880)	(2,040)	
Income before extraordinary item and cumulative effect of a change in accounting principle . . .	$ 8,500	$ 8,460
Extraordinary item, net of income taxes of $493 (Note 3)		1,224
Cumulative effect on prior years (to Dec. 31, Year 10) of changing to a different depreciation method; net of income taxes of $1,150 (Note 4)	1,250	
Net income	$ 9,750	$ 9,684
Per-share amounts:		
Income from continuing operations	$ 2.03	$ 1.60
Income from operations of discontinued Division X	.08	.10
Loss on disposal of Division X	(.41)	
Income before extraordinary item and cumulative effect of a change in accounting principle	$ 1.70	$ 1.70
Extraordinary item, net of income taxes		.24
Cumulative effect on preceeding years (to Dec. 31, Year 10) of changing to a different depreciation method	.25	
Net income	$ 1.95	$ 1.94
Pro forma amounts, assuming the new depreciation method is applied retroactively:		
Income from continuing operations	$10,130	$ 8,125
Per common share	2.03	1.63
Income before extraordinary item	8,500	8,595
Per common share	1.70	1.72
Net income	8,500	9,819
Per common share	1.70	1.96

* Adapted from Extraordinary Items, Prior Period Adjustments and Changes in Accounting Principles, Accountants International Study Group: 1974, Exhibit 1.

Note 1—Loss on Sale of Plant Facilities
Other expenses for Year 11 include $675,000 representing the loss incurred on the disposal of obsolete plant facilities. Based on provisions of **APB Opinion No. 30,** *this is not an extraordinary item.*

Note 2—Discontinued Operations
In October of Year 11, the company decided to dispose of its retail business which had consisted of 20 outlets in localities adjacent to its principal customers. Two of the outlets were closed in October and the remaining 18 were sold prior to December 31, Year 11. Charges resulting directly from the decision to dispose of this business, principally termination costs on long-term leases, severance pay, and losses on disposal of facilities and equipment related to the retail business, as well as provision for loss during the phase-out period beginning in October, Year 11, less reduction in income taxes of $1,880,000, are reported separately from the results of the company's continuing operations. The income statement for Year 10 has been reclassified to give effect to this presentation. Net sales of Division X were $920,000 in the phase-out period beginning in October, Year 11; $4,728,000 for the portion of Year 11 prior to phase-out period; and $5,207,000 for Year 10.

Note 3—Extraordinary Item
During Year 10, the Company received settlement from a state government for condemnation of land which had been held for future expansion of a manufacturing plant. The related gain, less income taxes of $493,000, is reported as an extraordinary item.

Note 4—Change to a Different Depreciation Method
Depreciation of plant equipment has been computed by the straight-line method in Year 11. Depreciation of plant equipment in prior years was computed by the sum-of-the-years'-digits method. The new method of depreciation was adopted to recognize . . . (state justification of change of depreciation method) . . . and has been applied retroactively to equipment acquisitions of prior years. The effect of the change in Year 11 was to increase income before extraordinary item by approximately $100,000 (or $0.02 per share). The adjustment of $1,250,000 (after reduction for income taxes of $1,150,000) to apply retroactively the new method is included in net income of Year 11. The pro forma amounts shown on the income statement have been adjusted for the effect of retroactive application on depreciation, the change in provisions for incentive compensation which would have been made had the new method been in effect, and related income taxes.

iation of the company's effective income tax rate with the statutory federal income tax rate.

5 Replacement cost of inventories and plant assets, as well as the amount of depreciation and cost of goods sold determined on the basis of replacement costs.

Some of these items of disclosure are illustrated in the financial statements for General Motors Corporation in the Appendix at the end of Chapter 4.

STATEMENT OF RETAINED EARNINGS

The statement of retained earnings is generally included with almost any set of financial statements, although it is not considered to be one of the major financial statements. Changing concepts of financial reporting in recent years have firmly established the all-inclusive income statement, thus tending to shorten and simplify the statement of retained earnings. Also significant has been the trend away from the use of appropriations of retained earnings. Consequently, the typical statement of retained earnings today merely lists the beginning balance of retained earnings, the net income for the period as an addition, the dividends (both cash and in the form of stock) as a deduction, and concludes with the ending balance of retained earnings. The information on dividends customarily shows the cash dividends per share as well as the total amount declared during the period. If operations for the latest period resulted in a loss, the beginning balance of retained earnings is reduced by the amount of the net loss. In addition, the beginning balance may be increased or decreased by a *prior period adjustment* (such as the correction of a material error) or the effect on prior years' operations resulting from certain types of changes in accounting principles.

Prior period adjustments

In contrast to extraordinary items described earlier in this chapter, prior period adjustments are excluded from the determination of net income for the current period and are reported (*net of any related income tax effect*) in the statement of retained earnings. Prior period adjustments were originally defined by the APB in *Opinion No. 9* as:

> . . . those material adjustments which (a) can be specifically identified with and directly related to the business activities of particular prior periods, and (b) are not attributable to economic events occurring subsequent to the date of the financial statements for the prior period, and (c) depend primarily on determinations by persons other than management and (d) were not susceptible to reasonable estimation prior to such determination. Such adjustments are rare in modern financial accounting.[19]

The interpretation of these guidelines proved to be difficult and unsatisfactory, particularly in relation to numerous out-of-court settlements of litigation. Such settlements were generally reported as prior period adjustments despite the fact that management must make a number of significant judgments, and hence the test that a prior period adjustment must "depend primarily on determinations by persons other than management" was not met. To correct the loose interpretations of the guidelines established by the APB, the FASB in 1976 issued an exposure draft of a proposed statement of financial standards which identified prior period adjustments as follows:

> Except as specified . . . below, all items of profit and loss recognized during a period, including accruals of estimated losses from loss contingencies, shall be included in the determination of net income for that period. Items of profit and loss related to the following shall be accounted for and reported as prior period adjustments and excluded from the determination of net income for the current period:

[19] *APB Opinion No. 9,* "Reporting the Results of Operations," AICPA (New York: 1966), p. 115.

a Correction of an error in the financial statements of a prior period discovered subsequent to their issuance and

b Adjustments that result from realization of income tax benefits of preacquisition operating loss carryforwards of purchases subsidiaries.[20]

Material errors in the financial statements might include arithmetical mistakes, the misuse or omissions of information, mistakes in the application of accounting principles or procedures, and failure to interpret properly the accounting aspects of major transactions. Another example of a correction of an error is in a change from an accounting principle that is not generally accepted to one that is. When a correction of an error is made as a prior period adjustment, the issuance of comparative financial statements will require restatement of the prior year's financial statements to reflect the correction of the error.

Early in 1977 the FASB announced that the necessary votes to adopt the proposed Statement were not obtained. Later in 1977 after a change in voting requirements for adoption of pronouncements by the FASB, the new standard was adopted in FASB *Statement No. 16*.[21]

Illustrations of statement of retained earnings

The basic format of a statement of retained earnings when a prior period adjustment has been recognized in the current period is illustrated below for Sample Corporation. The related income statement (multiple-step form) for Sample Corporation appears on page 103; the related balance sheet and statement of changes in financial position for Sample Corporation are presented in Chapter 4.

SAMPLE CORPORATION
Statement of Retained Earnings
For Year Ended December 31, Year 5
(In thousands of dollars)

Retained earnings, beginning of Year 5:		
As originally reported		$2,800
Less: Prior period adjustment—correction of error, net of applicable income tax effect of $240,000		360
Retained earnings at beginning of Year 5, as restated		$2,440
Add: Net income		1,057
Subtotal		$3,497
Less: Dividends on preferred stock ($6.00 per share)	$ 57	
Dividends on common stock ($0.50 per share)	400	457
Retained earnings, end of Year 5		$3,040

---

[20] Proposed *Statement of Financial Accounting Standards* "Prior Period Adjustments," FASB (Stamford: 1976), pp. 3–4.

[21] *FASB Statement No. 16*, "Prior Period Adjustments," FASB (Stamford: 1977).

As with other financial statements, the statement of retained earnings generally is presented in *comparative* form showing data for two years. This comparative form of retained earnings statement, which also includes an appropriation for contingencies, is illustrated below for FMC Corporation:

	Year ended December 31	
	1975	1974
FMC CORPORATION AND CONSOLIDATED SUBSIDIARIES		
Consolidated Retained Earnings		
Unappropriated at beginning of year	**$540,604,000**	*$493,240,000*
Net income	**108,166,000**	*80,887,000*
Cash dividends:		
Common stock—$0.94 per share in		
1975 and $0.92 per share in 1974	**(29,991,000)**	*(29,336,000)*
Preferred stock—$2.25 per share	**(4,187,000)**	*(4,187,000)*
Unappropriated at end of year	**614,592,000**	*540,604,000*
Appropriated for contingencies	**3,353,000**	*3,353,000*
Total retained earnings at end of year	**$617,945,000**	*$543,957,000*

Combined statement of earnings and retained earnings

A significant number of companies combine the income statement with the statement of retained earnings. Such a presentation has the advantage of displaying in one statement any prior period adjustments and extraordinary gains and losses, thus reducing the possibility that any of these items will be overlooked. One minor objection to this form of reporting is that the net income or net earnings figure appears in the middle, rather than as the final figure in the statement.

A combined statement of earnings and retained earnings showing comparative data for two years is presented on page 121 for Avon Products, Inc.

Note that in this illustration the per-share data appears within the body of the statement. An alternative approach, when there are no extraordinary items, is to show the earnings per share parenthetically on the line for net income or net earnings. When more complex per-share data are involved, the per-share amounts are presented at the end of the combined statement of earnings and retained earnings.

AVON PRODUCTS, INC. AND SUBSIDIARIES
Consolidated Statement of Earnings
and Retained Earnings

| | Year ended December 31 | |
	1975	1974
Net sales	$1,295,062,000	$1,260,292,000
Cost of goods sold	473,756,000	499,821,000
Selling and administrative expenses	540,312,000	521,733,000
Earnings before taxes	280,994,000	238,738,000
Taxes on earnings	141,990,000	126,983,000
Net earnings	139,004,000	111,755,000
Net earnings per share . . . . $	2.40	$ 1.93
Cash dividends—$1.51 and $1.48 per share .	87,594,000	85,827,000
Addition to retained earnings	51,410,000	25,928,000
Retained earnings, January 1	403,797,000	377,869,000
Retained earnings, December 31	$ 455,207,000	$ 403,797,000

REVIEW QUESTIONS

1 Ten accountants, if asked to measure the lifetime net income of a business and to assume no change in the purchasing power of the dollar, would probably agree within narrow limits on this long-run income measurement. The same ten accountants might vary over a wide range in their measurement of *periodic* net income for the same business. Why?

2 One of the basic standards recommended as a criterion to be used in evaluating accounting information is *verifiability.* Explain how you would expect this standard to be related to the accountant's search for objective evidence.

3 What is the distinction between *product* and *period costs?* Give an example of each type of cost.

4 What is the accounting principle of *revenue realization* and how does it affect the measurement of periodic income? What are two primary criteria used in determining when revenue has been realized?

5 Describe three stages in the earning process, other than the point of sale, at which revenue might be recognized. Give an example of a situation in which each of these three tests of realization might be appropriate.

6 The owner of an appliance store has just sold a refrigerator to a customer for $350. An employee recorded cost of goods sold of $240 relating to this sale. What elements are probably included in this cost figure? What elements of cost are probably omitted from the $240?

7 Would you expect a newly organized corporation engaged in the restaurant franchising field, having limited capital and attempting to secure capital from public investors and bankers, to favor accounting policies that would speed up the recognition of revenue or delay it? Explain.

8 Distinguish between a *functional* and a *natural* classification of expenses. What are the advantages of a functional classification for managerial purposes?

9 Distinguish between *expenses* and *losses,* and between *revenue* and *cost offsets.*

10 Explain the principal differences between the *single-step* and the *multiple-step* forms of income statement. Should earnings per share data be shown with either or both these forms of income statement?

11 What is the usual form of the *interim report of earnings?* Are such reports audited by independent CPAs?

12 What changes would you suggest in the content of income statements so that corporate earnings reports would better meet the objectives of financial statements?

13 In what ways would a *financial forecast* be useful to investors in making investment decisions?

14 Explain the meaning of *intraperiod tax allocation* and *interperiod tax allocation.*

15 Describe the criteria for *extraordinary items* as set forth in *APB Opinion No. 30.*

16 How are the results of a discontinued segment of a business for the period in which the segment is eliminated reported in the income statement? Is the loss or gain on the disposal of a segment of a business reported as an extraordinary item in the income statement? Explain.

17 Describe two types of *accounting changes* and indicate how each type is reported in the income statement.

18 What is the purpose of reporting *earnings per share* in the income statement? Under what circumstances is a *dual presentation* of earnings per share required in the income statement?

19 Give some examples of supplementary information relating to the income statement that may be disclosed in reports to the SEC or in the annual report to stockholders.

20 Define *prior period adjustments* and indicate how these are reported in a complete set of financial statements.

21 What is the major advantage of a combined statement of earnings and retained earnings? What disadvantage do you see in such a statement?

22 Briefly explain how each of the following material "losses" should be reported in the income statement or in the statement of retained earnings.
  a Shutdown expenses incurred during a major strike by employees.
  b A loss incurred upon the abandonment of outmoded equipment formerly used in the business.
  c A loss sustained as a result of damage caused by a tornado to the company's main warehouse. Tornadoes are an unusual and infrequent occurrence for the geographic area in which the company is located.
  d Reduction in carrying value of plant and equipment as a result of major error in recording the acquisition of these assets two years ago.

EXERCISES

Ex. 3-1 Yama Cigar Mfg. Corporation had inventories at the beginning and end of its current year as follows:

	Beginning	*End*
Raw materials	$22,000	$30,000
Goods in process	40,000	48,000
Finished goods	25,000	18,000
Total	$87,000	$96,000

During the year the following costs and expenses were incurred:

Raw materials purchased	$300,000
Direct labor cost	120,000
Indirect factory labor	60,000
Taxes and depreciation on factory building	20,000
Taxes and depreciation on salesroom and office	15,000
Sales salaries	40,000
Office salaries	24,000
Utilities (60% applicable to factory, 20% to salesroom, and 20% to office)	60,000

Prepare a single-step schedule to compute cost of goods sold for the current year.

Ex. 3-2 Select the best answer for each of the following multiple-choice questions:

  a Which of the following is an example of an extraordinary item in reporting results of operations?
  (1) A loss incurred because of a strike by employees
  (2) The write-off of equipment used in production believed to have no future benefit
  (3) A gain resulting from the devaluation of the U.S. dollar
  (4) A gain resulting from the state exercising its right of eminent domain on a parcel of land used as a parking lot

b Which of the following is **not** a generally practiced method of presenting the income statement?
   (1) Including prior period adjustments in the determination of net income
   (2) The single-step income statement
   (3) The consolidated statement of income
   (4) Including gains and losses from discontinued operations of a segment of a business in determining net income

c The accounting concept of matching is best demonstrated by:
   (1) Not recognizing any expense unless some revenue is realized
   (2) Associating effort (cost) with accomplishment (revenue)
   (3) Recognizing prepaid rent received as revenue
   (4) Establishing a Reserve for Possible Future Market Decline in Inventory account

d Conventionally accountants measure income:
   (1) By applying a value-added concept
   (2) By using a transactions approach
   (3) As a change in the value of owners' equity
   (4) As a change in the purchasing power of owners' equity

Ex. 3-3 Given below are selected account balances for Candy Corporation for the current year:

Beginning inventory	$ 35,600	Selling expenses	$52,800
Ending inventory	27,200	General and administrative	
Sales	374,000	expenses	32,400
Sales returns	6,480	Interest revenue	1,800
Sales discounts	5,360	Dividend revenue	4,000
Purchases	218,200	Interest expense	1,000
Transportation-in	25,320	Income taxes expense	22,000
Purchase discounts	4,840	Retained earnings, beginning	80,000
Purchase returns	7,320	Retained earnings, ending	88,000

From the foregoing information, compute the following:
a Total net revenue
b Total expenses, including cost of goods sold
c Net income
d Dividends declared during the year

Ex. 3-4 For the following list of events and transactions, you are to state for each one whether or not there is immediate realization of revenue or gain. Indicate briefly the reason supporting your conclusion.
a Sale for cash of a $200 gift certificate, which may be exchanged by the holder for merchandise in a subsequent period.
b Land purchased for $45,000 in 1970 has a current appraised value of $65,000.
c After receiving bids of $205,000 and $206,000 from independent contractors for construction of a new factory building, the X Company constructed the building itself for its own use at a cost of $190,000.
d Securities with a market value of $17,650 are received from a customer in settlement of an account receivable for $16,600 which was more than a year past due.
e Merchandise with a cost of $480 is sold under a 24-month installment contract for a 10% down payment of $60. Title to the merchandise remains with the seller until all installment payments have been collected.

f Land held for investment is planted in lettuce. If the crop is harvested successfully and demand remains strong, cash receipts are expected to exceed expenses by $20,000. The crop growth is halfway to maturity at this time.

g Services are rendered to a customer and a check drawn on a small out-of-state bank is received from the customer.

Ex. 3-5 Alfredo Company declared and paid cash dividends of $12,500 during Year 5. The company's records show that changes in account balances occurred as follows during Year 5.

	Increase	Decrease
Cash	$40,000	
Accounts receivable		$ 2,000
Inventory	15,000	
Equipment (net)	18,000	
Building (net)	30,000	
Accounts payable		15,000
Notes payable	50,000	
Capital stock, $5 par	30,000	
Paid-in capital in excess of par	10,000	
Retained earnings	?	

Assuming that there were no transactions affecting retained earnings except the cash dividend, calculate the net income for Year 5.

Ex. 3-6 Susan Swan Co. had general expenses of 10% of sales (or 20% of cost of goods sold). Selling expenses are an amount equal to 20% of sales. The beginning inventory was $100,000 and purchases amounted to 55% of sales. Income before taxes was $80,000. Assume an income tax rate of 40%. Prepare an income statement in good form for the year ended December 31, Year 2. (Give supporting computations.) **Suggestion:** (1) Compute the cost of goods sold as a percentage of sales by using the information given relating general expenses to cost of goods sold **and** to sales; (2) prepare an income statement in percentages, including all items from sales to income before income taxes, with sales representing 100%; (3) prepare an income statement in dollars, using the dollar amounts given and deriving the other dollar amounts from the percentage relationship.

Ex. 3-7 Using the following information, prepare a statement of retained earnings for Bonita Land Company for Year 5:

Total assets	$2,000,000
Total liabilities	600,000
Common stock, $1 par	300,000
Paid-in capital in excess of par	600,000
Prior period adjustment, net of income tax effect (understatement of liabilities in Year 4 as a result of major error)	100,000
Net income for Year 5	104,000
Dividends on common stock	63,00

SHORT CASES FOR ANALYSIS AND DECISION

Case 3-1 Six different companies recognized the following items in their accounting records during Year 10:

(1) A gain of $3.9 million was recognized by Soledad Gravel Corporation on early extinguishment of convertible bonds which were selling in the open market at a deep discount because of the deteriorated financial position of Soledad Gravel Corporation.

(2) An out-of-court settlement of litigation resulted in a payment by Exeter Corporation of $2 million to plaintiffs. The legal action was initiated two years ago.

(3) A pre-tax loss of $4 million resulted from the disposal of a chemical division operated by a grocery chain. In the year of disposal, the chemical division had sales of $10 million and operating expenses of $12 million. The income tax rate is 45%.

(4) A loss of $6 million from write-offs of receivables and inventories caused by a severe business recession was recognized by XY, Inc.

(5) A loss of $8 million was recognized from sale of all the assets (including the plant and equipment) related to the manufacture of men's woolen suits by an apparel manufacturer to concentrate activities in the manufacture of men's suits from synthetic products.

(6) A large diversified company sold a block of common stock from its portfolio of securities which it had acquired for investment purposes. This is the first sale from its portfolio and resulted in a material gain of $4.5 million before applicable income taxes.

Instructions Indicate how each of the items above should be reported in the respective company's financial statements at the end of Year 10. Give a brief explanation for each item.

Case 3-2 The financial statements of Right-on Publishing Company are presented to the board of directors for review upon completion of the annual audit. Sam Doll, a director, asks why the income statement is based on the assumption that an equal proportion of the revenue is earned with the publication of every issue of the company's magazine. He feels that the "crucial event" in the process of earning revenue in the magazine business is the cash sale of the subscription. He says that he does not understand why—other than for the smoothing of income—most of the revenue cannot be "realized" in the period of sale.

Instructions
a List three accepted methods for recognizing revenue in the accounts and explain when the methods are appropriate. Do not limit your listing to the methods for the recognition of revenue in magazine publishing.
b Discuss the propriety of timing the recognition of revenue in the Right-on Publishing Company's accounts with:
  (1) The cash sale of the magazine subscription
  (2) The publication of the magazine every month
  (3) Both events, by recognizing a portion of the revenue with the cash sale of the magazine subscription and a portion of the revenue with the publication of the magazine every month

Case 3-3 Creative Advertising Agency handles advertising for clients under contracts which provide that the agency shall develop advertising copy and layouts and place ads in various media, charging clients a commission of 18% of the media cost as its fee. The agency makes advance billings to its clients of estimated media cost plus its 18% commission. Later adjustments of these advance billings are usually minor. Often both the billings and receipt of cash from these billings occur before the period in which the advertising actually appears in the media.

In devising a system for measuring income, the agency considered the following possible points at which revenue and costs might be recognized and income measured: (1) At the time of the advanced billing; (2) when payment is received from clients; (3) in the month in which the advertising appears in the media; (4) when the bill for advertising is received from the media.

The agency chose (1) as the point at which it would recognize income, on the grounds that it has a contract with clients for specified advertising and thus income is earned when billed. At the time of billing, the agency establishes accounts receivable with clients and records the estimated liability to the media and its commission earnings. At this time the agency also estimates its expenses and establishes a liability for the estimated expense related to the client's billing. Adjusting entries are made to establish actual cost and revenue amounts when billings are received from media, when actual expenses are finally determined, and when final statements are sent to clients.

Instructions Discuss each of the four points at which the Creative Advertising Agency might recognize income, and state your opinion as to the proper basis for accounting for income in this case. If you disagree with the method followed by the agency, explain the basis for your disagreement and why you support an alternative occasion for income recognition.

Case 3-4 The combined statement of earnings and retained earnings shown below and on page 128 was prepared by New Styles Corporation. The company is in a retail business and makes most of its sales on credit. Accounts receivable are aged at the end of the period and the allowance for doubtful accounts is adjusted to the level required to value receivables at their estimated collectible amount.

NEW STYLES CORPORATION
Statement of Earnings and Retained Earnings
Years Ended December 31, Year 5, and December 31, Year 4

	Year 5	Year 4
Revenue:		
Gross sales including sales taxes	$876,900	$782,500
Less returns, allowances, and cash discounts	18,800	16,200
Net sales	$858,100	$766,300
Dividends, interest, and purchase discounts	30,250	18,300
Recoveries of accounts written off in prior years	11,800	3,000
Total revenue	$900,150	$787,600
Costs and expenses:		
Cost of goods sold, including sales taxes	$415,900	$332,200
Salaries and related payroll expenses	60,500	62,100
Rent	19,100	19,100
Freight-in and freight-out	3,400	2,900
Doubtful accounts expense	24,000	26,000
Total costs and expenses	$522,900	$442,300
Income before extraordinary items	$377,250	$345,300

Extraordinary items:		
Loss on discontinued styles (Note 1)	$ 24,000	$ 4,800
Loss on sale of marketable securities (Note 2)	52,050	
Loss on sale of warehouse (Note 3)	117,950	
Total extraordinary items	$194,000	$ 4,800
Net income	$183,250	$340,500
Retained earnings at beginning of year	312,700	163,100
Total	$495,950	$503,600
Less: Federal income taxes	$100,000	$170,000
Cash dividends on common stock	41,900	20,900
Total	$141,900	$190,900
Retained earnings at end of year	$354,050	$312,700
Net income per share of common stock	$ 1.83	$ 3.41

Notes to the Statement of Income and Retained Earnings:
(1) New styles and rapidly changing customer preferences resulted in a $24,000 loss on the disposal of discontinued styles and related accessories.
(2) The corporation sold an investment in marketable securities at a loss of $52,050, with no income tax effect.
(3) The corporation sold one of its warehouses at a loss of $117,950.

Instructions Identify and discuss the weaknesses in classification and disclosure in the single-step statement of earnings and retained earnings above. Your discussion should explain why you consider these treatments to be weaknesses and what you consider to be the proper treatment of items. Do not discuss form and terminology, and do not prepare a revised statement.

Case 3-5 At the beginning of the current year, Jason Moore, owner and operator of a large farm, had no inventories on hand. During the current year, he produced 8,000 bushels of soybeans, 10,000 bushels of barley, and 16,000 bushels of rye. During the year Moore sold one-half of each of his crops at the following prices: soybeans $6.50 per bushel, barley $3.25 per bushel, rye $2 per bushel. Moore followed the daily price quotations of these commodities very closely, and at the end of the year he noted that the market price per bushel for each of these commodities was as follows: soybeans $7 per bushel, barley $3.50 per bushel, and rye $2.20 per bushel.

The total expenses incurred in operating the farm during the year were $51,550, including depreciation of buildings and equipment. Moore estimates that his cost of selling and delivering these crops is 40 cents per bushel. The selling and delivering expenses applicable to the portion of the crops sold during the year are included in the total operating expenses given above.

Instructions
a Prepare an income statement for Moore for the current year. Explain the concept of revenue realization employed in your measurement of income and, in particular, the basis you used in assigning a valuation to the commodities on hand at the end of the year.
b In measuring income before income taxes for the current year, what consideration did you give to the possibility that the market price of these three commodities might change between the end of the current year and the time Moore finally sold them?
c What is the essential difference between the problem of measuring income for Moore and measuring income for a manufacturer of farm machinery?

PROBLEMS

Group A

3A-1 Gene Aldava began a small business early in 1975, investing $36,000 in cash and property (land and building) worth $90,000. In 1978, the business became a partnership with the admission of Chuck Bond as a partner. Bond invested $110,000 cash in the business at the time of his admission. By the end of 1980, the balance sheet of the business appeared as follows:

Cash	$ 26,200	Current liabilities	$ 43,160
Receivables (net)	57,820	Mortgage payable	100,000
Inventories	64,200	Aldava, capital	367,060
Plant & equipment (net)	492,000	Bond, capital	130,000
	$640,220		$640,220

At this date the partners disagreed over business policy and decided to liquidate the business. Inventories were sold for $50,000 and plant and equipment for $550,000. Of the receivables, $24,000 were collected; $32,000 were sold to a financing firm (without recourse) for $25,000; and $1,820 were written off as uncollectible. All debts were paid, including $400 of interest on the mortgage payable not accrued at the time of the above balance sheet. During the life of the business, Aldava had withdrawn $334,000 and Bond had withdrawn $79,740 from the business.

Instructions

a Compute the lifetime net income of this business on the basis of the above information. Income taxes are to be ignored, since a partnership is not a taxable entity.

b Explain whether there are any areas of uncertainty in your determination of lifetime net income of the business in this situation.

3A-2 Lubbock Corporation is engaged in the manufacture and sale of ethical drugs. Several years ago it acquired a book publishing business which has been operated at a loss since it was acquired. In Year 9, the board of directors of Lubbock Corporation sold the book publishing business. The results of operations for Year 9 are summarized below:

	Drugs	Books
Net sales	$14,900,000	$3,500,000
Cost of goods sold	9,500,000	2,700,000
Operating expenses	2,900,000	1,200,000
Loss on disposal of book publishing business (before income tax effect)		900,000
Extraordinary loss from earthquake (before income tax effect)	300,000	
Prior period adjustment, credit balance net of income taxes (correction of material error)	1,200,000	

The extraordinary loss is fully deductible for income tax purposes. The income tax rate for the company is 45%. There were 100,000 shares of common stock (the only capital stock issued) outstanding during Year 9.

Instructions Prepare an income statement for Year 9, including earnings per share data.

3A-3 General Clothiers, Inc., is a merchandising corporation with $5 par common stock, of which 25,000 shares are outstanding. In addition to its merchandising activities, the company obtains rental revenue of $28,324 a year for a part of its building leased to another company.

The following information is available concerning the merchandising activities for the current year:

Ending inventory (a decrease of $54,264 during the year)	$ 100,944
Purchases of merchandise (of which $11,224 was returned)	737,696
Transportation-in	63,504
Sales (of which $21,696 was returned by customers)	1,584,768
Selling expenses (salaries & wages, $182,340; purchased services, $41,248; supplies, $20,224)	243,812
Administrative expenses (salaries & wages, $120,688; purchased services, $38,048; supplies, $14,832)	173,568
Depreciation on buildings and equipment (75% selling and 25% administrative)	67,840

In addition to these operating revenue and expenses, General Clothiers, Inc., incurred interest expense of $13,568 and declared dividends of $50,000. The provision for income taxes was $119,368.

Instructions
a Prepare a multiple-step income statement for the current year. Include earnings per share.
b Prepare a single-step income statement for the current year, classifying expenses on a natural rather than a functional basis. Include data on earnings per share.
c Discuss the relative merits of the two forms of income statement.

3A-4 The following data were taken from the ledger of Formosa Export Company at the end of 1980. Income taxes for the current year applicable to ordinary income are $27,600. Income taxes applicable to the extraordinary gain are $10,500. Income tax credit applicable to the extraordinary loss is $28,500. Formosa Export Company has 20,000 shares of common stock issued and outstanding.

Cost of goods sold	$ 820,000
Depreciation expense	30,000
Cash dividends declared	32,000
Extraordinary gain	35,000
Insurance expense	7,000
Sales	1,200,000
Extraordinary loss	60,000
Salaries expense	195,000
Retained earnings, Jan. 1, 1980	265,500
Other operating expenses	62,400

Instructions
a Prepare a combined statement of earnings and retained earnings. Use the single-step form.
b Provide earnings per common share information.

3A-5 Sherman Oaks Lumber Co. had 100,000 shares of common stock throughout 1980. Selected information at December 31, 1980, is presented below:

Retained earnings balance, Jan. 1, 1980	$1,375,800
Inventory, Jan. 1, 1980	192,500
Extraordinary gain, before income taxes of $40,000	135,000
Purchases (continuing operations)	1,510,000
Sales (continuing operations)	2,195,000
Royalty revenue	24,100
Inventory, Dec. 31, 1980	208,000
Selling expenses (continuing operations)	120,400
Sales returns, allowances, and discounts	25,100
Purchase returns, allowances, and discounts	23,450
Dividends declared	200,000
Gain on disposal of equipment used in continuing operations	27,500
Income taxes applicable to results from continuing operations	192,500
General and administrative expenses (continuing operations)	197,550
Prior period adjustment: Decrease in retained earnings at Jan. 1, 1980,	
as a result of correction of error, net of income tax effect of $85,500 . .	110,000
Loss from disposal of a segment of a business: The company sold an	
unprofitable venture in a professional tennis team. The loss is net of	
income tax credit of $70,000 and includes all revenue and expenses	
relative to the tennis team for 1980	80,000

Instructions
a Prepare an income statement for the year ended December 31, 1980. The results from continuing operations should be in single-step form. (A number of accounts balances should be combined to obtain summary amounts to appear in the single-step format for the income statement.) Include per-share data in the income statement.
b Prepare a statement of retained earnings for the year ended December 31, 1980.

Group B

3B-1 In 1975 Alice Larry began a small business by investing $48,400 in cash and other property (land and a building) worth $92,000. In 1977, the business became a partnership with the admission of Jane Winningham as a partner. Winningham made a cash investment in the business of $99,000. At the end of 1980, the balance sheet of the business appeared as follows:

Cash	$ 31,240	Current liabilities	$ 44,670
Accounts receivable (net) . . .	56,910	Mortgage payable	92,000
Inventories	84,000	Larry, capital	333,480
Plant & equipment (net)	420,000	Winningham, capital	122,000
	$592,150		$592,150

At this point, the partners disagreed over business policies and decided to liquidate the business. Inventories were sold for $75,000 and plant and equipment for $540,000. Of the receivables, $30,200 were collected; $24,600 of receivables were sold to a financing firm (without recourse) for $20,000; and $2,110 were written off as uncollectible. All debts were paid, including $520 of interest on the mortgage payable not accrued at the date of the above balance sheet. During the life of the business (1975 through 1980), Larry had withdrawn $257,400 from the business and Winningham had withdrawn $69,450.

Instructions

a Compute the lifetime net income of the business on the basis of the above information. Since a single proprietorship and a partnership are not taxable entities, you are to disregard income taxes.

b Discuss any areas of uncertainty in your determination of lifetime net income of the business in this case.

3B-2 Gretchen Young, Inc., had 250,000 shares of a single class of capital stock outstanding throughout Year 5. During Year 5, the company sold a major line of business. The results of operations for Year 5 are summarized below:

	Continuing operations	Discontinued operations
Sales (net of returns, allowances, and discounts)	$8,600,000	$2,800,000
Cost and expenses:		
Cost of goods sold	5,700,000	2,000,000
Operating expenses	1,800,000	500,000
Gain on disposal of discontinued operations (before income taxes)		200,000
Extraordinary loss from early extinguishment of debt (before income tax effect)	100,000	
Prior period adjustment, debit balance before income tax effect (correction of material error applicable to Year 3)	777,000	

Income taxes at the rate of 45% apply to all items listed above.

Instructions Prepare an income statement for Year 5, including earnings per share data.

3B-3 The following information was compiled from the accounting records of Dion Corporation as a basis for preparation of an income statement for the current year:

Beginning inventory	$ 496,300
Ending inventory	542,700
Purchase returns & allowances	65,200
Common stock, $5 par	200,000
Sales	4,231,200
Sales returns & allowances	44,100
Depreciation on buildings and equipment (75% selling; 25% administrative)	220,000

Gain on sale of equipment	13,500
Rental revenue	18,200
Interest expense	12,840
Purchases	3,100,850
Transportation-in	123,400
Selling expenses:	
Salaries and wages	301,010
Purchased services	72,150
Materials and supplies	66,050
Administrative expenses:	
Salaries and wages	420,200
Purchased services	62,800
Materials and supplies	101,100

Assume that the company's income tax rate is 40% and that any loss can be carried back to obtain an income tax refund.

Instructions

a Prepare a multiple-step income statement for the current year. Include earnings or loss per share.

b Prepare a single-step income statement for the current year, using a natural classification of expenses. Include earnings or loss per share.

c Explain which form you prefer, giving reasons for your answer.

3B-4 Eastmont Company's capital structure consists solely of common stock, of which 200,000 shares are authorized and 50,000 shares were outstanding throughout 1980. At December 31, 1980, an analysis of the accounts and discussions with management revealed the following information:

Sales	$1,495,200
Sales discounts	22,000
Purchase discounts	21,050
Purchases	901,250
Earthquake loss, before income tax effect	120,000
Selling expenses	132,400
General and administrative expenses	163,500
Dividend revenue	12,000
Cash dividends declared	90,000
Interest expense	19,000
Inventory, Jan. 1, 1980	252,500
Inventory, Dec. 31, 1980	225,600
Retained earnings, Jan. 1, 1980	890,000
Reduction in retained earnings as of Jan. 1, 1980, resulting from prior period adjustment (no income tax effect)	137,000

The amount of income taxes applicable to ordinary income for 1980 was $113,200, but the tax effect of the loss from the earthquake amounted to $50,000, resulting in actual income taxes payable for the year of $63,200.

Instructions Prepare a combined statement of earnings and retained earnings for the year ended December 31, 1980. Use the single-step form and show earnings per share data in the combined statement.

3B-5 The information listed below was available for the Lin Metal Arts Corporation at December 31, 1980:

Sales	*$1,747,500*
Extraordinary gain	*200,000*
Income taxes applicable to extraordinary gain	*60,000*
Prior period adjustment (debit balance), before applicable income tax credit of $70,000	*150,000*
Dividends declared	*200,000*
Purchases	*1,392,000*
Purchase discounts	*20,000*
Inventory, Jan. 1, 1980	*146,000*
Income taxes applicable to ordinary income	*65,000*
Selling expenses	*100,000*
General and administrative expenses	*96,000*
Inventory, Dec. 31, 1980	*152,000*
Sales returns and allowances	*25,500*
Cumulative effect on prior years of change in accounting principle (credit balance), net of applicable income tax effect of $18,000	*30,000*

The retained earnings at January 1, 1980, amounted to $932,400. There were 25,000 shares of common stock outstanding throughout 1980.

Instructions
a Prepare a multiple-step income statement, including per share data.
b Prepare a statement of retained earnings.

CHAPTER 4

BALANCE SHEET AND STATEMENT OF CHANGES IN FINANCIAL POSITION

BALANCE SHEET: A REPORT ON FINANCIAL POSITION

A balance sheet presents the financial position of a business entity. The financial position of a business at a given date comprises the assets, liabilities, and owners' equity, and the relationship among them. An integral part of the balance sheet (or statement of financial position) consists of notes to the financial statements, which disclose contingencies, commitments, and other financial matters relevant to the business.

A balance sheet provides a historical summary of the following elements, as defined in *APB Statement No. 4:*[1]

1 *Assets.* Economic resources of an enterprise that are recognized and measured in conformity with generally accepted accounting principles. Assets also include certain deferred charges that are not resources but that are recognized and measured in conformity with generally accepted accounting principles.[2]

2 *Liabilities.* Economic obligations of an enterprise that are recognized and measured in conformity with generally accepted accounting principles. Liabilities also include certain deferred credits that are not obligations but that are recognized and measured in conformity with generally accepted accounting principles.

[1] *APB Statement No. 4,* "Basic Concepts and Accounting Principles Underlying Financial Statements of Business Enterprises," AICPA (New York: 1970), par. 132.

[2] An example of "deferred charges that are not resources" is deferred charges from income tax allocation. Deferred credits from income tax allocation are a prominent example of "deferred credits that are not obligations." Both these items are discussed in Chapter 21.

3 Owners' equity. The interest of owners in an enterprise, which is the excess of an enterprise's assets over its liabilities.

The balance sheet is basically a historical report, because it shows the cumulative effect of past transactions. It is often described as a detailed expression of the fundamental accounting equation:

Assets = Liabilities + Owners' Equity

The theoretical concept of an asset may readily be related to our discussion in Chapter 3 of revenue and expenses shown in the income statement. Assets are costs that have *not* been applied to past revenue; they represent *expected future economic benefits.* However, the rights to assets have been acquired by the entity as a result of past transactions. If no future economic benefit can reasonably be expected from a cost incurred by a business, then it follows that the cost in question does not qualify as an asset and should not be included in the balance sheet.

Liabilities also result from past transactions; they are obligations which require settlement in the future, either by conveying assets or by performing services.

Implicit in these concepts of the nature of assets and liabilities is the meaning of owners' equity as the residual interest in the assets of a business entity.

Uses and limitations of the balance sheet

At one time the balance sheet was considered the primary end product of the accounting process. However, experience pounded home the economic lesson that earning power is the prime determinant of the value of a going business, and users of financial statements gradually placed greater emphasis on the income statement. Today the balance sheet, supported by the statement of changes in financial position, is recapturing much of the respect it once had. Some evidence of this is found in the following excerpt from a leading business publication:

> A quiet, but potentially explosive, revolution is sweeping the U.S. business world as lenders, investors, regulators, accountants, and corporate managers rediscover what should never have been lost: the balance sheet.
> Behind the revolution is the inescapable fact that inflation, and all that goes with it, has made a shambles of the traditional income statement that shows only whether a company has made or lost money. Earnings-per-share growth may still captivate naive investors, but more critical observers now realize that it does not tell how much a company owes, or whether it can raise enough money to keep growing, or whether the earnings were real or simply the result of inflation and arcane accounting practices.
> Only by studying the balance sheet can a lender or an investor—or a regulator—measure a company's liquidity and its ability to generate profits and

pay debts and dividends year after year. . . . It shows whether the company will survive, how profitable it can be, and whether it has a major obstacle to profits, like a pile of debt coming due.

Because the balance sheet tells so much, it is astonishing that it could ever have gotten lost. . . . Then came the go-go years of the late 1960s and early 1970s, when the only thing that seemed to matter was how fast a company could grow, a game that the biggest, most sophisticated institutional investors played as avidly as the rankest amateur in for a fast kill.

But the go-go years ended in the inflation-recession agony of 1974–75, and people are focusing on the balance sheet as they have not in years.[3]

In addition to looking at earnings, investors and creditors are placing more emphasis on a company's current ratio, debt-to-equity ratio, and rate of return on investment. After recent experiences with the "liquidity crisis" triggered by high levels of interest rates and inflation, corporations are giving more attention to their balance sheets in order to preserve their ability to borrow or sell shares of stock. The accounting profession, cognizant of this growing emphasis on financial position, has taken significant steps to make the balance sheet more relevant and useful for decision makers. These steps have included a deliberate movement toward disclosure of replacement costs, immediate expensing of research and development costs, and the amortization of goodwill.

Balance sheets in **comparative form** provide a great deal of information to creditors, stockholders, management, prospective investors, and the public. For individuals with the ability to interpret comparative balance sheets, much can be learned as to the short-run solvency of a business, favorable or unfavorable trends in liquidity, commitments that must be met in the future, and the relative strength of the positions of creditors and equity investors.

In an ideal balance sheet the list of assets and liabilities would be all-inclusive and each would be reported at its current fair value. As a result the residual equity (assets minus liabilities) would reflect meaningful net worth of the business entity. The major **limitation** of the traditional balance sheet lies in the accountant's inability to measure the "current fair value" of the entire collection of net resources comprising the business entity.

The inability of accountants (or anyone else) to foresee future economic events forces us to prepare balance sheets on a different basis. It is necessary to use indirect methods of valuation to express some kinds of assets and liabilities on the balance sheet. Furthermore, we are unable to identify and provide a valuation for many factors that have a material bearing on the financial position of a business. The quality, morale, and character of management and company personnel, the market position of a firm and the reputation of its products, the growth potential implicit in the nature and diversity of its operations—all these

[3] *Business Week,* "Focus on Balance Sheet," June 7, 1976, p. 52.

are subjective and intangible factors of great importance in evaluating the financial position of a business entity at any given point in time. None is reported directly in the dollar and cents framework of the accounting process that leads to a balance sheet.

Some critics, in discussing the merits of various accounting concepts and procedures, take the position that because the balance sheet does not reflect "current fair value" it does not matter what figures appear in it. There is a serious defect in such thinking. To imply that *meaningful* income statements can be prepared as an adjunct to *meaningless* balance sheets shows a failure to understand the relation between these two financial statements. A consistently applied and meaningful set of assumptions governing the valuation of assets and liabilities is a prerequisite of meaningful income measurement.

Accounting principles underlying the balance sheet

A number of important basic principles of accounting impinge on the data appearing in balance sheets. Since all the principles discussed in the preceding chapters are relevant, we shall concentrate here only on their balance sheet implications.

The Valuation Principle Realization, which is a key factor in income measurement, also forms the basis for distinguishing methods of valuation used in reporting assets.

A general class of assets called *monetary assets* is usually carried on the balance sheet at figures closely approximating present value. Examples are cash, certificates of deposit, investments in bonds, and receivables; all these represent available purchasing power. *APB Opinion No. 21* stressed that notes receivable and notes payable which are non-interest-bearing or which carry an unreasonably low rate of interest are not to be valued at face amount, but at their present value. *Present value* may be determined by discounting all future payments on a note by using an imputed rate of interest reflecting prevailing market rates of interest. This requirement for discounting receivables and payables to their present value applies principally to notes and is not applicable to receivables and payables arising from transactions with customers or suppliers which are due within one year or less.[4]

Another broad category of assets, which might be termed *productive resources,* is reported at *cost,* that is, the original amount spent in acquiring the asset services that remain in potential at any given time. Inventories and prepayments are examples of short-term productive resources that will be realized (that is, contribute to revenue) at an early date. Buildings, equipment, patents, and investments in affiliated companies

[4] *APB Opinion No. 21,* "Interest on Receivables and Payables," AICPA (New York: 1971), par. 1–3.

are examples of long-term commitments of funds that will be realized over a number of accounting periods.

Until realization occurs, productive resources are measured and reported on the balance sheet on the basis of past or present exchange prices; after realization, valuations of quick assets generally approximate current value. These valuation assumptions govern the accounting for assets.

Since a liability is an obligation to convey assets or perform services, the appropriate valuation of liabilities on the balance sheet is in terms of the cash (or cash equivalent) necessary to discharge the obligation at the balance sheet date. If payment is to be made later, liabilities should be measured at the present discounted value (determined by using a yield or market interest rate) of the future payments necessary to discharge the obligation.[5] In the double-entry system of accounting, the present value of a debt at the time it is incurred determines the cash proceeds of the borrowing or the cost of the asset received in exchange for the contractual promise to make future payments. As the maturity of a debt approaches, its present value may increase or decrease and this change is a part of the computation of the interest cost of carrying the debt. This problem is considered in greater detail in Chapter 15.

The measurement of assets and liabilities in the balance sheet is closely related to the measurement of income in the income statement. Since revenue arises as the result of increases in assets or decreases in liabilities, and expenses result from increases in liabilities and decreases in assets, the problem of valuing assets and liabilities is inevitably linked to the problem of measuring income.

The Continuity or Going-Concern Principle The valuations used in a balance sheet and the classification of items into current and noncurrent groups are based on the continuity or going-concern principle previously discussed in Chapter 1. This principle, as specifically applied to the balance sheet, means an assumption that the business will continue operations long enough for assets to be used or sold according to plan. The going-concern principle is applicable to all cases except when specific evidence, such as inability to meet the demands of creditors, indicates that the assumption of continued operations is unreasonable.

The Monetary Principle The monetary principle was described in Chapter 1 as an assumption that the dollar is a useful standard measuring unit, and implications of this principle on income determination were discussed in Chapter 3. The principle is reflected on the balance sheet by

[5] The concept of present value as applied to liabilities has been expressed as follows: "If the creditor will not or cannot accept cash now in discharge of the liability, the appropriate amount is that sum which, if invested now (e.g., in a sinking fund), will provide the sums needed at maturity, even though in fact no explicit sinking fund or other investment device is actually used." *Accounting Research Study No. 3,* p. 39.

valuations expressed in dollars of different time periods, that is, dollars having different real values (if there have been changes in the general price level).

If the monetary assumption were changed and balance sheets were expressed in "current dollars," the two categories most affected would be productive assets and the ownership equity. As we have noted, monetary assets and liabilities are stated at approximately their current values and are thus automatically expressed in current dollars. However, the accounting valuation of productive assets is a mixture of historical costs. Similarly, paid-in capital and retained earnings in the stockholders' equity section of the balance sheet are expressed in dollars of past periods.

To illustrate this point, consider the case of Inflation Company which has operated for a period of 10 years, during which the general price level has risen steadily. Shown below is a balance sheet (in highly condensed and somewhat unorthodox form) for this company, expressed in both "mixed" dollars and "current" dollars. Compare the figures in the two columns.

INFLATION COMPANY
Balance Sheet
As of End of Current Year

		"Mixed" dollars (monetary assumption)	"Current" dollars (revised assumption)
Assets			
Monetary assets (cash, investments in debt securities, and receivables)		$200,000	$200,000
Productive resources (inventories, plant and equipment, and intangibles)		400,000	700,000
Total assets		$600,000	$900,000
Liabilities & Stockholders' Equity			
Liabilities (both short- and long-term)		$300,000	$300,000
Stockholders' equity:			
Capital stock	$200,000		$400,000
Retained earnings	100,000		60,000
Unrealized general price-level gain	–0–		140,000
Total stockholders' equity		300,000	600,000
Total liabilities & stockholders' equity		$600,000	$900,000

Note the upward revision of productive assets and stockholders' equity when expressed in current dollars. The decline in retained earnings when expressed in current dollars (from $100,000 to $60,000) occurs because the cost of goods sold, depreciation, and amortization of intangibles are higher when expressed in current dollars during a period of inflation. The "unrealized general price-level gain" ($140,000) is more complex. It results from the fact that productive resources were financed in part by debt. Creditors are entitled to a repayment of only a fixed number of dollars. Thus when unused productive resources are stated in terms of an increased number of current dollars, the company has gained at the expense of its creditors. Bear in mind that this illustration does not use current market prices, but historical costs adjusted for the change in the general price level.

Financial reporting in terms of constant dollars has been tried in a few countries where price inflation has been extreme. In the United States experiments with supplementary current-dollar statements have attracted considerable attention, but it appears unlikely that the monetary assumption will be abandoned in primary financial statements, barring a greater change in the value of the dollar than we have thus far experienced. The detailed procedures for converting mixed-dollar accounting data to current dollars are discussed in Chapter 22.

Other Accounting Principles and Concepts The *disclosure principle* and the closely related *concept of materiality,* which were discussed in Chapter 1, are especially applicable to the balance sheet. Adequate disclosure does not require the listing of precise dollar amounts. In the published financial statements of most large companies, all amounts are rounded off to the nearest thousand dollars. The extremely large companies go a step further; they omit digits for units, tens, and hundreds, and place the heading "amounts in thousands" at the top of the balance sheet and other financial statements. For example, if Sears, Roebuck and Co. has a ledger balance for accounts receivable of $5,278,501,329.71 and a related allowance for doubtful accounts of $100,000,000.00, the balance sheet would show among the current assets "Receivables. . . . $5,178,501." In reading these figures, one must bear in mind that five digits have been omitted. Supplementary information concerning credit operations, including the provision for doubtful accounts, would appear in notes to the financial statements.

In order that the balance sheet may provide a fair presentation of the financial position of a business, it is usually necessary to go considerably further than listing and classifying ledger account balances. Additional vital information, such as the existence of contingent liabilities and contingent assets, a summary of accounting policies, changes in accounting principles, and the occurrence of important events subsequent to the date of the balance sheet are most conveniently reported in the notes to financial statements.

FORM AND PRESENTATION OF THE BALANCE SHEET

Two objectives are dominant in presenting information in a balance sheet. One is clarity and readability; the other is disclosure of significant facts within the framework of the basic assumptions of accounting. Balance sheet classification, terminology, and the general form of presentation should be studied with these objectives in mind.

Balance sheet classification

The classifications, group headings, and number of items on a balance sheet will vary considerably depending on the size of the company, the nature of its operations, and whether the financial statements are intended for wide distribution or for the use of a few owners and creditors. As an example of the diversity encountered in published financial statements, public utility companies usually place plant assets at the top of the balance sheet followed by current assets. They may also use such distinctive group headings as "Assets and Other Debits," along with "Liabilities and Other Credits."

As a generalization subject to many exceptions, the following classification of balance sheet items is suggested as representative. However, alternative groupings will be used at times in this and following chapters to reflect acceptable alternatives.

        Assets:
            Current assets
            Investments (held for control or not readily marketable)
            Property, plant, and equipment
            Intangible assets
            Other assets (including deferred charges)
        Liabilities:
            Current liabilities
            Long-term liabilities (including deferred credits)
        Stockholders' equity:
            Capital stock
            Paid-in capital in excess of par
            Retained earnings

The above classification reflects only the three elements of the fundamental accounting equation, and in the opinion of the authors, is theoretically supportable. In practice, it is not unusual to find a fourth category placed between liabilities and stockholders' equity (often with the caption "Reserves" or "Deferred Credits"), to include such items as deferred income taxes, unamortized investment tax credits, reserves for overhaul of leased equipment, and minority interest in subsidiaries. The possibilities for elimination of this separate category are discussed later in this chapter and in Chapter 19.

Working capital

The **working capital** of a business entity is defined as the excess of current assets over current liabilities. This figure has always been of considerable interest to credit grantors as an easily interpreted measure of the short-run solvency of a business—the ability to finance current operations and to meet obligations as they fall due. The amounts of current assets and of current liabilities, and the relation between them (the **current ratio**), are widely quoted in financial circles and are often incorporated in contractual arrangements between a company and outsiders. It is therefore of some importance that there be a generally accepted and consistent basis for determining which items are included and which are excluded from the current asset and current liability categories.

Current Assets As a practical matter, the rough-and-ready difference between a current asset and a noncurrent asset is readily grasped. The border between these two categories, however, is hazy, and defining an exact boundary is not an easy task.

Five general types of assets are usually included in the current asset classification:

1 *Cash.* Money in any form—cash awaiting deposit, balances on deposit in checking accounts, established expendable cash funds.

2 *Secondary cash resources.* Various investments that are readily marketable. Any such funds with availability for current use restricted by contract or other formal arrangement are excluded.

3 *Short-term receivables.* Open accounts receivable and notes receivable with short-term maturities.

4 *Inventories.* Raw materials, supplies, goods in process, finished goods. This category includes items held for sale in the ordinary course of operations, items in process of production for sale, and items that will be currently consumed in production of goods or services that will be available for sale.

5 *Short-term prepayments.* The cost of various services, such as insurance, taxes, rent, that have been paid for in advance of use in operations. Short-term prepayments are sometimes referred to as **prepaid expenses.**

There is little question or difficulty about including cash, secondary cash resources, and short-term receivables in the current asset category. As might be expected, the troublesome area is the distinction between short- and long-term investments in productive goods and services.

The test usually applied in distinguishing current from noncurrent productive assets is whether the investment in these assets will be realized within the operating cycle of a business, or one year, whichever is the longer period of time.

The term **operating cycle** refers to the circulation of items within the current asset category. In a typical business, cash is invested in materials, supplies, labor, and various overhead services, and these costs are traced through and attached to inventories. Inventories are eventually realized by conversion into trade receivables, and receivables are in turn collected and become once more available in the form of cash. The average lapse of time between the investment in materials and services and the final conversion back to cash is the length of the operating cycle of a business. In most cases this is a matter of days or months; in some industries, where processing time is extensive, the cycle may extend beyond one year. Thus the conventional time test for current assets is realization within one year or one operating cycle, whichever is longer.

There are some theoretical flaws in the application of the time test. In a realistic sense all asset services that will be used in producing revenue during the immediately succeeding operating cycle or accounting period will be realized and converted into liquid resources. Some portion of the investment in plant assets will be realized in the same sense as will be the investment in raw materials. It may be argued, for example, that standing timber that will be manufactured into plywood in the next operating cycle has as good a claim to inclusion among current assets as the stock of glue that will bind the layers of wood. Thus the attempt to distinguish between assets that are consumed in definite physical installments and assets that yield services gradually through use has some logical stumbling blocks in its way. These conceptual niceties are largely ignored in reporting current assets in the balance sheet.

In any system of classification, there will be troublesome items that do not fit nicely into designated niches. For example, if money has been borrowed for the express purpose of constructing plant, it may be argued that its inclusion in working capital is misleading. The common practice of buying insurance for three- or five-year periods raises questions about the logical consistency of including the full amount of unexpired insurance as a current asset.

In resolving these difficulties, accountants find themselves at odds with a neat, logical statement of the characteristics that distinguish a current asset. They may explain their trouble as an inevitable conflict between theory and practice, but the result is that the practical distinction between current and noncurrent assets is based more on a rule-of-thumb than on a precise definition.

Current Liabilities The distinction between current and noncurrent liabilities is less troublesome than its counterpart on the asset side of the balance sheet. Current liabilities may be defined as obligations whose liquidation is reasonably expected to require the use of existing resources properly classifiable as current assets or the creation of other current liabilities.

Three main classes of current liabilities fall within this definition:

1 Obligations for goods and services which have entered the operating cycle.

These include trade payables and accrued liabilities such as wages, commissions, taxes, etc.

2 Other debt that may be expected to require payment within the operating cycle or one year. This includes short-term notes and the currently maturing portion of long-term obligations.

3 Collections received in advance of the delivery of goods or the performance of services. These advances are often described as "deferred revenues," but it is the obligation to furnish the goods or services or to refund the payment that puts them in the liability category.

Some liabilities that will be paid shortly after the balance sheet date are nonetheless excluded from the current liability category because of the requirement that a current liability must involve the use of current assets for its extinction. Examples are: (1) obligations due at an early date that will be retired by issuing new long-term debt securities, for example, bonds that will be refunded; (2) debts that will be paid from fund accumulations reported as noncurrent assets, for example, a life insurance policy loan that will be liquidated by cancellation against the cash surrender value of the policy or by deduction from the proceeds of the policy at maturity.

Noncurrent Assets The definition of current assets automatically determines by exclusion the assets that should be reported as noncurrent. There are at least three identifiable types of noncurrent assets:

1 *Long-term or restricted funds, investments, and receivables.* A variety of long-term commitments of funds do not qualify as secondary cash resources. Investments in the stock of subsidiaries made for the purpose of control would be included in this category. Also included are noncurrent receivables (such as long-term advances to affiliated companies), the **cash surrender value of life insurance,** and funds established for such purposes as the payment of pensions, retirement of capital stock, or repayment of long-term debt. Assets being held for sale but not includable in inventory are listed in this group. Raw land held for speculative purposes is an example. Another is plant and equipment items which have been retired from operating use and are being held for sale. A future plant site not presently in use is another example of an asset properly included in this category of noncurrent assets.

2 *Long-term tangible resources used in the operations of the business.* The distinguishing characteristics of assets of this type are that they are tangible (have physical substance) and are held for productive use in business operations. All kinds of business sites, natural resources subject to depletion, business structures, equipment, machines, tools, leased assets under capital leases, and leasehold improvements are included. Long-term prepayments for the use of physical assets, such as leaseholds, easements, or rights of way, may also be included in this category, though some accountants group these in the next class.

3 ***Long-term intangible resources.*** Long-term rights and privileges of an intangible nature may be of greater importance to a business than its tangible assets. Examples of such assets are patents, goodwill, trademarks, copyrights, organization costs, and franchises. However, under current accounting standards these items are recognized as assets only when an expenditure has been made to acquire an intangible right from outsiders.

A special category of assets labeled "long-term prepayments," "deferred charges," or "other assets" is sometimes found on balance sheets. These classifications may be useful in special cases, but it is difficult to think of a noncurrent asset that will not fit into one of the three categories just described.

Noncurrent Liabilities A noncurrent liability is an obligation that will not require the use of current assets within the next year or operating cycle, whichever is longer. There is some question whether there is any useful basis for subclassification within this category. In general practice a distinction is sometimes drawn between the following two classes:

1 *Long-term debt based on security issues or related contractual arrangements.* Included in this category would be notes, bonds, and mortgages, reported net of any unamortized discount and including any unamortized premium. The distinguishing characteristic is that there is a borrowing transaction supported by a contractual obligation to pay principal and interest.

2 *Other long-term obligations.* As the word "other" implies, this includes all long-term liabilities that do not fit into the previous category. An amount received in advance on a long-term commitment to furnish goods or services would be an example. Any portion of such advances that will be earned during the current period should be reported as a current liability. Other examples are long-term advances from affiliated companies, amounts payable under pension plan agreements, deferred revenue, and deferred income taxes.

Contingent Liabilities Liabilities that *may* come into existence as a result of transactions or activities that *have not yet been finalized* are not reported in dollar amounts on the balance sheet. Not only is the evidence with respect to such obligations too vague to be called objective, but the events necessary to bring the liabilities into existence have not yet been completed.

On the other hand, if, as a result of contracts or activities undertaken, there are possible liabilities whose existence is merely conditional upon the happening of some future event, these obligations, known as *contingent liabilities,* should be disclosed. The disclosure is usually made by means of a note to the financial statements. The obligation to reimburse a bank in case of default by the maker of a discounted note receivable, pending lawsuits that may result in an obligation to pay damages or other costs, taxes and other charges that are being contested, possible renegotiation refunds on government contracts—all are examples of contingent liabilities.

Management would be imprudent to provide dollar estimates on anticipated renegotiation refunds, or unfavorable results from pending lawsuits, since such disclosure might be considered an admission of the merits of the opposing case. If the item is material, however, disclosure in general terms is essential.

A common error is the failure to distinguish between contingent liabilities and obligations that exist but are not definite either as to amount, due date, or both. These latter may be called **estimated liabilities.** There are varying degrees of uncertainty about liabilities; some may be estimated with a high degree of accuracy; others may be subject to no more than an informed guess. The amount of income tax liability or the amount of payments due employees under pension plans are examples of estimated liabilities which can usually be established with reasonable precision on the basis of tentative tax returns or actuarial data. On the other hand, the cost to a company of making good its product guarantees is an existing obligation that can be estimated only within a fairly wide range of probability. When liabilities exist, accountants should make the best possible determination of their present value and include them on the balance sheet, even though the amounts are uncertain.

Contingent Assets Assets, as well as liabilities, may be contingent. A contingent asset is a property right whose existence is conditional on the happening of some future event. It is usually not appropriate to recognize contingent assets in the accounting records, because to do so would violate the principle of revenue realization. There is a lack of objective evidence and the earnings process has not been substantially completed. However, the disclosure of the existence of contingencies which may result in material gains or assets is useful.[6] An example of such disclosure in a recent annual report read as follows: ". . . the company had a tax loss carryforward of $15,200,000 which can be deducted from future taxable income. . . ."

Contra Asset and Liability Accounts The valuation of some asset and liability accounts is commonly reported in two amounts as a convenient means of disclosing more information about these items than would be afforded by a net valuation. For example, the net amount of accounts receivable is sometimes reported as the difference between the gross amount due from customers and an allowance for accounts estimated to be uncollectible. Similarly bond discount may be separately shown as a deduction from the face amount of the liability. The general criterion for determining whether to display a balance sheet item in one amount or two is the degree of usefulness of the added information. The amount of estimated uncollectibles may provide the reader with information about the expected collection experience on current accounts; showing the amount of accumulated depreciation on plant and equipment separately from original cost may give some information about the relative age of the plant or the company's depreciation policy. The disclosure may be made as a separate valuation account in the balance sheet, or by a parenthetical notation of the amount that has been deducted in arriving at a net valuation.

[6] *FASB Statement No. 5,* "Accounting for Contingencies," FASB (Stamford: 1975), p. 8.

Offsetting Assets and Liabilities The use of contra or valuation accounts should be carefully distinguished from an actual *offsetting* of asset and liability accounts. When valuation accounts are used, the amount deducted from an asset is not a liability, and the amount deducted from a liability is not an asset; the deductions represent modifications of the gross valuation of assets and liabilities.

Offsetting assets and liabilities is improper because it implies an association between the two that seldom exists. For example, if a company informally accumulates a special fund to meet a debt when it matures, the intention may be revoked before the fund is actually devoted to that purpose. The fund should be reported as an asset and the debt as a liability until payment is actually made.

There is a sound basis for the rule against offsetting assets and liabilities. A limited amount of offsetting in a few cases would probably not cause a material distortion in financial statements, but there is no obvious place to draw the line. The issue is disclosure in a manner that is not misleading, and there is little doubt that offsetting in general is likely to result in misleading information.

One recognized exception to the rule against offsetting occurs when a company purchases securities acceptable for the payment of taxes in circumstances such that the purchase is an advance payment of taxes otherwise due in the near future. This may occur as an accommodation to a governmental unit which issues securities specifically designated as acceptable for the payment of taxes.[7]

Ownership equity

The ownership equity in a business is the residual interest in assets, after liabilities have been deducted. The amount appearing in the owners' equity section of a balance sheet is thus directly dependent upon the valuations attached to assets and liabilities. When owners invest in a business, it is the asset valuation that determines the amount added to ownership equity. When operating results are summarized, the increase in net assets determines the amount of net income added to the owners' equity. This point is worth noting, because accountants are sometimes tempted to reverse this process and assume that if a figure (for example, the par value of stock) is associated with an element of ownership, there must be an asset to match.

Because of differences in the nature of the owners' equity in incorporated and nonincorporated businesses, there are variations in the balance sheet presentation of ownership equity for these two types of business organization.

Single Owner or Partnership Organizations The ownership equity in a proprietorship or partnership is usually reported on the balance sheet as a

---

[7] *APB Opinion No. 10,* "Omnibus Opinion—1966" AICPA (New York: 1966), p. 147.

single amount for each owner. There is no reason why the amount of capital invested by each owner should not be shown separately from the reinvested earnings, but because there is no legal restriction on the amounts proprietors or partners may withdraw from a business, such information is less significant than in the case of corporations.

The ownership rights of a partner are typically more complex than those of a corporate stockholder. Contractual arrangements among partners governing salaries, interest on capital, share of residual profits and losses, and investment and withdrawals make it important that the relative rights of each partner are accurately determined and fully reported on the balance sheet. A statement showing the change in each partner's equity for the current period may accompany or appear on the partnership balance sheet, as shown for the A B Partnership below.

A B PARTNERSHIP
Statement of Partners' Capitals
For Current Year

	Partner A	Partner B	Total
Ownership equity, Jan. 1	$25,000	$34,000	$59,000
Add: Net income for the year	12,600	18,200	30,800
Less: Withdrawals	(15,000)	(10,000)	(25,000)
Ownership equity, Dec. 31	$22,600	$42,200	$64,800

Corporations The presentation of stockholders' equity on a corporate balance sheet is strongly influenced by legal considerations. As a result there are a number of classifications (particularly within the "invested capital" section) that have no particular accounting significance. Below is an outline of the main elements of corporate ownership equity:

1 *Invested capital*
    a *Stated capital.* The amount contributed for or assigned to shares of stock outstanding to the extent of their par or stated value is known legally as the stated capital of a corporation. This amount usually appears under the heading **capital stock.** For each class of stock, the amount of par or stated value per share; the number of shares issued, outstanding, and held in the treasury; and any dividend or liquidating preference should be disclosed.
    b *Additional capital.* This category includes all amounts contributed for or assigned to shares in excess of par or stated value. The terms **paid-in-capital in excess of par,** and **paid-in capital in excess of stated value** are used throughout this book. Another alternative term used in a considerable number of published financial statements is **additional paid-in capital.** The annual editions of **Accounting Trends & Techniques,** a survey of accounting practices followed in 600 stockholders' reports, published by the AICPA, show a continuing trend away from the term **surplus** either standing alone or in such combinations as **capital surplus** or **paid-in surplus.** Use of the term **surplus** has long been discouraged by the AICPA. The word is generally unsuitable in a stockholders' equity section of a balance sheet be-

cause its popular meaning—something over and above what is necessary—gives it a misleading connotation.

Capital in excess of par or stated value may include both positive and negative amounts. If a corporation receives less than par or stated value for its stock, the contra-capital account Discount on Capital Stock belongs in this section of the balance sheet. Positive items include any amount in excess of par or stated value arising from the sale of unissued stock, the sale of treasury stock at more than cost, donations of assets to the corporation, or transfers from retained earnings through stock dividends by authorization of the board of directors. Similarly, the cost of **treasury stock** (a debit balance) is a negative stockholders' equity item.

2 *Increase in stockholders' equity through the retention of net income*

  a *Retained earnings.* Net income on past periods that has been retained in the business and is legally available as a basis for dividends falls in this category. The term **retained earnings** is used far more widely than any other to describe this element of stockholders' equity. Alternative terms are **earnings retained for use in the business, retained earnings invested in the business,** and **earnings retained for growth.** The term **earned surplus,** although still used by a few companies, is gradually becoming obsolete.

  b *Appropriated retained earnings.* A corporate board of directors may sometimes wish to indicate that a portion of a company's retained earnings has been appropriated. A formal segregation of retained earnings is an indirect means of disclosing that future dividend payments are restricted to some degree, either because of legal or contractual agreements or by management intent. The use of appropriations of retained earnings as a means of disclosure is gradually disappearing; other more effective means of indicating the restriction of retained earnings are available, principally the use of notes to the financial statements.

3 *Unrealized appreciation in value of productive assets; and unrealized loss in value of noncurrent investments.* Under unusual circumstances a company may report unrealized appreciation or decline in the value of its assets in the balance sheet to disclose a serious discrepancy between carrying value and current value. This procedure is an **exception** to the basic accounting assumption that only realized increases in asset values are recognized in the accounts. The offsetting increase or decrease in ownership equity should therefore be separately shown and clearly designated as an unrealized element of the owners' equity if unrealized appreciation or decline in value of noncurrent investments is recorded.

Use of the term "reserve"

In the past the term **reserve** has been used by accountants in a number of different and somewhat misleading ways. A reserve, in nonaccounting usage, is usually thought of as something held for a specific purpose, often for emergencies. This popular connotation leads to misinterpretation when the word "reserve" is included in the title of an asset valuation or estimated liability account. The trend in modern accounting terminology is to avoid the use of the word "reserve," although a significant number of companies continue to use it in the asset or liability sections of the balance sheet.

The term **reserve,** when used to describe an appropriation of retained earnings, is considered acceptable, although its use continues to decline. Such titles as Reserve for Plant Expansion are more likely to be misunderstood than Retained Earnings Appropriated for Plant Expansion. If used at all, the term *reserve* should appear only in the stockholders' equity section of the balance sheet. Since its principal purpose is to indicate a restriction of retained earnings, the nature of the restriction can be set forth more clearly in a parenthetical comment or in a note to financial statements than by an appropriation of retained earnings.

Standards of disclosure

The accountant should apply the adequate disclosure test as a basis for resolving a number of questions that arise in the preparation of balance sheets.

Account Titles In providing titles for general ledger accounts, considerable leeway is permissible, in deference to convenience and economy of space. The persons involved in the accounting function understand the nature of the item and thus short titles are a matter of convenience. However, in preparing financial statements, the user of the information must be kept in mind, and a clearly worded description of each item is desirable. For example, the title Accounts Receivable may be converted to Accounts Due from Customers in the balance sheet. In the choice between brevity and clarity, the latter should control in the preparation of financial statements. Of course, several ledger accounts may be combined into a single financial statement item, such as Inventories.

Basis of Valuation Informed readers of balance sheets are presumed to be familiar with the general assumption governing the accounting valuation of assets and liabilities. However, variations in accounting procedures in applying this assumption often produce balance sheet figures whose significance is difficult to interpret unless the procedure used is disclosed. The choice of "fifo" or "lifo" cost in inventory valuation, for example, results in materially different asset figures. An acceptable standard of disclosure requires that the basis of valuation be indicated in the caption of all balance sheet items, unless it is obvious (as in the case of cash, for example).

Notes to Financial Statements Explanatory comments and supplementary disclosure are made in "Notes to financial statements." Often a note may be applicable to both the balance sheet and the income statement, and the list of notes in its entirety may occupy several pages. As explained in Chapter 1 (page 19), a note summarizing significant accounting policies is prescribed as essential by *APB Opinion No. 22,* "Disclosure of Accounting Policies." For such matters as stock option plans, pension plans, lease agreements, and acquisitions, the only reasonable way to provide an adequate explanation is by using notes to financial statements. A complete set of notes accompanying the financial statements of General Motors Corporation appears on pages 162–166.

Supporting Schedules If the detail involved in a full picture of a section of the balance sheet interferes with a concise presentation, it may be desirable to summarize the item on the balance sheet and show the detail in a supporting schedule. For example, inventories might be reported as one figure and the detailed amounts of raw materials, goods in process, goods on consignment, and finished goods put in a supporting schedule attached to the balance sheet. Companies having a large number of debt issues outstanding find it convenient to show long-term debt as a single amount and include supporting schedules in which the details are furnished (see *Note 8* on page 164, for example). For the reader who

SAMPLE CORPORATION
Balance Sheet
December 31, Year 5
(In thousands of dollars)
Assets

Current assets:

Cash			$ 485
Marketable securities (at cost, market value $220,000)			210
Notes receivable and accrued interest			125
Amounts due from customers		$1,162	
Less: Allowance for doubtful accounts		50	1,112
Inventories (at lower of average cost or market)			580
Short-term prepayments			60
Total current assets			$ 2,572

Investments:

Stock of affiliated companies, not consolidated (at equity)		$1,250	
Fund for retirement of preferred stock		60	
Land held for future expansion		100	
Cash surrender value of life insurance		50	1,460

Plant and equipment:

	Cost	Accumulated depreciation	Carrying value	
Land	$ 3,060	$ –0–	$3,060	
Buildings	10,950	5,992	4,958	
Equipment	8,430	2,720	5,710	
Totals	$22,440	$8,712		13,728

Intangibles:

Goodwill (net of amortization)		$1,105	
Patents (net of amortization)		105	1,210
Total assets			$18,970

wants only "highlight" information, the balance sheet thus gives this in a concise and easily digestible manner. The analyst who desires more detailed information will find it in the supporting schedules.

Form of the balance sheet

Fairly standard ways of presenting balance sheet information have been developed in accounting, but there is no one stereotyped form. The objectives are clarity and adequate disclosure of all pertinent and material facts; there are various ways of meeting these objectives, and experimentation should be encouraged. The arrangement of the major sections of the balance sheet also may vary. We shall illustrate the basic feature of three forms of of presentation: the *account form,* the *report*

Liabilities & Stockholders' Equity		
Current liabilities:		
Accounts payable to trade creditors		$ 390
Accrued liabilities		130
Income taxes payable		200
Dividends payable		125
Advances by customers		20
Employees' retirement benefits payable currently		40
Total current liabilities		$ 905
Long-term liabilities:		
7% bonds payable, due Dec. 31, Year 15	$4,000	
Less: Discount on bonds payable	20	
Net bonds payable	$3,980	
Employees' retirement benefits payable in future years	250	
Deferred income taxes	300	
Total long-term liabilities		4,530
Total liabilities		$ 5,435
Stockholders' equity:		
6% cumulative preferred stock, $100 par (callable at $105 per share, authorized 10,000 shares, outstanding 9,500 shares)		$ 950
Common stock, no par, stated value $5 (authorized 1,000,000 shares, outstanding 800,000 shares)		4,000
Paid-in capital in excess of par or stated value:		
On preferred stock	$ 95	
On common stock	5,450	5,545
Total paid-in capital		$10,495
Retained earnings		3,040
Total stockholders' equity		$13,535
Total liabilities & stockholders' equity		$18,970

form, and the *financial position form.* Within the framework of these three patterns a number of variations are possible. In a recent survey of 600 large companies, 409 used the account form, 180 used the report form, and only 11 used the financial position form.[8]

Account Form A model balance sheet for Sample Corporation in the traditional balancing form appears on page 152 and 153. The distinguishing characteristic of this form is that all assets are listed on the left-hand side and liabilities and stockholders' equity are "balanced" against them on the right-hand side. The illustrative balance sheet, includes typical accounts in each classification and follows modern standards of disclosure and terminology. The appropriate degree of condensation in financial statements depends on the nature of the audience. A statement prepared for stockholders will be more condensed than one prepared for management. Notes relating to the balance sheet are purposely omitted from this illustration, because an actual set of notes to financial statements is presented in the Appendix at the end of this chapter.

Report Form The report form of balance sheet differs from the account form only in that the liability and stockholders' equity sections are listed below rather than to the right of the asset section.

Financial Position Form Both the account form and report form of the balance sheet express the equation *Assets* $=$ *Liabilities* $+$ *Stockholders' Equity.* A few companies, however, prefer to use a format which emphasizes working capital; this usually carries the title Statement of Financial Position. This is a *vertical* format in which current assets are listed and totaled; then current liabilities are listed next and the total deducted from the total of current assets to derive an amount for working capital. Other assets are then added and other liabilities deducted, leaving a residual amount as the stockholders' equity.

Comparative balance sheet

The illustrated balance sheet on pages 152–153 is only for one point in time, December 31, Year 5. Comparative figures for the previous year are presented in almost every published balance sheet. Such a *comparative balance sheet* is illustrated on pages 160–161 for General Motors Corporation. Many companies also publish 10- or 15-year summaries which bring out quite clearly important trends affecting the business and thus aid the reader in judging long-run financial performance.

---

[8] *Accounting Trends and Techniques,* 30th ed., AICPA (New York: 1977), p. 77.

Statement of stockholders' equity

As stated in Chapter 3 a statement of retained earnings explains the changes which have occurred in retained earnings during an accounting period. However, changes calling for explanation may also occur in the other stockholders' equity accounts. The explanation may take various forms, as suggested below by the APB:

> When both financial position and results of operations are presented, disclosure of changes in the separate accounts comprising stockholders' equity (in addition to retained earnings) and of the changes in the number of shares of equity securities during at least the most recent annual fiscal period and any subsequent interim period presented is required to make the financial statements sufficiently informative. Disclosure of such changes may take the form of separate statements or may be made in the basic financial statements or notes thereto.[9]

To achieve such disclosure, an increasing number of companies prepare a *statement of stockholders' equity.* Typical of such a statement is one illustrated below for Esmark, Inc.

Consolidated Statement of Stockholders' Equity
(In thousands of dollars)

	Preferred stock	Common stock	Other paid-in capital	Accumulated earnings	Cost of common stock in treasury	Total
Balance October 28, 1973	$36,485	$12,177	$137,858	$306,535	$ (208)	$492,847
Net earnings				68,066		68,066
Cash dividends paid:						
Preferred stock				(1,733)		(1,733)
Common stock				(11,883)		(11,883)
Purchases of common stock					(10,427)	(10,427)
Other changes			4		60	64
Balance October 26, 1974	36,485	12,177	137,862	360,985	(10,575)	536,934
Net earnings				79,685		79,685
Cash dividends paid:						
Preferred stock				(1,310)		(1,310)
Common stock				(19,227)		(19,227)
Issuance of stock in Doric acquisition		936	24,335			25,271
Conversion of preferred stock	(36,485)	1,173	35,312			
Five-for-four common stock split		3,563		(3,563)		
Other changes–net			10		418	428
Balance October 25, 1975	$ 0	$17,849	$197,519	$416,570	$(10,157)	$621,781

[9] *APB Opinion No. 12,* "Omnibus Opinion—1967," AICPA (New York: 1967), p. 190.

STATEMENT OF CHANGES IN FINANCIAL POSITION

Along with the income statement and the balance sheet, the statement of changes in financial position is included in the annual reports of publicly owned corporations and must be covered by the auditors' report. The objectives of the statement of changes in financial position are (1) to summarize the financing and investing activities of the entity, including the extent to which the entity has generated funds from operations during the period, and (2) to complete the disclosure of changes in financial position during the period.[10] In this context the term *funds* may be interpreted to mean *cash* or its equivalent, or it may mean *working capital*.

SAMPLE CORPORATION
Statement of Changes in Financial Position (Working Capital Basis)
For Year Ended December 31, Year 5
(In thousands of dollars)

Sources of working capital:		
Operations:		
Net income		$1,057
Add: Charges not requiring use of working capital:		
Depreciation expense	$186	
Amortization of goodwill, patents, and bond discount	64	
Employee retirement benefits payable in future years	40	
Deferred income taxes	20	
Less: Investment income from affiliated companies in excess of dividends received	(110)	200
Working capital provided from operations		$1,257
Issuance of preferred stock on January 3, Year 5		250
Disposal of investments in exchange for land		323
Disposal of equipment		100
Total sources of working capital		$1,930
Uses of working capital:		
Dividends on preferred and common stock	$457	
Deposit in fund for retirement of preferred stock	30	
Acquisition of land in exchange of investments	323	
Increase in cash surrender value of life insurance policies	10	
Purchase of patents	120	
Total uses of working capital		940
Increase in working capital		$ 990

---

[10] *APB Opinion No. 19,* "Reporting Changes in Financial Position," AICPA (New York: 1971), p. 372.

	End of Year 5	End of Year 4	Increase or (decrease) in working capital
Composition of working capital:			
Current assets:			
Cash	$ 485	$ 200	$285
Marketable securities	210	150	60
Notes receivable and accrued interest	125	–0–	125
Amounts due from customers	1,112	800	312
Inventories	580	1,000	(420)
Short-term prepayments . . .	60	20	40
Total current assets	$2,572	$2,170	
Current liabilities:			
Acc'ts pay.-trade	$ 390	$ 790	400
Accrued liabilities	130	80	(50)
Income taxes payable	200	350	150
Dividends payable	125	100	(25)
Advances by customers	20	138	118
Ret. benefits currently payable	40	35	(5)
Total current liabilities . . .	$ 905	$1,493	
Working capital	$1,667	$ 677	
Increase in working capital			$990

Most companies prepare the statement of changes in financial position on a working capital basis. However, either the cash or working capital basis should include in the statement the impact of financing and investing activities which do not directly affect cash or working capital. For example, the issuance of long-term bonds in exchange for land valued at $1 million should be reported as a $1 million source of funds from issuance of bonds and a $1 million use of funds to acquire land.

A complete discussion of the statement of changes in financial position is found in Chapter 24. At this point we shall only illustrate the statement without further explanation. The statement of changes in financial position on a working capital basis for Sample Corporation appears above. The related income statement and statement of retained earnings for Sample Corporation appear on pages 103 and 119 in Chapter 3, and the related balance sheet was presented earlier in this chapter (pages 152–153). Note that the statement is prepared in two parts— the first part shows the sources and uses of working capital, and the second part shows the composition of working capital at the beginning and end of Year 5. A more comprehensive statement of changes in financial position in comparative form appears in the Appendix (page 159).

APPENDIX: FINANCIAL STATEMENTS FOR GENERAL MOTORS CORPORATION

Statement of Consolidated Income

General Motors Corporation
and Consolidated Subsidiaries

for the years ended December 31, 1975 and 1974

	1975	1974
Net Sales	$35,724,911,215	$31,549,546,126
Equity in earnings of nonconsolidated subsidiaries and associates (dividends received amounted to $67,649,945 in 1975 and $65,649,711 in 1974)	136,577,410	114,423,643
Other income less income deductions (net deduction in 1975) (Note 2)	(147,695,735)	6,667,025
Total	35,713,792,890	31,670,636,794
Costs and Expenses		
Cost of sales and other operating charges, exclusive of items listed below	29,889,729,147	26,918,749,752
Selling, general and administrative expenses	1,333,720,820	1,363,921,772
Depreciation of real estate, plants and equipment	906,114,752	846,574,978
Amortization of special tools	1,180,070,069	858,369,689
Provision for the Incentive Program (Note 11)	32,866,137	5,851,240
United States, foreign and other income taxes (Note 3)	1,118,200,000	727,100,000
Total	34,460,700,925	30,720,567,431
Net Income	1,253,091,965	950,069,363
Dividends on preferred stocks	12,928,265	12,928,266
Earned on Common Stock	$ 1,240,163,700	$ 937,141,097
Average number of shares of common stock outstanding	286,838,592	286,289,679
Earned Per Share of Common Stock (Note 12)	$4.32	$3.27

Statement of Changes in Consolidated Financial Position
for the years ended December 31, 1975 and 1974

General Motors Corporation
and Consolidated Subsidiaries

	1975	1974
Source of Funds		
Net income	$1,253,091,965	$ 950,069,363
Depreciation of real estate, plants and equipment	906,114,752	846,574,978
Amortization of special tools	1,180,070,069	858,369,689
Deferred income taxes, undistributed earnings of nonconsolidated subsidiaries and associates, etc.—net	65,699,596	106,373,163
Total current operations	3,404,976,382	2,761,387,193
Proceeds from disposals of property	97,765,120	66,990,959
Proceeds from issuance of long-term debt (less discount)	752,795,190	241,968,490
Total	4,255,536,692	3,070,346,642
Application of Funds		
Dividends paid to stockholders	701,323,876	986,249,412
Expenditures for real estate, plants and equipment	1,200,889,262	1,458,453,166
Expenditures for special tools	1,035,592,727	1,095,595,289
Retirements of long-term debt	406,294,171	121,922,737
Investments in nonconsolidated subsidiaries and associates	13,067,137	13,586,495
Other—net	46,275,003	49,462,195
Total	3,403,442,176	3,725,269,294
Increase (Decrease) in working capital	852,094,516	(654,922,652)
Working capital at beginning of the year	5,541,928,523	6,196,851,175
Working capital at end of the year	$6,394,023,039	$5,541,928,523
Increase (Decrease) in Working Capital by Element		
Cash, government securities and time deposits	$2,044,458,667	($1,707,744,933)
Accounts and notes receivable	341,880,452	(81,686,584)
Inventories	(713,809,482)	1,227,805,771
Prepaid expenses	116,757,773	(14,582,233)
Accounts, drafts and loans payable	(181,124,894)	(270,297,335)
United States, foreign and other income taxes payable	(484,294,987)	247,504,236
Accrued liabilities	(271,773,013)	(55,921,574)
Increase (Decrease) in working capital	$ 852,094,516	($ 654,922,652)

Reference should be made to notes on pages 162 through 166.

Certain amounts for 1974 have been reclassified to reflect comparability with classifications for 1975.

Consolidated Balance Sheet
December 31, 1975 and 1974

Assets	1975	1974
Current Assets		
Cash	$ 357,470,570	$ 400,626,489
United States and other government securities and time deposits— at cost, which approximates market:		
Held for payment of income taxes	787,972,833	303,389,424
Other	2,237,373,575	634,342,398
Accounts and notes receivable (Note 4)	3,342,697,338	3,000,816,886
Inventories	5,690,892,746	6,404,702,228
Prepaid expenses	423,086,553	306,328,780
Total Current Assets	12,839,493,615	11,050,206,205
Investments and Miscellaneous Assets		
Equity in net assets of nonconsolidated subsidiaries and associates (Note 5)	1,498,852,038	1,416,857,436
Other investments and miscellaneous assets—at cost (less allowances)	125,361,365	134,704,509
Total Investments and Miscellaneous Assets	1,624,213,403	1,551,561,945
Common Stock Held for the Incentive Program (Note 6)	62,641,489	86,698,431
Property		
Real estate, plants and equipment (Note 7)	17,503,583,496	16,808,456,667
Less accumulated depreciation (Note 7)	11,091,109,004	10,592,991,565
Net real estate, plants and equipment	6,412,474,492	6,215,465,102
Special tools—less amortization	673,405,801	817,883,143
Total Property	7,085,880,293	7,033,348,245
Deferred Charges		
Goodwill—less amortization	26,061,688	32,468,434
Deferred income taxes and other deferred charges	26,594,106	119,266,754
Total Deferred Charges	52,655,794	151,735,188
Total Assets	$21,664,884,594	$19,873,550,014

Reference should be made to notes on pages 162 through 166.

Certain amounts for 1974 have been reclassified to reflect comparability with classifications for 1975.

General Motors Corporation
and Consolidated Subsidiaries

Liabilities, Reserves and Stockholders' Equity	1975	1974
Current Liabilities		
Accounts, drafts and loans payable	$ 3,187,012,203	$ 3,005,887,309
United States, foreign and other income taxes payable	842,097,047	357,802,060
Accrued liabilities	2,416,361,326	2,144,588,313
Total Current Liabilities	6,445,470,576	5,508,277,682
Long-Term Debt (less unamortized discount) (Note 8)	1,223,064,579	876,563,560
Other Liabilities	396,716,921	430,385,378
Deferred Credits and Reserves		
Deferred investment tax credits	241,049,345	189,115,478
Contingent credits under Stock Option Plan	8,100,000	11,443,157
General reserve applicable to foreign operations	141,667,396	141,667,396
Other deferred credits and reserves (Note 9)	126,451,110	185,500,785
Total Deferred Credits and Reserves	517,267,851	527,726,816
Stockholders' Equity (Notes 10 and 11)		
Capital stock:		
Preferred:		
$5.00 series	183,564,400	183,564,400
$3.75 series	100,000,000	100,000,000
Common	479,361,735	479,361,735
Total capital stock	762,926,135	762,926,135
Capital surplus (principally additional paid-in capital)	766,979,178	766,979,178
Net income retained for use in the business	11,552,459,354	11,000,691,265
Total Stockholders' Equity	13,082,364,667	12,530,596,578
Total Liabilities, Reserves and Stockholders' Equity	$21,664,884,594	$19,873,550,014

Notes to Financial Statements

Note 1. Significant Accounting Policies

Principles of Consolidation

The consolidated financial statements include the accounts of the Corporation and all domestic and foreign subsidiaries which are more than 50% owned and engaged principally in manufacturing or wholesale marketing of General Motors products. General Motors' share of earnings or losses of nonconsolidated subsidiaries and of associates in which at least 20% of the voting securities is owned is generally included in consolidated income under the equity method of accounting. Intercompany items and transactions between companies included in the consolidation are eliminated and unrealized intercompany profits on sales to nonconsolidated subsidiaries and to associates are deferred.

Translation of Foreign Currencies

Real estate, plants and equipment, accumulated depreciation and the provision for depreciation are translated into United States dollars at exchange rates in effect at the dates the related assets were acquired. Other assets, liabilities and deferred credits and reserves are translated at exchange rates in effect at the date of the balance sheet; other items of income and expense are translated at average exchange rates for the months in which the transactions occurred. Accumulated unrealized net loss from translation of foreign currency accounts of any foreign subsidiary is charged to income and accumulated unrealized net gain is deferred. Gains or losses on significant exchange contracts are included in costs and expenses currently.

Income Taxes

Investment tax credits allowable under the income tax laws are deducted in determining taxes estimated to be payable currently and are deferred and amortized over the lives of the related assets. The tax effects of timing differences between pretax accounting income and taxable income (principally related to depreciation, benefit plans expense, sales and product allowances and undistributed earnings of subsidiaries and associates) are deferred, except that the tax effects of certain expenses charged to income prior to 1968 have not been deferred but are recognized in income taxes at the time such expenses become allowable deductions for tax purposes. Provisions are made for estimated United States and foreign taxes, less available tax credits and deductions, which may be incurred on remittance of the Corporation's share of subsidiaries' and associates' undistributed earnings included in the consolidated financial statements.

Inventories

Inventories are stated at the lower of cost or market. Cost is determined substantially by the first-in, first-out or the average cost method. Market value is current sales price less distribution cost for finished product and replacement cost for other inventories. Physical inventories are taken at all locations.

Common Stock Held for the Incentive Program

Common stock in treasury is held exclusively for payment of liabilities under the Incentive Program and is stated substantially at cost.

Property, Depreciation and Amortization

Property is stated at cost. Maintenance, repairs, rearrangement expenses and renewals and betterments which do not enhance the value or increase the basic productive capacity of the assets are charged to costs and expenses as incurred.

Depreciation is provided on groups of property using, with minor exceptions, an accelerated method which accumulates depreciation of approximately two-thirds of the depreciable cost during the first half of the estimated lives of the property. The annual group rates of depreciation are as follows:

Classification of Property	Annual Group Rates
Land improvements	5%
Buildings	3½%
Machinery and equipment	8⅓ % (Average)
Furniture and office equipment	6% (Average)

In 1974, a modification of depreciation policies, which had the effect of depreciating the cost of certain groups of property more nearly over the service lives of the assets, reduced depreciation expense by $97 million.

Expenditures for special tools are amortized, with the amortization applied directly to the asset account, over short periods of time because the utility value of the tools is radically affected by frequent changes in the design of the functional components and appearance of the product. Replacement of special tools for reasons other than changes in products is charged directly to cost of sales.

Goodwill

Goodwill represents the excess of the cost over the value ascribed to the net tangible assets of businesses acquired and is amortized over ten years with the amortization applied directly to the asset account. Amortization amounted to $6,415,146 in 1975 and $6,427,346 in 1974.

Incentive Program

A reserve is maintained for purposes of the Bonus Plan and Stock Option Plan to which may be credited each year a maximum amount which the independent public accountants of the Corporation determine in accordance with the provisions of the Bonus Plan; however, for any year, the Bonus and Salary Committee may direct that a lesser amount be credited. Bonus awards under the Bonus Plan, contingent credits under the Stock Option Plan and such other amounts arising out of the operation of the Incentive Program as the Committee may determine are charged to the reserve. As a result of tentative determinations of awards by the Committee, the amount provided is transferred to current liabilities, other liabilities and deferred credits at December 31.

If Bonus and Stock Option Plan participants fail to meet conditions precedent to receiving undelivered instalments of bonus awards and contingent credits, the amount of any such instalments is credited to income. Upon the exercise of stock options, the related contingent credits are proportionately reduced and the amount of the reduction is credited to income.

General Reserve Applicable to Foreign Operations

The general reserve applicable to foreign operations was established in 1954. There has been no change in this reserve since its establishment.

Notes to Financial Statements (continued)

Note 1. Significant Accounting Policies (concluded)

Pension Program

The Corporation and its subsidiaries have a number of pension plans covering substantially all employes. Benefits under the plans are generally related to an employe's length of service, wages and salaries, and, where applicable, contributions. The costs of these plans are determined on the basis of actuarial cost methods and include amortization of prior service cost over periods not exceeding 30 years. With the exception of certain overseas subsidiaries, pension costs accrued are funded.

Product Related Expenses

Expenditures for advertising and sales promotion and for other product related expenses are charged to costs and expenses as incurred; provisions for estimated costs related to product warranty are made at the time the products are sold.

Accounting Statements

The Financial Accounting Standards Board issued Statements on Accounting for Contingencies, in March 1975, and Accounting for the Translation of Foreign Currency Transactions and Foreign Currency Financial Statements, in October 1975, which, for General Motors, are effective for the 1976 calendar year. General Motors is reviewing these Statements which are not expected to have a material effect upon the financial statements.

Note 2. Other Income Less Income Deductions

	1975	1974
Other income:		
Interest income		
Other	$ 132,686,194	$ 166,989,616
	47,248,884	29,606,184
Income deductions:		
Interest and related charges on long-term debt		
Other interest	(103,550,876)	(77,940,292)
Net loss on translation of financial statements in foreign currencies (a)	(190,384,838)	(84,802,411)
Other	(27,113,414)	(45,582,291)
	(6,581,685)	18,396,219
Net	($ 147,695,735)	$ 6,667,025

(a) In addition, net translation losses of $40,899,173 in 1975 and $14,770,612 in 1974 were charged to Other Deferred Credits and Reserves.

Note 3. United States, Foreign and Other Income Taxes

	1975	1974
Taxes estimated to be payable currently (b):		
United States Federal	$ 856,986,220	$ 329,664,925
Foreign	143,611,800	126,916,078
Other ($51,500,000 for 1974 largely offset by adjustments to prior years' accruals)	140,200,000	600,000
Total	1,140,798,020	457,181,003
Taxes deferred—net:		
United States Federal	(92,958,220)	248,334,075
Foreign	35,626,333	(17,997,320)
Other	(17,200,000)	29,300,000
Total	(74,531,887)	259,636,755
Investment tax credits deferred—net of amortization:		
United States Federal	52,272,000	10,101,000
Foreign	(338,133)	181,242
Total	51,933,867	10,282,242
Total	$1,118,200,000	$ 727,100,000

(b) Investment tax credits deducted in determining taxes estimated to be payable currently amounted to $95,301,093 in 1975 and $57,450,800 in 1974.

Note 4. Accounts and Notes Receivable

	1975	1974
General Motors Acceptance Corporation and subsidiaries (relating to current wholesale financing of sales of General Motors products, etc.)	$1,639,392,955	$1,359,792,896
Other trade and sundry receivables (less allowances)	1,703,304,383	1,641,023,990
Total	$3,342,697,338	$3,000,816,886

Note 5. Equity in Net Assets of Nonconsolidated Subsidiaries and Associates

	1975	1974
Nonconsolidated subsidiaries:		
General Motors Acceptance Corporation and subsidiaries (See page 21)	$1,250,617,638	$1,187,332,411
Dealerships operating under dealership assistance plans (retail companies)	118,421,744	108,581,712
Other domestic and foreign subsidiaries	46,170,125	30,229,903
Associates (interests in overseas companies)	83,642,531	90,713,410
Total	$1,498,852,038	$1,416,857,436

Notes to Financial Statements (continued)

Note 6. Common Stock Held for the Incentive Program	1975		1974	
	Shares	Amount	Shares	Amount
Balance at beginning of the year	1,223,166	$86,698,431	1,886,888	$137,407,501
Acquired during the year	233,326	12,957,656	70,900	3,556,657
Delivered to participants during the year	(514,513)	(37,014,598)	(734,622)	(54,265,727)
Balance at end of the year:				
Held for instalment deliveries of bonus awards and contingent credits related to prior years	530,445	37,984,308	950,415	68,351,323
Available for contingent credits related to outstanding stock options	91,452	6,643,873	153,288	11,443,157
Available for current bonus awards and contingent credits . . .	320,082	18,013,308	119,463	6,903,951
Total	941,979	$62,641,489	1,223,166	$ 86,698,431

Note 7. Real Estate, Plants and Equipment and Accumulated Depreciation	1975	1974
Real estate, plants and equipment:		
Land	$ 248,044,679	$ 247,778,103
Land improvements	589,474,841	546,176,357
Leasehold improvements—less amortization	28,389,540	25,061,275
Buildings	4,291,868,155	4,070,429,327
Machinery and equipment	11,586,565,467	10,957,876,467
Furniture and office equipment	157,253,016	238,842,532
Construction in progress.	601,987,798	722,292,606
Total	$17,503,583,496	$16,808,456,667
Accumulated depreciation:		
Land improvements	$ 352,770,784	$ 327,117,831
Buildings	2,446,730,325	2,308,058,108
Machinery and equipment	8,149,394,667	7,737,842,390
Furniture and office equipment	92,883,098	170,643,106
Extraordinary obsolescence	49,330,130	49,330,130
Total	$11,091,109,004	$10,592,991,565

Note 8. Long-Term Debt (Less Current Portion)		1975	1974
General Motors Corporation—United States dollars:			
8.05% Notes	1985	$ 300,000,000	$ —
8⅜% Debentures	2005	300,000,000	—
Other	1977-2000	127,141,261	122,563,832
Consolidated subsidiaries:			
United States dollars	1977-86	354,980,556	376,107,628
Canadian dollars		—	50,450,000
German marks	1977-79	72,628,100	184,675,000
Swiss francs		—	61,480,000
British pounds	1977-92	52,624,000	46,920,000
French francs	1977-81	7,515,200	5,069,300
Brazilian cruzeiros	1977-81	4,469,700	16,852,000
Venezuelan bolivars	1977-80	2,416,700	5,170,700
Other currencies	1977-2004	8,597,500	7,275,100
Total		1,230,373,017	876,563,560
Less unamortized discount		7,308,438	
Total		$ 1,223,064,579	$ 876,563,560

Maturities of long-term debt at December 31, 1975 for each of the five years through 1980 are: 1976—$251,939,988 (included in current liabilities); 1977—$216,675,701; 1978—$49,812,998; 1979—$129,297,364; and 1980—$27,867,670.

Note 9. Other Deferred Credits and Reserves	1975	1974
Deferred intercompany profits arising from sales to nonconsolidated subsidiaries	$ 65,256,838	$ 72,659,832
Deferred gains on translation of foreign currency accounts of foreign subsidiaries	47,330,924	88,230,097
Other deferred income	6,857,233	3,809,221
Miscellaneous reserves	7,006,115	20,801,635
Total	$ 126,451,110	$ 185,500,785

Notes to Financial Statements (continued)

Note 10. Stockholders' Equity	1975	1974
Capital Stock:		
Preferred Stock, without par value (authorized, 6,000,000 shares), no change during the year:		
$5.00 series, stated value $100 per share, redeemable at $120 per share (issued, 1,875,366 shares; in treasury, 39,722 shares; outstanding, 1,835,644 shares)	$ 183,564,400	$ 183,564,400
$3.75 series, stated value $100 per share, redeemable at $100 per share (issued and outstanding, 1,000,000 shares)	100,000,000	100,000,000
Common Stock, $1⅔ par value (authorized, 500,000,000 shares; issued, 287,617,041 shares), no change during the year	479,361,735	479,361,735
Total capital stock	762,926,135	762,926,135
Capital Surplus (principally additional paid-in capital), no change during the year	766,979,178	766,979,178
Net Income Retained for Use in the Business:		
Balance at beginning of the year	11,000,691,265	11,036,871,314
Net income	1,253,091,965	950,069,363
Total	12,253,783,230	11,986,940,677
Cash dividends:		
Preferred stock, $5.00 series, $5.00 per share	9,178,220	9,178,220
Preferred stock, $3.75 series, $3.75 per share	3,750,045	3,750,046
Common stock, $2.40 per share in 1975 and $3.40 per share in 1974	688,395,611	973,321,146
Total cash dividends	701,323,876	986,249,412
Balance at end of the year	11,552,459,354	11,000,691,265
Total Stockholders' Equity	$13,082,364,667	$12,530,596,578

Note 11. Incentive Program

For the year 1975, the Bonus and Salary Committee directed a credit to the Reserve for Bonus Plan and Stock Option Plan of $32,866,137 (the maximum permitted under the Bonus Plan formula as set forth on page 20). In addition, the Committee has directed that $930,000 of the unawarded balance in the reserve carried forward from 1974 be made available for the distribution related to 1975. Subject to final determination, the Committee has tentatively directed that the total of individual awards shall approximate the amount of the credit to the reserve related to 1975 plus the aforementioned $930,000. As a result, $33,796,137 was transferred to current liabilities, other liabilities and deferred credits. The balance of the unawarded bonus reserve carried forward from 1974 in the amount of $621,173 was, in accordance with action taken by the Bonus and Salary Committee, restored to income in 1975, but was not included in net earnings for that year in determining the provision for the Bonus and Stock Option Plan.

Changes during 1975 in the status of options granted under the Stock Option Plan are shown in the following table.

The option prices are 100% of the average of the highest and lowest sales prices on the New York Stock Exchange on the dates the options were granted. The options outstanding at December 31, 1975 expire ten years from date of grant. All options are subject to earlier termination under certain conditions.

The Corporation intends to deliver newly issued stock upon the exercise of any of the outstanding options. The maximum number of shares for which additional options might be granted under the Plan was 2,449,363 at January 1, 1975 and 2,657,593 at December 31, 1975.

		Shares Under Option		
			Changes During Year	
Year Granted	Option Price	Jan. 1, 1975	Exercised	Terminated	Dec. 31, 1975
1970	$69.82	162,786	—	162,786	—
1973	73.38	261,168	—	31,272	229,896
1974	50.00	332,988	—	14,172	318,816
Total		756,942	—	208,230	548,712

Note 12. Earnings Per Share

Earnings per share of common stock are based on the average number of shares outstanding during each year. The effect on earnings per share resulting from the assumed exercise of outstanding options and delivery of bonus awards and contingent credits under the Incentive Program is not material.

Note 13. Foreign Operations

Net assets, sales and income attributable to operations outside the United States and Canada, included in the consolidated financial statements, are summarized in the table on page 19. Net sales include sales to United States and Canadian operations. Net income is after provisions for deferred income taxes on unremitted earnings of such foreign operations and other consolidation adjustments and, in 1975, includes earnings (loss) attributable to the major overseas manufacturing subsidiaries, as follows: Adam Opel AG, $54 million; General Motors-Holden's Limited, $26 million; and Vauxhall Motors Limited, ($17 million).

Notes to Financial Statements (concluded)

Note 13. Foreign Operations (concluded)

Net Assets Attributable to Operations Outside the United States and Canada

	Western Europe	United Kingdom, Australia, New Zealand and South Africa	Other, Principally Mexico and South America	Total	December 31, 1974 Total
			December 31, 1975		
			(In Millions)		
Assets:					
Total current assets	$ 993	$ 933	$ 790	$2,716	$2,633
Real estate, plants and equipment	1,401	1,003	507	2,911	2,769
Accumulated depreciation	(934)	(746)	(191)	(1,871)	(1,768)
Special tools—less amortization	130	103	23	256	297
Other assets	25	20	164	209	223
Total assets	1,615	1,313	1,293	4,221	4,154
Liabilities:					
Bank borrowings and notes payable	176	247	314	737	798
Other current liabilities	437	367	232	1,036	919
Total current liabilities	613	614	546	1,773	1,717
Long-term debt of subsidiaries	166	70	171	407	674
Other liabilities and reserves	274	79	24	377	371
Total liabilities	1,053	763	741	2,557	2,762
Balance	$ 562	$ 550	$ 552	1,664	1,392
Less General Reserve Applicable to Foreign Operations .				142	142
Attributable to Operations Outside the United States and Canada:					
Net Assets				$1,522	$1,250
Net Sales				$7,227	$5,969
Net Income				$ 72	$ —

Note 14. Research and Development

Expenditures for research and development are charged to expenses as incurred and amounted to $1.1 billion in 1975 and $1.1 billion in 1974.

Note 15. Pension Program

The total pension expense of the Corporation and its consolidated subsidiaries amounted to $969 million in 1975 and $819 million in 1974. Based on a review of the Employee Retirement Income Security Act of 1974, it is expected that this law will have no material effect upon the cost of the pension plans. The actuarially computed value of vested benefits of all plans exceeded the total of pension funds, at market, and balance sheet accruals as of December 31, 1975, by about $2.9 billion.

Note 16. Contingent Liabilities

There are various claims and pending actions against the Corporation and its subsidiaries in respect of commercial matters, including warranties and product liability, governmental regulations including environmental and safety matters, civil rights, patent matters, taxes and other matters arising out of the conduct of the business. Certain of these actions purport to be class actions, seeking damages in very large amounts. The amounts of liability on these claims and actions at December 31, 1975 were not determinable but, in the opinion of the management, the ultimate liability resulting will not materially affect the consolidated financial position or results of operations of the Corporation and its consolidated subsidiaries.

──────── Accountants' Report ────────

Haskins & Sells
Certified Public Accountants

1114 Avenue of the Americas
New York 10036

General Motors Corporation, its Directors and Stockholders:

February 11, 1976

We have examined the Consolidated Balance Sheet of General Motors Corporation and consolidated subsidiaries as of December 31, 1975 and 1974 and the related Statements of Consolidated Income and Changes in Consolidated Financial Position for the years then ended. Our examination was made in accordance with generally accepted auditing standards, and accordingly included such tests of the accounting records and such other auditing procedures as we considered necessary in the circumstances.

In our opinion, these financial statements present fairly the financial position of the companies at December 31, 1975 and 1974 and the results of their operations and the changes in their financial position for the years then ended, in conformity with generally accepted accounting principles consistently applied.

Haskins & Sells

REVIEW QUESTIONS

1 What are three major limitations of the balance sheet as a source of information useful to management and investors?

2 In describing the accounting valuation assumptions, assets may be classified into two groups: monetary assets and productive resources. What is the relationship between the method of valuation applied to these two classes of assets and the measurement of revenue and expenses?

3 Barna Corporation issued $100 million of 8% bonds, receiving proceeds of $98 million. The bonds are callable at any time at 103. An argument has arisen over the proper valuation of these bonds in the company's balance sheet. One official supports $98 million; another argues for maturity value, $100 million; a third argues that $103 million is the proper figure since the bonds may be called at any time. What basic accounting principle should govern the decision? Which position would you support, and why?

4 A partnership earned $25,000, divided equally between two partners. Each partner will pay income taxes of $3,600 on his share of the partnership income. One partner argues that a liability of $7,200 should appear in the partnership balance sheet, since both partners plan to withdraw from the partnership an amount sufficient to pay their income taxes. What accounting principle is at issue? What is your position, and why?

5 As a supplement to its regularly published balance sheet, a company prepared a **comparative balance sheet** expressed in **current dollars.** On the supplementary statement the amount of liabilities was the same as on the historical-dollar balance sheet. One company officer commented, "We know that the general price level has been rising in recent years. Why should our liabilities be the same on these two statements?" Explain.

6 Dallas Smith is a member of the American Institute of Certified Public Accountants. In auditing the records of X Corporation, Smith found that the company followed an accounting principle with which he agrees but which has not been accepted by the Accounting Principles Board or the Financial Accounting Standards Board. Assuming that the difference in treatment has a material effect on the financial statements of the company, what are the alternatives facing Smith in preparing his audit opinion on the financial statements of X Corporation?

7 What is the distinction between an **estimated** and a **contingent** liability? Give an example of each.

8 How is the definition of a **current liability** related to the definition of a **current asset?**

9 What is the basis for the rule against offsetting assets and liabilities?

10 In practice, the term **reserve** has been used to describe a contra-asset account, an estimated liability, and an appropriation of retained earnings. Why are these uses of the term **reserve** in account titles objectionable? In which of the three uses is the term least misleading?

11 The financial statements prepared by a corporation include several items which taken together represent the excess of assets over liabilities. What are these items and what is the term used to describe them as a group?

12 Taylor Corporation issues its note payable at 8% interest to obtain a bank loan, but concurrently it issues a three-year note payable to a supplier at an annual interest rate of only 3%. Should both the notes payable be recorded at their face amount? Explain.

13 Could the current liability section of a balance sheet properly include an obligation for which no specific creditor could be named and no cash payment was required? Explain.

14 In the published financial statements of a large corporation, would you expect to find a summary of the **significant accounting policies** followed by the company? Explain.

15 Explain the term **operating cycle** and its significance in the classification of balance sheet items as current or noncurrent.

16 Indicate circumstances under which liabilities falling due within a month or two after the date of the balance sheet should be excluded from the current liability classification.

17 A balance sheet may be prepared in different forms. List these forms and indicate which is most widely used.

18 What is the purpose of a statement of stockholders' equity?

19 a Briefly state the functions of a statement of changes in financial position.
b What are the two basic approaches that may be used to prepare such a statement?

20 "The statement of changes in financial position is superfluous when a comparative balance sheet is made available to users of financial statements." Comment on the validity of this assertion.

EXERCISES

Ex. 4-1 The balance sheet of Rock Music Company contains the following group headings:

A Current assets	F Current liabilities
B Investments and restricted funds	G Long-term liabilities
C Property, plant, and equipment	H Deferred credits
D Intangible assets	I Invested capital
E Other assets (including deferred charges)	J Retained earnings

For each of the following items, indicate the preferable balance sheet classification by listing the appropriate letter from the listing above.

1 Accrued interest on bonds payable	11 Allowance for doubtful accounts
2 Premium on preferred stock	12 Cash surrender value of life insurance policies
3 Mortgage payable (outstanding for 19½ years; due in six months)	13 Premium on bonds payable
4 Raw land held for speculation	14 Accumulated depreciation
5 Payroll bank account	15 Paid-in capital in excess of par
6 Patents	16 Short-term prepayments
7 Discount on bonds payable	17 Machinery retired from use and held for sale
8 Unexpired insurance	18 Accrued payroll
9 Cost of moving home office (including employees) from New York to California	19 Sears Roebuck and Co. common stock (100 shares owned 10 years)
10 Leasehold improvements	20 Advance payments by customers

Ex. 4-2 Prepare a skeleton balance sheet for Z Company in account form, showing only major classifications (approximately ten topics or group headings).

Ex. 4-3 You have been asked to assist the chief accountant of the Julie Corporation in the preparation of a balance sheet. The outline presented below represents the various classifications suggested by the chief accountant for the balance sheet; classification "M" has been added for items to be excluded from the balance sheet. (You are not asked to approve or disapprove the various classifications set forth below.)

A Current assets
B Investments
C Plant and equipment
D Intangibles
E Other assets, including deferred charges
F Current liabilities
G Long-term liabilities, including deferred credits

H Preferred stock
I Common stock
J Paid-in capital in excess of par
K Retained earnings
L Appraisal capital
M Items excluded from the balance sheet

The 24 accounts listed below are to be classified according to the preferred classification group from the preceding list.

1 Dividend payable (on Julie Corporation's preferred stock)
2 Plant construction in progress
3 Factory building (retired from use and held for sale)
4 Premium on bonds payable
5 Land (held for possible future building site)
6 Merchandise inventory (held by Julie Corporation on consignment)
7 Stock dividend to be distributed, stated at par (in common stock to common stockholders)
8 Office supplies inventory
9 Sinking fund cash (First National Bank, Trustee)
10 Reserve for retirement of preferred stock
11 Installment sales accounts receivable (average collection period 18 months)
12 Premium on preferred stock
13 Advances to officers (indefinite repayment date, non-interest-bearing)
14 Unredeemed merchandise coupons issued to customers
15 Discount on bonds payable
16 Inventory of small tools
17 Contingent liability on notes receivable discounted
18 Liability for loss on merchandise purchase commitments
19 Allowance to reduce inventory to market
20 Matured capital stock subscriptions (called by the board of directors and considered collectible)
21 Common stock subscribed (Julie Corporation's stock)
22 Unrealized loss in market value of noncurrent securities
23 Securities held as collateral for loan to officer of Julie Corporation
24 Contracts payable, retained percentage

Using the letters representing the various balance sheet classifications, identify each of the 24 items according to the preferred balance sheet presentation. If an account is an offsetting or valuation account, mark an "X" before the letter. For example, "Allowance for Doubtful Accounts" would be "X–A."

Ex. 4-4 From the following balances, compute *(a)* the amount of working capital and *(b)* the stockholders' equity (book value) per share of capital stock:

Investment in affiliated companies (at equity)	$100,000
Cash surrender value of life insurance policies	10,000
Organization costs	5,000
Interest receivable	2,000
Other current assets	198,000
Other current liabilities	88,000
Reserve for contingencies	50,000
Retained earnings–unappropriated	170,000
Capital stock, $5 par	300,000
Paid-in capital in excess of par	200,000
Deferred income taxes payable	40,000
Construction in progress (for customers)	150,000
Cash in bond sinking fund	80,000
Product warranties outstanding	6,000
Creditors' accounts with debit balances	4,500

Ex. 4-5 The December 31, Year 5, balance sheet of Borg Corporation is presented below. These are the **only** accounts in Borg's balance sheet. Amounts indicated by a question mark (?) can be calculated from the additional information given.

Assets

Cash	$ 25,000
Accounts receivable (net)	?
Inventory	?
Property, plant, and equipment (net)	294,000
Total assets	$432,000

Liabilities & Stockholders' Equity

Accounts payable (trade)	$?
Income taxes payable (current)	25,000
Long-term debt	?
Common stock, $1 par	300,000
Retained earnings or deficit	?
Total liabilities & stockholders' equity	$432,000

Additional information:

Current ratio at end of Year 5	1.5 to 1
Total liabilities divided by total stockholders' equity	0.8
Turnover of ending inventory based on sales	15 times
Turnover of ending inventory based on cost of goods sold	10.5 times
Gross profit on sales for Year 5	$315,000

Instructions Compute the amount of each of the following accounts at December 31, Year 5:
a Inventory
b Accounts receivable (net)
c Accounts payable (trade)
d Retained earnings (or deficit)
e Long-term debt

SHORT CASES FOR ANALYSIS AND DECISION

Case 4-1 The **complete set** of financial statements issued by Joann Corporation for the year ended August 31, Year 5, is presented below:

JOANN CORPORATION
Balance Sheet
August 31, Year 5
(In thousands of dollars)

Assets

Cash		$ 103
Securities, at cost which approximates market value		54
Trade accounts receivable (net of $65,000 allowance for doubtful accounts)		917
Inventories, at cost		775
Property, plant, and equipment	$3,200	
Less: Accumulated depreciation	1,475	1,725
Prepayments and other assets		125
Total assets		$3,699

Liabilities & Stockholders' Equity

Accounts payable		$ 221
Accrued taxes		62
Bank loans and long-term debt		1,580
Total liabilities		$1,863
Capital stock, $10 par (authorized 50,000 shares, issued and outstanding 42,400 shares)	$ 424	
Paid-in capital in excess of par	366	
Retained earnings	1,046	
Total stockholders' equity		1,836
Total liabilities & stockholders' equity		$3,699

JOANN CORPORATION
Statement of Income and Retained Earnings
For Year Ended August 31, Year 5
(In thousands of dollars)

Product sales (net of $850,000 sales returns and allowances)		$10,700
Cost of goods sold		8,700
Gross profit on sales		$ 2,000
Operating expenses:		
Selling expenses	$1,500	
General and administrative expenses	940	2,440
Operating loss		$ (440)
Interest expense		150
Net loss		$ (590)
Retained earnings, Sept. 1, Year 4		1,700
Subtotal		$ 1,110
Dividends:		
Cash—$1 per share	$ 40	
Stock—6% of shares outstanding	24	64
Retained earnings, Aug. 31, Year 5		$ 1,046
Average market price of capital stock during the year		$ 15

Instructions List and briefly discuss deficiencies and omissions in Joann Corporation's **complete set** of financial statements. Consider each deficiency or omission separately, and do **not** consider the cumulative effect of the deficiencies and omissions. There are **no** arithmetical errors in the financial statements.

Case 4-2 Kevin Chen, a consulting engineer, developed and patented a device for measuring temperatures encountered in space travel. He offered to sell the patent rights to Dymo Company. An agreement was signed under which Dymo Company acquired the patent rights and gave Chen in exchange $500,000 in cash and a note for $500,000. The note provided for payment only in shares of the common stock of Dymo Company, at the rate of 4,000 shares of the company's $25 par value common stock per year for each of the next five years.

The accountant for Dymo Company included $100,000 among the current liabilities labeled Note Payable in Stock, and $400,000 among the long-term liabilities similarly labeled. He attached a footnote to the financial statements explaining the terms of the agreement with Chen.

The president of the company, who was about to present the company's financial statements to a bank in support of a loan application, objected to this treatment, contending that the company's liabilities were overstated. The accountant replied that liabilities were obligations to convey something of value and that the company's common stock had value.

Instructions
a Discuss the appropriate balance sheet treatment of the note, giving reasons for your conclusions.
b Suppose that under the terms of the note, Chen had the option of accepting each year $100,000 in cash or 4,000 shares of common. Would this change your answer? Why?

Case 4-3 Delphine Lee owns a resort located on an excellent fishing lake. Her busy season begins May 15 and extends through mid-fall. During the winter she engaged a contractor to build a boathouse and boat dock for a total price of $50,000. The contract called for completion by May 15, because the resort was completely reserved for the week of May 15 to 22, the opening week of the fishing season. Because the completion date was so important to Lee, she specified in the contract that if the construction was not completed by May 15 the price would be adjusted downward by a penalty of $200 per day, until completed.

The construction was not completed until June 9, at which time Lee paid the contract price of $45,000, deducting $200 for each of the 25 days of delay. Lee is convinced that she lost goodwill because her facilities were inadequate and that several of her clients reduced their stay because the facilities were still under construction.

In her balance sheet prepared at September 30, the end of her fiscal year, Lee included the boathouse and dock as assets valued at $50,000. Included in her revenue was an item "Penalty payments received in lieu of lost revenue, $5,000."

The auditor who examined Lee's report objected to this treatment and insisted that the facilities be recorded at their actual cost, $45,000. Lee stated that she could not understand the logic of this position. "Accounting principles are out of tune with reality," she complained. "What if the contract had been 250 days late and the boathouse and dock had cost me nothing; would you record in my balance sheet that I had no asset? I lost at least $200 per day in revenue because of the construction delay."

Instructions At what amount should these facilities be reported in the balance sheet at September 30? (You may ignore any question of depreciation from June 9 to September 30.) Explain your position in terms of accounting principles.

PROBLEMS

Group A

4A-1 A condensed income statement prepared by Blue Waters Company for the current year follows:

BLUE WATERS COMPANY

Income Statement

For Current Year

Revenue		$890,000
Costs and expenses:		
Cost of goods sold	$620,000	
Depreciation expense	28,000	
Amortization of intangibles	7,000	
Other operating expenses (including loss on sale of equipment)	112,000	
Income taxes (including deferred taxes of $10,000)	45,000	812,000
Net income		$ 78,000
Earnings per share		$ 3.90

20,000 shares

Additional information
(1) Dividends of $25,000 were paid in cash. ✓
(2) Equipment of $40,000 was acquired in exchange for common stock.
(3) Equipment was sold for $14,500, its carrying value. ✓
(4) The common stock was split 2 for 1.
(5) Long-term investments were acquired for $60,000 cash. ✓
(6) Treasury stock was purchased for $8,500 cash. ✓
(7) A $90,000 note was issued to Fidelity Insurance Company as evidence of a long-term loan. Cash received as proceeds on the note was $90,000. ✓
(8) The working capital at the beginning of the current year was $425,400; working capital at the end of the current year was $559,400.

Instructions Prepare a statement of changes in financial position on a working capital basis for the current year. Use the form illustrated on page 156, but do not list the composition of working capital since the information for this section of the statement is not available.

4A-2 The controller of International Sales, Inc., must prepare at June 30, the close of the company's current fiscal year, a statement of working capital. The purpose of this required reporting procedure is to demonstrate that the company's working capital exceeds $800,000, the amount International agreed to maintain under the terms of a loan agreement which defines **working capital** as the excess of current assets over current liabilities. The statement below, based on information taken from the accounts at June 30, was prepared by an assistant.

Current assets:		
Cash		$ 117,330
Notes and securities		480,000
Receivables		542,500
Inventories and prepayments		562,300
Total		$1,702,130
Current liabilities:		
Notes and accounts payable	$411,530	
Payroll taxes and pension liabilities	495,000	
Reserve for contingencies	200,000	
Total		1,106,530
Working capital		$ 595,600

The controller, after some investigation, has made the following notes on the items included in the above statement:

(1) *Notes and securities.* Includes $280,000 of notes receivable, of which $100,000 has been discounted at a bank. Also, $250,000 face amount of U.S. Treasury notes (current market value $236,000) purchased for $216,000, on which $8,500 of interest has accrued since the last interest date. International Sales, Inc., holds $84,000 in five-year notes receivable from a subsidiary company, on which $5,200 of interest is accrued at June 30 and is payable annually.

(2) *Receivables.* A single controlling account is used for receivables. The balance of the controlling account, $542,500, includes trade receivables of $394,040, a current receivable from a subsidiary company of $40,000, current advances to employees of $28,460, and an installment note of $80,000 received in payment for the sale of a warehouse, due in four installments of $20,000 per year; accrued interest on this note at June 30 was $4,800. Certain customers

have credit balances in their accounts, totaling $35,000, because they have made advances prior to the shipment of goods ordered. Of the trade receivables, $12,000 are worthless and should be written off; it is estimated that $20,000 of the remainder will prove uncollectible.

(3) *Inventories and prepayments.* The inventory of merchandise on June 30 on a lifo cost basis amounted to $320,750; its current replacement cost is estimated to be $470,750. Included in the $562,300 balance shown in the above statement is $98,000 of equipment that is rented to customers and $19,750 of merchandise on order for delivery during the next six months, the full cost of which is included in accounts payable. Also included in this balance are short-term prepayments of $94,800 and $29,000 representing a defalcation loss, of which $25,000 is expected to be recovered from the insurance company.

(4) *Current liabilities.* Current accounts payable amount to $261,530, and the company owes $150,000 on a 90-day note to the bank, on which unrecorded interest of $900 has accrued. Amounts withheld from employees for various payroll taxes amount to $70,000; the company's required contribution to such taxes of $28,700 has not been recorded. A provision for employee pensions amounts to $425,000, of which $53,400 will be paid within the coming fiscal year. The reserve for contingencies was set up to provide for **possible** losses that may arise from the obsolescence of plant and equipment.

Instructions

a On the basis of this information, prepare in good form a statement of working capital of International Sales, Inc., at June 30. List current assets in detail, followed by a detailed list of current liabilities. Provide supporting schedules as needed to show how specific items are computed. Is the company complying with the terms of the loan agreement as to the maintenance of working capital?

b Compute the current ratio at the end of the current year.

4A-3 The following information (listed in random order) is available for Bellanca Company at December 31, 1980:

Income taxes payable (*current*)	$ 36,625
Cash surrender value of life insurance policies	10,800
Accounts receivable (*net of credit balances of $10,000 arising from advance payments by customers*)	92,000
Allowance for doubtful accounts	5,800
Cash on hand	800
Cash in National Bank of Toledo	44,025
Cash in Bank of Trenton	26,000
Short-term prepayments	3,500
Retained earning	232,800
Current installment of long-term debt	20,000
7% long-term note payable (*including current installment of $20,000*)	250,000
Accounts payable	220,000
Inventories, at fifo cost	332,600
Marketable securities (at cost, market value, $58,500)	51,800
Buildings and equipment	400,000
Accumulated depreciation	109,600
Paid-in capital in excess of par	155,200

Organization costs	$ 26,500
Capital stock, $2 par, authorized 100,000 shares	60,000
Long-term advance to affiliated company	50,000
Patents (net of accumulated amortization of $18,950)	32,000

Instructions Use the information given to prepare a balance sheet in report form. Use two money columns with rulings as necessary under subtotals. Notes accompanying the balance sheet are not required.

4A-4 In January of the current year, Roy Atkins and Nelson Mamey organized a partnership known as the Reliable Service Center. Atkins, who had been in business for himself, contributed data-processing equipment having a current fair value of $30,000. This equipment had originally cost him $40,000 and had been depreciated by $16,200 on his records. Mamey contributed $15,000 in cash, a set of data-compiling forms which he had developed and which the partners agreed were worth $5,000, and land valued at $27,200 which will be used to construct a building. The two partners agreed to share profits equally.

The firm immediately acquired a small computer for $250,000, paying $25,000 down and signing a 8% note for the balance, promising payments of $45,000 per year plus interest. The first payment on this contract is due shortly after the end of the current year.

During the first year the firm collected $106,500 in cash for computer rentals and had receivables of $12,200 at the end of the year. Mamey borrowed $2,000 from the firm on October 1 to meet some emergency medical bills. He has agreed to pay this back at the rate of $100 per month, starting six months from the date of the loan, with interest at 10% on the unpaid balance of the loan.

The firm paid rent on a building and other operating expenses totaling $36,250. Atkins withdrew $700 per month from the business, while Mamey withdrew $800 per month. As of December 31, one month's rent ($650) on the building had been paid in advance. The partners agreed to depreciate the new computer at the rate of 10% per year, and the used equipment at the rate of 20%, using the straight-line method of depreciation and assuming no residual value. The systems forms developed by Mamey were to be amortized over a four-year period.

The firm had unpaid bills for operating expenses of $3,470 at December 31.

Instructions
a Prepare a balance sheet for Reliable Service Center at December 31 of the current year; also prepare a separate statement of partners' capitals.
b Prepare three separate supporting schedules to explain the computation of amounts in the balance sheet and statement of partners' capitals, as follows: (1) a schedule of cash receipts and payments concluding with the December 31 balance of cash; (2) a schedule showing the computation of depreciation on the computer and related equipment; and (3) a schedule listing revenue and expenses and concluding with the net income of the partnership. References to the first two of these supporting schedules should appear in the balance sheet on the lines for cash and for accumulated depreciation. Reference to the schedule of revenue and expenses should appear on the line for net income in the statement of partners' capitals.

4A-5 The financial position of Viking Company at the end of the current year is indicated by the highly condensed balance sheet prepared by the company's accountant:

Current assets	$1,000,000	Current liabilities	$ 510,000
Noncurrent assets	6,660,000	Long-term liabilities	2,500,000
		Paid-in capital	3,800,000
		Retained earnings	850,000
	$7,660,000		$7,660,000

Below is listed a series of comments, taken from an auditor's notes, describing certain components of the above balance sheet. Some of these comments indicate that the accountant has handled certain items improperly.

(1) Included in the long-term liabilities is an installment payable of $250,000 due within one year from the date of the balance sheet.
(2) A $125,000 dividend to be distributed in common stock of the company appears among the current liabilities.
(3) Included in the amount of current liabilities is a $42,000 contingent liability for possible legal suits.
(4) Included among noncurrent assets is $87,000 in cash surrender value of life insurance on officers of the company. Included among the current liabilities is a $60,000 loan made against this cash surrender value. The company intends to renew this borrowing at the maturity date.
(5) Discount on long-term debt of $161,500 is included among the noncurrent assets.
(6) Included in long-term liabilities is a $500,000 appropriation of retained earnings for retirement of preferred stock.
(7) The corporation purchased some of its own common stock for $400,000, its par value. This amount is included among the noncurrent assets.
(8) Rent received in advance in the amount of $74,800 is included in retained earnings.
(9) A cash dividend of $80,000 declared prior to the end of the year, but not payable until after the end of the current year, has not been recorded in the accounts.
(10) A fully depreciated asset was sold for $40,000 and the proceeds were credited to the Equipment account.
(11) Deposits of $38,000 made with suppliers in advance of the delivery of ordered goods have been netted against the accounts payable controlling account.
(12) An investment in 18% of the stock of an affiliated company, at a cost of $750,000, is included among current assets.
(13) Research and development costs of $417,500, incurred in developing a new product that will shortly go on sale, have been charged to expense. The new product is expected to be a successful revenue-producing item for three years or more.

Instructions
a List the dollar amounts of each of the six categories of the company's balance sheet on the first line of a six-column working paper. On separate lines below show the effect of any necessary corrections to the accountant's figures as a result of the information contained in the auditor's notes. Show as an end result the corrected balance sheet data as of the end of the current year. If the information contained in any of the auditor's notes does not indicate an erroneous treatment, explain why no adjustment is necessary in each case. Ignore any possible effect on income taxes as a result of your corrections.
b Would your interpretation of the company's financial position be substantially changed as a result of the revised data? Explain.

Group B

4B-1 The income statement for Glasgow Steel Corporation for the year ended June 30, 1980, follows:

GLASGOW STEEL CORPORATION
Income Statement
Year Ended June 30, 1980

Revenue from sales and miscellaneous sources		$4,200,000
Less: Costs and expenses:		
Cost of goods sold	$2,500,000	
Depreciation expense	120,000	
Amortization of goodwill and discount on bonds payable	12,000	
Other expenses	750,000	3,382,000
Income before income taxes		$ 818,000
Income taxes (including $30,000 deferred income taxes to be paid in future years)		388,000
Net income		$ 430,000
Earnings per share:		
Primary		$ 3.20
Fully diluted		$ 3.05

The following additional information also is available:

(1) Issued 8,000 shares of convertible preferred stock for $810,000 cash.
(2) Retired bonds payable of $500,000. Paid $502,200, including $2,000 accrued interest to date of retirement.
(3) Acquired land valued at $150,000 in exchange for common stock.
(4) Issued 10% stock dividend on 200,000 shares of $1 par value common stock when the market price of stock was $42 per share.
(5) Purchased machinery for $320,000 cash.
(6) Paid $220,000 in dividends on the preferred and common stock.
(7) Transferred $80,000 to a sinking fund for retirement of preferred stock.
(8) The working capital was as follows:

June 30, 1979	$643,200
June 30, 1980	925,000

Instructions Prepare a statement of changes in financial position on a working capital basis for the year ended June 30, 1980. Use the form illustrated on page 156, but do not present the composition of working capital since the information for this section of the statement is not given above.

4B-2 The following memorandum contains information concerning the financial position of Baja Air Lines, Inc., at December 31 of the current year.

Our properties and equipment *presently in use* consist of aircraft and other flight equipment acquired at a cost of $10,880,000, on which we have recognized depreciation to date of $2,431,200. In addition, we have one other aircraft which has been withdrawn from use and is being held for sale. The carrying value of this aircraft is $750,000 and we are currently negotiating for its sale at a price of $600,000. The negotiations for this sale will soon be completed.

When we acquired Mexicali Transport, we paid $550,000 for goodwill, of which $48,000 has been amortized to expense.

We have cash in checking accounts amounting to $880,600 and certificates of deposit for $801,600 which bear interest at rates from 6 to 9%. The general ledger controlling account for accounts receivable shows a debit balance of $1,660,000, but this total includes a credit balance of $120,000 from a customer who made an advance payment. The allowance for doubtful accounts amounts to $44,400. Our inventories are carried at average cost and amount to $91,200. Short-term prepayments of several types aggregate $42,000. The cash surrender value of life insurance policies, naming the company as beneficiary, amounts to $147,600.

Among our liabilities are $3,000,000 in 8% long-term notes payable, of which $300,000 falls due within the coming year. Accounts payable total $2,220,000, accrued liabilities $100,000, and income taxes $385,200.

We have 5 million shares of $1 par value capital stock authorized, of which 1,440,000 shares are outstanding. They were issued at a price of $4 per share. Our earnings which we have reinvested in the business represent a total of $1,664,200.

Instructions Use the above information to prepare a balance sheet in report form. Use two money columns, with rulings as necessary under subtotals. Notes to accompany the balance sheet are not required.

4B-3 Presented below is an alphabetical list of account balances taken from the ledger of Arizona Corporation at December 31, 1980:

Accounts payable	$ 803,900
Accounts receivable	1,016,000
Accumulated depreciation: Buildings	1,104,000
Accumulated depreciation: Leased equipment	220,000
Allowance for doubtful accounts	36,000
Buildings (at cost)	3,951,800
Cash	224,600
Cash surrender value of life insurance	115,000
Common stock, $50 par, authorized 100,000 shares	2,500,000
Dividends, common stock	55,000
Dividends, preferred stock	45,500
Goodwill	62,400
Income summary (credit balance)	195,000
Income taxes payable	92,600
Insurance claim receivable*	250,000
Inventories (lower of fifo cost or market)	1,146,000
Land	800,000
Leased equipment under capital leases	1,400,000
Marketable securities (market value $202,000)	200,000
9% note payable, due Oct. 1, 1988	1,000,000

Obligation under capital leases, including current portion
*   of $120,000* . . . . $1,050,000 ⌐
Paid-in capital in excess of par, common stock . . . .   295,000 ⌄
Preferred stock, 7%, $100 par, authorized 10,000 shares . . . .   650,000 ⌄
Premium on 9% note payable . . . .   30,000 ⌐
Retained earnings, Jan. 1, 1980 . . . .   ?
Unamortized issue costs on note payable . . . .   10,000 ⌄
Unearned rental revenue . . . .   25,000 ⌐

> ** Settlement in this amount has been agreed upon by the insurance company.*

Instructions
a Prepare a properly classified balance sheet as of December 31, 1980.
b Prepare a statement of retained earnings for the year ended December 31, 1980.

4B-4 A highly condensed balance sheet of Fullerton Corporation at the end of the current year is shown below:

FULLERTON CORPORATION
Balance Sheet
End of Current Year

Cash	$100,000	*Current liabilities*	$142,000
Receivables	138,000	*Long-term debt*	350,000
Inventories	78,000	*Capital stock, $1 par*	225,000
Plant and equipment (net)	650,000	*Retained earnings*	249,000
	$966,000		$966,000

During a discussion by the board of directors concerning the above balance sheet, Director John Ray raised a question as to what effect inflation had on the financial position of the company. He pointed out that the general price level had **doubled** since the organization and original sale of the company's capital stock and that there had been a substantial increase in prices after the company had acquired much of its plant and equipment.

The president felt that an answer to this question would require some study, and therefore asked the controller of the company to restate the company's balance sheet on the basis of current dollars as of the end of the year, using a general price index to measure the change in the value of money. After considerable analysis, the controller determined that the carrying value of the plant and equipment, stated in terms of its equivalent in current dollars, would be $910,000 and that the equivalent of $90,000 in current dollars had been invested in inventories. Realized retained earnings stated in current dollars were computed by the controller to be $192,000.

Instructions
a Using the information compiled by the controller, restate the balance sheet data of the Fullerton Corporation in terms of current dollars. Prepare a comparative balance sheet showing both mixed-dollar and current-dollar amounts.
b Write a report to the board of directors explaining the significance of the sup-

plementary data expressed in current dollars which appear in your comparative statement.

4B-5 Gilles Company is seeking a short-term loan to enable it to meet heavy payments to suppliers arising from a seasonal buildup of inventories. The company is also in need of cash to pay an impending installment on its serial bonds payable. Steven Jeppson, the loan officer of the Utah National Bank, is reviewing the loan application from Gilles Company. Included in the file is the balance sheet below prepared by the company at December 31, Year 10:

GILLES COMPANY

Balance Sheet

December 31, Year 10

Assets		Equities	
Cash	$ 78,700	Accounts payable	$ 175,500
Receivables	294,300	Accrued expenses	23,800
Inventories	376,200	Reserve for current	
Land, buildings, and		income taxes	50,000
property	940,000	Bonds payable, 9%	450,000
Marketable securities	88,600	Reserve for depreciation	420,000
Prepaid expenses	18,400	Reserve for bad debts	1,800
Notes receivable	43,000	Reserve for guarantees	10,900
Patents	75,000	Capital stock, common	225,000
Bond discount	12,000	Capital stock, preferred	206,000
Organization costs	35,000	Earned surplus	398,200
Total assets	$1,961,200	Total equities	$1,961,200

After some study of this balance sheet, Jeppson decided to ask Gilles Company to have an audit by a CPA firm. During the course of the audit, the CPA firm discovered the following additional information:

(1) Cash includes demand deposits of $59,000, cash change funds of $800, and an IOU signed by the company president for $18,900. (The IOU was collected three days later.)

(2) The balance of receivables is composed of the following items:

Balances in trade customers' accounts	$331,500
Advances to employees for expenses, to be covered by expense account reports which are submitted semimonthly	12,800
Claim for insurance recovery	35,000
Less: Customers' deposits on goods not yet manufactured	(85,000)
Total receivables	$294,300

(3) It is estimated that approximately $4,700 of the customers' accounts will prove uncollectible.

(4) The original cost of land owned by the company was $40,000, of buildings $750,800, and of equipment $299,200. The Buildings account has been re-

duced by $150,000, representing 6% mortgage note due in 10 years on which interest of $750 is accrued but unrecorded at December 31, Year 10. Accumulated depreciation on buildings is $240,000, on equipment $180,000.

(5) Marketable securities consist of the following:

	Cost	Market value
U.S. Treasury bonds	$20,000	$ 20,800
Second mortgage note on building of R Company, a supplier	66,390	?
Accrued interest:		
U.S. Treasury bonds	$ 250	
Second-mortgage note	1,960	2,210	2,210
		$88,600	

(6) Inventories consist of the following, at lower of average cost or market:

Raw materials	$207,380
Goods in process	17,530
Finished goods	151,290
	$376,200

(7) Notes receivable are short-term and were acquired in connection with sales; unrecorded accrued interest at December 31, Year 10, is $870. It is estimated that $2,400 of the notes may prove uncollectible.

(8) In Year 9, the company sold $500,000 of 6% serial bonds, due in annual installments, to a major stockholder. Of the total, $50,000, plus unrecorded accrued interest of $13,500, is due on January 4, Year 11. The bond discount applies to these serial bonds and has been correctly amortized during the year. Ignore any discount that may be applicable to the current portion of serial bonds payable.

(9) The reserve for guarantees represents the estimated amount of the company's obligation to service its products for a period of six months following sale.

(10) Common stock represents 15,000 shares of $10 par value stock originally sold at $15 per share; 2,000 shares of 7%, $100 par value preferred stock callable at $102 were originally sold at $103 per share; 25,000 shares of each class of stock are authorized to be issued.

(11) The company is the defendant in a lawsuit with the potential for a loss to the company in excess of its insurance coverage. Attorneys for the company are of the opinion that the outcome of the litigation will probably not have a material effect on the company's financial position.

Instructions Prepare in good form with modern terminology a revised balance sheet for Gilles Company, utilizing the information made available by the audit. Use a separate supporting schedule to show your computation of the revised ending balance of retained earnings. Make adequate disclosure, by means of a note attached to the balance sheet, of the status of litigation against the company.

CHAPTER **5**

THE CONCEPT OF PRESENT VALUE; ACCOUNTING APPLICATIONS

Quite apart from inflation, a dollar today is worth more than the assurance of receiving a dollar a year from now. In other words, we would all prefer to receive a given sum of money now rather than at some distant future date. This preference rests on the *time value of money.* We use the term *interest* to describe the price charged for using money over time. When we make payments for the time value of money, we incur interest expense. When we receive payments for the time value of money, we earn interest revenue.

Business decisions often involve receiving money or other assets *now* in exchange for a promise to make payments after one or more periods. A common example is a decision to borrow money. Another important group of business decisions involves investing money now in order to receive money or other goods and services in future periods. A common example is to lend money or to invest in an asset which will produce returns in future periods.

Inflows of dollars at various future dates must not be added together as if they were of equal value. These future dollar inflows must be restated at their *present values* before they are aggregated. The concept of the time value of money tells us that the more distant dollar inflows have a smaller present value than dollar inflows to be received within a shorter time span.

Similar reasoning applies to dollar outflows. Before we can add together dollar outflows at various future dates, we must restate these outflows at their present value. The more distant the date of a dollar out-flow, the smaller is its present value.

As a very simple example of this concept of present value, assume that you are trying to sell your automobile and you receive offers from three prospective buyers. Buyer A offers you a price of $2,000 to be paid immediately. Buyer B offers you a price of $2,050 to be paid to you one year from now. Buyer C offers the highest price, $2,300, but this offer provides that payment will be made after five years. Assuming that the offers by B and C involve absolutely no credit risk, which offer would you accept? You would surely accept the offer of $2,000 to be received immediately, because the *present value* of both the other offers is less than $2,000. If you were to invest $2,000 today, even at a very modest rate of interest such as 5%, your investment would grow and be worth more than $2,050 in one year and more than $2,300 within five years.

This example suggests that the timing of receipts and payments has an important effect on the economic worth and the accounting values of both assets and liabilities. Consequently, investment and borrowing de-cisions should be made only after a careful analysis of the relative present values of the prospective cash inflows and outflows.

The accountant finds many situations in which an objective measure-ment of a transaction depends upon the present value of future cash in-flows and future cash outflows. For example, the amount received for a bond issue by the issuing company reflects the present value of the company's promise to make a series of future interest payments and to repay the principal when the bonds reach maturity. Some other ex-amples of the need for measuring future dollar inflows and outflows are listed below.

1 Measuring and reporting leases and pension plans
2 Measuring and reporting notes receivable and notes payable when the inter-est rate is not specified or differs from the current market rate
3 Measuring and reporting plant assets acquired by issuance of long-term debt when the interest rate is not specified or differs from the current market rate
4 Accumulation of sinking funds for retirement of long-term debt or preferred stock
5 Computation of periodic depreciation using the sinking fund or annuity method of depreciation

Measuring the values implicit in these transactions involves the use of compound interest formulas and tables. In this chapter we shall illus-trate the basic principles of compound interest in a format which will be useful throughout this book. We will stress the use of compound inter-est tables (presented in Appendix A) as a basis for solving a wide range of accounting and financial reporting problems.

Simple interest and compound interest

Interest is the growth in a principal sum representing the fee charged for the use of money for a given time period. Since the concept of economic earnings is periodic, we typically think of return on investment in terms of return per year.

Simple interest is the return on a principal sum for one time period. We may also think of simple interest as a return for more than one time period if we assume that the interest itself does not earn a return, but this kind of situation occurs rarely in the business world. Simple interest is usually applicable only to short-term investment and borrowing transactions involving a time span of one year or less.

Compound interest is the return on a principal sum for two or more time periods, assuming that the interest in each time period is added to the principal sum at the end of the period and earns a return in all subsequent periods. Because many important investment and borrowing transactions involve more than one time period, business executives evaluate investment opportunities in terms of periodic returns, each of which is assumed to be reinvested to yield additional returns.

Because interest is generally expressed in terms of the annual rate, the simple interest formula is $I = prt$ (interest = principal × annual rate of interest × number of years or fraction of a year that interest accrues). For example, interest on $10,000 at 8% for one year is expressed as follows:

$$I = prt$$
$$I = \$10,000 \times .08 \times 1$$
$$I = \underline{\$800}$$

In contrast, if interest were compounded quarterly for one year, the total interest would be $824.32, determined as follows:

Period	Principal	× Rate	× Time =	Compound interest	Accumulated amount
1st quarter	$10,000.00	× 0.08	× ¼	$200.00	$10,200.00
2d quarter	10,200.00	× 0.08	× ¼	204.00	10,404.00
3d quarter	10,404.00	× 0.08	× ¼	208.08	10,612.08
4th quarter	10,612.08	× 0.08	× ¼	212.24	10,824.32
Interest on $10,000 at 8% compounded quarterly for one year				$824.32	

In the computation of compound interest, the accumulated amount at the end of each period becomes the principal sum for purposes of computing the interest for the following period.

Amount of 1

The accumulated **amount** (small a) of a single sum invested at compound interest can be computed period by period by a series of multiplications, as illustrated above for the $10,000 invested for one year at 8% compounded quarterly. If n is used to represent the number of periods that interest is to be compounded, i is used to represent the interest *per period,* and p is the principal sum invested, the series of multiplications to compute the accumulated amount a in the example above can be determined as follows:

$$a = p(1 + i)^n$$
$$a = \$10,000 (1 + 0.02)^4$$
$$a = \$10,000 (1.02)^4$$
$$a = \underline{\$10,824.32}$$

It is important to observe that i is the **rate of interest for each time period** that interest is **compounded.** For example, the formulas for the compound amount (a) of 1 at 12%, assuming different compounding patterns, would be:

Interest at 12% per year compounded annually $= a_{\overline{n}|i} = (1 + 0.12)^1$
Interest at 12% per year compounded semiannually $= a_{\overline{n}|i} = (1 + 0.06)^2$
Interest at 12% per year compounded quarterly $= a_{\overline{n}|i} = (1 + 0.03)^4$
Interest at 12% per year compounded monthly $= a_{\overline{n}|i} = (1 + 0.01)^{12}$

The symbol $a_{\overline{n}|i}$ is the amount to which $1 will accumulate at i rate of interest per period for n periods. This symbol is read as "small a angle n at i." If annual interest of 8% is compounded quarterly for one year, the rate of interest per time period (one-fourth of a year) would be 2%, and the number of interest periods (n) would be 4. Thus the amount of 1 formula at 8% compounded quarterly for one year is:

$$a_{\overline{n}|i} = (1 + i)^n \quad \text{or} \quad a_{\overline{4}|2\%} = (1 + 0.02)^4$$

Tables are available which give the value of $a_{\overline{n}|i}$. Use of these tables involves reference to a line showing the number of periods and a column showing the rate of interest per period. For example, Table 1 in Appendix A in the back of this book shows that $a_{\overline{4}|2\%}$ is equal to 1.082432, which means that $10,000 would accumulate to $10,824.32 in one year at 8% compounded quarterly. Compound interest tables are generally prepared for $1 and **the dollar sign is omitted.** This provides a convenient means of finding the accumulated amount of any number of dollars by multiplying the amount of 1 at i interest for n periods by the number of dollars involved in a problem.

Summary and Examples The amount of 1 formula, $a_{n\,i}$, is used to compute the future amount a of a principal sum p which earns compound interest at a specified interest rate i per period for n periods. A diagram for the amount of 1 is shown below:

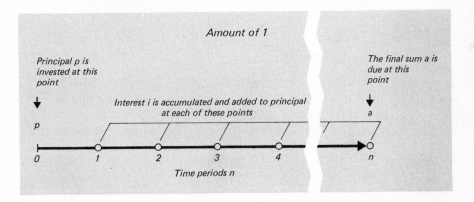

Amount of 1

Principal p is invested at this point

The final sum a is due at this point

p

Interest i is accumulated and added to principal at each of these points

a

0   1   2   3   4 n

Time periods n

Example 1: Finding the interest rate If $1,000 is deposited at compound interest on January 1, Year 1, and the amount on deposit at December 31, Year 10, is $1,806.11, what was the semiannual interest rate accuring on the deposit?

Answer The amount of 1 for 20 periods at an unstated rate of interest is 1.80611 ($1,806.11 ÷ $1,000 = 1.80611). Reference to Table 1 in Appendix A indicates that 1.806111 is the amount of 1 for 20 periods at 3%. Therefore, the semiannual interest rate was 3%.

Example 2: Amount accumulated when interest rate changes Marie deposited $10,000 in a fund which will earn 8% interest compounded quarterly for four years, and 10% interest compounded semiannually for the next six years. How much will Marie have in the fund at the end of 10 years?

Answer Using Table 1 in Appendix A, we have the following amount at the end of four years:

$$\$10,000 \times a\,\overline{_{16}}\,_{2\%} = \$10,000\,(1 + 0.02)^{16}$$
$$\$10,000 \times a\,\overline{_{16}}\,_{2\%} = \$10,000\,(1.372786) \quad \text{or} \quad \$13,728$$

And for the next six years, we have

$$\$13,728 \times a\,\overline{_{12}}\,_{5\%} = \$13,728\,(1 + 0.05)^{12}$$
$$\$13,728 \times a\,\overline{_{12}}\,_{5\%} = \$13,728\,(1.795856) \quad \text{or} \quad \underline{\$24,654}$$

In this case the interest rate **per period** changed at the end of four years from 2% to 5%. Therefore, it was first necessary to compute the amount on deposit at the end of four years ($13,728) and then to accumulate compound interest on this sum for six additional years at 10% compounded semiannually.

Present value of 1

In financial accounting many measurement and valuation problems require the computation of the discounted present value of a principal sum to be paid or received at a fixed future date. As the diagram below illustrates, the present value of 1 is closely related to the procedures used to compute the amount of 1:

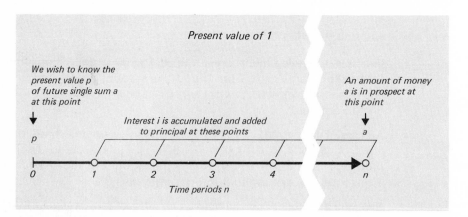

Present value of 1

We wish to know the present value p of future single sum a at this point

p

Interest i is accumulated and added to principal at these points

An amount of money a is in prospect at this point

a

0   1   2   3   4 n

Time periods n

From this diagram we see that finding the present value of a single future sum is a **reversal** of the process of finding the amount to which a present sum will accumulate. For example, we have seen that since $(1 + 0.02)^4 = 1.082432$, the principal sum p of $10,000 will accumulate to $10,824.32 in one year if interest is compounded quarterly. To find the principal p that must be invested now at 8% compounded quarterly to give us $10,824.32 in one year, we can proceed as follows: We know that $a = p(1 + i)^n$. If we solve for p by dividing both sides of the equation by $(1 + i)^n$, we have the following:

$$p = \frac{a}{(1 + i)^n}$$

And if we substitute $(1 + 0.02)^4$ for $(1 + i)^n$ and $10,824.32 for a, we have

$$p = \frac{\$10,824.32}{(1 + 0.02)^4} = \frac{\$10,824.32}{1.082432} = \underline{\underline{\$10,000}}$$

It should be clear that we can determine the present value of p of any future amount a by dividing the future amount a by $(1 + i)^n$. Thus the formula for the present value of 1 due in n periods at i rate of interest per period is:

$$p_{\overline{n}|i} = \frac{1}{(1 + i)^n}$$

The symbol $p_{\overline{n}|i}$ is read "small p angle n at i." The present value of 1 formula at 8% compounded quarterly for one year would be:

$$p_{\overline{4}|2\%} = \frac{1}{(1 + 0.02)^4}$$

It should be apparent that a table showing values for $1 \div (1 + i)^n$ at different interest rates (i) and different number of periods (n) would be useful. Table 2 in Appendix A provides such values. The value for $p_{\overline{4}|2\%}$ in this table is 0.923845; therefore, the present value of $10,824.32 discounted for one year at 8% compounded quarterly also can be computed as follows:

$$\$10,824.32 \times 0.923845 = \underline{\underline{\$10,000}}$$

Summary and Examples The present value of 1 formula, $p_{\overline{n}|i}$, is used to compute the discounted present value p of a given sum a due at some future date, discounted at a specified interest rate i per period for n periods.

Example 1: Finding the approximate interest rate by interpolation If the present value of $100,000 discounted at an unstated rate of interest for 20 periods is $64,162.10, what was the approximate interest rate per period used in computing this present value?

Answer From Table 2 in Appendix A and the information given above, we have:

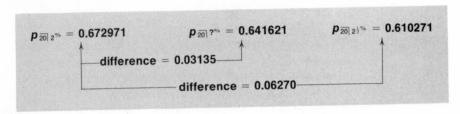

$$p_{\overline{20}|2\%} = 0.672971 \qquad p_{\overline{20}|?\%} = 0.641621 \qquad p_{\overline{20}|2\frac{1}{2}\%} = 0.610271$$

difference = 0.03135

difference = 0.06270

Therefore, the approximate interest rate per period is:

$$2\% + \tfrac{1}{2}\% \left(\frac{0.03135}{0.06270}\right) \quad \text{or} \quad 2\% + (\tfrac{1}{2}\% \times \tfrac{1}{2}) = 2\tfrac{1}{4}\%$$

Example 2: Present value when interest rate changes Dudley wants to deposit a lump sum at the beginning of Year 1 in a savings account so that he will have $50,000 at the end of Year 6. How much must he deposit at the beginning of Year 1 if the interest rate is 6% compounded semiannually for the first three years and 8% compounded quarterly for the last three years?

Answer Using Table 2 in Appendix A, we have the following present value at the beginning of Year 4 of the $50,000 required at the end of Year 6:

$$\$50,000 \times p_{\overline{12}|2\%} = \$50,000 \times 0.788493 = \$39,425$$

And at the beginning of Year 1, we have:

$$\$39,425 \times p_{\overline{6}|3\%} = \$39,425 \times 0.837484 = \underline{\$33,018}$$

Thus, Dudley must deposit $33,018 at the beginning of Year 1 to have $50,000 at the end of Year 6. Because the interest rate per period changed at the beginning of Year 4, it was necessary to prepare the solution in two separate steps.

Relationship of amounts of 1 and present value of 1 to *n* and *i*

In dealing with computations of accumulations and present values, it is useful to have some general idea of relationships as a basis for verifying the reasonableness of results. We can reason, for example, that $a_{\overline{n}|i}$ should grow *larger* for increasing rates of interest *i* and for an increasing number of periods *n*, since the longer a principal sum accumulates the larger it grows, and the higher the rate of interest the larger the future amount. The reverse situation is true of present values. The longer the time period *n* or the higher the rate of interest *i*, the *smaller* will be the present value of any future sum. This squares with our intuition that a far-distant prospect is worth less than one in the near future, and that the higher the rate of interest that can be earned on a present-dollar amount, the less valuable is the prospect of receiving an amount of money in the future.

Annuities

Many measurement situations in financial accounting involve periodic deposits, receipts, withdrawals, or payments (called *rents*), with interest at a stated rate compounded at the time that each rent is paid or received. These situations can be treated as *annuities* for computational purposes if all the following conditions are present:

1 The periodic rents are equal in amount
2 The time period between rents is constant, such as a year, a quarter of a year, or a month
3 The interest rate per time period remains constant
4 The interest is compounded at the end of each time period

When rents are paid or received at the end of each period and the total amount on deposit is determined at the time the final rent is made, the annuity is an *ordinary annuity.* Other types of annuities, that is, an *annuity due* and a *deferred annuity,* will be defined and illustrated in subsequent sections of this chapter.

Amount of ordinary annuity of 1

The amount of an ordinary annuity consists of the sum of the equal periodic rents and compound interest on the rents immediately after the final rent. The amount *A* to which an ordinary annuity of *n* rents of *R* dollars each will accumulate in *n* periods at *i* rate of interest per period is illustrated on page 192.

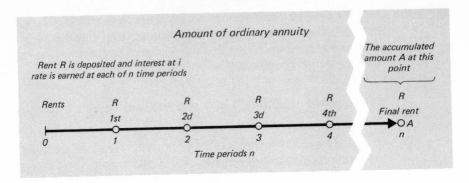

The amount (A) of an ordinary annuity of n rents of 1 at i interest rate per period is determined by **dividing the compound interest** that accumulates on a single deposit of 1 for n periods at i interest **by the interest rate per period.** This is expressed as follows:

$$A_{\overline{n}|i} = \frac{(1 + i)^n - 1}{i}$$

For example, the amount of an ordinary annuity of 16 rents at 2% is determined below:

$$A_{\overline{16}|\,2\%} = \frac{(1 + 0.02)^{16} - 1}{0.02} = \frac{1.372786 - 1}{0.02} = \frac{0.372786}{0.02} = \underline{\underline{18.6393}}$$

Tables, such as Table 3 in Appendix A, have been prepared which give the amount of ordinary annuities for different number of rents at varying interest rates. Note that in Table 3 the value for $A_{\overline{16}|2\%}$ is 18.64 (rounded to two decimal places). Table 3 in Appendix A is used to compute the amount of an ordinary annuity for rents of any dollar amount by the process of multiplication. For example, since the amount of an annuity of 16 rents of 1 at 2% is 18.64, the amount of an ordinary annuity of 16 rents of $500 would be $9,320 ($500 × 18.64 = $9,320).

Other applications of amount of an ordinary annuity of 1 formula

In the example above the amount of an ordinary annuity of 16 rents of 1 at 2% (18.64) and the periodic rent ($500) were known. From the information available we were able to compute the amount of the ordinary annuity of 16 rents of $500 at 2% as $9,320. Thus, four variables were involved:

1 The number of rents (16)

2 The interest rate per period (2%)

3 The amount of each periodic rent ($500)

4 The accumulated amount of the ordinary annuity immediately after the last rent ($9,320)

If any three of these values are known, the missing value can be determined by using Table 3 in Appendix A as illustrated below:

1 Question How many quarterly rents of $500 are required to accumulate $9,320 if the amount on deposit earns interest at 8% compounded quarterly?

Answer $9,320 ÷ $500 = 18.64, the amount of an ordinary annuity of 1 at 2% for unknown number of rents. The 2% column in Table 3 in Appendix A shows that the required number of rents is 16 because the amount of an ordinary annuity of 16 rents at 2% is 18.64 (rounded to two decimal places).

2 Question If an amount of an ordinary annuity of 16 rents of $500 equals $9,320 immediately after the sixteenth rent, what is the interest rate?

Answer $9,320 ÷ $500 = 18.64, the amount of an ordinary annuity of 16 rents of 1 at an unstated interest rate per period. The line for 16 rents in Table 3 in Appendix A shows that the interest rate per period is 2%.

3 Question If the required amount of an ordinary annuity of 16 rents at 2% is $9,320, what periodic rents are required to accumulate this sum?

Answer Table 3 in Appendix A shows that the amount of an ordinary annuity of 16 rents at 2% is 18.64 (rounded). The periodic rent is $500 ($9,320 ÷ 18.64 = $500).

Summary and Example The amount of an ordinary annuity of 1 formula, $A_{\overline{n}|i}$, is used to compute the future value A of n equal periodic rents of R dollars which earn compound interest i at a fixed rate per period. The periodic rent is computed by dividing the dollar amount to be accumulated by the amount of an ordinary annuity of 1 at the given interest rate for the number of periods equal to the number of rents (deposits).

Example: Accumulation of a fund to retire debt Bombary Company wants to accumulate $600,000 at December 31, Year 5, to retire a long-term note payable. The company intends to make five equal annual deposits in a fund which will earn interest at 6% compounded annually. The first deposit is made on December 31, Year 1. Compute the amount of the periodic deposits and prepare a fund accumulation table to prove that $600,000 will be available at December 31, Year 5.

Answer The amount of the periodic deposits is $600,000 ÷ 5.637093 (the amount of an ordinary annuity of five rents of 1 at 6% from Table 3 in Appendix A), or $106,438 (rounded). The fund accumulation table appears below:

	Fund Accumulation Table		
End of year	**Annual deposit**	**Interest earned at 6%**	**Fund balance**
1	$106,438	$ –0–	$106,438
2	106,438	6,386	219,262
3	106,438	13,156	338,856
4	106,438	20,331	465,625
5	106,438	27,937*	600,000

* Adjusted for slight rounding error.

Amount of an annuity due

The amount of an *annuity due* is the total amount on deposit **one period after the final rent.** This is illustrated below for an annuity due of 16 rents:

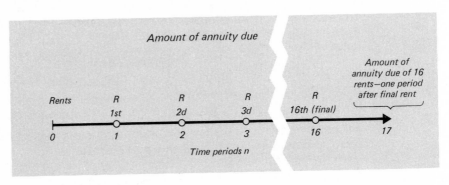

This diagram suggests that there are two ways of computing the amount of an annuity due of 16 rents of 1 at, say, 2% interest per period of time, as follows:

1 Take the amount of an ordinary annuity of 16 rents of 1 at 2% from Table 3 in Appendix A and accrue interest at 2% for one additional period: $18.639285 \times 1.02 = 19.01207$.

2 Take the amount of an ordinary annuity of 17 rents of 1 at 2% from Table 3 in Appendix A and subtract 1, the rent not made at this point in time: $20.01207 - 1 = 19.01207$.

The application of the amount of an annuity due is illustrated in the following example.

Example Adams Corporation needs $200,000 on March 31, Year 5. This amount is to be accumulated by making 16 equal deposits in a fund at the end of each quarter, starting March 31, Year 1, and ending on December 31, Year 4. The fund will earn interest at 8% compounded quarterly. Compute the periodic rents.

Answer The balance in the fund on March 31, Year 5, represents the amount of an annuity due of 16 rents at 2% per period. Therefore, the periodic rents are: $200,000 ÷ 19.01207 = $10,519.63.

> **Proof:** Amount of **ordinary annuity** of 16 rents of
> $10,519.63 at 2% on December 31, Year 4:
> $10,519.63 × 18.639285 . . . . $196,078
> Add: Interest for first quarter of Year 5: $196,078 × 2% 3,922
> **Balance in fund on March 31, Year 5** $200,000

Amount of deferred annuity

When the amount of an ordinary annuity remains on deposit for a number of periods beyond the final rent, the arrangement is known as a **deferred annuity.** The diagram on page 194 shows that the amount of an annuity due of 16 rents is also the amount of an ordinary annuity deferred for only one period. Thus, when the amount of an ordinary annuity continues to earn interest for an additional period, we have an annuity due situation; when the amount of an ordinary annuity continues to earn interest for more than one additional period, we have a deferred annuity situation.

The amount of a deferred annuity may be computed by multiplying the amount of the ordinary annuity by the amount of 1 for the period of deferral to accrue compound interest. Alternatively, we can take the amount of an ordinary annuity for all periods (including the period of deferral) and subtract from this the amount of the ordinary annuity for

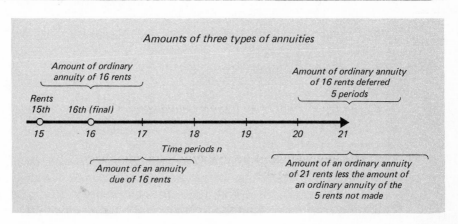

Amounts of three types of annuities

the deferral period when rents **were not made** but interest continued to accumulate. The diagram on page 195 illustrates the relationship of an ordinary annuity of 16 rents, an annuity due of 16 rents, and an ordinary annuity of 16 rents deferred for five periods.

Using Appendix A and assuming a 2% rate of interest per period, the amount of an ordinary annuity of 16 rents of 1 deferred for 5 periods (at time period 21) can be computed two ways as follows:

Future Amount Table

1 $A_{\overline{16}|\,2\%} \times (1 + 0.02)^5 = 18.639285 \times 1.104081 = \underline{20.57928}$

2 $A_{\overline{21}|\,2\%} - A_{\overline{5}|\,2\%} = 25.783317 - 5.204040 = \underline{20.57928}$

Although deferred annuity situations are relatively rare in the business world, accountants should understand the concepts illustrated here.

Present value of ordinary annuity of 1

Present values of annuities are more frequently used in financial accounting than any of the concepts discussed to this point. For example, the computation of (1) proceeds on a bond issue, (2) assets acquired through capital leases, (3) past service pension costs, (4) debt or receivables under installment contracts, and (5) mortgage debt or investments in mortgage notes all require the application of the present value of annuity concept.

A diagram depicting the present value (*P*) of an ordinary annuity of five rents (*R*) is given below:

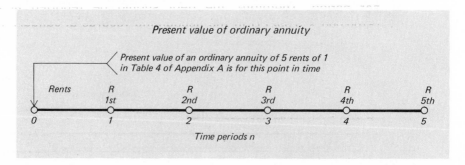

The present value of an ordinary annuity of five rents depicted above is the value of the rents, discounted at compound interest, at a point in time one period **before** the first rent. The present value of an ordinary annuity may be computed as the sum of the present values of the individual rents, but the use of a table, such as Table 4 in Appendix A, is considerably more efficient.

The present value (*P*) of an ordinary annuity of *n* rents at *i* rate of interest can be computed by dividing the compound discount on 1 for *n* periods at *i* rate of interest by the interest rate per period *i*. This is illustrated below in the computation of the present value of an ordinary annuity of five rents at 8% per period:

$$P_{\overline{n}|i} = \frac{1 - \dfrac{1}{(1 + i)^n}}{i} = \frac{1 - \dfrac{1}{(1 + 0.08)^5}}{0.08} = \frac{1 - 0.680583}{0.08}$$

$$= \frac{0.319417}{0.08} = \underline{\underline{3.99271}}$$

The present value of 1 at 8% for five periods (0.680583) is taken from Table 2 in Appendix A. Dividing the compound discount of 0.319417 by 8% gives the present value of an ordinary annuity of five rents of 1 at 8%. In Table 4 of Appendix A, the present value of an ordinary annuity of five rents of 1 at 8% is given as 3.992710, thus substantiating our computation above.

To illustrate the application of the present value of an ordinary annuity of 1, assume the following: Evans Company has outstanding five $100,000 non-interest-bearing notes payable, due at the rate of $100,000 per year for five years starting on December 31, Year 1. What is the present value of this debt on January 1, Year 1, for financial reporting purposes if 8% compounded annually is considered a fair rate of interest? The present value of the debt on January 1, Year 1 is equal to the present value of an ordinary annuity of five rents of $100,000 at 8% per period. Therefore, the debt should be reported at $399,271 ($100,000 × 3.99271) in the accounting records at January 1, Year 1. The payment schedule for this debt is summarized below:

Payment Schedule for Debt of $399,271 at 8% Interest

Date	Interest expense at 8% per year	Repayment at end of year	Net reduction of debt	Balance of debt
Jan. 1, Year 1				$399,271
Dec. 31, Year 1	$31,942	$100,000	$68,058	331,213
Dec. 31, Year 2	26,497	100,000	73,503	257,710
Dec. 31, Year 3	20,617	100,000	79,383	178,327
Dec. 31, Year 4	14,266	100,000	85,734	92,593
Dec. 31, Year 5	7,407	100,000	92,593	–0–

As illustrated in our earlier discussion of the amount of an ordinary annuity, Table 4 in Appendix A can be used to compute other variables in the formula for the present value of an ordinary annuity. For example, if we know that $P_{\overline{5}|8\%} = 3.99271$ and the present value of an ordinary annuity of five rents at 8% per period is $399,271, we can compute the periodic rent of $100,000 by dividing $399,271 by 3.99271.

Summary and Example The present value of an ordinary annuity of 1 formula, $P_{\overline{n}|i}$, is used to compute the sum P that would settle a debt one period before the first rent of n equal rents of R dollars discounted at compound interest rate i per period. Stated differently, $P_{\overline{n}|i}$ is used to compute the value one period before the first rent of a series of equal cash inflows or outflows discounted at a constant interest rate per period.

Example: Proceeds on issuance of bonds at a discount Rainbow Company issued $5 million face amount of 9%, five-year bonds on June 30, Year 5. The bonds pay interest on June 30 and December 31 and were issued to yield 10% compounded semiannually. Compute the proceeds on this bond issue.

Answer Since the 9% interest rate on the bonds is less than the 10% market rate of interest, the bonds were sold at a discount equal in amount to the present value of the semiannual interest **deficiency** (interest which will not be received by bondholders) of $25,000— [$5,000,000 × (0.050 − 0.045)] for 10 semiannual periods discounted at the 5% **market rate of interest per period.** Therefore, the proceeds on the bonds are determined as follows:

Face amount of bonds	$5,000,000
Less: Present value of ordinary annuity of 10 rents of $25,000 discounted at 5% per period: $25,000 × 7.721735	193,043
Proceeds on bonds	$4,806,957

Alternatively, the proceeds on the bonds may be determined as the sum of (1) the present value of the $5 million to be paid at maturity, discounted at the 5% semiannual market rate of interest for 10 periods, plus (2) the present value of an ordinary annuity of 10 rents of $225,000 semiannual interest payments, also discounted at 5% per period. This approach is illustrated on page 199.

Present value of $5 million discounted at 5% for 10 six-month periods:

$5,000,000 × 0.613913 . . . . $3,069,565

Add: Present value of ordinary annuity of 10 rents of $225,000 dis-

counted at 5%: $225,000 × 7.721735 1,737,390

Proceeds on bonds $4,806,955*

* $2 discrepancy between this amount and the amount computed above is caused by rounding in present value tables.

The proceeds on issuance of bonds at a premium (when the interest rate paid on the bonds is larger than the market rate of interest) would be computed similarly.

Present value of annuity due

The present value of an ordinary annuity falls one period before the first rent. In contrast, the present value of an annuity due *falls on the date the first rent is deposited or withdrawn,* as illustrated below:

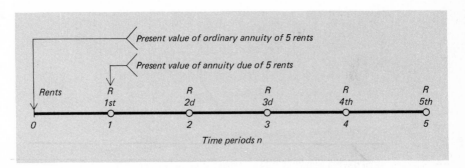

For example, we would need the present value of an *annuity due* of *n* rents of 1 to compute the periodic rental payments on an equipment contract or a lease when the first payment is due at the beginning of the period. The diagram above indicates that the present value at time period 1 of an annuity due of five rents can be computed (1) by adding interest for one period to the present value of an ordinary annuity of five rents or (2) by obtaining the present value of an ordinary annuity of four rents and then adding 1, representing the "extra" rent on this date (time period 1). These two approaches are illustrated on page 200, using Table 4 in Appendix A, to compute the present value of an annuity due of five rents of 1 at 8% per period.

> **1** *Present value of ordinary annuity of five rents of 1 at 8%, plus interest*
> *at 8% on this present value for one period: 3.99271 × 1.08* . . . . . <u>*4.312127*</u>
>
> **2** *Present value of ordinary annuity of four rents of 1 at 8%, plus 1, the*
> *fifth rent on this date: 3.312127 + 1* . . . . <u>*4.312127*</u>

To illustrate the application of the present value of an annuity due of 1, assume the following: On January 1, Year 1, Fernando, Inc., acquired a plant asset for $64,682. The company contracted to make five equal annual payments starting on January 1, Year 1, and ending on January 1, Year 5, at 8% compounded annually. The annual payments are determined below:

$64,682 ÷ 4.312127 = $15,000

The payment schedule for this contract is shown below:

		Payment Schedule for Liability of $64,682 at 8% Interest			
Jan. 1, year	*Liability at beginning of year*	*Payment at beginning of year*	*Balance accruing interest*	*Interest at 8%*	*Liability at end of year*
1	*$64,682*	*$15,000*	*$49,682*	*$3,975*	*$53,657*
2	*53,657*	*15,000*	*38,657*	*3,093*	*41,750*
3	*41,750*	*15,000*	*26,750*	*2,140*	*28,890*
4	*28,890*	*15,000*	*13,890*	*1,110**	*15,000*
5	*15,000*	*15,000*	*–0–*	*–0–*	*–0–*

* Adjusted for $1 discrepancy due to rounding of computations.

Present value of deferred annuity

When periodic rents are postponed for more than one period, the present value of such an annuity at some date prior to the first rent may be computed as follows: (1) <u>Discount the present value of the ordinary annuity portion at compound interest for the periods the annuity is deferred, or (2) determine the present value of an ordinary annuity equal to the total number of periods involved and subtract from this the present value of the "missing" ordinary annuity for rents equal in number to the number of periods the annuity is deferred.</u> To illustrate, assume that we wish to know the sum at time period 0 which would pay off a debt of five payments of $100,000 each, payments starting at time period 4 and interest compounded at 8% per time period. First it would be helpful to diagram the scheduled payments as follows:

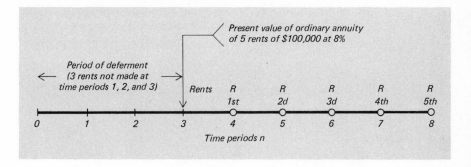

Using Tables 2 and 4 in Appendix A, we can compute the present value of the ordinary annuity of five rents of 1 deferred for three periods as follows:

1 *Present value of ordinary annuity of five rents of 1 at 8% at time period 3, discounted at 8% for three periods: 3.992710 × 0.793832* <u>3.169541</u>

2 *Present value of an ordinary annuity of eight rents of 1 at 8% at time period 0, less the present value of an ordinary annuity of three rents of 1 (the rents not made) at 8% at time period 0: 5.746639–2.577097* <u>3.169542*</u>

* Slight discrepancy due to rounding of present values in Appendix A.

Thus it would take $316,954 ($100,000 × 3.169542 = $316,954) at time period 0 to pay off the debt diagramed above.

Concluding comments

Many complex situations involving compound interest may be encountered in the business world. An understanding of the concepts discussed in the preceding pages should enable the student to analyze and solve problems requiring the application of compound interest principles. Since money can be readily invested to earn a return, there is a universal service charge (interest) for its use and any given amount of money available on a stated date has a different value at all other points in time. Compound interest procedures are a means of moving money inflows and outflows forward and backward in time on a basis that permits a comparison of values in equivalent terms.

For example, if we are given a choice of receiving $20,000 in two years or $30,000 in eight years, the choice is not obvious. These two sums of money can no more be subtracted in a meaningful sense than we could subtract X apples from Y trucks and obtain a meaningful result. Assuming that money is worth 10% per annum, we can compare these two sums at any point in time only by measuring their value at that particular point. If we choose *now* (time point zero), the following analysis would show that the $20,000 in two years is preferable to receiving $30,000 in eight years:

$$\$20,000(p_{\overline{n}|i}) = \$20,000(p_{\overline{2}|10\%}) = \$20,000 \times 0.826446 = \underline{\$16,529}$$

$$\$30,000(p_{\overline{8}|10\%}) = \$30,000 \times 0.466507 = \underline{\$13,995}$$

We can reach the same conclusion by comparing values *at the end of eight years* as follows:

$$\$20,000(a_{\overline{6}|10\%}) = \$20,000 \times 1.771561 = \underline{\$35,431}$$

$30,000 at the end of eight years obviously is equivalent to $\quad \underline{\$30,000}$

The receipt of $20,000 in two years is again shown to be preferable to the receipt of $30,000 in eight years because if $20,000 is invested at 10% at the end of the second year, it would accumulate to $35,431 by the end of the eighth year. We could choose any other point in time at any rate of interest and make a similar comparison without changing the validity of the decision in favor of the option calling for the receipt of $20,000 in two years.

REVIEW QUESTIONS

1 Briefly explain the difference between simple interest and compound interest.

2 a Explain the meaning of $(1 + i)^n$ and define the symbols i and n.
  b Give the formula for each of the following:
      (1) Present value of 1
      (2) Amount of an ordinary annuity of 1
      (3) Present value of an ordinary annuity of 1

3 Define each of the following:
  a Present value of an annuity due
  b Present value of a deferred annuity
  c Amount of an annuity due
  d Amount of a deferred annuity

4 Give the formula, including the numerical value for i and n, for computing the compound amount of $500 invested for five years
  a at 10% compounded semiannually

 b at 8% compounded quarterly
 c at 12% compounded monthly
 d at 6% compounded annually

5 The following values are taken from compound interest tables for the same number of periods *n* and at the same rate of interest *i*:
 a 13.180795   table 3   10 periods 6%
 b 1.790848   table 1
 c 0.558395   table 2
 d 7.360087   table 4
 What does each of the four values represent? Explain.

6 Indicate the compound interest table that would be used in solving each of the following problems:
 a Sheila Jones wants to know how much she would have in her savings account at the end of five years if she deposits a single sum and leaves it to accumulate interest.
 b Eva Smith owes Olson $5,000 due in two years at no interest. Smith wants to know how much she should pay Olson now if they can agree on a fair rate of interest.
 c Joe Harrison owes money to Andersen which is payable in semiannual installments of $2,000 each. The first installment is due today. Harrison wants to know the lump-sum amount he should pay to Andersen today to eliminate his liability.
 d Adam Kirkpatrick wants to know what equal annual deposits he should make at the beginning of each of 10 years so that he will have $20,000 to buy a cabin cruiser at the end of the tenth year. Interest at a fixed rate will be compounded annually on the cumulative amount in Kirkpatrick's "cruiser fund."

7 From the compound interest tables in Appendix A, compute the following values at 4%:
 a Amount of 1 for 10 periods
 b Present value of 1 for 20 periods
 c Amount of ordinary annuity of 15 rents of 1
 d Amount of annuity due of 15 rents of 1
 e Amount of ordinary annuity of 15 rents of 1 deferred for 10 periods
 f Present value of ordinary annuity of 25 rents of 1
 g Present value of annuity due of 25 rents of 1
 h Present value of ordinary annuity of 25 rents of 1 deferred for 5 periods

EXERCISES

Ex. 5-1 Abner Carr sold a parcel of land for $44,000. He received $12,000 cash at the date of sale and 16 notes of equal amount due serially, one each six months starting six months from the date of sale. It was agreed that the notes will include interest in their face amount at 12% compounded semiannually. Using Appendix A, compute to the nearest dollar the face amount of each note.

Ex. 5-2 Z Company acquired $10,000 face amount 10% noncallable bonds which have a remaining life of 12 years. The bonds pay interest every six months. Compute the price paid for the bonds if the market rate of interest for bonds of comparable quality is 8% compounded semiannually. The present value of 1 at 4% for 24 periods is 0.390121, and the present value of 1 at 5% for 24 periods is 0.310068. The present value of an ordinary annuity of 1 at 4% for 24 periods is 15.246963, and the present value of an ordinary annuity of 1 at 5% for 24 periods is 13.798642.

Ex. **5-3** George deposited $1,000 starting on June 30, Year 1, in a savings account which earned interest at 8% compounded quarterly. He has already made six deposits, the last one on December 31, Year 2. Using the tables in Appendix A, compute the amount George should have on deposit on each of the following dates (assuming that George made no withdrawals from his savings account and that deposits are made quarterly):

a December 31, Year 2

b March 31, Year 3

c June 30, Year 5, assuming that George made the last deposit on March 31, Year 5

Ex. **5-4** On January 2, Year 3, Shell Manufacturing Company leased equipment from Werner Corporation. This lease was noncancelable and was in substance an installment purchase. The initial term of the lease was 12 years, with title passing to Shell at the end of the twelfth year at no additional cost. Annual rental to be paid by Shell is $10,000 at the beginning of each year. The first rental payment was made on January 2, Year 3. The equipment has an estimated economic life of 20 years, with no anticipated residual value. The prevailing interest rate for Shell on similar financing arrangements was 8%. The present values of an *annuity due* of 1 at 8% are:

11 rents	7.710081
12 rents	8.138964
19 rents	10.371887
20 rents	10.603599

Compute the cost of the equipment for financial accounting purposes.

Ex. **5-5** Given below are the present values for 1 discounted at 8% for one to five periods. Each of the values is based on 8% interest compounded annually from day of deposit to day of withdrawal.

Periods	Present value of 1 discounted at 8% per period
1	0.926
2	0.857
3	0.794
4	0.735
5	0.681

Choose the best answer for each of the following four questions:

1 What amount should be deposited in a bank today to grow to $5,000 three years from today?

a $\dfrac{\$5,000}{0.794}$

b $5,000 × 0.926 × 3

c ($5,000 × 0.926) + ($5,000 × 0.857) + (5,000 × 0.794)

d $5,000 × 0.794

2 What amount should Bill Riley have in his bank account today before withdrawal if he needs $5,000 each year for four years with the first withdrawal to be made today and each subsequent withdrawal at one-year intervals? (He is to have exactly a zero balance in his bank account after the fourth withdrawal.)

a $5,000 + ($5,000 × 0.926) + ($5,000 × 0.857) + ($5,000 × 0.794)

b $\dfrac{\$5,000}{0.735}$ × 4

c ($5,000 × 0.926) + ($5,000 × 0.857) + ($5,000 × 0.794) + ($5,000 × 0.735)

d $\dfrac{\$5,000}{0.926}$ × 4

3 If an individual put $8,000 in a savings account today, what amount of cash would be available two years from today?

a $8,000 × 0.857

b $8,000 × 0.857 × 2

c $\dfrac{\$8,000}{0.857}$

d $\dfrac{\$8,000}{0.926}$ × 2

4 What is the present value today of $2,000 to be received six years from today?

a $2,000 × 0.926 × 6

b $2,000 × 0.794 × 2

c $2,000 × 0.681 × 0.926

d Cannot be determined from the information given.

Ex. 5-6 Hideaway Ranch wants to accumulate a fund of $80,000 at the end of Year 10 to retire a debt. The fund will be accumulated by making 20 equal deposits starting on June 30, Year 1. If the fund will earn interest at 6% compounded semiannually, compute the amount of the periodic deposits to the nearest dollar. Use Appendix A.

Ex. 5-7 Herman Abrams has a 6% loan with an unpaid balance of $17,169. The principal and interest are payable quarterly at the rate of $1,000. Abrams has 20 more payments to make, having just made the payment due December 31, Year 5. The lender approaches Abrams and offers to reduce the principal of the debt from $17,169 to $16,500 if he would take out a new loan for $16,500 at 10% (the current market rate), payable quarterly for the next five years. Should Abrams refinance the loan? Present computations (to the nearest dollar) in support of your answer. Ignore any possible income tax effects.

SHORT CASES FOR ANALYSIS AND DECISION

Case 5-1 While on an audit with a large CPA firm at the end of Year 5, Frank Swan observed the following deferred compensation contract signed by the client:

"In lieu of any salary and bonus for Year 5, Alex Hardwood will receive $25,000 at the end of Year 6 and each year thereafter through December 31, Year 11. Alex Hardwood will not be required to perform any services after December 31, Year 5."

The client recorded this contract as follows:

Executive Salaries	. . . .	150,000
Notes Payable	. . . .	150,000

To record salary and bonuses payable to Alex Hardwood.

The junior accountant working under Swan stated: "This entry is proper. The expense is applicable to Year 5, and the notes meet all the traditional tests of a liability. Hardwood's salary and bonus had been over $130,000 per year for several years, therefore the amount of the salary and bonus for Year 5 is reasonable."

Swan pointed out that there is no mention of interest in the contract and that the client had to pay 8% interest on most of its bank loans in the last quarter of Year 5. He agreed that the notes were genuine liabilities, but hastened to add that an auditor not only must ascertain whether a liability exists but also that the amount of the liability at the balance sheet date is correctly stated.

Instructions Use the appropriate table in Appendix A in arriving at your conclusions.

a Evaluate the positions taken by the junior accountant and by Swan.

b What correcting entry, if any, would you recommend at December 31, Year 5, assuming that notes payable are carried net of any discount?

c What entry should be made on December 31, Year 5, to record the first payment to Alex Hardwood?

Case 5-2 Martin Lee's godfather, M. V. Chai, decided to make him a gift of $27,000 with an option to receive the cash in any of the following three patterns:

(1) One thousand dollars at the end of each of the first three years, starting one year from now, $3,000 at the end of each of the next three years; and $5,000 at the end of each of the last three years. Chai suggests that this arrangement might be preferable because Lee is young and will need more money as he grows older, not only because he will learn to spend more but also because inflation will increase his cost of living.

(2) Three thousand dollars at the end of each of the next nine years, starting one year from now. Chai pointed out that this option offers the advantage of a steady cash flow for Lee.

(3) Five thousand dollars at the end of each of the first three years, starting one year from now; $3,000 at the end of each of the next three years; and $1,000 at the end of each of the last three years. Chai points out that he would not recommend this option to Lee because it would give him an excess of cash flow during the first three years which would be invested at a rate of interest lower than he (Chai) could earn. Lee had told Chai that he would invest all this money in San Francisco at 6% compounded annually; Chai had responded that he invests his money at 10% compounded annually in a Hong Kong bank.

After discussing these alternatives with friends in the Philosophy Department at Western University, Lee said to Chai: "All three options are the same; obviously, I will get an average of $3,000 at the end of each of the nine years, so it makes no difference." Chai responded, "I am happy to know that you are in school; there is much to learn."

Instructions

a Did Martin Lee make the right decision? Why?

b What is the present value of each option at 6% interest compounded annually, given the following values at 6%?

Periods	Present value of 1	Present value of ordinary annuity of 1
3	.8396	2.6730
6	.7050	4.9173
9	.5919	6.8017

c Briefly evaluate each point made by Chai.

Case 5-3 The following letter was mailed by Generous Finance Company to residents of a large city:

> Dear Mr. Reliable:
> You are one of a select group of creditworthy individuals in your community who qualify for a unique opportunity. Without additional credit references or time-consuming technicalities, you are guaranteed a Generous Prestige Loan of $10,000 now.
> Because you are financially responsible, and you've always handled your financial obligations with efficiency, your loan **has already been approved.** The enclosed Certificate entitles you to a loan of $10,000 any time you'd like to have it. So please call or come to our office now.
> Sincerely,
Chris Lewis

The certificate referred to in the letter indicated that the repayment of the loan was to be made in 24 equal monthly payments of $534 each.

Instructions
a What is the total amount a borrower would have to pay to Generous Finance Company over the two-year period of this installment loan?
b Compute the approximate **annual rate** of interest (as a percentage) compounded monthly, using Table 4 in Appendix A.
c Is the rate of interest attractive for "creditworthy" borrowers?

PROBLEMS

Group A

5A-1 This problem consists of four unrelated situations for Riverfront Corporation. Compute the answer (to the nearest dollar) for each situation by using the compound interest tables in Appendix A.

Situation A Riverfront Corporation wants to accumulate $100,000 at December 31, Year 10, to retire preferred stock. The company deposits $25,000 in a savings account on January 1, Year 1, which will earn interest at 6% compounded quarterly. The company wants to know what additional amount it has to deposit at the end of each quarter for 10 years to have $100,000 available at the end of Year 10. The periodic deposits also will earn interest at 6% compounded quarterly.

Situation B Riverfront Corporation wants to make five equal annual deposits beginning June 1, Year 4, in order to be able to withdraw $50,000 at six annual intervals beginning June 1, Year 9. The amount on deposit will earn interest at 5% annually until the savings fund is exhausted. Compute the equal deposits that should be made.

Situation C On June 30, Year 1, Riverfront Corporation purchased a machine for $80,000. The down payment was $10,000 and the balance will be paid in 48 equal monthly payments, including interest at 18% compounded monthly. What is the amount of the monthly payment if the first payment is due one month from the date of purchase?

Situation D On April 1, Year 2, Riverfront Corporation made a deposit of $100,000 in a fund and left the fund undisturbed for four years to earn compound interest at a rate which did not change during the four-year period. At the end of four years, the fund had accumulated to $132,088.60. If interest was compounded quarterly, what was the rate of interest earned each quarter?

5A-2 As a summer intern with Jamison and Turkel, Certified Public Accountants, you are presented with the following situations.

(1) Client A called to inquire whether a proposed transaction made economic sense. The client sold a parcel of land for $51,000 and was given the choice of receiving $51,000 cash or $17,000 per year for four years starting one year from now. The client does not need cash but would like to earn 12% before income taxes annually on idle cash resources; consequently, the client wants to know what interest rate (to the nearest tenth) would be earned if the installment payment option is taken.

(2) Client B wanted to know how much to pay for $100,000 face amount of 8% bonds which mature in five years if interest is payable semiannually and if 10% compounded semiannually is a fair return on this type of investment.

(3) Client C was negotiating to purchase a going business and was uncertain whether the asking price for goodwill (present value of future superior earnings) was reasonable. The seller asked $50,000 for goodwill but the client did not want to pay more than the present value of projected superior earnings for the next three years discounted at 15% annually. Superior earnings (to be realized at the end of each year) were estimated as follows:

At end of first year $25,000

At end of second year 20,000

At end of third year 15,000

(4) On June 1, Year 1, Client D wanted to make the first of four equal annual deposits in a fund which will earn 6% and which will amount to $100,000 immediately after the last deposit on June 1, Year 4. The client wanted to know the amount of each deposit and "proof" that $100,000 would be available on June 1, Year 4.

Instructions Prepare appropriate computations and schedules which would give each of the four clients the information requested. Carry all computations to the nearest dollar.

5A-3 As an accountant for Bluebird Rice Company, you find the following memo on your desk from Genny Walters, controller of the company:

(1) On December 31, Year 1, we will sign a non-interest-bearing note for $100,000 due in five years. The lender wants to earn 10% compounded annually on the amount advanced to us. Please compute the proceeds on this borrowing transaction and prepare a table showing our interest expense and net liability for each of the five years of the loan. Round all computations to the nearest dollar.

(2) Also on December 31, Year 1, the installment sale of the land on the East Side will be completed. The buyer will pay us $100,000 per year for ten years starting a year from now. Our agreement included interest at 10% per year in the face amount of the notes. The land is carried in our

accounting records at $400,000. I want you to prepare a journal entry to record the sale of the land and to prepare a table which will show interest revenue for each year and the net carrying value of the notes receivable at the end of each year. Round all computations to the nearest dollar.

Instructions Prepare a memo to the controller which includes the information she asked you to assemble. Use Table A in making required computations.

5A-4 This problem consists of three independent parts relating to Companies X, Y, and Z:

Company X invested $37,368 at the beginning of Year 1. The amount on deposit earned interest at 10% per year. The company plans to withdraw the amount on deposit in three equal annual installments starting on December 31, Year 4.

Company Y wishes to accumulate a fund of $58,666 at the end of five years by making five equal annual deposits starting one year from now. The fund will earn interest at 8% compounded annually.

Company Z invested $199,635 at the beginning of Year 1 at 8% compounded annually. The amount invested and accrued interest are to be withdrawn in five equal installments starting on December 31, Year 1.

Instructions (Use Appendix A and carry computations to the nearest dollar.)
a Compute the three equal amounts that Company X can withdraw and prepare a table which shows that the entire amount on deposit will have been withdrawn by December 31, Year 6.
b Compute the annual deposits that Company Y should make and prepare a fund accumulation table for the five-year period.
c Compute the amounts Company Z can withdraw each year and prepare a table which illustrates that the funds on deposit will be completely exhausted by December 31, Year 5.

Group B

5B-1 This problem consists of four unrelated situations for Thrifty Products Company. Determine the answer for each situation by using the compound interest tables in Appendix A.

Situation A On July 1, Year 1, Thrifty Products Company issued $10 million in 20-year, 8% bonds which paid interest semiannually. The bonds were issued to yield 9% compounded semiannually. What were the proceeds on this bond issue?

Situation B On April 1, Year 1, Thrifty Products Company purchased a plant asset by paying $5,000 down and agreeing to pay $5,000 at the beginning of each of the next 19 quarters. What was the cost of the plant asset for financial accounting purposes if the rate of interest agreed upon was 16% compounded quarterly?

Situation C Thrifty Products Company holds a promissory note of $300,000 issued by Gorman Corporation. The note calls for payment of principal of $100,000 at the end of each year starting in exactly three years, plus interest on the unpaid balance at the rate of 12% per year. Only interest is due at the end of the first two years. Thrifty Products Company discounts this note with a finance company at 10% interest compounded annually. How much did Thrifty Products Company receive for the $300,000 note?

Situation D Thrifty Products Company wants to accumulate a $5 million fund for the retirement of bonds in exactly 10 years. The company wants to make 20 equal deposits starting in six months to accumulate the $5 million fund. An officer for Michigan Trust Company informed Thrifty Products that the semiannual deposits will be $186,078.54. What semiannual interest rate will be earned on the fund deposits?

5B-2 In the course of your audit engagement for Sunrise Company, the following situations required you to apply compound interest principles:

(1) A non-interest-bearing note receivable in the face amount of $120,000 and maturing in three years was received on December 31 in partial payment of an account receivable. The accountant for the company credited the customer's account for $120,000 despite a written agreement that the customer was to receive credit for the "present value of the note discounted at 8% for three years, interest compounded semiannually."

(2) The company signed an agreement with an executive who retired during the year calling for payment of $10,000 per year for five years to the executive starting three years from the end of the current year. These payments were in lieu of a year-end bonus which would have been taxed at a combined federal and state income tax rate of over 60%. The company regularly borrows money for periods of three to five years at a 9% annual rate of interest.

(3) The company wants to accumulate a fund of $100,000 in six years to retire a long-term note. Three years ago, the board of directors had passed a resolution instructing the treasurer to make ten equal annual deposits in a fund earning interest at 8% compounded annually. Because no one knew how to compute the equal deposits, the treasurer decided to deposit $10,000 at the end of each year. The fourth deposit was made at December 31 of the current year. What equal annual deposits should be made during the next six years, starting a year from now, if exactly $100,000 is to be accumulated six years from now?

(4) The company recently purchased a barge for $500,000. The purchase contract calls for 20 payments of $32,629 every three months starting immediately. You have been asked by the president of the company to compute the approximate rate of interest charged on this contract every three months.

Instructions Prepare journal entries with supporting computations, to correct the accounts for situations (1) and (2) above, and compute the answers for situations (3) and (4). Carry computations to the nearest dollar.

5B-3 Jim Donner was recently hired by his uncle as an accountant for Donner Iron Works, Inc. Jim Donner's first assignment was given to him verbally by his uncle as follows:

"To get your feet wet and to give you some practice with the desk calculator, I want you to prepare tables summarizing our interest expense or revenue and the liability or asset balance for these two transactions:

(1) Today we purchased a machine for $54,173. We paid $5,000 down and agreed to make six equal payments, including interest at 12% compounded semiannually, every six months starting six months from now.

(2) We will need $200,000 five years from now to reline our furnaces. I want to deposit five equal amounts in a fund starting one year from now so that we will have the money we need in five years. I have arranged to invest the money with Fontana Trust Company at 8% compounded annually."

Instructions

a Compute (1) the amount of the semiannual payments on the contract for the purchase of the machine and (2) the amount of the annual deposits in the furnace relining fund.

b Prepare (1) a loan amortization table for the installment debt on the purchase of the machine and (2) a fund accumulation table for the deposits to the furnace relining fund.

5B-4 Monte Nevada Mining Company has a debt for $250,000 maturing on June 30, Year 10. The company wishes to deposit $20,000 in a debt retirement fund on June 30 each year starting June 30, Year 3. In addition, the company wants to deposit a lump sum on June 30, Year 2, which will be sufficient to repay the debt on June 30, Year 10. The funds on deposit earn interest at 7% compounded annually.

Monte Nevada Mining Company also has made annual deposits of $20,000 in a special fund at the end of each of the last four years. The balance in the fund after the fourth deposit on December 31, Year 4, was $90,122. Interest is compounded annually.

Instructions (Use Appendix A and carry computations to the nearest dollar.)
a Compute the lump-sum amount that must be deposited on June 30, Year 2, if $250,000 will be available on June 30, Year 10, in the debt retirement fund.
b What was the annual rate of interest earned on the special fund through December 31, Year 4?
c Compute the amount that can be withdrawn from the special fund at the end of each year for ten years, starting on December 31, Year 5, assuming that the amount on deposit earns interest at 6% annually from January 1, Year 5, through December 31, Year 14.

CHAPTER 6

CASH AND MARKETABLE SECURITIES

CASH

Cash is a medium of exchange which a bank will accept for deposit and immediate credit to the depositor's account. Cash includes currency and coin, personal checks, bank drafts, money orders, and cashiers' checks, as well as money on deposit with banks. Items which are usually under the control of the cashier and are sometimes confused with cash include postage stamps, postdated checks, and IOU's. Postage should be classified as a short-term prepayment; postdated checks and IOU's should be classified as receivables.

Deposits with a trustee, for example, a bond sinking fund which is not under the control of management, should not be included in cash. As another example, many airline companies have millions of dollars in cash deposits with manufacturers for purchase of flight equipment. Such deposits do not qualify as current assets since they are not available for payment of current liabilities.

Certificates of deposit are properly classified as short-term investments rather than as cash because they are not available for immediate withdrawal. Strictly speaking, savings deposits also may not be withdrawn without prior notice to the bank, but banks very seldom enforce this requirement. Consequently, savings deposits are usually considered as a part of the cash balance. Petty cash funds and change funds are minor elements of cash under the control of management even though these funds are usually intended to be used for very specific purposes. The limitations placed on the use of these funds do not remove them from the category of cash but simply aid in the overall control of the cash resources.

In summary, the criteria generally used in defining cash are that the item be a medium of exchange, be immediately available for the payment of current debts, and be free from any contractual restriction which would prevent management from using it to meet any and all obligations.

Management of cash

The management of cash is of major importance in any business because cash is the means of commanding goods and services. In addition, careful scrutiny of cash transactions is required because this asset may be readily misappropriated.

The management of cash generally is centered around two areas: cash budgeting and accounting controls. The responsibility of management with respect to cash is (1) to ensure that there is sufficient cash to carry on the operations, (2) to invest any idle cash which is not distributed to the owners, and (3) to prevent loss of cash due to theft or misappropriation. Cash budgeting is necessary for the proper planning of future operations and to assure that cash is available when needed but that cash balances are not excessive. Accounting controls are necessary to provide a basis for the planning function, and in addition to assure that the cash is used for proper business purposes and not wasted, misused, or stolen. Management is responsible for controlling and protecting all assets of a business. Special problems exist in controlling cash, however, because of its liquid nature and universal attractiveness.

Internal control

The purpose of a system of internal control is to assure that assets which belong to the enterprise are received when tendered, are protected while in the custody of the business, and are used only for business purposes. The system of internal control consists of *administrative control* and *accounting control,* which were defined by the AICPA as follows:

Administrative control includes, but is not limited to, the plan of organization and the procedures and records that are concerned with the decision processes leading to management's authorization of transactions. Such authorization is a management function directly associated with the responsibility for achieving the objectives of the organization and is the starting point for establishing accounting control of transactions.

Accounting control comprises the plan of organization and the procedures and records that are concerned with the safeguarding of assets and the reliability of financial records and consequently are designed to provide reasonable assurance that:

a Transactions are executed in accordance with management's general or specific authorization.

b Transactions are recorded as necessary (1) to permit preparation of financial statements in conformity with generally accepted accounting principles or any other criteria applicable to such statements and (2) to maintain accountability for assets.

c Access to assets is permitted only in accordance with management's authorization.

d The recorded accountability for assets is compared with the existing assets at reasonable intervals and appropriate action is taken with respect to any differences.[1]

Administrative and accounting controls are not designed primarily to detect errors but rather to reduce the opportunity for errors or dishonesty to occur. In an effective system of internal control, no one person should handle all phases of a given transaction from beginning to end. For example, if one person were permitted to order merchandise, receive it, write a check in payment, and record the transaction in the accounts, there would be no protection against either fraud or errors. In larger organizations separate and independent departments are established for such functions as purchasing, receiving, selling, finance, and accounting, which assures that no one department handles all phases of a transaction.

In many cases the system of internal control is improved by physical safeguards. Business machines help to improve the efficiency and accuracy of the record-keeping function. Cash registers, safes, and prenumbered business forms are very helpful in safeguarding cash and establishing responsibility for it. Any system of internal control must be supervised with care if it is to function effectively.

If an attempt is made to design a foolproof system, it should be remembered that management's primary responsibility is profitable operation of the business. The cost of the system of internal control must be balanced against the benefit to be derived in preventing errors and losses. When the cost of adding an additional safeguard cannot be justified in terms of its contribution to the overall performance, the risk of errors and losses may be accepted with full knowledge of the circumstances.

Controlling cash receipts and payments

The objective sought in the control of cash receipts is to ensure that all cash due to the business is collected and recorded without loss. The system of controlling cash payments should be designed to ensure that no unauthorized disbursements are made. Control is accomplished by division of responsibility so as to achieve independent verification of

[1] *Statement on Auditing Standards No. 1,* "Codification of Auditing Standards and Procedures," AICPA (New York: 1973), p. 20.

cash transactions without duplication of effort. Cash is safeguarded by depositing it in banks and through the use of special cash funds.

Imprest cash fund (petty cash fund)

The term *imprest cash* refers to a fund of fixed amount used for making small expenditures that are most conveniently paid in cash. The imprest fund is restored to its original amount at frequent intervals by writing a check on the general bank account payable to Petty Cash. The replenishment check is equal in amount to the expenditures made from the fund. Imprest cash funds placed in the custody of responsible employees thus serve to maintain control over cash without involved procedures for small disbursements.

The size of the fund should be sufficient to meet the normal need for small cash payments for a period of two or three weeks. As each cash payment is made, a voucher or receipt is placed in the fund in lieu of the cash removed. These vouchers are reviewed and canceled when the fund is replenished.

Illustration of the Use of a Petty Cash Fund On December 1, Seahawk Corporation established a petty cash fund of $250 for the purpose of paying certain bills. On December 21, the cashier requested reimbursement for bills paid during the intervening period. The following itemized list of disbursements was presented on December 21 for reimbursement and on December 31 in connection with the year-end audit:

Composition of Petty Cash Fund		
	Dec. 21	**Dec. 31**
Cash in fund	$ 9	$150
Office supplies expense	175	77
Miscellaneous selling expenses	65	25
Cash over and short	1	(2)
Total	$250	$250

The petty cash fund should also be replenished at the end of the accounting period so that the expenses paid from the fund will be recorded in the proper period and the year-end cash balance will be accurately stated. The entries required to account for the petty cash fund for the month of December are as follows:

Dec. 1	Petty Cash Fund	....	250
	Cash	....	250
	To record the establishment of a petty cash fund.		

Dec. 21	Office Supplies Expense	....	175
	Miscellaneous Selling Expenses	....	65
	Cash Over and Short	....	1
	Cash	....	241
	To reimburse the petty cash fund and to record expenses		
	incurred.		

Dec. 31	Office Supplies Expense	....	77
	Miscellaneous Selling Expenses	....	25
	Cash Over and Short	....	2
	Cash	....	100
	To record the expenses incurred since December 21 and		
	to reimburse the petty cash fund.		

If for any reason the petty cash fund is not replenished at the year-end, it is still desirable that the expenses be recorded before the accounts are closed. In this situation the December 31 entry illustrated above would be changed in only one respect: the credit of $100 would be to Petty Cash Fund rather than to Cash. The effect on the year-end financial statements is the same as if the fund had actually been replenished.

Change fund

A change fund is an imprest fund used to facilitate the collection of money from customers. The amount of the change fund is deducted from the total cash on hand at the close of business each day to determine the daily collections. The cash should be counted and checked against the cash register tape daily as a step in the internal control system. In general, change and petty cash funds are combined with cash on hand and in the bank for balance sheet purposes.

Reconciliation of bank balances

The cash balance indicated on the monthly bank statement will seldom agree with the cash balance indicated by the depositor's ledger account for cash. These two balances do not agree even though they purport to measure the same quantity, because there is a lag between the time that transactions are recognized by the two parties, the bank and the depositor. For example, the depositor will credit the ledger account, Cash, when writing a check in payment of a bill. The bank will not reduce the depositor's account until the check is presented for payment by the creditor. Another common difference between the two balances results when the deposit of cash receipts is made after the bank closes its records for the month. Both of these differences are self-correcting over time; the outstanding checks will be presented for payment and the deposit will be entered by the bank within a few days.

There are also time lags in transactions initiated by the bank. For example, a depositor is generally not notified of the bank's charges for servicing the account or for collecting a note receivable until the monthly bank statement is received.

In addition to items which involve merely a lag in the recording process, there are occasionally errors made by the depositor or by the bank. The process of reconciling the balances forces a careful review of all transactions involving cash and provides a means of proving the accuracy of the depositor's records. The value of this review stems from the fact that two independent agents have recorded the same transactions and that their records are being compared. When differences arise they must be explained. Those differences which are self-correcting require no further consideration. Corrections must be made, however, for omissions or other errors in recording transactions in the ledger. Errors made by the bank should be called to its attention for correction.

Two forms of bank reconciliation are in common usage: (1) both the bank balance and the balance per depositor's records are reconciled to a correct balance, and (2) the bank balance is reconciled to the balance in the depositor's records (or the balance in the depositor's records to the bank balance). The first form is generally preferred by accountants and is illustrated on page 218.

Illustration The Cash in Bank ledger account for Crossland Company shows a debit balance of $10,592.66 on December 31, Year 5. The bank statement indicates a balance on deposit of $12,269.02 on December 31. Receipts of December 31 in the amount of $1,144.60 were left in the night depository on December 31 but were not included on the bank statement. The December bank statement included a debit memorandum for $13.50 for service charges for November. A credit memorandum included with the statement indicated that a note receivable in the amount of $2,000, left with the bank for collection, had been collected and credited to the Crossland Company account by the bank for $2,030, including interest revenue of $30. Comparison of the paid checks with the check stubs indicated that check no. 821 for $463.90 on December 15, for the purchase of office equipment, had been erroneously entered in the cash payments journal as $436.90. In addition, it was learned that the following checks, all written in December, had not been paid by the bank:

No. 811	$421.96
No. 814	93.00
No. 822	250.00
No. 823	116.50

Also included with the bank statement was a check for $50 from Robert Davis, a customer of Crossland Company. This check was marked NSF (not sufficient funds). Finally, an examination of the accounting records indicated that the bank collected cash of $10,000 on December 31, Year 5, representing the maturity value of a U.S. Treasury bill; the bank did not credit the company's account until January 2, Year 6; the U.S. Treasury bill had been purchased by the bank for Crossland Company at a discount for $9,652 and had been recorded at cost in the Marketable Securities account by Crossland Company.

A reconciliation of both the balance per depositor's records and the balance per bank statement to the correct cash balance at December 31, Year 5, is given below:

CROSSLAND COMPANY
Bank Reconciliation
December 31, Year 5

Balance per depositor's records			$10,592.66
Add: Note collected by bank		$ 2,000.00	
Interest on note collected by bank		30.00	
Proceeds of U.S. Treasury bill which had been purchased for $9,652.00 (interest revenue = $348) .		10,000.00	12,030.00
Subtotal			$22,622.66
Less: Bank service charges for November	$	13.50	
NSF check received from Robert Davis		50.00	
Error in recording check no. 821		27.00	90.50
Correct cash balance			$22,532.16
Balance per bank statement			$12,269.02
Add: Deposit in transit		$ 1,144.60	
Proceeds of U.S. Treasury bill		10,000.00	11,144.60
Subtotal			$23,413.62
Less: Outstanding checks:			
No. 811	$	421.96	
No. 814		93.00	
No. 822		250.00	
No. 823		116.50	881.46
Correct cash balance			$22,532.16

The bank reconciliation serves three functions: (1) to arrive at the correct cash balance to be reported in the balance sheet, (2) to uncover errors made in recording cash transactions, either by the bank or the company's personnel, and (3) to provide information necessary to bring the accounting records up to date. The journal entry required to adjust the accounts for errors and omissions is taken from the top section of the bank reconciliation. All the items appearing on the reconciliation as additions to or deductions from the "balance per depositor's records" must be reflected in the journal entry. The journal entry required to adjust the accounting records of Crossland Company follows:

Cash	11,939.50	
Office Equipment	27.00	
Accounts Receivable: Robert Davis	50.00	
Miscellaneous Expense	13.50	
Interest Revenue ($30.00 + $348.00)		378.00
Notes Receivable		2,000.00
Marketable Securities (U.S. Treasury bill)		9,652.00
To adjust Cash account to correct balance as shown on December bank reconciliation.		

The balance per depositor's records, $10,592.66, plus the debit of $11,939.50 in the journal entry, equal the correct cash balance of $22,532.16.[2] If there had been arithmetic errors in balancing the Cash account, these would be corrected and the balance per depositor's records on the reconciliation would also be changed. Errors of this type are seldom found in bank reconciliation procedures if a trial balance of the general ledger has been properly prepared prior to the time the reconciliation is prepared.

The deposit in transit and the outstanding checks will be processed by the bank in the regular course of business during January.

Reconciliation of cash receipts and cash payments

Cash balances per the bank statement and the company's ledger are reconciled to establish the accuracy of the cash records. A full reconciliation of cash receipts and payments (known as a *proof of cash*) may also be made in establishing the accuracy of the cash balance and the effectiveness of internal controls over cash.

To illustrate a reconciliation of cash receipts and cash payments for Crossland Company, we need, in addition to the information already provided for the month of December, the bank reconciliation for No-

[2] As a general rule, the entry resulting from a bank reconciliation is the only example of an adjusting or correcting entry which involves the Cash account.

vember and cash receipts and payments data for December from both the bank's and the company's records. This information is provided below:

(1) The following bank reconciliation was prepared on November 30, Year 5:

CROSSLAND COMPANY
Bank Reconciliation
November 30, Year 5

Balance per depositor's records		$7,399.61
Less: Bank service charges for October	$ 3.25	
NSF check received from James Price	75.00	78.25
Correct cash balance		$7,321.36
Balance per bank statement		$6,947.26
Add: Deposits in transit		1,055.52
Subtotal		$8,002.78
Less: Outstanding checks: Nos. 760, 762, 763, and 764		681.42
Correct cash balance		$7,321.36

(2) The adjusting journal entry on November 30, Year 5, based on the bank reconciliation above, was as follows:

Miscellaneous Expense	3.25	
Accounts Receivable: James Price	75.00	
Cash		78.25

To adjust Cash account to correct balance as shown on November bank reconciliation.

(3) The cash receipts journal showed total cash received during December of $22,640.50 and the cash payments journal showed cash payments during December of $19,369.20. Thus the unadjusted cash balance in Crossland Company's accounting records at December 31, Year 5, was $10,592.66, determined as follows:

Unadjusted balance in Cash account at Nov. 30	$ 7,399.61
Add: Cash receipts during December	22,640.50
Subtotal	$30,040.11
Less: Adjustment per journal entry based on	
November bank reconciliation . . . . $ 78.25	
Cash payments during December 19,369.20	19,447.45
Unadjusted balance in Cash account at Dec. 31	$10,592.66

(4) The bank statement for December indicated that the total deposits of cash during December were $24,581.42 and that the total checks paid, together with bank charges, amounted to $19,259.66. This resulted in an unadjusted bank balance at December 31, Year 5, of $12,269.02 ($6,947.26 + $24,581.42 − $19,259.66 = $12,269.02).

The cash receipts, cash payments, and the cash balances reflected in the bank statement and in the ledger of Crossland Company can be reconciled to the correct balances for December as illustrated below:

CROSSLAND COMPANY
Reconciliation of Cash Receipts and Cash Payments for December, Year 5, and Cash Balance at December 31, Year 5

	Balance, Nov. 30	Receipts	Payments	Balance, Dec. 31
Balances per depositor's records .	$7,321.36	$22,640.50	$19,369.20	$10,592.66
Bank service charges			13.50	(13.50)
Proceeds of note collected		2,030.00		2,030.00
Proceeds of U.S. Treasury bill . . .		10,000.00		10,000.00
NSF check		(50.00)		(50.00)
Error in recording check no. 821 .			27.00	(27.00)
Correct balances	$7,321.36	$34,620.50	$19,409.70	$22,532.16
Balances per bank statement . . .	$6,947.26	$24,581.42	$19,259.66	$12,269.02
Deposits in transit:				
Nov. 30	1,055.52	(1,055.52)		
Dec. 31		1,144.60		1,144.60
Proceeds of U.S. Treasury bill . . .		10,000.00		10,000.00
Outstanding checks:				
Nov. 30	(681.42)		(681.42)	
Dec. 31			881.46	(881.46)
NSF check		(50.00)	(50.00)	
Correct balances	$7,321.36	$34,620.50	$19,409.70	$22,532.16

The proof of cash schedule for Crossland Company for December, Year 5, is explained below:

1 *Reconciliation of cash receipts per depositor's records.* The $2,030 proceeds of the note collected by the bank and the $10,000 proceeds from the U.S. Treasury bill must be recorded in the accounting records; the $50 NSF check must be deducted from the receipts as recorded in the accounts of Crossland Company because the check was not honored.

2 *Reconciliation of cash receipts per bank statement.* The $1,055.52 deposit in transit at November 30 is deducted from the deposits recorded by the bank in December because it was a receipt of cash in November. The $1,144.60 deposit in transit at December 31 is a receipt of cash in December and should be included in total cash receipts for December. The proceeds of $10,000 from the U.S. Treasury bill are added to the receipts because the bank failed to record this amount on December 31. The NSF check was included as a receipt when deposited but was later returned by the bank to Crossland Company. To reflect actual receipts, the NSF check for $50 is deducted from total receipts as recorded by the bank.

3 *Reconciliation of cash payments per depositor's records.* The unrecorded bank service charge of $13.50 in the December bank statement and the recording error of $27 must be added to cash payments as recorded in the accounts of Crossland Company to reflect actual cash payments for December.

4 *Reconciliation of cash payments per bank statement.* The outstanding checks of $681.42 on November 30 are included in the bank debits for December. These do not represent cash payments during December but rather were shown properly as cash payments in November. The outstanding checks of $881.46 on December 31 did not include any checks which were outstanding on November 30; therefore, this total is properly classified as a cash payment by the bank during December. The NSF for $50 was included in cash payments by the bank when it was charged back to Crossland Company. To correct the cash payments in the bank statement, $50 must be deducted because the amount of the NSF check was also deducted from the cash receipts in the bank statement (see 2 above).

5 *Reconciliation of bank and ledger cash balances.* The last column of the reconciliation is identical to the reconciliation of the bank and ledger balances to the correct cash balance illustrated on page 218. The journal entry required to adjust the accounting records of Crossland Company is the same as that illustrated on page 219.

Cash overdraft

The issuance of checks in excess of the balance on deposit will create an **overdraft** in the bank account. Banks often (but not always) refuse to pay a check which exceeds the amount of the depositor's account. Such refusal of course prevents an overdraft from occurring. In the rare situation in which a company maintains only one bank account and that account is overdrawn at the balance sheet date, the overdraft should be shown as a current liability. However, if a company has other bank accounts with larger positive balances, it is reasonable to present the net balance of cash as a current asset. This treatment is based on the reasoning that users of financial statements are interested primarily in a company's cash position rather than the status of individual bank accounts.

In rare instances, the accountant will encounter a situation in which checks are written (and recorded) in excess of the amount on deposit, but the checks are not mailed to the payees. In preparing financial statements, the credit balance in the Cash account should be eliminated by an entry debiting Cash and crediting Accounts Payable (or other liability accounts) by the amount of the checks written but not released.

Disclosure of compensating cash balances

The Securities and Exchange Commission requires that companies filing financial statements with the Commission disclose compensating cash balances.[3] A *compensating balance* generally is defined as that portion of any demand deposit maintained by a depositor which constitutes support for existing borrowing arrangements with banks.

Disclosure of compensating-balance arrangements is required because such cash balances are not readily available for discretionary use by management at the balance sheet date. Also, the maintenance of compensating cash balances affects liquidity and the effective cost of borrowing from banks. Users of financial statements may find such information relevant.

MARKETABLE SECURITIES

Investment of idle cash

To achieve efficient use of all resources, management frequently turns unproductive cash balances into productive resources through investment in marketable securities. In some cases we find that corporations follow a policy of holding, more or less continuously, securities which can be converted into cash whenever the circumstances demand.

Marketable securities (usually short-term notes or bonds and occasionally common stocks) held by a business for the purpose of earning a return on cash resources are characterized by their salability at a readily determinable market price. Stocks and bonds which are not widely held or frequently traded usually do not meet the marketability test; consequently, securities of this latter type are not considered in this discussion.

Investments in securities of other companies purchased as a means of exercising control over the operations of such companies are of a quite different character and should not be considered as temporary investments. If the holding is for the purpose of exercising control, the effective operation of the enterprise may be hampered by the liquidation of the investment. Investments of this nature are discussed in Chapter 11.

[3] *Accounting Series Release No. 148,* SEC (Washington: 1973).

In summary, marketable securities which are classified in the balance sheet as current assets must be readily salable and should not be held for purposes of bolstering business relations with the issuing corporation. On the other hand, there is no requirement that the securities be held for a limited time only or that management express its intent as to the duration of the holding. The objectives of investments in marketable securities are twofold: (1) to maximize the return on invested capital and (2) to minimize the risk of loss from price fluctuations.

When excess cash is available for short periods, the investment media typically used are *certificates of deposit, commercial paper,* and *bonds* (both government and corporate) with near-term maturities (in order to minimize price fluctuations). *Commercial paper* is the term used in the money market for short-term unsecured promissory notes issued by corporations and sold to investors, generally other companies. Longer-term bonds and common stocks, although occasionally used as a medium for investing idle cash, do not meet the objective of limited price fluctuation. Long-term bond prices fluctuate with changes in the level of interest rates, as do prices of bonds with short-term maturities; the degree of fluctuation is greater for bonds with longer maturities. On the other hand, common stocks are subject to wide and erratic price movements because of changes in investor sentiment, corporate earnings, and other business and economic factors which are difficult to predict.

Recording transactions in marketable securities

At acquisition, marketable securities are recorded at cost, the price of the security in the market *plus any cost incident to the acquisition,* such as brokerage commission and transfer taxes. Bonds acquired between interest dates are traded on the basis of the market price plus the interest accrued since the most recent interest payment. The accrued interest is a separate asset which is purchased simultaneously with the bond. The cost of these two assets should be separated to achieve a clear picture of the results of the security transaction.

Illustration On January 31, Year 5, Sawyer Company placed an order with a broker to buy 100, $1,000, 9% Atlantic Railroad bonds which mature on November 30, Year 8, with interest dates May 31 and November 30. The bonds were purchased on the same day at 103, plus accrued interest of $1,500 for two months. The brokerage commission was $500. The total cost of the bonds and the total cash outlay are computed on page 225.

Market price of bonds ($1,030 × 100)	$103,000
Add: Brokerage commission	500
Total cost of bonds	$103,500
Add: Accrued interest for two months on $100,000, at 9% per year . .	1,500
Total cash outlay	$105,000

The journal entry required to record the purchase of the bonds is as follows:

Marketable Securities	103,500	
Accrued Interest Receivable	1,500	
Cash		105,000
To record purchase of 100 bonds at 103 plus accrued interest		
of $1,500 and brokerage commission of $500.		

On April 30, Year 5, Sawyer Company sold the Atlantic Railroad bonds at 104¾ plus accrued interest for five months. The cash received upon sale of the bonds, assuming the brokerage commission to be $500, is computed as follows:

Market price of securities ($1,047.50 × 100)	$104,750
Less: Brokerage commission	500
Proceeds on sale of bonds	$104,250
Add: Accrued interest for five months on $100,000, at 9% per year . .	3,750
Total cash received	$108,000

The following journal entry is required in the accounts of Sawyer Company on April 30, Year 5, to record the sale of the bonds and to recognize interest revenue:

Cash	108,000	
Marketable Securities		103,500
Accrued Interest Receivable		1,500
Interest Revenue		2,250
Gain on Sale of Marketable Securities		750
To record sale of Atlantic Railroad bonds at 104¾, less broker-		
age commission of $500, plus accrued interest of $3,750.		

The gain of $750 realized on the sale of the Atlantic Railroad bonds is the result of a change in the market price of the bonds, which may have occurred for any number of reasons. The two most likely causes of such a gain are (1) a decline in the level of interest rates, or (2) a more favorable appraisal of this particular bond issue. If the level of interest rates had risen since January 31, Year 5, these bonds probably would have been sold at a loss. The $1,500 of accrued interest on the bonds acquired on January 31, Year 5, might at that time have been recorded as a debit to the Interest Revenue account. This procedure would require that the $3,750 of accrued interest received on April 30 be credited to the Interest Revenue account. The net effect would be to show $2,250 as interest revenue for the three months the bonds were owned.

Discount or Premium on Short-Term Investments in Bonds   In accounting for temporary investments in bonds, it is usually unnecessary to amortize premiums or to accumulate discounts. Bonds purchased as temporary investments generally have near-term maturities; consequently, any premium or discount is likely to be negligible. The holding period by the investor is also likely to be very short, which means that any change in market price is usually attributable to the two causes mentioned above rather than to the approach of the maturity date. In theory the amortization of premium or the accumulation of discount is always proper, but as a practical matter such amortization or accumulation would add little to the accuracy of income measurement on temporary investments in short-term bonds.

Computation of Interest on Investment in Bonds   Accrued interest on notes and bonds issued by business firms is generally computed on the basis of a 360-day year.[4] Any full month expired, whether it has 31 days, 30 days, or only 28 days, would be viewed as one-twelfth of a year. Additional interest is determined on the basis of the number of days elapsed. For example, interest from April 25 to August 10 would be computed for three months (May, June, and July) and 15 days (5 days in April and 10 days in August), or 105/360 of a year.

Interest on U.S. government securities is computed on the basis of a 365-day year; thus the *exact number of days* for the interest computation period must be determined. Interest on a U.S. Treasury bond from April 25 to August 10, for example, would be 107/365 of a full year's interest.

---

[4] Not long ago, Chairman Wright Patman of the House Banking Committee accused banks of manipulating the calendar to collect about $150 million of extra interest a year. According to Mr. Patman, "The banks are charging interest over the full 365 days (in a year) but are giving the customer the use of the money for only 360 days. In short, on a 12-month loan, the borrower pays five days of extra interest, and over a five-year period he will pay almost a full extra month's interest." As a result of widening criticism, many banks now compute interest on the basis of a 365-day year.

Cost Selection The cost of securities sold is not always as definite as in the preceding illustration. If there are several purchases of the same security at different dates and prices, and it is then decided to sell a portion of the holdings, some procedure of cost selection must be employed. Among the methods commonly used are specific identification, first-in, first-out, and average cost. For income tax purposes only specific identification and first-in, first-out are acceptable.

Stock and bond certificates generally have serial numbers which make it easy to identify the cost of specific acquisitions. By using the specific identification method, management may influence the amount of realized gain or loss by deliberately selecting the certificates to be sold from a high-cost lot or a low-cost lot. As an example, assume that Kane Company buys 100 bonds of American Telephone at a total cost of $96,000 and a few months later buys another 100 bonds at a cost of $99,000. A month later Kane Company decides to sell 100 American Telephone bonds. The market value is then $98,000. The sale will show a profit of $2,000 or a loss of $1,000, depending on whether Kane Company elects to deliver bonds from the first or the second purchase.

Price fluctuations and valuation of marketable securities

Since marketable securities are in a sense an extension of the cash account, the current market prices of these securities are important both to management and to other users of financial statements. These securities are secondary cash resources which can be converted into cash when the need arises.

Normally an asset is recorded at cost and this cost is associated with the revenue which arises from the use of the asset. If the asset loses its value without producing revenue, the cost is written off as a loss. The principle of *revenue realization* usually allows recognition of increases in the value of an asset only when it is sold. Whether realization should be limited to the point of sale for marketable securities is a question worth considering. By definition, marketable securities are readily salable at a quoted market price. This same characteristic is not usually found in inventories or plant assets. This basic difference between these types of assets suggests that the test of revenue realization should not control the valuation of marketable securities.

The consistent use of market prices in setting a valuation on marketable securities at the end of any accounting period has some advantages: (1) The income statement will show the results of decisions to hold or sell such securities period by period. For example, if the market price rises in one period and falls in the next, the gain from holding securities in the first period and the loss sustained by failure to sell at the higher price will be revealed. (2) Valuation at market eliminates the anomaly of carrying otherwise identical securities at different amounts because they were acquired at different prices. (3) The market value is more meaningful to the creditor, who studies the current section of a balance sheet to judge the debt-paying ability of the company.

The following example illustrates the issues that would arise if market value were used as the basis for valuation. At the close of business on December 31, Dixon Foundry had a portfolio of marketable securities which cost $148,000 and which had a market value of $151,500. The question at issue is whether on December 31 there has been a gain of $3,500. If we follow the traditional test of revenue realization, no gain would be recognized until the securities are sold. If valuation at market is accepted, the following journal entry would be recorded:

Marketable Securities—Increase in Market Value	*3,500*	
Gain in Market Value of Marketable Securities		*3,500*
To record appreciation in value of marketable securities.		

Thus the gain would be recognized in the period in which the price changed rather than in the period in which securities are sold.

Subsequently, on March 28, the securities are sold for $149,800. Has there been a gain or a loss on the sale of securities? If traditional revenue realization rules were followed, the gain in market price was not recognized earlier; since a sale has now taken place, a gain of $1,800 should be recorded. If the securities were valued at market on December 31, the entry to record the sale would show a loss of $1,700 sustained since the end of the preceding year.

The question which must be answered is, "What event in the life of the enterprise gives rise to the recognition of gains and losses from holding marketable securities in lieu of cash?" The traditional answer has been "Sale of the securities," but the logic of this answer is questionable.

In the early 1970s, the Accounting Principles Board attempted to issue an opinion which would have required the reporting of marketable securities at market value. The Board encountered considerable difficulty in finding a satisfactory method for reporting unrealized gains and losses on marketable securities and as a result the issuance of a formal opinion was abandoned. In the opinion of the authors, the current market value of investments in marketable securities is the most relevant valuation because it is most likely to aid users in making the types of decisions for which they use financial statements. The APB in **Statement No. 4** identified **relevance** as the primary qualitative objective of financial accounting.[5] It seems reasonable to anticipate that accoun-

[5] *Statements of the Accounting Principles Board, No. 4,* "Basic Concepts and Accounting Principles Underlying Financial Statements of Business Enterprises," AICPA (New York: 1970), p. 36.

tants will eventually find a satisfactory method of applying current market value to the various aspects of accounting for marketable securities.

Valuation at cost versus valuation at lower of cost or market

Despite the forcefulness of the arguments in favor of reporting marketable securities at market value, most companies reported marketable securities at cost[6] until the FASB issued *Statement No. 12* in December 1975.[7] However, valuation at lower of cost or market was required when the decline in market value was substantial and was not "due to a mere temporary condition."[8] Recoveries in the market value of securities which had been written down generally were not recognized in the accounts. When the market value of securities was below cost, generally accepted accounting and auditing principles required that:

> The auditor should examine evidence to determine whether management properly classified the marketable securities as current or noncurrent assets and whether the amounts at which they are carried in the financial statements are appropriate. The auditor should evaluate the reasons for the market decline when market value is below cost. . . . The classification of marketable securities as either current assets or noncurrent assets is an important consideration in evaluating their proper carrying amounts. Whether marketable securities are properly classified depends to a large extent on management's intent. If management intends to dispose of the securities in the next fiscal year, the securities are classified as a current asset. Marketable securities that represent an excess of funds available for operations, but which management does not intend to dispose of, are often classified as current assets since management can sell them at any time at their option. . . . Marketable securities, such as stocks and bonds, properly classified as current assets should be written down to market at the balance sheet date to reflect declines that are not temporary. . . . When marketable securities classified as a current asset have a market value lower than cost, retention of the cost basis requires persuasive evidence that indicates a recovery in the market value will occur before the earlier of the scheduled maturity or sale date of the securities or within a one-year period from the balance sheet date. Generally, such evidence would be limited to substantial recovery subsequent to the year end.[9]

The 1975 edition of *Accounting Trends & Techniques,* which covered financial statements issued prior to the effective date of *FASB Statement No. 12,* showed that 364 of the 600 companies included in the study re-

[6] There are notable exceptions to the general approach. Insurance companies, securities brokers and dealers, mutual funds, and others used special methods based on market value to account for investments in securities. For example, a stock brokerage firm recently reported marketable securities at market value of $42,879,231; in contrast, a bank reported common stock owned in Coca-Cola Co. at a cost of $110,000 and presented the pre-tax market value of $88,363,000 in a note to the financial statements.

[7] *FASB Statement No. 12,* "Accounting for Certain Marketable Securities," FASB (Stamford: 1975).

[8] *Accounting Research and Terminology Bulletins, Final Edition,* AICPA (New York: 1961), chap. 3A, p. 23.

[9] *AICPA Professional Standards,* vol. 3, AICPA (New York: 1975), Sec. 9332.

ported marketable securities in their balance sheets. Of this total, 276 used cost, 15 used lower of cost or market, seven used market value, and 66 did not disclose the basis of valuation used. Of the 276 companies using cost, 267 companies referred to market value, as illustrated below for Carnation Company:

Short-term commercial obligations, at cost (approximately market)	$66,808,202
Other marketable securities, at cost (quoted market value $7,888,000)	3,990,774

For most companies, the reporting of marketable securities in financial statements for periods ending on or after December 31, 1975, had to conform to *FASB Statement No. 12.*

Purpose and Applicability of FASB Statement No. 12 Because of the wide diversity of accounting practices applied to marketable securities, the FASB in December of 1975 issued *Statement No. 12,* "Accounting for Certain Marketable Securities," in an attempt to provide answers to several questions, including the following:

1 Under what circumstances should marketable equity securities be written down below cost?

2 Should marketable equity securities which have been written down be written back up?

An important reason for the issuance of *Statement No. 12* is stated briefly as follows:

> During 1973 and 1974, there were substantial declines in market values of many securities. As a result, in many enterprises where securities are carried at cost, the carrying amount is in excess of current market value. In other enterprises where carrying amounts were written down to reflect the market decline, the partial recovery in the market in 1975 has given rise to a situation in which securities are being carried at amounts which are below both original cost and current market value.[10]

FASB Statement No. 12 deals with marketable *equity* securities classified as current assets as well as marketable equity securities classified as noncurrent assets. In this section we are concerned primarily with the provisions of the Statement applicable to marketable equity securities carried in the current portfolio; provisions of the Statement applicable to noncurrent marketable equity securities are discussed in Chapter 11. *Statement No. 12* is applicable to most business enterprises as well as to personal financial statements. It does not apply to investments accounted for by the equity method (see Chapter 11), nor to

---

[10] *FASB Statement No. 12,* pp. 1–2.

not-for-profit entities, mutual life insurance companies, and employee benefit plans. The Statement for the most part does not apply to enterprises in industries having specialized accounting practices with respect to marketable equity securities. Such industries include investment companies, brokers and dealers in securities, stock life insurance companies, and fire and casualty insurance companies.

Definition of Terms For purposes of applying *Statement No. 12,* the FASB defined the terms listed below:

1 *Equity securities* include instruments representing ownership shares or the right to acquire or dispose of ownership shares at fixed or determinable prices. The following are not equity securities: preferred stock that by its terms either must be redeemed by the issuing enterprise or is redeemable at the option of the investor; treasury stock; and convertible bonds.

2 *Marketable* means that sales prices (or bid and ask prices) are currently available for an equity security on a national securities exchange or in the publicly reported over-the-counter market.

3 *Market price* refers to the price of a single share or unit of a marketable equity security.

4 *Market value* refers to the aggregate of the market price times the number of shares or units of each marketable equity security in the portfolio.

5 *Cost* refers to the original cost of a marketable equity unless a new cost basis has been assigned on recognition of an impairment of value that was deemed other than temporary. In such cases, the new cost basis shall be the cost.

6 *Valuation allowance* for a marketable equity securities portfolio represents the net unrealized loss in that portfolio.

7 *Carrying amount* of a marketable equity securities portfolio is the amount at which that portfolio of marketable equity securities is reflected in the balance sheet.

8 *Realized gain or loss* represents the difference between the net proceeds from the sale of a marketable equity security and its cost. (Such gain or loss results only upon sale of a security).

9 *Net unrealized gain or loss* on a marketable equity securities portfolio represents at any date the difference between the aggregate market value and aggregate cost. (Such gain or loss is recognized only at the end of an accounting period and is not a factor in the computation of taxable income).[11]

Accounting for Current Marketable Equity Securities The FASB stated that the carrying amount of a marketable securities portfolio should be the lower of its aggregate cost or market value, as determined at each balance sheet date. The amount, if any, by which the aggregate cost of the portfolio exceeds market value is accounted for by using a valuation allowance. The treatment of changes in the valuation allowance depends upon whether the securities are considered current or noncurrent assets. In the case of a classified balance sheet, marketable equity securities are grouped into separate current and noncurrent portfolios for the purpose of comparing aggregate cost and market value. In the case of an unclassified balance sheet, marketable equity securities

[11] Ibid., pp. 3–5.

should be considered as noncurrent assets. Generally, the current marketable equity securities portfolios of all entities included in consolidated financial statements are to be treated as a single consolidated portfolio; noncurrent portfolios are treated similarly.

Realized gains and losses from sale of current or noncurrent marketable equity securities are included in the determination of net income of the period in which they occur. Changes in the valuation allowance for a marketable equity securities portfolio included in current assets also are included in the determination of net income of the period in which they occur. Changes in the valuation allowance result in **unrealized** losses and gains. A recovery in the aggregate market value of securities which had been written down to a market value below cost requires the recognition of an unrealized gain which is included in the determination of net income. However, increases in the aggregate market value of the current portfolio of marketable equity securities above aggregate cost are not recognized in the accounts. Unrealized losses on securities held in the noncurrent portfolio are not included in the determination of net income of the period in which they occur; such losses are reported as direct reductions in stockholders' equity. In the balance sheet, the adjusted valuation allowance is deducted from aggregate cost of marketable equity securities.

If there is a change in the classification of a marketable equity security between current and noncurrent, the security should be transferred between the corresponding portfolios at the lower of its cost or market value at date of transfer. If market value is less than cost, the market value becomes the new cost basis, and the difference is accounted for as if it were a realized loss and included in the determination of net income.

Unrealized gains and losses on marketable securities are not taken into account in the determination of taxable income of the reporting entity. Such gains and losses result in **timing differences** between taxable income and pre-tax income reported in the income statement. Interperiod tax allocation procedures, described briefly in Chapter 3 and more completely in Chapter 21, should be applied to determine whether a net unrealized gain or loss should be reduced by the applicable income tax effect. However, a tax effect should be recognized on a net unrealized capital loss only when there exists **assurance beyond a reasonable doubt** that the benefit will be realized by an offset of the unrealized capital loss against future capital gains.

Illustration To illustrate the application of **FASB Statement No. 12** to the current portfolio of marketable equity securities, assume the following changes in the portfolio from December 31, Year 5, through December 31, Year 7:

	Cost	Market	Unrealized Gain (Loss)
Dec. 31, Year 5			
Security A	$100,000	$ 80,000	$(20,000)
Security B	200,000	160,000	(40,000)
Security C	50,000	75,000	25,000
Totals	$350,000	$315,000	$(35,000)
Dec. 31, Year 6			
Security A	$100,000	$ 75,000	$(25,000)
Security B	100,000*	70,000	(30,000)
Security C	50,000	60,000	10,000
Totals	$250,000	$205,000	$(45,000)
Dec. 31, Year 7			
Security A	$100,000	$ 80,000	$(20,000)
Security B	100,000	90,000	(10,000)
Security C	50,000	65,000	15,000
Totals	$250,000	$235,000	$(15,000)

*On March 1, Year 6, one-half of the holdings of Security B (cost, $100,000) was sold for $75,000. There were no other sales of securities in Year 6 or Year 7.

December 31, Year 5, the date of initial application A valuation allowance of $35,000 is required for marketable equity securities included in current assets to reflect the excess of cost, $350,000, over market value, $315,000. The corresponding charge for the unrealized loss should be reflected in the net income for Year 5, and ultimately is closed to retained earnings. The entry to establish the valuation allowance is:

Unrealized Loss in Value of Marketable Securities 35,000
    Valuation Allowance to Reduce Marketable Securities to
      Market Value 35,000
To establish valuation allowance for decline in market value of
current portfolio.

March 1, Year 6, sale of security at a loss The sale of one-half of the holdings of Security B resulted in a *realized loss* of $25,000. The loss should be reflected in the determination of net income for Year 6. The entry to record the sale is:

```
Cash . . . . . . . . . . . . . . . . . . . . . . . . . . . . . . .  75,000
Realized Loss on Sale of Marketable Securities . . . . . . . .  25,000
      Investment in Security B  . . . . . . . . . . . . . . .         100,000
To record sale of Security B at a realized loss.
```

December 31, Year 6, increase in valuation allowance A valuation allowance of $45,000 is required for securities included in current assets to reflect the excess of cost, $250,000, over market value, $205,000. Since the balance in the valuation allowance account is $35,000, an increase of $10,000 is required. The entry to record the increase in the valuation allowance is:

```
Unrealized Loss in Value of Marketable Securities . . . . . . .  10,000
      Valuation Allowance to Reduce Marketable Securities to
      Market Value . . . . . . . . . . . . . . . . . . . . . . . .       10,000
To record increase in valuation allowance as a result of further
decline in market value of current portfolio.
```

December 31, Year 7, recovery in market value of portfolio There has been a market recovery during Year 7, as evidenced by the need to reduce the valuation allowance for current securities from $45,000 to $15,000. This difference constitutes an "unrealized gain" and should be included in the determination of net income for Year 7. The entry to record the reduction in the valuation allowance is:

```
Valuation Allowance to Reduce Marketable Securities to Market
   Value . . . . . . . . . . . . . . . . . . . . . . . . . . . . . .  30,000
      Unrealized Gain in Value of Marketable Securities  . . .       30,000
To reduce valuation allowance as a result of recovery in market
value of current portfolio.
```

Note that in Year 6, the amount of the realized loss recognized in the accounts was based on the actual cost of Security B ($100,000), not the carrying amount at the time of sale ($80,000) and that the **valuation allowance is adjusted only at the end of the accounting period.** It should also be observed that the valuation of the entire current portfolio on the basis of lower of cost or market results in the recognition of the unrealized gain on Security C in Year 5 which, in effect, defers the recognition of the losses relating to Securities A and B. The current versus noncurrent portfolio approaches taken in *FASB Statement No. 12* can also result in possible manipulative practices to avoid recognition of unrealized losses in the current portfolio. This can be achieved by transferring a security with a market value above cost from the noncurrent portfolio to the current portfolio.

Disclosure Requirements of FASB Statement No. 12 The following information with respect to marketable equity securities owned in the current portfolio shall be disclosed either in the financial statements or in notes accompanying the financial statements:

1 As of the date of each balance sheet presented, aggregate cost and market value, with identification as to which is the carrying amount.

2 As of the date of the latest balance sheet presented, the gross unrealized gains representing the excess of market value over cost for all marketable equity securities in the portfolio.

3 For each period for which an income statement is presented:
  a Net realized gain or loss included in the determination of net income.
  b The basis on which cost was determined in computing realized gain or loss (that is, average cost or other method used).

4 Financial statements should not be adjusted for realized gains or losses or for changes in market prices when such events occur after the date of the financial statements but prior to their issuance. However, significant net realized and net unrealized gains and losses arising after the date of the financial statements, but prior to their issuance, applicable to securities owned at the date of the most recent balance sheet should be disclosed.[12]

Presentation of cash and marketable securities in the balance sheet

Cash is the most liquid asset which a business owns, in the sense that it is most easily converted into other assets and services. This characteristic justifies its position as the first item in the current asset section of the balance sheet. There is seldom any reason to be concerned about the valuation of cash. There are few sources of possible loss except for theft, which cannot be anticipated. Loss due to bank failure has all but disappeared in recent years with the institution of the Federal Deposit Insurance Corporation. This agency of the United States government insures accounts with banks which are covered under provisions of its charter. Cash is, therefore, reported on the balance sheet at the value which represents its exchange value.

As stated earlier, banks often require that borrowers maintain **compensating balances** of cash on deposit as a condition for borrowing money. The net effect of such arrangements is to increase the effective interest rate on loans because the full amount of the loan is not available to the borrower. Compensating-balance agreements with banks should be disclosed in financial statements to give more information about the effective cost of borrowing and the relationship between business entities and banks.

[12] Ibid., pp. 7–8.

An investment in marketable securities ranks next to cash in liquidity and should be listed in the current asset section of the balance sheet immediately after cash. Marketable securities represent highly liquid assets, regardless of how long they have been held or how soon they may be sold. Whether marketable securities are reported at cost or at the lower of cost or market, disclosure of the current market value is required by generally accepted accounting principles.

The AICPA has expressed the opinion that U.S. government securities specifically designated as acceptable in payment of taxes may be offset against the liability for income taxes. This exceptional procedure may not be extended to other assets or liabilities. **APB Opinion No. 10** described this **rule of offset** as follows:

1 It is a general principle of accounting that the offsetting of assets and liabilities in the balance sheet is improper except where a right of setoff exists. Accordingly, the offset of cash or other assets against the tax liability or other amounts owing to governmental bodies is not acceptable except in the circumstances described in paragraph 3 below.

2 Most securities now issued by governments are not by their terms designed specifically for the payment of taxes and, accordingly, should not be deducted from taxes payable on the balance sheet.

3 The only exception to this general principle occurs when it is clear that a purchase of securities (acceptable for the payment of taxes) is in substance an advance payment of taxes that will be payable in the relatively near future, so that . . . the purchase is tantamount to the prepayment of taxes. This occurs at times, for example, as an accommodation to a local government and in some instances when governments issue securities that are specifically designated as acceptable for the payment of taxes of those governments.[13]

The presentation of cash and marketable securities in the balance sheet is illustrated below:

Current assets:

Cash, including $1,000,000 certificate of deposit (Note 1)		$21,100,000
Short-term corporate and U.S. government obligations, at cost which approximates market		9,000,000
Marketable equity securities, at cost (Note 2)	$12,000,000	
Less: Valuation allowance to reduce current equity securities to market value	1,500,000	10,500,000

Note 1: The company maintains lines of credit with a group of domestic banks for borrowing funds on a short-term and long-term basis. The company has agreed to maintain an average compensating balance of 10% of the unused lines of credit and 15% of the amounts borrowed. At December 31, Year 4, the aggregate compensating-balance requirement was approximately $11,250,000.

Note 2: The gross unrealized loss at December 31, Year 4, was $4,000,000 and the gross unrealized gain was $2,500,000. At February 15, Year 5, the gross unrealized loss was $3,200,000 and the gross unrealized gain was $2,950,000.

---

[13] APB Opinion No. 10, "Omnibus Opinion—1966," AICPA (New York: 1966), p. 147.

REVIEW QUESTIONS

1 What are the normal components of **cash?**

2 How would you classify the following items on a balance sheet?
   a Travel advances to employees
   b Cash deposited with a trustee for the repayment of bonds
   c Undeposited cash representing receipts of the prior day
   d Customer's check returned by the bank marked NSF
   e A nonreturnable deposit with a real estate broker to pay for an option on a tract of land
   f Deposit in foreign banks where exchangeability is limited
   g U.S. Treasury bills temporarily held until cash is needed to make payments on building under construction
   h A petty cash fund composed of the following:

Coin and currency	$110
Vouchers:	
Selling expenses	61
General expenses	29

3 What is **management's responsibility** with respect to cash? What techniques are used to aid in carrying out this responsibility?

4 a What is a system of **internal control?**
   b Differentiate between **administrative control** and **accounting control.**
   c Why is internal control over cash and marketable securities particularly important?

5 Collins Corporation has developed a reasonably effective system of internal control over cash transactions; however, the controller has decided she needs a petty cash fund to expedite the payment of small bills. The controller cannot decide whether she will use the regular cashier or the typist who has a desk near the cashier's window. Which would you recommend and why?

6 Parr Company has a change fund of $100. The cash sales tickets for May 25 total $2,049.60 and cash in the cash register, verified by count, totals $2,154.25. Prepare the journal entry necessary to record the day's sales.

7 Why are adjusting entries usually not made to reflect outstanding checks as liabilities or deposits in transit as cash on hand?

8 a What are three functions of the bank reconciliation?
   b What function does the reconciliation of cash receipts and cash payments serve?

9 How should a material **cash overdraft** be reported in the balance sheet? Explain.

10 Define **compensating cash balances** and state the reasons for disclosure of such balances in financial statements.

11 Why is management concerned with investing cash, which is only temporarily in excess of actual requirements, in marketable securities? What can be done to eliminate or minimize the risk of loss from temporary fluctuations in the market price of securities?

12 Can you justify a departure from the **cost principle** in accounting for marketable securities held as temporary investments?

13 What two questions relative to marketable equity securities held in the current portfolio did the FASB attempt to answer in **Statement No. 12?**

14 Define the following terms relating to the accounting for marketable equity securities:
   a Equity securities
   b Valuation allowance
   c Carrying amount
   d Realized gain or loss
   e Net unrealized gain or loss

15 Briefly state the accounting treatment of the valuation allowance to reduce marketable equity securities to market value. Include in your answer the treatment of realized gains and losses and changes in market value in subsequent periods.

16 What information with respect to marketable equity securities should be disclosed in the financial statements or in the notes accompanying the financial statements?

17 Under what circumstances would it be appropriate to offset U.S. government securities against income taxes payable?

EXERCISES

Ex. 6-1 The petty cash fund for Grant Company is $100. During March $15.00 was spent on entertainment, $18.10 was spent on office supplies expense, $26.50 was spent on postage expense, $20.00 was spent for merchandise, $16.45 was spent on miscellaneous items, and $3.95 remained on hand. What journal entry is required to replenish the petty cash fund at the end of the month?

Ex. 6-2 From the following data, **(a)** compute the cash balance in the accounting records before adjustments are recorded and **(b)** give the journal entry required to bring the accounts up to date:

Balance per bank statement	*$15,500*
Checks outstanding	*6,400*
Receipts recorded not yet deposited	*1,920*
Bank service charges not recorded in the accounts	*12*
Note collected by bank not recorded in the accounts (includes interest of $40)	*4,040*

Ex. 6-3 The following bank reconciliation was prepared for Zurn Company at June 30, Year 6:

Balance per bank statement		$ 8,308
Add: Deposit in transit	$ 1,690	
Check incorrectly charged to Zurn Company by bank	250	
Bank service charges	10	
NSF check from customer returned by bank	120	2,070
Subtotal		$10,378
Less: Proceeds of bank loan arranged on June 29, Year 6	$10,000	
Outstanding checks	2,940	
Error in recording check in payment of invoice	18	12,958
Balance per accounting records		$(2,580)

Compute the correct cash balance at June 30, Year 6, and prepare the journal entry necessary to adjust the Cash account to the correct balance. Interest on the bank loan is payable at maturity and all payments on invoices are debited to Accounts Payable.

Ex. 6-4 Prepare journal entries to record the following transactions relating to marketable securities:

June 11 Purchased $50,000 face amount $7\frac{1}{2}$% bonds issued by Lamar Company. Total purchase price was $52,175, which included accrued interest of $625 from April 11.

Oct. 11 Received semiannual interest on Lamar Company bonds, $1,875.

Dec. 11 Sold $20,000 face amount Lamar Company bonds for total consideration of $20,250, which included accrued interest of $250 from Oct. 11.

Dec. 31 Recorded accrued interest for 80 days on remaining Lamar Company bonds.

Ex. 6-5 Given below is a condensed version of the bank reconciliation prepared by the Edgewood Company on March 31, Year 1:

Balance per bank statement		$11,120
Add: Deposits in transit	$1,390	
Service charge	8	1,398
Subtotal		$12,518
Less: Outstanding checks		2,008
Balance in Cash account (before adjustment)		$10,510

Cash receipts and payments recorded in the accounts during the month of April are listed below:

Cash receipts	$29,400
Cash payments	26,950

On April 30, Year 1, checks outstanding amounted to $2,950 and deposits in transit amounted to $1,911. There was no service charge for April and no error was made either by the bank or by the company.

Prepare a four-column reconciliation of cash receipts and cash payments for the month of April. An analysis of outstanding checks and deposits in transit at the end of March and April, together with the cash receipts and cash payments recorded by the company, should be made to determine the cash receipts and cash payments recorded by the bank during April.

Ex. 6-6 Tarbet Company began investing idle cash in marketable equity securities in Year 3. The cost and market value of the securities held in its current portfolio at the end of its fiscal years were as follows:

End of Year	Cost	Market
3	$200,000	$210,000
4	310,000	260,000
5	280,000	220,000
6	400,000	425,000

Prepare journal entries at the end of each year to adjust the valuation allowance to reduce marketable equity securities to market value.

Ex. 6-7 In auditing the accounting records of the Hilltop Company for Year 10, you find the following account:

Marketable Securities—Kewanee Industries, Inc.

Purchased 200 shares @ 26¼	5,250	Dividend received	80
		Dividend received	80
		Proceeds on sale of 100 shares	2,940

You find that a commission of $106 on the purchase of the 200 shares was debited to the Other Income account. Prepare a correcting journal entry required at December 31, Year 10.

SHORT CASES FOR ANALYSIS AND DECISION

Case 6-1 The management of Sweetwater Company foresees a period of three to five years of reduced operations. During this period the management does not expect to replace any plant assets. Management presents the board of directors with a plan (1) to maintain the current ratio of dividends to net income at 60%, and (2) to invest all cash which accumulates in excess of normal operating needs in a diversified list of high-quality common stocks. Management also proposes that the stocks be carried in the balance sheet at current market value at the balance sheet date. Any change in market value from date of purchase or the most recent evaluation for financial statement purposes is to be reflected in the income statement.

Instructions
a What are the advantages of accounting for and reporting this investment holding in this manner?
b What objections might be made to this method of reporting the investment?
c Should this investment be reported as a current or a noncurrent asset? Why?

Case 6-2 Ellmore Brick Company is projecting an increased level of operations for the coming year, which will require an additional investment in inventory and accounts receivable. The minimum cash balance required is $50,000. After a detailed review of the prospects for the coming year, the following forecast of monthly cash balances is prepared (brackets indicate projected cash deficit):

January	$110,000	July	$395,000
February	50,000	August	450,000
March	(100,000)	September	80,000
April	(230,000)	October	(250,000)
May	(150,000)	November	(290,000)
June	150,000	December	(50,000)

Investment decisions are made and loans are negotiated on the fifteenth of each month in an amount equal to the projected cash surplus or deficiency for the month. Changes in the investment or loan position are made in multiples of $5,000.

Assume that excess cash can be invested in short-term U.S. government bonds bearing 5% interest and that borrowed funds cost $7\frac{1}{2}$%.

Instructions

a Prepare a schedule of the net cost (interest expense less interest revenue on temporary investments) of short-term borrowing to finance the operations for the year ended December 31. Carry computations to nearest dollar.

b If Ellmore Brick Company is to avoid short-term borrowing, how much long-term or permanent capital must be raised? Would you recommend that the company attempt to raise the capital or follow a policy of short-term borrowing? Why?

Case 6-3 Since the issuance of *FASB Statement No. 12,* Front & Loading Company has intended to follow the practice of valuing its temporary investments in marketable equity securities at the lower of cost or market. At December 31, Year 10, the account Marketable Equity Securities (Current Portfolio) had a balance of $260,000 and the account Valuation Allowance to Reduce Marketable Equity Securities to Market Value had a balance of $40,000. The valuation allowance account had been unchanged during Year 10; the balance of $40,000 was based on the following facts relating to the securities owned at December 31, Year 9:

Security	Cost	Market	Valuation allowance required
X Company common stock	$150,000	$120,000	$30,000
Y Company common stock	80,000	70,000	10,000
Z Company warrants to purchase common stock.	30,000	75,000	–0–
Total	$260,000	$265,000	$40,000

During Year 10 the Y Company common stock was sold for $65,000, the difference between the $65,000 and the cost of $80,000 being charged to Loss on Sale of Marketable Equity Securities. The market values of the securities remaining on December 31, Year 10, were X Company common stock, $90,000; Z Company warrants to purchase common stock, $40,000.

Instructions (Ignore income tax considerations.)

a What argument is there for the use of the lower-of-cost-or-market rule in valuing marketable securities?

b Did the Front & Loading Company properly apply the lower-of-cost-or-market rule at the end of Year 9?

c What adjusting journal entry should be made on December 31, Year 10, assuming that any error made in Year 9 was corrected as a prior period adjustment?

d Assume that the president does not wish to recognize any unrealized loss in the value of marketable equity securities at the end of Year 10. Instead, the president wants to transfer a block of K Company common stock from the noncurrent portfolio to the current portfolio. The stock of K Company is listed on the New York Stock Exchange with a market value of $200,000. K Company is a major customer and its stock was acquired many years ago at a cost of $100,000 to maintain good business relations between Front & Loading Company and K Company. Would you approve the president's proposal? Explain.

PROBLEMS

Group A

6A-1 On September 30, Year 5, the marketable securities owned by Escondido Company are shown below:

	Cost
6% U.S. Treasury notes, $400,000 face amount, due June 1, Year 8	*$394,000*
1,500 shares of $8 preferred stock of Tesla Power Company, $25 par value	*156,000*
Total	*$550,000*

Accrued interest receivable on the U.S. Treasury notes on this date was $7,956. This amount has been recorded in the Accrued Interest Receivable account. Transactions relating to marketable securities for the three months ended December 31, Year 5, are summarized below:

Oct. 15 Purchased $40,000 face amount, 7½% bonds of General Corporation at a price of 104, plus commission of $200 and accrued interest of $375 from September 1. Record interest acquired in the Accrued Interest Receivable account.

Oct. 30 Received quarterly dividend on Tesla Power Company $8 preferred stock.

Nov. 10 Sold entire holdings of Tesla Power Company $8 preferred stock for $152,600, net of commission.

Dec. 1 Received semiannual interest on the 6% U.S. Treasury notes, $12,000.

Dec. 31 Sold $200,000 face amount of 6% U.S. Treasury notes at 101, net of commission, plus accrued interest of $986.

Instructions
a Record the transactions in general journal form, including the adjusting entry to accrue interest on bonds owned at December 31, Year 5. Do not amortize premium or accumulate discount on bonds owned. Compute accrued interest (to the nearest dollar) on the U.S. Treasury notes for 30 days on the basis of a 365-day year.
b Assuming that the market value of the notes and bonds owned is $236,000, show three alternative ways that marketable securities might be presented in the balance sheet at December 31, Year 5.

6A-2 The bank statement for Pearblossom Corporation showed a balance of $70,694.88 on December 31, Year 9. In comparing the bank balance with the balance in the accounting records, the corporation's accountant discovered the following:

(1) Checks amounting to $18,830 had not cleared the bank.
(2) A check in payment of an account payable was recorded in the accounts for $857.20; the correct amount on the check was $875.20.
(3) A customer's check for $739.90 was returned marked NSF. No entry has been made on the accounting records to record this bad check.
(4) A deposit of $12,565.70 had not been recorded by the bank.
(5) The charge for printing checks was $5.95.

Instructions
a What is the balance in the accounting records before any of the foregoing corrections and adjustments are made?
b Prepare a bank reconciliation which shows the correct cash balance.
c Prepare a single journal entry to bring the accounting records up to date.

6A-3 Red Rover Mining Company was organized early in Year 2. During the next four years it completed the following transactions in the current portfolio of marketable equity securities:

Year 2: Purchased the following equity securities:

	Total Cost
Security A	$100,000
Security B	50,000
Security C	75,000

Year 3: Sold Security A for $140,000, net of brokerage commission and other charges.
Year 4: Purchased Security D for $80,000.
Year 5: Sold Security B for $37,500, net of brokerage commission and other charges. Purchased Security E at a total cost of $180,000.

The market values of the current portfolio at December 31 of each year were as follows:

	Year 2	Year 3	Year 4	Year 5
Security A	$125,000			
Security B	30,000	$ 45,000	$ 35,000	
Security C	50,000	90,000	70,000	$ 55,000
Security D			85,000	80,000
Security E				175,000
Totals	$205,000	$135,000	$190,000	$310,000

Instructions
a Prepare journal entries to record the transactions in marketable equity securities listed above for the four-year period, including appropriate adjustments to the valuation allowance account at the end of each year. Ignore income tax considerations.
b Show how the current portfolio of marketable equity securities would be presented in the balance sheet at the end of each of the four years. Supplementary disclosure pursuant to **FASB Statement No. 12** is not required.

6A-4 During the audit of the financial statements of Longwood, Inc., for the year ended November 30, Year 10, you find a new account titled "Miscellaneous

Date	Posting reference	Entries in Miscellaneous Assets account	
		Debit	**Credit**
(1) Compudata common stock			
Mar. 31 Purchased 500 shares	CD 5	$24,000	
July 31 Received cash dividend of $2 per share	CR 7		$ 1,000
July 31 Sold 100 shares @ 60 . . .	CR 7		6,000
Nov. 15 Pledged 100 shares as security for $4,000 bank loan payable Feb. 15, Year 11 .	CR 11		4,000
Nov. 30 Received 150 shares by donation from stockholder whose cost in Year 3 was $10 per share (Donated Capital was credited) . . .	JE 9	1,500	
(2) Standard Atomic common stock			
Mar. 31 Purchased 900 shares . .	CD 5	23,400	
June 30 Received dividend ($0.25 per share in cash and 1 share Standard Atomic preferred for each 5 shares common owned)	CR 6		225
(3) Standard Atomic preferred stock			
June 30 Received 180 shares as stock dividend on Standard Atomic common	MEMO		
July 31 Sold 80 shares @ 17	CR 7		1,360
(4) Interstate Airlines bonds (due November 30, Year 20, with interest at 6% payable May 31 and November 30)			
June 30 Purchased 25 $1,000 bonds @ 102	CD 8	25,625	
Nov. 30 Received interest due . . .	CR 12		750
Nov. 30 Sold 25 bonds @ 101 . . .	CR 12		25,250
(5) Other			
July 31 Sold 40 shares of Longwood, Inc., treasury stock @ 82 (purchased in Year 8 at $80 per share—carried at cost)	CR 7		3,280
Nov. 9 Paid rental charge on safe deposit box used for investments	CD 10	35	
Totals		$74,560	$41,865

Assets." Your examination reveals that in Year 10 Longwood, Inc., began investing surplus cash in marketable securities and the company's accountant entered all transactions related to such investments in this account. Information summarized from the Miscellaneous Assets account for Year 10 appears on page 244.

All security purchases include brokers' fees and sales are net of brokers' fees and transfer taxes when applicable. The fair market values (net of brokers' fees and transfer taxes) for each security as of the Year 10 date of each transaction and at the end of the fiscal year were as follows:

Security	3/31	6/30	7/31	11/15	11/30
Compudata common stock	48		60	50	40
Standard Atomic common stock	26	30			25
Standard Atomic preferred stock		16⅔	17		14
Interstate Airlines bonds		102			101
Longwood, Inc., common stock			82		80

Instructions
a Prepare a separate journal entry at November 30, Year 10, to correct the accounting treatment for each of the five securities entered in the Miscellaneous Assets account. Assume that $2,340 of the cost of Standard Atomic common should be allocated to the Standard Atomic preferred acquired on June 30, Year 10. Ignore income taxes in your solution. Each entry should be supported by appropriate computations.
b Prepare a summary of the current portfolio of marketable equity securities at November 30, Year 10 to determine whether a valuation allowance to reduce marketable securities to market value is necessary. If a valuation allowance is required, prepare the appropriate journal entry at November 30, Year 10.

6A-5 Palmdale, Inc., received the bank statement for the month of September shown below and on page 246.

PALMDALE, INC.
In Account with Valley Bank
Waco, Texas

Checks			Deposits	Date	Balance
				Sept. 1	3,658.75
310.00	35.48	130.00	820.00	Sept. 2	4,003.27
60.00	31.15	510.00	72.80	Sept. 5	3,474.92
70.00	515.00		361.00	Sept. 7	3,250.92
90.00			280.00	Sept. 8	3,440.92
13.30	62.50		510.00	Sept. 9	3,875.12
28.00			205.60	Sept. 12	4,052.72
650.00			180.14	Sept. 14	3,582.86
			345.00	Sept. 16	3,927.86
85.00			427.50	Sept. 19	4,270.36
24.10	125.06			Sept. 20	4,121.20
40.00	65.00		90.00	Sept. 21	4,106.20
162.40			360.00	Sept. 23	4,303.80

PALMDALE, INC.

In Account with Valley Bank

Waco, Texas

Checks			Deposits	Date	Balance
15.00			625.00	Sept. 26	4,913.80
355.00	270.00	225.00	130.25	Sept. 28	4,194.05
7.50s			280.50	Sept. 30	4,467.05

s = Service charge

The entries in the cash journals for the month of September are shown below:

<table>
<tr><td colspan="3" align="center">Cash Recipts Journal</td><td colspan="4" align="center">Cash Payments Journal</td></tr>
<tr><td colspan="2">Date</td><td>Cash
(debit)</td><td colspan="2">Date</td><td>Check
no.</td><td>Cash
(credit)</td></tr>
<tr><td>Sept</td><td>1</td><td>72.80</td><td>Sept</td><td>1</td><td>65</td><td>130.00</td></tr>
<tr><td></td><td>3</td><td>361.00</td><td></td><td>1</td><td>66</td><td>90.00</td></tr>
<tr><td></td><td>6</td><td>280.00</td><td></td><td>1</td><td>67</td><td>35.48</td></tr>
<tr><td></td><td>8</td><td>510.00</td><td></td><td>2</td><td>68</td><td>31.15</td></tr>
<tr><td></td><td>10</td><td>205.60</td><td></td><td>4–19</td><td>69–78</td><td>1,648.86</td></tr>
<tr><td></td><td>13</td><td>180.14</td><td></td><td>20</td><td>79</td><td>24.10</td></tr>
<tr><td></td><td>15</td><td>345.00</td><td></td><td>21</td><td>80</td><td>38.60</td></tr>
<tr><td></td><td>17</td><td>427.50</td><td></td><td>22</td><td>81</td><td>65.00</td></tr>
<tr><td></td><td>20</td><td>90.00</td><td></td><td>22</td><td>82</td><td>162.40</td></tr>
<tr><td></td><td>22</td><td>360.00</td><td></td><td>23</td><td>83</td><td>150.00</td></tr>
<tr><td></td><td>24</td><td>625.00</td><td></td><td>26</td><td>84</td><td>15.00</td></tr>
<tr><td></td><td>27</td><td>130.25</td><td></td><td>28</td><td>85</td><td>270.00</td></tr>
<tr><td></td><td>28</td><td>280.50</td><td></td><td>28</td><td>86</td><td>105.20</td></tr>
<tr><td></td><td>29</td><td>1,710.10</td><td></td><td>28</td><td>87</td><td>225.00</td></tr>
<tr><td></td><td>30</td><td>315.25</td><td></td><td>28</td><td>88</td><td>355.00</td></tr>
<tr><td></td><td></td><td>5,893.14</td><td></td><td>30</td><td>89</td><td>25.00</td></tr>
<tr><td></td><td></td><td></td><td></td><td>30</td><td>90</td><td>645.29</td></tr>
<tr><td></td><td></td><td></td><td></td><td>30</td><td>91</td><td>155.00</td></tr>
<tr><td></td><td></td><td></td><td></td><td></td><td></td><td>4,171.08</td></tr>
</table>

The cash balance in the depositor's records as of August 31 agreed with the balance per bank statement, although a deposit was in transit and two checks were outstanding.

Instructions

a Prepare a bank reconciliation statement as of September 30.

b Prepare the necessary journal entry to adjust the Cash account as of September 30.

6A-6 The following information was obtained in an audit of the cash account of Hermit Ridge Lodge as of December 31, Year 4. Assume that the CPA was satisfied as to the validity of the cash book, the bank statements, and the returned checks, except as noted.

(1) The company's bank reconciliation at November 30 is presented below:

Balance per bank statement		$ 19,400
Add: Deposit in transit		1,100
Subtotal		$ 20,500
Less: Outstanding checks:		
2540	$140	
1501	750	
1503	480	
1504	800	
1505	130	2,300
Balance per cash book		$ 18,200

(2) A summary of the bank statement for December, Year 4, follows:

Balance brought forward	$ 19,400
Deposits	148,700
Subtotal	$168,100
Charges	132,500
Balance, Dec. 31, Year 4	$ 35,600

(3) A summary of the cash book for December, Year 4, before adjustments, follows:

Balance brought forward	$ 18,200
Receipts	149,690
Subtotal	$167,890
Disbursements	124,885
Balance, Dec. 31, Year 4	$ 43,005

(4) Included with the canceled checks returned with the December bank statement were all the November 30 outstanding checks except nos. 2540 and 1504. The following facts were noted about selected checks returned with the bank statement:

Number	Date of check	Amount of check
1501	November 28	$75

This check was in payment of an invoice for $750 and was recorded in the cash book as $750.

1528	December 12	$800

This check replaced no. 1504 that was returned by the payee because it was mutilated. Check no. 1504 was not canceled in the accounting records.

	December 19	$200

This was a counter check drawn at the bank by the president of the company as a cash advance for travel expense. The president overlooked informing the accountant about the check. The president had cashed the check but postponed the trip until January.

	December 20	$300

This check had been stolen, presented for payment, and paid although it lacked any signature. A bank error.

1575	January 5	$10,000

This check was given to the payee on December 30 as a postdated check with the understanding that it would not be deposited until January 5. The check was not recorded in the accounts in December.

(5) Hermit Ridge Lodge discounted its own 60-day note for $9,000 with the bank on December 1. The discount rate was 6% per year. The company's accountant recorded $9,000 as a cash receipt, forgetting that the bank would deduct $90 as interest and would deposit only $8,910 to the company's account. Interest expense for December has not been recorded.

(6) The company's accountant enters customers' dishonored checks as a reduction of cash receipts. When the dishonored checks are redeposited they are recorded as a regular cash receipt. Two NSF checks for $180 and $220 were returned by the bank during December. The $180 check was redeposited but the $220 check was still on hand at December 31. Cancellations of checks are recorded by Hermit Ridge Lodge as a reduction of cash payments.

(7) December bank charges were $20. In addition a $10 service charge was made in December for the collection of a foreign draft in November. These charges were not recorded in the accounts.

(8) Check no. 2540 listed in the November outstanding checks was drawn three years previously. Since the payee cannot be located, the president of Hermit Ridge Lodge agreed to the CPA's suggestion that the check be written back into the accounts by a journal entry.

(9) Outstanding checks at December 31 totaled $4,000, excluding check nos. 2540 and 1504.

(10) Inquiry at the bank disclosed that the bank had recorded a deposit of $2,400 on January 2. The accountant had recorded this deposit in the accounting records on December 31 and then mailed the deposit to the bank.

Instructions

a Prepare a four-column reconciliation of the cash receipts and cash payments recorded on the bank statement and on the company's accounting records for the month of December. The reconciliation should agree with the cash figure that will appear in the company's balance sheet.

b Prepare a journal entry to bring the accounting records up to date.

Group B

6B-1 On February 1, Year 1, Crown Valley Development Company had cash in excess of its immediate needs. The management decided to invest this cash, and any other cash which appeared to be temporarily in excess of current needs, in short-term U.S. government securities. The following transactions occurred during the following fiscal year ending January 31, Year 2:

Year 1

Feb. 2 Purchased for $96,938, including accrued interest of $438, U.S. Treasury 5% bonds, due in two years, $100,000 face amount, with interest payable June 30 and December 31. Debit Accrued Interest Receivable for $438.

May 31 Sold for $49,792, including accrued interest of $1,042, one-half of the U.S. Treasury 5% bonds acquired February 2.

June 30 Received interest on U.S. Treasury 5% bonds, $1,250.

Aug. 1 Purchased 40 U.S. Treasury 6% $1,000 bonds, interest payable April 1 and October 1, at 102 plus accrued interest of $800 and a commission of $125. These bonds mature three years after the next interest date.

Oct. 1 Received interest on U.S. Treasury 6% bonds, $1,200.

Dec. 15 Sold for $48,201, including accrued interest of $1,151, the remainder of the U.S. Treasury 5% bonds acquired February 2.

Year 2

Jan. 16 Purchased $100,000 face amount U.S. Treasury 7% notes for a net price of $102,250. Interest is paid on these notes on January 16 and July 16.

Jan. 31 Adjusted the accounts to reflect interest accrued to the end of the fiscal year. The management decided that the premium on bonds and notes purchased will not be amortized. Interest on U.S. Treasury obligations is computed based on the exact number of days elapsed, using a 365-day year. Compute interest on each issue to the nearest dollar.

Instructions

a Record the above transactions in general journal form.

b The market quote for the U.S. Treasury 6% bonds and the U.S. Treasury 7% notes at the close on January 31 was 101½ and 104, respectively. Prepare a partial balance sheet showing all data for marketable securities. Assume that marketable securities are reported at cost and that market value is shown parenthetically.

6B-2 The bank reconciliation for Soledad Sand & Gravel Corporation at November 30, Year 3, included deposits in transit of $9,600 and outstanding checks of $12,000. The following additional information is available at December 31, Year 3:

	Per accounting records	Per bank statement
Deposits during December	$ 98,400	$ 84,700
Payments during December	111,200	116,000
Collection of note by bank, including $100 interest revenue		
not recorded in the accounts		8,100
Bank service charges (including $60 consulting fee)		80
Cash balance at Dec. 31	40,800	32,720

Instructions

a From the foregoing information, prepare a bank reconciliation arriving at corrected balances at December 31, Year 3.

b Prepare a single journal entry to bring the accounting records up to date at December 31, Year 3.

6B-3 The following information pertains to marketable equity securities in the current portfolio of Modern Plastics Corporation at December 31, Year 3:

	Cost	Market value
1,000 shares of M Company common	$ 50,000	$ 55,000
2,000 shares of N Company common	125,000	120,000
500 shares of P Company convertible preferred	60,000	62,000

The company was organized on March 4, Year 3, and did not establish a valuation allowance to reduce marketable securities to market at the end of Year 3 because the aggregate market value of the current portfolio exceeded aggregate cost.

During Year 4, the company completed the following transaction in equity securities carried in its current portfolio:

Feb. 10 Purchased 1,000 shares of Q Company common at a total cost of $32,000.

June 19 Sold 500 shares of P Company convertible preferred for $66,000, net of brokerage commission and other charges.

Sept. 5 Purchased 800 shares of R Company common at a total cost of $47,500.

Market values of the equity securities held in the current portfolio at December 31, Year 4, were as follows:

1,000 shares of M Company common	$ 60,000
2,000 shares of N Company common	110,000
1,000 shares of Q Company common	25,000
800 shares of R Company common	50,000
Total market value	$245,000

On May 1, Year 5, the 800 shares of R Company common were sold for a net consideration of $44,000. There were no other purchases or sales through December 31, Year 7. The market values of the equity securities held in the current portfolio at December 31 of each of the succeeding three years were as follows:

	Year 5	Year 6	Year 7
1,000 shares of M Company common	$ 52,000	$ 48,000	$ 65,000
2,000 shares of N Company common	90,000	120,000	125,000
1,000 shares of Q Company common	30,000	24,000	40,000
Totals	$172,000	$192,000	$230,000

Instructions

a Prepare journal entries to record transactions relating to marketable equity securities for the four years (Year 4 through Year 7), including appropriate entries (if any) to the valuation allowance account at the end of each year. Ignore income tax considerations.

b Indicate the balance sheet presentation of current marketable equity securities at the end of each year (Years 4 through 7).

6B-4 On June 1, Year 2, Via Verde Corporation adopted a petty cash fund procedure for paying small bills. Also on June 1, Year 2, the company made an initial investment of idle cash in marketable equity securities. The fiscal year ends on June 30. The operations of the fund for the last month of the fiscal year and the first month of the following fiscal year, and the purchase of marketable equity securities, are summarized below:

June 1 Petty cash fund was established by cashing a company check for $2,500 and delivering it to the petty cash cashier.

June 1 Purchased 1,000 shares of Data Processing Associates, Inc., common stock at 40½, plus a negotiated commission of $825, as a short-term investment.

June 19 A request for replenishment of the petty cash fund was received by the accounts payable department, supported by appropriate signed vouchers summarized as follows:

Selling expenses	$ 468
Administrative expenses	678
Factory overhead costs	383
Special tools	192
Telephone, telegraph, and postage	48
Miscellaneous expenses	308
Total	$2,077

June 20 A check for $2,077 was drawn payable to the petty cash cashier.

June 30 The company's independent certified public accountant counted the fund in connection with his year-end audit work and found the following:

Cash in petty cash fund		$1,010
Employees' checks with July dates (postdated checks).		180
Expense vouchers properly approved as follows:		
Selling expenses	$249	
Administrative expenses	387	
Factory overhead costs	89	
Office supplies	96	
Telephone, telegraph, and postage	56	
Miscellaneous expenses	428	1,305
Total		$2,495

The petty cash fund was not replenished at June 30, Year 2.

June 30 The certified public accountant also noted that the closing price of the Data Processing Associates, Inc., stock on June 30 was $35 per share.

July 15 The employees' checks which were held in the petty cash fund at June 30 were cashed and the proceeds were held in the petty cash fund.

July 31 A request for replenishment of the petty cash fund was received by the accounts payable department and a check was drawn to restore the fund to its original balance of $2,500. The support vouchers for July expenditures are summarized on page 252.

Selling expenses	$ 149
Administrative expenses	164
Factory overhead costs	349
Telephone, telegraph, and postage	35
Miscellaneous expenses	338
Total	$1,035

Instructions

a Record the above transactions in general journal form, including any adjustment required at the end of the fiscal year, June 30, Year 2. Ignore any income tax effects.

b Evaluate the apparent policy of Via Verde Corporation in using the petty cash fund.

6B-5 The following data pertaining to the cash transactions and bank account of Sunrise Summit Company for September, Year 4, are available to you:

(1) Cash balance per accounting records	$18,104.50
(2) Cash balance per bank statement	24,090.80
(3) Bank charges for previous month's service	9.00
(4) Debit memo for checkbook delivered by the bank; the charge was not recorded in the accounting records	5.00
(5) Deposit of Sept. 30 not recorded by bank until Oct. 1	3,870.00
(6) Outstanding checks	8,128.30
(7) Proceeds of a bank loan on Sept. 30 not recorded in ledger (interest payable at maturity)	2,970.00
(8) Proceeds from customer's note, principal amount $800, collected by the bank; collection fee of $3 charged by the bank	810.00
(9) Check no. 1086 to a supplier had been entered in the accounts as $1,879.10; it was deducted from the bank statement in the correct amount of	1,789.10
(10) A stolen check lacking an authorized signature had been deducted from the account by the bank in error	867.50
(11) A customer's check was returned by the bank marked NSF, indicating that the customer's balance was not adequate to cover the check; no entry has been made to record the returned check	1,260.50

Instructions

a Prepare a reconciliation of the cash balances to the correct cash balance at September 30, Year 4.

b Prepare the journal entry required to adjust the accounting records at September 30, Year 4.

6B-6 In connection with an audit of cash of Holiday Hill Ski Resort as of December 31, Year 15, the following information has been obtained:

(1) Balance per bank statement:

Nov. 30	$ 195,700
Dec. 31	313,674

(2) Balance per accounting records:

Nov. 30 . . . . $ 164,826

Dec. 31 287,598

(3) Receipts for the month of December:

Per bank $1,670,450

Per accounting records 2,751,445

(4) Outstanding checks:

Nov. 30 . . . . $ 63,524

Dec. 31 75,046

(5) Dishonored checks are recorded as a reduction of cash receipts. Dishonored checks which are later redeposited are then recorded as a regular cash receipt. Dishonored checks returned by the bank and recorded by Holiday amounted to $6,250 during the month of December; according to the accounting records, $5,000 of dishonored checks were redeposited. Dishonored checks recorded on the bank statement but not in the accounts until the following months amounted to $250 at November 30 and $2,300 at December 31.

(6) On December 31, a $2,323 check on which a stop-payment order was in force was charged to the Holiday account by the bank in error.

(7) Proceeds of a note from Capp Company, collected by the bank on December 30, were not entered in the accounts.

Principal amount of note $2,000

Interest, $20, less collection charge of $5 15

Net proceeds $2,015

(8) The company has pledged its accounts receivable with the bank under an agreement whereby the bank lends the company 80% on the pledged accounts receivable. Accounting for and collection of the accounts are performed by the company, and adjustments of the loan are made from daily sales reports and daily cash deposits.

The bank credits the Holiday account and increases the amount of the loan for 80% of the reported sales. The loan agreement states specifically that the sales report must be accepted by the bank before Holiday is credited. Sales reports are forwarded by Holiday to the bank on the first day following the date of sales. The bank allocates 80% of each deposit to the payment of the loan and 20% to Holiday's account. Thus, only 80% of each day's sales and 20% of each collection deposit are entered on the bank statement.

The accountant for Holiday records the pledge of new accounts receivable (80% of sales) as a debit to cash and a credit to the bank loan as of the date of sales. Of the collections on accounts receivable, 100% is recorded as a cash receipt; 80% of the collections is recorded in the cash payments journal as a payment on the loan. In connection with the agreement, the following facts were determined:

(a) Included in the deposits in transit is cash from the pledged accounts receivable. Sales were $40,500 on November 30 and $42,250 on December 31. The balance of the deposit in transit at December 31 was made up from collections of $32,110, which were entered in the accounts in the manner indicated above.

(b) Collections on accounts receivable deposited in December other than deposits in transit totaled $1,320,000.

(c) Sales for December totaled $1,600,000.

(9) Cash receipts from other sources which were deposited intact during December totaled $120,835.

(10) Interest on the bank loan for the month of December charged by the bank but not recorded in the accounts amounted to $6,140.

Instructions

a Prepare a four-column reconciliation of beginning and ending cash balances, receipts, and disbursements for December. The first half of the reconciliation should begin with balances per bank statement and proceed to the correct cash balances; the lower half of the reconciliation should begin with balances per accounting records and should also proceed to the correct cash balances.

b Prepare adjusting journal entries as required to correct the Cash account at December 31.

CHAPTER 7

RECEIVABLES

The term *receivables* includes a variety of claims that will generally result in the future inflow of cash. Receivables come into existence as a result of transactions such as sale of goods or services, loans made, subscriptions obtained from investors for stocks or bonds, claims for tax refunds, claims for damages to property, and amounts due from leasing properties to others.

Receivables from customers frequently represent a substantial part of a company's liquid resources. Poor screening of applicants for credit or an inefficient collection policy can result in large losses. Consequently, the accounting methods and internal controls for receivables are important factors in achieving profitable operations.

Valuation of receivables

For most receivables the amount of money to be received and the due date can be reasonably estimated. The accountant is thus faced with a relatively certain future inflow of cash, and the problem is to determine the value of this inflow.

A number of factors must be considered in valuing prospective cash inflow. One factor is the probability that a receivable will actually be collected. For any single receivable, the probability of collection might be difficult to establish; however, for a large group of receivables a reasonably accurate estimate of doubtful accounts is usually possible.

The uncertainty of collectibility of receivables has been cited by the

FASB as an example of a *loss contingency*, because a future event (inability to collect) confirming the loss is *probable* and the amount of the loss can be *reasonably estimated*.[1] If the estimate of possible uncollectible accounts can be made within a range but no single amount appears to be a better estimate than any other amount within the range, the Board recommended that the minimum amount in the range be accrued as a contingency loss.[2] In the measurement of the amount of loss or the range of possible loss, the Board stated:

> Whether the amount of loss can be reasonably estimated . . . will normally depend on, among other things, the experience of the enterprise, information about the ability of individual debtors to pay, and appraisal of the receivables in light of the current economic environment. In the case of an enterprise that has no experience of its own, reference to the experience of other enterprises in the same business may be appropriate. Inability to make a reasonable estimate of the amount of loss from uncollectible receivables . . . precludes accrual and may, if there is significant uncertainty as to collection, suggest that the installment method, the cost recovery method, or some other method of revenue recognition be used. . . .[3]

Another factor to be considered in the valuation of receivables is the length of time until collection. As stated in Chapter 5, a sum of money due at some future time is not worth as much as the same sum due immediately. The longer the time to maturity, the greater the difference between the *maturity value* and the *present value* of a receivable. When the time to maturity is long, most contracts between debtors and creditors call for the payment of interest to compensate for the time value of money, and the present value of such a contract may correspond to its face amount. The present value of any non-interest-bearing receivable is less than the amount that will be received at the due date. If the lapse of time to maturity is short, this difference is usually ignored. For example, an ordinary 30-day unsecured account is almost always recorded at its face amount. The difference between present value and face amount of receivables should always be considered because this difference may be significant.

Receivables from sale of goods and services

The most common receivables are those that result from revenue-producing activities, such as the sale of goods and services. The unsecured *open account*, or *trade account*, is the most important of these. Contracts governing open accounts are typically informal and are supported by such documents as sales orders, specifications, invoices, and delivery contracts. Most open accounts are not interest bearing. In the retail trade, however, the addition of an interest or service charge to re-

---

[1] *FASB Statement No. 5,* "Accounting for Contingencies," FASB (Stamford: 1975), p. 4.
[2] *FASB Interpretation No. 14,* "Reasonable Estimation of the Amount of a Loss (an interpretation of *FASB Statement No. 5*)," FASB (Stamford: 1976), p. 2.
[3] *FASB Statement No. 5,* pp. 11–12.

volving charge accounts or installment receivables is a common practice. Manufacturers and wholesalers use cash discounts as a form of interest charge if payment is made after the discount period.

Trade receivables are also represented by various commercial credit instruments such as promissory notes, time bills of exchange, and conditional sales contracts. Such contracts have a stronger legal status than open accounts, and because the terms are clearly specified in writing, the holder finds it somewhat easier to borrow against them.

A customer who requests an extension of time on an open account is often asked to sign a note so that the holder can discount the note and receive cash immediately. Most notes and commercial credit instruments bear interest because they involve credit for longer periods of time. Amounts due from employees and owners of a business may be included among trade receivables if they result from sales of goods and services and are subject to the usual credit terms.

Receivables from miscellaneous sources

Some receivables result from transactions not directly related to the sale of goods and services. For example, a short-term advance to an affiliated company, to a subcontractor, or to a customer, is in essence a lending transaction made in anticipation of future benefits. A claim against an insurance company and a claim based on a legal suit for damages are other examples of miscellaneous receivables. Prospective refunds of amounts previously paid, such as a claim for refund of income taxes, represent receivables whenever the outcome of the claim is reasonably certain. Sale of stocks and bonds to subscribers and sales of plant and equipment items also represent sources of miscellaneous receivables. Any type of receivable which is sufficiently material in amount should be listed separately in the balance sheet. If miscellaneous receivables will probably be collected within one year, they should be classified as current assets; long-term receivables are reported as Investments or as Other Assets.

Accruals of interest, dividends, rent, and royalties are current receivables that represent a prospective inflow of cash. Rent and interest receivable accrue as a function of time. Dividends are usually not recognized as a receivable prior to the ex-dividend date. Royalties usually accrue as a function of the manufacture or sale of products or the extraction of natural resources.

Occasionally a receivable arises out of a debit balance in accounts payable when, for one reason or another, overpayment has been made to a creditor. If the buyer expects a cash refund the amount involved is clearly a receivable. The rule against offsetting assets and liabilities requires that any sizable debit balance be treated as a receivable rather than as an offset against other accounts payable. Similarly, a large credit balance in customers' accounts should be reported as a current liability. An advance payment on a purchase contract is properly reported as a prepayment for goods rather than as a receivable.

Receivables arising from certain types of leasing transactions are discussed in Chapter 16.

CUSTOMERS' ACCOUNTS

A large portion of retail trade in the United States involves credit in some form; at the wholesale and manufacturing level almost all business is transacted on a credit basis. Terms on ordinary open accounts range from the 10 days typically allowed in taking cash discounts to as long as six months or a year in some cases.

Accounting System and Internal Control Companies having a large volume of credit transactions usually adapt their recording procedures to the use of accounting machines or computers. A relatively simple machine system will enable the operator to record the credit sale, post to the controlling account, and post to subsidiary ledger accounts in a single operation. Modern electronic data-processing equipment makes possible a system that is highly automated. All information pertaining to a credit sale may be recorded on cards, tapes, or memory drums. The computer prepares a sales journal, posts to the controlling account and to customers' ledger accounts, prepares monthly statements, and issues a list of receivables at required intervals.

A procedure known as *cycle billing* eases the receivable systems problem of large department stores and public utilities when accounts with 100,000 or more customers are found. Accounts receivable subsidiary ledgers are divided into a number of groups on the basis of geographical location, type of customer, or alphabetically, with each group having its own subcontrol account. The customers in each subcontrol group are then billed at different times during the month. This procedure has the advantage of spreading the work of preparing customer statements more evenly through the month and assuring a more uniform cash flow from operations.

It is possible to reduce detailed record keeping by eliminating subsidiary receivable ledgers altogether. Invoices for credit sales are first sorted by subcontrol groups and the total amount is entered directly in the controlling account. The individual invoices are then filed according to customer. At the end of the month or cycle billing period, the amount due from each customer is summarized on a statement, the duplicate copy of which becomes the subsidiary ledger record for that customer. Invoices are reproduced (to provide a record for the company) and are then mailed to each customer along with the statement of his or her account. At the billing date, customers' statements can be reconciled with the amount shown by the appropriate subcontrol account to disclose any discrepancies.

Effective internal control over the sale of goods and related cash collections is an integral part of the system for handling trade accounts receivable. The responsibility for recording sales and collections in customers' accounts should not be assigned to individuals who handle cash receipts or who prepare bank deposit slips and bank reconciliations. Without such segregation of duties, a dishonest employee could abstract cash collections from customers and conceal the theft by recording the collection as a debit to Sales Returns and Allowances, or by writing off the receivable against the Allowance for Doubtful Accounts.

Recognition of trade receivables

Two important questions faced by accountants in recording trade receivables are:

1 At what point in the stream of business activities between a company and its customer does a trade account receivable warrant recognition in the accounts as a valid asset?

2 How should the amount of trade accounts receivable be measured so that this asset and also the related revenue and doubtful accounts expense will be properly stated?

Trade accounts receivable are generally recorded in the accounting records when the sale is made and title to the goods has passed. Receivables for services should be recognized only as services are performed. Receivables should not be recorded when a customer's order is received, or when goods are produced. Shipments on consignment are not sales since title to the goods does not pass until sales agents (consignees) actually sell the consigned goods. Receivables should be recognized for work completed on long-term construction contracts or on cost-plus-fixed-fee contracts.[4]

When it is determined that revenue has been earned and recognition of the claim against a customer is warranted, the question of measuring the amount of the receivable (and the revenue) still remains. For example, assume that a parcel of land is sold by a land developer for $5,000. The buyer can pay $5,000 in cash or pay $1,000 down and $1,100 at the end of each year for five years. If the sale is made on the deferred payment plan, should the receivable be reported at $4,000 ($5,000 cash price less the $1,000 down payment) or at $5,500, the face amount of the five remaining payments of $1,100 each? Is the revenue realized in the current year $5,000, $6,500, or some other amount? One of the objectives of this chapter is to explore these and similar questions.

[4] Accounting problems relating to consignment sales are covered in *Modern Advanced Accounting* of this series; procedures relating to long-term construction contracts are covered in Chapter 9.

Valuation of customers' accounts

The valuation assigned to accounts receivable is directly linked with the amount of revenue ultimately realized. There is no way of measuring revenue independently of the value of the claims resulting from revenue transactions.

The problem of valuation of accounts receivable centers on three issues: (1) the amount due, (2) the time of collection, and (3) the estimate of the probability that the receivable will be collected. A number of problems in these three areas are discussed in the following sections.

Determining the amount due

Trade Discounts In some industries it is customary to bill customers a gross price subject to one or more trade discounts. The gross price is usually the suggested price for resale and the trade discount represents the difference between gross or list price and the price to the buyer before cash discounts. The use of a fixed list price and varying trade discounts enables the seller to change prices, or to grant special discounts to large buyers, without reprinting catalogs or price lists. For accounting purposes these discounts should be recognized for what they are: a convenient means of pricing. The amount that a given customer will pay is the net price after trade discount, and this is the amount at which the receivable and the related revenue should be recorded.

Cash (or Sales) Discounts Cash discounts are widely used to establish a *cash* price when payment is received shortly after the delivery of the goods, as distinct from a higher *time payment* price. For example, if an invoice for $10,000 provides for terms of 2/10, n/30, the customer company is faced with two alternatives. It may pay $9,800 within 10 days or wait the full 30 days and pay $10,000. The differential of $200 represents an effective interest rate of 36.7% for the use of the $9,800 for the extra 20-day period, and thus offers a strong incentive for payment within the 10-day period.[5]

A theoretical valuation of receivables subject to cash discounts should allow for the probability that discounts will be taken. In the case cited above, for example, if the probability is high that the customer company will take the discount, the receivable is ultimately worth only $9,800; if it is expected that the customer will pay the face amount, the receivable will be worth $10,000.

In dealing with a large number of receivables, past experience is usually a good guide in estimating customer reaction to proffered discounts. In view of the generous saving inherent in the cash price, the as-

---

[5] Since there are eighteen 20-day periods in one year, the annualized rate earned can be computed as follows: ($200 × 18) ÷ $9,800, or 36.7%.

sumption that most customers will take the discount is reasonably justified.

Three alternative methods by which the seller may account for cash discounts are briefly described below:

Method A Accounts Receivable and Sales are recorded at gross, and discounts taken by customers are reported as debits to Sales Discounts. No entry is made at the end of the period to anticipate discounts that will probably be taken on outstanding accounts receivable. This method is simple and is widely used.

Method B Same procedure as in method A, except that an adjusting entry is also made at the end of the accounting period to accrue discounts that will probably be taken on outstanding accounts receivable. Sales Discounts is debited and Allowance for Sales Discounts is credited for the potential discounts on accounts receivable at the end of the period. The Allowance for Sales Discounts is deducted from Accounts Receivable in the balance sheet as a step in valuing the receivables at estimated net realizable value.

Method C Accounts Receivable are recorded at gross, Sales are recorded net of estimated discounts and the Allowance for Sales Discounts is credited at the time of sale and debited as discounts are taken or as discounts expire. In the latter case, Sales Discounts Not Taken would be credited and reported in the income statement as a revenue item.

Using method A, accounts receivable and net income will be overstated by the amount of estimated sales discounts not accrued. The overstatements inherent in method A do not exist in methods B and C. Both methods B and C yield identical net income amounts and are consistent with the objective of reporting accounts receivable and revenue at *net realizable amounts* in the financial statements. However, it should be pointed out that the anticipation of sales discounts is not allowed for income tax purposes. Perhaps for this reason, the anticipation of discounts is not often encountered in practice.

Credit Card Fees and Other Collection Expenses The fees charged to businesses by credit card companies on sales made to customers using credit cards represent a combination of cash discount, doubtful accounts expense, collection fees, and other costs. Credit card fees generally range from 3 to 7% of sales price. Since there is no uncertainty whether the fees will be charged, the sound accounting procedure is to accrue fees as soon as sales to credit card customers are recognized as revenue. Receivables from the credit card company are recorded net of the fees, an expense account is debited for the amount of the credit card fees, and the Sales account is credited by an amount equal to the retail price of goods or services sold. A less satisfactory procedure is to record both the receivable and sales net of the credit card fees. This procedure offsets material costs of doing business against revenue and may distort income statement statistics.

Valuation of receivables, other than those arising from credit card customers, should also take into account expected collection expenses, as illustrated below for a publicly owned corporation:

Accounts receivable:	
Customers' installment accounts, substantially all of which are due	
within one year	$58,216,135
Other	926,889
Total face amount of receivables	$59,143,024
Less: Allowance for returns, losses in collection, and **collection**	
expenses	13,563,641
Total net accounts receivable	$45,579,383

Sales Returns and Allowances The value assigned to accounts receivable should also recognize the probability that some customers will return goods that are unsatisfactory or will make other claims requiring reduction in the amount due. Potential sales returns and allowances reduce the amount that will ultimately be collected from customers and thus reduce the net realizable value of accounts receivable. If the amounts are material, periodic income measurement will be improved by an adjustment for estimated returns and allowances.

To illustrate, assume that experience shows that sales returns will average 5% of accounts receivable as of the end of any period and that an average of 60% of the original selling price is ultimately realized from the returned goods, after allowing for the cost of restoring the goods to salable condition. If gross receivables at the end of the period amount to $100,000, the appropriate adjusting entry would be as shown below:

Inventory—Anticipated Sales Returns (net realizable value) ...	3,000	
Sales Returns (contra Sales)	2,000	
Allowance for Sales Returns (contra A/R)		5,000
To record anticipated sales returns, net of the estimated net realizable value of returned goods.		

The effect of this entry is to reduce current assets and net sales by $2,000—the difference between the original sale price and the estimated net realizable value of anticipated sales returns. This adjusting entry can be reversed on the first day of the new period; then, as sales returns are made by customers, the normal entry of debiting Sales Returns and Allowances and crediting Accounts Receivable can be made.

Since the issuance of **Statement of Position 75-1** by the Accounting Standards Division of the AICPA in 1975, the accrual of sales returns has been widely used in industries experiencing material amounts of returns.[6] The anticipation of sales returns (as in the case previously discussed of anticipating sales discounts) is not allowed for income tax purposes.

Freight Allowances Occasionally goods are sold on terms "F.O.B. destination" with the understanding that the customer will pay the transportation charges and then deduct that amount from the remittance. In such instances, accounts receivable should be valued at the net amount to be collected. The easiest way to deal with this problem is to record the sale net of the transportation charge. If it is difficult or inconvenient to estimate the actual freight charges that will be incurred, it may be preferable to record the receivable at the gross amount and to set up an estimated allowance for freight. This allowance account is deducted from accounts receivable and the offsetting debit to Freight Paid by Customers may be deducted from sales or reported as a selling expense.

Sales and Excise Taxes Many governmental units impose sales and excise taxes on particular products or on the sales transaction itself. Usually the seller is responsible for the remittance of these taxes to the government. In theory an excise tax imposed on the manufacture of a product is a part of the cost of production, while an excise tax on the sale of the product is imposed upon the buyer of the goods and collected by the seller.

If sales and excise taxes are collected as separately disclosed additions to the selling price, they should not be confused with revenue but should be credited to a liability account. Whether this is done at the time of each sale or as an adjustment at the end of the period is a matter of accounting convenience.[7] It is generally preferable to record the tax liability at the time of sale. For example, if a day's sales amount to $8,000

---

[6]*Statement of Position 75-1*, "Revenue Recognition when Right of Return Exists," AICPA (New York: 1975), p. 5. See also discussion on page 99 in Chapter 3.

[7] Companies account for sales and excise taxes in a variety of ways: Some do not report such taxes either in sales or in expenses; others include such taxes in gross sales then deduct them in arriving at net sales; still other companies report sales and excise taxes either as part of cost of sales or as operating expenses. The amounts of excise taxes can be staggering: For example, a few years ago American Distilling Co. reported gross sales of $145 million less excise taxes of $110 million, leaving net sales of only $35 million; Philip Morris, Incorporated, reported operating revenues of $1.5 billion and federal and foreign excise taxes of $519 million, which were included under cost of sales.

and are subject to a 5% sales tax, the sales tax payable will be $400, and the journal entry to record sales would be:

Accounts Receivable (or Cash)	8,400	
Sales Tax Payable		400
Sales		8,000
To record sales and sales tax liability.		

Container Deposits Customers may be charged for deposits on containers, with the understanding that the deposit will be refunded when the container is returned. If the container deposit is collected in cash, the only problem is the correct accounting for the refund obligation. When the container is returned, the liability will be canceled by the refund of the deposit. If the container is not returned, the liability no longer exists and the difference between the amount of the deposit and the cost of the containers not returned represents a gain or loss which should be combined with the account reporting the depreciation on containers. When no time limit is set for the return, an estimate should be made of the number of containers that will not be returned, and adjustments should be made periodically on the basis of the company's experience.

In some cases, the container fee is charged to customers' accounts. This creates an uncertainty with respect to the amount that will actually be collected. Until the uncertainty is resolved, accounts receivable should show as a separate item the amount charged to the customer for containers, and a liability should be established for the refund obligation.

Time of collection and valuation of receivables

Mention has previously been made of the need to consider the length of the collection period and the need to assign a present value to receivables. The procedure is particularly significant when the collection period is long and interest is not charged to customers. For example, if a receivable of $5,500 is expected to be collected one year hence and the prevailing interest rate is 10%, the receivable and sales should be recorded at $5,000 ($5,500 ÷ 1.10) and interest revenue of $500 should be recognized during the period the receivable is outstanding.

Estimating probability of collection

Thus far we have considered the problem of determining the amount due and the time of collection under the terms of a credit sale. A third major valuation problem is to evaluate the probability that customers will be willing and able to pay their accounts. Since a business does not make a credit sale unless ultimate collection is reasonably assured, the probability of loss with respect to any given sale is presumably low. Even the best efforts of a capable credit department, however, cannot eliminate all uncollectible accounts. Furthermore, the managerial objective is not to minimize this expense but to maximize net income. Too stringent a credit policy may cause loss of sales which more than offsets the reduction in the doubtful accounts expense.

Receivables that will never be collected have a zero present value, and the corresponding revenue will not be realized. The accountant's objective in attempting to anticipate doubtful accounts expense, therefore, is to prevent an overstatement of assets and revenue in the period in which sales are made.

In the balance sheet, the estimate of doubtful accounts is carried as a credit balance in a valuation account titled Allowance for Doubtful Accounts or Allowance for Uncollectible Accounts. A separate valuation account is used because it is not known which specific accounts will prove uncollectible, and the Accounts Receivable controlling account should agree with the subsidiary ledger detail. The allowance account is deducted from gross receivables to arrive at the net realizable value of the claims against customers. Under no circumstances should the Allowance for Doubtful Accounts, or any asset valuation account, be shown among liabilities or elsewhere on the credit side of the balance sheet.[8]

The doubtful accounts expense can be classified several ways on the income statement. Logically, doubtful accounts expense should be classified as an offset against gross sales, on the grounds that it represents revenue that will not be collected. In practice, doubtful accounts expense usually appears among operating expenses rather than as an offset against sales. Finally, some consider doubtful accounts expense as a financial management item and report it as "other expense." Since each of these reporting practices produces the same net income, the issue is not a major one.

Two kinds of evidence are used in making estimates of doubtful accounts expense: (1) the average relationship between sales and uncollectible accounts in past years and (2) an analysis of the quality and age of outstanding receivables at the end of an accounting period.

Estimate of Doubtful Accounts Expense Based on Sales The average percentage of credit sales not collected in past periods is a logical basis for estimating the portion of current credit sales that will prove uncollectible. This approach, often referred to as the *income statement approach,* is simple to apply and makes possible an estimate of doubtful accounts expense as soon as credit sales are recorded. It results in a logical matching of costs and revenue, and is especially appropriate in preparing interim reports. For example, if sales for the first quarter of the

[8] *APB Opinion No. 12,* "Omnibus Opinion—1967" AICPA (New York: 1967), p. 188.

current year are $250,000 and doubtful accounts expense is estimated at 2% of sales, the following entry would be required:

Doubtful Accounts Expense *5,000*
    Allowance for Doubtful Accounts *5,000*
To record estimated doubtful accounts expense at 2% of sales for
first quarter of year.

If the ratio of cash sales to credit sales is relatively constant, estimating doubtful accounts expense as a percentage of **total sales** may produce reasonably accurate results. Strictly speaking, however, the estimate of doubtful accounts expense should be based on **credit sales** only. The estimate may be further refined by analyzing the experience for different classes of customers or in different geographical locations, if the necessary information is available.

Applying the appropriate percentage to the credit sales for any period provides an estimate of the sales of that period that will not be collected. The degree of error in the estimate cannot be determined until the record of collection experience is in. It is useful, therefore, to make periodic tests to determine the adequacy of the provision for doubtful accounts in the light of actual experience and business conditions.

Estimate of Doubtful Accounts Expense Based on Receivables A good way to test the adequacy of the allowance for doubtful accounts and to recognize the current charge against revenue is to make an analysis of accounts by age group and probability of collection. This procedure is known as the **balance sheet approach** to measuring doubtful accounts expense. Generally a strong correlation exists between the length of time an account is past due and its collectibility. A schedule classifying the balances of all accounts receivable according to whether the amounts are not yet due, or past due by varying lengths of time, is known as an **aging of accounts receivable.**

The number of different age classes to be used depends on company experience and the terms of sale. An estimate of the average collection experience for each age class provides a basis for estimating the portion of outstanding accounts receivable that may be uncollectible.

The following summary of an accounts receivable aging for Midwest Grain Company is illustrative:

MIDWEST GRAIN COMPANY
Aging of Accounts Receivable
June 30, 19___

Classification by due date	Balances in each category (summarized from analysis of individual accounts)	Estimated uncollectibles, %	Estimated doubtful accounts
Not yet due	$2,400,000 (75.0%)	1	$24,000
Under 30 days past due	416,000 (13.0%)	3	12,480
30–60 days past due	208,000 (6.5%)	5	10,400
61–120 days past due	96,000 (3.0%)	10	9,600
121–180 days past due	48,000 (1.5%)	30	14,400
Over 180 days past due	32,000 (1.0%)	Individual analysis	25,000
Totals	$3,200,000 (100.0%)		$95,880

If an aging of receivables is used as a basis for estimating doubtful accounts expense, the current provision will be an amount sufficient to bring the Allowance for Doubtful Accounts up to the amount indicated by the aging analysis. For example, if the balance in the Allowance for Doubtful Accounts for Midwest Grain Company at June 30 is $80,000 after interim provisions and write-offs, the analysis above calls for the following entry to bring the allowance account to the required $95,880:

```
Doubtful Accounts Expense  . . . . . . . . . . . . . . . . . . .  15,880
     Allowance for Doubtful Accounts  . . . . . . . . . . . . .          15,880
To adjust allowance to required balance of $95,880.
```

A simpler method sometimes followed is to increase the allowance *to a given percentage* of receivables or to increase the allowance *by a given percentage* of receivables. These latter procedures are not recommended; the results they produce are only rough approximations.

In the process of aging the accounts receivable, management should evaluate current financial statements of major customers in order to make a better assessment of the probability of collection. The credit department in many companies is assigned responsibility for a continuing analysis of the financial statements of customers and prospective customers so that it may prevent credit sales to customers who represent excessive risk of nonpayment.

Estimated uncollectibles and income measurement

It is most unlikely that estimated uncollectibles will agree with actual write-offs applicable to each year's revenue. So long as there is a reasonably close correlation between the annual estimate and actual experience, minor discrepancies year by year may be ignored.

A major adjustment to reduce or increase the Allowance for Doubtful Accounts may involve receivables originating in prior periods. Such adjustments should be made to doubtful accounts expense for the current period or listed separately in *computing income before extraordinary items;* they should not be treated as prior period adjustments, as extraordinary items, or as changes in *accounting principle* (discussed in greater detail in Chapter 23).

In rare situations, an unusual and infrequent event may take place, such as the destruction of a customer's business by a major earthquake, which results in a material write-off of accounts receivable. In such a situation, the effect of the write-off should be included in the computation of the extraordinary item if the write-off was a direct result of the earthquake. However, any portion of the write-off which would have resulted from a valuation of accounts receivable on a going-concern basis should not be included in the determination of the extraordinary item.[9]

A major adjustment to the allowance for doubtful accounts or a revision of the method used to compute doubtful accounts expense is viewed as a *change in accounting estimate* in *APB Opinion No. 20,* which states:

> Future events and their effects cannot be perceived with certainty; estimating, therefore, requires the exercise of judgment. Thus accounting estimates change as new events occur, as more experience is acquired, or as additional information is obtained.[10]

> The Board concludes that the effect of a change in accounting estimate should be accounted for in (a) the period of change if the change affects that period only or (b) the period of change and future periods if the change affects both. A change in an estimate should not be accounted for by restating amounts reported in financial statements of prior periods or by reporting pro forma amounts for prior periods.[11]

The effect of a change in the accounting estimate on income before extraordinary items, net income, and earnings per share of the current period should be disclosed *if material* in amount. Estimates made each period in the ordinary course of accounting for doubtful accounts expense need not be disclosed.

In preparing income tax returns, a change in estimates may be treated differently from the method used for financial reporting pur-

[9] *APB Opinion No. 30,* "Reporting the Results of Operations- . . . ," AICPA (New York: 1973), p. 566.

[10] *APB Opinion No. 20,* "Accounting Changes," AICPA (New York: 1971), p. 338.

[11] Ibid., p. 397. See Chapter 23 for a more complete discussion of changes in accounting estimate.

poses. Income tax regulations presently provide that an excessive or inadequate balance in the allowance account may be corrected by adjusting the rate used in estimating doubtful accounts expense in subsequent years—in effect overstating or understating taxable income in future years until the allowance is brought into line with actual experience.

Collection of accounts previously written off

When the decision is made to charge off an uncollectible account, the charge against the allowance account and credit to Accounts Receivable has no effect on either the carrying value of accounts receivable or on the net income of the period in which the write-off occurs. If an account that has been written off is later collected, a common procedure is to debit Accounts Receivable and credit Allowance for Doubtful Accounts. This reverses the entry erroneously made, and the collection is then recorded in the usual manner. This method has the advantage of providing in the customer's account a complete record of credit experience with that customer.

Direct charge-off method of recognizing doubtful accounts expense

Some businesses may elect to recognize doubtful accounts expense only as specific accounts become worthless. While this practice gives the appearance of being more objective, it overstates the net realizable value of receivables and does not properly match doubtful accounts with the revenue from which they originate, as required by the accrual concept of accounting. Under this procedure, for example, an account representing a sale in Year 1 may be recognized as an expense in Year 2, and accounts originating in Year 2 may be charged off against revenue of Year 3 or Year 4. In applying this method, subjective judgment is still required in determining when an account becomes worthless. The direct charge-off method is therefore likely to be less objective than it appears at first glance. Uncollectible accounts under this method are written off by a charge to Doubtful Accounts Expense and a credit to Accounts Receivable. Collection of an account written off in a previous period is credited to Doubtful Accounts Recovered; recovery of an account written off earlier in the current period is recorded as a credit to Doubtful Accounts Expense, thus eliminating the expense which was prematurely recorded.

Either the allowance or the direct charge-off method can be used for income tax purposes, but the method adopted must be consistently followed. The allowance method is generally more advantageous for income tax purposes since deductible expenses are anticipated and income taxes are not paid on revenue which may never be collected.

Sale and assignment of receivables

In the normal operating cycle of a business, cash needed for current operations is provided through the collection of accounts receivable. It is possible to accelerate this process by selling receivables or by borrowing money and pledging accounts receivable as collateral. In some industries such procedures are quite common; in other industries this may be done only in times of financial stress.

Sale of Receivables without Recourse The purpose of selling accounts receivable is to shift the risk of credit, the effort of collection, and the waiting period in granting credit to the buyer. Accounts receivable are usually sold *without recourse.* As a result, the discount on the sale may be quite high, depending on the quality of the receivables. The discount on sale of accounts receivable should be reported as a financing expense in the income statement.

Persons or financial concerns making a business of buying receivables are known as *factors,* and the process of selling receivables is often called *factoring.* A factor may buy receivables outright, with or without recourse, or may extend credit to a company needing money and take the collections on accounts receivable in repayment.[12] Customers are generally notified and are instructed to make payment directly to the factor.

Factoring arrangements vary widely. If the factor advances money with the expectation of obtaining accounts receivable from the borrower, interest is charged on the amount advanced plus a commission of from 1 to 3% of the net amount of receivables purchased, depending upon the size of the transaction, the terms of the sale, and the credit standing of the customers involved. Often it is agreed that the selling company will withdraw cash only as needed and will pay interest only on cash withdrawals made.

Factoring transactions raise no special accounting problems for the seller. Accounts receivable are converted into cash and the factor's commission and interest are recorded as expenses. The factor may hold back from 5 to 10% of the agreed amount as a margin of protection against sales returns and allowances. This amount should appear in the accounts as a receivable from the factor unless experience indicates that the probability of receiving it is small, in which case an allowance for sales returns and allowances should be established.

Sale of Receivables with Recourse When receivables are sold *with recourse,* the seller in effect guarantees the receivables and the company buying the receivables is assured of earning a stipulated rate of return on its investment. The sale of receivables on a recourse basis

---

[12] "With recourse" means that the factor is protected by the seller against loss, "without recourse" means that the factor assumes full risk of failure to collect the accounts purchased.

should be viewed as a financing transaction rather than as a sale transaction that gives rise to immediate profit or loss.

Generally, the sale of ordinary receivables on a recourse basis results in receipt of proceeds less than the face amount of receivables sold. Similarly, the sale of installment receivables which bear a lower interest charge than the discount rate used in the "sale" of the receivables would produce less than the carrying value of the receivables. For example, a sale on a recourse basis of accounts receivables of $20,000 for $19,000 would be recorded as follows:

Cash	19,000	
Deferred Financing Charges	1,000	
Accounts Receivable		20,000
To record sale of accounts receivable on a recourse basis.		

The Accounting Standards Division of the AICPA recommended that the deferred financing charges (differential) be amortized as interest expense over the period during which the receivables are collected.[13] This **delayed recognition method** would also be applied to the sale of receivables on a recourse basis for more than the carrying value of receivables. Installment receivables which require the payment of interest by the debtor at a rate higher than the rate used to compute the proceeds on sale would result in an excess of proceeds over the carrying value of the installment receivables. For example, assume that Dodson Company has the following installment receivable:

Installment receivable, including deferred interest at $1\frac{1}{2}$% per month, payable at the rate of $723 per month for 36 months commencing in one month	$26,028
Less: Unearned interest charges	6,028
Carrying value of receivable	$20,000

If this receivable is sold on a recourse basis at a price which would yield to the buyer a 1% rate of return per month, the proceeds would be $21,768, determined as follows:

Present value of ordinary annuity of 36 payments of $723 per month with interest at 1% per month: $723 × 30.107505 (Table 4 in Appendix A) .	$21,768

[13] *Statement of Position 74-6,* "Recognition of Profit on Sales of Receivables with Recourse," AICPA (New York: 1974), p. 13.

The sale of this receivable on a recourse basis would be recorded as follows:

```
Cash  . . . . . . . . . . . . . . . . . . . . . . . . . . . . . . . . . .   21,768
Unearned Interest Charges  . . . . . . . . . . . . . . . . . . . .    6,028
    Installment Receivable  . . . . . . . . . . . . . . . . . . .              26,028
    Unearned Interest Revenue  . . . . . . . . . . . . . . .                    1,768
To record sale of receivable on a recourse basis. The receiv-
able bears interest at 1½% per month but was sold on a 1% per
month yield basis.
```

A sale of receivables on a recourse basis is similar to financing transactions in which funds are borrowed and assets are pledged as collateral for the loan. In our example, the sale of the installment receivable on a recourse basis has not reduced Dodson Company's risk in any way, and the differential of $1,768 has the characteristics of deferred revenue from financing activities. The $1,768 is the difference between the present value of future interest receipts on the receivable sold and the present value of the interest charged by the buyer on the funds advanced.[14] Consequently, Dodson Company should recognize this deferred financing revenue as realized revenue only as the outstanding balance of the receivable is reduced.

Assignment of Receivables Instead of selling receivables, management may prefer to borrow money using accounts receivable as collateral. This may involve an informal pledge of accounts receivable under an agreement that the proceeds from their collection will be used to retire the loan. Alternatively, receivables may be *assigned* under a more formal arrangement whereby the business *(assignor)* pledges the receivable to the lender *(assignee)* and executes a note. Assignment gives the lender the same right to bring action to collect the receivables that the assignor possesses. The assignor assumes its own credit risk and collection effort, and promises to make good any accounts that cannot be collected. The customer company is usually not notified of the assignment and makes payments directly to the assignor; it may, however, be instructed to make payments to the assignee. The assignor has some equity in the receivables, since the financing company usually advances less than 100% of the face amount of receivables assigned.

The primary accounting problem raised by assignment of receivables is to measure the company's equity in the assigned accounts and its liability to the assignee. Assigned accounts should be transferred to a separate account, Assigned Accounts Receivable, and a liability to the assignee should be established. As collections are received, assigned

[14] Ibid., p. 24.

receivables will be reduced and the liability to the assignee will be correspondingly reduced as cash is remitted by the assignor. Commissions and interest charges will be included in the remittance and will be recorded as expenses.

To illustrate, assume that on January 2, Year 1, the Adams Company assigns accounts receivable of $50,000 to the Finance Corp. and receives $45,000, less a financing charge of 2% on the advance. Interest of 1% of the unpaid balance of the loan is to be paid monthly. The journal entries required in the accounts of Adams Company to record the assignment and subsequent transactions are shown below.

Transaction	Entry on assignor's records		
Jan. 2. Assigned accounts receivable of $50,000. Finance Corp. remitted 90% of account balances, less 2% financing charge.	Assigned Accounts Receivable	50,000	
	Accounts Receivable . .		50,000
	Cash	44,100	
	Financing Expense	900	
	Notes Payable to Finance		
	Corp.		45,000
Jan. 31. Collected $30,150 on assigned accounts. Paid this amount to Finance Corp., including interest at 1% per month on unpaid balance of loan, $45,000.	Cash	30,150	
	Assigned Accounts		
	Receivable		30,150
	Notes Payable to Finance Corp.	29,700	
	Financing Expense	450	
	Cash		30,150
Feb. 28. Collected $17,000 on assigned accounts. Paid balance owed to Finance Corp., plus interest at 1% per month on unpaid balance of loan, $15,300.	Cash	17,000	
	Assigned Accounts		
	Receivable		17,000
	Notes Payable to Finance Corp.	15,300	
	Financing Expense	153	
	Cash		15,453
Transferred balance of assigned accounts to Accounts Receivable.	Accounts Receivable	2,850	
	Assigned Accounts		
	Receivable		2,850

The assignor's interest in assigned receivables may be shown by deducting the obligation to the assignee from the amount of the assigned receivables. Offsetting the liability against the asset is appropriate in this case because collections on assigned receivables are contractually earmarked to liquidate the loan. This treatment is illustrated below for Adams Company at January 31, Year 1:

```
Current assets:
  Accounts receivable  . . . . . . . . . . . . . . . . . . . . . . . . . . . . . . . . .     $200,000
  Assigned accounts receivable  . . . . . . . . . . . . . . .    $19,850
  Less: Notes payable to Finance Corp. . . . . . . . . . . . .     15,300
  Equity in assigned accounts receivable  . . . . . . . . . . . . . . .        4,550
    Total receivables  . . . . . . . . . . . . . . . . . . . . . . . . . . . . . .     $204,550
```

Adequate disclosure should be made of accounts receivable pledged, assigned, or sold, including any related contingent liabilities.

Installment receivables

Many individuals and businesses find it convenient to buy certain items on the installment plan. The installment contract, in essence a note providing for payment over a period of time, is a widely used credit instrument. Some companies selling on an installment basis have adequate financial resources to carry their own contracts and thus earn interest in addition to other service charges included in the contract. Many companies, however, sell or discount their installment contracts receivable to finance companies.

Installment receivables from sale of goods or services in the ordinary course of business, including those not falling due for more than one year from the balance sheet date, are included in current assets. In valuing installment receivables, the unearned interest and service charges included in the contract are excluded both from installment receivables and from sales. For example, Sears, Roebuck and Co. recently reported the details of its receivables as follows:

RECEIVABLES	$ in thousands
Customer installment accounts receivable	
Easy payment accounts	$2,488,609
Revolving charge accounts	2,559,657
Other customer accounts (net of $60,967 accounts sold)	67,225
Miscellaneous accounts and notes receivable	163,010
	$5,278,501
Less—unearned finance charges	(205,308)
allowance for uncollectible accounts	(93,838)
	$4,979,355

Interest and service charges should be recognized as revenue only as earned and should be disclosed separately. Deferred income taxes related to installment receivables are also reported as current. For example, in a recent annual report, Sears, Roebuck and Co. included "Deferred Income Taxes" of $782 million under current liabilities. Accounting for installment sales is covered in *Modern Advanced Accounting* of this series.

NOTES RECEIVABLE

The term *notes receivable* is used in accounting to designate several types of credit instruments. The distinguishing characteristic common to all is that they are written contractual agreements containing an unconditional promise to pay a certain sum of money under terms clearly specified in the contract. Most credit instruments used as a basis for business transactions are *negotiable,* which means in essence that a *holder in due course* is free of certain equity defenses that might otherwise be available to prior parties. Negotiability is a valuable characteristic which makes the instrument freely transferable and thus enhances the ability of the holder to sell it, discount it, or borrow against it.

Notes receivable are often used when the goods sold have a high unit or aggregate value and the buyer wants to extend payment beyond the normal 30- to 90-day period of trade credit. In the banking and commercial credit field, notes are the typical form of credit instrument used to support lending transactions. Notes receivable may also result from sale of plant and equipment items or a variety of other business transactions, including the investment of idle cash.

Valuation of notes receivable

As in the case of accounts receivable, the proper valuation of notes and similar credit instruments is their fair value (present value) at the time of acquisition. The accountant can value notes because the terms of the note generally provide sufficient and clear evidence of the rights inherent in it. Except for questions of collectibility, there is little uncertainty with respect to the amount that will be received and the date on which it will be received.

Notes, like trade accounts, may prove to be uncollectible. If a company uses notes as a regular credit medium and has a large volume outstanding, the amounts of probable uncollectible notes may be estimated, and an allowance for such notes established using procedures similar to those discussed for accounts receivable.

Strictly speaking, there is no such thing as a non-interest-bearing note; there are only notes that contain a stated provision for interest and notes that do not. The time value of money is present in any case since the present value of a promise to pay money at some future date is not as great as the amount to be paid at maturity. The so-called non-interest-bearing note has a present value smaller than its face amount by an amount equivalent to an interest charge. On the other hand, if a note bears a fair rate of interest, its *face amount* and *present value* are the same at the date of issuance.

This point may be illustrated by an example. Suppose that two notes are received in connection with the sale of goods. In settlement of the first sale, Customer A gives a one-year, 6% note, with a face amount of $24,000. In settlement of the second sale, Customer B gives a one-year note with a face amount of $25,440 with no interest provision specified in the note. If accountants look only at face amounts, they might be tempted to record these notes as follows:

Customer A		*Customer B*	
Notes Receivable . 24,000		Notes Receivable . 25,440	
Sales	24,000	Sales	25,440

A careful examination of the evidence indicates that the two contracts are identical, assuming that 6% is a reasonable rate of interest. Both customers have promised to pay $25,440 at the end of one year, and both notes have a present value of $24,000 ($25,440 ÷ 1.06). A logical method of accounting would be to record both notes at $24,000 and to record interest of $1,440 as it is earned. Thus, the note received from Customer B may be recorded in the same way as the note from Customer A, or by using a Discount on Notes Receivable account as illustrated below:

Notes Receivable	25,440	
Discount on Notes Receivable		1,440
Sales		24,000
To record sales in exchange for notes receivable.		

The discount on notes receivable is transferred periodically to Interest Revenue and the balance in the discount account should be reported as a deduction from Notes Receivable in the balance sheet.

In practice, non-interest-bearing, short-term notes received from customers often are recorded at the outset at face amount (maturity value). The foregoing analysis shows that this procedure overstates assets and fails to recognize interest revenue. Although *APB Opinion No. 21* requires that notes be recorded at present value, the provisions of this Opinion do not apply to receivables arising from transactions with customers in the normal course of business which are due within one year. When the amount of the unearned implicit interest is substantial, this treatment would result in a significant overstatement of assets, stockholders' equity, and net income.

Discounting notes receivable

Negotiable notes receivable may be sold or discounted. The term *sale* is appropriate when a note is endorsed to a bank or finance company on a *nonrecourse* basis; that is, in the event the maker of the note defaults, the bank or finance company has no recourse against the company selling the note. The term *discounted* applies when a company borrows against notes receivable and endorses them on a *recourse* basis, which means that the borrowing company must pay the note if the original maker does not.

The *proceeds* received when a note is discounted are computed by deducting from the maturity value of the note the amount of interest or discount charged by the bank or other financing source. Banks sometimes compute the discount on the *maturity value* of the note rather than on the proceeds or amount borrowed, which in effect gives the bank a higher effective rate of interest than the quoted discount rate.

To illustrate these points and the accounting involved, assume that Lynn Company wishes to discount two notes receivable arising from the sale of merchandise. Both notes have a face amount of $100,000 and are due in one year. Note C carries no provision for interest; Note D is to be paid with interest at 6%. The bank also charges a 6% discount rate.

If we assume that the notes are discounted immediately upon receipt, the proceeds and the difference between the proceeds and the present value would be determined as follows:

	Note C (no interest)	Note D (6% interest)
Face amount of notes	$100,000	$100,000
Interest to maturity	–0–	6,000
Maturity value of notes	$100,000	$106,000
Bank discount (6% of maturity value for one year)	6,000	6,360
Proceeds	$ 94,000	$ 99,640
Present value @ 6% (maturity value ÷ 1.06) . . .	94,340	100,000
Difference between proceeds and present value .	$ 340	$ 360

The difference between the proceeds and the present value of each note on a 6% basis represents additional interest charged by the bank due to the fact that the 6% discount is computed on maturity value rather than on the amount actually borrowed (proceeds). The additional interest should be recognized as expense over the remaining life of each note. The entries to record the receipt and the discounting of these notes are as shown below:[15]

Note C			Note D		
At time of sale:					
Notes Receivable	100,000		Notes Receivable	100,000	
Discount			Sales . . .		100,000
on Notes					
Rec.		5,660			
Sales . . .		94,340			
At time notes are					
discounted:					
Cash	94,000		Cash	99,640	
Discount on			Interest Expense	360	
Notes Rec. . .	5,660		Notes		
Interest Expense	340		Receivable		100,000
Notes					
Receivable		100,000			

An alternative procedure for recording the discounting of notes receivable includes a credit to Notes Receivable Discounted (a contra-asset account) rather than a credit to Notes Receivable. If a Notes Receivable Discounted account is used, it should be deducted from Notes Receivable in the current asset section of the balance sheet, thus disclosing the contingent liability to the bank. However, it should be pointed out that the full contingent liability on Note C is $100,000 (not $94,340) and on Note D it is $106,000 (not $100,000).

When a Notes Receivable Discounted account is used, the amount credited thereto must be transferred to Notes Receivable when the contingency is ended by either the payment or dishonor of the note. Since most discounted notes are paid at the maturity date, the more efficient procedure is to credit the Notes Receivable account at the time the note is discounted and thus avoid the need for a subsequent entry. The contingent liability created by the discounting of notes receivable may be maintained on a memorandum basis, and disclosure of the contingency may be made in a note to the financial statements.

---

[15] An alternative approach is to view the proceeds received from the bank as the "true" present value of the notes. This interpretation would call for the recording of the two notes and related sales at $95,000 and $99,640, respectively, thus eliminating the need to recognize interest expense when the notes are discounted.

If Lynn Company had held these notes for some time before discounting them, interest earned prior to the time the notes were discounted should be recorded. The discounting of the notes would then be recorded in the manner previously illustrated.

If the discounted notes are dishonored, Lynn Company would be required to pay the bank. The amount that would be due in such an event, however, is not the present value at the time the note was received but rather the maturity value of the note plus any protest fees charged by the bank.

Notice of the dishonor of a discounted note must be given promptly; therefore, the borrower may assume that payment has been made if no notice is received within a few days after maturity date. If notes are dishonored, the total amount paid to the bank should be debited to Accounts Receivable (or Dishonored Notes Receivable). Subsequent collection would be recorded as a credit to this account; failure to collect would require that the receivable from the maker of the note be charged off to the Allowance for Doubtful Accounts.

A company discounting notes receivable is contingently liable if the maker of the note fails to pay at maturity. The contingent liability can be disclosed in the balance sheet as follows: (1) note to the financial statements, (2) parenthetical note, or (3) by using a Notes Receivable Discounted account and deducting it from Notes Receivable. Disclosure by means of a note to the financial statements is by far the most common practice. A more detailed discussion of contingent liabilities is presented in Chapter 10.

APB Opinion No. 21, "Interest on Receivables and Payables"

Opinion No. 21 issued by the Accounting Principles Board, is applicable if the face amount of a receivable (especially a note) does not reasonably represent the present value of the consideration given in exchange. This situation may arise if no interest is explicitly stated or if the stated rate of interest is not appropriate. Recording the receivable at an amount in excess of its fair present value, for example, overstates the sales price and gross profit recorded by the seller and understates the interest earned in subsequent periods.

As a highly simplified example, assume that A buys a tract of land for $6,000 cash and immediately sells it to B for $10,000 with payment consisting solely of a 10-year, non-interest-bearing note for $10,000. It would be improper for B to record this transaction as producing a $4,000 gain, because the non-interest-bearing, 10-year note has a present value far less than its $10,000 face amount.

APB Opinion No. 21 applies to secured and unsecured notes, debentures, bonds, mortgage notes, equipment obligations, and some accounts receivable and payable. It is not intended to apply to "receivables and payables arising from transactions with customers or suppliers in the normal course of business which are due in customary trade terms not exceeding approximately one year."[16] A brief summary of **APB Opinion No. 21** as it relates to receivables follows.

Notes Received for Cash Interest on a cash loan is generally equal to the excess of the amount the borrower agrees to repay over the amount of cash he receives. The stated interest rate may differ from the prevailing rate for similar notes and the proceeds may differ from the face amount of the note. These differences indicate that the present value of the note at the time of issuance differs from the face amount. The difference between the face amount and the proceeds is recorded as a premium or as a discount to be amortized over the life of the note.

Notes Received in Exchange for Cash and Other Rights or Privileges Instead of issuing a note solely for cash, the parties may agree to exchange other rights or privileges (stated or unstated). These rights and privileges should be given accounting recognition by taking into account any implicit discount or premium on the note. For example, assume that on December 31, Year 1, L Corporation lends $108,000 to a supplier payable in one year, without interest, even though the going rate of interest for this type of loan is 8%. The parties agree that all of L Corporation's inventory needs in Year 2 will be met at favorable prices by the supplier. This loan should be recorded by L Corporation on December 31 of Year 1 as follows:

Notes Receivable	108,000	
Property Rights in Contract with Supplier	8,000	
Discount on Notes Receivable		8,000
Cash		108,000
To record non-interest-bearing loan to supplier.		
Present value of note, $108,000 ÷ 1.08 = $100,000.		

The account Property Rights in Contract with Supplier would be classified as a current asset because it is similar to an advance on merchandise purchases. In this example we assumed that the note received by L Corporation was non-interest-bearing; if the note stipulated an unreasonably low rate of interest, the present value of the note would be less than $108,000 but more than $100,000, thus reducing the amount recorded in the Property Rights in Contract with Supplier account.

When payment is received on the note at December 31 of Year 2, the following entry would be required for L Corporation:

[16] APB Opinion No. 21, "Interest on Receivables and Payables," AICPA (New York: 1971), p. 418.

Cash	108,000	
Purchases	8,000	
Discount on Notes Receivable	8,000	
Notes Receivable		108,000
Property Rights in Contract with Supplier		8,000
Interest Revenue		8,000

To record proceeds and implicit interest earned on note receivable and to recognize value assigned to the contract with supplier as an additional cost of purchases.

The foregoing procedure properly recognizes interest revenue in Year 2, $8,000 ($100,000 × 8%) and the full cost of purchases through the recognition of the implicit interest on the note receivable as an additional cost of purchases from the supplier. (See Chapter 10 for parallel entries for this transaction in the accounts of the supplier.)

When notes are received in exchange for assets or services, and interest is either not stated or is unreasonably low, the notes and the sales price should be recorded at the fair value of the assets or services or at the market value of the note, whichever is the more clearly determinable. In the absence of exchange prices for the assets or services or evidence of the market value of the note, the present value of a note should be determined. This determination should be made at the time the note is acquired; any subsequent changes in interest rates should be ignored.[17]

Determining an Appropriate Interest Rate and Present Value of Note The appropriate interest rate for finding the present value of a note receivable depends on factors such as the credit standing of the issuer, terms of the note, the quality of collateral offered by the issuer, and the general level of interest rates. The interest rate selected for this purpose should approximate the rate at which the debtor could obtain similar financing from other sources. Therefore, the interest rate selected would represent an arm's-length negotiated rate for the borrower and the lender.

To illustrate the computation of the present value of a note, assume that on January 1, Year 1, Software Associates sends a $39,930 invoice for services to Z Corporation. The president of Z Corporation protests the amount of the invoice and asks that as a compromise it be allowed to pay it in three annual installments of $13,310, starting in one year. Software Associates agrees to this arrangement and receives three non-interest-bearing notes for $13,310 each. How should these notes be recorded in the records of Software Associates if an interest rate of

[17] Ibid., pp. 421–422.

10% is considered appropriate? It is first necessary to compute the present value of the notes using Table 4 in Appendix A as follows:

Amount of annual receipts (notes)	$13,310
Mulitply by present value of ordinary annuity of $1 at 10% interest ..	2.486852
Present value of three annual receipts of $13,310 at 10% interest ...	$33,100

The entries to record the receipt of the notes by Software Associates on January 1, Year 1, and the three annual collections from Z Corporation are illustrated below. We have assumed that no prior entry was made to record the receivable from Z Corporation and that the three notes are recorded at the face amount of $39,930:

January 1, Year 1:

Notes Receivable	39,930	
Discount on Notes Receivable		6,830
Revenue		33,100

Receipt of non-interest-bearing note for $39,930 payable in three annual installments. The note is recorded at its **present value** based on an interest rate of 10% per year.

End of Year 1:

Cash	13,310	
Discount on Notes Receivable	3,310	
Notes Receivable		13,310
Interest Revenue		3,310

To record collection of first note. Interest for first year: ($39,930 − $6,830) × 10% = $3,310.

End of Year 2:

Cash	13,310	
Discount on Notes Receivable	2,310	
Notes Receivable		13,310
Interest Revenue		2,310

To record collection of second note. Interest for second year: ($26,620 − $3,520) × 10% = $2,310.

End of Year 3:

Cash	13,310	
Discount on Notes Receivable	1,210	
Notes Receivable		13,310
Interest Revenue		1,210

To record collection of third note. Interest for third year:
($13,310 − $1,210) × 10% = $1,210.

In the journal entries above, the discount on notes receivable of $6,830 was recognized as interest revenue over the three-year life of the note using the **effective interest rate** of 10% applied to the carrying amount of the notes receivable **at the beginning of each year.**

Analysis of accounts receivable

Accounts receivable are an important factor in analyzing financial liquidity and projecting cash flows. Changes in the length of the average collection period or the number of days' sales in receivables, for example, should be carefully watched and action initiated to correct unfavorable trends. A discussion of analytical techniques for receivables appears in Chapter 25.

Presentation of receivables in the balance sheet

Within the current asset section of the balance sheet the amounts of the following classes of receivables should be separately reported: (1) notes and other receivables based on written negotiable contracts, (2) ordinary trade receivables, (3) installment accounts receivables, and (4) other current claims. Negotiable notes and contracts have a special status because of the ease with which they can be converted into cash through discounting. Users of financial statements may be interested in the percentage relationship between trade receivables and credit sales as an indication of a company's collection experience.

Any discount or premium relating to notes receivable should be reported in the balance sheet as a direct deduction from or addition to the face amount of the note. The description of notes receivable should include the effective interest rate.[18]

Receivables that have been pledged should be identified, and any receivables that will not be collected within a year or the operating cycle should be excluded from the current asset category. A credit balance in an individual account receivable, if material, should be shown as a current liability. Receivables from officers, employees, and stockholders

[18] Ibid., p. 423.

are generally classified as noncurrent unless current collection is definitely assured.

The balance sheet presentation of various kinds of receivables and related accounts is illustrated below:

Included in Current Assets

Receivables:	
Trade notes receivable (net of notes discounted of $50,000 and unearned discounts of $5,000)	$ 205,000
Trade accounts receivable (net of allowances of $45,000 for doubtful accounts, returns, and sales discounts)	620,000
Installment receivables (net of unearned interest and carrying charges)	400,000
Current amount due from affiliated company, interest at 9½% . . .	45,000
Miscellaneous (including $4,000 debit balance in accounts payable)	10,000
Total receivables	$1,280,000

Included in Investments or Other Assets

Receivable from sale of equipment (due with interest at 8% in 3 years)	$ 150,000
Notes due from officers and employees (due with interest at 7½% in installments over 10 years)	85,000
Dishonored notes receivable (net of allowance for doubtful notes of $6,000)	12,000

Included in Current Liabilities

Container deposits by customers	$ 17,500
Accounts receivable with credit balances	4,250

REVIEW QUESTIONS

1 Briefly discuss the significance of accounts receivable in analyzing the financial position of a business unit.

2 What is meant by **valuation of receivables?** If accountants generally require that assets be recorded at **cost**, why are accounts receivable not recorded at the cost of the merchandise sold?

3 What is the distinction between **trade receivables** and **miscellaneous receivables?** Give two examples of each.

4 At what point should trade receivables be recorded? Are shipments to consignees or sales agents recorded as receivables?

5 Describe a **cycle billing system** and state its advantages.

6 Describe how the following items affect the valuation of receivables: **trade discounts, sales discounts, returns and allowances, freight allowances, sales and excise taxes,** and **container deposits.**

7 Briefly describe three methods of accounting for cash (sales) discounts.

8 Some accountants classify Doubtful Accounts Expense as an operating expense while others classify it as a contra-revenue account. Discuss the reasoning behind these alternative positions. What objection, if any do you have to the account title "Loss from Bad Debts?"

9 What is an *aging of accounts receivable?* Describe how such an analysis may be used in estimating doubtful accounts expense and in analyzing the quality of accounts receivable.

10 According to *APB Opinion No. 20,* how should a change in estimating doubtful accounts expense and a major increase or decrease in the allowance for doubtful accounts be reported in the income statement?

11 Briefly discuss the logic of basing the estimate of doubtful accounts expense on **(a)** total sales, **(b)** credit sales, and **(c)** a fixed percentage of receivables at the end of the period.

12 Discuss the accounting procedures necessary to record recoveries of accounts previously written off **(a)** if an allowance for doubtful accounts is used, or **(b)** if the direct charge-off method is used.

13 Explain the distinction between *factoring* and *assigning* accounts receivable.

14 Explain the *delayed recognition method* of accounting for the excess of proceeds received over the carrying amount of receivables sold on a *recourse* basis.

15 City Equipment Company sells certain merchandise having a list price of $10,500 on an installment plan covering 24 months. Payments of $500 are to be made by the customer each month. Interest of $1,300 and service charges of $200 are added to the listed sales price in arriving at total installment receivables. The company records the sale by a debit to Installment Contracts Receivable and a credit to Sales for $12,000. Evaluate this procedure.

16 What error is introduced into the accounting records when a non-interest-bearing note receivable due in one year is recorded at face amount? Explain.

17 Describe various ways that the contingent liability relating to notes receivable discounted can be presented in the balance sheet.

EXERCISES

Ex. 7-1 On September 30 of the current year, the following notes receivable are discounted at the bank. The bank charges a 6% discount rate on the maturity value of the notes. Compute the proceeds of each note, using 360 as the number of days in the year.
a Customer's 60-day, $1,000, 6% note dated September 30
b Customer's 90-day $10,000, non-interest-bearing note dated August 15
c Customer's 45-day, $4,000, 4% noted dated September 15
d Customer's 6-month, $12,000, 8% note dated August 1

Ex. 7-2 Rea Corporation started in business in Year 1 and had outstanding accounts receivable of $300,000 at the end of the year. In arriving at the valuation of receivables at the end of the year, management wished to take into account the following:

Estimated doubtful accounts	$6,240
Estimated collection costs	1,800
Estimated price adjustments and other allowances on outstanding receivables (no returns are anticipated)	3,000
Estimated cash (sales) discounts	3,600

a Prepare a compound adjusting entry to recognize management's estimate of the net realizable value of accounts receivable at the end of Year 1. No accounts were written off in Year 1.

b Show how accounts receivable should be reported in the balance sheet at the end of Year 1.

Ex. 7-3 Myracle Company acquired merchandise having a cost of $4,000. The merchandise was offered for sale by Myracle Company at a list price of $6,500, before a trade discount of 20% and a cash discount of 2% if the invoice is paid within 10 days. Myracle Company billed customers net of the trade discount, and recorded accounts receivable and sales at the invoice price.

Prepare journal entries to record **(a)** the sale and the cost of the goods sold, and **(b)** the collection of the account within 10 days, assuming that the company uses a perpetual inventory system.

Ex. 7-4 From the following information, compute the doubtful accounts expense for Year 1: Beginning balance in Accounts Receivable was $80,000; beginning balance in Allowance for Doubtful Accounts was $6,000; ending balance in Accounts Receivable was $110,000, of which 4% was estimated to be uncollectible. During the year, $7,490 of accounts receivable were written off as uncollectible.

Ex. 7-5 Certain information relative to the operations of Mejia Company for Year 6 follows:

Accounts receivable, Jan. 1, Year 6	$16,000
Accounts receivable collected	52,000
Cash sales	10,000
Inventory, Jan. 1	24,000
Inventory, Dec. 31	22,000
Purchases	40,000
Gross profit on sales	18,000

Compute the balance in accounts receivable at December 31, Year 6.

Ex. 7-6 Your accounts receivable clerk, to whom you pay a salary of $650 per month, has just purchased a new Cadillac. You decide to test the accuracy of the accounts receivable balance of $30,400 as shown in the ledger.

The following information is available for your first year in business: Collections from customers, $125,000; payments for merchandise purchases, $130,000; ending inventory, $40,000; and ending accounts payable to merchandise suppliers, $30,000. All goods purchased were marked to sell at 40% above cost (sales price equals 140% of cost).

Compute an estimate of any apparent shortages in accounts receivable at the end of the year.

Ex. 7-7 The following accounts appear in the ledger of Betty Company at the end of the current year:

Sales	Accounts Receivable	Allowance for Doubtful Accounts
$1,200,000	$500,000	$2,000—debit balance

Prepare an entry to recognize doubtful accounts expense for each independent assumption below:

a The Allowance for Doubtful Accounts is increased to a balance of $15,000, thus requiring an additional debit of $17,000 to Doubtful Accounts Expense.

b The company recognizes 2% of sales as doubtful accounts expense.

c By aging the accounts, $24,750 of accounts receivable is considered doubtful.

Ex. 7-8 On March 1, Beckman Company assigned accounts receivable of $60,000 to Rec-Fin Co. and received $54,000 less a 2% financing charge. Interest is charged at the rate of 1% per month of the unpaid balance. Beckman Company made collections on the assigned accounts and remitted the proceeds at the end of each month to Rec-Fin Co. Collections in March were $30,000.

Prepare journal entries in the accounts of Beckman Company to record the transactions for March relating to the assignment of accounts receivable.

Ex. 7-9 You are auditing the accounts of Kelly Corporation at the end of its fiscal year. Your review of accounts receivable and discussions with the client disclose that the following items are included in the accounts receivable (both controlling account and subsidiary ledgers):

Customers' accounts with credit balances, $2,950

Receivables from officers, $12,500

Advances to employees, $2,200

Accounts that are definitely uncollectible, $2,880

Prepare a correcting journal entry to reclassify items which are not trade accounts receivable and to write off uncollectible accounts.

Ex. 7-10 According to **APB Opinion No. 21,** how would you record a low-interest, one-year loan for $250,000 by Company A to a supplier who agrees to sell raw materials to Company A at a favorable fixed price during the period of the loan?

Explain the approach used in recording this transaction. Prepare an entry on Company A's accounts to record the loan, assuming that the present value of the note is $225,000.

Ex. 7-11 Excelsior Corporation sold an old machine having a cost of $20,000 and a carrying value of $2,000 for $9,000, payable $1,014 down and $2,662 at the end of each of the next three years. No interest was mentioned in the contract, although 10% interest per year would have been a fair rate for this type of transaction.

Compute (without using compound interest tables) the present value of the $7,986 to be received over the next three years and record the sale of the machine as recommended in **APB Opinion No. 21.** Confirm your answer by using Table 4 in Appendix A.

Ex. 7-12 The information on page 288 is available for Sara Willson, Inc.:

| | Amounts in thousands | | |
	Year 1	Year 2	Year 3
Sales on account	$ 900	$1,100	$1,000
Cash sales	600	800	700
Total sales	$1,500	$1,900	$1,700
Accounts receivable (end of year)	$ 170	$ 230	$ 220
Allowance for doubtful accounts (end of year)	47	30	56
Accounts written off as uncollectible during the year . .	2	50	4

Assuming there was **no** change in the method used for estimating doubtful accounts during the three-year period, compute the balance in the allowance for doubtful accounts at the beginning of Year 1.

SHORT CASES FOR ANALYSIS AND DECISION

Case 7-1 Business transactions often involve the exchange of property, goods, or services for notes or similar instruments that may stipulate no interest rate or an interest rate that varies from prevailing rates.

Instructions
a When a note is exchanged for property, goods, or services, what value should be placed upon the note:
  (1) If it bears interest at a reasonable rate and is issued in a bargained transaction entered into at arm's length? Explain.
  (2) If it bears no interest and/or is not issued in a bargained transaction entered into at arm's length? Explain.
b If the recorded value of a note differs from the face amount
  (1) How should the difference be accounted for? Explain.
  (2) How should this difference be presented in the balance sheet? Explain.

Case 7-2 During the audit of accounts receivable of Daley Co., the president Robert Daley, asked why the current year's expense for doubtful accounts is charged merely because some accounts may become uncollectible next year. He then said that he had read that financial statements should be based upon verifiable, objective evidence, and that it seemed to him to be much more objective to wait until individual accounts receivable were actually determined to be uncollectible before charging them to expense.

Instructions
a Discuss the theoretical justification of the allowance method as contrasted with the direct write-off method of accounting for doubtful accounts.
b Describe the following two methods of estimating doubtful accounts. Include a discussion of how well each accomplishes the objectives of the allowance method of accounting for doubtful accounts.
  (1) The percentage of sales method
  (2) The aging method
c Of what merit is the president's contention that the allowance method lacks the objectivity of the direct write-off method? Discuss in terms of accounting's measurement function.

Case 7-3 As a result of earthquake losses, River Company, one of the oldest and largest customers of Barge Transport, Inc., suddenly and unexpectedly became bankrupt. Approximately 30% of the total sales of Barge Transport, Inc., have been made to River Company during each of the past several years.

The amount due from River Company—none of which is collectible—equals 25% of total accounts receivable, an amount which is considerably in excess of what was determined to be an adequate allowance for doubtful accounts at the close of the preceding year.

Instructions How should Barge Transport, Inc., record the write-off of the River Company receivable, if it is using the allowance method of accounting for doubtful accounts? Justify your suggested treatment.

Case 7-4 The annual report for Year 10 of Systems Corporation, which operates a group of correspondence and resident schools, includes the following relating to contracts receivable and sales:

Under current assets:

Contracts receivable, less allowance for doubtful accounts of $3,228,180 (Note 2)	$ 6,599,399

Under current liabilities:

Estimated costs to service contracts	$ 264,281
Unearned tuition revenue (Note 2)	1,074,226

In income statement:

Sales, net of discounts and allowances of $2,076,911	$14,350,698
Provision for doubtful contracts	3,863,800

Note 2—Contracts receivable:

Students in home study courses enter into contracts which contain various payment plans, generally for a term of one to three years. Similarly, home study courses are generally completed over a term of one to three years. Revenue on home study courses and estimated cost to service the contracts are recorded when the contract is received.

Many of the contracts receivable are due from resident students and represent advance registrations for classes which will begin subsequent to December 31, Year 10. Tuition revenue on these contracts and a portion of tuiton applicable to the class in progress at December 31, Year 10, net of an allowance for cancellations, have been deferred and will be credited to income as earned over the period of attendance.

It is estimated that gross contracts receivable of approximately $1,900,000 at December 31, Year 10, were not expected to be realized within one year. It is not practical, however, for the company to state separately the long-term portion of contracts receivable in the accompanying consolidated balance sheet because of the difficulty in determining the allowance for doubtful contracts relating to the long-term contracts receivable.

Instructions Briefly evaluate the accounting practices of Systems Corporation. Your answer should refer to such accounting concepts as revenue realization, matching of costs and revenue, conservatism, objectivity, and classification of contracts receivable as current based on the length of the operating cycle.

PROBLEMS

Group A

7A-1 The following information is taken from the trial balance for Allen's Glass and Screen at September 30, Year 10, the end of its fiscal period:

	Debit	Credit
Notes receivable from customers (due within one year, 9% interest)	$ 50,000	
Accounts receivable	220,000	
Allowance for doubtful accounts and notes	3,300	
Allowance for sales discounts		$ 800
Allowance for sales returns		–0–
Sales—cash		150,000
Sales—on account		630,000
Sales returns	6,500	
Sales discounts	8,900	

Accounts written off during the year were debited to the Allowance for Doubtful Accounts; merchandise returns by customers were recorded in the Sales Returns account; and sales discounts allowed to customers were recorded in the Sales Discounts account.

Instructions
a Prepare journal entries to adjust the Allowance for Doubtful Accounts and Notes, the Allowance for Sales Discounts, and the Allowance for Sales Returns based on the following information:
 (1) Aging of accounts and notes receivable indicates that the following balances are required at the end of the fiscal year:

Allowance for doubtful accounts and notes	$13,000
Allowance for sales discounts	2,900

 (2) Based on many years of experience, management estimated that of the $220,000 in accounts receivable at September 30, Year 10, $12,000 will be returned. The net realizable value of the returned merchandise was estimated at $7,200. The company follows the practice of establishing an inventory account for the merchandise expected to be returned by customers.
b Assuming that the allowance accounts are properly adjusted at September 30, Year 10, show how sales, doubtful accounts expense, and receivables will appear in the financial statements for the fiscal period ended September 30, Year 10. Doubtful accounts expense is reported as an operating expense in the income statement.

7A-2 In auditing the records of Antall Corporation for Year 5, you discover the following information:
 (1) On April 30, Year 5, the company received a non-interest-bearing note for $15,000 maturing in one year, as payment for a consulting fee. The fee was originally established at $13,800 but, because the client was short of cash, the company agreed to accept the note. The note was recorded at $15,000 by a debit to Notes Receivable and a credit to Fees Revenue. A discount account representing unearned interest revenue is used by the company.
 (2) The company sold a parcel of real estate on June 30, Year 5, for $10,000 in cash and a non-interest-bearing note of $40,000 due in three years. The land had a cost basis of $29,100 and Gain on Sale of Land was credited for $20,900. You ascertain that the present value of the note at June 30, Year 5, discounted at 10% compound interest, was $30,053.
 (3) A note receivable of $5,000, on which interest receivable of $180 had been recorded in the Accrued Interest Receivable account, was discounted at a

bank at a rate of interest higher than the rate on the note. Proceeds of $5,155 were credited to Notes Receivable. The policy of the company is to use a Notes Receivable Discounted account. The note matures early in Year 6.

(4) The company has recognized doubtful accounts expense only as specific receivables were deemed to be worthless. You ascertain that an allowance for doubtful accounts of $8,500 is required at the end of Year 5.

(5) Interest accrued on investment in bonds at the end of Year 5 amounts to $3,125.

(6) Accounts receivable in the amount of $1,240 are considered worthless at the end of Year 5.

Instructions Prepare an adjusting or correcting entry at December 31, Year 5, for each item (1) through (6) above. The accounts are still open for Year 5. Ignore income tax considerations and round all computations to the nearest dollar.

7A-3 In Year 3, Everett Company adopted a policy of providing for doubtful accounts at the rate of 2% of credit sales. A record of the company's experience for the past three years follows:

	Year 5	Year 4	Year 3
Credit sales	$515,000	$380,000	$320,000
Cash collected on credit sales:			
Year 3			$211,580
Year 4		$318,420	85,000
Year 5	$370,000	50,000	14,000
Accounts written off as uncollectible:			
Year 3			500
Year 4		5,180	6,800
Year 5	2,200	6,400	2,120
		$380,000	$320,000
Balance in accounts receivable at Dec. 31, Year 5	142,800		
	$515,000		

The company's accountant made no entries or adjustments affecting receivables other than those necessary to record sales, collections from customers, the annual provision for doubtful accounts, and the write-offs of individual accounts against the allowance account.

The company engaged you at the end of Year 5 to make an examination of its records for the purpose of supporting a loan application. You have the above information available as a basis for determining the adequacy of the allowance for doubtful accounts. You decide to adjust the allowance to conform to the actual experience relating to doubtful accounts expense during Years 3 and 4.

Instructions

a Set up ledger accounts for Accounts Receivable (Controlling Account), Doubtful Accounts Expense, and Allowance for Doubtful Accounts and post all entries as the company's accountant made them.

b Prepare in journal entry form, and post to these accounts, any adjusting entries you deem necessary as of the end of Year 5, assuming that the accounts have not yet been closed. Explain briefly the reasons for your adjustments and the basis for your determination of the proper allowance for doubtful accounts at December 31, Year 5. The company follows the accepted practice of recording corrections of prior years' doubtful accounts expense in the current year's doubtful accounts expense.

7A-4 Welder Company started in business on January 4, Year 3, and reported net income of $25,000 in Year 3, $33,000 in Year 4, and $50,000 in Year 5. The accounts for the year ending December 31, Year 5, are closed.

Welder Company did not use accrual accounting for some items. It was agreed that adjustments should be made in the accounts to report the assets, liabilities, and owners' equity on the accrual method of accounting.

Accounts receivable at the end of each year consisted of the following:

	Year 3	Year 4	Year 5
Relating to sales made in:			
Year 3	$20,000	$ 6,000	$ 3,000
Year 4		24,000	7,500
Year 5			35,000

Doubtful accounts expense was recorded when accounts were deemed uncollectible. Based on an aging of accounts, an allowance for doubtful accounts should be established at the end of Year 5 and should be recognized as follows: Current accounts, 5%; accounts relating to sales of Year 4, 10%; accounts relating to sales of Year 3, 20%. Doubtful accounts expense previously recorded and years of sale were:

	Doubtful accounts expense recorded		Doubtful accounts expense recorded for sales made in	
Year	Amount	Year 3	Year 4	Year 5
3	$1,500	$1,500		
4	2,000	1,400	$ 600	
5	5,500	500	2,000	$3,000
Totals	$9,000	$3,400	$2,600	$3,000

Salaries and insurance were recorded as expense when paid. The amounts of accrued salaries and unexpired insurance at the end of each year were:

	Dec. 31		
	Year 3	Year 4	Year 5
Accrued salaries payable	$ 800	$ 1,050	$ 1,420
Salaries paid in cash	20,000	25,000	26,500
Unexpired insurance	600	800	950
Insurance premiums paid	2,500	2,000	2,200

Instructions

a Determine the required balance in the Allowance for Doubtful Accounts at December 31, Year 5.

b Compute net income for Year 5, using the accrual method of accounting. First prepare schedules computing each of the following expenses for Year 5, using the accrual method of accounting. (Ignore income taxes.)
(1) Uncollectible accounts expense
(2) Salaries expense
(3) Insurance expense

c Prepare a journal entry required to restate the accounts to the accrual basis at December 31, Year 5. Close the net adjustment to net income for the three-year period to the Retained Earnings account.

7A-5 Cohen Factoring Associates was incorporated in December 1979. The capital stock of the company consists of 50,000 shares of $10 par value, all of which was paid in at par. The company was organized for the purpose of factoring (purchasing) accounts receivable.

Cohen Factoring Associates charges a commission to its clients of 5% of all receivables factored and assumes all credit risks. Besides the commission, an additional 10% of gross receivables is withheld on all purchases and is credited to the Liability to Clients account. This account is used for merchandise returns, etc., made by customers of the clients for which a credit memo would be due. Payments are made to its clients by Cohen Factoring Associates at the end of each month to adjust the Liability to Clients account so that it equals 10% of the uncollected receivables as of the end of the month.

Based on the collection experience of other factoring companies in this area, officials of Cohen Factoring Associates decided to make monthly provisions to Allowance for Doubtful Accounts based on 1% of all receivables purchased during the month.

The company also decided to recognize commission revenue on only the factored receivables which have been collected; however, for accounting simplicity all commissions are originally credited to Commissions Revenue and an adjustment is made to Unearned Commissions Revenue at the end of each quarter, based on 5% of accounts receivables then outstanding.

Operations of the company during the first quarter of 1980 resulted in the following:

Accounts receivable factored: January	*$400,000*
February	*500,000*
March	*800,000*

Collections on the above accounts receivable totaled $950,000.

General and administrative expenses paid during the period were as follows:

Salaries expense	*$19,500*
Office rent expense	*9,500*
Advertising expense	*800*
Equipment rent expense	*1,600*
Miscellaneous expenses	*1,450*

On January 31, 1980, a six-month 6% bank loan was obtained for $200,000, with interest payable at maturity.

For the first three months of the year, the company rented all its office furniture and equipment; however, on March 31, 1980, it purchased various office furniture and equipment at a cost of $10,200, payable within 10 days. This purchase was not recorded in the financial records.

Instructions

a Prepare a working paper to summarize the activities of the company for the quarter ended March 31, 1980. (Disregard all withholding taxes and the company's liability for FICA and income taxes.)

b Prepare a balance sheet for the company at March 31, 1980.

7A-6 You are examining East Slope Corporation's financial statement for the year ended December 31, 1980. Your analysis of the 1980 entries in the Notes Receivable account is presented below:

Date 1980	Analysis of transactions	Notes Receivable Debit	Notes Receivable Credit
Jan. 1	Balance	$118,000	
Feb. 28	Received 6%, $25,000 note due Oct. 28, 1980, from Daley, whose account was past due. Memorandum entry only.		
Feb. 28	Discounted Daley note at 6% for 8 months		$ 24,960
Mar. 29	Received non-interest-bearing demand note from Edge, the corporation's treasurer, for a loan	$ 6,200	
Aug. 30	Received principal and interest due from Allen and, in accordance with agreement, two principal payments in advance		34,200
Sept. 4	Paid protest fee on note dishonored by Charnes . . .	5	
Nov. 1	Received check dated Feb. 1, 1981, in settlement of Bailey note. The check was included in cash on hand on Dec. 31, 1980		8,120
Nov. 3	Paid protest fee and maturity value of Daley note to bank. Note discounted Feb. 28, 1980, was dishonored	26,031	
Dec. 27	Accepted fixtures with a fair value of $24,000 in full settlement from Daley		24,000
Dec. 31	Received check dated Jan. 3, 1981, from Edge in payment of Mar. 29, 1980, note. (The check was included in petty cash until Jan. 2, 1981, when it was returned to Edge in exchange for a new demand note for the same amount.)		6,200
Dec. 31	Received principal and interest on Charnes note . .		42,437
Dec. 31	Accrued interest on Allen note for six months	1,200	
	Totals	$151,436	$139,917

The following additional information is available:

(1) Balances at January 1, 1980, were a debit of $1,400 in the Accrued Interest Receivable account and a credit of $400 relating to Bailey's note in the Unearned Interest Revenue account. The $118,000 debit balance in the Notes Receivable Account consisted of the following three notes:

a Allen note dated Aug. 31, 1976, payable in annual installments plus accrued interest at 6% each Aug. 31 . . . . $70,000

b Bailey 6% note dated Nov. 1, 1979, due Nov. 1, 1980 8,000

     c Charnes note for $40,000 plus 6% interest, dated Dec. 31, 1979,
       due on Sept. 1, 1980 . . . . *$40,000*

(2) No entries were made during 1980 to the Accrued Interest Receivable account or the Unearned Interest Revenue account, and only one entry for a
credit of $1,200 on December 31 appeared in the Interest Revenue account.

(3) All notes were from trade customers unless otherwise indicated.

(4) Debits and credits offsetting related credit and debit entries to Notes Receivable were correctly recorded unless the facts indicate otherwise.

Instructions Prepare a working paper to adjust or correct each entry and to
properly reclassify it, if necessary. Enter your adjustments in the proper columns to correspond with the date of each entry and use a Notes Receivable Discounted account when notes are discounted. Do not combine related entries for
different dates. Your completed working paper will provide the basis for one
compound journal entry to correct all entries to Notes Receivable and related
accounts for 1980. Use the following headings for your working paper:

Date 1980	Analysis of transactions	Notes Receivable		Adjustment or reclassification required				
				Notes Receivable	Accounts Receivable	Interest Revenue	Other accounts	
		Debit	Credit	Debit (Credit)	Debit (Credit)	Debit (Credit)	Account title	Debit (Credit)

Group B

7B-1 The accountant for Michael Chase & Co. was hired at the beginning of the current year. At the end of the year, before making any adjusting entries, the accountant prepared a trial balance which included the following items:

	Debit	Credit
Accounts receivable	$240,000	
Notes receivable (received in exchange for accounts receivable)	30,000	
Allowance for doubtful accounts	7,080	
Sales		$1,830,000
Sales returns and allowances	8,850	
Sales discounts	15,540	

Instructions Prepare the appropriate adjusting entry to provide for estimated
doubtful accounts under each of the following independent assumptions. Explain the basis for each entry:

a Company experience indicates that 80% of all sales are credit sales and that
on the average 2% of gross credit sales prove uncollectible.

b An analysis of the aging of accounts receivable indicates that potential uncollectibles at the end of the year amount to $15,000.

c Company policy is to maintain an allowance for doubtful accounts equal
to 4% of outstanding trade receivables, including notes received from customers.

d The allowance for doubtful accounts is increased by 1% of gross sales, and an
allowance for sales discounts of $3,000 on outstanding accounts receivable is
to be established.

7B-2 The following information appears in the balance sheet for El-Badawi Corporation at December 31, Year 4:

Notes receivable		$ 60,000	
Less: Notes receivable discounted		36,000	$ 24,000
Accrued interest receivable (R Company note)			800
Accounts receivable		$280,000	
Less: Allowance for doubtful accounts	$11,200		
Allowance for sales returns	4,000	15,200	264,800

The notes receivable consist of the following:

Six-month 8% note from R Company dated July 31, Year 4	$ 24,000
60-day 6% note from P Company dated Nov. 15, Year 4. This note was discounted at Royal Bank on Nov. 30, Year 4	36,000

A summary of transactions relating to notes and accounts receivable during January of Year 5 are as follows:

Jan. 11 Received a 90-day, 6% note from a customer, Alex Cobb, in exchange for an account receivable of $7,200.
Jan. 13 Collected from Alice Tapp an account receivable written off in Year 4, $868.
Jan. 15 Notice was received from Royal Bank that P Company paid the $36,000 note due January 14.
Jan. 20 Worthless accounts of $4,800 from several customers were written off.
Jan. 30 Received payment on R Company note, including interest of $960.
Jan. 31 Sales on account for the month, $688,600.
Jan. 31 Collections on accounts receivable, excluding Tapp account:
    (1) From balance outstanding on December 31, Year 4, after $3,000 in sales discounts, $240,000.
    (2) From current month's sales, after $5,400 in sales discounts, $368,000.
Jan. 31 Recorded accrued interest for 20 days on note from Alex Cobb.
Jan. 31 Aging of accounts receivable shows that $14,000 is required in the Allowance for Doubtful Accounts and $5,600 is required in the Allowance for Sales Returns.

Instructions
a Record the transactions and other information given for the month of January in journal entry form. The company does not reverse any adjusting entries.
b Show how the information relating to notes and accounts receivable should appear in the balance sheet at January 31, Year 5.

7B-3 The Allowance for Doubtful Accounts in the accounting records of Guttrey Auto Supply for Year 5 is summarized below:

Allowance for Doubtful Accounts

Mar. 31	Write-off, Year 3 accounts	6,650	Jan. 1	Balance	22,500
June 30	Write-off, Year 4 accounts	9,100	Mar. 31	Provision	7,850
Sept. 30	Write-off, Year 4 accounts	6,840	June 30	Provision	9,720
Dec. 31	Write-off, Year 5 accounts	14,190	Sept. 30	Provision	14,200
			Dec. 31	Provision	12,550

The company sells on 30-day credit and has followed a practice of charging Doubtful Accounts Expense in an amount equal to 4% of sales. The accountant regularly prepares quarterly income statements and makes adjusting entries at the end of each quarter in order to measure accurately the interim net income. At the end of Year 5, the accountant suggests that an aging be made of accounts receivable to test the adequacy of the Allowance for Doubtful Accounts. The aging of accounts receivable at December 31, Year 5, follows:

Classification by due date	Amount
Current accounts, outstanding 30 days or less	$260,000
31–60 days old	85,200
61–120 days old	50,000
121 days–6 months old	31,000
Over 6 months old	16,800
Balance in controlling account at Dec. 31, Year 5	$443,000

After discussion with the sales manager of the company, the accountant estimated that the following percentages represented a reasonable estimate of the doubtful accounts in each category: current accounts, 2%; 31 to 60 days old, 5%; 61 to 120 days old, 10%; 121 days to 6 months old, 15%; over 6 months old, 25%.

Instructions
a On the basis of this information, test the adequacy of the balance in the company's Allowance for Doubtful Accounts at December 31, Year 5.
b Prepare any adjusting journal entry that should be made as a result of your analysis. The accounting records have not been closed for Year 5. You should adjust the Doubtful Accounts Expense for Year 5 for any required increase or decrease in the Allowance for Doubtful Accounts.

7B-4 Oak Furniture Company operates a furniture manufacturing business in Alabama. Although sales have been growing rapidly, the company has not been able to earn a consistently satisfactory net income because of price competition, losses as a result of excessive inventories, inability to collect on several large accounts, and ineffective controls over manufacturing costs. The company likes to pay bills promptly, but its customers do not. As a result, the company is short of cash and cannot start production of a new line of dining room furniture.

In an effort to obtain seasonal financing, Charles, the president of the company requests a working capital statement from his accountant with instructions to "make it look good." The accountant prepared the following statement:

OAK FURNITURE COMPANY
Summary of Working Capital
April 1, 1980

Current assets:

Cash	$ 3,150
Accounts receivable (net of $12,000 received from customers as deposits on special orders. Allowance for doubtful accounts, sales discounts, and sales returns have not been used)	73,000
Inventories, at cost	49,150
Receivable from U.S. Treasury for tax refund filed (net of income taxes payable of $4,000, which were due on Mar. 15, 1980)	2,800
Receivable from subsidiary company (no due date)	34,000
Miscellaneous current assets	8,250
Total current assets	$170,350

Less: Current liabilities:

Accounts payable	$50,450	
Accrued wages payable	5,000	
Notes and miscellaneous current liabilities, including property taxes of $1,800 due on Apr. 10, 1980	15,000	70,450
Working capital (current ratio 2.42 to 1)		$ 99,900

Charles presented this statement to three bankers, hoping to obtain a loan of $50,000 for one year. Each turns him down, giving reasons as follows:

Banker A "We do not extend credit on the basis of partial balance sheets and without an income statement. We also like to see a cash forecast for the coming year. Incidentally, you should hire a certified public accountant who understands generally accepted accounting principles."

Banker B "You have an exceptionally strong working capital position and do not need a loan. Besides, we are fully loaned up at the present time."

Banker C "Since you do not need the money immediately, I would suggest that you take the following action before we make a final decision on your loan request:

(1) Make a stronger effort to collect your receivables, write off the worthless accounts, and provide an allowance for additional uncollectibles.
(2) Cut production until inventories are reduced, auction some slow-moving items to raise cash, and postpone payments on payables as long as possible.
(3) Obtain the services of an accountant who can help you reduce costs, improve inventory controls, and reduce credit losses.

Instructions
a Evaluate the position taken by each of the three bankers.
b Assuming that $8,000 of the accounts are definitely uncollectible, that an allowance of 6% of the remaining receivables is considered adequate, and that the market value (replacement cost) of inventories is approximately $41,200, prepare a revised summary of working capital for Oak Furniture Company as of April 1, 1980.
c Prepare a reconciliation of the difference between the $99,900 working capital determined by the accountant and your computation of working capital in part **b** above.

7B-5 Denim Garment Corporation finances some of its current operations by assigning accounts receivable to Belmont Finance Company. On May 1 of the current year, it assigned accounts receivable amounting to $300,000, Belmont Finance Company advancing 80% of the accounts assigned, less a commission charge of 2% of the total accounts assigned. Customers are instructed to make payment directly to Belmont Finance Company. Collections in excess of the loan and finance charges will be remitted to Denim Garment Corporation. At this time, the accountant for the Denim Garment Corporation transfers any balance in Assigned Accounts Receivable to the regular Accounts Receivable account.

The status of assigned accounts receivable at the end of May and June follows:

May 31 Denim Garment Corporation received a statement that Belmont Finance Company had collected $180,000 of the assigned accounts receivable and had made an additional charge for interest of 1% of assigned accounts outstanding at May 31, this charge to be deducted from the first remittance of cash by Belmont Finance Company to Denim Garment Corporation.

June 30 Denim Garment Corporation received a second statement from Belmont Finance Company, together with a check for the amount due. The statement indicated that Belmont Finance Company had collected an additional $66,000 and had made an additional charge for interest of 1% of assigned accounts outstanding at June 30.

Instructions
a Prepare the journal entries necessary to record the above transactions in the accounts of Denim Garment Corporation.
b Show how the information regarding assigned receivables should be presented in the balance sheet of Denim Garment Corporation (1) at May 31 and (2) at June 30.

7B-6 Hill & Nutter, equal partners in a merchandising firm, have not prepared financial statements for three years, since December 31, Year 1. The partnership used the accrual method of accounting and reported income on a calendar-year basis prior to Year 2. During the past three years (Years 2, 3, and 4), the partnership has maintained cash records and has entered sales on account in an accounts receivable ledger; however, no general ledger postings have been made.

The balances at the beginning and end of the three-year period accumulated as a result of your examination are presented below:

	Dec. 31	
	Year 4	Year 1
Aging of accounts receivable:		
Less than 1 year old	$14,562	$7,700
1–2 years old	1,900	600
2–3 years old	2,138	
Over 3 years old (known to be uncollectible)	1,100	
	$19,700	$8,300
Inventories	$ 9,400	$5,800
Accounts payable: merchandise purchases	$ 6,500	$4,305

Other information compiled from the accounting records follows:

	Year 4	Year 3	Year 2	Total
Cash received on account, relating to:				
Current year's collections	$103,938	$80,900	$74,400	$259,238
Accounts of the prior year	8,400	7,500	6,700	22,600
Accounts of two years prior	262	200	300	762
Total cash received in Years 2–4 . .	$112,600	$88,600	$81,400	$282,600
Accounts to be written off in addition to				
the $1,100 which are over 3 years old	$ 1,062	$ 820	$ 1,988	$ 3,870
Of receivables remaining at end of Year 4,				
estimated uncollectible percentage .	10%	50%	80%	
Cash sales	$ 15,600	$13,200	$13,500	$ 42,300
Payments for merchandise purchases .	$ 86,900	$70,600	$62,500	$220,000

No accounts receivable have been written off during the three-year period. The partners estimate that the rate of gross profit remained relatively constant from year to year.

Instructions

a Prepare a schedule showing the gross profit on sales for Years 2, 3, and 4. First compute cost of goods sold as a percentage of sales for the three-year period.

b Prepare the adjusting entry necessary to write off the accounts known to be uncollectible and then set up an adequate allowance for estimated doubtful accounts at the end of Year 4. Debit current year's expense account for the full amount required to establish the allowance for doubtful accounts.

c The partners wish to know what percentage of credit sales would be reasonable as an estimate of yearly doubtful accounts expense in the future, based on the experience of the past three years. Support your recommendation with an orderly schedule.

8

INVENTORIES: COST AND COST FLOW ASSUMPTIONS

Nature of inventories

Inventories consist of goods held for sale to customers, partially completed goods in production, and materials and supplies to be used in production. Inventory items are acquired and sold continuously in a merchandising business; or acquired, placed in production, converted into a finished product, and sold in a manufacturing business. The sale of merchandise or finished products is the primary source of revenue for most business enterprises.

In a retail or merchandising operation, inventories consist principally of products purchased for resale in their existing form. A retail business may also have an inventory of supplies such as wrapping paper, cartons, and stationery. A manufacturing business, on the other hand, has several types of inventories: materials, parts, and factory supplies; goods in process; and finished goods.

Materials and parts are basic commodities or other products obtained directly from natural resources or acquired from others, which will be physically incorporated into finished goods. *Factory supplies* are similar to materials, but their relation to the end product is indirect. For example, in the manufacture of shirts, the bolts of cloth are inventoried as materials, whereas the cleaning materials and the oil to lubricate the machines are classified as factory supplies. *Goods in process* is the title given to the inventory of partially completed product. The goods in process inventory includes the cost of materials, direct labor, and factory overhead assigned to the partially completed units. *Finished goods* are items which are complete and ready for sale. The cost of finished goods is composed of the same elements as those found in goods in process, the difference being that *all* necessary production costs have been incurred and allocated to finished goods.

Inventory procedures

Two methods may be employed to ascertain the inventory quantities on hand, the periodic system and the perpetual system. Both systems may be employed simultaneously for various parts of the inventory.

The *periodic system* relies on a periodic physical count of the goods on hand as the basis for control, management decisions, and financial reporting. Although this procedure may give very accurate results at a given time, there is no continuing record of the inventory. The *perpetual system* requires a continuous record of all receipts and withdrawals of each item of inventory. The perpetual record is generally kept in terms of quantities only. This procedure provides a better basis for control than can be obtained under the periodic system. When a perpetual system is used, a physical count of the goods on hand must be made periodically to verify the accuracy of the inventory as shown in the accounting records. Any discrepancies discovered must be corrected so that the perpetual record reflects the physical count.

COST AND QUANTITY ACCUMULATION

Timing errors in recording purchases and sales

When the cost of goods available for sale during a particular period is being accumulated, decisions frequently must be made as to whether certain goods become the property of the company in the current or in the succeeding period. If acquisitions of goods are not recorded in the period in which they become the property of the buyer, errors in the financial statements will result:

Three common types of timing errors in recording inventory acquisitions may occur. The errors and their effect on financial statements are:

1 The purchase is recorded properly but the goods are not included in the ending inventory. The result is to understate current assets and net income.
2 The purchase is not recorded but the goods are included in the ending inventory. The result is to state the assets properly but to understate current liabilities and to overstate net income.
3 The purchase is not recorded and the goods are not included in the ending inventory. Net income in this case is unaffected since purchases and ending inventory are understated by the same amount, but current assets and current liabilities are both understated.

The first two errors are most likely to occur when the periodic inventory system is used; the third type may occur under either system, but it is more likely when the perpetual system is used. In most cases timing errors will be corrected automatically in the following period; however, the fact that the errors may be self-correcting does not remove the need for correct presentation of financial position and results of operations for each period.

The valuation of inventories has important effects on both the balance sheet and the income statement. The investment in inventory is frequently a major part of a business entity's total assets, and the valuation of inventory has a direct effect on the determination of the cost of goods sold. The role of inventory valuation on the balance sheet and on the income statement is illustrated below:

Beginning inventory (current asset in balance sheet at end of Year 9)	$200,000
Add: Purchases (or cost of goods manufactured) during Year 10 . . .	700,000
Total cost of goods available for sale during Year 10	$900,000
Less: Ending inventory (current asset in balance sheet at end of Year 10)	150,000
Cost of goods sold during Year 10	$750,000

In this illustration the cost of goods available for sale is $900,000, composed of the beginning inventory and the costs incurred during Year 10. The cost of goods available for sale is allocated between (1) the inventory on hand at the end of the period which will be economically useful in future periods, $150,000, and (2) the cost of goods which have been sold during the current period, $750,000. The cost of goods sold is the difference between the total cost of goods available for sale and the cost assigned to the ending inventory. Any failure to determine accurately either the cost of goods available for sale or the ending inventory can have a material effect on financial statements.

Goods in transit

Orders for goods which have not been filled by the seller present little difficulty for the account. Those orders which have been filled by the seller but not received by the buyer are the crucial ones. The problem which must be resolved in these cases is to determine whether the goods in transit are the property of the buyer or of the seller. The passage of title from the seller to the buyer marks the time when the legal responsibility for the goods changes from one party to the other.

Purchase contracts usually specify which party is responsible for the goods and the exact location when the responsibility changes. This point is usually indicated by the letters *"F.O.B.,"* meaning *"free on board,"* followed by the designation of a particular location, for example,

"F.O.B. Denver." This means that title is held by the seller until the goods are delivered to a common carrier in Denver who will act as an agent for the buyer.[1] The following example illustrates this concept:

Kansas Shirt Shop orders 200 shirts from Denver Fashions Co. to be shipped "F.O.B. Denver," the bill to be paid within 10 days after shipment. When Denver Fashions Co. delivers the goods in Denver to a common carrier who acts as an agent of Kansas Shirt Shop, the title to the goods passes to the buyer. At this time Kansas Shirt Shop should make an entry debiting Purchases (or Inventory) and crediting Accounts Payable. Of course the freight charges in this case must be paid by Kansas Shirt Shop; however, this liability does not arise until the agent delivers the goods to Kansas Shirt Shop.

Suppose at the same time Kansas Shirt Shop also orders 1,000 shirts from the Cub Co. in Chicago, delivered "F.O.B. Kansas City." In this case the shirts are the property of Cub Co. until they are delivered, and Kansas Shirt Shop does not recognize an asset or a liability until the shirts are actually received.

Goods on consignment and installment sales

Goods may be transferred by one party to another without the typical sale and purchase agreement. The party receiving the goods, the **consignee,** agrees to accept the goods without any liability, beyond that of providing reasonable protection from loss or damage, until the goods are sold to a third party. At this time the consignee must remit to the shipper, the **consignor,** the sales price less a selling commission and expenses incurred in connection with the sale. The consignor has retained title to the goods until the time of sale to the third party and the consignee, acting only as an agent, has never taken title to the goods. Therefore, until the goods are sold by the consignee, they remain the property of the consignor and must be included as a part of the consignor's inventory at cost, including the handling and shipping costs involved in the transfer to the consignee. The consignee does not own the consigned goods and, therefore, should not include them in inventory.

When goods are sold on the installment plan, the seller usually retains legal title to the goods until full payment has been received; however, such goods are excluded from inventory of the seller. The expectation is that customers will make payment in the ordinary course of business; therefore strict adherence to the "passing-of-title" rule is not considered a realistic approach to recording installment sales transactions. Problems that arise in recording consignments and installment sales are discussed in **Modern Advanced Accounting** of this series.

---

[1] Other important F.O.B. designations are "F.O.B. point of destination" and "F.O.B. point of shipment," meaning that title passes at buyer's plant and at seller's plant, respectively.

Inventoriable costs

The two most important functions in accounting for inventories are (1) to determine the quantity of goods to be included in inventory and (2) to determine the proper cost of the inventory on hand. The first function involves the *taking of inventory,* the second a *valuation of inventory.*

After the quantity of goods on hand has been determined, the starting point in the valuation process is to ascertain the inventoriable cost elements of merchandise purchased or products manufactured. For inventory items purchased from outsiders, the net invoice cost is generally considered as the inventoriable cost. *Net invoice cost* is the invoice price of the item less any cash (purchase) discount *available* to the buyer. Cash discounts should not be included as part of inventory cost, regardless of whether the buyer takes advantage of the discount or fails to do so.

In theory, if a given cost is expected to contribute to the production of future revenue, this cost should be associated with the goods acquired. Thus a theoretical justification exists for adding the indirect costs of ordering, freight-in, handling, and storing merchandise to the net invoice cost to determine the total cost of goods acquired. However, the work involved in allocating these costs to inventory often is greater than the benefits to be derived from increased accuracy of inventory valuation. Furthermore, the allocation of some indirect costs to goods acquired may be highly subjective.

Although the assignment to inventory of all costs incurred in readying goods for sale is desirable, unrealistic allocations of indirect costs should be avoided to prevent conveying a false implication of certainty and precision in the measurement of inventory costs. When costs are incurred which are necessary to the acquisition or production of goods but which are not expected to produce future benefits or are not material in amount, the costs are usually not included in inventories. Instead, such costs are considered period costs to be deducted from revenue of the current period. The foregoing discussion is summarized in a diagram on page 306.

Merchandise Inventories All costs incurred in ordering, securing, handling, and storing merchandise are as much a part of the total cost of the merchandise as the net invoice cost itself. The following example involving the purchase of merchandise by Kansas Shirt Shop described on page 304 illustrates the determination of the cost of goods acquired.

Assume that the invoice from Denver Fashions Co. indicates the price of the 200 shirts to be $10 each, with terms 2/10, n/30. This means that Kansas Shirt Shop must pay Denver Fashions Co. $1,960 within 10 days of the date of the invoice or pay $2,000 within 30 days after the date of the invoice. The net invoice cost is therefore $1,960. If payment is not made within 10 days, the $40 cash discount lost should be treated as a financing expense of the period rather than as a cost of inventory.

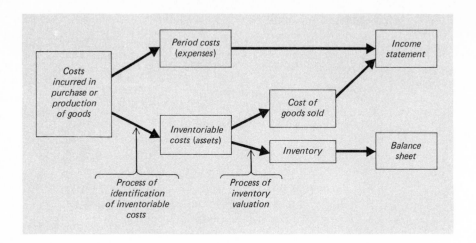

The cost of deciding to order these particular shirts, the actual cost of ordering them, the transportation cost, and the handling and storage cost incurred after receipt of the shirts, are all costs which logically might be added to the net invoice cost.

Manufactured Inventories In many ways the problems of measuring inventory costs are the same in a manufacturing concern as they are in a retail establishment. This is particularly true of raw materials and other purchased inventoriable items. The major difference is found in measuring the cost of finished goods and goods in process. Tracing the movement of goods and costs through the production process is often difficult, but if done with reasonable care, the resulting information is useful to both management and outsiders.

As stated earlier, three classes of inventory are usually found in a manufacturing business: (1) materials, parts, and factory supplies, (2) goods in process, and (3) finished goods. The cost of these inventories emerges as a part of the general process of measuring the cost of the resources (materials, direct labor, and factory overhead) that flow through the manufacturing process and of tracing these costs to specific quantities of partially finished and finished product as illustrated below:

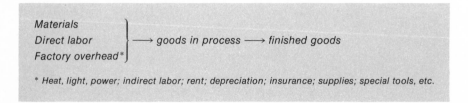

There are basically two *cost systems* that are used to accumulate product costs for a manufacturing enterprise, the job order cost system and the process cost system.

A *job order cost system* is used when the enterprise is manufacturing several distinct products. For example, a job order system would be used for a construction firm or a specialty product firm. Each product or group of products is distinct in some way and the production costs are identified with the specific job. *Job order cost sheets* are used to accumulate the cost of material, direct labor, and factory overhead incurred on each job. Costs entered in job order cost sheets make up the goods in process inventory until the jobs are completed. The cost of completed jobs is a part of the finished goods inventory until the title to goods passes to customers.

A *process cost system* is used when large numbers of similar units are produced on an assembly-line type of operation. The production process is typically divided into *cost centers* or departments, based on logical divisions for the assignment of responsibility. Material, direct labor, and factory overhead costs are then accumulated by cost center and the goods in process inventory is the sum of all costs incurred on the uncompleted units in the various cost centers. The finished goods inventory is composed of all costs incurred through the entire manufacturing operation.

When a process cost system is used, the cost of producing a complete unit of product is usually determined from departmental *cost of production reports.* Such reports show how the total costs incurred were assigned to any *by-products* (or scrap) and to the *main product.* By-products are usually priced at net realizable value; if the value is immaterial, no cost need be assigned to by-products.

Accountants frequently encounter situations in which production costs in a given manufacturing process relate to two or more products. The allocation of these *joint costs* is necessary to determine the unit cost of each product and is frequently made on the basis of the *relative sales value* of the *joint products.* By dividing the total joint costs by the total sales value of the joint products, the *cost percentage* is determined and is then applied to the unit selling price of each product to determine the estimated unit cost of each product.

Many companies engaged in manufacturing activities use standard costs as an integral part of their cost systems. *Standard costs* are estimates of what costs *should be* under relatively ideal conditions. The basic purpose of standard costs is to aid in measuring the efficiency of an operation, but standard costs are also sometimes used for inventory valuation. The factors that make standard costs a good control mechanism serve to reduce their usefulness for inventory valuation purposes. To be a good control device, a standard cost of a product should represent what cost *ought to be,* not what it *is* or *has been.* When standard costs are used for inventory valuation, accountants should ascertain that the standard costs are a reasonable approximation of costs actually incurred.

COST FLOW ASSUMPTIONS

The term *cost flow* refers to the inflow of costs when goods are purchased or manufactured and the outflow of costs when goods are sold. The cost remaining in inventory is the difference between the inflow and outflow of costs. During a given period such as a year or a month, identical goods may be purchased or manufactured at different costs. Accountants then face the problem of determining which costs apply to items in inventory and which to items that have been sold. The critical issue in accounting for inventories is summarized below:

> A major objective of accounting for inventories is the proper determination of income through the process of matching appropriate costs against revenues.
>
> Cost for inventory purposes may be determined under any one of several assumptions as to the flow of cost factors (such as, first-in, first-out, average, and last-in, first-out); the major objective in selecting a method should be to choose the one which, under the circumstances, most clearly reflects periodic income.[2]

The *assumed flow of costs* to be used in assigning costs to inventory and to goods sold need not conform to the physical flow of goods. *Cost flow assumptions relate to the flow of costs rather than to the physical flow of goods.* The question of which physical units of identical goods were sold and which remain in inventory is not of any particular importance in the accounting problem of income determination.

All methods of inventory valuation are based on the *cost principle;* no matter which method is selected, the inventory is considered to be stated at cost. In selecting an inventory valuation method (or cost flow assumption), we are matching costs with revenue, and the ideal choice is the method that "most clearly reflects periodic income." The methods of inventory valuation in wide use at the present time are:

1 First-in, first-out method (fifo)
2 Last-in, first-out method (lifo)
3 Weighted-average method
4 Specific identification method

A recent survey of 600 corporate annual reports indicated that fifo was used by 376 companies; lifo was used by 315 companies; average cost was used by 235 companies; and 118 companies applied a variety of other methods to the valuation of inventories. Obviously, many of the companies included in the survey used more than one method.[3]

---

[2] *Accounting Research and Terminology Bulletins—Final Edition,* AICPA (New York: 1961), chap. 4, pp. 28–29.
[3] *Accounting Trends & Techniques, 30th ed.,* AICPA (New York: 1976), p. 89.

First-in, first-out method

The first-in, first-out method assumes a flow of costs based on the assumption that the oldest goods on hand are sold first. This assumption about cost flow generally conforms to reality; management usually finds it desirable to keep the oldest goods in the inventory moving out to customers in order to keep fresh goods on hand. The method is systematic and is easy to apply; it adheres to the cost principle; and the cost assigned to inventory is likely to be in close harmony with the current prices being paid for inventory replacements.

To understand the application of the fifo method, assume the following data for the month of January relating to item X in the inventory of West Company:

WEST COMPANY			
Record of Purchases during January			
Jan. 1	Inventory on hand	200 units @ $ 7	$ 1,400
Jan. 8	Purchase	1,100 units @ $ 8	8,800
Jan. 25	Purchase	300 units @ $ 9	2,700
Jan. 30	Purchase	400 units @ $10	4,000
	Total	2,000	$16,900

A physical inventory taken on January 31 shows 700 units on hand. The inventory could be composed of any combination of 700 units on hand at the beginning of the period or purchased during the period. If we follow the fifo procedure, however, we assume that the inventory is composed of the items which were acquired most recently. The calculation of the inventory cost at January 31 based on fifo assumption is illustrated below:

WEST COMPANY		
Inventory: First-In, First-Out Method		
Jan. 30 (last purchase)	400 units @ $10	$4,000
Jan. 25 (next to last purchase)	300 units @ $ 9	2,700
Total	700	$6,700

The cost of goods sold is $10,200 (total goods available, $16,900, less ending inventory, $6,700). The cost of goods sold for the period has been charged with the earliest costs incurred for the goods. The fifo method will give the same result whether the periodic or perpetual inventory system is used. Each withdrawal of goods is from the oldest stock. For example, if the perpetual inventory system is used and the cost of units sold is determined on a daily basis, the cost of goods sold would be computed as shown below. The cost of the inventory on the fifo basis using a perpetual inventory system, therefore, is also $6,700 ($16,900 goods available for sale less $10,200 cost of goods sold).

WEST COMPANY
Cost of Goods Sold: First-In, First-Out Method

Jan. 6	100 issued @ $7	$ 700
Jan. 9	200 issued $\begin{cases} 100 @ \$7 \\ 100 @ \$8 \end{cases}$	1,500
Jan. 15	400 issued @ $8	3,200
Jan. 27	600 issued @ $8	4,800
Total	1,300	$10,200

Last-in, first-out method

The last-in first-out method assumes a flow of inventory costs based on the assumption that the most recently acquired goods on hand are sold first because current costs are incurred to make current sales and maintain an adequate inventory on hand. Under this view the latest costs are most closely associated with current revenue, and thus the matching principle of income determination is carried out. In the balance sheet, however, inventory under the lifo method tends to be valued at the earliest costs of accumulating a minimum level of inventory.

The following data for the month of January relating to item X in the inventory of West Company are the same as those used for the fifo illustration, except for the addition of dates sales were made:

WEST COMPANY
Record of Purchases and Sales during January

Purchases					Sales	
Date		Units	Price	Total	Date	Units sold
Jan. 1	Inventory on hand . .	200	$ 7	$ 1,400	Jan. 6	100
Jan. 8	Purchase	1,100	8	8,800	Jan. 9	200
Jan. 25	Purchase	300	9	2,700	Jan. 15	400
Jan. 30	Purchase	400	10	4,000	Jan. 27	600
	Total	2,000		$16,900	Total	1,300

The cost assigned to the ending inventory using lifo depends on whether the periodic or perpetual inventory system is used.

Periodic Inventory System Based on the information presented above, the cost of the 700 units on hand at January 31 is computed as follows under the lifo periodic inventory system:

WEST COMPANY		
Inventory: Last-In, First-Out Method (Periodic Inventory System)		
Jan. 1 (beginning inventory)	200 units @ $7	$1,400
Jan. 8 (first purchase)	500 units @ $8	4,000
Total	700	$5,400

The lifo inventory at January 31 is composed of two layers: the 200 units on hand on January 1, plus the layer of 500 units added during January. Should sales exceed purchases in any subsequent period, the cost of units comprising the most recently added layer or layers would be removed from inventory and transferred to cost of goods sold. The cost of the original layer would not be reduced until all subsequently added layers had been assigned to cost of goods sold. The cost of goods sold for January is $11,500 ($16,900 cost of goods available for sale less $5,400 cost of inventory at January 31) and comprises the most recent costs incurred for purchases.

Perpetual Inventory System Unlike the first-in, first-out method, the last-in, first-out method will not produce the same result if the perpetual inventory system is used. When a perpetual inventory system is used, each withdrawal must come from the most recent purchase; however, this may mean that under certain conditions items will be withdrawn from the beginning inventory or early purchases. If we assume the same record of purchases and sales as occurred under the fifo procedure above, the costs applicable to the goods sold using the lifo perpetual inventory system would be $10,600, as computed on page 312.

WEST COMPANY		
Cost of Goods Sold: Last-In, First-Out Method (Perpetual Inventory System)		
Jan. 6	100 issued @ $7	$ 700
Jan. 9	200 issued @ $8	1,600
Jan. 15	400 issued @ $8	3,200
Jan. 27	600 issued { 300 @ $9	2,700
	{ 300 @ $8	2,400
Total	1,300	$10,600

The ending inventory using the lifo perpetual inventory system amounts to $6,300 ($16,900− $10,600) and consists of the following:

WEST COMPANY		
Inventory: Last-In, First-Out Method (Perpetual Inventory System)		
Jan. 1 (Balance of beginning layer not sold) . . .	100 units @ $ 7	$ 700
Jan. 8	200 units @ $ 8	1,600
Jan. 30	400 units @ $10	4,000
Total	700	$6,300

Thus it becomes apparent that the results of the lifo method of valuing the inventory under the perpetual inventory system may vary somewhat, depending on the timing of sales.

Unit-lifo Method The practical problems of determining the cost of inventory using the lifo procedure occasionally are overwhelming, especially without the aid of a computer. When there are large numbers of similar items and numerous transactions, the weighted-average unit cost of the items purchased during the period is considered the cost for purposes of calculating additions to inventory for the period. Such a procedure eliminates the need for identifying the cost of particular units. This adaptation is used in conjunction with a periodic inventory system and is called the **unit-lifo method.** Using the data presented on the bottom of page 310 for West Company, the unit-lifo inventory at January 31 is computed as illustrated on page 313.

WEST COMPANY
Inventory: Unit-lifo Method

Beginning inventory	200 units @ $7.00	$1,400
Layer added in January	500 units @ $8.61*	4,305
Total	700	$5,705

* Calculation of weighted-average unit cost for units acquired in January:

Cost of purchases	$15,500
Total units purchased in January	1,800
Weighted-average unit cost of purchases: $15,500 ÷ 1,800	$ 8.61

The unit-lifo method would be applied only when there is an increase in the inventory during the period. The layer added in January would retain its identity in subsequent months as long as the inventory consists of 700 units or more. However, if the inventory decreased to 400 units in February, the inventory would consist of 200 units at $7 and only 200 units at $8.61.

Dollar-Value Lifo   The *dollar-value lifo* method is another procedure designed to facilitate the calculation of inventory. Under dollar-value lifo, the inventory can be priced at current costs, which eliminates the need for identification of the specific costs of units in inventory. The total current costs of the inventory is then restated, by means of a specific price index, to the cost prevailing when lifo was adopted. The ending inventory in terms of base-year dollars is compared with the beginning inventory also priced at base-year dollars to determine the physical change in the inventory on hand. Increases or decreases in the inventory are then assigned costs prevailing at the end of the period in which the items were acquired.

Simple Example of Dollar-Value Lifo   The essence of the dollar-value method can be observed in the following simplified example. If the beginning inventory cost $10,000 and the ending inventory cost $11,000, there has been an apparent increase in the number of units on hand of 10%. If the unit cost of the goods is unchanged, there would be a 10% increase in the quantity on hand; if there were originally 1,000 units, there are 1,100 units now. However, if the unit cost of goods had increased by 10%, there would have been no increase in the number of units on hand despite the 10% increase in dollar amount of inventory. *If the quantity of goods on hand is unchanged, the lifo inventory valuation stated in dollars also should remain unchanged.* In valuing lifo inventory by the dollar-value method, the *actual* increase or decrease in the physical inventory is first ascertained and then an appropriate current cost is assigned to the increase or decrease.

Any increase in the inventory quantity should be valued at costs prevailing during the current year. In practice the index of costs as of the **end of the current year** is often used to value the added layer. Although the use of the year-end cost index implies the use of the fifo method, practical limitations of computing several indices during a given year have led to acceptance of the year-end cost index for this purpose. A decrease in the inventory is deducted from the most recent layer added to the inventory at the costs prevailing in the year when the layer was added.

Comprehensive Illustration of Dollar-Value Lifo The following data concerning ending inventories and the specific cost index for the inventory at the end of each year are used to illustrate the application of the dollar-value lifo method for Doval Company:

Year ended	Inventory at year-end costs	Cost index at end of year
Dec. 31, Year 1	$36,000	100
Dec. 31, Year 2	57,500	125
Dec. 31, Year 3	60,000	150
Dec. 31, Year 4	65,800	140

Computation of dollar-value inventories for Doval Company is summarized on page 315.

Explanation of inventory computations

Year 2 The ending inventory is converted to a valuation of $46,000 at base-year costs by dividing the year-end cost of $57,500 by the year-end cost index of 1.25. The increase in the inventory is determined to be $10,000. This increase is then converted to year-end costs by multiplying the increase, stated in base-year costs, by the cost index at the end of the year. Thus the dollar-value inventory at the end of Year 2 is $48,500, the beginning inventory of $36,000 plus the layer of $12,500 added in Year 2.

Year 3 A decrease in inventory of $6,000 ($46,000 − $40,000 = $6,000) took place in Year 3. This decrease should be considered a reduction in the most recent addition to the inventory. The most recent addition was $10,000 (in terms of base-year costs), which took place in Year 2. The decrease of $6,000 from the $10,000 layer leaves only $4,000 of the Year 2 increase in inventory. This $4,000 is then converted to the cost level at the end of Year 2, when this layer was added. Thus the ending inventory at the end of Year 3 is $41,000, consisting of the base-year layer of $36,000 plus the remaining portion of the layer added in Year 2, $5,000.

Year 4 The inventory of $47,000 at base-year costs shows an increase of $7,000 ($47,000 − $40,000 = $7,000) during Year 4. This increase is multiplied by 1.40, the cost index at the end of Year 4, to convert it to the year-end

DOVAL COMPANY
Dollar-Value Lifo Method
Years 1 through 4

Year	Inventory at year-end costs	÷	Deflator (cost index at year-end)	=	Inventory at base-year costs	Determination of inventory layers	Dollar-value inventory at year-end
1 (base)	$36,000	÷	1.00	=	$36,000	——$36,000 × 1.00 ————	$36,000
2	$57,500	÷	1.25	=	$46,000	$36,000 × 1.00 = $36,000 10,000 × 1.25 = $12,500 $46,000	$48,500
3	$60,000	÷	1.50	=	$40,000	$36,000 × 1.00 = $36,000 4,000 × 1.25 = $ 5,000 $40,000	$41,000
4	$65,800	÷	1.40	=	$47,000	$36,000 × 1.00 = $36,000 4,000 × 1.25 = $ 5,000 7,000 × 1.40 = $ 9,800 $47,000	$50,800

cost of $9,800. The increase is then added to the beginning inventory of $41,000 to arrive at the ending inventory of $50,800.

The key feature of the dollar-value lifo method is the conversion of both beginning and ending inventory to base-year costs. The difference between the two converted inventory figures indicates the increase or decrease in the inventory expressed in terms of base-year costs. The lifo layers must then be valued at costs prevailing when the layers were added to the inventory.[4]

Cost Index Specific cost indices such as the index for nonferrous metals or for department store prices are often used in making inventory cost adjustments to arrive at dollar-value lifo data.

In the absence of an appropriate cost index, the accountant can take a *sample* of the inventory and value this sample at both current year's costs and at the base period's costs. The total cost in terms of the current year's prices is then divided by the total cost in terms of the base period's prices. The cost index so determined is used to value the entire

[4] For an excellent illustration of dollar-value inventory computation, see A. Jay Hirsch, "Dollar-Value and Retail LIFO: A Diagrammatic Approach," *The Accounting Review* (October 1969), vol. 44, pp. 840–842.

inventory. In calculating this index, discontinued and new products deserve special consideration. The best approach is to eliminate these items from the general calculation. They in turn must be valued separately, and in many cases the only feasible way is to refer to particular invoice costs.

The cost index for a sample of inventory items can be computed as follows:

Item	Inventory quantity	Unit costs		Total costs	
		End of current period	Base period	End of current period	Base period
A	150	$40.00	$36.00	$6,000	$5,400
B	60	15.00	13.00	900	780
C	200	4.00	4.10	800	820
				$7,700	$7,000

Cost index: $7,700 ÷ $7,000 = 110%

This computation indicates that current prices have risen on the average by 10% from base-period prices.

Base Stock Method The *base stock method* is similar to lifo but because it is not acceptable for income tax purposes and has little theoretical support, it is seldom used in practice. This method assumes a continuous existence of a minimum stock of goods and inventory is considered to be a permanent asset. Any excess over the base stock is considered a temporary increase and is priced at current replacement cost; any decrease in the base stock is considered to be temporary and is charged against revenue at the current replacement cost.

The base stock method differs from lifo in that it uses *current replacement cost* as an element in pricing inventory; on the other hand, lifo relies exclusively on actual costs.

Weighted-average method

The weighted-average method of valuing inventory is based on the assumption that all the goods are commingled and that no particular batch of goods is retained in the inventory. The inventory is thus priced on the basis of average prices paid for the goods, weighted according to the quantity purchased at each price. Using the information for West Company, the ending inventory and cost of goods sold are determined under the weighted-average method as follows:

WEST COMPANY

Inventory and Cost of Goods Sold: Weighted-Average Method (Physical System)

Cost of goods available for sale $16,900
Total units available for sale 2,000
Unit price = cost ÷ number of units ($16,900 ÷ 2,000) . . . . $ 8.45
Inventory valuation: 700 × $8.45 . . . . $ 5,915
Cost of goods sold ($16,900 − $5,915) $10,985

This method produces a result, both for inventory valuation and income determination, which lies between the results achieved under fifo and those achieved under lifo. The assumption on which the method is based may be attacked on the theory that few businesses withdraw goods from stock completely at random. The method will not produce an inventory value consistent with the current cost of the items in the inventory; by its very nature it will lag behind the market prices. During a period of rising prices the inventory cost will tend to be below market price and during a period of falling prices it will tend to be above market price.

If a perpetual system is used, the weighted-average method will give the result of a *moving weighted average.* Under a perpetual system, a new weighted-average unit cost is computed after each purchase and for this reason is known as the moving weighted average. Issues are priced at the latest weighted-average unit cost. Using the information for West Company, this effect is demonstrated on page 318.

Specific identification method

At first thought one might argue that each item of inventory should be identified with its cost and that the sum of these amounts should constitute the inventory value. While such a technique might be possible for a company handling a small number of items, for example, an automobile retailer, it becomes completely inoperable in a complex manufacturing company when the identity of the individual item is lost. Practical considerations thus make specific identification inappropriate in most cases.

Even when specific identification is a feasible means of valuation, it may be undesirable from a theoretical point of view. The method opens the door to income manipulation when there are like items acquired at varying prices. By choosing to sell the item which was acquired at a specific cost the management can cause material fluctuations in income. For example, assume that Jane Grain Company acquires 1 million bushels of wheat in four equal lots of 250,000 bushels each, at costs of $2.50, $3, $3.50, and $4 per bushel. Jane Grain receives an

WEST COMPANY

Inventory: Moving Weighted Average (Perpetual System)

	Units	Amount
Jan. 1 inventory	200 @ $7.00	$1,400
Less: Jan. 6 issue	(100) @ $7.00	(700)
Balance, Jan. 6	100 @ $7.00	$ 700
Jan. 8 purchase	1,100 @ $8.00	8,800
Balance, Jan. 8 (new unit cost computed) . .	1,200 @ $7.92	$9,500*
Less: Jan. 9 issue	(200) @ $7.92	(1,584)
Balance, Jan. 9	1,000 @ $7.92	$7,916*
Less: Jan. 15 issue	(400) @ $7.92	(3,168)
Balance, Jan. 15	600 @ $7.92	$4,748*
Jan. 25 purchase	300 @ $9.00	2,700
Balance, Jan. 25 (new unit cost computed) . .	900 @ $8.28	$7,448*
Less: Jan. 27 issue	(600) @ $8.28	(4,968)
Balance, Jan. 27	300 @ $8.28	$2,480*
Jan. 30 purchase	400 @ $10.00	4,000
Balance, Jan. 31 (inventory at new unit cost) .	700 @ $9.26	$6,480*

* Slight discrepancy due to rounding of average cost to nearest cent.

order to sell 250,000 bushels at $3.75 per bushel. If the management is accounting for inventory in accordance with specific identification, then it can determine the income reported for the period by selecting that batch of wheat which will produce the desired objective. The results of the transaction could range from a profit of $312,500, if the $2.50 wheat were sold, to a loss of $62,500 if the $4 wheat were sold. If an assumption regarding the flow of goods were adopted, for example, the first goods purchased are the first goods sold, the effect of such arbitrary decisions on reported income would be removed.

The total profit or loss derived from the sale of the 1 million bushels of wheat will be the same, ignoring tax effects, regardless of the order in which the batches are sold. The important consideration here is the periodic report of income and financial position, which may be changed as a result of varying assumptions regarding the flow of goods through the business. Consequently, a systematic inventory flow assumption is desirable in the interests of objective financial reporting.

Summary of inventory valuation methods

The inventory valuation and cost of goods sold for West Company as determined in the preceding illustrations are summarized on page 319. Results using the specific identification method are not shown because we did not identify the composition of the units in inventory by date of purchase.

WEST COMPANY
Inventory and Cost of Goods Sold: Various Cost Flow Assumptions

Cost flow assumption	Goods available for sale	Inventory	Cost of goods sold
First-in, first-out method . . .	$16,900	$6,700	$10,200
Last-in, first-out method:			
Periodic inventory system .	16,900	5,400	11,500
Perpetual inventory system	16,900	6,300	10,600
Unit lifo	16,900	5,705	11,195
Weighted-average (periodic)			
system	16,900	5,915	10,985
Moving-weighted-average			
(perpetual) system	16,900	6,480	10,420

In the West Company example in which prices were rising, the costs assigned to inventory range from a high of $6,700 using the fifo method to a low of $5,400 when the lifo method is used in conjunction with the periodic inventory system. The disparity in inventory valuation under the various cost flow assumptions depends on the trend and volatility of prices paid for new purchases and, of course, the length of time the lifo method has been in use.

INVENTORY VALUATION AND INFLATION

Although both lifo and fifo are accepted methods, they may lead to significant differences in the financial statements during a period of inflation. Since neither method achieves an entirely satisfactory reporting of both the inventory and cost of goods sold when prices are going up, it is not surprising that a controversy has evolved around the relative importance of the working capital and net income. But in an inflationary period, this controversy is somewhat overshadowed by the managerial and income tax implications underlying inventory valuation.

Effect on working capital and net income

As illustrated earlier, the fifo method has the effect of assigning the most recently incurred cost to the inventory, whereas the lifo assumption assigns the first costs incurred to inventory. During periods of rising price levels, inventory valued on the fifo basis will more closely approximate the current replacement cost of the inventory; the cost of items valued on the lifo basis will be less than the current replacement cost. The difference between the inventory value at lifo and current replacement cost will depend on the magnitude of the price increase. The lifo method produces a seriously distorted inventory valuation when it is used over a long period during which the price level increases steadily or when the price level increases very rapidly.

The understatement of inventory resulting from the use of the lifo method is objectionable because of the effect on working capital, current ratio, and inventory turnover rate. The problem is rather serious when no indication is included in the financial statements of the degree of understatement. The advocates of lifo minimize the importance of this understatement by their insistence that the income statement is more important than the balance sheet. They argue that a more accurate measure of net income may justify a less meaningful balance sheet.

Proponents of the lifo method argue that realized revenue should be matched with the cost of acquiring goods at or near the time the revenue is realized. They contend that during periods of rising prices, for example, two types of profits, inventory profits (or holding gains) and operating profits (or trading profits), are likely to be included in the determination of net income unless diligence is exercised to avoid the inclusion of inventory profits. **Inventory profits** arise as a result of holding inventories during periods of rising prices and **operating profits** are the result of selling a product at a price above current cost. Since the lifo method matches the most recently incurred costs with realized revenue, it tends to exclude inventory profits from net income. Supporters of lifo favor the excluding of inventory profits from net income, on the premise that inventory which is sold must be replaced and that income is not earned unless the revenue realized exceeds the cost of replacing the inventory sold.

Those supporting the fifo method of inventory valuation agree that there may be two types of profits, but they consider both to be an element of periodic income realized at the time of sale. They argue that if the proponents of lifo are truly interested in measuring *real,* as opposed to *monetary,* income, they should extend their proposal to use replacement cost to all assets. The cost of goods sold should not be the most recently incurred costs but rather those costs which will be incurred to replace the items which have been sold. This method has been referred to as the *next-in, first-out (nifo)* method of inventory valuation. At the present time it is not acceptable because it is considered a departure from the cost principle.

The measurement of *real income* poses another problem during a period of general inflation. To illustrate, assume that an inventory item was purchased for $100 when the general price-level index stood at 120 and was sold for $150 when the general price-level index stood at 132 and when the replacement cost of the item was $124. The apparent profit of $50 ($150 − $100) on the sale of the item may be allocated between the (1) general price-level adjustment, (2) holding gain, and (3) operating profit as follows:

> *General price-level adjustment: ($100 × 132/120) − $100 (original cost) . . $10*
> *Holding gain: $124 (replacement cost) − $100 (original cost) − (general price-*
> *level adjustment)* *14*
> *Operating profit: $150 (selling price) − $124 (replacement cost)* *26*
> *Total difference between selling price and original cost ($150 − $100)* . . *$50*

The holding gain of $14 is the increase accruing as a result of *owning* the item while the *specific* price (replacement cost) of the item was rising. The holding gain does not include the $10 increase in price of the item caused by general inflation. Finally, the operating profit is the real economic reward to the seller for distributing the unit to customers.

Managerial and income tax implications

The proponents of lifo argue that this method is an invaluable aid to management since it excludes inventory profits from the determination of net income. External factors which are beyond the control of management are often significant in creating inventory profits. Moreover, inventory profits are reinvested in inventory, which means that disposable income is measured more accurately by the use of lifo.

Fifo advocates agree that management may need information about replacement cost of the inventory and its effect on net income; however, they maintain that this information can be compiled without distorting working capital and net income. Moreover, they argue that if the inventory profits are excluded from net income, then similar profits derived from other investments should be excluded. If in fact management decisions regarding dividend declaration, wage negotiations, and prices are based on the concept of disposable income, then a more extensive modification of the determination of net income is needed than that achieved by lifo.

Despite the theoretical arguments in support of lifo, the dominant reason for its popularity appears to be the income tax benefits that result from the use of this method. During periods of rising prices, taxable income and income taxes are reduced through the use of lifo. If prices later fall to the level at the time lifo was adopted, this reduction is simply a deferral of the tax. If prices continue to rise the reduction will be permanent. In either case the lifo user gains, since a postponement of taxes has economic value. The federal income tax law requires that lifo be used for financial reporting if it is adopted for income tax purposes.

The income tax benefits of lifo are not guaranteed. If prices fall below levels at the time lifo is adopted, or if the quantity of inventory is reduced below the amount on hand at the inception of lifo, it is conceivable that the lifo method could produce a tax disadvantage. Before adopting lifo solely for tax reasons, management should consider such factors as the expected course of prices, future income tax rates, inventory fluctuations, the company's net income pattern, and the existence of provisions in the tax law (such as operating loss carryforwards) which even out the tax burden over periods of income and loss. Finally, when lifo is used and prices decline, the inventory cannot be valued on the basis of lower of cost or market for income tax purposes.

Disclosure of inventory profits

The Securities and Exchange Commission has urged publicly owned companies to disclose the amount of profit included in the income statement which is not repeatable due to increased replacement costs of inventory caused by inflation.[5] The disclosure may be made in the financial statements, the notes to the financial statements, or in textual material accompanying the financial statements. Included in the Commission's reasons for recommending the disclosure of inventory profits was the following paragraph:

> The most significant and immediate impact of price fluctuations on financial statements is normally felt in cost of goods sold in the income statement. In periods of rising prices, historical cost methods result in the inclusion of "inventory profits" in reported earnings. "Inventory profit" results from holding inventories during a period of rising inventory costs and is measured by the difference between the historical cost of an item and its replacement cost at the time it is sold. Different methods of accounting for inventories can affect the degree to which "inventory profits" are included and identifiable in current income, but no method based upon historical cost eliminates or discloses this "profit" explicitly. Such "profits" do not reflect an increase in the economic earning power of a business and they are not normally repeatable in the absence of continued price-level increase. Accordingly, where such "profits" are material in income statements presented, disclosure of their impact on reported earnings and the trend of reported earnings is important information for investors assessing the quality of earnings.[6]

An example of disclosure of inventory profits by a large oil company a few years ago follows: "Included in the net income of $1,292,400,000 is an estimated inventory profit of $422,000,000, related to consolidated worldwide inventories."

In 1976, the Securities and Exchange Commission issued *ASR No. 190* which required companies to disclose, among other things, the estimated current replacement cost of inventories and the approximate amount of cost of goods sold based on replacement cost for the two most recent fiscal years.[7] *ASR No. 190* is discussed in detail in Chapter 22.

---

[5] *Accounting Series Release No. 151,* SEC (Washington: 1974).
[6] Ibid., p. 1
[7] *Accounting Series Release No. 190,* SEC (Washington: 1976).

VALUATION OF INVENTORY AT LOWER OF COST OR MARKET

Pricing an inventory includes tabulating the number of units, determining the unit cost, and computing the total cost. We shall now consider another possibility: that of a decrease in the value of inventory prior to its sale. If some items of inventory are used for display or demonstration, a part of the cost of these units should be absorbed prior to their sale. Whenever an asset contributes to the production of revenue and a part of the usefulness of the asset is consumed in so doing, a part of the cost of the asset should be charged against the revenue produced.

Assume, for example, that the owner of Delphine's Dress Shop wants her store to have a reputation as *the* fashion shop in her area. To accomplish her objective she knows that she must stock the extreme styles in sufficient volume to satisfy a substantial part of her clientele. In many cases she will buy more dresses than she expects to sell in order to maintain her reputation. To obtain a proper measure of income and to value her inventory properly, a part of the cost of the excess supply of dresses will have to be charged against revenue prior to the sale of these dresses. The problem is one of ascertaining the amount of the cost that should be charged off. The loss of economic value is believed to have contributed to the production of revenue and the selling price of dresses on hand will have to be reduced. The expired costs of dresses still on hand may be added to the cost of goods sold.

Obsolescence of inventory

In other situations part of the cost of inventory must be charged against revenue even though no benefit has accrued to the business. Inventory items frequently become unsalable at regular prices because of obsolescence, damage, or deterioration. If items which are to become a part of a manufactured article are damaged or spoiled in the ordinary production process, the loss need not be segregated but may become a part of the cost of the completed product. This procedure is acceptable provided the damage or loss is expected as a part of the normal operation of the plant. On the other hand, unusual loss or damage should not be included in the cost of goods manufactured.

Damaged or obsolete goods are frequently valued at **net realizable value,** estimated selling price less direct costs of completion and disposal. A more severe standard is to write the goods down to replacement cost—the price that the present owners would pay for the goods in their present condition if they were considering buying the goods for resale. In some cases an arbitrary percentage of the cost is written off; this is difficult to defend but in some cases no more objective basis is available. Finally, when there is doubt about the existence of any net realizable value, the cost of the goods should be reduced to scrap value, or to zero in the absence of scrap value.

Price fluctuation and inventory valuation

Price changes which result in loss of economic usefulness of the inventory should be recognized as a deduction from revenue in the period in which the loss accrues. Since the cost of the inventory is determined by negotiation between the buyer and supplier based on the expectation by the buyer of earning a normal gross profit margin upon resale, a significant decline in the selling price of the inventory may be just cause for recognizing a reduction in the carrying value of the inventory. When accountants are attempting to value the inventory, they are in search of some measure of this reduction. The inventory value which is most appropriate in such situations is *replacement cost* (or a "derived market" value), that is, the value which will allow the business to recover the adjusted cost of the inventory and still earn a normal (or reasonable) gross profit margin.

At present, generally accepted accounting principles hold that gains attributable to price increases should not be recognized until the goods are sold. However, losses resulting from a decline in the prices of the inventoriable goods should be recognized in the period in which the price decline occurs. The basis for this rule, *the lower of cost or market,* can be found in the doctrine of conservatism which has guided accounting policy for a long time.

Lower-of-cost-or-market procedures

The lower-of-cost-or-market rule requires that the accountant price the inventory at the lower of these two values: cost price or market price. The benefits attributed to this method of inventory valuation are (1) the loss, if any, is identified with the period in which it occurred, and (2) goods are valued at an amount that measures the expected contribution to revenue of future periods. The following statement supports this practice:

> A departure from the cost basis of pricing the inventory is required when the utility of the goods is no longer as great as its cost. Where there is evidence that the utility of goods, in their disposal in the ordinary course of business, will be less than cost, whether due to physical deterioration, obsolescence, changes in price levels, or other causes, the difference should be recognized as a loss of the current period. This is generally accomplished by stating such goods at a lower level commonly designated as *market.*[8]

The measurement of utility is almost impossible and the adoption of the lower-of-cost-or-market price is a practical means of approximating the decline in utility.

What is meant by "market" in the expression "lower of cost or market"? Is it the price the item will bring when it is sold, or is it the price that would be paid to purchase the item? Current practice requires the use of the purchase price, that is, *replacement cost,* with certain limitations. Replacement cost is a broader term than purchase price

[8] *Accounting Research and Terminology Bulletins—Final Edition,* chap. 4, p. 30.

since it can be held to include incidental acquisition costs, such as freight, handling, and storage. Replacement cost can also be applied to manufactured inventories with reference to the prevailing prices for raw materials, direct labor, and factory overhead. In cases where replacement cost is not reasonably determinable or exceeds the amount expected to be realized by the sale of the items, the *net realizable value* should be used in place of replacement cost. The net realizable value is determined by subtracting from the expected selling price all prospective direct costs of completing and selling the item. The following limits (*ceiling* and *floor*) have been placed on "market."

> As used in the phrase *lower of cost or market* the term *market* means current replacement cost (by purchase or by reproduction, as the case may be) except that:
> *1* Market should not exceed the net realizable value (i.e., estimated selling price in the ordinary course of business less reasonably predictable costs of completion and disposal); and
> *2* Market should not be less than net realizable value reduced by an allowance for an approximately normal profit margin.[9]

Thus the ceiling is selling price less estimated cost of completion and selling expenses; the floor is selling price less completion cost, selling expenses, and a normal gross profit. *Replacement cost is used as market if it falls between the ceiling and the floor; the ceiling figure is used for market when replacement cost is above the ceiling; and the floor figure is used for market when replacement cost is below the floor.* This general rule is diagramed below for a unit costing $40, three different assumptions as to replacement cost ($38, $34, and $28), a ceiling limit on market value of $36, and for a floor limit on market value of $30.

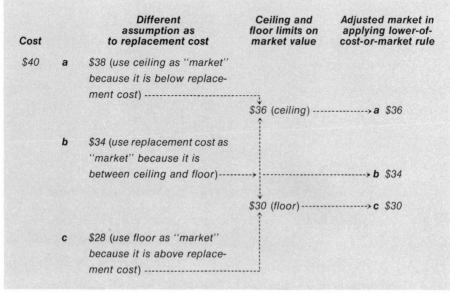

Cost		Different assumption as to replacement cost	Ceiling and floor limits on market value	Adjusted market in applying lower-of-cost-or-market rule
$40	a	$38 (use ceiling as "market" because it is below replacement cost)		
			$36 (ceiling) ----------→ a $36	
	b	$34 (use replacement cost as "market" because it is between ceiling and floor)		→ b $34
			$30 (floor) ----------→ c $30	
	c	$28 (use floor as "market" because it is above replacement cost)		

9 Ibid., p. 31.

Once the adjusted figure for market has been determined, **the final step is to compare the cost of the inventory item with the adjusted market** in arriving at a lower-of-cost-or-market valuation. In each of the three assumptions in the diagram on page 325, the adjusted market value is less than cost and would be the value assigned to inventory under the rule of lower of cost or market. This adjusted market value is treated as the "cost" for future comparisons with market value.

Federal income tax regulations state that: "Under ordinary circumstances and for normal goods in an inventory, market means the current bid price prevailing at the date of the inventory for the particular merchandise in the volume in which usually purchased by the taxpayer."[10] The "volume" restriction is relevant when prices vary depending on the quantity purchased. As stated earlier, current income tax rules do not permit the use of the lower-of-cost-or-market rule when cost is determined by the last-in, first-out method.

Illustrations of Selection of "Market" and "Lower of Cost or Market" The following additional examples illustrate the application of the lower-of-cost-or-market rule. The inventory value for each item is indicated by a double line. Completion and selling expenses are $6 for each item and the normal gross profit margin is 25% of the selling price.

	Inventory items				
	A	**B**	**C**	**D**	**E**
Selling price	$20	$20	$28	$36	$36
Cost (determined by specific identification, fifo, average, etc.)	16	15	20	25	20
Selling price less $6 completion and selling expenses (ceiling)	14	14	22	30	30
Sales price less completion and selling expenses and normal gross profit margin of 25% of selling price (floor)	9	9	15	21	21
Replacement cost at inventory date	15	16	17	20	19

Explanation

Item A Replacement cost of $15 exceeds the ceiling of $14; ceiling of $14 is the adjusted market value; since cost is $16, the inventory value is $14, the lower of cost or adjusted market.

Item B Replacement cost of $16 exceeds the ceiling of $14; ceiling of $14 is the adjusted market value; inventory value is $14 even though replacement cost of $16 exceeds the cost of $15.

Item C Replacement cost of $17 is between the ceiling-floor limit ($22 to

---

[10] Regulations, Sec. 39.22(e)4.

$15); replacement cost is the adjusted market value; inventory value is $17 because it is less than the cost of $20.

Item D Replacement cost of $20 is below the floor of $21; floor is the adjusted market value; the inventory value is $21 because it is less than the cost of $25.

Item E Replacement cost of $19 is below the floor of $21; floor is the adjusted market value; the inventory value is $20 or cost because cost is lower than adjusted market value. In this case the normal gross profit margin will be earned when the unit is sold and therefore no loss in value is recognized.

Application of Lower of Cost or Market The lower-of-cost-or-market rule can be applied to (1) each individual item in the inventory, (2) major categories of inventory, or (3) the inventory as a whole. Regardless of which of the three methods is adopted, each item in the inventory should be priced at cost and at market as a first step in the valuation process. The item-by-item method produces the lowest inventory value and the application of the lower-of-cost-or-market rule to the inventory as a whole produces the highest valuation. For income tax purposes, the item-by-item method must be used. For financial reporting purposes, the authors favor the application of the lower-of-cost-or-market rule to the inventory as a whole. This approach is consistent with the rule established for marketable equity securities in *FASB Statement No. 12.* The illustration below demonstrates the variation in lower-of-cost-or-market figures that will result from the application of these three methods.

Determination of Inventory Value Using Lower of Cost or Market—End of Year 1

Inventory categories	Cost	Market	(1) Item by item	(2) Category of inventory	(3) Inventory as a whole
No. 1: Item A	$ 6,000	$ 9,000	$ 6,000		
Item B	10,000	9,500	9,500		
Subtotal	$16,000	$18,500		$16,000	
No. 2: Item C	$15,000	$17,000	15,000		
Item D	20,000	14,000	14,000		
Subtotal	$35,000	$31,000		31,000	
Total	$51,000	$49,500			$49,500
Inventory valuation			$44,500	$47,000	$49,500

In valuing manufacturing inventories, the accountant must adjust goods in process and finished goods for any decline in the price of materials as well as for declines in direct labor and factory overhead costs.

Subsequent Valuation Problems Suppose that at the end of Year 2, item D in the illustration on page 327 is still on hand and that the market value has risen from $14,000 to $19,000. What is the inventory value of item D at the end of the next period? Generally, accountants have held that, once an inventory has been written down, this lower value *is considered cost* for future periods. Therefore, in the application of the item-by-item method the value of item D would be $14,000 because the item was written down to this amount in the previous period.

For *interim reporting purposes,* this rule has been modified by the APB as follows:

> Inventory losses from market declines should not be deferred beyond the interim period in which the decline occurs. Recoveries of such losses on the same inventory in later interim periods of the same fiscal year through market price recoveries should be recognized as gains in the later interim period. Such gains should not exceed previously recognized losses. Some market declines at interim dates, however, can reasonably be expected to be restored in the fiscal year. Such *temporary* market declines need not be recognized at the interim date since no loss is expected to be incurred in the fiscal year.[11]

Valuation allowance for write-down of inventory

When inventories are written down below cost, the reduction may be credited to an inventory valuation account. This procedure accomplishes the objective of a write-down while permitting the original cost of the inventory to be reported. The use of the valuation account is especially beneficial to a business using a perpetual inventory system in terms of dollar cost since it eliminates the necessity of adjusting the detailed inventory records to a lower-of-cost-or-market basis.

The journal entry to record the reduction of inventory at the end of Year 1 from a cost of $100,000 to a market valuation of $92,000 is illustrated below:

Cost of Goods Sold	8,000	
Allowance for Inventory Price Decline		8,000
To record the reduction of value in the inventory caused by declining prices.		

In the balance sheet at the end of Year 1 the inventory is listed at cost and is reduced to a lower market by deducting the allowance for inventory price decline from cost. This procedure is illustrated on page 329.

[11] *APB Opinion No. 28,* "Interim Financial Reporting," AICPA (New York: 1973), pp. 524–525.

Current assets:

Inventory, at cost $100,000

Less: Allowance for inventory price decline . . . . <u>8,000</u> $92,000

In the income statement for Year 1, the ending inventory may be shown in the cost of goods sold section at the carrying value of $92,000. If the write-down in inventory is material, it may be shown separately in the income statement. Such a write-down should be included in arriving at income from operations; under no circumstances should the write-down be reported as an extraordinary item.

The inventory valuation allowance is not needed after the goods in question are sold. Therefore, at the time the cost of the beginning inventory is transferred to Income Summary (or to the Cost of Goods Sold account), the allowance account should also be closed, thus reducing the cost of the beginning inventory to market price. For example, the following journal entry would be made at the end of Year 2 to close the beginning inventory, assuming that the periodic inventory system is used:

Income Summary 92,000

Allowance for Inventory Price Decline 8,000

    Beginning Inventory, at cost   100,000

To close beginning inventory to Income Summary.

If the market value of the inventory at the end of Year 2 is below cost, an allowance for inventory price decline should again be established.

An inventory allowance account similar to the one illustrated above is used by some companies to reduce inventory costs to a lifo basis. Such an account is established by a debit to Cost of Goods Sold or Income Summary and a credit to Allowance to Reduce Inventory to Lifo Basis. This valuation allowance, sometimes improperly referred to as **lifo reserve account,** is used to preserve inventory cost on the fifo or average cost basis for **internal** purposes while obtaining the advantages of using lifo for income tax purposes.

Valuation of purchase commitments at lower of cost or market

If at the end of an accounting period a company has a firm contract to purchase inventory at a fixed price and the contract price is higher than the current price of the inventory, a loss should be recognized. In other words, the outstanding purchase commitment should be valued on a lower-of-cost-or-market basis by recognition of a current loss and the accrual of a current liability. These accounting procedures are described in Chapter 10 dealing with current liabilities and contingencies.

Appraisal of the lower-of-cost-or-market rule

The lower-of-cost-or-market rule originated in an era of emphasis on balance sheet conservatism. It exemplifies an old accounting axiom: "Anticipate no profit and provide for all possible losses." In following this axiom the accountant assumes that purchase prices and selling prices move in the same direction. Therefore if the price of purchased goods declines, the selling price of the goods will decline also. By reducing the inventory to market, the income for the current period is reduced; however, presumably the business is enabled to earn a *normal* profit in the next period. On the other hand, if the price of the goods rises, accounting principles do not permit the value of the inventory to be increased. Such action would result in the recognition of income before revenue is realized.

The treatment of damaged and obsolete goods was discussed earlier in accordance with the principle of valuing inventory at cost less an amount which measures any deterioration in usefulness. Also, the argument has been presented that a decline in prices casts a shadow over a part of the inventory cost because the revenue in future periods may not be adequate to provide a normal margin of profit. Thus accountants have been led to the conclusion that the goods have lost a part of their economic value and that the unrecoverable portion of cost should be charged to current revenue.

One should not dismiss such an argument lightly; unrecoverable costs are not assets. On the other hand, every price decline does not necessarily mean that the cost of goods on hand will not be recovered. The price system is not so sensitive that it transmits related price movements quickly and uniformly throughout the economic system.

The indiscriminate application of the lower-of-cost-or-market rule should never be allowed to replace sound judgment in the valuation of inventories. There are cases when recognition of losses prior to sale is justified. However, a careful evaluation of the particular circumstances is necessary before the amount of the loss can be determined. The ceiling and floor limits on "market" clearly serve a useful function in making such an evaluation.

Anticipation of price declines

The lower-of-cost-or-market rule is applicable to price declines which have actually occurred, not to possible future price declines. The AICPA has made the following distinction between inventory losses which can be measured by objective evidence, and thus recorded in the accounts, and those which are measured by mere conjecture as to possible future losses:

> It has been argued with respect to inventories that losses which will have to be taken in periods of receding price levels have their origins in periods of rising prices, and that therefore reserves to provide for future price declines should be created in periods of rising prices by charges against the operations of those periods. Reserves of this kind involve assumptions as to what future price levels will be, what inventory quantities will be on hand if and when a major price decline takes place, and finally whether loss to the business will be measured by the amount of the decline in prices. The bases for such assumptions are so uncertain that any conclusions drawn from them would generally seem to be speculative guesses rather than informed judgments.[12]

Only actual losses on goods included in inventory which arise from price declines should enter into the determination of net income; *possible* future losses should not be recorded in the accounts.

REVIEW QUESTIONS

1 What features distinguish inventory costs from other costs which should be allocated into deferred and expired portions?

2 There are two methods of maintaining inventory records: (*a*) *periodic system* and (*b*) *perpetual system.* What are the basic differences and under what circumstances should each be used?

3 Why is the valuation of inventories critical to financial reporting? What criteria should the accountant use in deciding between alternative methods of valuation?

4 At the end of the period, the following purchase invoices dated December 27 are on hand but the goods have not been received. How would you handle each in the determination of the ending inventory?
   a Invoice amount $12,670; terms, 2/10, n/30; "F.O.B. shipping point."
   b Invoice amount $14,860; terms, 1/5, n/30; "F.O.B. destination."

5 Indicate the effects on the financial statements for the current and succeeding years of each of the following types of errors in accounting for the inventory. Simply indicate the direction of error—overstatement, understatement, or no effect.
   a An invoice for goods shipped "F.O.B. shipping point" has been received but no entry has been made to record the purchase. The items have not been received and are not included in the ending inventory.
   b An invoice for goods shipped but not received has been recorded properly to indicate that the goods legally belong to the buyer but the items have not been included in the ending inventory.
   c Goods which have been received but the purchase of which has not been recorded in the accounts are included in the ending inventory.
   d The ending inventory does not include goods shipped on consignment. The transfer of these goods has been recorded as a sale by the consignor

---

[12] *Accounting Research and Terminology Bulletins—Final Edition,* chap. 6, p. 42.

even though they remain in the consignee's inventory at the end of both the current year and the succeeding year.

6 What costs should be included in the cost of inventories? What objectives are considered when one is deciding what costs are going to be added to inventory?

7 Midtown Faucet Company is licensed to manufacture and sell a certain product under a patent owned by Alan Bella. A royalty of 10 cents is payable to Bella for each unit sold. For costing purposes, Midtown Faucet Company treats royalty payments as a selling expense and does not accrue a royalty liability on the unsold faucets in inventory. The property tax assessor claims that 10 cents should be treated as a production cost and included in the valuation of inventory of faucets. Do you agree with the tax assessor? Explain.

8 If two or more *joint products* are produced in a given department, how would the total production cost incurred in the department be allocated to the various joint products?

9 The identification of the cost of **specific units sold** has been supported by some accountants as the ideal method of achieving a matching of cost and revenue. What objections may be raised to the use of this method as a practical means of valuing inventory?

10 Differentiate between the **weighted-average** method and the **moving-weighted-average** method of determining cost of inventory.

11 Joe Doe tells you that he is considering changing from the fifo to the lifo method of inventory valuation and that he would like your advice on the matter. He admits that his primary objective is to reduce his tax bill, and his friends tell him this is a good way to do it. What factors would you want to consider in advising Doe?

12 In the application of the **dollar-value lifo** method of valuing the inventory, it is considered necessary to convert both the beginning and ending inventory figures to base-year prices. Why? Why would a conversion of end-of-year prices to beginning-year prices not serve equally as well?

13 Under what conditions may a portion of the inventory cost be written off prior to the actual disposal of the items comprising the inventory?

14 Define the term **market** as used in the inventory valuation procedure usually referred to as the lower-of-cost-or-market rule.

15 What are the arguments against the use of the lower-of-cost-or-market method of valuing inventories?

16 Is there any difference, insofar as inventory valuation is concerned, between an item having a cost of $50 which regularly sells for $75 but which has been so physically damaged that it can be sold for no more than $55 and the same item when there is no physical damage but the cost of replacing the item has declined to $30?

17 Under what conditions, if any, is it permissible to recognize anticipated price declines in the accounts?

18 Under what conditions, if any, should losses arising out of price declines involving future purchase commitments be recognized in the accounts?

19 A recent balance sheet for Copperweld Corporation included the following:

Inventories	$62,062,774
Less: Allowance to reduce carrying value of certain inventories to	
last-in first-out basis	12,398,448
Net inventories	$49,664,326

Give the probable reason for the use of the inventory valuation account by Copperweld Corporation.

EXERCISES

Ex. 8-1 The following information relates to commodity A for January:

Inventory, Jan. 1	100 units @ $5
Purchases, January	500 units @ $6
Inventory, Jan. 31.	200 units

a What cost should be assigned to the ending inventory, assuming the use of the first-in, first-out cost flow assumption?
b What is the cost of goods sold for January, assuming the use of the last-in, first-out cost flow assumption?

Ex. 8-2 Given below is the inventory activity for product Z for the month of April:

Date	Transaction	Units	Cost	Total	Units sold
Apr. 1	Inventory	1,200	$8.00	$ 9,600	
4	Purchase	800	8.25	6,600	
7	Sale				600
10	Purchase	400	8.10	3,240	
13	Sale				1,000
16	Purchase	700	7.90	5,530	
19	Sale				900
22	Purchase	300	7.90	2,370	
25	Purchase	600	7.80	4,680	
28	Sale				500
	Totals	4,000		$32,020	3,000

Assuming that a periodic inventory system is used, compute the inventory cost under each of the following cost flow assumptions:
a First-in, first-out
b Last-in, first-out
c Weighted-average

Ex. 8-3 Slumber Company sells beds. The perpetual inventory was stated as $19,600 in the accounts at December 31, Year 4. At the close of the year a new approach for compiling inventory was used and apparently a satisfactory cutoff for preparation of financial statements was not made. Some events that occurred near the end of Year 4 are listed at the top of page 334.

(1) Beds shipped to a customer January 2, Year 5, costing $2,000 were included in inventory at December 31, Year 4. The sale was recorded in Year 5.
(2) Beds costing $9,000 received December 30, Year 4, were recorded as received on January 2, Year 5.
(3) Beds received costing $1,900 were recorded twice in the perpetual inventory records.
(4) Beds shipped F.O.B. shipping point on December 28, Year 4, which cost $7,000, were not recorded as delivered until January 3, Year 5. The beds were included in the ending inventory.
(5) Beds on hand which cost $2,300 were not recorded in the accounts in Year 4.

Prepare a schedule showing the correct inventory at December 31, Year 4.

Ex. 8-4 Rider Corporation uses the dollar-value lifo method of pricing inventory. The inventory valued at end-of-year prices and the cost index are given below:

Year	Inventory at year-end costs	Cost index at end of year
1	$ 80,000	100
2	90,000	125
3	127,400	130

Prepare a schedule showing the calculation of the ending inventory at dollar-value lifo cost for Year 2 and Year 3.

Ex. 8-5 A company acquired goods for $4,000 when the general price-level index was 110. These goods were sold for $7,500 when the replacement cost of the goods was $5,400 and the general price-level index stood at 121. The "gain" of $3,500 on the sale of the goods may be attributed to three factors: change in the general price level, holding profit, and trading profit (margin to seller for distributing the goods to customers). Compute the portion of the total "gain" caused by each of the three factors.

Ex. 8-6 Given below are three different sets of assumptions relating to an item in inventory. Compute the inventory value at lower of cost or market for each case.

	Case 1	Case 2	Case 3
Actual cost	$12,400	$20,000	$28,000
Selling price	$30,000	$30,000	$30,000
Cost to complete and ship to customers	$ 4,000	$ 4,000	$ 4,000
Normal gross profit on selling price	25%	25%	10%
Replacement cost	$14,000	$18,000	$26,500
Inventory value at lower of cost or market	$_____	$_____	$_____

Ex. 8-7 You are given the following facts about four items included in the inventory of the Rebecca Corporation:

	Item			
	W	**X**	**Y**	**Z**
Actual cost	$50	$62	$29	$46
Replacement cost	52	48	25	40
Sales price less selling and completion expense	53	59	23	42
Sales price less selling and completion expense and less normal profit	47	51	20	38

Indicate which figure would be used in pricing the ending inventory in accordance with the rule of lower of cost or market.

Ex. 8-8 The inventory for Farmer's Supply Company consists of two major categories listed below:

	Quantities	**Unit cost**	**Market**
Category A:			
Item XP	80	$ 6	$ 5
Item XQ	40	8	9
Item XR	30	10	8
Category B:			
Item YS	100	$ 4	$ 3
Item YT	150	9	8
Item YU	300	12	14

Prepare a schedule similar to the one illustrated on page 327 computing inventory value using the lower-of-cost-or-market rule applied on (1) each item, (2) separate inventory categories, and (3) the inventory as a whole.

Ex. 8-9 Ridge Company buys and sells land. On January 1, Year 1, a tract of land was bought for $100,000. Costs of leveling the land were $25,000. The land was sub-divided as follows:

25 Class A lots to sell for $4,000 each
30 Class B lots to sell for $3,000 each
10 Class C lots to sell for $1,000 each

On December 31, Year 1, the unsold lots consisted of 15 Class A lots, 6 Class B lots, and 3 Class C lots.
Prepare a schedule computing the cost of unsold lots at December 31, Year 1. Total cost is allocated to the lots on the basis of relative sales value.

SHORT CASES FOR ANALYSIS AND DECISION

Case 8-1 K Manufacturing Company purchased 10,000 pounds of raw material at an in-voice cost of $50,000 with terms 3/5, 2/10, net 30. The freight cost applicable to this shipment was $4,500. The total cost of handling and storing raw material was $50,000 a year, and the quantity handled each year was about 500,000 pounds. This $50,000 handling and storage cost was not controllable; that is, it was fixed in amount and did not vary in relation to variations in the quantity of raw material in storage. The quantity of raw material on hand fluctuated widely during the year. K Manufacturing Company is debating whether this $50,000 should be treated as an expense or included in inventory.

Instructions
a Under what circumstances should handling and storage costs be included in inventory? Do these circumstances prevail in the case of raw material at the K Manufacturing Company?
b Determine the cost per pound of this purchase of raw material.
c Would the cost per pound be different if the company did not pay the invoice within the first 15 days? What would the cost per pound be if the invoice were paid between the fifth and tenth day? State the accounting principle underlying your answers.

Case 8-2 In order to effect an approximate matching of current costs with related sales revenue, the last-in, first-out (lifo) method of pricing inventories has been developed.

Instructions
a Describe the establishment of and subsequent pricing procedures for each of the following lifo inventory methods:
  (1) Lifo applied to units of product when the periodic inventory system is used.
  (2) Application of the dollar-value method to a retail lifo inventory or to lifo units of product. (These applications are similar.)
b Discuss the specific advantages and disadvantages of using the dollar-value lifo applications. Ignore income tax considerations.
c Discuss the general advantages and disadvantages claimed for lifo methods. Ignore income tax considerations.

Case 8-3 Paul Dunn, a partner in the law firm of Dunn, Ekker, and Finley, wants to withdraw from the partnership effective on April 1, Year 1. Because the partnership keeps its accounts on a cash basis, no recognition is given to accounts receivable and work (legal action suits) in process in the preparation of financial statements for the partnership. The partnership agreement includes the following provision relative to the withdrawal of a partner:

"A partner terminating his association with the firm shall be entitled to an immediate cash payment equal to his capital account increased by (1) his share of uncollected accounts receivable and (2) his equity in work in process. No diminution in the withdrawing partner's capital will be made for outstanding liabilities."

The senior partner computed the value of work in process at March 31, Year 1, as follows:

Direct reimbursable costs (travel, outside experts, etc.) chargeable to clients	$ 4,000
Salaries paid to staff attorneys working on cases	
(excluding time of any of the partners)	29,500
Total value of work in process	$33,500

Dunn objected to this procedure on grounds that it does not include the value of partners' time spent on work in process and the amount "represents a bare minimum value" of the work in process. He feels that the billable value of the work performed for clients to date amounts to at least $100,000 and that this amount represents the fair value of the work in process.

An accountant who was asked to arbitrate the dispute suggested that the senior partner's figure of $33,500 should be increased by $10,000, representing "general office overhead" applicable to the work in process. The accountant feels that partners' time should not be treated as an inventoriable cost because partners' salaries are not a cost of doing business for the partnership form of organization.

Instructions Briefly evaluate each of the three approaches to the valuation of work in process and recommend the procedure you consider equitable in this circumstance.

Case 8-4 Zinc Manufacturing Corporation had followed the practice of pricing the year-end inventory at the lower of fifo cost or market for many years. During this period prices had tended to move in a rather general upward trend. For the past three years the general trend of price movement has been very erratic and management has become concerned with the effect on reported income of the lower-of-cost-or-market inventory valuation. You have been requested to analyze the situation and make a recommendation to management supported by calculations and accounting logic. The beginning inventory on January 1, Year 1, was valued at both cost and market at $60,000; additional data are given below:

	Year 3	Year 2	Year 1
Sales	$425,000	$325,000	$375,000
Net purchases	300,000	225,000	260,000
Year-end inventory:			
At cost	75,000	70,000	60,000
At market	55,000	82,000	45,000

Instructions
a Prepare partial income statements for each of the three years using (1) cost and (2) lower of cost or market in the determination of cost of goods sold.
b Draft a report to management explaining the effect of their present procedure on reported profits. Assuming that this pattern of fluctuating profits is expected to continue, which method would you recommend? Why?

PROBLEMS

Group A

8A-1 The controller of Lubbock Corporation, a retail company, made three different schedules of gross profit for the first quarter ended March 31, Year 10. These schedules appear below:

	Sales ($10 per unit)	Cost of goods sold	Gross profit
Schedule 1 . . . LIFO	$280,000	$118,550	$161,450
Schedule 2 . . . Weighted Average	280,000	116,900	163,100
Schedule 3 . . . FIFO	280,000	115,750	164,250

The computation of cost of goods sold in each schedule is based on the following data:

	Units	Cost per unit	Total cost
Beginning inventory, Jan. 1	10,000	$4.00	$ 40,000
Purchase, Jan. 20	8,000	4.20	33,600
Purchase, Feb. 12	5,000	4.13	20,650
Purchase, Mar. 14	7,000	4.30	30,100
Purchase, Mar. 27	12,000	4.25	51,000
Totals	42,000		$175,350

Elaine Evans, president of the corporation cannot understand how three different gross profit amounts can be computed from the same set of data. As controller, you have explained to her that the three schedules are based on three different assumptions concerning the flow of inventory costs; that is, first-in, first-out; last-in, first-out; and weighted average. Schedules 1, 2, and 3 were not necessarily prepared in this sequence of cost flow assumptions.

Instructions Prepare a schedule computing the cost of goods sold and the composition of the ending inventory under each of the three cost flow assumptions.

8A-2 Modern Outlet began operations on January 1 with 150 units of item X at a cost of $1,350. The following data pertaining to purchase of item X were taken from the accounting records at the end of the first year's operations:

Lot No.	Number of units	Cost
1	24	$ 240
2	84	924
3	126	1,242
4	96	864
5	120	1,440
	450	$4,710

A physical inventory on December 31 reveals that 180 units of item X remain in stock.

Instructions Based on the data provided, compute **(a)** the inventory cost at December 31 and **(b)** the cost of goods sold during the year, using each of the following cost flow assumptions:
(1) Lifo
(2) Fifo
(3) Weighted-average

8A-3 In the process of determining the ending inventory at June 30, Year 5, for Lehigh Corporation, you are presented with the following summary relating to material J and finished part K.

	Material J (units)	Finished part K (units)
Inventory summary:		
(1) Units on hand in warehouse per physical count. Cost is $4 per unit for material J and $20.40 for finished part K . . .	7,500	5,000
(2) Units in receiving department, to be refused because of poor quality. Invoice cost is $4.20 per unit	1,000	
(3) Units stored in parking lot considered worthless. Cost of these units is $21 per unit		100
(4) Units in receiving department; no invoice has been received. Price on purchase order is $4.10 per unit	500	
(5) Units not received for which invoice marked "F.O.B. shipping point" has been received. Total cost in invoice, including freight, is $851	200	
(6) Units shipped on June 30, Year 5; invoice marked "F.O.B. shipping point" has been mailed to customer. Total cost of these units is $6,330		300
(7) Units completed in factory not yet transferred to warehouse. Cost is $21.50 per unit		150
(8) Units in shipping department; invoice marked "F.O.B. shipping point" has been mailed to customer. Cost of these units is $20 per unit		50
(9) Units in shipping department; invoice has not been mailed to customer. Cost of these units is $20.30 per unit		80
(10) Units in hands of consignees having a total cost of $2,448		120

Instructions Prepare a schedule similar to the summary above showing the cost of the various items comprising the ending inventory of material J and finished part K. Place amounts (in dollars) in the two columns at the right. Give the reason for including or excluding each item.

8A-4 During the first two years of operations, Clemson Corporation acquired widgets as follows:

	First year				Second year		
Lot No.	Number of widgets	Unit price	Total cost	Lot No.	Number of widgets	Unit price	Total cost
1	13,000	$4.00	$ 52,000	6	12,000	$3.25	$ 39,000
2	4,000	3.75	15,000	7	6,000	3.50	21,000
3	12,000	3.50	42,000	8	4,000	3.50	14,000
4	5,000	3.50	17,500	9	5,000	3.75	18,750
5	8,000	3.00	24,000	10	16,000	4.00	64,000
	42,000		$150,500		43,000		$156,750

The replacement cost of these widgets at the end of the first year is $3.15 and at the end of the second year $4.20. There are 16,000 widgets on hand at the end of the first year and 20,000 on hand at the end of the second year.

Instructions
a Compute the inventory cost and the cost of goods sold for each period (1) under the fifo method and (2) under the lifo method.
b If 800 widgets had been stolen during the second year and you wanted to separate the theft loss from the cost of goods sold, how would you determine the amount of the loss?

8A-5 Vanderbilt Company reported income before income taxes as follows:

Year 2	$125,000
Year 3	105,000
Year 4	115,000
Total	$345,000

The company uses the physical inventory system. An analysis of the inventories indicated the following:

(1) Inventory at December 31, Year 1, was correct.
(2) Merchandise, costing $340, was received in Year 2 and included in the ending inventory at the end of Year 2; however, the entry to record the purchase was made in January Year 3, when the invoice was received.
(3) The Year 2 ending inventory includes 1,000 units of item Z, which cost $7.30 per unit, erroneously priced at $3.70 per unit.
(4) Merchandise which cost $500 and which sold at $700 was shipped to a customer "F.O.B. shipping point" on December 31, Year 3, and was not included in the Year 3 ending inventory; however, the sale was not recorded until January 5, Year 4.
(5) Merchandise costing $2,000, shipped "F.O.B. shipping point," was recorded as a purchase in Year 3 when the invoice was received; however, it was not included in the ending inventory because it was not received until January 6, Year 4.
(6) Merchandise costing $2,750 was sold for $4,000 and billed on December 31, Year 3. This sale was recorded on December 31, Year 3, but the merchandise was included in the ending inventory because it had not been separated from regular stock and was not shipped until January 15, Year 4.
(7) The inventory at December 31, Year 4, was correct.

Instructions
a Calculate the corrected income before income taxes for each of the three years and the total for the three years.
b Give the entries required at the end of each year to correct the income before income taxes for that year, assuming that transactions of the succeeding year have not occurred and that those of the prior year are corrected.
c Give the entry required during Year 4 to correct the income before income taxes for Year 4, assuming that the entries in (b) were not made. Any correction to income of Year 3 should be made to "Restatement of Income for Year 3." Ignore income taxes.

8A-6 Baylor Department Store decided in December Year 1 to adopt the dollar-value lifo method for calculating the ending inventory for Year 2 and each year thereafter. Management feels that the published price indices are too general for its use; therefore, it intends to compute an index of price changes by sampling the stock of goods. The inventory at December 31, Year 1, was $75,000 and this is considered the base year for purposes of applying the dollar-value technique.

The following data have been accumulated as the basis for inventory valuation:

Inventory quantities (sample items)				Inventory prices (end of year)				
Item	Year 2	Year 3	Year 4	Item	Year 1	Year 2	Year 3	Year 4
M	40	80	40	M	$10.00	$12.00	$13.00	$13.00
N	80	100	102	N	12.00	13.75	14.40	15.00
O	30	40	43	O	8.00	9.00	10.00	10.00
P	100	120	100	P	14.00	14.50	16.00	17.30
				Total inventory cost at end-of-year prices ..	$75,000	$99,000	$117,000	$101,250

Instructions
a Calculate the index of inventory costs for Baylor Department Store.
b Compute the dollar-value lifo inventory for Years 2–4.

8A-7 Part A Company X manufactures two products: Yee and Zee. At December 31, Year 4, Company X used the first-in, first-out (fifo) inventory method. Effective January 1, Year 5, Company X changed to the last-in, first-out (lifo) inventory method. The cumulative effect of this change is not determinable and, as a result, the ending inventory of Year 4 for which the fifo method was used, is also the beginning inventory for Year 5 for the lifo method. Any layers added during Year 5 should be costed by reference to the first acquisitions of Year 5 and any layers liquidated during Year 5 should be considered a permanent liquidation.

The following information was available from the inventory records for the two most recent years:

	Yee		Zee	
	Units	Unit cost	Units	Unit cost
Year 4 purchases:				
Jan. 7	5,000	$4.00	22,000	$2.00
Apr. 16	12,000	4.50		
Nov. 8	17,000	5.00	18,500	2.50
Dec. 13	10,000	6.00		
Year 5 purchases:				
Feb. 11	3,000	$7.00	23,000	$3.00
May 20	8,000	7.50		
Oct. 15	20,000	8.00		
Dec. 23			15,500	3.50
Units on hand:				
Dec. 31, Year 4	15,000		14,500	
Dec. 31, Year 5	16,000		13,000	

Instructions Compute the effect on income before income taxes for the year ended December 31, Year 5, resulting from the change from the fifo to the lifo inventory method.

Part B Company Y manufactures one product. On December 31, Year 2, Company Y adopted the dollar-value lifo inventory method. The inventory on that date under the dollar-value lifo inventory method was $200,000. Inventory data are as follows:

Year	Inventory at respective year-end prices	Price index (base = Year 2)
3	$231,000	1.05
4	299,000	1.15
5	300,000	1.20

Instructions Compute the inventory at December 31, Year 3, Year 4, and Year 5, using the dollar-value lifo method.

Part C You are employed by Company Z as an accountant. The controller presents you with the following information about items included in the year-end inventory and asks you to indicate the proper unit price in accordance with the lower-of-cost-or-market rule.

Item	Original cost	Expected selling price	Replacement cost
1	$ 2.00	$ 2.40	$ 1.62
2	5.00	7.50	5.25
3	2.15	3.00	2.00
4	6.82	6.50	6.00
5	1.05	1.20	1.00
6	14.60	18.00	15.00
7	3.80	4.20	3.75
8	4.50	5.00	3.20
9	6.00	9.00	6.50
10	8.80	10.00	8.40

Assume that selling expense is 10% and normal profit is 25% of selling price.

Instructions Indicate the unit value which should be used to price each of the items in the inventory in accordance with the lower-of-cost-or-market rule and explain each selection.

Group B

8B-1 Drake Corporation uses the first-in, first-out method of arriving at the cost of its inventory at the end of the fiscal year. The physical inventory at the end of the current year is summarized on page 343.

Item No.	Unit cost*	Inventory count (units)	Freight applicable to inventory
101	$ 2	6,000	$ 915
102	5	9,000	675
103	6	4,500	1,110
104	10	2,400	960

* Before discount.

The company regularly takes a 2% discount on all purchases (excluding freight) and allocates an appropriate portion of freight charges to the ending inventory.

Additional information available at the end of the current year is presented below:

Beginning inventory	$100,500
Purchases (net of returns)	546,300
Purchase discounts	10,800
Freight charges on purchases	19,500
Sales (net of returns)	721,500
Sales discounts	9,300

Instructions

a Determine the appropriate valuation for the ending inventory.
b Prepare a partial income statement through gross profit on sales.

8B-2 Bradley Company sells a single product which has been steadily going up in price in recent months. The inventory at January 1, and the purchases and sales for the current year, are presented below:

	Number of units	Unit cost	Average sale price
Jan. 1, Inventory	8,000	$3.50	
Jan. 10, Purchase	3,000	4.50	
Jan. 21, Purchase	5,000	5.00	
Jan. 1–31, Sales for month	10,000		$ 8.00
Feb. 5, Purchase	4,000	6.00	
Feb. 18, Purchase	6,000	7.00	
Feb. 1–28, Sales for month	9,000		10.00
Mar. 5, Purchase	5,000	7.50	
Mar. 22, Purchase	10,000	8.00	
Mar. 1–31, Sales for month	13,000		12.00

The company uses the physical inventory system. Inventories are valued at the end of each month.

Instructions

a Compute the amount of inventory on hand at the end of each of the first three months of the current year using (1) the first-in, first-out cost flow assumption and (2) the last-in, first-out cost flow assumption.

b Prepare a comparative statement summarizing the gross profit on sales for each month, assuming that inventories are valued using (1) the first-in, first-out method and (2) using the last-in, first-out method. Use the following format:

	(1) Fifo			(2) Lifo		
	January	February	March	January	February	March
Sales						

8B-3 The perpetual inventory records of Yale Sales Company indicate that the purchases, sales, and inventory quantities for product KB-80 for the month of March are as follows:

	Purchases		Sales
Date	Units	Unit cost	(units)
Mar. 1 Inventory	800	$ 8	
6			500
10	700	9	
18			800
22	1,000	10	
30			500

Instructions

a Calculate the cost of the ending inventory and the cost of goods sold for March, assuming that the **perpetual inventory system** is used, using each of the following methods for inventory valuation. The following columnar headings are suggested: Date, Transaction, Units, Unit Cost, Inventory Balance.
  (1) First-in, first-out
  (2) Last-in, first-out
  (3) Moving-average
b Assuming that a **periodic inventory system** is used, compute the inventory cost and cost of goods sold, using each of the following methods:
  (1) First-in, first-out
  (2) Last-in, first-out
  (3) Weighted-average
c Where differences occur between **(a)** and **(b)**, explain why they exist. Under what conditions would you recommend the perpetual system? The periodic system?

8B-4 On June 30, Year 1, the end of the fiscal year, Ozark Wood Products, Inc., decided to adopt the dollar-value lifo method of pricing the ending inventory. The data on inventories valued at end-of-year prices and a cost index for the succeeding four years are provided as follows:

Date as of June 30	Inventory at end-of-year costs	Cost index at end of year
Year 1 (base year)	$105,000	100
Year 2	140,000	125
Year 3	196,000	140
Year 4	154,560	115
Year 5	109,200	120

Instructions

a Prepare a schedule showing the calculation of the ending inventory at lifo cost for the four years, Year 2–Year 5.

b Explain how the dollar-value method will facilitate the valuation of the inventory in terms of lifo cost.

8B-5 The following data were taken from the inventory records of Southwest Supply Company at December 31 of the current year:

Department	Item No.	Quantity (units)	Unit cost	Market (per unit)
Hardware	10	140	$24.00	$25.00
	11	350	12.10	11.70
	12	10	8.00	9.60
Power tools	20	60	4.00	3.00
	21	14	14.00	13.00
	22	8	36.00	37.00
Toys	30	70	2.40	2.00
	31	80	4.90	4.50
	32	110	1.20	1.30

Instructions

a Price the inventory using the lower-of-cost-or-market method applied to: (1) each individual item in the inventory, (2) major categories within the inventory, and (3) the inventory as a whole.

b Which value would you recommend for inclusion in the financial statements? Why is the value you choose preferred to the other two?

8B-6 **Part A** Karr Company manufactures and sells four products, the inventories of which are priced at the lower of cost or market. The company considers a gross profit margin of 30% of selling price to be normal for all four products. The following information was compiled as of December 31:

Product	Units	Original unit cost	Cost to replace	Estimated cost to dispose	Expected selling price
W	400	$35.00	$42.00	$15.00	$ 80.00
X	200	47.50	45.00	20.50	95.00
Y	480	17.50	18.00	4.00	21.00
Z	240	45.00	46.00	26.00	100.00

Instructions

a Why are expected selling prices important in the application of the lower-of-cost-or-market rule?

b Prepare a schedule containing unit values (including "floor" and "ceiling") for determining the lower of cost or market on an individual product basis. Underscore for each product the unit value for the purpose of inventory valuation resulting from the application of the lower-of-cost-or-market rule. The last column of the schedule should contain the extension for each product and the total valuation of inventory.

c What effects, if any, do the expected selling prices have on the valuation of the four products by the lower-of-cost-or-market rule?

Part B The following information was taken from the financial statements of the Yamamoto Company for the year ended April 30, Year 3:

Sales	$600,000
Beginning inventory (lifo basis)	50,000
Net purchases	340,000
Ending inventory (lifo basis)	60,000
Cash	45,000
Accounts receivable (net)	75,000
Marketable securities (at cost, which approximates current market value)	8,000
Short-term prepayments	2,000
Current liabilities	100,000

The inventory on the first-in, first-out basis was $120,000 at April 30, Year 2, and $132,000 at April 30, Year 3.

Instructions

a Compute the following amounts or ratios, assuming that inventories are valued on the (1) last-in, first-out basis and (2) first-in, first-out basis:
Current assets
Working capital
Current ratio
Cost of goods sold
Inventory turnover

b Does the use of the first-in, first-out method of inventory valuation give a more meaningful measure of the company's working capital, current ratio, and inventory turnover? Explain.

8B-7 The trial balance for Lynwood Tile Company shown on page 347 has been adjusted for all items except ending inventory and income taxes.

LYNWOOD TILE COMPANY
Trial Balance
December 31, Year 2

Cash	$ 46,000	
Accounts receivable (net)	40,000	
Inventory (at cost), at Dec. 31, Year 1	52,000	
Short-term prepayments	2,000	
Buildings	200,000	
Accumulated depreciation: buildings		$ 60,500
Equipment	225,000	
Accumulated depreciation: equipment		105,000
Accounts payable		55,000
Mortgage payable ($12,000 due in Year 3)		50,000
Capital stock, no par, 20,000 shares outstanding		90,000
Retained earnings, Dec. 31, Year 1		141,500
Dividends	25,000	
Sales		505,000
Sales returns and allowances	10,000	
Sales discounts	5,000	
Purchases, including freight charges	280,000	
Purchase discounts		3,500
Selling expenses	75,000	
General expenses	50,500	
Totals	$1,010,500	$1,010,500

Additional information

(1) Inventory at the end of Year 2 consists of the following:

	Cost	Replacement cost (net of freight and purchase discounts)
Inventory (cost includes freight charges but has not been reduced for 2% purchase discounts).	$87,000	$72,000

The controller for the company wants to recognize the decline in the market value of the inventory by setting up an Allowance for Inventory Price Decline; the write-down is included in the cost of goods sold in the income statement. The cost of the inventory should be reduced for purchase discounts which are normally taken. You also ascertain that the cost of ending inventory includes $4,700 of worthless goods and $2,300 of freight charges. Freight applicable to the worthless goods amounts to $65.

(2) Income taxes on corporate income are assumed as follows:

On first $25,000 of taxable income	22%
On taxable income over $25,000	48%

Instructions

a Determine the adjusted cost of the inventory at December 31, Year 2, and prepare a journal entry to record the estimated loss in a value of the inventory caused by declining prices. Assume that the closing inventory was recorded in the accounts by an appropriate closing entry.

b Prepare an income statement for the year ended December 31, Year 2. The write-down of inventory to market should be included in the cost of goods sold.

c Prepare a balance sheet at December 31, Year 2.

d Prepare a statement of retained earnings for the year ended December 31, Year 2.

9

INVENTORIES: SPECIAL VALUATION METHODS

Inventory valuation methods based on cost flow assumptions and the application of the lower-of-cost-or-market rule were described in Chapter 8. Special valuation methods, such as the retail method, the gross profit method, and percentage-of-completion method of inventory valuation for long-term construction contracts are discussed in this chapter.

THE RETAIL METHOD

The retail method is used primarily as a means of valuing the inventory of a retail business when there is an observable pattern between cost and selling price. Under periodic inventory procedures, the cost of the ending inventory is subtracted from the total cost of goods available for sale to arrive at the cost of goods sold. Under the retail method, a record is kept of the sales value of goods available for sale, and the sales for the period are deducted from this total to determine the ending inventory at selling price. The inventory valued at selling price is then reduced to estimated cost by applying the cost percentage for the period to the selling price.

Some uses of the retail method of estimating the cost of inventory are:

1 To verify the reasonableness of the inventory value at the end of the accounting period. By using a different set of data from that used in pricing the inventory, the accountant can establish that the value assigned is reasonable.

2 To estimate the inventory for interim reporting purposes without taking a physical count.

3 To permit the valuation of inventory when selling prices are the only accessible data. The use of this method allows management to mark only the selling price on the merchandise and eliminates the need for referring to purchase invoices.

Simple illustration of retail method

The retail method is illustrated in the following simplified example for Robinson Company:

	Cost	Retail
ROBINSON COMPANY		
Retail Method of Estimating Cost of Inventory		
End of Current Year		
Beginning inventory	$ 40,000	$ 50,000
Net purchases	150,000	200,000
Goods available for sale	$190,000	$250,000
Cost percentage ($190,000 ÷ $250,000) = 76%		
Less: Sales and normal shrinkage		220,000
Ending inventory, at retail		$ 30,000
Ending inventory, at estimated cost ($30,000 × 76%)	$ 22,800	

Although the retail method permits the calculation of inventory without a physical count of the items on hand, the accountant should insist that a physical inventory be taken periodically. Otherwise, shrinkage due to shoplifting, breakage, and other causes might go undetected and might result in an increasingly overstated inventory.

Normal shrinkage in the inventory is frequently estimated on the basis of the goods which were available for sale. The method which has received the most support in practice is to develop a percentage from the experience of past years, such as 1% of retail price of goods available for sale. This percentage is then used to determine the estimated shrinkage, which is deducted, along with sales, from goods available for sale at retail prices, to arrive at the estimated inventory at retail.[1] The cost of normal shrinkage should be included in the cost of goods sold; the cost of abnormal shrinkage (theft, unusual spoilage, etc.) should be reported separately in the income statement.

In the retail method the cost of the inventory is computed by using a *cost percentage,* that is, the relationship between the cost of goods avail-

[1] When sales are made to employees or selected customers at a special discount price, such discounts should be added to sales in arriving at the estimated inventory at retail.

able for sale and their retail value. The reliability of this procedure rests on the conditions that (1) there is a uniform relation between selling price and cost for all merchandise or (2) if the markup on the various items sold by the firm differs, the distribution of items in the ending inventory is roughly the same as the "mix" in the total goods available for sale. When one of these conditions is not present, the accuracy of the retail method is usually improved by applying it to the individual departments of the business, and adding the resulting departmental inventories to arrive at the estimated cost of the total inventory.

Retail trade terminology

The following terms, commonly used in retail business, should be understood by the accountant employing the retail method of estimating inventory.

Original selling price   The price at which goods are originally offered for sale to the customer.

Markup.   The initial margin between retail and cost. It is variously referred to as **gross margin** or **mark-on.**

Additional markup   An increase above the original selling price.

Markup cancellation   A reduction in the selling price after there has been an additional markup. The reduction does not reduce the selling price below the original selling price. Additional markups less markup cancellations are referred to as **net markups.**

Markdown   A reduction in selling price below the original selling price.

Markdown cancellation   An increase in the selling price, following a markdown, which does not raise the new selling price above the original selling price. Markdowns less markdown cancellations are referred to as **net markdowns.**

To illustrate these terms, assume that an item which cost $20 is priced to sell at $30. The **markup** is $10 (50% of cost or $33\frac{1}{3}$% of the selling price). In response to the great demand for the item, an **additional markup** of $3 is added, so that the selling price is raised to $33. As the demand slackens, the price is lowered to $31, a **markup cancellation** of $2. Subsequently, in order to dispose of the entire stock of the item, the price is reduced to $25, a markup cancellation of $1 and a **markdown** of $5. Finally management concludes that the remaining items can be sold at a price of $28, thus calling for a **markdown cancellation** of $3 to increase the selling price from $25 to $28 per unit.

Retail method—average-cost basis

A clear understanding of the meaning of each term defined above is important in applying the retail method to arrive at an estimate of inventory cost. The treatment of net markdowns, for example, significantly affects the valuation of ending inventory.

The following data for the Western Company will be used to illustrate the treatment of net markups and net markdowns in the application of the retail method at the end of Year 1:

	Cost	Retail
Beginning inventory, Year 1	$16,000	$ 27,000
Net purchases during Year 1	75,000	110,000
Additional markups		5,000
Markup cancellations		(2,000)
Markdowns		(10,875)
Markdown cancellations		875
Net sales during Year 1		(90,000)
Ending inventory, at retail		$ 40,000

The ending inventory at average cost, using the retail inventory method, is determined as follows:

WESTERN COMPANY

Estimate of Inventory Using Retail Method—Average-Cost Basis

End of Year 1

	Cost	Retail
Beginning inventory	$16,000	$ 27,000
Net purchases	75,000	110,000
Net markups ($5,000 − $2,000)		3,000
Less: Net markdowns ($10,875 − $875)		(10,000)
Goods available for sale	$91,000	$130,000
Cost percentage ($91,000 ÷ $130,000) = 70%		
Deduct: Net sales		90,000
Ending inventory, at retail		$ 40,000
Ending inventory, at estimated average cost ($40,000 × 70%)	$28,000	

The cost percentage (70%) is determined after adding net markups and deducting net markdowns to the goods available for sale at retail. This procedure results in valuation of the ending inventory at *average cost.*

The estimated cost of the ending inventory, $28,000, will be accurate only if the goods on hand consist of a representative sample of all goods available for sale during Year 1. For example, if the ending inventory does not include any of the goods on hand at the beginning of the year, the cost percentage should be computed without using the beginning inventory figures. Similarly, if all goods on which the net markups and net markdowns were made have been sold, both the net markups and the net markdowns should be excluded from the computation of the cost percentage. Under such circumstances, however, the net markups and net markdowns still would be used to arrive at the amount of the ending inventory at retail.

Retail method—lower of average cost or market

The retail inventory method can be adopted to produce inventory valuations approximating the lower of cost or market when there have been changes in the costs and selling prices of goods during the period. The crucial factor in the calculation of estimated cost of ending inventory by the retail method is the treatment of net markups and net markdowns in the computation of the cost percentage. The inclusion of net markups and the exclusion of net markdowns in the computation of the cost percentage produce an inventory valued at the *lower of average cost or market.* This is sometimes called the *conventional retail method* and is illustrated for the Western Company below:

WESTERN COMPANY

Estimate of Inventory Using Retail Method—
Lower of Average Cost or Market
End of Year 1

	Cost	Retail
Beginning inventory	$16,000	$ 27,000
Net purchases	75,000	110,000
Net markups ($5,000 − $2,000)		3,000
Goods available for sale	$91,000	$140,000
Cost percentage ($91,000 ÷ $140,000) = 65%		
Deduct:		
Net sales		(90,000)
Net markdowns ($10,875 − $875)		(10,000)
Ending inventory, at retail		$ 40,000
Ending inventory, at lower of average cost or market		
($40,000 × 65%)	$26,000	

Net markups and net markdowns change the relationship between the selling price and the cost of goods available for sale, and accordingly affect the dollar value of the ending inventory and the cost of goods sold computed by the retail method.

In the schedule above, the cost percentage is 65% and the ending inventory at estimated cost is $26,000. When both the net markups and net markdowns were used in the computation of the cost percentage, the percentage was 70% and the ending inventory at average cost was $28,000. The inclusion of net markups in computing the cost percentage assumes that the additional markups apply proportionately to items sold and to items on hand at the end of the period; however, net markdowns are assumed to apply only to the goods sold. Since the selling price of goods to which the markdowns apply is less than the original selling price, the net markdowns as well as sales must be deducted from goods available for sale at retail in order to determine the inventory at retail price. If these assumptions are correct, then the exclusion of net markdowns in the computation of the cost percentage will value the ending inventory at original cost.

In many cases, however, the net markdowns do not apply solely to goods sold; instead, they apply to both goods sold and those in the ending inventory. In such cases the exclusion of net markdowns from the computation of the cost percentage does not produce an inventory value in terms of actual cost but rather an inventory value below cost. Consequently, if net markdowns are excluded from the computation of the cost percentage, the inventory amount determined is the lower of cost or market.

As stated previously, the retail method is based on an assumption that the ending inventory is composed of the same mix of items as the total batch of goods from which sales were made. If there are markdowns for special promotions, then this assumption implicit in the retail method may not be valid. Some markdowns may apply to goods available for sale and to goods in ending inventory in equal proportions, but others may apply only to goods which have been sold. In essence we are saying that there are really two lines of merchandise, "special sale" items and regular items, on which the markup is different. These two different lines may not be held in equal proportions in the goods available and in the ending inventory. Attempts to handle the two items in one calculation are likely to prove inadequate as a means of deriving meaningfull inventory cost figures.

Retail method—lifo valuation

In the preceding discussion two variations of the retail method have been illustrated which produce an inventory valuation at *average cost* or at the *lower of average cost or market.* If the last-in, first-out method is used to estimate the cost of inventory, the conventional retail method must be modified. The retail method can be adapted to approximate lifo cost of the ending inventory by the calculation of a cost percentage only for purchases of the current period. The objective is to estimate the cost of any increase in inventory during the period.

Since lifo is a cost (not lower-of-cost-or-market) method, both net markups and net markdowns must be included in the calculation of the cost percentage for current purchases, in accordance with the discussion of the average-cost procedure on pages 351 to 353.

The modification of the retail method necessary to value inventory at lifo cost is illustrated below for General Dry Goods Company (not Western Company used in previous illustrations). For purposes of this illustration, assume that the selling prices have remained unchanged and that net markups and net markdowns apply only to the goods purchased during Year 1.

GENERAL DRY GOODS COMPANY
Estimate of Inventory Using Retail Method—Lifo Cost
End of Year 1

	Cost	Retail
Beginning inventory	$24,000	$ 40,000
Net purchases	74,200	100,000
Net markups ($10,000 − $2,000)		8,000
Less: Net markdowns ($5,000 − $3,000)		(2,000)
Goods available for sale, at retail		$146,000
Less: Net sales		96,000
Ending inventory, at retail		$ 50,000

Cost percentage for net purchases, including net markups and net markdowns ($74,200 ÷ $106,000*) = 70%

Ending inventory, at lifo cost:

$40,000 (beginning inventory layer)	$24,000
10,000 × 70% (layer added in Year 1)	7,000
$50,000 (ending inventory, at retail)	
Ending inventory, at estimated lifo cost (retail method)	$31,000

* $100,000 + $8,000 − $2,000 = $106,000.

The inventory is composed of the cost of the beginning inventory plus the cost of the layer which was added during Year 1. In the event that the inventory decreases in Year 2, the decrease would be taken from the layer added in Year 1, $7,000, and then from the layer on hand at the beginning of Year 1. For example, if the ending inventory for General Dry Goods Company totaled $45,000 at retail at the end of Year 2, the inventory at lifo cost would be computed as illustrated at the top of page 356.

Ending inventory, estimated at lifo cost—Year 2:

$40,000 (inventory layer at beginning of Year 1) $24,000

 5,000 × 70% (one-half of layer added in Year 1) 3,500

$45,000 (ending inventory, at retail)

Ending inventory, at estimated lifo cost (retail method) $27,500

The computation of the cost percentage for the current year's purchases is required **only when an increase in inventory at a retail price occurs during the current year.** The cost percentage is computed for the sole purpose of pricing the incremental layer in inventory. On the other hand, if a decrease in inventory takes place, the ending inventory will consist of a fraction of the beginning inventory cost. For example, if the ending inventory at retail for General Dry Goods Company at the end of Year 2 amounted to only $30,000, the lifo cost of this inventory would be determined as follows:

$$\$24,000 \times \frac{\$30,000}{\$40,000} = \$18,000$$

Retail method—fifo valuation

The cost of the inventory on a *fifo* basis can be determined from the data used in determining the lifo cost. For example, the cost of the inventory at the end of Year 1, for General Dry Goods Company on the first-in, first-out basis would be $35,000 ($50,000 × 70%). If the cost percentage for Year 2 is assumed to be 72% and the inventory at retail amounted to $45,000, the inventory at *fifo* cost would be $32,400 ($45,000 × 72%).

Changes in price levels and the retail lifo method

Let us now remove the simplifying assumption of the stability of selling prices. In reality, retail prices do change from period to period and this is particularly significant to pricing inventories at retail lifo. Because the procedure employed under these circumstances is similar to that used in the calculation of dollar-value lifo discussed in Chapter 8, this method is sometimes referred to as the **dollar-value retail lifo method.** The ending inventory at retail must be converted to beginning-year prices to ascertain the increase in the inventory at beginning-year prices. An appropriate index of price changes must be found to use in making the conversion from end-of-year prices to beginning-of-year prices. There are several indices published regularly by various governmental agencies which might be used. The portion of the *Consumers Price Index* concerned with changes in prices of consumer nondurables would probably be most appropriate for department stores.

The procedure for estimating the lifo cost of the ending inventory, using the retail method and assuming increasing selling prices, is illustrated below for Rising Company. The sales price index at the beginning of the period, *when lifo was adopted,* is assumed to be 100 and the index at the end of the period is assumed to be 110, an increase of 10%.[2] In order not to complicate the example, we have assumed that there were no net markups or net markdowns during the period.

RISING COMPANY

Dollar-Value Retail Lifo Method

End of Current Period

	Cost	Retail
Beginning inventory (date lifo was adopted)	$18,000	$ 30,000
Purchases during the period (cost percentage = 65%) . .	65,000	100,000
Goods available for sale during the period, at retail price .		$130,000
Less: Net sales during the period		75,000
Inventory at end of period, at retail prices		$ 55,000
Computation of inventory increase at end-of-period retail prices:		
Inventory, at beginning-of-period retail prices ($55,000 ÷ 1.10)		$50,000
Less: Beginning inventory, at retail prices		30,000
Inventory increase, at beginning-of-period retail prices .		$20,000
Inventory increase, at end-of-period retail prices, $20,000 × 1.10		$22,000
Ending inventory, at dollar-value retail lifo cost:		
Beginning inventory layer	$18,000	
Layer added in current period ($22,000 × 65%)	14,300	
Total	$32,300[3]	

[2] When the base-year index is other than 100, the percentage increase is determined by dividing the index at the end of the current year by the base-year index and subtracting 100. For example, if the base-year index is 125 and the index at the end of the current year is 150, the increase would be 20% [(150/125) − 100].

[3] Failure to recognize the increase in the price level would have resulted in an erroneous ending inventory cost of $34,250, as determined below:

	Lifo cost	Selling price
Beginning inventory layer	$18,000	$30,000
Incremental layer [lifo cost = ($55,000 − $30,000) × 65%]	16,250	25,000
Ending inventory	$34,250	$55,000

GROSS PROFIT METHOD

The gross profit method is useful for several purposes: (1) to control and verify the validity of inventory cost; (2) to estimate interim inventory valuations between physical counts; and (3) to estimate the inventory value when necessary information normally used is lost or unavailable for any reason. The procedure involved is one of reducing sales to a cost basis; that is, cost of goods sold is estimated. The estimated cost of goods sold is then subtracted from the cost of goods available for sale to arrive at the estimated inventory cost.

In the event that both inventory and records are destroyed by fire, the inventory value can also be estimated by the use of the gross profit method. The gross profit and cost of goods sold percentages are obtained from prior years' financial statements, which are presumably available. The beginning inventory for the current year is the ending inventory of the preceding year. Net purchases may be estimated by examining copies of the paid checks retained by the bank and through correspondence with suppliers. Sales may be computed by reference to cash deposits and by estimation of the uncollected receivables by direct correspondence with customers.

Determining the gross profit and cost of goods sold percentage

The crucial factor in applying the gross profit method is the development of an accurate and realistic measure of the gross profit percentage. Frequently the best available measure is an average of the gross profit percentages for recent years, adjusted for any changes which are known to have taken place in the current year. The cost of goods sold percentage (cost percentage) is determined by subtracting the gross profit percentage from 100%.

To illustrate the computation of ending inventory using the gross profit method, assume the following data for Marina Sea Store:

Beginning inventory, at cost	$ 40,000
Net purchases	200,000
Net sales	225,000
Average rate of gross profit on net sales for past three years	20%

Assuming that the average rate of gross profit for the current period remained at 20%, the inventory cost at the end of the period would be estimated as follows:

Beginning inventory, at cost		$ 40,000
Net purchases		200,000
Goods available for sale		$240,000
Less approximate cost of goods sold:		
Net sales	$225,000	
Cost percentage (100% − 20%)	80%	180,000
Approximate ending inventory, at cost		$ 60,000

The ending inventory computed by the gross profit method will be reasonably consistent with the usual method of pricing inventory. This follows from the fact that the gross profit percentage is based on historical records which have reflected the particular method of valuing the inventory. If the inventory is usually valued at lifo, the estimated inventory will approximate lifo cost; therefore, if the gross profit method is used as a basis for recovering an insured loss, the lifo inventory should be priced for insurance purposes at prevailing prices at the time of the loss.

In some cases the gross profit percentage is stated as a percentage of cost of goods sold. In such situations the gross profit percentage must be restated to a percentage of net sales. For example, if the gross profit is stated as 25% of cost of goods sold, the gross profit percentage can be restated to 20% of net sales as follows:

(1) $25\% = \frac{1}{4}$

(2) Add numerator of fraction to denominator to make $\frac{1}{5}$

(3) $\frac{1}{5} = 20\%$

When 20% is subtracted from 100%, we have the cost percentage of 80% of net sales. Alternatively, the cost percentage can be determined directly as follows:

Let X = **cost of goods sold as percentage of net sales (100%)**

$.25X$ = **gross profit percentage**

then $X + .25X = 100\%$

$1.25X = 100\%$

$X = \dfrac{100\%}{1.25}$

$X = 80\%$ **(cost percentage based on net sales)**

Applying the gross profit method to departments

If there are several classes of goods which have a different markup percentage, the gross profit method yields accurate results only if the inventory for each class is computed individually. The use of a combined cost percentage would require the unlikely assumption that the various classes of inventory are sold in the same relative proportions each year. To illustrate this point, assume that the gross profit percentage has averaged 50% for Department A and 30% for Department B. Thus the cost percentage is 50% for Department A and 70% for Department B; the combined cost percentage has averaged 65% in recent years. The cost of the ending inventory may be estimated as follows:

<table>
<tr><td colspan="4">Estimate of Cost of Departmental and Combined Inventories
For Current Year—Gross Profit Method</td></tr>
<tr><td></td><th>Dept. A</th><th>Dept. B</th><th>Combined</th></tr>
<tr><td>Beginning inventory, at cost . . . .</td><td>$ 20,000</td><td>$ 40,000</td><td>$ 60,000</td></tr>
<tr><td>Net purchases . . . .</td><td>90,000</td><td>95,000</td><td>185,000</td></tr>
<tr><td>Cost of goods available for sale . . . . . .</td><td>$110,000</td><td>$135,000</td><td>$245,000</td></tr>
<tr><td>Less: Approximate cost of goods sold:</td><td></td><td></td><td></td></tr>
<tr><td>Net sales . . . .</td><td>$150,000</td><td>$150,000</td><td>$300,000</td></tr>
<tr><td>Average cost percentage, prior years . .</td><td>50%</td><td>70%</td><td>65%</td></tr>
<tr><td>Approximate cost of goods sold . . . . .</td><td>$ 75,000</td><td>$105,000</td><td>$195,000</td></tr>
<tr><td>Approximate ending inventory . . . .</td><td>$ 35,000</td><td>$ 30,000</td><td>$ 50,000</td></tr>
</table>

Using the combined cost percentage (based on prior years' experience) produces an inventory estimate of $50,000, although the sum of the two departmental ending inventories is estimated at $65,000 ($35,000 + $30,000). The source of the error is clear when we note that the cost percentage for the current period, determined by combining the departmental results, is not 65 but 60%, because a higher-than-usual proportion of total sales *this year* was made in Department A. The actual combined cost percentage for the current year is determined below:

Total sales ($150,000 + $150,000) $300,000
Total estimated cost of goods sold ($75,000 + $105,000) $180,000
Combined cost percentage for current year ($180,000 ÷ $300,000) . . <u>60%</u>

If the cost percentage of 60% is used in the summary above for Departments A and B, the combined ending inventory would be $65,000 ($245,000 − $180,000 = $65,000).

Gross profit method and interim reports

The gross profit method is frequently used in the preparation of interim reports of earnings. It should be clear that the use of the gross profit method results in an *estimated cost* of inventory. If the reporting entity normally values inventory at lower of cost or market for annual reporting purposes, it must follow the same procedure for interim reporting purposes. Thus the estimated cost obtained by using the gross profit method must be compared to current replacement costs to determine whether a write-down to a lower "market" is required. The APB permitted the use of the gross profit method at interim dates even though annual inventories were determined using one of the cost flow assumptions described in Chapter 8. Companies using the gross profit method for interim purposes "should disclose the method used . . . and any significant adjustments that result from reconciliations with the annual physical inventory."[4]

OTHER VALUATION METHODS

Valuation of inventory at replacement cost

The valuation of inventories at replacement cost has been advocated by accountants who believe that the current asset section of the balance sheet should reflect current values. The cost methods of inventory pricing frequently understate the value of the inventory, particularly during periods of rising prices. The significance of replacement cost as a measure of inventory value varies considerably depending on the type of inventory involved. In the retail market the selling prices of staple commodities, such as sugar, wool, cotton, etc., tend to follow cost prices closely. In such situations replacement cost of the inventory is quite important to the manager and often to outside parties also.

Replacement cost valuation of inventories in the preparation of financial statements has not been widely adopted. Perhaps the closest practical approach is the fifo method. Unless prices are rising quite rapidly, the fifo method of pricing presents inventories in the balance sheet at or near current replacement cost without departing from the cost basis. The real need for disclosure of replacement costs of inventories arises when the lifo method is used in pricing the inventory.

The theoretical objection to the use of replacement cost as a method of inventory valuation is implicit in the arguments previously presented. Some of the advantages of inventory valuation at replacement cost can be achieved by the use of parenthetical notes in the balance sheet disclosing current replacement cost of inventories. Some accountants

[4] *APB Opinion No. 28,* "Interim Financial Reporting," AICPA (New York: 1973), p. 524. For an extensive discussion of the use of the gross profit method for interim reporting purposes, see Leonard Sorensen, "Gross Profit Method and Interim Financial Information." *Journal of Accountancy,* December 1975, pp. 56–64.

have argued for the adoption of replacement cost as a means of pricing inventory whether it is above or below cost. They base their argument on the fact that the utility of goods in inventory is indicated by the current cost of replacement by purchase or reproduction. A valid point made by proponents of replacement cost is that if replacement cost is objective, verifiable, and more useful when it is lower than cost, it also possesses those attributes when it is higher than cost.[5]

The consistent use of replacement cost as a basis of valuing inventories would require some broadening of the principle of revenue realization as presently applied. Under current accounting standards, revenue emerges at the time inventories are sold and converted into receivables, as indicated in the following diagram:

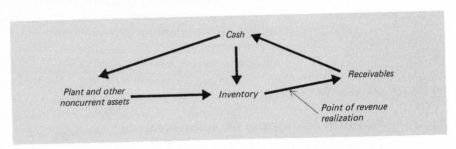

If replacement costs were adopted as the basis of inventory and plant asset valuation, gains and losses represented by the difference between cost and replacement cost would be recognized and included in income prior to the sale of finished products. The information resulting from such a procedure would be quite useful in periods when prices were changing significantly. The real issue is whether replacement costs can be determined with sufficient accuracy and objectivity to provide a reliable basis for financial reporting. At present, however, valuation of inventories at a replacement cost *higher* than actual cost cannot be considered a generally accepted accounting principle.

The Securities and Exchange Commission currently requires the disclosure of the replacement cost of inventories and of cost of goods sold as supplementary unaudited information accompanying the financial statements. Such disclosure was "designed to enable investors to obtain more relevant information about the current economics of a business enterprise in an inflationary economy than that provided solely by financial statements prepared on the basis of historical cost."[6] Restatement of inventory costs to a common measuring unit is another approach to the problem of changing prices; however, the elusiveness of the base unit, the purchasing power of the dollar, has thwarted most attempts in this direction. These subjects are considered in Chapter 22.

---

[5] Robert T. Sprouse and Maurice Moonitz, "A Tentative Set of Broad Accounting Principles for Business Enterprises," *Accounting Research Study No. 3*, AICPA (New York: 1962), p. 31.

[6] *Accounting Series Release No. 190*, SEC (Washington: 1976) p. 1.

Valuation of inventory at net selling price

The valuation of the inventory at *net selling price or net realizable value* (sales price less direct costs of completion and disposal) has some appeal, especially when one considers that in reality value is added as the goods are brought to market. For example, in a retail shop, goods are more valuable than they were at the wholesaler's warehouse; value has been added by the process of bringing the goods nearer the ultimate market. In a manufacturing concern, as materials, direct labor, and factory overhead costs are blended together, a product emerges which is normally more valuable than the sum of the three cost factors. However, this method of inventory valuation has not been widely adopted for two reasons: (1) lack of objectivity in determining the net selling price in many cases; and (2) the fact that the sales price has not been realized in terms of cash or cash equivalents. Accountants generally consider revenue to be realized at the time of sale, not at the time of manufacture.

The valuation of inventory at net selling price is appropriate for some types of businesses producing commodities which have an active and readily determinable market price. When the production of such commodities is complete, revenue may be considered realized. The completion of the sale transaction may be viewed as an anticlimax. In other businesses in which selling price is established by a firm contract, the sale follows production as a matter of course, and completed inventory might logically be valued at net selling price.

The use of net selling price in valuing inventories in effect moves the point of revenue realization back one step in the earning process. As costs are incurred during the process of bringing an item to market, income is earned in the most fundamental sense. Each activity necessary to advance the goods closer to the customer and ultimately to close the sale transaction adds an element of income—the increase in sales price over the added cost. Therefore, if there are costs still to be incurred, there is still an element of income to be earned. The valuation of inventories at net selling prices means that an element of income may be accrued before it is fully realized.

INVENTORY VALUATION FOR LONG-TERM CONSTRUCTION CONTRACTS

Contracts for construction of ships, bridges, dams, and similar projects often require several years to complete. Such contracts present special problems of inventory valuation and profit recognition. For a business engaged in long-term contracts, two approaches to inventory valuation and revenue recognition are available:

1 The completed-contract method
2 The percentage-of-completion method

Under the **completed-contract** method, inventory of construction in progress is valued at cost; no profit is recognized on the contract until the contract is completed and the work accepted by the customer. There may be some years in which no contracts are completed; consequently, in those years the company would have neither revenue nor profit on construction contracts. In fact, a loss would be reported to the extent of selling, general, administrative, and other expenses not chargeable to the inventories. In the year in which a long-term contract is finally completed, the entire profit created through several years of production would be recognized, even though only a small part of the work may have been performed in the final year of the contract.

To avoid such misleading reporting, most companies engaged in long-term contracts employ the **percentage-of-completion** method of accounting. This method (also known as the **production basis** of profit recognition) calls for accruing the revenue and profit over the life of the contract in accordance with the progress achieved each year. If the work performed in a given year is estimated to represent 10% of total performance under the contract, then 10% of the total estimated revenue and profit is considered earned. This accrual of profit is accomplished by increasing the carrying value of the inventory of construction in progress.

Accounting for long-term construction contract illustrated

A bridge is to be constructed by Regal Construction Company beginning in Year 1 at a contract price of $900,000 with estimated construction costs totaling $750,000. The bridge is expected to be completed in Year 3. The construction costs incurred, cost estimates, and other pertinent data are presented below in summary form for each of the three years:

	Year 1	Year 2	Year 3
Construction costs incurred	$125,000	$495,000	$145,000
Estimated cost to complete the contract . .	625,000	155,000	–0–
Amounts billed to customers	110,000	565,000	225,000
Collections from customers on billings . . .	90,000	520,000	265,000
Operating expenses incurred	15,000	30,000	22,500

Completed-Contract Method   Using the completed-contract method, the journal entries to record the transactions relating to the construction of the bridge are shown on page 365 for Regal Construction Company.

Direct costs incurred on the contract are accumulated in the Construction in Progress account and amounts billed to the customer are

REGAL CONSTRUCTION COMPANY
Journal Entries—Completed-Contract Method

Accounts and explanations of transactions	Year 1		Year 2		Year 3	
	Debit	Credit	Debit	Credit	Debit	Credit
Operating Expenses .	15,000		30,000		22,500	
Construction in						
Progress	125,000		495,000		145,000	
Materials, Cash,						
etc.		140,000		525,000		167,500
To record operating expenses and construction costs.						
Accounts Receivable .	110,000		565,000		225,000	
Partial Billings						
on Contract .		110,000		565,000		225,000
To record billings on contract.						
Cash	90,000		520,000		265,000	
Accounts						
Receivable . .		90,000		520,000		265,000
To record collections from customer.						
Partial Billings on						
Contract					900,000	
Construction Costs						
Applicable to Realized Revenue					765,000	
Construction						
Revenue . . .						900,000
Construction in						
Progress . . .						765,000
To record realized revenue and applicable construction costs upon final approval of project by customer.						

recorded in the Partial Billings on Contract account. These account titles may vary. When the project is completed and approved by the customer, the costs applicable to the project are transferred to an expense account (Construction Costs Applicable to Realized Revenue) and partial billings relating to the project are transferred to Construction Revenue.

The only closing entries required at the end of the first two years would be to close the Operating Expenses account, since no gross profit would have been recognized in these years. For cases in which operating expenses can be identified with particular projects, inclusion of these expenses in the cost of the construction is desirable. When a contract is expected to result in a loss, the loss should be recognized as soon as it is determinable by a debit to Loss on Long-Term Construction Contract and a credit to Construction in Progress. The credit to Construction in Progress eliminates from inventory the excess of the total estimated cost of the contract over the total contract revenue.

In Year 3, balances in the Operating Expense account, the Construction Costs Applicable to Realized Revenue account, and the Construction Revenue account are closed to the Income Summary account. The income statement for Year 3 for Regal Construction Company will show the following:

Construction revenue	*$900,000*
Less: Construction costs applicable to realized revenue	*765,000*
Gross profit on long-term construction contract	*$135,000*
Operating expenses	*22,500*
Income before income taxes	*$112,500*

The balance sheets for Regal Construction Company would include the amounts shown on page 367 when the **completed-contract method is used.**

Under the completed-contract method, the amount billed to customers may exceed the amount of construction costs incurred; therefore, when the Partial Billings on Contract account balance is deducted from the Construction in Progress account balance, a credit balance results. The AICPA offers the following guidelines in reporting such a balance in the balance sheet:

When the completed-contract method is used, an excess of accumulated costs over related billings should be shown in the balance sheet as a current asset, and an excess of accumulated billings over related costs should be shown among the liabilities, in most cases as a current liability. If costs exceed billings on some contracts, and billings exceed costs on others, the contracts should ordinarily be segregated so that the figures on the asset side include only those contracts on which costs exceed billings, and those on the liability side include only those on which billings exceed costs. It is

	End of Year 1	End of Year 2	End of Year 3
Current assets:			
Accounts receivable	$20,000	$65,000	$25,000
Inventories:			
Construction in progress	$125,000		
Less: Partial billings on contract	110,000		
Costs of uncompleted contract in excess of billings	$15,000		
Current liabilities:			
Partial billings on contract		$675,000	
Less: Construction in progress		620,000	
Billings on uncompleted contract in excess of costs		$55,000	

suggested that the asset item be described as "costs of uncompleted contracts in excess of related billings" rather than as "inventory" or "work in process," and that the item on the liability side be described as "billings on uncompleted contracts in excess of related costs."[7]

In our illustration of the bridge construction contract, the $15,000 excess of construction costs over partial billings on contracts at the end of Year 1 appears as a current asset in the balance sheet; at the end of Year 2, however, the $55,000 excess of partial billings on contracts over construction costs to date is included under current liabilities. These accounts are considered current because they arise in the normal operating cycle of a construction company. The balance in Accounts Receivable at the end of Year 1, $20,000, is composed of billings of $110,000 less collections to date of $90,000; at the end of Year 2, the balance in Accounts Receivable is $65,000, consisting of cumulative billings to date of $675,000 less total collections to date of $610,000; and at the end of Year 3, only $25,000 ($900,000 − $875,000) remains to be collected from the customer.

---

[7] *Accounting Research and Terminology Bulletins—Final Edition, ARB No. 45,* AICPA (New York: 1961), p. 6.

Percentage-of-Completion Method   The percentage of completion represented by each year's work may be based on (1) *engineering estimates* of the work performed to date relative to the total work required under the contract or (2) the *relationship between the cost incurred to date and the total estimated cost to complete the contract.* The percentage of completion determined by either of these two methods is applied to the contract price to determine the amount of revenue and gross profit earned to date.

In choosing between these two methods of establishing the percentage of completion, it is well to recognize that performance under some contracts will require that a substantial part of the material to be used for the entire contract be ordered before any actual construction takes place. These costs incurred for material can constitute a large part of the total costs of the contract, although little or no actual progress has been made toward the completion of the project. When these conditions exist, a percentage of completion based on engineering and architectural estimates may be superior to that based on relative costs for purposes of recognizing realized contract revenue and gross profit. The AICPA has suggested that during the early stages of a contract, costs of items such as materials and subcontracts should be excluded from the total cost incurred in calculating the percentage of completion.[8] Mere acquisition of materials or making a deposit with a subcontractor does not give rise to the realization of revenue.

The AICPA has sanctioned the percentage-of-completion method under certain circumstances as follows:

> It is . . . a generally accepted accounting procedure to accrue revenues under certain types of contracts and thereby recognize profits, on the basis of partial performance, when the circumstances are such that total profit can be estimated with reasonable accuracy and ultimate realization is reasonably assured. Particularly when the performance of a contract requires a substantial period of time from inception to completion, there is ample precedent for pro-rata recognition of profit as the work progresses, if the total profit and the ratio of the performance to date to the complete performance can be computed reasonably and collection is reasonably assured.[9]

If Regal Construction Company determines the percentage of completion on the basis of cost incurred to date as a fraction of the total estimated cost to be incurred on the contract, the journal entries for the three-year period would be as shown on page 369. The calculation of realized construction revenue on the basis of costs incurred to date related to total estimated costs on the contract is presented on page 370.

---

[8] Ibid., p. 4.
[9] *Accounting Research and Terminology Bulletins—Final Edition,* AICPA (New York: 1961), chap. 11A, p. 95.

REGAL CONSTRUCTION COMPANY
Journal Entries—Percentage-of-Completion Method

Accounts and explanations of transactions	Year 1		Year 2		Year 3	
	Debit	Credit	Debit	Credit	Debit	Credit
Operating Expenses .	15,000		30,000		22,500	
Construction in Progress	125,000		495,000		145,000	
Materials, Cash, etc.		140,000		525,000		167,500
To record operating expenses and construction costs.						
Accounts Receivable	110,000		565,000		225,000	
Partial Billings on Contract .		110,000		565,000		225,000
To record billings on contract.						
Cash	90,000		520,000		265,000	
Accounts Receivable		90,000		520,000		265,000
To record collections from customer.						
Construction Costs Applicable to Realized Revenue	125,000		495,000		145,000	
Construction in Progress	25,000		75,000		35,000	
Construction Revenue ...		150,000		570,000		180,000
To record realized revenue estimated on the basis of cost incurred to total estimated cost. (Calculations appear on p. 370).						
Partial Billings on Contract					900,000	
Construction in Progress ...						900,000
To record approval of project by customer.						

Calculation of Realized Construction Revenue
Years 1, 2, and 3

Year 1: Construction costs incurred in Year 1 . . . . $125,000
Estimated remaining costs to complete contract . 625,000
Total estimated costs of completing contract . . $750,000

Realized construction revenue in Year 1:
Contract price, $900,000 × ($125,000/$750,000) $150,000

Year 2: Construction costs incurred to date ($125,000
+ $495,000) $620,000
Estimated remaining costs to complete contract . 155,000
Total estimated costs of completing contract . . $775,000

Contract price, $900,000 × ($620,000/$775,000) . $720,000
Less: Realized construction revenue in Year 1 . . (150,000)
Realized construction revenue in Year 2 570,000

Year 3: Contract price $900,000
Less: Realized construction revenue in Year 1 and
Year 2 ($150,000 + $570,000) 720,000
Realized construction revenue in Year 3 180,000
Total realized construction revenue Years 1–3 . . . . $900,000

The first three entries on page 369 are the same as illustrated on page 365 for the completed-contract method. However, when the percentage-of-completion method is used, two nominal accounts are used at the end of each of the first two years and when the contract is completed in Year 3—the Construction Costs Applicable to Realized Revenue and the Construction Revenue accounts. The excess of realized construction revenue and the related costs represents the gross profit earned on the contract for each year and is debited to the Construction in Progress account. When the contract is completed in Year 3, the Partial Billings on Contract account is debited and the Construction in Progress account is credited to eliminate the balances in these accounts relating to the contract completed.

Although the percentage-of-completion method allows for the recognition of revenue and gross profit as the work progresses, this same calculation may in some cases indicate that a loss is probable. In the event that a loss can be foreseen, **ARB No. 45** requires that "in most circumstances provision should be made for the loss on the entire contract. If there is a close relationship between profitable and unprofitable contracts, . . . the group may be treated as a unit in determining the necessity for a provision for loss."[10] The loss would be recorded by a

[10] Accounting Research and Terminology Bulletins—Final Edition, ARB No. 45, p. 5.

debit to Loss on Long-Term Construction Contract and a credit to Construction in Progress. Thus, both the completed-contract and the percentage-of-completion methods of accounting for a given long-term contract produce identical results when it appears that a loss will be incurred on a given contract.

The presentation of construction revenue and construction costs applicable to realized revenue in the income statement is illustrated below for Regal Construction Company:

	Year 1	Year 2	Year 3
Construction revenue	$150,000	$570,000	$180,000
Less: Construction costs applicable to realized revenue	125,000	495,000	145,000
Gross profit on long-term construction contract	$ 25,000	$ 75,000	$ 35,000

The balance sheet for Regal Construction Company would include the following amounts when the **percentage-of-completion** method is used:

	End of Year 1	End of Year 2	End of Year 3
Current assets:			
Accounts receivable	$20,000	$65,000	$25,000
Inventories:			
Construction in progress . .	$150,000	$720,000	
Less: Partial billings on contract . . .	110,000	675,000	
Costs and profit on uncompleted contract in excess of billings . . .	$40,000	$45,000	

When the percentage-of-completion method of accounting is used, Construction in Progress is shown in the balance sheet as part of inventories (the same as under the completed-contract method). The inventory is valued at the cumulative construction costs incurred, plus the gross profit earned to date, less partial billings on the contract to date. The $150,000 balance in the Construction in Progress account at the end of Year 1 consists of construction costs of $125,000 plus the $25,000 gross profit earned in Year 1. At the end of Year 2, the balance of $720,000 in the Construction in Progress account consists of construction costs of $620,000 incurred in Years 1 and 2 plus $100,000 gross profit earned in Years 1 and 2.

Special problems relating to long-term contracts

Income tax laws permit the use of either the completed-contract method or the percentage-of-completion method. For income tax purposes, expenses of the contractor which are not directly related to the project under construction are expenses of the year in which they are incurred. And, finally, the contractor is required to use one of the two methods consistently. A change in the method of valuing the construction in progress for income tax purposes requires the approval of the Internal Revenue Service.

If the percentage-of-completion method is used for financial reporting purposes and the completed-contract method for income tax purposes, deferred income taxes should be recorded to give effect to the timing difference in income recognition. This problem is considered in Chapter 21. A change in the method of accounting for long-term contracts for financial reporting purposes requires the retroactive restatement of prior years' financial statements currently issued. The accounting for changes in accounting principles is discussed in Chapter 23.

The Securities and Exchange Commission requires the extensive disclosure of accounting policies for long-term contracts (extending over a period longer than 12 months). The SEC stated that such disclosure is necessary because long-term contracts "involve inventories and receivables with unique risk and liquidity characteristics."[11] The disclosure required includes the amount of inventoried costs, the nature of cost elements included in inventory, and the principal assumptions used to determine total contract costs.

Inventory of supplies and short-term prepayments

In addition to inventories of merchandise, finished goods, materials, and finished parts, a business enterprise may also have several types of supplies on hand. For example, inventory of supplies may include office supplies, promotional materials, shipping supplies, and factory supplies. The problems of determining cost and valuation of supplies are similar to those for inventories discussed earlier in Chapter 8. Supplies are purchased for use in the business and any quantities remaining on

[11] *Accounting Series Release No. 164,* SEC (Washington: 1974).

hand at the end of the period should be included among current assets. A business which finds that important amounts of supplies must be carried in stock should plan for acquisition and should control supplies on hand in the same manner as major inventory items.

The term *prepaid expenses* is widely used to describe unexpired costs which are expected to be consumed within a relatively short period of time. However, this term is somewhat of a misnomer and should be replaced by a more descriptive title such as *short-term prepayments.* A prepaid expense is a cost incurred to acquire an economically useful good or service that has not yet been consumed in the revenue-earning process. Strictly speaking, both depreciable plant assets and inventories fall within this definition. Plant assets are classified separately because their services are performed over relatively long time periods; inventories require separate designation because of their materiality and importance. There is a general presumption that a substantial portion of any good or service treated as a short-term prepayment will be consumed within one year or within the company's operating cycle; this is the reason for including these items among the current assets in the balance sheet.

Inventories and financial reporting standards

The objectives of reporting inventories on the balance sheet are to reveal the type, the relative liquidity, and the basis of valuation of the inventories. Accountants, in reporting the investment in inventories, as in reporting other assets, are concerned with disclosing all significant information; they are particularly concerned that the investment in inventories has been determined on a basis consistent with that of preceding years. If a change is made in the method of calculating inventory cost, the change should be explained fully as to its effect on the current year's statements and the corresponding effect for the prior year (or years). The accounting problems of reporting a change in the inventory valuation method are illustrated in Chapter 23 in the section dealing with "Accounting Changes."

When an inventory valuation account is used as a means of valuing the inventory at the lower of cost or market or at the last-in, first-out basis, this account should be subtracted from inventory cost in the balance sheet.

Financial reporting standards require that the various categories of inventories be indicated under the general caption "Inventories" and that the basis of valuation and the method of tracing costs be disclosed. Inventory profits and the replacement cost of the inventory also should be disclosed as required by the SEC.

Goods on order and advance payments to suppliers should not be considered a part of the inventory unless title to the goods has passed to the buyer in accordance with the legal tests described in Chapter 8.

Inventories which have been pledged as collateral for loans should be included in the inventory section rather than being offset against the loans secured by the inventory. Firm purchase commitments should be disclosed in a note to the financial statements.

Most companies report inventories in highly condensed form accompanied by an explanatory note. An example from a recent annual report issued by Potlatch Corporation follows:

	Year 10	Year 9
Inventories (Note 3)	$75,863,808	$79,407,280

Note 3. Inventories
Inventory components are valued at the balance sheet dates as follows:

	Year 10	Year 9
Logs, pulpwood, chips, and sawdust	$14,808,908	$10,337,848
Lumber and other manufactured wood products . .	9,092,589	9,759,782
Pulp, paper, and converted paper products	33,522,887	41,204,047
Materials and supplies	18,439,424	18,105,603
	$75,863,808	$79,407,280

Valued at lower of cost or market:

	Year 10	Year 9
First-in, first-out basis	$ 9,525,121	$ 9,423,818
Last-in, first-out basis	17,128,752	16,049,015
Average cost basis	49,209,935	53,934,447
	$75,863,808	$79,407,280

If the last-in, first-out inventory had been priced at current replacement cost, the values would have been $11,404,000 higher at December 31, Year 10, and $12,637,000 higher at December 31, Year 9. There was no significant liquidation of prior years' lifo layers in inventory during Year 10 or Year 9.

The above inventory balances were used in calculating cost of sales. The opening balance for Year 9 was $52,484,190.

REVIEW QUESTIONS

1 For what purposes may the **retail method** of inventory valuation be used?

2 Distinguish between **(a) markup** and **additional markup, (b) markup cancellation** and **markdown, (c) markdown cancellation** and **additional markup.**

3 Briefly describe the computation of the cost percentage when inventory is determined at average cost using the retail inventory method.

4 Briefly describe the computation of the cost percentage when inventory is determined at the lower of average cost or market in applying the retail inventory method.

5 What is the basic assumption as to the composition of the ending inventory when the retail inventory method is applied on the basis of average cost or on the basis of the lower of average cost or market?

6 Describe the application of the retail inventory method when cost is determined on a last-in, first-out basis.

7 Describe the special procedure to be followed in estimating inventory on the *retail lifo* basis after retail prices have increased.

8 List three uses that may be made of the *gross profit method.*

9 **(a)** Distinguish between gross profit as a percentage of sales and as a percentage of cost of goods sold. **(b)** Convert the following gross profit percentages based on sales to gross profit percentages based on cost of goods sold: $16\frac{2}{3}\%$, 25%, and 50%. **(c)** Convert the following gross profit percentages based on cost of goods sold to gross profit percentages based on sales: 25%, 50%, and 150%.

10 Explain the possible limitations of using an average cost of goods sold percentage for prior years to estimate the inventory under the gross profit method.

11 There are two accepted procedures of accounting for operations involving long-term construction contracts. What are the two methods? What criteria are used in choosing between the methods? How can you justify a departure from the accepted practice of recognizing revenue only at the time of sale?

12 When a business adopts the percentage-of-completion method of accounting for long-term contracts, there are two generally used methods of estimating the portion completed. What are these two methods and under what circumstances might each be used?

13 During the early stages of a construction project, some material costs and subcontract costs are not included in the total cost incurred when computing the percentage of completion. Why are these costs not included?

14 Under the percentage-of-completion method of accounting for long-term contracts, anticipated gross profits are recognized as the construction progresses but anticipated losses are recognized as soon as they can be reasonably ascertained. Why does this seeming inconsistency exist?

15 In view of the variety of procedures available for valuing the inventory and the diverse solutions that are produced by the various methods, how can the user of financial statements be assured that comparability exists between financial statements of the same company over a period of years?

16 What objections can you give to the use of the term "prepaid expenses"? Can you offer a better alternative?

17 What objectives is the accountant seeking to achieve in reporting inventories in the balance sheet?

EXERCISES

Ex. 9-1 Hupp Company uses the gross profit method for estimating monthly inventory balances. During recent months gross profit has averaged 30% of net sales. The following data for January are available:

Inventory, Jan. 1	$ 25,550
Purchases	120,000
Purchase returns	5,000
Freight-in	6,000
Gross sales	175,000
Sales returns and allowances	10,000

Compute the estimated cost of the inventory at January 31, using the gross profit method.

Ex. 9-2 Paul Reese computed the cost of his inventory at the close of business on July 20, Year 10, at $20,500. His fiscal year ends on June 30; therefore you find it necessary to establish an inventory figure at June 30, Year 10. You find that during the period July 1–20 sales were $70,500; sales returns, $1,800; goods purchased and placed in stock, $61,000; goods returned to vendors, $1,200; freight-in, $600.

Calculate the inventory at June 30, Year 10, assuming that goods are sold at 25% above cost.

Ex. 9-3 The following information is taken from the records of Payless Drug Company for the current year:

	At cost	At retail
Beginning inventory	$ 25,000	$ 46,200
Purchases	120,000	191,800
Net markups		12,000
Sales		190,000
Net markdowns		3,800

You are to assume that all net markups and net markdowns apply to purchases of the current year, and that it is appropriate to treat the entire inventory as a single department with no markdowns having occurred during the prior year.

Compute the ending inventory at lower of average cost or market using the retail method.

Ex. 9-4 Using the information given in Ex. 9-3 for Payless Drug Company, compute the ending inventory using the retail lifo method.

Ex. 9-5 Assuming that sales for Payless Drug Company in the current year were $209,240 instead of $190,000 and that all other facts are identical to those given in Ex. 9-3, compute the ending inventory using the retail lifo method.

Ex. 9-6 During the current year the index of selling prices for merchandise handled by the Stever Company increased from 90 to 108. From the information on page 377, compute the ending inventory at estimated lifo cost, taking into account the increase in selling prices.

	Cost	Selling price	Cost-selling price ratio
Beginning inventory (date lifo was adopted) . .	$ 40,000	$ 50,000	80%
Purchases during the year	150,000	200,000	75%
Goods available for sale	$190,000	$250,000	
Less: Net sales during the year		178,000	
Inventory at end of year, at selling price		$ 72,000	

Ex. 9-7 In Year 1, Gene Corporation began construction work under a three-year contract. The contract price is $800,000. Gene uses the percentage-of-completion method for financial accounting purposes. The revenue to be recognized each year is based on the proportion of cost incurred to total estimated costs for completing the contract. The balance sheet presentation relating to this contract at December 31, Year 1, follows:

Accounts receivable—construction contract billings	$18,000
Construction in progress $200,000	
Less: Partial billings on contract 188,000	
Costs and profit on uncompleted contract in excess of billings	12,000

In the income statement for Year 1, a gross profit of $20,000 was recognized on this contract.

a How much cash was collected on this contract in Year 1?

b What was the initial estimated gross profit on this contract?

Ex. 9-8 Reseda Construction Co. began operations in Year 3. By year-end, the first project was finished and a second project was under way, as follows:

	Project No. 1	Project No. 2
Cost incurred during the year	$ 80,000	$105,000
Portion of estimated total cost	100%	60%
Total contract price	$100,000	$200,000
Billings on contract during the year	$100,000	$115,000
Collections from customers during the year	$ 92,000	$ 75,000

Prepare journal entries for Year 3 (excluding closing entries) to record the transactions relating to the two projects if (1) the completed-contract method of accounting for long-term contracts is used, and (2) the percentage-of-completion method of accounting for long-term contracts is used.

Ex. 9-9 Refer to Ex. 9-8. Show how the account balances relating to long-term construction contracts will appear in the balance sheet of Reseda Construction Co. at the end of Year 3 if (1) the completed-contract method of accounting is used, and (2) the percentage-of-completion method of accounting is used.

SHORT CASES FOR ANALYSIS AND DECISION

Case 9-1 Inglewood Department Store uses the conventional retail method as a means of controlling the investment in inventory at its branch stores. Monthly the central accounting office summarizes the recorded activity at each branch and estimates the ending inventory. The estimate is then compared with a normal inventory investment based on expected volume. Store managers are asked to explain deviations of 5% or more from the expected normal inventory. The following data have been accumulated for the Compton Branch:

	Cost	Retail
Net sales		$630,000
Beginning inventory	$150,000	222,000
Net purchases	560,000	823,000
Net markups		20,000
Net markdowns		10,000
Estimated shrinkage		5,000

Instructions

a The normal inventory of the Compton Branch should be $200,000 at cost. Compute the amount of the ending inventory at retail and at cost, and indicate the nature of the inquiry to be made of the store manager.

b What effect, if any, would the following events have on the effectiveness of the retail method as a control device?
(1) A widely fluctuating shrinkage factor
(2) A shift in the volume of goods handled at various markups
(3) The additional markups related to goods which are entirely sold out by year-end
(4) Markdowns included as markup cancellations
(5) Additional markups included as markdown cancellations

Case 9-2 Jensen & Company has been using the lifo method of valuing inventory. Robert Jensen, the owner, is interested in the possibility of using the retail method to estimate his investment in inventory periodically, but he is not familiar with all the implications of this method and questions whether the retail method would be applicable to his situation.
You obtain the following data for the current year:

	Units	Cost	Retail
Beginning inventory	1,000	$ 6,000	$12,000
Purchases	5,000	40,000	60,000
Net markups			6,000
Net markdowns			3,000
Sales	4,500		56,250

Instructions

a Using the retail method, compute the ending inventory at (1) lifo average cost and (2) lower of average cost or market, assuming that net markups and markdowns apply proportionately to beginning inventory and purchases.

b Compute the inventory at lifo cost using units and unit costs.

c Explain the principles of the retail method to Jensen.

d Why is it desirable to know to which goods net markups and markdowns apply?

Case 9-3 Edgemar Company has used the gross profit method for estimating the investment in inventory and as a check on the physical count at the end of each year. The company has two lines of merchandise which have produced gross profit margins of 25 and 35%, respectively, on selling price over the past several years. The gross profit margin for the business as a whole has averaged 30% of sales. The operating data for the current year are as follows:

	Economy line	Quality line	Total
Sales	$100,000	$200,000	$300,000
Beginning inventory	10,000	25,000	35,000
Purchases	80,000	130,000	210,000
Gross profit margins on selling price	25%	35%	30%

A physical count of the merchandise reveals inventory to be $40,000, but the estimate using the gross profit method indicates ending inventory should be $35,000. The manager is of the opinion that the discrepancy is too great to accept without explanation. A test sample is selected and reveals that the gross profit margins on the two lines are unchanged at 25 and 35%.

Instructions
a Show how the manager computed the ending inventory using the gross profit method.
b Compute the ending inventory using the gross profit method in the manner in which you think it should be used in this situation.
c Explain to the manager why the difference exists between the physical count and the estimate of the inventory value.

Case 9-4 Norton Construction Company has three contracts in progress at December 31, the data for which are presented below:

Contract No.	Contract price	Total estimated cost	Cost incurred to date (all in current year)	Billings to date	Collections to date
1	$ 750,000	$ 600,000	$400,000	$450,000	$405,000
2	1,000,000	1,050,000	525,000	400,000	380,000
3	900,000	675,000	202,500	225,000	202,500

Instructions
a Prepare partial financial statements for Norton Construction Company reporting the details of the above contracts using (1) completed-contract method and (2) percentage-of-completion method, using estimated total cost and actual cost incurred to determine the degree of completion to date. Show total construction revenue and applicable costs in the partial income statement.
b What are the essential differences between the two sets of financial statements?
c Which set of financial statements do you think presents the more meaningful data about the long-term contracts of Norton Construction Company?

PROBLEMS

Group A

9A-1 Economy Stores, Inc., uses the retail inventory method to estimate ending inventory for its monthly financial statements. The following data pertain to a single department for the month of May, Year 5:

Inventory, May 1, Year 5:	
At cost	$ 22,000
At retail	30,000
Purchases (exclusive of freight and returns):	
At cost	98,151
At retail	146,495
Freight-in	5,100
Purchase returns:	
At cost	2,100
At retail	2,800
Additional markups	2,500
Markup cancellations	265
Net markdowns	800
Normal spoilage and breakage (at retail)	2,930
Sales (net of sales returns)	138,200

Instructions
a Using the conventional retail method, prepare a schedule computing estimated lower-of-cost-or-market inventory for May 31, Year 5.
b A department store using the conventional retail inventory method estimates the cost of its ending inventory as $30,000. An accurate physical count reveals only $24,000 of inventory at lower of cost or market. List the factors that may have caused the difference between the computed inventory and the physical count.

9A-2 **Part A** Company E uses the lifo retail inventory method. Information relating to the computation of the inventory at December 31, Year 5, follows:

	Cost	Retail
Inventory, Jan. 1, Year 5	$ 30,200	$ 45,000
Purchases	120,000	172,000
Freight-in	22,000	
Net sales		180,000
Net markups		40,000
Net markdowns		12,000

Instructions
Assuming that there was no change in the price index during the year, compute the inventory at December 31, Year 5, using the lifo retail inventory method.

Part B Company F prepares quarterly financial statements. The inventories at the retail stores are estimated by the gross profit method since the relationship of selling prices and costs remains relatively stable during the year. The ending inventory is always determined by a physical count of the goods on hand at December 31. The following data for the first three quarters of the fiscal year ending December 31 have been taken from the accounting records.

	March 31	June 30	Sept. 30
Purchases	$695,000	$735,000	$665,000
Freight-in	9,500	9,100	8,210
Purchase returns and allowances	500	2,400	4,630
Sales	993,600	963,000	808,500
Sales returns	13,000	20,000	8,000
Sales discounts	600	3,000	500
Selling and administrative expenses	102,000	103,000	94,400

The physical inventory at December 31 of the previous year was $105,000.

Instructions Assuming that the gross profit rate for the prior fiscal year was 25% of net sales and that this rate is expected to prevail throughout the current year, prepare quarterly income statements for the first three quarters. Assume income taxes are 40% of income before income taxes.

9A-3 Southland Retail Outlet converted from the conventional retail method to the retail lifo method on January 1, Year 1, and is now considering converting to the dollar-value retail lifo method. Management requested during your examination of the financial statements for the year ended December 31, Year 3, that you furnish a summary showing certain computations of inventory costs for the past three years.

Available information follows:

(1) The inventory at January 1, Year 1, had a retail value of $45,000 and a cost of $27,500, determined on the lower-of-cost-or-market retail method.
(2) Transactions during Year 1 were as follows:

	Cost	Retail
Gross purchases	$282,000	$490,000
Purchase returns	6,500	10,000
Purchase discounts	5,000	
Gross sales		467,000
Sales returns		5,000
Employee discounts granted (add to gross sales)		3,000
Freight-in	26,500	
Net markups		25,000
Net markdowns		10,000

(3) The retail value of the December 31, Year 2, inventory was $84,150; the cost to retail percentage for Year 2 under the retail lifo method was 62%; and the regional price index was 102% of the January 1, Year 2, price level.
(4) The retail value of the December 31, Year 3, inventory was $72,450; the cost percentage for Year 3 under the retail lifo method was 61%; and the regional price index was 105% of the January 1, Year 2, price level.

Instructions
a Prepare a schedule showing the computation of the cost of inventory on hand at December 31, Year 1, using the retail inventory method applied on the lower-of-cost-or-market basis.
b Prepare a schedule showing the computation of the cost of inventory on hand on December 31, Year 1, using the retail lifo method. Southland Retail Outlet does not consider beginning inventories in computing its lifo cost percentage. Assume that the retail value of the December 31, Year 1, inventory was $75,000.
c Without prejudice to your solution to part **(b)**, assume that you computed the December 31, Year 1, inventory (retail value $75,000) under the retail lifo method at a cost of $42,000. Prepare a schedule showing the computations of the cost of the Year 2 and Year 3 ending inventories under the dollar-value retail lifo method.

9A-4 Liquid Fuel Corporation is a small manufacturing company producing a highly flammable fluid. On March 31, Year 6, the company had a fire which completely destroyed the factory building and the inventory of goods in process; some of the equipment was saved.

After the fire a physical inventory was taken. The raw materials were valued at $35,000, the finished goods at $62,000.

The inventories on January 1, Year 6, consisted of:

Raw materials	$ 15,500
Goods in process	60,500
Finished goods	85,000
Total	$161,000

A review of the accounts showed that the sales and gross profit on sales for the last three years were:

	Sales	Gross profit on sales
Year 3	$400,000	$120,000
Year 4	380,000	110,500
Year 5	250,000	88,800

The sales for the first three months of Year 6 were $148,000. Raw material purchases were $60,000, transportation-in on purchases was $5,000, and direct labor for the three months was $50,000. For the past two years factory overhead has been 80% of direct labor.

Instructions Compute the cost of inventory of goods in process lost, using the weighted-average gross profit for the preceding three years. Include calculations as a part of your answer.

9A-5 Delmar Construction Company started operating in Year 4. Under long-term contracts, the company constructs waste water treatment plants for small communities throughout the United States. All its long-term contracts are appropriately recorded for accounting purposes under the percentage-of-completion method except for two contracts which are appropriately recorded for accounting purposes under the completed-contract method because of a lack of dependable estimates at the time of entering into these contracts.

The following information is available for the year ended December 31, Year 5:

Long-Term Contracts–Percentage-of-Completion Method

Long-term contracts recorded under the percentage-of-completion method aggregate $6,050,000. Costs incurred on these contracts were $1,500,000 in Year 4 and $3,000,000 in Year 5. Estimated additional costs of $1,000,000 are required to complete these contracts. Revenue of $1,750,000 was recognized in Year 4 and a total of $4,800,000 has been billed, of which $4,600,000 has been collected. No long-term contracts recorded under the percentage-of-completion method were completed in Year 5.

Long-Term Contracts–Completed-Contract Method

The two long-term contracts recorded under the completed-contract method were started in Year 4. One is a $5,000,000 contract. Costs incurred were $1,400,000 in Year 4 and $1,600,000 in Year 5. A total of $3,100,000 has been billed and $2,800,000 collected. Although it is difficult to estimate the additional costs required to complete this contract, indications are that this contract will prove to be profitable.

The second contract is for $4,000,000. Costs incurred were $1,200,000 in Year 4 and $2,600,000 in Year 5. A total of $3,300,000 has been billed and $2,900,000 collected. Although it is difficult to estimate the additional costs required to complete this contract, indications are that there will be a loss of approximately $150,000.

Other information

Selling, general, and administrative expenses, exclusive of amounts specified earlier, were $200,000 in Year 5. Other income, exclusive of amounts specified earlier, was $40,000 in Year 5.

Instructions Prepare an income statement for Delmar Construction Company for the year ended December 31, Year 5, stopping at income (or loss) before income taxes. Show supporting schedules and computations in good form. Ignore income tax and deferred tax considerations. Notes are not required.

9A-6 The board of directors of Stoller Construction Company is meeting to choose between the completed-contract method and the percentage-of-completion method of accounting for long-term contracts for reporting in the company's financial statements. You have been engaged to assist Stoller's controller in the preparation of a presentation to be given at the board meeting. The controller provides you with the following information:

(1) Stoller commenced doing business on January 1, Year 2.
(2) Construction activities for the year ended December 31, Year 2:

Project	Total contract price	Billings through Dec. 31, Year 2	Cash collections through Dec. 31, Year 2	Contract costs incurred through Dec. 31, Year 2	Estimated additional costs to complete contracts
A	$ 520,000	$ 350,000	$ 310,000	$ 424,000	$106,000
B	670,000	210,000	210,000	126,000	504,000
C	475,000	475,000	395,000	315,000	–0–
D	200,000	70,000	50,000	112,750	92,250
E	460,000	400,000	400,000	370,000	30,000
	$2,325,000	$1,505,000	$1,365,000	$1,347,750	$732,250

(3) All contracts are with different customers.
(4) Any work remaining to be done on the contracts is expected to be completed in Year 3.

Instructions

a Prepare a schedule by project computing the amount of revenue and income (or loss) before selling, general, and administrative expenses for the year ended December 31, Year 2, that would be reported under:

(1) The completed-contract method

(2) The percentage-of-completion method (based upon estimated costs)

b Following is a balance sheet which compares balances resulting from the use of the two methods of accounting for long-term contracts. For each numbered blank space on the statement, supply the correct balance [indicating dr. or (cr.), as appropriate] next to the corresponding number on your answer sheet. Do not recopy the statement but show how amounts were determined. Disregard income taxes.

STOLLER CONSTRUCTION COMPANY

Balance Sheet

December 31, Year 2

	Completed-contract method	Percentage-of-completion method
Assets		
Cash	$XXXX	$XXXX
Accounts receivable on contracts	(1)	(5)
Cost of uncompleted contracts in excess of billings	(2)	–0–
Costs and profits on uncompleted contracts in excess of billings	–0–	(6)
Other assets	XXXX	XXXX
Total assets	$XXXX	$XXXX
Liabilities & Stockholders' Equity		
Accounts payable and accrued liabilities	$XXXX	$XXXX
Billings on uncompleted contracts in excess of costs	(3)	–0–
Billings in excess of costs and profits	–0–	(7)
Estimated losses on uncompleted contracts	(4)	–0–
Notes payable	XXXX	XXXX
Common stock	XXXX	XXXX
Retained earnings	XXXX	XXXX
Total liabilities & stockholders' equity	$XXXX	$XXXX

Group B

9B-1 Data concerning the operations of the sportswear department of Calexico Clothiers are presented below:

	Cost	Retail
Beginning inventory	$ 56,000	$ 93,600
Purchases	257,800	406,900
Freight-in	10,400	
Purchase returns	4,200	7,000
Additional markups		15,000
Markup cancellations		8,500

	Cost	Retail
Markdowns		$ 8,000
Markdown cancellations		1,600
Gross sales		396,500
Sales returns		6,700
Estimated shrinkage from theft and spoilage		3,200

Instructions

a Compute the ending inventory at the lower of average cost or market by the retail method. Calculations should be presented in good form.

b Compute the ending inventory using the retail lifo method.

9B-2 Part A Company K lost all its inventory by fire on January 1, Year 10. A physical inventory was not taken on December 31, Year 9. The following data are available for the three preceding years:

	Year 9	Year 8	Year 7
Inventory, Jan. 1	$170,160	$168,000	$161,600
Purchases	720,000	656,000	644,000
Purchase returns	40,000	32,000	36,000
Sales	812,000	788,000	724,000
Sales returns	12,000	8,000	12,000
Operating expenses	240,000	221,000	198,000
Accounts receivable	60,000	50,000	55,000
Accounts payable	40,000	35,000	28,000

Instructions Assuming that the gross profit percentage in Year 9 was estimated to be two percentage points below the weighted-average gross profit percentage for Year 7 and Year 8, compute the estimated cost of inventory destroyed by fire.

Part B Company L uses the retail method to value its merchandise inventory. The following information is available: ·

	Cost	Retail
Beginning inventory	$ 40,500	$ 70,000
Purchases (net of returns)	290,000	400,000
Freight-in	2,000	
Net markups		5,000
Net markdowns		9,000
Employee discounts		1,000
Net sales		400,000

Instructions Compute the estimated ending inventory on the basis of lower of cost or market using the retail method.

Part C Company M is in the construction business. A long-term contract was entered into in Year 1. The contract price was $700,000 and the company expected to earn a gross profit of $80,000 on the contract. Following are data on experience to date:

Year ended Dec. 31	Cumulative costs incurred	Estimated cost to complete contract
Year 1	$ 49,600	$570,400
Year 2	172,800	467,200
Year 3	378,000	252,000

Instructions Prepare a schedule computing the gross profit earned in each of the three years by Company M under the percentage-of-completion method based on costs incurred to date and estimated cost to complete the contract.

9B-3 On January 1, Canyon Company installed the retail method of accounting for its merchandise inventory.

When you undertook the preparation of Canyon Company's interim report of earnings at June 30, the following data were available:

	Cost	Selling price
Inventory, Jan. 1	$ 76,200	$120,000
Markdowns		31,500
Additional markups		58,500
Markdown cancellations		19,500
Markup cancellations		13,500
Purchases	265,860	335,400
Sales		366,000
Purchase returns and allowances	4,500	5,400
Sales returns and allowances		18,000

Instructions

a Prepare a schedule to compute Canyon Company's June 30 inventory under the retail method of accounting for inventories. The inventory is to be valued at cost, using the lifo method. Assume that net markups and markdowns apply to purchases.

b Without prejudice to your solution to part (**a**), assume that you computed the June 30 inventory to be $132,300 at retail and the ratio of cost to retail to be 78%. The general price level has increased from 100 at January 1 to 105 at June 30. Round off figures to nearest dollar and percent. Prepare a schedule to compute the June 30 inventory at the June 30 price level, using the dollar-value retail lifo method.

9B-4 On April 15, Year 5, a fire damaged the office and warehouse of Dole Hardware Company. The only accounting record saved was the general ledger, from which the following trial balance was prepared:

DOLE HARDWARE COMPANY

Trial Balance

March 31, Year 5

	Debit	Credit
Cash	$ 20,800	
Accounts receivable	27,000	
Inventory, Dec. 31, Year 4	29,000	
Land	24,000	
Building and equipment	120,000	
Accumulated depreciation		$ 46,000
Other assets	3,600	
Accounts payable		23,700
Miscellaneous accrued liabilities		7,200
Capital stock, $2.50 par		100,000
Retained earnings		47,700
Sales		125,400
Purchases	103,000	
Other expenses	22,600	
Totals	$350,000	$350,000

The following information has been gathered:

(1) The fiscal year of the company ends on December 31.
(2) An examination of the April bank statement and canceled checks revealed that checks written during the period April 1 to 15 totaled $11,600: $5,700 paid to accounts payable as of March 31, $2,000 for April purchases, and $3,900 paid for other expenses. Deposits during the same period amounted to $10,650, which consisted of receipts on account from customers, with the exception of a $450 refund from a vendor for goods returned in April.
(3) Correspondence with suppliers revealed unrecorded obligations at April 15 of $3,500 for April purchases, including $1,300 for shipments in transit on that date.
(4) Customers acknowledged indebtedness of $26,400 at April 15. It was also estimated that customers owed another $5,000 which will never be acknowledged or recovered. Of the acknowledged indebtedness, $600 will probably be uncollectible. All sales were on account.
(5) Assume that the weighted-average gross profit percentage for the past two years was in effect during the current year. The company's audited financial statements disclosed the following:

	Year ended	
	Dec. 31, Year 4	Dec. 31, Year 3
Net sales	$400,000	$300,000
Net purchases	226,000	174,000
Beginning inventory	45,000	35,000
Ending inventory	29,000	45,000

(6) Inventory with a cost of $6,250 was salvaged and sold for $3,150. The balance of the inventory was a total loss.

Instructions Prepare a schedule computing the amount of the inventory fire loss. The supporting schedule of the computation of the cost of goods sold percentage should be in good form.

9B-5 Blue River Construction Company commenced doing business in January Year 10. Construction activities for Year 10 are summarized below.

Project	Total contract price	Contract costs to Dec. 31, Year 10	Estimated additional costs to complete contracts	Cash collections to Dec. 31, Year 10	Billings to Dec. 31, Year 10
100	$ 310,000	$187,500	$ 12,500	$155,000	$160,000
101	415,000	195,000	248,000	210,000	249,000
102	350,000	320,000	–0–	300,000	350,000
103	300,000	16,500	183,500	–0–	4,000
	$1,375,000	$719,000	$444,000	$665,000	$763,000

The company is your client. The president has asked you to compute the amounts of revenue for the year ended December 31, Year 10, that would be reported under the completed-contract method and the percentage-of-completion method of accounting for long-term contracts.

The following information is available:

(1) All contracts are with different customers.
(2) Any work remaining to be done on the contracts is expected to be completed in Year 11.
(3) The company's accounts have been maintained on the completed-contract method.

Instructions
a Prepare a schedule computing the amount of gross profit by project for the year ended December 31, Year 10, that would be reported under
   (1) The completed-contract method
   (2) The percentage-of-completion method
b Prepare a schedule under the completed-contract method computing the amounts that would appear in the company's balance sheet at December 31, Year 10, for
   (1) Costs in excess of billings
   (2) Billings in excess of costs
c Prepare a schedule under the percentage-of-completion method that would appear in the company's balance sheet at December 31, Year 10, for
   (1) Costs and profits in excess of billings
   (2) Billings in excess of costs and profits

9B-6 Dudley Contractors, Inc., undertakes long-term large-scale construction projects and began operations on October 15, Year 4, with contract No. 1 its only job during Year 4. A trial balance of the company's general ledger at December 31, Year 5, follows:

DUDLEY CONTRACTORS, INC.
Trial Balance
December 31, Year 5

Cash	$ 68,090	
Accounts receivable	136,480	
Construction in progress	421,320	
Plant and equipment	35,500	
Accumulated depreciation		$ 8,000
Accounts payable		70,820
Deferred income taxes		1,908
Partial billings on contracts		459,400
Capital stock, $5 par		139,000
Retained earnings		2,862
Selling and administrative expenses	20,600	
Totals	$681,990	$681,990

The following additional information is available:

(1) The company has the approval to determine income on the completed-contract basis for income tax purposes and on the percentage-of-completion basis for financial reporting purposes.

(2) At December 31, Year 5, there were three contracts in progress, the contract prices of which had been computed as follows:

	Contract No. 1	Contract No. 2	Contract No. 3
Labor and material costs	$169,000	$34,500	$265,700
Indirect costs	30,000	5,500	48,000
Total costs	$199,000	$40,000	$313,700
Add: Gross profit in contract ..	40,000	3,000	30,300
Total contract price	$239,000	$43,000	$344,000

During the year, billings are credited to Partial Billings on Contracts; at year-end this account is charged for the amount of revenue to be recognized as realized in the current year, which is credited to the Construction Revenue account. Construction costs applicable to realized contract revenue are transferred from Construction in Progress to the Construction Costs Applicable to Realized Revenue account.

(3) All contract costs are charged to Construction in Progress. Cost estimates are carefully derived by engineers and architects and are considered reliable. Data on costs to December 31, Year 5, are given on page 390.

Contract No.	Original estimate	Costs incurred to date		
		Total	Labor & materials	Indirect
1	$199,000	$115,420	$ 92,620	$22,800
2	40,000	32,000	26,950	5,050
3	313,700	313,700	265,700	48,000
Totals	$552,700	$461,120	$385,270	$75,850

(4) At December 31, Year 4, accumulated costs on contract No. 1 were $39,800, or 20% of the total; no costs had accumulated on contract No. 2 and contract No. 3. All work on contract No. 3 was completed on December 30, Year 5.

(5) Assume that the company is subject to an income tax rate of 30%.

Instructions

a Prepare a schedule computing the percentage of completion of contracts at December 31, Year 5.

b Prepare a schedule computing the amounts of revenue, related costs, and gross profit to be recognized in Year 5, from contracts in progress at December 31, Year 5.

c Prepare a schedule computing estimated income taxes and the income tax liability at December 31, Year 5.

d Give the adjusting journal entries that are necessary at December 31, Year 5, to record realized revenue to date, cost of realized revenue, and income taxes.

CHAPTER 10

CURRENT LIABILITIES AND CONTINGENCIES

A *liability* is an obligation, based on a past transaction, to convey assets or perform services in the future. Liabilities are recorded when obligations are incurred, and are measured at the amounts to be paid or at the present value of these amounts.[1] The distinction between current and long-term liabilities is important in evaluating the financial position of a business and in forecasting its ability to meet maturing obligations. Some liabilities are definitely determinable, both as to existence and as to amount; other liabilities definitely exist but the amount of the liability must be estimated. Finally, some contingent obligations may or may not be subject to accrual in the accounts. This chapter deals with the problems of accounting for current liabilities and contingencies; long-term liabilities are discussed in Chapters 15 and 16.

The distinction between current and long-term liabilities

Traditionally, one year marked the accounting boundary between current and long-term liabilities. The maturity-within-a-year rule was simple and easy to follow, but arbitrary. When strictly applied it sometimes caused a misleading financial picture, particularly when the operating cycle of a business exceeded one year.

The modern viewpoint is that current liabilities include: (1) all obligations for which payment will require the use of existing current

[1] These guidelines for recording and measuring liabilities are taken from *Statement of the Accounting Principles Board, No. 4,* AICPA (New York: 1970), pp. 73–74.

assets or the creation of other current liabilities, and (2) all other obligations that will probably be paid from current assets within one year. The definition of current liabilities is logically correlated with the definition of current assets. Thus current liabilities include obligations for items which have entered into the operating cycle, such as payables to suppliers and employees, collections received in advance of the delivery of goods or performance of services, and accruals for rentals, taxes, etc. Obligations incurred outside of the operating cycle and payable more than one year hence are considered long-term liabilities; obligations which definitely will be liquidated by the issuance of additional shares of capital stock are not liabilities and should be included in stockholders' equity.

The importance of current liabilities

Short-term credit is an important source of financing for most businesses. In part, its use is involuntary; current obligations such as accounts payable and other accrued liabilities regularly arise from business operations. An important element, however, results from a conscious decision by management to obtain credit from suppliers and to borrow from banks and others to meet cash needs during periods of expanding or peak activity.

   Financial analysts keep a close watch on the amount of current liabilities, the relationship of current assets to current liabilities, and the relationship between cash balances and current liabilities. These relationships are considered by many analysts to be important indicators of financial stability and *solvency* (ability to pay debts as they mature).

Valuation of current liabilities

A logical measure of any liability at the time it is incurred is the *present value* of the required future outlay of money.[2] In practice, however, current liabilities are usually carried in accounting records at face amount. The difference between the present value of a current liability and the amount that will ultimately be paid at maturity is usually not large because of the short time period involved. Thus the slight overstatement of liabilities that results from recording current obligations at face amount may often be excused as a compromise of accuracy in favor of convenience.

[2] The present value of a liability is the sum of expected future payments discounted to the present date at an appropriate rate of interest. *APB Opinion No. 21* states that presentation of liabilities at their discounted present value is not required for "payables arising from transactions with customers or suppliers in the normal course of business which are due in customary trade terms not exceeding approximately one year." The Opinion is also not intended to apply to estimates of warranty obligations assumed in connection with sales of property, goods, or services.

When is a prospective future outlay a liability?

Every going business faces the prospect of a wide variety of future cash outlays in order to continue in operation. It must, for example, buy materials, pay wages, pay for services, replace equipment, and pay taxes. We might take an extreme view and consider the present value of all these future outlays as the total debt of the company at any given time. This would correspond to the concept of assets as the present value of all future cash inflows. These theoretical extremes, however, are beyond the accountant's powers of measurement; as a practical matter, we need a basis for establishing some practical limits on the liability concept.

A logical starting point is to say that the amounts of all legally enforceable debts should appear as liabilities in the balance sheet. But what about legal obligations that are highly uncertain in amount? Since accounting liabilities must be measured, the ability to determine valuation with reasonable accuracy is important. Then we must consider whether a strict legal test excludes any obligations to convey assets that are significant in an economic sense. The process of determining periodic income may require that a valuation be placed on future outlays that result from past transactions, because the cost incurred should be deducted from revenue.

These two elements, *measurability* and *relation to past events,* lead us to conclude that liabilities should be defined to include all future outlays that result from transactions or events of the past and that can be estimated with reasonable accuracy. Because we are dealing with a *future* payment, the element of uncertainty plays an important role in the problem of accounting for current liabilities. To emphasize the importance of the degree of uncertainty, we shall discuss some of the specific problems relating to current liabilities under the following headings: (1) definitely determinable liabilities, (2) liabilities dependent on operating results, and (3) contingencies.

DEFINITELY DETERMINABLE LIABILITIES

Liabilities in this category are the result of contracts or the operation of legal statutes such that the amount of an obligation and its due date are known with reasonable certainty. The accounting problems are to ascertain that an obligation exists, to measure it accurately, and to record it properly in the accounting records.

Trade accounts payable

The accounting procedures for recording and controlling the payments for the purchase of goods and services are usually systematized so that the existence, amount, and due date of such liabilities are readily deter-minable. The accountant should give particular attention to transac-tions occurring near the end of one accounting period and at the begin-ning of the next period to see that the record of goods and services received is consistent with that of the liability. For example, if goods are received near the end of the period but an invoice has not arrived, the goods may have been counted as part of the ending inventory but the recording of the liability may have been overlooked.

As in the valuation of accounts receivable, cash discounts applicable to accounts payable should be anticipated and recognized by a debit to Allowance for Purchase Discounts and a credit to Purchase Discounts. The Allowance for Purchase Discounts should be deducted from Ac-counts Payable on the balance sheet. As an alternative, Accounts Pay-able may be recorded net of purchase discounts and only Purchase Dis-counts Lost recorded in the accounts.

Loan obligations

In this category are included short-term notes (including *commercial paper*[3]) issued as evidence of borrowing transactions, and any portion of long-term indebtedness that matures currently. If long-term debt cur-rently maturing will be retired from sinking funds, from the proceeds of new long-term indebtedness, or through conversion into stock, current funds are not required and the debt should be reported as noncurrent, accompanied by a note disclosing the plan for its liquidation.

No-Interest Loan with Other Obligations Attached No special problems arise in accounting for the issuance of short-term notes payable bearing the prevailing rate of interest. Cash or Accounts Payable is debited and Notes Payable is credited at the time the notes are issued. If notes pay-able bear an unrealistically low interest rate or are non-interest-bearing, the notes should be recorded at no more than present value in order to recognize the actual cost of borrowing or any other obligations implicit in the borrowing contract.

To illustrate, refer to the situation on page 280 in which a supplier borrowed $108,000 on December 31, Year 1, from L Corporation at no interest when the going rate of interest was 8%. The supplier agreed to repay the note on December 31, Year 2, and to sell merchandise to L Corporation for one year at favorable prices. The borrowing by the sup-plier on December 31, Year 1, is recorded as illustrated on page 395.

---

[3] Commercial paper (as defined in Chapter 6) is the term used in the money market for short-term unsecured promissory notes issued by corporations and sold to investors, gen-erally other companies.

Cash	108,000	
Discount on Notes Payable	8,000	
Notes Payable		108,000
Contractual Obligation to Customer		8,000
To record non-interest-bearing note issued to customer. Present value of note, $108,000 ÷ 1.08 = $100,000.		

The account Contractual Obligation to Customer would be classified as a current liability because it represents a legal obligation to sell merchandise at favorable prices. This account represents, in effect, an advance from the customer (L Corporation). The customer paid $8,000 for the privilege of buying merchandise at favorable prices and the supplier received $108,000 in exchange for two promises: (1) to repay $100,000 plus interest at 8% one year hence and (2) to supply the customer's inventory needs at favorable prices during Year 2, an obligation valued at $8,000. When payment is made on the note at December 31, Year 2, the following entry would be required in the accounts of the supplier:

Notes Payable	108,000	
Contractual Obligation to Customer	8,000	
Interest Expense	8,000	
Cash		108,000
Discount on Notes Payable		8,000
Sales		8,000
To record payment on non-interest-bearing note, the implicit interest expense on the note, and to recognize obligation assigned to the contract with customer as additional revenue (sales).		

The procedure illustrated above for the supplier recognizes interest expense for Year 2, $8,000 ($100,000 × 8%), and the full implicit value of sales made pursuant to the borrowing contract with the customer.

Classification of Short-Term Debt Expected to Be Refinanced When a company expects to refinance a short-term debt (obligation) on a long-term basis, a question arises as to the proper classification of such a debt. The FASB has taken the position that a short-term debt must be classified as a current liability unless the company intends to refinance the debt on a long-term basis and can demonstrate its ability to carry out the refinancing.[4]

[4] *FASB Statement No. 6,* "Classification of Short-Term Obligations Expected to Be Refinanced. . . ," FASB (Stamford: 1975), p. 4.

Refinancing means either replacing short-term debt with long-term debt or with equity securities or renewing, extending, or replacing the short-term debt with other short-term debt for an uninterrupted period extending beyond one year (or the operating cycle, if applicable) from the date of the balance sheet.[5] *Ability to refinance* on a long-term basis must be demonstrated either (1) by actually having issued long-term debt or equity securities to replace short-term debt after the date of the company's balance sheet but before it is issued or (2) by having entered into a firm financing agreement that will enable the company to refinance short-term debt when it becomes due.[6]

Accountants generally agree that cash earmarked for the retirement of a debt should be excluded from current assets if the debt to be liquidated is reported as a noncurrent liability. Following the issuance of *FASB Statement No. 6,* the FASB was asked to clarify whether a short-term debt should be excluded from current liabilities if it is repaid after the balance sheet date and is then replaced by long-term debt before the balance sheet is issued. Because the repayment of a short-term debt before funds are obtained through a long-term refinancing requires the use of current assets, the Board concluded that:

> . . . if a short-term obligation is repaid after the balance sheet date and subsequently a long-term obligation or equity securities are issued whose proceeds are used to replenish current assets before the balance sheet is issued, the short-term obligation shall not be excluded from current liabilities at the balance sheet date.[7]

Dividends payable

Cash dividends are declared by action of the board of directors. At the date of declaration, the corporation incurs a legal obligation to pay the amount of the dividend at the specified time, and stockholders gain creditor status to the extent of the declared amount. Since the time between declaration and payment is short, dividends payable in cash are always a current liability. Dividends in arrears on preferred stock are normally disclosed by note because there is no legal obligation to pay dividends on preferred stock until they are declared. Undistributed *stock dividends* should not be included among current liabilities, because no cash outlay will be required; the account Stock Dividends to Be Distributed should be classified as part of the stockholders' equity, preferably as an addition to the common stock outstanding.

---

[5] Ibid., p. 1.
[6] Ibid., pp. 4–5.
[7] *FASB Interpretation No. 8,* "Classification of a Short-term Obligation Repaid Prior to Being Replaced by a Long-term Security (an Interpretation of FASB Statement No. 6)," FASB (Stamford: 1976), p. 2.

Advances from customers

When a customer makes payment in advance of performance by the seller, a liability is created. The selling company is obligated to perform by delivery of goods or services, or to refund the advance if it fails to perform. Generally, the cost of performance will not be as great as the advance, since there is an element of unrealized profit in the price charged. The profit element emerges only with performance by the selling company; prior to this time the selling company is essentially a trustee of the funds received from customers. As performance is made under the terms of the contract, the amount of the liability diminishes and should be transferred to a revenue account. The costs of performance are recorded as expenses and income (or loss) emerges.

Advances from customers which are expected to be realized as revenue within a year or within the company's operating cycle should be classified as current liabilities. Examples include deposits on sales orders received, magazine subscriptions received in advance, and billings in excess of costs incurred on long-term construction contracts. Advances from customers which are not expected to be realized as revenue within one year or the operating cycle should be classified as noncurrent liabilities. It may be argued that certain short-term unearned revenue, such as rentals and interest received in advance, should be classified as noncurrent liabilities because the realization of such revenue is not expected to require current expenditures. Although this position has some merit, it has not been widely accepted, because the amounts involved are generally immaterial and because it may be difficult to estimate the expenditures to be incurred in the process of realizing short-term unearned revenue items.

Deposits received from customers for containers normally are refunded when the containers are returned (usually within a short period); therefore, such deposits should be classified among current liabilities.

Accrued liabilities

The term *accrued liabilities* (sometimes referred to as *accrued expenses*) is used to designate obligations that come into existence as the result of past contractual commitments or as the result of tax legislation such as payroll, income, property, and sales tax laws. Because of their materiality, tax liabilities should be listed separately among the current liabilities. Most other accruals may be combined under one heading, or, as in the case of accrued interest, combined with the liability to which they relate. The problems involved in determining some types of accrued liabilities require special attention.

Liabilities relating to payrolls

The employer is by law a tax collector for the federal and state governments with respect to taxes withheld from employees' salaries. An employer may also withhold from salaries and wages amounts for such items as union dues, state disability insurance, group life insurance, pension plans, and for purchase of savings bonds. The accountant should be familiar with the general terms of payroll tax legislation.

Social Security Taxes (FICA) The Federal Insurance Contributions Act provides for old age and survivors' benefits for qualified employees and members of their families, and hospitalization insurance (Medicare) provides for medical costs. These payroll taxes are often referred to as *social security taxes* and are levied against both the employer and the employee at the same rate, based on the employee's gross earnings. Both the rates and base earnings have been increased many times in recent years and are scheduled to change in the future.[8] For purposes of discussion and problems in this chapter, we shall assume that a rate of 6% applies for both the employer and employee on earnings up to $16,500. FICA taxes apply to employers of one or more persons, with certain exceptions.

Federal Unemployment Tax The Federal Unemployment Tax Act (FUTA) provides for a system of unemployment insurance established in cooperation with state governments. Employers of one or more persons, with certain exceptions similar to those under FICA legislation, are subject to the federal unemployment tax. In 1978, the tax applied to the first $6,000 of earnings paid to each employee during the calendar year. The federal tax is levied only on employers at a rate of 3.4%. However, a credit against the federal tax up to 2.7% of taxable earnings is allowed for contributions which an employer makes to a state plan. Thus the effective federal unemployment tax is 0.7% of earnings up to $6,000 per employee. Employers are required to make quarterly deposits of unpaid taxes that exceed $100.

State Unemployment Tax The provisions of the various state laws governing unemployment compensation differ from the federal law, and differ among various states. Most state laws tax only employers, but a few apply taxes on employees as well. An important feature of all state unemployment tax laws is the merit rating provision, under which a reduction in the tax rate levied by the state is granted to employers whose unemployment experience is better than a specified standard. Thus employers whose employee turnover rate is low may be entitled to a lower state tax rate. To make this type of incentive toward stable em-

---

[8] For example, the actual FICA tax rate in 1976 was 5.85% on earnings up to $15,300 and in 1977 the tax was 5.85% on earnings up to $16,500.

ployment effective, the federal law provides that an employer who pays less than 2.7% to any state under a merit rating system is still entitled to the full 2.7% credit against the federal tax.

Income Tax Withholding Employers of one or more persons are required to withhold from an employee's earnings an amount approximating the federal income tax due on those earnings. A number of cities and states which levy income taxes also require that income taxes be withheld from employees' earnings. An employer is required to withhold income taxes only if the legal relationship of employer and employee exists; this excludes payments to persons who perform services as independent contractors. Certain other limited classes of wage payments are exempt from withholding.

The amount of income tax withheld is determined by formula or may be read from tables prepared by the government; it varies according to the length of the pay period, the amount of taxable earnings, and the marital status and the number of dependents of the employee. The employer makes payment of income taxes withheld and FICA taxes at regular intervals.

Vacation Pay Paid vacations are today a standard element of the employment contract of most employees. The right to a vacation with pay usually depends upon the length of employment; the length of vacation often increases after an employee has completed a specified number of years of service.

When does the liability for vacation pay come into existence for accounting purposes? Does it arise only when an employee has met all the conditions, or does it accrue through the employment period? From the standpoint of cost determination, it seems clear that an employee who earns $200 per week and is entitled to a two-week vacation is paid $10,400 for 50 weeks of actual productive services, or $208 per week. This reasoning suggests that vacation pay accrues at the rate of $8 per week during the 50 productive weeks prior to the vacation.

Whether a definite legal liability exists depends on the terms of the employment contract. If the paid vacation is contingent upon the employee remaining in service until his vacation period, the legal obligation does not arise until this condition has been met. However, an obligation exists that meets all the tests of a determinable liability, since a company may estimate its total liability for vacation pay on the basis of its employee turnover experience. Generally, the probability is high that a future outlay for vacation pay will be made and recognition of a liability is warranted.

Recording Payroll Liabilities The liability aspect of the problem of accounting for payroll centers on the amounts due employees, the liabilities associated with withholdings from employees' earnings, and the employer's share of payroll taxes and fringe benefits. There is also a cost side to the problem. The total costs incurred for employee services, including gross earnings, payroll taxes, and other fringe benefit costs, must be allocated to functions or departments to provide useful cost information for management.

To illustrate the recording of a payroll in the accounts, we have assumed some payroll data for a merchandising company for the month of May. Because this is the fifth month of the year, some employees will have received salaries in excess of the limits subject to payroll taxes, so that the amount subject to payroll taxes will be less than the total amount earned. We have also assumed that the company is entitled to a merit rate of 2% on the state unemployment tax. A summary of total salaries earned and earnings subject to payroll taxes for the month of May follows:

Classification of expense	Total salaries earned	Earnings subject to payroll taxes		
		FICA taxes, 6%	Federal unemployment tax, 0.7%	State unemployment tax, 2%
Sales salaries	$ 60,000	$50,000	$35,000	$42,000
Administrative salaries .	40,000	30,000	25,000	28,000
Total	$100,000	$80,000	$60,000	$70,000

The employer's total payroll costs, including fringe benefits, are summarized below:

Payroll costs	Total	Sales salaries	Administrative salaries
Total salaries earned	$100,000	$60,000	$40,000
FICA taxes	4,800	3,000	1,800
Federal unemployment tax	420	245	175
State unemployment tax	1,400	840	560
Vacation pay	4,000	2,300	1,700
Total payroll costs	$110,620	$66,385	$44,235

The amounts withheld from employees' salaries and the computation of employees' net take-home pay are summarized on page 401.

Total salaries earned		$100,000
Withholdings:		
FICA tax	$ 4,800	
Income tax withheld	13,200	
Hospital insurance premiums (private plans)	1,500	19,500
Employees' net take-home pay		$ 80,500

Assuming that payroll taxes are combined with gross salaries for accounting purposes, the following summary journal entry would be prepared to record the payroll for the month of May:

Selling Expense—Salaries	66,385	
Administrative Expense—Salaries	44,235	
FICA Taxes Payable		9,600
Liability for Income Tax Withheld		13,200
Hospital Insurance Premiums Payable		1,500
Federal Unemployment Tax Payable		420
State Unemployment Tax Payable		1,400
Vacation Pay Payable		4,000
Accrued Payroll		80,500
To record payroll for the month of May.		

Payroll taxes on employers become a legal liability when salaries and wages are actually paid, rather than at the time the services by employees are rendered. For example, if salaries and wages accrued at year-end amount to $1,500, payroll taxes would not be levied on these earnings until the following year.

Property taxes

Property taxes, based on the assessed value of real and personal property, usually represent the primary source of revenue for local governmental units. From the viewpoint of the business owning property, property taxes are a part of the cost of the services of such property. Legally property taxes arise as of a particular date, usually on the so-called *lien date,* the date established by law on which the taxes become a lien against the property. When property is sold or transferred, the lien date determines whether the buyer or the seller is liable for payment of the tax.

The accounting issues relating to property taxes are: (1) When should the liability for property taxes be recorded? (2) To which period does the tax expense relate? The legal liability for property taxes arises on the lien date, and there is thus a clear basis for recognizing the liability at this time. Some accountants argue that the liability accrues throughout the tax year. Since property taxes are expenses associated with the right to use property during the fiscal year of the taxing authority, it seems reasonable to charge the tax expense against revenue during this time period.

The following illustration will help to clarify the issues. Assume that a company has property subject to property taxes by city and county governmental units. The fiscal year of the city and county runs from July 1 to June 30. Property taxes of $36,000 were assessed on January 1, covering the fiscal year starting on the following July 1. The lien date is July 1 and taxes are payable in two installments of $18,000 each on December 10 and on April 10.

The accounting for property taxes for the period from July 1 to December 31 is illustrated below under two alternative methods. Using method A, the property tax liability is recorded on the lien date (July 1) and the deferred property taxes (an asset) are amortized monthly throughout the following 12-month period; using method B property taxes are accrued monthly during the fiscal year of the taxing authority.

Explanation	Method A		Method B	

July 1. Liability for property taxes of $36,000 comes into existence on July 1, the lien date.	Def. Prop. Taxes . 36,000
	  Prop. Taxes
	    Payable . . .
		36,000	No entry	

At the end of July, August, September, October, and November. To record monthly property taxes expense, $3,000.	Prop. Taxes Exp. . 3,000
	  Def. Prop.
	    Taxes . . .
		3,000	Prop. Taxes Exp. . 3,000
			  Prop. Taxes
			    Payable . .
				3,000

Dec. 10. Payment of first installment of property tax bill, $18,000.	Prop. Taxes Pay. . 18,000
	  Cash . . . .
		18,000	Prop. Taxes Pay. . 15,000
			Prepaid Prop. Taxes 3,000
			  Cash . . . .
				18,000

Dec. 31. To record monthly property taxes expense.	Prop. Taxes Exp. . 3,000
	  Def. Prop.
	    Taxes . . . .
		3,000	Prop. Taxes Exp. . 3,000
			  Prepaid Prop.
			    Taxes . . . .
				3,000

Under method A, deferred property taxes of $18,000 will appear as a current asset in the December 31 balance sheet, and this amount will be amortized at the rate of $3,000 per month during the first six months of the next calendar year; under method B, neither a prepayment nor a liability is reported in the balance sheet at December 31. Since the liability comes into existence on the lien date (July 1), method A provides a more complete record of the company's financial position and is preferred by the authors. However, the AICPA has taken the position that monthly accrual in the taxpayer's records during the fiscal period of the taxing authority for which the taxes are levied is generally the most acceptable method.[9]

Losses on firm purchase commitments

To assure a steady supply of merchandise or raw materials, a business may enter into a contract for the future delivery of such goods at a fixed price. It is assumed in this discussion that the contract is **not subject to cancellation** regardless of changes in market price. If the current price of the goods falls below the contract price, the lower-of-cost-or-market rule should be applied to the commitment and the loss recognized promptly. The AICPA sums up the situation as follows: "Accrued net losses on firm purchase commitments for goods for inventory, measured in the same way as are inventory losses, should, if material, be recognized in the accounts and the amounts thereof separately disclosed in the income statement."[10]

The AICPA also concluded that if no loss is sustained because of the price decline, then the decline need not be recognized in the accounts. "The utility of such commitments is not impaired, and hence there is no loss, when the amounts to be realized from the disposition of the future inventory items are adequately protected by firm sales contracts or when there are other circumstances which reasonably assure continuing sales without price decline."[11]

The loss should be recognized in the period during which the price decline occurred. The value of the goods to be purchased under the commitment has been reduced just as though these goods were currently included in inventory. The entries to record an assumed loss of $15,000 and the subsequent purchase at a fixed price of $100,000 are illustrated on page 404.

[9] *Accounting Research and Terminology Bulletins—Final Edition,* AICPA (New York: 1961), pp. 83–84.
[10] Ibid., p. 34
[11] Ibid., p. 35.

Year of price decline:

Loss on Purchase Commitments Due to Price Decline	15,000	
Liability Arising from Purchase Commitments		15,000

To record loss due to decline in price of goods ordered.

Year of purchase:

Inventory (or Purchases)	85,000	
Liability Arising from Purchase Commitments	15,000	
Accounts Payable		100,000

To record purchase of goods under contract on which a loss
due to price decline was recognized in an earlier period.

The liability recorded in the year of price decline is the estimated amount which the buyer would be required to pay the seller if the buyer canceled the contract. When the goods are purchased, this estimated liability is transferred to Accounts Payable. If the expectation is that the purchase will be made during the regular operating cycle of the business, the liability arising from the purchase commitment should be listed as a current liability in the balance sheet.

If contracts to purchase goods at fixed prices are subject to cancellation, no liability is recognized for declines in market prices because such unfavorable contracts generally would be canceled.

LIABILITIES DEPENDENT ON OPERATING RESULTS

The amount of certain obligations cannot be measured until operating results are known. These include income taxes, bonuses, profit-sharing distributions, royalties, and contributions to employee retirement plans. There is no particular accounting problem in determining such liabilities at the end of a fiscal year, when the operating results are in. For *interim* reporting purposes, difficulties may arise in estimating some of these obligations in advance of the final determination of annual income.

Income taxes

The most familiar example of a liability whose amount is dependent upon operating results is income taxes. Individual proprietors and members of a partnership are subject to personal income taxes on their share of the profits of the business entity. Business units organized as proprietorships or partnerships are not taxable entities, and income tax liabilities do not appear on their balance sheets.

Corporations, estates, and trusts are separate taxable entities and are subject to income taxes. Income tax liabilities therefore will appear in the balance sheets of such entities. In most cases, corporations are required to make payments in advance of the estimated income tax liability. If payments of the estimated tax are not made when due, a penalty is assessed. The remaining tax not covered by the estimated payments is payable on March 15 of the year following the taxable calendar year. Calendar-year corporations may elect to pay the remaining tax in two equal installments (on March 15 and June 15).[12]

The estimated tax payments can be recorded in a Prepaid Income Taxes account or as debits to Income Taxes Payable if the accrued tax liability had been previously recorded in the accounts. A credit balance in Income Taxes Payable would be reported as a current liability. If U.S. government securities are held which can be used to pay income taxes and are clearly intended to be used to pay income taxes, they may be deducted from the estimated tax liability in the balance sheet. Most securities now issued by governments are not designed specifically for the payment of taxes and therefore should not be deducted from the amount of income taxes payable.

Accounting for Income Taxes in Interim Periods When interim financial reports are prepared, an estimate of accrued income tax liability must be made before the actual income tax liability for the year is known. If income taxes were assessed at a flat rate, it would be a relatively simple matter to compute the tax on the income to date. However, the progressive feature of the corporate income tax raises the question whether the income to date should be annualized and the proportionate income tax accrued for the period to date, or whether the marginal approach could be used whereby the first amount of income earned is taxed at the lower rate.

A similar question arises in businesses having a seasonal income pattern. For example, high income experienced early in the year may be offset by losses during the latter part of the year. If we follow the marginal approach, the income tax liability (in terms of the actual amount that ultimately will be paid) will be overstated during the early part of the year and must be adjusted downward during the latter part of the year when losses are sustained.

The Accounting Principles Board provided the following answers to these questions:

At the end of each interim period the company should make its best estimate of the effective tax rate expected to be applicable for the full fiscal year. The rate so determined should be used in providing for income taxes on a current year-to-date basis. The effective tax rate should reflect anticipated investment tax credits, foreign tax rates, percentage depletion, capital gains rates, and other available tax planning alternatives. However, in arriving at this ef-

[12] These rules were applicable in 1977; frequent changes in tax rates as well as rules regarding estimated tax payments are made by Congress.

fective tax rate no effect should be included for the tax related to significant unusual or extraordinary items that will be separately reported or reported net of their related tax effect in reports for the interim period or for the fiscal year.

The tax effects of losses that arise in the early portion of a fiscal year (in the event carryback of such losses is not possible) should be recognized only when realization is assured beyond any reasonable doubt. . . . An established seasonal pattern of loss in early interim periods offset by income in latter interim periods should constitute evidence that realization is assured beyond reasonable doubt, unless other evidence indicates the established seasonal pattern will not prevail. The tax effects of losses incurred in early interim periods may be recognized in a latter interim period of a fiscal year if their realization, although initially uncertain, later becomes assured beyond reasonable doubt. When the tax effects of losses that arise in the early portions of fiscal year are not recognized in that interim period, no tax provision should be made for income that arises in later interim periods until the tax effects of the previous interim losses are utilized. Changes resulting from new tax legislation should be reflected after the effective dates prescribed in the statutes.[13]

Additional discussion of accounting for income taxes in interim periods appears in Chapter 21.

Interperiod Allocation of Income Taxes As stated in Chapter 3, a problem arises in accounting for income tax obligations because of differences between *taxable* income and *accounting* income. As a result of these differences, the amount of income tax liability incurred by a corporation in any given year may differ materially from the amount of income tax expense reported in the income statement. Many companies report Prepaid Income Taxes as an asset or Deferred Income Taxes Payable as a liability. These accounts may be current or noncurrent, depending on the reasons for the differences between taxable income and accounting income. A complete coverage of this topic is presented in Chapter 21.

Bonus and profit-sharing plans

Contractual agreements covering rents, royalties, or employee compensation sometimes call for conditional payments in an amount dependent upon revenue or income earned during the period. We shall use the term *bonus* to describe conditional payments of this type.

Conditional expenses based on revenue cause little difficulty. For example, if a rental contract calls for a fixed rent of $100 per month and 1% of all sales over $100,000 per year, the fixed rental obligation accrues at the rate of $100 per month and when sales reach $100,000 each additional dollar of sales creates an additional rent obligation.

Some bonus plans provide for a bonus based on income. The plans are generally drawn so that the income figure to be used in determining the bonus is clearly defined. For example, the bonus may be based on:

[13] *APB Opinion No. 28,* "Interim Financial Reporting," AICPA (New York: 1973), pp. 527–528.

(1) income before income taxes and the bonus, (2) income after the bonus but before income taxes, or (3) *net* income after both the bonus and income taxes.

To illustrate the calculations involved, assume that a company has an incentive compensation plan under which a branch manager receives 20% of the income over $20,000 earned by the branch. Income for a given branch amounted to $80,000 before the bonus and income taxes. Assume for purposes of illustration that income taxes are 40% of income before income taxes. The bonus under each of the three plans listed above is computed as follows:

Plan 1 Contract provides that bonus shall be computed on income in excess of $20,000 but before deducting income taxes and the bonus:

> Bonus = .2($80,000 − $20,000) = <u>$12,000</u>

Plan 2 Contract provides that the bonus shall be computed on income in excess of $20,000 after deducting the bonus but before income taxes have been deducted:

> B = **Bonus**
> B = .2($80,000 − $20,000 − B)
> B = $16,000 − $4,000 − .2B
> 1.2B = $12,000
> B = <u>$10,000</u>

The computation of the bonus can be proved by taking 20% of the amount by which the income after the bonus exceeds $20,000. Thus, 20% of $50,000 ($80,000 − $10,000 − $20,000) equals the bonus of $10,000.

Plan 3 Contract provides that the bonus shall be computed on *net* income in excess of $20,000 after deducting both the bonus and income taxes:

> Let B = **Bonus**
> and T = **Income taxes**
> Then B = .2($80,000 − $20,000 − T − B)
> and T = .4($80,000 − B)

Substituting for T in the first equation, we can compute B (bonus) as follows:

> B = .2[$60,000 − .4($80,000 − B) − B]
> B = $12,000 − $6,400 + .08B − .2B
> 1.12B = $5,600
> B = <u>$5,000</u>

The computation of the bonus can be proved by taking 20% of the amount by which the net income after the bonus of $5,000 and income taxes of $30,000 (40% of $75,000) exceeds $20,000. Thus, 20% of $25,000 ($80,000 − $5,000 − $30,000 − $20,000) equals the bonus of $5,000.

The entry to record the bonus under Plan 3 is shown on page 408.

Bonus Expense	. . . .	5,000
Bonus Payable	. . . .	5,000
To record liability for bonus to branch manager.		

Bonus Expense would be included as an operating expense in the income statement and Bonus Payable as a current liability in the balance sheet. The Securities and Exchange Commission requires disclosure (description and expense) of bonus and profit-sharing plans which "are not available to all employees on a pro rata basis."[14]

CONTINGENCIES

Contingent liabilities were defined in Chapter 4 as potential obligations the existence of which is conditional upon the happening of some future event. Until the issuance of *FASB Statement No. 5* in 1975, the distinction between contingent liabilities and estimated liabilities was not clear in the minds of many accountants.[15] Similarly, some confusion existed as to which contingencies required the accrual of a loss or expense, which contingencies simply called for disclosure in the financial statements, and which general risk contingencies inherent in a business neither required accrual in the accounts nor disclosure in the financial statements. Some companies accrued estimated losses or expenses from certain contingencies prior to the occurrence of the events expected to resolve the uncertainties while, under similar circumstances, other companies recognized such losses or expenses only when the contingent events occurred. The purpose of *FASB Statement No. 5* was to establish more definitive standards of financial accounting and reporting for loss contingencies.

FASB Statement No. 5, "Accounting for Contingencies"

A *contingency* is an existing condition, situation, or a set of circumstances involving uncertainty as to possible gain *(gain contingency)* or loss *(loss contingency)* to an enterprise that ultimately will be resolved when a future event or events occurs or fails to occur.[16] (The term *loss* is used by the FASB to include some items that are commonly referred to by accountants as *expenses*.) Resolution of the uncertainty surrounding a gain contingency generally results in an acquisition of an asset or the reduction of a liability; resolution of the uncertainty surrounding a loss contingency generally results in reduction of an asset or the incurrence

---

[14] *Regulation S-X, Rule 3-16*(j), Securities and Exchange Commission (Washington).
[15] *FASB Statement No. 5,* "Accounting for Contingencies," FASB (Stamford: 1975).
[16] Ibid., p. 1

of a liability. The likelihood that the future event or events will confirm the loss may be *probable* (likely to occur), *reasonably possible* (more than remote but less than likely), or *remote* (slight chance of occurring).

The FASB stated that "not all uncertainties inherent in the accounting process give rise to contingencies." The preparation of financial statements requires estimates for many business activities, and the use of estimates does not necessarily mean that a contingency exists. For example, the measurement of depreciation and income tax expense involves estimates but neither is a contingency. Neither the expiration of the cost of depreciable assets nor the incurrence of the obligation to pay income taxes is uncertain; however, the periodic amounts recognized in the accounts require the use of estimates.

Examples of Loss Contingencies   The FASB identified the following examples of loss contingencies:

1 Collectibility of receivables
2 Obligations related to product warranties and product defects
3 Risk of loss or damage of enterprise property by fire, explosion, or other hazards
4 Threat of expropriation of assets
5 Pending or threatened litigation
6 Actual or possible claims and assessments
7 Risk of loss from catastrophes assumed by property and casualty companies, including reinsurance companies
8 Guarantees of indebtedness of others
9 Obligations of commercial banks under "standby letters of credit"
10 Agreements to repurchase receivables or other assets that have been sold

Accrual of Loss Contingencies   According to the FASB, an estimated loss or expense from a loss contingency shall be accrued by a charge to income if *both* of the following conditions are met:

   a Information available prior to issuance of the financial statements indicates that it is probable that an asset had been impaired or a liability had been incurred at the date of the financial statements. It is implicit in this condition that it must be probable that one or more future events will occur confirming the fact of the loss.
   b The amount of the loss can be reasonably estimated.[17]

When the range of loss can be reasonably estimated but no single amount within the range appears to be a better estimate than any other amount within the range, the minimum amount in the range should be accrued.[18] For example, assume that at the balance sheet date a company had lost a court case but the amount of damages remains unresolved. A reasonable estimate is that the judgment will be for not less

[17] Ibid., p. 4.
[18] *FASB Interpretation No. 14,* "Reasonable Estimation of the Amount of a Loss. . . . " FASB (Stamford: 1976), p. 2.

than $2 million or more than $6 million. No amount between $2 million and $6 million appears to be a better estimate than any other amount. According to the FASB, $2 million should be accrued as a loss and the possibility of an additional loss of $4 million should be disclosed in a note to the financial statements. Both accrued and actual contingency losses should be included in the determination of income before extraordinary items, unless such losses meet the criteria for classification as extraordinary items.

The important points to keep in mind are: (1) a contingency loss should be accrued only when an asset has been impaired or a liability incurred; (2) it must be probable that a future event or events will confirm the existence of the loss; and (3) the amount of the loss can be reasonably estimated. The absence of insurance (sometimes improperly referred to as *self-insurance*) covering property losses or the possibility that injury claims will be made against a company, for example, does not indicate that an asset has been impaired or that a liability has been incurred. Mere exposure to risk does not require the accrual of losses.

Included in the category of accruable loss contingencies would be estimates of doubtful accounts expense and sales returns when the customers have a right to return goods. Both of these contingencies were discussed in Chapter 7. The accounting for other accruable contingencies such as product warranty expense, gift certificates and service contracts outstanding, and coupons and trading stamps outstanding are described in a subsequent section of this chapter.

Loss Contingencies Which Are Not Accrued   Certain loss contingencies which do not meet the two criteria for accrual, but which still are at least "reasonably possible," should be disclosed in notes to the financial statements. The disclosure should indicate the nature of the contingency and provide an estimate of the possible loss or state that such an estimate cannot be made. An example of such a contingency would be a legal action against the reporting entity in which an unfavorable outcome is possible but a reasonable estimate of loss cannot be made.

If the probability of loss from a nonaccruable contingency is remote, the contingency should be disclosed. Such contingencies would include guarantees of indebtedness of others, agreements to repurchase receivables, and obligations of commercial banks under "standby letters of credit." Disclosure is not required of a loss contingency involving claims or legal suits not yet filed unless it appears probable that a claim or legal suit will be filed and that an unfavorable outcome is reasonably possible. General or unspecified business risks do not meet the conditions for accrual and need not be disclosed.

Gain Contingencies   Those contingencies that might result in gains should not be recorded in the accounts until the gains are actually realized. This is consistent with the general principles of revenue realization. Although disclosure should be made of contingencies that might result in gains, care should be exercised not to give an impression that realization of such gains is likely. Examples of gain contingencies include probable favorable outcome of plaintiff litigation and future benefits of operating loss carryforward for income tax purposes.

Accounting for loss contingencies when liability has been incurred

The accrual of loss contingencies requires a debit to a loss or expense account and a credit to an asset (or asset valuation) account or to an estimated liability account. The term *estimated liability* is used to describe an obligation which definitely exists but which is uncertain as to amount and due date. The primary accounting problem is to obtain objective evidence on which to base a reasonable estimate of the amount of the liability. Estimated liabilities may be current or long term. The accounting for certain contingencies which require the recognition of estimated current liabilities is described in the following sections.

Product Warranties Estimating the liability that arises in connection with various kinds of product warranties often poses a difficult problem. Warranties to replace or repair a product if it proves unsatisfactory within some specified time period are made by most companies. Such liabilities arise at the time of sale and may be recorded in the accounts either at the time of sale or at the end of the accounting period. The following entries would be made if the liability is recorded at the time of sale:

Product Warranty Expense		*XXX*
Estimated Liability under Product Warranty		*XXX*
To record estimated liability under product warranty.		
Estimated Liability under Product Warranty		*XXX*
Cash (or Accounts Payable, Accrued Payroll, Inventory of Parts, etc.)		*XXX*
To record costs of servicing customer claims.		

The balance in the estimated liability account at the end of the accounting period should be carefully reviewed and adjusted if necessary to make certain that it reflects a reasonable measure of potential customer claims on outstanding product warranties.

An acceptable alternative would be to make no entry in the estimated liability account at the time of sale; Product Warranty Expense would be debited as actual costs are incurred in servicing customer claims and at the end of the period to recognize outstanding potential claims.

Income tax regulations allow a deduction for product warranty expense only when the cost has been incurred. In the past many companies followed the income tax regulations in their accounting records, thus overstating net income and understating current liabilities. When the outstanding liability under a product warranty is significant, neither tax laws nor the uncertainty of the amount of expense to be incurred is a valid excuse for failure to include the accrued expense and the related current liability in the financial statements. *FASB Statement No. 5* has made the latter procedure mandatory.

Gift Certificates and Service Contracts Some companies issue tickets, tokens, or gift certificates which are promises to perform services or to furnish goods at some later date. The measure of the liability is equal to the amount advanced by customers. As redemptions are made, the liability account is debited and a revenue account is credited. Examples of this type of transaction are meal tickets issued by restaurants, coupons issued by garages and gasoline stations, tickets and tokens issued by transportation companies, gift certificates issued by retail stores. Because such advances are in small individual amounts and relatively numerous, it is almost certain that some will never be presented for redemption. Estimating the amount of forfeited claims is simplified when there is an agreement that the obligation lapses after a stated time. When the offer is of indefinite duration, it is necessary to estimate the amounts of potential claims that will not be redeemed and to transfer this amount from the liability account to a revenue account.

Companies selling or servicing major household appliances often sell a service contract to customers under which the companies agree to service the appliance for a specified period of time. In this case, the price of the service contract constitutes unearned revenue, which is earned by performance over the period of the contract. To illustrate, assume that a company sells television service contracts for $50 each, agreeing to service customers' sets for one year. If 1,000 such service contracts are sold, the entry is:

Cash (or Accounts Receivable)	50,000	
Unearned Service Contract Revenue		50,000
To record sale of 1,000 service contracts at $50 per contract.		

During the ensuing 12-month period, the unearned service contract revenue will be converted into realized revenue, and actual costs of servicing the television sets will be debited to expense accounts. On the basis of experience, it is often feasible to establish a pattern of probable service calls as a guide in recognizing revenue. For example, if the bulk of the service calls tend to be made in the first part of the year covered by the contract, a policy of crediting realized revenue with, say, 30% of the contract price in the first month, 20% in the second, and 5% in each of the ten subsequent months might be reasonable. The entries below are illustrative of this procedure for the first month of the contract period if we assume that costs of $10,250 were incurred in servicing the contracts during the first month:

Unearned Service Contract Revenue	15,000	
Service Contract Revenue		15,000
To record 30% of unearned service contract as realized		
revenue for the first month of the contract period.		
Service Contract Expense	10,250	
Parts Inventory		4,000
Cash, Accrued Payroll, etc.		6,250
To record costs incurred under service contracts.		

At the end of the first month, the balance of $35,000 in the Unearned Service Contract Revenue would be presented as a current liability in the balance sheet.

Coupons and Trading Stamps In an effort to promote the sales of certain products, a company may issue coupons exchangeable for prizes in cash or merchandise. In such cases the company incurs an estimated liability equal to the cost of the prizes which are expected to be claimed by customers.

The estimated liability for prizes to be distributed should be based on the company's past and anticipated experience with redemptions of coupons. For example, assume that in Year 1 a company issues coupons which may be redeemed for prizes costing $2,500 if all the coupons are presented for redemption. If past experience indicates that only 80% of the coupons issued will be presented for redemption, the estimated liabilitity is $2,000 (80% of $2,500, the maximum cost of prizes that may actually be claimed by customers).

The purchase of prizes to be given, such as reproductions of famous paintings, toys, and kitchen utensils, is recorded as follows:

Inventory (Prize Merchandise)	2,800	
Cash (or Accounts Payable)		2,800
To record purchase of merchandise to be offered as prizes.		

Generally, the cost of the coupons is immaterial in amount and would not be accounted for separately; if the cost of coupons is material, the cost may also be recorded in an appropriate inventory account. Assuming that customers present coupons during Year 1 in exchange for prizes costing $1,500, the following entry would be made:

Promotional Expense	1,500	
Inventory (Prize Merchandise)		1,500
To record redemption of coupons by customers in exchange for		
prize merchandise costing $1,500.		

At the end of Year 1, an adjusting entry is required to recognize the promotional expense and the estimated liability relating to the coupons outstanding. In our example, the total cost of prizes expected to be claimed by customers was estimated at $2,000, and $1,500 of this amount has been redeemed during the year. Thus, an estimated liability of $500 at the end of Year 1 should be recorded as follows:

Promotional Expense	500	
Estimated Liability for Coupons Outstanding		500
To record estimated liability for coupons outstanding at the end of		
Year 1.		

At the end of Year 1, the inventory of prize merchandise is $1,300 ($2,800 − $1,500). This inventory should be listed among the current assets in the balance sheet. The liability for coupons outstanding, $500, should be included among current liabilities. The promotional expense for the year, $2,000, is classified as a selling expense in the income statement.

A slightly different situation exists when a retailer gives his customers **trading stamps** (Blue Chip Stamps, Green Stamps, etc.) to be redeemed by another company engaged in the sale and redemption of trading stamps. The retailer pays a fixed price for the trading stamps which are recorded in an Inventory of Trading Stamps account. When stamps are issued to customers, an operating expense account is debited and the Inventory of Trading Stamps account is credited. The obligation to redeem the stamps is assumed by the trading stamp company. The trading stamp company records the sale of stamps in a revenue account and recognizes an estimated liability for the cost of merchandise and related service costs to be incurred when stamps are redeemed.

Operating Reserves and Discontinued Operations Some companies debit an expense account and credit an *operating reserve* account for costs such as repairs or maintenance which have not yet been incurred. Also, estimated disbursements for deferred compensation, restoration of leased properties, plant closing and relocation costs, and provisions for discontinued operations are sometimes included in the current liability section of the balance sheet.

The recording of these estimated costs is presumably an effort to implement accrual accounting by recognizing an expense or loss when an obligation to incur a cost in the future can be identified with reasonable certainty. When such costs are incurred, they are debited to the operating reserve account.

There is some evidence that operating reserves have at times been used by management as "income-smoothing" devices. Accountants should analyze the nature of these reserves and determine whether a liability has been incurred (or an asset impaired) or whether the reserves simply relieve future periods of expenses and losses.

When a cost that is expensed for annual reporting purposes clearly benefits interim periods, each interim period should be charged for an appropriate portion of the expense by the use of accruals and deferrals.[19] Costs and expenses expected to be incurred in carrying out a disposal of a segment of business should be accrued and included in the measurement of the gain or loss on the disposal.[20] For example, a recent balance sheet for the Singer Company included a "Provision for discontinued operations" of $275.7 million in current liabilities. A note to the financial statements stated that Singer Company "decided to withdraw from the manufacture and sale of its Business Machines Division product lines over a period of 12 months." The total provision was for $325.2 million for "estimated expenses and write-downs . . . to be incurred subsequent to the date of the decision to discontinue these operations."

Disclosure of contingencies not accrued

If a loss contingency does not meet the two conditions for accrual described on page 409 and the likelihood of loss is reasonably possible or remote, the loss contingency should be disclosed in the financial statements. The disclosure should include the nature of the contingency and, if possible, an indication of the amount involved. Adequate disclosure may be accomplished in a number of ways: (1) by a parenthetical comment included in the heading of an item in the balance sheet, (2) by a note to financial statements, (3) by showing the item

[19] *APB Opinion No. 28,* p. 526.
[20] *APB Opinion No. 30,* "Reporting the Results of Operations— . . .," AICPA (New York: 1973), p. 563.

among the liabilities but not extending the amount to be included in the liability total, or (4) by an appropriation of retained earnings authorized by the board of directors. Disclosure by note is probably the most satisfactory procedure and is almost universally used. Some examples are discussed and illustrated in the following sections.

Guarantees of Indebtedness of Others A contingency may arise from discounting notes receivable with recourse, from assigning accounts receivable with recourse, and from accommodation endorsements added to the obligations of other parties such as customers, employees, or affiliated enterprises. In such cases little question exists as to the amount of the obligation or its due date. The central issue is whether the parties primarily liable will pay the liability. If the probability is strong that the original debtor will make payment, the chance of the endorser being required to pay is correspondingly low. An example of disclosure of this type of contingency is illustrated below:

> In connection with providing for its future bituminous coal supply, the Company . . . has guaranteed capital and other obligations of certain coal suppliers (including five owned and two controlled coal companies) aggregating $131.6 million.

Pending or Threatened Litigation If a company is the defendant in a lawsuit calling for the payment of damages, a contingent liability exists. The outcome of such litigation can seldom be predicted with any assurance. The decision of the court may release the company of any obligation or it may establish an enforceable claim against it. However, the possibility of an appeal to a higher court still may exist. Another very possible outcome is an out-of-court settlement between the parties, thus ending the litigation.

Even though the evidence available at the balance sheet date does not seem to favor the defendant company, it is hardly reasonable to expect the company to publish in its financial statements a dollar estimate of the probable outcome. Such publicity could influence unfavorably the chances of an out-of-court settlement or encourage the opposing party to intensify its efforts. As a generalization, then, we may say that contingency from pending litigation should be adequately disclosed in notes to the financial statements. This disclosure will seldom, if ever, reach the point of estimating the dollar amount of a future settlement. To do so would weaken the company's position in the dispute.

In the area of threatened litigation or unasserted claims against a client company, a letter of audit inquiry to the client company's lawyers is the auditor's primary means of obtaining confirmation of the information provided by management. This audit step has been a source of considerable controversy between independent accountants and lawyers. The issue boils down to a struggle between the accountants' quest for full disclosure and the lawyers' responsibility to preserve the confidentiality of the lawyer-client privilege. A compromise position was reached between the AICPA and the American Bar Association which resulted in the issuance of a pronouncement by the Auditing Standards Executive Committee of the AICPA.[21] An example of disclosure of an asserted claim is given below:

> In January, 1976 a purported class action was filed in the U.S. District Court for the Southern District of New York against the Corporation, certain of its present and former directors and its independent accountants. Plaintiff alleges that the Corporation's Annual Reports for 1973 and 1974 and other statements and reports failed to make proper disclosures with respect to the Corporation's consolidated financial condition and earnings resulting in violation of Section 10(b) of the Securities Exchange Act of 1934 and Rule 10b-5 thereunder and constituting common law fraud. Plaintiff seeks damages in an unspecified amount on behalf of the alleged class consisting of all persons who purchased the corporation's common stock during the period of the alleged wrongful conduct. Management denies the claims asserted.

Actual or Possible Claims and Assessments The Internal Revenue Service may disagree with the treatment of items in the computation of taxable income and (within the period of the statute of limitations) may assess additional taxes. Because this contingency is well-recognized and understood, no specific disclosure is required prior to the time that an actual assessment has been made. Except in cases of fraud or failure to file a return, the statute of limitations on federal income tax deficiencies is three years; thus at any given time it is only the income tax of the last three years that may be in doubt as to matters involving an interpretation of the law. A note reference is frequently attached to financial statements indicating that income tax returns have been examined and final determination of income taxes made for certain years. The following disclosure of a proposed tax deficiency by a publicly owned company is given as an example:

> The Internal Revenue Service issued a notice of deficiency of $823,000, plus interest, relating primarily to the allocation of the purchase price to the acquired assets of a subsidiary and the subsequent valuations of its LIFO inventories. The Company has petitioned the United States Tax Court; however, no trial date has been set. In the event any portion of the deficiency is sustained, the adjustments would represent timing differences which should result in tax deductions in future years; consequently, there would be no material adverse effect on the consolidated financial statements.

Future liabilities and commitments

Most businesses are continuously planning activities for some time in the future. In many instances, commitments may be made that will result in substantial liabilities in the near future. At any balance sheet date, a company ordinarily will have made certain commitments that are of a

---

[21] *Statement on Auditing Standards No. 12,* "Inquiry of a Client's Lawyer Concerning Litigation, Claims, and Assessments," AICPA (New York: 1976).

recurring nature and normal in amount; these do not require any special disclosure. However, when unusual commitments that are large in amount have been made, their nature and amount should be disclosed. Examples are commitments for an unusually large purchase of materials, a major expansion of plant, acquisitions of natural resources, additional payments to be made contingent on earnings of acquired companies, or unusually large commitments for advertising and product development costs. An example of disclosure of commitments is illustrated below:

> *Commitments*—The Company has commitments under contracts for the purchase of land and for the construction of buildings. Portions of such contracts not completed at year-end are not reflected in the financial statements. Such unrecorded commitments amounted to approximately $58,575,000 at year-end 1978 as compared to $83,757,000 for 1977.

Presentation of current liabilities in the balance sheet

Two questions arise in connection with the presentation of current liabilities in the balance sheet: (1) the order in which short-term debt is to be listed and (2) the extent of the detail necessary in disclosing different types of current liabilities. Current liabilities can be reported in the **order of maturity** or according to **amount** (largest to smallest). It is difficult to satisfy both objectives, and the usual compromise is to rank them in order of size unless differences in maturity dates are significant. However, bank overdrafts and notes maturing shortly after the balance sheet date are usually listed first in deference to their priority of maturity.

In reporting notes payable in the balance sheet, the discount or premium on the notes should be reported as a direct deduction from or addition to the face amount of the notes. The description of the notes should include the effective interest rate, and the face amount of the notes should be disclosed in the financial statements or in the accompanying notes.[22]

The matter of detail will depend to some extent on the purpose for which the balance sheet is prepared. In a balance sheet prepared in support of a loan application or for use in forecasting short-range financial requirements, a listing of current liabilities in greater detail is desirable. For financial reporting purposes, the classification illustrated on page 419 is recommended.

If the due date of any liability can be extended, the details should be disclosed parenthetically or in notes accompanying the financial statements. Any short-term obligation which definitely will be liquidated by the issuance of additional shares of capital stock should be reported under stockholders' equity.

---

[22] *APB Opinion No. 21,* "Interest on Receivables and Payables," AICPA (New York: 1971), p. 423.

Current liabilities:

Notes payable to banks (interest rate, 9%)		$ 600,000
Notes payable to trade creditors (effective interest rate, 8%)	$475,000	
Less: Discount on notes payable	30,000	445,000
Accounts payable to trade creditors		325,200
Current maturities of long-term debt (including bonds, mortgages, and equipment contracts payable)		150,500
Income taxes payable		112,500
Other accrued liabilities (payroll, interest, royalties, guarantees, etc.)		29,000
Dividends payable		25,000
Miscellaneous current liabilities (advances from customers, credit balances in customers' accounts, etc.)		21,800
Total current liabilities		$1,709,000

REVIEW QUESTIONS

1 Liabilities are sometimes referred to as "equities of outsiders in the assets of a business." Do you agree with this description of liabilities?

2 Distinguish between a **liability** and a **commitment.** Should the currently maturing installment of a deferred compensation agreement which is to be liquidated by issuance of stock be reported as a liability on the balance sheet? Explain.

3 What is the basis for distinguishing between a **current** and a **long-term liability?**

4 Distinguish the following: **definitely determinable liability, liability dependent upon operating results, estimated liability, contingent liability.** Give an example of each.

5 Under what circumstances would it be proper to report a currently maturing debt as a noncurrent liability?

6 When should deferred revenue (or unearned revenue) be reported as a current liability? When should deferred revenue be reported as noncurrent?

7 What are the usual liabilities that arise in connection with a payroll?

8 When should the liability for property taxes be recognized in the accounting records? Over what period should property taxes be charged to expense? Explain.

9 Where would the liability for current year's income taxes appear on the balance sheet of a partnership?

10 What recommendations did the APB make in **Opinion No. 28** regarding the accrual of income taxes for interim periods?

11 A company acquired certain patent rights in return for an agreement to pay royalties equal to "10% of the company's income." What difficulties may arise in interpreting this agreement?

12 *a* Define a **contingency** and differentiate between a **gain contingency** and a **loss contingency.**
 b Give some examples of gain contingencies and loss contingencies.
 c What two conditions must be met before a loss contingency is accrued in the accounts?

13 On December 31, Year 6, Exeter Company had an investment of $2 million in the bonds of Z Company which has filed for bankruptcy. A reasonable estimate of the possible loss is in the range between $600,000 and $900,000. No amount of the estimated loss in this range appears at the time to be a better estimate than any other amount. How should Exeter Company account for this contingency in its financial statements for the year ended December 31, Year 6?

14 Briefly describe the accounting for promotional plans involving coupons and prizes, product guarantees, and the sale of service contracts.

15 The Larson Co. does not carry workmen's compensation insurance but it does have its own plan. Should estimated obligations to employees under this plan be reported as a liability? Are potential losses on "self-insurance" plans properly reported as liabilities? Why?

16 Included among the current liabilities of American Beef Packers, Inc., is an item described as "Excess of Checks Outstanding over Balance in Bank Account, $506,041." The current liabilities of Liggett & Myers, Incorporated, include "Estimated Costs Relating to Closing of Richmond Plant, $3,430,041." Briefly explain the nature of these two liabilities.

17 Explain how each of the following items would be measured and reported in financial statements:
 a Bank overdraft
 b Customers' accounts having credit balances
 c Service guarantee on products sold
 d Bonds maturing in three months, to be paid from a sinking fund
 e Dividend payable in common stock of the issuing corporation
 f Dividends in arrears on preferred stock
 g Balance in account Allowance for Purchase Discounts
 h Interest on notes payable, deducted from the face amount of the note in determining the net proceeds
 i Estimated payments to workers under a three-year union contract
 j Potential payments to stockholders of an acquired company based on future profits of the acquired company.

18 Describe four ways in which a contingent liability may be disclosed in financial statements.

19 Under what circumstances should commitments for future expenditures be disclosed in financial statements? How should this disclosure be made?

20 List some general guidelines in reporting current liabilities in the balance sheet.

EXERCISES

Ex. 10-1 At December 31, Year 3, Albertson Company issued a two-year non-interest-bearing note with a face amount of $58,320 for some scrap metal. The transaction was recorded as follows:

Purchases 58,320

    Note Payable   58,320

    a Prepare a correcting entry at December 31, Year 3, assuming that a fair rate of interest is 8% per year and that the accounts for Year 3 are still open. Use Appendix A to determine the present value of the note.
    b Prepare an adjusting entry at December 31, Year 4, to recognize interest expense on the note.
    c Show how the note should be presented in the balance sheet at December 31, Year 4.

Ex. 10-2 The following information is taken from the records of the Marina Club for the first three months of its operations:

Month	Total salaries earned	Income tax withheld	FICA withheld (6%)	Remitted to Internal Revenue Service
January	$ 2,600	$ 290	$156	$ –0–
February	3,400	360	204	602*
March	4,000	410	240	768†
Totals	$10,000	$1,060	$600	$1,370

* Income and FICA tax withheld from employees' salaries in January and employer's FICA tax for January.
† Income and FICA tax withheld in February and employer's FICA tax for February.

    Entries to record the payroll for January and February, including taxes on the employer (FICA, 6%; state unemployment tax, 2.7%; and federal unemployment tax, 0.7%) were properly recorded. Remittances to the Internal Revenue Service were debited to the respective liability accounts. All salaries earned through March are subject to payroll taxes.
    a Prepare a compound journal entry to record the payroll for March. Record all payroll taxes on the employer in the Payroll Taxes Expense account.
    b Prepare an entry at the end of April to record payment of the balance of the amount due for income tax withheld, FICA taxes, and the full amount of state unemployment tax for the first quarter of the year. Federal unemployment tax is not payable until after the amount payable exceeds $100.

Ex. 10-3 Lee Bell has a contract with Pill Corporation in which he is to receive a bonus of 20% of any net income over $97,500. Income before the bonus and income taxes for the year is $250,000. Taxes are 50% of taxable income.
    Compute the amount of the bonus, assuming that it is computed on the net income in excess of $97,500 after deducting both the bonus and income taxes.

Ex. 10-4 Supreme Fuel Co. offers a coupon with each full gallon of gasoline sold. A customer who turns in 100 coupons is given a choice of prizes consisting of a football, a basketball, or a baseball glove. These prizes cost the company $2.50 each. The Promotional Expense account is debited as redemptions are made during the year and also at the end of the year when an estimate is made of outstanding coupons which will be redeemed. The following five summary transactions occurred in Year 1:

a Purchased for cash 800 coupon books, each containing 1,000 coupons, for a total cost of $800. Debit Inventory of Coupons.

b Issued 500,000 coupons to customers.

c Purchased for cash 2,200 pieces of prize merchandise (footballs, basketballs, and baseball gloves).

d Issued 1,500 prizes to customers.

e Of the coupons issued, it is estimated that an additional 120,000 will be redeemed.

Prepare journal entries to record these transactions.

Ex. 10-5 Easyride Company sells on account a machine early in the current year for $1,200 along with a one-year warranty. Maintenance on each machine during the warranty period averages $100.

Give entries to record the sale of the machine and the subsequent expenditure of $85 in cash to service the machine during the warranty period, assuming that the Product Warranty Expense account is debited at the time of sale. (The sale is recorded at $1,200.)

Ex. 10-6 In October of the current year Long Company agreed to purchase 7,500 tons of material next year at the fixed price of $100 per ton. The contract is not subject to cancellation. At the end of the current year the replacement cost of the material stands at $88 per ton.

Prepare the journal entry to recognize the loss on the purchase commitment at the end of the current year.

Ex. 10-7 Gourmet Company distributes coupons to consumers which may be presented (on or before a stated expiration date) to grocers for discounts on certain products of Gourmet Company. The grocers are reimbursed when they send the coupons to Gourmet Company. In Gourmet Company's experience, 50% of the coupons ultimately are redeemed, and generally two months elapse between the date a grocer receives a coupon and the date Gourmet Company receives it. During Year 5, Gourmet Company issued two separate series of coupons as follows:

Date of issue	Consumer expiration date	Total value	Amount disbursed on redemptions as of Dec. 31, Year 5
Jan. 1, Year 5	June 30, Year 5	$40,000	$18,200
July 1, Year 5	Dec. 31, Year 5	80,000	21,100

Compute the estimated liability for unredeemed coupons for Gourmet Company at December 31, Year 5.

Ex. 10-8 Z Company had $6 million of short-term commercial paper outstanding at June 30, Year 6, the end of its fiscal year. At this date Z Company intended to refinance the commercial paper by issuance of long-term debt. However, because the company had excess cash in July, it paid $2 million of the commercial paper. On August 10, Year 6, the company issued $12 million long-term bonds and on August 15, it issued financial statements for the year ended June 30. The proceeds of the bond issue were intended to be used as follows:

(1) To increase working capital, $2 million

(2) To pay off balance of commercial paper, $4 million

(3) To finance construction of new warehouse, $6 million

Indicate how the foregoing information should be presented in the financial statements for the year ended June 30, Year 6.

SHORT CASES FOR ANALYSIS AND DECISION

Case 10-1 An unclassified balance sheet of Sumerfield Corporation at December 31, Year 5, follows:

SUMERFIELD CORPORATION

Balance Sheet

December 31, Year 5

Assets

Current assets	$15,000,000
Other assets	25,000,000
Total assets	$40,000,000

Liabilities & Stockholders' Equity

Accounts payable and accrued liabilities	$ 5,000,000
Bank loan payable, 6%, due Feb. 1, Year 6	2,500,000
Note payable, 9%, due July 10, Year 6	1,500,000
Bonds payable, 8%, due Dec. 31, Year 25	12,500,000
Stockholders' equity	18,500,000
Total liabilities & stockholders' equity	$40,000,000

Before the company issues a classified balance sheet on March 1, Year 6, for the year ended December 31, Year 5, you ascertain that the company intends to refinance the bank loan and the note payable on a long-term basis. During December of Year 5, the company negotiated a financing agreement with a major bank for a maximum amount of $4 million at any time through December 31, Year 7. The terms of the agreement are as follows:

(1) Funds will be made available at the request of Sumerfield Corporation and any amount borrowed will mature three years from the date of borrowing. Interest at the prevailing bank prime rate will be due quarterly.
(2) An annual commitment fee of 1% will be charged by the bank on the difference between the amount borrowed and $4 million.
(3) The agreement is cancelable by the lender only if
   (i) The borrower's working capital, excluding borrowings under this agreement, falls below $6 million.
  (ii) The borrower becomes obligated under lease agreement to pay annual rentals in excess of $1 million.
 (iii) The borrower acquires treasury stock without the prior approval of the bank.
 (iv) The borrower guarantees indebtedness of other companies in excess of $200,000.

Instructions
a Is Sumerfield's intention to refinance sufficiently finalized to permit the classification of the bank loan and the note payable as noncurrent liabilities in a classified balance sheet at December 31, Year 5?
b Assuming that the bank loan and the note payable are properly excluded from current liabilities in the balance sheet at December 31, Year 5, draft an appro-

priate note relating to the refinancing which should accompany the financial statements.

Case 10-2 Dugan Company has a bank loan which is due within three months of the balance sheet date. The loan has been in existence for five years, although it is of short maturity, and it is the intent of both the company and the bank to renew the loan indefinitely. The loan is secured by the cash surrender value of a life insurance policy.

The company over a period of years has been offering to officers and employees the right to buy the company's 9% bonds which will be redeemed at the holder's request at any time after two years from the date of issue. In the past, certain bonuses have been paid to employees by issuing these bonds. All the bonds presently outstanding have or will have an issued status for two years within one year of balance sheet date. During the past 10 years, bonds redeemed amounted to less than 10% of bonds outstanding, and evidence indicates that no employee-bondholders intend to redeem their bonds within the coming year.

Instructions State how you would classify the cash surrender value of life insurance, the bank loan, and the bonds payable in the balance sheet of Dugan Company at the end of the current year. Give reasons for your answer.

Case 10-3 At the end of the current year, the balance sheet of the Howe Corporation, a medium-sized firm, did not include among the current liabilities the following items (all of which are material in amount):

(1) Notes payable to a group of stockholders, the notes to become due and payable on demand of at least eight of the group of twelve stockholders
(2) A note payable due three months after balance sheet date, in settlement of which the holder accepted 1,000 shares of preferred stock 15 days after balance sheet date
(3) Rent collected one year in advance
(4) Bonds payable maturing in 90 days

Instructions Assuming that in each case the exclusion from current liabilities was based on logical reasoning, give the arguments in support of the statement presentation used by this company. If your answer involves assumptions as to facts not given in the question, state your assumptions.

Case 10-4 Promo-Rex, Inc., was found early this year to sell trading stamps throughout the country to retailers who distribute the stamps gratuitously to their customers. Books for accumulating the stamps and catalogs illustrating the merchandise for which the stamps may be exchanged are given free to retailers for distribution to stamp recipients. Centers with inventories of merchandise have been established for redemption of the stamps. Retailers may not return unused stamps.

The schedule on page 425 shows the company's expectations as to percentages of a normal month's activity which will be attained. For this purpose, a "normal month's activity" is defined as the level of operations expected when expansion of activities ceases or tapers off to a stable rate. The company expects that this level will be attained in the third year and that sales of stamps will average $2,000,000 per month throughout the third year.

Promo-Rex, Inc., plans to adopt an annual closing date at the end of each 12 months of operations.

Instructions
a Discuss the accounting alternatives that should be considered by Promo-Rex, Inc., for the recognition of its revenue and related expenses.
b For each accounting alternative discussed in **(a)** above, give balance sheet accounts that should be used and indicate how each should be classified.

Month	Actual stamp sales, %	Merchandise purchases, %	Stamp redemptions, %
6th	30	40	10
12th	60	60	45
18th	80	80	70
24th	90	90	80
30th	100	100	95

PROBLEMS

Group A

10A-1 Guzik Corporation acquired a machine on July 1, Year 1, for $5,000 down and an 18-month $15,000 face amount note on which interest was payable at the annual rate of 4% on December 31 and June 30. The current fair rate of interest on a note of comparable quality was 10% compounded semiannually.

Instructions (Round all computations to the nearest dollar.)
a Compute the cost of the machine for financial reporting purposes and record the acquisition of the machine at July 1, Year 1. Use Appendix A to determine the present value of the note payable.
b Prepare journal entries to record the following:
    (1) Payment of interest on the note and adjustment of the Discount on Note Payable account at December 31, Year 1.
    (2) Payment of interest on the note and adjustment of the Discount on Note Payable account at June 30, Year 2.
    (3) Payment of the note (including interest) and adjustment of the Discount on Note Payable account at December 31, Year 2.
c Show how the note payable should be presented in the balance sheet at December 31, Year 1.

10A-2 While auditing the accounts of Blanc Paper Company, you found that the following contingencies have not been recorded in the accounts:

    (1) Doubtful accounts are estimated at $14,900 as a result of aging of the accounts. The unadjusted balance in the Allowance for Doubtful Accounts shows a debit balance of $3,200.
    (2) In prior years the company had not accrued estimated claims for injuries to customers as a result of using the company's products because such claims were covered by insurance. In the current year the company discontinued the insurance. A reasonable estimate of outstanding claims at the end of the current year is $25,000.
    (3) A former employee has sued the company for $500,000 because of age discrimination against him. Outside counsel does not think the suit has any merit but has suggested that the company pay the former employee an out-of-court settlement of $5,000, because the cost of defending the suit was estimated at $50,000. Blanc Paper agreed, and the former employee signed appropriate settlement papers.
    (4) The company has been sued for breach of contract. The plaintiff is seeking damages of $100,000. Management and legal counsel are of the opinion that the results of the litigation will be adverse and that the damages the court would find for the plaintiff would be a minimum of $10,000 and a maximum of $50,000. No amount within this range is a better estimate of potential damages than any other amount.
    (5) The company is a guarantor on notes receivable discounted at a bank in the amount of $150,000, including interest. The primary debtors on the notes are

financially sound companies, except one. The one debtor had issued a one-year 10% note of $20,000 to Blanc Paper Company. The note matures in 30 days, but the debtor's bankruptcy referee has estimated that only 40% of the maturity value of notes will be paid.

(6) A lower court has awarded $200,000 in damages to the Blanc Paper Company in a litigation in which the company was the plaintiff. The defendants have appealed the decision to a higher court, which is not expected to issue a decision for at least a year.

(7) During the current year the company discontinued collision coverage on its vehicles and has decided to be self-insured for this contingency. Actual losses of $15,000 during the year were debited to Delivery Expense. Because the premiums for collision insurance in past years averaged $45,000, the controller wants to set up a "reserve for self-insurance" by increasing the Delivery Expense account by $30,000.

(8) Management has requested you to record a provision for unspecified general business risks in the amount of $80,000 by a charge to an expense account.

Instructions For each contingency described above, prepare a journal entry to record the contingency or briefly explain why an entry would not be in accordance with generally accepted accounting principles.

10A-3 Account balances and other data relating to liabilities, obligations, and commitments of Gregory Corporation at December 31, Year 5, are as follows:

Accounts payable	$ 98,100
Notes payable	70,000
Discount on notes payable	4,100
Accounts receivable, excluding $40,000 which have been sold to a factor on a	
"recourse" basis	171,200
Bonds payable, $100,000 due at June 30 of each year	800,000
Retained earnings appropriated for general contingencies	45,000
Accrued payroll	4,280
Payroll taxes payable	620
Liability for income tax withheld	1,150
Property taxes payable	600
Allowance for purchase discounts	1,350
Stock dividends to be distributed (at par)	20,000
Income taxes payable	32,100
Deferred income taxes payable (resulting from use of accelerated depreciation	
method for income tax purposes)	145,000
Estimated liability for coupons outstanding	7,500
Unearned service contract revenue (contracts are for one year)	6,000
Loans from officers (renewed annually)	60,000

The company signed a contract on October 10, Year 5, to purchase merchandise in Year 6 at a fixed price of $60,000. This merchandise has a market value in excess of $62,400 on December 31, Year 5.

Instructions Prepare the current liability section of the balance sheet at December 31, Year 5, and list any contingent liabilities or commitments which should be disclosed.

10A-4 The general manager of Elliott Wood, Inc., wants to ask for a bonus based on income of the current period, which the general manager estimates will be approximately $495,000 before the bonus and before federal and state income taxes.

Instructions If the bonus rate is established at 10% and total income taxes amount to 50% of taxable income, compute the estimated amount of the bonus to the general manager under each of the following assumptions. (Round all answers to nearest dollar.)
a Bonus is based on income before both income taxes and the bonus.
b Bonus is based on income after the bonus but before income taxes.
c Bonus is based on income after both income taxes and the bonus.

10A-5 Selected transactions completed by Thomas Sales Company during the current year are described below:

(1) On February 20, the company had an opportunity to obtain for $60,000 a special stock of merchandise being closed out by a manufacturer. The company purchased the merchandise on February 23 and paid for it on March 1 by borrowing $60,000 from the Soho Bank, signing a note for $63,750, due on March 1 of next year. Assume that the company uses a periodic inventory system and that it records notes payable at face amount.

(2) On July 1, property taxes on the company's retail stores for the ensuing 12-month period became a lien against the property. The company treasurer estimated that property taxes for the year in the amount of $13,200 would be paid on November 1. (Do not record the payment of the tax on November 1 because the actual amount of the tax is not yet known.)

(3) On August 2, the company purchased $30,000 of merchandise from Y Company, terms 2/10, n/30; and $10,000 of merchandise from Z Company, terms 2/10, n/e.o.m. The company uses a periodic inventory system and records accounts payable net of cash discounts offered. The invoice from Y Company was paid on August 10, but the invoice from Z Company was not paid until August 25, and the cash discount was lost.

(4) On December 1, the sales department launched a special one-month promotion of one of the company's products. Included in each product package sold during December was a coupon which, if sent back to the company with $1 enclosed, entitled the customer to receive a toy. The sales manager estimated that 50% of the customers would accept the offer, which would cost the company 80 cents for each toy claimed plus 30 cents in packaging and shipping costs. The company purchased 50,000 toys for cash. During December, 100,000 of the products were sold for $3 each (debit Cash), and 30,000 coupons were presented for redemption. You should credit the Packaging and Shipping Expense account for 30 cents for each coupon redeemed because actual costs incurred in packaging and shipping were recorded in this account. At December 31, on the basis of experience to date, it was estimated that only 12,000 additional coupons will be presented by customers before the offer expires. Toys which will not be distributed as prizes can be sold for 40 cents each and the inventory of prize merchandise is written down accordingly by a charge to a Promotional Expense account.

Instructions
a Prepare journal entries to record the transactions described above.
b Assume that no entries have been made other than the entries to record the above transactions as they occurred. Prepare any necessary adjusting entries on December 31 relating to each of the four transactions.
c Prepare a list of accounts used in **(a)** and **(b)** and indicate the financial statement classification, that is, current asset, current liability, cost of goods sold, operating expense, etc., for each account.

10A-6 Canyon Mining Corporation started mining in the current year on certain land leased from Prairie Company. Canyon Mining had previously paid minimum royalties of $48,000 none of which was earned, during a three-year period prior to the current year. The royalty provisions in the lease are as follows:

(1) Minimum annual royalty is $16,000, with a minimum of $4,000 payable quarterly. Unearned minimum royalties may be recovered in any subsequent period from earned royalties in excess of minimum royalties.

(2) Earned royalty shall be 10 cents per ton shipped from the mine plus a per ton amount equal to 2% of the amount that the market value of the ore at the mine exceeds $4 per ton.

Operations for the current year are summarized below:

Quarter	Tons shipped	Market value at destination, per ton	Freight from mine to destination, per ton
1st	None		
2d	150,000	$11.50	$3.50
3d	300,000	12.50	3.50
4th	None		

Instructions

a Compute the amount of royalty to be paid to Prairie Company for the current year and the amount of unearned minimum royalty at the end of the current year.

b How should the unearned minimum royalty paid be reported on the balance sheet of Canyon Mining at the end of the current year?

10A-7 Household Distributing Company requests that you make an estimate of the company's product warranty obligation as of the end of the first six months of the current year.

The company manufactures television tubes and sells them under a six-month guarantee to replace defective tubes without charge. At the beginning of the year, the company reported a Liability for Product Warranty of $374,800. By June 30, this account had been reduced to $32,920 by charges for the net cost of defective tubes returned which had been sold in the previous year. The net cost of replacing defective tubes sold in the current year (January to May) was recorded in Product Warranty Expense.

The company began the current year expecting tube returns to equal 8% of the dollar volume of sales for the year. However, as a result of the introduction of new models during the year, this estimated percentage of returns was increased to 10% as of May 1. It is assumed that no tubes sold during a given month are returned in that month. Each tube is stamped with a date at the time of sale so that the warranty may be properly administered. The following table indicates the likely pattern of sales returns during the six-month period of the warranty, starting with the month following the sale of the tubes.

Month following sale	Percentage of total returns expected
First	20
Second	30
Third	20
Fourth–sixth (10% each month)	30

Gross sales of tubes for the first six months of the current year were:

January	$3,600,000	April	$2,850,000
February	3,300,000	May	2,000,000
March	4,100,000	June	1,960,000

The company's warranty also covers the payment of shipping cost on defective tubes returned and on new tubes sent out as replacement. This shipping cost averages approximately 10% of the sales price of the tubes returned. The manufacturing cost of the tubes is roughly 80% of the sales price, and the salvage value of returned tubes averages 20% of their sales price. Returned tubes on hand at the beginning of the year were thus valued in inventory at 20% of their original sales price.

Instructions
a Prepare a schedule in support of your estimate of the company's liability under its product warranty at June 30.
b Prepare the necessary adjusting journal entry at June 30. (Income tax considerations may be ignored.)

Group B

10B-1 Gallagher Company purchased from Cain, Inc., an office machine on December 31, Year 1, for the following consideration:

Cash	$ 4,350
Cancellation of an account receivable from Cain, Inc.	1,650
Note payable, non-interest-bearing, due on Dec. 31, Year 3	16,000
Total consideration	$22,000

The market rate of interest for transactions of this type was 10% compounded annually.

Instructions (Round all computations to the nearest dollar.)
a Prepare an entry to record the purchase of the office machine on December 31, Year 1. Use Appendix A to determine the present value of the note payable.
b Prepare an entry on December 31, Year 2, to record interest expense and on December 31, Year 3, to record interest expense and the payment of the note.
c Show how the note payable should be presented in the balance sheet at December 31, Year 2.

10B-2 At the end of the current period, the auditor for Madigan Toy Company found the following contingencies which have not been recorded in the accounting records:

(1) Doubtful accounts receivable are estimated at $6,000. The allowance for doubtful accounts had a credit balance of $1,110.
(2) Product warranty costs during the period have been debited to an expense account. The estimated liability for product warranty of $11,000 at the end of the preceding period was not changed during the current period. The estimated liability for product warranty costs at the end of the current period is $7,800.
(3) The company has been sued for industrial espionage and the damages sought by the plaintiff amount to $200,000. The company's outside counsel and management are of the opinion that the suit has merit and the amount of damages may range from a minimum of $25,000 to a maximum of $75,000. No amount within this range is a better estimate than any other amount.

(4) A former officer has threatened to sue the company for $1 million "to recover the contributions he made to the success of the company's marketing program" for which he was not compensated adequately. In the opinion of management and outside attorneys, the suit has absolutely no merit and probably will never be filed.

(5) The company has guaranteed a debt of $500,000 issued by certain affiliated companies. The affiliated companies are in a strong financial position and management does not consider that any of the companies will default on their debt.

(6) Management is of the opinion that $100,000 should be set aside for general business risks which cannot be identified at the present time.

(7) A foreign country in which the company has an investment with a carrying value of $350,000 has decided to expropriate all foreign-owned assets. This contingency is covered by insurance and the company expects to recover $800,000. The estimated fair value of the investment in the foreign country is $1 million.

(8) In the current year the company discontinued fire insurance coverage on its assets because the premiums of $195,000 per year were too high and because the company has never experienced a fire. Management has decided to be "self-insured" and wants to recognize insurance expense equal to the amount of annual premiums it had paid in recent years "in order not to distort the net income for the current year."

Instructions For each contingency described above, prepare a journal entry to record the contingency or explain why an entry would not be in accordance with generally accepted accounting principles.

10B-3 Listed below are selected transactions for Sabatini Corporation relating to current liabilities during the current fiscal year:

Jan. 10   Purchased merchandise for $25,000. A 2% discount is offered by suppliers. Sabatini Corporation records purchases and accounts payable net of discounts.

Jan. 19   Paid $16,660 on invoice of January 10. The invoice was billed to Sabatini Corporation for $17,000.

Jan. 31   Paid balance of January 10 invoice, $8,000, after the discount period.

Apr. 1   Issued one-year note to supplier in settlement of an invoice for $10,000 dated March 31. The invoice was recorded net of 2% purchase discount: that is, $9,800. The face amount of the note was $10,584, including interest at 8% on $9,800 for one year. The note was recorded at face amount.

Apr. 30   Wages for April were $8,000 before the following withholdings:

Income taxes $1,190

FICA, 6%   480

The company records payroll taxes at the end of each month in a Payroll Taxes Expense account. All wages for April are subject to 2.7% state unemployment tax and 0.7% federal unemployment tax.

May 20   The company declared dividends as follows:

Cash $18,000

Stock 5%

The dividends are scheduled for distribution to stockholders on June 25. There are 120,000 shares of $5 par value capital stock outstanding; the current market price of the stock is $30 per share. Debit Retained Earnings for total value of dividends.

June 25   Paid the cash dividend and distributed the stock dividend declared on May 20.

Dec. 31   The company sells service contracts on its products and credits Deferred Service Contract Revenue when payments from customers are received. For the current year, $7,400 of the service contract revenue is considered realized.

Dec. 31   Recognized interest expense for the current year on the note issued to supplier on April 1.

Instructions   Prepare journal entries to record the transactions listed above.

10B-4   Tuttle Imports, Inc., operates in a state which levies a 10% tax on corporate income after federal income taxes. The state income tax for any year is an allowable deduction in computing the federal income tax for that year, but is not allowable in computing the state income tax for that year. Federal income tax rates are 40% on all taxable income. During the current year, the corporation had $400,000 of income subject to both state and federal income taxes, before deduction for either state or federal income taxes.

Instructions

a   Compute the company's liability for both federal and state income taxes for the current year, and prepare a schedule proving that the computed amounts are consistent. (Round all amounts to the nearest dollar.)

b   Prepare a journal entry to record the income tax liabilities for the current year, and compute net income for the current year.

10B-5   Freshen-Up Corporation sells carbonated apple juice in six-packs, cases, and through vending machines. In order to promote the drink among teen-agers and others who might otherwise be indifferent to the product, the company inaugurated in Year 10 a promotional plan called "Drink-N-Win." For every 10 bottle caps and 10 cents turned in, customers receive an attractive ball-point pen and become eligible for a grand prize of $100 in cash, one of which is awarded for every 15,000 caps turned in. The company estimates that only 40% of bottle caps reaching the hands of customers will be presented for redemption. A summary of transactions for Year 10 follows:

(1)   Sold 3,000,000 bottles of apple juice for $1,510,600 cash.

(2)   Purchased 50,000 ball-point pens for $25,000 cash. Debit Inventory (Prize Merchandise).

(3)   Expenses paid in cash and directly attributable to the promotional plan, $4,100.

(4)   A total of 39,000 ball-point pens were distributed as prizes to customers and an appropriate number of grand prizes were awarded.

At the end of each year, the company recognizes a liability equal to the estimated cost of potential prizes outstanding. The 10 cents received for each pen is considered sufficient to cover the direct expenses of handling each request; therefore, neither the estimated direct expenses nor the potential remittances from customers are accrued in the accounts at the end of the year.

Instructions

a   Prepare journal entries, with appropriate explanations, to record the transactions relating to the promotional plan for Year 10. Expenses of the promotional plan are recorded in a Promotional Expense account.

b   Compute the balances in all accounts relating to the promotional plan and explain how each account would be reported in the financial statements for Year 10.

10B-6 Described below are selected transactions of Booker Clifton Company during the current year:

(1) The company is obligated under a rental contract calling for the payment of monthly rent of $1,000 in advance, plus an additional rent (payable by the tenth day of the following month) equal to 8% of the net income earned by its branch store, after both total rent and a 40% provision for income taxes have been deducted. Net operating income of the branch store during January (before rent and income taxes) was $20,000. Compute rent expense to the nearest dollar and debit Rent Expense for both the rent advance on January 1 and the accrual of rent on January 31. Income tax expense is recorded monthly.

(2) The company issues gift certificates in denominations of $5, $10, and $25. These certificates are redeemable in merchandise having an average gross profit of 25% of selling price. During March, the company sold $31,000 of gift certificates and redeemed certificates having a sales value of $27,400. It is estimated that 8% of the certificates issued will never be redeemed. The company uses a periodic inventory system and thus does not compute the cost of goods sold until the end of the fiscal year. The sales of gift certificates are recorded in an Estimated Liability for Gift Certificates Outstanding account.

(3) Sales during June totaled $310,800, of which $195,000 were on open account. The company operates in a state where there is a 6% sales tax. Included in the sales amount are sales taxes collected from customers on all items except food, which is exempt from sales tax. Food sales amounted to 40% of total sales before the sales tax was added.

(4) Salaries for November were $250,000, of which $80,000 represented amounts paid over $16,500, and $150,000 represented amounts paid over $6,000 to certain employees. Income tax withheld totaled $30,000, and FICA tax withholdings were at the rate of 6% (on wages up to $16,500 per year). The company is subject to a state unemployment tax rate of 2.7% and a federal unemployment tax rate of 0.7% (on wages up to $6,000 per year). Payroll taxes on the employer are recorded in separate expense accounts. The accrued payroll and related payroll tax liabilities are recorded in the same entry.

Instructions
a Prepare all necessary journal entries to record the transactions described above. An entry to record the accrual of income taxes for January should be made in part (1).
b Prepare a list of all current liability accounts involved in your journal entries in **a.**

10B-7 A descriptive summary of financial position of Irvine Produce Corporation at December 31, Year 8 is given on page 433.

Cash—includes an overdraft of $1,250 with Suburban Bank, receivables from
    employees of $300, and checks from customers of $3,500 dated January
    10, Year 9, which have been recorded as collections . . . . $ 40,300

Customers—includes notes of $20,000 (accrued interest of $800 has not been
    recorded), open accounts of $77,500 (including an uncollectible account of
    $1,200 which should be written off), and an allowance for doubtful accounts
    of $1,300. Aging of accounts indicates that an allowance of $4,200 is re-
    quired on December 31, Year 8. Customers' notes of $12,000 due in 90 days
    have been discounted at the bank 96,200

Inventory—includes worthless goods carried at $6,800, and goods held on
    consignment, $5,000, owned by P. F. Company 60,000

Prepayments—includes tools of $2,000, cash surrender value of life insurance
    of $3,100, long-term utility deposits of $1,000 12,500

Fixtures—net of $34,500 of accumulated depreciation 197,000

    Total assets $406,000

Current liabilities, recorded in a single account which includes the following:

  Note—due in three annual installments; interest at 7½% since
    Sept. 1, Year 8, has not been accrued in the accounts $45,000

  Accounts payable 46,000

  Payable to P. F. Company for consigned goods 5,000

  Estimated liability for coupons outstanding . . . . 1,500 $ 97,500

  (The company has been sued for damages of $25,000 but does
    not anticipate that any liability will result.)

Capital—125,000 shares of no-par stock issued for $120,000 (less 1,000 shares
    of treasury stock reacquired for $2,800) and retained earnings of $191,300 308,500

    Total liabilities & stockholders' equity $406,000

Instructions Prepare a revised balance sheet in good form, including notes. Ignore the income tax effect of any corrections to previously reported net income.
The use of a working paper to determine correct account balances is recommended. Use the following form:

Accounts	Unadjusted balances		Adjustments and corrections		Corrected balances	
	Debit	Credit	Debit	Credit	Debit	Credit

CHAPTER 11

LONG-TERM INVESTMENTS

In Chapter 6 we discussed investments in marketable securities, such as an investment in shares of General Motors stock or in American Telephone bonds. Such investments can readily be converted into cash and are classified as current assets. Many companies also make long-term investments in corporate securities to create close business ties with another company and thereby improve operating performance. These long-term investments should not be classified as current assets, because they do not represent liquid resources available to meet working capital needs.

The basis of distinction between the asset categories of marketable securities (Chapter 6) and long-term investments lies in the nature and purpose of the investment. Investments which are readily marketable and which can be sold without disrupting corporate policies or impairing the operating efficiency of the business should be classified as current assets. Investments made for the purpose of fostering operational relationships with other entities should be regarded as long-term investments. Also, investments which do not meet the test of ready marketability are usually classified as long-term investments, even if these investments do not promote operational relationships. Long-term investments are usually listed below the current asset section. The descriptive title often used in the balance sheet is "Investments" or "Investments and other assets."

Objectives of long-term investments

Companies may make long-term investments in the securities of other corporations for many reasons. For example, these investments may be used to create close ties to major suppliers or to retail outlets. The rights of ownership inherent in common stock investments give a company investing in such securities a degree of influence or control over the management of the owned company. Thus, many companies use investments in common stock as a means of gaining control of a competitor, acquiring ownership of a cash-rich company, or diversifying by acquiring an ownership interest in companies in other industries.

Consolidated financial statements

When one company acquires a controlling interest in the common stock of another, the controlling company is termed the *parent* and the controlled company the *subsidiary.* The investment in the common stock of the subsidiary is shown as a long-term investment in the separate balance sheet of the parent. In addition to the financial statements prepared by the parent company and by the subsidiary, *consolidated financial statements* may also be prepared. Consolidated financial statements ignore the legal concept that each corporation is a separate entity and treat the parent and subsidiary companies as a single economic entity.

Viewing both companies as a single economic entity is an alternative to treating the subsidiary as an investment owned by the parent company. The circumstances in which consolidated financial statements are appropriate and the manner in which they are prepared are topics discussed extensively in *Modern Advanced Accounting* of this series.

Cost at acquisition

The cost of an investment in securities includes the purchase price plus brokerage fees, transfer taxes, and any other expenditures incurred in the transaction. If assets other than cash are given in payment for the securities and the fair value of such noncash assets is unknown, the current market price of the securities may be used to establish the cost of the securities and the value of the noncash assets given in exchange. When neither a market price for the securities nor the fair value of the assets given in exchange is known, the accountant must rely on independent appraisals to establish dollar values for recording the transaction.

If two or more securities are acquired for a lump-sum payment, the total cost should be allocated between the two classes of securities. If the various classes of securities so purchased are traded in the market, the existing market prices serve as the basis for apportioning the total cost. This type of cost apportionment is termed a *relative sales value allocation.*

Assume, for example, that X Company acquires from Y Company 100 units, of five common shares and one preferred share each, at a price of $240 per unit, when the common is selling for $30 and the preferred for $100 per share. The portion of the cost allocated to the common stock is $24,000 × 150/250, or $14,400, and the part allocable to the preferred stock is $24,000 × 100/250, or $9,600. If only one class of the stock is actively traded, that class will usually be recorded at the market price and the remaining portion of the cost will be considered the cost of the other class. When neither class of stock has an established market, the apportionment of the cost may have to be delayed until a fair value of the securities can be established.

ACCOUNTING FOR INVESTMENTS IN STOCKS

Measuring return on investment

What is the "return" on an investment in common stock? One school of thought holds that the stockholder's return consists of the stream of dividends received from the investment. A second point of view is that the common stockholder's return consists of a proportionate share of the net income (minus preferred dividends, if any) of the owned company, without regard to whether this income is actually distributed during the period in the form of dividends. Supporting this second viewpoint is the fact that the earnings of the owned company which are not distributed as dividends are retained by the company, causing an increase in stockholders' equity. A third interpretation of the stockholder's return is the dividends received plus (or minus) the change in the market value of the investment.

Three different accounting methods exist, depending upon which return an investor wishes to measure. These methods are:

1 *Cost method.* Investment income consists only of dividends received.
2 *Equity method.* Investment income consists of the stockholder's proportionate share of the owned company's net income.
3 *Market value method.* Investment income includes dividends received and changes in the market value of the investment.

The market value method (as a logical alternative to the cost method) was illustrated for use with marketable securities in Chapter 6. However, the market value method is much less appropriate with respect to long-term investments. By definition, long-term investments are not held for purposes of taking advantage of short-term fluctuations in market prices. When the investor is committed to holding an investment in securities for longer periods of time, the daily changes in market price lose much of their significance. Therefore, it is the cost and equity methods which are generally used to account for long-term investments in common stock.

Accounting for dividends received

When a company owns only a small portion (for example, less than 20%) of the total outstanding common stock of another company, the company owning the investment (termed *investor*) has little or no control over the other company (termed *investee*). In this case, the investor cannot influence the investee's dividend policy, and the only portion of the investee's income which reaches the investor is the dividends paid by the investee. Thus, when the investor has little or no control over the investee, the dividends received represent the only return realized by the investor. Under these circumstances, the cost method of accounting for the investment is appropriate.

The payment of dividends on common stock is a discretionary act, requiring that the directors of a corporation first declare the dividend. For this reason, investors should not accrue dividend revenue, as they do with interest revenue on a bond. There are three acceptable alternatives for timing the recognition of dividend revenue: (1) when the dividend is declared (declaration date), (2) when the dividend will be received by the current stockholder even if the stock is subsequently sold (ex-dividend date), or (3) when the dividend is received (payment date). For the purpose of consistency, all illustrations in this chapter will recognize dividend revenue at the date the dividend is actually received.

Not all dividends received represent revenue to the stockholder. Sometimes corporations may pay dividends in excess of total profits. In such cases the amount by which the cash distribution exceeds total profits to date is considered a return of capital, termed a *liquidating dividend,* rather than dividend revenue.

Some accountants have suggested that from the viewpoint of any given stockholder, a liquidating dividend may be deemed to have occurred if dividends received exceed total profits earned subsequent to the date the investment was acquired. Practical application of such a concept would be difficult, because corporations do not measure profits on a daily basis, whereas the acquisition of shares by individual investors occurs every day in the year. Moreover, some large investors make a series of purchases of a given company's shares in order to acquire a desired position without disrupting the market. Only in very special circumstances would a stockholder be able to determine that a dividend received represented profits earned prior to the date of a specific acquisition of shares.

For income tax purposes, liquidating dividends are defined with respect to the company paying the dividend, rather than with respect to individual investors. Tax laws recognize liquidating dividends only to the extent that total dividends paid exceed total profits earned **over the** *life of the company* paying the dividend. Under this legal interpretation, a stockholder acquiring shares from a previous stockholder "steps into his shoes" with respect to the distinction between dividend revenue and return of capital.

Applying the cost method

When the cost method is used, the investment account is maintained in terms of the cost of the shares acquired. Revenue is recognized only to the extent of dividends received which do not exceed the cumulative earnings from the date the shares were acquired. Changes in the assets of the investee are ignored unless a *significant* and *permanent* impairment of value of the investment occurs. Finally, long-term investments in equity securities may be written down to a lower of cost or market as required by *FASB Statement No. 12.* The three events which may cause a departure from the cost basis are discussed below:

Liquidating Dividends When the cost method is used, ordinary dividends received from an investee are treated the same as dividends on any other investment. Ordinary profits or losses of the investee are recognized by the investor only when and to the extent that dividends are distributed or when realized as a gain or loss at the time the shares are sold. However, any liquidating dividends received are recorded by reducing the Investment account.

Permanent Impairment in Value of Investment Operating losses of the investee, which reduce the investee's net assets substantially and which seriously impair its future prospects, are recognized as losses by the investor. A portion of the long-term investment has been lost and this fact is recorded by reducing the carrying value of the investment account. The following excerpt from *FASB Statement No. 12* supports this approach:

> If the decline is judged to be other than temporary, the cost basis of the individual security shall be written down to a new cost basis and the amount of the write-down shall be accounted for as a realized loss. The new cost basis shall not be changed for subsequent recoveries in market value.[1]

The journal entry to record such losses is:

Realized Loss in Value of Long-Term Investments	*XXX*	
Investments in Common Stocks		*XXX*
To record a significant and permanent decline in value of long-term		
investments in common stocks.		

[1] *FASB Statement No. 12,* "Accounting for Certain Marketable Securities," FASB (Stamford: 1975), p. 11.

Although **FASB Statement No. 12** gave little guidance for the determination of the existence of a permanent impairment in the value of long-term investments, consideration should be given to the following:

1 The length of time the security has been owned

2 The length of time the security has been below cost and the extent of the decline

3 The financial condition and prospects of the investee company

4 The financial condition of the investor company

5 The materiality of the decline in value of the investment in relation to the net income and stockholders' equity of the investor company

Valuation at Lower of Cost or Market Special accounting procedures are required when the aggregate market value of a long-term portfolio of equity securities, accounted for by the *cost method,* is below cost. Such a portfolio should be valued at the lower of cost or market. However, in contrast to the valuation of the current portfolio of marketable equity securities discussed in Chapter 6, the unrealized loss in value of a noncurrent portfolio of equity securities *is not included in net income.* Instead such unrealized losses are reported as reductions in stockholders' equity.[2]

To illustrate the valuation of long-term investments on the basis of lower of cost or market, assume the following: Early in Year 1, Investor Company made a long-term investment of $100,000 in the common stock of a publicly owned corporation. The market value of the investment was $80,000 at the end of Year 1 and $92,000 at the end of Year 2. The journal entries to value the long-term investment at lower of cost of market are:

End of Year 1

Unrealized Loss in Value of Long-Term Investment in Equity Securities	20,000	
Valuation Allowance to Reduce Long-Term Investment to Market Value		20,000

To establish valuation allowance for decline in market value of long-term investment in equity securities.

End of Year 2

Valuation Allowance to Reduce Long-Term Investment to Market Value	12,000	
Unrealized Loss in Value of Long-Term Investment in Equity Securities		12,000

To reduce the valuation allowance for decline in market value of long-term investment in equity securities to a balance of $8,000 required at the end of Year 2.

---

[2] Ibid., p. 7.

The balance sheets at the end of each year would include the following information:

	Year 1	Year 2
Investments:		
Long-term investment in equity securities, at cost .	$ 100,000	$ 100,000
Less: Valuation allowance to reduce long-term		
investment to market value	20,000	8,000
Long-term investment in equity securities, at lower		
of cost or market	$ 80,000	$ 92,000
Stockholders' equity:		
Total paid-in capital and retained earnings	$XXX,XXX	$XXX,XXX
Unrealized loss in value of long-term investment in		
equity securities	(20,000)	(8,000)
Total stockholders' equity	$XXX,XXX	$XXX,XXX

If the long-term investment is sold at a price below cost, a **realized loss** is recorded and the unrealized loss account and the allowance account are eliminated. For example, assume that in Year 3 Investor Company sold the investment described above for $75,000. The sale would be recorded as follows:

Cash	75,000	
Realized Loss on Sale of Long-Term Investment	25,000	
Valuation Allowance to Reduce Long-Term Investment to		
Market Value	8,000	
Long-Term Investment in Equity Securities		100,000
Unrealized Loss in Value of Long-Term Investment		
in Equity Securities		8,000
To record sale of long-term investment.		

Applying the equity method

When the investor owns enough stock in the investee to exercise significant control over the investee's management, the dividends paid by the investee may no longer be a good measure of the return on the investment. This is because the investor may control the investee's dividend policy. In such a case, dividends paid by the investee are likely to reflect the **investor's** tax considerations and cash needs, rather than the profitability of the investment.

For example, assume that one company owns all the stock in another company. For two years the subsidiary is very profitable but pays no dividends, because the parent company has no need for additional cash. In the third year, the subsidiary has operating losses but pays a large dividend to the parent company. Clearly, it would be misleading to report no investment income for the parent company while its fully owned subsidiary was operating profitably, and then to show large investment income in a year when the subsidiary operated at a loss.

The investee need not be fully owned for the investor to have a significant degree of control. When the stock of the investee is widely held, an investor with much less than 50% of the stock may have effective control, since it is doubtful that the remaining outstanding shares will vote as an organized block.

When the equity method is used, an investment is initially recorded at the cost of the shares acquired but is then adjusted for changes in the net assets of the investee subsequent to acquisition. The investor's proportionate share of the investee's net income is recognized as investment income, causing an increase in the investment account. If the investee's net income includes extraordinary items, the investor company should treat its share of such items as extraordinary (if material in amount to the investor), rather than as ordinary investment income. Dividends paid by the investee are treated by the investor as a conversion of the investment into cash, causing the investment account to decrease.

For example, assume that Par Company purchases 40% of the common stock of I Company for $300,000, which corresponds to the underlying carrying value. During the subsequent period, I Company reports a net income of $70,000 (including a $10,000 extraordinary gain) and pays dividends of $30,000. Par Company would account for its investment as follows:

Investment in I Company	300,000	
Cash		300,000
To record acquisition of 40% of the common stock of		
I Company at carrying value.		
Investment in I Company	28,000	
Investment Income (ordinary)		24,000
Investment Income (extraordinary)		4,000
To record 40% of net income of I Company (40% × $60,000		
= $24,000; 40% × $10,000 = $4,000).		
Cash	12,000	
Investment in I Company		12,000
To record dividends received from I Company (40% ×		
$30,000 = $12,000).		

Note that the net effect of Par Company's accounting for I Company's net income and dividends was to increase the investment account by $16,000. This corresponds to 40% of the increase reported in I Company's net assets during the period [40% × ($70,000 − $30,000) = $16,000].

Special Problems in Applying the Equity Method Two special problems often arise in applying the equity method. First, intercompany profits and losses resulting from transactions between the investor and investee must be eliminated until realized by a transaction with an unaffiliated entity. This special problem is discussed in *Modern Advanced Accounting* of this series. Second, when the acquisition cost of an investment differs from the carrying value of the underlying net assets, adjustments may have to be made to the investment income recognized by the investor.

Cost in Excess of Carrying Value Often an investor will pay more than the underlying carrying value of an investment because current fair values of the investee's assets may be greater than their carrying values, or because the investee possesses unrecorded goodwill. In either case, this excess of cost over the underlying carrying value will benefit the investor only over the economic lives of the undervalued (or unrecorded) assets.

To the extent that the excess of cost over carrying value was paid to acquire an interest in specific undervalued assets, this amount should be amortized over the economic lives of those assets. The journal entry to reflect the amortization would be:

Investment Income	XXX	
Investment in Partially Owned Company		XXX
To adjust investment income for amortization of excess of cost		
over carrying value.		

To the extent that the excess cost was incurred because of implied goodwill, the amount should be amortized over the estimated economic life of the goodwill. The Accounting Principles Board has taken the position in *Opinion No. 17* that amounts paid for goodwill should be amortized over a period of not more than 40 years.[3] As a practical matter, if the excess of the cost over the underlying carrying value is small, it is usually amortized as goodwill, rather than attempting to associate it with specific assets.

---

[3] *APB Opinion No. 17,* "Intangible Assets," AICPA (New York: 1970), p. 340.

Cost Less than Carrying Value In some cases, an investor may acquire an investment in common stock at a cost less than the underlying carrying value. In this event, it should be assumed that specific assets of the investee are overvalued. If these assets are depreciable, the investor should amortize the excess of carrying value over cost into investment income over the economic lives of the assets. The journal entry to reflect this amortization would be:

Investment in Partially Owned Company XXX
    Investment Income XXX
To adjust investment income for amortization of excess of carrying value over cost.

Note that this adjustment increases investment income. The rationale for this action is that the investee's reported net income is actually understated, because the investee has recorded depreciation or amortization based on overstated asset values.

Summary of Procedures under the Equity Method Accounting procedures under the equity method may be summarized as follows:

1 The investment is initially recorded at cost.

2 The investor subsequently records its proportionate share of the investee's reported net income (after elimination of intercompany profits) by debiting the investment account and crediting Investment Income. In event of a loss, Investment Loss would be debited and the investment account credited.

3 The investor views its share of dividends paid by the investee as a conversion of the investment into cash. Thus, the investor debits Cash and credits the investment account.

4 The investor adjusts the income or loss it has recognized by the amortization of any excess of cost over underlying carrying value associated with depreciable assets or goodwill. This adjustment consists of debiting Investment Income (or Loss) and crediting the investment account.

5 The investor adjusts the income or loss it has recognized by the amortization of any excess of underlying carrying value of assets over cost by debiting the investment account and crediting Investment Income (or Loss).

Illustration of the cost and equity methods

To illustrate the differences in the cost and equity methods, assume that on January 1 of the current year P Company buys 4,000 shares (20%) of the common stock of S Company for $1,000,000. At the date of acquisition, the carrying value of S Company's net assets was $4,550,000. P Company was willing to pay more than carrying value for the investment because it was estimated that S Company owned land worth $100,000 more than its carrying value, depreciable assets worth $150,000 more than their carrying values, and enough goodwill to make a 20% interest in S Company worth the $1,000,000 purchase price.

The excess of the cost of the investment over the underlying carrying value may be evaluated as follows:

Cost of investment	$1,000,000
Underlying carrying value (20% × $4,550,000)	910,000
Excess of cost over carrying value	$ 90,000
Composition of the excess:	
20% interest in undervalued land (20% × $100,000)	$ 20,000
20% interest in undervalued depreciable assets (20% × $150,000)	30,000
Implied purchase of goodwill ($90,000 − $20,000 − $30,000)	40,000
Excess of cost over carrying value	$ 90,000

The undervalued depreciable assets have an average remaining life of 10 years, and P Company's policy with respect to goodwill is to amortize over 40 years.

During the current year, S Company reported net income of $430,000, including an extraordinary loss of $50,000, and paid dividends at year-end of $200,000. P Company's accounting for its investment in S Company during the year is illustrated below, using both the cost and equity methods:

Step 1 To record acquisition on January 1 of 4,000 shares of S Company stock:

Cost Method		
Investment in S Company Stock	1,000,000	
Cash		1,000,000

Equity Method		
Investment in S Company Stock	1,000,000	
Cash		1,000,000

Step 2 To record on December 31 P Company's $86,000 share (20% × $430,000) of S Company's reported net income, consisting of a $96,000 share of income before extraordinary items, and a $10,000 share of the extraordinary loss:

Cost Method

No entry.

Equity Method

Investment Loss (extraordinary) 10,000
Investment in S Company Stock 86,000
           Investment Income (ordinary) 96,000

Step 3 To record on December 31 a $40,000 dividend (20% × $200,000) received from S Company:

Cost Method

Cash 40,000
      Dividend Revenue 40,000

Equity Method

Cash 40,000
      Investment in S Company Stock 40,000

Step 4 To amortize on December 31 a portion of investment cost over carrying value representing (1) a 20% interest in S Company's undervalued depreciable assets ($30,000 ÷ 10 years = $3,000 per year) and (2) a 20% interest in S Company's implied goodwill ($40,000 ÷ 40 years = $1,000 per year):

Cost Method

No entry.

Equity Method

Investment Income (ordinary) 4,000
      Investment in S Company Stock 4,000

Note that no adjustment is made under either method for the $20,000 excess of cost over carrying value representing P Company's 20% interest in S Company's undervalued land. This is because land is a permanent asset, and its cost is not depreciated. The results for the current year are illustrated for both methods on page 446.

	Cost method	Equity method
Investment in S Company stock (ending balance)	$1,000,000	$1,042,000
Investment income recognized by P Company:		
Ordinary	$ 40,000	$ 92,000
Extraordinary loss		$ (10,000)

Selecting the appropriate method

When the investor has a significant degree of control over the investee, the equity method better describes the benefits accruing to the investor than does the cost method. When the investor has little or no control over the investee, the benefits received by the investor may be limited to the dividends received, indicating the cost method to be more appropriate. The key criterion in selecting between the methods is the *degree of control* the investor is able to exercise over the investee.

The Accounting Principles Board recognized that the point at which an investor has a significant degree of control may not always be clear. To achieve a degree of uniformity in accounting practice, the APB took the position in *Opinion No. 18* that "an investment (direct or indirect) of 20% or more of the voting stock of an investee should lead to a presumption that in absence of evidence to the contrary an investor has the ability to exercise significant influence over an investee."[4] Thus, investments representing 20% or more of the voting stock are usually accounted for by the equity method, and investments of less than 20% by the cost method. Investments in preferred stock should be accounted for by the cost method, because preferred stockholders usually do not have voting rights and also do not have a residual interest in net income.

ACCOUNTING FOR INVESTMENTS IN BONDS

A bond contract represents a promise to pay a sum of money at maturity and a series of interest payments during the life of the contract. Investors buy corporate bonds to earn a return on investment. The effective rate of return (yield) on fixed-income securities to the investor is determined by the price investors pay for the securities (since the terms of the contract are fixed); it may differ from the effective interest cost to the borrower since the securities may have been issued at an earlier date at a different price.

[4] *APB Opinion No. 18,* "The Equity Method of Accounting for Investments in Common Stock," AICPA (New York: 1971), p. 355.

Computing the present value of an investment in bonds

The cost of an investment in bonds is the present value of the future money receipts promised in the contract, measured in terms of the market rate of interest prevailing at the time of purchase. The stated rate of interest in the bond contract measures the cash to be received semi-annually by the investor. If the rate of return demanded by investors is exactly equal to the coupon rate, the bond can be purchased at the face amount. If the market rate of interest has risen, the bond contract can be purchased at a *discount* because the buyer is demanding a higher return than the contract offers; therefore, to equate the yield on the bond with the market rate of interest, the contract is purchased at a price below face amount. If the market rate of interest is below the rate stated in the bond, the investor will be willing to pay a *premium* for the bond, that is, a price above face amount.

To illustrate the computation of the purchase price of bonds, assume that $200,000 of 7% bonds maturing in 15 years are purchased by Kane Company to yield 8% compounded semiannually. The bonds pay interest semiannually starting six months from date of purchase. Because the yield rate exceeds the coupon rate, the bonds are purchased at a discount, as determined below using Appendix A:

Present value of $200,000 discounted at 4% for 30 six-month periods:
$200,000 × 0.308319 . . . . $ 61,664
Add: Present value of ordinary annuity of 30 rents of $7,000
       (semiannual interest payments) discounted at 4%: $7,000 ×
       17.292033   121,044
Purchase price of bonds (discount of $17,292) $182,708*

* Alternative computation: $200,000 − ($1,000 semiannual interest deficiency × 17.292033) = $182,708.

If the current market rate of interest was only 6% compounded semi-annually, the bonds would be purchased at a premium as determined below:

Present value of $200,000 discounted at 3% for 30 six-month periods:
$200,000 × 0.411987 . . . . $ 82,397
Add: Present value of ordinary annuity of 30 rents of $7,000 dis-
       counted at 3%: $7,000 × 19.600441   137,203
Purchase price of bonds (premium of $19,600) $219,600*

* Alternative computation: $200,000 + ($1,000 × 19.600441) = $219,600.

Acquisition between interest dates

Interest on bond contracts accrues with the passage of time in accordance with the provisions of the contract. The issuing corporation pays the contractual rate of interest on the stated day to the person holding the bond on that day. The investor who buys a bond between interest dates must pay the owner the market price of the bond plus the interest accrued since the last interest payment. The investor is paying the owner of the bond the interest applicable to the first portion of the interest period and will in turn collect that portion plus the additional interest earned by holding the bond to the next interest date.

Illustration On July 1, Capitol Company acquired 10 bonds of Ray Company which were issued several years ago. The bond contract provides for interest at 8% per annum payable semiannually on April 1 and October 1. The market rate of interest is higher than 8% at the present time and the bonds are currently quoted at $97\frac{3}{4}$ plus accrued interest for three months. The entry to record the acquisition of the 10 bonds is:

Investment in Ray Company Bonds	*9,775*	
Accrued Interest Receivable	*200*	
Cash		*9,975*
To record the purchase of 10 bonds plus accrued interest of		
$200 for three months.		

Discount and premium on bond investments

At the date of acquisition, the investment account is usually debited for the cost of acquiring the bonds, including brokerage and other fees but excluding the accrued interest. The use of a separate discount or premium account as a valuation account is acceptable procedure; however, it is seldom used. The subsequent treatment of the investment might conceivably be handled in any one of three ways: (1) The investment might be carried at cost, ignoring the accumulation of discount or amortization of premium; (2) the investment account might be revalued periodically to conform to market conditions; (3) the discount or premium might be systematically accumulated or amortized to reflect the change in the carrying value of the bonds based on the effective rate of interest prevailing at the time of purchase.

The first alternative (the cost basis) is used primarily in accounting for temporary investments, as discussed in Chapter 6, for convertible bonds, and for other bonds for which the discount or premium is insignificant. The discount or premium on convertible bonds is seldom related to the level of interest rates but rather reflects the effect of the price of the security into which the bond may be converted. These securities are subject to wide price movements related to changes in the market price of common stocks; therefore, the amortization of premium or accumulation of discount does not seem appropriate.

The second alternative (valuation at market) is not in accord with the present interpretation of the realization principle or the doctrine of conservatism, especially during periods of rising bond prices. Changes in market prices of bonds held as long-term investments may be of less significance to the investor than changes in prices of short-term investments since the long-term investments are frequently held to maturity, at which time market price and face amount of the bonds are equal. When the investment in bonds is in jeopardy because of serious cash shortages by the issuing corporation, it is generally acceptable to write the investment down to its expected realizable value and recognize the loss.

The third alternative (the systematic accumulation and amortization) is the preferred treatment for long-term investments in bonds. This approach recognizes the fact that the revenue represented by the discount, or the reduction in revenue represented by the premium, does not come into being instantaneously at maturity but accrues over the life of the bonds. The revenue earned should be consistent with the circumstances surrounding the bonds at the date of purchase. This method is also consistent with the principle that assets should be accounted for at cost.

Interest revenue

The periodic interest payments provided for in a bond contract will represent the total investment revenue to an investor holding a bond to maturity only if the investor purchased the bond for its face amount. If an investor purchases a bond at a premium, the amount received upon maturity of the bond will be less than the amount of the initial investment, thus reducing the cumulative investment revenue by the amount of the premium. Similarly, if the bond is purchased at a discount, the maturity value will be greater than the initial investment, thereby increasing the cumulative investment revenue by the amount of the discount.

When a bondholder intends to hold an investment in bonds to maturity, there is little logic in treating the discount or premium as a gain or loss occurring instantaneously on the maturity date. Rather, the increase in bond value as a discount disappears should be viewed as part of the compensation accruing to the bondholder over the entire period the bonds are owned. Similarly, the decrease in value when a premium disappears is a cost the investor is willing to incur over the entire holding period to receive periodic interest payments higher than the market rates prevailing when the investment was acquired. Thus, the amount of the discount or premium should be viewed as an integral part of the periodic interest revenue earned by the investor. The accumulation of a discount increases periodic interest revenue, and amortization of a premium decreases periodic interest revenue.

An extreme illustration of this concept has occurred in certain government savings bonds which provided no periodic interest payments at all. Instead, these bonds sold at a large discount, and the gradual growth in the redemption value of the bonds toward their maturity value (accumulation of the discount) was the bondholder's only return. Although the bondholder received no cash proceeds until the bonds matured, interest revenue was still being earned. To measure the periodic interest revenue, the accumulation of the discount had to be recognized as interest revenue over the life of the bonds.

Methods of discount accumulation or premium amortization

The methods of discount and premium amortization for the issuing corporation are discussed in Chapter 15. These methods present precisely the same problem for the investor as for the issuer. The purpose of accumulating the discount or amortizing the premium systematically is to reflect accurately the interest revenue derived from the investment in bonds.

Straight-Line Method Under the straight-line method, the discount or premium is spread uniformly over the life of the investment. Although the bonds may be sold by the investor or redeemed by the issuer prior to maturity, the accumulation or amortization is always based on the years remaining to maturity. The straight-line method is simple to apply and avoids the necessity for determining the yield rate. The primary objection to this method is that it produces a constant interest revenue each period, which results in a variable rate of return on the investment.

Interest Method The interest method produces a constant rate of return on the investment. That is, the periodic interest revenue will always represent the same percentage return on the carrying value of the investment. Thus, when a discount is being accumulated and the investment account is increasing, the interest revenue recognized each period will also have to increase. This is accomplished by accumulating an ever-increasing portion of the discount each period. To apply the method, the interest revenue is computed every period by multiplying the balance of the investment account by the effective interest rate. The accumulation of the discount (or amortization of the premium) will then be the difference between the periodic cash receipt and the computed interest revenue.

Illustration The computation of periodic discount to be accumulated or premium to be amortized and the related journal entries will be illustrated using the examples for Kane Company given on page 447. The Kane Company examples involved (1) the purchase of $200,000 face amount of 7% bonds maturing in 15 years (or 30 semiannual periods) to yield 8% compounded semiannually and (2) the purchase of the same bonds to yield 6% compounded semiannually. The journal entries to record the investment, receipt of interest for the first year, and the related accumulation or amortization using the straight-line and interest methods are presented on pages 452 and 453. (All computations are rounded to the nearest dollar.)

When the bonds were acquired at a discount, the investment account was increased to $183,016 at the end of the first six-month period; therefore, the interest revenue for the second six-month period was computed at $7,321 ($183,016 × 4% = $7,321), which required $321 of the discount to be accumulated. When the bonds were acquired at a premium, the investment account was reduced to $219,188 at the end of the first six-month period; therefore, the interest revenue for the second six-month period was computed at $6,576 ($219,188 × 3% = $6,576), which required $424 of the premium to be amortized.

The interest earned on bond investments, like interest earned on any other investment, is accrued only at significant dates. The significant dates are: (1) interest payment dates, (2) the end of the investor's accounting period, and (3) the time of any transaction involving the particular investment which does not coincide with a regular interest payment date.

The interest on bond investments must be accrued, therefore, at the end of the accounting period and before the bonds are sold. The discount should be accumulated or the premium amortized in accordance with whatever method is being used. Regardless of whether the straight-line method or the interest method is used, amortization between interest dates may be allocated on the straight-line basis for the fractional period as a matter of convenience.

SPECIAL PROBLEMS IN ACCOUNTING FOR SECURITIES

Cost identification

Securities, like inventories, may pose a problem as to which costs should be offset against revenue in the period of sale. Assume, for instance, that Y Company buys 1,000 shares of Z Company common stock at a price of $80 per share, and that later it acquires another 1,000 shares at $90 per share. Several years later, Y Company sells 1,000 shares of Z Company common stock for $84 per share. Should Y Company recognize a $4,000 gain or a $6,000 loss?

The solution to this problem requires making a *cost flow assumption,* as with inventories. Since securities are usually identified by a certifi-

	Straight-line method		Interest method	
Bonds purchased to yield 8% compounded semiannually:				
Investment in 7% Bonds	182,708		182,708	
Cash		182,708		182,708
To record purchase of bonds at a discount of $17,292 to be accumulated over 30 six-month periods.				
Cash	7,000		7,000	
Investment in 7% Bonds	576		308	
Interest Revenue		7,576		7,308
To record receipt of interest at the end of the first six-month period: $200,000 × 7% × ½ = $7,000. Accumulation of discount: Straight-line method: $17,292 ÷ 30 = $576. Interest method: ($182,708 × 4%) − $7,000 = $308.				
Cash	7,000		7,000	
Investment in 7% Bonds	576		321	
Interest Revenue		7,576		7,321
To record receipt of interest at the end of the second six-month period: $200,000 × 7% × ½ = $7,000. Accumulation of discount: Straight-line method: $17,292 ÷ 30 = $576. Interest method: [($182,708 + $308) × 4%] − $7,000 = $321.				
Bonds purchased to yield 6% compounded semiannually:				
Investment in 7% Bonds	219,600		219,600	
Cash		219,600		219,600
To record purchase of bonds at a premium of $19,600 to be amortized over 30 six-month periods.				

	Straight-line method		Interest method	
Cash	7,000		7,000	
Investment in 7% Bonds . . .		653		412
Interest Revenue		6,347		6,588

To record receipt of interest at the
end of the first six-month period:
$200,000 \times 7\% \times \frac{1}{2} = \$7,000$.
Amortization of premium:
  Straight-line method: $19,600 ÷
  30 = $653.
  Interest method: $7,000
    ($219,600 \times 3\%) = $412.

	Straight-line method		Interest method	
Cash	7,000		7,000	
Investment in 7% Bonds . . .		653		424
Interest Revenue		6,347		6,576

To record receipt of interest at the
end of the second six-month
period: $200,000 \times 7\% \times \frac{1}{2} = \$7,000$.
Amortization of premium:
  Straight-line method: $19,600 ÷
  30 = $653.
  Interest method: $7,000 −
    [($219,600 − $412) \times 3\%] = $424.

cate number, it would be possible to use specific identification of stock
certificates in establishing the cost of the 1,000 shares sold. However,
some alternative cost flow assumption might be adopted. These alternative methods of cost flow include: (1) fifo—the first shares acquired are
assumed to be the first ones sold: (2) lifo—the last shares acquired are
assumed to be the first ones sold; and (3) weighted-average cost—each
share of a given security investment is assigned the same cost basis.

Income tax rules require the use of either the specific identification
method or the fifo method in measuring **taxable gain or loss.** Neither lifo
nor weighted-average cost is an acceptable method for income tax purposes. The specific identification method is usually more advantageous
for income tax purposes, because it allows the taxpayer to select for
sale those particular certificates which will lead to the most desirable
tax consequences. For accounting purposes, most firms use the same
method of cost selection used for income tax purposes in order to simplify record keeping. From a theoretical viewpoint, however, weighted
average is the only flow assumption that recognizes the economic

equivalence of identical securities. In our above illustration of successive purchases of the stock of Z Company at different prices, it is undeniable that each share of Z Company stock owned has exactly the same economic value regardless of the price paid to acquire it. The weighted-average flow assumption recognizes the economic reality that, except for tax purposes, it really makes no difference which 1,000-share certificate is sold and which is retained.

Accounting for stock dividends and stock splits

Stock dividends and stock splits do not result in income to investors. The income tax regulations are in agreement with financial accounting standards on this point.

> Since a shareholder's interest in the corporation remains unchanged by a stock dividend or split-up except as to the number of share units constituting such interest, the cost of the shares previously held should be allocated equitably to the total shares held after receipt of the stock dividend or split-up. When any shares are later disposed of, a gain or loss should be determined on the basis of the adjusted cost per share.[5]

The accounting procedure by the investor to record receipt of additional shares from a stock dividend or stock split is usually confined to a memorandum entry which indicates the number of shares received and the new cost per share.

Property dividends

When a company distributes a dividend in the form of merchandise, securities of other companies, or other noncash assets, the investor records the property received at its current fair value. Income tax regulations also require this use of current fair value for property dividends received.

Stock purchase warrants and stock rights

A *stock warrant* is a certificate issued by a corporation conveying to the holder *rights* to purchase shares of its stock at a specified price within a specified time period. A single right attaches to each share of outstanding stock and several rights are usually required to purchase one new share at the stipulated price. For example, when rights are issued, the owner of 100 shares of common stock will receive a warrant representing 100 rights and specifying the number of rights required to purchase one new share of stock. The life of these rights is usually limited to a few weeks. They must be exercised or sold before the expiration date or they become worthless.

[5] *Accounting Research and Terminology Bulletins—Final Edition,* AICPA (New York: 1961), chap. 7b, p. 51.

Accounting for Stock Warrants Acquired by Purchase The accounting problems involved when an investor buys warrants are similar to those relating to the acquisition of any security. The purchase price, plus brokerage fees and other acquisition costs, is debited to Investment in Warrants and the credit is to Cash. When warrants are acquired as a part of a package, the total cost must be allocated to the various securities included in the package.

When the warrants are used to acquire stock, the initial cost of the warrants used plus the cash required to complete the purchase is the cost of the stock. The Investment in Stock is debited; Cash and the Investment in Warrants are credited. If the market price of the stock is greater or less than this combined cost, this fact is ignored until the stock is sold, at which time a gain or loss is recognized.

Accounting for Stock Rights Stock rights are distributed to the stockholders of a corporation in proportion to their holdings. The receipt of a stock right can be compared to the receipt of a stock dividend. The corporation has not distributed any assets; instead, the way has been opened for an additional investment by the stockholders. Until the stockholders elect to exercise or sell their rights, their investment in the corporation is represented by (1) shares which have been purchased and (2) the right to acquire other shares at a specified price, usually below the market price. The cost of the original investment is therefore the cost of the share and the right. The cost of the original investment should be apportioned between these two parts of the investment on the basis of relative market prices. The stock will trade in the market on a "rights-on" basis until the ex-rights date, at which time the stock sells "ex rights" and the rights have a market of their own. Relative market value allocation may be used to apportion the cost between the original shares and the rights as follows:

$$
\begin{aligned}
&\text{Cost assigned to rights} \\
&= \frac{\text{market value of one right}}{\substack{\text{market value of} \\ \text{one share of} \\ \text{stock ex rights}} + \substack{\text{market value} \\ \text{of one right}}} \times \text{cost of investment in stock}
\end{aligned}
$$

Illustration Banner Corporation owns 100 shares of Warner Corporation common stock, acquired at a cost of $10,000. Warner Corporation announces that additional shares will be sold to present stockholders at $104 per share, at the rate of one new share for each 15 shares held. On the date that the stock sells ex rights, the market price of the right is $2 and of the stock $123. The cost of the investment in Warner Corporation stock may be allocated between the rights and the stock as follows:

Cost of 100 shares owned $10,000
Market values at date of issue of rights:
   One share of stock . . . . $ 123
   One right   2
Allocation of cost of $10,000:
   $10,000 × 2/125 = $160 cost of 100 rights, or $1.60 per right.

The journal entry to record the cost allocation is:

Investment in Warner Corporation Rights   160
   Investment in Warner Corporation Stock   160
To allocate portion of investment cost to rights.

Subsequently, Banner Corporation exercised 90 of the rights and sold the remaining 10 rights for net proceeds of $21. Assuming that Banner Corporation uses a first-in, first-out cost flow assumption and therefore must keep track of the basis of each lot of Warner Corporation stock, the entries to record the transactions are:

Investment in Warner Corporation Stock—Lot No. 2   768
   Investment in Warner Corporation Rights   144
   Cash   624
To record acquisition of six additional shares at $104 per share
through exercise of 90 rights.

Cash   21
   Investment in Warner Corporation Rights   16
   Gain on Sale of Rights   5
To record sale of 10 rights.

The original 100 shares of stock now have a cost of $9,840, or $98.40 per share, and the six shares purchased with the rights have a cost of $128 per share.

In the case of Banner Corporation all rights were exercised or sold; however, in the event that the rights were allowed to lapse, the investor should recognize a loss to the extent of the cost applicable to the rights. If the rights are not sold or exercised, a portion of the interest in the corporation has been lost; therefore, the cost of that part of the investment is a loss.

Income Tax Rules If the market value of the rights is less than 15% of the market value of the securities, the taxpayer is not required to apportion the cost of the investment. The taxpayer may, however, allocate the cost if desired, in which case the cost of the stock so acquired is the subscription price plus the cost of the old shares apportioned to the rights. The new shares acquired are considered to have been purchased on the date the rights are exercised.

Convertible securities

A corporation may invest in bonds or preferred stocks that are convertible into the common stock of the issuing company at the option of the holder. The characteristics of convertible securities are discussed in Chapters 15 and 18. At this point we shall consider the action to be taken by an investor who exercises the conversion privilege and receives common stock in exchange for convertible bonds or convertible preferred stock.

The *market value* of the common stock received may differ materially from the *cost* or carrying value of the converted securities. However, it is virtually universal practice to use the cost or carrying value of the convertible security as the carrying value of the common stock acquired. Thus, *no gain or loss is recognized at the time of conversion.* This treatment is required for income tax purposes and is also supported by the theoretical argument that investors contemplate the conversion transaction when they purchase a convertible security and thus no gain or loss should be recognized until the stock acquired by conversion is sold.

The following journal entry illustrates the conversion of an investment in bonds with a carrying value of $96,720:

Investment in ABC Company Common Stock	96,720	
Investment in ABC Company Convertible Bonds		96,720
To record conversion of bonds into common stock.		

OTHER LONG-TERM INVESTMENTS

Investments in special-purpose funds

Occasionally a corporation will accumulate a fund of cash, usually invested temporarily in securities, for a special purpose. The creation of the fund may be by voluntary action on the part of the management or it may be required by contract. Funds are generally created to pay off a liability or to acquire specific assets. In general, funds are treated as long-term investments only when they are created as a part of a contractual arrangement and the use of the money so invested is not available to management for general operating needs. A fund may be classified as a current asset if it is created voluntarily and the management may liquidate it for operating purposes.

Accounting for funds

The transactions which must be accounted for in connection with fund accumulation and administration are: (1) the transfer of assets to the fund, (2) the investment of the assets in corporation-managed funds, (3) the collection of revenue and payment of expenses if managed by the corporation, and (4) the use of fund resources for the intended purpose.

There are two methods of handling funds: (1) The fund may be created and managed by the corporate personnel; or (2) the assets may be deposited with a trustee who is charged with receiving the deposit, investing the assets, collecting the revenue, paying the expenses, and accounting to the responsible officials for the receipts and disbursements.

Typically, the funds which are created voluntarily are administered by the corporate personnel, whereas those created by contract are handled by a trustee. The periodic deposit to the fund is generally set in advance. It may be related to the level of operations; it may be set as a stated amount each period, or as a stated amount less earnings of the fund for the period. The method of determining the amount and time for the deposit can generally be found by referring to the document authorizing the creation of the fund. In cases when the fund is irrevocably committed for the purpose designated and the cash is actually deposited with a trustee, the fund itself may not appear among the assets of the corporation and the liability which is to be paid from fund assets may be excluded from the liabilities. This procedure is used most often when the liability does not exceed the fund balance, which means that the corporation has no liability other than that for the periodic deposits as stipulated in the contract. Most employee benefit plans, such as pension plans and supplemental unemployment benefit plans, are of this type.

Bond sinking funds are usually included among the assets and bonds outstanding are shown as a corporate liability. The sinking fund should not be offset against the bond liability. This particular fund and other similar funds are usually included in the balance sheet as an asset even though they are irrevocable and are held by trustees. To omit the fund balance from the balance sheet and include the net liability could conceal a significant amount of the company's liabilities, thus understating the extent to which the company was using borrowed capital.

One of the most common methods of accumulating a fund, particularly for purposes of retiring a bond liability, is to deposit a given sum each period. The periodic deposit is computed, using a compound interest formula for determining the periodic deposits required to total a certain sum in a definite period at an assumed rate of interest. The details of this calculation are covered in Chapter 5. The assumption of this calculation is that the funds deposited each period will be invested to yield the assumed rate of interest. Subsequent deposits and interest earned are both invested accordingly.

The transactions relating to the purchase and sale of securities, and the accrual and collection of income for the sinking fund, are accounted for in the same manner in which transactions in the general investments account are recorded.

Cash surrender value of life insurance policies

When a company is particularly dependent on certain officers for direction and management, life insurance policies may be purchased on the lives of these officers with the company named as the beneficiary. Certain types of insurance policies combine a savings program and an insurance plan. When these are purchased, the savings portion of the premium should be reflected in the balance sheet as an investment.

The savings part of the plan is generally referred to as the **cash surrender value** of the policy. This is the amount of money which the company would receive in the event that the policy were canceled; this same amount frequently serves as collateral for a loan by a bank or the insurance company. As the savings value (cash surrender value) of an insurance policy increases, the actual insurance coverage implicit in the policy decreases. This is depicted in the diagram below:

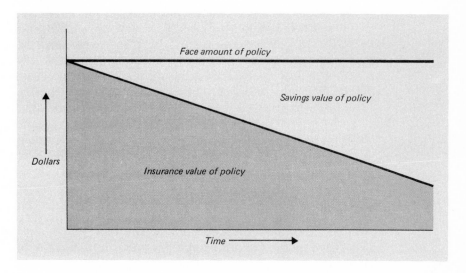

The following data represent the first four years' experience of White Co. with a $100,000 life insurance policy carried on one of its officers.

Year	Gross premium	Less dividend	Premium paid	Cash value increase	Insurance expense
1	$2,959	$–0–	$2,959	$–0–	$2,959
2	2,959	424	2,535	264	2,271
3	2,959	490	2,469	2,279	190
4	2,959	558	2,401	2,292	109

From this limited data, we can readily see the increase in the asset and the decreasing annual cost of insurance. The journal entries for the first two years are as follows:

```
Year 1  Insurance Expense  . . . . . . . . . . . . . . . . . . . . .   2,959
            Cash  . . . . . . . . . . . . . . . . . . . . . . . . .            2,959
        To record the payment of life insurance premium.

Year 2  Insurance Expense  . . . . . . . . . . . . . . . . . . . .    2,271
        Cash Surrender Value of Life Insurance Policy  . . . . .      264
            Cash  . . . . . . . . . . . . . . . . . . . . . . . . .            2,535
        To record the payment of life insurance premium.
```

In the event of death of the insured officer, White Co. would collect the face amount of the insurance policy. The entry to record this event, assuming death occurs at the end of the fourth year, would be as follows:

```
Cash  . . . . . . . . . . . . . . . . . . . . . . . . . . . . . . .   100,000
        Gain on Settlement of Life Insurance Policy  . . . . . .           95,165
        Cash Surrender Value of Life Insurance Policy   . . . .            4,835
    To record collection of insurance on life of officer.
```

For financial reporting purposes, the gain is included in income before extraordinary items. For income tax purposes, the premiums paid on life insurance policies in which the company is the beneficiary are not deductible. Similarly, the gain on the settlement pursuant to the death of the insured is not taxable income.

The procedures adopted in accounting for life insurance policies often sacrifice theory for expediency. For example, the dividends on life insurance policies actually accrue at the end of the policy year, so that in effect they are reductions of premiums already paid instead of those being paid. Prepaid insurance might be debited when the premium is paid, with subsequent entries to write off the prepaid amount as time passes. These are refinements that can be considered when the materiality of the expense justifies a more theoretical treatment.

Presentation in financial statements

Long-term investments which cannot readily be sold without impairing corporate relationships are classified as noncurrent assets. The classification of the investment on the balance sheet varies in practice. The materiality of the item appears to be of prime importance in the choice between placing it immediately following or preceding plant assets. If investments are a large amount relative to other asset groups, the item, Investments, is generally found immediately following the current assets; however, if the amount involved is relatively insignificant, this item may follow the plant asset group, or it may be combined with other assets that are not included in the major classifications, under a heading such as Other Assets.

Dividends and interest earned are normally listed under the caption Other Income and are included in the determination of income before extraordinary items. When the equity method is used, ordinary investment income (or loss) should also be included in Other Income, but the investor's share of any material extraordinary item should retain its character and be classified as an extraordinary item by the investor.

Because of the nature of long-term investments, gains and losses from sales occur relatively infrequently. A company with numerous long-term investments can expect occasional gains and losses from sales of these investments and should generally include such gains and losses in income before extraordinary items, under the caption of Other Income.

REVIEW QUESTIONS

1 Distinguish between the asset categories of marketable securities and long-term investments. Could the same securities constitute marketable securities to one company and long-term investments to another? Explain.

2 What is the cost of a security purchased for cash? Acquired in exchange for assets for which market value is not readily determinable? Acquired as part of a group purchase?

3 Explain three concepts of the "return on investment" to a common stockholder, and identify the appropriate accounting method for each concept of return on investment.

4 Why should dividend revenue not be accrued by an investor as is interest revenue? What are the alternatives for the timing of dividend revenue?

5 XYZ Corporation acquires 1,000 shares of ABC Company on May 15 for $75 per share when the carrying value of the ABC Company stock is composed of the following:

100,000 shares

Capital stock, $10 par	$1,000,000
Capital paid-in in excess of par	2,000,000
Retained earnings	4,500,000
Total stockholders' equity	$7,500,000

300,000

On May 16, ABC Company declares a dividend of $3 per share. What is the nature of this distribution from the point of view of XYZ Corporation? Of ABC Company? What is the legal interpretation of this distribution to XYZ Corporation?

6 Distinguish between the **cost** and **equity** methods of accounting for a long-term investment in common stock. When is each appropriate?

7 Identify three events which will cause a write-down of the investment account under the cost method.

8 How can the acquisition price of an investment affect subsequent investment income under the equity method?

9 Why does the effective yield of an investment in bonds often differ from the interest rate stated in the bond contract? Explain the effect of interest rate fluctuations on bond prices.

10 Why is the discount or premium on bond investments treated as an adjustment of the interest revenue rather than as a gain or loss upon sale, redemption, or maturity?

11 Distinguish between the **straight-line** and **interest** methods of accumulating a discount and amortizing a premium.

12 What is the theoretical support for using weighted average as a basis for determining cost when units of the same security are acquired at different dates and prices? What methods are allowed for income tax purposes?

13 From the investor's point of view, is there any significant difference between a stock dividend and a stock split? Does either represent income?

14 What are **stock rights?** How should they be accounted for by an investor?

15 When a convertible bond is converted into common stock, what entry should the investor make? Would your answer be different if the market price of the common stock were known? If the market price were not known? Explain.

16 Why is the **cash surrender value** of an insurance policy on the life of a company official carried as an asset in the balance sheet of the company?

EXERCISES

Ex. 11-1 On January 1, Year 5, Sampson Company purchased at carrying value 200,000 shares (25%) of the voting common stock of Kay, Inc., for $2,500,000. Direct costs associated with the purchase were $60,000. On December 1, Year 5, the board of directors of Kay, Inc., declared a dividend of $1.50 per share payable to holders of record on December 20, Year 5. The net income of Kay, Inc., for the year ended December 31, Year 5, was $2,200,000.

What should be the balance in Sampson's Investment in Kay, Inc., account at December 31, Year 5?

Ex. 11-2 Ann Company owns 300 shares of the outstanding common stock of Haggard Corporation, which has several hundred thousand shares publicly traded. These 300 shares were purchased by Ann in Year 3 for $105 per share. On June 20, Year 5, Haggard distributed stock rights to its stockholders to buy one new share of Haggard common stock for $120 cash and three rights. On June 20, Year 5, each share of stock had a market value of $134 ex-rights, and each right had a market value of $6. What cost should be recorded for each new share that Ann acquires by exercising the rights?

Ex. 11-3 The following events relate to Seaboard Corporation's long-term investment in Century Development Co.:

Apr. 10 Purchased 500 shares of common stock at $22 per share, plus broker-age commission and transfer costs of $400.

June 15 Purchased 1,000 shares of common stock at $29 per share, plus bro-kerage commission and transfer costs of $712.

Aug. 31 Century Development Co. distributed a 20% stock dividend.

a Prepare entries for Seaboard Corporation to record the events.

b Compute the basis per share of the investment in Century, assuming (1) the two purchases are treated as separate lots (to permit the use of fifo), and (2) a weighted average is computed for the investment as a whole.

c Prepare a journal entry to record the sale of 800 shares at $21 per share, assuming the cost of the shares sold is determined by (1) fifo, and (2) weighted average.

Ex. 11-4 At the beginning of the current year, Riley Corporation acquired 20% of the 100,000 outstanding shares of Stroud Company capital stock. During the year, Stroud Company reported net income of $140,000.

Compute the carrying value per share of Stroud Company stock and the basis per share of Riley Corporation's investment at the end of the current year under each of the following independent assumptions:

a Riley Corporation acquired the shares at their carrying value of $12 per share, and accounts for the investment by the cost method. Stroud Company paid dividends during the year of $80,000.

b Same facts as case **a**, except that Stroud Company paid dividends during the year of $160,000.

c Same facts as case **a**, except that Riley Corporation uses the equity method to account for the investment.

d Same facts as case **c**, except that Riley Corporation acquired the shares at a price of $15 per share, although their carrying value was only $12 per share. The excess of cost over carrying value was paid because a certain patent with a remaining life of 12 years was undervalued in Stroud's accounting records.

Ex. 11-5 Using the information in Exercise 11-4, prepare all journal entries in Riley Cor-poration's accounting records relating to the investment in Stroud Company during the current year, under each of the four assumptions. (Omit closing en-tries and entries to record the initial acquisition of stock.)

Ex. 11-6 Prepare journal entries in the accounts of Southland Company to record the fol-lowing events:

Feb. 10 Southland Company purchased 1,000 shares of Commuter Airlines common stock at $88 per share.

Mar. 31 Commuter Airlines issued a 10% stock dividend to common stock-holders.

June 30 Commuter Airlines issued rights to common stockholders, enabling the purchase of one additional share at $90 for every five shares held. The stock was trading ex rights at $114 per share and the rights had a market value of $6 each.

July 18 Southland Company exercised 1,000 rights to acquire new shares.

July 20 The remaining 100 rights were sold for $5.50 each.

Oct. 12 Southland Company sold 400 shares of Commuter Airlines stock for $44,000. The shares sold were specifically identified as being from those acquired on February 10.

Ex. 11-7 The following data are the beginning of an amortization table prepared by D Company to account for its investment in $80,000 face amount Sable Co. bonds, maturing in 17 years, which pay interest annually:

Year	Payment received	Interest revenue	Accumulation of discount	Carrying value of investment
				$61,132.08
1	$4,000.00	$4,584.91	$584.91	61,716.99
2	4,000.00	4,628.77	628.77	62,345.76
3				

a Is the discount being accumulated by the straight-line or the interest method?

b What is the contract rate of interest paid on the bonds?

c What is the effective yield on the investment?

d Prepare a journal entry to reflect D Company's interest revenue in Year 2.

e Compute the amounts to be entered in each column of the table for Year 3.

f What would be the interest revenue recognized per year if the discount were accumulated by the straight-line method?

g Compute the percentage return on the carrying value of the investment in Years 1 and 3, assuming that the discount was accumulated by the straight-line method.

SHORT CASES FOR ANALYSIS AND DECISION

Case 11-1 Paradise Investment Company purchased 2,000 of the 50,000 outstanding shares of Patio Products capital stock on March 15 at $40 per share.

On April 1, Patio Products declared a cash dividend of 75 cents per share payable April 20 to stockholders of record April 12. The operations of Patio Products were extremely unsuccessful during the first three quarters of the year and operating losses exceeded the accumulated retained earnings. On November 20 Patio Products declared a liquidating dividend of 50 cents per share payable December 20 to stockholders of record December 10.

Instructions

a Record these two dividend distributions by Patio Products in the accounting records of Paradise following the legal assumption.

b From the viewpoint of Paradise, do you favor the legal or economic treatment of these dividends? Give your reasons.

Case 11-2 Chen Systems, Inc., a chemical processing company, has been operating profitably for many years. On March 1, Year 4, Chen purchased 50,000 shares of Kelvin Company stock for $2,000,000. The 50,000 shares represented 25% of Kelvin's outstanding stock. Both Chen and Kelvin operate on a fiscal year ending August 31.

For the fiscal year ended August 31, Year 4, Kelvin reported net income of $800,000, earned ratably throughout the year. During November Year 3, and February, May, and August, Year 4, Kelvin paid its regular quarterly cash dividend of $125,000.

Instructions

a What criteria should Chen consider in determining whether its investment in Kelvin should be classified as (1) a current asset (marketable equity security) or (2) a noncurrent asset (investment) in Chen's August 31, Year 4, balance sheet? Confine your discussion to the decision criteria for determining the balance sheet classification of the investment.

b Assume that the investment should be classified as a long-term investment in Chen's balance sheet. The cost of the investment equaled its equity in the recorded values of Kelvin's net assets; recorded values were not materially different from current fair values (individually or collectively). How much investment income should Chen report as a result of its investment in Kelvin for the year ended August 31, Year 4? Explain.

Case 11-3 Dunlap Laser, Inc., acquired 45,000 of 150,000 outstanding shares of R Co. on January 2 at $30 per share. The carrying value of R Co. stock as of December 31, two days earlier, was $22.75 per share. During the year following the acquisition of the stock by Dunlap, R Co. earned $325,000 and paid dividends of $1.10 per share. The management of Dunlap is concerned about the appropriate method of presenting the investment in R Co. in the financial statements. The controller argues that Dunlap has earned 30% of R Co. profit by virtue of the fact that it holds 30% of R Co. common stock. The vice president of finance argues that the investment must be carried at cost as are all other assets and that the earnings of Dunlap should include only the dividends received from R Co.

Instructions

a Attempt to resolve this debate by pointing out the relevant issues on both sides of the argument.

b The vice president counters your points in favor of the controller's position with the statement that, "What you say makes sense until you try to explain what the dollar amount of the investment represents. It is not market value of the stock, since the current market value is $29 per share, and it most certainly is not cost." Present your answer to the vice president.

Case 11-4 On April 1, Year 9, Century Financial Company acquired 6% convertible debenture bonds with face amount of $1.5 million for $1,818,000 plus accrued interest for two months. The debentures pay interest semiannually on February 1 and August 1 and mature in 8 years and 10 months from date of acquisition. Each $1,000 bond is convertible on any interest date into 40 shares of common stock at the option of the holder.

On August 1, Year 9, 500 bonds were converted into common stock. At the date of conversion the common stock was selling for $40 per share. On September 1, Year 9, a 10% stock dividend was declared on the common stock to be distributed on October 10 to stockholders of record on September 20. On December 1, Year 9, 5,500 common shares were sold for $35 per share.

Instructions

a Record the above transactions, including receipt of interest and the accrual of interest at December 31, in journal entries, assuming that the conversion of the bonds is recorded at cost.

b Justify your reason for amortizing or not amortizing the premium on the investment in convertible bonds.

PROBLEMS

Group A

11A-1 North Salem Company has supplied you with information regarding two investments which were made during the current year as follows:

(1) On January 1, North Salem purchased for cash 40% of the 500,000 shares of voting common stock of the Yorktown Company for $2,400,000, representing 40% of the net assets of Yorktown. Yorktown's net income for the current year was $750,000. Yorktown paid dividends of $0.50 per share in the current year. The market price of Yorktown's common stock was $14 per share on December 31 of the current year. North Salem exercised significant influence over the operating and financial policies of Yorktown.

(2) On July 1, North Salem purchased for cash 15,000 shares representing 5% of the voting common stock of the Mahopac Company for $450,000. Mahopac's net income for the six months ended December 31 of the current year was $350,000; for the year ended December 31, net income was $600,000. Mahopac paid dividends of $0.30 per share each quarter during the current year to stockholders of record on the last day of each quarter. The market price of Mahopac's common stock was $32 per share on January 1 and $34 per share on December 31.

Instructions

a As a result of these two investments, what should be the balance in the Investments account for North Salem at December 31 of the current year? Show supporting computations in good form. Ignore income taxes and deferred tax considerations in your answer.

b As a result of these two investments, what should be the investment income reported by North Salem for the year ended December 31 of the current year? Show supporting computations in good form. Ignore income taxes and deferred tax considerations in your answer.

11A-2 At the beginning of Year 1, Catalina Corporation acquired 10,000 shares of Ellwood Company's common stock for $300,000 as a long-term investment. At the end of Year 1, the market value of the investment was $258,000. Late in Year 2, Catalina Corporation sold 2,000 shares of Ellwood's common stock for $55,000. At the end of Year 2, the market value of the remaining 8,000 shares of Ellwood's common stock was $225,000.

Instructions

a Prepare journal entries to record realized and unrealized losses relating to the investment in Ellwood Company's common stock in the accounts of Catalina Corporation.

b Show how the investment in Ellwood Company's common stock and the unrealized loss should be presented in the balance sheet of Catalina Corporation at the end of Year 1 and Year 2.

11A-3 On July 1 of the current year, Western Realty Company acquired 25% of the outstanding shares of K Development Company at a total cost of $720,000. The carrying value of the stock purchased by Western was only $600,000, according to K's accounts. Western was willing to pay more than carrying value for the shares for the following reasons:

(1) K owned depreciable assets (10-year remaining life) with a fair value $60,000 greater than their carrying value.

(2) K owned land with a fair value $300,000 greater than its carrying value in K's accounts.

(3) Western believed that K possessed enough goodwill to justify the remainder of the purchase price. Western's accounting policy with respect to goodwill is to amortize it over 40 years.

K Development Company earned a net income of $540,000 uniformly over the current year ended December 31. On December 31, K paid a cash dividend of $360,000. Both companies close their accounts on December 31.

Instructions
a Compute the total amount of goodwill Western believes K to possess, based on the price paid by Western for K stock.
b Prepare all journal entries in Western's accounts relating to the investment for the year ended December 31, using the cost method.
c Prepare all journal entries in Western's accounts relating to the investment for the year ended December 31, using the equity method.

11A-4 Reasoner Corporation acquired $500,000 of Deli Company bonds on September 30. The bonds carry a 7% coupon with interest payable semiannually on March 31 and September 30. The remaining life of the bonds is ten years with an effective yield to maturity of 8% compounded semiannually.

Instructions (Carry all computations to the nearest dollar.)
a Using the tables in Appendix A, compute the amount that Reasoner Corporation paid for the Deli Company bonds.
b Assuming that the bonds were purchased for $466,025, prepare tables for the first two years to show the accumulation of the discount and interest revenue, using both the straight-line method and the interest method.
c Prepare the journal entries required to record the first year's transactions, excluding the purchase of the bonds and closing entries, using both the straight-line method and the interest method. Assume that Reasoner Corporation's fiscal year ends on September 30.

11A-5 Nemo Company had just acquired 25,000 of the 250,000 outstanding shares in Aqua Corporation when Aqua Corporation issued nontransferable rights to all stockholders to buy an additional share of stock at $30 for every two shares owned. If not exercised, the rights will lapse in 90 days. At the time of the rights offering, the market price of Aqua Corporation stock was equal to its carrying value of $35 per share. Nemo's cost per share also was $35.
Nemo's vice president of finance is concerned about whether to exercise the rights or let them lapse, being reluctant to immediately increase Nemo's cash investment in Aqua, but also worried that if other stockholders exercise their rights, Nemo's 10% equity in Aqua Corporation will be diluted.

Instructions
a Compute the percentage of Aqua Corporation stock that will be owned by Nemo after the rights expire, if (1) all stockholders, including Nemo, exercise their rights; (2) all stockholders, except Nemo, exercise their rights; and (3) 60% of all rights are exercised and 40% lapse, but all of Nemo's rights are exercised. (Round to the nearest tenth of a per cent.)
b Compute the total cost and total market value of Nemo's investment in Aqua for each of the three situations described in **(a)** above, assuming that the market price of Aqua stock is equal to its carrying value ***after*** the exercise date.
c Assuming that Nemo Company intends to acquire additional shares of Aqua later and that it has enough cash available to exercise the rights if such action appears advantageous, draft a summary of your findings and your recommendations to Nemo's vice president of finance.

11A-6 Pomeroy Company issued at face amount $500,000 of 8%, 10-year bonds, interest to be payable annually. A sinking fund was established to accumulate the $500,000 at the end of 10 years. Pomeroy Company will make payments of $37,934 to the fund at the end of each year. The fund balance will be invested to earn 6% per annum.

In addition to the sinking fund, Pomeroy Company acquired a $100,000 life insurance policy on Redd Pomeroy, the company's president. The terms of the insurance policy were follows:

Year	Gross premium paid	Dividend on policy	Cash surrender value
1	$2,123		
2	2,123	$277	
3	2,123	313	$ 1,689
4	2,123	350	3,462
5	2,123	387	5,255
6	2,123	426	7,066
7	2,123	465	9,440
8	2,123	503	11,291
9	2,123	542	13,164
10	2,123	581	15,059

Instructions

a Prepare a fund accumulation table for the sinking fund for the first three years. Carry all computations to the nearest dollar.

b Prepare a table determining the net cash outlay, and the effect upon net income, of the insurance contract for each of the first three years.

c Prepare journal entries for all transactions involving the bonds, the sinking fund, and the insurance contract for each of the first three years.

11A-7 Excelsior Corporation has two investments acquired prior to the current year. Three years ago, Excelsior acquired 60% of the 30,000 shares of V Co. at a total cost of $1,440,000. This cost exceeded the underlying carrying value by $160,000, which Excelsior considered to be a purchase of unrecorded goodwill. Excelsior has adjusted the investment income it recognizes from V Co. for the amortization of this amount over a 40-year period. During the last three years, V Co. has reported earnings of $2,060,000 and has paid dividends of $1,950,000. Excelsior accounts for the investment in V Co. by the equity method.

Two years ago, Excelsior acquired 5% of the 200,000 shares of W Co. at a cost of $600,000. During those two years, W Co. has reported earnings of $1,200,000 and has paid dividends of $1,000,000. Excelsior accounts for this investment by the cost method.

The following events relate to Excelsior's long-term investments during the current fiscal year ending June 30:

July 31   Purchased $70,000 face amount of X Co. 9% bonds for $72,320 plus accrued interest for two months. The bonds pay interest on December 1 and June 1 and mature 116 months from the date of purchase.

Sept. 30   V Co. paid a $1 per share dividend; W Co. paid a $1.50 per share dividend.

Dec. 1   Received the interest payment on the X Co. bonds.

Dec. 31   V Co. paid a $1 per share dividend.

Mar. 31   V Co. paid a $1 per share dividend; W Co. paid a $1.50 per share dividend.

June 1 Received the interest payment on the X Co. bonds.
June 30 V Co. reported a net loss of $40,000, consisting of an income of $180,000 before extraordinary items and an extraordinary loss of $220,000; it paid a $1 per share dividend. W Co. reported a net income of $150,000.

Instructions
a Illustrate the balance sheet presentation of all items relating to Excelsior's long-term investments at the beginning of the current year. The market value of the W Co. common stock at the beginning of the current year was $625,000. (Round to the nearest dollar throughout the problem.)
b Compute the total earnings reported and dividends paid by V Co. and by W Co. from the date Excelsior acquired an interest in each to the end of the current year.
c Prepare journal entries in Excelsior's accounting records for all the transactions and adjustments relating to long-term investments during the current year. All amortization is recorded using the straight-line method. The market value of the W Co. common stock at June 30 was $550,000.
d Illustrate the balance sheet presentation of all items relating to Excelsior's long-term investments at the end of the current year.

Group B

11B-1 In Year 5, Investor Corporation acquired 1% of the common stock of Daley Company as a long-term investment. The accountant for Investor Corporation was inexperienced and made the following errors in recording the transactions relating to the investment in the common stock of Daley Company: (1) Shares received as a 10% stock dividend were valued at the market price and recorded as a debit to the Investment account and as a credit to Dividend Revenue; (2) the net cash proceeds on the sale of shares of stock and stock rights were credited to the Investment account; and (3) a cash dividend was credited to the Investment account.

The activity in the Investment account during Year 5 is presented below:

Investment in Daley Company Common Stock

Jan. 18	Acquired 4,000 shares	374,000	Mar. 6	Sale of 400 shares received as a 10% stock dividend		38,000
Feb. 28	Received 400 shares as 10% stock dividend (credited Dividend Revenue by amount equal to market value of shares)	40,000	May 25	Cash dividend		4,400
			June 27	Sale of 4,000 rights		7,850
			Dec. 20	Sale of 3,200 shares after a 4 for 1 split effective Oct. 10		88,800
(Balance, Dec. 31, $274,950)						

On June 27, Year 5, the common stock of Daley Company was selling ex rights at $98 and the rights were selling at $2.

Instructions
a Prepare a working paper summarizing the transactions in the Investment in

Daley Company Common Stock account as the transactions should have been recorded. Use the following column headings:

Date	Transactions	Number of shares	Cost	Proceeds on sale	Gain (or loss)
1/18					

b Prepare a single journal entry to correct the accounting records as of December 31, Year 5. Assume that the accounts have not been closed for Year 5.

11B-2 The following transactions and adjustments relate to long-term investments of Safford Company: 800 Int.

Apr. 30   Purchased $60,000 face amount 8% bonds issued by Disc Company at a cost of $61,880 plus accrued interest. Bonds pay interest semiannually on March 1 and September 1, and mature 94 months from the date of acquisition.

July 10   Purchased for the lump sum of $155,000 a package of 500 shares of 6%, $100 par, preferred stock and 1,000 shares of common stock in Pyramid Corporation. The preferred and common stock were trading at $80 per share and $120 per share, respectively.

Sept. 1   Received semiannual interest payment on the Disc Company bonds. (Premium is amortized only at year-end.)   2400

Oct. 15   Received the quarterly dividend on the Pyramid Corporation preferred stock.

Oct. 25   Received new shares from a 2 for 1 stock split of the Pyramid Corporation common stock.

Dec. 31   Adjusting entries are made for the end of the fiscal year. Premium is amortized by the straight-line method.

Instructions   Prepare journal entries to record the transactions listed above.

11B-3 On June 30, Year 2, Diversified Investment Co. purchased 20% of the 100,000 outstanding shares of Z Company. The net assets of Z Company on the date of purchase were as follows:

Common stock, $10 par	$1,000,000
Paid-in capital in excess of par	1,750,000
Retained earnings	2,350,000
Total stockholders' equity	$5,100,000

Diversified paid $1,410,000 cash for the shares of Z Company. The excess of the cost over the underlying carrying value was paid because (1) the land owned by Z Company had a fair value $550,000 greater than its carrying value in the accounts of Z Company, (2) the depreciable assets of Z Company were worth $450,000 more than their undepreciated cost, and (3) Z Company had at least the amount of goodwill imputed by the price paid for the 20% interest. Diversified's accounting policy with respect to goodwill is to amortize over 40 years. The depreciable assets have a remaining economic life of 12 years.

During the last six months of Year 2, Z Company earned a net income of $270,000, including an extraordinary loss of $45,000, and paid dividends of $1 per share. In Year 3, Z Company reported a net loss of $90,000 but paid dividends of $2 per share. Both companies end their fiscal years on December 31.

Instructions

a Compute the total imputed amount of Z Company's goodwill based on the price paid by Diversified for a 20% interest in Z Company.

b Prepare all journal entries for Year 2 and Year 3 in Diversified's accounts relating to the investment in Z Company, using the cost method. Assume that all adjustments are made and that dividends are received at the end of each year.

c Prepare all journal entries for Year 2 and Year 3 in Diversified's accounts relating to the investment in Z Company, using the equity method.

d On January 2, Year 4, Diversified decided that Z Company's goodwill no longer had any value and that the investment account should be reduced by Diversified's portion of unamortized goodwill. Prepare a journal entry to reflect this revaluation, assuming that the equity method has been in use.

11B-4 On November 30, Davis Corporation purchased $400,000 of Avalon Dock Co. 9% bonds maturing in eight years. The bonds pay interest on May 31 and November 30, and the investment shows an effective yield of 8% compounded semiannually.

Instructions (Carry all computations to the nearest dollar.)

a Using the tables in Appendix A, compute the amount that Davis Corporation paid for the Avalon Dock Co. bonds.

b Assuming that the bonds were purchased for $423,304, prepare tables for the first two years to show the amortization of the premium and the interest revenue, using the straight-line method and the interest method.

c Prepare the journal entries necessary to record the transactions for the first year, excluding the purchase of the bonds and closing entries, using each method of amortization. Assume that Davis Corporation's fiscal year ends on November 30.

11B-5 Bloomington Company purchased three blocks of Hanna Company common stock as follows:

Lot no.	Number of shares	Price per share	Brokerage and other costs
1	2,000	$28	$600
2	800	36	300
3	1,200	30	400

Hanna Company issued a 10% stock dividend on May 10 and stock rights on August 15 entitling common stockholders to purchase at $40 one new share for every 10 shares held. Shortly after the rights were issued, the common stock was trading ex rights at $49 and the rights at $1 per right. Bloomington sold 1,000 rights at $1.125 with brokerage and other costs of $45. The remaining rights were exercises.

Instructions

a Compute the gain or loss on the sale of rights using (1) fifo, (2) lifo, and (3) average cost to determine the cost of the rights sold. Round off cost per right to the nearest tenth of a cent.

b Prepare a schedule showing the number of shares in each lot, the total cost of each lot, and the unit cost of each lot (to the nearest cent), assuming the use of fifo in part **a** and considering the shares bought through the exercise of rights as lot No. 4.

11B-6 Demeter Corporation is required, in accordance with the terms of a long-term debt contract, to create a sinking fund with a trustee to pay off $100,000 of the obligation at the end of five years. The trustee offers Demeter two plans: (1) Pay $18,098 at the end of each year for five years to the trustee, plus expenses of administering the trust; (2) pay $18,463 at the end of each year for five years to the trustee, with the expenses of the trust being paid out of the resources of the trust fund. The trustee expects to earn 5% before expenses on the funds on deposit. The expenses of administration, payable at the end of each year, are estimated as follows:

Year 1	$-0-
Year 2	200
Year 3	365
Year 4	570
Year 5	780

The trustee does not guarantee the accumulation of $100,000. Demeter will be expected to make up any deficit or have refunded to it any excess accumulated in the fund at the end of the fifth year.

Instructions
a Prepare a fund accumulation table for each of the two alternatives, based on the stated assumptions.
b Prepare journal entries to record the transactions of the fifth year for each plan, including replayment of the obligation, assuming that the estimates were correct.
c Which alternative is Demeter likely to prefer? Why?

11B-7 The following transactions relate to the long-term investments of San Andreas Associates:

Jan. 2   Purchased 30,000 of 100,000 outstanding shares of D Company common stock for $15 per share. Carrying value was $12 per share; San Andreas Associates attributed the excess of cost over carrying value to goodwill, to be amortized over 30 years. The acquisition gave San Andreas Associates a significant degree of control over D Company.

Jan. 5   Purchased $100,000 of B Company first mortgage 9% bonds at face amount plus accrued interest for 36 days. Interest is payable semiannually on December 1 and June 1 with maturity 10 years from this past December 1. The bonds are callable at 106.

Feb. 15   Purchased 1,000 shares of C Company $10 par common stock for $65,280.

May 5   Received cash dividend on C Company common stock of 65 cents per share.

June 1   Received semiannual interest on B Company bonds.

Aug. 5   Received cash dividend on C Company common stock of 65 cents per share and a 2% stock dividend.

Sept. 30   Sold the shares of C Company common received as a stock dividend for $70 per share and purchased 50, $1,000, 8% subordinated debenture bonds of Z, Inc., at 94 (94% of face amount), with interest payable semiannually on March 31 and September 30, and with maturity 10 years from date of purchase. The bonds are callable at 102.

Oct. 1   Received a cash dividend of 75 cents per share from D Company. (Dividend paid from earnings.)

Nov. 5 Received cash dividend on C Company common of 70 cents per share.

Dec. 1 Received semiannual interest on B Company bonds and surrendered to B Company 60 of the $1,000 bonds at the call price in accordance with the provisions of the bond indenture.

Dec. 31 D Company reported net income for the year of $164,000, including a $24,000 extraordinary gain.

Instructions

a Record the above transactions in journal form and record any adjustments required at December 31. Accumulate the discount on the bonds of Z, Inc., to the nearest month, using the straight-line method. The market value of C Company common stock at December 31 was $75,000.

b Prepare a schedule of investments as they would appear in the balance sheet at December 31.

CHAPTER 12

PLANT ASSETS; ACQUISITION AND RETIREMENT

The terms *plant assets, plant and equipment, property, plant, and equipment,* or *fixed assets* are often used to describe the entire complex of tangible long-lived assets used by a business in its operations. Active use in operations distinguishes these assets from other tangible assets which are reported as investments. Land held as a prospective building site, for example, is an investment; when the building has been constructed and is in service, the same land should be classified as a plant asset. A characteristic common to all plant assets is that they yield services over a period of years. All plant assets except land have a limited economic life; consequently, their cost must be allocated to the periods receiving the services.

Classification of assets used in business

Assets used in business operations may be divided into a number of separate classes and subclasses:

I *Tangible assets.* Tangibility is the characteristic of bodily substance, as exemplified by a tract of timber, a bridge, or a machine.
  A *Plant and equipment.* Included in this category are all long-lived physical properties acquired for use in business operations. Examples are land, buildings and structures of all types, machinery, equipment, furniture, carpeting, tools, orchards, returnable containers, breeding animals, and leasehold improvements. Assets

falling in this category have two distinguishing qualities: **(a)** In yielding services over a number of periods the asset does not change in physical characteristic; that is, it does not become physically incorporated in the finished products. For example, a building or machine wears out and eventually loses the ability to perform its function efficiently, but its physical components remain relatively unchanged. In contrast, raw materials are incorporated into the finished products. **(b)** Plant assets are normally acquired for use rather than for resale.

1 *Land.* In contrast to the other kinds of physical property, land has an indefinite economic life. In general it does not deteriorate with the passage of time, and, unlike wasting natural resources, land is not physically exhausted through use. There are, of course, exceptional cases. Agricultural land may suffer a loss of service usefulness through erosion or failure to maintain fertility. Building sites may be damaged or destroyed by slides, floods, or earthquakes. In general, however, land is treated for accounting purposes as a nondepreciable asset.

2 *Property having a limited economic life.* With the exception of land, all other plant assets have limited economic lives. The investment in such assets is assigned through the process of **depreciation** to the goods and services produced.

B *Wasting assets.* This term includes all natural resources that are subject to exhaustion through extraction. The principal types of wasting assets are **(a)** mineral deposits, **(b)** oil and gas deposits, and **(c)** standing timber. In essence, wasting assets are large-scale, long-term inventories acquired for piecemeal resale or physical use in production over a number of years. The cost of acquiring and developing wasting assets is transformed into periodic charges (known as **depletion**) against revenue.

II *Intangible assets.* Intangibility denotes a lack of physical existence or substance. Examples of intangible assets include patents, copyrights, trademarks, franchises, organization costs, and goodwill. The cost of intangible assets should be **amortized** over their estimated economic life, but not in excess of 40 years.[1]

Basis of reporting in accounting records

In essence a plant asset is a **bundle of future services.** The cost of acquiring such assets is a measure of the amount invested in future services that will be provided by the asset. At the time of acquisition, cost is also an objective measure of the exchange value of assets. The market price represents the simultaneous resolution of two independent opinions (the buyer's and the seller's) as the the current fair value of the asset changing hands. There are cases where the buyer pays too high a price

[1] See Chapter 14 for a more complete discussion of intangible assets.

because of errors in judgment or excessive construction costs, and it is sometimes possible to acquire plant assets at bargain prices. These, however, are exceptional cases; the accountant seldom has objective evidence to support either "unfortunate" or "bargain" acquisitions. Accountants use cost as the basis of recording and reporting plant assets because it is objective and because it is a measure of the entity's investment in future services.

The problem of determining *carrying value* (often referred to as *book value*) subsequent to acquisition is also important. As a given plant asset is used in operations, a portion of the original bundle of service potential is used up. This can be illustrated as follows:

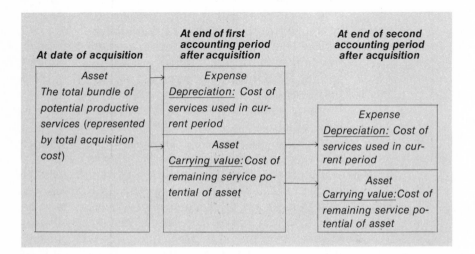

The carrying value of a plant asset is thus reduced by depreciation, since a smaller bundle of potential service remains at the end of each period. The problem of measuring depreciation and the carrying value of assets is discussed in Chapter 13.

Because plant assets generally have long economic lives, it is possible that their fair value may rise above or fall below carrying value between the time of initial acquisition and the time the services are used. When such price movements are material, serious questions may be raised about the continuing significance of historical cost. This issue is discussed in Chapter 22.

DETERMINING THE COST OF PLANT ASSETS

The total cost of a plant asset is the cash outlay, or its equivalent, made to acquire the asset and put it in operating condition. This is a clear and simple statement of the principle involved; however, problems arise in applying this principle to practical situations. In essence these issues may be divided into three categories: (1) What is included in the cost of plant assets? (2) How is cost of plant assets measured? and (3) How are costs subsequent to acquisition recorded? Each of these questions will be examined in the following sections.

What is included in the cost of plant assets?

Until a plant asset is ready to perform the services for which it was acquired, it is not complete. Some assets, for example a truck or an adding machine, are complete and ready to function at acquisition. The cost of such assets may be measured by combining the invoice price (including sales tax) and transportation costs. Other assets, for example an automobile assembly line or the machinery for a paper mill, must be assembled, installed, and tested. All expenditures connected with the assembling, installing, and testing are logically viewed as a part of asset cost.

Capital versus Revenue Expenditures Initial expenditures that are included in the cost of assets are called *capital expenditures,* and such expenditures are commonly said to be *capitalized;* expenditures treated as expenses of the current period are called *revenue expenditures.* This terminology, while not ideal, is satisfactory and is widely used.

The distinction between capital and revenue expenditures is important in arriving at a proper measure of periodic income. If the cost of acquiring plant assets is treated as a current expense, income of the current period is understated, and income of future periods, when the asset services are used, will be overstated.

The theoretical test to distinguish a capital from a revenue expenditure is simple: Have the services acquired been entirely consumed within the current period, or will there be a carryover of beneficial services into future periods? As we shall see, this test is not always easy to apply. At the outset, however, matters of accounting convenience should be distinguished from questions of principle. Many companies follow an arbitrary procedure of charging all asset expenditures of relatively small amounts (for example, those under $100) to expense, to avoid excessive accounting effort. Unless these small expenditures are significantly large in the aggregate, such practices, if consistently followed, are reasonable and efficient. They are condoned as a matter of expedience, since they do not materially distort periodic income.

Specific types of capital and revenue expenditures after acquisition, such as additions, betterments, replacements, and repairs, are covered in a subsequent section of this chapter.

Land Special problems arise in determining what to include in the initial cost of land. Normally the acquisition cost of land includes: (1) the purchase price; (2) all costs of closing the transaction and obtaining clear title, such as commissions, legal fees, escrow fees, title investigations, and title insurance; (3) all costs of surveying, clearing, draining, or filling to make the property suitable for the desired use; and (4) costs of land improvements that have an indefinite economic life.

It is sometimes necessary to examine the terms of the purchase agreement to determine the price paid for land. Suppose, for example, that a buyer agrees to pay $80,000 for a parcel of land and agrees to pay delinquent property taxes of $5,000 and to make up past-due mortgage payments in the amount of $1,500. The purchase price of the land in this case clearly includes this additional consideration and is $86,500, not $80,000.

When newly acquired land is not in the condition necessary for the contemplated use, the buyer will incur certain costs which should be recorded as part of the cost of the land. For example, the cost of clearing trees, or of leveling hills or filling low spots, is properly chargeable to the land. Any salvage realized in the process of clearing land should be treated as a reduction in cost.

Land improvement costs are capital expenditures; they can be treated as a part of land cost or recorded in a separate Land Improvements account. Such improvements as landscaping and drainage have indefinite economic lives and are properly added to land cost. The cost of such improvements as sidewalks, streets, and sewers may or may not have indefinite economic lives. In many localities, the cost of streets, sewers, and similar improvements are charged against the owners of the benefited property, but the local governmental unit agrees to maintain and replace them if they are built to standard specifications. In such cases the special assessment expenditure is a part of land cost, since it is permanent in nature. If the property owner is responsible for eventual replacement, however, land improvements have a limited economic life and should be recorded in a separate account to facilitate depreciation accounting.

Land held as a potential building site or for other speculative or investment purposes is not currently used in operations and should therefore be treated as an investment rather than as a part of the plant asset category. The carrying charges, such as property taxes, interest, and weed control, prior to the time that the land is put to use, should be capitalized (added to the cost of the land). When the site is put to use, the land should be reclassified from the investment category to the plant asset category, and future property taxes and carrying charges should be treated as operating expenses.

Buildings The distinction between land and building costs may be of considerable importance because of the potential effect on net income. For example, suppose that a parcel of land is acquired as the site for a new building. On the land is an old building that must be razed before the new structure can be built. Is the cost of tearing down the old building (net of any salvage recovery) a current expense, a part of the cost of the new building, or an element of land cost? If it is a current expense, it will be charged against revenue immediately; if a part of the cost of the new building, it will be depreciated over the economic life of the structure; if a part of land cost, it will not be depreciated. What are the guiding standards to be used in resolving these and similar questions?

The primary issue is the nature of the relationship between the expenditure and a particular plant asset. We must ask: What is the asset that we have acquired, and is the particular cost at issue reasonably related to the acquisition of this particular asset? If a parcel of land is acquired for a building site, the entire cost of bringing the land into suitable condition as a building site is allocable to the land; on the other hand, the cost of excavating and surveying in order to construct the foundation for the new building is a part of the cost of the building.

The line of reasoning outlined above can be applied in resolving a number of similar issues that may arise in determining building, construction, or acquisition costs. The examples below are illustrative:

Cost incurred	*Treatment and reason*
1 Cost of temporary buildings used for construction offices or to house tools and materials during construction of a new building.	Record as cost of new building. This is a necessary cost of constructing the **new** building.
2 Cost of tearing down a building previously used in operations in order to construct a new building. Building was no longer serviceable.	Recognize as part of loss on retirement of the old building. This cost is related to the services of the **old** building, not the new building.
3 Cost of insurance against risk of claims for accidents or damages while constructing a new building.	Record as cost of new building. This is an ordinary and necessary cost of constructing the **new** building.

When a building is being constructed, all costs necessary to complete the construction should be included in the cost of the building. This may include architects' fees, building permit, and a variety of overhead costs. When a building is purchased, all charges clearly relating to the building (termite inspection, for example) and considered applicable to future revenue should be capitalized. Separate accounts may be used for the building shell (foundation, walls, and floors), partitions, air-conditioning units, roof, wiring, siding, etc.

The accountant should be careful, however, not to capitalize any costs which will not benefit future periods. For example, suppose that immediately after the purchase of a used building it is found that extensive repairs will be necessary. The proper treatment of such costs must rest on evidence as to the circumstances of the purchase. If the buyer recognized the need for these repairs at the time he negotiated the purchase price, their cost is clearly a part of the cost of placing the building in serviceable condition and should be capitalized. The reasoning is that paying $100,000 for a rundown building and $50,000 for renovation is equivalent to paying $150,000 for a renovated building. If, on the other hand, a building is purchased for $150,000 under the assumption that it is in condition for occupancy and it is later discovered that there are serious defects requiring an expenditure of $50,000 to correct, any portion of the $50,000 expenditure that does not either result in an improved structure or add to the economic life of the building should be treated as a loss or expense of the current period.

A similar line of reasoning can be used to reject proposals to treat the undepreciated costs of assets replaced because of inadequacy and obsolescence either as costs of new plant assets acquired or as deferred charges. It is difficult to see how the new asset can have greater value, or how future periods will receive greater service benefit, because of inadequacy and obsolescence of assets no longer in service. Future periods will benefit from the ownership and use of *new* assets and not from the retirement of the old asset or from the failure to depreciate the *old* asset fast enough.

Leaseholds and Leasehold Improvements A *leasehold* is a personal property right granting to the *lessee* the use of real property for a specified length of time. The contract under which this right is granted is called a *lease,* and the owner of the property is known as the *lessor.* A lease contract usually calls for periodic rental payments. On rare occasions, leases provide for a lump-sum payment of the entire rental in advance.[2]

Since the lease contract gives the lessee the right to use the property in exchange for a contractual obligation to make future rental payments, it may be appropriate to record both the leased asset and the corresponding rental obligations in the accounts of the lessee. This topic will be discussed in Chapter 16.

Leasehold improvements in the form of buildings or structural alterations are sometimes made on leased property. Accounting for leasehold improvements by the lessee is comparable to accounting for similar owned property, except that economic life should be related to the duration of the lease. A building expected to last 20 years which is built on land leased for 15 years with no renewal provision has a 15-year economic life insofar as the lessee is concerned, and a residual value that is determined by the amount, if any, that the lessor agrees to pay upon the termination of the lease. When the lease agreement contains a provision to renew at the option of the lessee, the length of economic life becomes uncertain, except in terms of the present intentions of the lessee. In the above example, if the lease contract contained a renewal option for an additional 5-year period, the economic life for the building should be either 15 or 20 years, depending on the intention of the lessee with respect to renewal.

The lessor generally does not record leasehold improvements made by the lessee. However, if the lessor pays for any of the improvements,

---

[2] The lump-sum leasehold is almost extinct, largely because of the income tax law, which requires the lessor to include the entire sum received in taxable income in the year of receipt, without regard to the time period covered by the lease.

the cost should be recorded in a plant asset account by the lessor and depreciated over the economic life of the improvements.

Machinery and Equipment This category may encompass a wide variety of items, including all types of machinery, furniture, fixtures, ships, vehicles of all types, tools, containers, patterns and dies, computers, and office equipment. Cost of machinery and equipment items should be carefully determined and allocated to revenue through the process of depreciation. This is the essence of the matching principle as used in accounting.

Several topics relating to the acquisition of machinery, equipment, and buildings are discussed below.

Self-constructed Assets Occasionally a building, a machine, or equipment may be constructed by the business that intends to use it, either because this is an economical method of acquisition or because the quality and specifications of the asset can be better controlled if the asset is self-constructed. Determining the cost of the completed asset in this situation raises a number of issues.

Accountants generally agree that all direct costs incurred in construction activities should be capitalized. *Direct costs* are defined as those that can be specifically identified with the construction project in the sense that they would not have been incurred otherwise. Direct costs include the cost of materials, labor, design, engineering, etc. Whether any overhead should be included in the cost of the self-constructed asset is a debatable question.

The basic issue is whether overhead costs that will not change as the result of a self-construction project should be charged to the new asset. Some companies have engineering and construction departments that regularly engage in new construction. The overhead costs assignable to these departments are clearly allocable between ordinary maintenance work and new construction. But what about the overhead costs of a regular producing department that occasionally undertakes the construction of a plant asset? It is difficult to imagine a situation in which any significant self-construction project could be undertaken without increasing overhead to some extent. However, there are a number of fixed costs in overhead that will not increase as a result of construction activities. If these fixed costs are allocated between regular production and self-construction projects, the result may be that the average manufacturing cost for units produced will be reduced during periods in which significant self-construction activities are undertaken. Pretax income during the construction period would thus be increased by the amount of the fixed overhead assigned to the self-constructed asset. The three possible approaches to this issue are summarized below:

1 *Allocate no overhead to the self-constructed asset.* This approach has little to recommend it. At least some overhead is the direct result of new construction, and charging this incremental overhead to current operations is a clear case of distortion of income by failing to recognize a capital expenditure.

variable

2 *Allocate only incremental overhead to self-constructed assets.* This approach may be defended on the ground that incremental overhead represents the relevant cost which management considered in making the decision to construct the asset. Fixed overhead costs, it is argued, are period costs; since they would have been incurred in any case, there is no relationship between the fixed portion of overhead and the self-constructed project. This method has been widely used in practice because, its supporters argue, "it does not distort the cost of normal operations."

3 *Allocate a portion of all overhead to the self-constructed asset.* The argument for this approach is that the proper function of cost allocation is to relate all costs incurred in a given period to the output of that period. If a company is able to construct an asset and still carry on its regular activities, it has benefited by putting to use some of its **idle capacity,** and this fact should be reflected in higher income. To charge the entire overhead to only a portion of the productive activity is to ignore facts and to understate the cost of the self-constructed asset. The authors feel that this line of reasoning is sound and is supported by the Cost Accounting Standards Board as follows:

> Tangible capital assets constructed for a contractor's own use must be capitalized at amounts which include general and administrative expenses when such expenses are identifiable with the constructed asset and are material in amount. When the constructed assets are identical with or similar to the contractor's regular product, such assets must be capitalized at amounts which include a full share of indirect costs.[3]

Profit on Self-Construction Suppose that a company has aksed for bids on a plant asset and that the lowest bid is $50,000. Management finds that the same asset can be constructed in the company's own plant at a total cost, including materials, labor, and incremental overhead, of $40,000. If the company chooses to construct the asset, it might be argued that the asset should be recorded at $50,000 and that the company should recognize a profit of $10,000. Although there may be some support for this view, the facts do not meet the accounting test of realization. Profits are generated from asset **use and disposal** and not from asset acquisition; the $10,000 is a **saving** which will be realized through lower depreciation charges as the asset is used.

Interest during Construction During the time it takes to complete a self-construction project, money is tied up in materials, labor, and other construction costs. Is the interest cost incurred in borrowing funds for this purpose a part of the cost of the constructed asset? This is a controversial question in accounting theory.

Generally, accountants regard interest as a cost of financing and not as a cost of obtaining asset services. If Company X pays cash for an asset while Company Y borrows money to buy an identical asset, there is no logical basis for claiming that Company Y has a more valuable asset simply because it has paid interest on borrowed funds. This reasoning, carried over into the self-construction area, leads to the conclu-

[3] *Standard 404,* "Capitalization of Tangible Assets," CASB (Washington: 1973).

sion that interest on funds borrowed and used in construction should not be capitalized.

The opposing view is that interest during construction is a cost of acquiring future asset services. Funds are immobilized during the construction period. In deciding to construct the asset, management must have determined that the value created would be sufficient to cover all costs, including interest. Furthermore, interest on investment would be included in the asking price of the asset if it were purchased in finished form. Therefore, it is argued, accountants should not charge off as expense the interest on funds employed in construction of an asset prior to the time that the asset is ready to produce revenue.

Until 1974, an increasing number of companies were capitalizing interest actually paid on loans to finance projects during the construction period.[4] However, the Securities and Exchange Commission, in *Accounting Series Release No. 163,* placed a moratorium on such practice for all companies, except public utilities, savings and loan associations, and land development companies. The Commission's position may be summarized as follows:

> . . . companies . . . which had not, as of June 21, 1974, publicly disclosed an accounting policy of capitalizing interest costs shall not follow such a policy in financial statements filed with the Commission covering fiscal periods ending after June 21, 1974. At such time as the Financial Accounting Standards Board develops standards for accounting for interest cost, the Commission expects to reconsider this conclusion. Until such time, companies which have publicly disclosed such a policy may continue to apply it on a consistent basis but not extend it to new types of assets.
>
> In addition, the Commission has amended Regulation S-X to require that all companies which capitalize interest costs make disclosure in the face of the income statement of the amount capitalized in each year an income statement is presented and, in addition, that companies other than electric, gas, water and telephone utilities disclose the effect on net income of this accounting policy as compared to a policy of charging interest to expense as accrued.[5]

The position of the SEC was based on the following reasoning: (1) Interest or cost of capital is extremely difficult to measure; (2) any allocation of interest to particular assets is inherently arbitrary; and (3) interest costs are generally of a continuing nature and should be treated

---

[4] In the 1976 edition (30th ed.) of *Accounting Trends & Techniques* published by the AICPA, 47 of the 600 companies included in the survey disclosed the practice of capitalizing interest. An example of such disclosure by a large publicly owned corporation follows:

Income statement:

Interest expense (net of interest capitalized of $3,278,000). $174,949,000*
* *Capitalized Interest*—The company follows the practice of capitalizing interest costs incurred relating to construction in progress, since such interest is considered an integral part of the cost of the property. If these costs had not been capitalized, net earnings would have been reduced by $1,466,000.

[5] *Accounting Series Release No. 163,* "Capitalization of Interest by Companies Other than Public Utilities," SEC (Washington: 1974), pp. 2–3.

as period costs. Allocation of interest to construction is especially difficult when a company is continuously engaged in construction activities
and internally generated cash is used to finance such activities.

How is cost of plant assets measured?

We have just reviewed some of the problems that arise in determining
what is included in the cost of plant assets. Now let us examine the
problems that arise in measuring the cost of plant assets, when the
method of acquisition obscures the purchase price. The objective in
measuring cost is to determine the cash outlay or its equivalent necessary to obtain the asset. In general, the problems that arise in this area
center around the meaning of the term *cash equivalent.*

Cash Discounts When assets are purchased under terms that allow the
deduction of a discount for the payment of cash within a specified
period of time, the term "cash equivalent" is logically interpreted to
mean the invoice price, net of the discount. For example, if equipment is
purchased for $5,000, terms 2/10, n/30, the buyer has the choice of
either paying cash (within a 10-day grace period) of $4,900, or of defer-
ring payment for an additional 20 days, at an added cost of $100. If pay-
ment is made within the 10-day period, the cost of the equipment is only
$4,900; if payment is deferred for 20 days, the additional $100 paid is a
penalty for late payment and should not be viewed as a part of the cost
of the equipment.

Deferred Payment Contracts In many cases payment for an asset is delayed for longer time periods. For example, suppose that equipment is
purchased under an agreement calling for payments at $1,490 at the
end of each year for 10 years. To assume that the present value of the
liability, and thus the cost of the equipment, is $14,900 (10 × $1,490), is
to ignore the fact that there is an interest charge included in the contract. To arrive at a basis for recording this purchase, the accountant
should look for evidence of the cash-equivalent price of the equipment.
If this or similar equipment can be purchased for $10,000 in cash, this
amount becomes the measure of cost. If no conclusive evidence of a
cash price is available, the rate of interest implicit in the contract price
should be determined. The present value of 10 payments of $1,490 each
at 8% interest per year is approximately $10,000.[6] Assuming that an 8%
rate of interest is reasonable, the purchase and the first two payments
should be recorded as illustrated on page 485.

When payment is deferred for relatively short time periods, the
amount of interest implicit in the purchase price may not be material
and can be ignored. However, if the length of time and the amount of

[6] The computation of this amount requires the use of the present value of an ordinary
annuity formula as illustrated in Chapter 5.

interest involved are material, a reasonable estimate of the cash-equivalent purchase price is required.[7]

Journal Entries

At acquisition:

Equipment	10,000	
Discount on Equipment Contract Payable	4,900	
Equipment Contract Payable		14,900

Purchased equipment under contract requiring payment of
$1,490 at the end of each of 10 years. Present value of liability
at 8% is $10,000.

Payment on contract at end of first year:

Interest Expense	800	
Equipment Contract Payable	1,490	
Cash		1,490
Discount on Equipment Contract Payable		800

Interest on equipment contract for first year: 8% of $10,000 =
$800.

Payment on contract at end of second year:

Interest Expense	745	
Equipment Contract Payable	1,490	
Cash		1,490
Discount on Equipment Contract Payable		745

Interest on net carrying value of equipment contract for second
year: 8% of $9,310 ($13,410 − $4,100) = $745.

Property, plant, and equipment items are often acquired by assuming a purchase-money obligation. A **purchase-money mortgage,** for example, is a loan created at the time property is acquired, secured by such property, and having priority over any subsequently created lien on the property.

Lump-Sum Acquisitions A single negotiated price may be paid for two or more assets. If the assets in question have different economic lives, it is necessary to allocate the total lump-sum cost among them in order to provide a proper basis for computing depreciation. The most common example of this situation is the purchase of real property—land and building—for a single price. Since the economic life of land is indefinite

---

[7] *See APB Opinion No. 21,* "Interest on Receivables and Payables," AICPA (New York: 1971).

and the economic life of a building is limited, an allocation of cost is necessary. Assume, for example, that a building and the land on which it is located are acquired by Mills Company for $250,000 (see escrow statement on page 487). How is the accountant to determine how much of the $250,000 applies to the land and how much to the building? An examination of the negotiations that preceded the transaction may show that the price was settled upon under the assumption that $200,000 applied to the building and $50,000 to the land. If such evidence is not available or is considered to be unrealistic, the accountant must look elsewhere for more objective evidence of relative values as a basis for cost allocation. If, for example, the assessed valuation for property tax purposes is $161,000 for the building and $69,000 for land, the allocation of the total cost of $250,000 may be made as follows:

	Assessed valuation	Relative value	×	Total cost	=	Allocation of cost
Building	$161,000	70%				$175,000
				$250,000		
Land	69,000	30%				75,000
Totals	$230,000	100%				$250,000

The Escrow Statement Buyers and sellers generally engage an agent (a bank or an escrow company) to handle the details of a real estate transaction. When the transaction is closed, each party receives an *escrow statement* which shows the complete details of the transaction. The escrow statement will show as charges and credits) such items as the selling price, mortgage assumed by the buyer, transfer taxes, commission charged to seller, escrow fees, cash received from buyer, final amount paid to buyer or seller to complete the transaction, etc. The allocation of property taxes, interest on mortgage, insurance, rents, and other items is also summarized in the escrow statement. A condensed example of an escrow statement for the Mills Company (the *buyer* of the property discussed in the preceding section) is illustrated on page 487.

The escrow statement for Mills Company (the buyer) shows that the agreed price for the property was $246,700, a debit on the buyer's escrow statement. The Mills Company was also charged $240 for unexpired insurance, and additional costs allocable to the property of $3,300 ($1,490 + $290 + $20 + $1,500). Thus the total cost of the property is $250,000 ($246,700 + $3,300). The Mills Company was credited for $104,000 representing the unpaid balance of the mortgage assumed, $260 of accrued interest on the mortgage, $2,200 of accrued property taxes and $143,830 which was previously deposited in escrow to apply on the purchase price. (The cash deposit was recorded by Mills Company in the Escrow Deposit account.) The "check to balance" of $50 is the amount of cash returned to Mills Company to close the escrow on November 1, Year 1.

WESTERN ESCROW COMPANY

Escrow Statement

Date: November 1, Year 1
Escrow No.: 01-879

Statement of buyer: Mills Company

Items	Charges	Credits
Consideration (selling price)	$246,700	
Balance of mortgage payable		$104,000
Interest @ 6% from Oct. 17, Year 1 to Nov. 1, Year 1 . . .		260
Tax pro rata $6,600 per year, from July 1, Year 1 to Nov. 1, Year 1		2,200
Fire insurance pro rata $1,440 for three years, Nov. 1, Year 1, to May 1, Year 2	240	
Deposited in escrow by buyer		143,830
Title policy (buyer agreed to pay full amount)	1,490	
Revenue stamps (tax on transaction)	290	
Recording fee	20	
Commission (paid by seller)		
Escrow fee (buyer agreed to pay full amount)	1,500	
Check to balance	50	
Totals	$250,290	$250,290

The escrow statement provides the information needed to record the purchase of the property in the accounts of the Mills Company as shown below.

Journal Entry Based on Escrow Statement

Cash	50	
Building	175,000	
Land	75,000	
Unexpired Insurance	240	
Interest Payable		260
Property Taxes Payable		2,200
Mortgage Payable		104,000
Escrow Deposit		143,830

To record purchase of building and land per Escrow Statement No. 01-879. The total cost of $250,000 ($246,700 + $1,490 + $290 + $20 + $1,500) is allocated on the basis of property tax valuation of building and land (see allocation schedule on page 486).

A similar escrow statement prepared for the seller would provide the required information to record the sale of the property.

Securities Issued in Exchange for Assets When a company issues shares of its own capital stock in payment for assets, the proper basis for recording such a transaction is not always clear. The fair value of the asset acquired is the cash equivalent received by the company for its shares of stock.[8] On the other hand, the market value of the shares given in exchange is a measure of the consideration given for the asset. Accountants are thus faced with the problem of obtaining independent evidence of (1) the fair value of the asset and (2) the fair value of the shares given in exchange. We should expect that these two values would be roughly equivalent; if they are not, a choice between them must be made based on the factors considered by management in making the purchase and on the validity of each valuation.

Shares of stock represent an interest in the net assets of a business, including the asset being acquired. The market price of the shares issued is thus not an entirely independent variable, since it depends to some extent on the value of the asset received in exchange. This reasoning indicates that our first choice should be independent evidence of the fair value of the asset acquired, by appraisal, previous bid prices, or other objective sources. For example, if a machine which was independently appraised at $180,000 is acquired in exchange for 2,000 shares of $50 par value capital stock, the exchange would be recorded as follows:

Machinery	180,000	
Capital Stock, $50 par		100,000
Paid-in Capital in Excess of Par		80,000
Exchange of 2,000 shares of $50 par value capital stock for machine appraised at current value of $180,000.		

In some cases evidence of the market value of shares of stock is easier to get and more reliable than evidence as to the fair value of an asset. This is particularly true if the company's shares are listed on a stock exchange and daily quotations of market price are available.

Assets Acquired by Gift Normally there is a presumption against the idea that anyone dealing with a business makes a gift to it. There are occasions, however, where corporations receive property under conditions that are reasonably interpreted as the receipt of a gift. For example, as-

[8] Procedures for recording assets acquired pursuant to mergers interpreted as **purchases** and as **pooling of interests** are discussed briefly in Chapter 19. A more extensive treatment of this subject is found in the **Modern Advanced Accounting** text of this series.

sume that the City of Stillwater is trying to attract industry to its area. In order to induce S Company to locate a manufacturing plant in its city, the City Council agrees to donate a building site and erect a suitable building for the company, in return for which the company promises to operate a plant employing 200 persons for a period of 10 years. The land has a fair value of $400,000 and the building has a fair value of $2,000,000.

How should accountants record such transactions? If we adopt the view that the sole responsibility of accountants is to keep track of costs incurred, we might argue that no cost is involved in the receipt of the land and building in this instance, and therefore no entry is required. This is, however, too narrow a view of the scope of accounting. A primary justification for recording asset acquisitions at cost is that cost at that time represents more satisfactory evidence of fair value than any other basis. When cash outlay is no longer a reasonable basis for asset accountability or income measurement, accountants should be prepared to deal with the problem on its merits rather than bury their heads, ostrichlike, in the sands of cost. If a business receives an asset at no cost, the asset should be recorded at its fair value, determined on the basis of the best evidence obtainable. Referring to the S Company example, the donation of the land and building results in an increase in the net assets of the company and should be recorded as follows:

Land	400,000	
Building	2,000,000	
Donated Capital		2,400,000
To record at fair value property donated by City of Stillwater.		

Conditions are sometimes attached to a gift of property so that title is not transferred until the conditions are met (for example, continuing operations for a specified number of years). So long as indications are that the company intends to comply with the conditions, depreciation should be taken in the regular manner, both before and after title is acquired, in order that the value of the services obtained from the use of the asset (whether purchased or donated to the company) is recognized in the measurement of income.

Investment Tax Credit Tax legislation in recent years has provided for a reduction of federal income taxes by an amount known as the *investment tax credit.* The investment tax credit is subject to a number of limitations and has been frequently amended and even suspended. The credit generally has ranged from 4 to 10% of the cost of depreciable property other than buildings and their structural components. To illustrate, if a company purchased equipment with an economic life of seven years or more for $100,000, it would be entitled to a $10,000 (10% of $100,000), reduction in its tax bill. Despite this tax reduction, the full $100,000 cost may be depreciated for income tax purposes over the economic life of the equipment. Two methods have been used to recognize the effect of the investment tax credit in the accounting records.

Most Common Method

1 The **flow through method,** which reduces income tax expense by the amount of the investment tax credit in the year the asset is acquired. This method is favored by most business executives on grounds that immediate tax reduction is the intent of the tax law. Because income tax expense is reduced in the year depreciable assets are acquired, this method allows businessmen to increase net income by simply buying certain types of depreciable assets.

2 The **deferral method,** which calls for the amortization of the benefit arising from the investment tax credit over the economic life of the depreciable asset acquired. Under this method the investment tax credit is viewed as a reduction in the effective cost of the asset, although it is generally reported as a deferred credit in the balance sheet and is amortized by periodic reduction to Income Taxes Expense. The deferral method is favored by most accountants because it avoids an immediate increase in net income as a result of **buying** an asset and thus provides a more meaningful measurement of income.[9]

Costs subsequent to acquisition

Expenditures relating to plant assets will normally be made throughout the economic life of such assets. Whether these are expenses to be charged against current revenue or whether they should be capitalized is often a difficult question. The general approach in dealing with these expenditures may be stated as follows: Expenditures that result in additional asset services, more valuable asset services, or extension of economic life applicable to future revenue should be capitalized; expenditures to maintain assets in good operating condition are viewed as expenses of the period in which they are incurred. This approach is consistent with the principle of matching costs and revenue and should be applied to any expenditure of significant amount. Future benefit is a characteristic of all capitalized costs relating to plant

[9] Because this discussion of the investment tax credit is brief, the student should not conclude that the related tax law is not complex or that the accounting issues are not controversial. The APB in *Opinion No. 2* took the position that the investment tax credit should be reflected in net income over the productive life of assets on which the credit is allowed and not in the year in which the asset is acquired. Because of strong opposition from the business community and because the SEC permitted either approach, the APB issued *Opinion No. 4,* in which it stated that even though the deferral method was preferable, the alternative method of treating the credit as a reduction in income tax expense in the year in which the credit arises was also acceptable. Subsequently, the APB issued an exposure draft of an opinion which would have eliminated this alternative treatment by requiring the deferral method. However, strong pressure on Congress by some business groups resulted in a provision in the Revenue Act which **legally** permitted taxpayers to choose the method of accounting for the Investment tax credit. The method adopted must be used consistently and must be disclosed.

assets; costs which are applicable to current or past revenue should be recognized as expenses or losses.

Although the general approach outlined in the preceding paragraph enables accountants to distinguish between capital and revenue expenditures incurred subsequent to acquisition, a brief discussion relating to different types of these expenditures should be useful.

Additions An *addition* is a new and separate asset or an extension of an existing asset. The construction of a new wing on an existing building is an example of an addition to buildings. The installation of two-way communication radios in a fleet of company cars is an example of an addition to equipment. The addition of entirely new units is identical in nature to the acquisition of new assets and raises no accounting problems not previously discussed. When the addition involves an enlargement or extension of an existing asset, the only problem is to determine whether any portion of the service potential of the existing asset has been removed or lost in the process. For example, in connection with construction of a building addition, if it is necessary to remove the old central heating unit and install one with a larger capacity, the old unit should be retired. The recording of the asset addition should be accompanied by an entry removing the cost of the old heating unit and its related accumulated depreciation account from the accounting records and recognizing any resulting loss. The loss should not be treated as part of the cost of the new unit.

Improvements, Renewals, and Replacements Improvements (or betterments), renewals, and replacements are nonrecurring expenditures that in some way add to the service potential of plant assets. The additional value may be the result of extending the economic life, increasing the rate of output, or lowering the cost of operation per unit of output. Such expenditures are, therefore, properly related to future services and charged against revenue in the period in which the services are used. Improvements and renewals may be accomplished through the substitution of better component parts and hence may be labeled as replacements. The distinction between these different expenditures is obscure and is not germane to the basic accounting issues involved. Costs of this type are often referred to as cost of *plant renovation* or *plant modernization,* particularly when such costs are incurred as a part of a large-scale program of plant rejuvenation.

To the extent that renovation or modernization involves the substitution of new parts for old, the proper accounting is to remove the cost of the old part from the asset account (and the appropriate amount from the related accumulated depreciation account) and to substitute the cost of the new part. If renovation or modernization does not involve a substitution but results only in some modification of the asset, the costs incurred should be added to the carrying value of the asset by a debit either to the asset account or to the accumulated depreciation account. These three procedures are explained below.

The substitution procedure A considerable improvement in accounting for plant assets is possible if property units are defined in terms of major components and separate economic lives are used in depreciating these components. To illustrate, suppose that a glass-lined food storage tank is constructed at a cost of $200,000, of which $40,000 is estimated to be the cost of the glass lining. The estimated economic life of the tank is 20 years; the lining must be replaced approximately every five years. If a single asset account, Storage Tanks, is used, there will be a problem of dealing with the periodic replacement of the lining. A better procedure would be to use two asset accounts, Storage Tanks and Tank Linings, and to depreciate the former over 20 years and the latter over five. Now assume that at the beginning of the fifth year the glass lining had to be replaced, at a cost of $54,000, but a new material was used that is expected to last six years. The entries to record the lining replacement would be:

Accumulated Depreciation: Tank Linings	32,000	
Loss on Retirement of Tank Linings	8,000	
Tank Linings		40,000
To record removal of old tank linings. Undepreciated cost of		
tank linings is treated as a loss.		
Tank Linings	54,000	
Cash		54,000
To record replacement of old linings with new materials.		

Depreciation on the new lining will be recorded at $9,000 ($54,000 ÷ 6) in each of the next six years, and the record of the asset Storage Tanks is undisturbed by these events.

A debit to the asset account An expenditure which does not replace an existing part may enlarge the capacity or improve the efficiency of an asset without prolonging its economic life. Such expenditures should be recorded in the asset account and depreciated over the remaining economic life of the asset. This treatment is similar to the procedure previously suggested for additions.

A debit to the Accumulated Depreciation account The cost of asset renovation is often debited directly to Accumulated Depreciation. The rationale for this procedure is that such expenditures extend the economic life of the asset and thus restore some of the cost of service previously written off. Reducing Accumulated Depreciation means that additional time will be required to depreciate the asset, and it is assumed that this period will correspond to the increased economic life of the asset. This procedure is sound in theory and may be used for income tax purposes but it should not be followed blindly, particularly when additions and replacements are involved.

Rearrangements and Moving Costs Costs of rearranging machinery and equipment to secure a more efficient plant layout may be recorded in a separate account and amortized over the period of time expected to benefit from the rearrangement (usually a short period because of the possibility of further rearrangements). Costs of moving the entire plant or office may be similarly treated, unless the moving results from some unusual and infrequent event, in which case the costs of moving would be included as part of the related extraordinary loss. However, most companies recognize moving costs as current expenses.

Ordinary Repairs and Maintenance Minor repair and maintenance expenditures are usually required throughout the economic life of an asset in order to keep it in efficient operating condition. The distinguishing characteristic of such expenditures is that they neither add to the value of the property nor materially prolong its economic life. The usual procedure is to treat these costs as current expenses since maintenance activities are recurring and the cost is related to current revenue. However, any unusual or extraordinary repairs arising from fire or other casualties should be recognized as losses if not covered by insurance.

A somewhat questionable approach to the problem of dealing with repair costs which vary widely from period to period and are significant in amount is to anticipate such costs and spread them over the economic life of the asset. Under this procedure the total expected repair costs are estimated at the time each asset is acquired, and repair expense is debited each period for a portion of the estimated lifetime repair cost. The offsetting credit is to an account titled Allowance for Estimated Repairs. Actual repair expenditures are debited to the allowance account. However, only the actual expenditures are allowed for income tax purposes in the year incurred.

To illustrate, assume that for a particular item of equipment, repair costs are expected to average $250 per year, and that repair costs of $400 are incurred in the second year. The entries to be made during the first two years are given at the top of page 494.

At the end of the second year the allowance account would have a credit balance of $100 ($500 − $400). Conceivably, a debit balance might appear in the allowance account if major repairs occurred early or if the estimate of repair costs was too low.

A number of criticisms of this method have been raised. Some accountants argue that it is merely an income-smoothing device and that

End of Year 1:

Repair Expense 250

    Allowance for Estimated Repairs 250

To record estimated repair expense.

During Year 2:

Allowance for Estimated Repairs 400

    Cash, Parts, Accrued Payroll, etc. 400

To record actual repair costs.

End of Year 2:

Repair Expense 250

    Allowance for Estimated Repairs 250

To record estimated repair expense.

it tends to obscure the fact that repair costs may increase as an asset gets older. Others question whether reliable estimates of repair costs can be made. Finally, the classification of the Allowance for Estimated Repairs poses difficulties. A credit balance in the allowance account cannot be classified as a part of stockholders' equity since it is clearly illogical to debit an expense and increase stockholders' equity. Classification as a liability may be questioned because no legal obligation exists. Treating the allowance as an asset valuation account (to be deducted from or added to the cost of the related asset) assumes that the "accrued repairs" represent additional depreciation and thus reduce the carrying value of the asset. This is probably the least objectionable alternative, particularly since treating a debit balance in the allowance account as an asset—in the nature of a prepayment of repair expenditures—is consistent.

Anticipation of repair costs does not fit well into the generally accepted measurement concepts of accounting and this practice should be discouraged. Year-to-year accrual of estimated repairs lacks sufficient objectivity and might well encourage management to engage in other income-smoothing practices.

RETIREMENT, SALE, AND EXCHANGE OF PLANT ASSETS

Whenever a plant asset is retired, sold, or exchanged, the first step is to bring depreciation expense on the asset up to date. The next step is to remove from the accounting records all accounts relating to the asset. The second step generally requires the recognition of any consideration (proceeds) and gain or loss from the disposition of the asset. Some of the more common situations involving the retirement, sale, or exchange of plant assets include the following:

1 A fully depreciated plant asset is *retired* without receipt of any consideration; no gain or loss is recognized on such retirement.

2 A partially depreciated plant asset is *retired* without receipt of any consideration; a loss is recognized on such retirement.

3 A fully or partially depreciated plant asset is *retired* or *sold* with some recovery of residual or resale value; a gain or loss is recognized on such a retirement or sale.

4 A fully or partially depreciated asset may be *exchanged* for other assets without any cash being received or paid; the guidelines for the recognition of a gain or loss for financial reporting purposes on such *nonmonetary exchange transactions* are:

    a If a loss is indicated by the terms of the transactions, the *loss is always recognized.*

    b If a gain is indicated in an *exchange of dissimilar assets* which *result in the completion of the earning process* (such as the exchange of an inventory item held for sale which cost $1,000 for a plant asset with a fair value of $1,500), the *gain is recognized.*

    c If a gain is indicated in an *exchange of similar assets* which *does not complete the earning process* (such as an exchange of an inventory item held for sale for another inventory item or an exchange of a plant asset not held for sale for a similar plant asset), the *gain is not recognized.*

5 A fully or partially depreciated plant asset may be exchanged for a *similar asset* with cash being paid or received by the parties to the transaction. The guidelines for the recognition of gains and losses are the same as in **4** above, except that a *partial gain is recognized* on the exchange of similar plant assets *by the party receiving cash.*

The accounting procedures for these situations are described in the following sections.

Retirement and sale of plant assets

When a fully depreciated plant asset is retired and no proceeds are received, the retirement is recorded by a debit to accumulated depreciation and a credit to the plant asset; when a partially depreciated plant asset is retired and no proceeds are received, a loss is recognized equal in amount to the difference between cost and accumulated depreciation; when a fully or partially depreciated plant asset is retired or sold with some recovery of residual value or sales proceeds, a gain or loss is recognized equal to the difference between the carrying value of the asset and the proceeds received. For example, assume that equipment costing $6,000 has been depreciated at an annual rate of 10% for eight years. In the middle of the ninth year the equipment is sold for $1,750 cash (net of any direct costs incurred on the sale). The journal entries to record this sale are shown at the top of page 496.

The proper interpretation of any gain or loss that may arise upon the retirement or sale of an asset is often uncertain. To the extent that it stems from errors in estimating economic life or residual value, the "gain" or "loss" is in reality an adjustment of previously reported income. To the extent that it is due to changes in the price of the asset, the

```
Depreciation Expense ................................  300
        Accumulated Depreciation: Equipment ...........              300
To record depreciation at 10% for six months on machine
costing $6,000.

Cash ...............................................  1,750
Accumulated Depreciation: Equipment ................  5,100
        Gain on Sale of Equipment ....................              850
        Equipment ....................................            6,000
To record sale of equipment.
```

gain or loss is also an element of income for the current year. In most cases a combination of these factors is present. Material gains and losses (or provisions for losses) from the sale or abandonment of plant assets are included in the determination of income before extraordinary items.

Plant assets are sometimes retired from active service and are neither sold nor abandoned but are kept on a standby status for use in emergency or to meet peak-load requirements. When this occurs, an estimate of standby or residual value should be made and the asset should be written down to this amount. When the amount of standby equipment is significant, it should be separately reported in the balance sheet.

Exchanges of plant assets

Prior to the issuance of *APB Opinion No. 29,* exchanges of plant assets for similar plant assets were recorded in a variety of ways. Such transactions were frequently recorded using income tax requirements, that is, the asset acquired was recorded at the carrying value of the asset given in exchange plus any cash paid or less any cash received, and no gain or loss was recognized on the exchange. Alternatively, a gain or loss was recognized when the fair value of the asset given in exchange was used to record the transaction, and the asset acquired generally was recorded at the fair value of the asset exchanged plus any cash paid or less any cash received.

Provisions of APB Opinion No. 29 This opinion differentiated *monetary exchanges* involving cash and receivables or payables from *nonmonetary exchanges* involving, for example, inventories, investments in common stocks, and plant assets. An *exchange* was defined as a transfer between entities that results in one entity receiving assets or services or satisfying obligations by surrendering other assets or services or incurring other obligations.[10] The portion of the "basic principle" in **APB Opinion No. 29** which relates to exchanges of plant assets follows:

> The Board concludes that in general accounting for nonmonetary transactions should be based on the fair values of the assets (or services) involved which is the same basis as that used in monetary transactions. Thus, the cost of a nonmonetary asset acquired in exchange for another nonmonetary asset is the fair value of the asset surrendered to obtain it, and a gain or loss should be recognized on the exchange. The fair value of the asset received should be used to measure the cost if it is more clearly evident than the fair value of the asset surrendered.[11]

The APB modified this basic principle in several important respects. First, the accounting for exchanges should not be based on the fair values of assets unless such values are reasonably determinable.[12] If fair values are not reasonably determinable, the asset acquired is recorded at the carrying value of the asset given in exchange plus any cash paid, and no gain or loss is recognized. Second, when an exchange transaction does not result in the completion of the earning process (realization), the asset acquired also should be recorded at the carrying value of the asset surrendered. An example of such a transaction is an exchange of a plant asset not held for sale for a similar plant asset. However, if the terms of the transaction indicate that the asset surrendered has a fair value which is less than the carrying value of the asset, a loss is recognized. Finally, when cash (or other monetary consideration) is received in an exchange of plant assets, the recipient of the cash is deemed to have realized a gain on the exchange equal in amount to the excess of the cash received over the proportionate share of the carrying value of the asset given in exchange.[13] In other words, a transaction in which a plant asset and cash are received in exchange for another plant asset is viewed as a **sale** to the extent of cash received and an **exchange** to the extent of the fair value of the asset received.

The steps to be followed in recording exchanges of plant assets may be summarized as follows:

1 Compute the indicated gain or loss on the exchange. The gain or loss is equal to the difference between the fair value of the asset surrendered and its carrying value.

2 If the computation above results in a loss, the entire loss is recognized for financial reporting purposes and the asset acquired is recorded at the fair value of the asset surrendered plus any cash paid (or less any cash received). A loss is always considered realized.

3 If the computation in **1** above results in a gain and the earning process is completed, the full gain is recognized; if the earning process is not completed and

---

[10] *APB Opinion No. 29*, "Accounting for Nonmonetary Transactions," AICPA (New York: 1973), p. 541.

[11] Ibid., p. 547.

[12] Ibid., p. 548.

[13] Ibid., p. 549.

cash is paid (or no cash is involved in the exchange), no gain is recognized; if cash is received in the exchange, the gain is partially recognized as follows:

$$\text{Gain} \times \frac{\text{cash received}}{\text{cash received} + \text{fair value of asset acquired}} = \text{gain recognized}$$

Illustrations The steps for recording exchanges of plant assets are illustrated in the six examples below. The old asset exchanged has a carrying value of $6,000 (cost of $20,000 less accumulated depreciation of $14,000). Each of the six examples involves similar assets with comparable fair values (FV), adjusted for any cash paid or received.

Exchange transaction	*Journal entry*		

1 *Loss of $2,000 is indicated, no cash is involved:* FV of old asset is $4,000. (Cost of of new asset is FV of old asset.)	New Asset . . . .
	Accum. Depr.: Old Asset .
	Loss on Exchange of
	  Assets . . . .
	    Old Asset . . . . .
		4,000
		14,000
		
		2,000
			
			20,000

2 *Loss of $2,500 is indicated, cash of $1,000 is paid:* FV of old asset is $3,500. (Cost of new asset is FV of old asset plus cash paid.)	New Asset . . . .
	Accum. Depr.: Old Asset .
	Loss on Exchange of
	  Assets . . . .
	    Cash . . . .
	    Old Asset . . . . .
		4,500
		14,000
		
		2,500
			
			1,000
			20,000

3 *Loss of $1,000 is indicated, cash of $200 is received:* FV of old asset is $5,000. (Cost of new asset is FV of old asset less cash received.)	Cash . . . .
	New Asset . . . .
	Accum. Depr.: Old Asset .
	Loss on Exchange of
	  Assets . . . .
	    Old Asset . . . . .
		200
		4,800
		14,000
		
		1,000
			
			20,000

4 *Gain of $6,500 is indicated, no cash is involved:* FV of old asset is $12,500. (Cost of new asset is the carrying value of old asset.)	New Asset . . . . Accum. Depr.: Old Asset . Old Asset	6,000 14,000	 20,000

5 *Gain of $6,500 is indicated, cash of $1,000 is paid:* FV of old asset is $12,500. (Cost of new asset is the carrying value of old asset plus cash paid.)	New Asset . . . .
	Accum. Depr.: Old Asset .
	    Cash . . . .
	    Old Asset . . . .
		7,000
		14,000
			
			1,000
			20,000

6 *Gain of $4,000 is indicated,*	Cash	. . . .	1,000	
cash of $1,000 is received: FV	New Asset	. . . .	5,400	
of old asset is $10,000, indicat-	Accum. Depr.: Old Asset	.	14,000	
ing a FV of new asset of $9,000.	Old Asset	. . . . .		20,000
The portion of indicated gain	Gain on Exchange			
recognized is:	of Assets	. . . .		400

$$\$4000 \times \left(\frac{\$1,000}{\$1,000 + \$9,000}\right) = \$400$$

(The cost of new asset is the
carrying value of the old asset,
less cash received, plus gain
recognized.)

The indicated losses in each of the first three examples are recognized for financial reporting purposes. In the next two examples, no gain is recognized because cash was not involved in Example 4 and because cash was *paid* in Example 5. However, in Example 6, a partial gain is recognized because 10% of the total consideration received was in the form of cash.

If the exchanges in the last three examples involved dissimilar assets, the entire indicated gain would be recognized for financial reporting purposes because the earning process would be considered completed.

Exchanges of plant assets which are material in amount, either individually or in the aggregate, should be disclosed in financial statements. Such disclosure should include the nature of the exchanges, the basis of accounting for the assets transferred, and the amounts of gains and losses recognized on the exchanges.[14]

Involuntary conversions

The services of assets are occasionally lost through condemnation, fire, or other involuntary means. In recording such events, the amount of any loss or gain should be reported, and all amounts relating to such assets should be removed from the accounts. For example, assume that certain land and buildings owned by a business are condemned by the state as the site for a highway, and an agreed price of $140,000 is set as the condemnation award by the state. Accumulated depreciation on the building is $120,000, and its original cost was $160,000. The cost of the land was $40,000. The entry to record this involuntary conversion is given on page 500.

[14] Ibid., pp. 550–551.

Cash	140,000	
Accumulated Depreciation: Building	120,000	
Building		160,000
Land		40,000
Gain on Condemnation of Property		60,000
To record disposal of property condemned by state.		

The income tax rule on involuntary conversion is similar to that for exchanges. In most cases no gain is recognized for income tax purposes at the time of disposal if the owner of the property uses the funds received to replace the involuntarily converted asset.

When depreciable assets or merchandise are destroyed by fire or other casualties, accountants often assist in measuring and recording the losses sustained. Inventories on hand at the time of fire, for example, may have to be estimated through the use of the gross profit method described in Chapter 9.

Insurance on Plant Assets Most companies insure assets for possible losses resulting from fire, theft, explosion, and other insurable events. A *deductible clause* usually limits recovery to losses in excess of a certain amount, such as $100.

Insurance policies provide for recovery of loss based on the current fair value of the asset destroyed. The carrying value of an asset, although irrelevant in determining the amount of recovery from insurance companies, is used to measure the loss (or gain) as a result of the casualty. For example, if $10,000 is collected from an insurance company upon complete destruction of an asset with a carrying value of $7,500, a gain of $2,500 would result.

The amount of insurance carried on an asset should never exceed the current fair value of the asset because the amount recovered cannot be greater than the asset is worth. When inadequate insurance is carried on an asset, the insured in effect becomes a "coinsurer" with the insurance company. For example, if an asset worth $5,000 is insured for only $4,000 and is totally destroyed, the insurance company would bear $4,000 of the loss and the owner would absorb the remaining $1,000 of the loss.

Coinsurance Clause in an Insurance Policy If it were possible to obtain insurance coverage for only a fraction of value of an asset, the owner could benefit by receiving full reimbursement of most losses with a minimum insurance coverage and cost. In practice, however, insurance companies usually employ a *coinsurance clause* to prevent this approach to low-cost insurance protection. A coinsurance clause requires that an asset be insured for a certain minimum amount, usually 80% of current fair value, if a loss is to be fully absorbed by the insurance company. If the insurance purchased is below the stipulated percentage, the owner absorbs a portion of the loss even though the loss does not exceed the face amount of the insurance policy.

To illustrate the application of a coinsurance clause in a fire insurance policy, assume the following:

Insurance carried (face amount of policy)	$ 60,000
Coinsurance required by policy	80% of current fair value
Carrying value of machinery damaged (cost, $140,000)	$ 55,000
Current fair value of asset on date of fire	$ 100,000
Amount of fire loss (based on current fair value)	$ 40,000

The recovery of loss from the insurance company is determined by using the **coinsurance formula** as follows:

$$\frac{\$60,000 \text{ (amount of insurance)}}{\$80,000 \text{ (coinsurance requirement)}} \times \$40,000 \text{ (loss)} = \underline{\$30,000}$$

Several observations may be made at this point. The amount of insurance carried need not be limited to the carrying value of the asset (which, like cost, is irrelevant for purposes of measuring either the amount of insurance that can be carried or the amount of recoverable loss). Recovery on the loss is dependent on the current fair value of the asset, on the amount of insurance carried, and on the provisions of the coinsurance clause. If insurance equal to or in excess of the amount required by the coinsurance clause is carried, any loss up to the face amount of the policy is fully recoverable; if less than the required amount is carried, the loss will be partly absorbed by the **insured.** If the amount of insurance exceeds the coinsurance requirement, there is no need to apply the coinsurance formula. Studying the coinsurance formula indicates that the recoverable portion of the loss is always the lower of (1) the amount of the loss adjusted by the coinsurance formula, or (2) the face amount of the policy.

Two or More Insurance Policies When an asset is insured under two or more policies which do not have coinsurance clauses, any loss would be shared by the insurance companies in proportion to the amount of insurance written by each company; the same procedure applies when the insurance policies contain identical coinsurance requirements. If two or more insurance policies cover the same asset and the policies carry *different* coinsurance clauses, the coinsurance formula should be applied to each policy. However, the loss absorbed by any insurance company cannot exceed its proportion of the total insurance carried with all insurance companies. For example, assume that a building with a fair value of $40,000 is insured under two policies as follows:

Policy A: $15,000 with an 80% coinsurance clause
Policy B: $15,000 with a 70% coinsurance clause

Assuming that a fire causes damage of $24,000 to the building, how much of the loss would be recovered under each policy? If neither policy has a coinsurance clause, each would absorb 50% of the loss ($12,000) because each represents 50% of the total insurance ($30,000). If both policies had a 70% coinsurance requirement, each would absorb $12,000 of the loss because the total insurance carried ($30,000) exceeds the minimum insurance required by the coinsurance clause ($40,000 × 70% = $28,000). However, because policy A has an 80% coinsurance clause in this case the recovery under each policy is determined as follows:

Policy A:

$$\frac{\$15,000 \text{ (insurance under policy A)}}{\$32,000 \text{ (coinsurance requirement for policy A)}} \times \$24,000 \text{ (loss)} = \underline{\underline{\$11,250}}$$

Policy B:

$$\frac{\$15,000 \text{ (insurance under policy B)}}{\$30,000 \text{ (total insurance on building)}} \times \$24,000 \text{ (loss)} = \underline{\underline{\$12,000}}$$

The recovery under policy A is $\frac{15}{32}$ of the loss, which is less than the pro rata coverage of $\frac{15}{30}$, because the coinsurance requirement under this policy was not met. On the other hand, the recovery under policy B is $\frac{15}{30}$ of the loss because the total insurance on the building ($30,000) exceeds the minimum required under policy B ($28,000) and hence the coinsurance formula is not applicable to policy B.

Insurance contracts vary in form and complexity. The discussion here is brief and oversimplified. Although accountants need not be experts in insurance contracts, they should have a basic understanding of insurance to be able to account properly for premiums paid and proceeds received, and to help management formulate a sound insurance program.

REVIEW QUESTIONS

1 Define the following terms: *tangible asset, wasting asset, intangible asset.* Give an example of each.

2 What are the arguments in favor of using original cost as the basis for asset accounting? Can this logically be referred to as an asset valuation procedure?

3 How should the cost of a plant asset be determined for accounting purposes? What three issues are involved in accounting for the cost of plant assets?

4 What is meant by the terms **capital expenditure** and **revenue expenditure?** How are they related to the accounting concepts of realization and matching of costs and revenue?

5 Which of the following are capital expenditures? Indicate the proper treatment of items which are not capital expenditures.
a Cost of grading land prior to construction
b Cost of installing equipment, including cost of spoiled material during test runs
c Tax assessment for street paving
d Delinquent property taxes on land just acquired
e Cost of maintaining equipment in good running condition
f Cost of moving and reinstalling equipment to another part of factory
g Cost of repairs to used equipment; need for repair discovered immediately after acquisition
h Cost of tearing down an old building in preparation for new construction (old building used for 24 years and fully depreciated)
i Cost of insurance policy covering claims for damages that may arise during construction of a new building
j Excess of operating expenses over revenue during first year of operations
k Cost of removing soil to build foundation for new building

6 W Company has constructed a special-purpose machine for its own use. Direct labor and material costs were $10,000. Variable overhead is 10% of direct costs, and fixed overhead allocable to the constructed machine is $2,400. Company engineers estimate that an equivalent machine would cost $15,000 if purchased outside the company. At what figure should the equipment be recorded? Why? Is there a profit on the self-construction? Assuming that the machine could have been acquired for $8,000, how should the machine be recorded?

7 Capitalizing interest during construction may be an accepted accounting procedure; adding interest on an installment contract to the cost of the asset acquired is not. Explain the distinction between these two situations.

8 What position did the SEC take in **ASR No. 163** on capitalization of interest during the construction period?

9 Discuss the accounting problem that arises in dealing with each of the following situations, and explain the proper procedure:
a Assets are acquired on a deferred payment plan.
b A group of assets is acquired for a lump-sum price.
c Assets are acquired in exchange for capital stock or bonds issued by the buyer.
d Assets are acquired by gift.

10 What is the **investment tax credit** and how, in your opinion, should it be treated for accounting purposes?

11 Briefly describe the accounting procedures appropriate for the following:

    a Additions
    b Improvements, renewals, and replacements
    c Ordinary repairs and maintenance
    d Extraordinary repairs as a result of fire damage

12 The accountant for X Company follows a policy of estimating annual repair costs on equipment and making an entry each year debiting Repair Expense and crediting Allowance for Repairs, which sometimes shows a credit balance and sometimes a debit balance. What is the appropriate classification of this account in the balance sheet? Why?

13 Y Company charges the cost of major repairs against Accumulated Depreciation. Evaluate this procedure.

14 How should gains and losses on the retirement, sale, or exchange of plant assets be reported in the income statement? Should gains and losses on involuntary conversions be considered as realized even though they have been "forced" on the company?

15 *a* Describe the basic principle developed by the APB in *Opinion No. 29* relating to accounting for exchanges of plant assets.
    b List three modifications of the basic principle developed by the APB.

16 Describe the conditions in which exchange transactions involving plant assets require the recognition of gains and losses for financial accounting purposes.

17 What is meant by **coinsurance?** Describe the coinsurance formula. Can a gain result from the destruction of insured property? Explain.

EXERCISES

Ex. 12-1 A company replaced an old machine with a new one having a list price of $10,000, subject to a 2% cash discount if paid promptly. Net cost of removing the old machine to make way for the new one amounted to $800. Installation of the new machine cost $400. Costs of testing the new machine were $250 for operator's time and $125 in wasted materials. The discount was lost through late payment of the invoice. What is the cost of the new machine for financial accounting purposes?

Ex. 12-2 The costs incurred in acquiring land and constructing a building in 1980 are as follows:

Land (*including miscellaneous acquisition costs*)	$150,000
Construction insurance	1,500
Building contract (*excluding excavation*)	220,000
Architectural fees	2,000
Street and sidewalk (*maintained by the city*)	4,000
Costs of excavation for foundation	3,100
Property taxes on land (*prior to construction*)	1,600
Advertising costs to attract tenants	1,250
Interest during construction on loan to pay contractor	2,600

The company started operations in 1979 and is required to file financial statements with the SEC. Determine the cost of (**a**) land and (**b**) building for financial accounting purposes.

Ex. 12-3 Pandora Company acquired land having a market value of $590,000 in exchange for $200,000 face amount of 7% bonds payable and 20,000 shares of its $5 par value common stock. The stock was selling at $20½ on the New York Stock Exchange at this time.

Give the entry to record the acquisition of land. (You should record a premium or a discount on bonds payable.)

Ex. 12-4 In Year 2, Peter Saul sold a parcel of land for $55,000 which cost $30,000. The contract called for a down payment of $15,000 and a non-interest-bearing note for $40,000 due in four years.

Record the sale of land in Saul's accounts assuming that the present value of the note (discounted at compound interest at 6% for four years) was $31,684 and that 6% was a fair rate of interest on this type of note. Record the note receivable at face amount.

Ex. 12-5 On June 30, Year 10, Crane Company acquired equipment at a bankruptcy auction for the following consideration:

Cash down payment	$ 72,150
Four non-interest-bearing notes in the face amount of $50,000 payable annually on June 30, commencing in Year 11	200,000
Total consideration	$272,150

Record the acquisition of the equipment in the accounts of Crane Company, assuming that a fair rate of interest is 10% compounded annually. Use the appropriate table in Appendix A and carry computations to the nearest dollar.

Ex. 12-6 T. F. Sells sold a parcel property to Mary Beyer. The property had cost Sells $39,000, including $10,000 allocated to land. Depreciation of $3,500 had been recorded on the building by Sells. At the close of escrow, the following escrow statements were submitted to Sells and Beyer:

	To Sells		To Beyer	
	Charges	**Credits**	**Charges**	**Credits**
Sale price		$40,300	$40,300	
Deposit placed in escrow				$10,400
Pro rata property taxes	$ 120			120
Pro rata interest	70			70
Pro rata insurance		200	200	
Mortgage assumed by buyer . . .	30,160			30,160
Commission	2,370			
Title search fee	150		150	
Escrow fee	110			
Cash to seller	7,520			
Cash to buyer			100	
Totals	$40,500	$40,500	$40,750	$40,750

a Prepare a journal entry to record the sale in Sells' accounting records.

b Prepare a journal entry to record the purchase in Beyer's accounting records. The value assigned to land is $15,500. Beyer had recorded the cash placed in escrow, $10,400, in an Escrow Deposit account.

Ex. 12-7 Thomas Kowal, sole proprietor, has been doing the accounting work for the business. At the end of Year 3, after the accounts were adjusted but before they were closed for the year, you are engaged to review the records. Among the items which require correction are the following:

(1) Installation costs for fixtures, $1,200, were charged to Maintenance Expense. The fixtures have a five-year life and were installed at the beginning of Year 3. Assume the use of straight-line depreciation.

(2) A machine acquired on January 6, Year 1, at a cost of $5,000 has been depreciated on a straight-line basis over a five-year period. This machine was sold on June 20, Year 3, Kowal debited Cash and credited Machinery for $2,100, the proceeds on the sale. No depreciation was recorded on this machine in Year 3, but you conclude that one-half year's depreciation should be recognized.

Prepare a correcting entry for each of the two items described above.

Ex. 12-8 a F T Corporation acquired new machinery by trading in similar used machinery and paying $5,000 cash. The old machine originally cost $90,000 and had accumulated depreciation of $20,000 at the date of exchange. The new machinery could have been purchased for $80,000 cash. Record the exchange of the old machinery for the new machinery following the provisions of *APB Opinion No. 29.*

b Assume the same facts as in **a**, except that instead of paying $5,000 cash, FT Corporation received $20,000 cash. Record the exchange of the old machinery for the new machinery following the provisions of *APB Opinion No. 29.*

c Assume the same facts as in **a**, except that instead of paying cash of $5,000, F T Corporation received cash of $5,000 and the new machinery could have been purchased for $50,000 cash. Record the exchange of the old machinery for the new machinery following the provisions of *APB Opinion No. 29.*

Ex. 12-9 A building has a carrying value of $11,000 and a current fair value of $20,000. Determine the amount recoverable from the insurance company in each case below, assuming that the insurance policy in each case contains an 80% coinsurance clause:

Case	Insurance coverage	Loss
A	$10,000	$12,000
B	12,000	12,000
C	14,000	12,000
D	16,000	12,000
E	18,000	12,000

Ex. 12-10 Dodson, Inc., purchased three machines at an auction for a lump-sum price of $14,500 and paid $500 to have the machines delivered to their place of business. The estimate of the fair value of the three machines is shown at the top of page 507.

Machine X	$ 9,000
Machine Y	6,000
Machine Z	5,000
Total	$20,000

Determine the cost that should be assigned to each machine using the relative fair value of the machines as a basis of allocating the lump-sum price.

SHORT CASES FOR ANALYSIS AND DECISION

Case 12-1 Caliri Pipe Company has just constructed a new building at a cost of $2 million. After reviewing the contracts and cost data, the controller suggests that the company use the following classifications in future accounting for this building: (1) foundation, framing, and sheathing, (2) outside finish, (3) interior finish, (4) roof, (5) electric wiring and fixtures, (6) partitions, (7) acoustical ceiling, (8) furnace and boiler, and (9) plumbing system.

Instructions Discuss the advantages and the disadvantages of following such a system of accounting for this asset, particularly its effect on accounting for maintenance, depreciation, and retirement.

Case 12-2 Your client found three suitable sites, each having certain unique advantages, for a new plant facility. In order to investigate thoroughly the advantages and disadvantages of each site, one-year options were purchased for an amount equal to 5% of the contract price of each site. The costs of the options cannot be applied against the contracts. Before the options expired, one of the sites was purchased at the contract price of $60,000. The option on this site had cost $3,000. The two options not exercised had cost $3,500 each.

Instructions Present arguments in support of recording the cost of the land at each of the following amounts: (1) $60,000; (2) $63,000; (3) $70,000.

Case 12-3 Electro-Age Company manufactures electrical appliances, most of which are used in homes. Company engineers have designed a new type of blender which, through the use of a few attachments, will perform more functions than any blender currently on the market. Demand for the new blender can be projected with reasonable probability. In order to make the blenders, Electro-Age needs a specialized machine which is not available from outside sources. It has been decided to make such a machine in Electro-Age's own plant.

Instructions
a Electro-Age's plant may be operating at capacity or below capacity. Compare and contrast the problems in determining the cost to be assigned to the machine at these different levels of operations.
b Discuss the effect of projected demand in units for the new blenders (which may be steady, decreasing, or increasing) on the determination of a depreciation method to be used for the machine.

Case 12-4 Plant assets generally represent a material portion of the total assets of most companies. Accounting for the acquisition and use of such assets is, therefore, an important part of the financial reporting process.

Instructions
a Distinguish between *revenue expenditures* and *capital expenditures* and explain why this distinction is important.

b Identify six costs that should be capitalized as the cost of land. For your answer, assume that land with an existing building is acquired for cash and that the existing building is to be removed in the immediate future in order that a new building can be constructed on the site.

c At what amount should a company record a plant asset acquired on a deferred payment plan?

d In general, at what amount should plant assets received in exchange for other nonmonetary assets be recorded? Specifically, at what amount should a company record a new machine acquired by exchanging a similar machine and paying cash?

PROBLEMS

Group A

12A-1 This problem consists of five independent situations relating to plant assets for Horwath Corporation. Each situation contains specific instructions.

(1) The company has two fire insurance policies. Policy A with Ace Fidelity covers the office building at a face value of $360,000 and the furniture and fixtures at a face value of $108,000. Policy B with Bravo Indemnity covers only the office building at an additional face value of $140,000. A fire caused losses to the office building and the furniture and fixtures. The relevant data are summarized below:

	Furniture and fixtures	Office building	
Insurance policy	A	A	B
Appraised fair value of the property before			
the fire	$150,000	$700,000	$700,000
Appraised fair value of the property after			
the fire	$ 20,000	$420,000	$420,000
Face value of insurance policy	$108,000	$360,000	$140,000
Coinsurance requirement	80%	80%	75%

Compute the amount due from each insurance company for the loss on each asset category. Show computations in good form. Carry computations to the nearest dollar.

(2) One of the trucks owned by the company had just come in for its periodic inspection when it was noticed that the diesel engine, which normally lasts four years, was unexpectedly in need of an overhaul and that the trailer needed replacement. The engine cost $2,000 new and was two and a half years old. However, with a $500 overhaul, it was expected to last two more years. The old trailer cost $5,000 and had a carrying value of $750. The price of new trailers had increased by $1,000 since the old one was purchased. The company accounts for each truck component separately and records depreciation on a straight-line basis.

Prepare journal entries to record the overhaul of the engine and the replacement of the trailer.

(3) The company exchanged a business automobile. The old automobile had an original cost of $6,500, an undepreciated cost of $2,400, and a current fair value of $2,000 when exchanged. In addition, the company paid $5,200 cash

for the new automobile. The list price of the new automobile was $7,300 and the cash price was $7,200. Prepare a journal entry to record the exchange.

(4) The company exchanged 100 shares of treasury stock (its $50 par value common stock) for land to be used in the business. The treasury stock had cost $60 per share, and on the exchange date, it had a market price of $65 per share. The company received $1,200 for scrap when an existing building was immediately removed from this land. At what amount should this land be capitalized?

(5) The company received $20,000 in cash and a used computer with a current fair value of $180,000 from Chee Corporation for the company's old computer having a current fair value of $200,000 and an undepreciated cost of $160,000 recorded in the accounts.

Compute the gain (if any) that the company should recognize on this exchange transaction and the cost basis for financial accounting purposes of the used computer acquired from Chee Corporation. Your answers should be consistent with provisions of **APB Opinion No. 29.**

12A-2 In auditing the records of Big Valley Feed Co. for the fiscal year ended December 31, Year 5, you discover the following:

(1) Machine W with a cash selling price of $18,800 was acquired on April 1, Year 5, in exchange for $20,000 face amount of bonds payable selling at 94 and maturing on April 1, Year 15. The accountant recorded the acquisition by a debit to Machinery and a credit to Bonds Payable for $20,000. Straight-line depreciation was recorded, based on a five-year life and amounted to $2,400 for nine months. In computing depreciation, residual value of $4,000 was used.

(2) Machine X listed at a cash price of $6,400 was purchased on January 2, Year 5. The company paid $1,000 down and $500 per month for 12 months. The last payment was made on December 30, Year 5. Straight-line depreciation, based on a five-year life and no residual value, was recorded at $1,400 for the year. Freight of $200 on Machine X was charged to Transportation-in.

(3) Machine Y was recorded at $5,100, which included the carrying value of $1,100 of a machine accepted as a trade-in and cash of $4,000. The cash price of Machine Y was $4,250 and the trade-in allowance was $250. This transaction took place on December 28, Year 5.

(4) Machine Z was acquired on January 10, Year 5, in exchange for a past-due account receivable of $14,000 on which an allowance of 20% was established at the end of Year 4. The fair value of the machine on January 10 was estimated at $11,000. The machine was recorded by a debit to Machinery and a credit to Accounts Receivable for $14,000. No depreciation was recorded on Machine Z because it was not used in operations. In March, Machine Z was exchanged for 100 shares of the company's own stock having a market value of $105 per share. The Treasury Stock account was debited for $14,000, the carrying value of Machine Z.

Instructions Record any correcting entries required as of December 31, Year 5, for each transaction (1) through (4) above. Assume that revenue and expense accounts have not been closed for Year 5.

12A-3 Minahan Corporation received a $400,000 low bid from a reputable manufacturer for the construction of special production equipment needed in an expansion program. Because its factory was not operating at capacity, Minahan Corporation decided to construct the equipment there and recorded the following production costs related to the construction:

Services of consulting engineer	$ 17,500
Work subcontracted	20,000
Materials	200,000
Plant labor normally assigned to production	65,000
Plant labor normally assigned to maintenance	100,000*
Total	$402,500

* Included in factory overhead costs.

Management prefers to record the cost of the equipment under the incremental cost method. Approximately 40% of the corporation's production is devoted to government supply contracts, which are all based in some way on cost. The contracts require that any self-constructed equipment be allocated its full share of all costs related to the construction.

The following information is also available:

(1) The above production labor was for partial fabrication of the equipment in the plant. Skilled personnel were required and were assigned from other projects. The maintenance labor would have been idle time of nonproduction plant employees who would have been retained on the payroll whether or not their services were utilized.

(2) Payroll taxes and employee fringe benefits are approximately 30% of labor cost and are included in factory overhead costs. Total factory overhead costs for the year were $5,630,000.

(3) Factory overhead costs are approximately 50% variable and are applied on the basis of production labor cost. Production labor cost for the year for the corporation's normal products totaled $6,810,000.

(4) General and administrative expenses include $22,500 of executive salary costs and $10,500 of postage, telephone, supplies, and miscellaneous costs identifiable with this equipment construction.

Instructions

a Prepare a schedule computing the amount which should be reported as the full cost of the constructed equipment to meet the requirements of the government contracts. Any supporting computations should be in good form.

b Prepare a schedule computing the incremental cost of the constructed equipment.

c What is the largest amount that should be capitalized as the cost of the constructed equipment? Why?

12A-4 Dane Corporation offered Evon Company $200,000 cash for some used machinery. Evon replied that the price offered was acceptable but for tax reasons it did not want an all-cash transaction. Evon then offered to sell the machinery to Dane for a $50,000 cash down payment with the balance payable in five equal annual installments of $30,000 each, with interest payable annually at 6% on the unpaid balance. In addition, Dane agreed to sign a contract to purchase certain raw material from Evon during the following year.

Dane's management decided that, while Evon's raw material prices were in excess of current market prices, the 6% interest rate on the note was sufficiently below the 10% that Dane would have to pay to borrow elsewhere to make the contract appealing. Accordingly, on July 1, Year 7, Dane accepted Evon's proposal, made the down payment, signed the 6% note and the contract for the purchase of the raw material, and accepted delivery of the used machinery.

Instructions

a Record the acquisition of the machinery in the accounts of Dane Corporation at July 1, Year 7. At that date the discounted value of the five-year, 6% note, based on a market interest rate of 10%, was $135,490.

    b Prepare entries for Dane Corporation at December 31, Year 7, to record the following:

      (1) Interest expense for six months. Use the "interest method" of amortizing the discount on the note payable.

      (2) Depreciation for six months. Assume a five-year life for the used machinery, no residual value, and the straight-line method of depreciation.

      (3) Any required adjustment to cost of goods sold. Assume that one-half of the raw material contracted for with Evon had been purchased and that the goods incorporating this material had been sold by December 31, Year 7.

12A-5 Arthur Pate keeps his accounting records on a cash basis. On February 28, Year 10, he sold property, purchased 17 years earlier for $110,000, to Anna Smith for $150,000. The cost allocated to the building was $70,000 and the accumulated depreciation to the date of the sale was $42,500.

    The escrow statements as of February 28 for the buyer and the seller are shown below:

Seller's Escrow Statement (City Escrow Co., Escrow No. 911)

Sale price		$150,000
Title fee (one-half)	$ 430	
Drawing deed and recording	15	
Taxes for period Jan. 1 to Feb. 28, Year 10, accrued and unpaid	200	
Interest accrued on mortgage	185	
Lease deposits	850	
Pro rata rent	340	
Mortgage, assumed by buyer	73,460	
Fire insurance, pro rata		1,430
Revenue stamps (tax on real estate transfers)	150	
Commission	9,000	
Cash to seller, Arthur Pate	66,800	
Total	$151,430	$151,430

Buyer's Escrow Statement (City Escrow Co., Escrow No. 911)

Deposit of cash by buyer on Jan. 30 and recorded in Escrow Deposit account		$ 76,900
Sale price	$150,000	
Title fee (one-half)	430	
Recording deed	15	
Fire insurance, pro rata	1,430	
Mortgage, assumed by buyer		73,460
Taxes for period Jan. 1 to Feb. 28, Year 10, accrued and unpaid		200
Lease deposits		850
Pro rata rent		340
Interest accrued on mortgage		185
Balance paid to buyer, Anna Smith	60	
Total	$151,935	$151,935

Instructions
a Prepare a schedule showing how Pate should determine the gain or loss on this transaction. Ignore income taxes.
b Prepare a journal entry to record the above transaction in Pate's accounting records.
c Prepare a journal entry to record the above transaction in Smith's accounting records. Assuming that $80,000 of total cost is allocated to land and that items representing future expense or revenue are recorded in nominal accounts.

12A-6 On the evening of September 20, Year 8, a fire damaged the office and warehouse of Wilson Merchandising Corporation, whose fiscal year ends on December 31. The only accounting record saved was the general ledger, from which the following information was obtained as of August 31, Year 8:

	Debit	Credit
Accounts receivable	$25,000	
Inventory, Dec. 31, Year 7	60,920	
Accounts payable		$ 27,500
Sales to Aug. 31		100,000
Purchases to Aug. 31	80,000	

The following additional data are available:

(1) The September bank statement and canceled checks revealed that checks written during the period September 1 to 20 totaled $15,000: $8,000 to liquidate the accounts payable as of August 31, $2,000 for September purchases, and $5,000 paid for other expenses. Deposits during the same period amounted to $11,500, which consisted of receipts on account from customers, with the exception of a $1,300 refund from a vendor for goods returned in September.
(2) Correspondence with suppliers revealed unrecorded obligations of $7,200 on September 20 for purchases during September.
(3) Customers acknowledged indebtedness of $29,500 as of the close of business on September 20, Year 8.
(4) The following insurance was in effect on inventory at the date of the fire:

Insurance company	Amount of coverage	Coinsurance requirement
Allied Mutual	$30,000	80%
Blue Regional	20,000	70%
Claim Free	10,000	None

(5) The insurance companies agreed that the fire loss claim should be based on the assumption that the overall gross profit rate of 40% of sales for the past two years was in effect during the current year and that the cost of inventory so determined is a reasonable estimate of the current fair value of the inventory.
(6) Inventory with a cost of $22,400 was recovered and is in good condition. The balance of the inventory was a total loss. The office and the warehouse building were not insured. It cost the company $4,150 to repair the damage to the office but the warehouse was a total loss. The warehouse (excluding land) cost $50,000 to construct, was fully depreciated, and had a current fair value of $10,000 at the date of the fire.

Instructions

a Prepare a schedule computing the approximate cost of inventory lost in the fire.

b Prepare a schedule computing the pro rata claim to be filed with each insurance company.

c Assuming that Wilson Merchandising Corporation is indemnified as determined in part **b**, what is the loss or gain from fire that should be reported in its income statement for Year 8? Ignore income tax effect on the loss or gain.

Group B

12B-1 Six situations relating to plant assets are described below for Costello Corporation for Year 16. Specific instructions are given for each situation.

(1) A building was appraised at $100,000 when a fire occurred causing $60,000 damage. The loss was insured under an Erie Insurance Company fire insurance policy in the amount of $60,000 which contained an 80% coinsurance clause. Compute the amount that will be recovered by Costello Corporation under the policy.

(2) Land, buildings, and equipment were acquired in Year 16 from a bankrupt company at a lump-sum price of $90,000. At the time of acquisition, the company paid $6,000 to have the assets appraised. The appraisal disclosed the following current fair values:

Land	$60,000
Buildings	40,000
Equipment	20,000

Determine the cost that should be assigned to the land, buildings, and equipment for financial accounting purposes.

(3) Equipment for use in the company's regular manufacturing departments was built in Year 16 by the company's machine shop. The costs recorded by the machine shop for the equipment are shown below:

Materials and purchased parts	$ 6,000
Freight on materials and purchased parts	300
Insurance in transit on purchased parts	60
Implicit interest on capital used in building equipment	140
Labor to build	5,000
Labor to test	500
Factory overhead costs	2,000
Total costs	$14,000

The cash price for the equipment if purchased from outsiders would have been $20,500. Compute the cost of the equipment for financial reporting purposes.

(4) The company purchased a new machine on May 1, Year 7, for $50,000. At the time of acquisition, the machine was estimated to have an economic life of ten years and an estimated residual value of $2,000. The company has recorded monthly depreciation using the straight-line method. On March 1,

Year 16, the machine was sold for $3,500. Compute the gain or loss on the sale of the machine.

(5) At the beginning of Year 6, the company purchased a tooling machine for $30,000. The machine was being depreciated by the straight-line method over an estimated economic life of 20 years, with no residual value.

At the beginning of Year 16, when the machine had been in use for 10 years, the company paid $3,000 to overhaul it. As a result of this improvement, it was expected that the economic life of the machine would be extended an additional two years. What should be the depreciation expense recorded on the machine for Year 16.

(6) On January 4, Year 16, the company traded in an old delivery truck for a newer model. Data relative to the old and new trucks follow:

Old truck:

Original cost	$ 8,000
Accumulated depreciation on Jan. 4, Year 16	6,000
Average published retail value	1,700

New truck:

List price	$10,000
Cash price without trade-in	9,000
Cash paid with trade-in	7,800

Record the exchange transaction for financial accounting purposes following the guidelines established in *APB Opinion No. 29.*

12B-2 Jack Corporation recently purchased a new machine and retired an old machine which cost $16,000 and had a carrying value of $2,000 at the time of retirement. The company had received two offers to sell the new machine as follows:

(1) M Company offered its machine at $18,000 and agreed to allow $1,000 on the old machine as a trade-in.
(2) N Company offered an equivalent machine for $17,500, terms 2/10, n/30, but would not accept a trade-in.

Jack Corporation accepted N's offer and sold its old machine for $700 after incurring $220 in labor costs to remove it from the building. Additional costs incurred in placing the new machine in use were:

Freight (paid in cash)	$750
Installation:	
Materials	50
Labor	240
Travel expenses paid to N Company's engineer who supervised the installation	
(There was no charge for the engineer's time.)	210
Costs incurred in testing new machine:	
Operator's wages	60
Spoiled materials	100

As a result of an error in the treasurer's department, the N Company invoice was not paid until 30 days after invoice date, and therefore the cash discount could not be taken.

In the process of removing the old machine, a section of the factory floor was damaged, which had to be repaired at a cost of $285 paid to an independent contractor.

Instructions Prepare journal entries, together with supporting computations, to record the retirement of the old machine and the purchase of the new. Credit Materials Inventory for the cost of materials used and Accrued Payroll for labor costs incurred.

12B-3 Farrell Company was incorporated in January of the current year but was unable to begin manufacturing activities until July 1 because plant facilities were not finished until that date.

On December 31, the company's record of the construction and accounting for the plant appears in a Plant Assets account as follows:

Plant Assets

Jan. 31	Land and old sawmill	$325,000
Feb. 28	Cost of removing old sawmill	7,400
May 1	Partial payment on contract for construction of new building . . .	175,000
May 1	Legal fees	4,000
June 1	Second payment on construction contract	175,000
June 1	Insurance premium paid (effective date of policy is May 1)	3,600
June 1	Special tax assessments	5,000
June 30	General expenses	24,000
July 1	Final payment on construction contract	175,000
Dec. 31	Asset write-up	40,000
	Total debits to account	$934,000
Dec. 31	Less: Depreciation at 4% for six months	18,680
	Account balance at Dec. 31	$915,320

Additional information

(1) On January 31 the company paid $25,000 in cash and gave 3,000 shares of 8% cumulative preferred stock, par value $100 per share, for land and building. On January 30 a large block of these shares had been sold for $105 per share. The preferred stock was recorded at par value.

(2) An old sawmill was on the land when acquired. The demolition company charged $7,400 for removal and retained all usable materials.

(3) Legal fees covered the organization of the company $1,500; purchase of land, $2,000; and construction contract, $500.

(4) Insurance on the new building was taken out on May 1. The three-year premium was paid on June 1, upon receipt of the invoice.

(5) General expenses are for the period from January 2 to June 30 and include president's salary, $12,000; salary of plant superintendent who supervised construction of new building, $10,000; and office salaries, $2,000.

(6) The special tax assessments covered street improvements.

(7) During the six months' construction period, a new union contract for construction workers was negotiated calling for an increase of 15% in wages, and there were increases in construction material prices. On the basis of these facts, the plant superintendent suggested that the building be written up by $40,000 to recognize the increase in the replacement cost of the building. The credit was made to the Retained Earnings account.

(8) The new building is to be depreciated at the rate of 4% per year; depreciation for six months was debited to the Depreciation Expense account.

Instructions

a Prepare a work sheet classifying the transactions of Farrell Company in proper accounts. Allow separate columns for Land and for Building; other accounts should be analyzed in a Miscellaneous column.

b Prepare a single entry which would restate the accounting records to an acceptable basis. The accounts are still open for the current year.

12B-4 Hill Corporation completed six transactions in the current year aimed at simplifying the company's operations, improving its competitive position, and resolving business disputes.

The following three transactions involved transfers of mining claims to stockholders of Hill Corporation:

(1) Claim No. 1, carried in the accounts at a cost of $5,000, was sold for cash of $12,000.

(2) Claim No. 2, carried in the accounts at a cost of $3,000, was exchanged for 200 shares of Hill Corporation common stock. The common stock of Hill Corporation, which is publicly owned and widely traded, was selling for $125 a share at the time of the exchange. Record the stock acquired in the Treasury Stock account.

(3) Claim No. 3, carried in the accounts at a cost of $20,000, was transferred to Alice Joy, a stockholder, in consideration of her withdrawal of a patent infringement suit against Hill Corporation. When asked for an estimate of the current fair value of the mining claims, the president answered that it was "anyone's guess." Further question elicited the reluctant response, "Well, the first claim was probably worth about $15,000 and the other two were each worth about twice that." You have concluded that no more precise valuation data can be obtained.

The following three exchanges were made with Obispo Corporation, a competitor:

(4) Hill Corporation exchanged its 5% common stock interest in Z Co. carried at cost of $80,000, for a plant site owned by Obispo Corporation reliably appraised at $200,000.

(5) Hill Corporation traded certain inventory items located in Kansas City for similar items held by Obispo Corporation in Seattle. To equalize trading values, Obispo paid Hill an additional $2,000 cash. The cost of the inventory given up by Hill was $8,200; the current fair value of the inventory items was $10,000. Hill uses a perpetual inventory system.

(6) Hill Corporation obtained production jigs and dies from Obispo Corporation, giving in exchange a used milling machine and cash of $1,700. The milling machine was carried in Hill's accounts at its original cost of $20,000; accumulated depreciation was $12,000. Obispo would have been equally willing to pay Hill the $10,500 appraised value of the milling machine in cash, but Hill insisted on making the exchange for the jigs and dies.

Instructions Prepare journal entries for Hill Corporation to record each of the six transactions described above in accordance with provisions of **APB Opinion No. 29.**

12B-5 On July 10, Year 5, Flora Sternberg your client, sold a building to Peter Salomon. The escrow statements for the seller and the buyer are presented side by side on page 517.

Sternberg's accounting records are maintained on the accrual basis. When you undertake the September 30, Year 5, quarterly audit for your client, the following information is available to you:

(1) A "Suspense" account was opened for cash received in connection with the sale, including monthly receipts on the purchase-money mortgage. The

	Flora Sternberg, Seller		Peter Salomon, Buyer	
	Charges	*Credits*	*Charges*	*Credits*
Sale price		$310,000	$310,000	
First mortgage assumed by buyer . .	$120,000			$120,000
Purchase-money mortgage—6% . . .	80,000			80,000
Prorations:				
Property taxes from July 1	250			250
Insurance prorated		200	200	
Interest accrued	350			350
Fees:				
Escrow	100		100	
Title insurance . . . . : .			790	
Recording and legal	40		60	
Revenue stamps (taxes)			550	
Funds deposited in escrow account on July 10				111,100
Items paid from escrow account— commission	18,600			
Remit to Flora Sternberg	90,860			
Totals	$310,200	$310,200	$311,700	$311,700

"Suspense" account shows a credit balance of $93,655 on September 30, Year 5.

(2) The purchase-money mortgage payments are $1,000 per month, plus accrued interest on unpaid balance. The first payment was received on August 10 and amounted to $1,400; the second payment was received on September 9 and amounted to $1,395. Both amounts were credited to the "Suspense" account.

(3) The building and land were purchased on July 1, Year 1, for $270,000. The building was depreciated over a 40-year life by the straight-line method. Accumulated depreciation at December 31, Year 4, was $17,500. A half-year's depreciation has been consistently recorded for assets purchased or sold during the year. No depreciation has been recorded by Sternberg for Year 5.

Instructions

a Determine the net proceeds to the seller on the land and on the building. The sales price and expenses of sale are allocated by the seller as follows: land, 30%; building, 80%.

b Prepare the adjusting journal entries to record the sale and related transactions in Sternberg's accounting records. Prepare a supporting schedule showing the gain or loss on the sale of land and the gain or loss on the sale of building. Ignore income taxes.

c Prepare the entry to record the purchase of land and building in Salomon's accounting records. The purchase price, including all fees, is allocated 30% to land and 70% to building.

12B-6 Monterey Manufacturing Corporation manufactures patio furniture. On August 31, Year 2, the company had a fire which completely destroyed its building, the goods in process inventory, and machinery. Additional data follow:

(1) The cost of plant assets destroyed and the related accumulated depreciation accounts at August 31, Year 2, were:

	Cost	Accumulated depreciation
Building	$40,000	$17,500
Machinery	15,000	4,500

At present prices the cost to replace the destroyed property would be: building, $80,000; machinery, $37,500. At the time of the fire it was estimated that the building was 50% depreciated, and the destroyed machinery was one-third depreciated. Insurance companies agreed that the insurable value of the building and machinery was $65,000 on the date of fire.

(2) After the fire a physical inventory was taken. The raw materials were valued at $26,000 and the finished goods at 52,000.

(3) The inventories on December 31, Year 1, were: raw materials, $20,000; goods in process, $48,000; and finished goods, $54,000.

(4) The sales of the first eight months of Year 2 were $150,000 and raw material purchases were $55,000. Direct labor for the eight months was $40,000; for the past five years factory overhead has been applied at the rate of 80% of direct labor cost. The gross profit for the last five years has averaged 30% of sales price.

(5) Insurance is carried with two companies, each with an 80% coinsurance clause. The amount of insurance carried with each company is as follows:

	Building and machinery	Inventories
Acme Insurance Company	$42,000	$64,800
Zenith Indemnity Company	20,000	21,600

Instructions

a Compute the estimated cost of the goods in process lost in the fire.

b Compute the expected recovery from each insurance company, assuming that the estimated cost of inventory lost is accepted as a measure of current fair value on the date of the fire.

c Assuming that Monterey Manufacturing Corporation is indemnified as determined in part **b,** what is the loss or gain from fire that should be reported in its income statement prepared at the end of Year 2? Ignore the tax effect on the loss or gain.

CHAPTER 13

PLANT ASSETS: DEPRECIATION AND DEPLETION

In Chapter 12 we described plant assets as a "bundle of future services" and considered the problem of determining the acquisition cost of the future services embodied in such assets. This chapter is concerned with the problem of measuring the cost of asset services "withdrawn from the bundle" and consumed in business operations.

Depreciation is the portion of the cost of plant assets that is deducted from revenue for asset services used in the operations of a business. In practice the term *depreciation* is used to describe the cost of the expired services of tangible plant assets such as buildings and equipment. Recording the expired service cost of such intangible assets as patents and goodwill is called *amortization. Depletion* for accounting purposes refers to the estimated cost of natural resources such as oil, gas, timber, and iron ore that have been removed from their source.

DEPRECIATION

The concept of depreciation is closely linked to the concept of business income. Since part of the service potential of depreciable assets is exhausted in the revenue-generating process each period, the cost of these services must be deducted from revenue in measuring periodic income; the expired cost must be recovered before a business is considered "as well off" as at the beginning of the period. Depreciation is a measure of this cost.

Depreciation is one of the most controversial and troublesome areas in accounting. In the early history of accounting, it was necessary to convince users of accounting information that depreciation was actually a cost of doing business. Business executives tended to view depreciation as a matter of "setting aside something" during prosperous periods for the replacement of depreciable assets. When earnings were high, large amounts of depreciation might be recorded; when earnings were low or losses were incurred, depreciation was not recorded. Today it is universally agreed that depreciation is an expense that must be recorded whether or not revenue is sufficient to absorb it.

Accounting for depreciation is a process of cost allocation, not valuation. The acquisition of plant assets means that asset services have been purchased in advance of their use. Between the time of acquisition and the time of use, the value of these services may change materially, because of supply and demand factors or changes in price levels. Therefore, the accountant's measure of the historical cost of the asset services that are used may be significantly different from the current cost of acquiring similar services. This difference is germane to a variety of managerial decisions; however, the question of revaluing depreciable assets (in effect, revaluing the remaining unused services) at some time subsequent to acquisition should not be confused with the cost allocation problem. In this chapter we shall deal only with the allocation of the cost of plant assets; revaluation of assets for accounting purposes in response to increases in replacement costs and the general price level is considered in Chapter 22.

Factors in estimating periodic depreciation

The estimate of periodic depreciation is dependent on three separate variables:

1 *Economic life.* This involves choosing the unit in which economic life is to be measured and then estimating how many units of service are embodied in each asset.

2 *Depreciation base.* An asset may be sold by a business before its service value is completely consumed. The depreciation base is the cost of asset services that will be used by a given firm, and it is usually less than the original investment in the asset.

3 *Method of cost apportionment.* The problem here is to determine the amount of services that has expired in each accounting period. A corollary issue is to decide whether all units of service have an equal cost, or whether some units of service have a higher or lower cost than others.

Estimating economic life

The economic life of an asset is the total units of service expected to be derived from that asset. Business managers commonly measure economic life in terms of time units, for example, months or years. Economic life may also be measured in terms of output or activity and expressed in such physical units as tons, miles, board feet, gallons, or machine-hours. We may, for example, describe the estimated economic life of an automobile as *four years* or *100,000 miles.* Forces which tend to limit the economic life of an asset should be considered in determining the type of *unit of service* to use for a given asset or group of assets. The causes of decrease in economic life may be divided into two broad classes: (1) physical causes (including casualties) and (2) functional or economic causes.

Physical deterioration results largely from wear and tear due to operating use, and rust, rot, or decay due to the action of the elements. These physical forces terminate the usefulness of plant items by rendering them incapable of performing the services for which they were intended and thus set the maximum limit on economic life. Unusual events such as accidents, floods, earthquakes, etc., also serve to terminate or reduce asset usefulness.

Functional or *economic factors* may render an asset in good physical condition no longer useful because it is not economical to keep it in service or because of legal or other limits on the use of an asset. Two primary causes of functional depreciation are obsolescence and inadequacy. *Obsolescence* refers to the effect of innovations and technical improvements on the economic life of existing assets. An inevitable result of industrial research and development activities is to make existing plant assets obsolete. The jet airliners, for example, made propeller-driven aircraft uneconomical for major airlines to operate. Obsolescence thus terminated the economic life of many piston aircraft and sent them to the used plane market even though they had a physical potential of many more miles of service.

Inadequacy refers to the effect of growth and changes in the scale of a firm's operation in terminating the economic life of assets. A warehouse may be in sound condition, but if more space is required which cannot economically be provided by adding a separate building, the old warehouse has become inadequate and its economic life, from the owner's standpoint, is terminated. In a general sense, any plant asset whose capacity is such that it cannot be operated with optimum results, or which does not fit the requirements of the business, is inadequate.

In a highly developed industrial society, functional causes of depreciation probably have a greater influence on economic lives than physical wear and tear, particularly with respect to special-purpose equipment. Estimates of economic life are therefore strongly influenced by these factors.

The problem of choosing an appropriate *unit* of economic life also calls for search for the causes of depreciation. The objective is to choose the unit most closely related to the cause of service exhaustion. When economic life is limited largely by the effect of operating wear and tear, a unit that reflects physical use is appropriate. For example, hours of service might be chosen as the unit of economic life for an electric motor, or miles of service for a truck. On the other hand, the physical causes that predominate in limiting the economic life of buildings are probably related more closely to the passage of time than actual usage; therefore, an estimated economic life in terms of years would be more appropriate.

No estimate of economic life can be made with high precision. The best procedure is to start with an estimate of physical economic life as a maximum, modify this by considering the probable effects of obsolescence and inadequacy, and then be prepared to adjust these estimates in the light of actual experience. When the estimated economic life of an asset is revised, the undepreciated cost is allocated to the remaining years of service.

Establishing the depreciation base

The depreciation base (or "depreciable cost") of an asset is the portion of its cost that should be charged against revenue during its economic life. Since the owner of an asset may sell it before its serviceability is ended, the initial cost of a plant asset, as determined using the guidelines established in Chapter 12, is not necessarily its depreciation base. For example, a car rental company may pay $4,000 for a new car and sell it at the end of two years for $1,500, even though its economic life is much longer. The depreciation base is $2,500, the difference between cost and resale value.

Scrapping or removing buildings, structures, and heavy equipment may involve substantial cost in the year of retirement; theoretically, removal costs should be estimated and included in the depreciation base. Including removal cost in the depreciation base means that the entire cost involved in obtaining the services will be charged to the services provided by the assets, without regard to the timing of the expenditure. In practice, however, removal costs either may be ignored or netted against the estimated net residual value of the asset. The formula for arriving at the depreciation base thus becomes:

Depreciation base = acquisition cost − estimated net residual value

In some instances, net residual value (gross residual minus estimated removal costs) is likely to be so small or uncertain that it may be ignored in establishing the depreciation base.

Depreciation methods

When the economic life of an asset has been estimated and its depreciation base established, there remains the problem of determining the portion of cost that will expire with each unit of economic life. There are two major variables to be considered in reaching a systematic and rational solution to this problem:

1 The *quantity* of services "withdrawn from the bundle" may be equal or may vary during each period of economic life.

2 The *cost* of various units of service may be equal or may differ per unit during each period of economic life.

Because of the relatively high degree of uncertainty that surrounds estimates of economic life and service use, the distinction between these two variables may become blurred. We may illustrate by reference to a situation that is generally familiar—the depreciation of an automobile used for business purposes. Assume that the auto in question costs $6,600, has an expected net residual value of $600, and is estimated to have an economic life of 100,000 miles. The average depreciation expense per unit of service (1 mile) is 6 cents [($6,600 − $600) ÷ 100,000]. The miles of service used in each accounting period, however, may vary. If 20,000 miles are driven during the first year and 30,000 miles during the second year, there has been a variation in the *quantity* of service used, and depreciation of $1,200 for the first year and $1,800 for the second will recognize this fact.

On the other hand, even if the automobile is driven 20,000 miles in each year for five years, there may be a difference in the *cost* of the miles of service in each of these five periods. The miles of service when the auto is new and operating at top efficiency may be more valuable (and thus presumably more costly) than service miles during later years. Therefore, the assumption that each service mile bears the same depreciation expense may not be reasonable, and we might compute depreciation on the assumption that early miles cost more than later miles. For example, depreciation might be computed at 8 cents per mile for the first 20,000 miles, 6 cents for the next 20,000 miles, etc.

There are a number of systematic depreciation methods that attempt to recognize these factors in varying degrees. They may be classified as follows:

1 Straight-line method (based on expiration of time)
2 Accelerated methods (based on expiration of time)
  a Fixed-percentage-of-declining-balance
  b Sum-of-the-years'-digits
3 Units-of-output method (based on physical service or production)
4 Retirement and replacement methods
5 Interest methods

Depreciation under the straight-line and accelerated methods is a function of time rather than use. On the other hand, depreciation under the units-of-output method is a function of actual usage rather than the passage of time.

Depreciation may be computed to the nearest month, although other procedures consistently applied may be acceptable. A description of the most widely used depreciation methods follows.

Straight-Line Method The distinguishing characteristic of the straight-line method of depreciation is that each year of service absorbs an equal portion of acquisition cost. Depreciation per year is thus computed as follows:

$$\text{Depreciation per year} = \frac{\text{acquisition cost} - \text{estimated net residual value}}{\text{years of economic life}}$$

To illustrate the straight-line method of depreciation, assume that a machine is acquired at the beginning of Year 1 for $7,000 and that the net residual value of the machine at the end of four years of economic life is estimated at $1,000. The depreciation expense, accumulated depreciation, and carrying value of the machine over its economic life are presented below:

	Depreciation expense for year	Accumulated depreciation	Carrying value of machine
Beginning of Year 1			$7,000
End of Year 1	$1,500	$1,500	5,500
End of Year 2	1,500	3,000	4,000
End of Year 3	1,500	4,500	2,500
End of Year 4	1,500	6,000	1,000

At the end of each year, depreciation expense on this machine would be recorded as follows:

```
Depreciation Expense  . . . . . . . . . . . . . . . . . . . . . . .   1,500
        Accumulated Depreciation: Machinery  . . . . . . . . . .            1,500
To record depreciation for the year.
```

Accelerated Methods The assumption that plant assets yield either a greater quantity of service or more valuable services in early years of economic life has led accountants to devise methods of depreciation that will result in larger amounts of depreciation in early years of economic life, and smaller amounts in later years. These are known as *accelerated methods* of depreciation, and there are a number of different approaches.

Fixed-percentage-of-declining-balance method Under this method, a percentage depreciation rate is computed which, when applied to the carrying value of the asset as of the beginning of each period, will result in writing the asset down to estimated net residual value at the end of its economic life. Since the rate computed is applied on a constantly declining carrying value, the amount of depreciation decreases each year. The formula for computing the required rate per year (when *n* = years of economic life) is:

$$\text{Depreciation rate} = 1 - \sqrt[n]{\frac{\text{net residual value}}{\text{acquisition cost}}}$$

Net residual value greater than zero must be estimated, since it is impossible to reduce any amount to zero by applying a constant percentage to the successively declining remainder. The depreciation rate for an asset costing $10,000, having a net residual value of $1,296 and an economic life of four years, would be computed as follows:

$$\text{Depreciation rate} = 1 - \sqrt[4]{\frac{\$1,296}{\$10,000}} = 1 - \frac{6}{10} = 40\%$$

If the application of this formula yields a rate of, say, 39.69, rounding the rate to 40% would not be objectionable, from either a practical or a theoretical point of view, since measurement of depreciation is only a rough estimate.

The tabulation at the top of page 526 shows depreciation expense for the four-year period using a fixed percentage of 40% on declining carrying value.

It should be noted that the carrying value at the end of the fourth year is equal to the estimated net residual value, $1,296, and that annual depreciation expense decreases rapidly. (In this example, since the depreciation rate is 40%, the depreciation expense in the second and each of the succeeding years is only 60% of the expense reported a year earlier.)

Federal income tax law provides that for certain assets the fixed percentage may be as high as twice the applicable straight-line rate. For example, the straight-line rate for an asset with an estimated economic life of four years is 25% and the fixed-percentage rate would be 50% (25% × 2). This approach is referred to as the *double-declining-balance*

Year	Carrying value at beginning of year	Depreciation expense		Accumulated depreciation
		Amount (40% of carrying value at beginning of year)	Percentage of total	
1	$10,000	$4,000	46.0	$4,000
2	6,000	2,400	27.6	6,400
3	3,600	1,440	16.5	7,840
4	2,160	864	9.9	8,704
Balance	1,296			
		$8,704	100.0	

(or 200%-declining-balance) method. For some assets the rate may not exceed 150% of the straight-line rate. Current tax regulations require that residual value be taken into account only as a limiting factor in applying these rates; that is, the asset cannot be depreciated below net residual value.

Sum-of-the-years'-digits method Under this method, a decreasing depreciation expense is computed by a simple mathematical procedure relating to arithmetic progressions. The sum of a series of numbers representing the years of economic life becomes the denominator of the depreciation fraction in any year.[1] The numerator of the depreciation fraction for each year is the remaining years of economic life taken from the beginning of the year. Since the denominator remains constant and the numerator declines each year, the result is a decreasing depreciation charge. Furthermore, since the total of the numerators of the depreciation fractions is equal to the denominator, the sum of all the fractions is 1 and 100% of the depreciation base ultimately will be charged to expense.

The tabulation at the top of page 527 illustrates the application of this method to an asset costing $22,000, having a net residual value of $2,000, and an economic life of four years.

Fractional-period depreciation under accelerated methods Under accelerated methods, depreciation is determined for each full unit of economic life. A question of mechanics arises when assets are acquired during the year and less than a full year's depreciation is to be taken during the

---

[1] The formula for determining the sum of any arithmetic progression of n consecutive numbers is $n\left(\dfrac{n+1}{2}\right)$. Thus the sum of all numbers from 1 to 15 is $15\left(\dfrac{16}{2}\right)$, or 120. Tables are available which provide the decimal equivalent of the depreciation rate for each year of economic life.

Year	Deprecia-tion fraction	Deprecia-tion base ($22,000 − $2,000)	Deprecia-tion expense	Accu-mulated depre-ciation	Carrying value
					$22,000
1	$\frac{4}{10}$	$20,000	$8,000	$ 8,000	14,000
2	$\frac{3}{10}$	20,000	6,000	14,000	8,000
3	$\frac{2}{10}$	20,000	4,000	18,000	4,000
4	$\frac{1}{10}$	20,000	2,000	20,000	2,000
Sum 10					

first and last years of economic life. The logical solution to this problem follows:

1 *Double-declining-balance method.* Compute depreciation expense for a fraction of year in the year of acquisition and apply the appropriate percentage to the beginning carrying value of the asset to compute depreciation for subsequent fiscal years.

2 *Sum-of-the-years'-digits method.* Compute the depreciation for each full year of economic life, and then allocate each full year's depreciation charge between two different fiscal years. To illustrate, assume the following data:

Cost of asset, April 1, 1980 . . . . $8,000
Estimated economic life . . . . 5 years
Rate using double-declining-balance method 40%
Estimated net residual value $500

The computation of depreciation for the first partial year (1980) and the next full year (1981) under the two accelerated methods is demonstrated in the tabulation at the top of page 528.

The depreciation for the remaining $3\frac{1}{4}$ years would be determined in a similar manner.

Units-of-Output Method A more realistic allocation of the cost of some plant assets can be obtained by dividing the depreciable cost by the estimated units of output or production (machine-hours, units of product produced, or miles driven) rather than by the years of economic life. A bus company, for example, might compute depreciation on its vehicles by a mileage basis. If a bus costs $30,000 and is estimated to have an economic life of 200,000 miles, the depreciation rate per mile of operation will be 15 cents ($30,000 ÷ 200,000). At the end of each year, the amount of depreciation will be determined by multiplying the 15-cent rate by the number of miles the bus was operated during the year.

Double-declining balance		Sum-of-the-years' digits	
Full year of economic life	**Depreciation**	**Full year of economic life**	**Depreciation**
Year 1 (40% × $8,000) . .	$3,200	1 ($\frac{5}{15}$ × $7,500)	$2,500
Year 2 [40% × ($8,000 − $3,200)]	1,920	2 ($\frac{4}{15}$ × $7,500)	2,000
Depreciation for period from Apr. 1, 1980 to Dec. 31, 1980:			
$\frac{3}{4}$(9 mo.) × $3,200	$2,400	$\frac{3}{4}$(9 mo.) × $2,500	$1,875
Depreciation for 1981:			
40% × $5,600 ($8,000 −		$\frac{1}{4}$(3 mo.) × $2,500	$ 625
$2,400 taken in		$\frac{3}{4}$(9 mo.) × $2,000	1,500
1980)	$2,240	Total	$2,125

The estimated economic life of an asset using the units-of-output method is measured in terms of potential physical services or units of production and periodic depreciation is based on the actual use of the asset. As a result, *total* depreciation expense for a fiscal period varies if use varies, but the *depreciation per unit of output is constant.* The units-of-output method of depreciation is particularly appropriate when asset use fluctuates widely from period to period and depreciation is deemed to be more closely related to physical usage of the asset rather than to functional obsolescence.

Some accountants have suggested that certain assets be depreciated on the basis of periodic appraisal of the assets. This method may result in periodic depreciation charges for certain assets which closely parallel the units-of-output method, because the value of an asset depends to a considerable extent on the amount of wear and tear. The *appraisal method* requires a determination of the value of services that *remain in the asset* at the end of each period. Periodic depreciation is estimated by appraising assets on hand at the end of the period, and charging off an amount sufficient to reduce the carrying value to this appraised valuation. The appraisal method of depreciation is particularly appropriate for short-lived assets such as small tools, dies, utensils, and containers.

The most serious objection to the appraisal method is the fact that the going-concern value of specific plant assets can seldom be determined with sufficient precision to make this an objective measure of the cost of asset services consumed.

Retirement and Replacement Methods The methods of depreciation discussed thus far represent an attempt to measure the expiration of asset cost as it occurs. An alternative approach, advocated by some public utilities and railroads, is to recognize depreciation only at the time assets reach the end of their economic lives.

The **retirement method** is a system whereby the cost of plant units (net of residual value) is charged to expense in the year in which the asset is retired from service. Under the **replacement method** the original cost of all items of plant is retained in asset accounts and the cost of all replacements is charged to expense when they are acquired. Under the replacement method the asset account includes the cost of the first units of each type of property acquired. Under the retirement method, the property accounts include the full cost of all assets currently in use.

There are two objections to these depreciation methods. The first is that no depreciation will be charged against revenue until retirement occurs. Not only is income overstated in the early years of economic life, but also the original asset cost appears in the balance sheet, despite the fact that a portion of cost has expired. The second objection is that depreciation expense is determined by the number of assets replaced and the nature of the replacements. The probability that the cost of replacements or retirements in any period will coincide with the cost of asset services used during that period is rather slim. The force of this objection is increased when it is noted that managerial replacement policy is likely to vary in response to the availability of funds for capital expenditures, the stage of the business cycle, and earnings prospects.

Despite these rather obvious flaws, retirement and replacement methods have been used and supported in the public utility industry. This may be explained in part by the fact that utility plants are typically composed of large numbers of interrelated items such as rails, ties, poles, pipe sections, rail cars, transformers, etc., whose individual cost is small. Under these conditions, economic life is extremely difficult to estimate, and the distinction between maintenance and replacement is often difficult to make.

Compound Interest Methods The **annuity** and **sinking fund** methods call for application of compound interest concepts in measuring periodic depreciation. These methods are discussed and illustrated in the appendix at the end of this chapter.

Composite Depreciation Method Many companies find it expedient to account for depreciation of certain kinds of assets on a **composite** or **group** basis. The Internal Revenue Service allows economic lives to be applied to broad classes of assets rather than to detailed items of depreciable property. Composite or group depreciation is a process of averaging the economic lives of a number of property units and taking depreciation on the entire lot as if it were an operating unit. The term **composite** generally refers to a collection of somewhat dissimilar assets; the term **group** usually refers to a collection of similar assets. The procedure for determining the periodic depreciation charge is essentially the same in either case.

Several methods may be used to develop a composite or group depreciation rate to be applied to the total cost of a group of assets. The computation of a straight-line composite depreciation rate for a group of machines is illustrated in the schedule below:

Computation of Composite Depreciation Rate

Machine	Acquisition cost	Estimated residual value	Amount to be depreciated	Estimated economic life (years)	Annual depreciation expense
W	$ 6,000	$ -0-	$ 6,000	5	$1,200
X	10,000	1,200	8,800	8	1,100
Y	15,000	1,000	14,000	10	1,400
Z	19,000	1,000	18,000	12	1,500
Totals	$50,000	$3,200	$46,800		$5,200

Composite depreciation rate on acquisition cost: $5,200 ÷ $50,000 = 10.4%
Composite economic life of machines: $46,800 ÷ $5,200 = 9 years

This schedule also indicates that the composite life of the assets is nine years. In other words, the application of the 10.4% composite rate to the acquisition cost of $50,000 will reduce the composite residual value of the assets to $3,200 in exactly nine years [$50,000 − ($5,200 × 9) = $3,200].

Once the composite depreciation rate is computed, it is continued in use until a material change in the composition of plant assets or in the estimate of their economic lives occurs. The assumptions underlying the use of composite depreciation methods are that (1) plant assets are regularly retired near the end of their economic lives, (2) plant assets are regularly replaced with similar assets, and (3) proceeds on retirement are approximately equal to the net residual value used in computing the composite depreciation rate. If assets are not replaced, for example, the use of the 10.4% rate computed above would eventually result in excessive depreciation charges.

In determining yearly depreciation, the average rate of 10.4% is applied to the balance in the asset account at the beginning of the year, which balance excludes the original cost of all units retired prior to the beginning of the year. Thus for each of the first five years, annual depreciation would be $5,200 and in the sixth year (assuming machine W was replaced at the end of the fifth year with a similar machine costing $8,000), depreciation would be $5,512 ($53,000 × 10.4%). The composite depreciation rate is not revised when assets are replaced with reasonably comparable assets. The group of machines would not, of course, be depreciated below residual value at any time prior to retirement.

When composite procedures are employed, a record is not maintained for accumulated depreciation on individual assets. When an asset is retired from use or sold, an entry is made removing the original cost from the asset account and the difference between original cost and the proceeds received, if any, is debited to Accumulated Depreciation; a gain or loss is not recognized. To illustrate, if machine W were sold at the end of the fourth year for $2,230, the entry to record the sale would be:

Cash	2,230	
Accumulated Depreciation: Machinery	3,770	
Machinery		6,000
To record sale of machine W. Composite depreciation method is used, therefore no gain or loss is recognized.		

The primary disadvantage of the composite depreciation method is that the averaging procedure may obscure significant variations from average. The accuracy of the straight-line composite depreciation rate can be checked by recomputing depreciation on the straight-line basis for individual assets. Any significant discrepancies between the two results would require a change in the composite depreciation rate.

The advantages claimed for the composite method are simplicity, convenience, and a reduction in the amount of detail involved in property records and depreciation computations. The advent of computers has obviously reduced the force of this argument. In many cases unit property records are now feasible, although previously composite methods were considered a necessity.

The requisites for the successful operation of composite depreciation procedures are that there be a large number of homogeneous assets, of relatively small individual value, with similar life expectancies. Telephone and electric transmission poles, underground cable, railroad track, and hotel furniture are examples of situations in which composite depreciation may give satisfactory results.

Depreciation methods and management decisions

In highly industrialized nations, plant assets play a large part in the productive process. It is easy to see that the costs of materials and direct labor become a part of finished product. It is not always so clearly recognized, however, that a business also sells to its customers the services of the assets used in manufacturing and marketing its products.

The primary importance of depreciation stems from the various management decisions that are affected by it. To the extent that depreciation is a rather significant part of operating costs, and that operating costs are relevant in business decisions, the relative merits of various depreciation methods are a significant issue.

Depreciation is of particular importance in three decision areas:

1 Decisions relating to income measurement, and the impact of inflation
2 Decisions relating to income tax determination
3 Decisions relating to investment of capital

The effect of different depreciation methods in relation to each of these decision areas is briefly discussed in the following sections.

Depreciation, income measurement, and the impact of inflation

The purpose of depreciation accounting is to measure the amount that must be recovered from revenue to compensate for the portion of asset cost that has been used up. This idea is embodied in the phrase "maintenance of capital," which is so often used in relation to income measurement.

The wide use of the straight-line time method of depreciation can be traced to the fact that it is simple and convenient. Three basic objections may be leveled against the straight-line method, each of which becomes a supporting argument for some other method of depreciation.

1 It tends to report an increasing rate of return on investment.
2 It does not allow for the fact that productivity of plant assets may decline with age.
3 It does not take into account variations in the rate of asset utilization.

Let us consider each of these objections to the straight-line method of depreciation.

Increasing Rate of Return Argument The point of this objection can best be demonstrated by an example. Assume that John Adams acquires a business airplane for $300,000, which he plans to rent on a charter basis. He expects to keep the plane in service for four years and estimates that the net residual value will be $60,000. Anticipated rental revenue is $150,000 per year and operating expenses, exclusive of depreciation, are estimated at $54,000 per year. The effect of the use of straight-line depreciation, assuming that Adams' expectations are fully realized, is shown in the following tabulation:

Year	Revenue	Other operating expenses	Depre- ciation	Total expenses	Net income	Carrying value at beginning of year	Rate earned on carrying value at begin- ning of year, %
1	$150,000	$54,000	$60,000	$114,000	$36,000	$300,000	12
2	150,000	54,000	60,000	114,000	36,000	240,000	15
3	150,000	54,000	60,000	114,000	36,000	180,000	20
4	150,000	54,000	60,000	114,000	36,000	120,000	30
Residual value						60,000	

The use of straight-line depreciation results in reporting rates of return on carrying value that ranges from 12% in the first year to 30% in the last, because income remains constant in the face of a declining carrying value.[2] The fact that, after distributing the net income at the end of the first year, Adams has $60,000 in cash and $240,000 invested in his airplane does not alter the situation. The $60,000 may be reinvested in some other asset and will earn an additional return.

The idea of an increasing rate of return on investment as an asset approaches retirement does not square with reality. Reason suggests that rate of return should remain constant or actually decrease somewhat as an asset ages. The cause of the difficulty in our example is a failure of the straight-line method to take into account the factor of interest that is implicit in a lump-sum investment to be recovered piecemeal over a long period of time. The increasing rate of return argument has particular force in situations where operations focus on a single depreciable asset, for example, a toll bridge, a hydroelectric dam, or an office building.

The assumption that other operating expenses remain constant at $54,000 per year may be questioned on the grounds that repair, maintenance, and fuel costs are likely to increase as the airplane ages. Similarly, the assumption of a constant rental revenue throughout the economic life may not hold true. Thus the earning power of many assets tends to decline with age because of increasing operating expenses, decreasing revenue, or both. If this decrease in earnings parallels the decline in carrying value, the straight-line method may tend to produce a constant rate of return on the carrying value of an asset.

[2] The use of any of the accelerated methods of depreciation would actually exaggerate the apparent increase in the rate of return as long as the earnings before depreciation remain constant. The use of the sum-of-the-years'-digits method, for example, would produce rates of return on the declining carrying value of the airplane of approximately 0, 12, 36, and 86% over the four-year period.

Declining Productivity Argument Many business managers suggest that the decline in productivity of many assets is so pronounced that the value (and thus the cost) of asset services in the early stages of economic life is materially greater than in later years. If this is true, accelerated methods of depreciation may match costs and revenue more closely than the straight-line method. Originally the declining productivity argument centered on a rising curve of repair and maintenance costs as assets aged. In recent years greater weight has been given to the effects of obsolescence. The period of high earnings on new plant assets is often short because of the inroads of innovation and competition.

Variation in the Rate of Utilization Argument The use of the straight-line time depreciation method makes depreciation a fixed period cost by assumption and thereby fails to allow for the loss of service potential related to wear and tear through usage. If an asset is used twice as heavily in one period as another, it may be unrealistic to assume that the amount and cost of the services consumed is the same in both periods. This objection to straight-line depreciation becomes a case for using a measure of output or productivity as the unit of economic life, which would make depreciation a variable cost.

Impact of Inflation During an inflationary period any depreciation method based on historical cost will understate the amount of capital consumed (depreciation). Thus a part of reported income essentially represents return of capital. Users of financial statements should consider this shortcoming in the traditional income measurement model and should make appropriate adjustments to restate depreciation and income in terms of plant replacement costs. The impact of inflation on depreciation accounting is considered in greater detail in Chapter 22.

Depreciation policy and income taxes

Probably the strongest influence on depreciation policy in practice is the income tax law. The direction of the influence is toward accelerated depreciation. Depreciation expense reduces taxable income and income tax expense. Taxpayers cannot deduct more than the actual cost of a depreciable asset over its economic life, but income taxes can be postponed by accelerating depreciation deductions, and deferred taxes represent an interest-free loan for the period of the postponement. The only possible tax disadvantage to large initial depreciation deductions is that income tax rates might increase sufficiently to more than offset the implicit interest savings.

Tax factors encourage the use of minimum estimates of economic life and the adoption of accelerated depreciation methods, without regard to issues of accounting theory or economic reality. If such practices applied only to the computation of taxable income, no damage would be done to the validity of financial statements. For many businesses, however, the convenience of keeping only one set of depreciation records is such that the accounting records generally are made to conform to the income tax requirements.

If tax depreciation and accounting depreciation are substantially equivalent, there are practical advantages in keeping the accounting records on a tax basis. Tax deductions, however, are shaped by matters of public policy and the need for revenue by the government and are not necessarily related to the objectives of sound accounting. Material divergence between tax and accounting data is possible. Many companies, for example, follow a policy of using accelerated depreciation methods for income tax purposes but continue to use a straight-line method for financial reporting purposes.

Allowing relatively large depreciation deductions for income tax purposes is a means of subsidizing business investment. As a result, proposals for extraordinary depreciation allowances as a means of stimulating investment or encouraging certain kinds of investment are frequently made before Congress.[3] The pressure to increase depreciation provisions for maximum tax advantage is not likely to wane. Therefore, the continued usefulness of accounting data for managerial and investment purposes may depend upon maintaining a healthy state of independence between sound accounting measurements and income tax rules.

Depreciation and capital investment decisions

The two most important questions relating to the role of depreciation in a capital investment decision are: (1) Is depreciation a relevant cost in making the decision? (2) How does depreciation affect the cash flows from the investment?

Depreciation Expense May Be a Differential Cost or a Sunk Cost In essence, two kinds of costs are relevant to the decision to invest capital in productive assets: (1) *future costs,* that is, costs that will be incurred as the result of this decision; and (2) *differential costs,* that is, costs that will change as the result of the investment decision. The expense represented by depreciation on existing assets is attributable to an expenditure made at some time in the past. Except to the extent that an existing asset can be sold and some portion of the past investment recovered, no present decision can change the amount of cost that has been sunk into that facility. In many instances depreciation is aptly referred to as a *sunk cost.*

[3] Despite the numerous steps taken by the U.S. Congress in the last 25 years to liberalize depreciation policies, the United States still lags far behind other industrialized nations in this respect. Business firms in the United States, for example, are permitted to recover on the average less than 70% of the cost of assets over the first seven years of asset life. In contrast, business firms in the United Kingdom, France, Italy, Germany, and Switzerland are allowed to deduct 90% or more of the investment in plant assets over the first seven years of asset life.

A decision to invest in productive facilities should be based on an analysis of differential costs and revenue. The carrying value of existing assets, a sunk cost that cannot be changed in the short run, is an irrelevant factor and should be ignored (except for income tax consideration). Most managerial decisions as to alternative actions such as buying or leasing, buying or making, accepting or not accepting a special order, depend upon an analysis of differential costs and revenue. Depreciation may or may not represent a differential or relevant cost in comparing such alternative courses of action. Depreciation on special equipment which must be purchased specifically for a given activity is always a differential cost to that activity, but depreciation on existing assets would be a differential cost only if the use of the assets for the specific activity reduces their economic life.

We have oversimplified the problem in this discussion, but a valid generalization may be drawn. Whether or not depreciation should be regarded as a differential cost depends on whether the limiting factor in asset life is obsolescence or use, and whether the facility in question is now being used to capacity. For this reason, depreciation expense as computed for purposes of income determination generally is not a relevant figure for management to use in decision making.

Effect of Depreciation on Cash Flows Investment decisions are most frequently made on the basis of the expected rate of return on the investment. In computing the rate of return, *net cash flow* from the investment is generally a more useful concept than net income from the investment. Depreciation expense does not directly generate cash; it is simply an expense which does not currently reduce cash but which may be deducted in arriving at taxable income. Thus depreciation expense indirectly generates greater cash flows from operations by reducing the current income tax expense. For this reason, depreciation is universally viewed as a powerful instrument for speeding up cash flows and improving *payback* calculations on new investments in plant assets.

To illustrate the relationships between depreciation and cash flows, assume the following annual results for an asset owned by a leasing company and rented out to customers on a per diem basis:

Amount of cash received from rentals	$5,000
Less: All expenses (except income taxes) paid in cash	1,200
Net cash received	$3,800
Income taxes, 50% of income after depreciation of $2,000: ($3,800 − $2,000) × 50%	900
Net cash flow per year	$2,900

The net cash flow of $2,900 per year may also be determined by adding back the depreciation expense of $2,000 to the accounting net income of $900 earned on the asset. Determining the net cash flow from an investment is an important step in the complex area frequently referred to as *capital budgeting.*

Depreciation procedures and records

Accumulated Depreciation Account In theory depreciation could be recorded as a credit to the asset account, since depreciable assets are basically long-term prepaid costs. The direct write-off procedure is often followed in dealing with large numbers of small-value assets when periodic inventories are taken to determine the portion of asset cost remaining on hand. For larger property units, the almost universal practice is to credit a contra-asset account titled Accumulated Depreciation, Allowance for Depreciation, or Reserve for Depreciation.[4] The primary argument for the use of a separate account is to preserve information about the original cost in plant assets and the proportion of cost that has expired. Also it is convenient when analyzing account balances to be able to distinguish plant additions and retirements from adjustments in accumulated depreciation.

The Accumulated Depreciation account is frequently (but improperly) referred to as a *valuation account.* The Accumulated Depreciation account represents the portion of the acquisition cost of a plant asset which has been allocated to revenue through the process of depreciation. Its purpose is not to arrive at a valuation of a plant asset in terms of current realizable value but rather to determine the unallocated cost (or carrying value) at a given date.

Property Records The typical business employs many different kinds of property, having varying characteristics and economic lives. Precision in accounting for the use of such property is facilitated by detailed and complete property records. Property records may be maintained on ledger cards, tabulating cards, magnetic tapes, or in computer memory systems.

An ideal system is to maintain a record for each asset. The record should show, for each asset, its original cost, capital additions, estimated economic life, estimated residual value, date of installation, location, basis and amount of periodic depreciation, and any other information, such as serial numbers. In addition to providing thorough support for depreciation and retirement entries, such property records are

---

[4] The 1976 edition of *Accounting Trends & Techniques,* published by the AICPA, reported that of the 600 companies surveyed, 480 companies used the terms *accumulated depreciation* and *accumulated depreciation and amortization (or depletion),* 75 companies used the terms *allowance for depreciation* and *allowance for depreciation and amortization* (or *depletion),* and 45 companies used other captions.

		Depreciation (Lapsing) Schedule—Finishing Department				
Date acquired (or retired)	Type of asset	Machinery account		Accumulated depreciation		
		Debit or (Credit)	Balance	Debit or (Credit)	Balance
Jan. 3, Year 1	A	$3,100	$ 3,100		
Jan. 4, Year 1	B	6,000	9,100		
July 1, Year 1	C	4,800	13,900		
Depreciation for Year 1				$(2,740)	$(2,740)
April 1, Year 2	D	2,900	16,800		
Aug. 15, Year 2	E	4,000	20,800		
Dec. 29, Year 2 (retired)	B	(6,000)	14,800	(2 yrs) 3,600	860
Depreciation for Year 2				(3,940)	(3,080)
Depreciation for Year 3				(2,620)	(5,700)

useful in maintaining good internal controls and accountability over plant assets.

Depreciation Schedules When the number of individual items of property within each class of assets is not large, a *depreciation schedule* (sometimes known as a *lapsing schedule*) may be used. Lapsing schedules may take many forms and are often prepared by computer if the number of assets is large. A depreciation schedule is a means of keeping unit property records with a minimum of effort. Its purpose is to facilitate the computation of periodic depreciation and to provide a continuing record of asset costs and the related accumulated depreciation. An example of a depreciation schedule for a department of a factory appears above and on page 539.

When new property is acquired, the acquisition cost is entered on one line of the schedule and the prospective depreciation charges throughout its economic life are extended in the annual depreciation columns. If the asset is retired at the end of its economic life, the original cost is credited to the asset account, and depreciation to date is debited to Accumulated Depreciation. The gain or loss would be recorded in the general journal or the cash receipts journal. If an asset is retired prematurely, it is not necessary to erase or change the originally scheduled depreciation amounts. It is more convenient simply to cancel the depreciation charges by extending appropriate **deductions** on the line used to record the retirement. This is illustrated in the case of asset B. It was originally estimated that asset B would serve for three years, but it

Estimated residual value	Depre- ciation base	Estimated economic life, years	Depreciation expense (straight-line)		
			Year 1	Year 2	Year 3, etc.
$400	$2,700	5	$ 540	$ 540	$ 540
600	5,400	3	1,800	1,800	1,800
–0–	4,800	6	($\frac{1}{2}$) 400	800	800
			$2,740		
500	2,400	3		($\frac{3}{4}$) 600	800
160	3,840	8		($\frac{5}{12}$) 200	480
					(1,800) adj.
				$3,940	
					$2,620

was sold for $2,300 on December 29, Year 2, at the end of only two years of service. The removal of $6,000 from the asset account and $3,600 (two years at $1,800 per year) from Accumulated Depreciation is recorded on one line of the schedule. On the same line, in the Depreciation Expense columns, is entered a cancellation of the $1,800 depreciation which was originally scheduled for Year 3. Journal entries to record annual depreciation on all machines and the sale of machine B are shown on page 540.

Disclosure of depreciation in financial statements

Because of the significant effects on financial position and results of operations from depreciation expense and the depreciation methods used, the following disclosures should be made in the financial statements or in the notes accompanying the financial statements:

1 Depreciation expense for the period
2 Balances of major classes of depreciable assets, by nature or function
3 Accumulated depreciation, either by major classes of depreciable assets or in total
4 A general description of the method or methods used in computing depreciation with respect to major classes of depreciable assets[5]

The 1976 edition of *Accounting Trends & Techniques,* published by the AICPA, showed that 567 of the 600 companies surveyed used the

[5] *APB Opinion No. 12,* "Omnibus Opinion—1967," AICPA (New York: 1967), p. 188.

Year 1
Dec. 31   Depreciation Expense 2,740
         Accumulated Depreciation   2,740
        To record depreciation for Year 1.

Year 2
Dec. 29   Cash 2,300
        Accumulated Depreciation 3,600
        Loss on Sale of Machinery   100
         Machinery   6,000
        To record sale of machine B.

Dec. 31   Depreciation Expense 3,940
         Accumulated Depreciation   3,940
        To record depreciation for Year 2.

Year 3
Dec. 31   Depreciation Expense 2,620
         Accumulated Depreciation   2,620
        To record depreciation for Year 3.

straight-line method and 199 companies used one or more of the accelerated depreciation methods; only 38 companies used the unit-of-output method. If a change in the method of computing depreciation is made, the effect of the change on the current year's net income should be disclosed. Similarly, the effect of any unusual depreciation charges should be disclosed. Accounting for changes in depreciation methods, changes in economic lives of depreciable assets, and corrections of errors in recording depreciation are discussed in Chapter 23.

DEPLETION

A depreciable asset usually retains its physical characteristics as it performs services. In contrast, a wasting asset is in essence a long-term inventory of raw materials that will be removed physically from the property. In either case—whether the accountant is dealing with a "bundle of services" or a "store of raw materials"—the basic problem is to determine the cost of the units of services or materials that are consumed during each accounting period. The portion of the cost (or other valuation) assigned to property containing natural resources that is applicable to the units removed from the property is known as *depletion.*

The depletion base

The depletion base of any wasting asset is the entire cost of acquiring the property less the estimated residual value of the land after the natural resources have been removed. The estimated cost of restoring mined properties may be taken into account in determining residual value of the land or it may be "accrued ratably as minerals are produced."[6]

Acquisition cost logically includes expenditures for exploring, drilling, excavating, and construction preparatory to the removal of the resources. These are known as *development costs* and should be amortized in proportion to the removal of the natural resource. Structures and equipment used in extracting natural resources may have an economic life shorter than the time required to complete the removal, in which case the amortization of these assets should be made over their economic lives.

What if the expenditures made in acquiring, exploring, and developing natural resources prove unproductive? If each specific property is viewed as a separate venture, the logical interpretation is that no asset exists and a loss has therefore occurred. On the other hand, from the viewpoint of the company as a whole, particularly if it is seeking constantly to maintain its natural resource base by exploration and acquisition of new deposits, a certain amount of unproductive effort may be viewed as a normal hazard (expense) of discovering new deposits. If, for example, 10 dry holes are drilled on the average for each producing well brought in, the argument that 11 drillings are necessary to bring in a "producer" and that the cost of a producing well includes the cost of 10 unsuccessful efforts has considerable merit. The problem is analogous to that of accounting for spoilage in manufacturing. If a certain amount of spoilage is ordinary and necessary, it is treated as a part of the cost of the good units produced; if the amount of spoilage is abnormal, it is treated as a loss.

In the lumber industry, substantial costs are incurred for fire protection, insect and disease control, property taxes, and other maintenance costs applicable to standing timber that will be harvested for a considerable length of time. These costs, known as *carrying charges,* should be capitalized while the property is being developed. For example, if carrying charges of $40,000 are applicable to a given tract of timber and during the current accounting period 20% of the timber is cut, 80% of the $40,000 in carrying charges is applicable to uncut timber and should be capitalized.

---

[6] Robert E. Field, *Accounting Research Study No. 11,* "Financial Reporting in the Extractive Industries," AICPA (New York: 1969), p. 74.

Estimating recoverable units

Forecasting economic life for plant and equipment is a relatively simple undertaking when compared with the uncertainties encountered in estimating recoverable units of natural resources. The quantity of ore in a vein or the recoverable deposit in oil- and gas-producing property is often extremely difficult to determine, and revisions are constantly necessary as production takes place and new evidence becomes available. Adding to the problem is the fact that changes in the method of extraction may make it possible to work deposits that were originally deemed uneconomic.

Ideally, the recoverable deposit should be measured in units of *desired* product, such as an ounce of silver or a pound of nickel, rather than in units of *mined* product, such as a ton of ore. If depletion is based on tons of mined ore, the same charge will be applied to a ton of high-grade ore as to a ton of low-grade ore. This treatment is hardly logical in terms of the way mining property is valued and in terms of the accountant's efforts to attain a sound matching of costs and revenue.

Cost depletion

Any of the methods of depreciation previously discussed could be applied in a comparable manner to the computation of depletion. The straight-line method, however, is of doubtful applicability since the exhaustion of natural resources is a matter of physical output rather than the passage of time. Accelerated methods have not been commonly used in measuring depletion, despite the fact that the productivity of wasting assets may decline rapidly when the cost of recovery per unit increases as production moves from richer to poorer veins.

By far the most common method of depletion for accounting purposes is the units-of-output method, which produces a constant depletion charge per unit removed. To illustrate, assume that wasting-asset property cost $720,000. It was estimated that there were 1.2 million recoverable units and that the land would have a net residual value (after restoration costs) of $60,000 when the resource was exhausted. The depletion per unit of output would be computed as follows:

$$\text{Depletion} = \frac{\text{cost} - \text{net residual value}}{\text{total recoverable units}}$$

$$= \frac{\$720,000 - \$60,000}{1,200,000 \text{ units}} = \$0.55 \text{ per unit}$$

If 300,000 units were removed during the current year and 200,000 of these were sold, the cost of goods sold would be determined as follows:

	Total	Unit cost
Cost of goods sold:		
Depletion (300,000 units × $0.55)	$165,000	$0.55
Materials, labor, and overhead	237,000	0.79
Depreciation of equipment	15,000	0.05
Total cost of production (300,000 units)	$417,000	$1.39
Less: Ending inventory (100,000 units @ $1.39)	139,000	
Cost of goods sold (200,000 units @ $1.39)	$278,000	

When additional costs are incurred in developing mining properties or estimates of recoverable units are revised, the depletion rate should be redetermined. Depletion previously recorded, however, should not be revised. The new depletion rate is computed by dividing the unamortized cost of the mining property (including any additional development costs) by the new estimate of recoverable units. The issues relating to changes in accounting estimates are covered in greater detail in Chapter 23.

Percentage depletion for income tax purposes

For income tax purposes, a special depletion method known as *percentage* or *statutory depletion* can be used by taxpayers engaged in most mining activities. Under this procedure the depletion deduction may be computed as a percentage of the gross income received, without regard to the cost of the property or the number of units produced. Some examples of percentage depletion (subject to change at any time) follow:

Gold, silver, oil shale, copper, and iron ore	15%
China clay, rock asphalt, borax, and bauxite	14%
Coal and sodium chloride	10%
Gravel, peat, sand, and magnesium chloride	5%

The Tax Reduction Act of 1975 repealed the 22% depletion allowance for major oil- and gas-producing companies. However, the allowance was retained in significantly limited form for small producers and royalty recipients. The Act provided that the 22% depletion would continue for such taxpayers through 1980; the percentage rate would then be phased down to 20% in 1981, 18% in 1982, 16% in 1983, and 15% in 1984 and beyond.

Taxpayers have the option of using either cost depletion or percentage depletion, whichever is more advantageous. The only limit on percentage depletion is that it cannot exceed 50% of the taxable income from the property, before the allowance for depletion. To illustrate, assume the following facts for Arizona Copper Company for the current year:

Sale of copper ore (200,000 tons)	$15,000,000
Expenses (excluding depletion)	$ 6,500,000
Depletion base (cost) of ore-bearing property	$ 4,000,000
Estimated tons of ore recoverable from property	1,000,000
Cost depletion per ton of ore ($4,000,000 ÷ 1,000,000)	$ 4
Income tax rate	40%

The taxable income and net income for financial reporting purposes for Arizona Copper Company are determined below:

	Taxable income	Net income for financial reporting purposes
Sale of copper ore	$15,000,000	$15,000,000
Expenses (excluding depletion)	(6,500,000)	(6,500,000)
Income before depletion	$ 8,500,000	
Depletion:		
Percentage basis for income tax purposes, $15,000,000 × 15%.	(2,250,000)	
Cost basis for financial reporting purposes, 200,000 tons of ore @ $4 per ton		(800,000)
Taxable income	$ 6,250,000	
Income taxes, $6,250,000 × 40%		(2,500,000)
Net income		$ 5,200,000

The percentage depletion for the current year in computing taxable income is $2,250,000 (15% of $15,000,000) because this amount exceeds cost depletion ($800,000) and is less than 50% of the $8,500,000 income before depletion. If expenses excluding depletion amounted to $12,000,000, for example, percentage depletion would be limited to $1,500,000 (50% of $3,000,000, the income before depletion). For those properties to which the percentage method applies, depletion should be computed using both the cost method and the percentage method, and the larger deduction taken for income tax purposes.

The primary advantage of percentage depletion arises not because it may be larger than cost depletion in any given year, but because the cumulative amount of depletion deductions is not limited by the depletion base. There is no cost "base" for percentage depletion and taxpayers may thus take depletion deductions on their income tax returns many times over the cost of the property. *Percentage depletion is not recorded in the accounting records;* it simply represents a special income tax benefit granted to certain natural resource industries as a matter of public policy.

APPENDIX: INTEREST METHODS OF DEPRECIATION

For many years the *annuity* and *sinking fund* methods of depreciation have received attention from accounting theorists because of their focus on cost recovery and rate of return on the investment in depreciable assets. A depreciable asset represents a bundle of future services to be received periodically over the economic life of the asset. The cost of such an asset logically may be viewed as the present value of the approximately equal periodic rents (services) discounted at a rate of interest consistent with the risk factors surrounding the investment in the asset.

Annuity Method The annuity method of depreciation would be appropriate when the periodic cost (depreciation) of using a long-lived asset is considered to be equal to the total of the expired cost of the asset and the interest on the unrecovered investment in the asset. Depreciation Expense is debited and Accumulated Depreciation and Interest Revenue are credited periodically, as explained in the example below.

Assume that a computer with an economic life of five years and a net residual value of $67,388 at the end of five years is acquired for $800,000. If the fair rate of interest for this type of investment is 10% compounded annually, annual depreciation would be computed as illustrated at the top of page 546.

A schedule summarizing the results of the annuity method of depreciation and the journal entries to record depreciation for the first two years are presented at the bottom of page 546.

The schedule on page 546 shows that: (1) Depreciation computed by the annuity method is debited for $200,000 each year; (2) interest revenue is credited each year with 10% of the unrecovered investment (carrying value of the computer); (3) the difference between annual depreciation expense and interest revenue is credited to Accumulated Depreciation; and (4) the carrying value of the computer at the end of

$$\text{Depreciation} = \frac{\text{cost of asset less present value of net residual value}}{\text{present value of ordinary annuity of 5 rents at 10\%}}$$

$$\text{Depreciation} = \frac{\$800,000 - (\$67,388 \times 0.620921^*)}{3.790787\dagger}$$

$$\text{Depreciation} = \frac{\$800,000 - \$41,843}{3.790787}$$

$$\text{Depreciation} = \underline{\$200,000}$$

*Present value of $1 for five periods at 10% (Table 2 in Appendix A).
† See Table 4 in Appendix A.

Year 5 is $67,388, the net residual value at the end of its economic life. The total depreciation expense over the economic life of the computer exceeds its depreciable cost by $267,388 ($1,000,000 − $732,612), an amount equal to the interest revenue recorded during the economic life of the computer. The net charge to revenue over the five-year period is equal to the depreciable *cost* of the computer and *increases* each year. The annuity method of depreciation thus tends to produce

				Annuity Method of Depreciation		
Year	Depreciation expense	Interest revenue (10% of carrying value)	Credit to Accumulated Depreciation account	Balance in Accumulated Depreciation account	Carrying value of computer
0					$800,000
1	$ 200,000	$ 80,000	$120,000	$120,000	680,000
2	200,000	68,000	132,000	252,000	548,000
3	200,000	54,800	145,200	397,200	402,800
4	200,000	40,280	159,720	556,920	243,080
5	200,000	24,308	175,692	732,612	67,388
	$1,000,000	$267,388	$732,612		

Journal entries:	Year 1	Year 2
Depreciation Expense	200,000	200,000
Interest Revenue	80,000	68,000
Accumulated Depreciation .	120,000	132,000
To record depreciation using the annuity method.		

a more constant rate of return on investment than, say, the straight-line method of depreciation. Consequently, the use of the annuity method of depreciation for assets acquired under capital leases has been advocated by some accountants in recent years.

Sinking Fund Method The sinking fund method of depreciation might be used when a fund is to be accumulated to replace an asset at the end of its economic life. Under the sinking fund method, the amount of annual depreciation is equal to the increase in the asset replacement fund. The increase in the fund would consist of the equal periodic deposits (rents) plus the interest revenue at the assumed rate on the sinking fund balance.

We shall illustrate the sinking fund method of depreciation using the same example as we used to illustrate the annuity method, that is, a computer purchased for $800,000 with an economic life of five years and a net residual value of $67,388 at the end of five years. If we again assume a 10% annual compound rate of interest, the annual deposits to the sinking fund may be determined as follows:

$$\text{Sinking fund deposits} = \frac{\text{cost of asset less net residual value}}{\text{amount of ordinary annuity of 5 rents at 10\%}}$$

$$\text{Sinking fund deposits} = \frac{\$800,000 - \$67,388}{6.1051^*}$$

$$\text{Sinking fund deposits} = \underline{\$120,000}$$

*See Table 3 in Apppendix A.

A schedule summarizing the results of the sinking fund method of depreciation and the journal entries for the first two years are presented at the top of page 548.

The schedule on page 548 shows that: (1) Depreciation computed by the sinking fund method is debited each year for *increasing* amounts equal to the total increase in the sinking fund; (2) interest revenue is credited each year with earnings at 10% on the fund balance; (3) the net charges to revenue (depreciation less interest earned) each year remain constant at $120,000; and (4) the carrying value of the computer at the end of Year 5 is $67,388, the net residual value at this date.

The sinking fund method of depreciation may be used without accumulating a sinking fund. However, depreciation would still be recorded equal to the hypothetical fund increases as illustrated on page 548. The sinking fund method of depreciation is actually used by some utility companies.

Sinking Fund Method of Depreciation

		Sinking fund			Depreciation and carrying value		
Year	Annual deposit	Interest revenue (10% of fund balance)	Total fund increase	Fund balance	Depreciation expense	Balance in Accumulated Depreciation account	Carrying value of computer
0							$800,000
1	$120,000	$ –0–	$120,000	$120,000	$120,000	$120,000	680,000
2	120,000	12,000	132,000	252,000	132,000	252,000	548,000
3	120,000	25,200	145,200	397,200	145,200	397,200	402,800
4	120,000	39,720	159,720	556,920	159,720	556,920	243,080
5	120,000	55,692	175,692	732,612	175,692	732,612	67,388
	$600,000	$132,612	$732,612		$732,612		

Journal entries:	Year 1		Year 2	
Sinking Fund	120,000		132,000	
Depreciation Expense	120,000		132,000	
Cash		120,000		120,000
Interest Revenue		–0–		12,000
Accumulated Depreciation .		120,000		132,000
To record depreciation using the sinking fund method.				

REVIEW QUESTIONS

1 Some companies, particularly those in the real estate business, report an intermediate figure on their income statement and refer to it as "net income before depreciation." Comment on this practice.

2 Distinguish the terms **depreciation, amortization,** and **depletion.** How is depreciation accounting related to the replacement of an asset at the end of its economic life?

3 What are the three variables in estimating periodic depreciation? Is depreciation more properly referred to as a valuation procedure or a cost allocation procedure?

4 The manager of an electric utility stated, "Our transmission lines are kept in good operating condition by regular repairs and maintenance, and their efficiency is relatively constant—they just don't depreciate!" Do you agree with this statement? Explain.

5 What is meant by the term **estimated economic life** of an asset and how is it measured?

6 What are the main causes of a decrease in the economic life of an asset? How reliably can the causes be estimated?

7 Jordan Company buys delivery trucks for $8,000. These trucks have an economic life of six years and a residual value of $800. The company typically sells a truck for $3,000 after running it 50,000 miles. What should be the depreciation base for this delivery truck? What should be its estimated economic life?

8 The quantity of asset services used each period and the relative value of the asset services are both factors in choosing a method of depreciation. Explain.

9 List the various methods that may be used to compute depreciation.

10 **a** State three basic objections against the straight-line (time) method of depreciation.
  b What are the advantages of the straight-line (time) method of depreciation?

11 Many depreciable assets exhibit a declining productivity with advancing age. Explain how this fact may be used both as an argument for and an argument against the straight-line method of depreciation.

12 During the current year a strike halted manufacturing operations of Arcadia, Inc., for four months. Depreciation of its spinning and weaving machines for the full year using the straight-line method is $216,000. Its operations for the current year resulted in a loss of $132,000 (after deducting depreciation). The president suggests that the depreciation deduction should be reduced because of the low volume of operations. Do you agree?

13 Describe a situation in which the use of the units-of-output method of depreciation would be appropriate.

14 What is meant by **composite** or **group** depreciation method? What are the advantages and limitations of this method?

15 Explain why the use of accelerated depreciation methods is advantageous for income tax purposes, even though depreciation for income tax purposes cannot exceed original cost reduced by net residual value.

16 Explain why periodic depreciation on existing equipment is not a relevant factor in arriving at a decision to replace the equipment.

17 What principle should be applied in determining whether depreciation is a fixed or a variable expense for income measurement purposes? Explain the statement: "Depreciation is a noncash expense."

18 What disclosure relating to depreciation and depreciation methods should be made in the financial statements or in the accompanying notes?

19 Bronze Corporation has purchased property for $600,000 from which it expects to extract 1 million tons of 60% concentrate ore and 2 million tons of 30% concentrate ore. Compute the depletion charge per ton of ore extracted. Explain the term **percentage depletion.**

20 Plant assets or natural resources donated to corporations generally are recorded in the accounts and depreciation or depletion on them is charged against revenue. Justify this practice?

EXERCISES

Ex. 13-1 Southern Company leased a building and immediately purchased equipment of $430,000 and spent $35,000 to have special platforms and supporting encasements built. The lease agreement provides that when the lease expires Southern Company must remove the equipment, tear up the platforms and encasements, and restore the property to its original condition, an operation that is expected to cost $20,000. What should be the depreciation base of this equipment?

Ex. 13-2 An asset cost $58,000, has an economic life of seven years, and an estimated net residual value of $2,000.
    a Compute depreciation for the first year of asset life under the sum-of-the-years'-digits method of depreciation.
    b Assume that this asset was acquired on April 1, Year 1. Compute depreciation for the full year beginning on January 1, Year 2, under the sum-of-the-years'-digits method of depreciation.

Ex. 13-3 A machine with an estimated life of five years, or 100,000 units of output, was acquired on October 4, Year 1. The machine sells for $9,000 and will be paid for as follows:

Old machine accepted as trade-in	$ 500
Cash	1,500
Four installments payable at the rate of $2,000 every six months (includes	
$1,000 of interest and financing charges)	8,000
Total	$10,000

    Compute depreciation for the three months in Year 1 and for Year 2, assuming that the net residual value of the machine is $1,500, using each of the following methods:
    a Straight-line
    b Sum-of-the-years'-digits
    c Double-declining-balance
    d Units-of-output (8,000 units were produced in Year 1 and 30,000 units in Year 2)

Ex. 13-4 Clemente Company purchased an asset at the beginning of Year 1 for a total cost of $16,000. The asset has an economic life of four years and an estimated net residual value of $1,000.
    Compute the depreciation on the asset for Year 1, using each of the following methods:
    a Straight-line
    b Sum-of-the-years'-digits
    c Fixed-percentage-of-declining-balance (Compute the theoretically correct rate.)

Ex. 13-5 Y Co. purchased equipment on Jan. 3, Year 1. The equipment has an estimated economic life of 10 years and a net residual value of $10,000. The depreciation expense for Year 5 was $6,000 using the sum-of-the-years'-digits method. What was the original cost of the asset?

Ex. 13-6 The controller of Technitronics Company, an electronics manufacturer, maintains records of small equipment items used in manufacturing on the composite basis. A list of assets acquired at the beginning of Year 1 follows:

Assets	Cost	Estimated net residual value	Estimated economic life (years)
A-101	$4,000	$400	3
A-102	1,500	300	4
A-103	7,000	750	5

a Compute the composite depreciation rate.

b If at the end of Year 3, the A-101 assets are sold for $400, what entry would be made to record this sale?

Ex. 13-7 At the beginning of Year 1 a firm acquired for cash 20 similar machines for $4,000 each and developed a composite depreciation rate of 30% based on these expectations:

	Year 2	Year 3	Year 4
Number of machines to be retired at end of year	5	10	5
Net residual value of machines to be retired	$6,000	$4,000	$ –0–

The retirements and proceeds realized were exactly as expected. You may assume that the 30% rate is correct.

Record all transactions for the four-year period in T accounts and explain the balance in the Accumulated Depreciation account at the end of Year 4.

Ex. 13-8 Salt Lake Ore Company acquired mining property for $1.2 million. The mine was expected to yield 600,000 tons of ore, after which the property would have a net residual value of $200,000. During the first year, 60,000 tons of ore were mined and sold for $800,000. Operating expenses other than cost depletion amounted to $350,000. The ore mined is eligible for a 15% percentage depletion for income tax purposes. Income taxes are 45% of taxable income.

Compute the amount of *(a)* cost depletion on the mining property, *(b)* income tax expense, and *(c)* net income for financial reporting purposes.

Ex. 13-9 An analysis of the Machinery account of Brigham Corporation for the current year appears below:

Jan. 2	Acquired four machines with an economic life of five years	$12,000
Jan. 6	Installation costs	400
	Total debits	$12,400
Dec. 28	Less: Credit representing proceeds on sale of one machine (debit recorded in the Cash account)	2,100
	Balance in Machinery account	$10,300

a Prepare a journal entry to record depreciation expense for the current year on the four machines. The estimated net residual value of each machine is $350. Use the straight-line method of depreciation.

b Prepare an entry to correct the accounts at December 31, including the recognition of the gain or loss (which was not recorded on December 28) on the sale of the one machine.

Ex. 13-10 Volcanic Products Company acquired a tract of land containing an extractable natural resource. The company is required by its purchase contract to restore the land to a condition suitable for recreational use after it extracts the natural resource. Geological surveys estimate that recoverable reserves will be 3 million tons, and that the land will have a value of $600,000 after restoration. Relevant cost information follows:

Land	$6,000,000
Restoration of land	900,000
Geological surveys	300,000

If the company maintains no inventories of extracted material, compute the depletion charge per ton of material extracted.

SHORT CASES FOR ANALYSIS AND DECISION

Case 13-1 The controller of Daryl Manufacturing Corporation is preparing a set of accounting policies for the company in the first month of its operations. The company has a wide variety of plant assets, including a significant investment in highly specialized equipment. You have been asked to assist the controller on this project.

Instructions
a Briefly define ***depreciation*** as the term is used in accounting.
b Identify the factors that are relevant in the measurement of annual depreciation on plant assets and explain whether these factors are determined objectively or whether they are based on judgment.
c Explain why depreciation usually is shown in the Financial Resources Provided section of the statement of changes in financial position.

Case 13-2 Outland Steel Corporation computes depreciation based on the level of the company's operations. In the third quarter of a given fiscal year, the company, according to a financial news story, "returned to profit a sum equal to 25 cents per share that had been written off as depreciation in the previous six months but that it determined had not been needed."

Instructions
a Briefly evaluate the company's depreciation policy.
b Does it seem to you that this company is smoothing its net income through its depreciation policy or simply trying to match the service potential (cost) of its assets with the economic benefits derived (tons of steel produced)?

Case 13-3 Doug Company owned an old factory building that had a carrying value of $200,000. Machinery and equipment in the building had a carrying value of $300,000. In 1975 the company built a new building at a cost of $1.2 million and installed new equipment costing $650,000. Some of the equipment in the old building was replaced, and both plants were operated at near capacity from 1975 to 1980. Depreciation was taken on a straight-line basis.

In 1980 the company was forced to shut down the old plant because of a decline in sales. President Douglas proposes to stop taking depreciation on the old building and machinery, stating that while the old plant is useful, it is not wearing out; furthermore, depreciating the old plant increases costs, overstates the inventory, and places the company in a poor position to bid for business since its costs are high.

Instructions Discuss the president's position and evaluate these arguments. What recommendation would you make to the company?

Case 13-4 A news story appeared in a financial periodical which stated that the net income for Tulsa Oil Company has decreased from $2 million a year ago to only $500,000 in the current year, largely because of increased charges for depletion and depreciation. These additional charges were necessary because an independent engineering firm prepared new estimates of oil and gas reserves and these turned out to be substantially lower than the company's previous estimates of these reserves. As a result, it was necessary to increase the charges for depletion and depreciation in the current year. The story further stated that these revised estimates do not affect the company's revenue or cash flow, and that revisions in estimates of oil and gas reserves are not unusual in the petroleum industry. The president of the company was quoted as saying, "Because we are a relatively small company, these revisions affect us more seriously than they would larger companies."

Instructions

a How do you suppose the revised depletion and depreciation figure was determined? Should understatements in depletion and depreciation in prior years result in understating income in subsequent years?

b How can the independent auditor confirm the estimates of deposits of natural resources?

c Explain why increased depletion and depreciation charges do not affect revenue or cash flow.

d Why would revisions in estimates of oil and gas reserves affect a small company "more seriously" than they would larger companies? Would such revisions affect the percentage depletion allowed for income tax purposes?

PROBLEMS

Group A

13A-1 The cash price of a machine acquired by Maggie Manufacturing Corporation on September 30, Year 1, was $61,000, including sales taxes; it was paid for as follows:

In cash—down payment	*$ 5,000*
600 shares of company's capital stock with a current market price of $42 per	
share	*25,200*
Notes payable in 24 equal monthly installments, including interest	*36,000*
Total (paid or payable)	*$66,200*

The following additional costs were incurred before the machine was ready for use:

Installation costs	*$2,600*
Direct costs of trial runs	*1,000*

The machine was expected to produce 100,000 units of output during its economic life. It was placed in service on October 4, Year 1.

Instructions

a Determine the cost of the machine for financial accounting purposes. Assume that the discount on the notes is equal to the difference between the total payments to be made and the cash price of the machine.

b Assuming that the estimated net residual value of the machine is $4,600 and that the economic life is estimated to be five years, compute depreciation on the machine for Year 1 (3 months) and Year 2 using:
(1) Straight-line method
(2) Sum-of-the-years'-digits method
(3) Rate of 40% applied to declining net carrying value
(4) Units-of-output method (The machine produced 10,000 units in Year 1 and 25,000 units in Year 2.)

13A-2 A two-year record of the Equipment account in the accounting records of Strata Company is shown below. The company follows a policy of taking one-half year's depreciation in the year of acquisition and one-half year's depreciation in the year of retirement.

		Estimated		Sales or retirements	
Year	Cost of equipment	Economic life	Net residual value	Year acquired	Cost
1	$110,000	10	20% of cost		
2	84,000	6	20% of cost	1	$13,750

Instructions Prepare a schedule showing beginning balances, additions, reductions, and ending balances for the Equipment account, and for the related Accumulated Depreciation account, using the following depreciation methods:
a Straight-line
b Sum-of-the-years'-digits
c Percentage-of-declining-balance (double straight-line rate)

13A-3 In auditing the records of Rainbow Corporation, you observe the following entries in the Machinery account:

Debits:	Jan. 3, Year 3 Purchased Machine A	$22,000	
	Jan. 10, Year 3 Installation of Machine A	2,000	
	Sept. 28, Year 3 Purchased Machine B	30,000	
	Mar. 31, Year 4 Purchased Machine C	16,000	
	July 1, Year 5 Repairs due to flooding	4,500	$74,500
Credits:	Dec. 31, Year 3 Depreciation for year	$10,800	
	Dec. 31, Year 4 Depreciation for year	11,840	
	April 1, Year 5 Proceeds on sale of Machine A	10,560	
	Dec. 31, Year 5 Depreciation for year	7,460	40,660
Balance in account, Dec. 31, Year 5			$33,840

Depreciation at the end of each year was taken at 20% of the balance in the account. Residual value is estimated at 10% of invoice cost and economic life is estimated to be five years.

Instructions
a Prepare a depreciation (lapsing) schedule through December 31, Year 6, for machinery, using straight-line depreciation. Use the form illustrated on pages 538 and 539.
b Using the information from the lapsing schedule, prepare a single compound

entry to restate the accounts of the company in accordance with good accounting practice at December 31, Year 5. The income and expense accounts for Year 5 are still open. Any errors in computing depreciation for Years 3 and 4 should be recorded in a Correction in Prior Years' Depreciation account.

13A-4 Dehn Corporation, a manufacturer of steel products, began operations on October 1, Year 2. The accounting department of Dehn has started the depreciation schedule given on page 556. You have been asked to assist in completing this schedule. In addition to ascertaining that the data already on the schedule are correct, you have obtained the following information from the company's records and personnel:

(1) Depreciation is computed from the first of the month of acquisition to the first of the month of disposition.

(2) Land L and Building B were acquired from a predecessor corporation. Dehn paid $812,500 for the land and building together. At the time of acquisition, the land had an appraised value of $72,000 and the building had an appraised value of $828,000.

(3) Land LL was acquired on October 2, Year 2, in exchange for 3,000 newly issued shares of Dehn's common stock. At the date of acquisition, the stock had a par value of $5 per share and a fair value of $25 per share. During October of Year 2, Dehn paid $10,400 to demolish an existing building on this land so it could construct a new building.

(4) Construction of Building BB on the newly acquired land began on October 1, Year 3. By September 30, Year 4, Dehn had paid $210,000 of the estimated total construction costs of $300,000. Estimated completion and occupancy are July, Year 5.

(5) Certain equipment was donated to the corporation by the city of Pineridge. An independent appraisal of the equipment when donated placed the fair value at $16,000 and the residual value at $2,000.

(6) The total cost of $110,000 for Machinery M includes installation costs of $550 and normal repairs and maintenance of $11,000 incurred through January 31, Year 4. Machinery M was sold on February 1, Year 4.

(7) On October 1, Year 3, Machinery MM was acquired with a down payment of $3,760 and the remaining payments to be made in ten annual installments of $4,000 each beginning October 1, Year 4. The prevailing interest rate was 8%. The following data were taken from present value tables:

Present value of 1 at 8%

10 years	0.463
11 years	0.429
15 years	0.315

Present value of ordinary annuity of 1 at 8%

10 years	6.710
11 years	7.139
15 years	8.559

Instructions For each lettered item on the schedule on page 556, supply the correct amount. Round each answer to the nearest dollar. **Do not recopy the schedule.** Show supporting computations in good form.

DEHN CORPORATION

Depreciation Schedule

For Fiscal Years Ended September 30, Year 3, and September 30, Year 4

Assets	Acquisition date	Cost	Residual value	Depreciation method	Esti-mated life, years	Depreciation expense, year ended Sept. 30, Year 3	Year 4
Land L	Oct. 1, Year 2	$ (a)	*	*	*	*	*
Building B ..	Oct. 1, Year 2	(b)	$47,500	Straight-line	(c)	$14,000	$ (d)
Land LL ...	Oct. 2, Year 2	(e)	*	*	*	*	*
Building BB .	Under construction	210,000 to date	–0–	Straight-line	30	–0–	(f)
Donated equipment	Oct. 2, Year 2	(g)	2,000	150% de-clining-balance	10	(h)	(i)
Machinery M .	Oct. 2, Year 2	(j)	5,500	Sum-of-the-years'-digits	10	(k)	(l)
Machinery MM	Oct. 1, Year 3	(m)	–0–	Straight-line	12	–0–	(n)

* Not applicable

13A-5 Intermountain Freight Company purchased a fleet of 100 fully equipped trucks on January 2, Year 1, for $600,000. The controller of the company decided to use composite depreciation procedures of these trucks, and estimated the composite rate at 21% ($126,000 ÷ $600,000) as follows:

Year	Number of trucks to be retired	Acquisition cost	Estimated residual value	Amount to be depre-ciated	Estimated economic life, years	Annual depre-ciation expense
1	5	$ 30,000	$ 21,000	$ 9,000	1	$ 9,000
2	20	120,000	72,000	48,000	2	24,000
3	30	180,000	59,400	120,600	3	40,200
4	30	180,000	36,000	144,000	4	36,000
5	15	90,000	6,000	84,000	5	16,800
	100	$600,000	$194,400	$405,600		$126,000

At the end of Year 7 when the last truck had been retired, the controller prepared a summary of the company's actual experience as shown on page 557.

The company had followed composite depreciation procedures and recorded no gain or loss when the trucks were retired.

Year	Actual number of trucks retired	Actual proceeds received on retirement
1	4	$ 17,200
2	11	32,800
3	28	74,700
4	42	49,600
5	8	5,000
6	5	1,800
7	2	800
	100	$181,900

Instructions
a Reconstruct the Trucks and Accumulated Depreciation accounts as they would have appeared had the controller's estimates been exactly realized and the computed rate of 21% used as a basis for recording depreciation. Would the controller's rate have produced accurate results if the assumptions had turned out to be correct? Why?

b On the basis of hindsight, that is, the actual record of experience with this fleet, compute the composite depreciation rate that should have been used in depreciating this fleet of trucks. Also determine the composite economic life of the trucks.

c Using the rate computed in **b,** reconstruct the Trucks and the Accumulated Depreciation accounts. Explain any balance in the Accumulated Depreciation account at the end of Year 7 and state why this balance, if any, differs from the balance in Accumulated Depreciation obtained in **a.**

Group B

13B-1 The following entries are found in an improperly established Real Property account in the accounting records of Helena Company at the end of Year 1:

Debit entries:

Feb. 1	Amount paid to acquire building site	$ 25,000
12	Cost of removing old building from site	2,000
15	Contract price for new building which was completed on Apr. 5 . .	80,000
Apr. 1	Insurance and other cost directly connected with construction of	
	new building	4,000
	Total debits	$111,000

Credit entries:

Feb. 12	Proceeds from sale of material obtained from dismantling	
	of old building	$3,000
Dec. 31	Depreciation expense for Year 1—5% of balance in Real	
	Property account, $108,000 (Debit was recorded in the	
	Depreciation Expense account)	5,400
	Total credits	8,400
Balance in Real Property account at Dec. 31, Year 1	$102,600

Instructions
a Prepare a compound correcting entry at December 31, Year 1, assuming that the estimated economic life of the new building is 20 years and that depreciation using the straight-line method is to be recorded for nine months in Year 1. The accounts have not been closed at the end of Year 1.
b Compute depreciation on the building for Year 1, Year 2, and Year 3 using the following methods: (1) straight-line, (2) double-declining-balance, and (3) sum-of-the-years'-digits.

13B-2 Snyder Corporation has made a study of its five-year experience with a group of heavy trucks. The appraised values of these trucks at the end of each year and average miles driven per year per truck during a typical five-year period are as follows:

Year	Miles driven	Appraised value (% of cost)
1	40,000	75
2	60,000	55
3	40,000	40
4	30,000	30
5	30,000	25

Instructions On the basis of this information, compute the depreciation each year during the five-year economic life of a truck that cost $18,000 and is expected to have a residual value of $4,500 under each of the following depreciation methods (round all computations to the nearest dollar):
a Appraisal
b Straight-line
c Units-of-output
d Sum-of-the-years'-digits
e Fixed-percentage-of-declining-balance, using a 30% rate (Ignore any limitation imposed by income tax regulations.)

13B-3 On July 1, Year 15, Corpus Cristi Company established a new manufacturing department which requires a number of different types of machinery. The company uses the sum-of-the-years'-digits method of depreciation and closes its accounts annually on December 31. The transactions involving the machines in this department for a period of three years are described below:

July 5, Year 15 Purchased the following machines:

Machine No.	Cost	Estimated net residual value	Economic life, years
100	$40,000	$8,500	6
101	15,300	1,300	7
102	47,500	2,500	5

Jan. 2, Year 16 Purchased machine No. 103 for $60,000. Estimated economic life 10 years; estimated net residual value $5,000.
May 1, Year 17 Sold machine No. 100 for $20,000 and replaced it with machine No. 104, which was purchased for $54,000 and has an esti-

mated net residual value of $10,800 at the end of eight years of economic life.

Oct. 1, Year 18   Exchanged machine No. 102 for a new machine (No. 105), paying $45,000 in cash and receiving a trade-in allowance (equal to fair value) of $15,000. Machine No. 105 has an estimated economic life of 10 years and *no* estimated net residual value.

Instructions

a Prepare a depreciation (lapsing) schedule (illustrated on pages 538 and 539) showing the computation of depreciation for each of the years 15, 16, 17, and 18 and the balances in the Machinery account and Accumulated Depreciation: Machinery account during this period.

b Prepare general journal entries to record the sale of machine No. 100 and the trade-in of machine No. 102. Show computation of the carrying value of these machines at the time of sale or exchange. Any gain or loss should be recognized consistent with the provisions of *APB Opinion No. 29* as summarized in Chapter 12.

13B-4 Plateau Natural Resources, Inc., paid $1,850,000 for a tract of land containing valuable ore and spent $450,000 in developing the property during Year 1, preparatory to beginning mining activities on January 1, Year 2. Company geologists estimated that the mineral deposit would produce 8 million tons of ore, and it is assumed that the land will have a residual value of $300,000 after the ore deposit is exhausted.

A record of capital investment during the last half of Year 1, exclusive of the development costs previously mentioned, is as follows:

Asset	Estimated economic life, years	Cost
Mine buildings	30	$200,000
Railroad and hoisting equipment	20	600,000
Miscellaneous mine equipment	10	250,000

The buildings, railroad, and hoisting equipment cannot be economically removed from the mine location, but the miscellaneous equipment is readily movable and has alternative uses.

Operations during Year 2 are summarized below:

Tons of ore mined	1,000,000
Tons of ore sold at $5.10 per ton, F.O.B. the mine	950,000
Mining labor and other operating costs (exclusive of depreciation and depletion)	$2,400,000
Administrative and selling expenses	$ 625,750

Income taxes for the year, after deducting percentage depletion, were $543,000.

Instructions

a Prepare an income statement for Plateau for Year 2, showing the computation of depletion and depreciation per ton of ore mined in supporting schedules. The company has 250,000 shares of common stock outstanding.

b Early in Year 3, Plateau received an offer from a foreign firm to buy a single order of 500,000 tons of ore at a price of $3.70 per ton delivered in the foreign country. The company estimates that it will cost $1.40 per ton to ship the ore, and feels that accepting this order will not affect the domestic price. It is estimated that the cost of acquiring and developing additional ore property has not increased. One-fourth of the company's "mining labor and other operating costs" are fixed so long as at least 600,000 tons of ore are produced annually. Would you recommend that the company accept this order? Present data in support of your conclusion.

13B-5 Knowlton Company acquired 15 used machines on January 2 of Year 1 for $60,000. The machines are not identical but perform similar manufacturing functions. The machines have an average economic life of four years and the residual value for each machine will approximately equal the removal costs. A composite depreciation method (straight-line) is used to allocate the cost of the machines to revenue. Depreciation on assets retired or sold is computed for the full year.

Machines are retired from service as follows:

End of year	Machines retired or sold	Proceeds on sale
3	3	$ 700
4	10	1,200
5	2	100

New machines of this type are not acquired as replacements.

Instructions

a Prepare a cost allocation schedule using the composite depreciation method for the five-year period during which the assets are used. The schedule should have the following headings:

End of year	Depreciation expense	Machinery account		Accumulated depreciation		Carrying value
		Debit (Credit)	Balance	Debit (Credit)	Balance	

b Prepare a similar schedule but assume that nothing is received on the sale of the machines, that two machines are retired at the end of Year 3, and that 11 machines are retired at the end of Year 4.

c Comment on differences between the results obtained in **a** and **b**.

CHAPTER 14

INTANGIBLE ASSETS

Nature of intangibles

The basic characteristic that distinguishes intangible from tangible assets is that the former are not physical in nature. In legal terminology this distinction is consistently maintained, the term *intangibles* being applied to all nonphysical properties, including cash, accounts and notes receivable, and investments in corporate securities. In accounting terminology, however, intangible assets do not include current assets. Intangible assets for accounting purposes include patents, copyrights, trademarks, trade names, secret formulas, organization costs, franchises, licenses, leasehold costs, and goodwill (the excess of cost of an acquired business over the sum of identifiable net assets acquired). Some examples of intangibles included in balance sheets of corporations are presented at the top of page 562.

Some of these companies list other intangibles in their balance sheet. Generally, a note explaining the nature of the intangibles and the amortization policy relating to intangibles accompanies the financial statements.

Intangible and tangible assets have some important similarities since both derive their value from their revenue- and income-generating potential. Mere physical existence (obsolete machinery, for example) is no guarantee of economic value, nor does the absence of physical existence (the Listerine formula, for example) preclude economic value. In some businesses the value of intangibles may be greater than the value of the tangible assets.

Combined Communications Corporation

   Intangibles representing broadcast licenses, network affiliations
   and goodwill (excess of purchase over value ascribed to
   identifiable net assets):

Not subject to amortization	$ 8,849,000
Subject to amortization (over 40 years)	31,600,000
Other intangibles (amortized over 5–20 years)	172,000
Total intangibles	$40,621,000

Oscar Mayer & Co.

Patents, trade names, and other intangibles, less amortization ..	$ 1,496,000

Oxford Industries

Patents and non-compete agreements, at cost, less amortization	$ 1,723,000

Twentieth Century-Fox Film Corporation

Excess of cost over net assets acquired	$ 1,016,000
Music copyrights	1,903,000
Television station licenses, contracts, and network affiliation	
agreements	12,344,000

One reason for distinguishing between tangible and intangible assets is that it is often more difficult to identify intangible property rights. Because you can "stub your toe" on a tangible asset, it is relatively easy to know when you have one. Evidence of the existence of intangible assets is sometimes vague and the relationship between an expenditure and the emergence of an asset is difficult to establish objectively. The economic value of both tangible and intangible assets is dependent on their ability to generate future revenue and earnings, and this is often as difficult to measure for tangible assets as it is for intangibles.

Cost of intangible assets

A business may acquire intangible assets from others or it may develop certain types of intangible assets. The general objectives in accounting for intangible assets are comparable to those for tangible assets; the initial cost should be determined and allocated to the revenue which the intangibles help to generate. A significant and permanent decline in the value of an intangible asset should be charged to expense in the year the decline occurs. Such a write-off should not be reported as an extraordinary item in the income statement.

When an intangible asset is acquired by **purchase**, its cost can be measured with little difficulty. It may be necessary to estimate the value of nonmonetary assets given in exchange for intangibles or to allocate the total cost among various assets acquired as a group. The principles used in dealing with these problems, as previously described in relation to plant assets, are equally applicable to intangibles.

Accounting for intangibles which are *developed* by a company is more difficult. Distinguishing between capital and revenue expenditures (discussed in Chapter 12) applicable to the development of intangible assets is a challenging problem for both management and independent accountants. In *Opinion No. 17,* the Accounting Principles Board classified intangibles as *identifiable* and *unidentifiable,* and took the following position on the recognition of intangible assets:

> The Board concludes that a company should record as assets the costs of intangible assets acquired from other enterprises or individuals. Costs of developing, maintaining, or restoring intangible assets which are not specifically identifiable, have indeterminate lives, or are inherent in a continuing business and related to an enterprise as a whole—such as goodwill—should be deducted from income when incurred.
>
> Intangible assets acquired singly should be recorded at cost at date of acquisition. Cost is measured by the amount of cash disbursed, the fair value of other assets distributed, the present value of amounts to be paid for liabilities incurred, or the fair value of consideration received for stock issued. . . .
>
> Intangible assets acquired as part of a group of assets or as part of an acquired company should also be recorded at cost at date of acquisition. Cost is measured differently for specifically identifiable intangible assets and those lacking specific identification. The cost of identifiable intangible assets is an assigned part of the total cost of the group of assets or enterprise acquired, normally based on the fair values of the individual assets. The cost of unidentifiable intangible assets is measured by the difference between the cost of the group of assets or enterprise acquired and the sum of the assigned costs of individual tangible and identifiable intangible assets acquired less liabilities assumed. Cost should be assigned to all specifically identifiable intangible assets; cost of identifiable assets should not be included in goodwill.[1]

The Accounting Principles Board thus placed all intangible assets into two categories: (1) those that are specifically *identifiable* and (2) those that are *unidentifiable.* The costs of developing, maintaining, or restoring intangible assets which are not specifically identifiable (such as goodwill) should be deducted from revenue as incurred. Some years later, the Financial Accounting Standards Board wrestled with one of the most troublesome areas related to intangibles, namely, research and development costs, and reached the conclusion that "all research and development costs . . . shall be charged to expense when incurred."[2]

Amortization of intangible assets

The process of systematically writing off the cost of intangible assets is called *amortization.* For many years accountants approached the ques-

---

[1] *APB Opinion No. 17,* "Intangible Assets," AICPA (New York: 1970), p. 339.
[2] *FASB Statement No. 2* "Accounting for Research and Development Costs," FASB (Stamford: 1974), p. 6

tion of amortization by classifying intangibles into two categories: (1) those having a *limited* term of existence and (2) those with an *indefinite* or *unlimited* term of existence. Those with a limited economic life were amortized; those with an indefinite or unlimited economic life were maintained intact until they became worthless, at which time they were written off. This gave management considerable leeway in accounting for intangibles. However, in *Opinion No. 17* the Accounting Principles Board established the following amortization policy for intangibles acquired after October 31, 1970:

> The Board believes that the value of intangible assets at any one date eventually disappears and that the recorded costs of intangible assets should be amortized by systematic charges to income over the periods estimated to be benefited.[3]

According to the APB, then, all intangible assets acquired after October 31, 1970, and those with a limited term of existence acquired before October 31, 1970, must be amortized. The factors which should be considered in estimating the economic lives of intangible assets include:

1 Legal, regulatory, or contractual provisions when they place a limit on the maximum economic life.
2 Provisions for renewal or extension of rights or privileges covered by specific intangible assets.
3 Effects of obsolescence, customer demand, competition, rate of technological change, and other economic factors.
4 Possibility that economic life of intangibles may be related to life expectancies of certain groups of employees.
5 Expected actions of competitors, regulatory bodies, and others.
6 An apparently unlimited economic life may in fact be only *indefinite* and future benefits cannot be reasonably projected.
7 An intangible asset may be a composite of many individual factors with varying estimated economic lives.[4]

The period of amortization for intangible assets should be determined after a careful review of all relevant factors. This should enable management to make a reasonable estimate of economic life of most intangible assets. The cost of intangible assets should not be written off in the period of acquisition unless some unusual circumstances caused the intangible to become worthless. According to *Opinion No. 17,* the period of amortization *should not exceed 40 years,* and if a longer economic life is expected, the amortization period should be 40 years rather than an arbitrarily set shorter period.

In the opinion of the authors, the maximum period of amortization of 40 years is much too long for some companies. During the current era of major technological innovations and rapid changes in consumer tastes, few intangible assets can be expected to retain their usefulness for 40

[3] *APB Opinion No. 17,* pp. 339–340.
[4] Ibid., p. 340.

years. Consequently, many companies probably overstate their net income by choosing a policy of amortizing unidentifiable intangibles over the maximum period allowed. On the other hand, mandatory amortization of some types of intangibles which tend to increase in value over time (such as licenses to operate radio or television stations and trucking routes) may be unrealistic. Amortization of such intangibles may result in an understatement of assets and periodic net income.

The accounting procedures for the amortization of intangibles are comparable to those employed for depreciable assets. The cost of intangibles should be amortized in a systematic manner over their estimated economic life. A *straight-line* method of amortization is usually employed unless management presents a convincing case that some other systematic method is more appropriate. For example, if there is evidence that the value of services expiring in early periods is significantly higher, an accelerated method of amortization may be used.

The amortization of intangibles may be credited directly to the asset account, leaving a balance representing the unamortized cost. This is a matter of custom rather than accounting logic. The journal entry to record the amortization of intangibles is illustrated below:

Amortization Expense . . . . *XXX*		
Intangibles (or Accumulated Amortization: Intangibles) . . .		*XXX*
To record amortization of intangibles for current year.		

The amortization of intangible assets may be either a factory overhead cost or an operating expense, depending on the nature of the intangible. For example, the expired cost of a patent on a manufacturing process is logically a part of factory overhead, while the amortization of a trademark used to promote the product is a selling expense.

Disclosure of the method of amortization and the estimated economic life of intangibles, as well as the amount of amortization, should be made in the financial statements. The period used to amortize intangible assets should be continually reviewed to determine whether changing circumstances call for a change in the estimate of economic life. If a change is made in the estimated economic life of intangibles, the unamortized cost should be allocated over the **remaining economic life** of the intangibles. The remaining period of usefulness may be higher or lower than the original estimate. The revised economic life, however, cannot exceed 40 years from the date the intangibles were acquired. A review of the amortization policy may also indicate that a material amount of unamortized cost should be written off. However, a single loss year or even several loss years does not necessarily justify a write-off of all or a large part of the unamortized cost of intangible assets.[5]

IDENTIFIABLE INTANGIBLE ASSETS

Certain intangibles, such as patents, copyrights, and franchises, can be identified as distinct and separable property rights; others, such as goodwill, are very difficult to identify and thus to account for properly. The more common intangibles which can be identified are discussed in the following sections.

Patents

A patent is a grant by the federal government giving the owner the exclusive right to manufacture and sell a particular invention for a period of 17 years. Patent rights may be assigned in part or in the entirety. Agreements are frequently made under which royalties are paid to the owner of a patent for the right to use or to manufacture a patented product. Legally, patents cannot be renewed, but in practice their effective life is often extended by obtaining patents on slight variations and improvements near the end of the legal life of the original patent.

A patent has economic value only if the protection it affords against competition results in increased earnings through an ability to operate at a lower cost, to manufacture and sell a product, or to obtain a higher price for goods and services. The economic life of a patent is generally much shorter than its legal life; therefore amortization over the period of usefulness usually is necessary.

If a patent is purchased outright, its cost is measured by the purchase price and related expenditures. The purchase of an existing patent would be recorded as follows:

Patents	60,000	
Cash		60,000
To record purchase of patent.		

A patent does not include automatic protection against infringement; owners must prosecute those who attempt to infringe their patents and defend against infringement suits brought by owners of similar patents. The cost of successfully establishing the legal validity of a patent should be capitalized because it will benefit revenue over the remaining economic life of the patent. However, a patent infringement suit may take

[5] Ibid., p. 341.

years to resolve and the accounting treatment of legal costs during this period should recognize the uncertainties involved by expensing such costs. If the legal decision is favorable legal costs may be paid by the losing party; if the legal decision is adverse, both the cost of the infringement suit and the unamortized cost of the patent should be written off because no further economic benefits are expected to result from the patent.

The right to use a patent owned by others under a licensing agreement should not be recorded as an intangible asset unless a lump-sum payment is made at the outset of such an agreement. The periodic royalty payments are recorded as factory overhead or as operating expense, depending on the use made of the patent.

If a patent is developed as a result of the company's research and development efforts, the cost assigned to the patent would include only the direct legal and other costs incurred in obtaining the patent. No research and development costs incurred in the company's laboratory would be assigned to the patent because all such costs must be expensed as incurred. Accounting for research and development costs is covered in a subsequent section of this chapter.

Copyrights

A copyright is a grant by the federal government giving an author, creator, or artist the exclusive right to publish, sell, or otherwise control literary or artistic products for the life of the author plus 50 years. Until January 1, 1978, a copyright was good for a period of 28 years, subject to renewal for an additional 28 years. The rights granted under copyrights may be acquired by paying royalties, by outright purchase, or by obtaining a copyright on a product developed within a business. The problems that arise in measuring the cost of copyrights are comparable to those already discussed in connection with patents.

Although a copyright has a very long legal life, its economic life is limited to the period of time for which a commercial market exists for the publication. In order to achieve a proper matching of costs and revenue, copyright costs should be amortized against the total revenue that is anticipated from the copyright. Because of the difficulty encountered in estimating copyright revenue and because experience indicates that such revenue generally results over only a few years, copyrights are typically amortized over relatively short periods of time. On occasion, copyrights thought to be valueless may bounce back to life with renewed vigor. An outstanding example is old movies: Their production and copyright costs had long since been amortized, but these films suddenly became extremely valuable with the invention of television and the apparent incidence of insomnia among the American people. However, this increase in the value of copyrights was not reflected in the balance sheets of film companies.

License rights and agreements

Many companies invest considerable sums of capital to obtain licenses to engage in certain types of business or to acquire rights to use copyrighted materials owned by others. For example, a Federal Communications Commission license, network affiliation agreements, and film rights are probably the most valuable assets of a company engaged in the broadcasting industry. Without an FCC license, it would be impossible for a broadcaster to earn revenue; a network-affiliated station is more valuable than an independent station because of network-supplied programming; the rights to use old movies produced by motion picture companies is an important source of revenue for television broadcasters.[6]

The cost of license rights and agreements is recorded in the accounts and amortized over the periods expected to benefit. An FCC license generally is amortized over a period of 40 years; a network affiliation agreement is amortized over the period specified in the agreement; and film rights generally are amortized on an accelerated basis because first showings generate more advertising revenue than reruns.[7]

Trademarks, trade names, and secret formulas

Trademarks, trade names, secret formulas, and various distinctive labels are important means of building and holding customer acceptance for the products of a company. The value of such product identification and differentiation stems from its contribution to revenue by enabling a business to sell products in large volume and at prices higher than may be obtained for unbranded products.

Trademarks, trade names, secret formulas, and labels are property rights that can be leased, assigned, or sold. Their economic life continues so long as they are used, and their cost is amortized over their estimated economic life or 40 years, whichever is shorter.

The value of a trademark, trade name, or secret formula is often enhanced as the company succeeds in building consumer confidence in the quality of products distributed under a particular brand. Presumably this growth in value is not without cost, since companies typically spend large sums in advertising and otherwise promoting trade names. The relationship between promotional expenditures and the increase in the value of trade names is nebulous; therefore, accountants do not assign a cost to this intangible asset except when it is acquired by purchase.

---

[6] *Statement of Position 75-5,* "Accounting Practices in the Broadcasting Industry," AICPA (New York: 1975), p. 3

[7] Ibid., p. 8.

Organization costs

The organization of a business enterprise usually requires a considerable amount of time, effort, and cost. Compensation must be paid to those who conceive, investigate, and promote the idea; legal fees relating to drafting of corporate charter and bylaws, accounting fees, and incorporation fees will be incurred; and costs may be incurred in conducting initial meetings of stockholders and directors. All these expenditures are made with the expectation that they will contribute to future revenue. It is clear, therefore, that the cost of organizing a business enterprise logically should be treated as an asset and not as a shrinkage in stockholders' equity before activities commence. On the other hand, items such as losses from operations in the early years, bond discount and issue costs, large initial advertising expenditures, or discount on stock issues, should be recorded in separate accounts and not included in organization costs. Expenditures for issuing shares of stock, such as underwriting commissions, professional fees, and printing costs, generally should be deducted from the proceeds. Similar expenditures relating to issuance of bonds or mortgages should be deferred and amortized over the life of such obligations.

Theoretically the costs of organization have an economic life as long as the business remains a going concern and is generating revenue. Since the life of most businesses is not specifically limited, organization costs may be viewed as a permanent asset that will continue in existence until the business is terminated. Despite the logic of this position, organization costs generally are amortized over a five-year period, probably because the federal income tax law permits amortization over a period of "not less than five years."

Franchises

A *franchise* is a right or privilege received by a business entity for the exclusive right to conduct business in a certain geographic area. The franchise may be granted by a governmental unit or by one business entity to another. For example, public utilities generally receive a franchise from state or federal agencies and are subject to specific regulations; a retailer may obtain an exclusive right from a manufacturer to sell certain products within a specified territory; an operator of a restaurant may obtain the right to utilize trade names and recipes developed by another company.

Some franchises granted by manufacturers or retail chains may cost very substantial amounts. The amount paid for such a franchise is recorded by the *franchisee* as an intangible asset and amortized over its expected economic life. If the right to operate under a franchise is limited to 10 years, for example, the amortization period should not exceed 10 years. Although some franchises prove to be worthless within a short period of time, others may increase substantially in value if the location and product prove successful.

The proceeds received by the grantor of the franchise (called the *franchisor*) represent revenue which is recognized as earned only as contractual commitments to the franchisee are fulfilled.[8]

Leasehold costs

The purchase of an existing lease right and a lump-sum payment to acquire rights to explore for oil and minerals on land are valuable property rights which are frequently included under intangible assets in the balance sheet. Because such assets in effect represent rights in tangible assets, they may be included under plant assets.[9]

UNIDENTIFIABLE INTANGIBLE ASSETS: GOODWILL

Thus far we have discussed the major types of identifiable intangibles. However, the earning power of most prosperous companies is attributable to a variety of factors which cannot be specifically identified either as tangible or intangible assets. Accountants, business executives, and lawyers often refer to these factors collectively as goodwill.

In ordinary usage the term *goodwill* is associated with a kindly feeling or benevolence. However, in business and law goodwill has a different meaning. The *most acceptable evidence* of goodwill is the ability of a business entity to earn a rate of return on *net assets* (owners' investment) in excess of a normal rate for the industry in which the business entity operates. *Goodwill is the difference between the value of a business entity taken as a whole and the sum of the valuations attaching to all its identifiable tangible and intangible net assets.* Goodwill is in essence a "master valuation account"—the missing link that reconciles the current fair value of a business entity as a going concern with the current fair value of the sum of its parts.

The nature of goodwill

The first obstacle in the path toward an understanding of goodwill is the problem of estimating the current fair value of a business entity as a

---

[8] For a complete discussion on this topic, see *Accounting for Franchise Fee Revenue,* AICPA (New York: 1973).

[9] For example: United Brands Company recently showed the cost of a leasehold acquired for $3,117,000 under an intangible caption "Trademarks and Leaseholds"; Texas gulf, Inc., included the costs of contract rights, unproved properties, and exploration projects under "Property, Plant and Equipment"; Union Oil Company capitalized leasehold costs of exploratory acreage and intangible drilling expenditures and included them under "Property" labeled "Exploration and Production."

going concern. The current fair value of the business entity may be greater than the amount of identifiable tangible and intangible assets because of the presence of unidentifiable intangible assets. A simple example may help clear this initial obstruction. Assume that Parke Company is to be sold at the end of Year 10 and that the condensed balance sheet below is presented as a basis for negotiating an exchange price:

PARKE COMPANY
Balance Sheet
December 31, Year 10

Cash and receivables . . .	$130,000	Liabilities	$100,000
Inventories	90,000	Capital stock, $1 par	250,000
Plant assets (net)	280,000	Retained earnings	150,000
		Total liabilities & stock-	
Total assets	$500,000	holders' equity	$500,000

Without regard to the question of evidence, we shall assume that Parke Company is expected to earn an average of $60,000 per year indefinitely into the future. Since the current fair value of net assets depends directly on their earning power, it is clear that under the assumed conditions of certainty we can value the business as a going concern, without reference to its balance sheet, by determining the present value of future earnings of $60,000 per year. A logical way of appraising this is in terms of the rate of return on alternative investment opportunities of comparable risk. We shall assume this rate to be 10%. If it is possible to earn a 10% return on similar investments, the current value of the prospect of receiving $60,000 per year *in perpetuity* may be computed by determining the amount which must be invested at 10% to earn an annual return of $60,000. This procedure is commonly called *capitalizing income,* and the result in this case is a value for the net assets of the company of $600,000 ($60,000 ÷ .10 = $600,000) compared to a carrying value of only $400,000.

We might inquire why, if total assets of this company are apparently worth $700,000, they are shown in the balance sheet at only $500,000. One possibility is that Parke Company's accounting records do not reflect the current fair value of net assets. Inventories and plant assets, for example, may be worth considerably more than carrying value and liabilities may be overstated. If these discrepancies are brought to light during the negotiations, appropriate adjustments should be made.

It is entirely possible, however, that the carrying value of each asset and liability included in the balance sheet closely approximates its current fair value, and still the Parke Company is worth $200,000 more than the carrying value of net assets. Is this an accounting exception to the mathematical truism that the whole can be no greater or smaller than the sum of its parts? Or is it simply the case that some of the parts are not included in the balance sheet? The latter is obviously the more likely explanation, and it is apparent that the missing parts are those characteristics of the business that enable it to earn $60,000 per year (10% of $600,000) rather than $40,000 per year (10% of $400,000). The company apparently has intangible assets that are not recorded in the accounts. Any of the identifiable intangible assets we have previously discussed in this chapter are possible sources of the unexplained $200,000 in the current fair value of the business enterprise as a going concern.

For purposes of this illustration, we shall assume that Parke Company has a patent worth $50,000 which is not recorded in the accounting records because it was internally developed or has been fully amortized. After all identifiable assets, both tangible and intangible, have been appraised, only $150,000 ($200,000 − $50,000) now remains unexplained and we have isolated the imputed value of all unidentifiable assets, that is, goodwill. Goodwill exists as an asset, therefore, only because it is impossible to trace and identify separately all sources of the prospective earning power of a business entity. The foregoing analysis may be summarized as follows:

Value of Parke Company's assets		$700,000
Less: Fair value of tangible assets	$400,000	
Fair value of patent not recorded in accounts	50,000	
Liabilities	100,000	550,000
Unidentifiable intangibles: goodwill		$150,000

If patents of $50,000 and goodwill of $150,000 were added to the assets of Parke Company, the carrying value of its **net assets** then would be $600,000 (assets of $700,000 less liabilities of $100,000). Then if the company earned $60,000, its earnings would no longer be large in relation to the carrying value of its net assets. Thus the ability to earn a **superior** rate of return on net assets which **do not include** goodwill is evidence that goodwill exists; the ability to earn a normal rate of return on assets which **include** the goodwill and all identifiable intangibles is evidence of the existence of goodwill in the amount computed.

Negative goodwill

Goodwill, as we have defined it, can be either positive or negative in amount. Suppose, for example, that the prospective earnings of Parke Company had been estimated at only $30,000 per year indefinitely into the future and that its identifiable net assets are fairly stated at $400,000. On a 10% basis, the capitalized value of these earnings is $300,000 ($30,000 ÷ .10), and it is evident that the carrying value of the net assets exceeds the current fair value of the company as a whole by $100,000. This $100,000 may be referred to as **negative goodwill.**

When the earning potential of a business is such that the business as a whole is worth less than its net assets, the owners would be better off to dispose of the assets piecemeal, pay the liabilities, and terminate the business. In reality this may not be done because of concern for the welfare of employees, willingness of the owners to continue operating an unprofitable business, optimism about future prospects, or other considerations. Since the presence of negative goodwill suggests that liquidation is the best course of action, positive goodwill is more likely to be found in going concerns than negative goodwill. Although negative goodwill exists in many unsuccessful businesses, it is not isolated and reported in the balance sheet; the only evidence of its existence is a *low rate of return* on net assets.

If a business with negative goodwill is sold as a going concern, the value assigned to the net assets acquired by the buyer should not exceed the **cost actually paid.** The total appraised value of identifiable assets acquired less the liabilities assumed occasionally may exceed the price paid for the acquired business. According to **APB Opinion No. 16,** such an excess over cost should be allocated to reduce the values assigned to noncurrent assets in determining their "fair values." If this allocation reduces noncurrent assets to zero value, the remaining excess of net assets acquired over cost should be classified as a deferred credit and amortized over a period not exceeding 40 years.[10]

Recognition of goodwill (excess of cost over net assets acquired)

The high degree of certainty about the future assumed in measuring the goodwill of the Parke Company, in the example cited, does not exist in the real world. Assessing the earnings potential of a business is a most uncertain process, and any resulting estimate of goodwill is a matter of judgment and opinion.

In the face of this uncertainty, accountants have adopted a rule of caution with respect to goodwill. It is generally accepted that goodwill should be recognized in accounting records only when its amount is substantiated by an arm's-length transaction. Since goodwill cannot be either sold or acquired separately, accounting recognition of goodwill is restricted to those occasions in which the entire net assets of a business, or a substantial interest in the net assets representing a clearly defined segment of a business, are purchased and goodwill can be estab-

[10] *APB Opinion No. 16,* "Business Combinations," AICPA (New York: 1970), p. 321.

lished with reasonable objectivity.[11] In such cases goodwill is frequently labeled as *Excess of Cost over Net Assets Acquired.*

Limiting recognition to *purchased goodwill* is admittedly not a perfect solution to the problem. *Nonpurchased goodwill* may actually exist in a business and not be recorded; on the other hand, goodwill acquired in the past may appear in the accounting records when there is no current evidence (in terms of earning power) that it actually exists. The financial statements of companies that have changed hands will appear to be inconsistent with those of companies that have had a continuing existence. For example, assume that Parke Company, which was discussed earlier, has identifiable net assets of $450,000 and that a new company is formed to take over its net assets for $600,000 in cash. The opening balance sheet of the new company would show goodwill of $150,000. Is there any justification for a rule that refuses recognition of $150,000 goodwill in the accounts of Parke Company but permits recording this amount in the balance sheet of the new company?

On balance, an affirmative answer is warranted. Specific assets represent resources in which the capital of a business entity is invested, to the extent that it has been possible to determine them. The periodic adjustment of these asset valuations by a variable amount labeled "goodwill" to a level consistent with the present value of future earnings would not only be a highly subjective undertaking but would also obscure the significant relationship between actual investment and earning power. If $150,000 of goodwill had been recorded in the accounts of Parke Company, not only would there be a serious question as to the validity of this amount, but the high level of earnings on investment that Parke Company had been able to attain would be concealed. The investment of the new owners, on the other hand, was not $450,000 but $600,000. The new owners paid $150,000 for anticipated earnings in excess of normal, and if *only* $150,000 of excess earnings should materialize, this amount will not represent income to the new owners but a recovery of their investment. The position that goodwill should be recognized in the accounts only when it is evidenced by a purchase transaction appears to be consistent with the basic assumptions underlying the determination of accounting income.

Estimating the amount of goodwill

The price to be paid for a business is established as the result of bargaining between independent parties. The bargaining process will

[11] Cases in which goodwill is recognized in connection with the transfer of partnership interests and in the preparation of consolidated financial statements are presented in *Modern Advanced Accounting* of this series. Our discussion at this point will be limited to goodwill arising out of the *purchase* of the entire business for cash. When a going business is acquired in exchange for shares of stock, the transaction generally would be treated as a *pooling of interests.* Goodwill may be recognized in a purchase-type transaction but not in a pooling of interests. This subject is briefly discussed in Chapter 19.

take into account the possible existence of goodwill. The amount of goodwill **to be recorded,** however, will be determined after the terms of the contract are set by deducting all identifiable net assets from the total purchase price. Accountants are interested in the process of estimating goodwill because they are often called upon to aid in establishing the fair value of a business entity at the time of negotiations for the purchase or sale of a business, in court cases, and in similar circumstances.

Steps generally followed in estimating the fair value of a business entity, and thus the amount of goodwill, are as follows:

1 Estimate the current fair value of all identifiable tangible and intangible assets of a business entity, and deduct from this total the amount of all liabilities. This gives the current fair value of the identifiable net assets of the business.
2 Forecast the average annual earnings that the business entity expects to earn in future years with present facilities.
3 Choose an appropriate rate (or rates) of return to estimate the normal annual earnings the business entity **should earn** on its identifiable net assets.
4 Compute the amount of expected annual superior earnings, if any.
5 Capitalize the expected annual superior earnings, if any, at an appropriate rate of return to arrive at an estimate of the present value of such earnings. The present capitalized value of any expected annual superior earnings is the estimated value of goodwill.

In the following sections, an estimate of goodwill will be developed for the Reed Company (which is for sale) to serve as a basis for a discussion of the problems that arise in connection with each of the five steps listed above.

Estimating the Current Fair Value of Identifiable Net Assets Since carrying values and current fair values of assets seldom correspond, an appraisal of identifiable assets is necessary to establish the fair value of the business (excluding goodwill) and to identify the assets which generate the earnings of the business.

The fair value of current assets, such as cash and receivables, will usually approximate carrying value. Inventories, if carefully taken and priced on a fifo or average-cost basis, may also be reasonably stated. Lifo inventories, however, are probably stated in terms of costs incurred many years earlier and should be adjusted to current fair value. The carrying values of plant assets are not likely to approximate current fair value. Various methods of indirect valuation may be employed in making an appraisal of such assets on a going-concern basis. The fair value of any identifiable intangible assets known to exist should be estimated, even if these assets do not appear in the accounting records. The liabilities of the firm should be carefully reviewed, and any unrecorded liabilities should be estimated and recorded. Liabilities which will not be assumed by the new owners should be ignored, unless payment from present assets is contemplated before the business changes hands. Assets at appraised values, less liabilities to be transferred, gives the adjusted amount (estimated current fair value) of net assets for purposes of estimating the value of goodwill.

The following assumed data for the Reed Company illustrate the process of estimating the current fair value of identifiable net assets of a business as described above.

Items	Carrying value	Adjustments	Estimated current fair value
Cash, receivables, marketable securities	$142,000	$ (2,000)	$140,000
Inventories (lifo)	178,000	42,000	220,000
Plant assets (net)	480,000	120,000	600,000
Patents and secret formulas	–0–	30,000	30,000
Total assets	$800,000	$190,000	$990,000
Less: Liabilities	160,000	10,000	170,000
Net assets	$640,000	$180,000	$820,000

REED COMPANY
Carrying Value and Current Fair Value of Net Assets—December 31, Year 10

Forecasting Expected Average Annual Earnings The aggregate value of any business depends upon its future earnings, not its past earnings. Thus, the key step in any estimate of the fair value of a going business is a forecast of the future earnings, a process which, unfortunately, can never be more than an intelligent guess. Because the immediate past history of a business ordinarily affords the best available evidence and is most relevant, the usual procedure is to compute the average annual earnings of the business during the past three to six years and to project them into the future, adjusting for any changing conditions that can be foreseen. The estimate of future conditions and earnings is generally made by the parties to the transaction and not by accountants. A single year's performance is clearly not a sufficient basis for judgment; on the other hand, little may be gained by reaching too far into the past because both the internal and external conditions influencing business operations may have changed radically.

In attempting to compile a record of past earnings suitable for use in estimating earnings potential, two points should be kept firmly in mind:

1 We are not interested in establishing what past earnings were, but in learning what past experience can tell us about probable future earnings.

2 Our objective is to obtain an estimate of future earnings that is consistent with the adjusted current fair values of specific identifiable tangible and intangible assets.

It is seldom possible to obtain satisfactory data by simply taking an average of past reported earnings. A more reasonable approach is to work from actual revenue and expense figures, since changes in revenue and expenses are more likely to be related to projected economic and operating conditions. The effect on earnings of a 10% increase in revenue and a 15% increase in operating expenses, for example, may need to be determined. Past data should be adjusted for changes in the value of assets. For example, if inventories and equipment have been understated in terms of current fair values, adjustments of past cost of goods sold and depreciation expense must be made. Extraordinary items generally should be omitted from past earnings. In view of the subjectivity of estimates and income measurement, minor adjustments can be ignored.

In evaluating an average of past data, particular attention must be given to *significant trends.* For example, two companies may have the same five-year average sales, but if the sales of one company have increased in each of the past five years, while the sales of the other have steadily declined, the average sales figure should be interpreted differently.

An important point, often overlooked in adjusting past earnings in the light of future expectations, is that improvements in earnings expected as a result of the efforts of new owners and management should be carefully distinguished from prospective improvements that can be traced to existing conditions. If the buyer of a business expects to make changes in management, production methods, products, and marketing techniques that will increase earnings in the future, these changes should not be considered in valuing the business since they will flow from the efforts of the new owners. Of course, the final price paid for goodwill in any transaction is a matter of bargaining between the buyer and seller.

The schedule shown on page 578 is a continuation of the Reed Company example. It represents an assumed computation at December 31, Year 10, of estimated future earnings, based upon an average of the results experienced over the past five years. This estimate might be interpreted by the prospective buyer to indicate a probable range of future annual earnings for the Reed Company of, say, between $90,000 and $120,000 per year. However, for illustrative purposes, we shall use the figure of $106,000.

Choosing an Appropriate Normal Rate of Return The rate of return used in capitalizing future earnings and in separating superior from ordinary earnings is determined on the basis of the risks and alternatives involved. The objective is to approximate the rate necessary to attract capital to this particular business under the existing risk conditions. The cost of capital, like other costs, varies in relation to a wide variety of factors. The primary cause of differences in the rate of return necessary

REED COMPANY
Estimate of Average Future Earnings

Revenue:
Average annual revenue for past five years, which is expected to be
typical of future years (extraordinary gains and losses have been
excluded) $920,000

Expenses:
Average cost of goods sold and operating expenses for
past five years, excluding depreciation and income
taxes $635,600

Add: Anticipated annual increase in wages and fringe
benefits as the result of a new contract 45,800

Less: Average of the five-year increase in inventory valuation not included in the lifo basis of pricing inventories
($42,000 ÷ 5) . . . . (8,400)

Depreciation and amortization:
Average depreciation on carrying value of assets 24,000

Add: Increase in depreciation on the basis of current fair
value (25% increase in value) 6,000

Amortization of patents and secret formulas, not previously carried in the accounts ($30,000 over economic
life of 6 years) 5,000   708,000

Expected average future earnings before income taxes $212,000
Less: Estimated income taxes (50%)   106,000
Estimated average future earnings $106,000

to attract capital to different kinds of investment at any given time is the
amount of risk involved.

Data on average earnings rates for companies in particular industries
are available in financial services, trade association surveys, and government publications. Care should be exercised in using such figures to
be sure that they are being applied to comparable situations, for example, that the earnings rate is consistently assumed to be either before
or after income taxes. We shall assume for purposes of illustration that a
reasonable normal rate of return for the Reed Company is 10% *after income taxes.*

Computing Estimated Future Superior Earnings The amount of estimated
future superior earnings may be defined as the amount of earnings expected in excess of that which constitutes normal earnings on the current fair value of identifiable tangible and intangible net assets.

All variables necessary to compute the estimated future superior
earnings of the Reed Company have been discussed and can now be il-

lustrated. The current fair value of Reed Company's net assets is $820,000 (see schedule on page 576), and its average future earnings are estimated at $106,000. Since a 10% after-tax rate of return is enough to attract an investment in this company, estimated future superior earnings can be determined as follows:

Estimated average future earnings	$106,000
Less: 10% return on current fair value of identifiable net assets,	
$820,000 × 10%	82,000
Estimated future superior earnings	$ 24,000

This computation shows that $82,000 ($820,000 × 10%) per year is necessary to support a valuation of $820,000 for the identifiable net assets of the Reed Company. Since the company's prospects are for earnings in excess of $82,000, the source of this excess earning power must be unidentifiable intangibles (goodwill) which enable the company to earn a higher-than-normal rate of return.

Estimating the Present Value of Superior Earnings—The Final Step A number of different methods can be used in valuing the estimated future superior earnings and thus arriving at an estimate of goodwill. Four methods are illustrated below:

Method 1 *Estimated future superior earnings are capitalized at the normal rate of return.* One assumption is that the superior earnings of $24,000 per year, as determined above, will continue unimpaired into the future and that this prospect is entirely attributable to the existing resources of Reed Company. The annual superior earnings are **capitalized** in answering the following question: How much capital should be invested if the annual return on the investment is $24,000 in perpetuity and the desired rate of return is 10% per year? Under this approach, goodwill would be estimated at $240,000, as follows:

Value of estimated annual average earnings of $106,000 capitalized	
at 10% in perpetuity, $106,000 ÷ .10	$1,060,000
Less: Estimated current fair value of identifiable net assets	820,000
Goodwill	$ 240,000
Alternative computation:	
Value of estimated future superior earnings capitalized at 10% in	
perpetuity (goodwill): $24,000 ÷ .10	$ 240,000

There are serious flaws in the assumptions on which this method rests. It may be reasonable to forecast that a business entity will be able to earn a 10% return on its net assets over a very long period of time, but the assumption that superior earning power will persist in perpetuity in the face of competitive pressures and the hazards of free enterprise is optimistic, to say the least. Furthermore, even if superior earnings do continue, it will seldom be possible to trace their lineage to a condition present in the business at the time of acquisition. The frictions that erode superior earnings are such that a persistent ability to earn a higher-than-normal rate of return will ultimately be due to some additional propellant in the form of research, innovations, efficiency, and business acumen on the part of the new ownership and management.

Method 2 *Estimated future superior earnings are discounted for a limited number of years to determine the present value of such earnings.* The estimate of goodwill may be modified in several ways to allow for the fragile and ephemeral nature of superior earnings. One approach is to assume that any estimated future superior earnings will continue for a *limited period,* say, three, five, or ten years. The *present value* of a given series of superior earnings at a given rate of return can be computed by the use of compound interest principles as described in Chapter 5. In the Reed Company example, if estimated future superior earnings of $24,000 will continue for a five-year period, the present value of this prospect on a 10% basis is approximately $91,000, determined as follows:

Estimated future superior earnings (assume receipt at end of each year)	$24,000
Present value of ordinary annuity of five payments of $1 each, discounted at 10%	× 3.790787
Present value of estimated future superior earnings (goodwill)	$90,979

Method 3 *Estimated future superior earnings are capitalized at a higher-than-normal rate of return.* A variation of method 1 is to use a higher discount rate to capitalize estimated future superior earnings than is used to capitalize normal earnings. For example, if the normal rate of return is considered to be 10%, then a rate of, say, 20, 30, or 40% may be used to capitalize superior earnings. The higher assumed rates of return would allow for greater risk, since the prospect that superior earnings will continue unimpaired into the future is *much more uncertain* than the prospect of continued normal earnings. Referring once more to the Reed Company illustration, if superior earnings of $24,000 per year are capitalized at 30%, for example, goodwill is estimated at $80,000, as follows:

Estimated future superior earnings $24,000
Discount rate 30%
Capitalized value of estimated future superior earnings discounted at
  30% in perpetuity (goodwill): $24,000 ÷ .30 . . . . $80,000

Under this approach, the earnings prospects of Reed Company have been divided into two layers—$82,000 of normal earnings, and $24,000 of superior earnings—and a different discount rate has been used to value each layer. Any number of different layers and any number of different discount rates might be used in estimating the value of goodwill.

Method 4 *Estimated future superior earnings for a given number of years are purchased.* Another rule-of-thumb approach to the calculation of goodwill is to multiply estimated future superior earnings by a number of years and to refer to the result as a "number of years of estimated future superior earnings purchased." For example, a goodwill estimate of $120,000 is sometimes described as "the purchase of five years of estimated future superior earnings of $24,000 per year." Loose statements of this kind may obscure the real issues involved. As noted previously, the present value of five years of estimated future superior earnings of $24,000 discounted at 10% is not $120,000 but approximately $91,000; therefore, no reason exists for paying $120,000 for five years of estimated future superior earnings totaling $120,000 to be received over a five-year period if money is worth 10% compounded annually.

Summary of methods Uncertainty and subjectivity surround each of the variables involved in estimating goodwill. The probable amount of future earnings, the part that represents superior earnings, the length of time, and the appropriate rate of return to be used in valuing superior earnings—all are variables not subject to objective verification. They can be estimated only within a reasonable range of probability. The illustrated methods indicate the following possible range (from highest to lowest) in the estimated value of goodwill for the Reed Company:

Estimated future superior earnings of $24,000 are capitalized at 10%
  in perpetuity $240,000
Estimated future superior earnings of $24,000 for five years are
  purchased 120,000
Estimated future superior earnings of $24,000 for five years are discounted at 10% (rounded) 91,000
Estimated future superior earnings of $24,000 are capitalized at 30%
  (to recognize a much higher risk factor) in perpetuity 80,000

In a transaction involving the purchase of this business, the value assigned to goodwill would probably be set somewhere between $240,000 and $80,000, depending on the relative bargaining power of the buyer and seller. Inability to agree on a specific value for goodwill frequently results in an agreement to pay a minimum amount for goodwill, to be supplemented by additional payments *contingent* on future superior earnings of the acquired company. Such agreements may raise numerous accounting problems. For example, (1) How should the future payments be recorded? (2) How should the earnings be measured on which the contingent payments are based? (3) How should future contingent payments be disclosed in the balance sheet of the company which may be required to pay them? An attempt to answer these questions is beyond the scope of this discussion.

It is sometimes suggested that the market value of the shares of stock outstanding provides a basis for estimating the fair value of a corporate enterprise. Thus if the Reed Company, whose net assets have a current fair value of $820,000, has 200,000 shares of stock outstanding, quoted on the market at $6 per share, this suggests that the business is worth $1,200,000 and that goodwill should be estimated at $380,000. This contention would have some merit if the market price per share applied to the entire issue of 200,000 shares or to a block representing a substantial and controlling interest in the company. However, only a small fraction of the total shares outstanding is normally offered for sale on the market at any given time. The market prices of this floating supply of stock can fluctuate widely within relatively short periods of time and are strongly influenced by short-run factors that may be unrelated to the long-run prospects of the company. Furthermore, there is no quoted market price for the shares of the vast majority of small businesses. Stock prices may be useful as evidence of *relative* values in negotiating a merger through an exchange of stock, and they may also substantiate or cast doubt upon estimates of goodwill reached independently, but they are seldom useful in arriving at a direct valuation of goodwill.[12]

Non-compete agreement or goodwill?

When a going business is purchased, the buyer may pay an amount in excess of the current fair value of the identifiable assets acquired. Typically the excess would be recorded as goodwill. There are situations, however, in which a part of the purchase price may be attributable to a restriction placed on the seller not to engage in a competing business for a specified period of time. The purchaser of a retail store or a restaurant, for example, would not want the former owner to open a competing business in the same vicinity soon after selling the business.

---

[12] For an extensive coverage of the procedures to be followed in placing a value on a going concern, see *Valuing a Company: Practices and Procedures* by George D. McCarthy and Robert E. Healy, The Ronald Press Company (New York: 1971).

A **non-compete agreement** would be incorporated in the purchase agreement, as for example, "the seller agrees not to engage in the restaurant business in the City of Lee for a period of five years." Such an agreement obviously has value to the buyer, and a portion of the purchase price should be assigned to it. Although the value of a non-compete agreement is difficult to determine, the buyer and seller should be able to come up with a reasonable price. The value assigned to goodwill should be reduced by the value assigned to the non-compete agreement since it represents an **identifiable** intangible asset. For example, if a business with net assets of $100,000 at current value is purchased for $150,000, it would appear that the buyer is paying $50,000 for goodwill. If, however, the parties agree to place a value of $30,000 on a non-compete agreement for five years, the purchase of the business would be recorded as follows:

Net Assets	100,000
Non-Compete Agreement	30,000
Goodwill	20,000
Cash	150,000

To record the purchase of a going business with non-compete agreement and goodwill valued separately.

The advantage of reducing the recorded value of goodwill is that the non-compete agreement can be amortized at the rate of $6,000 per year, and this amortization is a deductible expense for income tax purposes; amortization of goodwill is not a deductible expense in computing taxable income.

Controversy over amortization of goodwill

Whether goodwill arising out of the purchase of a business entity should be amortized has been a controversial issue for many years. Even following the issuance of **Opinion No. 17,** which required the amortization of goodwill acquired after October 31, 1970, many business executives and accountants have continued to question the wisdom of mandatory amortization of purchased goodwill and certain other intangibles.

It has been argued that goodwill has an indefinite life and therefore should not be written off until there is evidence that it no longer exists. Supporters of this view maintain that so long as earnings are sufficiently high to indicate that goodwill is unimpaired, it is a permanent asset. To amortize goodwill in the absence of decline in earnings, it is argued, would obliterate the superior earnings which called for the recording of goodwill in the first place.

The argument against the amortization of purchased goodwill is particularly strong when earnings continue at a level which indicates that goodwill continues to exist. It is doubtful that continuing goodwill stems solely from conditions existing at the time of purchase. A more likely situation is that goodwill is maintained through the successful efforts of the new owners and management to keep ahead of competition. It is, of course, unlikely that the exact amount of original goodwill which has dissipated will be supplanted by a new layer of internally developed goodwill. Keeping purchased goodwill in the financial records would be an attempt to compensate for the accounting inconsistency of recording purchased goodwill and not recording internally developed goodwill. As a practical matter, expenditures for research, development, advertising, etc., necessary to maintain superior earning power are charged to expense. If purchased goodwill were amortized, there would be a duplication of charges—the write-off of the various costs incurred to build and maintain goodwill, and the periodic amortization of purchased goodwill.

The opposing view is that the amount paid for goodwill actually represents the purchase of a group of unidentifiable intangible assets and superior earnings for a limited number of years. It is argued that goodwill does not last forever and that the realization of superior earnings is not income to the new owners but merely a recovery of investment. Amortization of purchased goodwill is supported on practical grounds because its value is likely to become zero at some future date. Thus the investment in goodwill should be accounted for on the same basis as any other productive asset having a limited economic life. If expectations were exactly realized, that is, if earnings continued unchanged for the period of years used in estimating and amortizing purchased goodwill, the result of amortization might be the reporting of less than normal earnings on the investment of new owners during the amortization period. This squares with reality since the payment for superior earnings makes their ultimate emergence a return of investment, not income.

Both sides in this controversy agree that goodwill should be written down in the face of clear evidence that it is overstated. If superior earnings are gradually eroded by competitive pressures and other economic conditions, the consequent disappearance of goodwill should be charged to expense.

ACCOUNTING FOR RESEARCH AND DEVELOPMENT COSTS

Many companies spend large sums of money on research aimed at the discovery and development of improved processes and products. Some research expenditures result in patentable discoveries and some produce nonpatentable benefits of a general nature in the form of better production methods and techniques. However, significant amounts of research and development costs produce no measurable benefits to future revenue. As these expenditures bulk larger in corporate budgets, their impact on financial statements becomes more significant.

Corporate managements had almost complete discretion in deferring or expensing research and development costs until 1970 when the Accounting Principles Board stated that "a company should record as expenses the costs to develop intangible assets which are not specifically identifiable."[13] But this accounting principle was vague and did not prevent the accumulation of vast sums of deferred research and development costs in the balance sheets of numerous companies. In some instances such costs could not logically be related to specific future revenue and were often written off in a "year of the big bath" because of "deterioration in demand for the company's products."

The AICPA recognized the need to develop sharper accounting standards for research and development costs, and in 1973 published *Accounting Research Study No. 14,* "Accounting for Research and Development Expenditures." *ARS No. 14* recommended, among other things, that costs incurred in continuing research programs should be recognized as expenses immediately and that costs of any substantial development projects should be deferred and amortized over the future periods that they are intended to benefit.[14] This study provided background material for the Financial Accounting Standards Board in the development of *FASB Statement No. 2,* the current accounting standard for research and development costs.[15]

FASB Statement No. 2, "Accounting for Research and Development Costs"

FASB Statement No. 2 was issued in an effort to reduce the diversity of accounting practices and to establish standards of disclosure for research and development (R & D) costs. The Statement specified the activities that should be identified as R & D for financial accounting and reporting purposes, and the elements of costs that should be included in R & D.

The main conclusion of *FASB Statement No. 2* was that all R & D costs, other than fully reimbursable costs incurred for others under contract, *shall be charged to expense when incurred.*[16] R & D costs previously deferred were required to be written off as a prior period adjustment, net of the income tax effect. For example, if $240,000 of R & D costs had

[13] *APB Opinion No. 17,* p. 334.

[14] Oscar S. Gellein and Maurice S. Newman, *Accounting Research Study No. 14,* "Accounting for Research and Development Expenditures," AICPA (New York: 1973), pp. 6–8.

[15] *FASB Statement No. 2,* "Accounting for Research and Development Costs," FASB (Stamford: 1974).

[16] Ibid., p. 6.

been previously deferred, and related income taxes of $110,000 had been deferred, the write-off would be recorded as follows:

Deferred Income Tax Liability	110,000	
Prior Period Adjustment (Retained Earnings)	130,000	
Deferred Research and Development Costs		240,000
To write off deferred R & D costs, net of tax effect.		

When financial statements were presented for the periods before the write-off of R & D costs, the financial statements and summaries based on such statements were *restated retroactively to reflect the prior period adjustment.* The nature of the restatement and its effect on net income and earnings per share for each period presented were disclosed in the period of change. The FASB also required disclosure of total R & D costs charged to expense in each period for which an income statement is presented.

The FASB defined research and development as follows: *Research* is aimed at discovery of new knowledge with the hope that such knowledge will be useful in developing new products or processes or in bringing about improvements in existing products or processes. *Development* is the translation of research findings into a plan or design for new or improved products or processes; it includes the conceptual formulation, design, and testing of product alternatives, construction of prototypes, and operation of pilot plants; it does not include routine or periodic alterations to existing products and processes or market research and market testing activities.[17]

Activities that typically would be *included* in R & D are listed below:

1 Laboratory research aimed at discovery of new knowledge
2 Searching for applications of new research findings
3 Conceptual formulation and design of possible new products or processes
4 Testing in search for or evaluation of new products or processes
5 Modification of the formulation or design of a product or process
6 Design, construction, and testing of preproduction prototypes and models
7 Design of tools, jigs, molds, and dies involving new technology
8 Design, construction, and operation of a pilot plant that is not of a scale economically feasible to the enterprise for commercial production
9 Engineering activity required to advance the design of a product to the point that it meets predetermined specifications and is ready for manufacture[18]

Activities that typically would be *excluded* from R & D are: (1) engineering follow-through, quality control, and troubleshooting during commercial production; (2) routine efforts to improve products and

---

[17] Ibid., pp. 2–3.
[18] Ibid., p. 4.

adapt to changing customer needs; (3) routine design (or changes in design) of tools, jigs, molds, and dies; and (4) legal work in connection with patent applications or litigation, and the sale or licensing of patents.[19] Costs incurred in these activities normally are expensed, except legal costs incurred in connection with patent applications or litigation which are expected to benefit future revenue.

Elements of costs that should be *identified* as R & D costs are:

1 Materials consumed in R & D activities and depreciation and amortization on assets used in R & D activities. Materials and long-lived assets acquired for a particular R & D project that have no alternative uses should be treated as R & D costs as incurred.

2 Salaries, wages, and other related costs of personnel engaged in R & D activities.

3 The cost of contract services performed by others in connection with R & D activities. Intangibles purchased from others that have alternative future uses should be capitalized and amortized over a period of 40 years or less.

4 A reasonable allocation of indirect costs; general and administrative costs that are not clearly related to R & D activities should not be included as R & D costs.[20]

Evaluation of FASB Statement No. 2

The main provision of *FASB Statement No. 2,* that is, "all research and development costs . . . shall be charged to expense when incurred," was a compromise solution to a very difficult financial accounting problem. Those who opposed the deferral of R & D were naturally pleased with the position of the FASB. On the other hand, some accountants and corporate executives questioned the logic of immediately writing off those R & D costs which have a high probability of contributing to future revenue.

Admittedly, there is a considerable degree of uncertainty about the future benefits of individual R & D projects. "Estimates of the rate of success of R & D projects vary markedly—depending in part on how narrowly one defines a 'project' and how one defines 'success'—but all such estimates indicate a high failure rate."[21] Because a direct relationship between R & D costs and specific future revenues generally is difficult to establish, the recognition of such costs as expenses is a conservative application of the matching principle. For income tax purposes, all R & D costs may be charged to expense as incurred, and most companies regularly expense such costs for income tax purposes. Thus the new accounting requirement eliminated a major difference between financial reporting and income tax rules.

---

[19] Ibid., p. 4.
[20] Ibid., pp. 5–6.
[21] Ibid., p. 15.

Deferred charges

The term *deferred charges* is frequently used in practice to describe long-term prepayments subject to amortization. For example, the costs of issuing bonds produce benefits by making new funds available for corporate use; however, the funds raised will contribute to revenue over the entire outstanding life of the bonds. Similarly, the cost of machinery rearrangements presumably results in a more efficient and valuable plant and should therefore be allocated to revenue over an appropriate number of years. Other examples of items sometimes classified in the balance sheet as deferred charges include the following: prepaid income taxes, preoperating (or start-up) costs, and certain pension costs.

The use of the term *deferred charges* may be criticized because all assets other than cash, receivables, securities, and land are forms of deferred charges to revenue. Most deferred charges may be classified either as plant assets (machinery rearrangement) or as intangible assets (oil exploration costs). If a deferrable cost cannot be classified under plant or intangible assets, it should be included under Other Assets in the balance sheet to avoid a separate category for deferred charges.

Deferring an expenditure can only be justified if a genuine asset with future service potential has resulted. If the future service potential of any expenditure is obscure, it should be recognized as expense in the period incurred.

Accounting for development-stage companies

In the early 1970s a special category of deferred charges received considerable attention. Costs incurred by companies in the development stage were designated as *preoperating* or *start-up costs.* Such costs generally were deferred and amortized over a relatively short period after the company emerged from the development stage and started generating revenue. Preoperating costs which were applicable to abandoned projects and other costs which were not expected to contribute to revenue in future periods were written off in the period in which the loss of service potential became apparent.

Accounting practices for companies in the development stage varied considerably. Consequently, the FASB issued *Statement No. 7,* which specified guidelines for identifying companies in the development stage and the standards of accounting and reporting applicable to such companies. A company is considered to be in a development stage if it is devoting most of its efforts to establishing a new business and planned principal operations have not begun or, if they have begun, no significant revenue has been realized. A development-stage company typically devotes most of its efforts to financial planning, raising capital, exploring for and developing natural resources, research and development, establishing sources of supply, acquiring plant assets, and starting up production.[22] A brief summary of the accounting and disclosure requirements under *FASB Statement No. 7* follows:

1 Financial statements issued by development-stage companies should present financial position, changes in financial position, and results of operations in conformity with generally accepted accounting principles that apply to established operating companies.

2 In issuing the same basic financial statements as an established operating company, development stage companies also should disclose the following information:

    a A balance sheet, including any cumulative net losses reported with a descriptive caption such as "deficit accumulated during the development stage" in the stockholders' equity section.

    b An income statement, showing amounts of revenue and expenses for each period covered by the income statement and, in addition, cumulative amounts from the company's inception.

    c A statement of changes in financial position, showing the sources and uses of financial resources for each period for which an income statement is presented and, in addition, cumulative amounts from the company's inception.

3 A statement of stockholders' equity, showing for each issuance of securities from the company's inception: (*a*) the date and number of shares of stock, warrants, rights, or other securities issued for cash and for other consideration; (*b*) the dollar amounts assigned to the consideration received; and (*c*) the nature of the noncash consideration and the basis for assigning fair value to noncash consideration.[23]

In addition, the financial statements must be identified clearly as those of a development-stage company and must include a description of the nature of the development-stage activities. The financial statements for the first fiscal year in which a company is no longer considered to be in the development stage should disclose that in prior years it had been in the development stage.

Plant assets and intangibles in the balance sheet

There is a noticeable trend in corporate financial reporting toward including all noncurrent assets (other than investments) under a single major heading labeled "plant assets," "plant and equipment," "property, plant, and equipment," or "fixed assets." Tangible and intangible assets should be shown separately, and plant assets held for resale should be included under Investments or Other Assets. The methods of depreciation and amortization used, as well as the amounts of depreciation and amortization for the latest period, should be disclosed.

In a recent survey of 600 industrial companies, 431 reported intangible assets being amortized and 211 reported intangible assets (presumably acquired before October 31, 1970) not being amortized.[24] The most

---

[22] *FASB Statement No. 7*, "Accounting and Reporting by Development Stage Enterprises," FASB (Stamford: 1975), pp. 3–4.

[23] Ibid., pp. 5–6.

[24] *Accounting Trends & Techniques,* 30th ed., AICPA(New York: 1976), p. 121.

common types of intangibles reported were goodwill (excess of cost over net assets acquired in a business combination), patents, trade-marks, brand names, copyrights, licenses, and franchises. The follow-ing example illustrates the presentation of plant and intangible assets in the balance sheet:

Plant assets:		
Land, at cost	$ 350,000	
Buildings (cost $1,640,000, less accumulated depre-		
ciation of $185,000)	1,455,000	
Equipment (cost $870,000, less accumulated depreci-		
ation of $150,000)	720,000	
Tools and patterns, at unamortized cost	25,000	
Total plant assets, net of depreciation		$2,550,000
Intangible assets:		
Patents, amortized over 12 years	$ 85,000	
Trademarks and trade names, amortized over 20		
years	100,000	
Organization costs, amortized over 5 years	15,000	
Goodwill, amortized over 40 years	180,000	
Total intangible assets, net of amortization		380,000

Note: Depreciation and amortization amounted to $310,000 for the latest period. The straight-line method is used to compute depreciation and amortization both for financial reporting and income tax purposes.

REVIEW QUESTIONS

1 Accountants use the term **intangible assets** in a more limited sense than the legal meaning of this term. Explain. What are two categories of intangible assets?

2 Why is it more difficult to identify and determine the cost of intangible assets than tangible assets? What are some similarities between tangible and intangible assets?

3 Michigan Corporation has just been organized. The cost of forming the corporation and selling its shares amounted to $85,000. One officer of the company suggests that this amount be charged immediately against the amount paid in by stockholders in excess of the par value of shares. Another suggests that the amount be amortized over a period of five years against retained earnings. Evaluate these two proposals.

4 In computing the carrying value of stock, security analysts generally elimi-nate intangibles. Can you defend this practice?

5 Lyle Company applied for and received a patent on a manufacturing process. The legal and patent application fees totaled $10,000. Research expenditures leading to the patent have been estimated at $60,000. Shortly after the patent was issued, the company spent $25,000 in legal fees in successfully defending against a suit in which it was claimed that the Lyle Company's patent infringed upon the rights of a competitor.

a At what amount should the patent be carried in Lyle Company's accounts?
b What is the legal life of this patent?
c What factors should be considered in determining its economic life?

6 What amortization policy should be followed for **copyrights, trademarks, secret formulas,** and **license rights and agreements?**

7 It has been argued, on the grounds of conservatism, that all intangible assets should be written off immediately after acquisition. Give the accounting arguments against this treatment.

8 What expenditures are properly included in **organization costs?**

9 What is meant by the term **goodwill?** What is the test of the existence of goodwill? What is meant by the term **negative goodwill?** Is negative goodwill reported in the balance sheet?

10 In negotiations for the sale of a going business, an intangible factor called **goodwill** is sometimes estimated by capitalizing average superior earnings, that is, by dividing average superior earnings by an assumed earnings-rate factor. Explain how the average superior earnings are determined and justify the capitalization of superior earnings in estimating the value of goodwill.

11 What is the distinction between **capitalizing** estimated future earnings and measuring the **present value** of estimated future earnings?

12 If all the individual assets and liabilities of a company are identified and properly valued, goodwill will not exist. Do you agree?

13 Purchased goodwill usually is recorded and reported in the balance sheet; internally developed goodwill is seldom, if ever, recorded. Explain the basis for this apparent inconsistency.

14 Outline five steps usually followed in estimating the value of goodwill in an existing business. Can the aggregate market value of shares of stock be used as a basis to estimate the value of goodwill?

15 Endo Company has identifiable net assets having an estimated current fair value of $1 million. The company has an indicated ability to earn $160,000 per year and the normal earning rate in this industry is 10%. Describe three methods that might be used to estimate the value of goodwill for the Endo Company.

16 What are the two major provisions of **FASB Statement No. 2,** "Accounting for Research and Development Costs"?

17 Iowa Company conducts research on the development of new products, improvement of existing products, and improvement of its manufacturing process. How should these research costs be treated for accounting purposes?

18 a Define **development-stage companies.**
b Briefly summarize the accounting and disclosure requirements for development-stage companies as required by **FASB Statement No. 7.**

EXERCISES

Ex. 14-1 Early in Year 2, Adam Corporation acquired a patent on a product with a remaining legal life of 15 years and an estimated economic life of 8 years. The cost of the patent was $12,400. Early in Year 6, the company paid $4,800 to Ted Dale who claimed that the patent acquired in Year 2 infringed on one of his inventions. Prepare journal entries to record the acquisition of the patent, the payment on the patent infringement suit and the amortization for Year 6. Amortization is recorded as a credit in the Patents account.

Ex. 14-2 From the following list of accounts, prepare the intangible asset section as it should appear in the balance sheet:

Deposits with advertising agency which will be used to promote goodwill	$ 4,500
Organization costs	5,000
Discount on bonds payable	15,500
Excess of cost over net assets of acquired business	40,000
Patents	24,400
Franchise to operate in state of Oklahoma	10,000
Marketing costs of introducing new products	15,000
Research and development costs expected to benefit future periods	42,000

Ex. 14-3 Barry Corporation purchased the entire business and assumed the liabilities of Acme Bricks for $400,000 in cash. The balance sheet of Acme Bricks on the date of purchase is shown below:

Assets	$480,000	Liabilities	$150,000
		Sam Summa, capital	330,000
Total	$480,000	Total	$480,000

Barry Corporation valued the tangible assets of Acme Bricks at $525,000 and restated the liabilities at $162,500. Included in the purchase contract is a restriction that Summa cannot operate a competing business for three years; the cash purchase price of $400,000 included $25,000 for this agreement not to compete.
Record the purchase of Acme Bricks in the accounts of Barry Corporation.

Ex. 14-4 The earnings (before income taxes) of Camm Company for Year 1 were $300,000 and included the following:

Extraordinary gains	$80,000
Extraordinary losses	35,000
Profit-sharing payments to employees	25,000
Amortization of goodwill	15,000
Amortization of identifiable intangibles	17,500
Depreciation on building	44,000

The building is worth three times as much as carrying value and the remaining economic life will be increased by 100% by the new owner. The new owner will continue the profit-sharing payments to employees. These payments are based on earnings before depreciation and amortization.

What would be the normal earnings for Year 1 for purposes of measuring the possible existence of superior earnings?

Ex. 14-5 Net income and stockholders' equity for a three-year period for Dover Restaurant are shown below:

Year	Net income	Stockholders' equity at end of year
1	$62,000	$180,000
2	75,000	200,000
3	91,000	250,000

Jim Earp agreed to purchase Dover Restaurant on the following basis:

(1) 20% is considered a normal return on restaurant investments.
(2) Payment for goodwill is to be determined by capitalizing at 40% the average annual net income that is in excess of 20% of average stockholders' equity for the past three years.
(3) Net assets, which do not include any goodwill, will be recorded by Earp at carrying value.

Give the journal entry in Earp's accounts to record the purchase of the restaurant at the end of Year 3.

Ex. 14-6 X Company is planning to purchase Y Company. The past earnings of Y Company have averaged $20,000 per year. It is forecast that Y Company's earnings will be 20% greater in the future. Normal earnings for Y Company are determined to be $16,000 per year.
Compute the amount that X Company should pay for goodwill, assuming that:
a Goodwill is equal to the sum of superior earnings for four years.
b Superior earnings are capitalized at 20%.

Ex. 14-7 Able Company has just acquired Baker Company for $100,000. In acquiring Baker Company, the owners of Able felt that there was unrecorded goodwill associated with Baker's business. They decided to capitalize the estimated annual superior earnings of Baker Company at 20% to determine the amount of goodwill. The computation to determine goodwill revealed $10,000 worth of this intangible asset. A rate of 10% on net assets before recognition of goodwill was used to determine normal annual earnings of Baker Company since it is the rate that is earned on net assets in similar industries. All other assets of Baker were properly recorded.
What are the estimated annual earnings of Baker Company?

SHORT CASES FOR ANALYSIS AND DECISION

Case 14-1 On June 30, Year 1, your client, Rados Corporation, was granted two patents covering plastic cartons that it has been producing and marketing profitably for the past three years. One patent covers the manufacturing process and the other covers the related products.
Rados executives tell you that these patents represent the most significant breakthrough in the industry in the past 30 years. The products have been marketed under the registered trademarks Safetainer, Duratainer, and Sealrite. Li-

censes under the patents have already been granted by your client to other manufacturers in the United States and abroad and are producing substantial royalties.

On July 1, Rados commenced patent infringement actions against several companies whose names you recognize as those of substantial and prominent competitors. Rados' management is optimistic that these suits will result in a permanent injunction against the manufacture and sale of the infringing products and collection of damages for loss of profits caused by the alleged infringement.

The financial vice president has suggested that the patents be recorded at the discounted value of expected net royalty receipts.

Instructions

a Explain the meaning of "intangible assets" and "discounted value of expected net receipts." How would discounted value of royalty receipts be computed?

b What basis of valuation for Rados' patents would be generally accepted in accounting? Give supporting reasons for this basis.

c Assuming no practical problems of implementation and ignoring generally accepted accounting principles, what is the preferable basis of valuation and amortization for patents?

d What recognition, if any, should be made of the infringement litigation in the financial statements for the year ending September 30, Year 1?

Case 14-2 Zip Corporation, a retail fuel distributor, has increased its annual sales volume to a level three times greater than the annual sales of a dealership it purchased in Year 1 to begin operations.

In Year 6 the board of directors of Zip Corporation received an offer to negotiate the sale of the corporation to a large competitor. The majority of the board wants to increase the recorded value of goodwill in the balance sheet to reflect the larger sales volume developed through intensive promotion and the favorable market price of fuel. However, a few of the board members would prefer to eliminate goodwill altogether from the balance sheet to prevent "possible misinterpretations." Goodwill was properly recorded in Year 1.

Instructions

a Define goodwill and list the techniques used to calculate its tentative value in negotiations to purchase a going concern. To what extent does the value of goodwill depend on sales volume?

b Why are the recorded and fair values for goodwill of Zip Corporation different?

c Discuss the propriety of increasing or eliminating the recorded value of goodwill prior to negotiations for the sale of a going business.

Case 14-3 The following footnote explaining the composition of "other assets" accompanied the balance sheet of Software & Research Corporation for Year 2:

Deferred development expenses	*$10,860,000*
Debt issuance expense, net of amortization	*372,000*
Other miscellaneous receivables, cash value of life insurance, etc.	*783,000*
Total other assets	*$12,015,000*

Deferred development expenses include $8,500,000 relating to a computerized reservations system. Although the computerized reservations system started producing revenue in Year 1, start-up and development operations will continue through Year 3. Costs during this period, net of revenue, are being deferred and will be amortized on a unit-of-revenue basis through Year 6. The deferred computerized reservations system expenses are detailed as follows:

Development expenses (principally software) $2,591,000
Expenses, net of revenue during start-up and development period 5,505,000
Interest capitalized 404,000
  Total $8,500,000

In addition to the deferred expenses, equipment (principally computer terminals) costing $6,840,000 is included in properties. The company believes that total costs related to the system will be recovered through future operations.

Instructions Evaluate the balance sheet presentation of the items included under "other assets" and comment on the capitalization and amortization policies for "deferred development expenses."

Case 14-4 A recent annual report of Combined Communications Corporation included the following message to stockholders:

Because amortization of intangible assets as required by the **Accounting Principles Board Opinion No. 17** is significant to CCC's earnings and because management of CCC does not agree with the amortization requirement of **APB Opinion No. 17,** we wish to make our views known in the hopes you will then be in a better position to analyze our financial statements and the performance of the company.

Intangibles represent the difference between the total amount paid in a purchase acquisition and the fair market value of the tangible assets acquired (also commonly referred to as goodwill). In the broadcasting industry, the amount paid for intangibles includes, among other things, the station's Federal Communications Commission broadcast license, its network affiliation contract, an established audience, established program format, and established advertising clients. In the newspaper industry, the amount paid for intangibles includes, among other things, the paper's established circulation lists, editorial reference library, established news development resources, community loyalty developed through editorial policies and support of local activities, and established advertising clients. The Accounting Principles Board, in issuing **APB Opinion No. 17** requiring the amortization of intangibles acquired after October 31, 1970, apparently made the assumption that purchased goodwill gradually loses its value over a period of years and established an arbitrary maximum life of 40 years.

Management is in absolute disagreement with the required amortization of the intangibles related to broadcast stations and newspapers where the intangibles are clearly marketable assets which retain their value and, in many instances, increase in value over the years. We believe there is a sufficient number of sale and purchase transactions each year in the broadcast and newspaper fields to clearly demonstrate this fact. We simply cannot accept a conclusion that one rule for the amortization of purchased intangibles fits all businesses.

It is management's opinion that intangibles should not be charged off (in whole or in part) until such time as it becomes apparent that there has been or will become a measurable diminution in their value. Should it become apparent in years subsequent to the acquisition that a downward adjustment is necessary, it should be the responsibility of management to determine the amount of the adjustment and the period or periods to which such adjustment should be applied. Such a determination should, of course, be subject to the approval of the certifying public accountants.

Instructions Do you agree with the management of Combined Communications Corporation? Explain your position.

PROBLEMS

Group A

14A-1 Seattle Space Research Corporation performs subcontracting work for several major aircraft manufacturers. Early in Year 3, the company purchased from Zeon Labs, Inc., an unused patent for a new type of navigational instrument. The patent is expected to have an economic life equal to its legal life, which expires on January 1, Year 18. The company intended to incorporate the technology covered by this patent into one of its major projects after addition of several new features to the patent purchased.

In January of Year 4, while auditing the accounting records of Seattle Space Research Corporation for Year 3, you find the following account summarizing the costs incurred in the development of the new and improved patent for the navigational instrument:

NAVIGATIONAL INSTRUMENT PROJECT

Date	Explanation	Debit	Credit	Balance
Year 3				
Jan. 10	Cost of patent purchased from Zeon Labs, Inc.	60,000		60,000
30	Legal costs incurred in connection with purchase of patent from Zeon Labs, Inc.	4,000		64,000
June 30	Costs of improving patent: Blueprints for improvements	300		64,300
	Assembly and testing of prototypes and models	25,400		89,700
	Other R & D costs incurred in work on patent	19,300		109,000
July 5	Cost of settlement of a threatened infringement suit on patent purchased from Zeon Labs, Inc.	5,000		114,000
Dec. 31	Proceeds on sale of unneeded R & D data developed in Year 3		7,500	106,500
31	Royalty received on license granted to competitor to use an old patent on a navigational instrument		3,100	103,400

The improved patent was ready for use on July 5, Year 3, but the new navigational instrument was not sold to aircraft manufacturers until Year 4.

Instructions
a Prepare a summary of the costs that should be included in the Patents account in accordance with generally accepted accounting principles.
b Prepare a single journal entry to eliminate the Navigational Instrument Project account and to record the items in this account in conformity with generally accepted accounting principles. Assume that the accounts have not been closed for Year 3.
c Prepare a journal entry, if any, to record the amortization of the patent for Year 3. If no entry is required, explain why.

14A-2 The following information was obtained from the accounting records of Elmo, Inc., and Peruvian Clay Co. on January 2, Year 6, in connection with a proposed merger of the two companies:

	Elmo, Inc.	Peruvian Clay Co.
Assets other than goodwill	$2,625,000	$1,593,000
Liabilities	975,000	720,000
Average income before income taxes for years 1 through 5	408,000	281,400

The values of assets, including goodwill, will be determined as follows: 20% is considered a reasonable pre-tax return on the net assets, excluding goodwill; average pre-tax income for Years 1 through 5 in excess of 20% on net assets at January 2, Year 6, are to be capitalized at 25% in determining goodwill. The following adjustments to average pre-tax income are required before determining the going-concern value of each company:

(1) At the beginning of Year 1, Peruvian Clay Co. charged the cost of a franchise to expense. The cost of the franchise was $54,000. The franchise was considered to have an estimated economic life of 10 years from date of acquisition. The current fair value of the franchise on January 2, Year 6, was $27,000.
(2) Equipment of Elmo, Inc., is estimated to be worth $150,000 more than carrying value; the equipment has a remaining economic life of 10 years.
(3) Included in the income of Peruvian Clay Co. for Years 1 through 5 are extraordinary gains of $46,500 and extraordinary losses of $99,000.

Instructions Prepare a schedule showing for each company the valuation of **a** net assets other than goodwill and **b** goodwill.

14A-3 Midland Mfg. Company is being audited at the end of Year 1, its first year of operations. The accountant for the company recorded numerous transactions in an account labeled Investment in Intangibles. You have been assigned to audit the Investment in Intangibles account, which includes the following entries for Year 1:

Debit entries:

Jan. 2	Incorporation fees	$ 6,500
Jan. 2	Cost of stock certificates (engraving, etc.)	2,100
Jan. 10	Legal fees in connection with organization of company	5,000
Mar. 1	Large-scale advertising campaign during first year	20,000
July 1	Operating loss for first six months of year	22,200
July 7	Research and development costs on abandoned products	45,000
Aug. 1	Goodwill set up by credit to Retained Earnings pursuant to estimates of future favorable earnings	50,000
Sept. 25	R & D costs of EDP program for payroll system	8,000
Oct. 10	General research and development costs	40,400
Nov. 1	Purchase of patent (remaining economic life of five years from Nov. 1)	25,200
Dec. 30	Bonus to design supervisor for his "creative contribution to the product lines for Year 1"	4,800
	Total debits	$229,200

Credit entries:

Jan. 15 *Proceeds on issuance of capital stock in excess of par* $80,500

Oct. 1 *Proceeds from sale of potentially patentable design of new product. The costs of developing this design have been charged to general research and development costs during Year 1 and probably exceeded $15,000* . 6,000 $ 86,500

Dec. 31 *Balance in Investment in Intangibles account* $142,700

Instructions

a Prepare journal entries to correct the accounts, assuming that the accounts have not been closed for Year 1. Any amount allocated to organization costs should be amortized over five years.

b Prepare the intangible assets section of the balance sheet at December 31, Year 1.

14A-4 Exotic Home Products Corporation is considering the acquisition of Teak Furniture Co. The data below are available to the management of Exotic Home Products Corporation relating to Teak Furniture Co.:

Net assets (stockholders' equity) . . . . $ 649,000

Total assets on latest balance sheet 1,000,000

Pre-tax earnings for prior three years ($141,000 + $140,000 + $115,000) . . 396,000

Dividends paid in cash during last three years 150,000

Teak Furniture Co. has a valuable patent which is not recorded in the accounts and which would be transferred to Exotic Home Products Corporation at $126,000. Other assets have a value equal to carrying value. The estimated remaining economic life of the patent is no more than five years. The earnings of Teak Furniture Co. during the next four years are expected to average 10% more than the average earnings of the past three years (before taking into consideration the amortization of patents).

Instructions Estimate the amount of goodwill under each of the following independent assumptions.

a Average estimated future pre-tax earnings are capitalized at 15% in arriving at the total value of the business.

b Pre-tax earnings at the rate of 14%, based on identifiable net assets at appraised value, are considered minimal for this type of business. Goodwill is estimated to be equal to average superior earnings capitalized at 20%.

c Minimum pre-tax earnings rate on identifiable net assets at appraised value is considered to be 12½% and goodwill is estimated at an amount equal to estimated superior earnings for three years.

d Pre-tax earnings of $95,000 are considered normal. Goodwill is estimated to be equal to the present value of average superior earnings (before income taxes) for four years, discounted at 20%. The present value of an ordinary annuity of four $100 payments, discounted at 20%, is $258.87. (See if you can compute the amount of goodwill without knowing the present value of the four payments of $100 each.)

14A-5 Albert Company was organized early in Year 1 to manufacture an electronic device patented by Henry Albert. Albert had been offered $75,000 for his patent, but at about this time he inherited $200,000 and decided to form his own company, issuing himself 40,000 shares of $5 par value capital stock in exchange for $190,000 cash and his patent, which he recorded at $10,000 on the company records. The only other changes in stockholders' equity through the end of Year 4 were from results of operations. The company's records, kept by Albert, show the following results of operations:

Year 1—Loss $15,000   Year 3—Income $12,000

Year 2—Loss $25,000   Year 4—Income $65,000

Albert had taken out a modest salary during this four-year period, but received no dividends on his stock. Albert Company has paid no income taxes because of operating loss carryforwards available in Years 3 and 4 and because an accelerated method of depreciation has been used for income tax purposes.

In the middle of Year 1, Albert established a research and development department in his business to improve the original device and to develop new electronic products. Total salaries and other operating costs allocated to this department were:

Year 1—$30,000   Year 3—$137,500

Year 2—$90,000   Year 4—$159,400

At the beginning of Year 3, a patent was obtained on an improvement of the original device, and in Year 4 the company patented a new electronic component. Because Albert did not have plant capacity to meet the demand for the new component, he licensed another company to manufacture the component.

At the beginning of Year 5, Albert became seriously ill and his attorney undertook to sell the company. Within a few days a potential buyer was found who offered to purchase the company at a price equal to stockholders' equity, adjusted pursuant to the following agreement:

> Results of operations for each year are to be restated giving retroactive recognition to the value of $75,000 for the original patent. Research and development costs reasonably attributable to improvements on the original patent, the new component, and the new molding process are to be capitalized for the purpose of this contract and amortized on a straight-line basis over an estimated economic life as follows: 10 years on the original patent, 8 years on the improvement, and 7 years on the new component. A full year's amortization is to be recorded in Year 1 on the original patent, a full year on the improvement starting in Year 3, and a full year on the new component starting in Year 4. No amortization is to be recorded for the new molding process under development. The unamortized cost of these intangibles is to be recorded in the accounting records of Albert Company, the net income or loss, as redetermined, for each year and the restated amount of net assets (stockholders' equity) will be paid in cash 20 days after receipt of the restated financial statements.

Albert's attorney has prepared an analysis of research and development costs and can demonstrate that costs directly related to the development of patents are as follows:

Improvements on original patent:

Year 2	$40,000
Year 3	10,400

New component:

Year 3	$45,000
Year 4	43,200

New molding process:

Year 4	$19,500

The potential buyer agreed with these cost allocations and was anxious to complete the purchase of Albert Company at the earliest possible date.

Instructions
a On the basis of this information, prepare a schedule showing the revised yearly income or loss (excluding income taxes) of Albert Company for Years 1 through 4.
b Prepare a journal entry on January 2, Year 5, to reflect the adjustments summarized in *a*. Ignore income taxes and assume that amortization is recorded as a credit to the Patents account. The net increase in the income for Year 1 through 4 as a result of the change in the accounting method for patents and research and development costs should be credited to Retained Earnings.
c Compute the price that the potential buyer will pay for Albert Company, assuming that your analyses in *a* and *b* are correct.

Group B

14B-1 Wealthy investor Doris Jamison is considering the purchase of three companies. The latest balance sheets and partial income statements of these companies appear below:

	Xero Company	Yee Company	Zee Company
Total assets	$1,500,000	$1,500,000	$1,500,000
Current liabilities	$ 300,000	$ 300,000	$ 300,000
Bonds payable—8%	–0–	300,000	900,000
Stockholders' equity	1,200,000	900,000	300,000
Total liabilities & stockholders' equity .	$1,500,000	$1,500,000	$1,500,000
Income from operations	$ 420,000	$ 420,000	$ 420,000
Less: Interest expense on bonds	–0–	24,000	72,000
Income before income taxes	$ 420,000	$ 396,000	$ 348,000
Income taxes—50%	210,000	198,000	174,000
Net income for latest year	$ 210,000	$ 198,000	$ 174,000

The companies are in the same line of business and are offered for sale. Net income in the foreseeable future will be approximately the same as reported for the latest year. The asking price for each company is equal to the total of (1) net assets as reported in the accounts and (2) goodwill equal to three times annual net income (after interest and income taxes) in excess of 18% of net assets.

Instructions
a What should be the asking price for each company?
b Explain carefully the reasons for any differences in the asking price.
c Why does Zee Company evidently have the largest goodwill? Is this logical?
d Assuming that the normal rate of return on net assets for each company is 15, 20, and 30%, respectively, because of the differences in capital structure and

the commensurate risks to stockholders inherent in the use of financial leverage, what would be the asking price for each company?

14B-2 West Hollywood Productions, Inc., operates two television stations. On August 31, Year 10, the company contracted with a film distributor for a series of films. The contract gave the company an option to run the films as follows:

40 initial weekly telecasts starting on September 1, Year 10
12 reruns of the best films during the summer of Year 11
50 more reruns during the period from September of Year 11 to August of Year 12

The company plans to run the original series during prime viewing hours, the summer reruns as a late show, and second-year reruns as a late-late show. The expected revenue from advertisers on both stations is estimated by the manager as follows:

Revenue from original 40 weeks $420,000
Revenue from 12 summer reruns 108,000
Revenue from 50 second-year reruns 72,000

The cost of the film rental rights is $240,000, which West Hollywood Productions, Inc., may elect to pay in installments over a two-year period at the rate of $18,000 per month during the first year (starting on September 30) and $3,745 per month during the second year. These payments include interest at 1% per month on the net carrying value of the outstanding liability.

Instructions

a Prepare a journal entry to record the film rental contract on August 31, Year 10, assuming that the company elects to make payments on the installment basis. Record a discount on contract payable.

b Prepare a schedule showing how you would amortize the film rental rights per telecast over the two-year period.

c Prepare entries to record
(1) The first payment on the contract on September 30, Year 10.
(2) Amortization of the film rental rights for the year ended December 31, Year 10 (after 17 telecasts have been run)

d If West Hollywood Productions, Inc., decided in August of Year 11 not to rerun the films during the second year, what entry should be made at this time to write off the unamortized film rental rights?

14B-3 Maxwell Manufacturing Company, a family-owned business, has not issued financial statements to the public since it was incorporated in 1968. You have been engaged to audit the accounting records of the company for the year ending December 31, 1980. Management of the company wishes to present a set of financial statements to an investment banker in conjunction with a preliminary discussion of the possibility of issuing stock to the public. Management would like to report the maximum net income for 1980 permitted by generally accepted accounting principles.

This problem related solely to your audit of the Intangibles account summarized on page 602.

Debit entries:

2/1/68	Organization costs	$ 8,000
3/1/68	Goodwill—purchased a going concern	40,000
12/31/68	Net loss incurred in development stage	55,500
6/1/70	Patent purchased from Y Company with estimated remaining economic life of 15 years	25,200
12/31/74	Goodwill—purchased a going concern	66,000
12/31/75	Non-compete agreement covering six-year period	12,000
12/31/76	Research and development costs resulting in new and improved products and processes	32,500
12/31/77	Financing costs and discount relating to five-year loan of $2 million from Rainbow Insurance Company, arranged on 12/31/77	33,000
12/31/79	Research and development costs—new product	45,000
12/31/80	Research and development costs—new process	61,000
	Total debits	$378,200

No credit entries have been made to the Intangibles account since the company was organized and no amortization has been recorded on any of the items included in the account. You ascertain that the dollar amounts for all debits to the Intangibles account were correctly determined. Management agreed with your suggestion that the organization costs should have been amortized over a five-year period and that there has been no shrinkage in the value of any goodwill acquired.

Instructions (Ignore income tax considerations)

a Observing management's desire of reporting the maximum net income for 1980 in conformity with generally accepted accounting principles, prepare a working paper analysis of the Intangibles account. Any unamortized balance in an intangible asset as of December 31, 1980, should be recorded in a separate account. Use the following format (disposition of organization costs is given as an example):

Description of item	Amount in Intangibles account	Prior period adjustment (debit)	Expense & factory overhead for 1980	Other accounts	
				Amounts (debits)	Name of account
Organization costs—should have been fully amortized prior to 1980	$8,000	$8,000			

b Prepare a single journal entry to eliminate the Intangibles account and to reflect properly the accounting records at December 31, 1980. Accounts have not been closed for 1980.

14B-4 You are investigating the possibility of buying Foreign Car Imports, a retail tire and auto store owned by Keith Capp. The audited balance sheet of the company at December 31, Year 7, is as follows:

Current assets	$161,500	Current liabilities		$130,000
Equipment	186,000	7% mortgage payable		400,000
Building	640,000	Total liabilities		$530,000
Accumulated depreciation:				
equipment and building	(92,500)			
Land	15,000	Keith Capp, capital		380,000
Total assets	$910,000	Total liabilities & capital		$910,000

You have examined the business thoroughly and have determined that all assets are fairly stated, except that land is worth at least $55,000. An accountant has examined the income statements of the company over the last five years and reports that income (before interest on the mortgage and income taxes) amounted to $82,000 for Year 7. The average unpaid balance of the mortgage payable during the next four years will be $370,000. Because of an expected increase in volume, the income before interest and income taxes for each of the next four years is expected to increase at a compound rate of 10% per year. The company's present facilities are sufficient to handle the expected increase in volume. The business is listed with a broker at an asking price of $525,000 in cash. You consider 15% a normal rate of return (before income taxes) for a business of this type.

Instructions
a Prepare an estimate of the goodwill of Foreign Car Imports at December 31, Year 7, under each of the following methods. Round estimate of expected average income (before income taxes) and goodwill to the **nearest hundred dollars.**
   (1) Capitalization of the average expected superior income (before income taxes) over the next four years at 15%.
   (2) Purchase of expected superior income (before income taxes) for the next four years.
   (3) The present value of average superior income (before income taxes) expected over the next four years, discounted at 15%. (The present value of an ordinary annuity of four rents of 1 at 15% per year is 2.855.)
   (4) Capitalization of the first $5,000 of expected average superior income (before income taxes) at $12\frac{1}{2}$%, the next $5,000 at 20%, and the balance at 25%.
b Would you pay the price Capp is asking? Explain.
c Suppose that your investigation had indicated that this business could expect to produce average income (before income taxes) of $69,000 per year for an indefinite period. What maximum price would you be willing to pay for the business? Prepare the journal entry to record the purchase in your accounting records (assume a single proprietorship), under the assumption that you purchased the business for this price.

14B-5 At the end of the current year, a buyer is negotiating for the purchase of Nutter Bolt Company, whose capital stock is closely held. As a consultant to the buyer, Mary Anderson, you have examined the accounting records and have compiled the data listed at the top of page 604.
   Depreciation has averaged $50,000 per year during the past four years; it is budgeted at $55,000 for next year, computed on the original cost of the assets. The estimated current fair value of the research and development data is based on a study of the costs incurred in developing a new package for the company's product. These costs were incurred and charged to expense during the current year; the buyer plans to amortize these costs on a straight-line basis over the next five-year period.

	Carrying value	Estimated current fair value
Cash, receivables, and marketable securities	$ 70,000	$ 68,000
Inventories (lifo)	48,000	92,000
Plant and equipment (net)	370,000	500,000
Deferred research and development costs	–0–	60,000
Total assets	$488,000	$720,000
Less: Liabilities	122,000	120,000
Net assets	$366,000	$600,000

Revenue:

Total revenue reported during last four years	$2,150,000
Budgeted revenue for the next year	650,000

Cost of goods sold and operating expenses (excluding depreciation and income taxes):

Total for the past four years	1,340,000
Budgeted for next year (inventories will be values on fifo basis)	380,000
Estimated portion of the current fair value of inventories not reflected in lifo valuation over the last four years (It is agreed that net income is to be increased for this item.)	40,000
Estimated increase in annual depreciation on the basis of the current fair value of plant and equipment	15,000

As a consultant to the buyer, you have studied the above information and believe it provides a sound basis for arriving at a fair offering price for the shares of stock of Nutter Bolt Company. The buyer has agreed that the company's average experience over the last four years and the budget for the next year provide the basis for a reasonable estimate of average annual earnings for the next five years. Income taxes may be estimated at 45% of average estimated income before income taxes. Mary Anderson has stated that she considers an after-tax return of 10% on net assets a normal return in this industry.

Instructions

a On the basis of the information available, compute an estimate of the average annual earnings (after income taxes) for the next five-year period.

b Make an estimate of the Nutter Bolt Company's unrecorded goodwill on the basis of each of the following approaches:

(1) The sum of estimated superior earnings for the next $3\frac{1}{2}$ years
(2) Superior earnings capitalized at 20%
(3) Superior earnings capitalized at 25%
(4) The first half of superior earnings capitalized at 20%, the second half at 28%.

c Assuming that Nutter Bolt Company has 10,000 shares of capital stock outstanding, recommend to Mary Anderson (based on the estimates of goodwill compiled in b) a range of price per share that she might reasonably be willing to pay for this stock. Explain the reasoning used to arrive at your recommendation.

CHAPTER 15

BONDS PAYABLE

Those liabilities that do not require the use of funds within one year (or the operating cycle) for their liquidation are designated *long-term liabilities.* Examples of long-term liabilities are: bonds, notes, mortgages, equipment purchase obligations, product warranties extending over a period of years, customer deposits, amounts payable to employees under pension and deferred compensation agreements, certain types of lease obligations, deferred income taxes, and some deferred revenue items.

Long-term debt may be *secured* by liens on business property of various kinds, for example, equipment (equipment notes), real property (mortgages), or other securities (collateral trust bonds). Many of the larger industrial companies issue *debenture bonds* which are backed only by the general credit standing of the issuing company. The title of a long-term debt obligation usually indicates the collateral, if any, upon which it is issued.

As noted in Chapter 10, some current liabilities involve no specific mention of interest payments. Since money has a time value, some amount of interest is probably included in the face amount of such liabilities, but it is often ignored because of the relatively small amounts involved. The interest factor in long-term debt, however, is significant and should be given careful accounting consideration. Accounting for bonds, notes, and mortgages payable is covered in this chapter; pensions and leases are discussed in Chapters 16; deferred income taxes are covered in Chapter 21.

Types of bonds issued by corporations

Bonds are a means of dividing long-term debt into a number of small units. Usually bonds are issued in $1,000 denominations, or in multiples of $1,000. Occasionally additional denominations of $100 or $500 are used. In this way a sum of money larger than could be obtained from a single credit source may be borrowed from a large number of investors. The terms of the borrowing are contained in a contract between the corporation and the bondholders, which is known as the **bond indenture.** This contract is usually held by a *trustee* who acts as an independent third party to protect the interests of both the borrower and the bondholders.

Bonds may be issued by corporations, by nations, by state and local governments, and by governmental agencies. They may be **registered** or **coupon bonds.** Interest on registered bonds is paid only to the owner of record, but interest on coupon bonds is paid to persons presenting the periodic interest coupon. Some bond issues, known as **serial bonds,** mature in installments; **term bonds** mature on a single fixed maturity date.

Some bonds may rank behind previously issued **senior bonds** and may be described as **subordinated debentures** or **second mortgage bonds.** Most bonds are **callable**[1] at the option of the issuing company. Bond issues in some cases are **convertible** into common stock of the issuer at the option of the bondholder. **Revenue bonds** (issued by municipalities, turnpikes, bridge authorities, etc.) pay interest only from specific revenue sources. Occasionally bonds are **guaranteed** by a company other than the issuer.

Bonds may be privately placed with a single institution or sold to investment bankers, who in turn retail the bonds in smaller lots to individual investors. Investment bankers may **underwrite** the bond issue, in which case they guarantee a certain price to the issuer and take the risk in selling the issue to the public. If a bond issue is underwritten, the entire issue will be recorded at the time of the sale to underwriters. When an entire bond issue is not sold at one time, both the amount of the bonds authorized and the amount issued should be disclosed in the balance sheet, because unissued bonds represent potential indebtedness which may be incurred without further authorization or additional pledge of properties. Authorized and unissued bonds may be reported in the balance sheet by parenthetical remark or in a note to financial statements.

---

[1] The call provision protects the issuer who may wish to pay off the debt in advance, particularly when interest rates have fallen and he can secure more favorable financing. Bondholders who are repaid at this time must reinvest their funds at a lower rate of interest, and therefore insist on a call premium to compensate them, at least in part, for the reduced interest rate. Call premiums are generally established on a decreasing scale as the bonds move closer to maturity. For example, the $10\frac{1}{8}$%, 30-year bonds issued by Youngstown Sheet and Tube Company are callable at $110\frac{1}{2}$ in the first year, at $105\frac{1}{2}$ in the tenth year, and at 100 during the last five years of outstanding life.

Financial management considerations

When top-level managers decide to borrow money by issuing bonds, they must resolve a number of questions before they offer the issue on the market. First they must relate the need for funds to the amount of long-term debt which can be safely undertaken, by studying the financial position and earning prospects of the company. They must forecast the ability of the company to meet bond sinking fund requirements or periodic maturities of bonds. A decision must be made regarding the features of the bonds, such as security to be offered, call provisions, convertibility, etc. It is apparent that a great deal of advance preparation and study by the controller and financial officers of the company, in consultation with outside investment advisors, precedes the actual offering of bonds to investors.

Issuance of bonds

In a typical bond contract, the corporation promises two essentially different kinds of future payments: (1) the payment of a fixed sum, called the *face amount* or *par value,* at a specified date; (2) the periodic payment of interest, usually at six-month intervals, in an amount expressed as a percentage of the face amount of the bond. In the light of expectations as to what interest rate will be necessary to attract the required funds, a rate of interest is set. It is important to note that the interest expense actually incurred on the bonds is determined by the price at which the bonds are sold; thus the *effective interest rate* (sometimes called the *yield rate*) is set by the money market. Interest on bonds expressed as a percentage of the face amount is referred to as the *nominal* or *coupon rate.* If the market is willing to take the bonds at a yield rate identical to the coupon rate, the bonds will sell at face amount. If the effective rate is in excess of the coupon rate, the bonds will sell at a *discount,* or less than face amount. Conversely, if the effective rate is less than the coupon rate, the bonds will sell at a *premium,* or more than face amount. Differences between the coupon rate and the yield rate are thus adjusted by changes in the price at which the bonds are sold, without the necessity of amending the bond contract.

To illustrate this point, assume that $100,000 of five-year, 7% bonds are offered for sale.[2] The bond contract, which promises $100,000 at the end of five years and $7,000 annual interest, is then offered to investment bankers or investing syndicates. The prices bid by these underwriters will depend on their expectations as to the effective (or yield) rate of interest for this type of bonds. Under two different assumptions

---

[2] Although bonds issued in amounts as small as $100,000, paying interest annually and maturing in five years, are not found in real life, these amounts are used to facilitate the illustration.

as to the effective annual interest rate, the price would be determined as follows, using the appropriate present value tables in Appendix A:

Amount bid for 7% bonds, assuming an effective rate of 8%:		Amount bid for 7% bonds, assuming an effective rate of 6%:	
Present value of $100,000 due in 5 years @ 8%, with interest paid annually ($100,000 × 0.680583)	$68,058	Present value of $100,000 due in 5 years @ 6%, with interest paid annually ($100,000 × 0.747258)	$ 74,726
Present value of $7,000 every year for 5 years @ 8% ($7,000 × 3.992710)	27,949	Present value of $7,000 every year for 5 years @ 6% ($7,000 × 4.212364)	29,487
Proceeds of bond issue	$96,007	Proceeds of bond issue	$104,213

The underwriters would expect to resell these bonds to the public at a higher price and thus a lower effective interest rate, to give them a margin to cover their costs and earn a profit. The yield rate to the issuing corporation, however, is determined by the price it receives from the underwriters. The journal entries to record the issuance of 7% bonds at a discount and at a premium are given below:

Issued at effective rate of 8%:			Issued at effective rate of 6%:		
Cash	96,007		Cash	104,213	
Discount on Bonds Payable	3,993		Premium on Bonds Payable		4,213
Bonds Payable		100,000	Bonds Payable		100,000
Issued bonds at a discount.			Issued bonds at a premium.		

Bonds paying 7% sold to yield 7% obviously would sell at face amount, determined as follows:

Present value of $100,000 due in 5 years @ 7%, with interest paid annually ($100,000 × 0.712986)	$ 71,299
Present value of $7,000 every year for 5 years @ 7% ($7,000 × 4.100197)	28,701
Proceeds of bond issue when yield rate equals coupon rate	$100,000

Bond interest expense

Since differences between the effective and coupon rate of interest are reflected in bond prices, the amount of premium or discount will influence the interest expense to the issuer. This can be demonstrated by comparing the five-year interest expense under each of the two assumptions as to effective interest rates:

Assuming an effective rate of 8%:		Assuming an effective rate of 6%:	
Coupon interest ($7,000 × 5 annual payments)	$35,000	Coupon interest ($7,000 × 5 payments)	$35,000
Add: Discount ($100,000 − $96,007)	3,993	Less: Premium ($104,213 − $100,000)	4,213
Five-year interest expense . .	$38,993	Five-year interest expense . .	$30,787

If the bonds are issued to yield 8%, the discount of $3,993 represents an additional amount of interest which will be paid in a lump sum at maturity. Similarly, if the bonds are priced to yield 6%, the premium of $4,213 represents an advance paid by bondholders for the right to receive larger annual interest checks and should be viewed as a reduction in the effective interest expense. (The premium is in effect "returned" to bondholders periodically in the form of more generous interest payments.)

Interest method of amortization

In theory, the recorded interest expense each period should equal the effective interest expense, that is, the effective rate of interest applied to the **carrying value** of the debt at the beginning of that period. This approach to computing interest expense is known as the **interest method** of amortization.

In the opinion of the authors, the effective interest method generally should be used to amortize the discount or premium on bonds payable. However, the straight-line method may be used as a matter of expediency if the difference in results between the two methods is not material.

In 1967 the Accounting Principles Board stated that "the interest method of amortization is theoretically sound and an acceptable method."[3] Subsequently, the Board took a more explicit stand in relation to the amortization of discount or premium on notes receivable and payable, but equally applicable to bonds payable, as follows:

. . . the difference between the present value and the face amount should be treated as discount or premium and amortized as interest expense or income

[3] *APB Opinion No. 12*, "Omnibus Opinion—1967," AICPA (New York: 1967), p. 194.

over the life of the note in such a way as to result in a constant rate of interest when applied to the amount outstanding at the beginning of any given period. This is the "interest" method. . . . However, other methods of amortization may be used if the results obtained are not materially different from those which would result from the "interest" method.[4]

Bonds Issued at Discount When bonds are issued at a discount, the carrying value of the debt increases as the bonds approach maturity; thus the dollar amount of the effective interest expense increases in each period. Effective interest expense over the life of the bonds and journal entries to record interest expense for the first two years are given below:

Bonds Issued at a Discount
Interest Expense Determined Using Interest Method of Amortization
($100,000, 5-year bonds, interest at 7%, payable annually,
issued at $96,007, to yield 8% compounded annually)

Year	(A) Interest paid (7% of face amount)	(B) "Effective" interest expense (8% of bond carrying value)	(C) Discount amortization (B − A)	(D) Bond discount balance (D − C)	(E) Carrying value of bonds, end of year ($100,000 − D)
At time of issue				$3,993	$ 96,007
1	$7,000	$7,681	$681	3,312	96,688
2	7,000	7,735	735	2,577	97,423
3	7,000	7,794	794	1,783	98,217
4	7,000	7,857	857	926	99,074
5	7,000	7,926	926	−0−	100,000

Journal entries:

	Year 1		Year 2	
Bond Interest Expense	7,681		7,735	
Cash		7,000		7,000
Discount on Bonds Payable		681		735

To record interest expense, including amortization of discount, for first two years.

Bonds Issued at Premium When bonds are issued at a premium, the carrying value of the debt decreases as the bonds approach maturity and the amount of periodic interest expense decreases over the life of the bonds. Annual interest expense and journal entries to record interest expense for the first two years are presented on page 611.

[4] *APB Opinion No. 21*, "Interest on Receivables and Payables," AICPA (New York: 1971), p. 423.

Bonds Issued at a Premium
Interest Expense Determined Using Interest Method of Amortization
($100,000, 5-year bonds, interest at 7%, payable annually,
issued at $104,213, to yield 6% compounded annually)

Year	(A) Interest paid (7% of face amount)	(B) "Effective" interest expense (6% of bond carrying value)	(C) Premium amor- tization (A − B)	(D) Bond premium balance (D − C)	(E) Carrying value of bonds end of year ($100,000 + D)
At time of issue				$4,213	$104,213
1	$7,000	$6,253	$747	3,466	103,466
2	7,000	6,208	792	2,674	102,674
3	7,000	6,160	840	1,834	101,834
4	7,000	6,110	890	944	100,944
5	7,000	6,056*	944	−0−	100,000

* Adjusted $1 for rounding.

Journal entries:

	Year 1	Year 2
Bond Interest Expense	6,253	6,208
Premium on Bonds Payable	747	792
Cash	7,000	7,000

To record interest expense, including
amortization of premium, for first two
years.

Straight-line method of amortization

The additional interest expense (discount) or reduction of interest expense (premium) may be allocated evenly throughout the life of the bonds. This method, known as the *straight-line method of amortization,* results in a uniform periodic interest expense. Although this method does not give the accurate results obtained by use of the interest method of amortization, it is frequently encountered in practice. As previously stated, the use of the straight-line method may not be objectionable if it is applied to immaterial amounts of discount or premium. In choosing the amortization method, the accountant's chief concern is to make certain that periodic income is not distorted.

Bonds Issued at Discount When bonds are issued at a discount, the carrying value of the debt increases as the bonds approach maturity and periodic interest expense remains constant over the life of the bonds. Annual interest expense over the life of the bonds and journal entries to record interest expense for the first two years are given on page 612.

Bonds Issued at a Discount

Interest Expense Determined Using Straight-Line Method of Amortization

($100,000, 5-year bonds, interest at 7%, payable annually, issued at $96,007 to yield 8% compounded annually)

Year	(A) Interest paid (7% of face amount)	(B) Discount amortization ($\frac{1}{5}$ of $3,993)	(C) "Average" interest expense (A + B)	(D) Bond discount balance (D − B)	(E) Carrying value of bonds, end of year ($100,000 − D)
At time of issue				$3,993	$ 96,007
1	$7,000	$799	$7,799	3,194	96,806
2	7,000	799	7,799	2,395	97,605
3	7,000	799	7,799	1,596	98,404
4	7,000	799	7,799	797	99,203
5	7,000	797*	7,797*	−0−	100,000

* $2 adjustment to compensate for rounding average interest expense to the nearest dollar.

Journal entries:

	Year 1	Year 2
Bond Interest Expense	7,799	7,799
Cash	7,000	7,000
Discount on Bonds Payable	799	799

To record interest expense, including amortization of discount, for first two years.

Bonds Issued at Premium When bonds are issued at a premium, the carrying value of the debt decreases as the bonds approach maturity and periodic interest expense remains constant over the life of the bonds. Annual interest expense and journal entries to record interest expense for the first two years are presented on page 613.

Comparing periodic interest expense under the interest method shown on pages 610 and 611 and the straight-line method shown above and on page 613 reveals the extent of the error involved in using a simple average. For example, if the bonds were issued at a discount, the effective interest expense per year ranges from $7,681 to $7,926; using the straight-line method results in a constant annual interest expense of $7,799. In the first year, for example, interest expense on a $100 million bond issue would be approximately $118,000 more under the straight-line method. In choosing the method to use, the accountant should balance the simplicity of the straight-line method against the materiality of the error involved. The longer the life of the bond issue and the greater the discount or premium relative to the face amount of the bonds, the larger will be the difference between straight-line "average" interest ex-

Bonds Issued at a Premium
Interest Expense Determined Using Straight-Line Method of Amortization
($100,000, 5-year bonds, interest at 7%, payable annually,
issued at $104,213, to yield 6% compounded annually)

Year	(A) Interest paid (7% of face amount)	(B) Premium amortization ($\frac{1}{5}$ of $4,213)	(C) "Average" interest expense (A − B)	(D) Bond premium balance (D − B)	(E) Carrying value of bonds, end of year ($100,000 + D)
At time of issue				$4,213	$104,213
1	$7,000	$843	$6,157	3,370	103,370
2	7,000	843	6,157	2,527	102,527
3	7,000	843	6,157	1,684	101,684
4	7,000	843	6,157	841	100,841
5	7,000	841*	6,159*	−0−	100,000

* $2 adjustment to compensate for rounding average interest expense to the nearest dollar.

Journal entries:

	Year 1	Year 2
Bond Interest Expense	6,157	6,157
Premium on Bonds Payable	843	843
Cash	7,000	7,000

To record interest expense, including amortization of premium, for first two years.

pense and the effective interest expense determined by the interest method of amortization.

When interest is paid semiannually or when interest payment dates do not coincide with the end of the fiscal year, a policy of amortizing the discount or the premium only at the end of the fiscal year can be adopted to minimize the routine work involved.

Presentation of discount and premium in the balance sheet

At the time of issue, the carrying value of the bonds payable is equal to the proceeds received since these proceeds were computed by determining the present value of all future payments at the yield rate set by the market. Bond discount and bond premium are therefore valuation accounts relating to bonds payable. This is stated in *APB Opinion No. 21* in relation to notes (but is equally applicable to bonds), as follows:

> . . . the discount or premium should be reported in the balance sheet as a direct addition to or deduction from the face amount of the note. It should not be classified as a deferred charge or deferred credit. The description of the

note should disclose the effective interest rate; . . . Issue costs should be reported in the balance sheet as deferred charges.[5]

Using the figures from the previous illustration, bonds payable on the date of issue would be reported in the balance sheet as follows:

Bonds issued at a discount:		Bonds issued at a premium:	
Long-term debt:		Long-term debt:	
7% bonds payable, due in		7% bonds payable, due in	
5 years (face amount)	$100,000	5 years (face amount)	$100,000
Less: Discount	3,993	Add: Premium	4,213
Net liability (carrying		Net liability (carrying	
value)	$ 96,007	value)	$104,213

At issue date these bonds have a present value smaller or greater than face amount because the market rate of interest is higher or lower than the periodic interest payments provided in the bond contract. The process of amortizing bond discount or premium is in reality, therefore, a means of recording the increase or decrease **in the value of the debt obligation as it approaches maturity.** In the bond discount case, the increase in the carrying value of the debt comes about indirectly through the decrease in bond discount. Similarly, in the bond premium case the decrease in the carrying value of the debt comes about directly through the decrease in bond premium. In either case, the carrying value of bonds payable will be $100,000 at maturity.

Some accountants argue that bonds payable should not be reported at less than face amount because the company would have to pay this amount if the debt were to be settled at the balance sheet date. There are two answers to this argument:

1 Most bond indentures include a call provision, specifying a penalty payment (call premium) over and above face amount if the bonds are called before maturity date. For example, a bond issue may be callable at 105, which means that $1,050 must be paid to retire any $1,000 bond prior to maturity. The argument that bonds payable should be shown in the balance sheet at the amount necessary to retire the debt at that date would therefore require valuation at call price, not face amount.

2 Financial statements are prepared on the assumption that the business entity is a going concern. Retirement of long-term debt at balance sheet date is not the normal expectation. There is always the possibility that debt may be retired prior to maturity, and this decision would change the value of the debt, since a liability that is to be paid immediately has a different value than one due a number of years in the future. If a decision to call the bonds has been made, the accountant should disclose this fact in the financial statements. But typically the most probable event is that the entity will meet its debts as

[5] Ibid.

they fall due, and the proper accounting valuation of the debt is its present value in terms of the effective rate of interest prevailing when the bonds were issued.

Bond issue costs

A number of costs are incurred in connection with a bond issue: fees paid to accountants, attorneys, underwriters, and other experts in connection with the preparation of the bond contract and prospectus; printing and engraving costs; and costs incurred in advertising the issue. These are costs of securing the use of the funds borrowed and thus of benefits which will accrue to the borrower over the entire period of the loan.

Bond issue costs are classified as an asset and amortized over the life of the bonds because revenue benefits from the use of the bond proceeds over this period. An alternative procedure is to add bond issue costs to the amount of discount or deduct them from bond premium. The latter treatment implies that the amount of funds made available to the borrower is equal to the net proceeds of the bond issue *after* deducting all costs of completing the financing transaction. In this view, bond issue costs simply increase the effective interest expense during the life of the bonds.

Bonds issued between interest dates

Bond interest payments are usually made semiannually on dates specified in the bond contract. Bonds are often sold, however, at a date other than an interest payment date. It would be possible to adjust for this factor by reducing the interest payment for the first "short" interest period. However, it is much more convenient simply to add to the price of the bond the amount of interest that has accrued since the last interest payment date. The investors, in effect, reimburse the borrowing company for the portion of the full six-month interest payment to which they are not entitled. They will then receive the full six-month interest payment on the next semiannual interest payment date.

Assume that Electronic Devices, Inc., issued $100,000 in 10-year, 6% bonds, with interest payable semiannually on April 1 and October 1 of each year. The bonds were issued on June 1 at $107,080 plus accrued interest for two months. The bonds were dated April 1 and various issue costs amounted to $2,360. Note that this borrowing actually runs for 9 years and 10 months, or 118 months, and the accounting for the debt and related issue costs should reflect this fact. Assuming that the straight-line method of amortization is used, the average interest expense per month would be determined as illustrated on page 616.

Actual interest paid to investors over 10-year period (10 × $6,000) . . .	$60,000
Less:	
Premium received on issuance of bonds	(7,080)
Accrued interest received from investors (Apr. 1–June 1)	(1,000)
Total interest expense (9 years and 10 months)	$51,920
Average interest expense per month ($51,920 ÷ 118 months)	$ 440

Since the monthly interest accrual will be $500 ($6,000 ÷ 12 months) and the average interest expense is $440, the monthly premium amortization will be the difference, or $60 ($7,080 ÷ 118 months). Issue costs would be amortized at the rate of $20 per month ($2,360 ÷ 118 months). Assuming that amortization of the issue costs and the premium is recorded only at the end of the year, the entries relating to the bond issue during the first calendar year would be as shown on page 617.

It would be possible to credit Bond Interest Expense (rather than Accrued Bond Interest Payable) for $1,000 on June 1 for the accrued interest for two months purchased by bondholders. On October 1, then, Bond Interest Expense would be debited for $3,000, thus leaving a balance of $2,000 in Bond Interest Expense representing interest incurred from June 1 to October 1. It would also be possible to amortize the premium and bond issue costs at the time interest is paid and also at the end of the fiscal year, but there is little point in following such an inefficient procedure when straight-line amortization is used.

Early extinguishment of debt

Bonds payable may be acquired by the issuing corporation prior to maturity. Such bonds may be held in the treasury or may be formally retired. The acquisition of bonds completes the "transaction cycle" relating to the borrowing and should be viewed as an *early extinguishment of debt.* The Accounting Principles Board defined early extinguishment of debt as follows:

> *Early extinguishment* is the reacquisition of any form of debt security or instrument before its scheduled maturity except through conversion by the holder, regardless of whether the debt is viewed as terminated or is held as so-called "treasury bonds." All open-market or mandatory reacquisitions of debt securities to meet sinking fund requirements are early extinguishments.[6]

A gain or loss is recognized equal to the difference between the amount paid to retire the bonds and their carrying value less bond issue costs. The amortization of bond discount, bond premium, and bond issue costs should, of course, be adjusted to the date of retirement *be-*

[6] *APB Opinion No. 26,* "Early Extinguishment of Debt," AICPA (New York: 1972), p. 495.

Entries for Bonds Issued between Interest Dates

June 1	Deferred Bond Issue Costs	2,360	
	Cash		2,360
	To record various costs of issuing bonds.		
June 1	Cash	108,080	
	Bonds Payable		100,000
	Accrued Bond Interest Payable		1,000
	Premium on Bonds Payable		7,080
	To record issuance of bonds and accrued interest for two months.		
Oct. 1	Accrued Bond Interest Payable	1,000	
	Bond Interest Expense	2,000	
	Cash		3,000
	To record interest payment for first six months.		
Dec. 31	Bond Interest Expense	1,080	
	Premium on Bonds Payable	420	
	Bond Issue Expense	140	
	Deferred Bond Issue Costs		140
	Accrued Bond Interest Payable		1,500
	To accrue interest expense for three months and record amortization of deferred bond issue costs and premium on bonds payable for seven months. Amounts determined as follows:		
	Accrued interest: $100,000 \times 6\% \times \frac{3}{12}$	$1,500	
	Less: Amortization of premium:		
	$7,080 \times 7/118	420	
	Bond interest expense (net)	$1,080	
	Amortization of deferred bond issue costs: $2,360 \times 7/118	$ 140	

fore the entry to record the retirement is made. To illustrate, assume that $20,000 (20%) of the Electronic Devices, Inc., bonds described in the previous example are retired on December 1 of the second year, or 18 months after the bonds were issued. If the bonds are acquired at 102$\frac{1}{2}$, plus accrued interest of $200 for two months, the two entries on page 618 would be required.

The balance of the premium and issue costs applicable to the $20,000 of bonds acquired is eliminated from the accounting records. Gains and losses on extinguishment of debt reflect the changes in interest rates,

Entries to Record Early Extinguishment of Debt

Dec. 1	Premium on Bonds Payable	132	
	Bond Issue Expense	44	
	Bond Interest Expense		132
	Deferred Bond Issue Costs		44

To bring amortization up to date on $20,000 (or 20%)
of bonds for period Jan. 1 to Dec. 1.
　Amortization of premium:
　　$7,080 × 20% × 11/118 = $132.
　Amortization of deferred bond issue costs:
　　$2,360 × 20% × 11/118 = $44.

Dec. 1	Bonds Payable	20,000	
	Premium on Bonds Payable ($1,416 − $216)	1,200	
	Bond Interest Expense	200	
	Cash		20,700
	Deferred Bond Issue Costs ($472 − $72)		400
	Gain on Extinguishment of Bonds		300

To record extinguishment of bonds at 102½ plus
accrued interest of $200 for two months. The gain
is determined as follows:

Original proceeds, $107,080 × 20%	$21,416
Less: Original portion of bond issue costs,	
$2,360 × 20%	472
Carrying value at issuance date	$20,944
Amortization for 18 months:	
Premium, $60 × 20% × 18 months	(216)
Bond issue costs, $20 × 20% × 18 months . .	72
Carrying value of bonds at date of	
extinguishment	$20,800
Amount paid to extinguish bonds	20,500
Gain on extinguishment of bonds	$　300

and perhaps changes in risk factors, since the bonds were issued. Material gains and losses (net of income taxes) should be reported as extraordinary items. On this point *FASB Statement No. 4* stated:

> Gains and losses from extinguishment of debt that are included in the determination of net income shall be aggregated and, if material, classified as an extraordinary item, net of related income tax effect. . . . The conclusion does not apply, however, to gains and losses from cash purchases of debt made to satisfy current or future sinking-fund requirements. Those gains and losses shall be aggregated and the amount shall be identified as a separate item.[7]

---

[7] *FASB Statement No. 4*, "Reporting Gains and Losses from Extinguishment of Debt, . . ." FASB (Stamford: 1975), pp. 3–4.

When bonds are retired at maturity, no gain or loss results since the carrying value of the bonds equals face amount. Gains on bond extinguishments represent taxable income; losses are deductible for income tax purposes.

When the entire bond issue is **called** for redemption, the entire unamortized premium or discount and bond issue costs are written off. A loss will generally result on such a transaction since the sliding call prices will ordinarily be in excess of bond carrying values on corresponding dates.

If bonds are acquired but not formally retired, a Treasury Bonds account may be debited for the face amount of the **treasury bonds** held, but a gain or loss should still be recognized as illustrated above. The Treasury Bonds account is not an asset and should be deducted from Bonds Payable in the balance sheet. Interest should not be paid on reacquired bonds unless they are held as an investment by a company-sponsored fund, such as an employee pension fund.

Serial bonds

Thus far we have considered bonds having a single fixed maturity. An alternative type of debt contract, known as a **serial bond**, provides for repayment of the principal in periodic installments. Serial bonds have the obvious advantage of gearing debt repayment to the periodic cash inflow from operations.

As in the case of term bonds, serial bonds may sell at a premium or a discount in response to differences between coupon and effective interest rates. The proceeds of a serial bond issue are somewhat more difficult to compute because of the varying maturities, but the approach is the same: The present value of the series of principal payments plus the present value of the interest payments, all at the effective rate of interest, equals the price that should be paid for the bonds.

At this point the question arises: Is there any **single** interest rate applicable to a serial bond issue? We often refer loosely to the rate of interest, when in fact in the market at any given time there are a number of interest rates, depending on the terms, nature, and length of the contract offered. In a given serial bond issue, the terms of all bonds in the issue are the same except for the differences in maturity. Since short-term interest rates often differ from long-term rates, however, it is likely that each maturity will sell at a different yield rate, so that there will be a different discount or premium relating to each maturity.

In accounting for an issue of serial bonds under these conditions, each maturity should be treated as a separate bond issue. Thus if $100,000 in five-year, 5% serial bonds are issued, to be repaid in the amount of $20,000 each year, and each maturity sells at a price reflecting a different yield rate, the problem would be treated as a summarized accounting for five separate bond issues of $20,000 each, maturing in one, two, three, four, and five years, respectively. Each maturity would have a related discount or premium, and interest expense on each maturity might be computed as previously illustrated for term bonds.

In many cases, however, this degree of precision in accounting for serial bond issues is not possible because the yield rate for each maturity is not known. Underwriters may bid on an entire serial bond issue on the basis of an average yield rate and may not disclose the particular yield rate for each maturity that was used in arriving at the bid price. In this situation we may have to assume that the same yield rate applies to all maturities in the issue, and proceed accordingly.

If the interest method is to be used in accounting for interest expense, the procedure is similar to that illustrated in connection with single-maturity bonds. The interest expense for each period will be an amount equal to the effective rate multiplied by the carrying value of the bonds outstanding during that period, and the difference between interest expense so computed and the actual interest payments will represent the amortization of the bond discount or premium. The result will be a constant rate of interest expense in relation to the carrying value of the bonds outstanding.

A variation of the straight-line method, known as the *bonds outstanding method,* results in a decreasing amount of premium or discount amortization each period proportionate to the decrease in the outstanding debt.

Accounting for Serial Bonds Illustrated To illustrate the variation in the pattern of interest expense under each of these methods, assume that the James Company issues $100,000 in five-year, 5% serial bonds, to be repaid in the amount of $20,000 each year. To simplify the illustration, assume that interest payments are made annually. If the bonds are issued to yield 6% per year, the proceeds will be $97,375, as determined below from the 6% column in Table 2 of Appendix A:

Principal and interest due at end of Year 1:	
($20,000 + $5,000) × 0.943396	$23,585
Principal and interest due at end of Year 2:	
($20,000 + $4,000) × 0.889996	21,360
Principal and interest due at end of Year 3:	
($20,000 + $3,000) × 0.839619	19,311
Principal and interest due at end of Year 4:	
($20,000 + $2,000) × 0.792094	17,426
Principal and interest due at end of Year 5:	
($20,000 + $1,000) × 0.747258	15,693
Present value of serial bonds at 6% yield basis	$97,375

The accounting problem is to determine how the discount of $2,625 should be prorated over the life of the serial bond issue. Schedules determining periodic discount amortization and interest expense using the *interest* and *bonds outstanding* methods are illustrated below:

Amortization of Discount on Serial Bonds—Interest Method

Year	(A) Carrying value of bonds ($100,000 −E − F)	(B) Effective interest expense (6% × A)	(C) Interest payment	(D) Discount amortization (B − C)	(E) Bond discount balance (E − D)	(F) Principal repayment
Issue	$97,375				$2,625	
1	78,217	$ 5,842	$ 5,000	$ 842	1,783	$20,000
2	58,910	4,693	4,000	693	1,090	20,000
3	39,444	3,534	3,000	534	556	20,000
4	19,811	2,367	2,000	367	189	20,000
5	–0–	1,189	1,000	189	–0–	20,000
		$17,625	$15,000	$2,625		

Amortization of Discount on Serial Bonds—Bonds Outstanding Method

Year	Bonds out-standing (face amount)	Fraction of total of bonds out-standing	(A) Amortization of discount ($2,625 × fraction)	(B) Interest payments (5% of bonds out-standing)	Interest expense (A + B)
1	$100,000	10/30	$ 875	$ 5,000	$ 5,875
2	80,000	8/30	700	4,000	4,700
3	60,000	6/30	525	3,000	3,525
4	40,000	4/30	350	2,000	2,350
5	20,000	2/30	175	1,000	1,175
	$300,000	30/30	$2,625	$15,000	$17,625

The bonds outstanding method in this case produces results that are a close approximation of the effective interest expense because of the short life of the issue and the relatively small discount. The longer the life of the bonds and the larger the discount or premium, the larger would be the discrepancy between the two methods.

Using the straight-line method, amortization would be $525 per year ($2,625 ÷ 5). The bonds outstanding method may also be viewed as a "straight-line" method since it results in a constant amortization of discount or premium *per $1,000 face amount of bonds outstanding.* In this example, the amount of discount amortization per $1,000 bond outstanding may be calculated by dividing the total discount by the sum of the bonds outstanding over the life of the issue: ($2,625 ÷ $300,000 = $8.75 per $1,000 bond). If the discount amortization per $1,000 bond is determined at the time of the issuance, it is a simple process to compute the appropriate amount of discount applicable to any amount of bonds in any given year throughout the life of a serial bond issue. Thus in the fourth year, when $40,000 of bonds were outstanding, the discount to be amortized would be computed: $40,000 of bonds times $8.75 per $1,000 face amount, or $350.

Early Extinguishment of Serial Bonds When serial bonds mature, Bonds Payable is debited and Cash is credited. Since the carrying value of the bonds in this case is equal to the amount paid, no gain or loss would be recognized. If serial bonds are acquired prior to the regularly scheduled maturity date, a price different from carrying value generally would be paid and a gain or loss would result. The carrying value of serial bonds is equal to the face amount plus the related unamortized premium (or less the related unamortized discount) and less any unamortized bond issue costs. All these account balances would have to be canceled at the time of extinguishment.

To illustrate the extinguishment of serial bonds prior to maturity, assume that $10,000 of James Company bonds described in the preceding example are retired at the end of Year 2, two years ahead of the scheduled retirement date. The bonds are retired at 101 and interest has been paid for Year 2. The discount applicable to the $10,000 of bonds being retired is determined as follows under the bonds outstanding method:

Discount applicable to Year 3: $\frac{10,000}{60,000} \times \$525^* \ldots \ldots \ldots \ldots \ldots$ $ 87.50

Discount applicable to Year 4: $\frac{10,000}{40,000} \times \$350^* \ldots \ldots \ldots \ldots \ldots$ 87.50

Total discount applicable to retired bonds $\ldots \ldots \ldots \ldots \ldots \ldots$ $175.00†

* From Column A in table at bottom of page 621.
† Since the discount amortization amounts to $8.75 per $1,000 per year, this amount can be determined as follows: $8.75 × 10 × 2, or $175. Similar procedures can be used to compute amortization on serial bonds when the "bond year" and the fiscal year of the issuer do not coincide.

The entry to record the extinguishment is given below:

Bonds Payable	10,000	
Loss on Extinguishment of Bonds	275	
Discount on Bonds Payable		175
Cash		10,100

To record extinguishment of serial bonds two years prior to scheduled maturity date.

Bonds with a carrying value of $9,825 have been retired for $10,100, resulting in a loss of $275.

Refunding a bond issue

Refunding is the process of retiring one bond issue with the proceeds of a new bond issue. When refunding occurs at the time the old debt matures, the carrying value of the old debt equals its maturity value; no gain or loss arises from the retirement of the old debt and the new obligation is recorded in the usual manner.

A problem arises when refunding occurs prior to the maturity of the old bonds. This usually happens when interest rates have declined and the borrowing company sees a chance to reduce its interest expense by canceling the old contract (paying the required penalty in the form of a call premium) and entering into a new one. If the two transactions (canceling old bonds and issuing new) are viewed as separate and unrelated events, no issues are raised that have not already been discussed. Retiring the old bonds results in a realized gain or loss equal to the difference between carrying value and call price; the new bonds are recorded in the usual manner. Some accountants have argued, however, that the recognition of loss on the refunding prior to maturity should be postponed and amortized over part or the entire period of the new bond issue.

For example, assume that the Cleve Corporation has outstanding $1,000,000 in 8% bonds having 10 years to run and a carrying value of $960,000 (face amount of $1,000,000, less unamortized discount of $40,000). The company has decided to call the bonds at 105, using for this purpose the proceeds of a new 20-year issue of $6\frac{1}{2}$% bonds (which we will assume can be sold at face amount). Debt having a carrying value of $960,000 is thus being refunded at a cost of $1,050,000, and a question arises as to the treatment of the $90,000 difference. Three solutions to this question have been proposed:

1 Write off $90,000 (net of tax effect) immediately as a loss.
2 Record the $90,000 (net of tax effect) as an asset and amortize it over the remaining life of the retired bonds (in this case 10 years).

3 Record the $90,000 (net of tax effect) as an asset and amortize it over the life of the new issue (in this case 20 years).

The first alternative has the clear weight of logic in its favor. The amount of unamortized bond discount at any time measures the liability for additional interest that will accrue during the remaining life of bonds to compensate for the fact that the coupon rate of interest is less than the effective rate of interest. In order to be relieved of the old contract, the company is required to pay this $40,000 of interest now rather than at maturity date, and in addition, to pay a $50,000 call premium. These costs of terminating an unfavorable contract are *related* to past periods but are *caused* by current economic forces (decline in the market rate of interest) and by management action (the decision to refund). To defer these costs would penalize future periods since the new $6\frac{1}{2}\%$ bonds could be sold even if the 8% bonds had not been outstanding.

The Accounting Principles Board did not make a distinction between refunding and a nonrefunding retirement; it required that losses or gains on refunding, net of the tax effect "should be recognized currently in income of the period of extinguishment. . . ."[8]

Arguments for the amortization over the remaining life of old bonds are based on the doctrine that when a cost is incurred, the benefits of which may reasonably be expected to be realized over a period of years, the cost should be charged against income over those years. It may be argued that the unamortized bond discount and call premium paid to refund an issue are costs incurred to obtain the benefit of lower interest expense during the remaining life of the refunded issue. The payment of a call premium necessary to cancel an unfavorable contract and the write-off of unamortized discount on the contract may be viewed as events relating to the old contract and not as benefits to be derived from the new bonds. Had a larger coupon rate been set on the old bonds, they would have sold originally at face value and there would be no unamortized discount at the refunding date.

The third method rests on the premise that since the new bonds are a continuation of the old, the costs of both the old and new borrowing should be prorated over the life of the new bonds. The life of the new bonds would generally be longer than the unexpired term of the refunded bonds. It was suggested that deferral of the "loss" was appropriate when the refunding takes place because of currently lower interest rates or anticipated higher interest rates in the future. This position assumes that the key reason for the refunding is to obtain a lower interest cost over the term of the new issue.

Although students should be familiar with the alternatives discussed above, it should be emphasized that only the first method (immediate recognition of losses or gains) is sanctioned by generally accepted accounting principles.

[8] *APB Opinion No. 26,* pp. 501–502.

Deciding When to Refund a Bond Issue A decline in interest rates is not in itself a sufficient basis for a decision to refund an old bond issue. The out-of-pocket costs of refunding must be compared with the present value of future interest savings. In addition, the tax impact of refunding and bond indenture features on both the old and new bonds must be considered. Unamortized discount and bond issue costs applicable to the old debt may be deducted for income tax purposes in the year of refunding. The call premium is immediately deductible for tax purposes, but the issue costs of the new bonds must be amortized over their life. Future interest rates should also be considered, since a further decline in rates may mean that refunding can be made under even more favorable conditions at a later date. A more detailed discussion of this topic is found in *Modern Advanced Accounting* of this series.

Convertible bonds

Current Practice A convertible bond may be exchanged for a stipulated number of shares of common stock. The conversion feature of a convertible bond enables the holders of such a security to enjoy the status of a creditor and at the same time participate in the price appreciation of the common stock. According to *APB Opinion No. 14,* "no portion of the proceeds from the issuance of . . . convertible debt securities . . . should be accounted for as attributable to the conversion feature."[9] Based on this principle, the accounting for the issuance and conversion of convertible bonds is illustrated below.

Assume that Brazos Corporation issued at face amount $10 million of 10-year, 6% convertible bonds. Interest on the bonds is paid semiannually. Each $1,000 bond is convertible into 30 shares of the company's $20 par value common stock. The journal entries to record the issuance and subsequent conversion of the bonds are as follows:

Cash	10,000,000	
6% Convertible Bonds Payable		10,000,000
To record issuance of 10-year, 6% convertible bonds.		
6% Convertible Bonds Payable	10,000,000	
Common Stock, $20 par		6,000,000
Paid-in Capital in Excess of Par		4,000,000
To record conversion of 10-year, 6% convertible bonds		
into 300,000 shares of $20 par value common stock.		

[9] *APB Opinion No. 14,* "Accounting for Convertible Debt and Debt Issued with Stock Purchase Warrants," AICPA (New York: 1969), p. 207.

When common stock is issued in exchange for convertible bonds pursuant to the conversion feature, the carrying value of the bonds is assigned to the common stock. Thus no gain or loss is recognized on a conversion of bonds into common stock. Additional discussion of convertible bonds is found in Chapter 18.

Evaluation of Current Practice Current practice for recording the issuance of convertible bonds does not, in the opinion of the authors, portray the real economic substance of such transactions. When convertible bonds are issued, a portion of the proceeds is logically attributable to the conversion feature, a factor that is reflected in a lower coupon rate of interest. Since the bondholder receives a "call" on the common stock, a portion of the proceeds attributable to the conversion feature should, theoretically be recorded as paid-in capital, and bond discount (or a reduced bond premium) should be recorded. The discount (or reduced premium) would be equal to the difference between the price at which the bonds were issued and the estimated price for which they would have been issued in the absence of the conversion feature.

To illustrate, assume that the $10 million of 10-year, 6% convertible bonds were issued by the Brazos Corporation (see page 625) when similar nonconvertible bonds were yielding 8% compounded semiannually. Present value tables indicate that 6% nonconvertible bonds would be issued for approximately $8,640,967 to yield 8% compounded semiannually. The entry to record the issuance of the bonds by Brazos Corporation, *if a value is assigned to the conversion feature,* would be:

Cash	10,000,000	
Discount on Convertible Bonds Payable	1,359,033	
6% Convertible Bonds Payable		10,000,000
Paid-in Capital in Excess of Par		1,359,033

To record issuance of 10-year, 6% convertible bonds valued at $8,640,967 (exclusive of conversion feature).

The discount would be amortized over the life of the bonds, thus increasing the dollar amount of interest expense. If the bonds were converted prior to maturity, the carrying value of the bonds would be transferred to the Common Stock and Paid-in Capital in Excess of Par accounts.

In *Opinion No. 10,* the Accounting Principles Board required the assignment of a value to the conversion feature of convertible bonds as illustrated above, but a few years later, in *Opinion No. 14,* it reversed its earlier position. The opposition expressed by corporate managements and investment bankers to the separate accounting for the debt and the conversion feature probably was responsible for this reversal of position by the APB. In the opinion of the authors, the position finally taken by the Board is difficult to support from a theoretical standpoint. However, the student is reminded that the earlier illustration on page 625 is in accord with generally accepted accounting principles.

Early Extinguishment of Convertible Bonds Should a gain or loss be reported on the retirement of convertible bonds before maturity or conversion? A convertible bond is a hybrid security, and a simple answer to this question is not easy to give. When convertible bonds sell at a large premium because of their conversion feature and management wants to retire the entire issue of bonds, it would probably call the bonds to force bondholders to convert. However, if management wishes to retire only a portion of the issue, it could not exercise the call privilege and would have to pay the going market price for the bonds.

Because convertible bonds which are selling at a very large premium are, in effect, an equity security, sound theory would suggest that the difference between the carrying value of the bonds and the amount paid to retire them should be charged against paid-in capital, and not recorded as a loss. Under these circumstances the early retirement of the convertible bonds may be viewed as equivalent to a purchase of common stock for retirement. When convertible bonds sell at a deep discount, not because of higher market rates of interest but because the common stock is selling at a low price, retirement of such bonds may be viewed as giving rise to paid-in capital. This line of reasoning is based on the fact that the intent of issuing convertible bonds is to raise equity capital, and the low price of the bonds is caused by the fact that the value of the bonds as an equity security has decreased. Despite arguments along these lines, the Accounting Principles Board in *Opinion No. 26* stated:

> The extinguishment of convertible debt before maturity does not change the character of the security as between debt and equity at that time. Therefore, a difference between the cash acquisition price of the debt and its net carrying amount should be recognized currently in income in the period of extinguishment as losses or gains.[10]

This requirement by the Accounting Principles Board may in some cases result in material gains and losses being reported in the income statement which are essentially increases or decreases in paid-in capital.

Bonds issued with warrants attached

If bonds payable are issued which are not convertible into common stock but, instead, include *detachable warrants* giving the bondholder the right to purchase a certain number of shares of common stock at a

[10] *APB Opinion No. 26,* p. 502.

fixed price, a separate value should be assigned to the warrants. Thus, if $10 million of bonds, with warrants attached which are valued at $500,000, are issued for a total consideration of $10 million, the issuance would be recorded as follows:

Cash	10,000,000	
Discount on Bonds Payable	500,000	
Bonds Payable		10,000,000
Paid-in Capital—Stock Purchase Warrants . . .		500,000
Issuance of bonds with stock purchase warrants attached.		

Since the warrants are valued at $500,000, the bonds in effect were issued at 95. The APB supported this approach in *Opinion No. 14* as follows:

> The Board is of the opinion that the portion of the proceeds of debt securities issued with detachable stock purchase warrants which is allocable to the warrants should be accounted for as paid-in capital. The allocation should be based on the relative fair values of the two securities at the time of issuance. Any resulting discount or premium on the debt securities should be accounted for as such. . . . However, when stock purchase warrants are not detachable from the debt and the debt security must be surrendered in order to exercise the warrant, the two securities taken together are substantially equivalent to convertible debt. . . .[11]

When the warrants are exercised, the value assigned to the warrants is viewed as additional proceeds from the issuance of common stock. This topic is discussed more fully in Chapter 18.

Bond sinking fund and appropriation of retained earnings

Some bond indentures require that a sinking fund be established for the retirement of bonds. Ordinarily a bond sinking fund would not be created in connection with the issuance of serial bonds; such bonds are retired periodically in lieu of making sinking fund deposits. A disadvantage inherent in bond sinking funds is that a portion of the money borrowed for use in the business is not being used for this purpose if cash is deposited in a sinking fund.

A formal restriction on the payment of dividends, which is common in bond indentures, does not require the appropriation of retained earnings; restrictions on retained earnings, however, should be fully disclosed in financial statements or accompanying notes. The appropriation of retained earnings was never an efficient means of disclosure and is no longer in common use.

[11] *APB Opinion No. 14,* p. 209.

Notes and mortgages payable

Other long-term liabilities such as notes payable, equipment contracts payable, purchase-money obligations, and mortgages payable are frequently found on financial statements of business units. The essential accounting problems relating to these liabilities are similar to those applicable to bonds. The important point to keep in mind is that all long-term liabilities should initially be recorded at the present value of the amounts to be paid. This is particularly important when debts are incurred in connection with acquisition of noncash assets or are assumed by the acquiring company in a business combination. In the acquisition of a going business, for example, if liabilities are not fairly valued, the amount of unidentifiable intangibles (goodwill) and the periodic amortization of such intangibles will be misstated.

As pointed out in earlier chapters, a variety of other "deferred credit" or "quasi-liability" items are sometimes included under long-term liabilities in condensed balance sheets. These may range from unearned revenue items to items such as "equity in net assets of subsidiary over cost," deferred investment tax credits, and deferred income taxes.

Distinguishing between liabilities and stockholders' equity

Since interest is tax deductible and a payment designated as dividends is not, it is inevitable that creative financial managers will devise liability contracts which bestow on the securities as many of the characteristics of ownership as possible without destroying their income tax status as debt. As a result, the dividing line between debt and stockholders' equity is often blurred. An extreme example on the liability side is the *subordinated income bond.* These bonds are secured only by the general credit standing of the issuer, and the bond contract provides that interest will be paid only when and if earnings are sufficient. Interest payments on such a bond are usually cumulative, but failure to pay interest does not give bondholders the right to interfere in corporate affairs. It is clear that a substantial amount of risk, comparable to that borne by stockholders, attaches to such securities. The basic characteristic distinguishing subordinated income bonds from preferred stock is that the bonds have a maturity date. The absence of a maturity provision would give the Internal Revenue Service grounds for holding that subordinated income bonds are preferred shares in disguise.

On the stockholders' equity side of the dividing line, some forms of preferred stock are very similar to debt. A preferred stock issue which has no voting rights, carries a stated cumulative dividend, and requires redemption at specified times represents only a very limited form of ownership. Such preferred stock, some accountants have argued, represents "a liability masquerading as stockholders' equity."

The question arises, in dealing with such cases, whether the distinction can be drawn with sufficient clarity to make a clear-cut division in accounting between liabilities and stockholders' equity. Some accountants have argued, for example, that the entire right side of the balance sheet should be labeled "equities" and that the distinction between liabilities and stockholders' equity may not be too important.

Accounting for restructured debt

Companies which encounter financial difficulties sometimes are able to renegotiate more favorable terms with creditors for currently existing debt. The result of such an arrangement in a troubled loan situation is referred to as a *restructuring of debt* and may include the following provisions:

1 Extension of the due date of principal and interest payments
2 Reduction in the rate of interest on existing debt
3 Forgiveness by creditors of a portion of loan principal or accrued interest

In considering the appropriate accounting for a restructured debt, the FASB initially suggested in an exposure draft of a proposed accounting standard that a gain or loss be recognized by the debtor "in an amount equal to the difference between (1) the net carrying amount of the debt before the restructuring and (2) the present value of the cash payments (both principal and interest) required to be made by the debtor after the restructuring discounted at the effective prerestructuring rate of interest."[12]

Most debt restructurings would have resulted in a gain to debtors and a loss to creditors. As a result, creditors (particularly banks) opposed this proposed standard and the Financial Accounting Standards Board issued *Statement No. 15* which suggested that no gain or loss be recognized by debtors when *only a modification of terms is involved* unless the carrying amount of the debt exceeds the total future cash payments specified by the new terms.[13] If the carrying amount of the debt exceeds future cash payments, the debtor reduces the carrying amount of the debt and all cash payments are recorded as reductions in the debt. Thus the debtor recognizes a gain equal to the reduction in the carrying amount of the debt and no interest expense is recorded between the date of restructuring and the maturity date of the debt.

To illustrate the accounting for a debt restructuring as a result of a modification of terms, assume that Paul Corporation has the following debt at December 31, Year 10:

---

[12] *Proposed Statement of Financial Accounting Standards,* "Restructuring of Debt in a Troubled Loan Situation," FASB (Stamford: 1975), p. 3.
[13] *FASB Statement No. 15,* "Accounting by Debtors and Creditors for Troubled Debt Restructurings," FASB (Stamford: 1977), p. 7.

12% note payable, due Dec. 31, Year 11	$5,000,000
Accrued interest payable on 12% note	600,000

On December 31, Year 10, the debt is restructured as follows: (1) $500,000 of the principal and the $600,000 of accrued interest are forgiven by creditors, (2) the maturity date is extended to December 31, Year 15, and (3) the interest rate is reduced from 12% to 8% a year. Because the total future cash payments under the new terms amount to $6,300,000 (principal of $4,500,000 and interest of $1,800,000 for five years at 8%), which exceeds the $5,600,000 carrying amount of the debt prior to the restructuring, no gain or loss is recognized. The excess of the total payments over the carrying amount of the debt, $700,000 ($6,300,000 − $5,600,000 = $700,000), would be recognized as interest expense at a computed effective interest rate on the restructured amount of the debt.

However, if the interest rate had been reduced from 12% to 4%, the total future cash payments under the new terms would be $5,400,000 (principal of $4,500,000 and interest of $900,000 for five years at 4%) which is $200,000 less than the $5,600,000 pre-restructuring carrying amount of the debt. In this case, the debtor would record the debt restructuring and the subsequent payments as follows:

12% Note Payable	5,000,000	
Accrued Interest Payable	600,000	
Restructured Debt (including interest of $900,000		
for five years)		5,400,000
Gain on Restructuring of Debt		200,000
To record restructuring of debt on Dec. 31, Year 10.		
Restructured Debt	180,000	
Cash		180,000
To record payment of interest at the end of **each year** for five years (Dec. 31, Years 11–15).		
Restructured Debt	4,500,000	
Cash		4,500,000
To record payment of principal on Dec. 31, Year 15.		

Debt restructurings may take many forms and involve complex accounting issues. The illustration above was designed to illustrate a relatively simple situation of a modification of terms without any consideration changing hands at the time of the restructuring.

Long-term debt in the balance sheet

All long-term debt should be fully described in the balance sheet or accompanying notes. Companies having large amounts of long-term debt in the form of numerous issues often show only one figure in the balance sheet and support this with supplementary schedules showing the details of maturity dates, interest rates, call provisions, conversion privileges, assets pledged to secure payment, and dividend or any other restrictions imposed on the borrower.

Unless an automatic right of offset exists, long-term debt should be reported in full, and any pledged assets intended for use in repayment should be shown in the asset section of the balance sheet. Reacquired debt should not be reported as an asset.

Any portion of long-term debt that matures within one year should be shown as a current liability, unless retirement will not require the use of current assets. If, during the ensuing year, debt is likely to be converted into stock, refunded, or repaid from a sinking fund already established, there is no reason to change its classification from long to short term so long as the expected method of retirement is clearly disclosed.

REVIEW QUESTIONS

1 Define the following: *debenture bonds, term bonds, serial bonds, convertible bonds, bond indenture, nominal or coupon rate, effective rate,* and *call premium.*

2 A bond carrying a coupon rate of 5% is sold to yield 5.75%. Will the bond sell at a premium or a discount? Explain.

3 A $1 million bond issue is sold for $960,000. A few months later the bonds are selling at 102. Give possible reasons for the increase in the value of the bonds and explain the significance of the increase to the issuing company.

4 Viking Company plans to issue $1 million in 6%, 10-year bonds. What will be the average annual interest expense if the bonds are issued at 104? At 97?

5 If bonds are issued at a premium and the *interest method* is used in amortizing the premium, will the annual interest cost increase or decline over the life of the bonds? Explain.

6 Ram Company has just issued $100 million of 15-year debenture bonds at a discount. At an annual stockholders' meeting, one of the stockholders asks the chairman to explain the nature of bond discount and issue costs included among the company's assets at $4,829,000. The chairman answers, "This represents prepaid interest of $4.7 million and issue costs of $129,000 on our bonds, which are being amortized over the life of the debt." Evaluate this answer.

7 Explain how the interest accrued on bonds can be handled when bonds are sold between interest dates.

8 How should discount and premium on bonds payable be classified in the balance sheet? How should bond issue costs be classified?

9 Describe the preferred treatment of the difference between the carrying value of bonds payable and the amount paid to retire the bonds. How is the difference handled in the accounts and in the financial statements when bonds are refunded?

10 List some factors that management should consider in deciding when to refund a bond issue.

11 What are the advantages to a growing company of issuing convertible bonds?

12 What is the generally accepted practice in regard to the assignment of a value to the conversion feature of convertible bonds? Give an argument in favor of assigning a part of the proceeds received on the sale of convertible bonds to the conversion feature.

13 Briefly describe the accounting for bonds which include detachable warrants to purchase common stock.

14 A top executive of Chicago Railroad Company was quoted as saying, "Debt management is a continuous process that is highly essential to good operations. As long as I live, I will never go into debt without a sinking fund." Comment on the executive's position.

15 Pardee Corporation has outstanding an issue of 6% **cumulative preferred stock,** callable at par, and an issue of 6% **subordinated debentures.** What is the basic distinction between these two securities that determines their balance sheet classification?

16 How should the restructuring of debt through a modification of terms be accounted for by the debtor if the carrying amount of the restructured debt exceeds the total payments to be made on the debt?

EXERCISES

Ex. 15-1 Jackson Corporation plans to issue $5 million, 8% bonds, due 20 years from date of issue. Interest is payable semiannually. Using the present value tables in Appendix A, compute the probable proceeds of the bond issue if the market rate of interest compounded semiannually is **(a)** 7% and **(b)** 9%.

Ex. 15-2 Fencil Corporation issued $2,000,000 of 6% 10-year convertible bonds on June 1, Year 1, at 98 plus accrued interest. The bonds were dated April 1, Year 1, with interest payable April 1 and October 1. Bond discount is amortized semiannually on a straight-line basis.

On April 1, Year 2, $500,000 of these bonds were converted into 20,000 shares of $20 par value common stock. Accrued interest was paid at the time of conversion.

a If the Accrued Bond Interest Payable account was credited when the bonds were issued, prepare a journal entry to record the first interest payment and to amortize the discount on October 1, Year 1. Carry computations to the nearest dollar.

b Prepare a journal entry to record the conversion of bonds on April 1, Year 2.

Assume that amortization of bond discount and payment of interest has already been recorded. Carry computations to the nearest dollar.

Ex. 15-3 On January 1, Year 5, a calendar-year corporation issued 8% bonds with a face amount of $1,000,000. These bonds mature in 10 years, and interest is paid semi-annually on June 30 and December 31. The bonds were issued for $934,960 to yield 9% compounded semiannually. Using the interest method, compute the amount that should be debited to Bond Interest Expense in Year 5.

Ex. 15-4 On October 1, 1978, Sue Company issued serial bonds calling for the payment of $1.2 million in principal per year for each of the five years.
a Explain how a $270,000 discount on this bond issue would be amortized if the bonds outstanding method were used.
b How much of the discount would be amortized in the fiscal year ending November 30, 1980?

Ex. 15-5 Suppose that the bond issue in Exercise 15-4 called for the payment of $1.2 million at the end of each of five years, starting at the end of the third year after issue date. How would this affect the schedule of discount amortization computed by the bonds outstanding method?

Ex. 15-6 On December 31 of the current year, City Corporation has outstanding $10 million of 4%, 20-year bonds due in seven years and nine months. The unamortized discount on these bonds at October 1 of the current year was $340,000. Give the journal entry (a) to record the accrual of interest and amortization of the discount for the three months ended December 31 of the current year and (b) to record the call of $1 million of these bonds on January 1 of the following year at 102 plus accrued interest for three months, assuming that discount is amortized on a straight-line basis and that reversing entries are not used.

Ex. 15-7 The balance sheet of Sarbonne Wine Corporation includes the following accounts at December 31, Year 4:

6% convertible bonds payable (due Dec. 31, Year 20)	$2,000,000
Discount on convertible bonds payable	40,000

No value was assigned to the conversion feature when the bonds were issued. Each $1,000 bond is convertible into 35 shares of $5 par value common stock. Using the theoretically preferable method, record the conversion of all bonds into common stock on January 2, Year 5, assuming a market price of the common stock of $40 per share.

Ex. 15-8 Selca Marble Company issued $1 million face amount bonds with detachable warrants attached. The bonds were issued for $1,015,000. Immediately upon issuance the bonds were quoted at 96 and the warrants had a total market value of $90,000. Prepare a journal entry to record the issuance of the bonds, assuming that no accrued interest was charged to buyers of the bonds and that total proceeds were allocated on the basis of the relative market values of the bonds and warrants.

Ex. 15-9 Garcia Furniture Company wants to finance the purchase of plant assets by issuing 8% bonds. Management projects the earnings **before** deducting bond interest expense and income taxes at $1,166,000 per year. Garcia's income tax rate is 40%. Management wants its net earnings **after** deducting bond interest and income taxes to be ten times the bond interest expense. Assuming that the bonds can be issued to yield 8%, compute the face amount of bonds that should be issued.

Ex. 15-10 Shaky Construction Company has a $10,000,000 loan payable outstanding on June 30, Year 8, which is due in one year. Interest at 10% a year has been paid through June 30, Year 8. The fiscal year of the company ends on June 30. Because of Shaky's poor financial condition creditors have agreed to restructure the loan on June 30, Year 8, as follows: The maturity date of the loan is extended to June 30, Year 10, $1,500,000 of the principal is forgiven, and the interest rate is reduced to 5% a year on the reduced amount of principal. Compute the gain on the restructuring of the debt and prepare journal entries in the accounts of Shaky Construction Company to record the restructuring of the debt and all payments on the loan through June 30, Year 10.

SHORT CASES FOR ANALYSIS AND DECISION

Case 15-1 The balance sheet for the Leverage Company at the end of Year 5 follows:

LEVERAGE COMPANY

Balance Sheet

End of Year 5

(in thousands of dollars)

Assets

Current assets:

Cash	$ 5,000
Marketable securities (at cost, market value $15.2 million)	15,000
Accounts receivable (net)	10,000
Inventory	24,000
Short-term prepayments	1,000
Total current assets	$ 55,000
Plant and equipment (net of accumulated depreciation)	40,000
Miscellaneous other assets	5,000
Total assets	$100,000

Liabilities & Stockholders' Equity

Current liabilities		$ 35,000
6% bonds payable, callable at 105, each $1,000 bond convertible into 25 shares		
of capital stock		40,000
Total liabilities		$ 75,000
Stockholders' equity:		
Capital stock, no par, 2,000,000 shares authorized, 1,000,000		
shares outstanding	$ 5,000	
Retained earnings	20,000	
Total stockholders' equity		25,000
Total liabilities & stockholders' equity		$100,000

The president, Ken Stabler, thinks that the company is facing a serious financing problem, which he outlines for you as follows:

"We must raise approximately $50 million dollars over the next two years in order to finance the expansion of our product lines and sales territories. My banker friends tell me that our balance sheet is not in good shape. They have pointed out repeatedly that our current ratio (current assets divided by current liabilities) is significantly below the industry standard of 2 to 1 and that approximately 75% of our assets are financed by borrowed capital. They consider this to be much too high, considering the type of industry we are in. We don't want to sell more stock to the public and apparently we can't issue additional bonds unless our balance sheet can be cleaned up. I wish we had paid more attention to the management of our assets: We have $15 million invested in low-yielding securities, our accounts receivable and inventory are twice as large as they ought to be, and we have been paying out too much in dividends. Our profits have been growing steadily and we pay a dividend of $3 per share on our stock. As a result our stock is selling at $55 per share and our bonds are currently trading close to 140 on the open market. I would appreciate your advice on this matter."

Instructions Briefly outline a course of action the president should follow in "cleaning up" the balance sheet and raising the $50 million needed for expansion. Ignore the effect of income taxes in your answer.

Case 15-2 Grambling Electronics Corporation was organized two years ago by two experienced business executives and several members of the faculty at a local university. The main product of the company consists of a line of medium-size computers and software for all lines of data-processing and information-gathering systems. The company's total assets amount to $15 million and the liabilities amount to $10.5 million, consisting of $3 million of short-term debt and $7.5 million of notes payable to an insurance company. There are 100,000 shares of common stock outstanding. In order to expand its activities, the company needs $5 million in permanent capital. Members of the board of directors have discussed various proposals for raising the capital and have asked for your advice regarding the following alternatives:
(1) Issue bonds bearing interest at $6\frac{1}{2}\%$ with a sinking-fund provision.
(2) Issue 5% bonds at face amount. The bonds would be convertible into 40,000 shares of the company's common stock at $125 per share. The current price of the common stock is $96.
(3) Issue $4\frac{1}{2}\%$ preferred stock at a par value of $100. The preferred stock would be callable at $105 and convertible into three-quarters of one share of common stock.
(4) Issue 60,000 shares of common stock at $85 per share through a rights offering. Stockholders would be given rights to buy one additional share for every 10 shares held.

Instructions Evaluate the advantages and disadvantages of each of the four proposals.

Case 15-3 The directors of Winter Corporation are contemplating the issuance of $15 million of bonds. The corporation does not need the money immediately but Director Alan, a former banker, has convinced the board that the bonds should be issued "while interest rates are low and credit is readily available."

Banker Krueger, representative of a leading investment banking firm, also recommended that bonds should be issued because interest rates are beginning to turn up and a coupon rate of 6% would probably command a modest premium. Krueger believes that the board is making a mistake in not considering the issuance of convertible debentures instead of regular bonds for the following reasons:
(1) It would be cheaper for the company (a rate of about $4\frac{1}{2}\%$ would probably be sufficient).
(2) The company's equity will need "beefing up" as it continues to expand its activities.

(3) It is a means of selling common stock at about 20% above the current market price.

Director Barney, vice president of finance, suggested that a $6\frac{1}{2}$% rate be assigned to nonconvertible bonds stating, "A large premium is a sign of financial strength of our corporation; if interest rates continue to advance, 6% bonds would sell at a discount and I don't want people thinking that our credit is so poor that we have to give a discount in order to sell our bonds."

Director Carla, a public relations executive, disagreed with Director Barney. She stated that investors are bargain hunters who would be more willing to buy bonds at a discount than at a premium. She would assign a $5\frac{1}{2}$% coupon rate to the bonds, stating "discount on bonds payable is prepaid interest and it will not hurt us to have a jump on our interest payments to bondholders."

Instructions Briefly evaluate each of the four viewpoints mentioned in this case.

Case 15-4 Jessie Company recently issued $1 million principal amount, 7%, 30-year subordinated debentures at 97. The debentures are redeemable at 103 upon demand by the issuer at any date upon 30 days notice 10 years after issue. The debentures are convertible into $10 par value common stock of the company at the conversion price of $12.50 per share for each $500 or multiple thereof of the principal amount of the debentures.

Instructions
a Explain how the conversion feature of convertible debt has a value to the
   (1) Issuer
   (2) Purchaser
b Management has suggested that in recording the issuance of the debentures a portion of the proceeds should be assigned to the conversion feature.
   (1) What are the arguments for according separate accounting recognition to the conversion feature of the debentures?
   (2) What are the arguments supporting accounting for the convertible debentures as a single element?
c Assume that no value was assigned to the conversion feature upon issue of the debentures. Assume further that five years after issue, debentures in the principal amount of $100,000 and carrying value of $97,500 are tendered for conversion on an interest payment date when the market price of the debentures is 104, the common stock is selling at $14 per share, and the company recorded the conversion as follows:

Bonds Payable	100,000	
Discount on Bonds Payable		2,500
Common Stock, $10 par		80,000
Paid-in Capital in Excess of Par		17,500

Discuss the propriety of the above accounting treatment.

PROBLEMS

Group A

15A-1 On July 1, Year 1, Sunset Corporation issued bonds with a face amount of $1,000,000 maturing in ten years. The stated interest rate on the bonds is 9%, payable semiannually on June 30 and December 31. The bonds were issued to yield 10% compounded semiannually.

On June 30, Year 2, Sunset Corporation issued $500,000 of bonds with warrants attached. These bonds carried an interest rate of 8%, payable semiannually, and were issued at 105. One detachable warrant to purchase common stock was attached to each $1,000 bond. The current fair value of each bond without the warrant was estimated at $966.

Instructions
a Using Appendix A, compute the proceeds received on the 9% bonds issued on July 1, Year 1.
b Prepare journal entries to record the following:
  (1) Issuance of bonds on July 1, Year 1
  (2) Payment of interest and amortization, using the interest method, on December 31, Year 1
  (3) Payment of interest and amortization, using the interest method, on June 30, Year 2
c Prepare a journal entry to record the issuance of the 8% bonds on June 30, Year 2.

15A-2 The balance sheet of Conrad Warehousing Corporation at June 30, Year 5, included the following accounts:

6% first mortgage bonds payable, maturing on June 30, Year 20	$20,000,000
Discount on bonds payable	600,000
Deferred bond issue costs	132,000

Instructions
a Compute the annual interest expense, including amortization of bond issue costs. Straight-line amortization is used.
b Prepare an entry to record the retirement of $2 million of bonds at 105 on July 1, Year 10. The company's fiscal year ends on June 30.
c Show how the accounts relating to bonds payable would appear in the balance sheet at June 30, Year 15.

15A-3 In July of the current year, the board of directors of Sporting Goods Corporation authorized the issuance of $50 million of 6%, 20-year bonds payable, dated September 1. Interest on these bonds is payable semiannually on March 1 and September 1. The bonds were issued to underwriters on November 1 of the current year. The corporation amortizes discount or premium only at the end of the fiscal year, using the straight-line method.

Instructions Prepare the journal entries necessary to record the issuance of these bonds, the adjusting entry at December 31 (the close of the company's fiscal year), the entries to record the first two semiannual interest payments, and the adjusting entry at the end of the following year, assuming that:
a The bonds were issued to the underwriters at 101.904, plus accrued interest which was recorded in Accrued Bond Interest Payable. (Round any computations to the nearest dollar.)
b The bonds were issued to the underwriters at 97.62, plus accrued interest which was recorded in Accrued Bond Interest Payable. (Round any computations to the nearest dollar.)

15A-4 Irving Company issued $2 million of 7% serial bonds for a total price of $2,072,000 on January 1, Year 1. The bonds mature at the rate of $400,000 per year starting on December 31, Year 1. Interest is payable on June 30 and December 31.

Instructions
a Prepare a schedule showing the amortization of the premium and total interest expense for each year through Year 5. Amortization is computed using the bonds outstanding method.
b Assume that on July 1, Year 2, $200,000 of the bonds, which were scheduled

to be retired on December 31, Year 4, were retired at 101¼. Prepare a journal entry to record the retirement, assuming that the amortization of the premium was recorded through June 30, Year 2, when the semiannual interest was paid.

15A-5 Cameron Rock & Gravel Corporation needed funds to finance the development of a new product. The company arranged to place privately with a pension fund $5 million face value of five-year, 6% bonds. Interest is payable annually on September 30. The bonds were issued on October 1 of Year 0, and the company received proceeds of $5,445,182. In the annual report, the president wrote, "Although the debt carries a coupon rate of 6%, the financing has been arranged so that the effective interest expense to the company is 4% per annum."

Instructions

a Prepare an amortization table, similar to that illustrated on page 611, showing the interest expense for each year on an effective interest basis. (Round all computations to the nearest dollar, and adjust the interest expense for the last period to compensate for any net rounding error.)

b Using the data in the amortization table in **a,** prepare journal entries to record the issuance of the bonds, the interest payments at the end of the first and fifth years, and the retirement of the bonds at maturity.

c Prepare the same entries called for in **b**, assuming that interest is recorded on a straight-line basis.

d Explain the reason for the difference in annual interest expense under the straight-line and interest methods.

15A-6 Jordan Pipe Co. issued $10 million of 10-year, 6% convertible bonds on September 30, Year 1, for $9,064,000, plus interest for three months. Bond issue costs of $23,400 were incurred and recorded in a separate account. No value was assigned to the conversion feature. Interest is payable semiannually on June 30 and December 31. The bonds are callable after June 30, Year 6, and until June 30, Year 8, at 104; thereafter until maturity, at 102; and convertible into $2.50 par value common stock as follows:

(1) Until June 30, Year 6, at the rate of six shares for each $1,000 bond

(2) From July 1, Year 6, to June 30, Year 9, at the rate of five shares for each $1,000 bond

(3) After June 30, Year 9, at the rate of four shares for each $1,000 bond

The bonds mature on June 30, Year 11. The company adjusts its accounts monthly and closes its accounts yearly on December 31. Bond premium (or discount) and bond issue costs are to be amortized on a straight-line basis.

The following transactions occurred in connection with the bonds:

July 1, Year 7: $2 million of bonds were converted into common stock.

Jan. 1, Year 9: $1 million of bonds were purchased on the open market at 98 and were immediately retired.

June 30, Year 9: The remaining $7 million of bonds were called for redemption. In order to obtain the necessary funds for redemption and business expansion, a $10 million issue of 5½% bonds was issued at face amount. These bonds were dated June 30, Year 9, and were due on June 30, Year 29.

Instructions Prepare journal entries necessary to record the above transactions, including monthly adjustments where appropriate, as of each of the following dates. (Do not prepare closing entries, and give supporting computations as part of journal entry explanations.)

a Sept. 30, Year 1. (Record bond issue costs in a separate entry.)

b Dec. 31, Year 1. (Record one month's interest and amortization in a separate entry before recording the payment of interest.)

c July 1, Year 7.
d Jan. 1, Year 9.
e June 30, Year 9. (Record the accrual of interest and amortization, the payment of interest, the retirement of $7 million of bonds, and the issuance of $10 million of bonds in separate journal entries.)

Group B

15B-1 On December 1, Year 5, Pushkin Company issued 10-year bonds of $2 million at 102. Interest is payable on June 1 and December 1 at the rate of 9%. On April 1, Year 7, Pushkin Company extinguished (retired) 600 of these bonds at 96, plus accrued interest. The accounting period for Pushkin Company ends on December 31.

Instructions Prepare journal entries to record the following:
a The issuance of the bonds on December 1, Year 5.
b Interest payments and amortization in Year 6. Amortization is recorded by the straight-line method only at the end of the year. The company does not follow the policy of preparing reversing entries for the accrual of bond interest.
c The early extinguishment of $600,000 of bonds on April 1, Year 7. (**Hint:** First amortize premium for three months on the bonds retired.)

15B-2 On July 1, Year 5, Samuelson Printing Corporation issued $5 million of 9%, 20-year bonds with interest payable on March 1 and September 1. The company received proceeds of $5,120,500, including the accrued interest from March 1, Year 5.

Instructions Prepare journal entries required on each of the following dates:
a July 1, Year 5 (issuance of bonds)
b September 1, Year 5 (payment of interest and amortization of discount for two months using the straight-line method)
c December 31, Year 5 (accrual of interest and amortization of discount from September 1 to December 31)

15B-3 Central Farm Products Corporation was authorized to issue $10 million of 10-year, 6% convertible bonds due December 31, Year 15. Each $1,000 bond is convertible into 40 shares of $10 par value common stock, and the bond indenture contained an antidilution provision. The bonds were issued to underwriters on March 1, Year 6, for net proceeds of $10,029,200, including accrued interest. Interest is payable semiannually on June 30 and December 31. Any discount or premium is amortized annually on December 31 using the straight-line method.

Late in Year 6 the company declared a 10% stock dividend on the common stock, and in Year 7 the common stock was split 2 for 1. The interest payments and the amortization of discount on a straight-line basis have been recorded to January 1, Year 8. On May 1, Year 8, bonds with a face amount of $500,000 were converted, and the accrued interest on these bonds was paid in cash.

Instructions
a Prepare the entry to record the issuance of bonds. No value was assigned to the conversion feature.
b Prepare a compound journal entry to record, for the first four months of Year 8, the payment of interest and the amortization of discount on the bonds converted.
c Prepare the entry to record the conversion of $500,000 face amount of bonds on May 1, Year 8. (An antidilution provision calls for a proportionate adjustment in the number of shares into which each bond can be converted if the common stock is split or if stock dividends are distributed.)

15B-4 Quixote Feed Company issued $5 million of 8% serial bonds on January 1, Year 1. The bonds mature at the rate of $1 million per year starting on December 31, Year 5. The bonds were issued for $5,105,000. Interest is payable annually on December 31.

Instructions

a Prepare the journal entry to record the issuance of bonds.

b Prepare a schedule (similar to the one illustrated on page 621) showing the amortization of the premium and the net interest expense for each year over the life of the bonds. The premium is amortized using the bonds outstanding method.

c Assume that on December 31, Year 7, the following bonds were extinguished:

$1,000,000 due on December 31, Year 7, at face amount
$50,000 due on December 31, Year 8, at $101\frac{1}{2}$
$100,000 due on December 31, Year 9, at $102\frac{1}{4}$

Prepare a compound entry to record the extinguishment of bonds. Assume that the interest due on December 31, Year 7, had already been recorded.

15B-5 Rembrandt Castings Corporation issued, in a private placement with an insurance company, $4 million face amount of three-year, 9% bonds. Interest is payable semiannually on June 30 and December 31. The bonds were issued on January 1 of the current year at a price which gave the company an effective interest cost of 5% semiannually.

Instructions

a Compute the proceeds of the bond issue and prepare an amortization table, similar to that illustrated on page 610, showing the interest expense for each six-month period on an effective interest basis. (Round all computations to the nearest dollar.)

b Using the data in the amortization table prepared in **a**, prepare journal entries to record the issuance of the bonds, the interest payments at the end of the first six months and the last six months of the bond issue, and the extinguishment of the bonds at maturity.

c What interest expense would have been recorded in the accounts of Rembrandt Castings Corporation each six months if the straight-line method of discount amortization had been used? Explain why the interest method produces a different interest expense per period than the straight-line method.

15B-6 In March of Year 1, Cornerstone Construction Co. was authorized to issue $4 million of 6% convertible bonds due March 31, Year 11. Interest is payable on March 31 and September 30. The company's fiscal year ends on September 30. The bonds are callable at any time prior to maturity at a diminishing call premium. Each $1,000 bond is convertible into eight shares of $10 par value common stock. An antidilution provision in the bond indenture provides for the adjustment of this conversion ratio in the event of stock dividends or stock splits.

The bonds were issued on April 30, Year 1, for $3,880,000 including accrued interest for one month. Bond issue costs of $98,000 were incurred and combined with the discount for amortization purposes. Amortization is computed by the straight-line method. No value was assigned to the conversion feature.

On May 1, Year 2, 400 of the bonds were purchased on the open market for a total consideration of $408,000, including accrued interest for one month. The bonds were formally retired.

On October 1, Year 9, the company called the remaining bonds for retirement. All bondholders, except one owning $8,000 face amount of bonds, converted their holdings into common stock. The one bondholder was mailed a check for $8,240, the call value of the bonds. The market price of the common stock, which had been split 3 for 1 in Year 4, was $68 per share on October 1, Year 9.

Instructions
a Prepare journal entries to record the issuance of bonds and the payment of issuance costs on April 30, Year 1.
b Prepare a journal entry to record payment of interest on September 30, Year 1. Assume that amortization is recorded only at the end of fiscal year.
c Prepare a journal entry to record the retirement of bonds on May 1, Year 2.
d Prepare a journal entry to record the conversion and retirement of bonds on October 1, Year 9.

CHAPTER 16

ACCOUNTING FOR LEASES AND PENSION PLANS

The accounting for leasing transactions and the measurement of periodic pension expense have been challenging problems for accountants in recent years. Leasing as a means of acquiring the use of assets has grown both in popularity and complexity as a result of capital shortages and income tax considerations.

Pension plans have been a prominent feature of employment contracts between corporations and their employees for many years. Amounts being accumulated in private pension funds in the United States are almost staggering. A knowledge of the accounting and disclosure requirements relating to these two topics is essential to the serious student of accounting.

LEASES

Assets used in business may be acquired by outright purchase or by renting the assets under a lease contract. Lease contracts today are an important means of obtaining the use or financing the acquisition of almost any kind of long-lived asset, ranging from a typewriter to a football stadium.

In some cases, a company constructs or buys property, sells it to an investor, and simultaneously leases the property from the investor in a *sale-leaseback transaction.* In other cases, a company leases existing property or property constructed to its specifications. A company which leases property for use in its business may agree to pay certain **executory costs** (such as property taxes, insurance, and maintenance) incident to use of the property.

Guidelines have been developed over the years to help accountants identify leases of similar economic substance so that they may be reported in a consistent and meaningful manner.[1] More recently, the FASB issued **Statement No. 13,** "Accounting for Leases," which supersedes all previous official guidelines for lease accounting. Future reference will be to this new **Statement.**[2]

A **lease** is an agreement conveying the right to use property, plant, or equipment, usually for a stated period of time. The owner of the property for which the right is transferred is known as the **lessor** and the party to whom the right is transferred is known as the **lessee.** A further transfer of the right to use an asset from a lessee to another lessee during the term of the lease is a **sublease** arrangement.

Thus the problem of accounting for leases is twofold—accounting for lessors and accounting for lessees. Lessors must report the transfer of rights to use property which they own and lessees must account for and disclose the fact that they are paying for the right to use property which they do not own. If all lease contracts were identical, the accounting for and disclosure of leases would be fairly straightforward. However, the situation is complicated by the fact that contracts which are in essence sales transactions may be structured as leases; other contracts provide for the lease to be converted to a sale at a later date, usually at the option of the lessee. Unfortunately, a simple model does not exist which can be used to identify a given transaction specifically as a lease or a sale. However, a set of guidelines has been developed which can be used in analyzing each transaction and in determining the appropriate accounting for it. The remainder of this section is devoted to a discussion and illustration of these guidelines.

Terminology

Like many other specialized areas, leasing has its own language. This short summary of the terminology used in leasing should be useful in understanding the accounting and reporting issues involved in lease transactions:[3]

[1] See John H. Myers, *Accounting Research Study No. 4,* "Reporting of Leases in Financial Statements," AICPA (New York: 1962); *APB Opinion No. 5,* "Reporting of Leases in Financial Statements of Lessee," AICPA (New York: 1964); *APB Opinion No. 7,* "Accounting for Leases in Financial Statements of Lessors," AICPA (New York: 1966); *APB Opinion No. 27,* "Accounting for Lease Transactions by Manufacturer or Dealer Lessors," AICPA (New York: 1972); *APB Opinion No. 31,* "Disclosure of Lease Commitments by Lessees," AICPA (New York: 1973).

[2] *FASB Statement No. 13,* "Accounting for Leases," FASB (Stamford: 1976).

[3] Adapted from *FASB Statement No. 13,* pp. 2–7.

Inception of lease Date of the lease agreement or commitment, or date of completion of construction, or acquisition of leased property by the lessor, whichever is later.

Fair value of leased property In a sales-type lease the fair value is the normal selling price of the leased property adjusted for any unusual market conditions. In a direct financing-type lease, the cost or carrying value of the property and the fair value should be the same at the inception of the lease, unless substantial time has passed since the lessor acquired the property.

Bargain purchase option A provision giving the lessee the right to purchase the leased property at a price so favorable that the exercise of the option appears vitually assured at the inception of the lease.

Bargain renewal option A provision giving the lessee the right to renew the lease at a rental so favorable that the exercise of the option appears virtually assured at the inception of the lease.

Lease term The fixed noncancelable term of the lease plus (1) any periods covered by bargain renewal options, (2) any periods for which failure to renew the lease places a heavy penalty on the lessee, (3) any periods covered by ordinary renewal options during which a guarantee by the lessee of the lessor's debt related to the leased property is expected to be in effect, (4) the periods, if any, covered by ordinary renewal options which precede the exercise date of a bargain purchase option, and (5) any periods during which the lessor has a right to renew or extend the lease. However, in no case shall the lease term extend beyond the date a bargain purchase option becomes exercisable.

Estimated economic life of leased property The estimated remaining period during which the property is expected to be usable for the purpose for which it was designed, with normal repairs and maintenance, without limitation by the lease term.

Estimated residual value of leased property The estimated fair value of the leased property at the end of the lease term. That portion of the estimated residual value which is not guaranteed by the lessee or by a third party unrelated to the lessor is known as the ***unguaranteed residual value.***

Minimum lease payments The payments that the lessee is obligated to make or can be required to make; such payments include (1) the minimum periodic rentals up to the date of a bargain purchase option, (2) any guarantee by the lessee of residual value, (3) any payment upon failure to review or extend the lease, and (4) the payment required by a bargain purchase option. Executory costs (such as insurance, maintenance, and property taxes in connection with the leased property) are excluded from minimum lease payments.

Interest rate implicit in the lease The discount rate (applied to the minimum lease payments and any unguaranteed residual value) that causes the aggregate present value to be equal to the fair value of the leased property to the lessor, minus any investment tax credit retained by the lessor.

Lessee's incremental borrowing rate The rate that, at the inception of the lease, the lessee would have incurred to borrow the funds necessary to buy the leased asset.

Initial direct costs Those costs (such as commissions, legal fees, and costs of processing documents) incurred by the lessor that are directly associated with negotiating and completing a leasing transaction.

Accounting by lessees

Leases are classified for accounting purposes by lessees as either capital leases or as operating leases. *Capital leases* are those possessing more of the characteristics of a purchase, and *operating leases* are those covering the use of an asset for a portion of its life. A capital lease must meet one of the following criteria at its inception:[4]

1 The lease transfers ownership of the property to the lessee at the end of the lease term.
2 The lease contains a bargain purchase option.
3 The lease term is equal to 75% or more of the estimated economic life of the property.
4 The present value of the minimum lease payments is at least 90% of the fair value of the leased property.

If the beginning of the lease term falls within the last 25% of the total estimated economic life of the leased property, the last two criteria are not used. In computing the present value of the minimum lease payments, the lessee entity uses its incremental borrowing rate, unless *(a)* the lessee knows the lessor's implicit rate and *(b)* the lessor's implicit rate is less than the lessee's incremental borrowing rate. If both these conditions are met, the lessee uses the lessor's implicit rate.

Leases that do not qualify as capital leases are accounted for as operating leases by the lessee; that is, the lease is *not capitalized* and periodic lease payments are recorded as expenses. Leases which start in the last 25% of an asset's estimated economic life generally are classified as operating leases, regardless of other terms such leases may have.

The lessee records a capital lease as both an asset and an obligation in the amount equal to the present value of minimum lease payments during the lease term. However, if the computed present value exceeds the fair value of the leased asset at the inception of the lease, the *amount capitalized is the fair value of the asset.*[5] The lease payments capitalized

[4] *FASB Statement No. 13*, pp. 9–10.
[5] Ibid., p. 11.

exclude any executory costs to be paid by the lessor. If the lease transfers ownership of the asset to the lessee or if the lease contains a bargain purchase option, the asset is depreciated in the same manner as other assets owned by the lessee. Other capital leases are treated similarly, but the depreciation period for the lessee should be equal to the period covered by the lease. An amount should remain in the leased asset account at the end of the lease term equal to any residual value to the lessee.

Periodic payments made by the lessee are allocated between a reduction of the lease obligation and interest expense. This allocation produces a constant periodic rate of interest on the carrying value of the lease obligation. Assets and obligations recorded under capital leases are shown as separate items in the lessee's balance sheet, and the obligation is segregated between current and noncurrent amounts.

Journal entries to record a capital lease in the accounts of the lessee are presented on pages 652 and 654, along with the journal entries for the lessor.

Accounting by lessors

Leases are classified for accounting purposes by lessors as *sales-type leases, direct financing leases,* or *operating leases.* Normally, sales-type leases arise when manufacturers or dealers use leasing as a means of marketing their products. Such leases give rise to a profit (or loss) to the lessor at the inception of the lease. A sales-type lease must meet one or more of the criteria for a capital lease (as described on page 646 for accounting by lessees) *as well as the following two additional criteria:* (1) the collectibility of the lease payments is reasonably assured, and (2) no important uncertainties surround the amount of unreimbursable costs yet to be incurred by the lessor under the lease. Important uncertainties might include commitments by the lessor to protect the lessee from obsolescence of the leased property.[6]

Leases that do not give rise to a profit (or loss) to the lessor at the inception of the lease but otherwise meet all the criteria for sales-type leases are treated as *direct financing leases* by lessors. Such leases are typically financing arrangements by lessors who normally are not involved in the direct sale of the assets leased. In direct financing leases the carrying value and the fair value of the leased property generally are the same at the inception of the lease. Leases that are not sales-type or direct financing leases are accounted for by lessors as *operating leases.*

Sales-Type Leases The accounting for sales-type leases by lessors may be summarized as follows:[7]

[6] Ibid., p. 10.
[7] Ibid., pp. 16–18.

Gross investment in the lease	XXX
Less: Unearned interest revenue	XXX
Net investment in the lease	XXX

The **gross investment** in the lease consists of the total of the minimum lease payments (net of any executory costs) and any unguaranteed residual value accruing to the lessor at the end of the lease term. The **net investment** in the lease is equal to the sum of the present values (at the implicit rate) of the minimum lease payments and any unguaranteed residual value. The difference between the gross investment and the net investment represents **unearned interest revenue** which is recognized as interest revenue over the lease term using the interest method. In the balance sheet the net investment is divided between the current and noncurrent categories.

A sales-type lease is recorded in the accounts of lessors as follows: (1) The net investment in the lease is recorded as a debit to Lease Receivables and a credit to Sales, (2) the cost (or carrying value) of the leased property is debited to Cost of Goods Sold and credited to Inventory (or to another appropriate account such as Equipment Held for Lease), and (3) any initial direct costs, less the present value of any unguaranteed residual value accruing to the lessor, are charged against revenue of the same period. Periodic rental receipts are recorded as credits to Lease Receivables and Interest Revenue.

Any estimated unguaranteed residual value should be reviewed periodically and if the estimate is determined to be excessive, the accounting for the transaction is revised and the resulting reduction in the net investment is recognized as a loss. An upward adjustment of estimated residual value is not made. In leases in which the lessee guarantees a minimum residual value of the property at the end of the lease term, or in which there is a penalty for failure to renew, the minimum lease receivables at the end of the lease term will be equal to the amount of the guarantee or penalty at that date. At the termination of the existing lease term of a lease being renewed, the net investment in the lease is adjusted to the fair value of the leased property to the lessor at that date and the net adjustment is charged or credited to unearned interest revenue. The accounting for a sales-type lease is covered on pages 653–655.

Direct Financing Leases In direct financing leases, the net investment in the lease also equals the difference between the gross investment in the lease and the unearned interest revenue.[8] *Any initial direct costs are charged against revenue as incurred and an equal portion of the unearned interest revenue is recognized as interest revenue in the same period.* The net investment in the lease currently recoverable is classified as a current

[8] Ibid., pp. 19–21.

asset and any contingent rentals are recorded as revenue when such rentals become receivable.

In leases containing a residual guarantee or a penalty for failure to renew, the lessor follows the same procedure described above for sales-type leases. Similarly, any estimated residual value should be reviewed periodically and, if necessary, adjusted as described for sales-type leases.

Operating Leases Leased property is included by the lessor with or near plant and equipment in the balance sheet.[9] The leased property is depreciated in accordance with the lessor's normal depreciation policy, and in the balance sheet the accumulated depreciation is deducted from the investment in the leased property.

Rent is reported as revenue by lessors over the lease term as it becomes receivable according to the provisions in the lease. However, if the rentals are not received in level amounts, the rent should be recognized on a straight-line basis unless another basis is considered more appropriate. An example of a basis which may be more appropriate than straight-line is hours of usage for a machine. Any initial direct costs in connection with an operating lease are deferred and allocated over the lease term.

Accounting for a capital lease illustrated

The accounting for a 30-month capital lease for the lessee and lessor is illustrated using the following information:

(1) The lessor's cost of the leased equipment is $10,006; this is also the lessor's fair value of the equipment at the inception of the lease, January 2, Year 1.
(2) The estimated economic life of the equipment is 60 months.
(3) The lease has a fixed noncancelable term of 30 months, with a rental of $270 payable at the beginning of each month. The monthly rental was determined using an interest rate of 1% per month. The lessee guarantees a residual value of $4,000 at the end of 30 months. The lessee pays executory costs and is to receive any excess of selling price of the equipment over the guaranteed residual value at end of lease term. The lease is renewable periodically based on a schedule of rentals and guarantees of the residual values, which decrease over time.
(4) The residual value at the end of the lease term is estimated to be $4,000. The lessee depreciates owned equipment on a straight-line basis. The lessee's incremental borrowing rate is $1\frac{1}{4}$% per month and the lessee knows that the lessor's implicit rate is 1% per month. There were no initial direct costs of negotiating and closing the lease.

[9] Ibid., p. 21.

(5) On July 2, Year 3, the end of the lease term, the equipment is sold by the lessor for $4,200.

(6) The fiscal years for the lessee and the lessor end on December 31.

Computations and Classification of the Lease The minimum lease payments for both the lessee and lessor are computed as follows:

Minimum rental payments over the lease term ($270 × 30 months) . . .	$ 8,100
Add: Lessee's guarantee of the residual value at the end of the lease term	4,000
Total minimum lease payments	$12,100

The **interest rate implicit in the lease** is that rate implicit in the recovery of the fair value of the equipment at the inception of the lease ($10,006) through the minimum lease payments (30 monthly payments of $270 and the lessee's guarantee of the residual value of $4,000 at the end of the lease term). That rate is 1% per month.

The lease does not meet the first three criteria listed on page 646. The lease does not transfer ownership to the lessee by the end of the lease term; the lease does not contain a bargain purchase option; and the lease term is not equal to 75% or more of the estimated economic life of the equipment. However, the fourth criterion on page 646 **is met** (because the present value of the minimum lease payments using the lessor's implicit rate exceeds 90% of the fair value of the equipment at the inception of the lease) and thus the **lessee classifies the lease as a capital lease.** The present value computations, using Appendix A at the implicit interest rate of 1% per month, are presented below:

Present value of minimum lease payments:	
Monthly lease rentals: $270 × present value of annuity due of 30 rents at 1%, or $270 × 26.065785	$ 7,038
Add: Residual guarantee by lessee: $4,000 × present value of 1 discounted for 30 periods at 1%, or $4,000 × 0.741923	2,968
Total present value of minimum lease payments	$10,006
Fair value of equipment at inception of the lease	$10,006
Present value of minimum lease payments as a percentage of fair value of equipment	100%

In this case the lessee uses the lessor's implicit rate of 1% per month because the implicit rate *is known to the lessee* and it is lower than the lessee's incremental borrowing rate of $1\frac{1}{4}$% per month.[10]

From the standpoint of the lessor, the present value of $10,006 of the minimum lease payments also exceeds 90% of the fair value of the equipment at the inception of the lease. Because the lease meets this test, *the lessor classifies the lease as a direct financing lease* (as opposed to a sales-type lease) because the cost and fair value of the equipment are the same at the inception of the lease. We are assuming that collectibility of the lease payments is reasonably assured and that no important uncertainties surround the amount of unreimbursable costs yet to be incurred by the lessor.

Journal Entries The journal entries in the accounts of the lessee and the lessor for the first two monthly payments, depreciation at the end of the first year, and the disposition of the equipment at the end of the lease term (July 2, Year 3) are illustrated on page 652.

Had the lessee elected on July 2, Year 3, to renew the lease, the renewal would be treated as a new agreement extending to the date of the next renewal option. The lessee would compare the present value of the minimum lease payments (rentals and guarantee of any residual value) over the renewal period with the $4,000 fair value of the equipment to the lessor at the inception of the renewal lease. Although the fair value of the equipment is $4,200, the value accruing to the lessor is limited to $4,000, the guaranteed amount.

From the lessor's standpoint, the present value of the minimum lease payments is computed using the rate of interest implicit in the renewal lease. The implicit rate is based on the recovery, through the minimum lease payments, of the $4,000 fair value of the equipment to the lessor at the inception of the renewed lease.

A lessor's investment in leases may be recorded in two ways, both of which produce the same effects on net assets and income. The first method, which is widely used in practice, is the "gross" method. Under this method the undiscounted sum of the minimum lease payments and the unguaranteed residual value are recorded in one or more asset accounts, and the credit for unearned interest is recorded in a contra-asset account, as illustrated on page 652. This method has the advantage of accumulating the amounts needed for required disclosures under *FASB Statement No. 13* in separate ledger accounts.

The second method is the "net" method, in which the present value of the minimum lease payments and the unguaranteed residual value are recorded as a single amount, as illustrated on page 654. In the interest of simplification, the "net" method is suggested for much of the end-of-chapter material; the student should be aware of the need under this method for additional analysis of the accounting records to obtain data for required disclosures in the financial statements.

[10] Ibid., p. 10.

Date	Accounts of Lessee		Accounts of Lessor	
Year 1				
Jan. 2	*Leased Equipment —*		*Minimum Lease Payments*	
	Capital Lease	10,006	*Receivable*	12,100
	Obligation under		*Equipment*	10,006
	Capital Lease		*Unearned Interest*	
	(net)	10,006	*Revenue*	2,094
	To record capital lease at		*To record investment in*	
	inception.		*direct financing lease.*	
Jan. 2	*Obligations under Capital*		*Cash*	270
	Lease	270	*Minimum Lease*	
	Cash	270	*Payments*	
	To record lease rental for		*Receivable* . . .	270
	first month.		*To record receipt of lease*	
			rental for first month.	
Feb. 2	*Interest Expense*	97	*Cash*	270
	Obligation under Capital		*Unearned Interest Revenue*	97
	Lease (net)	173	*Minimum Lease*	
	Cash	270	*Payments*	
	To record lease rental for		*Receivable* . . .	270
	second month; interest		*Interest Revenue* .	97
	expense for first month:		*To record receipt of lease*	
	($10,006 − $270) × 1% =		*rental for second month and*	
	$97.		*to recognize portion of un-*	
			earned interest revenue that	
			is earned during first month	
			of lease: ($12,100 − $270 −	
			$2,094) × 1% = $97.	
Dec. 31	*Depreciation Expense* . . .	2,402	*No depreciation is recorded*	
	Leased Equipment—		*by lessor.*	
	Capital Lease . .	2,402		
	To record depreciation on			
	straight-line basis for first			
	year of lease: ($10,006 −			
	$4,000) × ⅛ = $2,402.			
31	*Interest expense is accrued*		*Interest revenue is accrued*	
	for the period Dec. 2–		*for the period Dec. 2–*	
	Dec. 31.		*Dec. 31.*	
Year 3				
July 2	*Cash*	200	*Cash*	4,200
	Obligation under Capital		*Minimum Lease*	
	Lease (net)	4,000	*Payments*	
	Leased Equip-		*Receivable* . . .	4,000
	ment—Capital		*Payable to Lessee*	200
	Lease	4,000	*To record sale of equipment*	
	Gain on Disposi-		*at the end of the lease term.*	
	tion of Leased			
	Equipment . . .	200	*Payable to Lessee*	200
	To record liquidation of ob-		*Cash*	200
	ligation under capital lease		*To remit excess of selling*	
	and the receipt of cash in		*price of equipment over*	
	excess of the residual		*residual guarantee to lessee.*	
	guarantee.			

Accounting for a sales-type lease illustrated

FASB Statement No. 13 requires that a lease which either transfers owner-ship of the property to the lessee by the end of the lease term or which contains a bargain purchase option should be accounted for as a capi-tal lease by the lessee and as a sales-type or direct financing lease by the lessor. For such leases, the lessee depreciates the leased asset over its estimated economic life rather than over the initial period of the lease. If the asset has a fair value which differs from its cost or carrying value at the inception of the lease, the transaction generally is recorded as a sales-type lease by the lessor, and *a profit or loss is recognized.* In a sales-type lease, the lessor's ability to collect the minimum lease pay-ments must be reasonably predictable and there must be no important uncertainties surrounding the amount of any additional costs to be in-curred by the lessor.

To illustrate the accounting for a sales-type lease, assume that on De-cember 31, Year 1, Orr Co. leased equipment (which had a cost of $11,500 and a fair value of $14,350) to LSE, Inc., for four years on the fol-lowing terms:

(1) LSE, Inc., agreed to make four annual rental payments of $4,000 starting on December 31, Year 1.[11] The estimated economic life of the equipment is six years with no residual value; LSE, Inc., planned to use the straight-line method of depreciation.
(2) LSE, Inc., agreed to absorb all maintenance costs, insurance, and property taxes; no initial direct costs were incurred by either party.
(3) LSE, Inc., was given an option to buy the equipment for $10 at the end of the lease term, December 31, Year 5.
(4) The effective rate of interest on December 31, Year 1, for this type of transaction was 8% a year.

The present value at December 31, Year 1, of the four rental payments consists of the total of (1) $4,000 due on December 31, Year 1, and (2) the present value of an ordinary annuity of three additional payments of $4,000 at 8% a year, as computed below:

Payment due on Dec. 31, Year 1	$ 4,000
Present value of ordinary annuity of 3 payments of $4,000 at 8% a year at	
Dec. 31, Year 2–Year 4: $4,000 × 2.577097 (see Table 4 in Appendix A)	10,308
Present value of 4 payments of $4,000 at 8% a year	$14,308

A table summarizing the payments and interest through December 31, Year 4, follows:

[11] Lease payments are generally made monthly; we have assumed annual payments to minimize computations in the accompanying table.

	(A)	(B)	(C)	(D)
		Lessor's interest revenue (or lessee's interest expense), 8% of (D)	Reduction in balance (A − B)	Balance of lessor's net receivable (or lessee's net obligation)
Date	Lease payments			
Dec. 31, Year 1	Balance			$14,308
Dec. 31, Year 1	$4,000	$–0–	$4,000	10,308
Dec. 31, Year 2	4,000	825	3,175	7,133
Dec. 31, Year 3	4,000	571	3,429	3,704
Dec. 31, Year 4	4,000	296	3,704	–0–

Summary of Lease Payments, Interest Revenue, and Interest Expense

The journal entries for the lessee and lessor for Year 1 and Year 2 to record this sales-type lease are illustrated below. (We have assumed that lease receivables and payables are recorded net of the deferred interest charges and credits.)

Date	Accounts of LSE, Inc. (Lessee)		Accounts of Orr Co. (Lessor)	
Year 1				
Dec. 31	Leased Equipment—Capital		Cash 4,000	
	Lease 14,308		Lease Receivables (net) . . 10,308	
	Cash	4,000	Cost of Goods Sold 11,500	
	Obligation under		Sales	14,308
	Capital Lease		Inventory (Eqpt.	
	(net)	10,308	Held for Lease) .	11,500
	To record capital lease, in-		To record sales-type lease,	
	cluding first lease payment.		including receipt of first	
			lease payment.	
Year 2				
Dec. 31	Obligation under Capital		Cash 4,000	
	Lease (net) 3,175		Interest Revenue .	825
	Interest Expense 825		Lease Receivables	
	Cash	4,000	(net)	3,175
	To record second lease		To record receipt of second	
	payment.		lease payment.	
	Depreciation Expense . . . 2,385		No depreciation is recorded	
	Leased Equipment—		by lessor.	
	Capital Lease (or			
	Accum. Depr.) .	2,385		
	To record depreciation for			
	first year: $14,308 ÷ 6 =			
	$2,385.			

It would be possible to record the lease receivables and payables at the gross amount of $12,000 ($4,000 × 3) and a discount of $1,692

($12,000 − $10,308) representing unearned interest revenue for the lessor and deferred interest expense for the lessee. Also we should emphasize that the lessee computes depreciation over the six-year economic life of the equipment and not over the four-year initial term of the lease.

If a sales-type lease is terminated before the end of the lease term by mutual consent without penalty, the lessee recognizes a loss. For example, assume that the lease in the illustration above is terminated on December 31, Year 3; the journal entry to record the termination in the accounts of LSE, Inc., is as follows:

Obligation under Capital Lease	*7,133*	
Depreciation Expense	*2,385*	
Loss on Termination of Lease	*2,405*	
Leased Equipment—Capital Lease (net)		*11,923*
To record termination of capital lease through mutual consent and		
depreciation for second year.		

Upon termination of the lease, the lessor records the equipment at the **lowest** of its original cost, present fair value, or present carrying amount, and recognizes any loss. The lessor does not recognize a gain on an early termination of a lease.

Illustration of accounting for a direct financing lease with initial direct costs

To illustrate the accounting for a direct financing lease, assume that Lessor Co. leased equipment to Lessee Co. with a cost and fair value of $11,127. The initial direct costs incurred by the lessor were $200. The lease was for seven years at an annual rental of $2,000 paid at the beginning of each year. The estimated economic life of the equipment was nine years and the estimated unguaranteed residual value at the end of seven years was $1,200. Lease payments were determined at an amount which will give Lessor Co. a 10% annual rate of return on its net investment, including the initial direct costs. The present value of the lease payments for the lessor, including the unguaranteed residual value, was $11,327. Lessee Co. knows Lessor's implicit interest rate. Lessee Co. agreed to pay all executory costs; the collectibility of the lease payments was reasonably assured and no additional costs were expected to be incurred by Lessor Co.

This lease meets the criteria for classification as a direct financing lease by Lessor Co. and a capital lease by Lessee Co. because (1) the lease term exceeds 75% of the economic life of the equipment, (2) the present value of the minimum lease payments is more than 90% of the fair value of the equipment at the inception of the lease, (3) the collectibility of the lease payments is reasonably assured and no additional costs were expected to be incurred by the lessor, and (4) there is no element of profit at the inception of the lease except for deferred interest revenue.

Using Appendix A, the net investment in the lease for the lessor is determined as follows:

> *Present value of annuity due of 7 rents of $2,000 at 10% (present value of*
> *minimum lease payments for lessee): $2,000 × 5.355261* $10,711
> *Add: Present value of unguaranteed residual value ($1,200 discounted*
> *at 10% for 7 years): $1,200 × 0.513158*   616
> *Net investment in the lease for the lessor* $11,327

Because the lessee does not obtain rights to the equipment at the end of the lease term, only the present value of the minimum lease payments is recorded by the lessee. The journal entries to record this lease in the accounts of the lessee and lessor, including the first lease payment, are as follows:

Accounts of Lessee			Accounts of Lessor		
Leased Equipment—			Cash	2,000	
Capital Lease	10,711		Lease Receivables (Net		
Cash		2,000	Investment in Direct		
Obligation under			Financing Lease) . .	9,327	
Capital Lease .		8,711	Operating Expenses . .	200	
To record capital lease,			Inventory (Equip-		
including first lease			ment Held for		
payment, at present			Lease)		11,127
value of minimum lease			Interest Revenue		200
payments.			Cash		200
			To record direct financ-		
			ing lease, including		
			receipt of first lease		
			payment, and initial		
			direct costs of $200.		

Note that the initial direct costs of $200 are recorded as operating expenses and that an equal amount of interest revenue is recognized as realized in the same period. This procedure is explicitly required by **FASB Statement No. 13.**

Sale-leaseback transactions

In certain cases an owner of an asset sells it and immediately leases it back from the buyer. Such *sale-leaseback transactions* give lessees use of assets in their business without a large investment of scarce capital and provide lessors with profitable investments. In addition, both lessors and lessees may derive significant income tax advantages from sale-leaseback arrangements.

Because the sale of the asset and the leaseback represents in effect a single transactions, neither the sale price of the asset nor the periodic rental payments can be evaluated separately from the other. Consequently, the FASB suggested the following standard to be used in accounting for sale-leaseback transactions:

> If the lease meets one of the criteria for treatment as a capital lease . . . , the seller-lessee shall account for the lease as a capital lease; otherwise, as an operating lease. Except as noted below, any profit or loss on the sale shall be deferred and amortized in proportion to the amortization of the leased asset, if a capital lease, or in proportion to rental payments over the period of time the asset is expected to be used, if an operating lease. However, when the fair value of the property at the time of the transaction is less than its undepreciated cost, a loss shall be recognized immediately up to the amount of the difference between undepreciated cost and fair value.[12]

Leveraged leases

A *leveraged lease* is an arrangement whereby a long-term creditor provides nonrecourse financing for a leasing transaction between the lessee and lessor. A leveraged lease is generally designed to provide maximum income tax benefits to the three parties involved in the transaction.

From the standpoint of the lessee, leveraged leases are classified and accounted for the same as nonleveraged leases. From the standpoint of the lessor, leveraged leases are treated as direct financing leases; sales-type leases cannot be classified as leveraged leases according to *FASB Statement No. 13.*[13] The lessor records the investment in a leveraged lease net of the nonrecourse debt. The amount recorded generally consists of (1) rentals receivable (net of portion applicable to the nonrecourse debt), (2) the amount of the investment tax credit to be realized on the transaction, (3) any estimated residual value of the leased asset, and (4) a reduction for any unearned revenue items.

Accounting for the various aspects of leveraged leases in the accounts of the lessor are quite complex and therefore will not be illustrated in this general discussion of leasing.[14]

---

[12] *FASB Statement No. 13*, p. 29.

[13] Ibid., p. 32.

[14] Appendix E of *FASB Statement No. 13* contains 19 pages of illustrations of accounting and financial statement presentation for leveraged leases.

Effective dates of FASB Statement No. 13

FASB Statement No. 13 was made effective for all leases entered into or revised on or after January 1, 1977. Earlier adoption was encouraged, including retroactive application for lease contracts completed prior to 1977. Retroactive application to leases entered into prior to 1977 was not required until fiscal years beginning after December 31, 1980. However, unless retroactive adoption is elected for leases existing or committed at December 31, 1976, disclosure of the effects of the new principles on financial statements is required in notes to financial statements. The required disclosure includes the amounts of assets and liabilities that would have been included in the balance sheet and the effect on net income that would have resulted if the leases had been classified and accounted for in accordance with *FASB Statement No. 13.*

Retroactive application of the new accounting principles to leases entered into prior to January 1, 1977, was delayed for four years to give companies time to accumulate the required information and to allow the investment community to digest the impact of *FASB Statement No. 13.* The Securities and Exchange Commission favored immediate retroactive application of *FASB Statement No. 13.* Consequently, the Commission issued a proposal early in 1977 which would require registrants to adopt *FASB Statement No. 13* by the end of 1977, unless loan agreement modifications or other legal matters could not be resolved by that time.

Prior to the issuance of *FASB Statement No. 13,* lessees were required to capitalize only those leases which were considered the equivalent to a purchase of property. Leases were often designed in such a way as to permit the lessor to record the lease as a sale but at the same time allow the lessee to account for the lease as an operating lease. Thus billions of dollars of leased assets were not included in the balance sheet either of the lessee or the lessor. Many lessees viewed leasing as an attractive source of "off-balance-sheet financing." However, users of financial statements and the Securities and Exchange Commission considered the accounting practices for leasing transactions unsatisfactory. *FASB Statement No. 13* changed all this. Under the new accounting standards, financial statements are more consistent with the conceptual framework of accounting, more informative, and more comparable between companies that lease assets and those that purchase assets outright.

Disclosure in financial statements

The disclosure requirements under *FASB Statement No. 13* for lessees and lessors are summarized in the following sections.

By Lessees The following information with respect to leases shall be disclosed in the lessee's financial statements or notes to the financial statements:[15]

[15] *FASB Statement No. 13,* pp. 15–16.

1 For capital leases:
  a The gross amount of assets recorded under capital leases as of the date of each balance sheet presented by major classes according to nature or function. This information may be combined with comparable information for assets owned by the lessee.
  b Future minimum lease payments as of the date of the latest balance sheet presented, in the aggregate and for each of the five succeeding fiscal years, with separate deductions from the total for the amount representing executory costs included in the minimum lease payments and for the amount of the imputed interest necessary to reduce the net minimum lease payments to present value.
  c The total of minimum sublease rentals to be received in the future under noncancelable subleases as of the date of the latest balance sheet presented.
  d Total contingent rentals (dependent on factors other than the passage of time) actually incurred for each period for which an income statement is presented.
2 For operating leases having initial or remaining noncancelable terms in excess of one year:
  a Future minimum rental payments required as of the date of the latest balance sheet presented, in the aggregate and for each of the five succeeding fiscal years.
  b The total of minimum rentals to be received in the future under noncancelable subleases as of the date of the latest balance sheet presented.
3 For all operating leases, rental expense for each period for which an income statement is presented, with separate amounts for minimum rentals, contingent rentals, and sublease rentals. Rental payments under leases with terms of a month or less that were not renewed need not be included.
4 A general description of the lessee's leasing arrangements including, but not limited to, the following:
  a The basis on which contingent rental payments are determined.
  b The existence and terms of renewal or purchase options and escalation clauses.
  c Restrictions imposed by lease agreements, such as those concerning dividends, additional debt, and further leasing.

By Lessors When leasing is a significant part of the lessor's business activities in terms of revenue, net income, or assets, the following information with respect to leases should be disclosed in the financial statements or notes to the financial statements:[16]

1 For sales-type and direct financing leases:
  a The components of the net investment in sales-type and direct financing leases as of the date of each balance sheet presented. The components include (1) future minimum lease payments to be received, with separate deductions for amounts representing executory costs included in the minimum lease payments, and the accumulated allowance for doubtful lease payments receivable; (2) the unguaranteed residual values accruing to the benefit of the lessor; and (3) the unearned interest revenue.
  b Future minimum lease payments to be received for each of the five succeeding fiscal years as of the date of the latest balance sheet presented.
  c The amount of unearned interest revenue included in income to offset initial direct costs charged against income for each period for which an income statement is presented. (For direct financing leases only.)
  d Total contingent rentals included in income for each period for which an income statement is presented.

[16] Ibid., pp. 23–24.

2 For operating leases:
  a The cost and carrying amount, if different, of property on lease or held for leasing by major classes of property according to nature or function, and the amount of accumulated depreciation in total as of the date of the latest balance sheet presented.
  b Minimum future rentals on noncancelable leases as of the date of the latest balance sheet presented, in the aggregate and for each of the five succeeding fiscal years.
  c Total contingent rentals included in income for each period for which an income statement is presented.

3 A general description of the lessor's leasing arrangements.

PENSION PLANS

Most medium and large companies incur continuing obligations under employee pension plans. A *pension plan* is a contract between the company and its employees whereby the company agrees to pay benefits to employees upon retirement. In some cases employees contribute to a pension fund; however, in most cases employers bear the full cost of a pension plan. Ordinarily, pension benefits consist of monthly payments to employees upon retirement and additional payments upon death or disability. Pension plans may be formal or may be implied from company policy. A company's practice of paying retirement benefits to selected employees in amounts determined on a case-by-case basis does not constitute a pension plan.[17]

Pension plans are a part of the total employment contract with employees and may be established for one or more of the following reasons:

1 To meet demands from employees and labor unions
2 To increase employee morale and productivity and to reduce employee turnover
3 To fulfill one of the social responsibilities of business enterprises

Assets of all private pension funds probably exceeded $260 billion at the end of 1977 and are expected to continue growing at a fast rate. Assets of private pension funds have been growing much faster than total assets of corporations and pension expense has been rising much faster than corporate earnings; over 40 million active workers were covered by private pension plans in 1977. As a result, accounting for pension costs has become one of the more important topics in financial accounting.

Funded and unfunded pension plans

A *funded pension plan* requires the company to make periodic payments to a funding agency (a designated trustee or an outside agency

[17] *APB Opinion No. 8,* "Accounting for the Cost of Pension Plans," AICPA (New York: 1966), p. 68.

such as an insurance company). The process of making payments to the funding agency is known as *funding.* Funding may be accomplished through an *insured plan* with a life insurance company or through a *trust fund plan.* Under an insured plan, individual policies providing death and retirement benefits may be purchased for each employee; alternatively, a group annuity contract may be purchased by the employer. Under a trust fund plan, the employer makes periodic contributions to a trustee who invests the fund assets and pays benefits to employees. If a pension plan is not administered by a funding agency or if assets are informally set aside for the payment of pensions, the plan is designated as an *unfunded pension plan.* Most corporate pension plans in the United States are fully or partially funded.

Prior to the Pension Reform Act of 1974 (ERISA), a company was able to assume the obligation for pension benefits without establishing a pension fund. However, under ERISA, all current pension costs must be funded. For pension plans which existed on January 1, 1974, past service pension costs must be fully funded in 40 years or less, and past service pension costs which arise after that date must be funded in 30 years or less.

To illustrate the basic accounting for a pension plan, assume that the pension expense for Napier Corporation for the current year amounts to $200,000, and that retired employees are paid $50,000. Journal entries required to record this information follow:

Transactions	Funded plan	Unfunded plan

Recognition of pension expense for current year.	Pension Expense . 200,000
	   Cash . . . 200,000
		Pension Expense 200,000
		   Liability
		   under
		   Pension
		   Plan . . . 200,000

Payment of benefits to retired employees during current year.	None (Funding agency makes payment directly to retired employees)	Liability under
		  Pension Plan . . 50,000
		   Cash . . . 50,000

The periodic contributions to the pension fund (or funding agency) made by employers may not equal the amount currently recognized as pension expense. If the contribution to the pension fund is less than the amount charged to pension expense, the difference should be recorded as a liability; if the contribution exceeds the amount charged to pension expense, the difference may be charged to a previously recorded liability or to a deferred pension cost account. On this point, *APB Opinion No. 8* stated:

The difference between the amount which has been charged against income and the amount which has been paid [to a fund or funding agency] should be shown in the balance sheet as accrued or prepaid pension cost. If the company has a legal obligation for pension cost in excess of amounts paid or accrued, the excess should be shown in the balance sheet as both a liability and a deferred charge.[18]

Pension plans are generally designed to meet federal income tax requirements of a "qualified" plan. A *qualified* plan has the following tax features: (1) The employer's contributions to the pension fund (within certain limits) are deductible for federal income tax purposes; (2) earnings on pension fund assets are not subject to federal income tax; and (3) generally, only the benefits received by retired employees represent taxable income to them.

General accounting guidelines for pension plans

Accountants are faced with three significant issues relating to pension plans, which are listed below:

1 **Timing** the recognition of pension costs **as expenses** in measuring periodic net income, particularly when pension plans cover employees who have already worked a number of years for the company at the time the plans are adopted

2 **Measuring the amount** of pension expense and any related deferred pension cost or accrued pension liability which should appear in the balance sheet

3 **Presenting** significant information relating to pension plans in the financial statements and the accompanying notes

In 1965 the Accounting Principles Board published **Accounting Research Study No. 8,** "Accounting for the Cost of Pension Plans."[19] A year later, **APB Opinion No. 8** was issued which provided guidelines for the measurement of periodic pension costs and for reporting relevant pension plan information in financial statements and the accompanying notes.

The measurement of pension costs involves numerous complexities, including the application of compound interest concepts, estimation of the life expectancy of employees, determination of the age of employees at retirement, future level of interest rates, probable employee turnover, gains and losses on pension fund investments, future salary levels of employees, pension benefits to be paid, and vesting provisions under the pension plan. These complexities, combined with the long-range nature of pension plans, cause significant uncertainties as to the amount of pension benefits ultimately to be paid and the amount of periodic pension expense to be recorded in the accounts.

Pension costs and the related costs of administering a pension plan should be allocated to revenue using the accrual basis of accounting. The amount of periodic expense should not be left to the whims of management. Ideally, the total pension cost relating to a particular employee should be recognized as expense over the period between the date the

---

[18] Ibid., p. 74.

[19] Ernest L. Hicks, *Accounting Research Study No. 8,* "Accounting for the Cost of Pension Plans," AICPA (New York: 1965).

employee is hired and the date he retires. All employees who may reasonably be expected to receive benefits under a pension plan should be included in the calculation of the periodic pension expense, with appropriate recognition of employee turnover rates.

Minimum-maximum range for pension expense

APB Opinion No. 8 recognized that different viewpoints exist as to the composition of pension cost, especially the extent to which pension expense should include the cost of employees' services prior to the adoption of a pension plan. The Opinion specified that the entire cost of benefit payments ultimately to be made should be charged to expense **subsequent** to the adoption or amendment of a plan and that no portion of such cost should be charged directly against retained earnings, that is, as a prior period adjustment.[20] The annual provision for pension expense should be determined in a consistent manner and the amount of the provision should be within the following prescribed range:

> a. *Minimum.* The annual provision for pension cost should not be less than the total of (1) normal cost, (2) an amount equivalent to interest on any unfunded prior service cost and (3) if indicated [under circumstances discussed below] . . . a provision for vested benefits. . . .
>
> b. *Maximum.* The annual provision for pension cost should not be greater than the total of (1) normal cost, (2) 10 per cent of the past service cost (until fully amortized), (3) 10 percent of the amounts of any increases or decreases in prior service cost arising on amendments of the plan (until fully amortized) and (4) interest equivalents . . . on the difference between provisions and amounts funded. The 10 per cent limitation is considered necessary to prevent unreasonably large charges against income during a short period of years.[21]

The APB expressed a preference for a method of measuring periodic pension expense which would include an appropriate portion of past service cost and prior service cost increments. However, any "rational and systematic" method which is consistently applied and which provides for periodic pension expense between the minimum and maximum range was considered acceptable.

The terminology used in the measurement of periodic pension expense within the minimum-maximum range is explained below:

> **Normal cost**   The cost of prospective retirement benefits accrued (on the basis of current service credits) during any year is known as a **normal cost** (or **current service cost**) of the pension plan. Normal cost is generally determined by professional actuaries using an acceptable actuarial cost method (see pages 665–666) for each year subsequent to the inception of the plan.
>
> **Past service and prior service costs**   The estimated cost of prospective retirement benefits considered to have accrued in the years prior to the adoption of a pension plan is known as **past service cost;** the estimated cost of

---

[20] *APB Opinion No. 8*, p. 73.
[21] Ibid., pp. 73–74.

employee services for years prior to the date of a particular actuarial valuation (including the past service cost) is known as *prior service cost.* Increases or decreases in prior service cost as a result of changes in the contractual provisions of the pension plan are referred to as *prior service cost increments.* (In the summary of components of the provision for pension expense shown on page 665, we can see that the minimum provision for pension expense includes only the interest charge on any unfunded prior service cost; the maximum provision may include 10% (based on the 10-year minimum amortization period allowed for income tax purposes) of the prior service cost. Once prior service cost is fully amortized, no further consideration would be given to such cost in applying the minimum-maximum guidelines.)

Vested benefits Earned pension benefits that are not contingent on the employee remaining in the service of the employer are known as *vested benefits.* Under some plans the payment of vested benefits begins only when an employee reaches a stated retirement age; in other cases the payment of vested benefits begins when an employee actually retires. The actuarially computed value of vested benefits at a given date consists of the present value of the sum of (1) the expected benefits to be paid to employees who have retired or who were terminated with vested rights, and (2) the benefits already earned and expected to become payable to active employees. A provision for vested benefits is required only when the pension expense (consisting of normal cost and interest on unfunded prior service cost) does not make a reasonable provision for vested benefits.

Interest equivalents The purpose of a pension fund is to accumulate amounts needed to pay retirement benefits. The fund generally is accumulated through the (1) periodic contributions by the employer and (2) the earnings on pension fund assets. If the employer's contributions exceed the actuarially determined pension expense, the earnings on the pension fund assets will be greater than required and the employer's future contributions should be correspondingly reduced; however, if the contributions are less than required by actuarial computations, the earnings which would otherwise have been realized on the pension fund assets must be made up in future years.

Under the minimum-maximum guidelines, the annual provision for pension expense should be adjusted by an amount equal to the interest on any difference between pension expense previously recorded and the amounts actually funded. (See amortization and funding tables on pages 669 and 670.)

In arriving at the *minimum* annual pension expense, provision must be made for interest on any unfunded prior service cost (or, in certain cases, on the difference between accounting provisions for normal pension costs and the amounts of normal costs actually funded). In arriving at the *maximum* annual pension expense, provision is made for interest on the unfunded prior service cost under the 10% limitation for such cost; in addition, a provision for interest must be made on the difference, if any, between the cumulative provisions for normal pension costs and the amounts of normal pension costs actually funded.

A summary of the components of the minimum and maximum annual provisions for pension expense appears on page 665.

Component of annual provision for pension expense	Minimum provision for pension expense	Maximum provision for pension expense
1 Normal cost	Full amount included	Full amount included
2 Prior service cost (which includes past service cost and prior service cost increments)	Only interest provision on unfunded portion is included	Include no more than 10% until fully amortized
3 Vested benefits	May be included in certain cases	Not applicable
4 Interest equivalents on the difference between provisions and amounts funded	Include (or deduct) in certain cases in connection with item (3) above	Include (or deduct)

Actuarial cost methods

The annual provision for pension expense should be based on one of the acceptable *actuarial cost methods.* The factors used in tentatively resolving uncertainties concerning future events affecting pension expense (such as mortality rates, employee turnover, compensation levels, and earnings on pension fund assets) are referred to as *actuarial assumptions.* An *actuarial valuation* of a pension plan is made by actuaries using these assumptions to determine the amounts an employer is to contribute to a pension fund. The first step in making an actuarial valuation is to determine the present value on the valuation date of benefits to be paid to employees over varying periods of time in the future. An actuarial cost method is then applied to this present value to determine the current contributions to be made by the employer.

Although actuarial techniques are primarily used to determine the periodic payments to be made to the pension fund (or funding agency), the same techniques are used to measure periodic pension expense. The amount of the pension expense recognized currently is the present value of future pension benefits which are estimated to have accrued during the current accounting period. Acceptable actuarial cost methods include (1) the *accrued-benefit-cost method* and (2) the *projected-benefit-cost methods.*

Accrued-Benefit-Cost Method Under the accrued-benefit-cost method (sometimes called the *unit-credit method*), the amount of pension expense assigned to the current year usually is equal to the present value of the increase in the employees' retirement benefits resulting from the services performed in the current year. Thus the normal annual pension expense under this method is the present value of the **units** of future benefits credited to employees for current services.

Projected-Benefit-Cost Methods Under the projected-benefit-cost methods, the amount of pension expense assigned to the current year usually represents a level amount that will provide for the total projected retirement benefits over the service lives of employees. Four projected-benefit-cost methods (entry-age-normal method, individual-level-premium method, aggregate method, and attained-age-normal method) may be used. A description of these methods is beyond the scope of this discussion.

In contrast to the two actuarial cost methods mentioned above, the terminal-funding method and the pay-as-you-go method are not considered acceptable. Under the **terminal-funding method,** provision (funding and recognition of pension expense) for future benefit payments is made only at the end of an employee's period of active service; under the **pay-as-you-go method,** pension expense is recognized only when benefits actually are paid to retired employees. The conclusion in **APB Opinion No. 8** relative to actuarial cost methods is summarized below:

> To be acceptable for determining cost for accounting purposes, an actuarial cost method should be rational and systematic and should be consistently applied so that it results in a reasonable measure of pension cost from year to year. . . . Each of the actuarial cost methods . . . , except terminal funding, is considered acceptable when the actuarial assumptions are reasonable and when the method is applied in conformity with the other conclusions of this Opinion. The terminal funding method is not acceptable because it does not recognize pension cost prior to retirement of employees. For the same reason, the pay-as-you-go method (which is not an actuarial cost method) is not acceptable.[22]

Actuarial gains and losses

We have seen that in measuring periodic pension expense it is necessary to make numerous assumptions based on estimates of future events. Actual events seldom coincide with previous estimates and the assumptions concerning the future may become invalid. As a result, periodic adjustments may be required to reflect actual experience and to revise the assumptions to be used in the future. These adjustments are commonly known as **actuarial gains and losses.** Actuaries normally compute the amount of the actuarial gains and losses and management determines the period of time to be used in recognizing such gains and losses in the accounts. Prior to the issuance of **APB Opinion No. 8,** three methods were used: (1) immediate recognition, (2) spreading over the current and future periods, and (3) averaging. **APB Opinion No. 8** considered the **spreading** and **averaging** methods acceptable:

> The Board believes that actuarial gains and losses, including realized investment gains and losses, should be given effect in the provision for pension

[22] Ibid., p. 77.

cost in a consistent manner that reflects the long-range nature of pension cost. Accordingly, . . . actuarial gains and losses should be spread over the current year and future years or recognized on the basis of an average. . . . Where spreading is accomplished by separate adjustments, the Board considers a period of from 10 to 20 years to be reasonable.

Actuarial gains and losses should be recognized immediately if they arise from a single occurrence not directly related to the operation of the pension plan and not in the ordinary course of the employer's business. An example of such occurrences is a plant closing, in which case the actuarial gain or loss should be treated as an adjustment of the net gain or loss from that occurrence and not as an adjustment of pension cost for the year.[23]

Accounting for the cost of a pension plan illustrated

Once a pension plan is adopted, actuaries are engaged to determine the present value of past service cost (if any) and to compute the normal pension expense for the current period using an acceptable actuarial cost method. Management then formulates a policy for the amortization and funding of the past service cost. At this point, it is necessary to ascertain that the computed amount of normal and past service pension expense falls between the minimum-maximum range described on page 663.

To illustrate the journal entries required to record annual pension expense, we shall assume that Penn Company adopted a pension plan at the beginning of Year 1. The company plans to fully fund the normal (current) pension cost, which is estimated at $60,000 per year. The company has a number of employees who have been working for the company for many years, and independent professional actuaries have determined the present value of the liability for past services applicable to such employees at $210,620. This present value of the past service cost was determined using a 6% annual interest rate.

Example 1. Past Service Cost Amortized and Funded over 15 Years If the management of Penn Company decides to amortize and fund the past service cost of $210,620 over a 15-year period by recognizing the expense and making equal payments to the funding agency *at the end of each year,* the annual amortization of past service cost and the annual payment to the funding agency are determined as follows:

$$\frac{\text{Present value of past service cost}}{\text{Present value of ordinary annuity of 15 payments of 1 at 6\%}} = \frac{\$210,620}{9.712249^*} = \underline{\underline{\$21,686}}$$

* See Table 4 in Appendix A.

[23] Ibid., pp. 79–80.

The entry at the end of each year to record the normal pension cost of $60,000, the amortization of the past service cost of $21,686, and payment to the funding agency follows:

Pension Expense (Normal and Past Service Cost) 81,686

    Cash   81,686

To record annual pension expense (including normal cost of $60,000 and past service cost of $21,686) and payment to the funding agency.

The pension expense of $81,686 falls between the minimum-maximum range and would appear as an additional payroll expense in the income statement. The balance sheet would not include **any** deferred pension cost of accrued pension liability because the entire current provisions for pension expense are fully funded at the end of each year. After the past service cost is fully amortized and funded at the end of the fifteenth year, only the normal (current) pension expense would be recorded and funded each year.

Example 2. Past Service Cost Amortized over a Period Longer than Funding Period Although management may elect to fund the past service cost over any number of years, the amortization of the past service cost cannot be less than 10 years or longer than 40 years. In order to minimize the computations in the table on page 669, we shall assume that Penn Company will amortize the past service cost over a period of eight years and will fund this cost by making five equal payments to the funding agency at the end of each of the first five years. The annual amortization and funding payments are computed below:

Amortization:

$$\frac{\text{Present value of past service cost}}{\text{Present value of ordinary annuity of 8 payments of 1 at 6\%}}$$

$$= \frac{\$210,620}{6.209794} = \$33,917$$

Payments:

$$\frac{\text{Present value of past service cost}}{\text{Present value of ordinary annuity of 5 payments of 1 at 6\%}}$$

$$= \frac{\$210,620}{4.212364} = \$50,000$$

A table showing the computation of the annual past service pension expense (column C) and the deferred pension cost balance (column F) is presented below:

PENN COMPANY
Past Service Pension Cost—Amortization and Funding

Year	Amortization (8 years)			Funding (5 years)	Deferred pension cost	
	(A) Computed annual amount at 6% interest	(B) Less interest (6% of previous balance in F)	(C) Debit to Pension Expense (A − B)	(D) Credit to Cash	(E) Increase or decrease (D − C)	(F) Asset balance (previous balance ±E)
1	$33,917	$ –0–	$33,917	$50,000	$16,083	$16,083
2	33,917	965	32,952	50,000	17,048	33,131
3	33,917	1,988	31,929	50,000	18,071	51,202
4	33,917	3,072	30,845	50,000	19,155	70,357
5	33,917	4,221	29,696	50,000	20,304	90,661
6	33,917	5,440	28,477	–0–	(28,477)	62,184
7	33,917	3,731	30,186	–0–	(30,186)	31,998
8	33,917	1,919*	31,998	–0–	(31,998)	–0–

* Adjusted for $1 discrepancy due to rounding of computations.

Because the payments to the funding agency during the first five years exceed the amount charged to expense, an asset (Deferred Pension Cost) is accumulated and reported as an asset in the balance sheet. Starting in Year 2, interest earned (column B) on the deferred pension cost balance (column F) **reduces** the annual debit to Pension Expense (column C).

Journal entries to record the amortization and funding of the past service cost for Year 1 and Year 8 are illustrated below:

Year 1	Pension Expense (Past Service Cost)	33,917	
	Deferred Pension Cost	16,083	
	Cash		50,000

To record payment to funding agency; amount paid exceeds amount currently recognized as expense.

Year 8	Pension Expense (Past Service Cost)	31,998	
	Deferred Pension Cost		31,998

To record amortization of deferred pension cost.

An additional entry would be made each year to record the normal cost of the pension plan. Keep in mind that *APB Opinion No. 8* does not permit the amortization of past service cost over a period less than 10 years; we have used eight years in order to simplify the computations in the example.

Example 3. Past Service Cost Amortized over a Period Shorter than Funding Period When the past service cost is amortized over a period shorter than the funding period, a pension liability (column F in the table below) is accumulated during the amortization period; this liability is gradually eliminated as payments are made to the funding agency in the years following the amortization period. Because the funding lags behind the recognition of the expense, interest on the fund deficiency (accrued pension liability) is *added* to the annual pension expense. A table illustrating the amortization of the past service cost over a three-year period and the funding of this cost over a five-year period by Penn Company is shown below:

PENN COMPANY
Past Service Pension Cost—Amortization and Funding

	Amortization (3 years)			Funding (5 years)	Accrued pension liability	
Year	(A) Computed annual amount at 6% interest	(B) Add interest (6% of previous balance in F)	(C) Debit to Pension Expense (A + B)	(D) Credit to Cash	(E) Increase or decrease (C − D)	(F) Liability balance (previous balance ± E)
1	$78,795*	$ –0–	$78,795	$50,000†	$28,795	$28,795
2	78,795	1,728	80,523	50,000	30,523	59,318
3	78,795	3,559	82,354	50,000	32,354	91,672
4	–0–	5,500	5,500	50,000	(44,500)	47,172
5	–0–	2,828‡	2,828	50,000	(47,172)	–0–

* $210,620 ÷ 2.673012 (*present value of ordinary annuity of 3 payments of 1 at 6%*) = $78,795.
† *Same as in example on page 669.*
‡ *Adjusted for $2 discrepancy due to rounding of computations.*

Journal entries to record the amortization and funding of the past service cost for Year 1 and Year 5 are illustrated on page 671.

The normal cost of the pension plan also would be recorded each year. Again, we should emphasize that the short amortization period was used only to simplify the computations. Attention should be focused on the basic principles involved and not on the amortization period used. In practice, the amortization period must exceed 10 years; generally a period of 15 to 30 years is used.

Deferred compensation contracts

Accrual accounting procedures applicable to pension plans also apply to other deferred compensation contracts. Such contracts generally

Year 1 Pension Expense (Past Service Cost) 78,795
            Cash 50,000
            Liability under Pension Plan 28,795
   To record payment to funding agency; amount paid is
   less than amount currently recognized as expense.

Year 5 Pension Expense (Past Service Cost) 2,828
   Liability under Pension Plan 47,172
            Cash 50,000
   To record payment to funding agency to eliminate balance in Liability under Pension Plan account and to
   recognize pension expense equal to 6% of liability
   balance.

stipulate that employees, to be eligible for benefits, must be employed for a specified period and that they should be available for consultation after retirement. The principle for the accrual of deferred compensation expense was formulated by the APB as follows:

> The estimated amounts to be paid under each contract should be accrued in a systematic and rational manner over the period of active employment from the time the contract is entered into, unless it is evident that future services expected to be received by the employer are commensurate with the payments or a portion of the payments to be made. If elements of both current and future services are present, only the portion applicable to the current services should be accrued.[24]

The Employee Retirement Income Security Act of 1974 (ERISA)

Until 1974, the statutes governing the creation and management of private pension plans and pension fund assets were somewhat vague and ineffective. An administrator could theoretically run a private pension fund by relying on personal judgment and intuition rather than on established standards. In order to give more protection to employees covered by private pension plans and to eliminate abuses in the management of such plans, Congress enacted the Employee Retirement Income Security Act of 1974 (ERISA), also known as the Pension Reform Act of 1974. The Act essentially attempted to protect employee pension rights through comprehensive minimum requirements for funding pension benefits, participation in the plan by employees, vesting of pension benefits, and detailed disclosure of pension plan activities. Under the Pension Reform Act of 1974, administrators of private pension plans are required to file annual reports with the Department of Labor which include a description of the plan, financial statements, and extensive supplementary schedules. Some examples of the type of information which

[24] APB Opinion No. 12, "Omnibus Opinion—1967," AICPA (New York: 1967), p. 189.

must be included in the annual report to the Department of Labor are given on page 673.

Shortly after the enactment of the Pension Reform Act of 1974, the Financial Accounting Standards Board issued *FASB Interpretation No. 3,* in which it stated that:

> A fundamental concept of *APB Opinion No. 8* is that the annual pension cost to be charged to expense for financial accounting purposes is not necessarily determined by the funding of a pension plan. Therefore, no change in the minimum and maximum limits for the annual provision for pension cost . . . is required as a result of the Act. Compliance with the Act's participation, vesting, or funding requirements may result, however, in a change in the amount of pension cost to be charged to expense periodically for financial accounting purposes even though no change in accounting methods is made. . . . *APB Opinion No. 8* requires that "the entire cost of benefit payments ultimately to be made should be charged against income subsequent to the adoption or amendment of a plan." Consistent with that requirement and within the minimum and maximum limits . . . of *APB Opinion No. 8,* any change in pension cost resulting from compliance with the Act shall enter into the determination of periodic provisions for pension expense *subsequent* to the date a plan becomes subject to the Act's participation, vesting, and funding requirements. That date will be determined either by the effective dates prescribed by the Act or by an election of earlier compliance with the requirements of the Act.[25]

The FASB also concluded that the Act did not create a legal liability for unfunded pension costs. However, if the employer company does not fund the minimum amount required by the Act and does not receive a waiver from the U.S. Secretary of the Treasury, the amount currently required to be funded shall be recognized as a liability and a charge to pension expense or deferred pension cost. Also, in the event of the termination of a pension plan, any excess of the estimated legal liability over pension fund assets had to be accrued.[26]

Presentation of pension plans in financial statements

The reporting guidelines for pension plans, as established in *APB Opinion No. 8,* are briefly summarized below:

1 A statement that a pension plan exists and a description of the employee groups covered by the pension plan.

2 A statement of the company's accounting and funding policies.

3 The amount of pension expense for the period.

4 The excess, if any, of the actuarially computed value of vested benefits over the total of the pension fund and any pension accruals in the balance sheet, less any pension prepayments or deferred charges.

5 Nature and effect of significant matters affecting comparability for all periods presented, such as changes in accounting methods, changes in actuarial as-

---

[25] *FASB Interpretation No. 3,* "Accounting for the Cost of Pension Plans Subject to the Employee Retirement Income Security Act of 1974 (an interpretation of *APB Opinion No. 8*)," FASB (Stamford: 1974), pp. 1–2.
[26] Ibid., pp. 2–3.

sumptions, or amendments to the pension plan. The effect on prior year cost of a change in the accounting method for pension cost should be applied prospectively to the current and future years, and should be disclosed.[27]

These reporting guidelines are quite limited in scope, which has led some critics to suggest that reporting of pension costs and pension funds in most cases tends to be inadequate, casual, and perhaps even misleading. At the very least, more information should be reported relative to the actuarial assumptions used in the computation of periodic pension expense, the composition of pension fund assets, and the earnings performance on pension fund assets. The Pension Reform Act of 1974 considerably expanded the pension plan disclosure requirements. Examples of the information required to be disclosed in annual reports of the pension plan (but not necessarily in the annual reports of the sponsoring company) under the Pension Reform Act of 1974 are the following:

1 Statements of pension plan assets and liabilities and changes in net assets available for the payment of pension benefits
2 Schedules of (a) pension plan investments, (b) transactions involving "parties in interest" such as officers and plan fiduciaries, (c) loans in default or exceeding 3% of the value of pension plan assets, and (d) transactions involving amounts exceeding 3% of the value of pension plan assets
3 A statement of the assets and liabilities of the trustee when pension fund assets are held in trust by a bank or insurance company
4 Statements of salaries, fees, and commissions paid by the pension plan
5 The number of employees covered by the plan, a periodic actuarial report, and an explanation of any changes of trustee, actuary, independent accountant, administrator, investment advisor, custodian, or insurance carrier

The following illustrative notes relating to pension plans are taken from the annual reports of three publicly owned corporations:

Esmark, Inc.

Pension and profit sharing plan expenses Pension expenses are accrued in amounts equal to the normal costs of the plans (including interest on the unfunded actuarial liabilities), amortization of prior service costs under certain of the plans over periods of not more than forty years, amortization of actuarial adjustments over periods of not more than twenty years and administrative expenses. The unit credit actuarial cost method is used for the major plans. Contributions to the pension trusts are made periodically in amounts authorized by the Board of Directors.

Profit sharing plan expenses are accrued in amounts equal to the stated percentages of earnings of Playtex.

Teledyne, Inc.

Pension program The total pension expense of the Corporation and its consolidated subsidiaries amounted to $969 million in 1975 and $819 million in 1974. Based on a review of the Employee Retirement Income Securitity Act of

---

[27] APB Opinion No. 8, pp. 84–85.

1974, it is expected that this law will have no material effect upon the cost of the pension plans. The actuarially computed value of vested benefits of all plans exceeded the total of pension funds, at market, and balance sheet accruals as of December 31, 1975, by about $2.9 billion.

Avon Products, Inc.

Retirement plan   Additional retirement plan expense of approximately $1,000,000 was incurred during 1976, as a result of changes in the U.S. retirement plan, which included compliance with the provisions of the Employee Retirement Income Security Act of 1974, improvements in benefits, and changes in actuarial methods and assumptions. These changes also caused an increase of approximately $13,000,000 in liability for vested benefits and $36,000,000 in unfunded prior service liability at January 1, 1976.

The liability for vested benefits under the U.S. retirement plan at December 31, 1976, exceeded the cost of the plan assets by approximately $11,800,000. The market value of the plan assets at December 31, 1976, was approximately $7,800,000 below the vested liability.

The unfunded prior service liability of all retirement plans at December 31, 1976, was approximately $45,800,000 compared with $49,900,000 at January 1, 1976.

Although much more extensive disclosure of pension plan information is made by many companies in their annual reports to stockholders, these examples are typical and satisfy current SEC and FASB requirements.

QUESTIONS

1 Define the following terms:
   a Lease
   b Sublease
   c Sale-leaseback transaction
   d Operating lease
   e Leveraged lease

2 Listed below are some terms used in *FASB Statement No. 13.* Give a short definition of each.
   a Inception of lease
   b Bargain purchase option
   c Unguaranteed residual value
   d Implicit interest rate
   e Initial direct costs

3 What are the components making up the *minimum lease payments* of a typical capital lease?

4 To be classified as a *capital lease* by the lessee, the lease must meet one of four criteria. List these four criteria.

5 Briefly describe the accounting procedures which are followed by the lessor and by the lessee for an *operating lease.*

6 Summarize the procedures followed by the lessee to account for a capital lease.

7 A **sales-type lease** (from the standpoint of the lessor) must meet one or more of the criteria of a capital lease as well as two additional criteria. What are these two special criteria?

8 Differentiate between the accounting procedures used by lessors to account for a **sales-type lease** and a **direct financing lease.**

9 What disclosures are required for leases in the financial statements of lessees?

10 What disclosures are required in the financial statements of lessors for various types of leases?

11 Ann Company leased a computer for three years at $25,000 a month, with an option to renew the lease for five years at $1,500 per month or to purchase the computer for $20,000 after the initial lease term of three years. How should this transaction be recorded in the accounts of Ann Company?

12 Ed Corporation leased an asset under a lease calling for the payment of $24,000 a year in rent. At the end of the current year, when the lease had a remaining term of 10 years, Ed Corporation subleased the asset for a rental of $36,000 a year for 10 years. When will the gain from this transaction be reported by Ed Corporation? Explain.

13 Define a **pension plan** and explain the difference between a **funded plan** and an **unfunded plan.**

14 What new funding requirements for pension costs were introduced in the Pension Reform Act of 1974?

15 What are the three main issues relating to the accounting for pension plans?

16 The total cost of contributions that must be paid ultimately to provide pensions for the present participants in a plan cannot be determined precisely in advance; however, reasonably accurate estimates can be made by the use of actuarial techniques. List some of the factors entering into the determination of the ultimate cost of a funded pension plan.

17 What is the purpose of the **minimum** and **maximum** limits established by the Accounting Principles Board in measuring the annual provision for pension expense?

18 Define each of the following in relation to the measurement of annual pension expense:
   a Normal cost
   b Past service cost, including amortization policy
   c Vested benefits
   d Interest equivalents

19 What purpose is served by **actuarial cost methods** in measuring pension expense? List two categories of actuarial cost methods which are considered acceptable for accounting purposes.

20 Define **terminal-funding** and **pay-as-you-go** methods of meeting a company's pension obligations. Why are these methods not considered acceptable?

21 Explain what is meant by **actuarial gains and losses** and describe the treatment of such gains and losses in measuring the annual provision for pension expense.

22 What were the major objectives of the Pension Reform Act of 1974 (ERISA)?

23 What information about a company's pension plan should be disclosed in financial statements according to *APB Opinion No. 8?*

24 Give some examples of the type of information required to be disclosed in the annual reports of a pension plan under the Pension Reform Act of 1974 (ERISA).

EXERCISES

Ex. 16-1 On January 2, Year 1, M Company (lessor) received a payment of $5,346 from N Company (lessee) representing an amount equivalent to the present value of three year-end rental payments of $2,000 discounted at 6%. The lease was classified as an operating lease. Carry computations to the nearest dollar.
  a Prepare journal entries to record the receipt of the $5,346 in the accounts of M Company at January 2, Year 1, and to record realized rental revenue and interest expense at December 31, Year 1. Record unearned rental revenue at net present value.
  b Prepare journal entries to record the payment of the $5,346 in the accounts of N Company at January 2, Year 1, and to record rent expense and interest revenue at December 31, Year 1. Record prepaid lease rental at net present value.

Ex. 16-2 The following information is available for a lease of a machine which is classified as a sales-type lease by the lessor and a capital lease by the lessee.

Cost of machine to lessor	$30,000
Initial payment by lessee at inception of lease	1,000
Present value of remaining 47 monthly payments of $1,000 each discounted at 1% per month	37,354

  a Record the lease (including the initial receipt of $1,000) and the receipt of the second installment of $1,000 in the accounts of the lessor. The lessor records unearned interest revenue in a separate account. Carry computations to the nearest dollar.
  b Record the lease (including the initial payment of $1,000) and the payment of the second installment of $1,000 in the accounts of the lessee. The lessee records the lease obligation at net present value. Carry computations to the nearest dollar.

Ex. 16-3 Dan Corporation leased a heavy crane to Ram, Inc., on July 1, Year 10, on the following terms:
  (1) 48 lease rentals of $1,500 at the end of each month to be paid by Ram, Inc.
  (2) The cost of the crane to Dan Corporation was $51,064.
  (3) Dan Corporation will account for this lease using the direct financing method; the difference between total rental receipts ($1,500 × 48 = $72,000) and the cost of the crane ($51,064) was computed to yield a return of $1\frac{1}{2}$% per month over the lease term.
  Prepare journal entries in the accounts of Dan Corporation (the lessor) to record the lease contract and the receipt of the first lease rental on July 31, Year 10. Record unearned interest revenue of $20,936 and carry calculations to the nearest dollar.

Ex. 16-4 On the first day of its fiscal year Orr, Inc., leased certain property to Lee Company at an annual rental of $100,000 receivable at the beginning of each year for 10 years. The first payment was received immediately. The leased property, which is new, had cost $650,000 and has an estimated economic life of 13 years and no residual value. The interest rate implicit in the lease is 8%. The present value of an annuity of 1 payable at the beginning of the period at 8% for 10 years is 7.247. Orr had no other costs associated with this lease. Orr should have accounted for this lease as a sales-type lease but mistakenly treated it as an operating lease.

Compute the effect on income before income taxes during the first year of the lease as a result of Orr's classification of this lease as an operating lease rather than as a sales-type lease.

Ex. 16-5 Mar Company retired a machine from active use on January 2, Year 5, for the express purpose of leasing it. The machine had a carrying value of $900,000 after 15 years of use and is expected to have four more years of economic life. The machine is depreciated on a straight-line basis. On March 1, Year 5, Mar Company leased the machine to Karr Company for $330,000 a year for a four-year period ending February 28, Year 9. Mar Company incurred total mainte-nance and other related costs under the provisions of the lease of $25,000 re-lating to the year ended December 31, Year 5. Karr Company paid $330,000 to Mar Company on March 1, Year 5. The lease was properly classified as an operating lease.

a Compute the income before income taxes derived by Mar Company from this lease for the year ended December 31, Year 5.

b Compute the amount of rent expense incurred by Karr Company from this lease for the year ended December 31, Year 5.

Ex. 16-6 On January 2, Year 4, Jordan Co., as lessor, leased machinery to Steven Co. for $1,000 per year for 10 years. The first payment is due on January 2, Year 4. The machinery is manufactured by Jordan Co. at a cost of $5,000 and has a list price of $6,500. Jordan Co. consistently uses an interest rate of 12% in establishing lease payment amounts. The estimated residual value of the machinery at the end of its 10 years of economic life is $1,000. The lease is not renewable but Steven Co. has an option to purchase the machinery at the end of the lease term for $1.

The present value of 1 for 10 periods at 12% per period is 0.3220.

The present value of an annuity due of 10 rents of 1 at 12% per period is 6.328.

Assume that this lease is treated as a sales-type lease by Jordan Co. Ignoring income taxes, compute the amount of gross profit which Jordan Co. should recognize at the date the lease is signed.

Ex. 16-7 Early in Year 10, Glacier Company adopted a pension plan for its employees which is to be administered by a funding agency. Unfunded past service cost was determined to be $3 million; this amount will be paid to a funding agency in 10 annual payments of $400,000, starting on December 31, Year 10. The past ser-vice cost will be amortized over a 20-year period; the amortization for Year 10 is computed at $265,000. Normal cost of the pension plan for Year 10 is $212,500; this amount is remitted to a funding agency at December 31, Year 10. Prepare a journal entry to record the foregoing information at the end of Year 10.

Ex. 16-8 Pasha Company has a contributory pension plan for all its employees. In Year 5, a total of $100,000 was withheld from employees' salaries and deposited into a pension fund administered by an outside trustee. In addition, Pasha deposited $200,000 of its own money into the fund in Year 5. Based on the report of outside actuaries which was received in December, Year 5, the actuarial cost of the pen-sion plan for Year 5 was $333,000. As a result of this report, Pasha deposited

$60,000 of its own money into the fund on January 12, Year 6. Compute the amount of pension expense to be included in Pasha's income statement for Year 5.

Ex. 16-9 The information given below relates to the past service pension cost of Delnora Company at the beginning of Year 1 when a pension plan was adopted:

Past service cost to be amortized over 10 years and funded over 20 years	$1,104,015
Annual payments at 6% sufficient to pay off a debt of $1,104,015 over 10 years	150,000
Annual payments at 6% sufficient to pay off a debt of $1,104,015 over 20 years	96,123

Prepare a partial table (similar to the one illustrated on page 670) summarizing the amortization and funding of the past service pension cost for the first two years of the pension plan.

Ex. 16-10 Using the data in the partial table prepared in Exercise 16-9, prepare the required journal entries for Years 1 and 2 and indicate the information that would appear in the balance sheet at the end of Year 2 relative to the past service pension cost.

SHORT CASES FOR ANALYSIS AND DECISION

Case 16-1 Wright Aircraft Company manufactures small single- and multiple-engine aircraft primarily for sale to individuals, flying clubs, and corporations. Wright is one of the pioneers in the industry and has developed a reputation as a leader in small-craft engineering and marketing innovations.

During the last few years Wright has leased profitably an increasing number of its aircraft to flying clubs. The leasing activity currently represents a significant portion of Wright's annual volume. Details of the leasing arrangements with flying clubs follow:

(1) The flying club signs a long-term lease agreement with Wright for the aircraft.
(2) The lease has a noncancelable term of six to eighteen years, depending on the aircraft's economic life. The lease term is set to be three-fourths of the normal economic life of the aircraft leased.
(3) The club is required to deposit with Wright an amount equal to 10% of the total lease rental for the term of the lease. The deposit is not refundable, but it is used in lieu of rent during last one-tenth of the lease term.
(4) A bank lends Wright an amount equal to the remaining 90% of the total lease rental, after deducting a discount of 14% per year. The net discounted amount is paid immediately to Wright. The bank-loan agreement requires Wright to use the lease rental payments from the flying club to pay off the loan to the bank.
(5) As a condition for the loan, the bank requires Wright to insure the leased aircraft for an amount equal to the loan.
(6) The flying club signs Wright's bank-loan agreement as a surety, thus obligating itself if Wright should default on the loan.
(7) When the bank loan is paid in full at the end of the lease term, the flying club may purchase the aircraft and receive title to it by paying Wright $100.

Instructions Discuss the criteria and other aspects of Wright's leasing activities which it should consider in determining whether to account for its flying club leases as operating leases or as sales-type leases. In your discussion, identify criteria which are clearly met in the facts presented in the question. For criteria which are **not** clearly met, indicate what additional information is needed to reach a conclusion with respect to each criterion.

Case 16-2 Atlantis Airlines recently purchased eight jetliners for a total cost of $180 million. It plans to depreciate the jets using the sum-of-the-years'-digits method over a 12-year period. It is estimated that the jets will have a resale value of $24 million at the end of 12 years. To finance the acquisition of the jets, Atlantis Airlines borrowed $180 million, payable at the rate of $20 million per year plus interest at 8% on the unpaid balance. The first payment is due one year after the loan is arranged.

Tripoli Airlines leased eight jetliners of the same type purchased by Atlantis Airlines for a 12-year period. Tripoli Airlines does not have an option to buy the jets at the end of the lease term and it classified the lease as an operating lease. Lease rentals are $22 million per year, payable at the end of each year. The lease rentals do not include property taxes, insurance, and maintenance of the jetliners; Tripoli Airlines pays all such expenses. The annual rental was computed to give the lessor slightly less than 8% return on investment, taking into account the $24 million resale value of the jets at the end of the 12-year lease period. The lease is noncancelable.

Instructions
a Prepare a schedule of annual expenses (depreciation and interest) for Atlantis Airlines in connection with the ownership of the eight jetliners. How do annual expenses for Atlantis Airlines compare with the annual lease rental incurred by Tripoli Airlines? What is the significance of the difference?
b Show the amounts relating to the jets and the related loan that would appear in the balance sheet of Atlantis Airlines at the end of the first year. In what respect is the balance sheet for Tripoli Airlines different?
c Do you believe that the classification of the lease as an operating lease by Tripoli Airlines was in conformity with the provisions of *FASB Statement No. 13?* State specific reasons for your conclusion.

Case 16-3 Pension plans have developed in an environment characterized by a complex interaction of social concepts, legal considerations, actuarial techniques, income tax laws, and accounting practices. *APB Opinion No. 8* delineates acceptable accounting practices for the cost of pension plans.

Instructions
a The following terms are relevant to accounting for the cost of pension plans. Define or explain briefly each of the following:
  (1) Normal cost
  (2) Past service cost
  (3) Prior service cost
  (4) Funded plan
  (5) Vested benefits
  (6) Actuarial gains and losses
  (7) Interest
b Identify the disclosures required in financial statements regarding a company's pension plan.

Case 16-4 Liberty, Inc., a calendar-year corporation, adopted a company pension plan at the beginning of Year 4. This plan is to be funded and noncontributory. Liberty used an appropriate actuarial cost method to determine its normal annual pension cost for Year 4 and Year 5 as $15,000 and $16,000, respectively, which was paid in the same year.

Liberty's actuarially determined past service costs were funded on December 31, Year 4, at an amount properly computed as $106,000. These past service costs are to be amortized at the maximum amount permitted by generally accepted accounting standards. The interest factor assumed by the actuary is 6%.

Instructions Prepare journal entries to record the funding of past service costs on December 31, Year 4, and the pension expenses for the Years 4 and 5. Under each journal entry, give the reasoning to support your entry. Round all amounts to the nearest dollar.

Case 16-5 On January 2, Year 8, the board of directors of Sammy Dong & Company approved the establishment of a pension plan for all employees. The pension is payable to employees when they reach age sixty-five if they have had three or more years of continuous service with the company. All employees currently on the payroll are eligible, thus requiring the recognition of past service cost over an appropriate number of years, starting in Year 8. The company was organized early in Year 1,

A summary of the active employees as of January 2, Year 8, who are eligible to participate in the pension plan is presented below:

Number of employees	Years of service as of Jan. 2, Year 8
20	7
18	6
32	5
25	4
40	3
45	2
20	1
200	

A partial list of benefits to be paid to retired employees on the basis of average annual earnings and the number of years of employment appears below:

Average annual earnings	Monthly pension benefits based on years of employment		
	3 years	10 years	25 years
$10,500	$30	$120	$360
12,000	40	160	480
13,500	50	200	600
16,000	60	240	720

The company plans to amortize and fund any past service cost over a 10-year period.

Instructions
a List some assumptions that would have to be made in computing the company's liability for past service cost at January 2, Year 8.
b List some additional facts that would be required to compute the liability for past service cost at January 2, Year 8.
c In reference to the work force of 200 employees at January 2, Year 8, what factors might cause the normal pension cost for Year 13 to increase over the normal pension cost for Year 8? What factors might cause the normal pension cost in Year 13 to be less than the normal pension cost in Year 8?

PROBLEMS

Group A

16A-1 On July 1, Year 4, Lesso Corporation leased equipment to See Corporation. The equipment had been carried by Lesso Corporation in the Inventory account at a cost of $225,000. Both corporations are on a June 30 fiscal year. There were no other significant costs associated with the lease and no residual guarantee by the lessee. Both the lessor and the lessee appropriately accounted for this transaction as a sales-type lease. The lease is for a noncancelable term of eight years, with $50,000 rent payable at the beginning of each fiscal year; title passes to See Corporation at the end of the lease term. See Corporation made the first payment on July 1, Year 4. The implicit interest rate is 10% and the present value of an annuity due of eight rents of 1 at 10% is 5.868419. The equipment is expected to have an economic life of 11 years, no residual value, and will be depreciated on a straight-line basis.

Instructions (Carry all computations to nearest dollar.)
a Prepare the journal entry for Lesso Corporation on July 1, Year 4, to record the lease transaction as a sales-type lease. Include the first lease payment in the journal entry and record the lease receivables net of the unearned interest revenue.
b Prepare the journal entry for Lesso Corporation on June 30 Year 5, to accrue interest for one year. Record the accrued interest in the Lease Receivables (net) account.
c Prepare the journal entry for Lesso Corporation on July 1, Year 4, to record the lease transaction, but for this part of the problem **assume that the transaction was classified as an operating lease.**
d Compute the expenses relative to the lease for See Corporation (lessee) for the fiscal year ending June 30, Year 5, assuming that it classified the lease (1) as an operating lease, and (2) as a capital lease.

16A-2 On January 2, Year 1, Ahead Racing, Inc., leased a "Formula-1" racing car from Formula Leasing Company. The fixed noncancelable term of the lease was 24 months, with an option to renew month by month based on a schedule of rentals and guarantees of the residual value which decrease over time. The cost, fair value, and estimated economic life of the racing car are listed below:

Lessor's cost of racing car (carried in Racing Equipment account of lessor)	$116,070
Fair value of racing car at inception of lease (Jan. 2, Year 1)	$116,070
Estimated economic life	36 months

The lease specified that Ahead Racing, Inc., will pay $4,125 on the first of each month and that it will guarantee a residual value of $35,000 to Formula Leasing Company at the end of 24 months (December 31, Year 2).

The lessee is to receive any excess over the guaranteed amount at the end of the lease term. Collectibility of lease rentals was reasonably assured and no unreimbursable costs were expected to be incurred by the lessor. The rentals were deemed to be fair and the residual value guarantee was expected to approximate actual realizable value. Ahead Racing, Inc., depreciates other racing cars it owns on a straight-line basis and its incremental borrowing rate generally is 1% per month, which is also the rate implicit in the lease. At the end of the lease term, December 31, Year 2, the racing car was sold by Formula Leasing Company for $39,500. The excess of proceeds received over the guaranteed residual value was paid to Ahead Racing, Inc.

Instructions
a How should this lease be classified by the lessor and the lessee? Explain in

terms of criteria required by **FASB Statement No. 13.** Use Appendix A to compute the present value of minimum lease payments.

b Prepare the journal entries required at the inception of the lease in the accounts of (1) the lessor and (2) the lessee. Prepare separate entries to record the lease and the first lease rental.

c Prepare the journal entry or entries required at the end of the lease term in the accounts of (1) the lessor and (2) the lessee. Assume that entries to record depreciation, interest revenue, or interest expense have been recorded on December 31, Year 2.

16A-3 Derrick Company leased equipment with an estimated economic life of 12 years to User Company for a period of 10 years. The normal selling price of the equipment was $288,256, and the unguaranteed residual value at the end of the lease term was estimated to be $20,000. User Company agreed to pay annual rentals of $40,000 at the beginning of each year and was responsible for all maintenance, insurance, and property taxes. Derrick Company incurred costs of $205,000 in manufacturing the equipment and $4,000 in negotiating and closing the lease. The collectibility of the lease payments was reasonably assured and no additional costs were expected to be incurred by Derrick Company. The implicit interest rate for Derrick Company was 9% per year and was known to User Company.

Instructions (Use Appendix A to obtain present values of 1 at 9%.)

a How should this lease be classified by Derrick Company? Explain.

b Assuming that Derrick Company classified this lease as a sales-type lease, compute the following at the inception of the lease:
(1) Gross investment in the lease
(2) Net investment in the lease
(3) Unearned interest revenue
(4) Selling price of the equipment
(5) Cost of goods sold (cost of equipment less present value of the unguaranteed residual value)

c Prepare a table summarizing the amortization of the net investment in the lease and the recognition of interest revenue over the lease term for Derrick Company.

d Prepare the journal entries for the first year of the lease in the accounts of Derrick Company.

16A-4 Chip Higgins & Co. (lessee) entered into a five-year noncancelable lease, with four renewal options of one year each, for machinery having an estimated economic life of 10 years and a fair value of $370,000 to the lessor (Paula Associates) at the inception date of the lease. The lessor's implicit interest rate is not available to Chip Higgins & Co. The company has an incremental borrowing rate of 1% per month and uses the straight-line method to depreciate plant assets. The lease contains the following provisions:

(1) Rental payments of $5,300 per month, including $300 for property taxes, payable at the beginning of the month. The lessee pays all insurance and maintenance on the machinery.

(2) A guarantee by the lessee of the lessor's seven-year bank loan obtained to finance the construction of the machinery.

(3) A termination penalty assuring renewal of the lease for a period of two years after the expiration of the loan guarantee.

(4) An option allowing the lessor to extend the lease for one year beyond the last renewal option exercised by the lessee.

(5) A guarantee by the lessee that the lessor will realize $5,000 from selling the machinery at the expiration of the lease.

Computations relevant to this lease are presented on page 683.

Lease term

Noncancelable period of lease	5 years
Additional period of debt guarantee	2
Additional period for which termination penalty assures renewal	2
Period covered by lessor's extension option	_1_
Lease term per **FASB Statement No. 13**	10 years

Minimum lease payments

Monthly rental less executory costs ($5,300 − $300)	$ 5,000
Lease term in months	×120
Subtotal	$600,000
Add: Residual guarantee	5,000
Total minimum lease payments	$605,000

Present value of minimum lease payments

Present value of annuity due of 120 monthly rents of $5,000 at 1% per month:

$5,000 × 70.3975	$351,988

Add: Present value of residual guarantee of $5,000 discounted at 1% per

month for 120 months: $5,000 × 0.3030	1,515
Total present value of minimum lease payments	$353,503

Lease obligation amortization on yearly basis

Year	Annual net rental payments (1)	Annual interest expense (2)	Lease obligation at end of year
Present value at inception			$353,503
1	$60,000	$40,786	334,289
2	60,000	38,349	312,638
3	60,000	35,605	288,243
4	60,000	32,509	260,752
5	60,000	29,023	229,775
6	60,000	25,095	194,870
7	60,000	20,668	155,538
8	60,000	15,679	111,217
9	60,000	10,059	61,276
10	60,000	3,724	5,000 (3)

(1) ($5,300 − $300) × 12 = $60,000
(2) Computed monthly
(3) Guaranteed residual value

The lease is a capital lease for Chip Higgins & Co. because its term of 10 years exceeds 75% of the estimated economic life (10 years) of the machinery and because the present value of the minimum lease payments of $353,503 exceeds $333,000 (90% of the $370,000 fair value of the machinery).

Instructions

a Prepare journal entries in the accounts of Chip Higgins & Co. to record (1) the lease at the beginning of Year 1, (2) aggregate rental payments for the first year (one entry), and (3) depreciation at the end of Year 1. (Assume that lessee will not realize anything from the sale of the machinery at the end of the 10-year lease term.)

b Prepare a table to compare the annual expenses for Chip Higgins & Co. relating to this capital lease with the annual costs that would be recognized if the lease were treated as an operating lease. Give the pre-tax effect on income as a result of treating the lease as a capital lease rather than an operating lease.

(Adapted from **Financial Reporting Developments,** "Accounting for Leases," published by Ernst & Ernst: 1977, pp. 13–16).

16A-5 On April 1, Year 5, Mori Corporation signed a five-year, noncancelable lease with San Jose Mfg. Corporation. The leased equipment was designed to meet the unique needs of Mori Corporation. Annual rent of $10,000 is payable in advance, starting on April 1, Year 5. The lease contract gave the lessee an option to purchase the equipment on March 31, Year 10, for $1, and is classified as a sales-type lease by the lessor and a capital lease by the lessee.

The estimated economic life of the equipment is 10 years, and management of Mori Corporation estimated that the residual value of the equipment at the end of its economic life will approximate the dismantling and removal costs. The straight-line method of depreciation is used by Mori Corporation, and its fiscal year ends on March 31.

The borrowing rate for Mori Corporation on April 1, Year 5, is 10% a year. The present value of an annuity due of five annual payments of 1 at 10% is 4.169865. San Jose Mfg. Corporation also considers 10% a year to be a fair rate of interest.

Instructions

a Prepare a summary of lease payments and lessee's interest expense (similar to the illustration on page 654) for the lease described above.

b Prepare journal entries for Mori Corporation (lessee) relating to the lease for the fiscal year ended March 31, Year 6. Record the lease obligation net of deferred interest.

c Assuming that the equipment is carried in the accounts of San Jose Mfg. Corporation (lessor) in the Inventory of Equipment account at $36,500, prepare a journal entry to record the lease in the accounts of San Jose Mfg. Corporation. Record lease receivables net of unearned interest revenue and include the receipt of the initial rental as part of your journal entry.

16A-6 Vista Palace, Incorporated, adopted a pension plan early in Year 4 and has regularly funded the full amount of its current pension expense. At the time the pension plan was adopted, the past service pension liability amounted to $1,472,020. The company has been amortizing the past service cost over a 15-year period and depositing $200,000 annually with a funding agency. The annual deposits are intended to provide an amount, plus interest at 6%, at the end of 10 years to enable the funding agency to pay the accrued past service pension liability when employees retire. Pertinent pension plan data for Year 6 and Year 7 are presented below:

	Year 6	Year 7
Normal pension expense	$380,200	$410,500
Past service cost:		
Amortization on 15-year basis	151,564	151,564
Interest at 6% on deferred pension cost	5,987	9,252
Annual payments to funding agency	200,000	200,000

Instructions

a Prepare journal entries to record the normal and past service pension expense for Year 6 and Year 7. Record normal and past service costs in a single Pension Expense account.

b Compute the balance in the Deferred Pension Cost account at the end of Year 7. (*Hint:* Remember that the plan was adopted in Year 4.)

16A-7 Actuaries have estimated the past service pension liability of Festus Corporation at the date it adopted its pension plan at $1,578,846. The actuaries estimate that 6% is a reasonable earnings rate on fund investments. The company plans to recognize the past service cost over 20 years, and to fund it over the next 30 years. The equal annual payment which will amortize $1,578,846 over 20 years at 6% is $137,650 ($1,578,846 ÷ 11.470, present value of 1 per year for 20 years at 6%); over 30 years it is $114,700 ($1,578,846 ÷ 13.765, present value of 1 per year for 30 years at 6%). The following partial table has been prepared:

Year	(A) 20-year amortization at 6%	(B) Add interest (6% of previous balance in E)	(C) Debit to Pension Expense (A + B)	(D) 30-year funding	(E) Accrued Pension Liability account*
1	$137,650	$ –0–	$137,650	$114,700	$ 22,950
2	137,650	1,377	139,027	114,700	47,277
20	137,650	46,461	184,111	114,700	844,203
21	–0–	50,652	50,652	114,700	780,155
29	–0–	12,617	12,617	114,700	108,208
30	–0–	6,492	6,492	114,700	–0–

* The previous year's balance in the Accrued Pension Liability account plus the difference between the pension expense and the payment to the funding agency for the current year.

Instructions

a Prepare journal entries to record the amortization and the funding of past service pension cost for Years 1, 2, 21, and 30.

b Assuming the same liability for past service cost ($1,578,846), amortization over 30 years, and funding over 20 years, the following partial table has been prepared:

Year	(A) 30-year amortization at 6%	(B) Less interest (6% of previous balance in E)	(C) Debit to Pension Expense (A – B)	(D) 20-year funding	(E) Balance in Deferred Pension Cost account*
1	$114,700	$ –0–	$114,700	$137,650	$ 22,950
2	114,700	1,377	113,323	137,650	47,277
20	114,700	46,461	68,239	137,650	844,203
21	114,700	50,652	64,048	–0–	780,155
29	114,700	12,617	102,083	–0–	108,208
30	114,700	6,492	108,208	–0–	–0–

* The previous year's balance in the Deferred Pension Cost account plus the difference between the payment to the funding agency and the pension expense for the current year.

Prepare journal entries to record the amortization and the funding of past service pension cost for Years 1, 2, 21, and 30.

c Explain the balance of $844,203 in the Deferred Pension Cost account at the end of Year 20 as presented in part **b** of the problem. (**Hint:** The present value of an ordinary annuity of 10 rents of 1 at 6% = 7.3601.)

(Adapted from Haskins & Sells CPA Preparation Course)

Group B

16B-1 Cannon, Inc., was incorporated in Year 1 to operate as a computer software service firm with a fiscal year ending August 31. Cannon's primary product is a sophisticated on-line inventory control system; its customers pay a fixed fee plus a usage charge for using the system.

Cannon has leased a large, BIG-I computer system from the manufacturer. The lease calls for a monthly rental of $30,000 for the 144 months (12 years) of the lease term. The estimated economic life of the computer is 15 years.

Each scheduled monthly rental payment includes $5,000 for the full-service maintenance on the computer to be performed by the manufacturer. All rentals are payable on the first day of the month beginning with August 1, Year 2, the date the computer was installed and the lease agreement was signed.

The lease is noncancelable for its 12-year term, and it is secured only by the manufacturer's chattel lien on the BIG-I system. On any anniversary date of the lease after August Year 7, Cannon may purchase the BIG-I system from the manufacturer at 75% of the then current fair value of the computer.

This lease is to be accounted for as a capital lease by Cannon, and it will be depreciated by the straight-line method with no expected residual value. Borrowed funds for this type of transaction would cost Cannon 12% per year (1% per month). Following is a schedule of the present value of 1 for selected periods discounted at 1% per period when payments are made at the beginning of each period.

Periods (months)	Present value of 1 per period discounted at 1% per period
1	1.000
2	1.990
3	2.970
143	76.658
144	76.899

Instructions Prepare, in general journal form, all entries Cannon should have made in its accounting records during August, Year 2, relating to this lease. Give full explanations and show supporting computations for each entry. Remember, August 31, Year 2, is the end of Cannon's fiscal accounting period and it will be preparing financial statements on that date. **Do not prepare closing entries.**

16B-2 Rocky Star Disco entered into a lease on April 1, Year 1, for the "ultimate sound system" from Big Sound Leasing Co. The fixed noncancelable term of the lease is four years with an option to renew at terms which represent expected fair value at the option date. The following information is available:

Cost of sound system to Big Sound Leasing Co. (carried in Inventory account) $19,996

Fair value of sound system at inception of lease $19,996

Estimated economic life of sound system . . . . 4 years

The lease specifies that Rocky Star Disco will pay $489 on the first of each month and that it will guarantee a residual value of $2,000 to Big Sound Leasing Co. at the end of 48 months. Rocky Star Disco is to receive any excess over the $2,000 guarantee at the end of the lease term.

The collectibility of the lease rentals is reasonably assumed and no unreimbursable costs are yet to be incurred. The rentals are deemed to be fair and the residual value guarantee is expected to approximate actual realizable value at the end of the lease term. Rocky Star Disco depreciates its other assets on a straight-line basis and has an incremental borrowing rate of 15% compounded monthly. The interest rate implicit in the lease is 1% per month and is known to Rocky Star Disco.

At the end of the lease term the sound system was sold by Big Sound Leasing Co. for $1,730 and the excess of the residual guarantee over the proceeds on sale was paid by Rocky Star Disco to Big Sound Leasing Co.

Instructions

a How should this lease be classified by the lessor and the lessee? Explain your conclusion in terms of the classification criteria required by **FASB Statement No. 13.** Use Appendix A to compute the present value of minimum lease payments.

b Prepare the journal entries required at the inception of the lease in the accounts of (1) Big Sound Leasing Co. and (2) Rocky Star Disco. Include the first lease rental in the entry to record the lease. Assume that the lessor records lease receivables at the "gross" amount and that the lessee records the lease obligation "net" of deferred interest.

c Prepare the journal entry or entries required at the termination of the lease in the accounts of (1) Big Sound Leasing Co. and (2) Rocky Star Disco. Assume that entries to record depreciation, interest revenue, or interest expense have been recorded on March 31, Year 5.

16B-3 On December 31, Year 0, Mimi Hermosa Company leased dredging equipment to Serbian Underground Industries. The equipment had a cost and fair value of $278,158. The term of the lease was for seven years with a $50,000 payment due at December 31 starting in Year 0. The unguaranteed residual value was estimated at $30,000 at the end of the lease term and the estimated economic life of the equipment was nine years. The terms were designed to give Mimi Hermosa Company a 10% annual rate of return on its net investment (including initial direct costs).

The lessee agreed to pay all property taxes, insurance, and maintenance; the lessor paid a commission of $5,000 to a broker for arranging the lease. Collectibility of the lease payments was reasonably assured and there were no additional costs to be incurred by the lessor.

Instructions   (Use Appendix A to obtain any present values of 1 at 10% which you may need to complete the following requirements.)

a How should this lease be classified by Mimi Hermosa Company? Explain.

b Assuming that Mimi Hermosa Company classified this lease as a direct financing lease and that initial direct costs are included in the gross investment in the lease, compute the following at the inception of the lease:
  (1) Gross investment in the lease
  (2) Unearned interest revenue on the lease
  (3) Net investment in the lease

c Prepare a table summarizing the amortization of the net investment in the lease and the recognition of interest revenue over the lease term for Mimi Hermosa Company.

d Prepare the journal entries in the accounts of Mimi Hermosa Company on December 31, Year 0, and on December 31, Year 1, relating to this lease.

16B-4 In Year 1, Roadking Company negotiated and closed a long-term lease contract for newly constructed truck terminals and freight storage facilities. The buildings were erected to the company's specifications on land owned by the company. On January 2, Year 2, Roadking Company took possession of the leased properties.

Although the terminals have a composite economic life of 40 years, the noncancelable lease runs for 20 years from January 2, Year 2, with a favorable purchase option available upon expiration of the lease. You have determined that the leased properties and related obligation should be accounted for as a capital lease by Roadking Company.

The 20-year lease is effective for the period January 2, Year 2, through December 31, Year 21. Advance rental payments of $1,000,000 are payable to the lessor on January 2 of each of the first 10 years of the lease term. Advance rental payments of $300,000 are due on January 2 for each of the last 10 years of the lease. The company has an option to purchase all these leased facilities for $1 on December 31, Year 21. It also must make annual payments to the lessor of $95,000 for property taxes and $155,000 for insurance; these payments also are due on January 2. The lease was negotiated to assure the lessor a 6% rate of return.

Instructions (Round all computations to the nearest dollar.)

a Prepare a schedule to compute for Roadking Company the discounted present value of the terminal facilities and related obligation at January 2, Year 2.

b Assuming that the discounted present value of terminal facilities and related obligation at January 2, Year 2, was $9,108,620, prepare journal entries for Roadking Company to record the:
  (1) Lease transaction and the payment to the lessor on January 2, Year 2 (separate entries). Record executory costs in expense accounts.
  (2) Depreciation of the leased properties for Year 2, using the straight-line method and assuming a zero residual value. Use an Accumulated Depreciation account.
  (3) Accrual of interest expense at December 31, Year 2, using the effective interest method. Accrue interest for a full year and record it in Accrued Interest Payable.
  (4) Payment to the lessor on January 2, Year 3.
  Selected present value factors are as follows:

Periods	For an ordinary annuity of 1 at 6%	For 1 at 6%
1	.943396	.943396
2	1.833393	.889996
8	6.209794	.627412
9	6.801692	.591898
10	7.360087	.558395
19	11.158116	.330513
20	11.469921	.311805

16B-5 Gunsmoke Chemicals, Inc., fully funds the current portion of its pension expense. When the company started its pension plan early in Year 1, it adopted a 10-year amortization period and a 12-year funding period for the past service cost of $350,000. The data on page 689 relate to the pension plan for Years 1–3:

	Year 1	Year 2	Year 3
Normal pension expense	$100,000	$103,900	$110,100
Past service cost:			
Amortization on 10-year basis	43,152	43,152	43,152
Interest at 4% on accrued pension liability . .	–0–	234	478
Annual payments to funding agency	37,293	37,293	37,293

Instructions
a Prepare journal entries to record the normal and past service pension expenses for the three-year period. Record normal and past service costs in a single Pension Expense account.
b Compute the amount of the accrued pension liability at the end of Year 3.

16B-6 Crete Company adopted a pension plan effective January 1, Year 5. Actuaries had determined that the past service pension liability applicable to active employees who were included in the pension plan was approximately $1,869,330. The company arranged to fund the past service pension cost by making 10 equal payments to a funding agency at the end of each year starting December 31, Year 5. The fund earns interest at 5% per year and past service pension cost is amortized over a 20-year period.

Instructions
a Compute the annual amortization amounts and the annual payments to the funding agency. The present value of an ordinary annuity of 20 annual payments of 1 at 5% is 12.462210 (see Table 4 in Appendix A); the present value of an ordinary annuity of 10 annual payments of 1 at 5% is 7.721735 (see Table 4 in Appendix A). Carry computations to the nearest dollar.
b Prepare a partial amortization and funding table (similar to the table illustrated on page 669) for the first four years of the pension plan.
c Prepare journal entries for Year 5 and Year 6 to record the amortization and funding of the past service pension cost.

16B-7 Dillon Corporation adopted a pension plan early in Year 5. The plan was to be administered by an insurance company and stipulated that the payments by Dillon Corporation to the insurance company would consist of three parts as follows:

(1) Annual payments of $10,000 beginning on January 2, Year 5, and ending on January 2, Year 14, covering the past service cost for qualified employees. These payments are to be adjusted periodically by mutual agreement because of changes in pension benefits to be paid to employees or because of separation from service of employees whose rights are forfeited. An interest rate of 6% per year was used in computing the amount of the annual payments.
(2) Payments for current service (normal) costs based on the number of employees, their birth dates, and the earnings rate that the insurance company is able to earn on the pension fund investments. These payments will be based on payroll data for the latest year and will be paid in two installments as follows: $25,000 on June 30 of each year and the balance (as determined at December 31 of each year) on January 5 of the following year.
(3) Payments for supplemental adjustments agreed upon by the insurance company and Dillon Corporation.

The payments made to the insurance company during the first three years of the pension plan are listed on page 690.

	Past service cost	**Current service (normal) costs**	
Year	**Jan. 2**	**Jan. 5**	**June 30**
5	$10,000	$ –0–	$25,000
6	10,000	27,010	25,000
7	10,000	29,460	25,000

Payments by the insurance company to retired employees for the first three years were: Year 5, $7,390; Year 6, $9,177; and Year 7, $12,380.

The management of Dillon Corporation considers the past service cost to be a legal obligation and wishes to follow the requirement of *APB Opinion No. 8* regarding the accounting for this cost, that is, "If the company has a legal obligation for pension cost in excess of amounts paid or accrued, the excess should be shown in the balance sheet as both a liability and a deferred charge." Current service (normal) costs are accrued only at the end of the fiscal year, which is the calendar year.

Instructions

a Prepare a partial amortization and funding table for the past service cost for Year 5 and Year 6. Assume that the present value of the 10 annual payments of $10,000 each, beginning on January 2, Year 5, and earning interest at 6% per year, is approximately $78,017. Dillon Corporation records $10,000 in Past Service Pension Expense each year.

b Prepare journal entries in the accounts of Dillon Corporation relating to the pension plan for Year 5 and Year 6.

c How should the information relating to the pension plan appear in the balance sheet for Dillon Corporation at December 31, Year 6?

CHAPTER 17

CORPORATIONS: PAID-IN CAPITAL

One of the striking features of our economy is the dominant role played by the business corporation. Corporations are responsible for the great bulk of our national output of goods and services; they are also the principal source of employment, a major medium for the investment of capital, and a leading factor in the research and development activities which are so rapidly altering our economy.

Efficiency of production and distribution in many industries require more capital than can be obtained by a single proprietor or a partnership. The large amounts of capital needed for successful entry into many fields of business are most easily acquired by selling stock (units of corporate ownership) to the public. The corporation has reached its present dominant role largely because of its efficiency as a device for concentration of capital. Because the typical business corporation has numerous stockholders who do not participate directly in management, complete accounting and internal control systems are of critical importance as a means of protecting the interests of these many absentee owners.

Several specific advantages of the corporate form of organization help explain why corporations are so successful in attracting capital. Among these advantages are the following:

1 *Limited liability.* A stockholder has no personal liability for the debts of the corporation. Creditors can look for payment only to the corporation itself and not to the personal resources of the owners. Freedom from personal liability is an important factor in encouraging both large and small investors to acquire stock in corporations.

2 *Liquidity of investments in corporate securities.* The owners of corporate securities (especially securities listed on a stock exchange) can sell all or part of their investment for cash at any time. The high liquidity of investments in securities is a major reason for their popularity.

3 *Continuity of existence.* The corporation is a separate legal entity with unlimited life, whereas a partnership may be terminated by the death or retirement of any one of the partners.

4 *Separation of the functions of management and ownership.* By attracting capital from a large number of investors and selecting management on a basis of executive ability, the corporation achieves expert direction of large amounts of economic and human resources.

Structure of the corporation

To form a corporation, one or more incorporators submit an application to the corporation commissioner or other designated official of a state government. The application identifies the incorporators, states the nature of the business, and describes the capital stock to be issued. After payment of an incorporation fee and approval of the application, *articles of incorporation* are issued by the state as evidence of the legal existence of the corporation. The incorporators, who must also be subscribers to shares of the corporation's stock, may now elect a *board of directors* and approve *bylaws* to serve as general guides to the operation of the corporation. The board of directors appoints officers to serve as active managers of the business. Corporate officers usually include a president, one or more vice-presidents responsible for such areas as manufacturing, sales, and industrial relations, a treasurer, a controller, and a secretary. The organization process is completed by issuing to the subscribers stock certificates evidencing their ownership of the corporation.

The corporate form of organization is not limited to stock companies organized for profit. The term *public corporation* is applied to government-owned units (such as the Federal Deposit Insurance Corporation), whereas the term *private corporation* includes all companies which are privately owned. Within the meaning of *private corporation* are both the *nonstock* corporations (churches, universities, and hospitals which are not organized for profit) and *stock* companies which operate to earn a profit and which issue shares of stock to the owners. In this book our attention is focused on the profit-oriented stock company. Within this group, one can also recognize subgroups such as *close corporations* with stock held by a small number of owners (perhaps a family), and *open corporations* with stock available for purchase by the public. Open corporations may be *listed* (traded on an organized stock exchange) or *over-the-counter* (a market in which securities dealers buy from and sell to the public). Listed corporations are also often referred to as *publicly owned* companies because the number of shareholders often runs into the hundreds of thousands. These large corporate enterprises with capital gathered from the public are to a considerable extent responsible for the present-day importance of financial statements and financial reporting.

Although the laws governing the formation and operation of a stock corporation vary among the several states, these state laws all emphasize certain basic concepts. Every state recognizes the corporation as a separate entity and provides for the issuance of shares of capital stock as units of ownership.

Elements of corporate capital

The word *capital* is used in a variety of meanings; consequently, accountants have developed the following more specific terms to describe important elements of corporate capital.

1 *Stated capital or legal capital.* Stated or legal capital is that portion of the stockholders' equity which the statutes require to be held in the business for the protection of creditors, as opposed to capital which is available for the declaration of dividends to owners.

2 *Paid-in capital.* Paid-in capital is that portion of the stockholders' equity which was invested or paid in by the stockholders, as opposed to capital arising from profitable operations. It includes legal capital.

3 *Stockholders' equity or proprietary capital.* Stockholders' equity represents the combined total of paid-in capital and all other increments in capital from profitable operations or other sources. It is the total equity of the owners.

4 *Enterprise capital.* Enterprise capital represents the combined interests of the stockholders and the creditors. It represents the total resources under the control of corporate management.

Components of stockholders' equity

The balance sheets of corporations show considerable variation in the terms applied to the different elements of stockholders' equity; in fact, it is unusual to find two balance sheets with identical wording. However the following classification illustrates the underlying theme of classification by source.

1 Paid-in capital
    a Capital stock, shown at the par or stated value
        (1) Preferred stock
        (2) Common stock
    b Paid-in capital in excess of par or stated value. Includes amounts paid in by owners in excess of the par or stated value of shares issued. (Formerly called *capital surplus,* which is becoming an outmoded term.[1]) In a few cases, includes amounts donated by non-

---

[1] The 1976 edition of *Accounting Trends & Techniques,* published by the American Institute of Certified Public Accountants, indicates a continuing decline in the use of *capital surplus.* The Committee on Terminology of the AICPA had previously recommended: "The use of the term *surplus* (whether standing alone or in such combination as *capital surplus, paid-in surplus, appraisal surplus,* etc.) be discontinued."

owners, such as a donation by a city to induce a corporation to establish a factory in the area.

2 Retained earnings. Represents the accumulated earnings of the corporation since the date of incorporation minus any losses and minus all dividends distributed to stockholders. (The older term **earned surplus** has largely disappeared, in accordance with the recommendation of the AICPA.) A portion of retained earnings may be appropriated, thus labeling it as unavailable for declaration of dividends. These appropriations are becoming much less common than in the past.

3 Unrealized appreciation in value of productive assets; and unrealized loss in value of noncurrent investments. An unrealized element of stockholders' equity arises when assets are written up to a valuation in excess of historical cost. Such upward revaluations are difficult to support except in unusual circumstances because of the current policy of adhering to historical cost for valuation of assets. Consequently, capital increments from appraisal increases are seldom encountered in published financial statements. It is more common to find an unrealized decrease in stockholders' equity in published financial statements. As explained in Chapter 11, such an unrealized decrease results from the decline in the market value of the equity securities (other than those accounted for by the equity method) held in a noncurrent investment portfolio.

Rights associated with stock ownership

If a corporation has only one class of capital stock, stockholders usually have certain basic rights to be exercised in proportion to the number of shares they own. These rights include: (1) a right to vote for directors and thus to be represented in management, (2) a right to share in dividends declared by the board of directors, (3) a preemptive right to purchase additional shares in proportion to one's present holdings in the event that the corporation increases the amount of stock outstanding, and (4) a right to share in the distribution of cash or other assets if the corporation is liquidated. Variations in these rights are of course encountered in individual cases. For example, the preemptive right attached to existing shares may prove inconvenient to a corporation interested in acquiring other companies by issuance of additional stock. Consequently, this preemptive right has been eliminated (with the approval of stockholders) by many corporations.

Common stock and preferred stock

When only one type of capital stock is issued, it has the basic rights described above and is called **common stock.** However, many corporations, in an effort to appeal to all types of investors, offer two or more classes of capital stock with different rights or priorities attached to each class. Stock that carries certain preferences over the common stock, such as a prior claim on dividends, is called *preferred stock.* Often a preferred stock conveys no voting rights or only limited voting rights to the holders. The characteristics of preferred stocks vary widely among companies; it is unsafe, therefore, to assume that a preferred stock has any particular rights or priorities without positive determination of its status. The special rights of a particular preferred stock are set forth in the articles of incorporation and in the contract between the corporation and its stockholders.

Class A and Class B stock

Companies issuing more than one class of stock may designate the various issues by letter, as Class A stock and Class B stock. In this case one of the issues is common stock and the other issue has some preference or restriction of basic rights. To determine the significant characteristics of stocks identified by letter, it is necessary to examine the stock certificates or other official statements issued by the company.

Characteristics of preferred stock

The following features are associated with most preferred stock issues:

1 Preference as to dividends at a stated rate or amount
2 Preference as to assets in event of liquidation
3 Callable at the option of the corporation
4 Absence of voting rights

A preference as to dividends does not give positive assurance that dividends will be paid; it signifies merely that the stated dividend rate applicable to the preferred stock must be paid before any dividends can be paid on the common stock. Unlike interest on bonds and notes payable, dividends do not accrue. A liability to pay a dividend arises only when the board of directors declares a dividend. Any dividend action by the board must take into consideration (1) whether the corporation is in a legal position to pay a dividend, and (2) whether the present cash position and future corporate plans make it expedient to pay a dividend.

Many preferred stocks have a par value, and this feature permits the dividend rate to be stated either as a percentage of par or as a fixed dollar amount. For example, Georgia-Pacific Corporation has issued a $5\frac{1}{2}$%, $100 par, preferred stock. On the other hand, Sperry Rand Corporation has a $4.50 preferred stock with a par value of $25 but with a prior claim of $100 in the event of redemption or liquidation. Preferred stocks of the no-par variety necessarily state the dividend as a fixed dollar amount. An example is National Gypsum Company's "$4.50 Cumulative Preferred Stock (without par value; callable at $103 a share)."

Cumulative and Noncumulative Preferred Stock   Most preferred stocks have a cumulative provision as to dividends. If all or any part of the stated dividend on a cumulative preferred stock is not paid in a given year, the unpaid portion accumulates and must be paid in a subsequent year *before any dividend can be paid on the common stock.*

A dividend is said to have been *passed* if the directors fail to declare a dividend at the established date for dividend action. Any omitted dividends on cumulative preferred stock constitute *dividends in arrears.* The amount in arrears is not a liability of the company because no liability exists until the board of directors declares a dividend. However, no dividends can be declared on common stock until dividends in arrears on preferred stock have been cleared up and the current period's preferred dividend paid. Consequently, the amount of any dividends in arrears on preferred stock is of importance to investors and always should be disclosed. The disclosure is usually made by a note accompanying the financial statements.

In the case of noncumulative stocks, a dividend omitted or passed in one year is lost forever to the shareholder. Most investors refuse to buy noncumulative preferred stocks; consequently, this type of preferred stock is seldom issued.

As an illustration of the significance of dividends in arrears (and the inherent weakness of a noncumulative preferred stock), assume that a corporation has three classes of capital stock as follows:

6% cumulative preferred stock, $10 par, issued and outstanding 200,000 shares	$2,000,000
7% noncumulative second preferred stock, $25 par, issued and outstanding 40,000 shares	2,000,000
Common stock, $10 par, issued and outstanding 200,000 shares	2,000,000

Assume also that operations were unprofitable in Years 1, 2, and 3 and no dividends were paid during these three years. In Year 4, however, large profits were earned and the company decided on December 31, Year 4, that the amount of $900,000 should be distributed as dividends. Despite the equal amounts of capital represented by the three stock issues, the dividend payments would heavily favor the cumulative preferred stock and the common stock. The holders of the noncumulative stock would receive relatively little, as shown by the schedule at the top of page 697.

	6% cumulative preferred stock	7% noncumulative preferred stock	Common stock
Dividends in arrears	$360,000		
Preferred dividends, current year	120,000	$140,000	
Remainder, to common stock	–0–	–0–	$280,000
Total dividends paid . .	$480,000	$140,000	$280,000

Participating and Nonparticipating Preferred Stock A *fully participating* preferred stock shares equally with the common stock in any dividends paid after the common stock has received a dividend at a rate equal to the preference rate on the preferred stock. Assume, for example, that X Corporation this year has paid the usual 5% dividend on its fully participating $100 par preferred stock and has also paid a dividend of $5 on the common stock. If any additional dividend is paid to the common stockholders, a corresponding additional amount must be paid on the preferred stock. A *partially participating* preferred stock is one with a ceiling established limiting the extent to which it participates with the common stock.

Actually, participating preferred stocks are extremely rare. The great majority of existing preferred stocks are of the nonparticipating variety. Consequently, even though a company enters a period of great prosperity and pays very large dividends on its common stock, it will typically pay only the stated rate to the preferred shareholders. A preferred stock is nonparticipating unless the stock certificate specifically provides for participation.

Convertible Preferred Stock Many corporations increase the attractiveness of their preferred stock to investors by including a *conversion clause* which entitles the holders to exchange their shares for common stock in a stipulated ratio. The holders of convertible preferred stock have the advantage of a preferred claim on dividends and also the option of switching into common stock which enjoys unlimited participation in earnings.

Preferred stock will tend to be converted into common if the dividend rate on the common stock is increased. As long as the conversion privilege is open, the preferred stockholder gains the benefit of any rise in market price of the common stock without actually converting because the price of the preferred will rise in proportion to any rise in the price of the common stock. It is sometimes said that the prices of a common stock and the related convertible preferred stock are "in gear." The primary determinant of when to convert may then be the relative yields of the shares on prevailing market price. In addition, consideration may be given to the greater assurance of continued dividend payments on the preferred stock. For some stocks the conversion ratio expires after a specified number of years; for others the conversion period is unlimited; and in some cases the conversion privilege is subject to change at specified future dates.

Callable Preferred Stock   Most preferred stocks can be called or redeemed at the option of the corporation. The *call price* is specified in the preferred stock contract and is usually set a few points above the issuance price. The existence of the call price tends to set a ceiling on the market price of nonconvertible preferred stock. Any dividends in arrears must be paid when a preferred stock is called for redemption.

If a convertible preferred stock is called, the owners have the privilege of converting the preferred shares into common stock rather than surrendering their investment in the company. Consequently, the market price of outstanding convertible preferred stock tends to move with the price of the common stock even though this amount is well above the call price.

Why does a corporation generally make its preferred stock callable? The call feature is advantageous to the corporation because the capital obtained through issuance of callable preferred stock will be available as long as needed and can be paid off whenever the corporation desires. In some cases the corporation decides to call the preferred stock after retained earnings are sufficient to finance the corporation adequately; in other cases the decision to call may be made because other sources of capital offering more attractive terms have become available.

Liquidation Preference   Most preferred stocks have preference over common as to assets in the event of liquidation. The claims of creditors of course take preference over both preferred and common stock. The preference of a preferred stock as to assets usually includes any dividends in arrears in addition to the stated liquidation value. It is not safe to assume that every preferred stock has a prior claim on assets; the status of the stock in the event of liquidation depends upon the specific provisions of the preferred stock contract.

The preference which a preferred stock has in the event of liquidation should be disclosed in the financial statements. In *Opinion No. 10,* the Accounting Principles Board stated:

> Companies at times issue preferred (or other senior) stock which has a preference in involuntary liquidation considerably in excess of the par or stated value of the shares. The relationship between this preference in liquidation and the par or stated value of the shares may be of major significance to the users of the financial statements. . . . Accordingly, the Board recommends that, in these cases, the liquidation preference of the stock be disclosed in

the equity section of the balance sheet in the aggregate, . . . rather than on a per share basis or by disclosure in notes.[2]

Preferred Stock Regarded as Stockholders' Equity The position of the preferred stockholder is in some respects more like that of a creditor than an owner. Typically the preferred shareholder provides capital to the corporation for an agreed rate of return and has no voice in management. If the company prospers it will probably increase the dividend rate on its common stock, but it will not even consider increasing the dividend on preferred stock. Preferred shares generally have no maturity date, but the preferred stockholder's relationship with the company may be terminated if the company chooses to call in the preferred stock. Despite this lack of some of the traditional aspects of ownership, the preferred stockholder is regarded as an owner, not as a creditor. It is universal practice to include all types of preferred stock in the stockholders' equity section of the balance sheet. If the corporation encounters financial difficulties, all claims of creditors take precedence over the equity of both preferred and common stockholders.

Par value and no-par value stock

In the early history of American corporations, all capital stock was required to have a par value, but now most state laws permit corporations to choose between par value and no-par value stock. A corporation which chooses to issue par value stock can set the par at any amount desired, such as $1, $5, or $100 a share. If a corporation subsequently splits its par value stock, the par value of each share is reduced accordingly. For example, General Motors common stock, which has been split many times, now has a par value of $1.66⅔ per share.

The par value of capital stock is the amount per share to be entered in the capital stock account. This portion of the value of assets originally paid in to the corporation must be kept permanently in the business. The par value of the shares issued thus signifies a "cushion" of equity capital for the protection of creditors.

The par value device was originally introduced for the protection of creditors but proved less effective than anticipated since the intent of the law could easily be circumvented by issuing stock in exchange for property rather than for cash. In the era before rigorous security laws, large amounts of stock were sometimes issued for mining claims, patents, goodwill, and other assets of unproved value. These assets were usually recorded at the par value of the stock issued in payment, with the result of gross overvaluation of assets and overstatement of stockholders' equity in the balance sheet.

To avoid this abuse of the par value concept and to reduce the incentive for corporations to overvalue assets received in exchange for capi-

[2] *APB Opinion No. 10,* "Omnibus Opinion—1966," AICPA (New York: 1966), p. 148.

tal stock, most states enacted legislation permitting corporations to issue stock without par value. It was argued that many investors had in the past assumed that any stock was worth as much as its par value, and that the use of no-par stock would force investors to consider more fundamental factors such as earnings, dividends, and current fair value of assets.

The trend for corporations to set par values at quite low amounts, such as $1 or $5 per share, has lessened the effectiveness of the arguments for no-par stock and has also reduced some of the significance attached to the term *par value.*

Stated (or legal) capital

From the viewpoint of stockholders, one of the advantages of the corporate form of organization is that of limited liability. Stockholders are not personally liable for the debts of the corporation; creditors of the corporation must look for payment to the corporation alone and not to the stockholders individually, no matter how wealthy they may be.

What would be the effect upon creditors if the stockholders should withdraw virtually all the cash and other liquid assets from the corporation? Such actions would leave the creditors with uncollectible claims against a "hollow corporate shell." To prevent such harsh treatment of creditors, state laws provide that corporations shall not make payments or distribute assets to stockholders which would reduce the stockholders' equity below a designated amount called *stated capital* or *legal capital.*

If a corporation issues par value stock, the stated capital is equal to the total par value of all shares issued or subscribed. Since it is common practice to set the par value as low as $1 or $5 per share and to issue the stock at perhaps $25 or more per share, it is apparent that the stated capital will often be far less than the total capital invested by stockholders.

If no-par stock is issued, a few states define the stated capital as the total amount received for the no-par shares. In most states, however, the law permits the board of directors to establish an arbitrary stated value for no-par shares; this stated value is often set at an amount far below the issuance price.

The paid-in capital of a corporation may be regarded as an accounting concept, whereas stated capital is a legal concept. The paid-in capital is often shown in the balance sheet divided into two portions:

1 Stated capital or legal capital, equal to the par or stated value per share times the number of shares issued

2 The excess of paid-in capital over and above the stated or legal capital.

In brief, the stated or legal capital concept requires that stockholders keep a permanent stake in the corporation. This cushion of ownership capital not subject to withdrawal stands between the creditors and any losses incurred by a corporation. Of course the stated capital provision does not fully protect the creditors; if losses incurred by a corporation are so large as to wipe out the stockholders' equity, the losses will then fall on the creditors. In other words, stated capital can be impaired by corporate losses but not by dividends or payments to reacquire the corporation's own shares. The reacquisition of shares of stock involves a payment from the corporation to one or more of its stockholders; if not restricted by law, it could be as injurious to creditors as unrestricted payment of dividends.

The corporation laws of the several states also make provision for formal reduction of stated capital through such procedures as a reduction in the number of issued shares, or by lowering the par or stated value per share. These procedures require formal approval by state regulatory authorities; such approval would presumably not be granted if injury to creditors appeared likely to result.

Accounting for capital stock transactions

A clear understanding of the following terms is necessary in accounting for capital stock transactions:

1 *Authorized capital stock* means the number of shares which the state has authorized a corporation to issue. Typically a corporation will obtain authorization for a much larger number of shares than it plans to issue in the foreseeable future. The securing of authority to issue shares of stock does not bring an asset into existence nor does it give the corporation any capital. Authorization merely affords a legal opportunity to obtain assets through the issuance of stock. Consequently, authorization of capital stock does not constitute a transaction to be recorded in the debit-credit structure of accounts. A notation of the event in the general journal and in the ledger account for capital stock is appropriate.

2 *Issued capital stock* is the cumulative total number of authorized shares that have been issued to date. The number of issued shares includes treasury stock, as defined below.

3 *Unissued capital stock* describes the authorized shares that have not as yet been issued to investors.

4 *Outstanding capital stock* is the number of authorized shares that have been issued and are presently held by stockholders.

5 *Treasury stock* means the corporation's own shares which have been issued, fully paid, and reacquired by the issuing corporation but not canceled. Treasury stock is included in issued capital stock as defined above, but is not part of outstanding capital stock.

6 *Subscriptions to capital stock* represent an asset, in the form of a receivable from investors who have promised to pay the subscription price at a future date.

7 *Subscribed capital stock* refers to authorized but unissued shares which are earmarked for issuance under existing contracts with subscribers. The subscribed stock is issued when a subscription contract is collected in full. If financial statements are prepared between the date of obtaining stock subscriptions and the date of issuing the stock, the subscribed stock will appear in the stockholders' equity section of the balance sheet.

Ledger accounts for paid-in capital

Investments of capital by stockholders usually require the use of two types of stockholders' equity accounts: (1) capital stock accounts and (2) accounts for paid-in capital in excess of par or stated value.

Capital Stock Accounts A separate ledger account is used for each class of capital stock. The number of shares authorized and the par or stated value may be recorded by a memorandum entry in the general journal and may also be indicated by a memorandum in the ledger accounts as shown below.

8% Cumulative Preferred Stock
(Authorized 10,000 shares, $100 par, callable at $105 per share)

Common Stock
(Authorized 1,000,000 shares, no-par, stated value $5)

Accounts for Paid-in Capital in Excess of Par or Stated Value Capital stock is often issued at a price well above the par or stated value. This additional paid-in capital is credited to an account with a descriptive title indicating the source of the capital, such as Paid-in Capital in Excess of Par: Preferred Stock or Paid-in Capital in Excess of Stated Value: Common Stock. In the preparation of financial statements, it is not necessary to use the exact titles of the ledger accounts as long as the sources of capital are disclosed. For example, the paid-in capital indicated by the preceding account titles might appear in the balance sheet as follows:

Stockholders' equity:

8% cumulative preferred stock, $100 par (callable at $105 per share), authorized 10,000 shares, outstanding 9,000 shares . . .		$ 900,000
Common stock, no-par, stated value $5, authorized 1 million shares, outstanding 600,000 shares		3,000,000
Paid-in capital in excess of par or stated value:		
On preferred stock	$ 18,000	
On common stock	6,000,000	6,018,000
Total paid-in capital		$9,918,000

Some accountants would prefer to list the paid-in capital applicable to the preferred stock immediately following the listing of preferred stock, and to place the paid-in capital applicable to the common stock immediately following the listing of common stock.[3]

Journal Entries for Issuance of Stock for Cash The following journal entries illustrate issuance of the capital stocks summarized in the above balance sheet.

```
Cash  . . . . . . . . . . . . . . . . . . . . . . . . . . . . . . . . . . . . . . . . . . .    918,000
        8% Cumulative Preferred Stock  . . . . . . . . . .                        900,000
        Paid-in Capital in Excess of Par: Preferred Stock  .                       18,000
    Issued 9,000 shares of $100 par, cumulative preferred
    stock for $102 per share.

Cash  . . . . . . . . . . . . . . . . . . . . . . . . . . . . . . . . . . . . . . . .    9,000,000
        Common Stock  . . . . . . . . . . . . . . . . . . . .                     3,000,000
        Paid-in Capital in Excess of Stated Value: Common
            Stock  . . . . . . . . . . . . . . . . . . . . . . . .                 6,000,000
    Issued 600,000 shares of no-par common stock with a
    stated value of $5 per share for $15 per share.
```

In the balance sheet, various sources of paid-in capital are frequently reported under a single caption such as Paid-in Capital in Excess of Par or Additional Paid-in Capital. Other sources of paid-in capital in excess of par (such as treasury stock transactions) will be discussed later.

Discount on capital stock

Many states now prohibit the issuance of capital stock at less than par value. In planning a stock issue, a corporation is free to set the par value per share as low as it pleases. Since par value is usually set at an amount considerably below the offering price, the question of discount on capital stock is no longer of much practical importance. The topic deserves brief consideration, however, because of its theoretical implications.

In the past some states required a par value of $100 a share, and some corporations were unable to issue shares at such a high price. Consequently, the issuance of stock at a discount was not unusual. Under the laws of some states, if a corporation became unable to pay its debts, the person to whom stock had been issued at less than par might be held personally liable to creditors of the corporation for an amount equal to the discount on the shares purchased.

[3] For a comprehensive treatise of accounting for stockholders' equity, see Beatrice Melcher, "Stockholders' Equity," *Accounting Research Study No. 15,* AICPA (New York: 1973).

If capital stock is issued at a price below par, the amount of the discount should be debited to an account entitled Discount on Capital Stock, which will appear as a deduction (or negative element of paid-in capital) in the stockholders' equity section of the balance sheet. The discount on capital stock should be carried in the accounts as long as the related stock issue is outstanding so that an accurate record of the original investment by stockholders is maintained.

Once stock has been issued, it may be sold by one investor to another at more or less than par without any effect on the corporation's accounts. In other words, discount on capital stock refers only to the original issuance of shares by a corporation at a price below par. To avoid any possibility of a contingent liability to the corporation's creditors, prudent investors may limit their investments to capital stock bearing the inscription "fully paid and nonassessable."

Assessments on capital stock

Although most states require that stock offered to the public be nonassessable, situations are occasionally found in which a corporation may make an assessment against its stockholders. If the stock was originally issued at a discount, the amount received by assessment may be credited to the Discount on Capital Stock account. If the debit balance in the discount account is thereby eliminated, any remaining portion of the assessment should be credited to a separate stockholders' equity account such as Paid-in Capital from Assessment of Stockholders. This account would be credited with the entire amount of the assessment if the shares were originally issued at a price equal to or in excess of par value.

Issuance price and subsequent market price of stock

The preceding discussion of the issuance of stock at prices above and below par raises a question as to how a corporation decides on the issuance price. For a new issue of stock, the corporation usually sets an issuance price based on such factors as (1) expected future earnings and dividends, (2) present financial condition and reputation of the company, and (3) current demand-supply relationships in security markets.

After a stock has been issued, the subsequent market price at which it is traded among investors will tend to reflect the progress and prospects of the company and such external factors as the state of investor confidence and the general trend of the economy. The current market prices of common stocks often bear no discernible relationship to par value or to original issuance price.

Subscriptions for capital stock

The preceding sections have illustrated the issuance of capital stock for cash, but often stock is issued under a subscription contract calling for payment by the subscriber at a later date. Generally the stock certificates are not issued until the subscription price has been collected in full.

From the corporation's viewpoint, a stock subscription contract in most states is regarded as an asset (a special type of receivable), and is recorded by debiting Subscriptions Receivable: Common Stock or Subscriptions Receivable: Preferred Stock. When there are a large number of subscribers, the subscriptions receivable accounts may become controlling accounts supported by subsidiary ledgers containing an individual account with each subscriber. In the balance sheet, stock subscriptions receivable may be included among the current assets, provided that early collection is anticipated.

Some accountants argue that stock subscriptions do not represent an asset, and should be shown as a contra item in the stockholders' equity section. Under this view a stock subscription receivable is contrasted with the ordinary trade receivable; and it is argued that a stock subscription is a dubious claim against the subscribers because the corporation has not delivered merchandise or rendered services to them. As a practical matter, however, stock subscriptions are usually collected promptly and in full. Moreover, they constitute valid legal claims. The market price of newly subscribed shares often changes rapidly; if the stock subscription contract were not binding, unethical investors might benefit by refusing to pay the balance of their stock subscription contracts unless market prices were rising.

The increase in assets caused by obtaining a stock subscription receivable is offset by an increase in stockholders' equity. The accounts to be credited (in the case of par value common stock) are Common Stock Subscribed and Paid-in Capital in Excess of Par. At a later date when the stock is issued, the Common Stock Subscribed account will be debited and the Common Stock account will be credited.

If financial statements are prepared between the date of obtaining subscriptions and the date of issuing the stock, the Common Stock Subscribed account will appear in the stockholders' equity section of the balance sheet. In most states persons who sign subscription contracts immediately acquire the legal rights and privileges of stockholders, even though they do not receive a stock certificate until full payment is made. Such privileges include the right to receive dividends and to vote.

Journal Entries for Stock Subscriptions Assume that subscriptions are received for 10,000 shares of $10 par common stock at a price of $50 per share. The journal entry to record these subscriptions follows.

Subscriptions Receivable: Common Stock 500,000
    Common Stock Subscribed   100,000
    Paid-in Capital in Excess of Par   400,000
Received subscriptions for 10,000 shares of $10 par common
stock at $50 per share.

All subscribers paid one-half of the amounts of their stock subscription contracts. The entry is:

Cash 250,000
    Subscriptions Receivable: Common Stock   250,000
Made partial collection on all stock subscription contracts.

Subscribers paid the balance due on their stock subscription contracts, with the exception of one individual who had subscribed for 100 shares.

Cash 247,500
    Subscriptions Receivable: Common Stock   247,500
Collected balance due on subscriptions for 9,900 shares.

Common Stock Subscribed 99,000
    Common Stock   99,000
Issued 9,900 shares after collection of subscriptions in full.

Defaults by subscribers to capital stock

If subscribers fail to pay all or part of their subscriptions, the disposition of the contracts and of any amounts paid in by the subscribers will depend upon the laws of the state and the policy of the corporation. If no payment has been made by the subscribers and nothing can be collected from them, the corporation may simply reverse the entries used to record the subscriptions. If the subscribers have made one or more partial payments prior to default, the entire amount paid in prior to default may be refunded. Or, as an alternative, the amount refunded may be the amount paid in minus any expenses or losses in reselling the shares. Another possible alternative calls for amending the subscription contracts to permit the issuance of a reduced number of shares corresponding to the cash collected. Still another alternative under some state laws calls for forfeiture by the subscribers of the amount paid prior to the default.

Default by a subscriber requires the writing off of the uncollectible subscription receivable; the entry will also include a debit to the account for Capital Stock Subscribed and usually a debit to the Paid-in Capital in Excess of Par account. If the corporation retains any amounts paid in on defaulted subscriptions without issuing shares, this increase in paid-in capital may be credited to a separate account with a descriptive title such as Paid-in Capital from Defaults on Stock Subscriptions or may be included in Paid-in Capital in Excess of Par.

Stockholders' ledger and stock certificate book

In addition to maintaining a general ledger account for each class of capital stock, a corporation must maintain detailed supporting records showing the identity of stockholders. A *stockholders' ledger* contains a separate account for each stockholder showing the number of shares each owns. When a stockholder sells shares to another investor, an entry must be made in the stockholders' ledger decreasing the number of shares held by the first stockholder and opening an account for the new stockholder. No entry would be necessary in the general ledger since the amount of stock outstanding remains unchanged. The stockholders' ledger is maintained in number of shares rather than in dollars.

A *stock certificate book* is also necessary to control the amount of stock outstanding. When a certificate is issued, the name of the owner and number of shares are listed on the certificate stub. When a stockholder sells shares to another, the original certificate is canceled and attached to the stub. A new certificate is issued to the new stockholder. The open stubs in the stock certificate book indicate the number of shares outstanding. Most large corporations retain an independent *stock registrar* and *transfer agent* to control stock certificates and ownership records. Such records are maintained by the use of computers when the volume of transactions is large.

Issuance of two types of securities as a unit

Corporations sometimes offer preferred and common shares as a unit, with no indication of the issuance price of either security considered separately. In other cases one or more shares of common stock may be offered as a so-called "bonus" to the purchaser of a bond payable. Such unit offerings raise a question as to how the proceeds should be divided between the two issues. The same question arises when a company issues two or more kinds of securities to acquire another business entity. The aggregate par value of preferred and common shares issued as a unit will usually be less than the fair value of the consideration received. How should the paid-in capital in excess of par be allocated between the two issues? If either security is concurrently being sold on a cash basis, the known market price of that security can be taken as evidence of the value received for that element of the unit sales; the remainder of the issuance price for a unit of preferred and common is applicable to the other class of stock.

It is also possible that units of preferred and common stock might be issued for a consideration less than the aggregate par or stated values of the shares. In such a case, reference to a known market price for either security would permit determination of the discount to be recorded on one or both of the two classes of capital stock.

Capital stock issued for property or services

When stock is issued for assets other than cash, the fair value of the property or the market value of the stock, whichever is more clearly evident, should be used to record the property received and the related amount of paid-in capital. In the absence of an arm's-length sale of property for cash, opinions often differ widely as to its fair value, especially in the case of intangible assets. Consequently, it is appropriate to consider how much the stock would have sold for if offered for cash. The underlying reasoning is that the exchange of capital stock for property is essentially the equivalent of selling these shares for cash and using the cash to buy property. The two separate transactions are in effect combined into one by the exchange transaction.

If the company's stock is actively traded, the cash price of the stock prevailing at the date of the exchange constitutes good objective evidence as to the values exchanged. However, if stock sales are infrequent and of small amount, there is no assurance that the company could have issued a large block of stock for cash without forcing the price down. In some cases of management fraud, the purchase or issuance of small quantities of stock for cash at an unrealistic price has been specially arranged to set the stage for an exchange of stock for property at an inflated value.

Either treasury stock or previously unissued stock may be given in exchange for property. However, the cost of treasury shares used for this purpose does not constitute a proper basis of valuation for the exchange unless by chance such cost is equal to the present market value of the stock.

The establishing of valuations for property acquired in exchange for capital stock is the responsibility of the corporation's board of directors. The decisions of the board and the use made of appraisals or other valuation techniques should be set forth in the corporate minutes. When certified public accountants perform an independent audit of the company, they will look for such supporting evidence for property values. It is also within the independent auditors' responsibility to challenge any unreasonable valuations even though these carry specific approval by the board of directors. Under no circumstances should the par value of the shares issued in exchange for property be regarded as the decisive factor in establishing the fair value of the assets acquired.

The valuation problem when a corporation issues capital stock for personal services by employees or outsiders, such as attorneys and accountants, parallels that previously described in Chapter 12 in the exchange of stock for property. The fair value of the services received is an entirely proper basis of valuation, but the market value of the stock is often more readily determinable and is also an acceptable basis for establishing the accounting basis for the exchange transaction.

Watered stock and secret reserves

A corporation's stock is said to be *watered* if the stockholders' equity is overstated because of a corresponding overvaluation of assets. The expression "watered stock" stems from the era when cattle raisers sometimes gave their herds quantities of salt and then all the water they could drink just before they were delivered to the markets. The "watered stock" weighed more and brought a higher price.

In a corporation, watered stock usually relates to inflated asset values, although capital stock can also be watered through understatement of liabilities. This factor is less common, however, since most liabilities are listed at contractual amounts or at the present value of future payments.

The most direct approach to eliminating water from a corporate capital structure is through writing down the overvalued assets. The reduction in carrying value of the assets may be accompanied by a reduction in retained earnings, or by reducing the par value per share or number of shares outstanding. Since such a write-down affects each shareholder proportionally, no real loss is involved; the proportionate equity in the net assets is unchanged.

The existence of *secret reserves* in a corporation is one way of saying that the stockholders' equity is understated. Such understatement of stockholders' equity may be achieved by using high depreciation rates, by excessive provision for doubtful accounts, by using lifo inventory procedures in periods of rising price levels, by charging capital expenditures to expense, or by any other step which understates assets or overstates liabilities. The deliberate creation of secret reserves is clearly inconsistent with the maintenance of integrity in financial reporting.

INCORPORATION OF A PARTNERSHIP

When a single proprietorship or a partnership grows into a large-scale enterprise, the owner or owners may consider incorporating so that they can enjoy such corporate advantages as limited liability and the availability of outside capital without loss of control. A new set of accounting records may be opened for the new corporate entity, or the records of the old organization may be adjusted to reflect the results of incorporation and continued in use. Since the unincorporated business is selling its assets, including any goodwill which deserves recognition, to the new corporation, the records of the old organization should be adjusted to reflect current values for the assets. A corresponding adjustment is made to increase or decrease the owners' capital accounts by the amount of gain or loss implicit in the adjustment of asset values.

To illustrate the incorporation of a partnership, assume that Blair and Benson, partners who share profits in an 80 to 20% ratio, organize the Blair-Benson Corporation to take over the partnership business. The balance sheet of the partnership on June 30, Year 1, the date of incorporation, appears at the top of page 711.

After an appraisal of the equipment and an audit of the accounts, it is agreed that the following adjustments are warranted:

1 Increase the allowance for doubtful accounts to $1,000.
2 Increase the inventories to current replacement cost of $30,000.
3 Increase the equipment to reproduction cost new of $70,000, less accumulated depreciation on this basis of $30,500.
4 Recognize accrued liabilities of $1,100.
5 Record goodwill of $10,000.

The Blair-Benson Corporation is authorized to issue 10,000 shares of $10 par capital stock. It issues 5,500 shares to the partnership, in exchange for which the corporation acquires all the assets of the partnership and assumes all the liabilities. (To avoid the need for issuance of fractional shares to a partnership, it is sometimes convenient for the partners to withdraw small amounts of cash so that their capital accounts may be rounded out.) The 5,500 shares received by the partnership are divided between the partners as indicated by their adjusted capital accounts. This step completes the dissolution of the partnership. Blair-Benson Corporation also issued 1,000 shares for cash to outsiders at $15 a share.

Establishing accounting records for the new corporate entity

Although the accounting records of the partnership could be modified to serve as the records of the new corporation, it is customary and more satisfactory to open a new set of records for the new corporate entity. The steps to be taken are as follows:

On partnership records:

1 Prepare adjusting entries for revaluation of assets, including recognition of goodwill if any.
2 Record any cash withdrawals necessary to adjust partners' capital accounts

BLAIR & BENSON PARTNERSHIP
Balance Sheet
June 30, Year 1
Assets

Cash		$12,000
Accounts receivable	$28,100	
Less: Allowance for doubtful accounts	600	27,500
Inventories		25,500
Equipment	$60,000	
Less: Accumulated depreciation	26,000	34,000
Total assets		$99,000

Liabilities & Partners' Capitals

Liabilities:		
Accounts payable		$35,000
Partners' capitals:		
Blair, capital	$47,990	
Benson, capital	16,010	64,000
Total liabilities & partners' capitals		$99,000

BLAIR-BENSON CORPORATION
Balance Sheet
June 30, Year 1
Assets

Cash		$ 27,000
Accounts receivable	$28,100	
Less: Allowance for doubtful accounts	1,000	27,100
Inventories		30,000
Equipment	$70,000	
Less: Accumulated depreciation	30,500	39,500
Goodwill		10,000
Total assets		$133,600

Liabilities & Stockholders' Equity

Liabilities:		
Accounts payable		$ 35,000
Accrued liabilities		1,100
Total liabilities		$ 36,100
Stockholders' equity:		
Capital stock, $10 par, authorized 10,000 shares, issued		
and outstanding 6,500 shares	$65,000	
Paid-in capital in excess of par	32,500	97,500
Total liabilities & stockholders' equity		$133,600

<u>Entries on partnership records</u>

Inventories	4,500	
Equipment	10,000	
Goodwill	10,000	
Allowance for Doubtful Accounts		400
Accumulated Depreciation		4,500
Accrued Liabilities		1,100
Blair, Capital		14,800
Benson, Capital		3,700

To adjust assets and liabilities to agreed amounts and to divide
net gain between partners in an 80 and 20% ratio.

Receivable from Blair-Benson Corporation	82,500	
Accounts Payable	35,000	
Accrued Liabilities	1,100	
Allowance for Doubtful Accounts	1,000	
Accumulated Depreciation	30,500	
Cash		12,000
Accounts Receivable		28,100
Inventories		30,000
Equipment		70,000
Goodwill		10,000

To record the transfer of assets and liabilities to Blair-Benson
Corporation.

Stock of Blair-Benson Corporation	82,500	
Receivable from Blair-Benson Corporation		82,500

Received 5,500 shares of $10 par stock valued at $15 a share
in payment for net assets transferred to corporation.

Blair, Capital	62,790	
Benson, Capital	19,710	
Stock of Blair-Benson Corporation		82,500

Distributed capital stock to partners; 4,186 shares to Blair
and 1,314 shares to Benson.

to round amounts. (In some instances the agreement may call for transfer to the corporation of all assets except cash.)

3 Record the transfer of assets and liabilities to the corporation, the receipt of capital stock by the partnership, and the distribution of this stock to the partners in settlement of the balances in their capital accounts.

On corporation records:

1 Record the acquisition of assets and liabilities (including obligation to pay for the net assets) from the partnership at current fair values.

2 Record the issuance of capital stock at current fair values in payment of the obligation to the partnership.

3 Record the issuance of capital stock for cash to other persons.

The journal entries to illustrate the recording of these steps in the incorporation of the Blair & Benson partnership appear on page 712 and below.

Entries on corporation records

Cash	12,000	
Accounts Receivable	28,100	
Inventories	30,000	
Equipment	70,000	
Goodwill	10,000	
Allowance for Doubtful Accounts		1,000
Accumulated Depreciation		30,500
Accounts Payable		35,000
Accrued Liabilities		1,100
Payable to Blair & Benson		82,500

To record acquisition of assets and liabilities from Blair & Benson.

Payable to Blair & Benson	82,500	
Capital Stock		55,000
Paid-in Capital in Excess of Par		27,500

Issued 5,500 shares of $10 par stock at price of $15 a share in payment for net assets acquired from Blair & Benson.

Cash	15,000	
Capital Stock		10,000
Paid-in Capital in Excess of Par		5,000

Issued 1,000 shares of $10 par stock at $15 a share.

The balance sheet of Blair-Benson Corporation after these transactions is shown at the bottom of page 711. The corporation could as an alternative have chosen not to transfer the Accumulated Depreciation account and to set up the net carrying value of the equipment at its cost to the corporation.

Tax aspects concerning incorporation of a partnership

For income tax purposes, no gain or loss is recognized on the incorporation of a partnership if the former partners hold control of the corporation immediately after the transfer. As a result of this rule, the basis of the property transferred is the same for the corporation as it was for the partnership. The depreciation program is continued for income tax purposes on the basis of the original cost of the depreciable assets to the partnership. Control of the corporation is defined for income tax purposes as ownership of 80% of the voting stock and also at least 80% of any other classes of stock outstanding.

A conflict evidently exists between the action required for income tax purposes and that indicated by accounting theory. From the viewpoint of accounting theory, the assets are appropriately recorded in the accounts of the corporation at the new cost basis established by the transfer of ownership and substantiated by the market (or fair) value of the stock issued for these assets. This line of reasoning would also indicate the possibility of a gain or loss to the selling entity. As a practical solution to this conflict between income tax requirements and theoretical considerations, the corporation may wish to maintain a separate set of supplementary records for depreciable assets to facilitate the computation of depreciation expense allowable for income tax purposes.

REVIEW QUESTIONS

1 Why do corporations often issue two or more types of capital stock?

2 What are the basic rights inherent in ownership of capital stock? What modification of these basic rights is usually found in the case of a preferred stock?

3 If a corporation with cumulative preferred stock outstanding fails to pay any dividend during a given year, what disclosure, if any, should be made in the financial statements?

4 Assume that a corporation has 10,000 shares of $5 cumulative convertible preferred stock of $100 par and 100,000 shares of common stock of $5 par. Net income amounts to $50,000 in the first year, $160,000 in the second year, and $300,000 in the third year. At the beginning of the third year, 1,000 shares of preferred stock are converted into common stock at the stipulated rate of four shares of common for one share of preferred. Assuming that the company follows a policy of paying dividends each year equal to 70% of net income, what will be the amount of annual dividends to each class of stock?

5 Distinguish between a convertible provision in a preferred stock and a callable provision. May a preferred stock be both convertible and callable? If so, may both provisions be exercised?

6 In what respects does the position of preferred stockholders resemble that of bondholders rather than common stockholders? How does preferred stock differ from bonds payable?

7 For what purpose was the par value concept originally required for capital stock?

8 What represents stated (or legal) capital in the case of par value stock and no-par stock?

9 State briefly the accounting principle to be followed in recording the issuance of capital stock in exchange for services or property.

10 What restrictions are commonly placed upon a corporation to guard against impairment of stated (or legal) capital?

11 From the following list of features which are sometimes found in preferred stock issues, list the three that you believe are most commonly encountered.

a Voting

b Fully participating

c Callable

d Cumulative

e Nonvoting

f Convertible

g Noncumulative

h Partially participating

12 Are most preferred stocks:

a Voting or nonvoting?

b Cumulative or noncumulative?

c Participating or nonparticipating?

d Callable or noncallable?

13 May a corporation with a deficit also have watered stock? If so, would the elimination of the water from the stock tend to eliminate the deficit? Explain.

14 May a corporation have both **watered stock** and **secret reserves**? Explain.

15 A partnership operated by Mann and Field decided to incorporate as the Manfield Corporation. The entire capital stock of the new corporation was divided equally between Mann and Field since they had been equal partners. An appraisal report obtained at the date of incorporation indicated that the land and buildings had increased in value by 50% while owned by the partnership. Should the assets be increased to appraisal value or kept at original cost to the partnership when transferred to the corporation's accounting records? If the assets are revalued, will the corporation be permitted to take depreciation for income tax purposes on the increased valuations? Explain.

EXERCISES

Ex. 17-1 Identify each of the following statements as True or False.

(1) Retained earnings can **never** be greater than the accumulated earnings of the company since the date of incorporation minus any losses incurred and dividends declared.

(2) Paid-in capital in excess of par or stated value is often larger than the amount in the capital stock account.

(3) In a company which has always operated at a profit and has distributed approximately half its earnings as dividends, the amount of paid-in capital will be less than the stockholders' equity.

(4) The amount of enterprise capital is increased when a corporation obtains a bank loan.

(5) Stated or legal capital cannot be less than net assets minus retained earnings.

(6) Stated or legal capital is usually less than paid-in capital, and paid-in capital is usually less than stockholders' equity or proprietary capital.

(7) A ledger account entitled Premium on Capital Stock may properly be included under the balance sheet caption of "paid-in capital in excess of par."

(8) A corporation is said to be "listed" if its capital stock has been designated by state officials as an approved investment by savings banks.

(9) A corporation in which stock ownership has always been limited to members of a single family is properly termed a "close corporation."

(10) General Motors Corporation is a "private corporation," but it is also a "publicly owned corporation."

Ex. 17-2 Toddy Corporation obtained authorization for 35,000 shares of common stock and promptly issued all the stock at $25 per share. For each of the following independent cases, prepare the stockholders' equity section of the balance sheet, including as complete as possible a description of the stock issued and making any appropriate change in terminology.

Case A:

Common Stock		Paid-in Capital in Excess of Stated Value	
	105,000		770,000

Case B:

Common Stock		Premium on Common Stock	
	245,000		630,000

Ex. 17-3 Given the following information, prepare in good form the stockholders' equity section of the balance sheet of Loretto Corporation.

Subscriptions receivable: common stock.	$ 55,000
Paid-in capital in excess of par: preferred stock.	50,000
Common stock, $5 par, authorized 40,000 shares, issued and outstanding 20,000 shares	100,000
Paid-in capital in excess of par: common stock	150,000
Retained earnings, unappropriated	327,000
Retained earnings appropriated for contingencies.	125,000
Common stock subscribed.	25,000
7% cumulative preferred stock, $50 par, authorized 20,000 shares, issued and outstanding 10,000 shares	500,000
Paid-in capital from donation of plant site	40,000

Ex. 17-4 Nick & Nick, Inc., a successful enterprise, received authorization to issue an additional 100,000 shares of no-par common stock with a stated value of $10 per share. The stock was offered to subscribers at a subscription price of $50 per share. Subscriptions were recorded by a debit to Subscriptions Receivable and a credit to Common Stock Subscribed and a paid-in capital account. A short time later, subscribers who had contracted to purchase 100 shares defaulted on their contracts after paying 40% of the subscription price.

The method used by Nick & Nick, Inc., in recording the default will depend upon the contractual and legal rights of the defaulting subscribers and especially upon the statutes of the state of incorporation. You are to identify four methods of accounting at the time of the default for the amount paid in prior to the default. Prepare a journal entry for each method to show how the default would be recorded.

Ex. 17-5 The balance sheet for the Dinka & Zane Partnership immediately before the partnership was converted to a corporation (DZ Corporation) follows:

DINKA & ZANE PARTNERSHIP
Balance Sheet
September 30, Year 5

Assets		Liabilities & Partners' Capitals	
Cash	$ 10,400	Accounts payable	$ 16,300
Accounts receivable	15,900	Dinka, capital	60,000
Inventories	42,000	Zane, capital	52,000
Plant assets (net of $18,000			
accum. depr.)	60,000	Total liabilities & partners'	
Total assets	$128,300	capitals	$128,300

The following adjustments to the balance sheet of the partnership are recommended by a CPA before opening a new set of accounting records for the DZ Corporation:

(1) An allowance for doubtful accounts in the amount of $1,200 should be established.
(2) Short-term prepayments valued at $800 are on hand.
(3) The current fair value of inventories is $48,000, and the current fair value of the plant assets is $72,000.
(4) Accrued liabilities are estimated at $750.

Prepare an opening balance sheet in good form for the DZ Corporation at October 1, Year 5, assuming that 400 shares of $5 par common stock are issued to the two partners in exchange for their equities in the partnership. Plant assets are recorded at current fair value; 1,000 shares of common stock are authorized to be issued.

SHORT CASES FOR ANALYSIS AND DECISION

Case 17-1 The outside auditor of Smokey Meat Company explained to the president that the use of the lifo inventory method during an extended period of rising prices and the expensing of all human resource costs are among the accepted accounting practices which help create **secret reserves.** The auditor also pointed out that **watered stock** is the opposite of a secret reserve.

Instructions
a What is a **secret reserve**? How can secret reserves be created or enlarged?
b What is the basis for saying that the two specific practices cited above tend to create secret reserves?
c Is it possible to create a secret reserve in connection with accounting for a liability? If so, explain or give an example.
d What are the objections to the creation of secret reserves?
e What is **watered stock**?
f Describe the general circumstances in which watered stock can arise.
g What steps can be taken to eliminate "water" from a capital structure?

Case 17-2 After the cancellation of some of its government contracts, Porterville Electronics Corporation began production under a new long-term government contract. During the period of operating losses the company had suspended dividend payments on all of its four stock issues. These four issues consisted of a $7 cumulative, $100 par, first preferred stock; a $2.50 noncumulative, convertible, $50 par, preferred stock; a 4%, $100 par, noncumulative Class B stock; and a

Class A stock without any dividend preference. Of each issue, 10,000 shares were outstanding. All indicated dividends had been paid through Year 3, but the company had been unable to pay any dividends in Year 4 or Year 5. During Year 6, the company's position improved greatly, and at a directors' meeting near the end of Year 6, a proposal was made to pay a dividend of $2.25 a share on the Class A common stock to stockholders of record December 31, Year 6.

Edward Cobb, who owned 100 shares of the $2.50 noncumulative, convertible, $50 par, preferred stock, had been considering converting these 100 shares into common stock at the existing conversion ratio of four shares of common for each share of preferred. The conversion ratio was scheduled to drop to $3\frac{1}{2}$ to one at the end of Year 6. Observing that the price of the common stock was rising rapidly, Cobb explained that he was "torn between a desire to retain his preferred stock until the indicated dividend was received and a desire to convert promptly before the common stock went higher and the conversion ratio was reduced."

Instructions
a Determine the amount of cash needed for dividend payments if the proposal to pay a $2.25 dividend on the Class A common stock is adopted. (Assume that there is no conversion of preferred stock.)
b Advise Cobb on the merits of converting the stock at this time as opposed to converting after the dividends have been paid and the conversion ratio decreased. Explain fully the issues involved.

Case 17-3 Exeter Company was organized on October 1, Year 2, with an authorized capital stock of $1 million par value. Shares with a par value totaling $300,000 were issued in equal amounts to A, B, and C in consideration of their transfer to the company of parcels of commercial real estate as of that date. The company planned to operate the properties as rental property. The Property account was debited and the Capital Stock account credited with $300,000 to record the transaction. No other stock was issued.

On December 31, Year 2, a journal entry was recorded, upon the basis of a resolution passed by the board of directors, increasing the Property account by $1.8 million and crediting a Capital Surplus account with a like amount to state the property at its fair value. The adjusted valuation of $2.1 million is equivalent to twice the assessed value for Year 2 property tax purposes, which is the average relationship of current quoted prices of similar property to their assessed value. The company has on file a report from a reputable real estate appraisal company which states that it considers the fair value at the date the property was transferred to the corporation to be in excess of $2.5 million.

Instructions You are engaged to examine a balance sheet of the company at December 31, Year 2.
a In indicating in the balance sheet the valuation of the property, would you recommend stating the valuation to be:
(1) At valuation appraised by the board of directors?
(2) At less than appraised valuation?
(3) At cost?
(4) At carrying value?
(5) At some other amount?
State briefly your reasons why your statement of the valuation is correct.
b State the exact description you think should be used in the balance sheet to explain what the "capital surplus" represents.

Case 17-4 The partnership of Bell, Owens, and Weston operated successfully until Paul Owens and Donald Weston retired. The partners then agreed to incorporate the business as the Bell Corporation with Ed Bell as president. Capital stock of $10 par value was authorized and issued as follows: Bell 12,000 shares, Owens 6,000 shares, and Weston 2,000 shares. Authorized but unissued stock totaling 30,000 shares remained available for future use. At December 31, Year 9, the stockholders' equity amounted to a total of $220,000, including $20,000 of retained earnings.

President Bell decided on January 2, Year 10, that more working capital was needed. Both the other stockholders were away on extended winter vacations at this time, so Bell decided to supply the needed capital. At the time of incorporating the former partnership, Bell had withdrawn $20,000 in cash because his equity was much larger than that of the other partners and the business had excess cash on hand. Bell had immediately invested this $20,000 in common stocks of industrial companies and these investments had increased in value to approximately $30,000. On January 3, Year 10, Bell sold these investments and deposited the proceeds of $30,000 in the bank account of Bell Corporation, arranging for an additional 3,000 shares of stock to be issued in his name in return for this investment.

After learning of this transaction, Owens protested that his basic rights as a stockholder had been violated. Weston also protested on the grounds that Bell should have taken 2,000 shares rather than 3,000, since this smaller amount would have corresponded to the $20,000 originally withdrawn from the business and invested in industrial stocks. Weston explained that if Bell had not made the cash withdrawal of $20,000, he (Bell) would have been entitled to 2,000 additional shares at the date of incorporation.

Bell denied any intent of wrongdoing but offered to reimburse the former partners for any inequity they could substantiate in a logical manner. There had been no trading in the stock of Bell Corporation at any time.

Instructions Evaluate the objections and arguments presented by Owens and Weston. If you think they have been unjustly treated, suggest a basis for remedying the injustice.

Case 17-5 A few months after the organization of the Mack Corporation, one of the largest stockholders, Hoyt, offered to transfer to the corporation a tract of land and a factory building in exchange for 11,000 shares of Mack Corporation's $10 par value capital stock. Under the terms of the offer, an existing mortgage of $28,000 on the land and buildings was to be assumed by Mack Corporation.

The board of directors of Mack Corporation determined that the property was well-suited to the corporation's needs. The board was informed by the secretary of the corporation that 15,000 authorized but unissued shares were available.

One member of the board, Sparks, opposed the idea of assuming the mortgage, on the grounds that long-term debt could prove burdensome for a new business without established earning power, and suggested making a counteroffer of 13,800 shares with the understanding that Hoyt pay the mortgage in full at date of transferring the property.

A second director, Brown, argued against further issuance of stock, pointing out that the company had just obtained $325,000 in cash from issuance of 26,000 shares of stock and that this cash should be used to the extent necessary to acquire plant and equipment. Brown proposed that the company offer Hoyt $110,000 in cash, assume the mortgage, and pay it in full immediately.

A third director, Benson, urged prompt acceptance of Hoyt's offer without modification. Benson produced documents showing that the property had been purchased by Hoyt 10 years previously at a total price of $206,000 and that Hoyt's accounting records indicated depreciation to date on the building of $36,000. In conclusion, Benson stated that these facts showed that the company would be saving $32,000 by accepting Hoyt's offer.

Instructions
a Comment on the logic and reasonableness of the views expressed by each of the three directors. Explain how each arrived at the amounts mentioned.

b Indicate which deal you believe would be most advantageous to the company, assuming that it was acceptable to Hoyt.

c Assuming that the company accepted the original offer by Hoyt, draft the journal entry to record the transaction, and explain fully the principles underlying the entry. Assume that the land is worth half as much as the building.

Case 17-6 Subscriptions receivable for capital stock under most circumstances have traditionally been regarded as an asset; however, the theoretical propriety of this treatment has been questioned. An alternative proposal is to treat subscriptions receivable as a deduction from stockholders' equity.

Instructions

a Discuss and justify the traditional treatment of stock subscriptions receivable for capital stock.

b Present arguments which question the theoretical propriety of the traditional treatment and, instead, lend support to the view that stock subscriptions receivable should be treated as a deduction from stockholders' equity.

PROBLEMS

Group A

17A-1 On January 4, Acme Storage Company was organized and authority received from the state to issue equity securities as follows:

$5 preferred stock, $100 par, 250,000 shares
Common stock, no-par, stated value $5 per share, 1,000,000 shares

After this authorization to issue securities, the following transactions affecting stockholders' equity occurred during the first quarter of the current year:

Jan. 15　Received subscriptions for 25,000 shares of preferred stock at $105 per share. A down payment of 40% accompanied each subscription; the balance was to be paid on March 15. (Record the full amount subscribed and then, in a separate entry, show the cash collection for 40% of this amount.)

Jan. 17　Received subscriptions for 125,000 shares of common stock at $20 per share, payable March 1.

Jan. 30　Issued 1,000 shares of common stock in payment for legal and accounting services relating to the organization of the corporation and valued at $20,000.

Mar. 1　Received payment in full of the amount due on common stock subscriptions.

Mar. 15　Received payment in full of the balance due on preferred stock subscriptions.

Mar. 30　Issued 5,000 shares of preferred stock for cash of $520,000.

Mar. 30　Issued 6,000 shares of common stock and 2,500 shares of preferred stock in exchange for assets for which the board of directors established the following fair values:

Land	$154,000
Building	190,000
Delivery equipment	20,000
Inventories	15,000

Mar. 31　Net income earned to March 31 amounted to $118,000. No dividends had been declared.

Instructions
a Prepare journal entries to record the transactions listed above.
b Prepare the stockholders' equity section of the balance sheet at March 31.

17A-2 On October 1 Marine Bio Corporation was organized with authorization to issue 25,000 shares of $100 par, 7% cumulative preferred stock and 500,000 shares of $10 par common stock. The first transaction by the new corporation was the acquisition of a going business in exchange for 12,500 shares of the preferred stock plus the assumption of a mortgage payable in the amount of $350,000. A firm of independent appraisers presented a report showing a valuation of $1,750,000 for the assets acquired in this transaction, which was completed on October 10.

Subscriptions for 25,000 shares of common stock at a price of $30 a share were obtained. All the subscriptions were collected with the exception of a subscription for 250 shares by Paul Trani. After paying $2,500, Trani defaulted on the subscription contract. Marine Bio Corporation resold the 250 shares for cash at a price of $29 a share. As required by state statutes, Marine Bio Corporation then refunded to Trani the amount paid in minus the loss incurred on the resale of the 250 shares. The last two transactions were completed on November 2.

From October 1 to December 31, the operations of the corporation produced net income of $88,125. A quarterly dividend of $1.75 per share on the preferred stock was declared on December 10 payable January 25 to stockholders of record on December 30. No dividends were declared on the common stock.

Instructions
a Prepare journal entries for all transactions relating to the stockholders' equity, including declaration of the dividend on the preferred stock.
b Prepare the stockholders' equity section of the balance sheet at December 31.

17A-3 Everett and Green, after several years of successful operation as a partnership, decided to incorporate and issue stock to outsiders to obtain the capital needed for expansion of their growing business.

At December 31, Year 5, an after-closing trial balance of the partnership of Everett and Green appeared as follows:

Cash	$ 15,240	
Accounts receivable	102,000	
Inventories	153,000	
Land	90,000	
Buildings	244,000	
Accumulated depreciation		$ 48,000
Accounts payable		42,000
Everett, capital		165,730
Green, capital		348,510
Totals	$604,240	$604,240

On January 2, Year 6, the business was incorporated as Evergreen Corporation with authorization to issue 200,000 shares of $10 par common stock. The corporation issued 20,000 shares for cash to public investors at $25 a share. Everett and Green agreed to accept shares at the same price in amounts equal to their respective capital accounts after making the adjustments indicated below and after making cash withdrawals sufficient to avoid the need for issuing fractional shares. In payment for the shares of stock to be issued to Everett and Green the partnership's assets were transferred to the corporation and the partnership's liabilities were assumed by the corporation. Stock certificates were then issued by the corporation in payment for the net assets of the partnership. A new set of accounting records is to be opened for the corporation.

The profit-sharing clause of the partnership agreement provided for Everett to receive 40% of net income and Green 60%. The partners agreed that the following adjustments were to be made in the partnership accounts at December 31, Year 5, as a preliminary step to incorporation on January 2, Year 6.

(1) Recognize accrued liabilities of $2,700 and miscellaneous short-term pre-payments of $3,615.
(2) Provide an allowance for doubtful accounts of $15,000.
(3) Increase the value of land by $30,000.
(4) Increase inventories to present replacement cost of $180,000.

Instructions
a Prepare journal entries necessary to adjust the accounts of the partnership to the agreed values. Also prepare all other journal entries needed to record the events described.
b Prepare journal entries in the accounts of the corporation necessary to record the events described.
c Prepare a balance sheet for the corporation at January 2, Year 6, after the transactions in **b** have been recorded.

17A-4 Coastal Dredging Corporation is authorized to issue 500,000 shares of $25 par value, 8% cumulative preferred stock, and 1,500,000 shares of no-par common stock with stated value of $2.50 per share.

Early operations of the company were profitable but a prolonged strike caused a net loss of $920,000 to be sustained for the current fiscal year ending June 30. Because of the loss, the company paid no dividends on its common stock during the current fiscal year. Dividends on preferred were paid in the amount of $120,000 but dividends were in arrears on the preferred stock at June 30, in the amount of $360,000.

A trial balance of the general ledger at May 31 of the current year included the following:

8% cumulative preferred stock, $25 par	$6,000,000
Common stock, no-par, $2.50 stated value	1,000,000
Subscriptions receivable: preferred stock	618,000
Retained earnings (June 30, prior year)	1,380,200
Paid-in capital in excess of par: preferred stock	198,000
Preferred stock subscribed	600,000
Paid-in capital in excess of stated value: common stock	1,375,000
Subscriptions receivable: common stock	525,000
Common stock subscribed	250,000
Dividends: preferred stock	120,000

Transactions during June relating to capital stock included the issuance on June 5 of 4,200 shares of common stock in exchange for a patent. An additional 30,000 shares of common stock were issued for cash on June 11 at a price of $6 per share. Cash was collected on June 21 representing payment in full for common stock subscriptions covering 20,000 shares. These subscriptions had been received and recorded prior to May 31. All common stock offerings by the company prior to May 31 had been at the same price.

Instructions

a Compute the average price at which the preferred stock was offered by the company.

b Compute the price at which the common stock was offered by the company prior to June of the current year.

c Prepare journal entries to record the transactions (including net loss and dividends) during June which affected the stockholders' equity accounts.

d Prepare the stockholders' equity section of the balance sheet at June 30, including any notes which should accompany the balance sheet.

17A-5 Westside Company, Inc., was organized on January 10 of the current year and received subscriptions immediately for 20,000 shares of preferred stock at par. Subscriptions for common stock were received on the same date. (The number of common shares subscribed and the subscription price can be determined from information given in the problem.) On May 15 an additional 4,000 shares of preferred stock were subscribed at $52 per share. Cash payments were received from subscribers at frequent intervals for several months after subscription and the company followed the policy of issuing stock certificates only when subscribers had paid in full. On December 12, common stock in the amount of 5,000 shares was issued in exchange for land having a fair value of $82,500. (Subscriptions were not used in this transaction.)

The balance sheet prepared at December 31 contained the following items, among others:

Subscriptions receivable: common stock	. . . .		$ 90,000
Subscriptions receivable: preferred stock	. . . .		52,000
Capital stock:			
Preferred, 7% cumulative, $50 par, authorized 40,000			
shares, issued and outstanding 22,000 shares	. . . . . .	$1,100,000	
Preferred stock subscribed, 2,000 shares	. . . .	100,000	1,200,000
Common, $5 par, authorized 50,000 shares, issued and out-			
standing 13,000 shares	. . . .	$ 65,000	
Common stock subscribed, 12,000 shares	. . . .	60,000	125,000
Paid-in capital in excess of par:			
On preferred stock	. . . .		8,000
On common stock	. . . .		257,500

Instructions

a Prepare journal entries showing all the transactions entered into by Westside Company, Inc., from January 10 to December 31, as suggested by the above account balances. Assume that the collections on the preferred stock subscriptions were made on a fifo basis.

b What is the dollar amount of paid-in capital for each class of stock at December 31? What is the amount of stated capital attributable to the common stock?

Group B

17B-1 Product Research Corporation was organized August 30, 19___, with authorization to issue capital stock as follows: 120,000 shares of $5 preferred stock, $100 par value; 480,000 shares of no-par common stock, stated value $5 per share.

During the remainder of the year the transactions affecting stockholders' equity were as follows:

Sept. 15 Received subscriptions for 12,000 shares of preferred stock at $103 per share. A down payment of 50% accompanied each subscription; the balance was to be paid on December 15. (Record the full amount subscribed and then in a separate entry show the cash collection for 50% of this amount.)

Sept. 17 Received subscriptions for 60,000 shares of common stock at $22 per share, payable December 1.

Sept. 30 Issued 600 shares of common stock in payment for legal and accounting services relating to the organization of the corporation and valued at $13,200.

Dec. 1 Received payment in full of the amount due on common stock subscriptions.

Dec. 15 Received payment in full of the balance due on preferred stock subscriptions.

Dec. 30 Issued 3,000 shares of preferred stock for cash of $312,000.

Dec. 30 Issued 4,000 shares of common stock and 1,500 shares of preferred stock in exchange for assets for which the board of directors established the following fair values:

Inventories	$ 30,000
Office equipment	8,400
Building	105,000
Land	101,000

Dec. 31 Net income earned to December 31 amounted to $104,000. No dividends had been declared.

Instructions

a Prepare journal entries to record these transactions in the accounts of Product Research Corporation.

b Prepare the stockholders' equity section of the balance sheet at December 31.

17B-2 Yaqui Yarn Corporation was organized on September 5, Year 2, with authorization to issue 600,000 shares of $5 par common stock and 22,500 shares of $50 par, 8% cumulative preferred stock. On September 15, a going business was acquired in exchange for 12,000 preferred shares plus the assumption of a mortgage liability of $276,000. The assets acquired in this manner were valued by a firm of independent appraisers at $900,000. On September 20, subscriptions were obtained for 30,000 common shares at a price of $15 per share.

All subscriptions were collected and recorded on October 5, except for a subscription by Nati Cano for 300 shares. Cano paid $1,500 but defaulted on the balance of the contract. On October 10, the 300 shares were resold for cash by the corporation at a price of $13 per share. In accordance with statutes of the state, Yaqui Yarn Corporation refunded the amount paid by Cano after deducting the loss incurred on the resale of the 300 shares.

No dividends were declared on the common stock. A quarterly dividend of $1 a share on the preferred stock was declared on November 9 payable December 15 to stockholders of record on December 1. Operations for the fractional year ended December 31 resulted in net income of $49,272.

Instructions

a Prepare journal entries relating to the capital stock transactions and the dividend declaration and payment.

b Prepare the stockholders' equity section of the balance sheet at December 31, Year 2.

17B-3 After several years of successful operation of a partnership business, the two owners, Engle and Hart, decided to incorporate the business and to sell stock to outsiders.

On January 4, Year 5, Englehart, Inc., was organized with authorization to issue 150,000 shares of $10 par common stock. It issued 20,000 shares for cash to public investors at $16 per share. Engle and Hart agreed to accept shares at the same price in amounts equal to their respective capital accounts after making the adjustments indicated below and after making cash withdrawals sufficient to avoid the need for issuing less than a multiple of 100 shares to either of the two partners. In payment for such shares, the partnership's net assets were transferred to the corporation and stock certificates were then issued. A new set of accounting records is to be opened for the corporation.

The post-closing trial balance of the partnership of Engle and Hart appeared as follows on December 31, Year 4:

Cash	$ 37,000	
Accounts receivable	30,000	
Inventories	56,000	
Land	28,000	
Buildings	50,000	
Accumulated depreciation		$ 17,000
Accounts payable		10,000
Engle, capital		63,000
Hart, capital		111,000
Totals	$201,000	$201,000

The partnership agreement provides that Engle is to receive 40% of the profits and Hart 60%. It is agreed that the following adjustments should be made to the partnership accounts at December 31, Year 4:

(1) Recognize short-term prepayments of $1,500 and accrued liabilities of $750.
(2) Provide an allowance for doubtful accounts of $12,000.
(3) Increase the value of land to $45,000.
(4) Increase inventories to present replacement cost of $75,000.

Instructions

a On the partnership accounting records, prepare the journal entries necessary to adjust the accounts to the agreed values. (One compound journal entry may be used to adjust the accounts to the agreed amounts.) Also prepare all other entries needed to record the events described.

b On the corporation accounting records, prepare the journal entries necessary to record the events described.

c Prepare the opening balance sheet for the corporation after the above transactions have been recorded.

17B-4 The capital structure of Cuco del Cid Corporation consists of an authorized issue of 400,000 shares of $60 par, 6% cumulative preferred stock and an authorized issue of 1 million shares of no-par common stock with a stated value of $10 per share. For both the preferred and the common stock, the number of shares issued at the time of organization was less than the amount authorized.

Although early operations of the company were profitable, a prolonged strike caused a net loss of $1,496,350 to be shown for the current fiscal year ended June 30. Because of this year's unprofitable operations, the company paid no dividends on its common stock during the current fiscal year. Dividends of $198,000 were paid this year on the preferred stock, but this limited payment left dividends in arrears at June 30 in the amount of $594,000.

A trial balance of the general ledger taken at May 31 (a month before the end of the fiscal year) included the following balances:

6% cumulative preferred stock, $60 par $13,200,000

Common stock, no-par, $10 stated value 3,500,000

Subscriptions receivable: preferred stock 1,518,875

Retained earnings (June 30, prior year) 2,531,600

Paid-in capital in excess of par: preferred stock 183,750

Preferred stock subscribed 1,500,000

Paid-in capital in excess of stated value: common stock 2,925,000

Subscriptions receivable: common stock 1,650,000

Common stock subscribed 1,000,000

Dividends: preferred stock 198,000

Cash was received on June 2 representing payment in full for common stock subscriptions covering 30,000 shares. These subscriptions had been received and recorded prior to May 31. All common stock offerings by Cuco del Cid Corporation prior to May 31 had been at the same price.

Other transactions during June were the issuance of an additional 10,000 shares of common stock for cash on June 9 at a price of $17\frac{1}{2}$. Another 2,000 shares of common stock were issued in exchange for a patent on June 24.

Instructions

a Compute the average price at which the preferred stock was offered by the company.

b Compute the price at which the common stock was offered by the company prior to June.

c Prepare journal entries to record the transactions (including net loss and dividends) during June which affected the stockholders' equity accounts.

d Prepare the stockholders' equity section of the balance sheet at June 30, including any notes which should accompany the balance sheet.

17B-5 On December 31, at the end of its first year of operations, Sunrise Breakfast Foods, Incorporated, presented a balance sheet containing the following items, among others:

Subscriptions receivable: preferred stock		$ 208,000
Subscriptions receivable: common stock		720,000
8% cumulative preferred stock, $100 par, authorized 200,000		
shares, issued and outstanding 44,000 shares	$4,400,000	
8% preferred stock subscribed 4,000 shares	400,000	4,800,000
Common stock, $10 par, authorized 400,000 shares, issued		
and outstanding 48,000 shares	$ 480,000	
Common stock subscribed 48,000 shares	480,000	960,000
Paid-in capital in excess of par:		
On preferred stock		32,000
On common stock		1,952,000

The corporation had been organized on January 2 of the current year and had immediately received subscriptions for 40,000 shares of preferred stock. Subscriptions for common stock were received on the same date. (The number of common shares subscribed and the subscription price can be determined from information given in the problem.) On May 5 subscriptions were received for an additional 8,000 shares of preferred stock at a price of $104 per share.

Cash payments were received from subscribers at frequent intervals for several months after subscription. The company followed a policy of issuing stock certificates only when subscribers had paid in full. On December 22, Sunrise Breakfast Foods, Incorporated, issued 16,000 shares of its common stock in exchange for a tract of land with a fair value of $512,000. (Subscriptions were not used in this transaction.)

Instructions
a Prepare journal entries for all the transactions carried out during the year by Sunrise Breakfast Foods, Incorporated, as indicated by the December 31 account balances. Assume that collections on the preferred stock were made on a fifo basis.
b Compute the amount of paid-in capital for each class of stock at the year-end. Also determine the amount of stated capital applicable to the common stock.

CHAPTER 18

STOCK RIGHTS, WARRANTS, OPTIONS, AND CONVERTIBLE SECURITIES

STOCK RIGHTS AND WARRANTS

As explained in Chapter 11, a *warrant* is a certificate issued by a corporation conveying to the holder rights to purchase shares of its common stock at a specified price. The term *stock right* means the privilege attaching to each outstanding share of stock to buy a fractional share or a specified number of shares of common stock. The holder of 100 shares of stock might therefore receive a warrant for 100 rights, which would permit him to purchase a specified number of new shares. For example, some years ago American Telephone & Telegraph Company issued rights to its stockholders permitting the purchase of one share of common stock in exchange for 20 rights and $86 cash. A.T.&T. stock was selling at that time for approximately $125. Thus a holder of 100 shares of A.T.&T. stock received 100 rights which could be used to buy five additional shares of common stock at a price of $86 a share.

The use of rights is not limited to the acquisition of additional shares of common stock; some companies in recent years have issued rights to their common stockholders entitling them to buy convertible debenture bonds at a stipulated price. The use of rights in buying bonds is considered later in this chapter. At this point we are concerned only with rights which entitle the holder to purchase common stock at a specified price.

Various forms of stock rights are often issued by corporations in the following three situations:

1 As a preliminary step to raising more capital through the issuance of additional shares of common stock or convertible bonds to existing stockholders. Such contractual privileges are generally called *stock rights.*

2 In combination with an offering of bonds, notes, or preferred stock, thus adding a speculative bonus for investors in these securities. Such rights are known as *stock warrants.* Warrants may also be issued to promoters and underwriters.

3 As additional compensation to officers and employees. These privileges are most frequently referred to as *stock options.*

When stock rights, warrants, or options are outstanding, the corporation's balance sheet should disclose the number of shares of stock being held in reserve to meet the contractual commitments to issue additional shares of stock. This disclosure may be made in the stockholders' equity section or in a note to the financial statements.

The special characteristics of the three major categories of stock rights listed above are discussed in the following sections along with recommended accounting treatment.

Rights granted to existing stockholders

When rights are granted to existing stockholders as a preliminary step to raising more capital through the issuance of additional shares of common stock, the corporation receives nothing in exchange for the rights when they are issued. Only when the rights are exercised does the corporation receive funds. This situation is a sharp contrast with the other two situations listed above involving the issuance of stock warrants and options. When warrants are issued in combination with an offering of bonds or preferred stock, a portion of the proceeds is in fact attributable to the warrants. When stock options are issued as additional compensation to corporate officers or key employees, the fact that the stock options constitute a part of a compensation plan and not a gift indicates that the company is receiving services in exchange for them.

Stock rights granted to existing stockholders as a preliminary step to raising more capital through the issuance of additional common stock usually expire within a few weeks. Consequently, the corporation can rapidly complete its program of raising capital through the issuance of additional common stock to present stockholders or other investors. Stock rights of this type are transferable and may be actively traded on the stock exchanges. Consequently, many investors acquire rights by purchase from other investors. When investors who have purchased rights from other investors decide to exercise such rights, the cost they incurred in buying the rights must be combined with their cash payments to the corporation to determine the total cost of their investment in shares of stock.

The purchase price specified in stock rights granted to existing stockholders is usually somewhat less than current market price. In the following illustration of a subscription warrant for common stock issued by Pacific Gas and Electric Company a few years ago, 15 rights were needed for each share of stock to be purchased at the subscription price (not shown) of $25.65. The market price of the common stock at the time the rights were issued was $27.62. The life of the rights was short—they were issued March 6 and expired on March 27. Through use of these rights the company sold over 4 million shares of stock and raised capital in excess of $102 million within the three-week life span of the rights. The rights were actively traded on the New York Stock Exchange throughout their brief life, with the price per right varying from a low of about one-eighth of a dollar to one-half dollar.

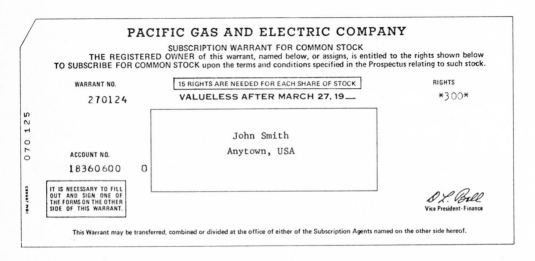

The issuance of rights to stockholders does not require debits or credits to any accounts of the issuing corporation, although a memorandum entry stating the number of rights issued normally would be used. When the rights are exercised by the holders, the corporation issues shares of stock at the stipulated price. This issuance of shares requires the usual entry for sale of stock.

Rights to purchase convertible bonds

The preemptive right of common stockholders to purchase additional shares in proportion to their present holdings in the event that the corporation increases the amount of stock outstanding was discussed in Chapter 17. This preemptive right logically applies also to any new issues of convertible bonds or convertible preferred stock because these securities may eventually be converted into common stock.

In recent years convertible bonds have been a popular form of financing. Rights have been issued to common stockholders entitling them to buy convertible bonds at a specified price, and usually with the provision that the rights will expire if not exercised within a month or two. For example, some years ago National Cash Register issued to its common stockholders rights to purchase $4\frac{1}{4}\%$ convertible bonds maturing in 1992. Ten rights and $100 cash were required to purchase $100 face value of bonds. The rights traded for several weeks on the New York Stock Exchange at prices varying between $1 and $2 per right, while the convertible bonds were concurrently trading on a **when-issued** basis at prices ranging from about $108 to $116 per $100 face value. (Sales of securities on a when-issued basis do not require delivery until after the scheduled date of issuance.)

The accounting procedures for rights to purchase convertible bonds are similar to the procedures described for rights to purchase common stock. The corporation need make no formal journal entry in its accounts when the rights are issued but must maintain memorandum records of the number of rights issued, exercised, and outstanding. When the rights are exercised, the entry usually required is to debit cash and credit the liability account for the convertible bonds. Usually the price stipulated by the right is par; hence no discount or premium is involved when the convertible bonds are issued.

Warrants issued in combination with bonds or preferred stock

A company may add to the attractiveness of its bonds or preferred stock by attaching a warrant to buy its common stock at a specified price.[1] The longer the life of the warrant the greater its speculative appeal; warrants often run for several years and some have no expiration date.

When bonds are issued with detachable warrants, the rate of interest on the bonds is usually less than if the bonds were offered alone. Similarly, preferred stock accompanied by detachable warrants for the purchase of common stock can attract investors even though the dividend rate on the preferred stock is lower than would otherwise be necessary. In other words, a part of the proceeds to the company from issuing bonds or preferred stock with warrants attached represents payment by investors for the warrants. Therefore, proper accounting for these "combination packages" of securities **requires that part of the proceeds be recognized as attributable to the warrants.**

Accounting for bonds payable issued with detachable warrants was illustrated in Chapter 15. At this time our discussion will be focused on the issuance of warrants in combination with preferred stock.

Warrants giving the holder the right to purchase common stock at a specified price at any time during a span of years have an economic value regardless of whether the specified exercise price is higher, lower, or equal to the market price of the stock when the warrants are issued. Since the detachable warrants are often traded separately from the pre-

[1] Warrants to purchase common stock are also sometimes offered in combination with the public issuance of common stock or in business combinations. For example, some years ago Tenneco, Inc., offered 5.5 million shares of common stock with detachable warrants entitling the holder to purchase additional shares of common stock at $24.25.

ferred stock or bond with which they were originally issued, objective evidence is available to aid in allocating the proceeds between the two types of securities.

In *APB Opinion No. 14,* the Accounting Principles Board stated that "the portion of the proceeds of debt securities issued with detachable stock warrants which is allocable to the warrants should be accounted for as paid-in capital. The allocation should be based on the relative fair values of the two securities at time of issuance."[2] Although this discussion related specifically to bonds issued with detachable stock purchase warrants, the reasoning also appears applicable to warrants issued with preferred stock.

Assume, for example, that Gulf, Inc., issues 1 million shares of $25 par value preferred stock at $26½ and gives with each share a warrant to purchase one share of common stock at $30 at any time during the next 10 years. The common stock has a par value of $5 and a current market price of $26. The warrants have a value because of the likelihood that the market price of the common stock will rise above $30 during the next 10 years. Assume also that immediately after issuance the warrants are traded in the market at a price of $1 each. The following entry should be made to record the proceeds of the stock offering:

Cash	26,500,000	
Preferred Stock		25,000,000
Paid-in Capital in Excess of Par: Preferred		
Stock		500,000
Common Stock Warrants		1,000,000
Issued 1 million shares of $25 par preferred stock at		
$25½ and 1 million warrants at $1 each.		

The account Common Stock Warrants would be classified in the stockholders' equity section of the balance sheet as an element of paid-in capital. If the warrants are exercised and the common stock issued at $30 a share, the journal entry would be:

Cash	30,000,000	
Common Stock Warrants	1,000,000	
Common Stock		5,000,000
Paid-in Capital in Excess of Par: Common Stock		26,000,000
Issued 1 million shares of $5 par common stock in ex-		
change for 1 million warrants and cash of $30 a share.		

---

[2] *APB Opinion No. 14,* "Accounting for Convertible Debt and Debt Issued with Stock Purchase Warrants," AICPA (New York: 1969), p. 209.

Assume, however, that the market price of the common stock consistently remained below $30 after the issuance of the warrants. Consequently, no warrants were exercised; the following journal entry would be made upon the expiration date of the warrants:

Common Stock Warrants 1,000,000
     Paid-in Capital from Expired Warrants   1,000,000
To record expiration of 1 million warrants originally
issued at a valuation of $1 each.

STOCK OPTION CONTRACTS

Stock option contracts with officers and key employees represent an important element of executive compensation in many corporations. A *stock option plan* gives officers and key employees the right to purchase the corporation's stock at a specified price. The option price is usually 100% of the fair (or market) value of the stock at the date of granting the option, and the life of the option is often five years. For example, assume that you, as an executive of X Corporation, receive today a five-year option to buy 1,000 shares of the company's stock at today's price of $20. If, during the next five years, the market price of the stock rises to, say, $70, you will be in the fortunate position of being able to purchase $70,000 worth of stock for $20,000. The option is in reality a *call* on the stock at a fixed price over a period of years with no risk to the holder. The opportunity for gain is unlimited; the chance of loss is zero. In the event of a stock split or stock dividend, the option price is reduced and the number of shares under option increased proportionately to avoid dilution to the option holder. By means of stock option contracts, corporate employees are not only rewarded by increases in the price of the company's stock, but the personal income obtained in this manner may be taxed in some cases as a capital gain rather than as ordinary income.

Impact of income tax requirements

Qualified Stock Option Plans In adopting stock plans for employees, corporations in the past have made extensive use of *qualified stock options* as defined in federal income tax legislation. However, the Tax Reform Act of 1976 generally repealed the qualified stock option rules for employee stock options granted after May 20, 1976, unless such options were granted under a plan adopted prior to that date. According to present law, option contracts must be exercised prior to May 21, 1981, to retain their qualified option status.

In a qualified stock option plan, the option price had to be set at not less than the market price of the stock on the date the options were granted. Furthermore, the options had to be exercised within five years after the date of grant. Among the income tax consequences resulting from a qualified stock option plan are the following:

1 No income (for federal income tax purposes) will result to optionees at the time they receive the options or when they acquire stock by exercising the options.

2 If the stock is held by optionees for three years after the exercise of the options, they may then sell the stock and treat any gain or loss as a long-term capital gain or loss for income tax purposes.

3 The corporation granting qualified stock options is not permitted to deduct as compensation expense any part of the value of stock delivered under the option plan.

4 No amount other than the price paid by optionees will be considered as received by the corporation for the shares issued under the option plan.

The widespread use of qualified stock option plans reflected the desire of many corporations to attract and retain competent executives by offering them rewards which were not subject to the higher rates of our graduated personal income tax structure. The opportunity to acquire stock under a stock option plan without recognizing taxable income at the time of acquiring the stock was a strong attraction to most executives. The possibility of selling the stock three years or more after acquisition and treating any gain as a long-term capital gain was especially attractive, since long-term capital gains generally are taxed at a lower rate than is ordinary income.

The impact of income tax rules upon the development of financial reporting standards is difficult to measure, but it clearly is important. For example, the fact that corporations do not record any compensation expense for the stock issued to executives under qualified stock option plans is at least partially due to the fact that no such compensation expense may be deducted in computing the *taxable income* of the corporation.

Nonqualified Stock Option Plans Most stock options currently granted to employees are *nonqualified* for income tax purposes. Among the income tax consequences resulting from a nonqualified stock option plan are the following:

1 The value of the options is treated as ordinary income to the employees when it is granted so long as it has a readily ascertainable market value at the time of grant. If the options have no readily ascertainable market value on the date of grant, the difference between the option price and the market value of the stock acquired is taxed as ordinary income when the employees exercise the options.

2 The options can be set at any price, can be effective for any number of years, and there is no limit on the length of time over which the options can be granted to employees.

3 The amount of compensation taxable to employees generally is allowed as a tax-deductible expense to the granting corporation.

Theoretical issues

From a theoretical viewpoint, the valuation of stock options is a difficult and challenging problem. In current practice, however, the problem of valuation of stock options is generally ignored, and the accounting procedures for the options are designed to comply with income tax rules. Present income tax rules state that the receipt of stock options does not constitute income to the recipient, and that no compensation expense may be deducted by the corporation when the option price is equal to or above the quoted market price of the common stock. Thus, the difficult problem of determining the fair value of stock options generally is avoided by assuming that the options have no value.

Although this treatment of stock options may be convenient for administration of the income tax laws, the current practice clearly has little theoretical support. Because stock options generally represent an important part of the total compensation cost to a corporation, it has been suggested that the options be valued at the amount for which options could be sold to the public at the time similar options are granted to employees. However, the accounting profession has not found this line of reasoning persuasive because stock options are designed to give employees additional compensation and not for sale to the public.

In the opinion of the authors, the current practice of not recording compensation expense for most stock option plans results in an understatement of compensation expense and a corresponding understatement of capital contributed for shares of stock issued under stock option plans. The basic accounting principle of matching costs with related revenue suggests that the compensation expense implicit in stock option plans should be accrued throughout the life of the option plans. Such accruals would require the use of estimates (perhaps based on the trend of market prices from year to year). Thus the two major accounting problems relating to stock option plans may be identified as (1) the measurement of any compensation cost implicit in the stock option plans and (2) the allocation of such compensation cost among accounting periods. The current generally accepted accounting principles addressing these two problems are found in *APB Opinion No. 25,* which is discussed in the following sections.[3]

APB Opinion No. 25, "Accounting for Stock Issued to Employees"

APB Opinion No. 25 provided a historical summary of the problems encountered in accounting for stock options and set forth the current accounting and reporting standards for stock option plans. Generally, the current accounting and disclosure requirements for all stock option

---

[3] *APB Opinion No. 25,* "Accounting for Stock Issued to Employees," AICPA (New York: 1972).

plans depend essentially on whether the plan is viewed as noncompensatory or compensatory in nature.

Noncompensatory Plans A *noncompensatory plan* is one not primarily designed as a form of compensation, but rather for such purposes as raising capital or inducing widespread ownership of the corporation's stock among officers and employees. Essential characteristics of a noncompensatory plan are (1) participation of all full-time employees; (2) offering of stock on an equal basis or as a uniform percentage of salary to all employees; (3) a limited time for exercise of the option; and (4) a discount from market price no greater than would be reasonable in an offering to stockholders. In such noncompensatory plans, no compensation is presumed to be involved. Consequently, the corporation records no compensation expense for financial accounting purposes and claims no deduction for income tax purposes.

The exercise of the option is recorded as an ordinary issuance of capital stock, as illustrated below:

Cash	40,000	
Common Stock, $5 par		5,000
Paid-in Capital in Excess of Par: Common Stock		35,000
To record issuance of 1,000 shares of common stock at $40 a share pursuant to exercise of noncompensatory stock options by employees.		

The noncompensatory type of stock option plan was apparently summarized in *APB Opinion No. 25* principally to clear the way for consideration of the more controversial issues of accounting for compensatory plans.

Compensatory Plans Any stock option plan not possessing the four specified characteristics of a noncompensatory plan is classified as a *compensatory plan.* The features of a compensatory plan may vary in an almost endless number of respects. For example, the *grantee* (employee granted the option) may be obligated to continue in the employment of the corporation or of its subsidiaries. The total number of shares specified in the option may be acquired at one time or only in a limited number during each year of the option plan. The consideration received by a corporation for stock issued through a stock option plan may include cash, notes receivable, or other assets, as well as services from the employee. In all compensatory plans, services from the grantee represent part of the consideration for the capital stock issued.

A key provision of *Opinion No. 25* is that compensation for services received as consideration for the stock issued shall be measured by the *quoted market price of the stock at the measurement date less the amount, if any, that the employee is required to pay.* In applying this policy, determination of the measurement date for determining compensation cost touches the theoretical center of the problem. The measurement date is stated to be the *first date on which are known both the number of shares to be received by each individual and the option price.* On the measurement date the corporation and the employees presumably reach agreement as to the amount of total compensation to be paid and the corporation forgoes any alternative uses of the stock reserved for the exercise of the options. In most plans, that early date is the date that the option is granted.

APB Opinion No. 25 then concludes that a corporation should recognize compensation cost for stock issued through compensatory stock option plans when the option price is less than the quoted market price of the stock at the measurement date. As previously indicated, qualified stock option plans set the option price at or above the market price of the stock at the date of grant. Consequently, no compensation cost is recognized for most qualified stock option plans.

When compensation cost is recognized, it should be allocated to the periods which are deemed to have received benefit from the services provided by the employees receiving the options. The following guidelines for accruing compensation cost are presented in *APB Opinion No. 25:*

> Compensation cost in stock option, purchase, and award plans should be recognized as an expense of one or more periods in which an employee performs services and also as part or all of the consideration received for stock issued to the employee through a plan. The grant or award may specify the period or periods during which the employee performs services, or the period or periods may be inferred from the terms or from the past pattern of grants or awards. . . .
>
> An employee may perform services in several periods before an employer corporation issues stock . . . for those services. The employer corporation should accrue compensation expense in each period in which the services are performed. If the measurement date is later than the date of grant or award, an employer corporation should record the compensation expense each period from date of grant or award to date of measurement based on the quoted market price of the stock at the end of each period.
>
> If stock is issued in a plan before some or all of the services are performed, part of the consideration recorded for the stock issued is unearned compensation and should be shown as a separate reduction of stockholder's equity. The unearned compensation should be accounted for as expense of the period or periods in which the employee performs service.
>
> Accruing compensation expense may require estimates, and adjustment of those estimates in later periods may be necessary. . . . For example, if a stock option is not exercised (or awarded stock is returned to the corporation) because an employee fails to fulfill an obligation, the estimate of compensation expense recorded in previous periods should be adjusted by decreasing compensation expense in the period of forfeiture.[4]

---

[4] Ibid., pp. 474–475.

The reporting of unearned (deferred) compensation cost as a reduction of stockholders' equity may be justified on grounds that the full recorded consideration relating to issuance of stock has not been received. When the services are performed, the debit balance in Deferred Compensation Cost is transferred to compensation expense.

Illustration of Compensatory Stock Option Plan: Measurement Date Is Date of Grant To illustrate the accounting for a compensatory stock option plan when the measurement date is the date of grant, assume the following facts: On January 2, Year 1, Clark Corporation granted certain employees options to purchase 10,000 shares of its $10 par common stock at $20 per share in exchange for services to be performed over the next three years. The quoted market price of the stock at this date was $23 per share. The options were exercised at December 31, Year 3, when the quoted market price of the stock was $31 per share. The journal entries for each year would be as follows:

Year 1

Jan. 1 Deferred Compensation Cost 30,000
  Common Stock Options 30,000
  To record compensatory stock options at grant date
  to purchase 10,000 shares of common stock at $20
  per share. Quoted market price of stock is $23 per
  share. Deferred compensation: 10,000 ($23 − $20) =
  $30,000.

Dec. 31 Compensation Expense 10,000
  Deferred Compensation Cost 10,000
  To record compensation expense for Year 1.

Year 2
Dec. 31 Same entry as at Dec. 31, Year 1.
Year 3
Dec. 31 Same entry as at Dec. 31, Year 1.
Dec. 31 Cash 200,000
  Common Stock Options 30,000
    Common Stock, $10 par 100,000
    Paid-in Capital in Excess of Par: Common
      Stock 130,000
  To record issuance of 10,000 shares of common
  stock at $20 per share pursuant to stock option
  plan.

The common stock options and deferred compensation cost would be included in the paid-in capital section of the balance sheet at December 1, Year 1, as follows:

Common stock options	$30,000	
Less: Deferred compensation cost	20,000	$10,000

Illustration of Compensatory Stock Option Plan: Measurement Date Is Two Years after Date of Grant To illustrate the accounting for a compensatory stock option plan when the measurement date is *subsequent* to the date of grant (because the option price and the number of shares that can be purchased have not been definitely fixed), assume the following facts: On January 2, Year 1, Dome Corporation adopted a stock option plan for key employees to purchase an estimated 20,000 shares of $1 par common stock at a price estimated at $20 per share. The number of shares to be issued and the option price will be determined on December 31, Year 2, the measurement date. The options were granted in consideration for services to be performed during Years 1 and 2, and can be exercised at any time starting in Year 3. The number of shares covered by the plan, the option price, and the quoted market price of the common stock at the relevant dates are as follows.

	January 2, Year 1	December 31, Year 1	December 31, Year 2
Number of shares optioned	20,000 (est.)	20,000 (est.)	21,000 (final)
Option price	$20 (est.)	$20 (est.)	$22 (final)
Quoted market price of common stock	$19	$25	$33

No journal entry would be required on January 2, Year 1, because estimated option price was less than the quoted market price of the common stock and because the final measurement date was December 31, Year 2.

On December 31, Year 1, estimated compensation expense would be recorded as illustrated at the top of page 740.

On the measurement date, December 31, Year 2, the second journal entry on page 740 would be required.

At the time the options are exercised, a journal entry similar to the last entry illustrated on page 738 would be required.

When compensation expense is reported by the corporation in a

```
Compensation Expense  . . . . . . . . . . . . . . . . . . . 100,000
     Common Stock Options . . . . . . . . . . . . . . . .           100,000
To record estimated compensation expense for Year 1 based
on quoted market price of common stock, estimated num-
ber of shares optioned, and estimated option price: 20,000 ×
($25 − $20) = $100,000.
```

```
Compensation Expense  . . . . . . . . . . . . . . . . . . . 131,000
     Common Stock Options . . . . . . . . . . . . . . . .           131,000
To record compensation expense for Year 2 at the meas-
urement date, determined as follows:
  Total compensation cost: 21,000 × ($33 −
     $22) . . . . . . . . . . . . . . . . . . . . . . . $231,000
  Less: Estimated compensation expense re-
     corded in Year 1 . . . . . . . . . . . . . .   100,000
  Compensation expense for Year 2  . . . . . . . $131,000
```

period other than that in which the expense is deductible for income tax purposes, a *timing difference* results which would require the application of interperiod income tax allocation procedures. This topic is covered in Chapter 21.

Stock option plans are complex and may involve difficult accounting problems. Our objective in this section was to illustrate the basic and more important accounting aspects of compensatory plans.

Accounting for employee stock ownership plans (ESOP)

Closely related to a stock option plan described in the preceding pages is an employee stock ownership plan (ESOP). Such a plan may be established under the provisions of the Employee Retirement Income Security Act (ERISA) of 1974. An employee stock ownership plan is a *qualified* stock bonus plan designed to invest primarily in the securities of the company sponsoring such a plan for its employees.[5] An ESOP acquires securities of the employer company either directly from the employer (as periodic contributions) or by using borrowed funds. The debt of an ESOP is usually secured by a pledge of the stock owned by the plan and by either a guarantee of the employer or a commitment by the employer to make periodic contributions to the fund. The periodic contributions are treated as deductible expenses in the computation of the employer's taxable income.

[5] *Employee Retirement Income Security Act of 1974,* Title II, Subtitle B, Sec. 2003.

In the accounting records of the employer, the periodic contributions to ESOP are recorded as compensation expense and any debt of the plan guaranteed by the employer should be reported as a liability in the balance sheet of the employer. However, assets held by the ESOP are not included in the balance sheet of the employer because such assets are owned by employees and not by the employer. When the liability for the guarantee of the debt of the plan is recorded by the employer, the offsetting debit should be recorded in an unearned (or deferred) compensation cost account. This account is reported as a deduction from stockholders' equity (similar to the treatment of deferred compensation cost recognized under stock option plans). When the ESOP reduces the debt guaranteed by the employer (presumably from contributions from the employer), both the liability and deferred compensation cost are reduced. The AICPA summarized these accounting requirements as follows:

> . . . the offsetting debit to the liability recorded by the employer should be accounted for as a reduction of shareholders' equity. Therefore, when new shares are issued to the ESOP by the employer, an increase in shareholders' equity should be reported only as the debt that financed that increase is reduced. . . . When outstanding shares, as opposed to unissued shares, are acquired by the ESOP, shareholders' equity should similarly be reduced by the offsetting debit until the debt is repaid. . . . The liability is initially recorded because the guarantee or commitment is in substance the employer's debt. Therefore, it should not be reduced until payments are actually made. Similarly, the amount reported as a reduction of shareholders' equity should be reduced only when the ESOP makes payment on the debt. These two accounts should move symmetrically.[6]

The amount charged to expense by the employer company should be the amount (cash or current fair value of stock) contributed to the stock ownership plan. In the computation of earnings per share, the employer company should treat all shares held by the ESOP as issued and outstanding.[7]

Disclosure requirements for stock option plans

Although differences of opinion exist as to the best method of measuring the amount of compensation expense implicit in stock options, there is general agreement as to the necessity of disclosing the significant information contained in the stock option plan. In each set of annual financial statements, information should be given as to the number of shares under option at a given option price and the time periods within which these options may be exercised. Often this disclosure will show that the corporation has stock options outstanding granted at various dates and at varying prices.

The note on pages 742 and 743 attached to the financial statements

---

[6] *Statement of Position No. 76-3,* "Accounting Practices for Certain Employee Stock Ownership Plans," AICPA (New York: 1976), pp. 3–4.
[7] Ibid., p. 5.

Note 12. Employee Stock Option Plans

Options to purchase common stock of the Company have been granted under various plans to officers and other key employees at prices equal to the fair market value of such stock on the dates the options were granted. Certain information for 1975 and 1976 relative to common stock options is summarized as follows (in millions, except for number of shares):

	Number of shares	Aggregate option price	Corresponding market value
Stock options, October 1, 1974:			
Outstanding	1,259,537	$31.5	$31.5(a)
Exercisable	914,023	22.5	
Available for future grant · · · ·	500,400		
Changes in stock options during 1975:			
Granted:			
Options	281,850	6.3	6.3(a)
Alternative options	417,250	8.8	8.8(a)
Became exercisable	239,135	6.1	5.0(b)
Exercised	241,933	4.3	5.5(c)
Expired	161,243	4.0	
Stock options, September 30, 1975:			
Outstanding	1,138,211(d)	27.0(d)	27.0(a)(d)
Exercisable	769,986(e)	20.7(e)	
Available for future grant · · · ·	265,300		
Changes in stock options during 1976:			
Granted	148,200	4.4	4.4(a)
Became exercisable	358,790	8.4	10.8(b)
Exercised	142,259	3.5	4.3(c)
Expired	118,581	3.3	
Stock options, September 30, 1976:			
Outstanding	1,025,571(d)	25.1(d)	25.1(a)(d)
Exercisable	874,997(e)	22.7(e)	
Available for future grant	181,500		

(a) As of dates granted.
(b) As of dates became exercisable.
(c) As of dates exercised.
(d) Based on alternative options, where applicable (see following paragraph).
(e) Based on previously granted matched options, where applicable (see following paragraph).

Certain stock options granted during 1975 were in the form of alternative options to options previously granted and outstanding (matched options) under the

Company's most recent option plan. Each such alternative option granted for which the number of shares that may be purchased is equal to the outstanding number of shares that may be purchased under a matched option, may not be exercised while the matched option remains outstanding, and the number of shares available for exercise under the alternative option is automatically reduced to the extent the matched option is exercised. Thus, an optionee has the alternative of either exercising all or part of the matched option or allowing the matched option or the unexercised part thereof to expire and thereby being entitled to exercise the alternative option or the remaining portion thereof. Such alternative options do not change the number of shares that may be purchased under outstanding options or available for future grant. Assuming future exercise of matched options in lieu of alternative options, the number of shares related to stock options outstanding would not change and such shares would have an aggregate option price of $27.1 million and $29.3 million at September 30, 1976 and 1975, respectively, which amounts are equal to their market values as of dates granted. A pending shareowner action seeks a determination that the outstanding alternative options be declared invalid.

Common stock options outstanding at September 30, 1976 have option prices ranging from $15.61 to $35.25 a share and expire at various dates from February 11, 1977 to July 14, 1985. Options available for future grant may not be granted after November 30, 1982.

of Rockwell International Corporation illustrates how detailed the disclosure of stock option plans may be.

The Securities and Exchange Commission has specified in some detail in Regulation S-X the information regarded as constituting adequate disclosure of stock option plans. The SEC requirement includes a statement of the basis of accounting for the plans and the charges to expense, if any, during the current period.

CONVERTIBLE SECURITIES

Characteristics of convertible preferred stock

Many preferred stocks are convertible into common stock at the option of the holders. The appeal of the convertible preferred stock lies in the fact that it combines certain attributes of both common and preferred stock in a single security. Because the convertible preferred stock may be exchanged for common shares in a fixed ratio, convertibles have the same appreciation potential as the related common stock. The status of the convertible preferred stock as a *senior security* with a stated annual dividend gives convertibles the same reduced risk possessed by non-convertible preferred stock. The extent to which one or the other of these attributes of potential appreciation and reduced risk is more influential varies from one preferred stock issue to another, and even for the same issue over a period of years.

Definitions applicable to convertible preferred stock

The *conversion ratio* indicates the number of common shares for which a convertible preferred stock may be exchanged. The basic ratio is set when the convertible preferred stock is issued, but the ratio is subject to adjustment in the event of a stock split or a stock dividend on the common stock. For example, each share of American Home Products Corporation's $2 cumulative convertible preferred stock was convertible into $1\frac{1}{2}$ shares of its common stock. When the common stock was split 3 for 1 several years ago, the conversion ratio increased to $4\frac{1}{2}$ shares of common for each share of the convertible preferred.

Conversion value is the value of the preferred stock if exchanged for common; it is calculated by multiplying the market price of the common stock by the conversion ratio.

Conversion premium is the excess, if any, of the market price of the convertible preferred stock over its conversion value. This dollar premium is usually expressed as a percentage, obtained by dividing it by the conversion value. The lower the conversion premium, the more closely the market price of the convertible stock tends to follow changes in the market price of the common stock.

Investment value is an estimated price, influenced by prevailing interest rates, at which the preferred stock would be likely to sell *if it were not convertible.* For example, assume that the prevailing rate of return in the market for securities of a given quality is 6%. It follows that a $4 convertible preferred stock in this particular quality group would have an investment value of $66.67, computed as follows: $4 annual dividend divided by 6% equals $66.67. At a price of $66.67, the $4 convertible preferred stock would provide a dividend yield of 6%. The stock would sell at this price only if its conversion feature were completely ignored. Those convertible preferred stocks which have risen greatly in price by moving "in gear" with a rising price trend in the related common stock often trade at a market price far above the investment value of the preferred stock.

Price risk for a convertible preferred stock is a term used to describe the difference between its current market price and its investment value as defined above. The dollar excess of market price over investment value may be expressed as a percentage by dividing the excess by the current market price of the stock.

To illustrate the application of these terms, we shall extend the previous example of the $2 cumulative convertible preferred stock of American Home Products Corporation. Prior to the split of the common stock, the convertible preferred stock was trading in the market at about $190 per share, while the market price of the common stock was about $127 a share. The *conversion ratio* of the preferred stock was 1.50 to 1;

therefore the **conversion value** of the preferred stock was $1\frac{1}{2}$ times $127, or approximately $190. Consequently, the conversion premium was zero; the market price of the preferred stock did not exceed its conversion value. The yield on the $2 preferred stock was only 1.1% at its $190 price; however, the prevailing rate demanded by investors in stocks of comparable quality without the conversion privilege was about 6.9%. We can compute the investment value of this $2 convertible preferred stock by dividing $2 by 6.9%, which gives the amount of $29. The **price risk** was naturally high, since the market price of the convertible was so largely based on its conversion value. To compute the price risk as a percentage, we first deduct the investment value of $29 from the market price of $190. The resulting $161 differential is divided by the market price ($190) to arrive at the price risk of approximately 85%. These relationships are typical of outstanding growth stocks in which current dividend yields are largely ignored because of an excellent record of capital appreciation.

Conversion of preferred stock into common stock

Many preferred stocks are convertible into common stock at the option of the holder. When such conversions are recorded, any paid-in capital in excess of par applicable to the preferred shares should be eliminated by transfer to the accounts representing the common shares being issued.

Assume, for example, a $100 par preferred stock convertible at the option of the holder into four shares of the company's $10 par common stock. All the preferred shares were issued at a price of $105 a share, and the account balances relating to the preferred stock are as follows:

Preferred stock	$1,000,000
Paid-in capital in excess of par: preferred stock	50,000

If 100 shares of preferred stock are presented for conversion, the entry will be as follows:

Preferred Stock	10,000	
Paid-in Capital in Excess of Par: Preferred Stock	500	
Common Stock		4,000
Paid-in Capital in Excess of Par: Common Stock		6,500
Issued 400 shares of $10 par common in exchange for 100 shares of $100 par convertible preferred stock.		

In the rare situation in which the par or stated values of the shares in a conversion transaction exceeded the par or stated value of the securities being converted, a debit to retained earnings would be necessary. Note, however, that retained earnings is *never* increased by a conversion transaction.

It may be assumed that the original purchasers of convertible preferred stock were influenced in their investment decision by the possibility that conversion would be advantageous at some future date. The paid-in capital received by the issuing corporation for convertible preferred stock may therefore logically be regarded as the appropriate amount of paid-in capital applicable to the common shares which the investors receive upon exercise of their conversion option.

Conversion of bonds into common stock

Bond contracts that allow investors to exchange their bonds for common stock are known as *convertible bonds,* and this feature is called a *conversion option.* Inclusion of the conversion feature makes bonds far more attractive to investors and may enable the issuing corporation to obtain funds at an interest rate well below that which would otherwise have to be paid on long-term borrowings. The conversion feature may also have the effect of providing a relatively automatic retirement of debt as the bondholders over the years elect to exchange their bonds for common stock. Thus by issuing convertible bonds, the corporation in effect sells common stock at a price substantially above the market price prevailing at the time the bonds are issued.

Investors favor the conversion option because they stand to gain if the company is extremely successful; at the same time they limit their risk by retaining preferential status as creditors in case the company suffers reverses. Some indication of the capital gain potential in convertible bonds is available in the current market prices quoted for issues of some highly successful companies. The 8% convertible bonds of Ramada Inns, scheduled to mature in 1995, have traded at prices in excess of $2,700 for each bond of $1,000 denomination. The $4\frac{3}{4}$% convertible bonds of PepsiCo, Inc., maturing in 1996, have increased in value by more than 50%, as have the convertible bonds and convertible preferred stocks of many other companies.

If a convertible bond or convertible preferred stock is called by the issuing company before the scheduled maturity date, the holders are given a limited period, such as 30 or 60 days, within which to exchange their convertible securities for common stock at the predetermined conversion ratio. Consequently, the investor who holds a convertible bond of preferred stock with a market price far above its face amount need not fear a loss caused by the issuing corporation deciding to call the convertible security at or near its par value. When a corporation calls a convertible security which has a market price well above par, the effect is to force investors to convert their holdings into common stock. Convertible securities are seldom called until they are selling well above the call price and probably at little or no premium above the conversion value.

The issuing company sometimes arranges a sliding scale of conversion prices so that the bondholder is encouraged to convert before a date when the conversion ratio is reduced. For example, a 10-year bond may be convertible during the first five years at the rate of 20 shares of stock for one $1,000 bond; during the next three years at 19 shares of stock for one bond; and during the last two years at a ratio of 18 shares of stock for one bond.

Whenever a company has convertible securities outstanding, the balance sheet should disclose the number of common shares held in reserve to meet demands for conversion. This concept was illustrated earlier in this chapter with reference to the disclosure required for outstanding stock options. The two situations are alike in that both pose the possibility that the corporation may be called upon to issue additional common shares if stock options are exercised or the holders of convertible securities decide to convert them.

When bonds are converted, the accountant faces the problem of recording the retirement of the debt and the issuance of additional stock. To illustrate, assume that R Corporation has outstanding $10,000,000 of 7% convertible bonds, carried in its accounts at $10,400,000, the $400,000 representing unamortized bond premium. The bonds at this time are convertible into $25 par common stock having a market price of $125 per share, at a conversion ratio of 10 shares of common for each $1,000 bond. Assume that the corporation calls the bonds; therefore all bondholders present their bonds for conversion.

The company has exchanged common stock having a total market value of $12,500,000 for bonded debt having a carrying value of $10,400,000. However, the market value of the stock and of the bonds is ignored. The conversion is recorded by assigning the carrying value of the bonds to paid-in capital, as shown by the following entry:

7% Convertible Bonds Payable	10,000,000	
Premium on Bonds Payable	400,000	
Common Stock, $25 par		2,500,000
Paid-in Capital in Excess of Par: Common Stock		7,900,000
To record conversion of bonds into 100,000 shares of common stock.		

At the original issuance date of the convertible bonds, the price received reflected the prospect that the bonds might be exchanged for common stock at some later time under favorable conditions. Thus the original proceeds represented the market value of the debt contract *and* the conversion feature. When the conversion is actually made, *the car-*

rying value of the debt measures the increase in paid-in capital which resulted from the additional issue of common stock.

APB Opinions and convertible bonds

The issuance of convertible bonds raises an interesting question as to whether the amount received by the issuing company should be recorded entirely as debt or should be divided between debt and an element of stockholders' equity representing the portion of the proceeds attributable to the convertible feature of the bonds. Accounting Principles Board *Opinions Nos. 10* and *14* bear on this issue. The rationale underlying these Opinions was discussed and evaluated in the sections devoted to convertible bonds in Chapter 15.

Protection against dilution of conversion rights

For both convertible preferred stocks and convertible bonds, it is standard practice to include a guarantee against dilution through common stock splits or stock dividends. Any increase in the number of common stock shares from splits or stock dividends causes a corresponding adjustment in the conversion ratio.

This protection against dilution is most essential in maintaining the relative positions of the holders of stock warrants, stock options, convertible preferred stock, and convertible bonds. For example, assume that you had invested in the $2 convertible preferred stock of American Home Products Corporation at a market price of $190 just prior to the 3 for 1 split of the common stock. (See page 744.) Each share of the convertible preferred stock you purchased was exchangeable for $1\frac{1}{2}$ shares of common stock which was selling for about $127 per share before the split. After the 3 for 1 split of the common stock, the total number of common shares outstanding was three times as large and the price per share was only one-third of the former price, or about $42 a share. If it had not been for the clause in the preferred stock contract protecting you against dilution, the market price of your convertible preferred stock would probably have declined overnight from $190 per share to about $63, the market price of $1\frac{1}{2}$ new common shares selling at $42. However, because of the guarantee against dilution, your conversion ratio has been increased from $1\frac{1}{2}$ to $4\frac{1}{2}$ as a result of the 3 for 1 split of the common stock. The conversion value of your preferred shares would therefore be little changed and would be computed at $4\frac{1}{2}$ times about $42, or a total of about $190 for each convertible preferred share.

Presentation of stockholders' equity in the balance sheet

An acceptable balance sheet presentation of stockholders' equity is shown on page 749. Note that this illustration discloses the following information:

1 The par value or stated value of each class of stock

2 Dividend preference, conversion privilege, and call price of the preferred stock

3 Number of shares authorized, issued, and outstanding for each class of stock

4 Number of common shares reserved for possible issuance upon conversion of preferred stock and exercise of stock option contracts

5 Additional paid-in capital applicable to each class of stock

6 Total amount of paid-in capital and the total amount of stockholders' equity

---

Stockholders' equity:

$4 convertible preferred stock, $100 par, callable at $106 per share,	
authorized, issued, and outstanding 100,000 shares	*$10,000,000*
Common stock, $2.50 par, authorized 2,000,000 shares, issued	
and outstanding 1,000,000 shares (Notes 1 and 2)	*2,500,000*
Paid-in capital in excess of par:	
On preferred stock	*400,000*
On common stock	*5,000,000*
Total paid-in capital	*$17,900,000*
Retained earnings	*4,100,000*
Total stockholders' equity	*$22,000,000*

Note 1. At December 31, 19___, 500,000 shares of common stock were reserved for conversion of the $4 convertible preferred stock on the basis of five shares of common stock for each share of preferred stock.

Note 2. Stock options. (See pages 742–743 earlier in this chapter for an illustration of disclosure of stock options.)

In published balance sheets of large corporations, the need for concise presentation may cause some of the data concerning paid-in capital to be disclosed in the notes to financial statements rather than in the body of the balance sheet. Information concerning stock options, conversion ratios, and subclassifications of additional paid-in capital, for example, may be disclosed by notes referenced to the financial statements.

Pro forma financial statements

When significant new financial changes are in prospect, accountants may be asked to prepare financial statements which will give effect to the planned transactions. These statements reflecting transactions not yet consummated are called **pro forma financial statements.** For example, when two or more corporations are planning to combine by forming a new corporation, the stockholders and management of each existing corporation will want pro forma financial statements for the planned new corporate entity to facilitate study of the relative position of each present organization in the planned new corporation.

Another use for pro forma financial statements arises after a business combination of two companies occurs *during* a fiscal year. A pro forma income statement for a full year may be prepared to show the operating results which *would have* resulted for the entire year *if* the combination of the two companies had taken place at the beginning of the fiscal year. An illustration of such a pro forma income statement appears below.

KING CORPORATION
Unaudited Pro Forma Combined Income Statement

The following pro forma income statement for the twelve-month period ended August 31, Year 2, which has not been examined by certified public accountants, includes the operations of King Corporation, combined with Western Land Company, acquired July 1, Year 2, as if Western Land Company had been acquired as of the beginning of the fiscal year ended August 31, Year 2:

Combined historical:	
Sales, less returns and allowances	$50,501,830
Cost of goods sold	47,712,775
Gross profit on sales	$ 2,789,055
Selling and administrative expenses	1,216,841
Operating income	$ 1,572,214
Other income (expense):	
Interest expense	$ (207,032)
Miscellaneous income (net)	48,937
Total other expenses	$ (158,095)
Earnings before taxes on income	$ 414,119
Taxes on income	729,162
Combined historical net income	$ 684,957
Pro forma adjustment:	
Annualized interest expense (net of tax effect) for debt incurred in connection with acquisition of Western Land Company	11,750
Pro forma combined net income	$ 673,207
Pro forma combined earnings per share of common stock (based on 600,000 shares outstanding)	$ 1.12

Pro forma financial statements also are useful in situations other than business combinations. For example, a corporation might be considering the issuance of preferred stock in order to obtain funds with which to call the bonds outstanding. In weighing the merits of this action, management will need pro forma financial statements to show the financial position of the company as it will appear if these financial changes are carried out. Since the substitution of preferred stock for bonds will eliminate interest expense and have a bearing on taxable income, it will also be desirable to prepare a pro forma income statement showing how the operating results of the past year would have been modified if the changes in the capital structure had been in effect.

Pro forma financial statements may be prepared on work sheets by using existing account balances as a starting point and making adjustments to reflect the assumed transactions. The headings of financial statements summarizing assumed transactions should indicate clearly their hypothetical nature, and the character or purpose of the assumed transactions to which the statements give effect. The balance sheet heading in the illustration below meets this requirement.

PANORAMA CORPORATION

Pro Forma Balance Sheet at September 30, Year 4

After Giving Effect to the Proposed Issuance of

150,000 Additional Shares of Common Stock in

Payment for the Net Assets of Virdon Chemical Company

REVIEW QUESTIONS

1 Rincon Corporation issued rights to the holders of its 600,000 shares of common stock on November 30, 1980, entitling them to buy one convertible $1,000 bond at par for each 100 shares of common stock owned. The rights expired on January 28, 1981. At December 31, 1980, bonds in the face amount of $2,500,000 had been issued through the exercise of rights. What disclosure should be made of these events in the balance sheet at December 31, 1980?

2 Is the *preemptive right* which is inherent in common stock ownership logically applicable only to additional issuance of common stock or should it also apply to preferred stocks and bonds? Explain.

3 Eamer Corporation issued 150,000 shares of $50 par preferred stock for $54½ a share. Included in this offering at no extra charge were separate stock warrants entitling the holders to purchase one share of common stock for each share of preferred upon presentation of a warrant and $25 cash. At the time of issuance the common stock was selling on a regional stock exchange at $23 a share. The warrants began trading on the stock exchange at a price of $3½ each and the preferred stock was trading at $51 a share. The warrants expire in five years.

Give the necessary journal entry for issuance of the preferred stock with warrants attached. How should the stock warrants be listed in the balance sheet?

4 If common stock warrants are assigned a value at the time of issuance, what action is necessary if the warrants are not exercised and expire?

5 What circumstances usually induce a corporation to adopt a *qualified* stock option plan?

6 What is the principal accounting problem relating to stock option plans?

7 Santana Company issued five-year options to its key executives on May 21,

1980, at 100% of the market price of the stock on that date. State arguments for and against recording compensation expense corresponding to the estimated current fair value of these options.

8 In discussing the establishment of a *nonqualified* stock option plan for Brutus Corporation, one director advocated a five-year plan with the grantees permitted to exercise only 20% of the option in any one year. What advantage and/or disadvantage can you see in such a provision?

9 What are the major differences between a *compensatory* stock option plan and a *noncompensatory* plan? Does the corporation record compensation expense applicable to either?

10 What date does *APB Opinion No. 25,* "Accounting for Stock Issued to Employees," stipulate for use in measuring compensation for services relating to stock option plans? How is the amount of compensation cost measured, and how does this apply to qualified stock options?

11 Upon the retirement of the vice president in charge of sales after 50 years' service with the company, the board of directors authorized the presentation of a certificate for 100 shares of the corporation's $50 par common stock "in appreciation of loyal services." The shares were part of the company's holding of treasury stock, acquired and carried at cost of $80 a share. Book value per share was $140 and market value $125. How should the presentation to the vice president be recorded in the company's accounts?

12 On July 18, Year 4, Wang Corporation granted nontransferable options to certain of its key employees as additional compensation. The options permitted the purchase of 10,000 shares of Wang's common stock at a price of $30 per share. On the date of grant, the market price of the stock was $38 per share. The options were exercisable beginning January 2, Year 5, and expired on December 31, Year 6. On February 3, Year 5, when the stock was selling for $45 per share, all the options were exercised. How much total compensation should Wang record from the issuance of these options? Explain.

13 Define an *employee stock ownership plan* (ESOP) and briefly describe the significant accounting requirements for the employer company relating to such a plan.

14 Should the financial statements of a corporation include disclosure of outstanding stock options? If so, how should the disclosure be made?

15 Define *pro forma financial statements* and give some examples of circumstances in which they may be prepared.

EXERCISES

Ex. 18-1 The $10 par common stock of Kapnick Corporation is listed on a major stock exchange and presently quoted at $30 a share. The company has 10 million authorized shares, of which 4 million are issued and outstanding. Because of a need for additional capital, the company issues to its common stockholders at this time rights permitting the purchase of one new share of common stock in exchange for five rights and $28 cash. The rights expire 21 days after the date of issuance.

a If you are the holder of 400 shares of Kapnick Corporation common stock and receive a warrant for 400 stock rights, what alternative courses of action are open to you? Which course of action would be least desirable?

b What journal entry, if any, should be made by the company to record the issuance of the stock rights?

c Assuming that all the stock rights are exercised, give the journal entry which should be made by the corporation to record the exercising of the stock rights.

d Assuming that only 90% of the stock rights are exercised before the expiration date, give the journal entry or entries to be made by the company.

Ex. 18-2 Kipper Corporation has outstanding three issues of securities: convertible bonds, convertible preferred stock, and common stock. All three securities are actively traded on the New York Stock Exchange. Assume that you bought 100 shares of the 8%, $100 par convertible preferred stock when it was originally issued by the company at price of $103. The preferred stock is convertible into four shares of $10 par common stock at any time. When you made your investment in the convertible preferred stock, the common stock had a market price of $22 a share. Now several years later the common stock has risen to a market price of $90 a share and you decide to convert your preferred stock into common stock.

a Prepare the journal entry which should be made by Kipper Corporation to record the conversion. Explain why you have or have not utilized the prevailing market prices of the convertible preferred stock and/or the common stock in recording the conversion in the company's accounts.

b As a separate case, assume that while you are still holding your 100 shares of convertible preferred stock and the common stock has reached a market price of $90 a share, you decide that the common stock is grossly overpriced. Under this assumption would you still be inclined to convert your preferred stock into the common stock? Explain.

Ex. 18-3 A corporation granted 10-year stock options to five executives. The options for 50,000 shares of $5 par common stock stipulated an option price of $25 a share. The current market price of the stock at the option date was $28. The five officers who were each granted 10,000-share options under the plan were given the right to exercise the options at any time within the 10-year period and could sell the shares acquired at any time. The corporation's stock is listed and actively traded every day.

In a discussion of the plan before its adoption, one executive suggested that the difference between the market price and the option price be charged to the Retained Earnings account since the cost to the corporation was attributable in large part to the past services of the five executives. Another executive expressed the view that there was no cost to the corporation since no payment of cash or other assets would be required of the corporation.

a Does the stock option plan described above meet the requirements for a "qualified" stock option plan? Explain.

b In the light of **APB Opinion No. 25,** is there a cost to the corporation which should be recognized? If so, should it be recognized at the time the options are granted, when they are exercised, or at some other time?

c Prepare the journal entry, if any, which you think should be made to record issuance of the stock options, and the entry which should be made to record the exercising of the options for 50,000 shares. The market price at the date the options were exercised was $40. Observe the concepts set forth in **APB Opinion No. 25** in your answer.

Ex. 18-4 The information at the top of page 754 applies to the convertible preferred stock and the common stock of Angeles Crest Corporation:

	Recent prices	Dividend	Conversion ratio
Convertible preferred stock	$96.50	$6.75	3.25
Common stock	$22.00	$1.50	0

a Compute the following for these securities:
  (1) Yield on the convertible preferred stock
  (2) Yield on the common stock
  (3) Conversion value of the preferred stock
  (4) Conversion premium of the preferred stock (as a percentage)
  (5) Investment value of the preferred stock (assume an interest rate of 7.5% for securities of this quality)
  (6) Price risk of the preferred stock expressed as a percentage of market price
b Would the holder of 200 shares of the convertible preferred stock of Angeles Crest Corporation increase or decrease dividend income by converting into common stock at this time? By what amount? Comment on the relationship of your answer to the conversion premium computed in part **a**.

Ex. 18-5 The following information applies to the securities of Titanium Mining Company:

	Recent prices	Dividend	Conversion ratio
Convertible preferred stock	$59	$1.20	1.40
Common stock	$42	$0.75	0

a Compute the following for these securities:
  (1) Yield on the convertible preferred stock
  (2) Yield on the common stock
  (3) Conversion value of the preferred stock
  (4) Conversion premium of the preferred stock (as a percentage)
  (5) Investment value of the preferred stock (assume the prevailing rate of return being demanded for investments of this quality is 8%)
  (6) Price risk of the preferred stock expressed as a percentage of market price
b Would the holder of 500 shares of the convertible preferred stock of Titanium Mining Company increase or decrease dividend income by converting into common stock at this time? By what amount? Comment on the relationship of your answer to the conversion premium computed in part **a**.

Ex. 18-6 Cyclops Company established an employee stock ownership plan (ESOP) in Year 1. Selected transactions relating to the plan during Year 1 were as follows:

  (1) Cyclops Company contributed $20,000 cash and 2,000 shares of the company's $5 par common stock to the plan. The quoted market price of the common stock at this time was $22 per share.
  (2) The plan borrowed $500,000 from East River National Bank and purchased an additional 20,000 shares of Cyclops Company's common stock at $23 per share. One-half of these shares were purchased in the open market and the other half directly from the company. Cyclops Company guaranteed the loan from the bank.
  (3) The plan repaid $25,000 of the loan from East River National Bank and also paid $10,000 interest accrued on the loan.

Prepare any journal entries required in the accounts of Cyclops Company as a result of the transactions described.

SHORT CASES FOR ANALYSIS AND DECISION

Case 18-1 Little Rock Lumber Company uses stock options as a form of compensation for its key employees. Since the options provide a call on the stock at a fixed price over a period of years with no risk to the holder, the opportunity for gain is unlimited and the chance of loss is zero. Despite the obvious value of such stock options and their importance in attracting and retaining competent employees, accountants have had great difficulty in agreeing on the most appropriate method of determining a dollar valuation, if any, to be assigned to executive stock options. Among the methods which have been proposed for determining the value of stock options granted to employees are the following:

(1) The probable fair value of the option to the recipients at the date of grant
(2) The cash value of the services to be received from employees and for which they are being compensated by the stock option plan
(3) The excess of the market price of the stock over the option price at the date the options are granted
(4) The excess of the market price of the stock over the option price at the date the options become exercisable, for example, after the grantees have completed the required period of employment
(5) The excess of the market price of the stock over the option price at the date the options are exercised

Instructions Discuss the conceptual merits of each of the five methods listed above for determining the value of stock options granted to employees.

Case 18-2 On January 2, Year 10, as an incentive to better performance in their duties, Rumford Corporation adopted a qualified stock option plan to grant corporate executives nontransferable stock options to 500,000 shares of its unissued $1 par common stock. The options were granted on May 1, Year 10, at $25 per share, the market price on that date. All the options were exercisable one year later and for four years thereafter, providing that the grantee was employed by the company at the date of exercise.

The market price of this stock was $40 per share on May 1, Year 11. All options were exercised before December 31, Year 11, at times when the market price varied between $40 and $50 per share.

Instructions
a What information on this stock option plan should be presented in the financial statements of Rumford Corporation at (1) December 31, Year 10, and (2) December 31, Year 11?
b It has been said that the exercise of such a stock option would dilute the equity of existing stockholders.
(1) How could this happen? Discuss.
(2) What condition could prevent a dilution of existing equities from taking place in this transaction?

Case 18-3 Thomas Smith, assistant to the president of Dockson Corporation, is responsible for answering letters received by the president from the company's stockholders. These letters often contain complaints or suggestions about the company's policies. The president has instructed Smith to draft answering letters (to be signed by the president) which would build favorable relations with stockholders and give them an understanding of the company's policies and actions. One of the letters from a stockholder, Mrs. Barbara Lee, requiring an answer to be drafted by Smith, read as follows:

I have learned that officers of Dockson Corporation exercised stock options last year for 30,000 shares. The average market price of our stock last year was $75 and at December 31 it was $90, but the option price was only $25. According to my calculations that cost the company at least $1,500,000, which is more than the entire salary expense for officers during the last year, according to some statements made in the annual meeting last week. So, I'd like to know where you buried this $1,500,000 expense in the financial statements.

I would also like to know why the stock option plan doesn't prohibit these officers from selling the stock they get through options. I saw an item in the paper that showed the president sold 8,000 shares last year. I have never sold any of my shares, and if every one else would follow this policy, the price would really go up. I would appreciate a prompt answer to these questions.

Instructions Draft the letter which Smith should prepare for the president's signature, answering each of the stockholder's questions as fully as possible. Assume that the stockholder's letter is correct with respect to details such as the number of shares for which options were exercised, the market prices, the sale of shares by the president, and related data.

Case 18-4 Lou Sabatella, president of Lou-Sab Company, finding that an excessive amount of time was being taken up by correspondence with stockholders, gave a staff assistant the following assignment:

"I get quite a few letters from our stockholders offering suggestions and making complaints about various policies of the corporation. I want you to draft appropriate letters to these people for my signature. Be sure to maintain the best possible stockholder relations. Here's one to answer now from a Ms Rose Sadowski who says she owns 50 shares of our new convertible preferred stock."

The letter from Ms Sadowski read as follows:

After purchasing 50 shares of your $4 convertible preferred stock at $104 a share, I discovered some very unfavorable factors about this stock. As you know, it is convertible into 10 shares of common for each share of preferred and I had hoped the common would go up, and then I could convert my shares at a good profit. Now I have discovered that you have just declared a 10% stock dividend on the common and have said you may continue to do so in future years. This is going to be very hard on me as a preferred stock holder. I can still convert my 50 shares into 500 shares of common but it won't be worth nearly as much, because in five years you will have increased the amount of the common stock by about 60%. You should only pay cash dividends on the common or you are injuring the convertible preferred shareholders.

Also I find my stock is callable at $110, so it can't go any higher than that because of the danger that you would call it in. In view of these facts I want a refund for my shares or I will be forced to take legal action.

Sincerely,
Ms Rose Sadowski

Instructions Put yourself in the position of the staff assistant and draft a reply to Rose Sadowski for signature by the president. Indicate clearly in your letter whether the points made by Sadowski are valid. You should assume that the terms of the company's stock issues and its policies are in accordance with customary business practice.

PROBLEMS

Group A

18A-1 The following notice of redemption of convertible subordinated debentures by Halliburton Company appeared in *The Wall Street Journal:*

Notice of Redemption of

Halliburton Company

4½% Convertible Subordinated Debentures Due September 15, 1987

Redemption Date: October 15, 1975

Conversion Rights Expire: October 15, 1975

Halliburton Company, a Delaware Corporation (the Company), would like to remind holders of Debentures that all of the Debentures have been called for redemption on October 15, 1975 and that as a consequence of such redemption, the right to convert Debentures into shares of Halliburton Company Common Stock will expire at the close of business on October 15, 1975.

IMPORTANT FACTS ABOUT REDEMPTION

	Halliburton Common Shares into which one $1,000 Debenture may be converted[1]	Market Value of Halliburton Common Shares into which one $1,000 Debenture is convertible[2]	Redemption Price[3]
$1,000 Principal Amount 4½% Halliburton Debenture due 1987	7.575 Shares	$1,234.75	$1,036.25

1 The conversion price is $132 per share. Cash based on the market value will be paid for fractional shares.
2 Based on September 16, 1975, closing price of $163 per share.
3 Includes 3½% premium and accrued interest from September 15, 1975, to date of redemption, October 15, 1975.

FAILURE TO ACT

Debentureholders who do not convert or sell their Debentures through usual brokerage facilities prior to the close of business on October 15, 1975, will be entitled to receive only the redemption price and interest accrued to October 15, 1975 as shown in the table. No interest will accrue on the Debentures after October 15, 1975.

Debentures presented for conversion were not entitled to receive any of the interest accrued to October 15, 1975. The company's common stock had a par value of $7.50 per share. The debentures were originally issued at face amount. Unamortized issue costs relating to the debentures may be ignored.

Assumed transactions relating to the redemption of the convertible subordinated debentures are summarized below:

(1) $20 million of debentures were exchanged for an even number of shares of common stock.
(2) $10 million of debentures were exchanged for 75,000 shares of common stock and cash was paid for fractional shares equivalent to 750 full shares at an average market value of $160 per share. Do not recognize a loss on any portion of this transaction.
(3) Holders of $2 million of debentures failed to act and received the redemption price of $1,036.25 per $1,000 bond, as stipulated in the notice of redemption. A loss on the redemption of these debentures should be recognized.

Instructions Record in journal entry form the three assumed summary transactions described above.

18A-2 On August 31, Year 10, the stockholders' equity section of Wabash Corporation appeared as follows:

Common stock, $2.50 par, authorized 5,000,000 shares, issued and out-standing, 3,000,000 shares	$ 7,500,000
Paid-in capital in excess of par: common stock	38,400,000
Retained earnings	28,200,000
Total stockholders' equity	$74,100,000

At this time Wabash Corporation completed arrangements for public sale of an issue of 200,000 shares of $3 preferred stock with a par value of $50 a share. Accompanying each preferred share was a detachable stock warrant entitling the holder to purchase one share of common stock at $40 a share at any time within the next 10 years. The common stock was currently being traded on the stock exchange at a price of $36. As soon as the terms of the preferred stock and rights offering were announced, the warrants began trading separately on the stock exchange at a price of $3.50 on a when-issued basis.

The entire issue of 200,000 shares of preferred stock with warrants attached was sold on September 1 at a price of $55 a share. During the next few months the price of the common stock rose rapidly, and on December 1 it was being traded at $66 a share. On that date, 40,000 warrants were exercised and Wabash Corporation issued the required 40,000 shares of common stock.

Instructions

a Prepare journal entries to record the issuance of the preferred stock and de-tachable stock warrants on September 1, and the issuance of common stock on December 1. (Entries are not required for dividend actions.)

b Prepare the stockholders' equity section of the balance sheet at December 31, Year 10, assuming that net income since August 31 has been $3,500,000 and that on December 1 a quarterly dividend of 75 cents a share was declared on the preferred stock, payable January 15 to stockholders of record on December 15. Dividends of $120,400 were declared on the common stock during Year 10.

c Prepare any appropriate note or notes to the financial statements based on the information provided.

18A-3 The fiscal year for Baseline Products Corporation ends on December 31. On March 1, Year 10, the company established a compensatory stock option plan for its key executives who have been with the company a minimum of five years. The number of shares of common stock initially included in the plan was approximately 100,000 at an estimated option price of $40 per share. The final determination of the number of shares to be offered and the option price will be made on December 31, Year 11, and will be based on a predetermined formula. The formula was designed to adjust the number of shares to be optioned and the final option price by taking into account the earnings of the company and the market price of the common stock during Years 10 and 11.

Options were granted in consideration for services performed through the end of Year 11 and were exercisable at any time after January 2, Year 12. The estimated number of shares included in the plan, the estimated option price, and the quoted market price of the common stock on March 1, Year 10, and on December 31, Year 10, were as follows:

	March 1, Year 10	December 31, Year 10
Estimated number of shares to be included in option plan	100,000	100,000
Estimated option price	$40	$40
Quoted market price of common stock	$39½	$44

The final contractual provisions of the stock option plan were determined on December 31, Year 11, as follows:

Number of shares included in plan 95,000

Option price $42

The quoted market price of the common stock on December 31, Year 11, was $52 per share.

On April 20, Year 12, executives exercised options for 30,000 shares. The company had 3,500,000 shares of $5 par common stock outstanding on December 31, Year 11.

Instructions
a What is the measurement date for this stock option plan?
b Compute the total compensation cost that should be recognized by Baseline Products Corporation as a result of this stock option plan. How should the compensation cost be allocated among accounting periods? Give supporting computations.
c Prepare journal entries required to record all transactions relating to the stock option plan for Year 10 through Year 12.

18A-4 Skyline Company has outstanding an issue of $15,000,000 of 6% convertible bonds with interest payment dates of June 1 and December 1. The conversion feature of the bond contract entitles the bondholders to receive 50 shares of $10 par common stock in exchange for each $1,000 bond.

On May 15, the annual dividend rate on the common stock was increased from $1 to $1.50. On June 1 the holders of $1 million face value of bonds exercised the conversion privilege. The quoted market price of the bonds at this date was $129½ per $100 face value; the price per share of common stock was $25½. The ledger balances pertaining to the bonds and the stock were as follows on June 1 prior to recording the conversion:

Bonds payable $15,000,000

Discount on bonds payable 600,000

Common stock, $10 par, authorized 1,000,000 shares, issued and outstand-

ing 400,000 shares 4,000,000

Paid-in capital in excess of par 3,400,000

Instructions
a Prepare the journal entry to record the conversion of bonds on June 1.
b Evaluate the effects of the conversion upon Skyline Company with respect to:
(1) Income before income taxes. (Disregard amortization of bond discount.)
(2) The amount of income taxes. Assume a marginal income tax rate of 48%.
(3) The total annual amount of payments to security holders.
c What effect would the conversion have upon the annual cash receipts of an investor who converted 25 bonds into common stock on June 1?

18A-5 Frank Caliri, president of Caliri Corporation, commented during the course of a directors' meeting that the corporation had achieved higher sales and higher net income during each of the last seven years. Also, the market price of both the common stock and the convertible preferred stock had been in a long-term definite uptrend. Caliri also stated:

"We have 50,000 shares of 6%, $100 par, convertible preferred stock outstanding, which was originally issued for cash of $5,100,000. This stock is callable at $106 and convertible at any time into our $5 par common stock in the ratio of three shares of common for each share of preferred. We have been paying $1 a year dividend on our common stock and do not plan any increase in the near future. Although our earnings have been rising, we need to reinvest these earnings to take advantage of opportunities for growth. Our common stock is now selling for $70 a share, so apparently our stockholders are more interested in earnings than in dividends."

After these comments, Caliri invited questions or suggestions from the directors. Director Larry Winningham offered the following suggestion:

"Our convertible preferred stock is too small an issue for a company of our present size. I propose that we call it all in at once and get rid of it. If everyone is forced to convert into common, the additional common dividend will go up by only $150,000 a year and we will be saving $300,000 a year in preferred dividends. Also we can transfer the $100,000 of paid-in capital in excess of par on preferred stock now in our accounts to our retained earnings or include it as an extraordinary gain on this year's income statement. If any preferred stockholders fail to convert, we will have a larger gain on those shares equal to the excess of the present market price over the call price. And if we want convertible preferred stock in the future we will be able to put out a larger issue at less than the 6% rate we're now paying. Consequently, calling this stock will give us several benefits and cost us nothing."

Instructions

a Evaluate point by point the proposal by Director Winningham. For each point indicate (and explain fully) your agreement or disagreement.

b What is the probable approximate market price of the convertible preferred stock? Explain.

c Prepare the journal entry (or entries) that would be necessary if Winningham's plan to call the preferred stock is carried out.

Group B

18B-1 El Rey Company, a large listed corporation, showed the following amounts in the stockholders' equity section of its balance sheet at May 31, Year 3:

Stockholders' equity:

Common stock, $10 par, authorized 6,000,000 shares, issued and outstanding, 2,500,000 shares	$25,000,000
Paid-in capital in excess of par: common stock	12,500,000
Retained earnings	15,775,000
Total stockholders' equity	$53,275,000

The company's operations had been profitable, but management had decided that additional capital was needed. Authorization was therefore obtained for 250,000 shares of $4 preferred stock with a par value of $50 a share. To help assure success of this financing, El Rey Company offered with each share of preferred stock a detachable stock warrant which entitled the holder to purchase one share of common stock at $40 a share at any time within the next 10 years. The common stock was selling at a price of $35 at this time. As soon as the terms of the offering were announced, the warrants began trading on the stock exchange at a price of $6 each.

The issuance of 250,000 shares of the $4 preferred stock with warrants attached was carried out on June 1 at a price of $60 per share (including the stock warrant). The price of the common stock rose rapidly during the next several months. On December 1, when the common stock was selling at $65 a share, 25,000 warrants were exercised and El Rey Company issued the required 25,000 shares of common stock.

Instructions

a Prepare journal entries to record the issuance of the preferred stock and the detachable common stock warrants on June 1, and the issuance of common stock on December 1 when 25,000 warrants were exercised. (Entries are not required for dividends on the preferred stock.)

b Prepare the stockholders' equity section of the balance sheet at December 31, Year 3, assuming that net income since May 31 was $7,500,000 and that dividend action on the preferred stock since that date has been as follows:

Sept. 1 Declared quarterly dividend of $1 per share on preferred stock.

Oct. 1 Paid quarterly dividend on preferred stock.

Dec. 1 Declared quarterly dividend of $1 per share on preferred stock, payable January 10 to stockholders of record December 15.

c Prepare any appropriate note or notes to the financial statements based on the information available in the problem.

18B-2 James & Pamela, Inc., has outstanding two issues of securities: (1) common stock, and (2) a 4.5% convertible bond issue in the face amount of $20,000,000. Interest payment dates of the bond issue are April 1 and October 1. The conversion clause in the bond contract entitles the bondholders to receive 30 shares of $5 par common stock in exchange for each $1,000 bond.

On March 15, the annual dividend rate on the common stock was raised from $1.50 to $2. On April 1 the holders of $2 million face value in bonds exercised the conversion privilege. The market price of the bonds at this date was quoted at $122 per $100 face value; the price per share of common stock was $39. The account balances pertaining to the bonds payable and the common stock were as follows on April 1, prior to the conversion:

Bonds payable (maturing in 10 years) $20,000,000

Discount on bonds payable 800,000

Common stock, $5 par, authorized 1 million shares, issued and outstanding

  750,000 shares 3,750,000

Paid-in capital in excess of par 11,830,500

Instructions

a Prepare the journal entry to record the conversion of bonds on April 1.

b Evaluate the effects of the conversion upon James & Pamela, Inc., with respect to

(1) Income before income taxes. (Consider amortization of bond discount.)

(2) The amounts of income taxes and net income. Assume an income tax rate of 48%.

(3) The total annual amount of payments to security holders.

c What effect would the conversion have upon the annual cash receipts of an investor who converted 10 bonds into common stock on April 1?

18B-3 Robert Bernard accepted a position as Assistant Vice President—Sales in Latimer Corporation and received a three-year contract at an annual salary of $70,000. Shortly thereafter Bernard learned that all executives at the level of vice president and above were to be granted five-year stock options for 5,000 shares each. Bernard was disappointed that the plan did not include assistant vice presidents.

After thinking the matter over, Bernard went to the president with the following proposal: "I would like to be included in the stock option plan and receive an option on 5,000 shares of our $10 par common stock at 100% of the present market price of $30. In consideration for my inclusion in the option plan, I am willing for my three-year salary contract to be amended to reduce my annual salary from $70,000 to $60,000."

The president discussed the proposal with the board of directors and received approval to include Bernard in the stock option plan. The plan as amended was then approved by vote of the stockholders.

One of the directors, who was also a large stockholder, commented as follows: "We will save $30,000 by the reduction in Bernard's salary for the next three years. If the price of the stock does not rise above its present level, the option for the extra 5,000 shares will never be exercised and will cost us nothing. If the stock does go up and Bernard exercises the option, we will issue an extra 5,000 shares but we will have no cash payment to make and no expense to recognize. So either way, we will be saving $30,000."

Instructions

a Under current standards of accounting for stock options, what journal entry, if any, should be made to record the granting of the stock option to Bernard. Explain the reasoning involved.

b Without regard to current income tax regulations or official pronouncements, what minimum compensation cost, if any, do you think should be assigned to the stock option granted to Bernard? Give the journal entry you would use to record issuance of the option.

c Assume that the market price of the stock rose to $50 a share within one year and Bernard exercised the option for 5,000 shares. Give the journal entry to record issuance of the 5,000 shares optioned to Bernard.

d Discuss the logic of the director's comments on the $30,000 saving by granting the 5,000-share option to Bernard in exchange for a reduction in salary.

18B-4 The following hypothetical example of the issuance to stockholders of rights to purchase a new issue of convertible debentures was included in an examination in financial accounting theory and practice.

Kerner Corporation recently announced the issuance to preferred stockholders of two rights for each share of preferred outstanding, and the issuance to common stockholders of one right for each share of common outstanding. The preferred stock is cumulative, but neither convertible nor participating. The announcement stated that 10 rights and $100 cash would be required to purchase $100 principal amount of the 5% convertible debentures and that the rights would expire in 60 days.

Some stockholders sold their rights immediately and active trading in the rights began on a regional stock exchange at prices approximating $3 per right. The convertible debentures, although not yet issued, were also traded on this exchange on a "when issued" basis, meaning that delivery would not be required until after the scheduled issuance date. All the 2 million rights issued were exercised before the stipulated expiration date and the convertible debentures were issued.

Instructions

a Was the distribution of stock rights by Kerner Corporation as described in this case typical of current practice? Explain.

b What was the approximate trading price of the convertible debentures on a "when issued" basis?

c Would a common stockholder, who sold the rights instead of exercising them, own a smaller share of the net assets of the company than before the rights were issued? Explain.

d Give the journal entry Kerner Corporation should record when the 2 million rights were exercised and the convertible debentures issued.

18B-5 Edmund Freed organized EF Corporation with a modest amount of capital and the business grew steadily during the next 22 years. Freed served as president of the company and was also the largest single stockholder, owning 50,000 shares of preferred stock and 200,000 shares of common stock at the time of retirement from the presidency in January Year 23. Freed was succeeded as president by Gordon Leisner who owned no stock in the company but was proposed for the position by another large stockholder, the M Corporation, which owned approximately 80,000 shares of EF Corporation's common stock.

The capital structure of EF Corporation consisted of two stock issues, as follows:

8% preferred stock, $100 par, cumulative, callable at 104; authorized, issued, and outstanding 80,000 shares	$8,000,000
Common stock, $1 par, authorized 3 million shares, issued and outstanding 2 million shares	2,000,000

The preferred stock had been issued at par and the common stock at $7 a share. The continued profitable operation of the company had caused retained earnings to grow to $10 million by the time of Freed's retirement in January Year 23. However, start-up expenses associated with bringing new facilities into operation in Year 22 had limited earnings in that year to approximately $2 a share. Freed, who continued as a director after retiring from the presidency, predicted that earnings would increase very rapidly once the new facilities were operating efficiently.

The change in management in January Year 23 was a thoroughgoing one. In addition to the new president, M Corporation also arranged for the appointment of two new vice presidents and a new treasurer, all of whom were former executives with M Corporation. Four members of the 10-man board of directors of EF Corporation were presently executives of M Corporation. The other board members, except Leisner and Freed, were "public members," who had been selected because of their prominence in the community rather than because of any particular interest in the affairs of EF Corporation.

One of the first acts of the new president, Gordon Leisner, was to propose a stock option plan "to aid the company in attracting and retaining executive personnel of outstanding ability." The stock option plan was designed to meet the requirements of the Internal Revenue Service for a "qualified stock option plan." The plan made available to executives and key employees a total of 100,000 shares. The option price was not to be less than 100% of the market price of the stock at the time of granting the option. Options were to run for a period of five years from date of grant but could not be exercised during the first two years from date of grant. The options were not transferable and expired upon termination of employment other than by reason of death. The plan called for options to be granted to key employees by the board of directors upon recommendation of a three-member stock option committee.

The stock option plan was bitterly opposed by Freed but was approved by the board of directors and subsequently by stockholders and became effective on May 1, Year 23. On May 15, Year 23, options to purchase 40,000 shares were granted to 10 officers and employees at a price of $35, the average price of the stock on the Boston Stock Exchange on the day of grant.

On the day of grant, Freed, who continued to oppose the stock option plan, made a formal offer to the company to purchase a five-year option on 40,000 shares at the existing price of $35. The price offered by Freed for this option was $280,000 cash. Freed simultaneously resigned from the board and threatened to file suit against the corporation and its directors if they "reject my cash offer and persist in robbing the stockholders by giving away stock to a gang of selfish insiders." In a news conference, Freed predicted that the earnings of the company would triple within the next two years and that "the price of the stock would hit $100 within two years."

Instructors

a If you were a member of the board of directors, would you favor accepting Freed's offer to purchase an option on 40,000 shares? Explain fully. If the offer were accepted, how should this action be reflected in the accounts and in the financial statements?

b Assume that the company accepted Freed's offer, that earnings after preferred dividend requirements amounted to $6 million in Year 23 and that no dividends were paid on common stock; prepare the stockholders' equity section of the balance sheet at December 31, Year 23. No options had been exercised to this date.

c Without regard to current practice or any official pronouncements, state what valuation, if any, should be assigned to the 40,000 shares optioned to key employees. Explain fully the reasoning involved and give the journal entry or entries, if any, to be made at the date of grant.

d Assuming that all the options issued to executives were exercised on July 1, Year 25, when the market price of the stock reached $100 a share, give the journal entry to record the issuance of these shares. Explain fully the reasoning supporting this entry.

e Assuming that the market price of the stock did not rise above $35 at any time during the option period and that no options were exercised, what recognition, if any, should be given in the accounts of EF Corporation for the expiration of the options issued to employees under the qualified stock option plan?

CHAPTER 19

RETAINED EARNINGS AND DIVIDENDS

RETAINED EARNINGS

Distinguishing between paid-in capital and earned capital

In the balance sheet of a single proprietorship, the owner's equity is customarily shown as a single amount. For a partnership, too, the equity of each partner is presented as a single figure without any distinction between paid-in capital and accumulated earnings. However, in the balance sheet of a corporation a basic objective in reporting the stockholders' equity is to distinguish clearly between paid-in capital and earned capital.

Why should the stockholders' equity be subdivided in the corporate form of organization? One reason is that stockholders and creditors have a right to know whether a corporation in paying dividends is actually distributing earnings or is returning invested capital. In the single proprietorship and partnership, the owners may withdraw capital from the business in any amounts they choose even though such withdrawals may exceed earnings. In a corporation, however, only the accumulated earnings are ordinarily regarded as available for withdrawal. This view reflects corporate policy and desire for continuity of existence as well as legal considerations. Consequently, accountants try to keep a clear distinction between paid-in capital and accumulated earnings. The maintenance of these two separate categories of capital is also desirable because stockholders are principally absentee owners not participating in management. They may regard the active management of the corporation as custodians of the paid-in capital and may judge the efficiency of management to some extent by the amount of earnings accumulated by the corporation.

From the standpoint of accounting theory, it is necessary to distinguish total paid-in capital from retained earnings. Any further classification of capital usually rests on legal requirements rather than on accounting concepts. The framers of corporation laws have attempted to protect creditors by creating the concept of *legal capital*—an amount of stockholders' equity not subject to withdrawal. In recognition of these legal requirements, accountants customarily make a further classification by subdividing paid-in capital between legal capital (capital stock) and paid-in capital in excess of par or stated value (additional paid-in capital). Legal capital generally is not subject to withdrawal; in some states, however, additional paid-in capital is legally available for dividends, provided that stockholders are notified of the source of the dividends. In still other states dividends may be paid from net assets in excess of capital stock, which means that dividends could be paid from additional paid-in capital without notice to stockholders. Although dividends can be declared in some states even when a deficit exists, corporate financial policy is usually far more cautious, and dividends from any source other than retained earnings are rare.

In recent years the accounting profession has been quite successful in substituting the term *retained earnings* for the older and somewhat ambiguous term *earned surplus,* but it is interesting to note that many state laws still speak of "surplus" as opposed to "capital." Consequently, corporate announcements, such as merger agreements, which are influenced by state statutes, continue to employ the terms *capital* and *surplus.* Even in financial statements the older terminology still appears occasionally.

The legal and accounting viewpoints as to necessary classification of stockholders' equity are thus somewhat at variance. Users of financial statements tend to view the entire paid-in capital as being permanently committed to the enterprise. But, more strictly speaking, only that portion of paid-in capital which is classified by statute as legal capital is definitely unavailable as a source of dividends.

Reasonable compliance with both accounting and legal considerations may be achieved in financial statements by showing the total paid-in capital as a major classification with legal capital as a component thereof. The other major classification should be retained earnings, regardless of whether this amount indicates the total legally available for distribution to stockholders. In fact, the balance sheet of a corporation usually does not purport to show the amount legally available for dividends. Such a determination would be a legal one, guided by the laws of the particular state in which the company was incorporated, and would ordinarily bear little or no relationship to actual dividend policy, since few if any corporations declare dividends up to the maximum amount legally allowable.

Even though the uses of financial statements outweigh the legal niceties involved, legal considerations have at times had considerable influence on the form and structure of the balance sheet. Much of what the accountant does in this area is purely and simply a matter of legal reporting, as opposed to economic reporting. In the balance sheets of some early-day corporations, the stockholders' equity section showed little more than a division between legal capital and "surplus." Surplus was then regarded merely as the excess of a corporation's total capital over its legal capital. Under such standards the category of surplus was a most confusing catchall, often including the portion of proceeds received on issuance of capital stock in excess of par or stated value, "gains" from treasury stock transactions, capital donated by outsiders, and retained earnings. Such a balance sheet presentation was quite unsatisfactory from the viewpoint of investors and bankers. To avoid the confusion caused by this lumping together of unlike elements in the "surplus" account, accountants began reporting stockholders' equity by source, and to show each classification as a separate item in the balance sheet.

Classifying corporate capital by source

The first step toward classifying surplus by source was to use the categories of *capital surplus* and *earned surplus.* The term *capital surplus* soon fell into disrepute, however, because it was used in several different meanings. Some companies limited capital surplus to paid-in capital in excess of par or stated value of shares issued; others included increments in capital arising from arbitrary write-up of asset values; still others added in extraordinary gains and losses. The caption of capital surplus is still encountered occasionally in published financial statements, but the term is no longer in good standing. *Paid-in surplus* was another term widely used for a time to distinguish paid-in capital in excess of par from accumulated earnings.

In an effort to develop more uniform and descriptive terminology for the elements of corporate capital, the AICPA suggested complete discontinuance of the term *surplus.* The AICPA proposed substituting terms which would distinguish clearly (1) legal capital, (2) capital in excess of legal capital, and (3) accumulated earnings.

Objections to the terms *surplus* and *capital surplus* stressed the prevailing connotations of surplus, such as excess, residue, or "that which remains when use or need is satisfied." No such meaning is intended in accounting. More descriptive terms indicating source such as "retained earnings," "retained income," and "earnings reinvested in the business" were recommended as replacements for "earned surplus."

Currently accepted terms for the stockholders' equity section

At present the following balance sheet classifications of corporate capital are widely used:

1 Capital stock (legal capital)
2 Paid-in capital in excess of par or stated value
3 Retained earnings (or deficit)

A subtotal entitled "total paid-in capital" should desirably be inserted in the stockholders' equity section of the balance sheet to show the aggregate of the capital stock and paid-in capital in excess of par or stated value.

The question of "appraisal capital" has little practical importance, as corporations have generally adhered to the cost principle of asset valuation. If any appreciation is included in the stockholders' equity, it should be shown separately and given a title such as "unrealized appreciation from revaluation of assets" or simply "appraisal capital."

Paid-in Capital in Excess of Par Paid-in capital in excess of par comes principally from the following sources:

1 Excess of issuance price over the par or stated value of capital stock
2 Conversion of convertible bonds or preferred stock into common stock
3 Excess of proceeds from reissuance of treasury shares over the cost of these shares
4 Reduction of par or stated value of capital stock
5 Donations of property to the corporation by stockholders or governmental units

Although capital from all these sources may be combined into the single balance sheet item of Paid-in Capital in Excess of Par or Stated Value, or Additional Paid-in Capital, a separate ledger account is needed for each in order to carry out the principle of classifying by source all elements of the stockholders' equity. If any part of paid-in capital is distributed by a dividend, management has a duty to inform the stockholders that the dividend is a return of capital and not a distribution of earnings.

Neither operating losses nor extraordinary losses of nonrecurring nature should be charged against paid-in capital. Examples of improper charges against paid-in capital to which the SEC has taken exception include the following:

1 Write-offs of purchased goodwill
2 Write-downs of plant and equipment which have lost usefulness because of obsolescence or unexpectedly rapid deterioration
3 Write-off of bond discount at the time of issuing the bonds
4 Losses on sale of investments

In all these situations the SEC has followed the principle that paid-in capital should under no circumstances be used to absorb losses which, if currently recognized, would have been chargeable against income. If paid-in capital were to be charged with such losses, it follows that net income and retained earnings would be relieved of the losses and would therefore be overstated.

Although charges against paid-in capital accounts are infrequent, they are warranted in such situations as the following:

1 Payment of a liquidating dividend.

2 Redemption of shares, originally issued for more than par, at a price in excess of par. For example, X Corporation redeems at the stipulated call price of $104 a portion of its preferred shares originally issued at a price of $105. The $4 per share redemption premium may be charged against paid-in capital in excess of par.

3 Absorption of a deficit as part of a quasi-reorganization.

Unrealized Appreciation (or Loss) from Revaluation of Assets Present accounting standards require that most assets such as plant and equipment be accounted for on the basis of cost, despite increases or decreases which occur in their fair value. However, in view of the large increases in the replacement cost of certain assets because of scarcity and inflation, much attention has been given to the possibility of writing up asset values.

There is general agreement among accountants that if assets are written up to appraisal values, the corresponding unrealized increment in stockholders' equity should be reported as a separate and distinct element of corporate capital. An appropriate title might be Unrealized Appreciation from Revaluation of Assets, or possibly Appraisal Capital. Since such increments in capital are unrealized, they should not be used as a basis for absorbing losses or for the declaration of dividends. If the laws of a given state permit dividends based on appraisal capital accounts, the accountant should insist upon full disclosure of the nature of the dividend action.

The opposite of Appraisal Capital is Unrealized Loss in Value of Long-Term Investments in Equity Securities. This account is reported as a deduction in stockholders' equity and is described in Chapter 11.

The Retained Earnings account

Retained earnings represents the accumulated net income of a corporation minus amounts distributed to stockholders and amounts transferred to paid-in capital accounts as a result of stock dividends. Extraordinary gains and losses, cumulative effect of a change in accounting principle, and operating earnings and losses are included in the determination of net income which is transferred to the Retained Earnings account. A negative amount (debit balance) in the Retained Earnings account is termed a *deficit.*

In many a large corporation, the amount of retained earnings shown in the balance sheet is actually far less than the total income earned and retained, because numerous large transfers have been made from the Retained Earnings account to the Capital Stock and Paid-in Capital accounts. Such transfers are legally permissible because they tend to strengthen the position of corporate creditors by increasing the cushion of capital between creditors and the threat of operating losses. In terms of maintaining a clear distinction between paid-in capital and retained earnings, however, such transfers pose a problem. These transfers will be discussed further in our consideration of stock dividends.

The illustration below indicates the kinds of debits and credits which may comprise a typical Retained Earnings account.

Retained Earnings	
1. Net loss	1. Net income
2. Dividends declared	2. Prior period adjustments (to correct
3. Prior period adjustments (to correct	material error made in prior
material error made in prior	period)
periods)	

As explained in Chapter 3, current practice requires that extraordinary gains and losses be included in the determination of net income rather than being entered directly in retained earnings. *Prior period adjustments* are entered directly in the Retained Earnings account and are not included in the determination of the current year's net income. As stated in *FASB No. 16,* the following items should be accounted for and reported as prior period adjustments and excluded from net income for the current period:

a Correction of an error in the financial statements of a prior period
b Adjustments that result from realization of income tax benefits of preacquisition operating loss carry forwards of purchased subsidiaries[1]

Prior period adjustments do not include normal recurring corrections and adjustments arising from the use of estimates in the accounting process. Thus, changes in depreciation because of revised estimates of economic life are not prior period adjustments; they are to be reflected in operations of the current period.

It is a common expression to say that a company pays dividends "out of its retained earnings" or that it "distributes its retained earnings in the form of dividends." These statements are inaccurate because in fact

---

[1] *FASB Statement No. 16,* "Prior Period Adjustments," FASB (Stamford: 1977), p. 5.

dividends are paid "out of cash" and from no other source. The expressions quoted above tend to create confusion in the minds of persons lacking a knowledge of accounting; such persons may acquire a mental picture of corporate retained earnings in the form of a pile of cash or other property which may be handed out to stockholders. They fail to recognize that retained earnings, like capital stock and other paid-in capital accounts, are not tangible things but merely an element of the stockholders' equity in the assets owned by the corporation. Retained earnings is that portion of stockholders' equity which is not paid-in capital. The existence of a retained earnings account with a balance of, say, $100,000 tells us nothing about the amount of cash or any other type of asset held by the company.

After listing the principal sources of retained earnings, it may be useful to mention a few items which *do not* belong in retained earnings but which are sometimes erroneously entered there. These are:

1 Treasury stock transactions which appear to result in a "gain"
2 Donations of property (such as the gift to a corporation or a plant site by a city seeking to attract new industries)
3 Increase in stockholders' equity resulting from writing up plant assets to an appraised current value in excess of carrying value based on historical cost

Let us consider briefly why each of these items does not belong in retained earnings. The reissuance of treasury stock at a price in excess of cost results in an increase in paid-in capital. The receipt of donated property should be recorded in a separate paid-in capital account with a descriptive title, in accordance with the principle of classifying capital by source. Such an account, perhaps entitled Capital from Donation of Plant Site, is one of the several types of paid-in capital. Increases in the carrying value of plant assets, if recorded at all, produce an unrealized increase in stockholders' equity and require separate classification.

DIVIDENDS

Cash dividends

The usual meaning of dividend is a distribution of assets to stockholders in proportion to the number of shares owned by each. The term *dividend,* when used by itself, is generally understood to mean a cash dividend; this usage is followed throughout this book. Corporations frequently distribute additional shares of their own capital stock to stockholders and call such distributions "stock dividends." Strictly speaking, a stock dividend is not a dividend at all because no assets are distributed to stockholders. However, stock dividends are of considerable practical importance and pose some challenging accounting questions which are discussed later in this chapter.

No obligation to pay a dividend exists until the board of directors has formally declared a dividend. This dividend action by the board consists of a resolution specifying the following points:

1 Date of declaration
2 Date of record
3 Date of payment
4 Amount per share

On the **date of declaration** of a cash dividend, the newly created liability is usually recorded by debiting Dividends and crediting Dividends Payable. The Dividends account is closed into Retained Earnings at the end of the accounting period. If the corporation has both common and preferred stock, a separate Dividends account should be used for each (Dividends: Common Stock, and Dividends: Preferred Stock).

The **date of record** is specified in the dividend declaration and usually follows the date of declaration by a few weeks. To qualify for the dividend, a person must be listed as a stockholder in the company's stockholders' ledger on the date of record.

The stocks of companies listed on the stock exchanges sell "ex-dividend" three business days before the date of record, thus facilitating compilation of the list of owners on the record date. An investor who buys shares before the ex-dividend date is entitled to receive the dividend; conversely, a stockholder who sells before the ex-dividend date is selling his right to receive the dividend as well as the shares of stock.

The **date of payment** of a dividend usually is set for a few weeks after the date of record. Payment is recorded by debiting Dividends Payable and crediting Cash.

After declaration of a cash dividend by the board of directors and notice of the declaration to stockholders, the dividend action cannot be rescinded by the directors. A declaration of a cash dividend generally is irrevocable except by the unanimous consent of stockholders. However, a board of directors may rescind a stock dividend at any time before the issuance of the new certificates.[2]

The declaration of a cash dividend creates a liability, classified in the balance sheet as a current liability, because the date for payment is ordinarily only a few weeks or months away. In the event that a corporation should become insolvent in the interval between the declaration date and payment date, the stockholders are in the same position with respect to their right to receive the dividend as any unsecured creditor.

In an accounting textbook emphasizing principles rather than mechanics, it is convenient to speak of dividends being recorded as a debit to Retained Earnings, rather than indicating that the Dividends account is debited and then later closed into Retained Earnings. Consequently, we shall as a matter of convenience sometimes illustrate the declaration

[2] Paul M. Van Arsdell, *Corporation Finance: Policy, Planning, Administration,* The Ronald Press Company (New York: 1968), p. 1203.

of a dividend by showing a debit directly to the Retained Earnings account.

As indicated in the preceding discussion, general requirements for payment of a cash dividend include (1) existence of retained earnings, (2) an adequate cash position, and (3) action by the board of directors.

Earnings and dividends

The net income earned during an accounting period results in an increase in net assets and an equal increase in the stockholders' equity. The board of directors must decide whether this net income is to be retained for use in the business or is to be distributed to stockholders as dividends. Many "growth companies" pay little or nothing as cash dividends because their rapid expansion creates an urgent need for working capital. In older, more stable companies, cash dividends often range from perhaps 40 to 80% of earnings, with a few industries such as public utilities noted for an even higher percentage distribution of earnings.

Most listed companies follow a policy of regular quarterly dividends with an "extra" being paid at year-end if earnings prove better than expected. Established annual dividend rates such as $4 per share or $1.60 per share thus become associated with certain stocks, and this reputation of stable dividends tends to add to the investment quality of these securities. Once such a rate has become generally known, a company is reluctant to lower the rate unless forced to do so by a sustained decline in earnings or a critical shortage of cash.

Dividends paid in form of nonmonetary assets (property dividends)

Most dividends are in cash but occasionally a company may choose to declare a dividend in the form of merchandise or other nonmonetary assets, such as securities of another company. When such **property** or **nonmonetary** dividends are declared, the current fair value (not the carrying value) of the nonmonetary asset distributed is the appropriate amount to be recorded by the issuing company as a dividend. Similarly, stockholders should record the receipt of the property dividend at the current fair value of the asset distributed.

APB Opinion No. 29 established the following principle for the accounting of property dividends by the issuing company:

> A transfer of a nonmonetary asset to a stockholder or to another entity in a nonreciprocal transfer should be recorded at the fair value of the asset transferred, and a gain or loss should be recognized on the disposition of the asset.[3]

If the fair value of the nonmonetary asset distributed is not objectively measurable at the time of the distribution, the only feasible alternative

[3] *APB Opinion No. 29,* "Accounting for Nonmonetary Transactions," AICPA (New York: 1973), pp. 547–548.

may be to record the property dividend at the carrying value of the non-monetary asset.

To illustrate the accounting for a dividend paid in the form of a non-monetary asset, assume that M Corporation owns 10% of the stock of Bliss Company with a carrying value of $400,000 in the accounts of M Corporation. At the end of Year 10, the current fair value of this investment is $750,000. At this time the board of directors of M Corporation distributes the Bliss Company stock as a dividend to the shareholders of M Corporation. The journal entries in the accounts of M Corporation to record the declaration and distribution of this nonmonetary dividend are as follows:

Dividends (or Retained Earnings)	*750,000*	
Dividend Payable in Stock of Bliss Company		*750,000*
To record declaration of nonmonetary dividend.		
Dividend Payable in Stock of Bliss Company	*750,000*	
Investments		*400,000*
Gain on Disposal of Investments		*350,000*
To record payment of nonmonetary dividend.		

It would be possible for M Corporation to record the unrealized gain on the investment in stock of Bliss Company before the declaration of the nonmonetary dividend is recorded. This procedure might be followed to avoid recording a liability in excess of the carrying amount of the asset which will be used to liquidate the dividend liability. If a balance sheet is prepared after the declaration but before the payment of the nonmonetary dividend, the asset to be distributed should be classified as a current asset because the dividend payable would normally be considered a current liability. However, if the asset to be distributed had been carried as a noncurrent asset and the amount is very large, both the asset and the dividend liability may be reported as noncurrent to avoid distortion of the company's current ratio.

Dividends in scrip (liability dividends)

In theory a corporation which is short of cash might obligate itself by declaring a dividend consisting of promissory notes to its stockholders calling for payment at some future date. In practice, however, such "scrip dividends" almost never occur, because corporations which are short of cash are usually careful not to incur any unnecessary liabilities. The accounting entry for a "scrip dividend" or "liability dividend" would be a debit to the Dividend (or Retained Earnings) account and a credit to a liability account with an appropriate title, such as Notes Payable to Stockholders or Scrip Dividends Payable.

Liquidating dividends

The term *liquidating dividend* may be used in reference to the following situations:

1 A pro rata distribution of assets to stockholders which reduces paid-in capital rather than retained earnings

2 A pro rata distribution to stockholders by a company having wasting assets such as mineral deposits or timberlands, representing a return of invested capital

3 A pro rata distribution to stockholders when a company is being liquidated

A liquidating dividend may be recorded as a debit to a specific paid-in capital account or to a separate account such as Liquidating Dividend Distributed. Any balance in this account would be deducted from total paid-in capital in the balance sheet.

Corporations must fully inform their stockholders when a dividend, or a portion of a dividend, represents a return of capital. Liquidating dividends should be reported by stockholders as reduction in the cost of their investment rather than as revenue. This procedure is generally applicable both for accounting and for income tax purposes.

A spin-off is closely related to a liquidating dividend, except that a spin-off may involve a reduction in accumulated earnings. A *spin-off* is a transfer by a corporation of selected assets to a new corporation in exchange for capital stock, which is then distributed pro rata to stockholders.

Generally, a gain is not recognized on a distribution of a liquidating dividend or on a transfer of assets to a new corporation in a spin-off, but a loss should be recognized. This point is covered in *APB Opinion No. 29* as follows:

> Accounting for the distribution of nonmonetary assets to owners of an enterprise in a spin-off or other form of reorganization or liquidation or in a plan that is in substance the rescission of a prior business combination should be based on the recorded amount (after reduction, if appropriate, for an indicated impairment of value) of the nonmonetary assets distributed, A prorata distribution to owners of an enterprise of shares of a subsidiary or other investee company that has been or is being consolidated or that has been or is being accounted for under the equity method is to be considered to be equivalent to a spin-off.[4]

Stock splits

When the market price of a company's stock reaches an inconveniently high trading range such as $100 a share or more, the company may decide to split the shares. A stock split of, say, 3 for 1 of a stock selling for $150 a share will cause the number of shares held by each stockholder to triple and should in theory cause the price to drop to approximately

[4] Ibid., p. 549.

$50 a share. (Since many cross currents are normally present in the stock markets, the actual movement of a security's market price is never precisely predictable.) One result of a stock split may be to achieve wider distribution of shares, because many investors are unwilling to purchase stock with a high price per share. The most popular price range with American investors, according to some students of the securities business, is around $30 to $50 a share. Those companies selling consumer products such as automobiles, gasoline, and household appliances have a particular interest in developing the widest possible distribution of their shares, since stockholders may be expected to favor the products sold by "their" company.

A stock split causes no change in the total dollar amount of stockholders' equity and no change in paid-in capital, retained earnings, or other components. The par or stated value per share is reduced in proportion to the increase in number of shares. For example, in a 4 for 1 split of a stock with par value of $10, the new shares would have a par value of $2.50 each.

When a stock is split, the old shares usually are *not* called in or exchanged for new ones. The company merely issues to shareholders a sufficient number of new shares to bring their total holdings up to the number indicated by the split. A stockholder who owned 100 shares prior to the previously mentioned 4 for 1 split of a $10 par stock would receive 300 new shares of $2.50 par value. The stockholder would continue to hold the original certificate for 100 shares of $10 par stock. Of course, the par value of all the shares is now $2.50 but it is not necessary for any exchange of certificates to be made. Eventually the old $10 par certificates will disappear from circulation; whenever such a certificate is sold, the new certificate issued in the name of the new owner will show the reduced par value of $2.50.

Since the only ledger account affected by a stock split is the Capital Stock account, the stock split may be recorded in a memorandum entry. Alternatively, a journal entry such as the following may be made to record the change in par value and number of outstanding shares.

Capital Stock, $10 par	10,000,000	
Capital Stock, $2.50 par		10,000,000
To record a 4 for 1 stock split carried out by reducing		
par value from $10 to $2.50 a share and issuing 3 million		
additional shares, thus increasing total outstanding		
shares from 1 million to 4 million.		

A *reverse stock split,* as the name suggests, is the opposite of a stock split. The number of outstanding shares is reduced proportionately for all stockholders. For example, the outstanding stock might be reduced from 3 million shares to 1 million shares in a 1 for 3 reverse stock split. All stockholders would surrender their existing shares in exchange for one-third as many new shares. A reverse stock split does not affect the assets or liabilities of the company and therefore does not change the total amount of stockholders' equity. Such transactions are rare; they are usually considered only by companies with stock which has dropped in market price to an extremely low level. The reverse split tends to increase the market price per share in inverse proportion to the reduction in number of outstanding shares.

Stock dividends

In recent years an increasing number of corporations *have* has elected to distribute stock dividends as well as cash dividends, or in some cases to distribute stock dividends only. A stock dividend is a distribution of additional shares, called **dividend shares,** to the stockholders in proportion to their existing holdings. "Common on common" is the usual type of stock dividend; such a distribution is also known as an **ordinary stock dividend.**

Distribution of a stock dividend causes no change in the assets or liabilities of a corporation; the only effect is a transfer between accounts in the stockholders' equity group. Since there is no decrease in the net assets of the corporation, a stock dividend does not give stockholders anything they did not have before. The number of shares held by each stockholder is increased but each share represents a smaller slice of ownership in the corporation. The net assets of the corporation are unchanged by a stock dividend and the proportionate interest of each stockholder in those net assets is unchanged.

Assume, for example, that X Corporation has total stockholders' equity of $120,000, represented by $60,000 of capital stock and $60,000 of retained earnings. There are 1,000 shares of stock outstanding; therefore, each share represents a 0.1% interest in the corporation, or $120 of net assets. The X Corporation now distributes a 20% stock dividend, so the total number of shares rises to 1,200. Since total net assets remain at $120,000, the net assets per share drop to $100. A stockholder who owned 100 shares (a 10% interest) before the stock dividend would now own 120 shares, but this still represents 10% of the shares outstanding. Also the net assets represented by 120 shares would be unchanged. Prior to the stock dividend 100 shares represented $12,000 of net assets (100 × $120); 120 shares after the 20% stock dividend also represent $12,000 of net assets (120 × $100).

The principal argument for stock dividends is that they enable a "growth company" to retain accumulated earnings in the business yet provide the stockholders with additional shares as evidence of their increasing equity in the corporation. This view was well-explained in a recent letter to stockholders by the president of a major corporation which read as follows:

> It is my pleasure to inform you of the action taken by the Board of Directors of our Company today declaring a 5% Common Stock dividend, which is at the rate of one share of Common Stock for each twenty shares of Common Stock you now hold.
>
> The Stockholders' equity in our company has been steadily enhanced in value by continuing large investments in all phases of the business. These large investments are being financed from current operations and cash available from undistributed earnings of prior years. Inasmuch as your equity in the working assets of the business thus has been increased, your Board of Directors now has considered it appropriate to recognize this increase by capitalizing a portion of the reinvestment by means of this stock dividend.

It may be argued that distribution of a stock dividend causes retained earnings to be understated on the corporation's subsequent balance sheets since a portion of the accumulated earnings becomes concealed in the paid-in capital accounts. One answer is that the decision of the board of directors, acting in behalf of the stockholders, to issue a stock dividend constitutes a dedication of earnings to the permanent capital of the corporation. This dedication of earnings for permanent use may be viewed as the equivalent of distributing earnings to stockholders and immediate return by them of such earnings to the corporation, thus increasing the paid-in capital.

What amount of retained earnings should be transferred to the paid-in capital accounts for each share issued in a stock dividend? Although the legal requirement in most states is merely the par or stated value of the dividend shares, current accounting standards call for capitalizing an amount equal to the **market price per share** prior to the dividend. Both the SEC and the AICPA support the use of market price as a measure of the amount of retained earnings to be capitalized for all stock dividends which increase the number of outstanding shares by less than 20 or 25%. For larger stock dividends, only the par or stated value per share is transferred from retained earnings to permanent capital. The reasons underlying this difference in treatment of small and large stock dividends is explained in a later section of this discussion.

Most recipients of stock dividends regard them as distributions of corporate earnings in an amount equal to the market value of the shares received. Such views are strengthened by the fact that small stock dividends often do not cause any apparent decline in the market price of the stock, and the total market value of the original shares held often remains unchanged. Stockholders are thus able, if they wish, to sell for cash the dividend shares received without any decrease in the market value of their stock investment. When stockholders are entitled to receive only a fraction of a dividend share, the company ordinarily will act as their agent in selling the fractional share and will remit the cash proceeds to individual stockholders.

One explanation for the fact that market prices often do not decline when the outstanding stock is increased by a small stock dividend is that the corporation will presumably continue to pay the established rate of cash dividend per share. Shareholders thus anticipate an increased amount of cash dividends on their investment.

Because of the prevalent belief among some investors that stock dividends constitute a distribution of corporate earnings, both the AICPA and the SEC require that corporations should in the public interest record stock dividends by transferring from retained earnings to the paid-in capital accounts an amount equal to the market value (generally as of the date of declaration) of the dividend shares. If any lesser amount is capitalized, some part of the earnings which stockholders believe to have been distributed to them would remain in retained earnings available for future dividends.

It should be observed that in many companies with stock selling at prices of $50 to $100 a share or more, the par value is often as low as $1 or less. Consequently, the legal requirement of capitalizing an amount of retained earnings equal to the par or stated value of the additional shares means very little. A company which wished to mislead its stockholders might do so by issuing frequent stock dividends having a market value significantly higher than current earnings. Practically no limitation would exist on the extent of such distributions if only a nominal amount of retained earnings were capitalized for each share issued as a stock dividend.

Securities which are convertible into common stock (such as convertible preferred stock, warrants, and stock option contracts) contain an *antidilution clause* which calls for adjusting the conversion ratio to compensate for the "reduced size" of a share of common stock after a stock dividend or a stock split. If, for example, a preferred stock is convertible into three shares of common, the conversion ratio would increase to 3.3 shares after a 10% stock dividend on the common stock.

Large stock dividends and stock splits

A large stock dividend, such as one increasing the number of outstanding shares by 25 or 50%, may be expected to cause a material decrease in the market price per share. Such dividends are in the nature of stock splits, and the arguments outlined in the preceding section as to small stock dividends do not apply. In other words, the amount of retained earnings to be capitalized in the case of large stock dividends is an amount equal to the par or stated value of the dividend shares. Let us use a somewhat extreme example to illustrate the probable reaction of the stockholder to a large stock dividend. Assume that Stockholder A owns 10 shares of stock in Snowpeak Company and current market price is $150 a share. A 100% stock dividend is distributed and the market price promptly drops to $75 a share. Stockholder A will no doubt recognize that the so-called "stock dividend" is not a distribution of earnings but is essentially similar to a splitting of the shares on a 2 for 1 basis.

The AICPA has recommended that corporations avoid the use of the word "dividend" in corporate notices relating to stock distributions of such magnitude that they will reduce materially the market price per share. If legal requirements demand use of the word "dividend," the transaction might well be described as a **split-up effected in the form of a stock dividend.** Large stock dividends are frequently debited to paid-in capital accounts rather than to retained earnings.

Illustrative Entries for Stock Dividends Assume that Oscar Company has 1 million authorized shares of $5 par common stock, of which 500,000 shares are outstanding. The market price is $80 a share and a cash dividend of 50 cents quarterly has been paid for several years. Current earnings are large and rising but the company wishes to conserve cash to permit expansion of plant. Consequently, the board of directors decides to issue a 2% stock dividend rather than to increase the established cash dividend per share. A condensed journal entry summarizing both the declaration and distribution of the 2% stock dividend is presented below to emphasize the end results of the transaction:

Retained Earnings	800,000	
Common Stock, $5 par		50,000
Paid-in Capital from Stock Dividends		750,000
Declared and issued a 2% stock dividend consisting of		
10,000 shares of $5 par common stock with a market price of		
$80 per share at the date of declaration.		

The $50,000 credit to Common Stock of course loses its identity on the balance sheet as part of the total of that account; also the $750,000 credit to Paid-in Capital from Stock Dividends is likely to be merged with other types of paid-in capital in the preparation of a condensed balance sheet. Consequently, the reader of a subsequent balance sheet may be unaware that much of the paid-in capital emerged from retained earnings by means of stock dividends.

The preceding illustration of a journal entry for a stock dividend could appear as three separate entries. The first entry would record declaration of the stock dividend by debiting Stock Dividends for the market value of the shares to be issued, crediting Stock Dividends to Be Distributed for the par value of the shares, and crediting Paid-in Capital from Stock Dividends for the excess of the earnings capitalized over the par value of the shares to be issued. The second entry would record issuance of the shares by debiting Stock Dividends to Be Distributed and crediting Common Stock. At the end of the year, the Stock Dividends account would be closed into Retained Earnings. If a balance sheet is prepared between the date of declaring the stock dividend and the date for distributing it, the account Stock Dividends to Be Distributed would be shown as part of stockholders' equity.

The announcement to stockholders that a stock dividend has been declared should include a statement as to the amount of retained earnings to be capitalized and the date of determining the market price of the dividend shares. The following language is typical:

> The Company's Board of Directors has declared a 2% stock dividend on the common stock (two common shares for each 100 shares held) to be distributed March 28 to holders of record of common stock at the close of business February 25. Retained earnings is being charged a total of $800,000 to reflect the dividend, computed at $80 per share, the closing price of the stock on January 25, the date of declaration.

If Oscar Company declared and distributed from retained earnings a large stock dividend, say 50%, the journal entry would be as follows:

```
Retained Earnings  . . . . . . . . . . . . . . . . . . . . . . . . .   1,250,000
      Common Stock, $5 par  . . . . . . . . . . . . . . .                        1,250,000
Declared and issued a 50% stock dividend consisting of
250,000 shares of $5 par common stock.
```

Dividing line between "large" and "small" stock dividends

Since current practice calls for quite different accounting treatment of large and small stock dividends, it is appropriate to ask "How large must a stock dividend be to qualify as a large distribution and thereby to avoid the requirement of capitalizing retained earnings in an amount equal to the market value of the additional shares issued?"

The AICPA, in *Accounting Research and Terminology Bulletins—Final Edition,* suggested 20 or 25% as a dividing line. Above this amount it may be assumed that the purpose of the distribution is to reduce the market price of the stock, as in the case of a stock split. Below this level it may be assumed that the dividend shares will be regarded by most shareholders as a distribution of earnings. (As previously explained, a stock dividend does not really constitute a distribution of earnings, but it is commonly regarded as such by many investors.) The appropriate accounting treatment of the two categories of stock dividends may be restated in concise form as follows: Small stock dividends are recorded by capitalizing retained earnings at the market price of the dividend shares; large stock dividends are recorded by capitalizing retained earnings at the par or stated value of the dividend shares. As stated earlier, large stock dividends may be debited to paid-in capital accounts.

Fractional shares

When a small stock dividend is declared, persons owning only a few shares will be entitled to receive only a fraction of a dividend share. For example, in the preceding illustration of a 2% stock dividend, the holder of less than 50 shares would be entitled to only a fraction of a share. To avoid the inconvenience of issuing fractional shares, most companies offer stockholders the alternative of receiving in cash the market value of the fraction of a share due, or of paying in sufficient cash to qualify for a full share.

Business combinations—purchase versus pooling of interests

In recent years many corporations have been brought together or combined to obtain the economies of large-scale operation and the financial strength arising from diversification in various industries. Business combinations are discussed at length in the *Modern Advanced Accounting* text of this series. Our purpose, at this point, is merely to call attention to the difference in impact upon retained earnings of the *purchase method* and the *pooling-of-interests method* in carrying out business combinations.

When the acquisition of one corporation by another is accounted for as a *purchase,* the acquiring corporation records its investment at the cost established by cash paid or market value of shares issued in exchange for shares of the acquired corporation. *The retained earnings of the corporation acquired do not become part of combined retained earnings.* Net incomes of the two corporations are combined only from the date of acquisition.

On the other hand, when a business combination has characteristics that require use of the *pooling-of-interests method,* the assets of the two corporations are combined at their recorded carrying values on the premise that no purchase has occurred. The current fair values of shares issued and of assets acquired are ignored. The pooling-of-interests method rests on an assumption of continuity of common ownership and the *retained earnings accounts of the two corporations are added together to arrive at the amount of retained earnings of the combined entity.* The earnings of the combined entity include the earnings of both corporations for the entire year in which the business combination occurs.

Prior to issuance of *APB Opinion No. 16,* "Business Combinations," in 1970 some "growth" companies made acquisitions on a pooling-of-interests basis primarily to maintain an illusion of ever-increasing earnings per share. The distortion of economic reality by such abuses of accounting principles was extreme in the 1960s. These abuses have been considerably restricted by the requirements imposed by *APB Opinion No. 16* for use of the pooling-of-interests method of accounting for business combinations.

STATEMENTS OF RETAINED EARNINGS AND STOCKHOLDERS' EQUITY

An income statement is sometimes described as the connecting link between successive balance sheets. However, an income statement does not explain fully the change in stockholders' equity from one balance sheet date to the next. Cash dividends, stock dividends, exercise of stock options, and treasury stock transactions are examples of events affecting the stockholders' equity along with the net income or loss for the period. Because users of financial statements are interested in such changes in stockholders' equity, most companies issue supplementary financial statements which may include:

1 A statement of retained earnings accompanied by a statement of paid-in capital, or alternatively,
2 A statement of stockholders' equity

Statement of retained earnings

As explained in Chapter 3, a *statement of retained earnings* shows the changes in retained earnings during the year, thus reconciling the beginning and ending balances of retained earnings.

The content and relative importance of the statement of retained earnings in portraying the year's financial developments have been somewhat reduced by the movement to the all-inclusive concept of income measurement. *FASB Statement No. 16* requires that all items of profit and loss recognized during a period be included in the determination of net income, except for *prior period adjustments*. As explained earlier, very few events meet the rigorous requirements for classification as prior period adjustments to be recorded in the Retained Earnings account. Thus, the typical statement of retained earnings is now relatively short and consists of the following:

1 The beginning balance of retained earnings
2 An addition of the year's net income (or deduction of the year's net loss)
3 A deduction for any dividends declared
4 The ending balance of retained earnings

An illustration of a statement of retained earnings in comparative form for Pacific Corporation appears at the top of page 784.

A comparative statement of retained earnings for Atlantic Lines, Inc. which includes a prior period adjustment appears at the bottom of page 784.

The widespread adoption of the all-inclusive income concept of net income has tended to reduce the significance of the statement of retained earnings as a reconciling device. The function of the statement has also been narrowed by the trend away from making appropriations of retained earnings. These trends tend to reduce the number of direct

PACIFIC CORPORATION
Statement of Retained Earnings
For Years Ended December 31, Year 5 and Year 4

	Year 5	Year 4
Retained earnings, beginning of year	$719,824	$640,000
Add: Net income	230,000	210,000
Subtotal	$949,824	$850,000
Less: Dividends declared:		
On preferred stock ($6 per share)	(30,000)	(30,000)
On common stock:		
In cash ($1 per share)	(41,600)	(40,000)
In common stock (4%)	(72,312)	(60,176)
Retained earnings, end of year	$805,912	$719,824

debits and credits to Retained Earnings and thus simplify the task of reporting changes in this account. Perhaps these trends are also responsible in part for the fact that many companies now prepare a **combined statement of earnings and retained earnings** such as the one shown for Handley Corporation on page 785.

Reporting changes in paid-in capital or stockholders' equity

Reporting of changes in the accounts for capital stock and paid-in capital in excess of par became a requirement with the issuance of **APB Opinion No. 12.** The Accounting Principles Board stated:

> When both financial position and results of operations are presented, disclosure of changes in the separate accounts comprising stockholders' equity (in

ATLANTIC LINES, INC.
Statement of Retained Earnings
For Years Ended June 30

	Year 10	Year 9
Retained earnings, beginning of year:		
As originally reported		$850,000
Less: Prior period adjustment—correction of error, net		
of applicable income tax effect of $250,000 . . .		280,000
Retained earnings, beginning of year (as restated for		
Year 9)	$675,000	$570,000
Add (or deduct): Net income or loss	(85,000)	205,000
Subtotal	$590,000	$775,000
Less: Dividends declared	25,000	100,000
Retained earnings, end of year	$565,000	$675,000

HANDLEY CORPORATION
Combined Statement of Earnings and Retained Earnings
For Years Ended December 31, Year 10 and Year 9
(dollars in thousands except per-share figures)

	Year 10	Year 9
Revenue:		
Sales to customers	$1,317,683	$1,140,485
Other revenue	18,886	15,753
Total revenue	$1,336,569	$1,156,238
Costs and expenses:		
Cost of products sold	$ 650,275	$ 567,206
Selling, general, and administrative expenses	416,699	362,968
Depreciation and amortization	41,597	35,862
Income taxes	103,339	83,747
Other expenses	3,953	4,634
Total costs and expenses	$1,215,863	$1,054,417
Net earnings (per share: Year 10, $2.15; Year 9, $1.82)	$ 120,706	$ 101,821
Retained earnings, beginning of year	469,647	391,850
Cash dividends paid	(25,136)	(24,024)
Retained earnings, end of year	$ 565,217	$ 469,647

addition to retained earnings) and of the changes in the number of shares of equity securities during at least the most recent annual fiscal period and any subsequent interim period presented is required to make the financial statements sufficiently informative. Disclosure of such changes may take the form of separate statements or may be made in the basic financial statements or notes thereto.[5]

Required disclosure of changes in capital accounts other than retained earnings may be explained by the practice by many corporations of issuing frequent small stock dividends. Such dividends cause a transfer from retained earnings to capital stock and to paid-in capital in excess of par. Another recent trend causing frequent changes in capital stock and paid-in capital in excess of par is the issuance of shares to employees under stock option plans. Still another factor affecting paid-in capital is the conversion of bonds or preferred stock. Because of these factors, a statement showing changes in paid-in capital, or in all elements of stockholders' equity, may be prepared. One approach is to prepare a statement of paid-in capital to accompany the statement of retained earnings similar to the statement illustrated on page 786.

An alternative approach is to prepare a statement of stockholders' equity, including retained earnings, as illustrated for Lin Corporation on page 787. In this example, the amounts for preferred stock and common stock are combined into one column headed "capital stock," and an

[5] *APB Opinion No. 12,* "Omnibus Opinion—1967," AICPA (New York: 1967), p. 190.

PUBLIC CORPORATION
Statement of Paid-in Capital
For Years Ended June 30, Year 4 and Year 5

	Preferred stock	Common stock	Additional paid-in capital	Treasury stock
Balance, July 1, Year 3: preferred shares issued 2,407,977, treasury 8,097; common shares issued 12,860,855, treasury 282,796	$10,104,023	$12,860,855	$17,597,766	$(5,376,858)
Exchange of subordinated debentures for preferred stock	(2,700,640)		(1,274,851)	
Additional shares issued 72,388 common treasury shares			(416,528)	416,528
Reacquired stock, 235,409 common shares				(1,295,454)
Other		(10)	(8,105)	
Balance, June 30, Year 4 . .	$ 7,403,383	$12,860,845	$15,898,282	$(6,255,784)
Reacquired stock, 181,102 common shares				(838,013)
Other, including conversion of 54 preferred shares into 318 common shares	(4,425)	318	(292,464)	
Balance, June 30, Year 5 . .	$ 7,398,958	$12,861,163	$15,605,818	$(7,093,797)

accompanying note describes in more detail the events of the year portrayed in the statement of stockholders' equity.

The financial statements which have been presented to illustrate methods of explaining changes in stockholders' equity show that many alternative forms are in use. Another method favored by many companies for disclosing capital changes is the use of an explanatory note to the financial statements. Selection of the most appropriate type of disclosure in a particular situation depends upon the number and the character of the changes which have occurred during the year and upon the amount of detailed information desired in the financial statements. In addition, there is the factor of personal judgment as to the most concise, effective, and forceful way of portraying the significant elements of the company's financial position.

APPROPRIATIONS OF RETAINED EARNINGS AND RESERVES

Restrictions on retained earnings

The board of directors of a corporation may restrict or appropriate a portion of the retained earnings by transfer to a separate account. For

LIN CORPORATION
Statement of Consolidated Stockholders' Equity
For Years Ended December 31, Year 4 and Year 5

	Capital stock	Paid-in capital in excess of par	Retained earnings
Balances, Dec. 31, Year 3	$ 5,966,000	$21,419,000	$16,161,000
Net income			9,938,000
Cash dividends ($0.10 per common share)			(1,229,000)
Transfer to common stock of amount equal to par value of common stock issued as a result of 100% stock dividend . .	6,266,000	(6,266,000)	
Exercise of common stock options and warrants	355,000	4,891,000	
Conversion of subordinated debt	144,000	3,667,000	
Acquisition of Butler Co. (preferred stock, $13,527,000; common stock, $1,465,000)	14,992,000	35,723,000	
Balances, Dec. 31, Year 4	$27,723,000	$59,434,000	$24,870,000
Net income			19,518,000
Cash dividends:			
Preferred ($1.50 per share) . .			(676,000)
Common ($0.12 per share) . .			(1,741,000)
Exercise of common stock options and warrants	525,000	5,171,000	
Conversion of subordinated debt and preferred stock	1,260,000	27,558,000	
Balances, Dec. 31, Year 5	$29,508,000	$92,163,000	$41,971,000

Note: Stockholders' Equity: The authorized capital stock of the company consists of 25 million shares of common stock and 2 million shares of preferred stock. The preferred shares outstanding at December 31, Year 5, are convertible into 315,561 shares of common stock and have liquidation preference of $13,524,000.

At December 31, Year 5, the company had reserved 710,000 shares of its common stock for issuance under outstanding common stock purchase warrants. The warrants are exercisable prior to May of Year 6 at $12.10 a share. The company has also reserved 525,000 shares of common stock for issuance upon conversion of the 6% subordinated notes and the convertible preferred stock, and 640,000 shares for issuance under stock option plans.

Common shares issued upon exercise of stock options during Year 4 and Year 5 amounted to 99,939 and 109,846, respectively. There were options outstanding at December 31, Year 4 and Year 5, for 280,561 and 383,053 common shares, respectively, and the aggregate purchase price of all outstanding stock options was $6,037,000 and $6,067,000, respectively.

Retained earnings of approximately $15,500,000 are available at December 31, Year 5, for payment of cash dividends under the most restrictive provisions of the company's indebtedness agreements.

example, appropriations of retained earnings (sometimes called *reserves*) may be made for expansion of plant, extinguishment of bonds, redemption of preferred stock, and for loss contingencies. Although the practice of appropriating retained earnings is not widely followed, generally accepted accounting principles sanction such practice. In *FASB Statement No. 5,* the Financial Accounting Standards Board stated:

> Some enterprises have classified a portion of retained earnings as "appropriated" for loss contingencies. In some cases, the appropriation has been shown outside the stockholders' equity section of the balance sheet. Appropriation of retained earnings is not prohibited by this Statement provided that it is shown within the stockholders' equity section of the balance sheet and is clearly identified as an appropriation of retained earnings. Costs or losses shall not be charged to an appropriation of retained earnings, and no part of the appropriation shall be transferred to income.[6]

A portion of retained earnings may be restricted and thus not available as a basis for dividend declaration for a variety of legal, contractual, or discretionary reasons. The almost universal practice is to disclose such a restriction in a note to financial statements, such as the following:

> The company's articles of incorporation and credit agreements with commercial banks contain restrictions limiting the payment of cash dividends. Retained earnings of $30 million dollars at December 31, Year 10, are not available for distribution to stockholders as a result of such restrictions.

It is essential to keep in mind that the appropriation of retained earnings has no effect whatsoever on the composition of the assets. Sometimes, concurrently with the appropriation of retained earnings, a corporation will also segregate assets to be used exclusively for the purpose indicated by the appropriation of retained earnings. Such a segregation of assets earmarked for a particular purpose is called a *fund;* an example is a fund for retirement of bonds.

In a few cases, the appropriation of retained earnings may be required by the terms of a contract with creditors or by statute, but most appropriations represent voluntary actions by the board of directors and usually are not accompanied by the establishment of a fund.

As a specific example of an appropriation of retained earnings, assume that a corporation during a period of growth and profitable operations decides to enlarge its plant. The new buildings and equipment are to be paid for without resorting to outside financing. In other words, cash accumulated through profitable operation and not distributed to stockholders as dividends is to be invested in new plant assets. Because of this decision, there may be relatively little cash available for dividends in the near future. To make this situation clear to stockholders, the board of directors may authorize the establishment of a Retained Earnings Appropriated for Expansion of Plant account by restricting

---

[6] *FASB Statement No. 5,* "Accounting for Contingencies," FASB (Stamford: 1975), p. 7.

$5,000,000 of retained earnings. The journal entry required by this action follows:

Retained Earnings 5,000,000
    Retained Earnings Appropriated for Expansion of
      Plant 5,000,000
To appropriate a portion of retained earnings per resolution of board of directors.

When the expansion of plant is completed and paid for and the restriction on retained earnings is no longer needed, the appropriation is eliminated by the following journal entry:

Retained Earnings Appropriated for Expansion of Plant 5,000,000
    Retained Earnings 5,000,000
To transfer appropriation of retained earnings to Retained Earnings account.

The board of directors could, of course, reduce or even eliminate dividends without appropriating retained earnings. The only argument for creating an appropriation of retained earnings is that it may communicate to stockholders the thinking of directors as to the use of funds generated by profits for expansion and the consequent limitation of dividends.

Reserves as a separate category in the balance sheet

For many years accounting literature has advocated that the term **reserve** be used only to describe appropriations of retained earnings. This viewpoint opposes the presentation of reserves in a separate section between the liabilities and the stockholders' equity section of the balance sheet.

Confusion over the meaning and balance sheet classification of reserves still persists despite efforts to limit this term to appropriations of retained earnings. A number of companies continue to publish balance sheets with a "Reserves" section between liabilities and stockholders' equity. Some of these reserves are merely appropriations of retained earnings; others have been created by charges to expense; for still others it is impossible for the reader to determine their origin or nature. Adding together these unlike elements creates further confusion.

For example, a recent balance sheet of a publicly owned company included on the right-hand side of the statement four group headings as follows: Current Liabilities, Long-Term Debt, Reserves, and Stockholders' Equity. The Reserves section included the following three items:

Reserves:	
Insurance and deferred liabilities	*$ 22,687,000*
Anticipated abandonments	*39,627,000*
Deferred income taxes	*66,458,000*
Total reserves	*$128,772,000*

One might infer from a balance sheet arranged in this format that the accounting equation should be revised to read: Assets = Liabilities + Reserves + Owners' Equity. Unfortunately, no established meaning of the term *reserves* as used in this context is available.

At the end of 1975 the balance sheet of General Motors Corporation showed between liabilities and stockholders' equity a section entitled Deferred Credits and Reserves which totaled $517 million and included an item "General reserve applicable to foreign operations" of $141,667,396. In the balance sheet at the end of 1976, this reserve was redesignated as an Allowance on Foreign Investments and classified as a liability.

Despite the practice of a number of prominent corporations in presenting reserves as a separate category on the right-hand side of the balance sheet, *there is no fourth dimension in the framework of accounting theory.* Assets are equal to the sum of the liabilities and the stockholders' equity. The uncertainties and complexities which surround certain business events are no justification for the publication of a balance sheet which leaves the reader to guess whether certain account balances represent liabilities or are part of stockholders' equity.

QUASI-REORGANIZATIONS

A *quasi-reorganization* occurs when a corporation in financial difficulties modifies its capital structure without being forced to do so by creditors and without coming under the supervision of a bankruptcy court.[7]

Typically, a quasi-reorganization involves writing off a deficit against paid-in capital; sometimes there is a reduction in the par or stated value of capital stock and a write-down of overvalued assets. Following a quasi-reorganization, the corporation is considered from an accounting standpoint to have a *fresh start* and the way is cleared for reporting profits and declaring dividends in future years. Although the write-down of asset values and the elimination of a deficit obscure historically signifi-

[7] The word *quasi* means resembling or seemingly, but not actually. Thus a quasi-reorganization resembles but is not a formal type of a corporate reorganization.

cant data, the procedure is generally accepted because it results in more relevant asset figures. Furthermore, a quasi-reorganization may help a corporation to regain its place as a profitable business unit without the stigma that attaches to a large deficit, continuous operating losses, and inability to declare cash dividends.

Typical steps in a quasi-reorganization

A quasi-reorganization typically involves the following procedures:

1 Assets which are considered to be overstated are written down to current fair value by charges to retained earnings. If the current fair value of any asset exceeds carrying value, increasing the carrying value of such an asset is generally discouraged.

2 The deficit in retained earnings following the asset write-downs is eliminated against paid-in capital. Gains or losses realized subsequent to the quasi-reorganization which are clearly attributable to the period prior to the quasi-reorganization should be recorded as increases or decreases in paid-in capital in excess of par or stated value.

3 If paid-in capital in excess of par or stated value at the time of the quasi-reorganization is insufficient to absorb the deficit, the par or stated value of capital stock is reduced in order to establish a paid-in capital account which can then be used to absorb the deficit.

4 Retained earnings following a quasi-reorganization must be identified (dated), generally for a period not exceeding 10 years, as accruing since the effective date of the quasi-reorganization. In subsequent balance sheets, this disclosure, called *dating the retained earnings,* may appear as follows:

Retained earnings accumulated since June 30, Year 8, when a deficit of $4,202,000 was written off against paid-in capital as a result of a quasi-reorganization $1,917,400

Illustration of a quasi-reorganization

To illustrate the accounting for a quasi-reorganization, assume that Quasar Corporation acquired plant assets and goodwill at extremely high prices and that several years of unprofitable operations resulted in the balance sheet (at the end of Year 15) shown on page 792.

The existence of the $1,600,000 deficit and the high historical cost of plant and goodwill would make it impossible for Quasar Corporation to report earnings or to pay dividends. To overcome these obstacles, let us assume that management proposes to effect a quasi-reorganization as of December 31, Year 15, as follows:

1 The carrying value of plant assets is reduced by $2,100,000, consisting of a $4,000,000 reduction in cost and a $1,900,000 reduction in accumulated depreciation; in addition, the entire goodwill of $1,000,000 is written off, thus increasing the deficit from $1,600,000 to $4,700,000.

QUASAR CORPORATION
Balance Sheet
December 31, Year 15
Assets

Current assets		$ 6,200,000
Plant assets	$12,500,000	
Less: Accumulated depreciation	5,700,000	6,800,000
Goodwill		1,000,000
Total assets		$14,000,000

Liabilities & Stockholders' Equity

Current liabilities		$ 3,900,000
Long-term debt		500,000
Stockholders' equity:		
Capital stock, $10 stated value	$10,000,000	
Paid-in capital in excess of stated value	1,200,000	
Retained earnings (deficit)	(1,600,000)	9,600,000
Total liabilities & stockholders' equity		$14,000,000

2 The stated value of capital stock is reduced from $10 per share to $5 per share, thus increasing the paid-in capital in excess of stated value from $1,200,000 to $6,200,000.

3 The deficit of $4,700,000 is written off against paid-in capital in excess of stated value, resulting in a zero balance in the Retained Earnings account and a $1,500,000 balance in the Paid-in Capital in Excess of Stated Value account.

The journal entries to record the quasi-reorganization of Quasar Corporation are illustrated below:

Retained Earnings	3,100,000	
Accumulated Depreciation	1,900,000	
Plant Assets		4,000,000
Goodwill		1,000,000
To write down carrying values of assets as the first step in quasi-reorganization.		

Capital Stock, $10 stated value	10,000,000	
Capital Stock, $5 stated value		5,000,000
Paid-in Capital in Excess of Stated Value		5,000,000
To reduce the stated value of capital stock from $10 to $5 per share as part of a quasi-reorganization.		

Paid-in Capital in Excess of Stated Value   4,700,000
  Retained Earnings   4,700,000
To eliminate accumulated deficit as part of a quasi-
reorganization.

Any retained earnings accumulated after December 31, Year 15, would be available as a basis for dividend declaration and should be dated in balance sheets prepared following the quasi-reorganization. For example, assume that Quasar Corporation reported a net income of $375,000 and declared cash dividends of $125,000 in Year 16; the stockholders' equity section of the balance sheet at the end of Year 16 would be presented as follows:

Stockholders' equity:
  Capital stock, $5 stated value $5,000,000
  Paid-in capital in excess of stated value   1,500,000
    Total paid-in capital $6,500,000
  Retained earnings, accumulated since Dec. 31, Year 15, at which
    time a deficit of $4,700,000 was written off against paid-in capital
    in excess of stated value as a result of a quasi reorganization . .   250,000
    Total stockholders' equity. $6,750,000

Because replacement costs of plant assets generally have been increasing for many years, quasi-reorganizations are seldom encountered in practice. Companies experiencing severe financial difficulties are more likely to undergo a formal reorganization under the supervision of a bankruptcy court. This subject is covered in **Modern Advanced Accounting** of this series.

REVIEW QUESTIONS

1 "In the classification of items comprising the stockholders' equity section of the balance sheet, the most important principle followed by accountants is to show clearly the amount which can legally be distributed as dividends." Do you agree? Give reasons for your answer.

2 Enumerate several types of transactions which would cause an increase in paid-in capital in excess of par or stated value. What types of transactions cause a decrease in paid-in capital in excess of par or stated value?

3 The ledger of Tupolo Corporation includes the following accounts, among others:

> *Land (at appraised value)* *$900,000*
>
> *Unrealized appreciation from revaluation of land* *660,000*

The land originally acquired as a building site was sold because its value has risen so greatly as to make it unsuitable for the company's use. The sales price was $850,000. Give the journal entry to record the sale of land.

4 Galaxy Company sustained a loss of $100,000 from flood damage. Because retained earnings amounted to only $75,000 and paid-in capital in excess of par was $150,000, the company charged one-third of the loss to the former account and two-thirds to the latter. Is this treatment of the loss in accord with generally accepted accounting principles? Explain.

5 List three types of events that may be viewed by nonaccountants as resulting in an increase in retained earnings.

6 List the significant information usually included in a resolution by a board of directors for the declaration of a cash dividend.

7 How should a dividend in the form of property be recorded by the issuing corporation?

8 Define each of the following:
   a Scrip dividend
   b Liquidating dividend
   c Spin-off

9 Distinguish between a **stock dividend** and a **stock split.**

10 Sprouse Corporation follows a practice of distributing a 3% stock dividend each year in addition to paying an annual cash dividend of $2 a share. How should the amount of the charge to retained earnings for the stock dividend be determined?

11 Stock splits and stock dividends may be used by a corporation to change the number of shares of its stock outstanding.
   a What is meant by a **stock split effected in the form of a stock dividend**?
   b From an accounting viewpoint, explain how a stock split effected in the form of a stock dividend differs from an **ordinary stock dividend**.
   c How should a stock dividend which has been declared but not yet issued be classified in a balance sheet? Why?

12 Would you, as a bondholder of a corporation, be willing to give management a free hand in deciding upon distributions of stock dividends or would you prefer to include in the bond indenture some limitation upon the extent of stock dividends?

13 The stock of Cardenas Corporation is widely distributed among several thousand investors, most of whom own less than 50 shares. The company is planning to distribute a 2% stock dividend. What should be done for those stockholders who own less than 50 shares?

14 The AB Corporation, a manufacturer of sporting goods, decided to merge with the CD Corporation, a retailer of sporting goods. Barajas Sports Corporation was formed and received 60% of its total assets from AB Corporation and 40% from CD Corporation. Capital stock was issued by Barajas in these same proportions in payment for its assets. The former officers of the AB Corporation and of the CD Corporation assumed similar positions in the new corporation. Should Barajas Sports Corporation have a Retained Earnings account at the beginning of its existence? Could the new corporation have a Retained Earnings account larger or smaller than those accounts of the predecessor corporations? Explain.

15 Briefly state the purpose of each of the following financial statements:
 a Statement of retained earnings
 b Statement of paid-in capital
 c Combined statement of earnings and retained earnings
 d Statement of stockholders' equity

16 Explain the disposition of the account "Retained Earnings Appropriated for Expansion of Plant" when the planned expansion is carried out. Would your answer be altered if the expansion of the plant was paid for from bank borrowings?

17 In what ways might a corporation offer bondholders protection against excessively generous cash dividend payments to stockholders?

18 The right-hand side of the balance sheet of Krinke Corporation shows a group heading of Reserves between the sections for liabilities and stockholders' equity. Under the Reserves heading appear the following items:

Reserve for expropriation of assets	*$12,800,000*
Other	*2,500,000*

 Can you determine from the titles of these reserves and their position on the balance sheet whether they were created by charges to expense or by appropriations of retained earnings? Comment on this method of reporting.

19 To eliminate a deficit of $700,000, Driscoll Corporation obtained approval from its stockholders for a "reverse split." One new share of capital stock with par value of $5 was issued for each two old shares of $10 par value. The entire issue of 100,000 old shares was retired. Give the journal entries to record the exchange of shares and elimination of the deficit.

20 Under what circumstances should the retained earnings be "dated?" Does dating of the retained earnings refer to an item in the balance sheet or to a ledger account?

EXERCISES

Ex. 19-1 Mohamed Company was organized on January 2, Year 5, and issued the following capital stock:

 200,000 shares of $5 par common stock at $12 per share (authorized 500,000 shares)

 50,000 shares of $10 par fully participating 4% cumulative preferred stock at $25 per share (authorized 150,000 shares)

 The net income for Year 5 was $420,000 and cash dividends of $72,000 were declared and paid in Year 5.
 Compute the dividends paid on the preferred and common stock during Year 5.

Ex. 19-2 The stockholders' equity section for Wharton Manufacturing Company at December 31, Year 2, appears on page 796.

Stockholders' equity:

Common stock, $10 par, authorized 500,000 shares, issued 90,000

shares . . . . *$ 900,000*

Paid-in capital in excess of par *20,250*

Retained earnings *424,680*

Less: Cost of 1,210 shares of common stock in treasury . . . . *(36,300)*

Total stockholders' equity *$1,308,630*

On January 5, Year 3, 650 shares of treasury stock were sold, and on January 20, Year 3, a 5% stock dividend was declared. The dividend shares were issued on March 10. The market price of the Wharton's common stock was $21 per share on January 20.

Prepare journal entries to record the declaration (debit Retained Earnings) and distribution of the stock dividend.

Ex. 19-3 X Company declared and distributed dividends as follows:

a The entire investment in the common stock of S Company, a wholly owned subsidiary accounted for under the equity method, was distributed to X Company's stockholders. The carrying value of this investment at the date of distribution was $725,000; the distribution was made instead of accepting a cash offer of $2,000,000 from General Conglomerates, Inc.

b The company's 5% common stock interest in T Company was distributed to stockholders. The investment in T Company was carried at a cost of $62,000; the quoted market value of this investment was clearly established at $90,000. Prepare journal entries in the accounts of X Company to record the declaration and distribution of the two dividends described above.

Ex. 19-4 The stockholders' equity section of the balance sheet of Oscar Jimenez Company at the beginning of the year contained the following items:

Convertible preferred stock, $100 par, authorized, issued, and outstanding

10,000 shares (Note A) *$1,000,000*

Common stock, $5 par, authorized 1 million shares, issued and outstanding

400,000 shares *2,000,000*

Retained earnings *6,000,000*

Total stockholders' equity *$9,000,000*

Note A: *The preferred shares are convertible at any time into common shares at a conversion ratio of four common shares for each preferred share, with the conversion ratio subject to adjustment for any dilution of the common stock.*

On January 10, a 5% common stock dividend was declared, to be distributed January 30 to stockholders of record January 15. On March 1 all the preferred stock was converted into common shares. Market price per share was as follows: January 10, $40; January 15, $42; January 30, $43; March 1, $45.

Post the transactions described above in appropriate ledger accounts and determine the dollar amount of the following accounts after giving consideration to all the listed transactions: **(a)** common stock, **(b)** paid-in capital in excess of par, and **(c)** retained earnings. Also compute the total stockholders' equity after giving effect to these transactions.

Ex. 19-5 Beresford Corporation has in its ledger a number of accounts established many years ago, but it is considering the adoption of more modern account titles. For each of the following accounts, you are to state (1) the balance sheet classification or account group and (2) an improved title if you consider the present one unsatisfactory.

a Reserve for depreciation
b Reserve for loss contingencies
c Earned surplus
d Capital surplus
e Reserve for bad debts
f Reserve for current income taxes
g Reserve for treasury stock purchased
h Reserve for bond sinking fund
i Reserve for vacation pay accrued

Ex. 19-6 Select information as appropriate from the items listed below and prepare the stockholders' equity section of a balance sheet. Combine items and revise titles if customary.

Unissued common stock (275,000 shares)	$2,750,000
Bond sinking fund	600,000
Premium on bonds payable	5,000
Appropriation for bond sinking fund	600,000
Appropriation for loss contingencies	250,000
Reserve for doubtful accounts	10,000
Common stock options outstanding	25,000
Common stock warrants outstanding	60,000
Paid-in capital from stock dividends	140,000
Unrealized loss in value of noncurrent investments	180,000
Authorized common stock, $10 par	5,000,000
Earned surplus (unappropriated)	350,000
Appraisal capital from revaluation of land (approved by board of directors)	150,000

Ex. 19-7 Select the best answer for each of the following multiple-choice questions:
  a The dating of retained earnings is associated with:
    (1) Earnings accumulated by a subsidiary company subsequent to date of acquisition of controlling interest
    (2) Earnings accumulated subsequent to a quasi-reorganization
    (3) The declaration of a stock dividend in excess of 25%
    (4) Earnings of a foreign subsidiary subsequent to the date of a major currency devaluation
  b A business combination that requires the pooling-of-interests method:
    (1) Involves the acquisition by one company of the assets of another company for cash
    (2) Causes the assets of the acquired company to be restated in the accounts of the combined entity at fair value at date of acquisition
    (3) Causes the retained earnings accounts of the two corporations to be added together in arriving at the amount of retained earnings of the combined entity
    (4) Causes the earnings of the combined entity to include the earnings of the constituent companies only after the date of the combination
  c The right-hand side of a corporate balance sheet should show all items clearly identified under group headings of:
    (1) Current liabilities, long-term liabilities, and stockholders' equity
    (2) Current liabilities, long-term liabilities, reserves, and stockholders' equity
    (3) Liabilities, reserves, and stockholders' equity
    (4) Liabilities, reserves and deferred credits, and stockholders' equity

Ex. 19-8 Obsolescence has become a major problem in the inventory of Ray Groves, Inc. Lack of attention to inventory turnover rates, combined with a change in product design to permit use of lighter-weight materials, has caused much of the existing inventory to become obsolete. A careful analysis of the inventory at December 31 of the current year indicated that inventory value should be reduced by $1,100,000 because of obsolescence.

The net earnings of the current year before considering the obsolescence loss were estimated to be $210,000. The stockholders' equity accounts before year-end adjusting entries showed the following balances:

Capital stock, $1 par	$1,000,000
Paid-in capital in excess of par	600,000
Retained earnings	400,000
Total stockholders' equity	$2,000,000

The board of directors informs you that it regards obsolescence as an extraordinary item and that a tentative decision has been made to write down the inventory by the full amount of the obsolescence loss; to charge $400,000 against retained earnings, $600,000 against paid-in capital in excess of par, and $100,000 against operations of the current year.

Evaluate the proposed treatment of the obsolescence loss in the light of generally accepted accounting principles. Disregard income tax considerations. State the amount of income before income taxes for the current year and explain how the obsolescence loss should be reported. Disregard other adjustments that may be required in the computation of income before income taxes.

SHORT CASES FOR ANALYSIS AND DECISION

Case 19-1 "Since my retirement I have switched my investments into stocks that pay cash dividends, because I need a regular income," said Kimmie Lee.

"A regular cash income from stocks is one of my requirements, too," replied Curtis Chee. "However, I find it works better to buy stocks that pay regular stock dividends, and then, in effect, to declare my own cash dividends. I have been getting a reasonable cash flow from my stock investments even though the companies don't pay cash dividends. Furthermore, my investments are retaining their value and some are appreciating."

Instructions How could Chee obtain a cash flow from investments in stocks that did not pay cash dividends? Evaluate his investment policy.

Case 19-2 After receiving a stock certificate for three shares, Roger Bell, a stockholder in Niagara Corporation, expressed this reaction:

"The Niagara Corporation has just declared another stock dividend despite that letter of protest I wrote to the president last year. I told her I hate to see a company declare a stock dividend because it causes a transfer of retained earnings into legal capital. Such a transfer obviously reduces the amount available for cash dividends."

"You are absolutely right," said Gene Green. "When I bought Niagara stock I was hoping for an increase in cash dividends per share over a period of time, but the declaration of stock dividends certainly reduces my expectations for cash dividends. Let's write her another letter."

Instructions Evaluate the opinions expressed by Bell and Green from the standpoint of accounting principles and also in the light of customary dividend practices. Identify any elements of truth in the statements and any lack of logic in the conclusions reached by Bell and Green.

Case 19-3 James McDermott, CPA, was asked by the president of a client corporation for an explanation of a "quasi-reorganization." The president is unfamiliar with the procedure and is concerned that a competitor might have an advantage since undergoing a quasi-reorganization.

Instructions Prepare the report McDermott should provide to the president explaining a quasi-reorganization. The report should include the following points:
a Definition and accounting features of the procedure.
b The purpose of the procedure. Under what conditions should it be considered?
c Authorization necessary.
d Disclosure required in the financial statements.
e Does the competitor have an advantage? Discuss.

Case 19-4 The stockholders' equity section of Orona Corporation at the beginning of the current year consisted of the following items:

$4 preferred stock, $50 par	*$ 6,000,000*
Common stock, $10 par	*3,000,000*
Paid-in capital in excess of par:	
On preferred stock	*300,000*
On common stock	*3,000,000*
Retained earnings	*1,500,000*
Total stockholders' equity	*$13,800,000*

During the current year Orona Corporation became aware of major unexpected obsolescence of much of its plant equipment because of the appearance on the market of new types of machinery far less bulky and far more efficient. Some difference of opinion existed among the corporate officials as to how the obsolescence loss, estimated at $2 million, should be reflected in the accounts, if at all.

The corporation had operated successfully during its early years, but it had been incurring losses in recent years and the market prices of its securities were quite depressed, although the company's cash position was still strong. The following suggestions were made by various executives.

(1) Purchase and cancel the company's outstanding preferred stock, which had a current market price of about half the par value. The loss on the obsolete machinery could then be charged against the additional paid-in capital created by purchase of the preferred shares below par.
(2) Write down the machinery by charging the additional paid-in capital accounts applicable to the preferred and common stock.
(3) Write down the machinery by charging retained earnings.
(4) Write down the machinery by a charge against current revenue.
(5) Acquire new machinery but retain the old as standby equipment and continue to depreciate it as in the past.

Instructions Evaluate each of the above five proposals in the light of generally accepted accounting principles.

PROBLEMS

Group A

19A-1 The board of directors of Flamson Corporation declared a 6% stock dividend on October 1, to be distributed on October 25 to stockholders of record October 15.

The market price of the company's capital stock was as follows on these dates: October 1, $63; October 10, $66; and October 20, $70. The accounting records of Flamson Corporation are maintained on the basis of a fiscal year ending September 30.

On October 28 the board of directors declared a cash dividend of $0.80 a share on the capital stock. The dividend was payable on December 1 to stockholders of record November 18.

The stockholders' equity section of the balance sheet at September 30 of the current year is shown below. During October the net income was $41,750.

Stockholders' equity:

Capital stock, $15 par, authorized 200,000 shares, issued and outstanding 60,000 shares	$ 900,000
Paid-in capital in excess of par	1,250,000
Total paid-in capital	$2,150,000
Retained earnings	2,260,000
Total stockholders' equity	$4,410,000

Instructions
a Prepare journal entries for the declaration and the distribution of the dividends which would be required during the month of October. Debit Retained Earnings for dividend declarations. Also prepare a journal entry to record the net income for October (debit Income Summary).
b Prepare the stockholders' equity section of the balance sheet at October 31.

19A-2 Clelland Company has only one issue of capital stock consisting of 5,000,000 authorized shares, of which 600,000 shares had been issued several years ago. There were only three items in the stockholders' equity section of the balance sheet at the beginning of the current year: common stock, $3,000,000; paid-in capital in excess of par, $8,250,000, and retained earnings, $5,600,000.

On May 1, the company declared a 3% stock dividend, distributable June 1 to stockholders of record on May 15. On July 1, a cash dividend of $1 a share was declared payable August 1 to stockholders of record on July 20. On October 1, a 2 for 1 stock split was carried out. (Assume that the stock split was authorized and carried out on the same day.) Net income for the year ended December 31 amounted to $3,200,000. Stock prices at selected dates during the current year were: May 1, $30; May 15, $31; June 1, $35; October 1, $45; December 31, $20.

Instructions
a What was the par value per share and the issuance price per share for the common stock issued in prior years? Show computations.
b What was the dollar increase or decrease in retained earnings as a result of the 3% stock dividend? Explain.
c What was the dollar increase or decrease in total stockholders' equity resulting immediately and directly from (1) the 3% stock dividend and (2) the stock split? Explain.
d Prepare journal entries to record the stock dividend, cash dividend, stock split, and net income. You may debit Retained Earnings directly for dividend declarations rather than using accounts for Dividends and Stock Dividends. Give separate entries for the declaration and distribution of dividends.
e Prepare the stockholders' equity section of the balance sheet at December 31.

19A-3 On January 1, Year 15, El Dorado Company had a balance in its Retained Earnings account of $24 million and paid-in capital in excess of par of $5.5 million. The company had outstanding 2 million shares of common stock with a par value of $5; authorized shares were 4 million.

During Year 15, the company's net income from operations was $7.6 million. A cash dividend of 40 cents was paid July 31, Year 15, and a 5% stock dividend was declared on October 15, Year 15, to be distributed November 20 to stockholders of record November 5.

Early in December of Year 15, a property dividend consisting of 210,000 shares of Investee Company's common stock was declared and paid. The stock was held as a long-term investment by El Dorado Company.

You are asked to advise on the proper accounting treatment of the stock dividend and the property dividend. Your inquiries produce the following information: The stock of the company is traded on a national stock exchange. The market price of the stock on October 15 was $32; on November 5 it was $44; and on November 20 it was $40. The investment in Investee Company represented 8% ownership interest in the common stock of Investee Company. The cost of the stock was $1,280,000, and the market value on the declaration date was $1,680,000. The gain recognized on the property dividend was not taxable.

On December 28, Year 15, the company issued 150,000 additional shares of common stock for net proceeds of $6,275,200.

Instructions

a Prepare a statement of retained earnings for Year 15 in a form suitable for inclusion in the annual report. The net income reported by the company did not include the effect of the property dividend.

b Prepare a statement of paid-in capital for Year 15 in a form suitable for inclusion in the annual report.

c Prepare the stockholders' equity section of the balance sheet at December 31, Year 15.

d Prepare a note to the financial statements setting forth the basis of accounting for the stock and property dividends and add separately appropriate comments or explanations regarding the bases chosen.

19A-4 The stockholders of Romeo Corporation have voted approval for the corporation to carry out a quasi-reorganization. The balance sheet appeared as follows at September 30, Year 3, the effective date of the reorganization:

Assets

Current assets		$1,080,000
Plant assets	$800,000	
Less: Accumulated depreciation	395,000	405,000
Goodwill		1,520,000
Total assets		$3,005,000

Liabilities & Stockholders' Equity

Current liabilities	$ 330,000
6% bonds payable	250,000
7% preferred stock, $100 par (dividends in arrears, $42,000)	200,000
Common stock, $10 par	2,200,000
Retained earnings	25,000
Total liabilities & stockholders' equity	$3,005,000

The company is engaged in the manufacture of space exploration equipment and has acquired numerous small businesses at amounts in excess of the fair value of their tangible net assets. The purchase price included, among other things, payment for research work and for the services of technically trained personnel. The value assigned to acquired assets was based on the par value of stock issued pursuant to the acquisition. The market value of stock was approximately equal to its par value.

In recent months several major research projects were abandoned and some key people left the company. As a result, many contracts were lost and the goodwill was deemed to be worthless. In order to get a "fresh start" for financial reporting purposes, the following actions were taken pursuant to a quasi-reorganization approved by stockholders:

(1) Inventories and net receivables were written down by $150,000 and $10,000, respectively.
(2) The net carrying value of plant assets was reduced to $250,000 by increasing accumulated depreciation.
(3) The goodwill was written off.
(4) The par value of common stock was reduced to $1 a share.
(5) The dividends in arrears on the preferred stock were paid in cash and 80,000 shares of $1 par common stock were issued to the preferred stockholders in exchange for their stock.
(6) Following the asset write-offs, the deficit was eliminated against paid-in capital in excess of par value.
(7) During the last quarter of Year 3, Romeo Corporation earned a net income of $65,000, and as a result, current assets increased by $95,000, current liabilities increased by $5,000, and accumulated depreciation increased by $25,000. Current liabilities also increased by $7,000 as a result of additional income tax assessed for Year 1.

Instructions
a Prepare journal entries necessary to record the quasi-reorganization and to summarize the activities for the final quarter of Year 3.
b Compute the balance in retained earnings on December 31, Year 3.

19A-5 The stockholders' equity section of Liz Company as shown in the December 31, Year 2, balance sheet follows:

Stockholders' equity:

Common stock, $10 par, authorized, 500,000 shares; issued, 75,000 shares	$ 750,000
Paid-in capital in excess of par	175,000
Total paid-in capital	$ 925,000
Retained earnings	725,000
Subtotal	$1,650,000
Less: 4,700 shares of common stock in treasury, at cost	11,500
Total stockholders' equity	$1,638,500

A note to the financial statements stated that 1,000 shares of authorized and unissued common stock were reserved for issuance at $22 per share to employees. The stock option contract contains a clause protecting the optionees against dilution of their interests. The options had not been recorded in the accounts.

During the year ended December 31, Year 3, the following events occurred:

Jan. 16   A cash dividend of $0.20 a share was declared, payable February 15 to stockholders of record on February 5.
Feb. 1   Stock options for 500 shares were exercised.
Mar. 1   A 2 for 1 stock split was declared. The additional stock was issued March 15 to stockholders of record on March 5. The par value of the stock was reduced to $5 a share.

Apr. 1   The stockholders of Butler Corporation exchanged all their stock for 25,000 shares of Liz Company unissued common stock. Butler Corporation's net assets at current fair value amounted to $450,000. The business combination was treated as a purchase for accounting purposes.

June 30   Stock options for 400 shares were exercised.

Nov. 1   A 10% stock dividend was distributed. The stock dividend was declared on October 3.

Nov. 15   In a business combination that was treated as a pooling of interests for accounting purposes, 100,000 shares of Liz Company common stock were exchanged for all the stock of Larry Corporation. At the date of the exchange the stockholders' equity of Larry Corporation consisted of $500,000 capital stock, $160,000 paid-in capital in excess of par, and $270,000 retained earnings.

Dec. 1   Stock options for 100 shares were exercised.

Dec. 31   Net income for Liz Company for the year December 31, Year 3, amounted to $410,700.

The market price and book value per share (computed from interim financial statements) of Liz Company common stock at certain dates during Year 3 follow:

Date	Market price	Book value
February 1	$30	$26.00
March 1	36	27.00
April 1	19	13.75
June 30	23	14.00
October 1	24	14.25
November 1	25	14.50
November 15	26	14.75
December 1	27	15.00

Instructions   Prepare a working paper summarizing the transactions for Year 3. The working paper should have the following column headings:

Common Stock (number of shares and amount)
Paid-in Capital in Excess of Par
Retained Earnings
Treasury Stock (number of shares and cost)
Options Outstanding (number of shares and price per share)

Group B

19B-1 The retained earnings of Cadre Company at January 1, Year 4, amounted to $18 million, and paid-in capital in excess of par was $9 million. Common stock outstanding at this date consisted of 2 million shares with a par value of $5 a share.

On January 30, Year 4, the company discovered an error which required the payment of an additional $3 million of income taxes applicable to an unusual transaction which had occurred in Year 2.

During Year 4, the net income amounted to $7.7 million. A cash dividend of $1.10 a share was paid June 30, Year 4, and a 5% stock dividend was declared October 10, Year 4, to be distributed December 10, Year 4, to stockholders of record November 25, Year 4.

The stock of the company was traded on a national stock exchange. Market price of the common stock was as follows: October 10, $46; November 25, $52; and December 10, $50.

Instructions

a Prepare a four-column statement of stockholders' equity for Year 4, with columns showing changes in common stock (number of shares and dollar amounts), paid-in capital in excess of par, and retained earnings.

b Prepare a note to the financial statements concerning the retroactive charge to retained earnings to correct the error applicable to Year 2.

19B-2 Knox Corporation maintains its records on the basis of a fiscal year ending March 31. The stockholders' equity section of the balance sheet at March 31 of the current year appears below:

Stockholders' equity:

Capital stock, $10 par, authorized 250,000 shares, issued and outstanding 100,000 shares	*$1,000,000*
Paid-in capital in excess of par	*2,675,000*
Total paid-in capital	*$3,675,000*
Retained earnings	*3,240,000*
Total stockholders' equity	*$6,915,000*

On April 1, the board of directors of Knox Corporation declared a cash dividend of $1 a share payable on April 29 to stockholders of record April 15.

On April 10, the board of directors of Knox Corporation also declared a 3% stock dividend distributable on May 31 to stockholders of record May 15. The market price of the stock on April 10 was $60 a share. The net income for April amounted to $78,500.

Instructions

a Prepare journal entries for the declaration and the distribution of the dividends and to record net income for April. Debit the declarations of dividends directly to the Retained Earnings account, and debit Income Summary to record the net income.

b Prepare the stockholders' equity section of the balance sheet at April 30, supported by a separate statement of retained earnings.

19B-3 The market price of Don Marcos Corporation's capital stock at June 30, Year 1, was $52 a share. The stockholders' equity at this date included substantial retained earnings in addition to 250,000 shares of $2 par capital stock, which had been issued at a price of $12 a share. A total of 500,000 shares was authorized to be issued.

A property dividend of $1.10 a share was declared on March 10, Year 2, payable April 25, Year 2, to stockholders of record March 31, Year 2. The carrying value of the marketable securities distributed as a property dividend was $180,000.

A cash dividend of $1.50 a share was declared on June 1, Year 2, payable July 20, Year 2, to stockholders of record July 1, Year 2; a 5% stock dividend was declared at the same time and with the same dates of record and distribution. The cash dividend was not applicable to the dividend shares. The market price of the stock was $55 on June 1, Year 2, and $58 on June 30, Year 2.

During the fiscal year ended June 30, Year 2, net income amounted to $1,512,500 (including the effect, if any, of the property dividend), which represented an earnings rate of 10% on total equity capital at the beginning of the year.

Instructions

a Record the transactions affecting stockholders' equity during Year 2 in the general journal. Debit Retained Earnings for declarations of dividends, and Income Summary to record the net income for Year 2

b Prepare a statement of retained earnings for the year ended June 30, Year 2.

c Prepare the stockholders' equity section of the balance sheet at June 30, Year 2.

19B-4 During the initial stages of your audit of Corona Company for the year ended December 31, Year 7, you are informed by the president that the company is insolvent and must declare bankruptcy unless a large loan can be obtained immediately. A lender who is willing to advance $500,000 to the company has been located, but will only make the loan if the company agrees to a quasi-reorganization, as follows:

(1) A $800,000, 6% mortgage payable on the company's land and buildings held by a major stockholder will be canceled along with four months' accrued interest. The mortgage will be replaced by 7,000 shares of $100 par, 6% cumulative (if earned), nonparticipating preferred stock.

(2) A $500,000, 8% mortgage payable over 15 years on the land and buildings will be given as security on the new loan from an insurance company.

(3) On May 1, Year 6, the company's trade creditors had accepted $360,000 in notes payable on demand at 6% interest in settlement of all past-due accounts. No payment has been made to date. The company plans to settle these notes at the rate of 75 cents per $1 owed or to replace the notes payable on demand with new notes payable for full indebtedness over five years at 6% interest. It is estimated that $200,000 face amount of the demand notes will be exchanged for the longer-term notes and that the holders of the remaining notes will accept the offer of a reduced cash settlement of 75 cents per $1 owed (including accrued interest). One-fifth of the new notes is due each year.

(4) A new issue of 500 shares of $100 par, 5%, noncumulative and nonparticipating, preferred stock will replace 500 outstanding shares of $100 par, 7%, cumulative and participating preferred stock. Preferred stockholders will repudiate all claims to $21,000 of dividends in arrears. The company has not formally declared the dividends.

(5) A new issue of 600 shares of $50 par, Class A common stock will replace 600 outstanding shares of $100 par, Class A common stock.

(6) A new issue of 650 shares of $40 par, Class B common stock will replace 650 outstanding shares of $100 par, Class B common stock.

(7) The deficit is eliminated.

The president of Corona Company asks that you determine the effect of the foregoing on the company and furnishes the following additional condensed account balances at December 31, Year 7, which you believe are fairly presented:

Bank overdraft	$ 25,000
Other current assets	620,000
Plant assets net of accumulated depreciation	840,000
Trade accounts payable	235,000
Other current liabilities	85,000
Paid-in capital in excess of par: common stock	125,000
Retained earnings (deficit)	(345,000)

Instructions

a Prepare pro forma journal entries that you would suggest to give effect to the quasi-reorganization as of January 2, Year 8. Entries should be keyed to numbered information in the same sequence as given in the problem.

b Prepare a pro forma balance sheet for the Corona Company at January 1, Year 8, assuming that the quasi-reorganization had been consummated.

19B-5 At the beginning of the current year, the stockholders' equity of Upmann Cigar Company was as follows:

$6 convertible preferred stock, $100 par, authorized 10,000 shares, issued and outstanding 5,000 shares (Note 1)	$ 500,000
Common stock, $2 par, authorized 1,000,000 shares, issued and outstanding 350,000 shares (Note 2)	700,000
Common stock subscribed, 8,000 shares	16,000
Paid-in capital in excess of par: common stock	3,500,000
Total paid-in capital	$4,716,000
Retained earnings	5,262,600
Total stockholders' equity	$9,978,600

Note 1: *Preferred shares were issued at par, are callable at $105, and are convertible into common shares at a rate of 3 for 1, subject to an antidilution provision.*
Note 2: *10,000 shares are reserved for stock options at a price of $33, subject to an antidilution provision.*

During the first quarter of the current year the following transactions were completed:

Jan. 7   Collected $310,000, representing payment in full for all outstanding common stock subscriptions; issued the stock.

Jan. 31   Declared the regular quarterly dividend on the preferred stock, to be paid March 3 to stockholders of record February 19.

Feb. 1   Declared a 10% common stock dividend to be distributed March 4 to common stockholders of record February 20.

Mar. 3   Paid quarterly dividend on the preferred stock.

Mar. 4   Distributed the 10% common stock dividend.

Mar. 15   All outstanding stock options were exercised at a price adjusted for the effect of the 10% stock dividend.

Mar. 30   All preferred stock was converted into common stock.

Mar. 31   Issued 100,000 shares of common stock in exchange for the net assets of Ipanima Corporation appraised at $4.5 million.

Mar. 31   Net income for the first quarter of the current year was $877,700. (Debit the Income Summary account.)

Market price per share of Upmann Cigar Company's common stock was as follows: January 9, $40; February 1, $38; February 20, $40; March 4, $42; March 15, $43; March 31, $45.

Instructions

a Prepare journal entries for the transactions described above. Debit Retained Earnings for declarations of dividends.

b Prepare a statement of stockholders' equity (including retained earnings) for the first quarter of the current year.

CHAPTER 20

TREASURY STOCK, BOOK VALUE, AND EARNINGS PER SHARE

Additional topics dealing with stockholders' equity which require special attention are (1) the acquisition and retirement or reissue by a corporation of its capital stock, (2) the computation of book value per share of capital stock, and (3) the computation of earnings per share of common stock. The acquisition of capital stock reduces total stockholders' equity and affects the computation of book value and earnings per share; book value per share is the net asset value of each share of capital stock outstanding; earnings per share is the amount of net income earned on each share of common stock and is considered by many investors as the most important financial measurement. These topics present challenging problems for accountants.

TREASURY STOCK

Treasury stock is the capital stock of a corporation which has been legally issued, fully paid for, and subsequently acquired by the corporation but not formally retired. All transactions by a corporation involving its own stock result in a contraction or an expansion of stockholders' equity. When a corporation acquires shares of its own capital stock, certain stockholders surrender their ownership interest in the corporation. Thus the acquisition of treasury stock by a corporation is logically viewed as a partial liquidation and no gain or loss results from such transactions.

Treasury stock may be acquired by corporations for a variety of reasons, including the following: (1) to buy out a particular stockholder, (2) to use the stock in connection with stock option and bonus plans or for acquiring other companies, (3) to settle claims against debtors who are also stockholders, (4) to increase earnings per share by reducing the number of shares outstanding, and (5) to support the market price of the stock.[1] There is little justification for a corporation to attempt to influence the market price of its stock through the acquisition and reissuance of treasury stock; such efforts necessarily create a conflict of interest between the corporation and its stockholders and may be illegal in some circumstances.

Treasury stock and stated (or legal) capital

Stated (or *legal*) capital, as explained in Chapter 17, is a statutory definition of the amount of capital to be held in the business for protection of creditors; it is not available for withdrawal by stockholders. Legal capital generally consists of the total par or stated value of stock issued. The acquisition of treasury stock is not regarded as a reduction in legal capital; however, such an acquisition involves an outflow of assets to stockholders and therefore certain legal restrictions are necessary to protect the corporation's creditors. Generally, a corporation is not permitted to acquire treasury stock if such acquisitions would cause the stockholders' equity to be reduced below legal capital. Furthermore, a portion of retained earnings becomes restricted and unavailable for dividends to the extent of the amount paid for treasury stock.

It should be emphasized that the retirement of capital stock reduces legal capital and the acquisition of treasury stock does not. In terms of economic significance, the retirement of capital stock and the acquisition of treasury stock are similar, because both transactions consist of a return of corporate assets to stockholders and a corresponding reduction in the amount of capital invested in the business.

Treasury stock is not an asset

A corporation cannot own a portion of itself, and for this reason treasury stock is not to be viewed as an asset. The holding of treasury stock does not give the corporation any right to receive cash dividends, to vote, to

---

[1] In the 30th edition of *Accounting Trends & Techniques* issued by the AICPA in 1976, 455 of the 600 companies included in the survey reported treasury stock, either common or preferred, in their balance sheets. For an additional discussion of the various aspects of treasury stock, see the following: Charles D. Ellis and Allan E. Young, *The Repurchase of Common Stock,* The Ronald Press Company (New York: 1971); and Guy J. Agrati, "Practical Considerations in Common Stock Repurchase," *Management Adviser* (May–June 1972), pp. 35–39.

exercise preemptive rights as a stockholder, or to receive assets when the corporation is liquidated. Corporations can and sometimes do formally cancel treasury stock; certainly this action would never be taken if such cancellation actually meant the destruction of genuine assets. If a corporation were to dissolve, any treasury stock held would contribute nothing in the process of converting assets into cash for distribution to shareholders.

The view that treasury shares are not assets is further strengthened by recognition that treasury shares are essentially much the same as unissued shares, and no one advocates that unissued shares be listed as assets.

The policy of carrying treasury shares as assets, if justified at all, must rest on grounds of expediency rather than accounting principles. Treasury shares of a very large publicly owned corporation are sometimes acquired with the intention of reissue in the near future under an employee stock-purchase program.[2] The company may have a liability to employees participating in the stock-purchase program; to meet this liability the company expends cash to acquire treasury shares and soon thereafter discharges the liability by delivery of the treasury shares to employees. If such shares are few in number as compared with outstanding shares, they may be treated much the same as an investment in securities of any other corporation. The Accounting Principles Board has given recognition to this situation as follows:

> When a corporation's stock is acquired for purposes other than retirement (formal or constructive), or when ultimate disposition has not yet been decided, the cost of acquired stock may be shown separately as a deduction from the total of capital stock, capital surplus, and retained earnings, or may be accorded the accounting treatment appropriate for retired stock, or in some circumstances may be shown as an asset. . . .[3]

The Securities and Exchange Commission stipulates the following reporting requirement for reacquired shares:

> Reacquired shares not retired shall be shown separately as a deduction from capital shares, or from the total of capital shares and other stockholders' equity, or from other stockholders' equity, at either par or stated value, or cost, as circumstances require.[4]

The reasons for refusing to recognize treasury stock as an asset are many and are generally recognized as valid, yet the issue is kept alive by the policy of a few corporations which persist in listing treasury stock among their assets.

---

[2] At the end of 1976, for example, General Motors Corporation reported as an asset 1,457,629 shares, costing $100 million, as "Common Stock Held for the Incentive Program."

[3] *APB Opinion No. 6,* "Status of Accounting Research Bulletins," AICPA (New York: 1965), p. 40.

[4] *Accounting Series Release No. 125* (Amendments to Regulations S–X, Rule 3-14), Securities and Exchange Commission (Washington: 1972), p. 10.

Alternative treatments of treasury stock

The two principal alternative treatments of treasury stock are (1) the *cost method* and (2) the *par* or *stated value method.* Although the par or stated value method still receives some theoretical support in accounting literature, practicing accountants have turned increasingly to the cost method in recent years.[5] Both methods come within the range of generally accepted accounting principles.

Under the cost method, the acquisition of treasury stock is regarded as a first step in a financial move which is completed by the reissuance of the treasury stock. Treasury stock is thus viewed as a "suspense" item of stockholders' equity, with the corporation acting as an intermediary between the former and new stockholders. When the cost method is used, the Treasury Stock account is debited for the cost of the stock acquired and this account is shown in the balance sheet as a deduction from the *total* stockholders' equity. With this arrangement of the stockholders' equity section of the balance sheet, there is no reduction in the legal or stated capital. Since the laws of most states indicate that the acquisition of treasury stock does not constitute a reduction in legal capital, this balance sheet presentation may be regarded as reflecting the prevailing legal concept of treasury stock.

Under the par or stated value method, the possibility of reissuance of the treasury stock is not given much weight. The relationship between the corporation and the former owners of shares now held in treasury has ended and therefore the account showing paid-in capital in excess of par relating to the treasury shares is reduced. If the corporation decides to retire the shares, the Capital Stock account also would be reduced; on the other hand, the reissuance of treasury stock would be treated as an original issuance of capital stock.

Illustration of Accounting for Treasury Stock—Cost Method   To illustrate the cost method of accounting for treasury stock transactions, assume that the balance sheet for Rae Corporation includes the following:

Stockholders' equity:
Capital stock, $100 par, authorized, issued, and outstanding
 10,000 shares $1,000,000
Paid-in capital in excess of par 200,000
Retained earnings 500,000
 Total stockholders' equity $1,700,000

---

[5] In the 30th edition of *Accounting Trends & Techniques* issued by the AICPA in 1976, common stock held in treasury was carried at cost by 364 companies and at par or stated value by 70 companies; preferred stock held in treasury was carried at cost by 45 companies and at par or stated value by 24 companies.

At this time Rae Corporation acquired 300 shares of treasury stock at $115 a share. The acquisition of treasury stock was recorded at cost as illustrated below:

Treasury Stock	*34,500*	
Cash		*34,500*
Acquired 300 shares of treasury stock at $115 a share.		

The stockholders' equity section of the balance sheet of Rae Corporation would appear as follows when treasury stock was recorded at cost:

Stockholders' equity:

Capital stock, $100 par, authorized and issued 10,000 shares of which 300 shares have been purchased and are held in treasury	$1,000,000
Paid-in capital in excess of par	200,000
Retained earnings (see note)	500,000
Subtotal	$1,700,000
Less: Cost of 300 shares of treasury stock	34,500
Total stockholders' equity	$1,665,500

Note: *The declaration of dividends and the acquisition of treasury stock are restricted to the amount of the retained earnings reduced by the cost of treasury stock, or $465,500.*

The presentation of stockholders' equity (when treasury stock is recorded at cost) has the weakness of failing to show the net amount of capital invested by stockholders; it thus does not achieve one of the more important objectives in the classification of corporate capital. However, the cost approach to treasury stock does have the merit of showing as capital stock an amount equal to the legal capital of the corporation.

Let us assume that Rae Corporation *canceled* the 300 shares of treasury stock recorded at cost. This action causes a reduction in legal capital and in paid-in capital in excess of par equal to the amount paid for treasury stock. The journal entry to record the cancellation of the treasury stock is given at the top of page 812.

The 300 shares were originally issued at $120 each ($1,200,000 ÷ 10,000), or for a total of $36,000. The shares were acquired at a cost of $34,500 or $1,500 *less* than the paid-in capital relating to these shares. Therefore, the cancellation of the 300 shares calls for a reduction of only $34,500 in the paid-in capital accounts; the excess of the amount originally paid in by stockholders over the cost of treasury

Capital Stock	30,000	
Paid-in Capital in Excess of Par	4,500	
Treasury Stock		34,500
To record cancellation of 300 shares of treasury stock carried at cost.		

shares, $1,500 ($36,000 − $34,500 = $1,500) remains in the Paid-in Capital in Excess of Par account.

If Rae Corporation, instead of canceling the 300 shares of treasury stock as previously illustrated, should reissue these shares at a price of $108 a share, or $2,100 *below cost,* the journal entry would be as follows:

Cash	32,400	
Paid-in Capital in Excess of Par	2,100	
Treasury Stock		34,500
Sold 300 shares of treasury stock at $108 a share, or $2,100 below cost.		

Under the cost method, the Treasury Stock account is credited for the cost of the shares being reissued. Cost may be computed on an average basis, on a first-in, first-out basis, or by specific identification. When the reissuance price is less than cost, as in the illustration above, the excess of cost over the proceeds upon reissuance is charged to Paid-in Capital in Excess of Par. This account was credited at the time the stock was originally issued; however, if such paid-in capital is insufficient, paid-in capital from previous treasury stock transactions or Retained Earnings can be debited for the excess of cost over the proceeds upon reissuance.

When treasury stock is reissued at a *price above cost,* the excess of the proceeds over cost of the treasury shares is credited to Paid-in Capital in Excess of Par, as illustrated below:

Cash	37,500	
Treasury Stock		34,500
Paid-in Capital in Excess of Par		3,000
Sold 300 shares of treasury stock at $125 a share, or $3,000 above cost.		

Illustration of Accounting for Treasury Stock—Par (or Stated) Value Method
To allow a ready comparison between the cost method and the par

(or stated) value method of accounting for treasury stock, we will use the same transactions illustrated above for Rae Corporation. Using the par value method, the entry to record the acquisition of treasury stock by Rae Corporation is shown below:

Treasury Stock	30,000	
Paid-in Capital in Excess of Par	4,500	
Cash		34,500
Acquired 300 shares of treasury stock at $115 a share.		

In this entry the reduction in the stockholders' equity amounts to $34,500, or $1,500 less than the $36,000 originally invested in the corporation by its stockholders. In other words, $1,500 of the capital originally invested by those stockholders who have relinquished their ownership equity in the corporation remains in the business.[6]

After the acquisition of treasury stock, the stockholders' equity section of Rae Corporation's balance sheet appears at the top of page 814.

This form for reporting the stockholders' equity section has the merit of showing the net amount for paid-in capital after the treasury stock acquisitions. However, it may be criticized on the grounds that the net figure shown for capital stock ($970,000) may be erroneously interpreted as the legal capital; the legal capital of $1,000,000 is not reduced by the acquisition of treasury stock.

If Rae Corporation should *cancel* all 300 shares of treasury stock, the cancellation would be recorded by a debit to Capital Stock and a credit to Treasury Stock for $30,000. After cancellation of the treasury stock, the stockholders' equity section would not include treasury stock and there would be no need to indicate a restriction on retained earnings.

---

[6] If the amount paid for treasury stock is more than the amount originally invested by stockholders, the excess is treated as a reduction in retained earnings. For example, if Rae Corporation paid $40,000 to acquire stock originally issued for $36,000, the transaction would be recorded using the par value method as follows:

Treasury Stock	30,000	
Paid-in Capital in Excess of Par	6,000	
Retained Earnings	4,000	
Cash		40,000

If treasury stock is acquired at a price below par value, the excess of par value over cost of treasury stock would be credited to Paid-in Capital in Excess of Par. For example, if Rae Corporation paid only $25,000 for the 300 shares of stock, the entry to record the acquisition would be:

Treasury Stock	30,000	
Paid-in Capital in Excess of Par		5,000
Cash		25,000

Stockholders' equity:

Capital stock, $100 par, authorized and issued 10,000 shares	$1,000,000	
Less: Treasury stock, 300 shares at par	30,000	$ 970,000
Paid-in capital in excess of par		195,500
Total paid-in capital		$1,165,500
Retained earnings (see note)		500,000
Total stockholders' equity		$1,665,500

Note: *Retained earnings is restricted to the extent of $34,500, the amount paid for treasury stock.*

The cancellation, in effect, has permanently reduced legal capital to $970,000.

If Rae Corporation, instead of canceling the 300 shares of treasury stock as previously illustrated, should resell the shares at a price *above par,* say $108 each, the journal entry would be:

Cash	32,400	
Treasury Stock		30,000
Paid-in Capital in Excess of Par		2,400

Sold 300 shares of treasury stock at $108 a share, or $2,400 above carrying (par) value.

Note that the journal entry for reissuance of treasury shares is similar to an entry for original issuance of stock. The difference between the issuance price of the treasury shares and the par value of the shares, as recorded in the Treasury Stock account, is credited to the Paid-in Capital in Excess of Par account. Under the par value approach, the acquisition of treasury shares is viewed as a temporary retirement of these shares; the reissuance of treasury shares then logically should be treated in the same manner as an original issuance of capital stock.

In the event that the treasury stock was reissued at *less than par,* it would not be appropriate to debit a Discount on Capital Stock account because no "discount liability" attaches to treasury stock reissued below par. Instead, the deficiency would be recorded by a debit to Paid-in Capital in Excess of Par if such paid-in capital were available. In the absence of sufficient paid-in capital in excess of par to absorb the deficiency, it should be charged to Retained Earnings.

Points of emphasis in accounting for treasury stock

Certain key points stand out from the rather involved procedures and alternative methods used in accounting for treasury stock:

1 Treasury stock is not an asset and is not entitled to receive cash dividends, to vote, or to share in the liquidation of the corporation.

2 No gain or loss is recognized on treasury stock transactions, either for accounting or for income tax purposes.

3 Retained earnings can never be increased through treasury stock transactions; however, retained earnings may be decreased through such transactions.

4 The total stockholders' equity would be the same regardless of the method used to account for treasury stock; however, some variations in the relative amounts of paid-in capital and retained earnings may arise, depending on the method used.

5 Retained earnings in an amount equal to the cost of treasury stock is unavailable as a basis for declaration of cash dividends.

Redemption of preferred stock

Most corporations issuing preferred stock include in the contract a provision that all or any part of the preferred stock may be called for redemption (retirement) at any time desired by the corporation. The call price is usually above the issuance price; it may be an unchanging amount or it may be a series of amounts on a sliding scale relating to specified time periods and eventually dropping to par value. When preferred stock is called for redemption, the stock is canceled and hence not available for reissuance. Redemption may be effected by calling the stock pursuant to the call provision, by purchase in the open market, or by making a special offer to stockholders to *tender* their shares at a price above the current market price of the stock.

The redemption of preferred stock is not to be confused with the acquisition of treasury stock, because *redemption* signifies both acquisition and cancellation (retirement) of the stock.

Preferred stock can also be acquired for subsequent reissuance and held as treasury stock. However, acquisitions of preferred stock generally are made for the purpose of retiring the stock.

To illustrate the redemption of preferred stock, assume that D Corporation had issued 10,000 shares of $100 par preferred stock at $102. The call price was $105 a share. If D Corporation called the entire issue at the call price of $105 a share, the journal entry to record the redemption is illustrated at the top of page 816.

This entry eliminates both the Preferred Stock and the Paid-in Capital in Excess of Par: Preferred Stock accounts; clearly this action is appropriate since the capital invested by the preferred stockholders has been returned in full and these investors no longer have any ownership equity in the company. The $30,000 paid to the preferred stockholders in excess of their original investment, referred to as *premium paid on the re-*

Preferred Stock, $100 par 1,000,000
Paid-in Capital in Excess of Par: Preferred Stock 20,000
Retained Earnings 30,000
    Cash 1,050,000
Redeemed 10,000 shares of preferred stock for $30,000
in excess of the original issuance price.

tirement of preferred stock, should be debited to Retained Earnings and not to any paid-in capital accounts applicable to other classes of capital stock.

When the preferred stock is selling at a price below call price, a company may wish to redeem a portion of the issue by purchase in the open market. Returning to the previous example, assume that D Corporation acquired 1,000 shares at $90. The entry to record the redemption would be:

Preferred Stock, $100 par 100,000
Paid-in Capital in Excess of Par: Preferred Stock 2,000
    Cash 90,000
    Paid-in Capital from Redemption of Preferred Stock . 12,000
Redeemed 1,000 shares of preferred stock at a cost $12,000
below the original issuance price.

By a payment of $90,000, the corporation has eliminated 1,000 shares of preferred stock representing $102,000 of paid-in capital. Recording the $12,000 excess of the original investment by preferred stockholders over the amount paid to redeem the 1,000 shares in the manner illustrated above results in an increase in the equity of the common stockholders. However, this increase should not be regarded as a gain to be reported in the income statement. It would also be unsound to credit to retained earnings the $12,000 difference between the carrying value of redeemed stock and the redemption price. The $12,000 was originally recorded as paid-in capital and it continues in that category with a descriptive title indicating the effect of the redemption of the preferred stock at a price below the original issuance price.

The two preceding examples illustrate the following general rules for interpreting the redemption of preferred stock:

1 When preferred stock is redeemed at a cost in excess of the original issuance price, the excess payment is usually treated as a reduction in retained earnings. Such an excess should **not** be recorded as an extraordinary loss or as a debit to any paid-in capital relating to outstanding shares of any other class of stock.

2 When preferred stock is redeemed for an amount less than the issuance price, the difference is treated as a paid-in capital item and **not** as an extraordinary gain or as an increase in retained earnings.

BOOK VALUE PER SHARE

The term **book value** is often used in negotiations for the sale of a going business. In closely held corporations, it is not unusual for a contract to be signed giving one of the stockholders the right to buy out another stockholder within a specified time period at a price equal to the book value per share of capital stock.

Book value when single class of capital stock is outstanding

Book value is based on going-concern value and not on the assumption of business liquidation. **Book value per share is the amount of net assets applicable to each share of outstanding capital stock.** In a corporation with only one class of capital stock outstanding, book value per share is computed by dividing the total stockholders' equity by the number of shares of stock outstanding. This is illustrated below:

$$\frac{\text{Total stockholders' equity}}{\text{Number of shares outstanding}} = \frac{\$2,500,000}{100,000} = \$25 \text{ book value per share}$$

If a corporation holds treasury stock, the debit balance in the Treasury Stock account is deducted in determining the total stockholders' equity and the number of shares outstanding does not include the treasury stock.

The formula for computing book value is deceptively simple, but the determination of book value per share under the terms of a contract for sale of stock may be highly controversial for such reasons as the following:

1 Carrying values for assets (especially inventories, depreciable assets, natural resources, and intangible assets) vary greatly according to the accounting principles and methods selected.

2 Changes in accounting principles may have been made since the signing of the contract, with significant impact upon the carrying values of assets and liabilities.

3 Accounting errors may have been made in current or past periods, thus providing a basis for arguing that the accounting records must be adjusted to show the proper valuation of assets and liabilities.

4 Investments in securities, land, plant assets, and intangible assets may have a current cash value far in excess of the cost valuation shown in the accounting records. Some valuable assets may not even be included in the balance sheet.

5 Certain assets may be overstated or contingent liabilities of large amount may exist without being reported in the accounting records. Similarly, large amounts of contingent assets (such as potential income tax benefits of operating loss carryforwards) may exist.

When the term "book value per share" is used in a contract for the sale of an interest in a business, the courts may interpret "book value" in accordance with what is believed to have been the *intent* of the contracting parties.

The purpose of accounting data is to present *meaningful* information about a business entity. In the opinion of the authors the computation of book value per share requires adjustment of the accounts to correct many types of errors, including mechanical errors, violations of generally accepted accounting principles, and inconsistencies in the application of accounting policies. However, these corrective measures still may result in an amount for book value far different from the *current fair value* of net assets. Substantial differences between book value and current fair value per share are inevitable when accounting records are maintained on a cost basis. The conclusion must be that contracts for the sale of an interest in a business should be more specific in prescribing how the price per share is to be computed. It is not enough to specify "book value per share."

Book value of common stock when preferred stock is outstanding

Book value is used to some extent as a guide to investors, but usually with recognition that some other concepts, such as earnings per share, may be more closely correlated with changes in market price. Even though common stocks often sell at prices far above and far below the book value per share, some investors feel that the book value per share should be taken into account along with other criteria in reaching investment decisions.[7]

The concept of book value per share is more meaningful and more widely used for common stock than for preferred stock; however, if a corporation has both types of stock outstanding, the book value of the preferred stock must be determined as a preliminary step to computing book value for the common stock, as shown in the example at the top of page 819.

The book value of the preferred stock in this example is $108 per share. In computing the book value of the preferred stock, consideration must be given to any *dividends in arrears* and other contractual limitations on the equity of preferred stockholders in the net assets of the corporation. On a going-concern basis, is it (1) par or stated value,

---

[7] One writer states that any investor who totally ignores book value of stock "can justifiably be accused of having his head in the sand." [Steven C. Leuthold, "Spotting Tops and Bottoms: Multiples of Normalized Earnings, Book Values Are Useful Guides," *Barron's* (June 19, 1972), p. 5.]

Book value per share of common stock—two classes of stock
  outstanding:

Total stockholders' equity (net of treasury stock)	$9,280,000
Less: Amount applicable to preferred stock: 10,000 shares, $100 par, 5% preferred stock, callable at $108	1,080,000
Equity applicable to common stock, consisting of 1,000,000 shares outstanding (not including treasury stock)	$8,200,000
Book value per share of common stock, $8,200,000 ÷ 1,000,000 shares	$ 8.20

(2) call price, or (3) liquidation price that is most significant in measuring the book value of the preferred stock? Nearly all preferred stocks issued in recent years contain a call provision; this call price is usually the maximum claim to net assets imposed by the preferred stock contract. Although there may be no immediate prospect that the preferred stock will be called, the call price is nevertheless of more significance from the viewpoint of the going concern than is the liquidation price. The authors therefore favor using the call price of the preferred stock as the most appropriate measure of the stockholders' equity applicable to the preferred stock.

Other factors influencing book value per share of common stock

When significant amounts of convertible securities, stock warrants, and stock options are outstanding, the potential effect on book value of common stock may be material. In such cases the computation of book value per share on a *pro forma* basis should accompany the book value figure determined under the existing capital structure. For example, assume the following capital structure for Bowman Company:

Stockholders' equity:

5% convertible bonds payable (each $1,000 bond is convertible into 40 shares of common stock and is callable at par)	$1,000,000
Common stock, $10 par	2,000,000
Retained earnings	600,000

What effect would the conversion of the bonds payable have on the book value per share of common stock? The answer to this question appears in the example at the top of page 820.

Effect of Conversion of Bonds Payable on Book Value per Share of Common Stock

	Before conversion	To record conversion	Pro forma (after conversion)
5% convertible bonds payable . .	$1,000,000	$ −1,000,000	$ −0−
Common stock, $10 par	$2,000,000	+400,000	$2,400,000
Paid-in capital from conversion of bonds payable		+600,000	600,000
Retained earnings	600,000		600,000
Total stockholders' equity	$2,600,000		$3,600,000
Number of shares of common stock outstanding	200,000		240,000
Book value per share of common stock	$ 13		$ 15

Since each additional share of common stock issued pursuant to the conversion of the bonds adds $25 ($1,000,000 ÷ 40,000 shares) to stockholders' equity, the book value per share of common stock increased from $13 to $15.

Other events which increase or decrease the book value per share of common stock are listed below:

1 *Increases in book value*   Net income, reverse splits, issuance of additional common stock at prices above book value, acquisition of common stock at prices below book value, and retirement of preferred stock at prices below book value of the preferred stock.

2 *Decreases in book value*   Net loss, cash dividends (including any accumulated dividends on preferred stock), stock dividends, stock splits, issuance of additional common stock at prices below book value, acquisition of common stock at prices above book value, and retirement of preferred stock at prices above book value of the preferred stock.

Other more complex situations, such as quasi-reorganizations and business combinations, may materially alter the book value per share of common stock.

EARNINGS PER SHARE

Because of the complexities of business activities and the need for a small number of comparative measurements to highlight financial analysis, earnings per share has become perhaps the most important figure for many investors. Probably no financial statistic is cited more widely than earnings per share. In the opinion of many investors, market prices of common stocks are closely related to earnings per share.

Earnings per share is the amount of net income earned on a share of common stock during a year or quarter of a year. Earnings per share is meaningful only with respect to common stock; it should not be computed for preferred stock because the participation in earnings by preferred stockholders is limited by contract. Assuming that only one class of capital stock is outstanding and that there was no change in the number of shares outstanding during the period, earnings per share would be computed as follows:

$$\frac{\text{Net income}}{\text{Number of shares of stock outstanding}} = \text{earnings per share}$$

When preferred stock is also outstanding, the current dividend requirement on the preferred stock (whether or not declared by the board of directors) would be deducted from net income to determine the earnings available for the common stock.

Investors in common stocks make extensive use of earnings per share in the evaluation of the profitability of corporations. By computing the *price-earnings* ratio (price of a share of stock divided by earnings per share), investors also attempt to determine whether the market price of the stock is reasonable or whether it might be too high or too low. However, financial statements are only one part of the total information that can be used in evaluating the company's past and predicting its future performance, and the earnings per share figure is a small piece of the total information available in financial statements. Excessive reliance on earnings per share data may result in failure to consider the totality of a company's operations, including a wide range nonfinancial data which may be far more important.

Historical perspective

The inclusion of earnings per share in the income statement became a generally accepted principle with the issuance of *APB Opinion No. 9* in 1966.[8] Three years later, the APB issued *Opinion No. 15,* "Earnings per Share," to: (1) recognize the importance of the increasingly complex capital structures of many corporations in which the distinctions between common stockholders' equity and other forms of capital were not clearly apparent; (2) provide guidelines and procedures for the computation of earnings per share in a consistent manner which would be meaningful to investors; and (3) specify procedures for reporting the potential dilution in earnings per share.[9] The Accounting Principles

---

[8] *APB Opinion No. 9,* "Reporting the Results of Operations," AICPA (New York: 1966).
[9] *APB Opinion No. 15,* "Earnings per Share," AICPA (New York: 1969).

Board recognized that it is difficult to identify all conditions that may be encountered in the computation of earnings per share.[10]

Computation of weighted-average number of shares outstanding; stock splits and stock dividends

The first step in the computation of earnings per share is to determine the number of shares outstanding for each period for which earnings data are to be presented. Earnings per share should be based on the *weighted-average* number of common shares outstanding during each period. (At this point of our discussion we will not be concerned with common stock equivalents or other complexities discussed later in this chapter.)

The weighted-average number of common shares is determined by relating the portion of time within a period that a given number of common shares were outstanding to the length of that period. For example, if 1,000 shares were outstanding during the first nine months of Year 1 and 1,400 shares were outstanding during the balance of the year as a result of the issuance for cash of 400 additional shares, the weighted-average number of shares outstanding during Year 1 would be 1,100, determined as follows:

1,000 shares × $\frac{3}{4}$ of a year	750
1,400 shares × $\frac{1}{4}$ of a year	350
Weighted-average number of shares outstanding during Year 1	1,100

The use of the weighted-average number of shares outstanding is necessary when additional shares are issued for cash or other assets in order to compute a more meaningful earnings per share figure. Assuming that 400 shares were sold for cash at the end of the ninth month in the example above, the proceeds on the sale would be available to generate earnings only during the last three months of the year. These 400 shares would be outstanding for one-fourth of a year, or an equivalent of 100 shares for a full year. In other words, the weighted-average number of shares outstanding consists of 1,000 shares during the entire year plus 100 full-year equivalent shares issued at the end of the ninth month of the year.

[10] Shortly after the issuance of *APB Opinion No. 15,* the AICPA published a 189-page monograph by J. T. Ball, "Computing Earnings per Share—Unofficial Accounting Interpretations of APB Opinion No. 15" (New York: 1970). *APB Opinion No. 15* has been criticized on grounds that it deals with financial analysis rather than accounting principles, that it contains some illogical assumptions, and that it is overly complex. However, *APB Opinion No. 15* has played an important role in standardizing the computation of earnings per share.

When the number of shares outstanding changes as a result of a stock split, stock dividend, or reverse split, the computation of the weighted-average shares outstanding should be adjusted *retroactively.* This is necessary to report earnings per share which are fully comparable in terms of the latest capital structure. If a stock split, stock dividend, or reverse split will become effective after the close of the latest period but before financial statements are issued, the per-share computations should be made on the basis of the *new capitalization.* When earnings per share data are computed on this basis, the method of computation should be disclosed in a note to the financial statements.

The computation of the weighted-average number of shares of common stock outstanding, showing retroactive adjustment for a stock dividend and a stock split, is illustrated on page 824 for Split Hotel Corporation.

In computing the retroactive weighted-average number of shares outstanding in Year 1, the 20% stock dividend declared in Year 2 was applied to the 650,000 weighted-average number of shares actually outstanding in Year 1; and the 3 for 1 split in Year 3 was applied to the 780,000 weighted-average number of shares after adjustment for the 20% stock dividend.

To continue the example, assume that the net income of Split Hotel Corporation for Year 3 was $5,040,000 and that net income and earnings per share were *originally reported* at the end of each of the preceding two years as follows:

	From income statement for Year 2	From income statement for Year 1
Net income	$3,780,000	$2,574,000
Earnings per share of common stock:		
Year 1: $2,574,000 ÷ 650,000 (weighted-average number of shares outstanding in Year 1, before retroactive adjustment for 20% stock dividend and 3 for 1 stock split)		$ 3.96
Year 2: $3,780,000 ÷ 840,000 (weighted-average number of shares outstanding in Year 2, before retroactive adjustment for 3 for 1 stock split)	$ 4.50	

A comparative income statement at the end of Year 2 would show earnings per share for Year 1 of $3.30 ($2,574,000 ÷ 780,000 shares outstanding after giving effect to the 20% stock dividend in Year 2). The

	Year 3	Year 2	Year 1
Analysis of changes in common stock outstanding:			
Number of shares outstanding, beginning of year	840,000	700,000	500,000
Increase as a result of issuance of additional shares for cash on April 1, Year 1			+200,000
Increase as a result of 20% stock dividend in August of Year 2		+140,000	
Increase as a result of 3 for 1 stock split in March of Year 3 (200% increase)	+1,680,000		
Number of shares actually outstanding at the end of each year	2,520,000	840,000	700,000
Computation of weighted-average number of shares of common stock outstanding for three-year period (giving retroactive recognition to stock dividend and stock split):			
Year 1: Outstanding, beginning of Year 1 (see above)			500,000
Add: Full-year equivalent of additional shares issued, 200,000 $\times \frac{3}{4}$ of a year			+150,000
Weighted-average shares outstanding before retroactive adjustment			650,000
Add: Effect of 20% stock dividend in Year 2 (650,000 × 20%) . . .			+130,000
Subtotal			780,000
Add: Effect of 3 for 1 stock split in Year 3 (200% increase) . . .			+1,560,000
Year 2: Outstanding, end of Year 2 (see above)		840,000	
Add: Effect of 3 for 1 stock split in Year 3 (200% increase) . . .		+1,680,000	
Year 3: Outstanding at end of Year 3 (per analysis above, no adjustment required)	2,520,000		
Weighted-average number of shares outstanding, as adjusted retroactively	2,520,000	2,520,000	2,340,000

comparative net income and earnings per share for Split Hotel Corporation, giving effect to the 20% stock dividend in Year 2 and the 3 for 1 split in Year 3, should be presented *at the end of Year 3* as follows:

	Year 3	Year 2	Year 1
Net income	$5,040,000	$3,780,000	$2,574,000
Earnings per share of common stock:			
Year 1: $2,574,000 ÷ 2,340,000			
shares (adjusted)			$ 1.10
Year 2: $3,780,000 ÷ 2,520,000			
shares (adjusted)		$ 1.50	
Year 3: $5,040,000 ÷ 2,520,000			
shares (adjusted)	$ 2.00		

Earnings per share are thus reported on a fully comparable basis in terms of the capital structure at the end of Year 3. For example, since one share of common stock outstanding in Year 1 is equal to 3.6 shares at the end of Year 3 as a result of the 20% stock dividend and the 3 for 1 split, the earnings for Year 1 are retroactively restated at $1.10 per share ($3.96, as originally reported in Year 1, divided by 3.6).

The difficulties encountered in computing earnings per share do not end with the computation of the weighted-average number of shares outstanding. For example: How are earnings per share computed for a company which has preferred stock (convertible or nonconvertible) or convertible bonds outstanding? How do outstanding stock options and warrants affect the computation of earnings per share? To answer these questions, our discussion will focus on two types of corporate capital structure as follows:

1 For companies that have a *simple capital structure*
2 For companies that have a *complex capital structure*
   a *Primary* earnings per share, which takes into account the potential dilutive effect of common stock equivalents outstanding
   b *Fully diluted* earnings per share, which takes into account the maximum potential dilutive effect of convertible securities, stock options, and stock warrants outstanding

Simple capital structure

The capital structure of a corporation may consist only of common stock; or the capital structure may include nonconvertible preferred stock, little or no potentially dilutive convertible securities, and small amounts of stock options and warrants. In such cases the corporation is said to have a *simple capital structure. Dilution* is the reduction in earnings per share that would occur if convertible securities were converted or if outstanding options and warrants were exercised. If the potential dilution in earnings per share is less than 3% (before taking dilution into account), potentially dilutive securities and options or warrants need not be considered in the computation of earnings per share. In such cases, a *single presentation* of earnings per share in the income statement is appropriate. This "single" presentation may include an extraordinary item, as illustrated below for Simplex Corporation:

	Year 2	Year 1
Data required to compute earnings per share of		
common stock:		
Income before extraordinary loss	$810,000	$750,000
Extraordinary loss net of income taxes	$140,000	
Dividend requirement on nonconvertible preferred		
stock	$ 50,000	$ 50,000
Shares of common stock outstanding:		
Beginning of year	400,000	300,000
Issued for cash on July 1, Year 1	–0–	100,000
End of year	400,000	400,000
Common shares reserved for employee stock		
options (1)	10,000	10,000
Weighted-average number of shares outstanding .	400,000	350,000 (2)
Presentation in the income statement:		
Earnings per share of common stock:		
Income before extraordinary loss	$1.90 (3)	$2.00 (4)
Extraordinary loss, net of income taxes	(0.35)(5)	–0–
Net income	$1.55	$2.00

(1) *Excluded from weighted-average number of shares because options represent less than 3% of weighted-average number of shares. This is below the limitations established by **APB** **Opinion No. 15.***
(2) *300,000 shares for the full year, plus 100,000 shares for one-half year (equivalent to 50,000 for a full year) = 350,000 shares.*
(3) *($810,000 − $50,000) ÷ 400,000 weighted-average number of shares = $1.90.*
(4) *($750,000 − $50,000) ÷ 350,000 weighted-average number of shares = $2.00.*
(5) *$140,000 ÷ 400,000 weighted-average number of shares = $0.35.*

The example for Simplex Corporation shows that the income per share before the extraordinary gain decreased in Year 2 despite the fact that the same number of shares were outstanding at the end of each year (400,000 shares) and that *total* income before the extraordinary gain actually increased in Year 2. This is attributed to the increase in the *weighted-average* number of shares outstanding; the 100,000 shares issued on July 1, Year 1, were outstanding for only 6 months in Year 1 and for 12 months in Year 2. In the absence of extraordinary items, only a single earnings per share figure would appear in the income statement for a company with a simple capital structure. When the income statement includes extraordinary items, results of discontinued operations, and a cumulative effect of a change in accounting principle, the presentation of earnings per share is more detailed (see page 116 in Chapter 3).

Complex capital structure

When a corporation has convertible securities, stock options, warrants, or other potentially dilutive contracts outstanding, its capital structure is viewed as *complex* for purposes of computing earnings per share. The Accounting Principles Board took the position in *Opinion No. 15* that earnings per share should reflect potential dilution when securities which are in substance the equivalent to common stock are outstanding. As a result, companies with a complex capital structure must report with equal prominence in the income statement *primary* earnings per share (which include the dilutive effect of common stock equivalents) and *fully diluted* earnings per share (which include the maximum potential dilutive effect of all convertible securities, stock options, and warrants outstanding); this is referred to as a *dual presentation* of earnings per share. (See page 835 for an example.) These reporting requirements for earnings per share do not change the legal rights of the various security holders or the presentation of other data in the financial statements. The computation of primary earnings per share is explained below; the explanation of fully diluted earnings per share starts on page 833.

Primary Earnings per Share and Common Stock Equivalents *Primary earnings per share* is the amount of earnings applicable to each share of common stock; the number of shares of stock consists of a weighted-average number of common shares actually outstanding plus any common stock equivalents. A *common stock equivalent* is a security which contains contractual provisions enabling its owner to exchange the security for common stock.[11] Such a security is considered equivalent to common stock because its holders have a right to participate in the appreciation of the value of the common stock. This participation is essentially the same as that of a common stockholder except for the fact that the security generally carries a specified dividend or interest rate. The market value of a security which is a common stock equivalent is dependent to a considerable degree on the market value of the common stock. Neither actual conversion nor the assumption that conversion is likely to take place is necessary before a security can be classified as a common stock equivalent. *Common stock equivalency is determined at the*

[11] *APB Opinion No. 15*, p. 225.

time the security is issued and does not change so long as the security remains outstanding.[12]

In a complex capital structure case, potentially dilutive securities may or may not qualify as common stock equivalents for purposes of computing primary earnings per share. However, common stock equivalents should not be used in computing primary earnings per share if doing so would be *antidilutive,* that is, have the effect of increasing earnings per share or reducing a loss per share. Common stock equivalents generally include convertible bonds, convertible preferred stock, and stock options and warrants.

Convertible Securities   A bond or preferred stock which at the time of issuance is substantially equivalent to common stock is treated as a common stock equivalent. Convertible stocks or bonds are considered common stock equivalents if at the time of issuance the cash yield, based on the market price, is less than $66\frac{2}{3}\%$ of the then current bank prime interest rate.[13] The *bank prime interest rate* is the rate banks charge on short-term loans to borrowers with the highest credit standing. If convertible *senior securities* (bonds payable and preferred stock) do not meet the test of a common stock equivalent at the date of issue, they would not be a factor in computing primary earnings per share but would be used (if dilutive) in computing fully diluted earnings per share.

A convertible security which qualifies as a common stock equivalent should be assumed to have been converted at the beginning of the earliest period for which earnings per share are being reported or at the time of issuance, whichever is the more recent date. For example, if convertible preferred stock was issued on April 1, the equivalent number of shares of common stock would be considered outstanding for nine months of the year even though some of the preferred stock might have been converted into common stock late in the year.

In computing primary earnings per share, net income is adjusted (increased) by the amount of interest (net of income taxes) on convertible bonds which qualify as common stock equivalents. In determining the net income available for common stock, net income is not reduced by the amount of the dividend requirement on convertible preferred stock which qualifies as a common stock equivalent. These adjustments are necessary because it is assumed that both the convertible bonds and the preferred stock are converted into common stock.

Example 1: Convertible preferred stock is a common stock equivalent   At the beginning of Year 1, X Corporation issued at $100 per share, 50,000 shares of $3 convertible preferred stock. At the time the preferred stock was issued, the bank prime interest rate was 6%. Each share of pre-

---

[12] *Ibid.,* p. 227.
[13] *Ibid.,* p. 229.

ferred stock is convertible into two shares of common stock; no shares have yet been converted. If the X Corporation has net income of $950,000 in Year 2 and 400,000 shares of common stock outstanding, compute the primary earnings per share for Year 2.

Solution: The convertible preferred stock qualifies as a common stock equivalent because its cash yield of 3% ($3 ÷ $100) is less than 4% (66⅔% of the 6% bank prime interest rate at the date the convertible preferred stock was issued). A convertible preferred stock is dilutive any time the dividend per share paid on the stock (calculated on the basis of the number of common shares which would be issued upon conversion) is less than the earnings per share of common stock before considering conversion. In this case the convertible preferred stock is dilutive, because the equivalent converted dividend on the preferred stock is $1.50 ($3 ÷ 2 shares), which is less than the earnings per share of common stock before the conversion is assumed, $2 ($950,000 net income − $150,000 preferred dividend ÷ 400,000 shares of common stock outstanding). The amount of primary earnings per share for Year 2 is computed below:

$$\frac{\text{Net income before preferred dividends}}{\text{Common stock outstanding + common stock equivalents}}$$

$$= \frac{\$950,000}{400,000 + 100,000} = \underline{\underline{\$1.90}}$$

The conversion of the preferred stock, if dilutive, would also be assumed in computing fully diluted earnings per share; this is illustrated in Example 6 on pages 833–835.

Example 2: Common stock equivalent is antidilutive Assuming the same facts as in Example 1 for X Corporation, except that net income for Year 2 amounts to only $350,000, compute primary earnings per share for Year 2.

Solution: Although the convertible preferred stock is a common stock equivalent, conversion would not be assumed in computing primary earnings per share because such an assumption would be antidilutive. This is illustrated below:

Earnings per share of common stock:
Conversion not assumed: $350,000 net income − $150,000 preferred dividends = $200,000 ÷ 400,000 shares *$0.50*
Conversion assumed: $350,000 net income ÷ 500,000 shares *$0.70*

Since earnings per share would be increased if the common stock equivalent was used in the computation, primary earnings per share would be reported at $0.50 per share, not $0.70 per share. Because the assumed conversion of the preferred stock is antidilutive (increases earnings per share), conversion would not be assumed in computing fully diluted earnings per share.

Example 3: Convertible bonds are not common stock equivalents On December 31 of Year 1, Y Corporation issued at par $1 million of 6% convertible bonds when the bank prime rate of interest was $7\frac{1}{2}$%. Each $1,000 bond is convertible into 25 shares of the corporation's common stock. In Year 2, Y Corporation earned $225,000 after interest expense and income taxes. The income tax is assumed to be 40% of taxable income. At December 31, Year 2, no bonds had been converted and 75,000 shares of common stock were outstanding. Compute the primary earnings per share for Year 2.

Solution: The cash yield of 6% ($60 ÷ $1,000) on the convertible bonds was *greater* than 5% ($66\frac{2}{3}$% of $7\frac{1}{2}$% bank prime interest rate at the date the bonds were issued); therefore, the convertible bonds are not common stock equivalents for computing primary earnings per share for Year 2. Primary earnings per share would be $3 ($225,000 ÷ 75,000 shares). However, conversion of the bonds would be assumed in computing fully diluted earnings per share, unless such an assumption would be antidilutive.

Example 4: Convertible bonds are common stock equivalents Assume the same facts as in Example 3 for Y Corporation, except that the interest rate on the convertible bonds is $4\frac{1}{2}$% rather than 6%. Compute primary earnings per share for Year 2 if net income is $225,000.

Solution: In this case the convertible bonds are common stock equivalents because the cash yield of $4\frac{1}{2}$% ($45 ÷ $1,000) was *less* than 5% ($66\frac{2}{3}$% of $7\frac{1}{2}$% bank prime interest rate at the date the bonds were issued). The computation of primary earnings per share is shown on page 831.

If conversion of the bonds were not assumed, the earnings per share would have been improperly reported at $3 per share ($225,000 ÷ 75,000 shares). Conversion would also be assumed (if dilutive) in computing fully diluted earnings per share.

Options or Warrants to Purchase Common Stock A corporation may issue options or warrants which give the holder the right to purchase common stock at a fixed price. Such options or warrants should be regarded as common stock equivalents at all times;[14] however, dilution of less than 3% would be ignored. Therefore, primary earnings per share

[14] *Ibid.,* p. 230.

Earnings to be used in computing primary earnings per share:		
Net income as reported		$225,000
Add back interest on convertible bonds, net of income taxes:		
Interest, $1,000,000 × 4½%	$45,000	
Less income taxes at 40%	18,000	27,000
Earnings to be used in computing earnings per share		$252,000

Number of shares to be used in computing primary earnings per share:	
Number of shares outstanding at end of Year 2	75,000
Number of shares to be issued, assuming conversion of bonds,	
1,000 × 25	25,000
Number of shares to be used in computing primary earnings per share	100,000
Primary earnings per share of common stock, $252,000 ÷ 100,000	
shares	$ 2.52

should reflect the impact from the exercise of options or warrants, including the possible **use of the proceeds** which would be received upon the exercise of the options or warrants. In computing primary earnings per share, an assumption should be made that the options or warrants are exercised **only** if such an assumption would result in a dilution of earnings per share.

When the exercise of options or warrants is assumed, any proceeds that would be received are assumed to be used to acquire treasury stock at the average market price during the period. This is known as the **treasury stock method.** For example, if options to purchase 10,000 shares of common stock at $5 per share are outstanding and the average market price during the period was $20 per share, the $50,000 that would be received by the corporation upon exercise of the options and issuance of 10,000 additional shares would be sufficient to acquire 2,500 shares of common stock ($50,000 ÷ $20 = 2,500). Thus, 7,500 (10,000 − 2,500) shares would be added to the number of shares of common stock already outstanding in computing primary earnings per share. The exercise of the options or warrants is assumed to have taken place at the **beginning of the period** or **at the time** the options or warrants were issued, whichever is the more recent date.

APB Opinion No. 15 recommends that the exercise of options or warrants should not be assumed until the common stock sells in excess of the exercise price for "substantially all of three consecutive months ending with the last month of the period to which earnings per share data relate."[15] Under the treasury stock method, options or warrants would have a dilutive effect on earnings per share only when the average market price of the common stock exceeds the exercise price

[15] *Ibid.*, pp. 230–231.

of the options or warrants. The computation of primary earnings per share using the treasury stock method is illustrated in the example below:

Example 5: Options to purchase common stock are outstanding Z Corporation has 200,000 shares of common stock and options to purchase 30,000 shares of common stock at $10 per share outstanding at the end of Year 2. The options were granted to employees several years ago. The average market price of the common stock during Year 2 was $30 per share. Net income for Year 2 was $550,000. Compute primary earnings per share for Year 2.

Solution:

Computation of number of shares of common stock to be used in determining primary earnings per share:		
Number of shares of common stock outstanding at end of Year 2 . . .		200,000
Add: Number of shares of common stock to be issued upon exercise of options	30,000	
Less: Assumed purchase of common stock using the proceeds received upon exercise of options [(30,000 × $10) ÷ $30] . .	10,000	20,000
Number of shares of common stock to be used in determining primary earnings per share		220,000
Primary earnings per share of common stock, $550,000 ÷ 220,000 shares		$ 2.50

APB Opinion No. 15 requires a departure from the procedure illustrated above when the number of additional shares of common stock that may be issued pursuant to outstanding options and warrants exceeds 20% of the number of common shares actually outstanding at the end of the period. In such cases, it should be assumed that **all** options and warrants were exercised and the total proceeds were used (1) to purchase 20% of the outstanding stock and (2) the balance was used to retire outstanding debt. However, if all debt is thus eliminated, it should be assumed that the remaining proceeds are used to purchase short-term investments. Appropriate recognition should be given to the income tax effects of the assumed use of the potential proceeds from the exercise of options and warrants.

Computation of fully diluted earnings per share when options to purchase common stock are outstanding is illustrated in Example 6 starting on page 833.

The reader should realize that it is virtually impossible to cover all situations which may arise in the computation of primary earnings per share; our objective has been to describe the basic issues involved. We now turn our attention to the second part of the **dual presentation** of earnings per share—the computation of fully diluted earnings per share.

Fully Diluted Earnings per Share   It is apparent from the foregoing discussion that primary earnings per share may include some potential dilution and that certain potentially dilutive securities are not considered common stock equivalents. However, in the computation of fully diluted earnings per share, *all* convertible securities, options, and warrants are assumed to have been converted or exercised in order to reflect the maximum potential dilution. As in the computation of primary earnings per share, conversion of securities or the exercise of options or warrants *should not* be assumed when the effect would be antidilutive (would have the effect of increasing earnings per share or reducing a loss per share).

The computation of fully diluted earnings per share differs from the computation of primary earnings per share in two essential respects.

1 All convertible securities, whether or not they qualify as common stock equivalents, which individually would decrease earnings per share if conversion had taken place, are included in the calculation of fully diluted earnings per share. All such conversions are assumed to have taken place at the beginning of the period (or at the time of issuance of the convertible security, if later).

2 To recognize the maximum potential dilution, the market price of the common stock at the end of the period, if higher than the average market price during the period, is used to determine the number of shares of common stock which could be acquired using the proceeds received upon the exercise of options or warrants. This procedure reduces the number of shares of common stock which could be acquired using the proceeds and thus has the effect of increasing the number of outstanding shares on a pro forma basis.

The computation of primary and fully diluted earnings per share is illustrated in the example below:

Example 6: Stock options and convertible preferred stock are outstanding Primary and fully diluted earnings per share for Year 10 are computed on page 834 from the information presented below for Dual Corporation:

Net income for Year 10	*$330,000*
Number of shares of common stock outstanding throughout Year 10	*95,000*
*Number of shares of $4 convertible preferred stock outstanding throughout Year 10; each share of preferred stock is convertible into three shares of common stock; the preferred stock is **not** a common stock equivalent, but is dilutive*	*3,000*
Outstanding options (issued in Year 6) to purchase common stock at $20 per share; average price of common stock during Year 10 was $40 per share and the price at the end of Year 10 was $50 per share	*10,000*

Solution:

	Primary	Fully diluted
Computation of number of shares of common stock to be used in computing earnings per share for Year 10:		
Number of shares of common stock outstanding at end of Year 10	95,000	95,000
For computing primary earnings per share:		
Shares of common stock to be issued upon exercise of options at $20 per share	10,000	
Less: Assumed purchase of common stock at average market price during Year 10 using proceeds received upon exercise of options [(10,000 × $20) ÷ $40]	5,000	5,000
For computing fully diluted earnings per share:		
Shares of common stock to be issued upon exercise of options at $20 per share	10,000	
Less: Assumed purchase of common stock at market price at end of Year 10 using proceeds received upon exercise of options [(10,000 × $20) ÷ $50]	4,000	6,000
Assume conversion of 3,000 shares of preferred stock into common stock (3 for 1)		9,000
Number of shares of common stock to be used in computing earnings per share for Year 10	100,000	110,000
Earnings per share for Year 10:		
Primary: $318,000* ÷ 100,000 shares	$ 3.18	
Fully diluted: $330,000 ÷ 110,000 shares		$ 3.00

* Net income of $330,000 less preferred dividend requirement of $12,000.

In computing fully diluted earnings per share for Dual Corporation, the proceeds of $200,000 from the issuance of 10,000 additional shares of common stock upon exercise of options is assumed to be used to acquire common stock at $50 per share, the market price of the common stock at the end of the year. Since only 4,000 ($200,000 ÷ $50) shares can be acquired using the proceeds of $200,000, the number of shares of common stock to be used in computing fully diluted earnings per share is increased by 6,000 (10,000 − 4,000). In addition, the 3,000 shares of convertible preferred stock which do not qualify as common stock equivalents in computing primary earnings per share are assumed to be converted into 9,000 shares of common stock. These adjustments fully recognize the maximum potential dilution in earnings per share.

It should be pointed out that in computing primary earnings per share, the amount of the dividend requirement on the convertible preferred stock ($12,000) was deducted from net income to arrive at the income available for common stock; however, when fully diluted earnings per share were computed, net income was *not* reduced by the preferred dividend requirement because the preferred stock was assumed to have been eliminated through conversion into common stock.

Summary of earnings per share computations

The foregoing discussion relating to the computation of earnings per share is summarized on page 836.

Presentation of earnings per share in the income statement

Shown below is an actual presentlation of earnings per share (including the accompanying note) by a large publicly owned company with a complex capital structure:

	Year ended December 31,	
	1978	1977
	(thousands)	
Net income	$342,936	$314,149
Preferred and preference stock dividends	29,387	35,549
Net income to common stock	$313,549	$278,600
Earnings per share of common stock (Note 1):		
Primary	$ 4.15	$ 3.98
Fully diluted	$ 3.63	$ 3.35

Note: Earnings per share
Earnings per share of common stock are based on the average number of shares of common stock outstanding during each period. Such average shares outstanding were 75,608,800 and 70,079,891 shares for the years 1978 and 1977, respectively. Earnings per share computations assuming full dilution additionally include the average common shares issuable for convertible or exchangeable securities, stock options and warrants during each period and the elimination of the related dividend and interest requirements, less applicable federal income taxes. Such average shares assuming full dilution were 92,583,448 and 91,964,825 shares for the years 1978 and 1977, respectively.

Additional examples of presentation of earnings per share appear in Chapter 2. See Chapter 23 for the presentation of earnings per share following changes in accounting principles.

Capital structure	Earnings per share in income statement	Explanation
1 Simple	Single presentation	Divide net income by the weighted-average number of shares of common stock outstanding for the period. Dilutive securities are ignored when the potential dilution in the aggregate is less than 3% of earnings.
2 Complex	Dual presentation: **a** Primary	Divide net income (increased by the after-tax effect of assumed conversion of bonds, if any) by the weighted-average number of shares of common stock and common stock equivalents outstanding for the period. Convertible securities may or may not qualify as common stock equivalents at date of issue; options and warrants are always treated as common stock equivalents. In no case should common stock equivalents be used to determine primary earnings per share if inclusion is antidilutive. Potential earnings dilution of less than 3% is ignored.
	b Fully diluted	Essentially the same procedure as above, except that all convertible securities are assumed to have been converted (at the beginning of the period or issue date, if later) if the effect of the assumed conversion is dilutive. The proceeds from the assumed exercise of options and warrants are applied to purchase common stock at years end market price if such price is higher than the average market price during the period covered. Potential earnings dilution of less than 3% is ignored.

REVIEW QUESTIONS

1 Define **treasury stock** and state briefly how it should be shown in the balance sheet.

2 For what reasons do companies acquire their own stock?

3 The president of Sierra Wood Company said, "We seek to purchase 8.4% of our stock in order to secure a ready and safe investment for excess cash." Comment on this quotation.

4 Does the acquisition and resale of its own stock by a corporation result in a profit or loss to the corporation?

5 In reviewing the Miscellaneous Revenue account of Great Divide Land Co., you find a credit for $200 representing a dividend of $1 per share on 200 shares of treasury stock. You determine that the dividend declaration covered the entire 10,000 shares originally issued, that Retained Earnings was charged for $10,000, and that $9,800 of cash was paid to stockholders. Discuss the propriety of this procedure.

6 a Discuss the propriety of declaring stock dividends on treasury stock.
b Should treasury stock be split?
c How would the issuance of treasury stock (recorded at cost) pursuant to a 2% stock dividend be recorded?

7 The Treasury Stock account of a corporation contained a debit balance of $54,000, representing the cost of 6,000 shares reacquired by the corporation. Later the corporation exchanged the 6,000 treasury shares for land which was listed in the balance sheet as "Land, at cost . . . $54,000." Do you approve of this treatment? Explain.

8 Most states place some restriction on the acquisition by a corporation of its own capital stock. What is the usual nature of this restriction? What is the purpose of such restrictions?

9 The majority stockholder in a closely held corporation had an option to buy all the stock of a minority stockholder at book value at any time during the first 10 years of operation. After four years, the method of inventory valuation was changed from fifo to lifo. At the end of the tenth year, the majority stockholder exercised this option. The minority stockholder objected, arguing that the change in inventory valuation was reducing the option price by thousands of dollars. Discuss.

10 What is the appropriate accounting treatment of the difference between original issuance price and the price paid to retire preferred stock?

11 What special steps are required in computing the book value of common stock in each of the following cases:
a Both preferred and common stock are outstanding.
b Treasury stock has been acquired.
c Convertible bonds, stock options, and warrants are outstanding.

12 The book value of 100,000 common shares is $40 per share. Indicate the effect of each of the following four transactions on book value per share:
a Sale of additional shares at $10 pursuant to stock option contract
b Sale of additional shares at $60 through rights offering
c Purchase of treasury stock at $75 per share
d Conversion of bonds, 20 shares for every $1,000 bond

13 Define **earnings per share** and indicate how this statistic is used by investors.

14 a How is the weighted-average number of shares outstanding for a given year computed?
   b What effect do stock dividends and stock splits have on the presentation of earnings per share for two or more years?

15 Differentiate between the following:
   a *Simple* and *complex* capital structure
   b *Primary* and *fully diluted* earnings per share
   c *Single* and *dual* presentation of earnings per share

16 Discuss the reasons why securities other than common stock may be considered *common stock equivalents* for the computation of primary earnings per share.

17 Explain how convertible securities are determined to be common stock equivalents and how those convertible senior securities which are not considered to be common stock equivalents enter into the determination of earnings per share data.

18 Explain the *treasury stock method* as it applies to options and warrants in computing primary earnings per share data.

19 For the first six months of the current year, Rialto Corporation reported primary earnings per share of $4.50 and fully diluted earnings per share of only $2. What factors may cause such a large difference between the two earnings per share figures? If the stock of Rialto Corporation sells for $36 per share, what is the price-earnings ratio?

20 In a recent article in *Financial Analysts' Journal,* an executive of the Chase Manhattan Bank stated that "any evaluation of corporate policies in terms of their impact on earnings per share (EPS) is fraught with danger. . . . If the leverage idea is sound, management can increase EPS without making any investment whatever, merely by borrowing to retire common shares." Do you agree with this observation? Explain.

EXERCISES

Ex. 20-1 The stockholders' equity section of Weston Company's balance sheet at December 31, Year 5, was as follows:

Stockholders' equity:

Capital stock—$100 par, authorized 50,000 shares, issued and outstanding	
10,000 shares	*$1,000,000*
Paid-in capital in excess of par	*500,000*
Retained earnings	*800,000*
Total stockholders' equity	*$2,300,000*

Early in Year 6, the company acquired 400 shares of its stock for $50,000. During the year it reissued 100 of the treasury shares at $140 per share, reissued 100 shares at $120 per share, and retired the remaining 200 shares of treasury stock. The company records treasury stock at cost.
   Prepare journal entries to record the purchase, the reissuance, and the retirement of the treasury stock.

Ex. 20-2 Belair Company has decided that since it has idle cash and since its $100 par value, 5% cumulative preferred stock (which was originally issued at $98) has been selling on the open market at around $85 per share, it should retire as many shares of the stock as possible in an effort to improve the earnings per share on the common stock. On March 2, the company acquired 5,000 shares of the preferred stock from one large shareholder at $84 per share.

What entry would be made to record the retirement of the 5,000 shares of preferred stock?

Ex. 20-3 Sylvester Corporation has a total stockholders' equity of $35,500,000, including $10,750,000 of paid-in capital in excess of par and retained earnings. The capital stock included in stockholders' equity follows:

7% preferred stock, $50 par, callable at $53 per share; 200,000 shares issued

and outstanding *$10,000,000*

Common stock, $10 par, 5,000,000 shares authorized; 1,550,000 shares were

issued and 1,500,000 shares are outstanding (50,000 shares costing

$750,000 are held in treasury) *15,500,000*

Compute the book value per share of common stock.

Ex. 20-4 At the beginning of Year 4, Sandler Company had 100,000 shares of common stock and 10,000 shares of $4 cumulative preferred stock outstanding. The preferred stock is callable at $55 per share. Sandler Company had not borrowed money since it was incorporated in Year 1.

Early in Year 5, the company retired the preferred stock at $55. The company used idle cash and the proceeds from the sale of surplus plant at carrying value to pay for the preferred stock.

At the beginning of Year 6, the company borrowed $1 million at 6% and used the proceeds to retire 20,000 shares of common stock.

The company reported operating income (before interest expense and income taxes at the rate of 50%) as follows:

Year 4 . . . . *$800,000*
Year 5 . . . . *750,000*
Year 6 . . . . *700,000*

Compute the earnings per share of common stock for each of the three years (Year 4–Year 6). Comment on the trend in earnings per share in the face of the decreasing operating income.

Ex. 20-5 A corporation had 500,000 common shares outstanding on January 1, issued 300,000 shares for cash on April 1, and had net income of $3,625,000 for the year ending December 31. Assuming that the corporation had no preferred stock or potentially dilutive securities outstanding, compute the earnings per share for the year.

Ex. 20-6 A newly organized corporation began business on January 2, Year 2, by issuing 2,000 shares of common stock for various assets. On July 1, Year 3, an additional 1,000 shares were issued for cash. On April 1, Year 4, a 10% stock dividend was issued. On July 1, Year 5, the stock was split 3 for 1.

Earnings and dividends per share of common stock for each of the four years of the company's history are to be reported on a comparable basis in the annual report to stockholders for Year 5.

Compute the current equivalent number of shares outstanding at the end of each of the four years, to be used in computing the earnings per share of common stock.

Ex. 20-7 The capital structure of Singer Corporation consists of the following:

$3 preferred stock, no-par, cumulative and nonconvertible, 20,000 shares issued and outstanding $1,000,000

$4 convertible preferred stock, no-par, convertible into three shares of common stock, 10,000 shares issued and outstanding 1,000,000

Common stock, no-par, 50,000 shares issued and outstanding 500,000

Neither preferred stock issue is a common stock equivalent. Compute primary and fully diluted earnings per share of common stock, assuming that net income for the current year was $220,000.

Ex. 20-8 Warrants exercisable at $20 each to purchase 12,000 shares of common stock were outstanding during a period when the average market price of the common stock was $25 and the ending market price was $30.

Determine the **increase** in the weighted-average number of outstanding common shares as a result of applying the "treasury stock method" for the assumed exercise of these warrants when computing **(a)** primary earnings per share and **(b)** fully diluted earnings per share.

Ex. 20-9 At December 31, Year 4, Debbie Company had 550,000 shares of common stock outstanding. On September 1, Year 5, an additional 150,000 shares of common stock were issued for cash. In addition, Debbie Company had $10,000,000 of 8% convertible bonds outstanding at December 31, Year 4, which are convertible into 200,000 shares of common stock. The bonds were not considered common stock equivalents at the time of their issuance and no bonds were converted into common stock in Year 5. The net income for the year ended December 31, Year 5, was $3,400,000 (after income taxes). Assuming that the income tax rate was 50%, compute the fully diluted earnings per share for the year ended December 31, Year 5.

SHORT CASES FOR ANALYSIS AND DECISION

Case 20-1 Running Springs Development Corporation purchased $180,000 of equipment for $120,000 cash and a promise to deliver an indeterminate number of treasury shares of its $10 par common stock, with a market value of $15,000, on January 1 of each year for the next five years. Hence $75,000 in "market value" of treasury shares will be required to discharge the $60,000 balance due on the equipment.

The corporation immediately acquired 3,000 shares of its own stock for $48,000 in the expectation that the market value of the stock would increase substantially before the delivery dates. A total of 2,500 of these shares were subsequently issued in payment of the balance due on the equipment contract.

Instructions
a Discuss the propriety of recording the equipment at
(1) $120,000 (the cash payment)
(2) $180,000 (the cash price of the equipment)
(3) $195,000 (the $120,000 cash payment plus the $75,000 market value of the treasury stock that must be transferred to the vendor in order to settle the obligation in accordance with the terms of the agreement)
(4) $160,000 (the $120,000 cash payment plus the $40,000 cost of the 2,500 treasury shares issued in payment for the equipment)
b Discuss the arguments for treating the balance due as
(1) A liability
(2) Treasury stock subscribed

c Assuming that legal requirements do not affect the decision, discuss the arguments for treating this corporation's treasury shares as
(1) An asset awaiting ultimate disposition
(2) A capital element awaiting ultimate disposition

Case 20-2 Oro Blanco Corporation was at one time quite successful, but in recent years had been operating at a loss. In reaction to these losses, the market price of the stock had dropped to an all-time low of $5 a share. The capital stock had originally been issued at par of $10 a share; present book value was $12 a share.

At this point, the three Jones brothers acquired control of the company by purchasing in small lots a total of 20,000 shares at a total cost of $130,000. Total stock outstanding was 100,000 shares but the remaining 80% of the stock was scattered among many small owners. By an aggressive proxy campaign, the Jones brothers were able to secure enough outside support to elect a full slate of directors.

The Jones brothers had no hopes for profitable operation of the company; sales were in a declining trend and the principal products were gradually becoming obsolete. The attraction of the company to the Jones brothers was its relatively high book value and strong cash position. They planned to recover their investment rapidly through stripping the company of its most salable assets and then selling their shares for whatever they would bring. Retained earnings of the company amounted to only $200,000 but cash, receivables, and marketable securities amounted to $500,000.

At the instruction of the Jones brothers, the new board of directors took the following actions:

(1) Issued optimistic statements to the press concerning planned acquisition of several profitable companies and resumption of cash dividends.
(2) Sold the receivables and securities, thus increasing cash to approximately $500,000.
(3) Borrowed $200,000 secured by pledge of the inventory, thus obtaining additional cash.
(4) Began purchasing the company's own stock at steadily increasing prices. After acquisition of 10,000 shares at an average cost of $9, the company offered to purchase up to 15,000 shares at $15. Stockholders sold 10,000 shares to the company at $15 per share.
(5) Sold the land and building to the Jones brothers for $450,000 more than book value. This gain was included in the quarterly earnings report and was widely publicized. The sale agreement called for payment partially in stock of another company controlled by the Jones brothers and partially in mining lands owned by them. No cash was involved.
(6) Purchased from the Jones brothers their entire holdings of 20,000 shares at a price of $20 a share. This transaction consumed nearly all the available cash. All members of the board then resigned for "personal reasons."

Instructions (Ignore income tax considerations)
a Prepare the stockholders' equity section of the balance sheet after these transactions.
b Did the purchase of treasury stock by the company violate the concept of limiting dividends and purchases of treasury stock to the amount of retained earnings?
c Were any of the actions by the board of directors improper? Explain.

Case 20-3 The owners of Crestline Company, a closely held corporation, have offered to sell their 100% interest in the company's common stock at an amount equal to the book value of the common stock. They will continue to own the company's preferred stock, which is convertible into common stock at a price substantially below book value.

Your audit clients would like to combine the operations of Crestline Company with their Cicero Division and they are seriously considering buying the common stock of Crestline Company. They question the use of book value as a basis for the sale, however, and have come to you for advice.

Instructions Prepare a memorandum to your clients covering the following points:
a Definition of book value. Explain its significance in establishing a value for a business that is expected to continue in operation.
b Description of the procedure for computing book value of common stock.
c Your advice to the clients regarding this proposed purchase.

Case 20-4 Bloom Blouse Corporation, a new audit client of yours, has not reported earnings per share data in its annual reports to stockholders in the past. The president requested that you furnish information about the reporting of earnings per share data in the current year's annual report in accordance with generally accepted accounting principles.

Instructions
a Define the term *earnings per share* as it applies to a corporation with a capitalization structure composed of only one class of capital stock. Explain how earnings per share should be computed and how the information should be disclosed in the corporation's financial statements.
b Explain the meanings of the terms (1) *senior securities* and (2) *common stock equivalents,* which are often used in discussing earnings per share, and give examples of the types of items which each term includes.
c Discuss the treatment, if any, which should be given to each of the following items in computing earnings per share of common stock for financial reporting purposes:
(1) The declaration of current dividends on cumulative preferred stock.
(2) The acquisition of some of the corporation's outstanding common stock during the current fiscal year. The stock was classified as treasury stock.
(3) A 2 for 1 stock split of common stock during the current fiscal year.
(4) A provision created out of retained earnings for a contingent liability from a possible lawsuit.
(5) Outstanding preferred stock issued at a premium with a par value liquidation right.

Case 20-5 Lorin Company had the following account titles on its December 31, Year 4, trial balance:

6% cumulative convertible preferred stock, $100 par
Paid-in capital in excess of par: preferred stock
Common stock, $1 stated value
Paid-in capital in excess of stated value: common stock
Retained earnings

The following additional information about Lorin Company was available for the year ended December 31, Year 4:

(1) There were 2,000,000 shares of preferred stock authorized, of which 1,000,000 were outstanding. All 1,000,000 shares outstanding were issued on January 2, Year 1, for $120 a share. The bank prime interest rate was 8.5% on January 2, Year 1, and was 10% on December 31, Year 4. The preferred stock is convertible into common stock on a 1 for 1 basis until December 31, Year 10; thereafter the preferred stock ceases to be convertible and is callable at $100 by the company. No preferred stock has been converted into common stock, and there were no dividends in arrears at December 31, Year 4.
(2) The common stock has been issued at amounts above stated value per share

since incorporation. Of the 5,000,000 shares authorized, there were 3,500,000 shares outstanding at January 1, Year 4. The market price of the outstanding common stock has increased consistently for the last four years.

(3) The company has an employee stock option plan under which certain key employees and officers may purchase shares of common stock at 100% of the market price at the date of the option grant. All options are exercisable in installments of one-third each year, commencing one year after the date of the grant, and expire if not exercised within four years of the grant date. On January 1, Year 4, options for 70,000 shares were outstanding at prices ranging from $47 to $83 a share. Options for 20,000 shares were exercised at $47 to $79 a share during Year 4. No options expired during Year 4 and additional options for 15,000 shares were granted at $86 a share during the year. The 65,000 options outstanding at December 31, Year 4, were exercisable at $54 to $86 a share; of these, 30,000 were exercisable at that date at prices ranging from $54 to $79 a share.

(4) The company also has an employee stock-purchase plan under which the company pays one-half and the employee pays one-half of the market price of the stock at the date of the subscription. During Year 4, employees subscribed to 60,000 shares at an average price of $87 a share. All 60,000 shares were paid for and issued later in September, Year 4.

(5) On December 31, Year 4, there was a total of 355,000 shares of common stock set aside for the granting of future stock options and for future purchases under the employee stock-purchase plan. The only changes in the stockholders' equity for Year 4 were those described above, net income, and cash dividends paid.

Instructions

a Prepare the stockholders' equity section of the balance sheet of Lorin Company at December 31, Year 4; substitute, where appropriate, Xs for unknown dollar amounts. Use good form and provide full disclosure. Write appropriate notes as they should appear in the published financial statements.

b Explain how the amount of the denominator should be determined to compute *primary* earnings per share for presentation in the income statement. Be specific as to the handling of each item. If additional information is needed to determine whether an item should be included or excluded or the extent to which an item should be included, identify the information needed and how the item would be handled if the information were known. Assume Lorin Company had substantial net income for the year ended December 31, Year 4.

PROBLEMS

Group A

20A-1 The following data are taken from the balance sheet of Paul Wilson, Inc., at the end of Year 5:

Assets

Current assets	$ 40,000,000
Plant assets (net)	55,000,000
Investment in common stock of K Corporation (at cost, market value, $25 million)	10,000,000
Investment in common stock of L Corporation (at cost, market value, $12 million)	15,000,000
Total assets	$120,000,000

Equities

Current liabilities	$ 29,000,000
5% bonds payable	40,000,000
Capital stock, $20 par, 1 million shares issued and outstanding	20,000,000
Retained earnings	31,000,000
Total equities	$120,000,000

The securities of Paul Wilson, Inc., are quoted currently on the open market as follows:

5% bonds payable	60½
Capital stock	$30 per share

The market value of the investment in the common stock of K Corporation is more clearly evident than is the quoted market value of the company's 5% bonds payable.

The investment in the common stock of K Corporation is exchanged for all bonds payable and the investment in the common stock of L Corporation is exchanged for 400,000 shares of the company's outstanding capital stock. These treasury shares were recorded at a cost of $12 million by Paul Wilson, Inc.

Instructions
a Prepare separate journal entries to record the two transactions described above. Ignore the income tax effect on the transactions.
b Compute the book value per share of Paul Wilson, Inc., capital stock (1) before the two transactions and (2) after the two transactions.

20A-2 The stockholders' equity section of Jeff Corporation's balance sheet at December 31, Year 7, is shown below:

Stockholders' equity:

$5 preferred stock, $100 par; callable at $104, authorized 50,000 shares, issued and outstanding 20,000 shares	$2,000,000
Common stock, $5 par; authorized 500,000 shares, issued and outstanding 300,000 shares	1,500,000
Paid-in capital in excess of par: preferred stock	70,000
Paid-in capital in excess of par: common stock	1,500,000
Retained earnings	4,200,000
Total stockholders' equity	$9,270,000

Early in Year 8 the company purchased 3,000 shares of its preferred stock at $99 a share. These shares were held by the estate of a deceased stockholder. Shortly thereafter, the remaining 17,000 shares were called for redemption and retired at the established call price. Net income for Year 8 was $925,000; cash dividends of $1 per share were paid on the common stock in Year 8.

Instructions
a Prepare journal entries to record the redemption of the preferred stock.
b Prepare the stockholders' equity section of the balance sheet at December 31, Year 8.
c Compute the effect of the redemption of preferred stock on the book value per share of the common stock. Ignore net income and dividends for Year 8.

20A-3 The balance sheet of Conrad Company at December 31, Year 2, shows the following items in the stockholders' equity section:

Stockholders' equity:

6% convertible preferred stock, $100 par, callable at $105 and convertible into four shares of common stock		$ 400,000
Common stock, $10 par, 300,000 shares authorized, 80,000 shares issued		800,000
Paid-in capital in excess of par:		
Preferred stock	$ 20,000	
Common stock	200,000	220,000
Total paid-in capital		$1,420,000
Retained earnings		980,000
Total stockholders' equity		$2,400,000

Following is a list of transactions completed by the company during Year 3:

Jan. 7   Two hundred shares of preferred stock are acquired and formally retired at a cost of $115 a share.

Mar. 1   A 10% stock dividend on common stock is declared and distributed. At the time of declaration the stock is quoted at $32 a share.

Apr. 1   The remaining preferred stock is called for redemption. Holders of all outstanding shares convert their holdings pursuant to the antidilution provision of the preferred stock contract. Dividends for the first quarter (not previously recorded) amounting to $5,700 are paid at the time of conversion.

Sept. 4   Two hundred shares of common stock are acquired at a cost of $35 a share. The company records treasury stock at cost. Of these, 100 are retired and the other 100 are held in the treasury.

Oct. 30   Fifty shares held in the treasury are sold for $42 a share and on the same date the remaining 50 shares are issued for a patent.

Dec. 31   Net income for the year amounted to $254,842 (debit Other Assets) and cash dividends amounting to $107,700 were paid during the year, including the $5,700 paid on preferred stock during the first quarter of Year 3.

Instructions

a Prepare journal entries to record the foregoing transactions.

b Prepare the stockholders' equity section of the balance sheet at December 31, Year 3.

c Compute the book value per share of common stock on December 31, Year 3.

20A-4 The following condensed balance sheet of Boyington Corporation was prepared at December 31, Year 5:

Assets

Current assets (net of allowance for doubtful accounts)	$ 600,000
Other assets	750,000
Total assets	$1,350,000

Liabilities & Stockholders' Equity

Current liabilities		$ 390,000
Stockholders' equity:		
$5 convertible preferred stock, par and liquidation value, $100		
per share	$200,000	
Common stock, $2.50 par	100,000	
Paid-in capital in excess of par: common stock	300,000	
Retained earnings	385,000	
Subtotal	$985,000	
Less: Treasury stock 2,000 shares of common stock, at cost	25,000	960,000
Total liabilities & stockholders' equity		$1,350,000

The preferred stock is convertible into common stock at any time in the ratio of 10 shares of common for each share of preferred. The bank prime rate of interest was 6% when the preferred stock was issued in Year 3.

The following transactions were completed during the fiscal year ended December 31, Year 6:

Jan. 2   200 shares of common stock were received in settlement of $4,390 in past-due accounts receivable. The treasury stock is considered to be worth an amount equal to the book value of common stock at this date.

Jan. 3   The 2,200 shares of treasury stock were reissued in exchange for land valued at $43,800.

Feb. 15   Cash dividends were declared and paid as follows: preferred, $2.50 per share; common, $0.40 per share. (Debit Retained Earnings and credit Cash.)

Aug. 15   Cash dividends were declared and paid as follows: preferred, $2.50 per share; common, $0.40 per share. (Debit Retained Earnings and credit Cash.)

Dec. 31   Net income for the year was $126,000. (Debit Income Summary and credit Retained Earnings.)

Instructions
a Prepare journal entries to record the transactions described above.
b Prepare a condensed balance sheet at December 31, Year 6. Assume that the amounts of current assets and current liabilities were unchanged from the balance sheet of the preceding year.
c Compute primary and fully diluted earnings per share on the common stock for Year 6. The market price of the common stock at the end of Year 6 is $25 per share.

20A-5 Selected data summarizing the earnings performance of Taylor Company for a five-year period are given at the top of page 847 (all figures in thousands).
Late in December of each of the five years, the company called 10,000 shares of its preferred stock, paying the call price of 102 plus the final quarter's dividends. During Year 2 the company split its common stock 2 for 1, and in Year 4 it issued a 20% stock dividend. On October 1, Year 3, 2½ million shares of common stock were sold for cash. On July 1, Year 5, the company purchased 5 million shares of common stock from a major stockholder who was unhappy with company profits. The company plans to use the shares for acquisitions. There were no common stock equivalents outstanding during the five-year period.

	Year 5	Year 4	Year 3	Year 2	Year 1
Operating income	$64,120	$38,680	$84,480	$69,940	$47,200
Bond interest expense	5,200	5,200	9,100	10,400	10,400
Income before income tax expense	$58,920	$33,480	$75,380	$59,540	$36,800
Income tax expense	24,400	15,000	37,040	28,940	15,140
Net income	$34,520	$18,480	$38,340	$30,600	$21,660
Number of common shares outstanding at end of year	13,000	18,000	15,000	12,500	6,250
6%, $100 par value preferred; number of shares at end of year	60	70	80	90	100

Instructions Earnings per share of common stock for the five-year period are to be reported on a comparable basis in the company's annual report as of the end of the fifth year. Determine the figures that should be reported for each of the five years.

20A-6 The controller of Warhawk Corporation has requested assistance in determining net income, primary earnings per share, and fully diluted earnings per share for presentation in the company's income statement for the year ended September 30, Year 5. As currently calculated, the company's net income is $2,000,000 for the fiscal year ending September 30, Year 5. The controller has indicated that the net income figure might be adjusted for the following transactions which were recorded by charges or credits directly to the Retained Earnings account. (The amounts are net of applicable income taxes.)

(1) The sum of $1,875,000, applicable to a breached Year 1 contract, was received as a result of a lawsuit. Prior to the award, legal counsel was uncertain about the outcome of the suit. Assume that **FASB Statement No. 16**, "Prior Period Adjustments," was not in effect in Year 5.

(2) A gain of $1,500,000 was realized on the sale of a subsidiary company.

(3) A special inventory write-off of $750,000 was made, of which $625,000 applied to goods manufactured prior to October 1, Year 4.

Your working papers disclose the following analysis for the year ended September 30, Year 5.

(1) Common stock (at October 1, Year 4, stated value $10, authorized 300,000 shares; effective December 1, Year 4, stated value $5, authorized 600,000 shares):

Balance, Oct. 1, Year 4—issued and outstanding, 60,000 shares.
Dec. 1, Year 4—60,000 shares issued in a 2 for 1 stock split.
Dec. 1, Year 4—280,000 shares (stated value $5) issued for cash at $39 per share.

(2) Treasury stock—common:

Mar. 1, Year 5—acquired 40,000 shares at $38 per share.
Apr. 1, Year 5—sold 40,000 shares at $40 per share.

(3) Series A warrants (each warrant was exchangeable at any time with $60 for one common share; effective December 1, Year 4, when the stock was split 2 for 1, each warrant became exchangeable for two common shares at $30 per share):

Oct. 1, Year 4—25,000 warrants issued at $6 each.

(4) Series B warrants (each warrant is exchangeable with $40 for one common share):

Apr. 1, Year 5—20,000 warrants authorized and issued at $10 each.

(5) First mortgage bonds, 5½%, due Year 20 (nonconvertible; priced to yield 5% when issued):

Balance Oct. 1, Year 4—authorized, issued and outstanding, the face value of $1,400,000.

(6) Convertible debentures, 6.8%, due Year 24 (each $1,000 bond was convertible at any time until maturity into 15 common shares; effective December 1, Year 4, the conversion rate became 30 shares for each bond as a result of the 2 for 1 stock split):

Oct. 1, Year 4—authorized and issued at their face value of $12,000,000.

The following table shows market prices for the company's securities and the bank prime interest rate for selected dates:

	Price (or rate) at			Average for year ended Sept. 30, Year 5
	Oct. 1, Year 4	Apr. 1, Year 5	Sept. 30, Year 5	
Common stock	60	40*	36¼*	37½*
First mortgage bonds, 5½% . . .	88½	87	86	87
Convertible debentures, 6.8% .	100	120	119	115
Series A warrants	6	22	19½	15
Series B warrants	0	10	9	9½
Bank prime interest rate	8%	7¾%	7½%	7¾%

* After 2 for 1 stock split.

Instructions
a Show how net income should be presented in the company's income statement for the year ended September 30, Year 5.

b Assuming that net income after income taxes for the year was $2,700,000 and that that there were no extraordinary items, prepare a schedule computing (1) the primary earnings per share and (2) the fully diluted earnings per share which should be presented in the company's income statement for the year ended September 30, Year 5. A supporting schedule computing the numbers of shares to be used in these computations should also be prepared. (Because of the relative stability of the market price of the common stock, the annual average market price may be used where appropriate in your calculations. Assume an income tax rate of 50%.)

Group B

20B-1 In Year 8, Corsair Company issued all shares of its outstanding capital stock at a price of $25 a share. At December 31, Year 11, the balance sheet included the following stockholders' equity section:

Stockholders' equity:

Capital stock, $10 par, authorized 500,000 shares, issued and outstanding 200,000 shares	$2,000,000
Paid-in capital in excess of par	3,000,000
Retained earnings	1,950,000
Total stockholders' equity	$6,950,000

On February 15, Year 12, the company acquired 10,000 shares of treasury stock at $49 a share. On December 9, Year 12, the company reissued 5,000 shares of treasury stock for $267,500, net of commissions.

Instructions
a Record the two transactions in journal entry form, assuming that treasury stock is recorded at cost.
b Record the two transactions in journal entry form, assuming that treasury stock is recorded at par value of stock.
c Compute the book value per share at December 31, Year 11, and after each of the two transactions is completed. Why did book value per share change?

20B-2 Following are the journal entries recorded in the Ownership Equity account of Avenger Air Travel, Inc., during Year 1, its first year of operations:

Ownership Equity

(1) Acquired 2,000 shares of		(5) Issuance of 10,000 shares		
treasury stock	32,000	of $10 par common stock		159,420
(2) Cash dividends declared,		(6) Issuance of 5,000 shares of		
payable in Year 2	10,000	common stock for land		
(3) Discount on bonds payable .	12,000	appraised at $80,000. The		
(4) Loss on sale of land	7,040	land was recorded at		
		$50,000, the par value of		
		the stock issued		50,000
		(7) Reserve for "contingencies"		
		debited to expense		2,000
		(8) Proceeds from reissuance of		
		1,000 shares of treasury		
		stock		21,000
		(9) Net income for Year 1		42,720

The bonds were issued on June 30, Year 1, and mature on June 30, Year 11. Avenger Air Travel, Inc., was authorized to issue 50,000 shares of $10 par common stock and 20,000 shares of $1 no-par preferred stock. None of the preferred stock has been issued.

Instructions
a Prepare correcting journal entries for each item (1) through (9). Any corrections to current year's income should be made to Income Summary; the balance in the Income Summary account should be closed to Retained Earnings. Record treasury stock at cost.
b Prepare the stockholders' equity section of the balance sheet at December 31, Year 1.
c Compute the book value per share of common stock at December 31, Year 1.

20B-3 Thunderbolt Corporation was organized on January 5, Year 4, with authority to issue 500,000 shares of $10 par capital stock. It issued 300,000 shares immediately for cash at a price of $25 a share. Operations were profitable from the beginning; earnings averaged over $40,000 a month, with a total of $480,500 for the first fiscal year ended December 31, Year 4. A dividend of $1 a share was declared on December 10, Year 4, payable January 15, Year 5, to stockholders of record December 31, Year 4.

Thunderbolt Corporation established a policy of encouraging all its employees to acquire stock in the company. During Year 4 the corporation acquired shares from several employee-stockholders who left the company; some of these shares were subsequently reissued to new employees. The following treasury stock transactions took place during Year 4:

Mar. 4	Acquired 200 shares at $29 a share.
Aug. 12	Reissued 100 shares at $34 a share.
Nov. 8	Acquired 500 shares at $32 a share.
Dec. 28	Reissued 100 shares acquired on March 4 at $28 a share.

The company records all sources of paid-in capital in excess of legal capital in an account titled Additional Paid-in Capital.

Instructions
a Assuming that treasury stock is recorded at cost, prepare:
(1) Journal entries for treasury stock transactions
(2) Stockholders' equity section of the balance sheet at December 31, Year 4
b Assuming that treasury stock is recorded at par value, prepare:
(1) Journal entries for treasury stock transactions
(2) Stockholders' equity section of the balance sheet at December 31, Year 4

20B-4 A comparative summary of the stockholders' equity for Hellcat Corporation, together with certain additional information, is given below:

	Dec. 31, Year 5		Jan. 1, Year 5
Stockholders' equity:			
Capital stock, authorized 250,000 shares;			
issued:			
At Dec. 31, Year 5, 70,000 shares, $8 par			
(1,000 held in treasury)	$ 560,000		
At Jan. 1, Year 5, 40,000 shares, $10 par			$ 400,000
Stock dividend to be distributed (6,900			
shares)	55,200	$ 615,200	
From issuance of capital stock, in-			
cluding $8,000 at Dec. 31, Year 5, from			
treasury stock transactions	$ 808,700		200,000
From issuance of stock dividends . . .	276,000	1,084,700	
Total paid-in capital		$1,699,900	$ 600,000
Retained earnings:			
Appropriated for acquisition of treasury			
stock	$ 37,000		
Unappropriated	1,232,600	1,269,600	1,420,200
Total paid-in capital and retained earnings		$2,969,500	
Less: Treasury stock, 1,000 shares, at cost		37,000	
Total stockholders' equity		$2,932,500	$2,020,200

In February of Year 5, the board of directors approved a 5 for 4 stock split which reduced the par value of the capital stock from $10 to $8 a share. The split was approved by stockholders on March 1 and distributed on March 25. A memorandum entry was used to record the stock split.

On April 1, Year 5, the company acquired 2,000 shares of its stock at $37 a share.

On June 30, Year 5, 1,000 shares of treasury stock were reissued at $45 a share.

On July 1, Year 5, 20,000 shares of $8 par capital stock were issued in exchange for the net assets of Holland Company. The total market value of the 20,000 shares issued was $760,700.

A cash dividend of $2 a share was declared on December 2, Year 5, payable on December 29, to stockholders of record on December 15; a 10% stock dividend was declared on December 20, to be distributed on January 25, Year 6. The market price of the stock on December 20 was $48 a share. Debit Retained Earnings to record cash and stock dividends.

The net income for Year 5 was $318,600, which included an extraordinary gain of $35,400 (net of income tax effect).

Instructions

a Prepare journal entries to record transactions relating to stockholders' equity that took place during the year ended December 31, Year 5. Debit Income Summary and Credit Retained Earnings to record net income for Year 5.

b Prepare the lower section of the income statement for the year ended December 31, Year 5, showing operating income and the extraordinary gain. Also illustrate how the earnings per share should be presented in the income statement, assuming that earnings per share are determined on the basis of the weighted-average number of shares outstanding during the year and that financial statements are issued before the 10% stock dividend is distributed.

c Prepare a statement of retained earnings for the year ended December 31, Year 5. Use two columnar headings: "Unappropriated" and "Appropriated for Acquisition of Treasury Stock."

d Compute the book value per share of capital stock at December 31, Year 5.

20B-5 On February 1, Year 6, when your audit and report are nearly complete, the financial vice president of Midway Company asks you to prepare statistical schedules of comparative financial data for the past two years for inclusion in the company's annual report. Your working papers include the following information:

(1) Income statements show net income as follows: Year 4, $2,880,000; Year 5, $2,400,000.
(2) On January 1, Year 4, there were outstanding 200,000 shares of common stock, $5 par, and 20,000 shares of 6% convertible preferred stock, $100 par. The preferred stock was issued at par. Each share of preferred stock is initially convertible into 2.5 shares of common stock, to be adjusted for any stock dividends and splits. The market price of common stock has ranged from $45 to $60 a share during the past two years. The prime bank rate of interest was $5\frac{1}{2}$% at the time the preferred stock was issued.
(3) On December 31, Year 4, a 20% stock dividend was distributed to common stockholders. On this date, the market price of the common stock was $50 a share.
(4) In June of Year 5, common stock was split 2 for 1.
(5) Cash dividends are paid on the preferred stock on June 30 and December 31. Preferred stock dividends were paid in each year; none of the preferred stock has been converted into common stock.

Instructions

a In connection with your preparation of the statistical schedule of comparative financial data for the past two years.

(1) Prepare a schedule computing the number of shares of common stock outstanding as of the respective year-end dates.

(2) Prepare a schedule computing the equivalent number of shares of common stock outstanding for each year for purposes of computing primary earnings per share. Equivalent shares means the number of shares outstanding in the respective prior periods in terms of the present capital structure.

(3) Prepare a schedule computing the equivalent number of shares of common stock outstanding for each year for purposes of computing fully diluted earnings per share.

b Prepare the lower section of the income statement, showing primary and fully diluted earnings per share for Year 4 and Year 5.

20B-6 The stockholders' equity section of Pearl Harbor Salvage Corporation's balance sheet as of December 31, Year 5, is presented below:

Stockholders' equity:

$1 cumulative convertible preferred stock ($25 par, authorized 1,600,000 shares, issued 1,400,000 converted to common 750,000, and outstanding 650,000 shares. Involuntary liquidation value, $30 a share, aggregating $19,500,000)	*$16,250,000*
Common stock ($0.25 par; authorized 15,000,000 shares; issued and outstanding 8,800,000 shares)	*2,200,000*
Paid-in capital in excess of par	*32,750,000*
Retained earnings	*40,595,000*
Total stockholders' equity	*$91,795,000*

Included in the liabilities of Pearl Harbor Salvage are 5½% convertible debentures issued at their face value of $20,000,000 in Year 4. The debentures are due in Year 24, and until then are convertible into the common stock of Pearl Harbor Salvage at the rate of 50 shares of common stock for each $1,000 debenture. To date none of these debentures has been converted.

On April 2, Year 4, Pearl Harbor Salvage issued 1,400,000 shares of convertible preferred stock at $40 per share. Quarterly dividends to December 31, Year 5, have been paid on these shares. The preferred stock is convertible into common stock at the rate of two shares of common for each share of preferred. On October 1, Year 5, 150,000 shares and on November 1, Year 5, 600,000 shares of the preferred stock were converted into common stock.

On July 2, Year 5, Pearl Harbor Salvage granted options to its officers and key employees to purchase 500,000 shares of the company's common stock at a price of $20 a share.

During Year 5, dividend payments and average market prices of Pearl Harbor Salvage Corporation's common stock were as follows:

	Dividend per share	*Average market price per share*
First quarter	*$0.10*	*$20*
Second quarter	*0.15*	*25*
Third quarter	*0.10*	*30*
Fourth quarter	*0.15*	*25*
Average for the year		*25*

The December 31, Year 5, closing price of the common stock was $25 a share.

Assume that the bank prime interest rate was 7% throughout Year 4 and Pearl Harbor Salvage Corporation's net income for the year ended December 31, Year 5, was $47,500,000. Assume that the income tax rate was 50%.

Instructions

a Prepare a schedule which shows the valuation of the common stock equivalency status of the (1) convertible debentures, (2) convertible preferred stock, and (3) employee stock options.

b Prepare a schedule which shows for Year 5 the computation of:
(1) The weighted-average number of shares for computing primary earnings per share
(2) The weighted-average number of shares for computing fully diluted earnings per share

c Prepare a schedule which shows for Year 5 the computation to the nearest cent of:
(1) Primary earnings per share
(2) Fully diluted earnings per share

CHAPTER 21

ACCOUNTING FOR INCOME TAXES

One of the more interesting areas of corporate accounting is the reporting problem created when accounting income in a corporation's income statement differs materially from taxable income reported in its income tax return. We have seen in previous chapters a number of situations which produce such differences. In preparing an income statement to be issued to the public, accountants are primarily concerned with measuring business operating results in accordance with generally accepted accounting principles. Taxable income, on the other hand, is a legal concept governed by law. In devising tax statutes, Congress is interested not only in meeting the revenue needs of government but in achieving other economic and social objectives. Because the rules for measuring accounting income and taxable income were developed with different objectives in mind, it is not surprising that the results are sometimes materially different.

The nature of the income tax allocation problem[1]

Why do differences between accounting and taxable income produce a reporting problem? To answer this question, consider the highly condensed income statement for American Company shown at the top of page 855.

[1] For a more extensive discussion of the income tax allocation problem, see the following: Homer A. Black, "Interperiod Allocation of Corporate Income Taxes," *Accounting Research Study No. 9,* AICPA (New York: 1966); David F. Hawkins, "Deferred Taxes: Source

AMERICAN COMPANY
Condensed Comparative Income Statement

	Year 2	Year 1
Sales and other revenue	$9,000,000	$9,000,000
Less:		
Cost of goods sold	(5,400,000)	(5,400,000)
Operating expenses	(2,600,000)	(2,600,000)
Income before income taxes (operating income) . .	$1,000,000	$1,000,000
Income tax expense	600,000	300,000
Net income	$ 400,000	$ 700,000

After examining this comparative income statement, the reader would want to know why the same operating income (pre-tax income) resulted in such a large difference in net income for the two years. Corporate tax rates are changed frequently, but in recent years the rates have been such that companies reporting operating income of $1 million pay about half of this amount in income taxes. Knowing this, the reader would expect American Company to pay about $500,000 of income taxes each year, and would want to know why taxes were so much smaller than this in Year 1, and so much larger in Year 2. It is apparent that the company's taxable income in each of the two years differed materially from its accounting income. By analyzing the source of the differences between accounting income as determined from the accounting records and taxable income as defined by tax statutes, we could determine whether income tax expense was reported in accordance with generally accepted accounting principles.

Another possible distortion between pre-tax income and income tax expense may result when extraordinary items are included in the income statement. To illustrate this point, consider the partial income statement for General Corporation on page 856.

The picture presented in this income statement is obviously distorted. The operating income absorbs a charge for income taxes at the rate of 180% while the extraordinary gain is reported at the full pre-tax amount of $300,000. An allocation of income taxes between operating income and the extraordinary gain at the effective tax rate of 45% would be more consistent with the matching concept and would correct the distorted relationship between operating income and income tax expense.

---

of Non-Operating Funds," *Financial Executive* (February 1969), pp. 35–44; Hugo Nurnberg, *Cash Movements Analysis of the Accounting for Corporate Income Taxes,* MSU Business Studies, Michigan State University (East Lansing: 1971); *APB Opinion No. 11,* AICPA (New York: 1967); *APB Opinion No. 23,* AICPA (New York: 1972); *APB Opinion No. 24,* AICPA (New York: 1972); *and FASB Statement No. 9,* FASB (Stamford: 1975).

GENERAL CORPORATION
Partial Income Statement for Year 1

Income before income taxes (operating income)	$100,000
Income tax expense (45% of $400,000 including extraordinary gain of	
$300,000)	180,000
Operating loss before extraordinary gain	$ (80,000)
Extraordinary gain (before income tax effect)	300,000
Net income	$220,000

Terminology used in accounting for income taxes

A brief definition of terms used in accounting for income taxes is necessary at this point.[2]

1 *Income taxes* Taxes based on income as determined under provisions of federal, state, and, in certain cases, foreign tax laws. This term is also used to describe the amount of income taxes (income tax expense) charged to an accounting period.

2 *Pre-tax accounting income* Income for an accounting period before deducting income taxes. **Accounting income** and **income before income taxes** are alternative terms for pre-tax accounting income.

3 *Taxable income* (or *loss*) The excess of taxable revenue over deductible expenses (or the excess of deductible expenses over taxable revenue) for an accounting period. For purposes of this definition, deductible expenses do not include operating loss carrybacks or carryforwards.

4 *Timing differences* Differences between pre-tax accounting income and taxable income for a fiscal period caused by reporting items of revenue or expense in one period for accounting purposes and in an earlier or later period for income tax purposes. Timing differences thus originate in one accounting period and "reverse" in future periods. Most timing differences reduce income taxes that would otherwise be payable currently, but a few timing differences increase the amount of income taxes payable currently.

5 *Permanent differences* Differences between pre-tax accounting income and taxable income arising from transactions that, under applicable tax laws and regulations, will not be offset by corresponding differences or reversals in future periods.

6 *Tax effects* Differences between actual income taxes payable currently and income tax expense for a period which are attributable to **(a)** revenue or expense transactions which enter into the determination of pre-tax accounting income in one period and into the determination of taxable income in another period, **(b)** deductions or credits that may be carried backward or forward for income tax purposes, and **(c)** prior period adjustments. A permanent difference between accounting and taxable income does not result in a tax effect.

7 *Deferred taxes* Tax effects which are postponed for allocation (either as increases or decreases) to income tax expense of future periods.

8 *Interperiod tax allocation* The process of apportioning income tax expense among accounting periods.

[2] Adapted with some modifications from *APB Opinion No. 11*, "Accounting for Income Taxes," AICPA (New York: 1967), pp. 158–160.

9 *Interim-period tax computation*   The computation of income tax expense for periods, such as fiscal quarters, within a year.

10 *Tax allocation within a period* (or *intraperiod tax allocation*)   The process of apportioning income tax expense applicable to a given period among income before extraordinary items, extraordinary items, and prior period adjustments.[3]

Assumptions underlying income tax allocation

Income tax allocation procedures are based on the assumption that income taxes represent an expense of doing business and that income taxes will continue in the future. Income measurement on a going-concern basis requires the application of the accrual concept of accounting. Accrual accounting calls for the matching of realized revenue with expired costs for specific accounting periods. Accordingly, income taxes applicable to income recognized currently in the income statement should be estimated and accrued currently without regard to the time of payment. Income taxes which must be paid currently but which are applicable to income to be reported at some future date should be deferred and recognized as an expense when the related income is included in the income statement. Income taxes (or tax reductions) applicable to extraordinary items are offset against the pre-tax extraordinary items so that the extraordinary items are reported in the income statement *net of the income tax effect.*

Sources of differences between accounting and taxable income

The major sources of differences between corporate accounting income and taxable income fall into three categories:

1 *Timing differences in the recognition of revenue and expense*   A number of provisions in the income tax law allow (or sometimes require) taxpayers to recognize revenue and expense at different times than would be appropriate under generally accepted accounting principles. When a corporation has an option, it is likely to choose accounting methods for income tax purposes that delay the recognition of revenue and accelerate the recognition of an expense.

2 *Differences due to carryback and carryforward of losses for income tax purposes*   The federal income tax law provides that an operating loss in one year may be offset against taxable income of specified previous and future tax years.[4] As a result, an **operating loss** in a given year may result in either

---

[3] Tax allocation within a period also applies to "income or loss from discontinued operations" and "cumulative effect on prior years of a change in accounting principle." Tax allocation treatment of these items parallels that accorded extraordinary items.

[4] The current tax law provides that an *operating loss* may be carried back to the third year before the loss and applied until exhausted against taxable income in successive years through the seventh year after the loss. The three-year carryback may be waived by the taxpayer and the entire loss carried forward. As in the case of taxable income, there are certain differences between the definition of an operating loss for tax purposes and the accounting concept of such a loss.

a refund of taxes previously paid or a potential reduction of income taxes in future years. For income tax purposes, **capital losses** incurred by corporations may be deducted only against capital gains, and capital losses in excess of capital gains in one year may be carried back and offset against net capital gains of the preceding three years. Any unused net capital loss may be carried over and deducted against net capital gains in the succeeding five years.

3 *Permanent differences caused by legal provisions* Some types of revenue and expense are recognized for accounting purposes but not for income tax purposes; some are recognized in computing taxable income but are not included in accounting income.

In the following sections we shall consider the accounting implications of each of these three categories. In all illustrations we shall assume an effective corporate tax rate of 45% on ordinary income and 30% on net capital gains to simplify the computations.

Timing differences

In some cases the period in which an item of revenue is taxable or an expense is deductible for income tax purposes differs from the period in which the revenue or expense is recognized in measuring accounting income. When accounting income in any period differs from taxable income as a result of *timing differences,* the divergence will be counterbalanced in future periods by opposite variations between accounting income and taxable income. When accounting income is *larger* than taxable income, a deferred income tax liability results; when accounting income is *smaller* than taxable income, a prepayment of income taxes results. Deferred income tax liabilities and prepaid income taxes are recognized through interperiod income tax allocation.

Accounting Income Exceeds Taxable Income: Deferred Income Tax Liability Most timing differences produce accounting income which is larger than taxable income. The two reasons for such a difference are described below:

Revenue or a gain is recognized in the accounting records in the current period but is not taxed until later periods An example of this situation occurs when a company sells merchandise on the installment basis and recognizes accounting income on the accrual basis when sales are made, but elects to compute taxable income on the basis of cash collections. Another example involves long-term construction contracts when accounting income is measured on the basis of construction in progress (the percentage-of-completion method described in Chapter 9), but taxable income is reported only when the contracts are completed (the completed-contract method described in Chapter 9). Finally, the use of the equity method of accounting for investments in common stocks generally results in timing differences between taxable income and accounting income.[5]

[5] See Chapter 11 and *APB Opinions No. 23 and No. 24,* AICPA (New York: 1972).

Expense or a loss is deducted for income tax purposes in the current period but is not recognized in the accounting records until later periods An example of this situation occurs when a business chooses an accelerated method to depreciate plant assets for income tax purposes but uses the straight-line method for accounting purposes.

To illustrate the accounting for a deferred income tax liability, assume that Slow Company acquired for $1 million an item of equipment with an economic life of four years. The company uses the sum-of-the-years'-digits method of depreciation for income tax purposes and the straight-line method for accounting purposes. Assuming that the company earns $800,000 each year (before depreciation expense and income taxes), the effect of these procedures on pre-tax accounting income and taxable income is shown below:

Year	Accounting income before depreciation and income taxes	Accounting depreciation	Tax return depreciation	Pre-tax accounting income	Taxable income
1	$ 800,000	$ 250,000	$ 400,000	$ 550,000	$ 400,000
2	800,000	250,000	300,000	550,000	500,000
3	800,000	250,000	200,000	550,000	600,000
4	800,000	250,000	100,000	550,000	700,000
Totals	$3,200,000	$1,000,000	$1,000,000	$2,200,000	$2,200,000

Note that the total pre-tax accounting income and taxable income are identical over the four-year period. The journal entries to record income taxes at the rate of 45% are presented below:

```
Year 1  Income Tax Expense ($550,000 × 45%) . . . . . . .   247,500
            Income Taxes Payable . . . . . . . . . . . .              180,000
            Deferred Income Tax Liability . . . . . . . . .           67,500


Year 2  Income Tax Expense  . . . . . . . . . . . . . . .   247,500
            Income Taxes Payable . . . . . . . . . . . .              225,000
            Deferred Income Tax Liability . . . . . . . . .           22,500


Year 3  Income Tax Expense  . . . . . . . . . . . . . . .   247,500
        Deferred Income Tax Liability . . . . . . . . . . .  22,500
            Income Taxes Payable . . . . . . . . . . . .              270,000


Year 4  Income Tax Expense  . . . . . . . . . . . . . . .   247,500
        Deferred Income Tax Liability  . . . . . . . . . . .  67,500
            Income Taxes Payable . . . . . . . . . . . .              315,000
```

A deferred tax liability of $90,000 ($67,500 + $22,500 = $90,000) arises during the first two years when pre-tax accounting income exceeds taxable income and is extinguished during the last two years when the reverse is true. In the income statement for Year 1, income tax expense should be divided between the amount currently payable and the amount deferred, as follows:

SLOW COMPANY

Partial Income Statement for Year 1

Income before income taxes (operating income)		$550,000
Income tax expense:		
Currently payable	$180,000	
Deferred	67,500	247,500
Net income		$302,500

Taxable Income Exceeds Accounting Income: Prepaid Income Taxes The two reasons why taxable income may exceed the amount of income for financial reporting purposes are explained below:

Revenue or a gain is taxed in the current period but is not recognized in the accounting records until later periods Congress is conscious of the fact that taxpaying ability arises when taxpayers have cash with which to pay the tax. Therefore, the tax law tends to make realization of income in liquid form the general test of tax timing. The accounting test of income recognition depends both on realization and on whether a business has earned the income. Revenue received in advance is not included in accounting income until the earning process is complete, but it must usually be reported for income tax purposes in the period received. For example, suppose that a corporation leases property for five years at $1,000 per year and receives the first and last year's rental in advance. For income tax purposes the entire $2,000 must be included in income in the year of receipt; for accounting purposes the $1,000 rent for the last year is carried as deferred revenue in the balance sheet until the fifth year, when it will be included in accounting revenue but will not be subject to income tax.

Expense or a loss is recognized for accounting purposes in the current period but is not deducted for income tax purposes until later periods In general, an expense or a loss is recorded when evidence that it has been incurred is reasonably clear. For income tax purposes, more definite evidence is sometimes required. For example, companies often guarantee their products against defect for a number of years. On the basis of experience, a company knows that despite its best efforts a certain portion of the goods sold will prove defective, and it may accrue an estimated liability for performance under the guarantee in order to match the estimated expense with revenue in the period of sale. For income tax purposes, however, this estimated expense is not deductible until it has actually been incurred. Accounting income will therefore be smaller than taxable income in the year the estimated expense is recorded, and counterbalancing will take place in the year in which customers make claims under the warranty.

To illustrate the accounting for prepaid income taxes, assume that Fast Company sells a product that requires frequent servicing. At the time of sale, therefore, the company agrees to furnish service by factory representatives over a five-year period without further charge. The company records estimated servicing expense as a percentage of the sales realized in any period. For income tax purposes, however, servicing expenses are deductible as incurred. During a given three-year period the estimated and actual servicing expenses were as follows:

Year	Accounting income before servicing expense	Estimated servicing expense	Pre-tax accounting income	Actual servicing expense	Taxable income
1	$ 600,000	$100,000	$ 500,000	$ 20,000	$ 580,000
2	600,000	100,000	500,000	150,000	450,000
3	600,000	100,000	500,000	70,000	530,000
Totals	$1,800,000	$300,000	$1,500,000	$240,000	$1,560,000

Using tax allocation procedures, Fast Company would accrue income tax expense each period on the basis of accounting income and would record the difference between the current income tax liability and the income tax expense as prepaid income taxes. Journal entries to record income taxes at the rate of 45% for the three years are shown below:

```
Year 1   Income Tax Expense ($500,000 × 45%) . . . . . . .   225,000
             Prepaid Income Taxes  . . . . . . . . . . . . .    36,000
                 Income Taxes Payable . . . . . . . . . . .              261,000


Year 2   Income Tax Expense  . . . . . . . . . . . . . . .   225,000
             Prepaid Income Taxes . . . . . . . . . . . .                 22,500
             Income Taxes Payable . . . . . . . . . . .                  202,500


Year 3   Income Tax Expense  . . . . . . . . . . . . . . .   225,000
             Prepaid Income Taxes  . . . . . . . . . . . . .    13,500
                 Income Taxes Payable . . . . . . . . . . .              238,500
```

In this illustration, accounting and taxable income are not identical over the three-year period, but there is a presumption that the $60,000 excess of estimated servicing expenses over actual servicing expense will counterbalance in future periods. The debit balance of $27,000 ($36,000 − $22,500 + $13,500 = $27,000) in the Prepaid Income Taxes account at the end of Year 3 represents the future tax benefits that will arise when the servicing costs are actually incurred and, although not reported as an expense for accounting purposes, will be deducted in computing taxable income.

In the income statement for Year 1, Fast Company will report a $225,000 income tax expense. To meet the standards of good financial reporting, however, the amount of taxes currently payable and prepaid income taxes applicable to future periods should be shown separately as follows:

FAST COMPANY

Partial Income Statement for Year 1

Income before income taxes (operating income)		$500,000
Income tax expense:		
Currently payable	$261,000	
Less: Prepaid income taxes	36,000	225,000
Net income		$275,000

Alternative Approaches to Interperiod Tax Allocation Three approaches to the accounting for timing differences have been suggested. These are summarized below:

1 *Deferred method* Under this method, the income tax effects of current timing differences are computed **using tax rates in effect when the deferral of taxes takes place.** No adjustments are made to the Deferred Income Tax Liability account or to the Prepaid Income Taxes account for subsequent changes in tax rates. The deferred taxes are then allocated to income tax expense when the timing differences reverse. The treatment of timing difference reversals is illustrated above in the Slow Company example (Years 3 and 4) and in the Fast Company example (Year 2).

2 *Liability method* This is essentially a balance sheet approach to interperiod tax allocation. Its main objective is the correct measurement of the deferred income tax liability. If the tax rates in the year the deferral takes place are different from the expected tax rates in the year in which the payment of taxes is anticipated, the latter rates are used to measure the deferred income tax liability. Furthermore, subsequent changes in income tax rates would require adjustment of the deferred income tax liability to reflect the new tax rates.

3 *Net-of-tax method* Interperiod tax allocation under the net-of-tax method views the income tax effects of timing differences as **valuation accounts** associated with the related assets and liabilities. The tax effects are applied to reduce specific assets or liabilities. For example, the deferred income tax "liability" arising from the use of an accelerated depreciation method for income tax purposes would be deducted from plant assets in the balance sheet; similarly the deferred income tax liability arising from the use of the installment method of accounting for income tax purposes would be deducted from installment receivables.

APB Opinion No. 11 required the use of the deferred method; the Opinion stated:

> The Board has concluded that the deferred method of tax allocation should be followed since it provides the most useful and practical approach to interperiod tax allocation and the presentation of income taxes in financial statements.[6]

A minority view of interperiod tax allocation calls for *partial allocation.* Supporters of partial allocation argue that when recurring differences between pre-tax accounting income and taxable income appear to cause an indefinite postponement of tax payments, tax allocation is not required for such differences. For example, assume that a company with a growing investment in depreciable assets uses straight-line depreciation for accounting purposes but accelerated depreciation for computing taxable income. Under the partial allocation approach, the income tax expense for the company would be the tax actually payable for the period.

Advocates of partial allocation thus make a general presumption that income tax expense for accounting purposes should be the tax payable for the period, except for cases in which nonrecurring differences between taxable income and pre-tax accounting income would cause material misstatement of income tax expense and net income. Such an exception is illustrated by the installment sale of a plant asset at a gain, which is reported in accounting income of the current period but is not taxable until future periods.

The more widely accepted position is that all timing differences between accounting income and taxable income require **comprehensive allocation** of income taxes. Under comprehensive allocation, income tax expense for a period includes all accruals, deferrals, and estimates necessary to adjust the income taxes actually payable for the period in order to recognize the tax effects of transactions included in accounting income for that period. Tax effects of initial timing differences are recognized and allocated to those periods in which the initial differences *reverse.* Comprehensive allocation thus associates tax effects with related transactions as they are reported in the income statement.

The Accounting Principles Board resolved the issue of partial as opposed to comprehensive tax allocation as follows:

> The Board has considered the various concepts of accounting for income taxes and has concluded that comprehensive interperiod tax allocation is an integral part of the determination of income tax expense. Therefore, income tax expense should include the tax effects of revenue and expense transactions included in the determination of pre-tax accounting income. The tax ef-

---

[6] *APB Opinion No. 11,* p. 169.

fects of those transactions which enter into the determination of pre-tax accounting income either earlier or later than they become determinants of taxable income should be recognized in the periods in which the differences between pre-tax accounting income and taxable income arise and in the periods in which the differences reverse.

The tax effect of a timing difference should be measured by the differential between income taxes computed with and without inclusion of the transaction creating the difference between taxable income and pre-tax accounting income. The resulting income tax expense for the period includes the tax effects of transactions entering into the determination of results of operations for the period. The resulting deferred tax amounts reflect the tax effects which will reverse in future periods. The measurement of income tax expense becomes thereby a consistent and integral part of the process of matching revenues and expenses in the determination of results of operations.[7]

Although *APB Opinion No. 11* established workable standards for interperiod tax allocation, it by no means eliminated the conceptual controversies associated with this subject. Many accountants and business executives continue to favor the liability method, partial allocation of income taxes, and the net-of-tax method for balance sheet presentation of deferred income tax accounts. Interperiod tax allocation will probably continue to be a controversial topic as long as taxes on business income continue to be levied at relatively high rates.

Carryback and carryforward of operating losses

To help lighten the tax burden of corporations that experience losses, the current federal tax law provides that operating losses may be carried back against the taxable income of the three preceding years and then forward against taxable income earned in the seven years following the loss. The effect of this provision is to create a receivable for a tax refund or potential future tax savings when an operating loss occurs. When an operating loss is carried back or forward, pre-tax accounting income and taxable income (after the operating loss is deducted) will differ for the fiscal period to which the loss is applied. Thus *operating losses create special kinds of tax timing differences.*

Operating Loss Carryback When an operating loss occurs following a period of profitable operations, a corporation has a claim for a refund of past income taxes that should be recognized in the accounting records in the year in which the loss occurs. On this point, *APB Opinion No. 11* stated:

> The tax effects of any realizable loss **carrybacks** should be recognized in the determination of net income (loss) of the loss periods. The tax loss gives rise to a refund (or claim for refund) of past taxes, which is both measurable and currently realizable; therefore the tax effect of the loss is properly recognizable in the determination of net income (loss) for the loss period.[8]

[7] Ibid.
[8] Ibid., p. 172.

To illustrate the accounting for an operating loss carryback, assume that W Company reports an operating loss of $100,000 for the current year. Because of certain technical adjustments required by tax laws, the company is able to carry back only $90,000 of this loss and offset it against taxable income of a prior year, thus claiming a tax refund of $40,500 (assuming a 45% corporate tax rate). The following journal entry recognizes the effect of the loss carryback:

Income Tax Refund Receivable	40,500	
Tax Benefit of Operating Loss Carryback		40,500
To record claim for income taxes previously paid: $90,000 × 45% = $40,500.		

The lower portion of the company's income statement for the year in which the operating loss is incurred would appear as follows:

W COMPANY
Partial Income Statement for Current Year

Operating loss before income tax effect of operating loss carryback	$(100,000)
Less: Tax benefit of operating loss carryback	40,500
Net loss	$ (59,500)

Operating Loss Carryforward If a corporation must depend on future earnings to use the operating loss as a tax deduction, the accounting for income taxes presents a more difficult problem. For example, suppose that X Corporation experienced a $200,000 operating loss in the first year of operations. A question arises as to whether the probability of future income tax benefit is sufficiently high to warrant an accounting treatment which **anticipates** the benefit of the loss carryforward. On this point, the APB took the following position:

> The tax effects of loss **carryforwards** also relate to the determination of net income (loss) of the loss periods. However, a significant question generally exists as to realization of the tax effects of the **carryforwards,** since realization is dependent upon future taxable income. Accordingly, the Board has concluded that the tax benefits of loss **carryforwards** should not be recognized until they are actually realized, except in unusual circumstances when realization is **assured beyond any reasonable doubt** at the time the loss **carryforwards** arise. When the tax benefits of loss **carryforwards** are not recognized until realized in full or in part in subsequent periods, the tax benefits should be reported in the results of operations of those periods as extraordinary items.[9]

[9] Ibid., p. 173.

In its first year of operations, then, X Corporation would report the full operating loss of $200,000 in its income statement without adjustment for the possible tax benefits in future years. Assuming that X Corporation had an operating income of $240,000 in the second year and that the income tax rate was 45%, the entry to record income tax expense and the tax benefit of the operating loss carryforward would be:

Income Tax Expense 108,000
    Income Taxes Payable   18,000
    Extraordinary Item: Tax Benefit of Operating Loss Carry-
       forward   90,000
To record income tax expense and effect of operating loss carryforward. Amounts are determined below:
  Income tax expense: $240,000 × 45% = $108,000.
  Income taxes payable: ($240,000 − $200,000) ×
    45% = $18,000.
  Tax benefit of operating loss carryforward: $200,000 ×
    45% = $90,000.

The lower section of the comparative income statements issued at the end of the second year would be presented as follows:

X CORPORATION
Partial Income Statement for Years 2 and 1

	Year 2	Year 1
Income (loss) before income taxes (operating income) .	$240,000	$(200,000)
Less: Income tax expense (only $18,000 is actually payable after deducting $90,000 tax benefit of operating loss carryforward)	108,000	–0–
Income before extraordinary item	$132,000	$(200,000)
Extraordinary item: Tax benefit of operating loss carryforward	90,000	–0–
Net income (loss)	$222,000	$(200,000)

If the realization of a potential tax benefit of an operating loss carryforward is "assured beyond any reasonable doubt," the tax benefit should be recognized in the period of the loss by recording an asset (potential tax benefit) and reducing the operating loss by the same amount. Because the prospect of future income is always uncertain, the recognition of a potential tax benefit of an operating loss carryforward in the year of the loss should be considered an exceptional approach. It might apply, for example, in the case of a well-established company with a history of steadily increasing earnings and good future prospects, which incurs a substantial loss because of an unprofitable venture that is not expected to recur. Under these circumstances the probability that the operating loss will produce a future tax benefit may be sufficiently high to warrant recognition of the carryforward tax benefit as an asset.[10]

The amount of the potential tax benefit recognized in the loss period should be computed using the tax rate expected to be in effect at the time of realization. The asset (potential tax benefit of operating loss carryforward) will be reduced by a debit to income tax expense in measuring the net income of future profitable periods.

As an example, assume that Y Corporation had pre-tax earnings of $50,000 in Year 1 (a year in which it was subject to income taxes at only a 20% rate), $200,000 in Year 2, and $400,000 in Year 3, but incurred a $50,000 pre-tax loss in Year 4 due to a labor dispute. The dispute was settled late in Year 4 and management was confident that taxable income for Year 5 would exceed $500,000. Because carryforward of the loss to the next year would create tax savings of $22,500 (applying the 45% rate expected in Year 5 to the $50,000 loss) while a carryback would create a refund of only $10,000 (based on the 20% rate that had applied in Year 1), Y Corporation elected to waive the carryback option and to apply the loss to future years.[11] The journal entry to record income taxes for Year 4 would be:

Current Asset: Potential Tax Benefit of Operating Loss		
Carryforward	22,500	
Tax Benefit of Operating Loss Carryforward (reduction		
of loss)		22,500

To record effect on income taxes of operating loss expected to be carried forward to Year 5, based on anticipated income tax rate for Year 5: $50,000 \times 45\% = \$22,500$.

---

[10] In 1976, the SEC (*Staff Accounting Bulletin No. 8*) stated that a loss carryforward should not be recorded as an asset unless the company has a very strong earnings history, the loss was not caused by a general economic or industry decline, the company has reasonable alternative tax strategies available, and a forecast based on reasonable assumptions indicates more than enough future income to offset the loss carryforward.

[11] Operating loss carrybacks must be applied first to the earliest year of the allowable carryback period—in this case to Year 1. However, the Tax Reform Act of 1976 added a provision allowing taxpayers to irrevocably relinquish the entire carryback period with respect to a given loss year. Because it will no longer be necessary for a corporation to have four consecutive loss years before being able to carry forward an operating loss, the conditions for recording the tax benefits of an operating loss carryforward as an asset at the end of a loss year may be met more frequently than before.

Assuming that taxable income in Year 5 was $500,000, the income tax for that year would be recorded as follows:

Income Tax Expense 225,000
    Current Asset: Potential Tax Benefit of Operating Loss
        Carryforward   22,500
    Income Taxes Payable   202,500
To record income tax expense: $500,000 × 45% = $225,000.
The amount currently payable is reduced by the operating
loss carryforward: ($500,000 − $50,000) × 45% = $202,500.

Permanent differences between taxable income and pre-tax accounting income

Accounting income may differ from taxable income because certain revenue is exempt from taxation and because allowable tax deductions differ from expenses recognized for financial reporting purposes. These differences are permanent in the sense that they arise not from differences in the timing of revenue and expense but because Congress has seen fit to use the tax law to accomplish certain public policy objectives. Some possible cases are listed below:

Nontaxable Revenue Examples of accounting revenue which is not subject to federal income taxation are: interest received on state or municipal bonds and life insurance proceeds received by a corporation upon death of its officers.

Nondeductible Expenses Examples of business expenses which are not deductible for tax purposes are: amortization of acquired goodwill, premiums paid on life insurance policies in which the corporation is the beneficiary, certain penalties, and illegal payments, such as those made for the purpose of influencing legislation or to obtain foreign business.

Tax Deductions That Are Not Expenses The tax law allows some deductions for tax purposes that do not represent actual business expenses. The special deductions (usually 85%) for certain dividends received by corporations and the excess of percentage (statutory) depletion over cost depletion allowed on certain natural resources are prominent examples.

A corporation that has tax-free revenue, nondeductible expenses, or percentage depletion in excess of cost depletion is taxed at an "average" tax rate that differs from the "normal" tax rate applicable to corporations. This is an economic and political fact which should be reflected in the accountant's measurement of income. Since permanent differences between taxable and pre-tax accounting income do not affect other periods, interperiod tax allocation is not required to account for such differences. Because tax laws are subject to change, a material permanent difference should be explained in notes to the financial statements.

Tax allocation within a period

The need for tax allocation within a period (also known as *intraperiod tax allocation*) may arise when extraordinary items are included in net income or a prior period adjustment is recorded in the current period. If extraordinary items and prior period adjustments are taxable or are deductible for tax purposes, income taxes (or tax refunds) should be apportioned between income before extraordinary items, extraordinary items, and prior period adjustments. Income taxes applicable to income before extraordinary items should be based on the difference between revenue and expenses before giving effect to the tax consequences of extraordinary items. Extraordinary items and prior period adjustments should be reported *net* of the taxes applicable to these items.

Extraordinary Gain To illustrate a situation involving an extraordinary gain and a prior period adjustment, assume that Z Company reported the following for Year 4:

Income before income taxes *(fully taxable at 45%)*	$300,000
Extraordinary capital gain *(taxable at 30%)*	800,000
Prior period adjustment—*increase in earnings for Year 1 as a result of an error (fully taxable at 45%)*	200,000

The presentation of these items in the income statement and the statement of retained earnings using intraperiod tax allocation and without intraperiod tax allocation is shown at the top of page 870.

Failure to apply intraperiod tax allocation procedures in this case would distort the results from normal operations and also understate net income by $90,000, the tax applicable to the prior period adjustment.

Assuming that the extraordinary gain and the prior period adjustment were previously recorded in the accounts (before recognizing the tax effects), income taxes at the end of Year 4, using intraperiod tax allocation, should be recorded by the Z Company as illustrated in the second table on page 870.

Extraordinary Loss To illustrate a situation involving an extraordinary loss, assume that in Year 5 Z Company reports a pre-tax income of $600,000 and incurs a fully deductible extraordinary loss of $500,000.

	Using intraperiod tax allocation	Without intraperiod tax allocation
Income statement:		
Income before income taxes	$300,000	$ 300,000
Income tax expense	135,000	465,000*
Income (loss) before extraordinary gain . . .	$165,000	$(165,000)
Extraordinary gain:		
Using intraperiod tax allocation, $800,000 −		
($800,000 × 30%)	560,000	
Without intraperiod tax allocation		800,000
Net income	$725,000	$ 635,000
Statement of retained earnings:		
Prior period adjustment—increase in		
beginning balance in retained earnings . .	$110,000	$ 200,000

```
* Income tax expense, $300,000 × 45%   . $135,000
  Tax on capital gain, $800,000 × 30%  . .   240,000
  Tax on prior period adj., $200,000 × 45%    90,000
  Total income tax currently payable  . . .  $465,000
```

```
Income Tax Expense . . . . . . . . . . . . . . . . . . . . . . .   135,000
Extraordinary Gain (Tax Effect) . . . . . . . . . . . . . . .   240,000
Prior Period Adjustment (Tax Effect) . . . . . . . . . . . .    90,000
        Income Taxes Payable . . . . . . . . . . . . . . . . . .            465,000
To record income tax effect on operating income, extra-
ordinary gain, and prior period adjustment (correction of
error).
```

The tax rate is 45%, and the company's income tax is $45,000 (45% of taxable income of $100,000). The comparative summary at the top of page 871 shows how Z Company's income statement would appear using intraperiod tax allocation and without intraperiod tax allocation.

The greater clarity obtained by using intraperiod tax allocation is apparent. This presentation shows the after-tax effect of the extraordinary loss and the normal impact of taxes on operating income. If tax allocation is not used, the reader of the income statement will question the relationship between the operating income of $600,000 and the disproportionately low income tax expense of $45,000. Without tax allocation, the amount of income before extraordinary loss and the amount of the extraordinary loss both would be overstated by $225,000

	Using intraperiod tax allocation	Without intraperiod tax allocation
Income before income taxes (operating income)	$600,000	$600,000
Income tax expense	270,000	45,000
Income before extraordinary loss	$330,000	$555,000
Extraordinary loss:		
Using intraperiod tax allocation: $500,000 − ($500,000 × 45%)	275,000	
Without intraperiod tax allocation		500,000
Net income	$ 55,000	$ 55,000

($500,000 × 45%), the tax effect of the extraordinary loss. Using intraperiod tax allocation, income taxes are recorded as follows:

Income Tax Expense ($600,000 × 45%)	270,000	
Extraordinary Loss (Tax Effect)		225,000
Income Taxes Payable		45,000
To record income tax effect on operating income and extraordinary loss.		

Note that the tax effect is recorded as an offset to the Extraordinary Loss account, which we have assumed was previously recorded in the accounts at $500,000; it would, of course, be possible to record the tax effect in a separate account. In either case, the extraordinary loss should be reported in the income statement net of taxes, that is, $275,000, with appropriate disclosure of the current income tax liability and the tax effect of the loss.

Because extraordinary items and prior period adjustments create certain tax consequences, tax allocation within a period is simply an effort to match income taxes (or tax credits) with these special items. In this way, extraordinary items and prior period adjustments are reported net of taxes—at amounts representing the net *economic impact* of such items.

Other situations requiring income tax allocation within the financial statements for a given period include recognition of the cumulative effect of a change in an accounting principle and reporting gain or loss on disposal of a segment of a business. Treatment of these items is similar to the treatment of extraordinary items and is discussed further in Chapter 23.

Presentation of tax accounts in financial statements

Thus far we have assumed that tax allocation which stems from differences in the timing of revenue and expense results in either a liability, Deferred Income Tax Liability, or an asset, Prepaid Income Taxes. Whether these accounts meet the definition of liabilities and assets is an issue worth considering.

A deferred income tax liability arises when a corporation recognizes income for financial reporting purposes before it is taxed, either because revenue has been reported as earned before it is subject to tax or because expenses not recognized in the accounts have been deducted in computing taxable income. There is, of course, no existing debt to the government for taxes on future earnings which may or may not materialize. However, we have previously defined liabilities to include future outlays that result from current or past events that can be measured with reasonable accuracy. Assuming continuing successful operation of a business, it is reasonable to include in this definition the increased taxes that will follow from having recognized income before it is taxed. Even though the deferred income tax liability may not be paid for many years, the APB stated that "deferred taxes should not be accounted for on a discounted basis."[12]

The classification of prepaid income taxes as an asset rests on the assumption that there will be a future tax benefit to the corporation. At some later time the corporation will realize revenue which will not be subject to tax, or it will have a tax deduction which will not be reported as an accounting expense. The asset represents the amount of tax that has already been paid on income to be reported in the income statement in future periods.

The APB emphasized the "deferred" characteristics of the tax accounts resulting from interperiod tax allocation procedures when it established the following guidelines for presenting such accounts in the balance sheet.

> Deferred charges and deferred credits relating to timing differences represent the cumulative recognition given to their tax effects and as such do not represent receivables or payables in the usual sense. They should be classified in two categories—one for the net current amount and the other for the net noncurrent amount. This presentation is consistent with the customary distinction between current and noncurrent categories and also recognizes the close relationship among the various deferred tax accounts, all of which bear on the determination of income tax expense. The current portions of such deferred charges and credits should be those amounts which relate to assets and liabilities classified as current. Thus, if installment receivables are a current asset, the deferred credits representing the tax effects of uncollected installment sales should be a current item; if an estimated provision

[12] *APB Opinion No. 10,* "Omnibus Opinion—1966," AICPA (New York: 1966), p. 145. This Opinion was issued prior to the adoption of discounting for long-term receivables and payables under *APB Opinion No. 21* (1971). Subsequent reluctance to require discounting for deferred tax items may be explained in part by the difficulty of specifying an appropriate interest rate.

for warranties is a current liability, the deferred charge representing the tax effect of such provision should be a current item.[13]

The Board did not permit the use of the net-of-tax method of reporting deferred tax accounts as elements of valuation of assets or liabilities. Claims for refunds of taxes previously paid or offsets to future taxes arising from the recognition of the tax effects of operating loss carrybacks or carryforwards should be classified either as current or noncurrent, depending on the expected period of realization.

The requirements for reporting income tax accounts in the balance sheet are summarized below:

Current assets:

1 *Prepaid income taxes (related to current liabilities such as estimated warranties outstanding which will be satisfied within one year or the operating cycle of the business)*
2 *Claim for refund of income taxes previously paid*
3 *Potential tax benefit of operating loss carryforward (if current benefits are assured beyond any reasonable doubt)*

Current liabilities:

1 *Deferred income tax liability (related to current assets such as receivables from installment sales or long-term construction in progress)*
2 *Current income tax liability (balance of tax due on income taxable currently)*

Noncurrent assets:

1 *Prepaid income taxes (related to noncurrent liabilities such as long-term warranties outstanding)*
2 *Potential tax benefit of operating loss carryforward (if benefits are assured beyond any reasonable doubt)*

Noncurrent liabilities:

1 *Deferred income tax liability (related to timing differences, such as those caused by use of an accelerated depreciation method for income tax purposes)*

The items listed first under each of the two current categories should be offset and reported as a single amount. Similarly, the items listed first under each of the two noncurrent categories should be offset.

In the income statement or in the accompanying notes, the taxes currently payable, the tax effects of timing differences, and the tax effects of operating losses should be disclosed. These amounts should be allocated to income before extraordinary items and to extraordinary items. The tax benefit of an operating loss carryforward not previously re-

---

[13] *APB Opinion No. 11,* p. 178. The importance of consistency in the classification of installment receivables and any related income tax credits is strongly emphasized in *ASR No. 102,* SEC (Washington: 1965).

corded should be reported as an extraordinary item in the period in which it is realized. In addition, notes to the financial statements should include disclosure of unused operating loss carryforwards (along with expiration dates), reasons for significant variations in the customary relationships between income tax expense and pre-tax accounting income, and any other factors relating to income taxes which users of financial statements would find helpful in evaluating current earnings and in forecasting future earnings of the company.[14]

Allocation to interim periods

Most publicly owned corporations issue earnings reports on a quarterly basis. Determination of income tax expense for such interim periods involves two classes of problems—estimation of appropriate income tax rates and the treatment of losses.

Estimation of appropriate tax rates includes (1) consideration of the effect of rate differentials, permanent differences between accounting and taxable income, expected investment tax credits, and other items; (2) selection of rates to be applied to ordinary income, extraordinary items, etc.; and (3) adjustment of these rates on the basis of legislation enacted during the fiscal year.[15]

For example, assume that Company A is subject to tax at 20% on the first $50,000 of taxable income and at 50% on taxable income over $50,000. Capital expenditures yielding $10,000 in investment tax credits are planned for the current year. Ordinary income before taxes for the first quarter was $20,000 and at the time the income statement for the first quarter was being prepared, ordinary income before taxes for the entire year was expected to be $100,000. There were no extraordinary items or timing differences. Income tax expense for the first quarter would be computed as shown at the top of page 875.

For subsequent quarters the year-to-date tax expense is computed using a current estimate of the effective tax rate. The tax for the quarter is the difference between the new year-to-date tax and the tax previously recognized up to the beginning of the quarter. If Company A had pre-tax ordinary income of $30,000 for the second quarter and now expected ordinary income for the year of $110,000 instead of $100,000 and

---

[14] For companies subject to its jurisdiction, the Securities and Exchange Commission provides more detailed disclosure rules. Additional SEC requirements include (1) breakdown of income tax expense into its U.S., foreign, and other components; (2) disclosure of amounts, if any, by which cash outlays for income taxes are expected to exceed reported income tax expense for any of the next three years; (3) reconciliation of any difference between reported total income tax expense and the expense that would result by applying the normal income tax rate to income before tax; and (4) the net timing difference due to deferral of investment tax credits.

[15] *FASB Interpretation No. 18,* "Accounting for Income Taxes in Interim Periods," FASB (Stamford: 1977), pp. 4–5; *APB Opinion No. 28,* "Interim Financial Reporting," AICPA (New York: 1973), pp. 527–528.

Estimated income tax expense for the year:

($50,000 × 20%) + ($50,000 × 50%) $35,000

Less: Anticipated investment tax credits 10,000

Net estimated income tax expense for the year $25,000

Estimated effective income tax rate for the year:

$25,000 ÷ $100,000 = 25%

Income tax expense for the first quarter ($20,000 × 25%) . . . . $ 5,000

investment tax credits of $9,200 instead of $10,000, the income tax expense for the second quarter would be:

Estimated income tax expense for the year:

($50,000 × 20%) + ($60,000 × 50%) $40,000

Less: Anticipated investment tax credits 9,200

Net estimated income tax expense for the year $30,800

Estimated effective income tax rate for the year:

$30,800 ÷ $110,000 = 28%

Income tax expense for the second quarter:

Year-to-date ordinary income, before income taxes $50,000

Estimated effective income tax rate . . . . × 28%

Year-to-date income tax expense $14,000

Less: Income tax expense accrued for first quarter 5,000

Income tax expense for the second quarter . . . . $ 9,000

Extraordinary items and other items not included in ordinary income are treated as marginal items for purposes of interim income tax allocation. Income tax expense is computed both with and without the extraordinary item and the difference is the tax applicable to the extraordinary item. In considering tax rate changes within a year, the effects on previous periods of new tax legislation should be reflected in the first interim period ending after the new legislation becomes effective; previously issued interim financial reports should not be restated to reflect the new legislation.[16]

Treatment of situations involving losses in interim periods is similar to the treatment of net operating loss carrybacks and carryforwards in annual reporting. A circumstance unique to interim reporting, however, is when seasonal earnings patterns establish the value of a loss carryforward beyond a reasonable doubt. When a seasonal loss is carried forward to a subsequent interim period within the same year, the tax

[16] *FASB Interpretation No. 18*, p. 10.

benefits are *not* treated as extraordinary items as is the case in annual financial statements.

Evaluation of income tax allocation

We have seen that differences between accounting and taxable income arise from several sources. No allocation problem arises from permanent differences between accounting and taxable income. The allocation of income taxes to extraordinary items and to prior period adjustments, and also the recognition of the income tax benefits of operating loss carrybacks as extraordinary gains, are almost universally accepted. Few accountants question the desirability of recognizing the income tax effect of operating loss carryforwards when the tax benefits are virtually certain. Therefore, the controversy over income tax allocation centers on interperiod tax allocation when there are differences in the timing of revenue and expenses.

Arguments in Favor of Interperiod Tax Allocation   The two major arguments in favor of interperiod tax allocation may be stated as follows:

1 The earning of income is the basic cause of an income tax levy. The tax expense to be applied in measuring periodic income is the tax caused by each period's earnings, independent of the time of payment. Failure to match income taxes against income as it is included in the income statement causes misleading fluctuations in net income.

2 Timing differences are temporary and create liabilities or assets. A tax saving attributable to a timing difference is only a postponement of tax and a highly probable future cash outlay based on a past event is created. Similarly, a tax payment based on income that will be recognized in the accounting records at some later date makes it highly probable that the corporation will earn tax-free income in future years, creating an expected future economic benefit. Consequently, these highly probable future outlays and benefits qualify as liabilities and assets within the accepted meanings of these terms. For these future outlays and benefits to be highly probable, it must be assumed that tax rates will remain at similar levels in the foreseeable future and that the company will earn taxable income in most future years. Experience in past years has tended to support the assumption as to tax rates; the assumption as to profitable continuity has proved applicable to most major corporations, especially with liberal loss carryback and carryforward provisions in the income tax law.

Arguments against Interperiod Tax Allocation   Opposition to tax allocation is based primarily on two points: (1) the nature of income taxes, and (2) the possibility that timing differences may not be temporary. These arguments are summarized below:

1 Income taxes by their nature differ from most expenses. First, income tax expense emerges only if income is earned; secondly, income tax expense is based on taxable income which differs from accounting income in a number of respects. This line of reasoning leads to the conclusion that income taxes are not an expense but an involuntary distribution because taxes are determined only after income emerges. Finally, opponents of tax allocation point

out that the amount of income taxes properly associated with the operations of any period should be the legal tax liability for that period because income taxes are based on the legal concept of taxable income rather than accounting income.

2 When we view the taxable income of a corporation as a whole, the shifting of income taxes in time (particularly the postponement of taxes) tends to be a permanent rather than a temporary shift, because when one deferral is reversed another arises to take its place. This argument is raised most frequently with respect to one area of tax timing differences—the case in which a corporation adopts accelerated depreciation methods for income tax purposes, but not in its accounts. For example, a stable company purchasing about the same amount of depreciable assets each year will realize a tax postponement in the year that accelerated depreciation is adopted and this postponement is never offset in future years as long as the company continues to replace its depreciable assets at a steady rate. If a company acquires a larger amount of depreciable assets each year, the total difference between tax depreciation and depreciation recorded in the accounts would continue to increase.

Neither position against interperiod tax allocation is without significant logical flaws. Consider the following: Companies A and B acquire identical plant assets. Both use straight-line depreciation and equal economic lives for financial reporting purposes, but Company A uses accelerated depreciation and Company B uses straight-line depreciation for income tax purposes. Barring unusual circumstances, Company A is clearly "better off" than Company B. Company B owes less tax *now,* and will enjoy interest-free use of the funds arising from this tax saving until the timing differences reverse. This advantage exists regardless of whether or not the assets are replaced or whether the total investment in plant assets increases. Yet present tax allocation requirements produce identical net incomes for both companies and Company A's relative economic gain is ignored.

However, this problem would not be resolved by failure to allocate income taxes. Nonallocation would show the entire deferral as a net income advantage to Company A. But in future years Company B will be able to deduct more than Company A from its taxable income with respect to these assets. To the extent that these future deductions have economic value, Company B is "better off" than Company A, yet this relative advantage would be ignored if there were no tax allocation.

There is no easy solution. Clearly in this tax deferral example, Company A has gained an advantage of using "tax dollars" without paying interest. A reasonable measure of Company A's economic gain would at first seem to be the difference between the gross tax deferral and its discounted value. This would be consistent with viewing the tax deferral as a long-term liability. But if the tax deferral is a liability, it is indeed a most unusual one. The "liability" would be repaid only if future taxable income is earned; it may be renewed indefinitely through the acquisition of more depreciable assets, or it may increase or decrease as Congress chooses to change income tax rates. As a result, both the estimate of the amount to be paid eventually and the selection of an appropriate interest rate for discounting this type of liability might be viewed as highly speculative and lacking in objectivity.

From a standpoint of traditional stewardship reporting, whereby net income is viewed as the critical measure of management performance, discounting the deferred tax items might achieve greater "fairness" than do present tax allocation procedures. However, from a standpoint of stock market evaluation of earnings potential, there is increasing evidence that the crucial elements are the *timeliness* and *completeness* of financial statement disclosures. Thus the present tax allocation procedures may represent the best practical solution from the standpoint of investors. Such procedures appear to be simpler and more objective than discounting and are less likely to create misleading fluctuations in net income than either partial allocation or nonallocation.

REVIEW QUESTIONS

1 What are the objectives of generally accepted accounting principles in their application to the income statement? What are the objectives of income tax laws?

2 Define *interperiod tax allocation, tax allocation within a period,* and *interim-period tax allocation.*

3 What fundamental assumptions are necessary in the implementation of income tax allocation?

4 What are three basic sources of differences between accounting income and taxable income?

5 Describe two situations which result, under tax allocation procedures, in a deferred income tax liability.

6 Describe two situations which result, under tax allocation procedures, in prepaid income taxes.

7 Explain the following interperiod tax allocation approaches:
   a Deferred method
   b Liability method
   c Net-of-tax method

8 What is meant by an *operating loss carryback* and an *operating loss carryforward?*

9 Explain the different accounting problems that arise in accounting for an operating loss carryback and an operating loss carryforward.

10 Describe three situations which produce a permanent difference between taxable income and pre-tax accounting income. Give an example of each.

11 Explain how each of the following accounts should be classified (for example, current assets or current liability) in the balance sheet:
   a Deferred Income Tax Liability

    b Prepaid Income Taxes
    c Receivable—Refund of Income Taxes Previously Paid
    d Potential Tax Benefit of Operating Loss Carryforward (debit balance, if recorded)

12 What kind of information regarding income taxes should be included in notes accompanying the financial statements?

13 Identify and briefly explain some of the problems involved in determining income tax expense for interim periods.

14 Briefly summarize the arguments for and against interperiod tax allocation.

EXERCISES

Ex. 21-1 In Year 5, Haley Corporation reported $200,000 of income before income taxes in its income statement but only $30,000 on its tax return. In Year 6, income before income taxes was $300,000 and taxable income was $400,000.
    Prepare the entry to record income tax expense and income taxes payable for Year 6, assuming that timing differences were responsible for the disparity between accounting income and taxable income. Assume a 45% corporate tax rate.

Ex. 21-2 Burt Company reported taxable income of $300,000 in Year 1 and $400,000 in Year 2. Income before income taxes was $200,000 in Year 1 and $500,000 in Year 2. The differences between taxable income and the income before income taxes resulted from the inclusion of $100,000 of income on the tax return for Year 1 which was not considered realized for accounting purposes until Year 2.
    Assuming that the corporate income tax rate is 45%, prepare the lower section of the income statement for Year 1 and Year 2, (1) using tax allocation and (2) without tax allocation.

Ex. 21-3 The accounting income and taxable income for Charles T. Andrews, Inc., for a three-year period were as follows:

Year	Accounting income before income taxes	Taxable income
1	$70,000	$60,000
2	70,000	70,000
3	70,000	80,000

The differences between accounting and taxable income were due solely to the use of sum-of-the-years'-digits depreciation for tax purposes and straight-line depreciation for accounting purposes on a special-purpose machine costing $70,000 and having a $10,000 residual value at the end of its three-year economic life. Tax rates are 20% on the first $50,000 and 50% on income in excess of $50,000.
    Prepare the journal entries required for each year to allocate income taxes resulting from timing differences in accounting for depreciation expense.

Ex. 21-4 The accounting and taxable income for Ossman Corporation over a three-year period are presented at the top of page 880.

Year	Accounting income before income taxes	Taxable income
1	$100,000	$134,000
2	100,000	98,000
3	100,000	98,000

The differences between accounting income and taxable income are explained as follows:
(1) Taxable income in Year 1 includes $36,000 of rental revenue which for financial reporting purposes was recorded as earned at the rate of $12,000 per year.
(2) Amortization of goodwill at the rate of $10,000 per year is recorded for financial reporting purposes but is not deductible in arriving at taxable income. Amortization of goodwill does not give rise to a timing difference for income tax allocation purposes.
 Prepare the journal entries required for each year to allocate income taxes. Assume that income taxes are 50% of taxable income.

Ex. 21-5 Income statements for El Paso Corporation show the following results for the first three years of its operations:

Year 1: Operating loss (before income taxes) . . . . $(100,000)
Year 2: Operating income (before income taxes) 240,000
Year 3: Operating loss (before income taxes) . . . . (200,000)

The company operates in a cyclical and highly competitive industry.
 Prepare the journal entries for each year to recognize the tax effects of operating loss carryforwards or carrybacks. Assume that operating losses as reported are fully allowed for income tax purposes and that the income tax rate is 45%.

Ex. 21-6 Kam Company reported income before income taxes of $600,000 and a fully deductible extraordinary loss of $450,000 for Year 1. Prepare a journal entry to record the tax effect on the pre-tax income and on the extraordinary loss. Show how the foregoing information should be presented in the income statement. Assume that corporate taxes are levied at the rate of 45% and that the tax effect of the extraordinary loss is credited directly to the loss account.

Ex. 21-7 Gear Corporation reported income before income taxes of $300,000 and a capital gain of $1.2 million. Prepare a journal entry to record the tax effect on the pre-tax income and on the extraordinary gain. (Record the tax effect on the extraordinary gain as a debit to the gain account.) Show how the foregoing information should be presented in the income statement. Assume that the tax rate is 45% on income before income taxes and 30% on the extraordinary gain.

Ex. 21-8 Prepare a schedule showing the computation of (a) the actual income tax liability and (b) income tax expense for Years 1, 2, and 3. Assume that the accounting income (before income taxes) computed after all adjustments and corrections was $280,000 for Year 1, $212,000 for Year 2, and $252,000 for Year 3. The income tax rate was 40% in each of the three years. Assume that depreciation expense, rent revenue, and interest revenue have been included in accounting income and taxable income for Year 1 through Year 3, as follows:

	Accounting income before income taxes	Taxable income
Depreciation expense:		
Year 1	$50,000	$70,000
Year 2	54,000	71,000
Year 3	58,000	68,000
Rent revenue:		
Year 1	9,000	9,500
Year 2	9,000	8,500
Interest revenue (tax-free municipal bonds):		
Year 1	8,000	–0–
Year 2	4,000	–0–
Year 3	3,800	–0–

Ex. 21-9 Baur Corporation issues financial statements on a quarterly basis. During Year 1, its actual quarterly results and its expectations were as follows:

	Taxable income		Expected for year	
	Quarter	Year to date	Taxable income	Investment tax credit
End of 1st quarter	$20,000	$ 20,000	$ 80,000	$5,000
End of 2d quarter	10,000	30,000	60,000	3,000
End of 3d quarter	40,000	70,000	90,000	6,600
End of year	30,000	100,000	100,000	6,000

Assuming that the corporate tax rate is 20% on the first $50,000 of taxable income and 50% thereafter, compute the **(a)** estimated income tax rate for each quarter, **(b)** year-to-date income tax expense as of the end of each quarter, and **(c)** income tax expense for each quarter.

SHORT CASES FOR ANALYSIS AND DECISION

Case 21-1 A partial income statement and related note for Regency Company is given below:

Income before provision in lieu of federal income tax	$7,277,326
Provision in lieu of federal income tax (**Note 3**)	3,490,000
Income before extraordinary gain	$3,787,326
Gain arising from utilization of operating loss carryforward (**Note 3**)	3,490,000
Net income	$7,277,326

Note 3—*Federal income tax:*
No federal income tax is payable with respect to results of operations because of available operating loss carryforward from prior years. However, in the income statement, a provision in lieu of the federal income tax that would have been required in the absence of the operating loss carryforward has been charged to income before extraordinary gain and the gain arising from utilization of the net operating loss carryforward has been reflected as an extraordinary item.

Instructions

a Give a supporting argument in favor of the procedure used to account for the tax effect of the operating loss carryforward.

b Prepare the journal entry that was required to reflect the tax effect of the operating loss carryforward. Use the account titles as they appear in the income statement for Regency Company.

c Assuming that Regency Company had recognized the full potential tax benefit of the operating loss in prior years, how would the income statement differ for the latest period?

Case 21-2 Levell Construction Company was organized early in Year 1 after Edson Levell was awarded a contract to build a major section of a highway in Alaska. The completion of the contract will take four years, and the company does not plan to bid on additional contracts. All costs incurred by the company will be directly chargeable to the highway contract; in other words, the company will not record any selling and general expenses.

The pre-tax net profit on the contract is estimated at $200,000. Under the percentage-of-completion method of accounting, $50,000 of the net profit would be recognized in each of the four years. Income taxes of $10,500 ($50,000 × 21% = $10,500) would be paid on March 15 of each year starting in Year 2 if the percentage-of-completion method were adopted for income tax purposes. If the completed-contract method were adopted for income tax purposes, a tax of $82,500 ($200,000 × 48% − $13,500 − $82,500) would be paid on March 15, Year 5.

Instructions

a Assuming that the company considers 8% a fair rate of return after income taxes, prepare a schedule showing whether the company should use the completed-contract or the percentage-of-completion method of accounting for tax purposes. Compute the net advantage of the method you recommend, in terms of dollar savings, at March 15, Year 5. The amount of an ordinary annuity of four rents of $1 invested at 8% is $4.5061.

b Assuming that the company had a large amount of income each year from other sources and that the profit on the long-term contract is taxed at the marginal rate of 48%, what method of accounting would you recommend for tax purposes? What would be the net advantage at March 15, Year 5, if money is worth 8%?

Case 21-3 Mono Metals Company received $50,000 in Year 10 as a rental advance on one of its mining properties. Under income tax law the advance is subject to federal income tax in Year 10, although the company did not report the advance as revenue in its accounting records until Year 11.

In Year 10, the company reported taxable income of $250,000, paying income taxes of $106,500 (21% on the first $50,000 of taxable income and 48% on the $200,000 remainder). The controller reported $200,000 as the company's operating income for Year 10 and showed the amount of income taxes applicable to the rental advance (48% of $50,000) as an asset under the heading "prepaid income taxes."

In Year 11, the company suffered a decline in income as a result of severe declines in world metal prices, and its operations resulted in an operating income of only $50,000, including revenue from the rental advance received in Year 10. When the controller of the company presented the company's Year 11 income statement to the president, the latter commented, "I thought you said the effect of income tax allocation was to show in each year a tax expense that bore a normal relation to reported operating income. You report operating income of $50,000 and show income taxes at $24,000. If we had taxable income of only $50,000 we would pay only $10,500 in taxes. I realize we broke even for tax purposes this year and won't actually pay any tax, but I think your tax allocation procedures are off someplace."

Instructions

a Prepare a partial comparative income statement for Year 10 and Year 11, starting with operating income and following the controller's approach.

b What is the issue implicit in the president's question? How would you reply if you were the controller?

PROBLEMS

Group A

21A-1 Chatfield Corporation has income before income taxes of $200,000 for the current year and is subject to income taxes of 45%. The following items are treated in one way in arriving at the $200,000 income before income taxes but are treated differently in computing taxable income.

(1) The company recorded $35,000 in product warranty expense; for income tax purposes only $22,000 of warranty expense actually incurred is deductible. The warranty liability account is classified as current.

(2) $40,000 in construction profit has been included in accounting income on a percentage-of-completion basis. Only one-fourth of this amount is taxable in the current year; the balance will be taxed next year when the remaining contracts are completed.

(3) A lease deposit of $20,000 was received and credited to a long-term liability account. It is subject to tax in the current year but will not be earned until the fifth year of the lease.

(4) The company has recorded $65,000 depreciation expense in its accounts using the straight-line method. Accelerated depreciation of $75,000 is allowable for income tax purposes.

Instructions

a Compute the income tax expense to be shown on the company's income statement and the amount of income tax currently payable.

b Prepare a journal entry to record the company's income tax expense and related liabilities and prepayments. Separate the deferred income tax items into current and noncurrent components.

c Prepare a partial income statement for the current year beginning with income before income taxes.

d Indicate the amount and classification of any income tax items in the balance sheet at the end of the current year. Deferred charges and credits should be classified in two categories—one for the **net** current amount and the other for the **net** noncurrent amount.

21A-2 Fast Freight, Inc., began business in Year 1. Anticipating a growth in traffic, the company has developed plans for the purchase of trucks over the next six years. The controller of the company is studying the question of depreciation policies, and feels that the sum-of-the-years'-digits method should be used for income tax purposes but that the straight-line method is preferable for financial reporting purposes. The controller has prepared the data at the top of page 884, using a five-year economic life for the trucks.

	Year 1	Year 2	Year 3	Year 4	Year 5	Year 6
Cost of new trucks acquired	$100,000	$220,000	$300,000	$ 50,000	$ 10,000	$ 25,000
Residual value	10,000	25,000	30,000	5,000	1,000	2,500
Sum-of-the-years'-digits depreciation	30,000	89,000	160,000	138,000	101,000	67,900
Straight-line depreciation	18,000	57,000	111,000	120,000	121,800	108,300
Excess of tax depreciation over depreciation recorded in the accounts	12,000	32,000	49,000	18,000	(20,800)	(40,400)

Instructions

a Verify the $49,000 excess of tax depreciation over recorded depreciation for Year 3 in the schedule above. Assume that a full year's depreciation is taken in the year of acquisition.

b Determine the balance that would appear in the Deferred Income Tax Liability account at the close of the sixth year if an income tax rate of 45% is applicable. State how this amount would be classified in the balance sheet.

c Assuming that the company's accounting records show pre-tax income of $150,000 in Year 1 and $190,000 in Year 6, prepare partial income statements (starting with income before income taxes) for these two years. In the statements or notes you are to show the tax currently payable, the tax effects of timing differences, and the reason for the timing differences.

d Compare the net incomes for Years 1 and 6 as calculated above with the net incomes that would result if income tax allocation procedures were not followed.

21A-3 Jim's Camera Shop, Inc., operated at a modest profit for its first five years, but in Year 6 a chain of discount camera stores opened a large outlet in a nearby shopping center. Primarily as a result of this new competition, Jim's Camera Shop sustained a loss before income taxes of $50,000 for Year 6. Only $40,000 of this operating loss can be carried back to the three preceding years; $10,000 can be carried forward to Year 7.

The president of Jim's Camera Shop expressed optimism concerning the company's future prospects, stating that more aggressive marketing policies, along with increasing population in the trading area, would bring a return to profitable operations within the next two years. In Year 7, the company reported an income before income taxes of $16,000.

Instructions

a Prepare a journal entry to record the effects of income taxes for Year 6. Assume that the rules for recognition (or nonrecognition) of the benefits of a net operating loss carryforward are strictly observed and that the rate of income tax for all years is 25%.

b Prepare a journal entry to record income tax expense and the tax benefit of the operating loss carryforward in Year 7.

c Prepare a partial comparative income statement for Years 6 and 7.

21A-4 The following comparative income statement was presented to Gene O'Connor, president of O'Connor Corporation, covering operations for a two-year period:

	This year	*Last year*
Net sales	$1,090,000	$1,000,000
Cost of goods sold	690,000	630,000
Gross profit on sales	$ 400,000	$ 370,000
Operating expenses	250,000	280,000
Income before income taxes (operating income)	$ 150,000	$ 90,000
Income tax expense	90,600	10,500
Net income	$ 59,400	$ 79,500

After examining the statement, Gene O'Connor frowned, "When I send this statement to my father, who owns 30% of the common stock, he will never understand why net income fell in the face of a substantial increase in operating income."

"There are two reasons," commented the controller. "You will remember that last year we took a $40,000 fully deductible earthquake loss on the East Bend warehouse, and this year we had a capital gain of $107,000 (taxed at 30%) when we sold our Global Company stock, our only investment, and used the proceeds to built a new warehouse. Both these transactions were reported in the statement of retained earnings."

"I'll have trouble getting that across to my father," Gene O'Connor replied. "He knows we're subject to federal tax of 48% on all income over $50,000 and 21% on the first $50,000. A ninefold increase in income taxes in the income statement is going to be confusing. Can't you revise the income statement so that the reasons for these odd tax figures will be apparent?"

Instructions Prepare a revised comparative income statement that will, in your opinion, meet the objections raised by Gene O'Connor. Assume that both the loss and the gain are extraordinary items.

21A-5 Lindvall Manufacturing Company presents you with the following information for the year ended December 31, Year 10:

Sales	$2,500,000
Cost of goods sold	1,500,000*
Operating expenses	410,000
Uninsured loss caused by first flood in 80 years, fully deductible for income tax purposes	200,000
Taxable prior period adjustment (material error)—income applicable to Year 9	150,000
Income tax expense for Year 10	?

* Includes depreciation of $100,000 on a straight-line basis; however, depreciation for income tax purposes was $140,000.

A corporate income tax rate of 45% is applicable on all items above.

Instructions
a Compute the amount of income taxes currently payable by Lindvall Manufacturing Company as a result of activities in Year 10.
b Prepare a compound journal entry to record income taxes for Year 10 (including allocation of taxes among operating income, the extraordinary items, and the prior period adjustment). Assume that the Flood Loss account shows a pre-tax debit balance of $200,000 and that the Prior Period Adjustment account shows a pre-tax credit balance of $150,000.

c Prepare an income statement and a separate statement of retained earnings for Year 10. The balance in retained earnings at the beginning of Year 10 was $1,221,000. Dividends amounting to $125,500 were declared during Year 10.

21A-6 In Year 5, Star Sulfur Co. had sales of $800,000 and income of $300,000 before income taxes. Straight-line depreciation expense of $80,000 was recorded in the accounts but accelerated depreciation for income tax purposes amounted to $124,000. Cost-based depletion of $100,000 was deducted in arriving at operating income but a deduction for depletion equal to 22% of sales was allowed on the income tax return.

Income before income taxes did not include a gain of $440,000 from the sale of land on the installment basis, which was reported properly as an extraordinary item. The gain from the sale of the land was reported as an extraordinary item because it resulted from sale of the only surplus parcel of land the company owned and because it was held for more than 30 years. Only one-fourth of the sales price was collected during the year, therefore only $110,000 of the gain was taxable at 30% in Year 5.

Ordinary income was taxed at 21% of the first $50,000 and 48% of the balance. An operating loss of $50,000 and a capital loss of $8,000 were carried forward from Year 4 and are available to reduce the income tax liability for Year 5; the capital loss is to be offset against the gain from the sale of land in Year 5.

Instructions

a Prepare a compound journal entry to record income taxes for Year 5. An asset has not been established for the loss carryforwards. Deferred taxes are recognized for the timing differences between accounting income and taxable income.

b Prepare an income statement for Year 5.

c Show how the deferred income tax liability will appear in the balance sheet at the end of Year 5. Assume that at the beginning of the year the Deferred Income Tax Liability—Noncurrent account showed a balance of $220,000 (there was no current balance) and that one-fourth of the selling price of the land will be collected in Year 6.

Group B

21B-1 Johnson-Yamashita, Inc., pays income taxes at 55% of taxable income and has made estimated income tax payments of $400,000 during the current year. No exact computation of taxable income has been made, but the accounting income before income taxes is correctly stated at $800,000. The following items require consideration in reconciling the accounting income before income taxes with taxable income:

(1) The company acquired another business in a prior year and recorded $80,000 goodwill; this is being amortized over the maximum allowable period of 40 years.

(2) Gross profit on installment sales has been recognized in the amount of $200,000 in the accounts; for income tax purposes only $150,000 gross profit will be recorded in the current year. All installment receivables are current.

(3) Pension expense accrued during the current year amounted to $40,000; only the $30,000 cash deposited with the pension trust is currently deductible. The related pension plan liability will be settled by a payment in the next year.

(4) Interest expense for the year of $120,000 includes the effect of $1,800 amortization of bond premium. The company does not amortize bond premium for income tax purposes.

(5) Straight-line depreciation for the year of $200,000 has been recorded in the

accounts; for income tax purposes $220,000 in declining-balance depreciation will be deducted.

Instructions
a Compute the additional income tax to be paid for the current year.
b Prepare a journal entry to record the remaining income tax expense for the year, assuming that the estimated tax payments were debited to the Income Tax Expense account during the year. Separate the deferred income tax items into appropriate current and noncurrent accounts.
c Prepare a partial income statement for the current year. Start with the $800,000 income before income taxes.
d Show the balance sheet presentation of all income tax items at the end of the current year. Show deferred charges and credits as one **net** current amount and another **net** noncurrent amount.

21B-2 Lockett & Co., a newly established department store, plans to use the installment method of recognizing gross profit on installment sales for income tax purposes. Under this method, the expected 40% gross profit on sales will be recognized only as cash payments are received; this serves to postpone until future periods taxable income equal to 40% of the year-end balance in installment accounts receivable. Because collection of the full sales price is reasonably assured, Lockett recognizes in its financial statements the entire gross profit at the time sales are made. The following information has been developed as a part of the company's income-planning activities:

	Year 1	Year 2	Year 3	Year 4	Year 5
Expected installment sales .	$1,000,000	$1,500,000	$1,800,000	$2,000,000	$2,000,000
Expected installment receivables at year-end . . .	200,000	400,000	500,000	550,000	525,000
Gross profit to be recognized:					
In the accounting records	400,000	600,000	720,000	800,000	800,000
In the income tax return	320,000	520,000	680,000	?	?

Instructions
a Compute the two missing items in the schedule above.
b Compute the balances that should appear in the Deferred Income Tax Liability account at the end of each of the five years, assuming an income tax rate of 50%. State how these balances will be classified in the balance sheet; remember the defined relationship between current assets and the operating cycle.
c Assume that the company's projections show income before taxes of $220,000 in Year 1 and $350,000 in Year 5. Prepare partial income statements for these two years (as if the projected events had actually occurred), showing in the statements or accompanying notes the provision for current income taxes and the provision for deferred income taxes.
d Assume that, at the beginning of Year 6, Lockett decided to stop selling on an installment basis, and that by the end of the year all installment receivables had been collected. If income before income taxes for Year 6 is assumed to be $360,000, prepare a journal entry to record Lockett's income taxes for Year 6.

21B-3 Roy Anderson is president and sole shareholder of The Prancing Pony, a successful restaurant and cocktail lounge. During Year 8, confident in the competence and integrity of the assistant manager, Anderson left for a six-month archaeological expedition. Upon returning he found that the assistant had been stealing from the business to cover gambling debts and that the quality (and patronage) of the restaurant had suffered seriously; as a result operations in Year 8 yielded a loss before income taxes of $200,000. On the basis of prior success, Anderson was confident that under his personal direction the restaurant could promptly be restored to profitability.

Instructions

a Prepare a journal entry to record the effects of income taxes for Year 8. Assume that (1) of the $200,000 operating loss for Year 8, only $140,000 may be carried back to preceding years; (2) no recognition is given to the potential tax benefit of the $60,000 loss carryforward in the financial statements for Year 8; and (3) the income tax rate is 40% for all years involved.

b Prepare partial comparative income statements for Year 8 and Year 9, assuming that income before income taxes was $80,000 in Year 9.

c Using the above assumptions, **except** that you are to assume that the potential tax benefit of the $60,000 loss carryforward was recognized in the financial statements for Year 8, prepare a partial comparative income statement for Year 8 and Year 9.

21B-4 Alice Paul, the controller of Continuous Casting Corporation, has summarized the following data with respect to the company's operations for Year 3:

Sales	$1,400,000
Extraordinary gain resulting from a successful antitrust suit for treble damages (taxable at ordinary income tax rates)	100,000
Cost of products sold	1,000,000
Operating expenses, including $5,000 amortization of goodwill	285,000
Correction of error resulting from double-counting items in inventory at the end of Year 2	30,000

Because Paul is busy with problems arising in connection with a newly installed computer system she has asked you, an independent consultant, to assist her in preparing the income statement for Year 3.

Instructions

a Compute the income tax for Year 3 applicable to current operations, to the extraordinary gain, and to the prior period adjustment. The corporate income tax rate for Year 3 is 48% and for Year 2 it was 40%.

b Prepare an income statement for Year 3.

c Prepare a statement of retained earnings for Year 3. The balance reported at the end of Year 2 (without correction for the error in inventories) was $418,000, and cash dividends of $25,000 were declared in Year 3.

21B-5 Daryl Jamison, the controller of Austin Company handed an assistant a sheet of paper on which appeared the information shown below, saying, "Here's the story on our accounting and taxable income for the current year; I'd like you to put these figures together into an income statement and a separate statement of retained earnings."

AUSTIN COMPANY
Computation of Accounting Income
For Current Year

	Debit	Credit
Sales (net)		$869,000
Interest revenue on municipal bonds (nontaxable)		10,000
Prior period adjustment—refund of income taxes as a result of error discovered by Internal Revenue agents		30,000
Cost of goods sold	$519,000	
Operating expenses	128,000	
Earthquake loss (not covered by insurance), before tax effect .	142,000	
Gain on early extinguishment of debt, before tax effect		90,000
Subtotal	$789,000	$999,000
Prior period adjustment	30,000	
Income taxes payable for year (see below)	46,000	
Net income	134,000	
Totals	$999,000	$999,000

AUSTIN COMPANY
Computation of Income Tax Liability
For Current Year

Sales (net)		$869,000
Gain on early extinguishment of debt (fully taxable)		90,000
Total revenue items		$959,000
Less: Cost of goods sold	$519,000	
Operating expenses	128,000	
Earthquake loss (fully deductible)	142,000	
Excess of accelerated depreciation over straight-line depreciation used for financial reporting purposes . . .	55,000	844,000
Taxable income		$115,000
Income tax rate		40%
Income taxes payable for current year		$ 46,000

The amount of income taxes payable for the current year has been computed correctly.

Instructions

a Prepare a journal entry to record income tax expense, deferred income tax liability, and intraperiod allocation of taxes. Assume that the earthquake loss and the gain on early extinguishment of debt qualify as extraordinary items for financial reporting purposes.

b On the basis of this information, and assuming income tax rates of 40% on ordinary income, prepare in suitable form for publication an income statement and a separate statement of retained earnings for the current year. Austin Company reported a balance in retained earnings at the close of the prior year of $1,917,200 and declared dividends of $75,000 during the current year.

21B-6 Nancy Morris, controller of Pacific Exports, Inc., was injured in a plane crash shortly after the end of Year 5. In her absence, the general ledger bookkeeper has prepared the following income statement for use in connection with the year-end audit:

PACIFIC EXPORTS, INC.
Income Statement
For Year 5

Sales	$2,000,000
Rental revenue (an additional $5,000 advance rental was received and is tax-	
able in Year 5 but will not be earned until Year 6)	45,000
Interest revenue (including $6,000 tax-free municipal bond interest)	14,000
Total revenue	$2,059,000
Cost of goods sold	$1,400,000
Operating expenses (including straight-line depreciation of $45,000; acceler-	
ated depreciation for income tax purposes is $60,000)	500,000
Loss on seizure of shipment of goods by foreign terrorists (fully deductible	
for income tax purposes)	250,000
Additional expense recognized this year attributable to errors in calculating	
depreciation in Years 3 and 4	49,000
Total expenses	$2,199,000
Loss before income taxes	$ (140,000)

The corporate income tax rate in effect for Years 1 through 5 is 40%; income before income taxes has amounted to more than $200,000 each year in Years 2, 3, and 4.

Instructions
a Compute all essential income tax amounts in connection with the income statement shown above.
b Prepare the journal entry to record income taxes at the end of Year 5. Assume that the operating loss for Year 5 is carried back to Year 2, and that amended returns are filed for Years 3 and 4.
c Prepare a combined statement of income and retained earnings for Years 5. The retained earnings balance as previously reported at the end of Year 4 was $843,000; cash dividends of $10,000 were declared during Year 5.

CHAPTER 22

ACCOUNTING AND INFLATION

One of the primary purposes of financial statements is to provide information for decision making. Decision makers such as investors, creditors, and management realize that financial statements prepared using "generally accepted accounting principles" may not reflect current economic realities. As a result, it has been suggested that financial statements would be more useful if historical costs were adjusted for the changing value of the dollar, or if historical costs were abandoned entirely and replaced with current fair values or replacement costs.

In this chapter we describe some conceptual issues which would be faced by accountants and users of financial statements if changes in the general price level or changes in the fair value of assets were incorporated into the accounting model. The final section of this chapter includes a discussion of SEC *Accounting Series Release No. 190,* which requires disclosure of *replacement cost* information by certain corporations filing financial statements with the Securities and Exchange Commission.

FINANCIAL STATEMENTS RESTATED FOR CHANGES IN THE GENERAL PRICE LEVEL

Needed: A stable unit of value

We have seen in preceding chapters that money is the common denominator used in the preparation of financial statements. The dollar, or any other monetary unit, represents a unit of value; it measures the amount of purchasing power available to obtain goods and services through exchange transactions. Implicit in the use of money as a measuring unit is the assumption that the dollar is a stable unit of value, just as the mile is a stable unit of distance and an acre is a stable unit of area. But unlike the mile and the acre, the dollar is not a stable measuring unit.

For many years the prices of goods and services in our economy have been rising. When the general price level rises the value of money decreases. The **general price level** is the weighted average of the prices of goods and services within the economy and is measured by an **index** with a base year assigned a value of 100. The reciprocal of the general price-level index represents the **purchasing power** of the dollar. Thus, if Year 1 = 100 and Year 5 = 125, the current purchasing power of the dollar amounts to only 80% (100 ÷ 125) of the base-year dollar; in other words, prices have risen 25% and purchasing power has decreased by 20%. The most common measurements of the general price level are: **Consumer Price Index, Wholesale Price Index,** and **Gross National Product Implicit Price Deflator.** The GNP Implicit Price Deflator is perhaps the most comprehensive index and is widely recognized as the best measure of the general price level in the United States economy. Prices as measured by the GNP Implicit Price Deflator increased more than 100% during the period 1958–1977, and nearly 45% during the five-year period 1972–1977.

Despite the steady erosion in the purchasing power of the dollar in the United States for more than 40 years, accountants generally have continued to assume that the value of the dollar is stable. Income tax laws also ignore changes in the purchasing power of the dollar. This unrealistic assumption is one of the reasons why traditional financial statements are sometimes considered by users to be potentially misleading. Consequently, proposals have been made to restate historical-cost financial statements to current dollars by using an appropriate general price-level index.

Historical costs versus current fair value

Even if historical-dollar financial statements were restated to reflect the changing value of the dollar, the resulting statements would still be presented in terms of historical costs and would not reflect the current fair value of assets. For example, a tract of land which cost $1 million would be restated at $1.5 million if the general price level had risen by 50%. However, the current fair value of the land might be $5 million because the price of land had risen more than the general price level. Historical cost reflects the fair value of an asset at the date of acquisition; but a significant change in the fair value of the asset after acquisition tends to make historical cost irrelevant for decision-making purposes. Consequently, many users of financial statements have argued that **current fair** *values* of assets should replace historical costs as a valuation basis used in the preparation of financial statements.

Effects of inflation on financial statements

As stated earlier, the United States economy has experienced persistent inflation (increase in the general level of prices) for many years. Stated another way, the value of the dollar has been falling. How does inflation affect the measurement of income and the presentation of financial position for a business? Suppose that a company acquired a building for $1 million early in Year 1 when the general price-level index was 100. The building has an estimated economic life of 20 years and has been depreciated at the rate of $50,000 per year. At the end of Year 5, assume that the general price-level index is 200, and a comparable building acquired new would cost $2 million. The higher current replacement cost of the building is attributed entirely to the decrease in the purchasing power of the dollar; a doubling in the general price-level index means that a dollar at the end of Year 5 can buy only half as much as in Year 1. Financial statements prepared in conformity with generally accepted accounting principles at the end of Year 5 would show the following information relating to the building:

Using historical cost:

	Balance sheet		*Income statement*	
Building	$1,000,000	*Depreciation expense*	$ 50,000
Less: Accumulated			
depreciation	250,000		
Carrying value of building	$ 750,000		

Is this a meaningful portrayal of economic facts? Clearly it is not. Giving effect to the 50% reduction in the purchasing power of the dollar (100% increase in the general price-level index), the information would be presented more meaningfully as shown at the top of page 894.

Both presentations are stated in terms of historical costs; however, in the latter the historical costs were adjusted to reflect the current general price-level index. The increase of $750,000 in carrying value of the building would be reflected in the stockholders' equity section of the balance sheet as an "inflation adjustment." When financial statements are not adjusted for changes in the general price-level index, carrying values of depreciable assets and depreciation expense may be significantly misstated; similarly, inventories, cost of goods sold, other assets, and various other expenses also may be misstated. When the effects of

Using historical cost restated to reflect 100% increase in
the general price-level index:

Balance sheet		Income statement	
Building	$2,000,000	Depreciation expense . . .	$100,000
Less: Accumulated			
depreciation	500,000		
Carrying value of building ·	$1,500,000		

changes in the general price-level index are ignored, net income is measured by matching costs and revenue expressed in dollars having **different purchasing power.**

Income Measurement and Maintenance of Capital Suppose you buy 1,000 pounds of sugar for $100 when the general price level is 100 and sell the sugar for $108 when the general price level reaches 110. How much profit did you make on the transaction? By comparing your cost of $100 with the proceeds of $108, you conclude that you earned a profit of $8. However, in arriving at this result, you are using different types of dollars. It would be more logical to say that your investment of $100 is now equivalent to $110 in terms of current purchasing power and that you actually lost $2 on the transaction because you cannot buy for $108 now what you could have bought for $100 when you made the investment. In other words, you failed to recover your full capital investment and thus suffered an economic loss of $2 on the transaction.

To illustrate this point with another example, suppose that a company acquired land in Year 1 for $100,000 and sold it for $200,000 in Year 11. If the general price-level index doubled during that 10-year period, thus cutting the value of money in half, the company is not "better off" from an economic standpoint as a result of these two transactions; the $200,000 received for the land in Year 11 is equal to the $100,000 invested in Year 1. In terms of the dollar as a measuring unit, however, accountants would record a gain of $100,000 ($200,000 − $100,000) in Year 11. Thus, by combining the Year 1 and Year 11 transactions in dollar terms, accountants conclude that the company is "better off" (by reporting a profit) if it recovers more than the original **number of dollars** invested in the land.

Failure to consider the changing value of money in the preparation of financial statements in a period of inflation means that what is reported as income may be in part, a recovery of capital. The amount of **original capital invested in the business would not be maintained** and taxable income, income tax expense, and net income may be overstated. Taxable income may be overstated because depreciation charges are not large enough to offset the inflation in the prices of plant assets. This characteristic of traditional financial statements is perhaps the major argument in favor of price-level accounting. However, failure to recognize the effect of price-level changes during a period of inflation does not necessarily result in an overstatement of net income, because there may be offsetting general price-level gains from borrowing. This point is expanded in the following section.

Monetary Items and General Price-level Gains and Losses In discussing the changing value of the dollar, balance sheet accounts are classified either as monetary or as nonmonetary items. Cash, certificates of deposit, notes receivable, accounts receivable, investment in nonconvertible bonds which will be held to maturity, and most liabilities are examples of *monetary items* because they represent current buying power or legal obligations to pay out a fixed number of dollars. All other balance sheet accounts (inventories, investments in common stocks, plant assets, intangibles, and stockholders' equity accounts) are examples of *nonmonetary items.*

Changes in the general price level give rise to gains and losses (known as *general price-level* or *purchasing-power gains and losses*) as a result of holding monetary items. The ownership of cash or claims to cash in the form of notes and accounts receivable result in a loss of purchasing power when the general price-level index is rising; a policy of borrowing during a period when the general price-level index is rising, on the other hand, results in a gain of purchasing power because fixed-dollar liabilities can be paid with cheaper dollars. We can summarize this point as follows: When the general price-level index is rising, it is advantageous to be in a *negative monetary position,* that is, to hold an excess of liabilities over monetary assets; a *positive monetary position* (excess of monetary assets over liabilities) results in a loss of purchasing power when prices are rising. To illustrate, assume the following balance sheets (in millions of dollars) for two companies:

	X Company	Y Company
Cash, notes, and accounts receivable	$600	$100
Inventories and plant assets (net)	300	800
Total assets	$900	$900
Liabilities (current and long-term)	$200	$650
Stockholders' equity	700	250
Total liabilities & stockholders' equity	$900	$900

If the general price-level index increased by 10% (from 120 to 132, for example) since the two companies acquired the nonmonetary assets (inventories and plant assets) and incurred the liabilities, the balance sheets restated to current dollars would be as shown on page 896.

	X Company	Y Company
Cash, notes, and accounts receivable .	$600	$100
Inventories and plant assets (net) . . .	330 ($300 × 1.1)	880 ($800 × 1.1)
Total assets	$930	$980
Liabilities (current and long-term) . . .	$200	$650
Stockholders' equity	770 ($700 × 1.1)	275 ($250 × 1.1)
Net general price-level (loss) or gain .	(40)*	55†
Total liabilities & stockholders' equity	$930	$980

* Loss from holding cash and receivables, $60 ($600 × .10), reduced by the gain from borrowing, $20 ($200 × .10) = $40. X Company has a positive monetary position.
† Gain from borrowing, $65 ($650 × .10), reduced by the loss from holding cash and receivables, $10 ($100 × .10) = $55. Y Company has a negative monetary position.

The nonmonetary items (inventories, plant assets, and stockholders' equity) are restated to current dollars by using a **conversion factor** of 1.1 (132 ÷ 120).[1] Stated another way, the current general price-level index is equal to 110% of the index at the date when inventories and plant assets were acquired. Monetary items are not restated because these items are already stated in terms of current dollars.

To illustrate the fundamental effects of inflation on the two companies, we used a somewhat static and oversimplified example; we assumed that all assets and liabilities remained unchanged while the general price-level index was rising by 10%. The effects of general price-level changes on revenue and expenses are illustrated in a subsequent section of this chapter.

Emergence of price-level accounting—summary of APB Statement No. 3

The restatement of financial statements to reflect the effects of changes in the general price level is known as **price-level accounting.** Price-level accounting is not new. Most nations around the world have experienced severe inflation in the twentieth century and have used various approaches to restate financial statements for the changing value of their currencies. Although the inflationary trend in the United States has been persistent, it generally has not been considered severe enough to warrant a departure from the basic assumption that the monetary unit is stable. As prices continue to rise, however, a change in this assumption

---

[1] The adjustment of financial statements for changes in the general price-level index is generally facilitated by computing the relationship between the current index and the base-year index as a conversion factor in decimal form. For example, a current index of 126.9 and a base-year (or date-of-transaction) index of 90 gives a conversion factor of 1.41 (126.9 ÷ 90).

will have to be made; some accountants and business executives think that already we have waited too long.

The first significant work on price-level accounting in the United States was published by Henry W. Sweeney in 1936. His book, *Stabilized Accounting,* established the conceptual framework for later studies and official pronouncements.[2] In 1961, the Accounting Principles Board authorized a study of the price-level problem which resulted in the publication in 1963 of *Accounting Research Study No. 6.*[3] *ARS No. 6* recommended that the effects of price-level changes should be disclosed as a supplement to the conventional financial statements. Six years later, the Board issued *Statement of the Accounting Principles Board No. 3,* which outlined detailed procedures for the restatement of financial statements to recognize changes in the general price level.[4] A summary of the recommendations of *APB Statement No. 3* is presented below:

1 General price-level financial statements or information may be presented in addition to the basic historical-dollar financial statements, but general price-level financial statements should not be presented as the basic financial statements. Price-level financial statements are *supplementary* in nature and are *not required* for fair presentation.

2 The same accounting principles used in preparing historical-dollar financial statements should be used in preparing general price-level financial statements, except that changes in the general purchasing power of the dollar are recognized in general price-level financial statements. Price-level financial statements are an *extension of* (not a departure from) *the historical-cost basis of accounting.*

3 An *index of the general price level,* not an index of specific prices, should be used to prepare general price-level financial statements. The GNP Implicit Price Deflator is the most comprehensive indicator of the general price level and normally should be used for this purpose.

4 General price-level financial statements should be prepared in terms of the general purchasing power of the dollar at the *latest balance sheet date.* Economic actions take place in terms of current dollars, and translating the accounts into current dollars expressed them in amounts used to make business decisions.

5 *Monetary* and *nonmonetary* items should be distinguished for the purpose of preparing general price-level financial statements. Monetary assets and liabilities (including taxes payable) in historical-cost balance sheets are stated in terms of dollars of current general purchasing power and appear in current general price-level financial statements at the same amounts. The amounts of nonmonetary items should be restated to dollars of current general purchasing power at the end of the period.

6 The amounts of *income statement items* (revenue and expenses) should be restated to dollars of current general purchasing power at the end of the period. Income tax expense in the general price-level income statements is based on the income tax expense as reported in the historical-dollar income

[2] Henry W. Sweeney, *Stabilized Accounting,* Harper & Brothers (New York: 1936). Reprinted in 1964 by Holt, Rinehart and Winston, Inc., New York.
[3] *Accounting Research Study No. 6,* "Reporting the Financial Effects of Price-level Changes," authored by the staff of the Research Division, AICPA (New York: 1963).
[4] *Statement of the Accounting Principles Board No. 3,* "Financial Statements Restated for General Price-level Changes," AICPA (New York: 1969).

statement and is **not** computed in direct relationship to the income before income taxes reported in the general price-level income statement.

7 **General price-level gains and losses** should be calculated by means of the general price-level index and included in current net income. The gain from holding liabilities during a period of inflation should be recognized as part of net income of the period in which the general price-level rises. Recognition of such gains should not be deferred until the related assets (if any) are consumed or sold. The net general price-level gain or loss should be reported separately in the general price-level income statement.

8 General price-level financial statements of **earlier periods should be updated** to the dollars of the general purchasing power at the end of the subsequent periods for which they are presented as comparative information. Financial statements of earlier periods are "rolled forward" by multiplying each item by the ratio of the current general price-level index to the general price-level index of the earlier period. All general price-level information presented should be based on complete general price-level calculations. Partial restatement (of depreciation, for example) is not acceptable.

9 General price-level information as a supplement to the basic historical-dollar financial statements should be designed to promote **clarity and minimize possible confusion.** Presentation in separate schedules, not in parallel columns, should be encouraged. Ratio and trend analyses based on price-level information are appropriate.

10 The basis of preparation of general price-level information and what it purports to show should be clearly explained in notes to the general price-level financial statements. For example, the explanation should include a note stating that the same generally accepted accounting principles used in preparing historical-dollar statements also are used in preparing general price-level financial statements and that the latter do not purport to represent current fair values of assets.

APB Statement No. 3 provided the basis for the issuance by the FASB of an exposure draft of a proposed **Statement** on price-level accounting.[5] The FASB withdrew the proposed **Statement** in 1976 when the SEC gave strong indications that it favored disclosure of replacement cost information rather than price-level-adjusted financial statements as a solution to the accounting problems created by inflation.

Illustration of price-level accounting

Data for Illustration A relatively simple set of financial statements for Baker Company will be used to illustrate the application of **APB Statement No. 3.** Baker Company was organized on December 31, Year 4, as a result of a merger of several separate businesses which were previously operated as partnerships or single proprietorships. All assets were recorded by Baker Company at current fair values. Changes in the Gross National Product Implicit Price Deflator during Year 5 are presented at the top of page 899.

---

[5] *Exposure Draft* (Proposed Statement of Financial Accounting Standards), "Financial Reporting in Units of General Purchasing Power," FASB (Stamford: 1974).

	GNP Implicit Price Deflator (general price-level index)	Conversion factor to restate to end-of-Year 5 dollars
End of Year 4 (and beginning of Year 5)	150.0	1.092*
Average for Year 5 (also at July 1)	157.5	1.040†
End of Year 5	163.8	1.000

* 163.8 ÷ 150.0 = 1.092.
† 163.8 ÷ 157.5 = 1.040.

The comparative balance sheet (before price-level adjustments) at the end of Year 5 for Baker Company is shown below:

BAKER COMPANY
Comparative Balance Sheet
End of Year 4 and Year 5

	End of Year 4	End of Year 5
Assets		
Monetary assets (cash and receivables)	$200,000	$260,000
Inventories (fifo method)	150,000	130,000
Land	40,000	40,000
Equipment	210,000	270,000
Less: Accumulated depreciation	–0–	(24,000)
Total assets	$600,000	$676,000
Liabilities & Stockholders' Equity		
Current liabilities	$ 80,000	$ 90,000
Long-term liabilities	100,000	116,000
Capital stock, $10 par	140,000	140,000
Paid-in capital in excess of par	280,000	280,000
Retained earnings	–0–	50,000
Total liabilities & stockholders' equity	$600,000	$676,000

The statement of income and retained earnings for Baker Company, before price-level adjustments, for Year 5 (the first year of operations) is shown at the top of page 900.

BAKER COMPANY
Statement of Income and Retained Earnings
For Year 5 (the first year of operations)

Sales (net)		$800,000
Cost of goods sold:		
Beginning inventories (fifo method)	$150,000	
Purchases (net)	500,000	
Cost of goods available for sale	$650,000	
Less: Ending inventories (fifo method)	130,000	
Cost of goods sold		520,000
Gross profit on sales		$280,000
Operating expenses (excluding depreciation)	$ 96,000	
Depreciation expense	24,000	120,000
Income before income taxes		$160,000
Income tax expense		70,000
Net income		$ 90,000
Less: Dividends paid		40,000
Retained earnings, end of Year 5		$ 50,000

Equipment costing $60,000 was acquired on July 1, Year 5, when the GNP Implicit Price Deflator stood at 157.5. Depreciation expense based on historical costs was computed as follows:

$210,000 × 10%	$21,000	
$60,000 × 5% (one-half of year)	3,000	$24,000

Net sales, net purchases, and operating expenses (excluding depreciation) took place evenly throughout the year. Inventories are priced on a first-in, first-out basis; goods in ending inventories were acquired evenly during the year. The dividend of $40,000 was declared and paid near the end of Year 5.

Exhibit 1—Statement of Income and Retained Earnings A working paper to restate the statement of income and retained earnings for Year 5, in terms of end-of-Year 5 dollars, is presented in Exhibit 1 on page 901.

A brief explanation of the procedures followed to restate the statement of income and retained earnings follows:

Sales Sales were made at a fairly uniform rate during Year 5; therefore, the amount of sales reported in the accounting records ($800,000) is stated in terms of the average general price-level index for the year. To restate sales in terms of end-of-Year 5 dollars, a conversion factor of

Exhibit 1

BAKER COMPANY
Statement of Income and Retained Earnings Restated for
General Price-Level Changes
For Year 5 (the first year of operations)

	Per accounting records	Conversion factor	Restated to end-of-Year 5 dollars
Sales (net)	$800,000	1.040 (A)	$832,000
Cost of goods sold:			
Beginning inventories (fifo method)	$150,000	1.092 (B)	$163,800
Purchases (net)	500,000	1.040 (A)	520,000
Cost of goods available for sale	$650,000		$683,800
Less: Ending inventories (fifo method)	130,000	1.040 (A)	135,200
Cost of goods sold . .	$520,000		$548,600
Gross profit on sales	$280,000		$283,400
Less: Operating expenses (excluding depreciation)	(96,000)	1.040 (A)	(99,840)
Depreciation expense .	(24,000)	(C)	(26,052)
Income before general price-level gain or loss	$160,000		$157,508
General price-level loss . . .		(Exhibit 2)*	4,800
Income after general price-level loss			$152,708
Income tax expense	70,000	1.040 (A)	72,800
Net income	$ 90,000		$ 79,908
Less: Dividends paid	40,000	1.000 (D)	40,000
Retained earnings, end of Year 5	$ 50,000		$ 39,908

(A) The general price-level index at the end of Year 5 (163.8), divided by the average general price-level index during Year 5 (157.5) = 1.040.

(B) The general price-level index at the end of Year 5 (163.8), divided by the general price-level index at the end of Year 4 (150.0) when inventories were acquired = 1.092.

(C) Depreciation expense is restated for the increase in the general price-level index as follows:

On equipment acquired at end of Year 4: $21,000 × 1.092 . . . . $22,932
On equipment acquired on July 1, Year 5: $3,000 × 1.040 . . . . 3,120 $26,052

(D) Dividends were declared and paid near the end of Year 5, and are therefore stated in terms of current dollars at the end of Year 5.

* See p. 903.

1.040 is used. This factor is computed by dividing the end-of-Year 5 index of 163.8 by 157.5, the average index for Year 5.

Beginning inventories The goods comprising the beginning inventories were acquired when the general price-level index was 150.0. The amount of the beginning inventories is restated by using a conversion factor of 1.092, the end-of-Year 5 general price-level index of 163.8 divided by 150.0, the index at the time the inventories were acquired.

Purchases Purchases took place at a fairly uniform rate during Year 5. Consequently, the restatement is accomplished by multiplying, by a conversion factor of 1.040, the end-of-Year 5 general price-level index of 163.8 divided by 157.5, the average index during Year 5.

Ending inventories Because inventories are priced on a first-in, first-out basis, it is assumed that the goods in the ending inventories were acquired at the average general price level for Year 5. Thus ending inventories are restated to current dollars by using the average general price-level index conversion factor of 1.040 (the same conversion factor used to restate purchases).

Operating expenses (other than depreciation) In our example we have assumed that operating expenses were incurred evenly throughout the year; therefore, operating expenses are restated to current dollars by applying the average general price-level index conversion factor of 1.040.

Depreciation Depreciation expense on the accounting records consists of two amounts: (1) depreciation of $21,000 on equipment acquired on December 31, Year 4, when the general price-level index was 150.0 and (2) depreciation of $3,000 on equipment acquired on July 1, Year 5, when the general price-level index was 157.5. Depreciation expense is therefore restated as follows:

$21,000 × 1.092 (163.8 ÷ 150.0)	$22,932
$3,000 × 1.040 (163.8 ÷ 157.5)	3,120
Total depreciation expense, as restated	$26,052

General price-level loss Any gain or loss resulting from the ownership of monetary assets or from borrowing activities is computed in a separate schedule and is added to or subtracted from income before general price-level gain or loss. The determination of the general price-level loss of $4,800 for Baker Company appears in Exhibit 2 on page 903.

Income tax expense Income taxes accrue throughout the year as revenue and expenses are recorded. Since sales and expenses accrued evenly throughout the year, income tax expense is adjusted to end-of-

Exhibit 2

BAKER COMPANY
Computation of General Price-Level Gain or Loss
For Year 5 (the first year of operations)

	Amounts per accounting records		Conversion factor	Restated to end-of-Year 5 dollars
Net monetary items at beginning of Year 5:				
Monetary assets (cash and receivables)	$200,000			
Current liabilities	(80,000)			
Long-term liabilities	(100,000)	$ 20,000	1.092 (A)	$ 21,840
Add: Sources of net monetary items during Year 5:				
Sales (net)		800,000	1.040 (B)	832,000
Subtotal		$820,000		$853,840
Less: Uses of net monetary items during Year 5:				
Purchases (net)	$500,000		1.040 (B)	$520,000
Operating expenses (excluding depreciation) . .	96,000		1.040 (B)	99,840
Income tax expense	70,000		1.040 (B)	72,800
Dividends paid	40,000		1.000 (C)	40,000
Purchase of equipment . .	60,000		1.040 (D)	62,400
Total uses		766,000		$795,040
Net monetary items as restated at the end of Year 5 if there were no general price-level gain or loss ($853,840 − $795,040)				$ 58,800
Net monetary items actually on hand at the end of Year 5:				
Monetary assets (cash and receivables)	$260,000			
Current liabilities	(90,000)			
Long-term liabilities	(116,000)	$ 54,000		54,000
General price-level loss during Year 5				$ 4,800

(A) The amount of net monetary items at the beginning of Year 5 is rolled forward by multiplying $20,000 by the conversion factor of 1.092, which is the ratio of end-of-Year 5 general price-level index to the index at the beginning of Year 5 (163.8 ÷ 150.0 = 1.092).

(B) Sales, purchases, operating expenses, and income tax expense are restated in the same manner as in Exhibit 1, that is, by using a conversion factor for the average general price-level index for Year 5 (163.8 ÷ 157.5 = 1.040).

(C) Dividends were declared and paid near the end of Year 5 and therefore are already stated in terms of current dollars.

(D) Equipment was purchased on July 1, Year 5, when the general price-level index was 157.5; this amount is restated by multiplying the cost of $60,000 by 1.040 (163.8 ÷ 157.5).

Year 5 dollars by multiplying the actual income tax expense of $70,000 by the average general price-level conversion factor of 1.040. As stated on pages 897 and 898, income tax expense in the general price-level income statement is based on the income tax expense as reported in the historical-dollar income statement and is not computed in direct relationship to the income before income taxes reported in the general price-level income statement.

Dividends paid Because dividends were declared and paid near the end of Year 5, the amount of dividends paid is stated in terms of current dollars and requires no restatement. (If dividends had been declared and paid on July 1, Year 5, for example, the amount of dividends would be restated by using a conversion factor of 1.040.)

Exhibit 1 shows that Baker Company earned a net income of $79,908 rather than $90,000 as shown in the conventional income statement. The difference of $10,092 is caused by three major factors: (1) an increase in the cost of goods acquired at the end of Year 4 and sold in Year 5; (2) an increase in depreciation expense because of an increase in the general price level since the equipment was acquired; and (3) a general price-level loss as a result of holding an excess of monetary assets over liabilities during a period when the general price level was going up. As a result of the difference in net income, the retained earnings will appear in the price-level balance sheet (see Exhibit 3 on page 906) at $39,908 ($50,000 − $10,092).

Exhibit 2—Computation of General Price-Level Gain or Loss The general price-level loss of $4,800 which appears in the statement of income and retained earnings restated for general price-level changes is presented in Exhibit 2 on page 903.

In the preparation of Exhibit 2, transactions (such as net sales) which caused an increase in monetary assets during Year 5 are added to the amount of net monetary items at the beginning of the year; those transactions which caused an increase in liabilities or a decrease in monetary assets are deducted. Included under deductions are net purchases, operating expenses other than depreciation, income tax expense for the year, dividends paid, and the purchase of equipment. Depreciation expense is not included in Exhibit 2 because it is a nonmonetary expense. The amount of net monetary items at the beginning of Year 5 (restated to end-of-Year 5 dollars), plus sources and less uses of net monetary assets (restated to end-of-Year 5 dollars) gives $58,800 as the amount of net monetary items that *should be* on hand if there were no general price-level gain or loss. Because net monetary items at the end of Year 5 amount to $54,000, the general price-level loss is $4,800 ($58,800 − $54,000).

Exhibit 3—Comparative Balance Sheet A working paper to restate the comparative balance sheet, in terms of end-of-Year 5 dollars, is presented on page 906. Note that the balance sheet amounts (as taken from the accounting records) at the end of Year 4 are *rolled forward*, in order to reflect end-of-Year 5 dollars, by multiplying each amount by 1.092

(163.8 ÷ 150.0). This rolling forward of the balance sheet amounts is necessary so that the balance sheet at the end of Year 4 can be meaningfully compared with the restated balance sheet at the end of Year 5. Thus, balance sheet amounts at both dates are stated in terms of current dollars having uniform purchasing power.

The restatement of the balance sheet accounts at the end of Year 5 is explained in the following paragraphs.

Monetary items Monetary assets (cash and receivables) and liabilities are already reported in terms of end-of-Year 5 dollars and require no restatement.

Inventories Inventories at the end of Year 5 are priced using the first-in, first-out method. Goods comprising the ending inventories were acquired evenly throughout the year and therefore are restated by using a conversion factor of 1.040, the general price-level index at the end of Year 5, 163.8, divided by the average index during Year 5, 157.5. This is consistent with the restatement of ending inventories in Exhibit 1 on page 901.

If inventories were priced on a last-in, first-out basis, the ending inventories in this illustration would consist entirely of the cost layer on hand at the beginning of Year 5 and would be restated by applying a conversion factor of 1.092 (163.8 ÷ 150.0).

Land Because land was acquired at the end of Year 4 when the general price-level index was 150.0, it is restated to $43,680 by multiplying the cost of $40,000 by 1.092 (163.8 ÷ 150.0).

Equipment and accumulated depreciation Equipment costing $210,000 was acquired at the end of Year 4 when the general price-level index was 150.0 and equipment costing $60,000 was acquired on July 1, Year 5, when the index was 157.5. One possible approach to the restatement of equipment and accumulated depreciation accounts at the end of Year 5 is presented below:

Equipment			Accumulated depreciation		
Per accounts ×	Conversion factor	= Adjusted	Per accounts ×	Conversion factor	= Adjusted
$210,000 ×	1.092 (163.8 ÷ 150.0) =	$229,320	$21,000 ×	1.092	= $22,932
60,000 ×	1.040 (163.8 ÷ 157.5) =	62,400	3,000 ×	1.040	= 3,120
$270,000		$291,720	$24,000		$26,052

The carrying value of the equipment at the end of Year 5 is $246,000 ($270,000 − $24,000) in terms of actual historical cost and $265,668 ($291,720 − $26,052) when actual cost is adjusted for general price-level changes. Thus if the equipment were sold for $250,000 at the

Exhibit 3

BAKER COMPANY
Comparative Balance Sheet Restated for
General Price-Level Changes
End of Year 4 and Year 5

	End of Year 4			End of Year 5		
	Per accounting records	Conversion factor	Rolled forward to end-of-Year 5 dollars	Per accounting records	Conversion factor	Restated to end-of-Year 5 dollars
Assets						
Monetary assets (cash and receivables) ..	$200,000	1.092 (A)	$218,400	$260,000	(B)	$260,000
Inventories (fifo method)	150,000	1.092	163,800	130,000	1.040 (E)	135,200
Land	40,000	1.092	43,680	40,000	1.092 (A)	43,680
Equipment	210,000	1.092	229,320	270,000	(C)	291,720
Less: Accumulated depreciation	–0–		–0–	(24,000)	(D)	(26,052)
Total assets	$600,000		$655,200	$676,000		$704,548
Liabilities & Stockholders' Equity						
Current liabilities ...	$ 80,000	1.092	$ 87,360	$ 90,000	(B)	$ 90,000
Long-term liabilities .	100,000	1.092	109,200	116,000	(B)	116,000
Capital stock, $10 par	140,000	1.092	152,880	140,000	1.092 (A)	152,880
Paid-in capital in excess of par	280,000	1.092	305,760	280,000	1.092 (A)	305,760
Retained earnings ..	–0–		–0–	50,000	(Exhibit 1)*	39,908
Total liabilities & stockholders' equity	$600,000		$655,200	$676,000		$704,548

(A) General price-level index at end of Year 5 (163.8) divided by the general price-level index at the end of Year 4 (150.0) = 1.092.

(B) Monetary items at the end of Year 5 are not adjusted because these are already stated in terms of end-of-Year 5 dollars.

(C) Equipment is adjusted for the increase in the general price-level index as follows:
Acquired at the end of Year 4: $210,000 × 1.092 .... $229,320
Acquired on July 1, Year 5: $60,000 × 1.04 (163.8 ÷ 157.5) 62,400
Total as restated $291,720

(D) Accumulated depreciation is adjusted for the increase in the general price-level index as follows:
On equipment acquired at the end of Year 4: $21,000 × 1.092 .... $ 22,932
On equipment acquired on July 1, Year 5: $3,000 × 1.04 3,120
Total accumulated depreciation as restated .... $ 26,052

(E) General price-level index at end of Year 5 (163.8), divided by the average general price-level index during Year 5 (157.5) = 1.040.

* See p. 901.

beginning of Year 6, a gain of $4,000 would result in terms of historical cost and a loss of $15,668 would result when general price-level accounting is applied.

Capital stock and paid-in capital in excess of par Paid-in capital accounts are carried in the accounting records at amounts invested by stockholders. These amounts should be restated to current dollars by multiplying each amount by a fraction (conversion factor) in which the current general price-level index is the numerator and the index at the time the paid-in capital was invested by stockholders is the denominator. Therefore, the conversion factor used to restate the paid-in capital accounts is 1.092 (163.8 ÷ 150.0).

Retained earnings The balance in retained earnings was previously determined in Exhibit 1 on page 901.

If the foregoing steps have been correctly applied, the total of assets, as restated, should equal the restated total of liabilities and stockholders' equity.

Similar procedures would be followed in subsequent years to adjust financial statements for changes in the general price-level index. For example, if comparative financial statements are presented at the end of Year 6, the amounts appearing in the statements for Year 5, as restated in terms of end-of-Year 5 dollars, would have to be rolled forward so that they are stated in end-of-Year 6 dollars.

Price-level information in practice

Financial statements adjusted for changes in the general price level are not generally accepted as primary reports to stockholders. The 1976 edition of *Accounting Trends & Techniques* disclosed that two of the 600 companies included in the survey presented supplementary information adjusted for price-level changes.[6] A few companies not included in this survey publish price-level financial statements.

The practice of presenting supplementary price-level financial statements has not been widely followed in the United States, perhaps because the business community considers the cost of providing such statements to be greater than the value to users. With modern computer technology, it is probably safe to conclude that the additional cost and effort required to prepare price-level financial statements would not be excessive.

FAIR-VALUE ACCOUNTING

Significance of changes in value

The restatement of historical-cost financial statements for price-level changes is an effort to recognize the fact that the value of the dollar is not stable. Such financial statements require no other departures from generally accepted accounting principles. Some accountants feel that an additional departure is needed to add greater relevance and usefulness to financial statements. In their view, historical costs and completed transactions should be replaced by *fair-value accounting.* They

[6] *Accounting Trends & Techniques,* 30th ed., AICPA (New York: 1976), p. 72.

argue that financial statements showing current fair values (or current replacement costs) of assets and the changes in such values would convey a more meaningful picture of a company's financial position and earning power.

To illustrate, suppose that a company purchased land for $100,000 and erected a factory building for $600,000, which is being depreciated over a 30-year life, or $20,000 per year. During the first 10 years the values of the land and building increased substantially. At the end of the 10-year period (during which the general price level remained stable), it was apparent that the land and building were worth considerably more than recorded carrying values. As a result, the financial statements for the company in the eleventh year would show: (1) Assets that are substantially below current fair value; (2) net income that is overstated because the full economic cost of using the building was not reflected in annual depreciation expense; and (3) rates of return on assets and stockholders' equity that are overstated, because what really amounts to capital recovery in terms of current prices is being reported as a part of net income.

Assuming that at the beginning of the eleventh year the current fair value of the land was $180,000 and the current fair value of the building was $1,000,000 (replacement cost new of $1,500,000 less depreciation to date of $500,000), the appraisal might be recorded as follows:

Land—Appraisal Increase	80,000	
Building—Appraisal Increase	900,000	
Accumulated Depreciation-Appraisal Increase		300,000
Appraisal Capital		680,000
To record appraisal of land and building to current fair value.		

The annual depreciation expense on the building would be $50,000 ($1,500,000 ÷ 30 years = $50,000) to reflect the current cost of building services being consumed. The balance sheet would now show land and building at amounts approximating current fair value, and reported net income would represent the amount by which the company was "better off" after recovering the current fair value of the remaining building services over the next 20 years (assuming that no further value changes occurred during that period).

Relationship between price-level and fair-value accounting

The use of fair-value accounting does not mean that changes in the general price level would be ignored. Price-level accounting and fair-value accounting are complementary responses to different measurement problems. The two approaches are not mutually exclusive alternatives.

Dealing with one is not a substitute for dealing with the other and either or both approaches may be adopted in a single set of financial statements. Restatement of financial statements for general price-level changes does not attempt to deal with specific price changes while fair-value accounting does not deal specifically with inflation. The different alternatives that may be followed in preparing financial statements are:[7]

1 Historical cost

2 Historical cost restated for general price-level changes

3 Current fair value, without separate identification of the effects of general price-level changes

4 Current fair value, with the effects of general price-level changes being shown separately

Financial statements adjusted for changes in the general price level are based on historical costs; however, the unit of measurement (the dollar) is adjusted to reflect changes in its general purchasing power. In contrast, fair-value accounting is a departure from historical cost because the current fair values for assets are derived from appraisals which reflect both changes in the general price level and changes in the relative price levels of specific goods. Thus fair-value accounting represents a clear break from historical cost for a particular company. For example, if M Company and N Company bought identical assets at different dates and price levels, price-level accounting would give different adjusted values for the assets of each company. However, fair-value accounting would give the *same value* for the assets of both companies, because fair-value accounting is not concerned with historical costs.

When changes in the general price level *are not* incorporated in fair-value financial statements, the difference between historical costs and appraised values of assets is referred to as an unrealized *holding gain or loss;* the unrealized holding gain or loss, net of the tax effect, would be reported as a separate item in the income statement. When changes in the general price level *are* incorporated in fair-value financial statements, the unrealized holding gain or loss (difference between historical costs and appraised values of assets) would consist of a net general price-level gain or loss and the net gain or loss resulting from changes in the relative values of specific assets; these two distinct types of net gains or losses would be reported separately in the income statement.

Use of fair values in the preparation of financial statements

Proposals to incorporate fair values in accounting measurements are not entirely of recent origin. For example, fair values are used in applying the lower-of-cost-or-market rule to the valuation of inventories and

[7] *APB Statement No. 3,* pp. 69–70.

marketable securities, and assets may be written down to fair value in a quasi-reorganization. In such cases the use of fair values results in a reduction in the carrying value of assets *below* cost (or carrying value in terms of historical cost). However, fair values also are used when such values exceed historical cost. For example, marketable securities held by mutual funds and inventories of certain metals and agricultural products are frequently reported at fair (or market) value. A significant number of companies increased the carrying value of plant assets during the inflation of the 1920s, only to write the same assets down during the depression of the 1930s. In response to a recommendation by the authors of *Accounting Research Study No. 3* for the use of current replacement costs for plant and equipment, a member of the Project Advisory Committee made the following observation: "Shades of the 1920s! Those of us who remember how impossible it was to determine the fairness or reasonableness of the results of an appraisal shudder at the idea of going through it all over again."[8] Past experience indicates that valuations not subject to independent verification can be manipulated to the possible disadvantage of users of financial statements.

Nevertheless, the idea persists. In *A Statement of Basic Accounting Theory,* issued in 1966 by the American Accounting Association, a recommendation was made that financial statements should be presented in two-column form; one column would present data in terms of historical costs and the other in terms of current costs.[9] This recommendation has been widely supported; some writers even have suggested that historical-cost financial statements should be *supplanted* by fair-value statements. Neither the AICPA nor the FASB has sanctioned the issuance of financial statements in which assets are stated at current fair value. For example, in *APB Opinion No. 6,* the Accounting Principles Board stated that it was "of the opinion that property, plant and equipment should not be written up by an entity to reflect appraisal, market or current values which are above cost to the entity."[10]

The meaning of value

The term *value* has many meanings and its use in the business world often conveys a deceptively reassuring message. Value is closely related to the economic concept of *utility.* Goods and services have utility because they are scarce and because they are demanded by users in a certain *form,* at a certain *time,* and at a certain *place.* In short, goods and ser-

---

[8] Robert T. Sprouse and Maurice Moonitz, *Accounting Research Study No. 3,* "A Tentative Set of Broad Accounting Principles for Business Enterprises," AICPA (New York: 1962), p. 62.

[9] *A Statement of Basic Accounting Theory,* American Accounting Association (Sarasota, Fla.: 1966), pp. 30–32.

[10] *APB Opinion No. 6,* "Status of Accounting Research Bulletins," AICPA (New York: 1965), p. 42.

vices have economic utility because they are capable of satisfying human wants. In our economy, goods and services are valued and exchanged through the price mechanism. Some goods and services which are widely used or regulated by governmental agencies have a readily ascertainable price or value; however, the price or value of other goods and services is difficult to pinpoint.

The basic purpose of a manufacturing or mechandising business is to create economic utility through the process of production and/or distribution. For example, raw materials are acquired by a manufacturer, the raw materials are converted into a finished product, and this product is then sold. The cost of a product may be $10 to the manufacturer; the wholesaler may purchase the product from the manufacturer for $15 and sell it to a retailer for $20; the retailer in turn may sell it to the ultimate consumer for $28. What is the fair value of this product? Obviously the question cannot be answered without asking: To whom? At what location? At what point in time? The same questions apply in attempting to determine the fair value of any asset. The value of almost any business asset depends on the use that is being made (or will be made) of the asset, the place where the asset is located, and the business and economic conditions at the time the valuation is made.

But the difficulties do not end here. For a long time courts of law have recognized that the current fair value of an asset (such as a patent or a going business) depends on the **purpose** for which the valuation is made. In addition, several different approaches may be used in arriving at current fair value. As a basic proposition, we can say that the economic worth of any asset is equal to the present value of the future earnings it can produce when it is put to its **most efficient use.** This is a somewhat idealistic definition of value, but it stems from the fact that the "current fair value" of an asset is directly dependent upon its expected earning power. However, earnings generated by specific assets are difficult to identify because earnings depend on a multitude of factors. Similar difficulties are encountered in arriving at an appropriate interest rate to be used in computing the present value of future earnings, and in identifying the "most efficient use" for the asset.

It may be useful to recall at this point that changes in value are caused by two major factors: (1) change in general price levels, and (2) changes in relative value of goods and services. A characteristic of inflation is that most prices move upward and thus the cost of replacing assets goes up; revenue from the sale of goods and services increases; and the **monetary** value of assets rises in response to these conditions.

The **relative** (or **comparative**) value of an asset changes when an asset becomes more or less valuable **in relation to other goods and services in the economy.** For example, if prices in general are holding steady and an asset rises in value from $10,000 to $15,000, the asset has become more valuable in relation to other goods and services.

In a competitive economy, the value of reproducible assets is closely tied in to the cost of manufacture or construction. Any evidence of higher value will presumably encourage the production of more assets of this type and thus bring their value down to levels consistent with cost of production. The possibility of wide and permanent change in the value of nonreproducible assets (such as land or natural resources) is much greater, because they cannot be duplicated.

Arriving at current fair value

Thus far, we have mentioned the possibility of replacing historical costs of assets with current fair values without specifying how these values might be determined. The concept of value most widely referred to in legal proceedings is *fair value,* defined as "an exchange price that a willing and well-informed buyer and an equally willing and well-informed seller would reach through negotiation." This should not be confused with *market value,* which is the price obtainable currently for any asset. No single method of estimating fair value is entirely satisfactory; therefore, in order to be able to evaluate intelligently the arguments for and against fair-value accounting, it may be helpful to identify some of the methods used in estimating fair value.

Capitalization of Net Cash Inflows In theory, the ideal way to estimate the fair or *economic value* of any asset would be to compute the present discounted amount of the probable future net cash inflows expected to result from the use of the asset. This is known as *direct valuation.* A limitation of the direct valuation approach is that estimates of future net cash inflows are likely to be highly subjective. More importantly, the earnings and cash inflows of a business entity are a joint product of all its resources, and it is virtually impossible to identify clearly the contribution to earnings and cash inflows of any particular asset. The concept of direct valuation, although somewhat impractical for valuing specific assets, is useful in appraising the merits of other *indirect valuation* methods discussed below.

Exit Values The *current exit value* of an asset is the amount that could be realized from its current sale; the *expected exit value* of an asset is the nondiscounted amount of cash into which the asset is expected to be converted in due course of business. Exit values may be viewed as fair values only for assets that are in fact offered for sale, and as minimum values for assets that are continued in use. However, in many cases the fair values of assets may be materially above exit values. Exit values are related to but are not identical to market values because exit values may imply an urgent need to sell. Although reasonable estimates of exit-values can be made for certain assets such as stocks and bonds and some items of inventory, estimates of such values for many types of special-purpose equipment and intangible assets may be quite difficult to obtain.

Replacement Cost Replacement cost of an asset is the estimated cost of acquiring *new* and substantially *equivalent* property at current prices, adjusted for estimated depreciation since acquisition. Replacement cost should be distinguished from *reproduction cost,* which is the estimated cost of producing *new* substantially *identical* assets, at current prices, adjusted for depreciation to date. Replacement cost may be approximated by applying an appropriate *specific-price index* to the historical cost of assets, particularly plant assets. Specific-price indices are available for broad classifications of equipment, buildings, and land. The application of specific-price indices is illustrated below:

Assets	Historical cost	Specific-price index at date of acqui-sition	Current specific-price index	Conversion factor	Current specific-price index replace-ment cost
Building	$200,000	100	125	125/100	$250,000
Less: Accumulated depreciation . . .	60,000	100	125	125/100	75,000
Carrying value . . .	$140,000				$175,000
Land	240,000	120	130	130/120	260,000

The building was acquired for $200,000 when the specific-price index for building construction in this industry was 100. Since the index is now 125, the historical cost of the building is restated to a current specific-price index replacement cost of $250,000 ($200,000 × 125/100); accumulated depreciation is similarly adjusted. The specific-price index of land costs in the geographic area where the land is located increased from 120 to 130 since the land was acquired; therefore, the historical cost of the land, $240,000, is multiplied by 130/120 to arrive at the current specific-price index replacement cost of $260,000.

This brief discussion should serve to point out that much sharper asset valuation techniques must be developed before fair-value accounting becomes a practical alternative for the preparation of financial statements.

Prospects for the use of fair-value accounting

Proposals for the implementation of fair-value accounting may be placed into four categories as follows:

1 Abandon traditional historical-cost accounting and adopt fair-value accounting, both for income measurement and valuation (balance sheet) purposes.

2 Issue fair-value financial statements as supplements to historical-cost statements, or issue historical-cost statements as supplements to fair-value statements.

3 Adopt fair values for assets as rapidly as reasonably objective measures for fair values can be developed; ultimately, all or at least most items in the financial statements would be stated on a fair-value basis.

4 Continue the traditional emphasis on historical costs and **disclose** fair values of assets in supplementary form when fair values can be determined with a reasonable degree of objectivity and when disclosure would be useful.[11]

Implicit in each of these proposals is the assumption that the current fair value of most assets is determinable, that the value of a company is equal to the sum of the value of its assets less its liabilities, and that fair-value financial statements are more useful than historical-cost statements. Although the current fair value of some assets may be readily determined, the current fair value of many others cannot be ascertained with any reasonable degree of precision. But even if the fair values of all identifiable assets could be determined with a reasonable degree of precision, the problems of valuing unidentifiable assets (goodwill) would still remain. Besides being subjectively determined in most cases, values based on future expectations change constantly. Finally, serious doubt has been expressed by some accountants and financial analysts that users of financial statements really want subjectively determined current fair values incorporated into the accounting model.

A switch to fair-value accounting would probably weaken the accounting model as a device for holding management responsible for the custody of economic resources entrusted to it by stockholders. Also, in an era of unprecedented litigation involving auditors, a change to fair-value accounting might enlarge the opportunities for charging that financial statements were misleading.

It seems doubtful, then, that proposals (1) and (2) listed above are feasible in the near future or that proposal (3) is desirable. As stated earlier, certain assets, such as cash, receivables, and inventories valued on a lower-of-cost-or-market basis, have been reported at fair value for many years. Extension of this practice to inventories when market exceeds cost, investments in listed securities, and plant assets may be possible in some situations.

Thus the last proposal, that is, "continue the traditional emphasis on historical costs and disclose fair values of assets in supplementary form when fair values can be determined with a reasonable degree of objectivity and when disclosure would be useful," may well represent the most logical course of action in the short run. Many accountants even question the usefulness of this proposal because estimates of current fair value generally lack objectivity. However, when assets increase significantly in value, it is useful to provide fair-value information in supplementary form despite the absence of precision and objectivity inherent in such information. It is probably safe to conclude that fi-

---

[11] *Additional Views on Accounting Objectives* (pamphlet), Ernst & Ernst (Cleveland: 1972), p. 8.

nancial reporting would be improved if more relevant information were made available to users even by sacrificing some precision and objectivity. The Study Group on Objectives of Financial Statements recommended in 1973 that "current values should also be reported when they differ significantly from historical cost."[12]

In December 1976 the FASB issued a *Discussion Memorandum* dealing with the conceptual framework for financial accounting and reporting in which it identified various alternatives to historical cost in measuring assets and liabilities. These included: (1) current cost, (2) current exit value, (3) expected exit value, and (4) present value of expected cash flows.[13] The selection of the most appropriate *measurement concept* or concepts promises to be a controversial undertaking. The Board also indicated that it will have to decide on what *unit of measure* to use, that is, whether to continue with the stable-monetary-unit assumption or whether to make adjustments for changes in the purchasing power of the dollar. As inflation continues to plague the economy of the United States and other industrialized nations, these issues probably will continue to receive considerable attention in the years ahead.[14]

DISCLOSURE OF REPLACEMENT COST INFORMATION

Methods for determining replacement costs

Replacement cost of an asset was defined on page 913 as the "estimated cost of acquiring *new* and substantially *equivalent* property at current prices, adjusted for estimated depreciation since acquisition." Four methods of determining replacement cost are described below:

1 *Direct pricing* The actual replacement cost of an asset is determined by **direct quotation** from suppliers, manufacturers, contractors, or other sources.

2 *Unit pricing* The replacement cost is determined by **direct pricing of component parts** of the asset being appraised.

3 *Functional pricing* The replacement cost is estimated by a **ratio** to the

---

[12] *Objectives of Financial Statements,* AICPA (New York: 1973), p. 64.

[13] *FASB Discussion Memorandum,* "Conceptual Framework for Financial Accounting and Reporting: Elements of Financial Statements and Their Measurement," FASB (Stamford: 1976), pp. 196–208.

[14] Additional references on the general topic of fair-value accounting are: Lawrence Revsine, *Replacement Cost Accounting,* Prentice-Hall, Inc. (Englewood Cliffs, N.J.: 1973); Howard J. Trienens and Daniel U. Smith, "Legal Implications of Current Value Accounting," *Financial Executive* (September 1972), pp. 44–47; Morton Backer, *Current Value Accounting,* Financial Executives Research Foundation (New York: 1973); Donald R. Brinkman and Paul H. Prentiss, "Replacement Cost and Current Value Accounting Comes of Age," *Financial Executive* (January 1976); Alfred M. King, "Replacement Cost Accounting: Developing the Information," *Financial Executive* (August 1976); *Current-Value Accounting, Economic Reality in Financial Reporting—A Program for Experimentation,* Touche Ross & Co. (New York: 1975).

replacement cost of a new and essentially equivalent type of asset which has a *different productive capacity.*

4 *Indexing* Replacement cost is established through the multiplication of the carrying value of the asset (in terms of historical cost) by an index which reflects price changes for a particular class of assets.[15]

The four methods that may be used to determine replacement cost are illustrated in the following simplified example:

Miklos Industries, Inc., is a producer of an expensive line of greeting cards. The company manufactures greeting cards only as orders are received, and therefore has no inventories other than paper. The only plant asset is a multicolor printing press acquired on January 2, Year 1, for $2 million. The capacity of the printing press is 2,000 greeting cards per hour. The estimated economic life for the printing press is 10 years with no residual value.

On December 31, Year 3, estimates of replacement costs for the printing press owned by Miklos Industries, Inc., were obtained as follows:

(1) Supplier A (the original manufacturer of the printing press) quoted a price of $2.8 million for a similar printing press with a capacity of 2,000 greeting cards per hour.

(2) Supplier B quoted a price of $3.0 million for a similar printing press with a capacity of 2,500 greeting cards per hour.

(3) Suppliers C & D presented separate bids aggregating $2.9 million to reproduce the several major component parts of the printing press.

The specific price index for a wide range of printing presses was 120 on January 2, Year 1, and 156 on December 31, Year 3.

The inventory of Miklos Industries, Inc., consists of 45 tons of paper valued at a lifo cost of $64,320. Under a long-term contract negotiated at the end of Year 3, Miklos Industries, Inc., will be able to purchase paper from a major supplier at $2,000 per ton.

The replacement costs at December 31, Year 3, for the inventory and the printing press, using the methods described above, are determined on page 917.

In practice, many difficulties may be encountered in making estimates of replacement costs for plant assets. For example, historical costs or acquisition dates may be difficult to determine and price indices may not be available for the specific type of plant asset owned by the reporting company. Furthermore, equipment currently available may not be comparable to existing equipment because of significant technological innovations, thus rendering the use of direct pricing or unit pricing impractical. As a result, management may have no choice but to use the functional pricing method. When more than one method for estimating replacement costs is feasible, management must either select the valuation method which most fairly measures replacement

[15] D. R. Brinkman, "Replacement Cost/Current Value Accounting," chap. 46, *Handbook of Modern Accounting,* 2d ed., edited by Sidney Davidson and Roman L. Weil, McGraw-Hill Book Company (New York: 1977).

Inventory: Quantity × long-term contract unit price – 45 tons × $2,000 per ton = $90,000

Printing press (in thousands of dollars):

	Historical cost	Direct pricing	Unit pricing	Functional pricing	Indexing
Printing press . . .	$2,000	$2,800 (2)	$2,900 (3)	$2,400 (4)	$2,600 (5)
Less: Accum. depr. (1) .	600	840	870	720	780
Carrying value, at replacement cost	$1,400	$1,960	$2,030	$1,680	$1,820

Explanations:

(1) For each method the accumulated depreciation is determined at 30% of historical cost or derived replacement cost because the printing press has an economic life of 10 years and has been used for three years.

(2) The quoted current price by supplier A for a similar printing press with the same capacity as the one currently owned.

(3) The quoted bids by suppliers C and D to reproduce the several major component parts of the printing press.

(4) On the basis of the quoted price of $3 million from supplier B for a similar printing press with a capacity of 2,500 greeting cards per hour, the replacement cost of the printing press currently owned (capacity of 2,000 greeting cards per hour) is determined as follows:
$3,000 × 2,000/2,500 = $2,400

(5) Because the specific price index for printing presses increased from 120 to 156 since the printing press was acquired on January 2, Year 1, the replacement cost at December 31, Year 3, is determined as follows:
$2,000 × 156/120 = $2,600

cost of plant assets or, alternatively, disclose a possible *range* of replacement costs.

SEC requirements

Most inflation accounting proposals were taken rather lightly by accountants and corporate managements until the threat of continuing double-digit inflation in the United States and the issuance by the Securities and Exchange Commission in 1976 of *Accounting Series Release No. 190* which required large corporations to disclose certain replacement cost information.[16]

The purpose of *ASR No. 190* was to provide information which would assist investors in obtaining an understanding of the current costs of operating the business. It was recognized by the SEC that such information would necessarily include subjective estimates and that such esti-

[16] *ASR No. 190*, SEC (Washington: 1976).

mates may be supplemented by additional disclosures to assist investors in understanding the meaning of the data in particular company situations. A secondary reason for requiring disclosure of replacement cost data was to provide information which would enable investors to determine the current economic investment in inventories and plant assets.

ASR No. 190 required the disclosure in supplementary form of certain replacement cost data by corporations registered with the SEC which have total inventories and gross property, plant, and equipment (that is, before deduction of accumulated depreciation, depletion, and amortization) of more than $100 million *and* these comprise more than 10% of total assets. The consolidated balance sheet at the *beginning* of the most recent fiscal year is used in determining whether these reporting requirements apply. A summary of the key requirements of *ASR No. 190* follows:

1 Companies are required to disclose their assets in terms of (a) the current replacement cost of inventories and (b) the current cost (gross and net of accumulated depreciation) of newly replacing the productive capacity (plant assets) on hand.

2 Companies should also disclose (a) the cost of sales for the two most recent years using the replacement cost of inventory items at the time of sale and (b) the amount of straight-line depreciation for the two most recent years based on the average current replacement cost of productive capacity.

3 The methods used in determining the amounts disclosed in **1** and **2** above should be described.

4 Management should furnish any additional information which it believes is necessary to prevent the replacement cost information from being misleading. For example, such information might include (a) customary relationship between cost changes and changes in selling prices and (b) the difficulty and related costs (such as those related to environmental regulations) which might be incurred in replacing productive capacity.

5 The replacement cost disclosure is to be presented in a note to financial statements and in the 10-K forms filed with the SEC. Published financial statements need not include all replacement cost information but should include comments relating to the effect of price-level changes and reference to the replacement cost data filed with the SEC.

6 Replacement cost disclosures are to be labeled "unaudited" but must be included as part of the annual statements. Although such replacement cost information is unaudited, independent auditors are "associated" with it. An amendment to *ASR No. 190* created a "safe harbor" rule, which protects the auditor against liability under the securities laws if the replacement cost information is prepared on a reasonable basis and is disclosed in good faith.

A wide range of methods of disclosure is possible under *ASR No. 190.* The method to be used in the determination of replacement costs was placed in the hands of management. Two examples of the presentation of replacement cost information are given in the Appendix at the end of this chapter for American Telephone and Telegraph Company and Alcan Aluminium Limited.

The initial implementation of replacement cost disclosure raised many practical questions which were addressed by the SEC in various *Staff Accounting Bulletins* (SAB).[17] Some examples of the clarifications included in these Bulletins are given below:

1 Productive capacity is a measurement of a company's ability to produce and distribute. The productive capacity of a manufacturer would be measured by number of units it can presently produce.

2 Replacement cost is the lowest amount that would have to be paid in the normal course of business to obtain a new asset of equivalent operating or productive capacity.

3 Fully depreciated assets still in use should be disclosed but no adjustment to depreciation should be made. Land should be excluded from productive capacity unless it is consumed (that is, depleted) in the production process. Intangible assets are not included in productive capacity; however, assets held under capital leases are to be included.

4 Companies with long-term (that is, more than two years) supply contracts should use the contract prices in determining the replacement cost of inventories.

Reactions to the disclosure of replacement cost information have been mixed. Some users of financial statements viewed *ASR No. 190* as the initial step in the adoption of fair-value accounting as the primary financial reporting model. They viewed the disclosure of replacement cost information as a positive step which provides investors and creditors with more relevant data for making business decisions.

On the other hand, some users of financial statements, public accountants, and corporate managements were less enthusiastic. They viewed such disclosure as costly, potentially misleading, and possibly dangerous because it would cast a long shadow on the validity of reported earnings and thus might make it more difficult for companies to raise capital. The following observation by a security analyst probably was shared by many who felt that disclosure of replacement cost information was premature: "The real question is how seriously the stock market will take the new set of data. It's to be hoped that it will just ignore it."[18] Only actual experience with replacement cost disclosure will enable us to evaluate the two sides of the issue.

---

[17] *Staff Accounting Bulletins* are not rules or interpretations of the Commission; they represent interpretations and practices followed in administering the disclosure requirements of the federal securities laws.

[18] Myron Simons, *Forbes* (Mar. 15, 1977) p. 134.

APPENDIX: NOTE TO FINANCIAL STATEMENTS—AMERICAN TELEPHONE AND TELEGRAPH COMPANY (1976 ANNUAL REPORT)

(N) Replacement Cost (Unaudited)—In response to Securities and Exchange Commission requirements, the following figures compare telephone plant investment as shown on the balance sheet at December 31, 1976, with the approximate cost to replace its productive capacity at that date. They also compare accumulated depreciation at that date with the amount that would have been provided had past depreciation accruals contemplated such replacement costs. Additionally, they compare depreciation expense for the year ended December 31, 1976, with depreciation expense computed (using historic depreciation assumptions) on these estimates of replacement costs.

	Millions of dollars		
	As stated	*At replacement cost*	*Difference*
Telephone plant investment:			
For which replacement cost has been determined	$90,660	$130,405	$39,745
Included at historic cost	3,507	3,507	—
Total	$94,167	$133,912	$39,745
Accumulated depreciation	18,245	32,634	14,389
Net telephone plant investment	$75,922	$101,278	$25,356
Depreciation expense	$ 4,484	$ 5,980	$ 1,496

These replacement cost figures are theoretical, based on the assumptions that, as of December 31, 1976: electronic switching systems would replace all electromechanical switching systems; most other telephone plant would be replaced in accordance with present replacement practices; and building space would be reduced because of the use of electronic switching systems. Certain telephone plant categories are included at historic cost: principally land, telephone plant under construction, and telephone plant held for future use.

The difference between historic and estimated replacement cost of net telephone plant investment does not represent additional book value for the Company's stock. The above replacement cost is an approximation of the amount of capital that could have been required were the Company to have replaced the entire productive capacity of such plant on December 31, 1976. Replacement actually will take place over many years and the funds needed will be derived from sources similar to those available during 1976.

Depreciation expense based on an estimate of replacement cost also is a theoretical figure and not deductible in determining income tax expense. The excess of depreciation on replacement cost over that determined on historic cost is a measure of the extent to which current operations have not been making provision for the higher replacement cost of present plant capacity. Such provision, if made, would provide funds which would be used in lieu of funds from other sources for plant construction.

It would be unrealistic to impute a reduced net income by the difference between depreciation based on historic cost and that based on estimates of replacement cost. New plant is likely to provide largely-offsetting additional revenue-generating services and operating efficiencies. Additionally, replacement of plant will take place over many years. It is true, however, that the earnings of the Company must be high enough to provide some equity capital from reinvested earnings and to attract additional debt and equity to provide funds for any replacement cost in excess of depreciation accruals based on the historic cost of the plant.

ALCAN ALUMINIUM LIMITED ANNUAL REPORT 1976

Inflation Accounting

International developments Inflation, although diminishing, continues to trouble most parts of the world, but no wholly satisfactory method of accounting and reporting the effects of inflation on the financial results of a business has yet been developed. However, in 1975, recognizing the need to provide its shareholders and investors with some appreciation of the impact of past inflation on its business, Alcan published a supplementary set of financial statements for 1974, using the current purchasing power method (CPP) of inflation accounting. This was being advocated at that time in several countries, and gave historical costs re-stated in current dollars by use of a consumer price index. Subsequently, it became apparent that in a number of countries this method was not considered adequate to meet the problem, and Alcan decided not to publish any supplementary statements last year. However, during 1976 the search for an appropriate method of accounting under inflationary conditions continued, and there have been significant developments in the United Kingdom, Australia and the United States.

In the United Kingdom, the Government-appointed Sandilands Committee proposed in September 1975 an inflation-accounting method described as 'current cost accounting' (CCA), and this was further refined by the Morpeth Committee in December 1976. The recommended effective date for the larger U.K. companies to adopt CCA is for periods commencing on or after 1 July 1978.

In Australia, a provisional standard issued in October 1976 by the accounting profession suggested that companies adopt 'current cost accounting' (CCA), a procedure carrying the same name but differing somewhat from the method proposed in the U.K., for periods starting on or after 1 July 1977. These statements would supplement the conventional historical cost statements. By July 1978 a formal standard is expected which would make CCA mandatory for financial reporting purposes.

In the United States, the Securities and Exchange Commission (SEC) announced in March 1976, in its Accounting Series Release No. 190, a requirement for the larger listed companies to provide the estimated 'current replacement cost' of productive capacity and inventories with depreciation expense and cost of sales based on those amounts, effective for the year 1976. Unlike the U.K. and Australian versions of CCA, which will call for audited financial statements, the SEC calls for supplementary information which need not be audited.

Replacement cost data In accordance with SEC requirements, Alcan's estimated replacement cost data are shown on pages 922–923, but within the framework of a consolidated balance sheet and income statement. The latter has only been taken to the 'Income before income tax' stage since no appropriate method of accounting for tax under these circumstances has been agreed.

Asset values and operating costs Alcan's major operating subsidiaries made detailed reviews of their assets, and calculated the replacement cost mainly by valuing specific assets or operating capacities. Valuations of the other assets and those of the remaining smaller subsidiaries were based on appropriate indices.

Generally, replacement costs for the major alumina, power and aluminum smelter facilities have been developed through engineering estimates of cost per unit of capacity, including appropriate technological improvements, and multiplied by existing capacity to arrive at the estimated total replacement cost.

No attempt has been made to re-engineer the entire productive capacity. Nor do the estimates take into account the manifold problems of relocation and consolidation of existing productive facilities, including availability of labour, sources of raw materials and proximity to customers, all of which would necessarily have to be considered in depth before undertaking actual replacement. These studies might significantly alter the cost and manner of replacement.

Furthermore, replacement would also alter the current level of operating costs, due to the greater efficiency in the use of labour and materials in new production facilities of more modern design. However, these cost changes cannot be quantified with any precision. Nevertheless, Alcan believes that they would significantly offset the additional depreciation on a replacement-cost basis.

Accumulated depreciation is estimated by the relationship of expired lives to total lives of the existing facilities, applied to the estimated replacement cost of the productive capacity. At this point no attempt has been made to re-estimate the useful lives of the assets for the replacement-cost depreciation calculations.

The annual depreciation charge based on replacement values is calculated on the straight-line method, using the historical-cost depreciation rates for existing facilities, applied to the average of the estimated replacement cost of productive capacity as at the beginning and at the end of the year.

Replacement cost of sales is estimated by adjusting historical costs for the inflation occurring during the period between production and sale.

Amounts on the replacement basis related to locations outside the United States have been compiled initially in local currencies and then translated into U.S. dollars at year-end exchange rates for productive capacity and inventories, and at average rates during the year for cost of sales and depreciation expense.

Consolidated Balance Sheet

31 December 1976	Estimated replacement cost basis	Historical cost basis
	(in millions of U.S. dollars)	
Current assets		
Inventories	$ 923	$ 817
Other	552	552
Property, plant and equipment(a) .	7,133	2,997
Less: Accumulated depreciation .		
and depletion	(4,233)	(1,596)
Other assets (b)	320	320
	$4,695	$3,090
Current liabilities	$ 595	$ 595
Debt not maturing within one year	837	837
Deferred income taxes and credits	225	225
Minority interests	207	163
Shareholders' equity		
Share capital	429	429
Retained earnings	841	841
Replacement reserve	1,561	
	$4,695	$3,090

(a) Land, water rights and mineral properties have not been revalued and are included in the estimated replacement cost at their historical cost of $83 million. Accumulated amortization and depletion relating to these assets of $8 million also have not been revalued and are included in the replacement data without change.

(b) Includes investments, in companies owned 50% or less, of $207 million which have not been revalued and are included in the estimated replacement cost at the same amount.

Consolidated Statement of Income

Year ending 31 December 1976	Estimated replacement cost basis	Historical cost basis
	(in millions of U.S. dollars)	
Revenues	$2,671	$2,671
Costs and expenses		
Cost of sales and operating expenses	2,198	2,155
Depreciation and depletion	278	116
Other	304	304
Income before income taxes	$ (109)	$ 96

Conclusions Some conclusions may be drawn. In particular:

1. The figures indicate that replacement of existing production capacity would not be justified by the 1976 price structure, even after allowing for the problems stated above (such as the greater efficiency that replaced assets would provide) and the fact that 1976 was a poor year for earnings because of work stoppages. This illustrates a fact that has been frequently stated. Of course, replacement might be justified by the price structure which would be in effect when any particular replacement could be completed.

2. Government treatment of capital-intensive business is not satisfactory where current-cost depreciation—although a measure of the current usage of assets—is not allowed as a cost for income tax purposes, and where in Canada and some other countries (although not the U.S. or the U.K.) inventory profits are taxed currently. Furthermore, in most countries exercising price controls, the basis of costing is average costing and not current costing, even though the price controls may thus be giving a negative real return.

3. The current replacement value of Alcan's assets is far higher than the historical cost in current dollars, showing that the inflation in machinery and construction costs has far exceeded the consumer price index. In a capital-intensive industry this leads to a very high current-cost depreciation charge, and a corresponding impact on current-cost earnings. However, cash flow is not affected.

4. Under the recommended guidelines, credit is not taken in the replacement-cost net income statement for gains experienced from having debt, or losses resulting from holding monetary assets, such as cash and receivables, in times of inflation. However, this omission seems questionable in a capital-intensive industry where leverage is of great importance to the capital structure. As Alcan has debt and other net monetary liabilities of about one billion dollars, an average inflation rate of 10 per cent in the countries where it operates would give an annual gain of about $100 million, greatly improving the current cost picture.

5. The replacement-cost method does not correct for the change in value of currency during the year. Also, it does not call for the restatement of previous years' accounts in current dollars. It, therefore, will not permit a direct comparison of the replacement value accounts of one year with those of prior years.

Summary of Alcan's view Because of the lack of established standards, the considerable degree of continuing experimentation and the many subjective judgments required in the compilation of the data, we consider that the figures provided cannot give more than a general impression of the values involved, and that specific comparisons with other reported data are unlikely to be valid.

Furthermore it is our view that an attempt to present a valuation of assets which might replace the existing assets is not sufficiently factual for a satisfactory accounting presentation. We would prefer to see a method which revalues in current dollars the assets which the company actually owns.

The whole problem of inflation accounting is still far from resolved. However, it is likely that considerable progress will be made in 1977 and, when a method is finally agreed, it will mark the most significant development in accounting practice in this century.

REVIEW QUESTIONS

1 What evidence can you offer in support of the assertion that "the dollar is not a stable unit of value?"

2 List three indices of the general price level in the United States. Which index is considered to be best measure of the general movement in prices?

3 Evaluate the following quotation: "If historical-dollar financial statements were restated to reflect the changing value of the dollar, assets would be stated at current fair value and net income would not be determined by matching realized revenue with expired costs."

4 Explain how the use of generally accepted accounting principles may result in reporting as a part of net income what is in reality a recovery of capital.

5 Explain each of the following:
   a Monetary items
   b Positive monetary position
   c Negative monetary position
   d General price-level gains and losses (or purchasing-power gains and losses)

6 What is meant by the expression *conversion factor?* Compute the conversion factor for land if the general price-level index was 80 on the date the land was acquired and is 144 today.

7 What is meant by *price-level accounting?*

8 a What suggestion was made in *APB Statement No. 3* for reporting price-level information as a supplement to the basic historical-dollar financial statements?
   b What points should be explained in the notes relating to the price-level information accompanying the basic historical-dollar financial statements?

9 To what extent have fair values been used by accountants in the preparation of financial statements?

10 What is the position of the Accounting Principles Board in *Opinion No. 6* regarding the reporting of plant assets at current fair value?

11 What are the causes of changes in the *relative* (or *comparative*) *value* of reproducible assets?

12 Distinguish between *relative* (or *comparative*) *value changes* for assets and *price-level changes.*

13 The basic method of valuation used in accounting for assets is actual costs

less depreciation. At various times during their economic life it is possible to estimate the current fair value of such assets by using one of the following methods:

a Capitalization of net cash inflows (or direct valuation)
b Exit values (both current and expected)
c Replacement cost
d Specific-price index replacement cost

Explain the meaning of the term **current fair value** and define each of the four methods of arriving at current fair value listed above.

14 Evaluate the following quotation: "Accounting is no more than the recording and reporting of transactions. Recognition of the current fair values of assets in the financial statements is neither feasible nor useful; besides, it lacks objectivity."

15 Proposals for the implementation of fair-value accounting may be placed into four categories. List the categories and indicate which one seems to be most feasible at the present time.

16 Describe four methods of determining replacement costs of plant assets.

17 Briefly state the objectives that the SEC attempted to achieve through the disclosure of replacement cost information as required by **ASR No. 190.**

18 List the key requirements of **ASR No. 190** issued by the SEC in 1976.

EXERCISES

Ex. 22-1 A building was acquired for $400,000 at the beginning of Year 1 when the general price-level index was 80 and has been depreciated at a straight-line rate of $2\frac{1}{2}\%$ per year. At the end of Year 30 the general price-level index is 220. Show how the building and the related accumulated depreciation would be shown at the end of Year 30 in a balance sheet restated for changes in the general price-level index.

Ex. 22-2 For each independent situation below, compute the general price-level gain or loss, assuming that assets and liabilities remained unchanged during the entire period. The general price level rose by 7% during the period:

a Monetary assets $110,000
    Current liabilities 60,000

b Monetary assets $250,000
    Current liabilities 100,000
    Long-term liabilities 300,000

c Cash . . . . $ 50,000
    Accounts receivable 60,000
    Notes receivable 90,000
    Inventories 100,000
    Investment in common stocks 200,000
    Plant and equipment (net of accumulated depreciation) 600,000
    Liabilities 475,000
    Stockholders' equity 625,000

Ex. 22-3 From the following year-end general price-level indices, compute the conversion factors to restate the financial statements for Year 1, Year 2, and Year 3 in terms of end-of-Year 4 dollars:

Year 1	90
Year 2	100
Year 3	120
Year 4	126

Ex. 22-4 At the beginning of Year 1, when the general price level was 100, Larry Bianchi had total assets of $100,000 consisting of $25,000 in cash and $75,000 in copper. At the end of Year 1, when the general price level was 140, the copper was sold for $100,000. Compute the general price-level gain or loss for Year 1. What was the "real" (economic) gain or loss on the sale of the copper?

Ex. 22-5 Antoci Reel Company was formed and began business operations in Year 1. The company adopted the lifo method of inventory pricing and has consistently used this method. At the end of Year 15, the composition of the inventory and the average general price-level index in the year of acquisition were as follows:

Acquired in Year 1 (index = 90)	$380,000
Year 3 layer (index = 100)	20,000
Year 10 layer (index = 120)	5,000
Year 15 layer (index = 135)	35,000
Total inventory at lifo cost, as shown on financial statements at Dec. 31, Year 15	$440,000

Prepare a schedule restating the inventory at December 31, Year 15, to reflect changes in the general price level.

Ex. 22-6 Wong's Rolls bought 10,000 bushels of wheat at $2 per bushel and later another 10,000 bushels of the same grade at $2.50 per bushel. The general price level has risen 10% since the first purchase and 5% since the second purchase, but because of bad weather the market price of wheat is now $4 per bushel. Both lots of wheat are included in the ending inventory. What is the value of each lot of wheat under (a) price-level accounting and (b) fair-value accounting?

Ex. 22-7 Given below is a balance sheet for Marangi & Associates at the beginning and end of Year 1, the first year of business:

	Beginning of Year 1	End of Year 1
Monetary assets	$60,000	$ 82,000
Office equipment (net)	20,000	18,000
Total	$80,000	$100,000
Liabilities	$10,000	$ 17,000
Tina Marangi, capital	70,000	83,000
Total	$80,000	$100,000

The income statement for Year 1 is presented below:

Fees earned		*$40,000*
Less:		
Operating expenses (excluding depreciation)	*$15,000*	
Depreciation expense	*2,000*	*17,000*
Net income		*$23,000*

Fees were earned and expenses were incurred evenly through the year. The owner withdrew $10,000 from the business at the end of Year 1. The general price-level index at the beginning of Year 1 was 100; at the end of Year 1 it was 120; and the average for the year was 109. Compute the general price-level gain or loss for Year 1. (Carry the computation of conversion factors to two decimal places.)

Ex. 22-8 **a** From the information given in Exercise 22-7, prepare a balance sheet for Marangi & Associates at the end of Year 1, restated for the change in the general price level.

b Prepare an income statement for Year 1 restated for the change in the general price level. Assume that the general price-level loss (computed in Exercise 22-7) is $12,500.

c Prepare a statement of owner's capital restated for the change in the general price level.

Ex. 22-9 Joan Roberts, the controller of the Roberts Company, is discussing a comment you made in the course of presenting your audit report.

". . . and frankly," Miss Roberts continued, "I agree that we, too, are responsible for finding ways to produce more relevant financial statements which are as reliable as the ones we now produce.

"For example, suppose we acquired a finished item for inventory for $40 when the general price-level index was 110. And, later, the item was sold for $75 when the general price-level index was 121 and the current replacement cost was $54. We could calculate and report a 'holding gain' of $10."

a Explain to what extent and how current replacement costs already are used **within** the generally accepted accounting principles to value inventories.

b Show how Miss Roberts computed the holding gain of $10.

Ex. 22-10 Valuation to reflect general price-level adjustments, as opposed to replacement cost, would yield differing amounts on a company's financial statements. Several transactions concerning one asset of Saunders Corporation, a calendar-year company, are summarized as follows:

Year 4   Purchased land for $40,000 cash on December 31.

Replacement cost at year-end was $40,000.

Year 5   Held this land all year.

Replacement cost at year-end was $52,000.

Year 6   October 31—sold this land for $68,000

General price-level index:

Dec. 31, Year 4	*100*
Dec. 31, Year 5	*110*
Oct. 31, Year 6	*120*

On your answer sheet, duplicate the schedules at the top of page 928 and complete the information required based upon the transactions described above:

Valuation of land in balance sheet	General price level	Replacement cost
Dec. 31, Year 4	$	$
Dec. 31, Year 5	$	$

Gain in income statement	General price level	Replacement cost
Year 4	$	$
Year 5		
Year 6		
Total	$	$

SHORT CASES FOR ANALYSIS AND DECISION

Case 22-1 Valuation of assets is an important topic in accounting theory. Suggested valuation methods include the following:

Historical costs (past purchase prices)

Historical costs adjusted to reflect general price-level changes

Discounted cash flow (future exchange prices)

Market prices (current selling prices)

Replacement costs (current purchase prices)

Instructions
a Why is the valuation of assets a significant issue?
b Explain the basic theory underlying each of the valuation methods cited above. Do not discuss advantages and disadvantages of each method.

Case 22-2 A common objective of accountants is to prepare meaningful financial statements. To attain this objective many accountants maintain that the financial statements must be adjusted for changes in the general price level. Other accountants believe that financial statements should continue to be prepared on the basis of unadjusted historical cost.

Instructions
a List arguments for adjusting financial statements for changes in the general price level.
b List arguments for preparing financial statements only on the basis of unadjusted historical cost.
c In their discussions about accounting for changes in the general price level and the methods of measuring them, uninformed individuals have frequently failed to distinguish between adjustments for changes in the price levels of specific goods and services and adjustments for changes in the general purchasing power of the dollar. What is the distinction? Which are "price-level adjustments"? Discuss.

Case 22-3 Chip Higgin, a small but growing road-building contractor, would like to bid on a contract to rebuild and surface 8 miles of road. The job is considerably larger than any he has attempted in the past and, if he wins the contract, he estimates that he will need a $200,000 line of credit for working capital.

Higgin's most recent balance sheet shows a capital of $180,000, of which $150,000 represents the carrying value of road-building equipment. Most of the equipment was acquired a few years ago at a bankruptcy sale. The equipment has a fair value several times as great as carrying value. Knowing that the bank will not extend a $200,000 line of credit on the basis of a balance sheet which shows capital at only $18,000, Higgin wants to adjust the accounting records to show the fair value of the equipment and to prepare a revised balance sheet.

Instructions

a List the factors that, alone or in combination, may have caused the difference between the carrying value and the fair value of the equipment.

b Discuss the propriety of adjusting the accounting records to show the current fair value of the equipment and preparing a revised balance sheet. Suggest a possible alternative approach. Your answer should take into consideration the factors that may have caused the difference between the carrying value and the current fair value of the equipment.

c Do bankers tend to place as much emphasis on the balance sheet prepared in conventional form as Higgin apparently thinks they do?

Case 22-4 Financial statements are tools for the communication of quantifiable economic information to readers who use them as one of the factors in making a variety of management and investment decisions and judgments. To fulfill this function accounting data should be quantifiable and should also be relevant to the kinds of judgments and decisions made. They should be verifiable and free from personal bias. There are many who believe that for some purposes current cost is a more useful measure than historical cost and recommend that dual statements be prepared showing both historical costs and current fair values.

Instructions

a Discuss the ways in which historical costs and current fair values conform to the standards of verifiability and freedom from bias.

b Describe briefly how the fair values of the following assets might be determined.

  (1) Inventory
  (2) Investments in marketable securities
  (3) Equipment and machinery
  (4) Natural resources
  (5) Goodwill

PROBLEMS

Group A

22A-1 Select the best answer for each of the following questions relating to price-level accounting. Choose only one answer for each question.

1 In the context of general price-level adjustments, which of the following is a nonmonetary item?

  a Receivables under capital leases
  b Obligations under capital leases
  c Patents
  d Unamortized discount on bonds payable

2 When does a general purchasing-power loss occur and when is it recognized?

  a It occurs when holding net monetary assets during inflation and is recognized in units-of-general-purchasing-power financial statements.
  b It occurs when holding net monetary liabilities during inflation and is recognized in units-of-general-purchasing-power financial statements.

c It occurs when holding net monetary assets during inflation and is recognized in units-of-general-purchasing-power and units-of-money financial statements.

d It occurs when holding net monetary liabilities during inflation and is recognized in units-of-general-purchasing-power and units-of-money financial statements.

3 Mock Company reported sales of $2,000,000 in Year 3 and $3,000,000 in Year 4. Sales were made evenly throughout each year. The general price-level index during Year 2 remained constant at 100, and at the end of Year 3 and Year 4 it was 102 and 104, respectively. What should Mock report as sales for Year 4 restated for general price-level changes?

a $3,000,000   b $3,029,126   c $3,058,821   d $3,120,000

4 On January 2, Year 5, Brazil Corporation mortgaged one of its properties as collateral for a $1,000,000, 7%, five-year loan. During Year 5, the general price level increased evenly, resulting in a 5% increase for the year.

In preparing a balance sheet expressing financial position in terms of the general price level at the end of Year 5, at which amount should Brazil Corporation report its mortgage note payable?

a $950,000   b $1,000,000   c $1,025,000   d $1,050,000

5 If land were purchased in Year 10 for $150,000 when the general price-level index was 100 and sold at the end of Year 19 for $240,000 when the index was 170, the general price-level income statement for Year 19 would show:

a A general price-level gain of $105,000 and a loss on sale of land of $15,000
b A gain on sale of land of $90,000
c A general price-level loss of $15,000
d A loss on sale of land of $15,000
e None of the above

6 A company was formed on January 2, Year 2. Selected balances from the historical-dollar balance sheet at December 31, Year 2, were:

Accounts receivable	$ 70,000
Accounts payable	60,000
Long-term debt	110,000
Common stock	100,000

At what amounts should these selected accounts be shown in a general price-level balance sheet at December 31, Year 2, if the general price-level index was 100 at December 31, Year 1, and 110 at December 31, Year 2?

	Accounts receivable	Accounts payable	Long-term debt	Common stock
a	$70,000	$60,000	$110,000	$100,000
b	$70,000	$60,000	$110,000	$110,000
c	$70,000	$60,000	$121,000	$110,000
d	$77,000	$66,000	$121,000	$110,000

7 If the base year is Year 1 (when the general price-level index = 100) and land is purchased for $50,000 in Year 5 when the general price-level index is 108.5, the cost of the land restated to Year 1 general purchasing power (rounded to the nearest whole dollar) would be:

a $54,250   b $50,000   c $46,083   d $45,750   e None of the above

8 Assume the same facts as in question 7 above. The cost of the land restated to

December 31, Year 10, general purchasing power when the general price-level index was 119.2 (rounded to the nearest whole dollar) would be:

a $59,600   **b** $54,931   **c** $46,083   **d** $45,512   **e** None of the above

9 If land were purchased at a cost of $120,000 in January of Year 13 when the general price-level index was 120 and sold in December of Year 19 when the index was 150, the selling price that would result in no gain or loss in price-level financial statements would be:

a $180,000   **b** $144,000   **c** $120,000   **d** $150,000   **e** None of the above

22A-2 The income statement for Anchor Chain Company for Year 1, in historical dollars, follows:

Sales (net)		$900,000
Cost of goods sold		690,000
Gross profit on sales		$210,000
Expenses:		
Depreciation	$ 15,000	
Other (including interest expense and income taxes)	120,000	135,000
Net income		$ 75,000

Sales per month generally averaged $75,000 and expenses (including income taxes) were incurred at a relatively even rate throughout the year. Both cost of goods sold and the ending inventory consist of a representative sample of goods purchased during the year.

A comparative balance sheet (in historical dollars) at January 1 and December 31, Year 1, follows:

ANCHOR CHAIN COMPANY
Comparative Balance Sheet

	Jan. 1, Year 1	Dec. 31, Year 1
Assets		
Monetary assets	$127,500	$ 22,500
Investment in common stock of Fertig Company	–0–	100,000
Inventory (fifo method)	–0–	160,000
Land	60,000	60,000
Building (net)	150,000	144,000
Equipment (net)	112,500	103,500
Total assets	$450,000	$590,000
Liabilities & Stockholders' Equity		
Current liabilities	$ 25,000	$135,000
Long-term notes payable	175,000	150,000
Capital stock, $5 par	200,000	200,000
Paid-in capital in excess of par	50,000	50,000
Retained earnings	–0–	55,000
Total liabilities & stockholders' equity	$450,000	$590,000

On April 30 of Year 1, the company invested $100,000 in the common stock of Fertig Company. Also on April 30, Anchor Chain Company declared a dividend of $20,000.

The changes in the general price-level index during Year 1 are summarized below:

	General price-level index	Conversion factor to restate to end-of-Year 1 dollars
Jan. 1	110	1.100
Apr. 30	112	1.080
July 1 (also the average for the year)	115	1.052
Dec. 31	121	1.000

Instructions

a Prepare a working paper to restate the income statement for Year 1 for changes in the general price level. Compute any general price-level gain or loss in a supporting schedule (Schedule A).

b Prepare a working paper to restate the balance sheets at January 1, Year 1, and at December 31, Year 1, for changes in the general price-level index. (Use the form illustrated on page 906).

c "Prove" the amount of retained earnings needed in part **b** to balance total assets (as restated) with total liabilities and stockholders' equity (as restated) by preparing a separate statement of retained earnings (adjusted for changes in the general price-level index).

22A-3 Ann Betty & Co. was organized on July 1, Year 1. Under the partnership contract, $900,000 was provided by Ann and $600,000 by Betty as initial capital; income and losses were to be shared in the same ratio as the initial capital contributions. No additional capital contributions have been made.

The December 31, Year 6, balance sheet appears below:

Assets

Cash and marketable securities	$ 200,500
Accounts receivable, net of allowance for doubtful accounts	950,000
Inventory (lifo method)	1,500,000
Unexpired insurance	18,000
Land	58,000
Machinery, net of accumulated depreciation	1,473,500
Total assets	$4,200,000

Liabilities & Capital

Current liabilities	$1,475,000
Ann, capital	1,615,000
Betty, capital	1,110,000
Total liabilities & capital	$4,200,000

Ann and Betty are considering selling their business but are concerned that the financial statements do not reveal its current worth. You have been requested to assist in determining the current fair value of the assets.

You compile the following information in addition to the asset section of the balance sheet:

(1) An aging of accounts receivable disclosed the following:

Year accounts originated	Gross amount	Allowance for doubtful accounts	Net valuation
Year 3	$ 40,000	$ 35,000	$ 5,000
Year 4	125,000	105,000	20,000
Year 5	160,000	67,500	92,500
Year 6	925,000	92,500	832,500
Totals	$1,250,000	$300,000	$950,000

A review of past experience shows that all receivables over two years old have been uncollectible; those over one year old have been 50% collectible; and those less than one year old have been 90% collectible.

(2) The inventory level has been increasing and its cost has been determined using the last-in, first-out cost flow assumption. The cost of the last-in, first-out layers at the average price for the indicated year of acquisition and the inventory specific-price increases have been as follows:

Last-in, first-out layers		Specific-price increases	
Year acquired	Cost	Period	Increase
Year 2	$ 60,000	Year 2–Year 6	20%
Year 3	150,000	Year 3–Year 6	18%
Year 4	240,000	Year 4–Year 6	15%
Year 5	350,000	Year 5–Year 6	11%
Year 6	700,000	Year 6	5%
	$1,500,000		

(3) Machinery was purchased in Year 2, Year 4, and Year 5 for $500,000, $850,000, and $660,000, respectively. The straight-line depreciation method and a 10-year estimated economic life have been used for all machinery, with a half-year of depreciation taken in the year of acquisition. The experience of other companies over the last several years indicates that the machinery can be sold at 125% of its carrying value.

(4) An independent appraisal made in December, Year 6, placed a current fair value of $100,000 on the land.

Instructions Prepare a comparative statement of assets showing historical costs and current fair values at December 31, Year 6. Supporting schedules should be in good form.

22A-4 Selca Corporation purchased a tract of land as an investment in Year 11 for $100,000; late in that year the company decided to construct a shopping center on the site. Construction began in Year 12 and was completed in Year 14; one-third of the construction was completed each year. Selca originally estimated the costs of the project would be $1,250,000 for materials, $750,000 for labor, $150,000 for variable overhead, and $600,000 for depreciation of plant assets used on this construction project.

Actual costs (excluding depreciation) incurred for construction were:

	Year 12	Year 13	Year 14
Materials	$420,000	$434,560	$462,000
Labor	236,250	274,400	282,000
Variable overhead	47,250	54,208	61,200

Shortly after construction began, Selca sold the shopping center for $3,040,000 with payment to be made in full on completion in December, Year 14. Of the total sales price, $150,000 was allocated for the land.

The transaction was completed as scheduled and now a controversy has developed between the two major stockholders of the company. One feels the company should have invested in land because a high rate of return was earned on the land. The other feels the original decision was sound and that changes in the general price level which were not anticipated affected the original cost estimates.

You were engaged to furnish guidance to these stockholders in resolving their controversy. As an aid, you obtained the following information:

(1) Using Year 11 as the base year, the general price-level indices for relevant years are: Year 8 = 90, Year 9 = 93, Year 10 = 96, Year 11 = 100, Year 12 = 105, Year 13 = 112, and Year 14 = 120.

(2) The company allocated $200,000 per year for depreciation of plant assets used on this construction project; of that amount $27,200 was for a building purchased in Year 8 and $172,800 was for equipment purchased in Year 10.

Instructions

a Prepare a schedule to restate in base-year (Year 11) dollars the actual construction costs, including depreciation, incurred each year. Disregard income taxes and assume that each year's price-level index was valid for the entire year. Use a fraction for the conversion factor, for example, 100/105, 100/112, etc.

b Prepare a schedule comparing the originally estimated costs of the project with the total actual costs for each element of cost (materials, labor, variable overhead, and depreciation) adjusted to the Year 11 general price level.

c Prepare a schedule to determine the gain or loss on the sale of the shopping center in terms of base-year (Year 11) purchasing power. The gain or loss should be determined separately for the land and the building. Briefly evaluate the results.

Group B

22B-1 Select the best answer for each of the following questions relating to price-level accounting. Choose only one answer for each question. The following information is applicable to questions 1 through 4:

Equipment purchased for $120,000 on January 1, Year 1, when the general price-level index was 100, was sold on December 31, Year 3, at a price of $85,000. The equipment originally was expected to last six years with no residual value and was depreciated on a straight-line basis. The general price-level index at the end of Year 1 was 120, at Year 2 was 150, and at Year 3 was 175.

1 The general price-level financial statements prepared at the end of Year 1 would include:

    a Equipment of $144,000, accumulated depreciation of $24,000, and a gain of $24,000

    b Equipment of $144,000, accumulated depreciation of $24,000, and no gain or loss

    c Equipment of $144,000, accumulated depreciation of $20,000, and a gain of $24,000

    d Equipment of $120,000, accumulated depreciation of $20,000, and a gain of $24,000

    e None of the above

2 In general price-level comparative financial statements prepared at the end of Year 2, the Year 1 financial statements should show equipment (net of accumulated depreciation) at:

    a $150,000   **b** $125,000   **c** $100,000   **d** $80,000   **e** None of the above

3 The general price-level financial statements prepared at the end of Year 2 should include depreciation expense of:

    a $35,000   **b** $30,000   **c** $25,000   **d** $20,000   **e** None of the above

4 The general price-level income statement prepared at the end of Year 3 should include:

    a A gain of $35,000   **d** A loss of $20,000

    b A gain of $25,000   **e** None of the above

    c No gain or loss

5 The valuation basis used in conventional (historical-dollar) financial statements is:

    a Fair value

    b Historical cost

    c Replacement cost

    d A mixture of historical costs and fair values

    e None of the above

6 An unacceptable practice for presenting general price-level information in annual reports of corporations is:

    a The inclusion of general price-level gains and losses on monetary items in the general price-level income statement

    b The inclusion of extraordinary items in the general price-level income statement

    c The use of charts, ratios, and narrative information

    d The use of specific-price indices to restate inventories and plant assets

    e None of the above

7 When a general price-level balance sheet is prepared, it should be presented in terms of:

    a The general purchasing power of the dollar at the end of the latest period presented

    b The general purchasing power of the dollar in the base period

    c The average general purchasing power of the dollar for the latest period

    d The general purchasing power of the dollar at the time the financial statements are issued

    e None of the above

8 The restatement of historical-dollar financial statements to reflect general price-level changes results in presenting assets at:

    a Lower-of-cost-or-market values

    b Current appraisal values

    c Historical costs adjusted for purchasing-power changes

    d Current replacement costs

    e None of the above

9 Following are four observations regarding the amounts reported in financial statements that have been adjusted for general price-level changes. Which observation is valid?

a The amount obtained by adjusting an asset's cost for general price-level changes usually approximates its current fair value.

b The amounts adjusted for general price-level changes are not departures from historical cost.

c When inventory increases and prices are rising, last-in, first-out (lifo) inventory accounting has the same effect on financial statements as amounts adjusted for general price-level changes.

d When inventory remains constant and prices are rising, lifo inventory accounting has the same effect on financial statements as amounts adjusted for general price-level changes.

22B-2 The latest income statement for Simca Soybean Corporation is given below (in historical dollars):

SIMCA SOYBEAN CORPORATION
Income Statement
For Current Year

Sales (net)		$700,000
Cost of goods sold:		
Inventory, Jan. 1 (lifo method)	$ 80,000	
Purchases (net)	450,000	
Cost of goods available for sale	$530,000	
Less: Inventory, Dec. 31 (lifo method)	95,000	435,000
Gross profit on sales		$265,000
Operating expenses:		
Selling (reducing net monetary assets)	$ 30,000	
General (reducing net monetary assets)	25,000	
Depreciation	35,000	90,000
Income before income taxes		$175,000
Income tax expense		70,000
Net income		$105,000

All items in the income statement were recorded at a fairly uniform rate throughout the year. The beginning inventory and depreciable assets were acquired when the general price-level index was 125. The lifo layer of $15,000 added to the inventory during the current year consists of goods acquired throughout the year. Changes in the general price-level index during the current year are summarized below:

Beginning of year (conversion factor = 1.200)	150
Average for the year (conversion factor = 1.078)	167
End of year (conversion factor = 1.000)	180

Instructions Prepare a working paper to restate the income statement in terms of the general price-level index at the end of the current year. Assume that the general price-level loss as a result of holding net monetary assets during the year was $8,880.

22B-3 Sitka-Alaska Corporation was organized on December 30, Year 4, by issuing

100,000 shares of $1 par capital stock for $500,000 in cash, and it started doing business early in Year 5. On January 2, Year 5, it completed the following trans-action:

Land	80,000
Buildings	200,000
Equipment	150,000
Cash	300,000
Long-term Notes Payable	130,000

Acquired assets in exchange for cash and long-term note payable.

The changes in the general price-level index during Year 5 are summarized below:

	General price-level index	Conversion factor to restate to end-of-Year 5 dollars
Dec. 31, Year 4 (also for beginning of Year 5) . .	100	1.232
July 1, Year 5 (also the average for Year 5)	110	1.120
Sept. 30, Year 5	115.5	1.067
Dec. 31, Year 5	123.2	1.000

On September 30, Year 5, the corporation declared and paid a dividend of 50 cents per share and issued 10,000 additional shares of capital stock at $8 per share.

The balance sheet at December 31, Year 5, and the income statement for Year 5 (in historical dollars) are summarized below:

SITKA-ALASKA CORPORATION
Balance Sheet
End of Year 5

Assets		Liabilities & Stockholders' Equity	
Monetary assets	$390,000	Current liabilities	$110,000
Inventory	100,000	Long-term notes payable . . .	130,000
Land	80,000	Capital stock, $1 par	110,000
Buildings (net)	192,000	Additional paid-in capital . . .	470,000
Equipment (net)	138,000	Retained earnings	80,000
	$900,000		$900,000

SITKA-ALASKA CORPORATION
Income Statement
For Year 5

Sales (net)		$1,260,000
Cost of goods sold		920,000
Gross profit on sales		$ 340,000
Expenses:		
Depreciation	$ 20,000	
Other (including interest expense and income taxes)	190,000	210,000
Net income		$ 130,000

Sales amounted to approximately $105,000 per month, and expenses accrued at the rate of $17,500 per month. Both cost of goods sold and the ending inventory consist of a representative cross section of merchandise acquired throughout the year.

Instructions

a Prepare a working paper to restate the statement of income and retained earnings for Year 5 for general price-level changes. Compute any general price-level gain or loss in a supporting schedule.

b Prepare a working paper to restate the balance sheet at December 31, Year 5, for general price-level changes.

22B-4 Osaka Silk Company was organized at the end of Year 9. The company's management has decided to supplement its Year 12 historical-dollar financial statements with general price-level financial statements. The following general ledger trial balance (historical-dollar basis) and additional information are available:

OSAKA SILK COMPANY

Trial Balance

December 31, Year 12

	Debit	Credit
Cash and receivables (net)	$ 540,000	
Marketable securities (common stocks)	500,000	
Inventory	440,000	
Equipment	650,000	
Accumulated depreciation		$ 164,000
Accounts payable		400,000
8% bonds payable, due in Year 30		500,000
Common stock, $10 par		1,000,000
Retained earnings, Dec. 31, Year 11	46,000	
Sales		1,900,000
Cost of goods sold	1,508,000	
Depreciation expense	65,000	
Other operating expenses, interest expense, and income taxes	215,000	
Totals	$3,964,000	$3,964,000

Additional information

(1) Monetary assets (cash and receivables) exceeded monetary liabilities (accounts payable and bonds payable) by $445,000 at December 31, Year 11. The amounts of monetary items are fixed in terms of numbers of dollars regardless of changes in specific prices or in the general price level.

(2) Net purchases ($1,840,000 in Year 12) and sales were made uniformly throughout Year 12.

(3) Depreciation expense was computed on a straight-line basis, with a full year's depreciation being taken in the year of acquisition and none in the year of retirement. The depreciation rate is 10% and no residual value is anticipated. Acquisitions and retirements have been made fairly evenly over each year, and the retirements in Year 12 consisted of assets purchased during Year 10. An analysis of the Equipment account follows:

Year	Beginning balance	Additions	Retirements	Ending balance
10	$ –0–	$550,000	$ –0–	$550,000
11	550,000	10,000	–0–	560,000
12	560,000	150,000	60,000	650,000

(4) The 8% bonds payable were issued in Year 10 and the marketable securities were purchased at regular intervals during Year 12. Other operating expenses and interest expense are assumed to be incurred evenly throughout Year 12.

(5) Assume that Gross National Product Implicit Price Deflators (Year 4 = 100) were as follows:

Annual averages	Index	Conversion factors* (Year 12, 4th quarter = 1.000)
Year 9	113.9	1.128
Year 10	116.8	1.100
Year 11	121.8	1.055
Year 12	126.7	1.014

Quarterly averages		Index	Conversion factors
Year 11	4th	123.5	1.040
Year 12	1st	124.9	1.029
	2d	126.1	1.019
	3d	127.3	1.009
	4th	128.5	1.000

* Average index for 4th quarter of Year 12 (128.5) divided by the index for any preceding period. For example, the conversion factor for Year 9 = 128.5 ÷ 113.9 = 1.128.

Instructions

a Prepare a schedule to restate the Equipment account balance at December 31, Year 12, from historical cost to general price-level adjusted dollars.

b Prepare a schedule to analyze in historical dollars the Accumulated Depreciation account for the Year 12.

c Prepare a schedule to analyze in general price-level dollars the Accumulated Depreciation account for Year 12.

d Prepare a schedule to compute Osaka Silk Company's general price-level gain or loss on its net holdings of monetary items for Year 12 (ignore income tax implications). The schedule should give consideration to appropriate items on or related to the balance sheet and the income statement.

CHAPTER 23

ACCOUNTING CHANGES; STATEMENTS FROM INCOMPLETE RECORDS

As accounting principles change in response to changes in the economic and social environment, accountants must find ways to implement the new principles into financial reporting. Putting new principles and new accounting estimates into the stream of annual reports may make current financial statements inconsistent with those of prior years. However, we cannot ignore new and improved principles and estimates merely to maintain consistency with the financial reporting of the past. In this chapter we shall explore some approaches to the adoption of new accounting principles and estimates with the goal of maintaining the maximum degree of comparability and, at the same time, gaining the advantages inherent in a change to new or improved accounting standards and measurements.

Also in this chapter we shall discuss methods of correcting and reporting errors which are discovered to exist in financial statements issued in prior years. Finally, we shall consider ways in which the accountant may develop financial statements from incomplete accounting records.

ACCOUNTING CHANGES

In the past, questions were often raised as to how certain accounting changes should be reported in the financial statements while at the same time the objectives of consistency and comparability of the statements were preserved. By changing its accounting practices, a company might affect significantly the presentation of its financial position and results of operations for an accounting period. The change might also distort the earnings trend shown in comparative income statements.

For example, suppose that Hester Company purchased equipment early in Year 1 for $500,000. The equipment had an expected economic life of eight years and an estimated residual value of $50,000. For two years the equipment was depreciated on a straight-line basis. Early in Year 3 the company revised its original estimates and concluded that the equipment had a remaining economic life of ten years and a revised residual value of $100,000. During Year 3, the company also changed from the straight-line method of depreciation to an accelerated method of depreciation and merged with Pool Company in a business combination which was accounted for as a pooling of interests. It should be evident that the financial statements prepared by Hester Company at the end of Year 3 would not be comparable with the financial statements issued in Years 1 and 2 unless the changes which took place were accounted for in a manner designed to preserve comparability.

In the illustration above we have examples of a change in accounting estimate (the revisions of estimated economic life and residual value of the equipment), a change in accounting principle (the change from the straight-line method to an accelerated method of depreciation), and a change in the reporting entity (the inclusion of Pool Company in the financial statements for Year 3). Thus, accountants must find appropriate methods of communicating these changes to users of financial statements so that the financial statements are not misleading and so that a meaningful comparison of earnings for the three-year period can be made.

For many years the disclosures of accounting changes were often incomplete and obscure and resulted in suggestions by some critics that such changes were "tools of management" used to manipulate reported earnings. Many users of financial statements not only misunderstood the reasons for accounting changes but also failed to grasp their full impact. In an effort to establish explicit guidelines for reporting the effects of accounting changes on financial statements, the APB in 1971 issued *Opinion No. 20,* which defined the different types of accounting changes and established guidelines for reporting such changes in financial statements.[1]

TYPES OF ACCOUNTING CHANGES

In *Opinion No. 20,* the APB was concerned with two issues: (1) the reporting of accounting changes and (2) the accounting for corrections of

[1] *APB Opinion No. 20,* "Accounting Changes," AICPA (New York: 1971).

errors in previously issued financial statements. The Board classified accounting changes into three categories—changes in accounting
principle, changes in accounting estimate, and changes in the reporting
entity.

A *change in accounting principle* can occur in two ways. The first results from the adoption of a generally accepted accounting principle
different from one used previously for financial reporting purposes. For
example, the issuance of a new accounting standard by the Financial
Accounting Standards Board would be sufficient support for a change
in accounting principle. The term "accounting principle" also includes
the various "methods" which may be used in applying accounting principles. Examples of changes in accounting principle include a change
in the method of computing depreciation, such as a shift to an accelerated depreciation method from a straight-line method; and a change in
the method of valuing inventory, such as a change from lifo to fifo.

A *change in accounting estimate* may be required as new events occur
and as better information becomes available about the probable outcome of future events. Examples of changes in accounting estimates include: An increase in the percentage used to estimate doubtful accounts expense from 2 to 5% of sales; a major write-down of inventory
because of obsolescence; a change in the estimated economic life of
tangible or intangible assets; a change in the estimated recoverable
units of natural resources; and a revision in the amount of estimated liability for outstanding product warranties.

A *change in the reporting entity* takes place when the group of companies comprising the reporting entity changes. For example, if one company combines with another company, the financial statements of the
current year (which combine the revenue, expenses, assets, liabilities,
and stockholders' equity) would not be comparable to those of previous
years without adequate disclosure of the change in the reporting entity
as well as the impact on the financial statements caused by the change.

A *correction of an error* is required when errors are discovered in previously issued financial statements. Such errors may result from mathematical computations, mistakes in the application of accounting principles, or oversight or misuse of facts that existed at the time the financial
statements were prepared. An example of a correction of an error is the
discovery that material amounts of depreciation were not recorded in
prior periods.

Introducing accounting changes in financial statements

Financial statements for a given entity are most useful when they are
prepared on a *consistent* basis, thus making comparisons between
periods meaningful. For this reason, many accountants argue that
financial statements for prior periods should be *restated retroactively* following an accounting change. Others would not restate previously is-

sued financial statements on grounds that such restatements would confuse users and reduce the credibility of financial statements.

Three approaches will be described for reporting the effect of accounting changes. These approaches are not alternatives for a given type of accounting change; instead, they represent methods of reporting different types of accounting changes. The three approaches are summarized below:

1 *Cumulative effect of the change is reported in the income statement of the current period.* The cumulative effect on the net income of prior periods of a change in an accounting principle is **reported in the income statement** of the period in which the change is made.

2 *Prior periods' financial statements are restated retroactively.* The financial statements for prior periods presented are **restated** to conform to the new basis of accounting. The balance of retained earnings at the beginning of the earliest period presented is adjusted for the cumulative effect of the change on net income for the periods prior to those being presented.

3 *The accounting change is viewed as affecting the net income for current and future periods.* The effect of the change **is not carried back** to prior periods and no recognition is given to the cumulative effect of the change in the current period. Thus, the financial statements presented for earlier periods are not restated retroactively and all accounting changes are viewed as **prospective** for financial reporting purposes.

The applications of these possible interpretations to the various types of accounting changes are described in the following sections.

Change in accounting principle

At first glance, a change in accounting principle would seem to violate the assumption that financial statements are prepared "in conformity with generally accepted accounting principles applied on a basis consistent with that of the preceding year." In the preparation of financial statements there is a presumption that accounting principles once adopted should not be changed, so that meaningful comparisons of successive financial statements can be made. Consequently, a change in accounting principle is appropriate only when the reporting entity adopts an **alternative** generally accepted accounting principle which is clearly preferable. A change from an unacceptable accounting principle to an accepted accounting principle is considered a correction of an error rather than a change in accounting principle.

As stated earlier in the chapter, a change in accounting principle is generally considered appropriate in two situations. The first is a change to a different method of applying a generally accepted accounting principle. For example, a change from the fifo method to the lifo method of inventory valuation would qualify. However, a company is justified in changing to a new method only if it can demonstrate that the new method is preferable in that it **more fairly presents** the financial position and the results of operations. The second situation in which a change in accounting principle is appropriate is the issuance of a pronouncement by the FASB which creates a new accounting principle, expresses a preference for an accounting principle, or rejects a specific accounting principle.

The reason for the change in accounting principle and the effect of the change on net income should be disclosed in the financial statements of the period in which the change is made.

In *Opinion No. 20,* the APB specifically excluded two events from being considered a change in accounting principle. These are: (1) the initial adoption of an accounting principle to report transactions occurring for the first time and (2) the adoption of a principle to report transactions that are substantially different from those previously occurring.

How should a change to a preferable accounting principle (or the selection of a different method of applying the principle) be handled in order to preserve the comparability between future financial statements and those issued in the past? The answer to this question depends on the type of change in accounting principle and the magnitude of its effect. A change that has a material effect on net income should be reported more completely than a change that has little effect on net income. Also, the effects of certain types of changes on the prior periods' financial statements may be more difficult to analyze than the effects caused by other types of changes. For this reason the APB stated that those changes which have a material effect on net income should be classified into one of the following categories: (1) those for which the cumulative effect of the prior years is included in the income statement in which the change is made, and (2) those which require the restatement of the prior years' financial statements.

Cumulative Effect of Change Reported in Current Period The Accounting Principles Board concluded that "most changes in accounting should be recognized by including the cumulative effect, based on a retroactive computation, of changing to a new accounting principle in net income of the period of the change. . . ."[2] The possibility that public confidence in financial statements would be reduced if financial statements of prior periods were restated retroactively was a major factor in reaching this conclusion. Examples of changes in accounting principle in this category are: A change in the method of computing depreciation expense on previously recorded assets (for example, a change from the sum-of-the-years'-digits method to the straight-line method),[3] and a change from the fifo to the lifo method of pricing inventory. The following guidelines should be followed for those changes in accounting principle which require recognition of the cumulative effect of the change:

1 Financial statements for prior periods included for comparative purposes should be presented as previously reported.

[2] Ibid., pp. 391–392.

[3] A change to the straight-line method at a specified point in the economic life of an asset may be planned at the time the accelerated depreciation method is adopted to fully depreciate the cost over the economic life of the asset. Consistent application of such a policy does not constitute a change in accounting principle under *APB Opinion No. 20.*

2 The **cumulative effect** of the change on the retained earnings balance at the beginning of the period in which the change is made should be included in the net income of the period of the change. The amount of the cumulative effect is the difference between **(a)** the **actual** amount of retained earnings at the beginning of the period of a change and **(b)** the amount of retained earnings that **would have been reported** at that date if the new accounting principle had been applied retroactively for **all** prior periods. In computing the cumulative effect, appropriate consideration should be given to income taxes. The total and per-share amount of the cumulative effect should be shown in the income statement immediately below any extraordinary items.

3 The total and per-share effect of the change on the income before extraordinary items and on the net income of the period of the change should be disclosed.

4 Income before extraordinary items and net income computed on a **pro forma basis**[4] should be shown on the face of the income statement for all prior periods presented as if the newly adopted accounting principle had been used in the prior periods. If an income statement is presented for the current period only, the actual and pro forma amounts (including earnings per share) for the immediately preceding period should be disclosed.

Let us now examine how a change in a company's depreciation method would be reported. Suppose that the Shift Company, which specialized in the ownership and management of office buildings, decided to change from a straight-line to an accelerated depreciation method. The accelerated method, which had been used for income tax purposes, was now considered preferable for financial reporting purposes because the revenue-producing capability of the buildings tended to decline as the buildings became older. Because most other companies in the industry used the accelerated method of depreciation, the change would also make the operating results of Shift Company more comparable with other companies in the office rental business.

If the accelerated method of depreciation had been used in past years for financial reporting purposes, the total depreciation charges would have been $600,000 higher and, therefore, income before income taxes would have been $600,000 lower. Assuming an income tax rate of 45%, the journal entry to record the change in accounting principle would be:

Cumulative Effect on Prior Years of Change in Accounting Principle	*330,000*	
Deferred Income Tax Liability	*270,000*	
Accumulated Depreciation		*600,000*
To record effect of change in accounting principle—the change from straight-line to accelerated depreciation method.		

---

[4] *Pro forma* means "on the assumption that certain transactions are completed or that different principles are used." In connection with our discussion of accounting changes, pro forma means that net income and earnings per share of earlier periods are restated retroactively to conform to the newly adopted accounting principle.

The debit to the Deferred Income Tax Liability account represents the amount of income taxes the company deferred in the past as a result of using the straight-line method of depreciation for financial reporting purposes while using an accelerated method for income tax purposes. The cumulative effect on prior years of change in accounting principle of $330,000 is the net amount by which Retained Earnings would have been **decreased** had the accelerated method of depreciation also been used for financial reporting purposes. The cumulative effect is reported in the income statement after income from operations but before any extraordinary items, as illustrated on page 947.

In the income statement for Shift Company the pro forma income before extraordinary item for Year 4 was decreased by $140,000 ($2,600,000 − $2,460,000), or $0.14 per share. Thus the pro forma amounts for Years 4 and 5 are fully comparable because they are stated in terms of the newly adopted accounting principle for depreciation.

In some situations, the determination of the cumulative effect of a change in accounting principle may be impossible. An example of this type of change is a change in inventory pricing method from the fifo to the lifo method. In such situations, the disclosure would be limited to showing the effect of the change on the net income and earnings per share of the period of change. The reason for not showing the cumulative effect of the change in accounting principle also should be stated.

Cumulative Effect in Interim Periods In *Opinion No. 28,* the APB stated that a cumulative effect type change in accounting principle adopted in an interim period "should be reported in the interim period in a manner similar to that to be followed in the annual report."[5] Subsequently, the FASB amended this rather general guideline in two important respects as follows:

1 If a cumulative effect type accounting change is made during the **first** interim period of an enterprise's fiscal year, the cumulative effect of the change on retained earnings at the **beginning of that fiscal year** shall be included in net income of the first interim period (and in last-twelve-months-to-date financial reports that include that first interim period).

2 If a cumulative effect type accounting change is made in **other than the first** interim period of an enterprise's fiscal year, **no** cumulative effect of the change shall be included in net income of the period of change. Instead, financial information for the pre-change interim periods of the fiscal year in which the change is made shall be restated by applying the newly adopted accounting principle to those pre-change interim periods. The cumulative effect of the change on retained earnings at the **beginning of that fiscal year** shall be included in restated net income of the first interim period of the fiscal year in which the change is made (and in any year-to-date or last-twelve-months-to-date financial reports that include the first interim period). Whenever financial information that includes those pre-change interim periods is presented, it shall be presented on the restated basis.[6]

[5] *APB Opinion No. 28,* "Interim Financial Reporting," AICPA (New York: 1973), p. 530.
[6] *FASB Statement No. 3,* "Reporting Accounting Changes in Interim Financial Statements . . . ," FASB (Stamford: 1974), p. 4.

SHIFT COMPANY
Partial Income Statement
Year Ended December 31

	Year 5	Year 4
Income before extraordinary item and cumulative effect on prior years of change in accounting principle	$3,000,000	$2,600,000
Add: Extraordinary item—tax benefit of operating loss carryforward	–0–	60,000
Less: Cumulative effect on prior years (to end of Year 4) of change in accounting principle (Note 1) . . .	(330,000)	
Net income	$2,670,000	$2,660,000
Earnings per share of common stock (1 million shares):		
Income before extraordinary item and cumulative effect of change in accounting principle	$ 3.00	$ 2.60
Add: Extraordinary item—tax benefit of operating loss carryforward		0.06
Add: Cumulative effect on prior years (to end of Year 4) of change in accounting principle (Note 1)	(0.33)	
Earnings per share (1 million shares)	$ 2.67	$ 2.66
Pro forma amounts, assuming the change in accounting principle is applied retroactively (Note 1):		
Income before extraordinary item	$3,000,000	$2,460,000
Earnings per share	$ 3.00	$ 2.46
Net income, including extraordinary item	$3,000,000	$2,520,000
Earnings per share	$ 3.00	$ 2.52

Note 1—Change in accounting principle: *During the year ended December 31, Year 5, the company changed its method of accounting for depreciation from the straight-line to an accelerated method. The new method is a generally accepted method used in the industry, and it is believed such a method will cause the company's results to be more comparable with other companies in the industry. The effect of the change for the year ended December 31, Year 5, was to decrease income before extraordinary item by $120,000 (or $0.12 per share). The adjustment of $330,000 (after reduction of $270,000 for deferred income taxes) to apply retroactively the new method is included in net income of Year 5. The pro forma amounts for Year 4 have been adjusted for the effect of retroactive application of the change on depreciation expense and related income taxes. The effect of the change for the year ended December 31, Year 4, was to decrease income before extraordinary item by $140,000 (or $0.14 per share).*

The FASB also required extensive disclosure of a cumulative effect type accounting change in interim financial reports, including the nature and justification for the change and the effect of the change on net income and related per-share amounts for all interim periods presented.

Change Requiring Restatement of Prior Years' Financial Statements In *Opinion No. 20,* the APB took the position "that a few specific changes in accounting principles should be reported by restating the financial statements of prior periods."[7] Examples of accounting changes that require the restatement of financial statements of prior periods include the following:

1 A change from the lifo method of inventory pricing to another method of inventory pricing such as the fifo method
2 A change in the method of accounting for long-term construction contracts
3 A change in the accounting for development costs in the extractive industries
4 A change in the reporting entity
5 A change from an acceptable accounting principle to another acceptable accounting principle for a closely held company issuing financial statements to the public for the first time

Why did the APB provide for these exceptions? Although a number of reasons might be cited, the main reason for the restatement of prior years' financial statements is that the amount of the cumulative effect of the accounting change might be so large as to render the income statement potentially misleading. Imagine the effect on a company changing from the lifo to the fifo method of inventory valuation in, say, 1978. If the company had been in business for 30 years and had valued inventories at the original base layer, the last goods in would be the first goods sold and the beginning inventory in 1978 would still approximate 1948 prices. Thus a change from the lifo method to the fifo method of inventory valuation could have such a material effect on net income that the cumulative effect approach would distort the earnings picture of the company in 1978.

When financial statements are restated, the nature of the change in accounting principle, as well as the justification for the change, should be disclosed in the financial statements for the period in which the change is made. Disclosure of the effect of the accounting change on income before extraordinary item, net income, and the related per-share amounts should be made for all periods presented. This disclosure may be in the income statement or in the accompanying notes and need not be repeated in the financial statements for the periods following the change.[8]

To illustrate the restatement of an income statement for a prior period as a result of a change in accounting principle, assume the following: Retro Company adopted the completed-contract method of accounting for long-term construction contracts when it was incorpo-

[7] *APB Opinion No. 20,* p. 392.
[8] Ibid., p. 396.

rated in Year 1. The company had reported net income of $137,500 in Year 1 and $330,000 in Year 2. In Year 3, the company decides to change to the percentage-of-completion method. The effect of this change in accounting principle, assuming an income tax rate of 45%, is summarized below:

	Operating income using		Differences		
Year	Completed-contract method	Percentage-of-completion method	Before tax effect	Tax effect, 45%	Increase in net income
1	$250,000	$550,000	$300,000	$135,000	$165,000
2	600,000	700,000	100,000	45,000	55,000
3	700,000	850,000	150,000	67,500	82,500

The partial comparative income statement at the end of Year 3, giving retroactive effect to the change in accounting principles, appears below:

RETRO COMPANY
Partial Income Statement

	Year 3	Year 2 (restated—see Note 1)
Operating income	$850,000	$700,000
Income tax expense	382,500	315,000
Net income	$467,500	$385,000
Earnings per share (100,000 shares outstanding) . .	$ 4.68	$ 3.85

Note 1—Change in method of accounting for long-term construction contracts: The company has accounted for long-term construction contracts by the percentage-of-completion method in Year 3, whereas in all prior years the completed-contract method was used. The new method of accounting was adopted to report the results of operations in a manner which more closely portrays the economic activity of the company. Financial statements of prior years have been restated to apply the new method of accounting retroactively. For income tax purposes, the completed-contract method will be continued. The effect of the accounting change on net income and earnings per share of Year 3, and on net income and earnings per share previously reported for Year 2, follows:

	Year 3	Year 2
Increase in:		
Net income	$82,500	$55,000
Earnings per share	$ 0.83	$ 0.55

The balances of retained earnings for Year 2 and Year 3 have been adjusted for the effect (net of income taxes) of applying retroactively the new method of accounting.

To illustrate the effect of the change in the presentation of retained earnings, the comparative statement of retained earnings for Retro Company is illustrated below. In this illustration we have assumed that the company has not declared any dividends since it was organized in Year 1.

	Year 3	Year 2
RETRO COMPANY		
Statement of Retained Earnings		
Balance at beginning of year, as previously reported . .	$ 467,500	$137,500
Add: Cumulative effect on prior years of applying		
retroactively the new method of accounting for		
long-term construction contracts	220,000	165,000
Balance at beginning of year, as restated	$ 687,500	$302,500
Net income	467,500	385,000
Balance at end of year, as restated	$1,155,000	$687,500

In some situations the pro forma effect on the net income of individual prior periods cannot be computed or reasonably estimated, although the cumulative effect on retained earnings at the beginning of the period of change can be determined. The cumulative effect in such cases should be reported in the income statement of the period of change and the reason for not restating prior years' results should be given.[9]

Change in accounting estimate

Much of the accountants' work involves the use of subjective judgment. That is, accountants are often relied upon to estimate such things as the economic life of a depreciable asset, its residual value at the end of that life, the amount of probable uncollectible accounts, and inventory obsolescence, and to make under uncertainty other decisions which require the estimate of the effects of future events. As time passes, the results of new events and better information about the probable outcome of future events may require, for example, that the original estimate of economic life or residual value of depreciable assets be revised to reflect these new developments.

For example, assume that management had estimated the economic life of a plant asset at 10 years, with no residual value at the end of that period. The cost of the asset, $20,000, has been depreciated at the rate of $2,000 per year for 7 years. At the beginning of the eighth year, management determines that the asset has a remaining economic life of 5 years and that it will have a residual value of $500 at the end of 12 years of economic life. The revised annual depreciation expense over the newly estimated remaining economic life of the asset is determined as follows:

Cost of plant asset	$20,000
Less: Depreciation for Years 1–7 @ $2,000 per year	14,000
Unrecovered cost at beginning of Year 8	$ 6,000
Less: Estimated residual value at end of Year 12	500
Amount to be depreciated in Years 8–12 (5 years)	$ 5,500
Revised annual depreciation for Years 8–12, $5,500 ÷ 5 years of remaining economic life	$ 1,100

The change in estimated economic life and residual value affects only the remaining years of economic life (Years 8 through 12); no correction to the previously reported net income for Years 1 through 7 is required. Because accounting measurements based on estimates are imperfect and some disparity between past and subsequent estimates cannot be avoided, retroactive restatements of previously reported earnings as a result of changes in accounting estimates may cast suspicion on both the original and the revised earnings figures. The information used to revise the service potential of the asset could not have been fully anticipated at the time the asset was acquired. Revised estimates are based on present economic facts and management decisions and for this reason, it seems logical to assign the unexpired cost of an asset over the remaining estimated economic life based on the latest evidence and conditions.

A change in an accounting estimate occurs because of new or better information which has come to light in the current period. Thus, it seems logical that the resulting change should affect the computation of operating income of the period in which the change is made; if the change has a continuing effect, it should be consistently applied to the periods following the period of the change. A change in accounting estimate **does not** require (as does a change in accounting principle) the recognition of the cumulative effect of the change in the current period **or** the retroactive restatement of financial statements for prior periods. Although disclosure of the effects on those income statement amounts is not necessary for estimates which are made in the ordinary course of accounting for items such as doubtful accounts or inventory obsolescence, any change in estimate which has a significant effect on net income and earnings per share should be disclosed in the notes to financial statements.

A revision in the estimated economic life or residual value of a plant asset, as described above, is a change in accounting estimate. A change in the method of computing depreciation on a previously recorded asset, for example a change from straight-line to accelerated method of depreciation on an asset acquired two years ago, would be a change in accounting principle. But what if a company acquired a new plant asset and decided that a units-of-output method would be the most appropriate depreciation method for this new plant asset? As long as it continued to depreciate its previously recorded assets using the same method as before, there would be no need for a cumulative adjustment in the income statement because there was no change in accounting principle on those assets. However, the effect of the new method of depreciation for newly acquired assets on the net income of the period of the change should be disclosed.

In certain instances a change in accounting principle may be accompanied by a change in accounting estimate. In such cases it is difficult to separate the effect of the change in accounting principle from the effect of the change in accounting estimate. For example, a company which has been deferring and amortizing certain costs might decide to change to a method of recording the costs as expenses because the future benefits of the costs have become doubtful. This type of change is often related to the process of obtaining new or additional information which calls for a revision of the original judgment that the costs would have future benefits. Because the new accounting method was adopted in partial or complete recognition of the change in estimated future benefits, **APB Opinion No. 20** suggested that such an accounting change be accounted for as a change in accounting estimate.[10]

Change in reporting entity and initial public issuance of financial statements

Certain events, such as a merger of two or more entities through a pooling of interests, result in financial statements that are in effect the statements for a *different reporting entity.* A change in the reporting entity is viewed as a special type of change in accounting principle which is reported by restating the financial statements of all prior periods as though the new entity had existed all along.

As pointed out earlier, certain changes from one acceptable accounting principle to another acceptable principle do not require the restatement of financial statements of prior periods. An exception is made for a closely held company *issuing securities publicly for the first time.* Potential investors in the securities of a company "going public" are better served by earnings summaries for a period of years prepared on the basis of the newly adopted accounting principle. Comparisons of operating results will be more meaningful because the newly adopted

[10] Ibid., p. 388.

accounting principle will also be used in future periods. Therefore, the financial statements issued in connection with the initial public offering of securities are restated retroactively for all periods for which financial statements are presented.[11]

CORRECTION OF ERRORS

In previous chapters we have noted the difficulties inherent in any attempt to determine the periodic income of a business. At best, accountants can only measure the impact of past transactions and events and make informed estimates of the present effect of probable future events. In addition, *errors* in financial statements may result from mathematical mistakes, mistakes in the application of accounting principles, or the oversight or misuse of facts that existed at the time the financial statements were prepared.[12] An example of a correction of an error is a change from an accounting principle that is not generally accepted to one that is generally accepted.

Correction of an error in previously issued financial statements

When a material error is discovered in previously issued financial statements, the correction of the error should be reported as a *prior period adjustment.*[13] The nature of the error and the effect of its correction on net income and earnings per share should be disclosed in the period in which the error is corrected. An example of such disclosure, generally presented in a note accompanying the financial statements, is illustrated below:

> **Note 1—Correction of error:** A major revision of labor standards in February Year 3 resulted in a charge to Year 2 earnings of $2,500,000 because of reduced labor and factory overhead costs included in the inventories at December 31, Year 2. In connection with the pricing of the December 31, Year 2, inventory in February Year 3, it was determined that **an error** had been made in applying factory overhead to the December 31, Year 1, inventory. The correction resulted in a reduction of the December 31, Year 1, inventory by $450,000. Earnings before income taxes for Year 1 were reduced from $1,500,000 to $1,050,000; net income was reduced from $816,000 to $600,000; and earnings were reduced from $0.41 to $0.30 per share.

If the error has a material effect on previously issued financial statements, retroactive revision of the statements for prior periods may be warranted. Whenever readers of financial statements make a serious analysis of the financial affairs of a company, they will, for example, want to see comparative income statement data for a series of years.

---

[11] Ibid., pp. 396–397.
[12] Ibid., p. 389.
[13] *FASB Statement No. 16,* "Prior Period Adjustments," FASB (Stamford: 1977), p. 5.

When such comparative income statements are prepared, it is always desirable to revise prior years' income statements to reflect material errors discovered after the original financial statements were issued. The Auditing Standards Executive Committee of the AICPA has made the following recommendation on this point:

> If the effect on the financial statements or auditor's report of the subsequently discovered information can promptly be determined, disclosure should consist of issuing, as soon as practicable, revised financial statements and auditor's report. . . . Generally, only the most recently issued audited financial statements would need to be revised, even though the revision resulted from events that had occurred in prior years.[14]

Anyone who attempts to assess probable future earnings and financial position relies heavily on information about the recent past. An error which causes a material misstatement of net income in any of the recent years results in a misleading picture of the earnings pattern of a business. This kind of distortion can affect the decisions of those who rely on financial statements for investment information.

Correction of financial statements illustrated

To illustrate the correction of a material error, assume that Errata Corporation purchased a machine early in Year 1 for $100,000. The machine had an economic life of 10 years and was being depreciated on a straight-line basis. The accountant incorrectly recorded annual depreciation expense for Year 1 through Year 4 at $1,000 per year rather than at the correct amount of $10,000 per year because of a clerical error. Thus depreciation expense was understated by $9,000 per year, or $36,000 for the four years ending with Year 4. The error is discovered early in Year 5, after the condensed financial statements shown on page 955 were prepared.

Ignoring the income tax effect of the error, the following correcting journal entry would be required in Year 5:

Prior Period Adjustment: Error in Computing Depreciation . .	36,000	
Accumulated Depreciation		36,000
To correct mechanical error in computing depreciation for		
Years 1 through 4.		

If corrected financial statements for prior periods were not issued in Year 5, the account Prior Period Adjustment: Error in Computing Depreciation would be closed directly to the Retained Earnings account; in

---

[14] *Statement on Auditing Standards No. 1*, "Codification of Auditing Standards and Procedures," AICPA (New York: 1973), p. 129.

the statement of retained earnings for Year 5, the prior period adjustment of $36,000 would be shown as a correction to retained earnings at the beginning of Year 5. When corrected financial statements are prepared in Year 5, the prior period adjustment would also be closed to the Retained Earnings account but the ending balances for retained earnings would be corrected retroactively for each prior year for which corrected financial statements are presented.

ERRATA CORPORATION
Comparative Income Statement (Before Correction)
For Years 3 and 4

	Year 4	Year 3
Sales	$300,000	$280,000
Cost of goods sold and expenses	270,000	260,000
Net income	$ 30,000	$ 20,000
Earnings per share	$ 3.00	$ 2.00

ERRATA CORPORATION
Comparative Balance Sheet (Before Correction)
End of Years 3 and 4

	Year 4	Year 3
Assets, excluding machinery	$260,000	$225,000
Machinery	320,000	290,000
Less: Accumulated depreciation	(80,000)	(65,000)
Total assets	$500,000	$450,000
Liabilities	$170,000	$150,000
Capital stock, $10 par	100,000	100,000
Retained earnings	230,000	200,000
Total liabilities & stockholders' equity	$500,000	$450,000

As an example, the corrected comparative financial statements for Year 3 and Year 4 are presented on page 956.

In the corrected income statement, "cost of goods sold and expenses" are increased retroactively by the $9,000 understatement in annual depreciation expense, thus reducing net income for each year by $9,000.

ERRATA CORPORATION

Comparative Income Statement (After Correction)

For Years 3 and 4

	Year 4	Year 3
Sales	$300,000	$280,000
Cost of goods sold and expenses	279,000	269,000
Net income	$ 21,000	$ 11,000
Earnings per share	$ 2.10	$ 1.10

ERRATA CORPORATION

Comparative Balance Sheet (After Correction)

	Year 4	Year 3
Assets, excluding machinery	$260,000	$225,000
Machinery	320,000	290,000
Less: Accumulated depreciation	(116,000)	(92,000)
Total assets	$464,000	$423,000
Liabilities	$170,000	$150,000
Capital stock, $10 par	100,000	100,000
Retained earnings	194,000	173,000
Total liabilities & stockholders' equity	$464,000	$423,000

The two balance sheet items requiring correction at the end of Year 4 and Year 3 are accumulated depreciation and retained earnings. Because depreciation was understated by $9,000 per year, the cumulative effect is $36,000 at the end of Year 4 and $27,000 at the end of Year 3. The corrected balance in accumulated depreciation at the end of Year 4 is $116,000 ($80,000 as originally reported plus $36,000 correction) and at the end of Year 3 it is $92,000 ($65,000 as originally reported plus $27,000 correction). The amount of retained earnings is restated to $194,000 ($230,000 − $36,000) at the end of Year 4 and to $173,000 ($200,000 − $27,000) at the end of Year 3.

Types of errors

Many accounting errors are automatically brought to light by the controls in the double-entry accounting system. Outside auditors, internal auditors, and Internal Revenue agents may uncover errors during an examination of the accounting records. The installation of an improved accounting system may cause the discovery of material errors resulting from the inadequacies of the previous system. Thus the necessity of correcting errors is more likely to occur in a small business than in a large publicly owned corporation.

The problem of dealing with errors of the same type can be generalized to some extent. Once the nature of the distortion created by a given class of error is understood, it is possible to determine the effect of similar errors.

Errors Affecting Only Balance Sheet Accounts An error that affects only balance sheet accounts may arise because journal entries were made to the wrong account, because transactions were omitted, or because the amounts of certain entries were wrong. For example, if Accounts Payable is debited instead of Accounts Receivable, assets are understated and liabilities are understated by the same amount. When the error is discovered, only balance sheet accounts will need correction.

Errors Affecting Only Income Statement Accounts An error that is confined to income statement accounts will have no effect on the amount of periodic income. Such errors may arise through misclassification; for example, an expense or revenue may be debited or credited to the wrong nominal account.

Errors Affecting Both Balance Sheet and Income Statement Accounts Errors that affect both the balance sheet and the income statement fall into two subclasses: (1) Those which will be counterbalanced in the next accounting period and (2) those which will not be counterbalanced in the next accounting period.

Some errors, if not discovered, **will be counterbalanced** in the regular course of the next period's accounting. The typical counterbalancing error causes a misstatement of the income of one period and the balance sheet at the end of that period, which is offset by a misstatement of income in the opposite direction in the following period. The balance sheet at the end of the second period and the income of subsequent periods are not affected by the error, which has in a sense "corrected itself" over two accounting periods.

An example of a counterbalancing error is the failure to record accrued wages at the end of a given year. The liability, accrued wages, is understated at the end of the year, and because wage expense is understated, income is overstated in the year the error is made. In the following year the payment of the unrecorded accrued wages will be debited to wage expense, thus overstating the expenses for the second year. As a result, income in the second year is understated by an amount exactly equal to the overstatement of the previous year. If proper wage accruals are made at the end of the second year, the liability account in the balance sheet at that date will be correct. Retained earnings also will be properly stated at the end of the second year.

Other errors affect both the balance sheet and the income statement accounts but *are not counterbalanced* in the next accounting period. For example, suppose a purchase of equipment is charged to expense by mistake. Since expenses are overstated in the year of the error, net income for that year will be understated. Net income will also be overstated in subsequent years by the amount of unrecorded depreciation on the equipment while it is in service. Equipment in the balance sheet will be understated throughout the economic life of the equipment.

Analyzing the effect of errors

When an error is discovered, the accountant must make a careful analysis of the effect of the error on financial data for previous, current, and subsequent accounting periods. Because it is not feasible to discuss every possible error that might occur, we shall illustrate the reasoning used in determining the effect of errors. The illustrations are designed to show corrections required to produce revised income statements of prior years, and do not purport to illustrate the application of any APB or FASB pronouncement. In other words, we are primarily concerned with omissions and other errors which may occur in a *small business which does not issue financial statements to the public.*

As an example, let us trace through the effect of an error in determining the amount of inventory on hand at the end of a given period. Assume that we discover that the ending inventory at December 31, Year 4, was overstated by $3,400. We can analyze the effect of this error (ignoring income taxes) as follows:

Income Statement		
Year 4	**Year 5**	**Year 6**
Income overstated by $3,400. (Cost of goods sold was understated, since ending inventory was too high.)	*Income understated by $3,400 (Cost of goods sold was overstated, since beginning inventory was too high.)*	*Error has fully counterbalanced; no correction is required.*
Balance Sheet		
Assets overstated by $3,400. (Ending inventory was too high.) Retained earnings overstated by $3,400. (Income was overstated.)	*Balance sheet items are properly stated since Dec. 31, Year 5, inventory is correct and overstatement of retained earnings in Year 4 has been offset by understatement of income in Year 5.*	*No correction required.*

The action to be taken upon discovery of this error depends on when the error is discovered and the extent of the revision of financial statements that is desired.

Discovery in Year 4 If the error were discovered in Year 4 before the accounts were closed, a separate correcting journal entry would not be necessary. The ending inventory typically is recorded in the accounts at the time closing entires are made, and it is a simple matter to use the revised inventory figure in making the closing entries. The ending inventory in the income statement for Year 4 would be decreased by $3,400 and reported income would be decreased by this amount.

Discovery in Year 5 If the error were discovered at any time up to the closing of the accounts in Year 5, the correcting entry would be:

> *Prior Period Adjustment: Correction to Net Income for Year 4* . *3,400*
>   *Inventory, Dec. 31, Year 4* *3,400*
> *To correct overstatement in beginning inventory.*

The purpose of this entry is to correct the financial statements for Year 5; both the income for Year 5 and the balance sheet at the end of Year 5 will be properly stated after the prior period adjustment is closed to the Retained Earnings account. In the statement of retained earnings for Year 5, the prior period adjustment is reported as a correction to the balance in retained earnings at the beginning of the year.

Discovery in Year 6 If the error in the inventory at the end of Year 4 were not discovered until Year 6, no entry would be required, since the error has been fully counterbalanced. If the Year 4 and Year 5 financial statements are to be corrected retroactively, this could be accomplished by simply changing the inventory and retained earnings figures on these statements or by the use of a separate working paper. As of the beginning of Year 6, however, all account balances are free of this particular error.

Working paper for analysis of errors

The first step in correcting discovered errors is to analyze the effect of the errors on financial data. The next is to prepare the necessary correcting journal entries. In the course of an audit or when an accountant is called upon to straighten out records that have been improperly kept, a substantial number of errors, affecting several accounting periods, may be discovered. In such cases it may be helpful to use a working paper as an orderly means of analyzing the extent to which errors have counterbalanced and their effect on financial statements. The working paper will also serve as the underlying support for a single correcting entry to bring the accounting records up to date. There is no standard form of working paper; one form that has proved useful for this purpose is illustrated in the following example:

Illustration An audit of the records of Small Trading Company early in Year 8 has revealed a number of errors affecting the financial statements for Year 6 and Year 7, as follows:

1 Unexpired insurance was omitted from the records; insurance premiums were charged to expense as paid. The proper amount of prepayment at the end of Year 6 was $550; at the end of Year 7, $980.

2 No entry had been made to accrue interest on notes payable at the end of the year. Interest was charged to expense at the time of payment. Accrued interest payable at the end of Year 6 was $1,700; at the end of Year 7, $480.

3 Interest on notes receivable was credited to Interest Revenue as received. At the end of Year 6, accrued interest receivable amounted to $450; at the end of Year 7, $840.

4 The company rented certain land, receiving rent in advance; receipts were credited to Rental Revenue. Unearned rental revenue at the end of Year 6 was $1,800; at the end of Year 7, $740.

5 The company is subject to state and federal income taxes at a rate of 20% of taxable income. There are no differences between taxable income and accounting income. It is assumed that Year 6 tax returns will be revised to reflect the foregoing errors, and that the company will claim a refund for excess taxes paid in Year 6 or will pay any tax deficiency.

Small Trading Company reported net income of $10,000 in Year 6, and net income of $6,000 in Year 7. We wish to determine the extent of the errors in the net income for Year 6 and Year 7 and to correct the accounting records at December 31, Year 7. The working paper on page 961 illustrates the procedure.

Let us assume that the accounting records *have been closed* at the end of Year 7. On the basis of our working paper analysis, the following journal entry will correct the accounting records at December 31, Year 7:

Unexpired Insurance	980	
Accrued Interest Receivable	840	
Tax Refund Receivable, Year 6	500	
Prior Period Adjustment: Correction to Net Income for Years		
6 and 7		480
Accrued Interest Payable		480
Unearned Rental Revenue		740
Income Taxes Payable		620
To correct errors revealed by audit in Year 8 after the accounts have been closed for Year 7.		

SMALL TRADING COMPANY
Working Paper for Analysis of Errors
December 31, Year 7

Explanation	Net income for Year 6 (Dr) Cr*	Net income for Year 7 (Dr) Cr*	Balance sheet accounts requiring correction at Dec. 31, Year 7 (Dr) Cr*	Account title
(1) Unexpired insurance omitted:				
Dec. 31, Year 6	$ 550	$ (550)		
Dec. 31, Year 7		980	$(980)	Unexpired Ins.
(2) Accrued interest on notes payable omitted:				
Dec. 31, Year 6	(1,700)	1,700		
Dec. 31, Year 7		(480)	480	Accrued Interest Payable
(3) Accrued interest on notes receivable omitted:				
Dec. 31, Year 6	450	(450)		
Dec. 31, Year 7		840	(840)	Accrued Interest Receivable
(4) Unearned rental revenue omitted:				
Dec. 31, Year 6	(1,800)	1,800		
Dec. 31, Year 7		(740)	740	Unearned Rental Revenue
Increase (or decrease) in income before income taxes	$ (2,500)	$3,100		
(5) Revision of income taxes (20%):				
Year 6 income taxes overstated	500		(500)	Tax Refund Receivable, Year 6
Year 7 income taxes understated		(620)	620	Income Taxes Payable
Increase (or decrease) in net income	$(2,000)	$2,480	480	Prior Period Adjustment
Net income as originally reported	10,000	6,000		
Corrected net income	$ 8,000	$8,480		

* Separate columns for debit and credit amounts may be used.

Trace the figures in this entry to the working paper and you will see that all the data necessary for the correcting entry were developed in the working paper. To prepare a corrected income statement for Year 7, it would be necessary to revise the individual expense and revenue accounts to reflect the total increase of $2,480 in Year 7 net income. If the accounts *had not been closed* at the time the correcting journal entry was made, it would be necessary to expand the above journal entry to include the correction of expense and revenue accounts for Year 7 as follows:

Unexpired Insurance	*980*		
Accrued Interest Receivable	*840*		
Tax Refund Receivable, Year 6	*500*		
Prior Period Adjustment: Correction to Net			
Income for Year 6	*2,000*		*Correction of*
Income Tax Expense, Year 7	*620*		*revenue and*
Insurance Expense ($980 − $550) .		*430*	*expense accounts*
Interest Expense ($1,700 − $480) . .		*1,220*	*to reflect*
Interest Revenue ($840 − $450) . . .		*390*	*$2,480*
Rental Revenue ($1,800 − $740) . .		*1,060*	*increase in net*
Accrued Interest Payable		*480*	*income for Year 7*
Unearned Rental Revenue		*740*	
Income Taxes Payable		*620*	
To correct errors revealed by audit in Year 8.			
Accounts not yet closed at Dec. 31, Year 7.			

The analysis of errors in the working paper indicates that net income for Year 7 was understated by $2,480. If Year 7 revenue and expense accounts are to be corrected, it is necessary to look at the details in the column headed "Net income for Year 7" and determine the individual revenue and expense accounts that require adjustment. All the necessary amounts appear in this column, but the working paper does not show the accounts involved. It would be possible to add a column or two to the working paper and enter the account titles at the time the working paper is prepared. It is usually easier, however, to determine the appropriate revenue or expense account by noting the description of the error in the explanation column. For example, when we see that unexpired insurance was omitted at the end of both Year 6 and Year 7, it is apparent that the adjustment involves insurance expense. Because unexpired insurance increased from $550 to $980 during Year 7, it is clear that insurance expense was overstated by the $430, since an increase in assets in this amount was charged to expense in error. This reasoning determines the credit of $430 to Insurance Expense in the correcting journal entry.

The working paper for analysis of errors illustrated on page 961 is very helpful in tracing through the effect of errors on net income for several years, and in providing the basis for the necessary journal entry or entries to correct general ledger account balances at the end of the current year. Once the necessary entries have been recorded, the balance sheet and income statement for the current year can be prepared in the usual way.

If comparative statements are to be prepared, there remains the problem of revising the income statements and balance sheets of prior years to reflect the correction of errors. A correcting journal entry will always revise a company's balance sheet accounts to their corrected balances as of the end of the current year, but it will not correct account balances as of any prior date. Similarly, once the revenue and expense accounts for any given year are closed, an entry to correct errors will have no effect on the particular revenue and expense items for that year.

If the number of errors affecting data for prior years is small, it is usually a simple matter to make the necessary changes in amounts appearing on financial statements for prior years. However, when there are a large number of errors or when the correcting entries are complex, it may be desirable to use a working paper to correct the financial statements for prior years. A working paper which provides two columns for the original balances, two columns for the correcting entries, and two columns each for the income statement and balance sheet amounts will serve the purpose, and will also constitute a record of the revision for the accounting files.

STATEMENTS FROM INCOMPLETE ACCOUNTING RECORDS

The heart of the double-entry accounting system is the process of analyzing the effect of each transaction on the basic accounting equation: Assets = liabilities + owners' equity. Many small organizations operate with varying degrees of success with only minimal records and without the benefit of a complete accounting system. A system (or lack of system) of record keeping in which transactions are not analyzed and recorded in the double-entry framework is sometimes called a *single-entry* system. The records of social clubs, civic organizations, and small business units are often maintained on a single-entry basis.

At some time after the data have been well muddled, an accountant is likely to be called on to sift through such records and gather enough information to complete an income tax return and to prepare a balance sheet and an income statement. The process of recasting single-entry information into the double-entry framework is thus a very practical analytical exercise.

Balance sheet from incomplete accounting records

A business having no formal accounting system would still find it necessary to record certain basic information to stay in operation. For example, a record of cash received and checks written and a record of amounts due from customers and amounts owed to creditors would be essential. It would be possible to prepare a balance sheet at any given date for such a business from various sources of information. Cash on hand could be determined by count and by examining bank statements. Amounts due from customers could be summarized from unpaid sales invoices. Inventory on hand could be counted and its cost determined from purchase invoices. The cost of land, buildings, and equipment owned could be similarly established. The amount owing to creditors could be determined from purchase invoices and monthly statements. Ownership equity would be the difference between the valuations assigned to assets and liabilities.

Determining net income from single-entry accounting records

One way to determine net income from single-entry accounting records is to analyze the change in owners' equity during any given period. We know that owners' equity is the residual interest in the net assets of a business and that it is increased by net income and additional investment, and decreased by losses and distributions of assets to the owners. By the process of elimination, if we know the beginning and ending balance of owners' equity and the amount of any additional investments or withdrawals by owners, we can arrive at the change in owners' equity attributable to the net income or loss from operations during the period under consideration, as follows:

	Case I (net income)	Case II (net loss)
Owners' equity at end of period	$22,000	$20,000
Owners' equity at beginning of period	18,500	25,000
Total increase or (decrease) in owners' equity	$ 3,500	$(5,000)
Add: Amounts withdrawn by owners	4,800	2,600
Less: Additional investment by owners	(1,000)	(500)
Net income or (loss) for the period	$ 7,300	$(2,900)

For many purposes a more complete picture of operations is needed than that conveyed by a single net income figure. The Internal Revenue Service insists on some details of revenue and expenses. For even the most elementary budgeting and managerial control purposes, information is required as to how net income was determined. The problem then is how to develop these operating details from single-entry accounting records.

Because money transactions are of major importance in any business, a detailed record of cash receipts and payments is a valuable source of information. This is demonstrated below.

From a detailed list of cash receipts we can determine:	*From a detailed list of cash payments we can determine:*
Cash receipts from sales and other revenue	Cash paid for purchases of merchandise and operating expenses
Collections on customers' accounts	Payments to creditors
Proceeds from sale of plant assets	Cash paid to acquire plant assets
Amounts borrowed	Payments on loans
Investments by owners	Cash withdrawals by owners

If, in addition to cash receipts and payments data, we have (1) a list of assets at the beginning and end of the period and (2) a list of liabilities at the beginning and end of the period, we can determine the owners' equity at the beginning and end of the period, and prepare comparative balance sheets.

From this basic information, plus some help from miscellaneous sources, we can reconstruct the major components (sales, other revenue, cost of goods sold, and operating expenses) of the income statement. In the sections that follow are some examples to illustrate how these various revenue and expense items can be derived, using the information available in single-entry accounting records.

Illustration: Income Statement from Incomplete Accounting Records To illustrate the preparation of an income statement, we shall assume a relatively simple situation. The balance sheet at the end of Year 1, summary of operations for Year 2, and other information for Joe's Place, a single proprietorship, is presented on pages 966 and 967 and will serve as a basis for our illustration.

JOE'S PLACE
Balance Sheet—End of Year 1
(Prepared from Incomplete Records)

Assets		Liabilities & Capital	
Cash	$ 4,680	Accounts payable	$ 9,400
Notes receivable from		Accrued salaries payable	1,100
suppliers	12,000	Unearned rental revenue	600
Accounts receivable	4,000	Total liabilities	$11,100
Accrued interest receivable	320		
Inventory	18,000	Joe Palermo, capital	55,900
Unexpired insurance	500		
Building and equipment	40,000		
Less: Accumulated			
depreciation	(12,500)		
Total assets	$67,000	Total liabilities & capital	$67,000

Summary of operations for Year 2 (from cash and supplementary records)

Cash receipts:		
Collections on accounts receivable	$35,000	
Sales on cash basis	42,000	
Interest revenue	540	
Rental revenue	3,600	$81,140
Cash payments:		
For merchandise (including freight)	$53,400	
Insurance premiums	940	
Salaries	10,700	
Other operating expenses	3,000	
Withdrawals by owner	6,000	74,040
Sales returns and allowances		1,800
Cash discounts taken by customers (sales discounts)		600
Accounts written off as uncollectible during the year		300
Cash discounts taken on purchases (purchase discounts)		1,100
Purchase returns and allowances		970

Account balances at end of Year 2 (from supplementary analyses)

Cash (verified through count and bank reconcillations)	$?
Notes receivable (no change during the year)	12,000
Accounts receivable	7,600
Accrued interest receivable	530
Inventory	25,000
Unexpired insurance	700
Accounts payable	8,500
Accrued salaries payable	1,900
Unearned rental revenue	450

Additional information

(1) No acquisitions or disposals of buildings or equipment took place during Year 2.
(2) Depreciation is computed by the accountant at $2,800 for Year 2.
(3) Payroll taxes and income tax withholdings are ignored in order not to complicate the example.
(4) The direct write-off method is used to recognize doubtful accounts expense.

Reconstructing Gross Sales Sales arise from two sources, cash receipts from customers and gross increases in accounts receivable. Since beginning receivables reflect revenue realized in prior periods, cash collections of these receivables during the current period have no connection with the revenue of the current period. Therefore, the beginning balance of accounts receivable must be deducted from the total cash collections to arrive at sales of the current period that were realized in cash. On the other hand, receivables at the end of the current period represent sales which are not reflected in cash receipts and which must be added in to convert a cash receipts figure into the sales figure. Receivables included in this computation should include only accounts and notes arising from the sale of goods and services.

Sales returns and allowances, sales discounts, and receivables written off as uncollectible during the period represent sales during the period that were not realized in cash and are not included in the accounts receivable balance at the end of the year. These amounts, however, should be included in the computation of gross sales. Applying this reasoning, we can reconstruct gross sales for Joe's Place as illustrated at the top of page 968.

JOE'S PLACE
Gross Sales for Year 2

Sales on account for Year 2:

Collections on accounts receivable	$35,000	
Receivables written off as uncollectible	300	
Sales returns and allowances	1,800	
Cash discounts taken by customers	600	
Accounts receivable at the end of Year 2	7,600	
Less: Accounts receivable at the beginning of Year 2 . .	(4,000)	$41,300
Cash sales		42,000
Gross sales for Year 2		$83,300

Reconstructing Other Revenue The amount of other revenue items such as interest revenue and rental revenue may be determined from comparative balance sheet and cash data as illustrated below for Joe's Place.

JOE'S PLACE
Other Revenue for Year 2

	Interest revenue	Rental revenue
Amount of revenue received in cash in Year 2	$540	$3,600
Less: Amounts included in cash receipts but not earned in Year 2:		
Advance payments by tenants at end of Year 2		450
Accrued interest receivable at beginning of Year 2 . . .	320	
Cash receipts representing revenue for Year 2	$220	$3,150
Add: Amounts earned in Year 2 but not included in cash receipts:		
Advance payments by tenants at beginning of Year 2 . .		600
Accrued interest receivable at end of Year 2	530	
Revenue for Year 2	$750	$3,750

Reconstructing Cost of Goods Sold The cost of goods sold is derived from information about purchases and inventories. Inventories at the end of a period can be determined by a physical count. Hopefully, beginning inventories were also determined by count at the end of the previous period; if not, an estimated amount must be used.

The purchases figure may be reconstructed from cash payments records and schedules of accounts payable at the start and end of the period. The balance of accounts payable at the beginning of the period reflects purchases during prior periods that are not germane to the operating results of the current year. Therefore, from total cash payments to merchandise creditors we must deduct the beginning balance of accounts payable to arrive at the cash outlays for merchandise purchases applicable to this period. Accounts payable at the end of the period represent credit purchases during the current year, which must be added in to arrive at an estimate of the total amount of purchases for the period. An analysis of invoices will supply information as to the cash discounts taken during the period and the credits received for purchase returns and allowances.

The following illustration for Joe's Place demonstrates how reasoning and a systematic organization of the available data enable the accountant to arrive at a cost of goods sold figure. The first step is to compute the amount of gross purchases for Year 2, as shown below:

JOE'S PLACE
Gross Purchases for Year 2

Payments on accounts payable during Year 2	$53,400
Cash discounts taken on purchases	1,100
Purchase returns and allowances	970
Accounts payable balance at end of Year 2	8,500
Less: Accounts payable balance at beginning of Year 2	(9,400)
Gross purchases for Year 2	$54,570

In deriving gross purchases, the accountant must be careful to include in accounts payable only accounts relating to merchandise purchases. This analysis, together with the inventory figures taken from comparative balance sheets, provides all the information necessary to compute cost of goods sold as shown below:

JOE'S PLACE
Cost of Goods Sold for Year 2

Beginning inventory			$18,000
Gross purchases (see above)		$54,570	
Less:			
Cash discounts taken on purchases	$1,100		
Purchase returns and allowances	970	(2,070)	
Net purchases			52,500
Cost of goods available for sale			$70,500
Less: Ending inventory			25,000
Cost of goods sold for Year 2			$45,500

Reconstructing Operating Expenses Expenses arise from cash payments, from purchases of goods and services on credit, and from the consumption of assets on hand. Since cash payments during any given period may involve the acquisition of assets or the payment of debts that relate to expenses of prior periods, reconstructing the expenses of the current period requires an analysis of both asset and liability accounts as well as cash payments.

The balance of any asset that is subject to amortization increases as a result of the acquisition of additional assets, and decreases as the asset is used up. The normal process of determining the ending balance of the asset is: Beginning asset balance, plus acquisitions, less assets consumed, equals the ending balance. In reconstructing expenses we usually are able to determine the beginning and ending balance of the related asset and the cost of new acquisitions during the period (through an analysis of cash payments and credit transactions). We can convert this information into the amount of expense for the period as follows:

Assets acquired during the period	*XX*
Less: Asset balance at the end of the period	*(XX)*
Add: Asset balance at the beginning of the period	*XX*
Equals expense for the period	*XXX*

The determination of expenses by analyzing accrued liability balances and related cash payments is a similar process. The beginning balance of the accrued liability is deducted from the total cash payments during the current period to arrive at the cash payments relating to current period's expense. Adding to this figure the accrued liability at the end of the period produces the expense for the current period. Reconstruction of operating expenses for Joe's Place is illustrated on page 971.

Working Paper for Preparation of Financial Statements from Incomplete Records The foregoing computations and other information derived from incomplete records can now be used to prepare a complete set of financial statements. Most accountants, however, prefer to summarize the information in working paper form, as illustrated on page 972 for Joe's Place. Formal financial statements may be prepared from the information in the last four columns of the working paper. Alternative forms of the working paper may be used; for example, a pair of columns for a trial balance at the end of Year 2 may be added following the "Transactions for Year 2" columns in the working paper illustrated for Joe's Place.

JOE'S PLACE
Operating Expenses for Year 2

	Insurance expense	Salary expense	Other operating expenses	Depreciation expense
Cash payments during Year 2	$940	$10,700	$3,000	
Less: Amounts included in payments but not expenses of Year 2:				
Prepayments at end of Year 2	(700)			
Accrued liability at beginning of year 2		(1,100)		
Add: Amounts not included in cash payments, but chargeable to operations of Year 2:				
Prepayments at beginning of Year 2	500			
Accrued liablility at end of Year 2 . . .		1,900		
Depreciation expense (as computed by accountant)				$2,800
Operating expenses for Year 2	$740	$11,500	$3,000	$2,800

JOE'S PLACE
Working Paper for Preparation of Financial Statements
from Incomplete Accounting Records
For Year 2

Accounts	Balances, beg. of Year 2 Debit	Credit	Transactions for Year 2 Debit	Credit	Income statement for Year 2 Debit	Credit	Balance sheet end of Year 2 Debit	Credit
Cash	4,680		(1) 42,000 (2) 35,000 (3) 4,140	(5) 53,400 (6) 14,640 (8) 6,000			11,780	
Notes receivable	12,000						12,000	
Accounts receivable	4,000		(1) 41,300	(2) 37,700			7,600	
Accrued int. rec.	320		(3) 210				530	
Beginning inv.	18,000				18,000			
Unexpired insurance	500			(6) 200			700	
Bldg. & equipment	40,000						40,000	
Accum. depreciation		12,500		(7) 2,800				15,300
Accounts payable		9,400	(5) 55,470	(4) 54,570				8,500
Accrued sal. pay.		1,100		(6) 800				1,900
Unearned rental rev.		600	(3) 150					450
J. Palermo, capital		55,900						55,900
J. Palermo, drawing			(8) 6,000				6,000	
Sales				(1) 83,300		83,300		
Sales ret. & allow.			(2) 1,800		1,800			
Sales discounts			(2) 600		600			
Doubtful accts. exp.			(2) 300		300			
Interest revenue				(3) 750		750		
Rental revenue				(3) 3,750		3,750		
Purchases			(4) 54,570		54,570			
Purchase ret. & allow.				(5) 970		970		
Purchase discounts				(5) 1,100		1,100		
Insurance expense			(6) 740		740			
Salary expense			(6) 11,500		11,500			
Other operating exp.			(6) 3,000		3,000			
Depreciation exp.			(7) 2,800		2,800			
Ending inventory						25,000	25,000	
					93,310	114,870	103,610	82,050
Net income					21,560			21,560
	79,500	79,500	259,780	259,780	114,870	114,870	103,610	103,610

Explanation of transactions for Year 2:
(1) Gross sales, $42,000 in cash and $41,300 on account.
(2) Collections on account, sales returns and allowances, sales discounts, and doubtful accounts expense.
(3) Collection of interest and rental revenue; adjust interest receivable and unearned rental revenue.
(4) Gross purchases.
(5) Payments on accounts payable; also to record purchase returns and allowances and purchase discounts.
(6) Payments for expenses; adjust unexpired insurance and accrued salaries payable.
(7) Depreciation expense (given).
(8) Owner's drawings.

REVIEW QUESTIONS

1 Briefly describe the purpose of **Opinion No. 20** issued by the Accounting Principles Board.

2 What are two types of **accounting changes?** Briefly describe each type.

3 List the three possible approaches that may be applicable to reporting the effect of an accounting change.

4 Describe a situation in which a **change in accounting principle** would be considered appropriate.

5 How is the **cumulative effect** of a change in accounting principle determined and reported in the income statement for the period in which the change is made?

6 List five examples of changes in accounting principle which would require the retroactive restatement of financial statements for prior periods.

7 Jefferson Pie Company wrote down its plant and equipment by $15 million in Year 2. The reasons given were:
a To reduce excess capacity by closing inefficient plants
b To recognize obsolescence attributed to new technological developments and a shift in the demand for the company's products
How should the write-off be reported in the financial statements?

8 Vermont Tile Corp. charged $87.9 million against operating income as a result of a write-down of its seagoing tanker fleet. Included in this amount was $65 million "for possible losses in the future." Evaluate the accounting treatment of this write-down.

9 How should a material error in previously issued financial statements be reported in the year the error is discovered?

10 What is the basis for distinguishing between an error in measuring the net income of a prior period that should be treated as a prior period adjustment, and an error whose correction should be considered a part of the determination of net income in the period in which it is discovered?

11 Which of the following errors should be treated as a prior period adjustment?
a A depreciable asset which was estimated to have an economic life of four years is now estimated to have an estimated economic life of six years.
b A substantial deficiency in income taxes relating to the income of two years ago is assessed by the Internal Revenue Service as a result of an error in the interpretation of tax laws.
c An analysis of credit experience indicates that doubtful accounts expense over the past three years has exceeded the provision for such expense made at the rate of 1% of sales.
d A substantial amount of merchandise in transit at the close of the previous year was included in purchases but was not included in the ending inventory.
e An audit reveals that a substantial purchase of a depreciable asset was inadvertently charged to expense last year.

12 Errors affecting both the balance sheet and the income statement may be classified into two major types. State and define each type.

13 Why is it important to correct material errors even after they have counterbalanced?

14 Explain what is meant by the term *single-entry accounting system.*

15 Briefly describe two general approaches that may be followed in arriving at the amounts required to prepare financial statements from incomplete accounting records.

EXERCISES

Ex. 23-1 During the year ended December 31, Year 3, Cathay China Company changed its method of accounting for property taxes during construction from expensing property taxes to capitalizing them as building costs. The company was organized in Year 1. The data below have been extracted from the accounting records.

	Year 3	Year 2	Year 1
Income before cumulative effect of accounting change in Year 3	$400,000	$270,000	$150,000
Property taxes during construction	125,000	75,000	24,500
Depreciation on buildings—based on accounting principle formerly followed	50,000	35,000	30,000
Depreciation on buildings—based on newly adopted accounting principle	59,000	39,000	30,980
Earnings per share as reported, before cumulative effect of accounting change in Year 3	$2.00	$1.35	$0.75

The income for Year 3 was determined using the newly adopted accounting principle. The number of shares of stock outstanding during the three-year period was 200,000 shares.

a Compute the cumulative effect of the change in accounting principle which should appear in the income statement for Year 3. Assume a 40% income tax rate.

b What was the effect of the change in accounting principle on earnings per share for each of the three years?

Ex. 23-2 From the data in Exercise 23-1, prepare a partial comparative income statement for Years 2 and 3. The income statement should include the cumulative effect on prior years of the change in accounting principle, the earnings per share, and pro forma amounts for Year 2, as illustrated on page 947.

Ex. 23-3 San Pedro Cork Co. included the following items on its balance sheet at the end of Year 5:

Equipment	$3,780,000	
Less: Accumulated depreciation	1,260,000	$2,520,000
Goodwill		1,225,000

Both assets were acquired early in Year 1. The equipment has been depreciated over an estimated economic life of 15 years and the goodwill has been amortized over a period of 20 years. Late in Year 6 the company decided that the total economic life of the equipment should be reduced to 12 years and that goodwill should be amortized over a period of 40 years from the date of acquisition. Compute the depreciation on the equipment and the amortization of goodwill for Year 6, assuming that the residual value of the equipment is estimated at $140,000.

Ex. 23-4 At the end of Year 1, Dehn Company's accountant recorded the cost of a patent purchased from Q Co., intending to amortize the cost over the next five years. At the end of Year 3 it was discovered that the sales manager's Year 1 salary of $25,000 had inadvertently been included in the patent cost at the end of Year 1. The company is subject to a 50% income tax rate and intends to file amended income tax returns for Years 1 and 2. Prepare a journal entry to correct this error at the end of Year 3, after normal adjusting entries have been made but before the accounts have been closed.

Ex. 23-5 The following errors in the accounting records of Dinko & Jozica, a partnership, were discovered in Year 4:

	Inventory overstated	Depreciation understated	Accrued rental revenue not recorded	Accrued interest expense not recorded
Year 1	$10,000	$-0-	$3,000	$-0-
Year 2	-0-	2,500	1,000	-0-
Year 3	4,000	-0-	-0-	500

The partners share profits and losses equally.
a Prepare a correcting entry in Year 4, assuming that the accounts were closed for Year 3.
b Prepare a correcting entry in Year 4, assuming that the accounts are still open for Year 3.

Ex. 23-6 During the current month the cash records of Pogoda Parts show that $27,400 was collected from credit customers and $12,400 was received from cash sales. The amount due from credit customers increased from $7,300 at the beginning of the month to $8,150 at the end of the month. During the month the credit manager had written off $790 of accounts receivable as uncollectible. From this information, determine the gross sales for the month.

Ex. 23-7 Lasers, Inc., sells TV cable services to customers, who may choose to pay $4 per month for the service or may pay in advance a yearly charge of $42 for 12 months of service. During the current year the company collected $150,700 from customers. Additional information for the current year follows:

	Beginning of year	End of year
Advance payments by customers	$3,500	$5,700
Accounts receivable from customers	6,820	6,930

From the information given, compute the total cable revenue earned during the year.

Ex. 23-8 The inventory of Jester Company increased by $17,500 during the year, and its accounts payable to merchandise suppliers increased by $9,500. During the year the company paid $130,200 to suppliers and $7,200 in transportation charges on merchandise. The company also purchased $4,100 of merchandise for cash. Determine the cost of goods sold for the year.

Ex. 23-9 The following information is taken from the records of Matilda Malt Company for Year 1:

	Jan. 1	Dec. 31
Stockholders' equity (no stock issued or retired)	$98,000	$117,000
Cash	6,000	12,400
Inventory	20,000	14,000
Payable to merchandise creditors	8,000	8,500
Receivable from customers	14,200	18,200
Cash paid to merchandise creditors		70,000
Operating expenses and income taxes paid in cash (including $800 prepaid at end of year)		32,000
Current year's sales written off as uncollectible (an additional allowance of $250 is required at Dec. 31)		500
Dividends declared and paid		20,000
Depreciation expense		6,200
Other assets	77,800	82,350
Other liabilities	12,000	12,000

Prepare an income statement on the accrual basis for Year 1 in good form. Show supporting schedules for sales, cost of goods sold, and total operating expenses and income taxes. (**Hint:** First compute net income and work back to sales.)

Ex. 23-10 Ken Company's year-end financial statements contained the following errors:

	Dec. 31, Year 3	Dec. 31, Year 4
Ending inventory	$2,000 understated	$1,800 overstated
Depreciation expense	400 understated	No error

Net income as determined by the company was $20,000 in Year 3 and $25,000 in Year 4. An insurance premium of $1,500 was prepaid in Year 3 covering Year 3, Year 4, and Year 5. The entire amount was charged to expense in Year 3. In addition, on December 31, Year 4, a fully depreciated machine was sold for $3,200 cash, but the sale was not recorded until Year 5. There were no other errors during Year 3 or Year 4, and no corrections have been made for any of the errors. Ignore income tax considerations.
a Compute the corrected amount of net income on the accrual basis for Year 4.
b Compute the total effect of the errors on the amount of Ken Company's working capital at December 31, Year 4.
c Prepare a single journal entry to correct the accounting records in Year 5. Assume that the accounts have been closed for Year 4. (Remember that the gain on the sale of the machine was recorded but in the wrong year.)

SHORT CASES FOR ANALYSIS AND DECISION

Case 23-1 Various types of accounting changes can affect the second reporting standard of generally accepted auditing standards. This auditing standard reads, "The report shall state whether accounting principles have been consistently observed in the current period in relation to the preceding period."

Assume that the following list describes changes which have a material effect on a client's financial statements for the current year.

(1) A change from the completed-contract method to the percentage-of-completion method of accounting for long-term construction contracts.

(2) A change in the estimated economic life of previously recorded plant assets based on newly acquired information.

(3) Correction of a mathematical error in inventory pricing made in a prior period.

(4) A change from prime costing to full absorption costing for inventory valuation.

(5) A change from presentation of financial statements of individual companies to presentation of consolidated financial statements for all companies.

(6) A change from deferring and amortizing preproduction costs to recording such costs as an expense when incurred because future benefits of the costs have become doubtful. The new accounting method was adopted in recognition of the change in estimated future benefits.

(7) A change to including the employer share of FICA taxes with "retirement benefits" on the income statement from including it with "other taxes."

(8) A change from the fifo method of inventory pricing to the lifo method of inventory pricing.

(9) A change from the lifo method of inventory pricing to the fifo method of inventory pricing.

Instructions Identify the type of change which is described in each item above and state whether the prior year's financial statements should be restated when presented in comparative form with the current year's statements.

Case 23-2 Given below is an abstract from a news item which appeared in the *Wall Street Journal:*

Libby McNeill & Libby said a change in its method of inventory valuation will contribute an extraordinary gain of about $15 million to results for the fiscal year ending July 3. The food company said it's changing to first-in, first-out from last-in, first-out inventories.

The company said it incurred losses in prior years and reported that it has about $18.8 million of these losses available to offset taxable income earned in the future.

While Libby didn't detail reasons for the change, industry sources said the switch to FIFO can be advantageous under certain circumstances. In the case of companies having large tax-loss carryforwards that may be due to expire, for example, the switch to FIFO permits the taxable gain realized to be offset by the tax-loss carryforward. This lessens, at least in part, the tax impact and, at the same time, permits utilization of the loss carryforward that otherwise might expire unused.

The industry source also stated that a change to FIFO from LIFO tends to improve earnings during periods of inflation. That situation arises because under the FIFO method, inventories are valued on a current cost basis while under LIFO they are valued as of an earlier date and presumably at a lower cost basis.

Instructions

a The news item uses the term *extraordinary gain* in reference to the change in inventory pricing method. Describe how the effect of this change should be reported in the financial statements and indicate whether an extraordinary gain results from a change from lifo to the fifo method of inventory pricing.

b Why would a company change from lifo to fifo if such a change results in a significant amount of back income taxes which may have to be paid to the government?

Case 23-3 Hills Company, which is closely held, plans to sell additional shares of stock to the public to finance an expansion program. The company has been in operation for five years and has never had an audit. To meet the requirements of the Securities and Exchange Commission in connection with its registration, the company has hired a firm of CPAs to audit its records for the first time, as of the end of Year 10.

In its financial statements for the past five years the company has reported the following earnings and stockholders' equity:

	Net income	Earned per share of common stock	Stockholders' equity
Year 6	$368,000	$1.84	$4,945,000
Year 7	390,000	1.95	5,195,000
Year 8	435,000	2.18	5,350,000
Year 9	470,000	2.35	5,620,000
Year 10	510,000	2.55	5,870,000

The auditors discovered in the course of their examination that the company had consistently omitted from its ending inventory in each of the five years an inventory of goods in a warehouse in Ohio. This warehouse operation had not proved successful and had been discontinued in Year 10; therefore, the inventory at the end of Year 10 was not affected by the error. Warehouse records show that the inventory of goods in the warehouse at the end of each year, stated at lower of average cost or market, was as follows: Year 6, $180,000; Year 7, $90,000; Year 8, $210,000; Year 9, $115,000. The auditors also discovered that because the sales report from the warehouse was late in arriving at the end of Year 7, $80,000 of sales applicable to Year 7 operations were not recorded as revenue until Year 8.

When the auditors insisted that these errors be corrected retroactively in presenting income data for the five-year period in the registration statement, the company treasurer objected. "The warehouse has been discontinued. There is no inventory there now. All these errors you have dug up have washed themselves out in the accounting records and there is no point in going back and raking over the dead coals of past history. There's nothing wrong with our balance sheet at the end of Year 10, or our income statement for Year 10, and that's what the people who buy our stock are interested in."

Instructions Determine the effect of the errors discovered by the auditors on the financial statements of Hills Company. You may ignore income taxes. What position would you take with respect to the treasurer's objection?

PROBLEMS

Group A

23A-1 Thomas Lin purchased merchandise for $19,700 in a bankruptcy sale early in the current year. With an additional investment of $4,000 cash, Lin opened a store near a college campus under the name of Lin's Dreams. During the first year of operations he paid $65,000 to merchandise suppliers and spent $16,750 for salaries and other operating expenses. During the year Lin withdrew $13,500 in cash from the business and $410 of inventory for personal use, including gifts to personal friends.

On New Year's Eve at the end of the first year of operations, while en route from the store to his apartment, Lin lost the briefcase containing the accounting records for the business. From bank records it was determined that cash totaled $4,130 at year-end. The accounts receivable ledger at the store showed total accounts receivable of $9,380, of which $280 were considered to be probably uncollectible. Lin had to retake the inventory of merchandise in the store, which totaled $13,150 at cost. Statements from suppliers showed that Lin owed $7,800 at the close of the year. Lin had prepaid expenses of $255 and accrued expenses of $395 at the end of the current year.

Instructions

a On the basis of the above information, prepare an income statement for Lin's Dreams for the first year of operations. Include supporting schedules which show how you determined sales and the cost of goods sold for the current year.

b Prepare a balance sheet for Lin's Dreams as of the end of the current year.

23A-2 Cossack Fur, Inc., has used the completed-contract method of accounting for long-term construction contracts for ten years. In Year 3, the company decided to change to the percentage-of-completion method in order to achieve a better matching of construction effort and realized construction profits reported in its income statement. The company recently added an expert in cost estimation, and management feels that it is now able to make reasonably accurate estimates of costs to be used in determining the percentage of completion on each contract. In addition, management thinks that it would be unfair to stockholders to report a decrease in earnings for Year 3, which can be attributed to two significant factors as follows:

(1) Several major contracts were completed in Year 2 which resulted in an unusually high net income for that year.

(2) Few contracts were completed in Year 3, although the company had 40% more work under construction in Year 3 than it did in Year 2 and had 30% more employees on the payroll.

A summary of results for the last two years using the completed-contract method follows:

	Year 3	Year 2
Contract revenue realized	$6,000,000	$18,600,000
Construction costs applicable to contract revenue realized	4,500,000	14,700,000
Operating expenses	1,050,000	900,000
Income tax expense, 45%	202,500	1,350,000
Net income	247,500	1,650,000

Application of the percentage-of-completion method to the operations of the last two years would have given the following results:

	Year 3	Year 2
Contract revenue realized	$17,400,000	$9,300,000
Construction costs applicable to contract revenue realized	14,100,000	7,500,000

Operating expense using the percentage-of-completion method would be the same as was reported under the completed-contract method. The completed-contract method will continue to be used for income tax purposes. Income tax allocation procedures for timing differences will be used in preparing revised financial statements giving retroactive effect to the change in accounting principle. Assume that income taxes are 45% of operating income.

Instructions Restate the comparative income statement for Year 2 and Year 3, giving retroactive recognition to the change in accounting principle. Assume that the company had 330,000 shares of capital stock outstanding during the two-year period. Prepare a note suitable for inclusion in the annual report which explains the reason for the change in accounting principle and the effect of the change on net income and earnings per share. (See illustrative note on page 949 describing this type of accounting change.)

23A-3 The financial statements of Cambio Company showed income before income taxes of $4,030,000 for the year ended December 31, Year 10, and $3,330,000 for the year ended December 31, Year 9. Additional information is as follows:

(1) Capital expenditures were $2,800,000 in Year 10 and $4,000,000 in Year 9. Included in the Year 10 capital expenditures is equipment purchased for $1,000,000 on January 1, Year 10, with no residual value. Cambio used straight-line depreciation based on a ten-year estimated economic life in its financial statements. As a result of additional information now available, it is estimated that this equipment should have only an eight-year economic life.

(2) Cambio made an error in its financial statements which should be regarded as material. A payment of $180,000 was made in January Year 10 and charged to expense in Year 10 for insurance premiums applicable to policies commencing and expiring in Year 9. No liability had been recorded for this item at December 31, Year 9.

(3) The allowance for doubtful accounts reflected in Cambio's financial statements was $7,000 at December 31, Year 10, and $97,000 at December 31, Year 9. During Year 10, $90,000 of uncollectible receivables were written off against the allowance for doubtful accounts. In Year 9 the provision for doubtful accounts was based on a percentage of net sales. The Year 10 provision has not yet been recorded. Net sales were $58,500,000 for the year ended December 31, Year 10, and $49,230,000 for the year ended December 31, Year 9. Based on the latest available facts, the Year 10 provision for doubtful accounts is estimated to be 0.2% of net sales.

(4) A review of the estimated warranty liability at December 31, Year 10, which is included in "other liabilities" in Cambio's balance sheet, has disclosed that this estimated liability should be increased $170,000.

(5) Cambio has two large blast furnaces that it uses in its manufacturing process. These furnaces must be periodically relined. Furnace A was relined in January Year 4, at a cost of $230,000, and in January Year 9, at a cost of $280,000. Furnace B was relined for the first time in January Year 10, at a cost of $300,000. These costs were expensed as incurred.

Because the relining will last for five years, a more appropriate matching of revenue and costs would have resulted if the cost of the relining was capitalized and depreciated over the economic life of the relining. Cambio has decided to make a change in accounting principle from expensing relining costs as incurred to capitalizing them and depreciating them over their economic life on a straight-line basis with a full year's depreciation in the year of relining. This change meets the requirements for a change in accounting principle under **APB Opinion No. 20,** "Accounting Changes."

Instructions
a For the years ended December 31, Year 10 and Year 9, prepare a work sheet to determine income before income taxes and cumulative effect of a change in accounting principle as adjusted for the above additional information. Show supporting computations in good form. ***Ignore income taxes and deferred tax considerations in your answer.*** The work sheet should have the following format:

| | Year ended December 31, | |
	Year 10	Year 9
Income before income taxes and before adjustments	$4,030,000	$3,330,000
Adjustments:		
	$	$
Net adjustments	$	$
Income before income taxes and cumulative effect of a		
change in accounting principle, after adjustments	$	$

b For the year ended December 31, Year 10, compute the cumulative effect, before income taxes, of the change in accounting principle from expensing to capitalizing furnace relining costs. *Ignore income taxes and deferred tax considerations in your answer.*

23A-4 J. Stanley started a business on July 10, Year 1, by investing $75,000 in cash and merchandise. Net income for the remainder of Year 1 was $30,000 and for Year 2 it was $56,250. Stanley has made no additional investments and has not made any withdrawals since July 10, Year 1. A comparative balance sheet prepared by Stanley's wife is shown below:

J. STANLEY

Balance Sheet

December 31

	Year 2	Year 1
Cash	$ 22,650	$ 16,650
Accounts receivable	67,500	48,750
Inventory	60,000	42,600
Equipment (at cost)	45,000	45,000
Total assets	$195,150	$153,000
Accounts payable	$ 33,900	$ 33,000
Note payable to bank	–0–	15,000
J. Stanley, capital	161,250	105,000
Total liabilities & capital	$195,150	$153,000

The following errors are discovered by the auditor who was engaged in January of Year 3 to review the accounting records of the business:

(1) Inventory was overstated by $4,500 at the end of Year 1.
(2) Accrued liabilities of $1,800 were not recorded at the end of Year 1.
(3) Inventory of supplies of $1,050 was not recorded as an asset at the end of Year 1, and inventory of supplies of $450 at the end of Year 2 was debited to an expense account.
(4) Accrued revenue of $1,200 at the end of Year 2 was not recorded as a receivable.
(5) An allowance for doubtful accounts equal to 4% of accounts receivable should be established at the end of each year. No accounts receivable were written off during the last two years.
(6) Depreciation of $1,500 was not recorded in Year 1 and depreciation of $3,000 was not recorded in Year 2.

Instructions
a Prepare a working paper for analysis of errors to correct the net income for Year 1 and for Year 2.

b Prepare a correcting journal entry early in Year 3, assuming that the accounts are closed for Year 2.

c Prepare a corrected comparative balance sheet for Year 1 and Year 2. (**Note to student:** Be sure that capital for Stanley at the end of Year 1 is equal to the original investment plus the corrected net income for Year 1. Similarly, the capital for Stanley at the end of Year 2 should equal the original investment plus the total corrected net income for Year 1 and Year 2.)

23A-5 Robert Day organized Bob's Confectionery in Year 1. A friend set up an accounting system for Day which showed that at the end of Year 1, Day's capital had grown from $46,000 to $51,000. A summary of the capital account for Years 2 and 3 is shown below:

Robert Day, Capital

	Debit	Credit	Balance
Balance, Jan. 1, Year 2			$51,000
Net income, Year 2		$10,400	61,400
Drawings, Year 2	$6,000		55,400
Net loss, Year 3	800		54,600
Drawings, Year 3	7,200		47,400

Discouraged by this record, Day is considering admitting a partner who can provide the business with more management talent. Early in Year 4, a CPA firm was engaged to audit the accounts of the company and prepare comparative financial statements for Years 2 and 3. The auditors discovered the following in the course of their examination:

(1) Accrued commissions payable to salespersons at the end of the year were not recorded. These amounted to $1,150 at the end of Year 1; $1,400 at the end of Year 2, and $960 at the end of Year 3.

(2) Delivery and installation costs of $1,200 on new baking equipment were charged to expense when they were incurred on September 30, Year 2. The machinery has an economic life of 10 years and negligible residual value.

(3) Personal drawings by Day in the amount of $750 were debited to the Purchases account in Year 3.

(4) Raw materials costing $7,800, which were received near the end of Year 2, were included in the ending inventory but were recorded as purchases early in Year 3.

(5) A three-year insurance premium of $1,570 paid in advance on December 31, Year 3, was charged to Year 3 expense.

(6) An analysis of accounts receivable indicated that accounts originating in the following years should have been written off: Year 1, $180; Year 2, $890; Year 3, $80. The auditors estimated that a provision for doubtful accounts of $500 at the end of Year 3 would have been adequate to cover uncollectible accounts originating in Year 3.

Instructions

a Prepare a working paper for analysis of errors to determine the corrected net income for Years 2 and 3.

b Assuming that the accounts had been closed at the end of Year 3, prepare the necessary correcting journal entry at the beginning of Year 4.

c Prepare a corrected statement of Day's capital account from the beginning of Year 2 to the end of Year 3.

d On the basis of the audited data, is Day's business significantly better or worse off than the accounting records indicated?

23A-6 Joseph Voss started Point Fermin Research Company several years ago. For a number of years his wife kept the accounting records, but early in the current year she became seriously ill. Voss got in touch with a bookkeeping service whose manager told him, "You keep a record of your cash receipts and payments, and a list of your assets and liabilities at the beginning and end of the year, and I'll prepare financial statements for you at the end of the year."

At the close of the current year Voss presented the following data to the manager of the bookkeeping service:

Analysis of Cash Receipts and Cash Payments

Cash receipts:		Cash payments:	
Jan. 1, balance	$ 18,460	Paid on accounts payable (net	
Proceeds of bank loan	40,000	of $6,480 cash discounts) . .	$225,650
Cash sales	87,300	Paid for equipment	25,000
Interest received	1,590	Operating expenses	47,610
Collected on notes receivable	13,000	Insurance policy premium . .	980
Received from equipment rental	7,000	Freight-in on purchases	12,400
Received from customers (net		Payment on bank notes (in-	
of $4,130 in cash discounts)	177,690	cluding interest of $600) . .	15,600
		Dec. 31, balance	17,800
Total cash receipts	$345,040	Total cash payments	$345,040

List of Assets and Liabilities

	Jan. 1	Dec. 31
Cash	$ 18,460	$ 17,800
Notes receivable	15,000	2,000
Accrued interest receivable	900	500
Accounts receivable	43,560	64,320
Inventory	38,900	43,400
Unexpired insurance	1,900	1,500
Equipment (net of depreciation)	124,000	136,000
Total	$242,720	$265,520
Notes payable	$ 10,000	$ 35,000
Accrued interest payable	500	1,750
Accounts payable	47,500	52,300
Other accrued liabilities	3,400	6,300
Unearned rental revenue	1,200	1,800
Total	$ 62,600	$ 97,150

Voss reported that all accounts and notes receivable arose from merchandise sales and that $1,400 of accounts receivable had been written off during the year, of which $850 were in the accounts before January 1. Voss estimated that $1,320 of the December 31 receivables will prove uncollectible. Only purchases of merchandise are recorded in accounts payable.

Instructions

a On the basis of the above information, prepare an income statement for Point Fermin Research Company for the current year. Show supporting schedules. It is the company's policy to deduct doubtful accounts expense and cash discounts allowed from gross sales in the income statement.

b Prepare a statement of changes in Voss' capital account during the year.

Group B

23B-1 The following fragmentary information relates to the affairs of Nada's Other Place during the current year:

	Beginning of year	End of year
Owner's equity (Nada Berzov, capital)	$81,900	$97,800
Inventory	15,800	27,320
Payable to merchandise creditors	40,000	25,000
Short-term prepayments	1,800	2,400
Accrued liabilities	3,150	2,850

A summary of checks written shows that $200,000 was paid to merchandise suppliers during the year, $66,000 was paid for operating expenses, and $17,400 was withdrawn in cash by Nada Berzov. Estimated depreciation on buildings and equipment for the year is $8,400, and a reasonable provision for doubtful accounts is 2% of gross sales.

Instructions On the basis of the above information, prepare an income statement for Nada's Other Place for the current year. Show all supporting computations. (Deduct the provision for doubtful accounts from gross sales in the income statement.)

23B-2 The accountant for Gold Coast Corporation has just completed the comparative income statement for Years 11 and 12. The income statement appears below:

	Year 12	Year 11
Sales	$605,000	$580,000
Less: Cost of goods sold (lifo basis)	365,000	350,000
Gross profit on sales	$240,000	$230,000
Less: Operating expenses	125,000	130,000
Operating income	$115,000	$100,000
Less: Income tax expense, 40%	46,000	40,000
Income before extraordinary item	$ 69,000	$ 60,000
Extraordinary item, net of income tax effect	(30,000)	(10,000)
Net income	$ 39,000	$ 50,000
Earnings per share:		
Income before extraordinary item	$3.45	$3.00
Extraordinary item, net of income tax effect	(1.50)	(0.50)
Net income	$1.95	$2.50

When the comparative statement was presented, the president said: "This is the year we should do what we have been talking about for years. Take this thing back downstairs and revise it using the fifo method of inventory pricing. We have kept careful records of our inventories so that restating the financial statements from the lifo basis to the fifo basis will not be difficult. The change would give us a more realistic working capital position and would make our financial statements more comparable with those of our competitors; all of them use fifo."

Within a few hours, the accountant was able to come up with the required data and recomputed the cost of goods sold for each year as follows:

	Year 12	Year 11
Cost of goods sold (fifo basis)	$325,000	$330,000

The company had 20,000 shares of a single class of capital stock outstanding throughout the two-year period.

Instructions Restate the comparative income statement giving retroactive recognition to the change in accounting principle. Prepare a note which should accompany the financial statements issued at the end of Year 12, including the effect of the change in accounting principle on net income and earnings per share. (See page 949 for illustrative note describing this type of an accounting change.)

23B-3 Condensed statements of income and retained earnings of Lee Company for the years ended December 31, Year 4, and December 31, Year 3, are presented below:

LEE COMPANY

Condensed Statements of Income

and Retained Earnings

	Years Ended December 31	
	Year 4	Year 3
Sales	$3,000,000	$2,400,000
Less: Cost of goods sold	1,300,000	1,150,000
Gross profit on sales	$1,700,000	$1,250,000
Less: Selling, general, and administrative expenses	1,200,000	950,000
Income before extraordinary item	$ 500,000	$ 300,000
Extraordinary item	(400,000)	–0–
Net income	$ 100,000	$ 300,000
Retained earnings, Jan. 1	750,000	450,000
Retained earnings, Dec. 31	$ 850,000	$ 750,000

Presented below are three **unrelated** situations involving accounting changes and classification of certain items as ordinary or extraordinary. Each situation is based upon the condensed statements of income and retained earnings of Lee Company shown above and requires revisions to these statements.

Situation A On January 1, Year 2, Lee Company acquired machinery at a cost of $150,000. The company adopted the double-declining-balance method of depreciation for this machinery, and had been recording depreciation over an estimated economic life of ten years, with no residual value. At the beginning of Year 4, a decision was made to adopt the straight-line method of depreciation for this machinery. Due to an oversight, however, the double-declining-balance method was used for Year 4. For financial reporting purposes, depreciation is included in selling, general, and administrative expenses.

The extraordinary item in the condensed statement of income and retained earnings for Year 4 relates to shutdown expenses incurred by the company during a major strike by its operating employees during Year 4.

Situation B At the end of Year 4, Lee's management decided that the estimated rate on uncollectible accounts receivables was too low. The rate used for the Years 3 and 4 was 1% of total sales, and due to an increase in the write-off of uncollectible accounts, the rate has been raised to 3% of total sales. The amount recorded in doubtful accounts expense under the heading of selling, general, and administrative expenses for Year 4 was $30,000 and for Year 3 was $24,000.

The extraordinary item in the condensed statement of income and retained earnings for Year 4 relates to a loss incurred in the abandonment of obsolete equipment formerly used in the business.

Situation C The extraordinary item appearing in the condensed statement of income and retained earnings for Year 4 represents a correction of a material error in the computation of the cost of goods sold. Of the total amount, $340,000 related to Years 1 and 2 and $60,000 related to Year 3.

Instructions For each of the three **unrelated** situations, prepare revised condensed statements of income and retained earnings of Lee Company for the years ended December 31, Year 4, and December 31, Year 3. Each answer should recognize the appropriate accounting changes and other items outlined in the situation. **Ignore all earnings per share computations and income tax considerations unless indicated to the contrary.**

23B-4 The office manager of Beran Banana Company has prepared the balance sheet shown below for the company at the end of Year 3:

BERAN BANANA COMPANY
Balance Sheet
End of Year 3

Assets		Liabilities & Stockholders' Equity	
Cash	$ 9,800	Accounts payable	$ 25,600
Accounts receivable (net)	37,000	Income taxes payable	2,700
Inventory	45,000	Capital stock, $1 par	40,000
Furniture & fixtures (net)	38,000	Retained earnings	61,500
		Total liabilities & stockhold-	
Total assets	$129,800	ers' equity	$129,800

The company began business early in Year 1, and income statements prepared by the office manager have shown the following net income (after income taxes) for the three-year period: Year 1, $26,000; Year 2, $19,200; Year 3, $16,300.

Walter Beran, the president, is concerned about this income trend, and asked a CPA firm to review the accounting records. This review revealed that the following errors and omissions had not been corrected during the applicable years:

End of	Inven-tory over-stated	Inven-tory under-stated	Prepaid rent omitted	Unearned revenue omitted	Accrued expense (misc. pay-ables) omitted	Accrued revenue (misc. receiv-ables) omitted
Year 1	$8,700		$ 950		$1,400	
Year 2	6,500		1,100	$ 800	1,200	$ 400
Year 3		$4,900	1,300	1,250	900	2,700

Combined federal and state income taxes are 30% of pre-tax income. The company will file amended tax income returns for Years 1 and 2; the income tax return for Year 3 had not yet been filed at the time the above errors were discovered. No dividends have been declared by the company in the first three years of its operations.

Instructions

a Prepare a working paper for analysis of errors to correct the net income for Years 1 to 3.

b Assuming that the accounts have been closed at the end of Year 3, prepare a journal entry to correct the accounting records at the end of Year 3.

c Prepare a corrected balance sheet at the end of Year 3.

d If you were presented with revised income statements for Beran Banana Company for the past three years, would your impression of its operating performance be substantially changed? Comment.

23B-5 Bill Dudley organized Dudley Corporation to manufacture an improved riveting gun he had invented. At the close of the third year of operations, Dudley found it necessary to apply for a bank loan. He showed the comparative three-year income statement to the bank loan officer and pointed out with some pride that net income had grown by about 25% in each year; the statement showed net income as follows: Year 1, $9,900; Year 2, $12,500; Year 3, $15,600. The bank officer suggested that Dudley have the records audited and present comparative statements backed by the opinion of a CPA. The audit revealed a number of errors, summarized in the schedule below. The auditor determined that all errors relating to Years 1 and 2 qualify as prior period adjustments.

The auditor recommended that amended income tax returns be filed for Years 1 and 2. Tax returns for Year 3 have not yet been filed. Assume that the corporation is subject in an income tax rate of 30%.

	Year 1	Year 2	Year 3
Ending finished goods inventory understated		$4,600	
Ending finished goods inventory overstated			$6,280
Customers' deposits on future sales recorded as revenue	$850	1,300	1,920
Accrued interest receivable omitted	480		150
Costs capitalized as deferred charges and amortized at 10% per year which should have been charged to selling expense in year costs were incurred		5,000	4,000

Instructions

a Prepare a working paper for analysis of errors showing the corrected net income (after income taxes) for each of the three years.

    b Prepare a correcting journal entry at the end of Year 3, assuming that the accounts have been closed for Year 3.

    c Prepare a correcting journal entry at the end of Year 3, assuming that the accounts are still open for Year 3 and that perpetual inventory records are used.

23B-6 Townsend Corporation was organized on July 1, Year 1, with authorized stock of 200,000 shares of $5 par common stock and 10,000 shares of $100 par, 6% preferred stock. Richard Townsend was given 200 shares of preferred and 2,000 shares of common for work and expenses in organizing and promoting the corporation. Attorneys' fees of $1,800, incurred in connection with the formation of the corporation, have not been paid as of September 30, Year 1.

Additional information

(1) On July 15, Year 1, Townsend transferred assets from his single proprietorship in exchange for 6,000 shares of preferred stock. The current fair values of these assets were as follows: notes receivable, $360,000; inventories $60,000; equipment, $180,000. The business did not begin operation until August 1, but interest of $900 accrued on the notes receivable between the time they were turned over to the corporation and July 31. This amount was recorded as Accrued Interest Receivable on July 31.

(2) On July 31, Year 1, 160,000 shares of common were sold at par for cash, $150,000 of which was used to buy land and $600,000 applied to the price of a building. The building cost $1,340,000; the balance was represented by a $7\frac{1}{2}$% mortgage due in 10 years. Interest on the mortgage payable did not begin until August 1 and is payable monthly.

(3) On September 30, Year 1, the accountant for the corporation prepared a summary of all transactions completed by the corporation during August and September in the form of "net" debit and credit **changes in ledger accounts.** This information, which includes all adjusting entries, except for ending inventory and income taxes, is shown below:

	Net changes in ledger accounts	
	Debits	Credits
Accounts showing changes during two months ended Sept. 30, Year 1:		
Cash		$ 28,350
Accounts receivable	$ 76,285	
Allowance for doubtful accounts		1,250
Accrued interest receivable	3,600	
Accumulated depreciation–building		8,375
Accumulated depreciation–equipment		6,500
Organization costs		1,060
Accounts payable		18,500
Retained earnings (first quarterly dividend on preferred stock)	9,300	
Sales		164,800
Purchases	110,000	
Operating expenses (includes depreciation, amortization of organization costs, and doubtful accounts expense)	24,000	
Interest expense	9,250	
Interest revenue (does not include $900 earned in July)		3,600
	$232,435	$232,435

The organization costs are being amortized over 60 months starting August 1, Year 1. The inventory on September 30, Year 1, amounted to $68,200.

Instructions
a Prepare the balance sheet of Townsend Corporation at July 31, Year 1. Income taxes should be accrued at the rate of 40% on the interest earned in July. This was the only item of revenue or expense through July 31, Year 1.
b Prepare an income statement for Townsend Corporation, summarizing its activities for the two months ending September 30, Year 1. Assume that income taxes are 40% of income before income taxes. Do not compute earnings per share.
c Prepare a balance sheet for Townsend Corporation at September 30, Year 1.
d Prepare a schedule for cash receipts and cash payments reconciling the decrease of $28,350 in the Cash account during the two-month period ended September 30.

24

STATEMENT OF CHANGES IN FINANCIAL POSITION

For many years the basic financial statements of a business were the balance sheet and the income statement. Many companies also prepared a third financial statement, called a *statement of source and application of funds* or simply a *funds statement.* This statement was originally developed as a means of explaining to creditors why net income was not accompanied by a corresponding increase in cash or working capital. The inclusion of such a financial statement in annual reports was an optional matter for many years, and even among those companies which prepared funds statements, the content and terminology varied greatly.

In 1963, *APB Opinion No. 3,* "The Statement of Source and Application of Funds," encouraged but *did not require* the presentation of a funds statement as supplementary information in financial reports.[1] *APB Opinion No. 3* recognized that the term *funds* was sometimes used to mean cash or cash equivalents. A funds statement based on this narrow definition of funds was really a statement of cash receipts and payments. Most companies, however, defined funds more broadly as *working capital* (current assets less current liabilities). A funds statement prepared on the working capital basis usually included only those transactions which directly affected current assets or current liabilities.

[1] *APB Opinion No. 3,* "The Statement of Source and Application of Funds," AICPA (New York: 1963), p. 16.

The all-financial-resources concept of "funds"

After considering the different prevailing concepts of funds and the varying forms of funds statements, the Accounting Principles Board in *Opinion No. 3* recommended that the concept of funds be broadened to include "all financial resources." Under this concept, a funds statement would not be limited to transactions affecting cash or working capital but would include the financial aspects of such significant exchange transactions as the issuance of capital stock for plant assets.

In 1971, *APB Opinion No. 19* made mandatory the inclusion of a funds statement in annual reports and recommended that it be given the new title of "Statement of Changes in Financial Position." The new title better describes the broader concept of "all financial resources" required by *APB Opinion No. 19.* The new requirements call for a business to "disclose all important aspects of its financing and investing activities regardless of whether cash or other elements of working capital are directly affected. For example, acquisitions of property by issuance of securities or in exchange for other property, and conversions of long-term debt or preferred stock to common stock, should be appropriately reflected in the Statement."[2]

Thus the issuance of 10,000 shares of capital stock with a market price of $60 a share in *exchange* for patents is reported in the statement of changes in financial position as follows:

Financial resources provided:
   Issuance of capital stock in exchange for patents $600,000
Financial resources applied:
   Acquisition of patents in exchange for capital stock $600,000

A *conversion* of $5 million of bonds payable into capital stock is reported as illustrated below:

Financial resources provided:
   Issuance of capital stock pursuant to conversion of bonds payable $5,000,000
Financial resources applied:
   Extinguishment of bonds payable through conversion into capital stock $5,000,000

---

[2] *APB Opinion No. 19,* "Reporting Changes in Financial Position," AICPA (New York: 1971), p. 374.

Other examples of exchange transactions are: refunding of bonds payable, exchanges of property, capitalization of leases by lessees, and donation of plant assets to the corporation. On the other hand, stock dividends, write-offs of noncurrent assets, and appropriations of retained earnings are not considered to be exchange transactions and their effect on noncurrent accounts would not be listed in the statement of changes in financial position.

Objectives of statement of changes in financial position

To summarize the impact of the developments described above, we can identify the basic objectives of a statement of changes in financial position as follows:

1 To provide information on all financing and investing activities of a business
2 To show the financial resources (funds) provided from operations and other sources during the period
3 To show the uses or applications of financial resources during the period
4 To disclose the amounts and causes of all other changes in financial position during the period

The statement of changes in financial position "cannot supplant either the income statement or the balance sheet but is intended to provide information that the other statements either do not provide or provide only indirectly about the flow of funds and changes in financial position during the period."[3]

The information shown in a statement of changes in financial position is relevant to users of financial statements in making economic decisions. Therefore the format of the statement and the definition of funds adopted should take into consideration the needs of those who will use the information to make decisions. For example, the statement is prepared on a cash basis for internal use and also when cash flow is considered to be of primary importance to creditors and investors. When a broader concept of liquid resources (funds) is considered to be more relevant to users of financial information, the statement is prepared on a working capital basis.

Format and content of the statement of changes in financial position

The APB recognized that the statement of changes in financial position may differ in form, content, and terminology to meet its objectives. For example, the working capital format generally would not be relevant to a business that does not classify assets and liabilities as current and noncurrent. Thus a business entity adopts the format that is considered most informative in its circumstances.

[3] Ibid., p. 372.

The ability of a business entity to generate working capital or cash from operations is an important factor in considering its financing and investing activities. The statement should therefore disclose working capital or cash provided from or applied in operations for the period, and the effects of any extraordinary items should be reported separately from the effects of recurring activities. Additional guidelines for the preparation of the statement were offered by the APB as follows:

> The Statement for the period should begin with income or loss before extraordinary items, if any, and add back (or deduct) items recognized in determining that income or loss which did not use (or provide) working capital or cash during the period. Items added and deducted in accordance with this procedure are not sources or uses of working capital or cash, and the related captions should make this clear, e.g., "Add—Expenses not requiring outlay of working capital in the current period." An acceptable alternative procedure, which gives the same result, is to begin with total revenue that provided working capital or cash during the period and deduct operating costs and expenses that required the outlay of working capital or cash during the period. In either case the resulting amount of working capital or cash should be appropriately described, e.g., "Working capital provided from [used in] operations for the period, exclusive of extraordinary items." This total should be immediately followed by working capital or cash provided or used by income or loss from extraordinary items, if any; extraordinary income or loss should be similarly adjusted for items recognized that did not provide or use working capital or cash during the period.
>
> Provided that these guides are met, the Statement may take whatever form gives the most useful portrayal of the financing and investing activities and the changes in financial position of the reporting entity. The Statement may be in balanced form or in a form expressing the changes in financial position in terms of cash, of cash and temporary investments combined, of all quick assets, or of working capital. The Statement should disclose all important changes in financial position for the period covered; accordingly, types of transactions reported may vary substantially in relative importance from one period to another.[4]

The Board also stated that net changes in each element of working capital should be disclosed for at least the current period, either in the statement or in a supporting exhibit. This disclosure applies whether or not working capital flow is presented in the statement. Thus, when the statement is prepared on the cash basis, changes in working capital accounts constitute sources and uses of cash and should be disclosed. The effects of other financing and investing activities should be presented individually; however, immaterial items may be combined.[5]

The statement of changes in financial position appears in a variety of forms in annual reports of publicly owned corporations. In a recent survey of 600 annual reports, 415 used a form in which the increase or decrease in working capital is highlighted; 69 companies "balanced" the statement by reporting the increase in working capital as a use of funds (or a decrease in working capital as a source of funds); 31 companies used "cash and cash equivalents" as the definition of funds, and 85

---

[4] Ibid., pp. 374–375.
[5] Ibid., p. 376

companies arrived at the ending balance in working capital.[6] An example in which the ending balance in working capital is presented appears for General Motors Corporation in the appendix at the end of Chapter 4.

Because the statement of changes in financial position may be prepared either on the working capital or cash basis, it is appropriate that we now consider these two approaches in greater detail.

Funds defined as working capital

One of the primary financial responsibilities of management is seeing that a business has sufficient liquid resources to meet obligations as they fall due and to take advantage of favorable investment opportunities as they arise. Managers and also those outsiders who evaluate managerial performance keep a sharp eye on the inflow and outflow of liquid resources and the prospective balance between funds available and funds required.

The *working capital* of a business is the amount by which current assets exceed current liabilities. The amount of working capital is a measure of the safety factor that exists for the protection of short-term creditors. Working capital may also be viewed as funds available for investment in noncurrent assets or to liquidate noncurrent liabilities. Increases in working capital occur when noncurrent assets are decreased (sold) and also when noncurrent liabilities and stockholders' equity are increased (as by additional investment in the business). Decreases in working capital occur when noncurrent assets are increased (acquired) and also when noncurrent liabilities and stockholders' equity are decreased (as by extinguishment of long-term debt and by payment of cash dividends to stockholders). The major sources and uses of working capital are summarized below:

Sources	*Uses*
1 *Revenue from operations*	1 *Operating expenses*
2 *Disposal of noncurrent assets*	2 *Acquisition of noncurrent assets*
3 *Long-term borrowing*	3 *Extinguishment of long-term debt, or*
4 *Issuance of equity securities*	*reclassification of it as current debt*
	4 *Distributions to stockholders, including cash dividends, purchase of treasury stock, and redemption of preferred stock*

---

[6] *Accounting Trends & Techniques,* 30th ed., AICPA (New York: 1976), p. 306.

Both managers and outsiders are vitally concerned with the flows of working capital because an adequate supply of working capital is essential to the health of any business. The ability of a business entity to generate working capital internally is also an important factor in forecasting cash flows and in estimating ability to pay liabilities at maturity. In the typical operating cycle of a business, the first step is the purchase of inventory (usually on short-term credit); the inventory is then converted into a larger amount of accounts receivable; these receivables are collected and the inflow of cash is used to retire current payables. The operating cycle then begins anew. The statement of changes in financial position depicts these dynamics of the operating cycle as well as the inflow and outflow of other economic resources.

The revenue and expenses shown in the income statement do not run parallel to the inflow of working capital. Consequently, the income statement alone does not call attention to the development of a shortage or an oversupply of liquid assets. In the preparation of budgets and planning for future growth, management must coordinate the expected flow of internally generated liquid assets with the inflow of funds obtained from external sources, as through borrowing or by the issuance of capital stock. Statements showing past and projected flows of working capital thus become basic tools of financial planning and analysis.

Working Capital Provided from Operations As stated on page 493, special problems arise in the determination of the amount of working capital provided from operations. Deductions from revenue which do not reduce working capital are added to net income (or loss) and revenue items and offsets to expenses which do not provide working capital are subtracted from net income (or loss) in computing the amount of working capital provided from operations during an accounting period. Examples of such items are given in the table on page 996.

Depreciation expense, an increase in the deferred income tax liability, the amortization of intangibles and deferred charges, and the amortization of bond discount and issue costs all reduce net income without reducing working capital and are therefore added to net income. Similarly, the amortization of a premium on investment in bonds and a loss accrued on investment in stock using the equity method reduce long-term investments and net income but have no effect on working capital; therefore, these items also are added to net income to measure the working capital provided from operations. The value assigned to stock options is charged to expense and credited to a stockholders' equity account, hence this is a nonfund expense and is added to net income.

A decrease in the deferred income tax liability, the amortization of investment tax credit or deferred revenue, and the amortization of premium on bonds payable all represent increases in net income and decreases in long-term liability accounts. Since these items increase net income but are not sources of working capital, they are deducted from

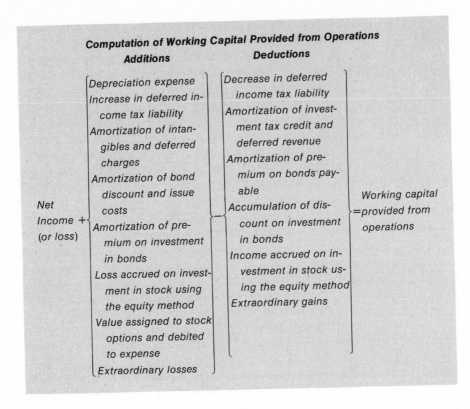

Computation of Working Capital Provided from Operations

Additions	Deductions
Net Income + (or loss)	

Additions:
Depreciation expense
Increase in deferred income tax liability
Amortization of intangibles and deferred charges
Amortization of bond discount and issue costs
Amortization of premium on investment in bonds
Loss accrued on investment in stock using the equity method
Value assigned to stock options and debited to expense
Extraordinary losses

Deductions:
Decrease in deferred income tax liability
Amortization of investment tax credit and deferred revenue
Amortization of premium on bonds payable
Accumulation of discount on investment in bonds
Income accrued on investment in stock using the equity method
Extraordinary gains

= Working capital provided from operations

net income. The accumulation of discount on investment in bonds and the income accrued on investment in stock using the equity method represent increases in long-term investments and net income but do not affect working capital; therefore, these items also are deducted from net income to measure the working capital provided from operations.

According to **APB Opinion No. 19,** the working capital or cash provided or applied from extraordinary items should be shown immediately below the amount of working capital provided (or used in) operations. However, in the opinion of the authors, it is preferable to eliminate extraordinary items, as well as other nonoperating gains and losses, from net income and report separately the full effect on working capital from all significant nonoperating transactions.

Funds defined as cash

As stated previously, the statement of changes in financial position may be prepared with emphasis on cash rather than working capital. When funds are viewed as cash, the statement of changes in financial position is more than a cash flow statement, that is, a listing of cash receipts and payments, because financing and investing activities which do not involve cash also are listed as financial resources provided and applied.

The "all-financial-resources" concept of the statement is equally applicable whether funds are defined as working capital or as cash.

Adoption of cash as the definition of funds can be justified on grounds that a statement of changes in financial position on a cash basis provides useful predictive information for decision makers. Management and outside users of financial statements are concerned with the ability of a business to meet maturing obligations and remain solvent. A statement of cash inflows and outflows which includes other significant financing and investing activities is viewed by many users of financial statements as a barometer of financial strength.

Cash Provided from Operations In the computation of the amount of cash provided from operations, the same additions and deductions to net income (or loss) illustrated on page 996 for computing the amount of working capital provided from operations are made. However, changes also must be considered in current accounts (except cash, marketable securities, loans receivable from others than customers, loans payable to others than suppliers, and dividends payable). The reason for this is apparent in the purchase of inventory for cash, for example. In this transaction cash is reduced but working capital is not. Thus the computation of cash provided from operations for an accounting period may be summarized concisely as follows:

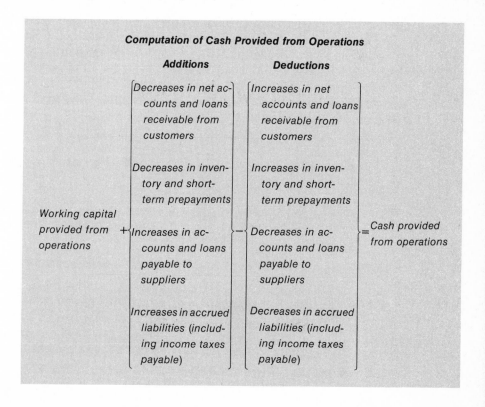

Computation of Cash Provided from Operations

Decreases in net accounts and loans receivable from customers during an accounting period indicate that more cash was collected from customers than was reported as revenue in the income statement; increases in these accounts indicate that less cash was collected from customers than was reported as revenue in the income statement.

Decreases in inventory and short-term prepayments indicate that a portion of the cost of goods sold and expenses resulted from the using up of assets previously paid for and not from current cash outlays; increases in inventory and short-term prepayments indicate that cash was used to accumulate inventory and prepayments.

Increases in accounts and loans payable to suppliers and accrued liabilities indicate that portions of cost of goods sold and expenses included in the income statement were not paid; decreases in accounts and loans payable to suppliers and accrued liabilities indicate that more cash was paid for these items than was included in the income statement.

The amount of cash provided from operations should not be viewed as a substitute for net income. Cash flow from operations is essentially the amount of net income on a cash basis; it is not a summary of revenue realized and expenses incurred. The profitability of a business is measured by comparing expired costs with realized revenue, not by computing income on a cash basis.

Reporting of Cash Flow per Share Reference has often been made by financial analysts to "cash flow per share," determined by adding depreciation and amortization charges to net income and dividing the result (income before noncash expenses) by the number of shares of common stock outstanding. Accounting authorities have consistently discouraged computations of this sort. *APB Opinion No. 19,* for example, contains a suggestion that:

> Terms referring to "cash" should not be used to describe amounts provided from operations unless all non-cash items have been appropriately adjusted. The adjusted amount should be described accurately, in conformity with the nature of the adjustments, e.g., "Cash provided from operations for the period." . . . The Board strongly recommends that isolated statistics of working capital or cash provided from operations, especially per-share amounts, not be presented in annual reports to stockholders. If any per-share data relating to flow of working capital or cash are presented, they should as a minimum include amounts for inflow from operations, inflow from other sources, and total outflow, and each per-share amount should be clearly identified with the corresponding total amount shown in the Statement.[7]

The Securities and Exchange Commission also has discouraged the inclusion of cash flow per share in registration statements filed with the Commission and in annual reports to shareholders. The SEC stated that presentation of cash-flow-per-share statistics "appear designed to decrease the credibility of conventional statements as a measure of busi-

---

[7] *APB Opinion No. 19,* pp. 377–378.

ness activity."[8] The Commission viewed the reporting of cash flow per share (whether based on the amount of cash provided from operations or the amount of net income before depreciation and amortization) to be both *misleading* and *irrelevant.* Accordingly, it urged that per-share data other than that relating to net income, net assets, and dividends should be avoided in reporting financial results. The position of the SEC is summarized below:

> If accounting net income computed in conformity with generally accepted accounting principles is not an accurate reflection of economic performance for a company or an industry, it is not an appropriate solution to have each company independently decide what the best measure of its performance should be and present that figure to its shareholders as Truth. This would result in many different concepts and numbers which could not be used meaningfully by investors to compare different candidates for their investment dollars.
>
> Where the measurement of economic performance is an industry-wide problem, representatives of the industry and the accounting profession should present the problem and suggested solutions to the Financial Accounting Standards Board which is the body charged with responsibility for researching and defining principles to financial measurement.[9]

Simple illustration of statement of changes in financial position

The income statement, the statement of retained earnings, and the comparative balance sheet provide the basic information for preparing a statement of changes in financial position. Using this information, the major movements of working capital or cash can be identified for the period under consideration.

When the working capital approach is adopted, the noncurrent assets of a business represent the financial resources in which working capital has been invested; the noncurrent liabilities and the stockholders' equity represent the financial sources from which working capital was provided. The first clue to an inflow or outflow of working capital, therefore, is a change in noncurrent accounts during the period. The income statement and the statement of retained earnings help to explain the change in financial position that resulted from operations and from distributions to stockholders. The difference between the inflow and outflow of financial resources during the period *must equal* the increase or decrease in working capital between the beginning and end of the period.

When the cash approach is adopted, changes in *all* balance sheet accounts represent potential inflow and outflow of cash. These accounts are analyzed to obtain specific amounts of cash inflows and outflows, thus reconciling the beginning cash balance with the ending cash balance.

---

[8] *Accounting Series Release No. 142,* "Reporting Cash Flow and Other Related Data," Securities and Exchange Commission (Washington: 1973).
[9] Ibid.

The data below and on page 1001 for Elwood Supply Company will be used to illustrate the preparation of a statement of changes in financial position first on a working capital basis and then on a cash basis, without using working papers. The use of working papers is illustrated in the comprehensive example starting on page 1009.

ELWOOD SUPPLY COMPANY
Income Statement
For Year Ended December 31, Year 2

Sales (net)		$107,000
Cost of goods sold:		
Beginning inventory	$40,000	
Purchases (net)	50,000	
Cost of goods available for sale	$90,000	
Less: Ending inventory	30,000	
Cost of goods sold		60,000
Gross profit on sales		$ 47,000
Expenses:		
Operating expenses (excluding depreciation)	$10,000	
Depreciation expense	7,500	
Interest expense	1,500	19,000
Income before incomes taxes		$ 28,000
Income tax expense		7,000
Net income		$ 21,000
Earnings per share (average of 10,500 shares outstanding)		$ 2.00

ELWOOD SUPPLY COMPANY
Statement of Retained Earnings
For Year Ended December 31, Year 2

Balance, beginning of year	$30,000
Net income	21,000
Subtotal	$51,000
Dividends declared	5,000
Balance, end of year	$46,000

Additional information for Year 2

(1) Equipment was acquired for $18,000 cash, and additional equipment with a fair value of $12,000 was acquired in exchange for 1,000 shares of capital stock on July 1.

ELWOOD SUPPLY COMPANY
Comparative Balance Sheet
December 31

	Year 2	Year 1	Net change Debit (Credit)
Assets			
Cash	$ 29,900	$ 14,000	$ 15,900
Accounts receivable (net)	33,000	27,000	6,000
Inventory	30,000	40,000	(10,000)
Short-term prepayments	1,600	1,000	600
Equipment	130,000	100,000	30,000
Less: Accumulated depreciation . . .	(19,500)	(12,000)	(7,500)
Total assets	$205,000	$170,000	$ 35,000
Liabilities & Stockholders' Equity			
Accounts payable	$ 15,500	$ 23,400	$ 7,900
Accrued interest payable	1,500	–0–	(1,500)
Income taxes payable	7,000	6,600	(400)
Dividends payable	5,000	–0–	(5,000)
Long-term notes payable, due Year 5	8,000	–0–	(8,000)
Capital stock, $10 par	110,000	100,000	(10,000)
Paid-in capital in excess of par	12,000	10,000	(2,000)
Retained earnings	46,000	30,000	(16,000)
Total liabilities & stockholders' equity	$205,000	$170,000	$(35,000)

(2) Cash of $8,000 was borrowed on a long-term basis (a note due in Year 5).

(3) Cash dividends of $5,000 were declared (but not paid) at the end of the year.

Statement of Changes in Financial Position on a Working Capital Basis
When the statement of changes in financial position is prepared on a working capital basis, it explains fully the reasons for an increase or decrease in working capital during the period. Referring to the comparative balance sheet for Elwood Supply Company above the increase in working capital during Year 2 can be determined as illustrated at the top of page 1002.

The increase in working capital for Elwood Supply Company can be viewed as a *result* which is to be explained by analyzing the changes in non-working capital accounts. In other words, the *causes* of the increase in working capital can only be found in the changes which have occurred in the noncurrent accounts. However, not all changes in noncur-

ELWOOD SUPPLY COMPANY
Change in Working Capital during Year 2

	End of Year 2	End of Year 1	Increase or (decrease) in working capital
Current assets:			
Cash	$29,900	$14,000	$15,900
Accounts receivable (net)	33,000	27,000	6,000
Inventory	30,000	40,000	(10,000)
Short-term prepayments	1,600	1,000	600
Total current assets	$94,500	$82,000	
Current liabilities:			
Accounts payable	$15,500	$23,400	7,900
Interest payable	1,500	–0–	(1,500)
Income taxes payable	7,000	6,600	(400)
Dividends payable	5,000	–0–	(5,000)
Total current liabilities	$29,000	$30,000	
Working capital	$65,500	$52,000	
Increase in working capital			$13,500

rent accounts cause changes in working capital. For example, distributions of stock dividends and exchange transactions cause changes in noncurrent accounts but do not change working capital. Exchange transactions, such as the issuance of capital stock for equipment by Elwood Supply Company, are financial resources provided and applied.

A statement of changes in financial position on a working capital basis for Elwood Supply Company is illustrated on page 1003. This form highlights the increase in working capital; some companies prepare the statement in "balancing form," showing an increase in working capital as a financial resource applied or a decrease in working capital as a financial resource provided.

Statement of Changes in Financial Position on a Cash Basis When the statement of changes in financial position is prepared on a cash basis, it contains a summary of all cash receipts and payments as well as significant exchange transactions. This form is a useful analytical tool for management and other users of financial statements because it provides answers to questions such as the following: How much cash was generated by recurring operations last period? What use was made of cash receipts? How much cash was received from nonrecurring sources? Why is the company short of cash? Can the current level of cash dividend payments be maintained? The statement of changes in

ELWOOD SUPPLY COMPANY
Statement of Changes in Financial Position (Working Capital Basis)
For Year Ended December 31, Year 2

Financial resources provided:
  Working capital provided from operations:
    Net income $21,000
      Add: Expense which did not reduce working capital—depreciation   7,500
      Working capital provided from operations $28,500
    Borrowing on long-term notes 8,000
    Issuance of capital stock in exchange for equipment 12,000
      Total financial resources provided $48,500
Financial resources applied:
  Purchase of equipment for cash $18,000
  Acquisition of equipment in exchange for capital stock . . 12,000
  Declaration of cash dividends 5,000
    Total financial resources applied 35,000
Increase in financial resources (working capital) $13,500

	End of Year 2	End of Year 1	Increase or (decrease) in working capital
Composition of working capital:			
Current assets:			
Cash	$29,900	$14,000	$15,900
Accounts receivable (net)	33,000	27,000	6,000
Inventory	30,000	40,000	(10,000)
Short-term prepayments	1,600	1,000	600
Total current assets	$94,500	$82,000	
Current liabilities:			
Accounts payable	$15,500	$23,400	7,900
Accrued interest payable	1,500	–0–	(1,500)
Income taxes payable	7,000	6,600	(400)
Dividends payable	5,000	–0–	(5,000)
Total current liabilities	$29,000	$30,000	
Working capital	$65,500	$52,000	
Increase in working capital			$13,500

financial position on a cash basis for Elwood Supply Company is illustrated on page 1004.

    The declaration of dividends is not shown in the cash-basis statement for Elwood Supply Company because it was not paid in Year 2. If the

ELWOOD SUPPLY COMPANY
Statement of Changes in Financial Position (Cash Basis)
For Year Ended December 31, Year 2

Financial resources provided:

Cash provided from operations:

Net income		$21,000
Add: Depreciation expense		7,500
Decrease in inventory		10,000
Increase in accrued interest payable		1,500
Increase in income taxes payable		400
Subtotal		$40,400
Less: Increase in net accounts receivable	$ 6,000	
Increase in short-term prepayments	600	
Decrease in accounts payable	7,900	14,500
Cash provided from operations		$25,900
Borrowing on long-term notes		8,000
Issuance of capital stock in exchange for equipment		12,000
Total financial resources provided		$45,900

Financial resources applied:

Purchase of equipment for cash	$18,000	
Acquisition of equipment in exchange for capital stock	12,000	
Total financial resources applied		30,000
Increase in financial resources (cash)		$15,900

(Composition of working capital, as presented on page 1003, generally should be included in the statement or in a supplementary exhibit.)

presentation of cash provided from operations is quite detailed, it may be presented in a separate accompanying schedule.

Alternative Approach: Cash-Basis Net Income   Instead of showing the cash provided from operations as illustrated above, the income statement may be converted from the accrual basis to a cash basis to show actual cash receipts and payments from operations. Receipts from customers, payments to suppliers, and payments for specific expenses are thus shown with other financial resources provided and applied in the statement of changes in financial position on a cash basis. This approach is illustrated on pages 1005 and 1006 for Elwood Supply Company.

Special problems

When a statement of changes in financial position is prepared from the detailed accounting records, all the necessary information may be obtained from the ledger accounts or computer printouts. The task is more

ELWOOD SUPPLY COMPANY
Conversion of Income Statement from Accrual to Cash Basis
For Year Ended December 31, Year 2

	Income statement (accrual basis)	Add (deduct)	Cash basis
Sales	$107,000		
Less: Increase in net accounts receivable		$ (6,000)	$101,000
Cost of goods sold	60,000		
Add: Decrease in accounts payable		7,900	
Less: Decrease in inventory		(10,000)	57,900
Gross profit on sales	$ 47,000		$ 43,100
Expenses:			
Operating expenses (excluding depreciation)	$ 10,000		
Add: Increase in short-term prepayments		600	$ 10,600
Depreciation expense	7,500	(7,500)	–0–
Interest expense	1,500	(1,500)	–0–
Income tax expense	7,000		
Less: Increase in income taxes payable		(400)	6,600
Total expenses	$ 26,000		$ 17,200
Net income—accrual basis.	$ 21,000		
Net income—cash basis (cash provided from operations)			$ 25,900

difficult when the statement must be prepared only from comparative balance sheets, the income statement, the statement of retained earnings, and other miscellaneous information. Some special problems involved in the preparation of the statement of changes in financial position *on a working capital basis* are described in the following sections.

Doubtful Accounts Expense Neither the recognition of doubtful accounts expense nor the actual write-off of uncollectible accounts requires any action in preparing a statement of changes in financial position on a working capital basis. The recognition of doubtful accounts expense reduces net accounts receivable and is reflected as a deduction from revenue in measuring working capital provided from operations; a write-off against the allowance account does not reduce net accounts receivable, hence has no effect on working capital.

ELWOOD SUPPLY COMPANY
Statement of Changes in Financial Position (Cash Basis)
For Year Ended December 31, Year 2

Financial resources provided:
Collections on accounts receivable	$101,000
Borrowing on long-term notes	8,000
Issuance of capital stock in exchange for equipment	12,000
Total financial resources provided	$121,000

Financial resources applied:
Merchandise purchases	$57,900	
Operating expenses	10,600	
Income tax expense	6,600	
Purchase of equipment for cash	18,000	
Acquisition of equipment in exchange for capital stock	12,000	
Total financial resources applied		105,100
Increase in financial resources (cash)		$ 15,900

(Composition of working capital is generally included here.)

Gain or Loss on Sale (or Write-Down) of Marketable Securities When marketable securities classified as current are sold at a gain, working capital is increased by the amount of the gain; if such securities are sold at a loss, working capital is reduced by the amount of the loss. Unrealized gains and losses recognized on marketable equity securities (pursuant to *FASB Statement No. 12*) and included in the determination of net income also have an effect on working capital. However, because marketable securities generally are acquired to obtain a return on cash not currently needed in operations, such gains and losses normally are included in net income when computing the amount of working capital provided from or applied to operations.

Purchase of a Going Business When a going business is acquired, the effect of the acquisition on financial resources requires careful analysis. For example, assume the following transaction:

Current Assets	200,000	
Noncurrent Assets	500,000	
Current Liabilities		50,000
Cash		150,000
Capital Stock, no-par value		500,000
To record purchase of a going business.		

The acquisition of current assets in the amount of $200,000 in this example does not affect working capital because current liabilities in the amount of $50,000 were increased and cash in the amount of $150,000 was paid; the net effect was to increase both the current assets and the current liabilities by $50,000. The exchange of capital stock for noncurrent assets is reported as financial resources provided and applied.

Reclassification of Current and Noncurrent Items When a long-term obligation matures within a year, it should be reclassified as a current liability. For example, serial bonds and mortgage notes due for payment within one year generally are reclassified from long-term debt to the current liability category. This reclassification decreases the amount of working capital and thus represents a financial resource applied. Similarly, a long-term receivable which matures within one year from the end of the current period is reclassified as a current asset, thus increasing working capital (a financial resource provided).

Reclassifications of current assets to the noncurrent category (such as an extension of maturity dates on receivables) or current liabilities to long-term debt (through a debt restructuring, for example) change the amount of working capital. Consequently, such reclassifications are reported as financial resources applied and provided.

Analysis of Changes in Plant Asset Accounts When a number of changes have occurred in plant asset accounts, it is helpful to prepare an analysis of such an account before isolating the effect on working capital. For example, assume that the following information relating to equipment is available from comparative financial statements:

	End of current year	End of previous year	Change Debit (Credit)
Equipment	$540,000	$620,000	$(80,000)
Accumulated depreciation . .	230,000	195,000	(35,000)
Depreciation expense	60,000		60,000
Loss on sale of equipment . .	40,000		40,000

Assume that equipment with a cost of $130,000 and a carrying value of $105,000 was sold during the current year. It may be helpful to develop the analysis given at the top of page 1008.

From this analysis we can identify the transactions that caused the changes in the two accounts and affected working capital. The journal entries made at the time of each transaction and the corresponding effect on the statement of changes in financial position prepared on a working capital basis are summarized on page 1008.

	Equipment	Accumulated depreciation
Balance, beginning of current year	$ 620,000	$(195,000)
Sale of equipment for $65,000*	(130,000)	25,000
Purchase of equipment for cash	50,000	
Depreciation expense for current year		(60,000)
Balance, end of current year	$ 540,000	$(230,000)

* $105,000 − $40,000 = $65,000.

Entries at time of transaction		Effect on statement of changes in financial position (working capital basis)
Cash 65,000		Financial resources pro-
Accumulated Depreciation . 25,000		vided: Sale of equipment,
Loss on Sale of Equipment 40,000		$65,000.
Equipment	130,000	The loss on sale of equip-
To record sale of equipment		ment, $40,000, is added to
		net income to measure the
		amount of working cap-
		ital provided from
		operations.
Equipment 50,000		Financial resources applied:
Cash	50,000	Purchase of equipment,
To record purchase of		$50,000.
equipment.		
Depreciation Expense . . . 60,000		Depreciation of $60,000 is
Accumulated		added to net income to
Depreciation	60,000	measure the amount of
To record depreciation		working capital provided
expense.		from operations.

The analyses above fully reconcile the changes in the Equipment and Accumulated Depreciation accounts, increase net income by $100,000 to cancel the effect of nonfund charges (loss on sale of equipment and depreciation), and explicitly report the financial resources provided and applied.

Capital Leases A lease contract which meets the criteria for a capital lease is recorded in the accounting records of the lessee by a debit to a noncurrent asset and a credit to a liability account, a portion of which is currently due. To illustrate, assume that Lessee Company recorded a capital lease in Year 5 as follows:

Leased Equipment under Capital Lease	100,000	
Obligation under Capital Lease ($15,000 due within		
one year)		100,000
To record capital lease.		

In a statement of changes in financial position on a working capital basis for Year 5, the lease contract would be reported as follows:

Financial resources provided:	
Long-term borrowing under capital lease	$ 85,000
Financial resources applied:	
Acquisition of equipment under capital lease	$100,000

In a statement of changes in financial position on a cash basis for Year 5, the lease contract would be reported as a financial resource provided and applied, both in the amount of $100,000.

COMPREHENSIVE ILLUSTRATION OF STATEMENT OF CHANGES IN FINANCIAL POSITION

The following illustration is designed to show how the reasoning discussed thus far can be applied to an analysis of *working capital flows* in a more complex situation. The data on which the analysis is based are contained in the comparative after-closing trial balances, an income statement for Year 5, a statement of retained earnings for Year 5, and the additional information for Haas Corporation listed below and on pages 1010 and 1011.

Additional information for Year 5

(1) Land was purchased for $150,000 cash.
(2) An analysis of the changes in the Building and Equipment account during Year 5 is given at the top of page 1012.
(3) During Year 5, Haas Corporation accrued its share, $13,250, of net income earned by Z Company. Haas Corporation owns 25% of the common stock of Z Company.
(4) At the beginning of Year 5, $50,000 of bonds payable were retired at 105. Unamortized premium of $2,500 ($10,000 × ¼) on bonds pay-

HAAS CORPORATION
Comparative After-closing Trial Balances

	Dec. 31, Year 5		Dec. 31, Year 4	
	Debit	Credit	Debit	Credit
Cash	$ 27,100		$ 52,800	
Notes receivable from				
customers	50,000		30,000	
Accounts receivable (net) .	36,900		50,400	
Inventory	96,050		57,300	
Short-term prepayments .	12,600		9,600	
Land	150,000			
Building and equipment .	554,000		826,000	
Accumulated				
depreciation		$185,000		$ 355,000
Investment in stock of Z				
Company (equity method)	53,250		40,000	
Accounts payable		22,150		31,300
Accrued liabilities		17,600		16,300
Income taxes payable . . .		42,800		17,000
Dividends payable		42,000		
Bonds payable, 8%, due				
Jan. 1, Year 15		150,000		200,000
Premium on bonds payable		6,750		10,000
Deferred income tax				
liability		45,000		80,000
Capital stock, $10 par . . .		150,000		100,000
Paid-in capital in excess				
of par		106,200		58,000
Retained earnings		229,900		198,500
Treasury stock, 1,000				
shares	17,500			
Totals	$997,400	$997,400	$1,066,100	$1,066,100

able was written off, resulting in neither a gain nor a loss. The balance in the Premium on Bonds Payable account, $7,500, is being amortized over a 10-year period, or $750 per year.

(5) During Year 5, Haas Corporation reacquired 1,000 shares of capital stock for $17,500. At a time when 9,000 shares of capital stock were outstanding and the market price was $15 a share, the company declared a 4% stock dividend. The board of directors authorized a transfer of $5,400 (360 shares × $15) from retained earnings to paid-in capital to record the stock dividend. Later in Year 5, 4,640

HAAS CORPORATION
Income Statement
For Year 5

Sales		$313,600
Cost of goods sold		158,000
Gross profit on sales		$155,600
Operating expenses:		
Depreciation expense	$30,000	
Other	28,000	58,000
Income from operations		$ 97,600
Nonoperating income and expense:		
Investment income from Z Company	$13,250	
Less: Interest expense	11,250	2,000
Income before income taxes		$ 99,600
Income tax expense (including $10,000 deferred)		48,300
Income before extraordinary items		$ 51,300
Extraordinary gain on condemnation of building, after taxes of $22,500		27,500
Net income		$ 78,800
Earnings per share		$ 6.19

HAAS CORPORATION
Statement of Retained Earnings
For Year 5

Retained earnings, beginning of year		$198,500
Less: Stock dividend (360 shares @ $15 a share)	$ 5,400	
Cash dividends	42,000	47,400
Subtotal		$151,100
Add: Net income		78,800
Retained earnings, end of year		$229,900

shares of capital stock, with a market price of $20 a share, were issued in exchange for equipment. A cash dividend of $3 a share was declared on the 14,000 (9,000 + 360 + 4,640) shares outstanding at the end of Year 5, payable in January of Year 6.

Schedule of changes in working capital

The first step in preparing a statement of changes in financial position on a working capital basis for Haas Corporation is to determine its working capital at the beginning and at the end of Year 5, and the increase or

	Building and equipment	Accumulated depreciation
Balance, Dec. 31, Year 4	$826,000	$355,000
Condemnation of building in Year 5	(400,000)*	(200,000)
Purchase of equipment in Year 5	128,000†	
Depreciation expense for Year 5		30,000
Balance, Dec. 31, Year 5	$554,000	$185,000

* The condemnation of the building in Year 5 was recorded as follows:

Cash	250,000	
Accumulated Depreciation	200,000	
Deferred Income Tax Liability	45,000	
Building		400,000
Extraordinary Gain (net of income taxes of $22,500)		27,500
Income Taxes Payable		67,500

To record proceeds received from condemnation of building.

† Acquired in an exchange transaction through issuance of 4,640 shares of capital stock with a fair value of $92,800 and $35,200 in cash, a total of $128,000.

decrease in working capital during the year. The composition of working capital is shown in the lower section of the statement of changes in financial position which appears on page 1018.

Working paper for statement of changes in financial position

After the schedule of changes in working capital is prepared, the beginning balance of working capital, $135,500 may be entered in the first column of a working paper. The use of a working paper to analyze changes in noncurrent accounts and to identify the financial resources provided and applied is not necessary for relatively simple problems; however, for more complex problems the use of a working paper is helpful. Similarly, the beginning balances in all other noncurrent accounts are recorded in the first column of the working paper. Transactions for Year 5 are then analyzed and the sources and uses of working capital are determined as described earlier in this chapter. The working paper for the statement of changes in financial position on a working capital basis for Haas Corporation is shown on page 1014.

Analysis of Transactions in the Working Paper By studying the changes in the noncurrent accounts, we are able to find the specific reasons for the $37,400 decrease in working capital during Year 5. As previously stated, only changes in the noncurrent accounts represent sources and uses of working capital. The analysis of the transactions completed by Haas Corporation during Year 5 are explained below. (The numbers correspond to the numbers used in the working paper.)

(1) The net income of $78,800 is closed to the Retained Earnings account and is shown under "Financial Resources Provided: Operations." Net income represents an increase in stockholders' equity and is one of the major sources of working capital for most companies. Net income, however, is only a tentative measure of the increase in working capital from operations because not all revenue and expense items represent sources and uses of working capital. Furthermore, any extraordinary items should be eliminated from net income because the transactions giving rise to such items should be **reported separately** if they affect working capital.

(2) Because depreciation expense does not reduce a current asset or increase a current liability, it has no effect on working capital. Therefore, the depreciation expense of $30,000 for Year 5 is added to net income and is credited to Accumulated Depreciation. In other words, because depreciation is a nonfund expense, the increase in working capital from operations exceeded net income.

(3) Depreciation was not the only expense which did not reduce working capital. The income tax expense of $48,300 includes $10,000 payable in future years and appears as an increase in the Deferred Income Tax Liability account. This portion of income tax expense is added to net income because it did not reduce working capital.

(4) Land was purchased for $150,000 cash in Year 5. This is a reduction in working capital and is listed in the working paper as a financial resource applied.

(5) The journal entry that was prepared to record the condemnation of the building in Year 5 appears on page 1012. In the working paper, the condemnation is recorded as a source of working capital of $182,500 because cash increased $250,000 and income taxes payable increased $67,500. The accumulated depreciation applicable to the building, $200,000, is debited to the Accumulated Depreciation account and the deferred tax of $45,000 relating to the building is debited to the Deferred Income Tax Liability account. The extraordinary gain of $27,500 is deducted from net income so that the net proceeds (after income taxes of $22,500) can be listed intact as a source of working capital. The original cost of the building, $400,000, is credited to the Building and Equipment account to complete the transaction in the working paper. Note that when the increase of $30,000 for depreciation and the decrease of $200,000 on the condemnation of the building are combined with the beginning balance of $355,000, we come up with the ending balance of $185,000 in the Accumulated Depreciation account.

(6) At the beginning of Year 5 bonds payable were retired at 105 as illustrated in the journal entry at the top of page 1015. This entry is recognized in the working paper by debits to Bonds Payable and to Premium on Bonds Payable (same as in the original entry); however, the reduction in cash is recognized as a financial resource ap-

HAAS CORPORATION
Working Paper for Statement of Changes in Financial Position (Working Capital Basis) For Year Ended December 31, Year 5

	Account balances at Dec. 31, Year 4	Analysis of transactions for Year 5		Account balances at Dec. 31, Year 5
		Debit	Credit	
Working capital	135,500		(x) 37,400	98,100
Land	–0–	(4) 150,000		150,000
Building and equipment . . .	826,000	(9)128,000	(5) 400,000	554,000
Investment in stock of Z Company (equity method)	40,000	(8) 13,250		53,250
Treasury stock, 1,000 shares	–0–	(10) 17,500		17,500
Totals	1,001,500			872,850
Accumulated depreciation .	355,000	(5)200,000	(2) 30,000	185,000
Bonds payable, 8%	200,000	(6) 50,000		150,000
Premium on bonds payable .	10,000	(6) 2,500 (7) 750		6,750
Deferred income tax liability	80,000	(4) 45,000	(3) 10,000	45,000
Capital stock, $10 par	100,000		(9) 46,400 (12) 3,600	150,000
Paid-in capital in excess of par	58,000		(9) 46,400 (12) 1,800	106,200
Retained earnings	198,500	(11) 42,000 (12) 5,400	(1) 78,800	229,900
Totals	1,001,500	654,400	654,400	872,850
Financial resources provided:				
Operations—net income		(1) 78,800		
Add: Depreciation expense		(2) 30,000		
Increase in deferred income tax liability		(3) 10,000		
Less: Amortization of premium on bonds payable			(7) 750	From operations, 77,300
Investment income from Z Company .			(8) 13,250	
Extraordinary gain .			(5) 27,500	
Proceeds on condemnation of building, net of taxes		(5)182,500		
Issuance of capital stock in exchange for equipment		(9) 92,800		
Financial resources applied:				
Extinguishment of bonds payable			(6) 52,500	
Purchase of land			(4)150,000	
Purchase of equipment . .			(9) 35,200	
Acquisition of equipment in exchange for capital stock			(9) 92,800	
Acquisition of treasury stock			(10) 17,500	
Declaration of cash dividends			(11) 42,000	
Total financial resources provided and applied		394,100	431,500	
Decrease in working capital		(x) 37,400		
		431,500	431,500	

Explanations of transactions for Year 5 start on page 1013.

Bonds Payable	50,000	
Premium on Bonds Payable	2,500	
Cash		52,500

plied of $52,500. At this point we have accounted for the decrease in the Bonds Payable account from $200,000 to $150,000.

(7) The amortization of the premium on bonds payable was recorded at the end of Year 5 as follows:

Premium on Bonds Payable	750	
Interest Expense		750

The working paper analysis of this adjusting entry is to debit the Premium on Bonds Payable account and to record the reduction in working capital provided from operations because the credit to Interest Expense increased net income without increasing working capital. The amount of bond interest paid in Year 5 was $12,000 ($150,000 × 8%) and not $11,250 reported as interest expense in the income statement. The debit of $750 to the Premium on Bonds Payable account, combined with the debit of $2,500 in entry (6), explains the decrease in this account from a balance of $10,000 at the beginning of Year 5 to a balance of $6,750 at the end of Year 5.

(8) The net income for Year 5 includes an accrual of $13,250 of income on the investment in the stock of Z Company. The investment income was recorded as follows:

Investment in Stock of Z Company (equity method)	13,250	
Investment Income from Z Company		13,250

In the working paper, this entry is recorded as a debit to the investment account and a credit (reduction) to "operations" because the investment income did not generate working capital. After this entry is entered in the working paper, the ending balance of $53,250 in the Investment in Stock of Z Company account may be determined by adding $13,250 to the balance of $40,000 at the beginning of Year 5.

(9) The purchase of equipment for cash and the issuance of 4,640 shares of capital stock were recorded as shown at the top of page 1016.

Building and Equipment	128,000	
Cash		35,200
Capital Stock, $10 par		46,400
Paid-in Capital in Excess of Par		46,400

Although this transaction actually reduced working capital by only $35,200, the full purchase price of the equipment should be shown as a financial resource applied. The reason for this is that the issuance of capital stock valued at $92,800 is viewed as both a financial resource provided and applied. The working paper analysis of this transaction follows:

Building and Equipment	128,000	
Issuance of Capital Stock in Exchange for Equipment	92,800	
Purchase of Equipment		35,200
Acquisition of Equipment in Exchange for Capital		
Stock		92,800
Capital Stock, $10 par		46,400
Paid-in Capital in Excess of Par		46,400

This analysis records the changes in the non-working capital accounts in the upper part of the working paper and the financial resources provided and applied in the lower part. The debit of $128,000 in the Building and Equipment account, less the credit of $400,000 in entry (5) above, explains the net decrease in this account in Year 5 from $826,000 to $554,000.

(10) The acquisition of treasury stock for $17,500 is recorded in the working paper as a debit to the Treasury Stock account, thus establishing the ending balance in this account, and as a credit to Financial Resources Applied: Acquisition of Treasury Stock.

(11) The declaration of cash dividends, $42,000, is entered in the working paper as a debit to Retained Earnings and a credit to Financial Resources Applied: Declaration of Cash Dividends. The declaration of the cash dividend creates a current liability and thus reduces working capital.

(12) The declaration of a stock dividend required a transfer from Retained Earnings to paid-in capital accounts; a stock dividend has no effect on working capital and is not considered as a financing and investing transaction under the all-financial-resources concept of funds. The working paper entry for the 4% stock dividend (360 shares valued at $15 per share) requires a debit to Retained

Earnings for $5,400, a credit to Capital Stock for $3,600, and a credit of $1,800 to Paid-in Capital in Excess of Par. After this transaction is entered in the working paper, the ending balances in the Capital Stock, Paid-in Capital in Excess of Par, and Retained Earnings accounts can be determined.

(X) After all changes in noncurrent accounts are analyzed in the working paper, the total ($394,100) of the financial resources provided column and the total ($431,500) of the financial resources applied column are obtained. At this point, the decrease in working capital during the year, $37,400, should be entered as a credit to "Working Capital" in the first line of the third column in the working paper and also as a balancing figure on the next to the last line of the second column in the working paper. The account balances at the end of Year 5 can now be determined in the last column of the working paper (including the ending working capital of $98,100) and the subtotals ($654,400) obtained for the "Debit" and "Credit" columns. If the totals ($872,850) for account balances at the end of Year 5 agree, it may be reasonably concluded that all transactions in noncurrent accounts have been analyzed and that the decrease in working capital has been explained.

Summary of Working Paper Procedures The procedures illustrated to develop the information needed to prepare a statement of changes in financial position on a working capital basis are summarized below:

1 Determine the amount of working capital at the beginning and end of the period under consideration.

2 Enter the amount of working capital and the amount of all noncurrent accounts at the beginning of the period in the first column of the working paper.

3 Enter in summary form all transactions which caused increases and decreases in working capital, listing the specific sources and uses of working capital in the lower part of the working paper. Certain transactions which involved only noncurrent accounts (stock dividends, for example) simply are entered in the accounts affected since these are neither sources nor uses of working capital. Exchange transactions (issuance of stock in exchange for plant assets, for example) are reported as both financial resources provided and applied.

4 Determine that the difference between the financial resources provided and applied is equal to the increase or decrease in the working capital during the period. The fact that the difference between the financial resources provided and applied is equal to the change in working capital does not necessarily prove that the working paper analysis is correct, but it does indicate that all account changes have been analyzed and that no arithmetic errors have been made. An error in classifying a current asset as noncurrent, for example, will not be disclosed.

5 Prepare a formal statement of changes in financial position, showing the financial resources provided and applied during the period, as well as the composition of working capital at the beginning and at the end of the period.

HAAS CORPORATION
Statement of Changes in Financial Position (Working Capital Basis)
For Year 5

Financial resources provided:
  Working capital provided from operations:
    Net income, including extraordinary gain . . . . $ 78,800
    Less: Net charges and credits not requiring use of working capital
      (see working paper on page 1014 for detail)   1,500
    Working capital provided from operations . . . . $ 77,300
  Proceeds on condemnation of building, net of taxes 182,500
  Issuance of capital stock in exchange for equipment   92,800
    Total financial resources provided $352,600
Financial resources applied:
  Extinguishment of bonds payable . . . . $ 52,500
  Purchase of land 150,000
  Purchase of equipment (cash) 35,200
  Acquisition of equipment in exchange for capital stock . 92,800
  Acquisition of treasury stock 17,500
  Declaration of cash dividends   42,000
    Total financial resources applied 390,000
Decrease in financial resources (working capital) . . . . $(37,400)

	Dec. 31, Year 5	Dec. 31, Year 4	Increase or (decrease) in working capital
Composition of working capital:			
Current assets:			
Cash	$ 27,100	$ 52,800	$(25,700)
Notes receivable from customers .	50,000	30,000	20,000
Accounts receivable (net)	36,900	50,400	(13,500)
Inventory	96,050	57,300	38,750
Short-term prepayments	12,600	9,600	3,000
Total current assets	$222,650	$200,100	
Current liabilities:			
Accounts payable	$ 22,150	$ 31,300	9,150
Accrued liabilities	17,600	16,300	(1,300)
Income taxes payable	42,800	17,000	(25,800)
Dividends payable	42,000	–0–	(42,000)
Total current liabilities	$124,550	$ 64,600	
Working capital	$ 98,100	$135,500	
Decrease in working capital			$(37,400)

Statement of changes in financial position on a working capital basis

The statement of changes in financial position on a working capital basis for Haas Corporation is presented on page 1018. The amounts are taken from the working paper on page 1014. Although it would be possible to list individual nonfund adjustments to net income, this generally is not necessary unless the amounts have some special significance.

Alternative Form Showing Revenue and Expenses An acceptable procedure, which gives the same result, is to begin with total revenue that provided working capital during the period and deduct operating costs and expenses that required the outlay of working capital during the period. This form is illustrated below for Haas Corporation.

HAAS CORPORATION
Statement of Changes in Financial Position (Working Capital Basis)
For Year 5

Financial resources provided:		
Sales		$313,600
Less: Cost of goods sold	$158,000	
Operating expenses (other than depreciation)	28,000	
Income tax expense	38,300	
Interest expense	12,000	236,300
Working capital provided from operations		$ 77,300
Proceeds on condemnation of building, net of taxes		182,500
Issuance of capital stock in exchange for equipment		92,800
Total financial resources provided		$352,600
Financial resources applied:		
Extinguishment of bonds payable	$ 52,500	
Purchase of land	150,000	
Purchase of equipment (cash)	35,200	
Acquisition of equipment in exchange for capital stock	92,800	
Acquisition of treasury stock	17,500	
Declaration of cash dividends	42,000	
Total financial resources applied		390,000
Decrease in financial resources (working capital)		$(37,400)
Composition of working capital: (same as on page 1018.)		

The impact of income taxes on working capital for Year 5 is equal to the income tax expense of $48,300 as reported in the income statement, less $10,000 deferred income taxes; the impact of interest expense on working capital is equal to the interest expense of $11,250 as reported in the income statement, plus $750 amortization of the premium on bonds payable, or $12,000 which is the amount of interest paid in cash during the year.

Statement of changes in financial position on a cash basis

The statement of changes in financial position on a cash basis for Haas Corporation is presented below. The amounts included in the statement are developed in the working paper on page 1021. This working paper is an extension of the one prepared on the working capital basis which appears on page 1014.

HAAS CORPORATION

Statement of Changes in Financial Position (Cash Basis)

For Year 5

Financial resources provided:

Cash provided from operations (see working paper on page 1021)	.	$ 47,000
Proceeds on condemnation of building, net of taxes		182,500
Issuance of capital stock in exchange for equipment		92,800
Total financial resources provided		$322,300

Financial resources applied:

Extinguishment of bonds payable	$ 52,500	
Purchase of land	150,000	
Purchase of equipment (cash)	35,200	
Acquisition of equipment in exchange for capital stock .	92,800	
Acquisition of treasury stock	17,500	
Total financial resources applied		348,000
Decrease in financial resources (cash)		$ 25,700

Composition of working capital: (same as on page 1014)

Alternative forms of working paper

The working paper for the statement of changes in financial position may be adapted to meet varying needs when the information for solving problems is given in somewhat different form. For example, assuming that only *changes* in account balances for Bider Corporation during Year 10 are given and that beginning and ending account balances are not available, the working paper for the statement of changes in financial position may take the form illustrated on page 1022.

In the analysis of transactions for Year 10, the objective is to *summarize the changes in noncurrent accounts* and to identify the financial resources provided and applied in the process. The credit changes in noncurrent assets ($10,000) and capital stock ($25,000) are explained by entries to record depreciation and the issuance of capital stock. Simi-

	Account balances at Dec. 31, Year 4	Analysis of transactions for Year 5		Account balances at Dec. 31, Year 5
		Debit	Credit	
Cash	52,800		(x) 25,700	27,100
Notes receivable from customers .	30,000	(5) 20,000		50,000
Accounts receivable (net)	50,400		(2) 13,500	36,900
Inventory	57,300	(6) 38,750		96,050
Short-term prepayments	9,600	(7) 3,000		12,600
Totals	200,100	(8) 9,150		222,650
Accounts payable	31,300			22,150
Accrued liabilities	16,300		(3) 1,300	17,600
Income taxes payable	17,000		(4) 25,800	42,800
Dividends payable	–0–		(9) 42,000	42,000
All noncurrent accounts (see page 1014)	135,500	(1) 37,400		98,100
Totals	200,100	108,300	108,300	222,650
Financial resources provided:				
Operations—working capital (see page 1014)		(1) 77,300		
Add: Decrease in accounts receivable (net)		(2) 13,500		
Increase in accrued liabilities		(3) 1,300		
Increase in income taxes payable		(4) 25,800		
Less: Increase in notes receivable from customers			(5) 20,000	Cash from operations, 47,000
Increase in inventory . . .			(6) 38,750	
Increase in short-term prepayments			(7) 3,000	
Decrease in accounts payable			(8) 9,150	
Proceeds on condemnation of building		(1)182,500		
Issuance of capital stock in exchange for equipment . . .		(1) 92,800		
Financial resources applied:				
Extinguishment of bonds payable			(1) 52,500	
Purchase of land			(1) 150,000	
Purchase of equipment (cash) .			(1) 35,200	
Acquisition of equipment in exchange for capital stock . .			(1) 92,800	
Acquisition of treasury stock . .			(1) 17,500	
Declaration of cash dividends .		(9) 42,000	(1) 42,000	
Total financial resources provided and applied . .		435,200	460,900	
Decrease in cash		(x) 25,700		
		460,900	460,900	

Explanations for analysis of transactions:

(1) All financial resources provided and applied from working paper for statement of changes in financial position on working capital basis (see page 1014) which involve cash or exchange transactions.

(2) through (8) Analysis of changes in all current accounts which have an effect on the amount of cash provided from operations.

(9) To eliminate effect of dividend declaration because it was not paid.

BIDER CORPORATION

Working Paper for Statement of Changes in Financial Position (Working Capital Basis) For Year 10

	Changes in account balances during Year 10		Analysis of transactions for Year 10	
	Debit	Credit	Debit	Credit
Increase in working capital .	80,000		(X) 80,000	
Noncurrent assets (net)		10,000		(2) 10,000
Long-term debt	5,000		(4) 5,000	
Capital stock		25,000		(3) 25,000
Retained earnings		50,000	(5) 15,000	(1) 65,000
Totals	85,000	85,000	100,000	100,000
Financial resources provided:				
Operations—net income . .			(1) 65,000	
Add: Depreciation				
expense			(2) 10,000	
Issuance of capital stock . .			(3) 25,000	
Financial resources applied:				
Extinguishment of long-term				
debt				(4) 5,000
Cash dividends declared . .				(5) 15,000
Total financial resources				
provided and applied .			100,000	20,000
Increase in working capital . .				(X) 80,000
Totals			100,000	100,000

Explanation of transactions for Year 10:
(1) Net income for the year, a tentative measure of working capital provided from operations.
(2) Depreciation expense added to net income to obtain working capital provided from operations, $75,000.
(3) Issuance of capital stock for cash, a source of working capital.
(4) Extinguishment of long-term debt, a use of working capital.
(5) Declaration of cash dividends, a use of working capital.
(X) Balancing entry—increase in working capital during Year 10.

larly, the net credit change of $50,000 in retained earnings consists of net income of $65,000 less cash dividends declared of $15,000; and the debit change of $5,000 in long-term debt represents the extinguishment of debt.

Instead of using a formal working paper to prepare a statement of changes in financial position, some students and instructors prefer to use T accounts, one for working capital and one for each noncurrent account. Such an approach may be more efficient, particularly for solving relatively simple problems. In practice, a working paper generally is used because it provides a more complete record for permanent files.

REVIEW QUESTIONS

1 What are some meanings that may be attached to the term *funds* in the preparation of a statement of changes in financial position?

2 Briefly describe the all-financial-resources concept of funds flows.

3 Briefly discuss the uses to which a statement of changes in financial position may be put by users of financial statements.

4 "Last year, Java Oil Company earned $8 per share on sales of $250 million. Its cash flow for the year, a generous $60 million, represented a high return on equity capital." Comment on the implications of this quotation.

5 What basic data are necessary to prepare a statement of changes in financial position?

6 In analyzing working capital flows, business transactions may be classified into three categories: Transactions which affect only current asset or current liability accounts, transactions which affect both current and noncurrent accounts, and transactions which affect only noncurrent accounts. Indicate the effect of each category on working capital.

7 Give an example of each of the following situations, assuming that a statement of changes in financial position is being prepared:
a A decrease in a noncurrent asset that *is not* a source of working capital
b A decrease in a noncurrent asset that *is* a source of working capital
c An increase in a noncurrent liability that *is not* a source of working capital
d A decrease in stockholders' equity that *is* a use of working capital
e An increase in stockholders' equity that *is not* a source of working capital
f An increase in a noncurrent asset that *is not* a use of working capital
g A decrease in a noncurrent liability that *is not* a use of working capital

8 The following transaction was recorded during the current year:

Land	35,000	
Building	450,000	
Mortgage Payable (long-term)		380,000
Marketable Securities		50,000
Cash		55,000

Describe two ways this transaction can be reported in a statement of changes in financial position on a working capital basis. Which do you prefer?

9 Golubac Company has outstanding a $5 million issue of serial bonds. The first series of bonds, in the amount of $500,000, mature in July of Year 10. In preparing a statement of changes in financial position for calendar Year 9, the accountant shows a use of working capital of $500,000 relating to these bonds. Is this correct? Explain.

10 Explain why the accumulation of a discount on bonds held as investments and the amortization of deferred revenue items would be deducted from net income in arriving at working capital provided from operations.

11 How would the extinguishment of bonds be reported in a statement of changes in financial position on a working capital basis, assuming that sinking-fund securities are liquidated and the proceeds used to retire the bonds?

12 What two approaches may be followed in arriving at working capital provided by operations in the statement of changes in financial position?

13 What useful information might management find in a **cash flow statement** for a fiscal year just ended? Would such a statement be helpful to outsiders?

14 Briefly outline the procedure for converting net income from the **accrual** to the **cash basis.**

15 Is **cash flow per share** a better measure of operating results than earnings per share?

EXERCISES

Ex. 24-1 Account balances relating to equipment during Year 8 follow:

	Dec. 31, Year 8	Jan. 1, Year 8
Equipment	$210,000	$96,000
Less: Accumulated depreciation	38,000	30,000

Equipment with a carrying value of $10,000 and original cost of $25,000 was sold at a gain of $3,000. Compute the following for Year 8:
a Working capital provided by sale of equipment
b Working capital used to acquire equipment
c Depreciation expense on equipment which should be added to net income in computing working capital provided from operations.

Ex. 24-2 Explain how each of the following transactions would be shown on a statement of changes in financial position for Year 10, prepared on a working capital basis.
a Cash dividends of $200,000 were declared on December 11, Year 10, payable on January 14, Year 11.
b A 5% stock dividend was distributed; the market value of the dividend shares, $1,020,000, was transferred from retained earnings to paid-in capital accounts.
c Mining properties valued at $380,000 were acquired on January 3, Year 10, in exchange for bonds payable with a face value of $400,000. The bonds mature on December 31, Year 19.
d An additional income tax assessment of $98,000 was charged to the Retained Earnings account as a prior period adjustment. The assessment resulted from a material error.
e Oil exploration costs of $200,000 were deferred in Year 9 for financial accounting purposes but were deducted in computing taxable income. As a result, the Deferred Income Tax Liability account was credited for $96,000. In Year 10, the deferred oil exploration costs were written off as follows:

Oil Exploration Expenditures	104,000	
Deferred Income Tax Liability	96,000	
Deferred Oil Exploration Costs		200,000

Ex. 24-3 Adams Printing Co. reported a net income of $80,400 for the fiscal year just ended. In arriving at the net income, the following items were included:

Compensation expense (value assigned to stock options)	$24,000
Amortization of premium on bonds payable	5,000
Investment loss from 25%-owned company	120,000
Depreciation expense	45,000
Doubtful accounts expense	11,200
Unrealized loss in value of marketable equity securities (current portfolio) . .	25,000
Amortization of organization costs	3,000
Write-down of obsolete inventory to cost of goods sold	18,000
Income taxes, of which $27,000 is payable two or more years hence	70,000
Realized profit on long-term construction contracts	35,000
Extraordinary gain	41,500

Compute the amount of working capital provided from operations in the fiscal year just ended.

Ex. 24-4 From the following data, compute the cash provided from operations during the past year:

	Dec 31	Jan. 1
Accounts receivable	$20,200	$15,200
Accounts payable	15,000	24,000
Accrued liabilities	3,600	1,600
Accumulated depreciation (no retirements during the year)	32,000	26,000
Inventory	30,000	27,500
Short-term prepayments	2,200	3,000
Net income (accrual basis)	41,225	

Ex. 24-5 The following data are taken from the latest comparative balance sheet of General Cotton Corporation:

	End of year	Beginning of year
Cash	$ 20,000	$ 15,000
Marketable equity securities (net of allowance) . . .	40,000	55,000
Accounts receivable	50,000	30,000
Inventory	70,000	60,000
Short-term prepayments	5,000	3,000
Noncurrent assets (net)	242,500	209,000
Accounts payable	60,000	30,000
Notes payable (due in 10 months)	25,000	40,000
Accrued liabilities	2,500	2,000
Long-term debt & stockholders' equity	340,000	300,000

Prepare a schedule of the composition of working capital as it would appear in the statement of changes in financial position.

Ex. 24-6 A summary of the financial position for W. Goodson Company at the beginning and end of the current year is given on page 1026.

	End of year	Beginning of year
Working capital	$ 87,500	$ 96,000
Noncurrent assets:		
Investment in stock of R Corporation (equity method)	82,500	75,000
Land	60,000	45,000
Buildings	120,000	100,000
Less: Accumulated depreciation	(50,000)	(46,000)
	$300,000	$270,000
Long-term debt & stockholders' equity:		
Notes payable, due in 5 years	$ 20,000	$ –0–
Capital stock, $1 par	200,000	200,000
Retained earnings	80,000	70,000
	$300,000	$270,000

The net income of $25,000 (after depreciation of $4,000) included unrealized investment income of $7,500 from R Corporation. A cash dividend was declared during the year.

Prepare a statement of changes in financial position on a working capital basis for the year, without using a working paper.

Ex. 24-7 The following data for Year 1 were obtained from the records of Right-On Company:

	Net changes during Year 1	
	Debits	**Credits**
Current assets	$ 98,100	
Plant assets (net)	30,000	
Goodwill (amortized over 25 years)		$ 1,500
Current liabilities		68,500
Bonds payable, 7%		100,000
Discount on bonds payable	1,900	
Preferred stock, $10 par	100,000	
Common stock, no-par value		50,000
Retained earnings		10,000
	$230,000	$230,000

Retained Earnings

Premium on retirement of preferred stock	5,000	Balance, Jan. 1	60,000
Stock dividend on common stock	50,000	Net income	80,000
Cash dividends paid	15,000		

Ten-year bonds of $100,000 were issued on July 1 at 98, proceeds being used for the retirement of preferred stock. Land with a cost of $55,000 was exchanged at an agreed value of $70,000 for a new building costing $95,000; the balance of $25,000 was paid in cash. Depreciation for the year amounted to $10,000.

Prepare a statement of changes in financial position on a working capital basis for Year 1. A working paper is not required.

Ex. 24-8 T. C. Roth Corporation reported net income of $40,000 and paid dividends of $15,000 in Year 2. Comparative balance sheets at the end of Year 2 and Year 1 follow:

Assets	Year 2	Year 1
Cash	$ 82,500	$ 12,500
Accounts receivable (net)	67,500	37,500
Inventory	80,000	100,000
Equipment (net)	380,000	300,000
Total assets	$610,000	$450,000

Liabilities & Stockholders' Equity		
Accounts payable	$ 40,000	$ 25,000
Bonds payable (due in Year 15)	80,000	100,000
Capital stock, no-par value	290,000	150,000
Retained earnings	200,000	175,000
Total liabilities & stockholders' equity	$610,000	$450,000

Equipment was purchased for $75,000 cash, additional capital stock was sold to the public for cash, and capital stock with a market value of $40,000 was issued for new equipment.

Prepare a statement of changes in financial position on a cash basis for Year 2. Compute the cash provided from operations in a separate schedule; do not include a summary of the composition of working capital in the statement.

Ex. 24-9 A comparative balance sheet for Hohman Company at December 31, Year 2, follows:

	Year 2	Year 1
Cash	$ 52,500	$ 65,000
Accounts receivable (net)	100,000	90,000
Inventory	97,500	40,000
Plant assets	260,000	155,000
Less: Accumulated depreciation	(80,000)	(50,000)
Total assets	$430,000	$300,000
Accounts payable	$ 70,000	$ 55,000
Capital stock, $10 par	280,000	200,000
Paid-in capital in excess of par	25,000	-0-
Retained earnings	55,000	45,000
Total liabilities & stockholders' equity	$430,000	$300,000

On June 15, Year 2, the company issued 8,000 shares of capital stock in exchange for equipment. There were no retirements of plant assets in Year 2. Dividends of $25,000 were paid to stockholders during Year 2. The allowance for doubtful accounts was reduced by $3,000 during Year 2 as a result of writing off accounts known to be uncollectible, and increased by $5,000 at the end of the year. The net income can be derived from the data given.

Prepare a statement of changes in financial position on a working capital basis for Year 2, without using a working paper. Do not include a summary of the composition of working capital in the statement.

Ex. 24-10 The following financial statements were prepared for Sue Smith, Inc.:

SUE SMITH, INC.

Balance Sheet

January 1, Year 1

Assets

Current assets	$ 37,000
Equipment	48,000
Less: Accumulated depreciation	(15,000)
Patents	5,000
Total assets	$ 75,000

Liabilities & Stockholders' Equity

Current liabilities	$ 12,000
Capital stock, no-par value	27,000
Retained earnings	36,000
Total liabilities & stockholders' equity	$ 75,000

SUE SMITH, INC.

Statement of Changes in Financial Position

For Year 1

Working capital, Jan. 1		$25,000
Working capital provided:		
Operations:		
Net income	$24,000	
Add: Depreciation expense	10,000	
Amortization of patents	1,000	
Less: Gain on sale of equipment	(4,000)	31,000
Issue of capital stock		13,000
Sale of equipment		7,000
Total working capital provided		$76,000
Working capital applied:		
Dividends paid	$12,000	
Purchase of land	14,000	
Purchase of equipment	30,000	56,000
Working capital, Dec. 31		$20,000

Total assets in the balance sheet at December 31, Year 1, are $110,000. Accumulated depreciation on the equipment sold was $6,000.

Based on the information available from the balance sheet at January 1, Year 1, and the statement of changes in financial position for Year 1, prepare a balance sheet for Sue Smith, Inc., at December 31, Year 1.

SHORT CASES FOR ANALYSIS AND DECISION

Case 24-1 Dixon Engineering Company is a young and growing producer of electronic measuring instruments and technical equipment. You have been retained by Dixon to advise it in the preparation of a statement of changes in financial position. For the fiscal year ended October 31, Year 2, you have obtained the following information concerning certain events and transactions of Dixon.

(1) The amount of reported earnings for the fiscal year was $800,000, which included a deduction for an extraordinary loss of $93,000 (see item 5 below).
(2) Depreciation expense of $240,000 was included in the income statement.
(3) Uncollectible accounts receivable of $30,000 were written off against the allowance for doubtful accounts. Also, $37,000 of doubtful accounts expense was included in determining earnings for the fiscal year, and the same amount was added to the allowance for doubtful accounts.
(4) A gain of $4,700 was realized on the sale of a machine; it originally cost $75,000 of which $25,000 was undepreciated on the date of sale.
(5) On April 1, Year 2, a freak lightning storm caused an uninsured inventory loss of $93,000 ($180,000 loss, less reduction in income taxes of $87,000). This extraordinary loss was included in determining earnings as indicated in (1) above.
(6) On July 3, Year 2, building and land were purchased for $600,000; Dixon gave in payment $100,000 cash, $200,000 market value of its unissued common stock, and a $300,000 purchase-money mortgage.
(7) On August 3, Year 2, $700,000 face value of Dixon's 6% convertible debentures were converted into $140,000 par value of its common stock. The bonds were originally issued at face value.
(8) The board of directors declared a $320,000 cash dividend on October 20, Year 2, payable on November 15, Year 2, to stockholders of record on November 5, Year 2.

Instructions For each of the eight items above, explain whether each item is a source or use of working capital and explain how it should be disclosed in Dixon's statement of changes in financial position for the fiscal year ended October 31, Year 2. If any item is neither a source not a use of working capital, explain why it is *not* and indicate the disclosure, if any, that should be made of the item in Dixon's statement of changes in financial position for the fiscal year ended October 31, Year 2.

Case 24-2 Information concerning the debt and stockholders' equity of Taiwan Imports Company appears below and on page 1030.

Short-term borrowings:

Balance at Dec. 31, Year 4	$ 1,200.000
Proceeds from borrowings in Year 5	1,500,000
Payments made in Year 5	(1,400,000)
Balance at Dec. 31, Year 5	$ 1,300,000

Current portion of long-term debt:

Balance at Dec. 31, Year 4	$ 5,500,000
Transfers from caption "Long-term debt"	6,000,000
Payments made in Year 5	(5,500,000)
Balance at Dec. 31, Year 5	$ 6,000,000

Long-term debt:

Balance at Dec. 31, Year 4	$ 42,500,000
Proceeds from borrowings in Year 5	18,000,000
Transfers to caption "Current portion of long-term debt"	(6,000,000)
Payments made in Year 5	(10,000,000)
Balance at Dec. 31, Year 5	$ 44,500,000

Stockholders' equity at Dec. 31, Year 4:

Convertible preferred stock $20 par. Each share convertible into 2 shares of common stock. Authorized 60,000 shares; issued and outstanding 55,000 shares	$ 1,100,000
Common stock, $10 par. Authorized 3 million shares; issued and outstanding 2 million shares	20,000,000
Additional paid-in capital: common stock	4,225,000
Retained earnings	10,650,000
Total stockholders' equity	$ 35,975,000

During Year 5, a total of 30,000 shares of the convertible preferred stock were converted into common stock. Also during Year 5, a total of 100,000 shares of common stock were issued for cash at $25 per share.

Instructions
a Assuming that *funds* are defined as working capital, show how the above information should be shown on Taiwan Imports Company's statement of changes in financial position for the year ended December 31, Year 5.
b Explain why each change in the accounts listed above is included in or excluded from the statement of changes in financial position for Year 5. Ignore net income and dividends paid for Year 5.

Case 24-3 The following statement of changes in financial position was *improperly* prepared by the accountant for Mal Preparado, Inc.:

MAL PREPARADO, INC.
Statement of Changes in Financial Position
December 31, Year 1

Funds provided:

Acquisition of land	$105,000
Cash dividends declared (to be paid on Jan. 21, Year 2)	30,000
Stock dividend distributed	50,000
Acquisition of equipment	15,000
Purchase of marketable securities as short-term investment	150,000
Total funds provided	$350,000

Funds applied:

Net income, including gain of $20,000 net of taxes	$120,000
Issuance of note payable—due Year 4	85,000
Depreciation and amortization expense	60,000
Sale of equipment—carrying value (sold at gain of $20,000 net of taxes) .	10,000
Issuance of capital stock pursuant to stock dividend	50,000
Decrease in working capital	25,000
Total funds applied	$350,000

Don White, the president, is upset because he had hoped to increase the working capital during Year 1 by at least $100,000. Furthermore, he is somewhat confused with the arrangement of the statement and wonders if he should plan to issue additional shares of capital stock early in Year 2 in order to "bolster working capital."

Instructions

a Identify and discuss the weaknesses in the presentation of the statement of changes in financial position for Mal Preparado, Inc., as prepared by the accountant. Your discussion should explain why you consider them to be weaknesses and suggest the proper treatment of any item improperly presented.

b Prepare a revised statement of changes in financial position and advise the president whether or not Mal Preparado, Inc., should issue additional shares of capital stock in order to improve its working capital position.

Case 24-4 The income statement for Plains Peach Company for Year 3 included the following items:

Net income, including miscellaneous gains and losses	$399,500
Deferred income tax expense	20,000
Depreciation expense	160,000
Accumulation of discount on investment in bonds	1,000
Amortization of discount on bonds payable	1,500
Doubtful accounts expense	7,600
Realized gross profit on installment sales made in Years 1 and 2	62,000
Gain on sale of factory site	102,000
Interest revenue accrued	4,800
Expenses for Year 3 which will be paid in Year 4	12,000
Amortization of deferred "investment tax credit"	4,000
Compensation expense—value of stock option contracts	15,000
Investment income accrued on investment in Q Co. stock (equity method) .	5,000

Instructions

a Determine the amount of working capital provided from operations, assuming that the effects of nonoperating transactions on working capital are separately reported.

b Briefly explain the effect on working capital of each item above.

Case 24-5 The consolidated statement of changes in financial position for Charter Flights, Inc., is shown below:

	Year 10 (in thousands)	
Financial resources provided:		
Operations:		
Income before gain on sale of aircraft	$ 3,770	(1)
Add: Charges against income not involving working capital:		
Depreciation	11,380	(2)
Deferred federal income tax, amortization of investment tax credit, and deferred debt expense	1,400	(3)
Net loss of unconsolidated subsidiaries	450	(4)
Total from operations	$ 17,000	(5)
Gain on sale of aircraft, including $1 million of deferred federal income tax	2,100	(6)
Addition to long-term debt	40,000	(7)
Sale of common stock, less expense of issue	5,800	(8)
Disposal of flight and other property—carrying value	1,800	(9)
Increase in current portion of contracts receivable on aircraft leases	1,200	(10)
Total financial resources provided	$ 67,900	

Financial resources applied:		
Dividends on common stock	$ 610 (11)	
Addition to long-term contract receivable, excluding aircraft reclassifications	3,205 (12)	
Investment of funds held for purchase of aircraft	4,785 (13)	
Additions to flight, other property and equipment, and deposits on purchase contracts	62,100 (14)	
Long-term debt refinanced	12,000 (15)	
Provision for current portion of long-term debt	8,500 (16)	
Investment in and advances to unconsolidated subsidiaries	2,250 (17)	
Total financial resources applied		93,450
Increase (decrease) in working capital		$(25,550) (18)
Working capital at end of year		$ 12,600 (19)

Instructions Briefly explain each item numbered (1) through (19) and comment on the propriety of the format of the statement and the terminology used by Charter Flights, Inc.

PROBLEMS

Group A

24A-1 Comparative balance sheets for Hun Smelting Corporation are presented on page 1033.

	December 31,	
	Year 4	**Year 3**
	Dr. (Cr.)	**Dr. (Cr.)**
Current assets	$ 237,000	$ 160,000
Equipment	740,000	600,000
Less: Accumulated depreciation	(218,000)	(210,000)
Goodwill	240,000	250,000
	$ 999,000	$ 800,000
Current liabilities	$(180,000)	$(80,000)
Bonds payable (due in Year 12)	(200,000)	(300,000)
Discount on bonds payable	–0–	4,000
Capital stock, no-par value	(675,000)	(550,000)
Retained earnings	56,000	126,000
	$(999,000)	$(800,000)

You have accumulated the following additional information:

(1) During Year 4, equipment with a carrying value of $38,000 was sold at no gain or loss and new equipment was purchased for $75,000 cash.
(2) During Year 4, bonds in the face amount of $100,000 were extinguished at 105. The bonds were **not** current liabilities prior to their extinguishment.
(3) The Retained Earnings account was affected only by the net income or loss for Year 4.
(4) Capital stock with a current fair value of $125,000 was exchanged for new equipment.

Instructions Prepare a statement of changes in financial position for Year 4 on a working capital basis, without using a working paper.

24A-2 The comparative balance sheet and income statement for the latest two years for Retail Plywood Company are presented below and on page 1034.

RETAIL PLYWOOD COMPANY
Balance Sheet
December 31

Assets	Year 5	Year 4
Current assets:		
Cash	$ 150,000	$ 100,000
Marketable securities	40,000	–0–
Accounts receivable (net)	420,000	290,000
Inventory	330,000	210,000
Short-term prepayments	50,000	25,000
Total current assets	$ 990,000	$ 625,000
Plant assets	565,000	300,000
Less: Accumulated depreciation	(55,000)	(25,000)
Total	$1,500,000	$ 900,000

Liabilities & Stockholders' Equity

Current liabilities:		
Accounts payable	$ 265,000	$ 220,000
Accrued liabilities	70,000	65,000
Dividends payable	35,000	–0–
Total current liabilities	$ 370,000	$ 285,000
Note payable due in Year 8	250,000	–0–
Total liabilities	$ 620,000	$ 285,000
Stockholders' equity:		
Common stock, no-par value	600,000	450,000
Retained earnings	280,000	165,000
Total	$1,500,000	$ 900,000

RETAIL PLYWOOD COMPANY
Income Statement
For Year Ended December 31

	Year 5	Year 4
Net sales (including service charges)	$3,200,000	$2,000,000'
Cost of goods sold	2,500,000	1,600,000
Gross profit on sales	$ 700,000	$ 400,000
Expenses (including income taxes)	500,000	260,000
Net income	$ 200,000	$ 140,000

Additional information available included the following:

(1) The only entries to Retained Earnings were for net income and declaration of cash dividends.
(2) No plant assets or common stock were retired during Year 5.
(3) All accounts receivable and accounts payable related to merchandise transactions. Cash discounts are not allowed to customers but a service charge is added to an account for late payment. Accounts payable are recorded net and always are paid to take all the discount allowed. The Allowance for Doubtful Accounts at the end of Year 5 was the same as at the end of Year 4; no receivables were written off in Year 5.
(4) The proceeds from the note payable were used to finance a new store building. Capital stock was issued to provide additional working capital.

Instructions
a Compute the following for Year 5:
  (1) Cash collected on accounts receivable
  (2) Cash payments on accounts payable
  (3) Cash paid for expenses (including income taxes)
  (4) Cash receipts which were not provided from operations
  (5) Cash payments which were not reflected in operations
b Prepare a statement of changes in financial position for Year 5 on a cash basis, showing a single figure for cash provided from operations.
c Prepare a statement of changes in financial position for Year 5 in support of the increase in working capital. Do not include the composition of working capital in the statement.

24A-3 Comparative financial data as of the close of Years 1 and 2 for Garnett Sales Corporation are shown below:

	As of Dec. 31, Year 2	Year 1
Cash	$ 44,220	$ 20,800
Receivables (net)	40,400	24,000
Inventory	37,600	36,800
Short-term prepayments	4,180	4,400
Land	69,000	19,000
Buildings	276,000	250,000
Equipment	381,600	360,000
Patents	32,000	40,000
Total debits	$885,000	$755,000
Accumulated depreciation: buildings	$ 92,000	$ 80,000
Accumulated depreciation: equipment	238,000	220,000
Accounts payable	64,000	30,000
Accrued liabilities	20,000	10,000
Long-term debt (due in Year 10)	65,000	95,000
Common stock, $25 par	230,000	200,000
Paid-in capital in excess of par	85,000	40,000
Retained earnings	91,000	80,000
Total credits	$885,000	$755,000

Early in Year 2 the board of directors of the company ordered that $25,000 be transferred from retained earnings to reflect a 5% stock dividend. In addition, cash dividends of $29,000 were paid. Common stock valued at $50,000 was issued in exchange for land. There were no sales or retirements of buildings and equipment during the year, and no new expenditures were made for patents. Net income for Year 2 was $65,000.

Instructions

a Prepare a statement of changes in financial position for Year 2 on a working capital basis, without using a working paper. Include the composition of working capital in the statement.

b Prepare a schedule to convert the net income for Year 2 from the accrual to the cash basis.

c Prepare a statement of changes in financial position for Year 2 on a cash basis, using the information generated in parts **a** and **b** above. Do not include the composition of working capital in the statement.

24A-4 The schedule on page 1036 showing net changes in balance sheet accounts at December 31, Year 10, compared to December 31, Year 9, was prepared from the records of Solace Company. The statement of changes in financial position for the year ended December 31, Year 10, has not yet been prepared.

	Net changes Increase (Decrease)
Assets	
Cash	$ 50,000
Accounts receivable (net)	76,000
Inventories	37,000
Short-term prepayments	1,000
Plant assets (net)	164,000
Total assets	$328,000
Liabilities	
Accounts payable	$ (55,500)
Notes payable to banks—current	(15,000)
Accrued liabilities	33,000
Bonds payable (long-term)	(28,000)
Unamortized bond discount (account with debit balance) . . .	1,200
Total liabilities	$(64,300)
Stockholders' equity	
Preferred stock, $50 par	$100,000
Common stock, $10 par	500,000
Paid-in capital in excess of par	200,000
Retained earnings	(437,700)
Appropriation of retained earnings	30,000
Total stockholders' equity	$392,300
Total liabilities & stockholders' equity	$328,000

Additional information
(1) The net income for the year ended December 31, Year 10, was $172,300. There were no extraordinary items.
(2) During the year ended December 31, Year 10, uncollectible accounts receivable of $24,200 were written off.
(3) A comparison of plant assets as of the end of each year follows:

	December 31, Year 10	December 31, Year 9	Net increase (decrease)
Plant assets	$670,500	$510,000	$160,500
Less: Accumulated depreciation	224,500	228,000	(3,500)
Plant assets (net)	$446,000	$282,000	$164,000

During Year 10 machinery was purchased at a cost of $45,000. In addition, machinery with a fair value of $100,000 was acquired in exchange for preferred stock on December 20. Machinery that was acquired in Year 3 at a cost of $48,000 was sold for $13,600. At the date of sale, the machinery had an undepreciated cost of $4,200. The remaining increase in plant assets resulted from the acquisition of a tract of land for a new plant site.
(4) The bonds payable mature at the rate of $28,000 every year.
(5) In January, Year 10, the company issued an additional 10,000 shares of its common stock at $14 per share upon the exercise of outstanding stock options held by key employees. In May, Year 10, the company declared and is-

sued a 5% stock dividend on its outstanding stock. During the year, a cash dividend was paid on the common stock. On December 31, Year 10, there were 840,000 shares of common stock outstanding.

(6) The appropriation of retained earnings for possible future inventory price decline was provided by a charge against retained earnings, in anticipation of an expected future drop in the market prices of goods in inventory.

Instructions

a Prepare a statement of changes in financial position (including the composition of working capital) for the year ended December 31, Year 10, based upon the information presented above. The statement should be prepared on a working capital basis. A working paper may be used but is not required.

b Adjust the working capital provided from operations (computed in *a*) to a cash flow basis and prepare a statement of changes in financial position on a cash basis. Do not include the composition of working capital in the statement.

24A-5 Caswell Brands, Inc., has prepared its financial statements for the year ended December 31, Year 3, and for the three months ended March 31, Year 4. You have been asked to prepare a statement of changes in financial position on a working capital basis for the three months ended March 31, Year 4. The company's balance sheet data at December 31, Year 3, and March 31, Year 4, and its income statement data for the three months ended March 31, Year 4, are presented at the bottom of the page and on page 1038. You have previously satisfied yourself as to correctness of the amounts presented.

Your discussion with the company's controller and a review of the financial records have revealed the following information.

(1) On January 8, Year 4, the company sold marketable securities for cash. These securities had been held for more than six months.

(2) The company's preferred stock is convertible into common stock at a rate of one share of preferred for two shares of common. The preferred stock and common stock have par values of $2 and $1, respectively.

(3) On January 17, Year 4, three acres of land were condemned. An award of $32,000 in cash was received on March 22, Year 4. Purchase of additional land as a replacement is not contemplated by the company.

(4) On March 25, Year 4, the company purchased equipment for cash.

(5) On March 29, Year 4, bonds payable were issued at face amount for cash.

(6) The investment in 30%-owned company included an amount attributable to goodwill of $3,220 at December 31, Year 3. Goodwill is being amortized at an annual rate of $480.

	Balance Sheet	
	Mar. 31, Year 4	*Dec. 31, Year 3*
Cash	$ 87,400	$ 25,300
Marketable investments	7,300	16,500
Accounts receivable (net)	49,320	24,320
Inventory	48,590	31,090
Total current assets	$192,610	$ 97,210
Land	18,700	40,000
Building	250,000	250,000
Equipment	81,500	–0–
Accumulated depreciation	(16,250)	(15,000)
Investment in 30%-owned company	67,100	61,220
Other assets	15,100	15,100
Total	$608,760	$448,530

Accounts payable	$ 17,330	$ 21,220
Dividend payable	8,000	–0–
Income taxes payable	34,616	–0–
Total current liabilities	$ 59,946	$ 21,220
Other liabilities	186,000	186,000
Bonds payable	115,000	50,000
Discount on bonds payable	(2,150)	(2,300)
Deferred income tax liability	846	510
Preferred stock	–0–	30,000
Common stock	110,000	80,000
Dividends declared	(8,000)	–0–
Retained earnings	147,118	83,100
Total	$608,760	$448,530

	Income Statement for Three Months Ended Mar. 31, Year 4
Sales	$242,807
Gain on sale of marketable investments	2,400
Equity in earnings of 30%-owned company	5,880
Gain on condemnation of land	10,700
Total revenue	$261,787
Cost of goods sold	$138,407
General and administrative expenses	22,010
Depreciation expense	1,250
Interest expense	1,150
Income taxes expense	34,952
Total expenses	197,769
Net income	$ 64,018

(7) The company's income tax rate is 40% for regular income and 20% for capital gains.

Instructions

a Prepare in good form a statement of changes in financial position, including any supporting schedules needed, on a working basis for the three months ended March 31, Year 4.

b Prepare a working paper to convert the income statement for the three months ended March 31, Year 4, to a cash basis. Assume that the gain on the sale of marketable investments is included in operations and that the proceeds on the condemnation of land is reported separately.

c Using the data in parts a and b, prepare a statement of changes in financial position on a cash basis for the three months ended March 31, Year 4. You need not include the composition of working capital in the statement.

24A-6 The financial statements of Grantland Corporation for Year 10 and Year 9 appear on pages 1039 and 1040. The company was formed on January 1, Year 7.

GRANTLAND CORPORATION
Comparative Balance Sheets
December 31, Year 10 and Year 9

	Year 10	Year 9	Increase (decrease)
Current assets:			
Cash	$ 3,500	$ 27,000	$ (23,500)
Accounts receivable (net of allowance for doubtful accounts of $2,900 and $2,000) . .	89,900	79,700	10,200
Inventories (fifo, lower of cost or market) . . .	136,300	133,200	3,100
Short-term prepayments	4,600	12,900	(8,300)
Total current assets	$234,300	$252,800	$ (18,500)
Investments: Land held for future plant site . . .	$ 35,000	$ -0-	$ 35,000
Plant and equipment:			
Land	$ 47,000	$ 47,000	$ -0-
Buildings and equipment (net of accumulated depreciation of $155,600 and $117,000) . . .	581,900	425,000	156,900
Total plant and equipment	$628,900	$472,000	$156,900
Other assets: Organization costs	$ 1,500	$ 3,000	$ (1,500)
Total assets	$899,700	$727,800	$171,900
Current liabilities:			
Accounts payable	$ 3,000	$ 7,800	$ (4,800)
Notes payable	8,000	5,000	3,000
Mortgage payable	3,600	3,600	-0-
Accrued liabilities	6,200	4,800	1,400
Income taxes payable	87,500	77,900	9,600
Total current liabilities	$108,300	$ 99,100	$ 9,200
Long-term liabilities:			
Notes payable	$ -0-	$ 18,000	$ (18,000)
Mortgage payable	70,200	73,800	(3,600)
Total long-term liabilities	$ 70,200	$ 91,800	$ (21,600)
Deferred investment tax credit	$ 16,800	$ 18,900	$ (2,100)
Stockholders' equity:			
Capital stock; $1 par; shares authorized, 300,000 in Year 10 and 200,000 in Year 9; shares issued and outstanding, 162,000 in Year 10 and 120,000 in Year 9	$162,000	$120,000	$ 42,000
Paid-in capital in excess of par	306,900	197,900	109,000
Retained earnings appropriated for contingencies	25,000	-0-	25,000
Retained earnings—unappropriated	210,500	200,100	10,400
Total stockholders' equity	$704,400	$518,000	$186,400
Total liabilities & stockholders' equity	$899,700	$727,800	$171,900

GRANTLAND CORPORATION

Statement of Income and Retained Earnings

For Years Ended December 31, Year 10 and Year 9

	Year 10	Year 9	Increase (decrease)
Sales	$980,000	$900,000	$ 80,000
Cost of goods sold	540,000	490,000	50,000
Gross profit on sales	$440,000	$410,000	$ 30,000
Selling and administrative expenses	262,000	248,500	13,500
Operating income	$178,000	$161,500	$ 16,500
Other expenses	3,000	1,500	1,500
Income before income taxes	$175,000	$160,000	$ 15,000
Income tax expense	85,400	77,900	7,500
Net income	$ 89,600	$ 82,100	$ 7,500
Retained earnings, Jan. 1	200,100	118,000	82,100
Stock dividend distributed, 10%	(36,000)	–0–	(36,000)
Cash dividends paid	(18,200)	–0–	(18,200)
Appropriation for contingencies	(25,000)	–0–	(25,000)
Retained earnings, Dec. 31	$210,500	$200,100	$ 10,400

The following information was given effect in the preparation of these financial statements:

(1) The 10% stock dividend was distributed on August 1, Year 10. The investment in land for a future plant site was obtained by the issuance of 10,000 shares of the corporation's capital stock on October 1, Year 10. On December 1, 20,000 shares of capital stock were sold to obtain additional working capital. There were no other transactions in Year 10 affecting paid-in capital.

(2) During Year 10 depreciable assets with a total cost of $17,500 were retired and sold as scrap for a nominal amount. These assets were fully depreciated at December 31, Year 9. The only depreciable asset acquired in Year 10 was a new building.

(3) When new equipment, with an estimated economic life of 10 years, was purchased on January 2, Year 9, for $300,000, the decision was made to defer the resulting investment tax credit, with the benefit of the credit being allocated over the economic life of the equipment by a reduction in income tax expense. The income tax rate is 50%.

(4) In Year 10, $10,000 was paid in advance on long-term notes payable. The balance of the long-term notes is due in Year 11.

(5) An appropriation of retained earnings for possible contingencies of $25,000 was established in Year 10.

Instructions

a Prepare a working paper for a statement of changes in financial position on a working capital basis for the year ended December 31, Year 10.

b Prepare a formal statement of changes in financial position for Year 10. You need not show a summary of the composition of working capital, which is generally included in the lower section of the statement. Report the amount of working capital provided from operations as a net figure taken from the working paper in part **a**.

Group B

24B-1 Given below are the *changes* in account balances of the retail business owned by Ralph Fox for the fiscal year ended July 31, Year 10:

Cash	$27,100
Accounts receivable	(8,000)
Allowance for doubtful accounts	(200)
Merchandise inventory	(15,000)
Equipment	28,400
Accumulated depreciation	10,000
Accounts payable	(5,000)
Accrued liabilities	400
Ralph Fox, capital	27,300

The parentheses denote a decrease in the debit or credit balance normal to a given account.

Accounts receivable of $1,000 were written off as uncollectible. Equipment costing $7,500 was sold for $2,000, resulting in a loss of $1,600. Net income, including the loss on sale of equipment, amounted to $47,300. The balance of the change in the owner's capital account represents drawings.

Instructions
a Prepare a statement of changes in financial position on a working capital basis, without using a working paper. The statement should include a schedule of the changes in working capital accounts.
b Prepare a statement of changes in financial position on a cash basis, without using a working paper. Do not include a schedule of the changes in working capital accounts.

24B-2 The operating data for Davis & Davis Groves, Inc., for the current year include the following:

Sales (net of returns and allowances)	$427,500
Purchases (including $6,000 acquired by issuance of stock)	240,000
Operating expenses, including $22,000 depreciation expense	100,000
Interest expense	4,100
Income tax expense	25,200
Cash dividends paid	24,000

The information below and on page 1042 is taken from comparative balance sheets:

	End of year	Beginning of year
Cash	$?	$ 4,800
Accounts receivable (net)	42,250	46,000
Inventory	61,000	70,000
Short-term prepayments	3,000	2,200
Furniture and equipment	178,000	165,000
Less: Accumulated depreciation	(135,000)	(108,000)
Land for future expansion	40,000	–0–
Totals	$?	$ 180,000

Accounts payable	$ 14,150	$ 25,000
Income taxes payable	25,200	10,000
Accrued interest payable	300	350
Equipment notes payable ($11,000 was current at beginning of		
year and $12,100 was current at end of year)	47,400	58,400
Capital stock, $10 par	80,000	55,000
Paid-in capital in excess of par	32,000	2,000
Accumulated earnings	?	?
Totals	$?	$ 180,000

Late in the current year, 2,500 shares of capital stock were issued in ex-change for assets with fair values as follows: land, $26,000; inventory, $16,000; furniture, $13,000. No plant assets were sold or retired during the year.

Instructions
a Prepare a reconciliation of the Accumulated Earnings account for the current year.
b Prepare a statement of changes in financial position on a working capital basis, supported by a schedule of changes in working capital accounts. The use of a working paper is optional.
c Prepare a schedule to determine the amount of cash provided from opera-tions during the current year.

24B-3 The adjusted trial balances of Andersen Company at the close of two recent years were as follows:

ANDERSEN COMPANY
Adjusted Trial Balance
December 31
(in thousands of dollars)

	Year 2	Year 1
Cash	$ 650	$ 440
Receivables (net)	830	700
Inventories	750	500
Supplies and unexpired insurance	210	250
Land	95	95
Buildings	1,050	915
Equipment	460	340
Cost of goods sold	1,600	1,500
Operating expenses	600	580
Income taxes expense	180	90
Dividends (cash)	75	40
Interest expense	20	25
Totals	$6,520	$5,475

Accumulated depreciation: buildings	$ 380	$ 340
Accumulated depreciation: equipment	200	170
Accounts payable (merchandise creditors)	590	690
Income taxes payable	80	50
Accrued liabilities	300	160
Bonds payable, 5%, maturity date Dec. 31, Year 10	400	500
Capital stock, $20 par	1,100	800
Capital in excess of par	340	100
Retained earnings (beginning of each year)	430	365
Sales (net)	2,700	2,300
Totals	$6,520	$5,475

Bonds payable were retired at face amount in Year 2. No disposal of plant assets took place in Year 2.

Instructions (All figures in your solution may be stated in thousands of dollars.)
a Prepare a comparative income statement for each year and determine the ending balances in retained earnings.
b Convert the income statement for Year 2 to a cash basis. Use the form illustrated on page 1005.
c Prepare a statement of changes in financial position on a cash basis for Year 2. Use the amount determined in **b** as cash provided from operations. Other cash receipts and payments can be obtained by analyzing the changes during Year 2 in the following accounts: Buildings, Equipment, Bonds Payable, Capital Stock, Capital in Excess of Par, and Retained Earnings.
d Prepare a statement of changes in financial position on a working capital basis for Year 2. Do not use a working paper. Do not include the composition of working capital as a formal part of the statement.

24B-4 The following information is obtained from the records of Harwell Hill Corporation for Year 5:

Net Changes in Account Balances

	Debit	Credit
Cash	$ 34,950	
Accounts receivable	90,000	
Allowance for doubtful accounts		$ 2,500
Inventories	35,050	
Equipment	150,000	
Accumulated depreciation		65,000
Goodwill		10,000
Income taxes payable		15,000
Accounts payable		5,000
Bonds payable—7% due Jan. 2, Year 25		250,000
Premium on bonds payable		9,500
Preferred stock, $100 par	240,000	
Common stock, no-par value		105,000
Retained earnings		88,000
	$550,000	$550,000

A summary of the activity in the Retained Earnings account during Year 5 follows:

Balance, Jan. 1, Year 5		$3,300,000
Add: Net income for year, after amortization of goodwill . . .	$402,500	
Refund received on Year 3 income taxes (caused by error)	12,500	415,000
Subtotal		$3,715,000
Less: Cash dividends	$210,000	
Stock dividends on common stock . . . . *.	105,000	
Retirement premium on preferred stock	12,000	327,000
Balance, Dec. 31, Year 5		$3,388,000

Accounts receivable of $20,000 were written off during the year. Equipment costing $200,000, which was 80% depreciated, was sold at carrying value and new equipment with larger capacity was acquired. The bonds were issued on January 2, Year 5, at 104. The bond interest checks were mailed on December 31, Year 5.

Instructions Prepare a statement of changes in financial position (working capital basis) for Year 5. A working paper is not required. If you use a working paper, the form illustrated on page 1022 would be appropriate for this problem. A summary of changes in working capital accounts should be prepared as a part of the statement of changes in financial position.

24B-5 Comparative financial data for Hale Henderson & Co., in millions of dollars, as of December 31, appear below and on page 1045.

	Year 2	Year 1
Cash	$ 11.0	$ 24.4
Marketable securities (lower of cost or market)	8.7	–0–
Trade receivables (net)	36.4	29.5
Income tax refund receivable	3.8	–0–
Inventories	17.5	11.3
Short-term prepayments	2.5	1.9
Investment in other companies, at cost	28.0	18.0
Land	26.0	15.2
Buildings	52.0	49.5
Accumulated depreciation: buildings	(25.0)	(24.0)
Equipment	82.5	76.8
Accumulated depreciation: equipment	(44.4)	(32.6)
Totals	$199.0	$170.0

Accounts payable	$ 33.6	$ 23.9
Notes payable (current)	28.0	20.0
Income taxes payable	–0–	9.7
Mortgage payable (noncurrent)	14.0	14.0
Preferred stock, $100 par	45.0	27.0
Common stock, $5 stated value	58.0	50.0
Capital in excess of stated value	16.1	14.1
Retained earnings	4.3	11.3
Totals	$199.0	$170.0
Sales	$245.0	$230.0
Cost of goods sold	188.3	148.2
Selling and administrative expenses	64.0	47.9
Interest expense	1.0	1.2
Income tax expense (credit)	(3.8)	15.8
Cash dividends paid	2.5	10.8

Short-term prepayments relate entirely to administrative costs. Depreciation on building is 80% applicable to manufacturing activities, and depreciation on equipment is entirely applicable to manufacturing. During Year 2, the company issued common stock in exchange for 18% of the common stock of a major supplier. Additional preferred stock was issued at par value.

Instructions

a Prepare a schedule of changes in working capital during Year 2. Assume that the income tax refund receivable is a current asset.

b Prepare a working paper for working capital flows for Year 2.

c Prepare a statement of changes in financial position in which the amount of working capital provided from operations is taken as a single figure from the working paper in *b.* Do not include a summary of changes in working capital accounts in the statement of changes in financial position.

d Prepare a statement of changes in financial position showing the revenue and expense items which provided or used working capital as a result of recurring operations.

24B-6 Comparative balance sheet data for Racecourse, Inc., at December 31 are shown below and on page 1046.

	Year 2	Year 1
Cash on hand and in banks	$ 76,000	$ 175,000
Marketable securities (at cost)	–0–	30,000
Accounts receivable, less allowances of $20,000 and $8,000		
for Year 2 and Year 1, respectively	435,000	260,000
Inventories	493,000	400,000
Investments (at cost)	520,000	610,000
Equipment (net of accumulated depreciation)	1,953,000	1,700,000
Discount on mortgage bonds payable	16,000	25,000
Totals	$3,493,000	$3,200,000

Bank overdraft	$ 5,000	$ –0–
Notes payable to banks (current)	350,000	40,000
Accounts payable	315,000	290,000
6% mortgage bonds payable	800,000	1,000,000
Preferred stock, $100 par, each share convertible into three		
shares of common	250,000	300,000
Common stock, $5 par	542,500	500,000
Paid-in capital in excess of par	655,500	340,000
Retained earnings	575,000	730,000
Totals	$3,493,000	$3,200,000

An analysis of account changes disclosed the following:

(1) Uncollectible accounts amounting to $11,299 were written off in Year 2.
(2) Some long-term investments were sold at a gain of $80,000. Marketable securities, however, were sold at a loss of $2,110. (Include the loss on sale of marketable securities in working capital provided from operations because marketable securities are acquired to invest temporarily idle cash.)
(3) Mortgage bonds mature on December 31, Year 6. On July 1, Year 2, bonds of $200,000 were extinguished at 102.
(4) Additional shares of common stock were issued during the year at $44 per share, and 1,500 shares were issued as a result of conversion of preferred stock.
(5) Equipment, cost $60,000, was sold at its carrying value of $30,000. Depreciation of $120,000 was recorded during the year. Additional equipment was purchased for cash.
(6) Net loss for Year 2, including nonoperating gains and losses, amounted to $110,000.
(7) Cash dividends paid during the year amounted to $45,000.

Instructions
a Prepare a schedule determining the change in working capital during Year 2.
b Prepare a statement of changes in financial position which explains the reasons for the change in working capital. Use of a working paper is recommended; if a working paper is not used, supporting schedules and computations should be presented. Do not include the composition of working capital in the statement because it has already been prepared in part **a.**
c Prepare a statement of changes in financial position on a cash basis for Year 2. Do not include a summary of working capital as required by **APB Opinion No. 19.**

CHAPTER 25

ANALYSIS OF FINANCIAL STATEMENTS

Many groups outside the business enterprise—creditors, investors, regulatory agencies, financial analysts, labor union leaders—are interested in its financial affairs. Management is also interested in the results and relationships reported in financial statements. Outsiders do not have access to the detailed data that are available to management and must therefore rely on published information in making decisions that relate to a business firm. In this chapter we shall consider the analysis of financial statements as a basis for decision making by outsiders.

Management makes operating and financial decisions based on a wide variety of reports which are generated by the company's own information system or which are available from other sources. Management's use of financial information for certain decision-making purposes has been mentioned in preceding chapters. More sophisticated analyses of profit-volume relationships, make or buy decisions, differential costs, budgets, product line profitability, gross profits, distribution costs, and rates of return on investments are usually covered in cost or management accounting courses and for that reason are not discussed in this book.

Sources of financial information available to outsiders

The first step in financial analysis is to obtain as much factual information as possible. The major sources of corporate financial information are described in the following sections.

Published Reports Corporations whose stock is publicly owned issue annual and quarterly reports. Annual reports generally contain comparative financial statements and the accompanying notes, supplementary financial information, and comments by management on the year's operations and prospects for the future. They are made available to the public as well as to stockholders.

Securities and Exchange Commission (SEC) Publicly owned corporations are required to file annual reports with the SEC, copies of which may be acquired at normal cost. These reports (Form 10-K) are particularly valuable sources of financial information because the SEC prescribes a standard format and terminology and because they typically contain more detailed information than reports to stockholders. Listed corporations generally indicate in their annual reports to stockholders that a copy of Form 10-K as filed with the Securities and Exchange Commission may be obtained free of charge by writing to the corporate secretary. A quarterly report filed with the SEC (Form 10-Q) also is a valuable source of timely information.

Credit and Investment Advisory Services Organizations such as Moody's Investors Service and Standard & Poor's Corporation compile financial information for investors in annual volumes and periodic supplements. A wide variety of data on companies, particularly small and medium-sized businesses, is published by such organizations as Dun & Bradstreet, Inc., and Robert Morris Associates. Many trade associations collect and publish average ratios for companies in an industry. Major brokerage firms and investment advisory services compile financial information about publicly owned companies from all sources and make it available to their customers. In addition, such firms maintain a staff of analysts who study business conditions and review published financial statements; make plant visitations and talk with executives to get information on new products, industry trends, and management changes; and interpret all this information for investors.

Audit Reports When a CPA firm performs an audit, its report is addressed to the board of directors, and frequently to the stockholders, of the audited company. The CPA firm's opinion on financial statements is included in annual reports. Frequently the audit report consists only of the opinion; however, when dealing with smaller businesses, the CPA firm may prepare a "long-form report" which contains rather detailed financial information and comments. Banks and other lending institutions rely heavily on this type of audit report for financial information about businesses applying for loans.

What is financial analysis?

Knowing what to look for and how to interpret it is the essence of the art of analysis. Financial analysis is a process of *selection, relation, and evaluation.* The first step is to select from the total information available about a business the information relevant to the decision under consideration. The second is to arrange the information in a way that will bring out significant relationships. The final step is to study these relationships and interpret the results.

Financial statements themselves are organized summaries of detailed information, and are thus a form of analysis. The type of statements accountants prepare, the way they arrange items on these statements, and their standards of disclosure are all influenced by a desire to provide information in convenient form. In using these financial statements, analysts focus their attention on key figures and relationships. They may then extend their investigation to find out why the conditions revealed by the financial statements exist.

Procedures of analysis

Financial analysis is not primarily a matter of making computations. The important part of the analytical process begins when the computational task is finished. There are, however, some analytical procedures that are useful in highlighting important relationships and reducing masses of detail into brief, convenient numerical form so that the essential facts can be readily grasped.

Ratios Ratios may be expressed as percentages, as fractions, or as a stated comparison between simple numbers. For example, we might describe the relationship between $120 million of sales and $24 million of operating income as: (1) operating income is 20% of sales; (2) operating income is $\frac{1}{5}$ of sales; (3) the ratio of sales to operating income is 5 to 1; (4) for every dollar of sales the company earned 20 cents in operating income. Each of these ratios describes concisely the relationship between sales and operating income. Computing a ratio does not add any information not already inherent in the figures under study. A useful ratio can be computed only when a significant relationship exists; a ratio of two unrelated figures is meaningless.

Component Percentages The ratio of one item in a financial statement to the total that includes that item is called a *component percentage.* Reducing data to component percentages helps the analyst visualize quickly the relative importance of any item on financial statements and of significant changes from period to period.

Financial statements expressed in component percentages are sometimes called "common size" financial statements. Two examples, one for Company A and one for Companies A and B, are presented below.

COMPANY A
Common Size Income Statements

	Year 2	Year 1
Net sales	100.0%	100.0%
Cost of goods sold	63.2	66.4
Gross profit on sales	36.8%	33.6%
Operating expenses	23.2	24.2
Operating income	13.6%	9.4%
Income tax expense	5.0	3.2
Net income	8.6%	6.2%

COMPANIES A AND B
Common Size Balance Sheets
December 31, Year 1

	Company A	Company B
Assets:		
Current assets	56.4%	43.2%
Plant assets (net)	38.7	50.1
Other assets	4.9	6.7
Total assets	100.0%	100.0%
Liabilities & stockholders' equity:		
Current liabilities	36.2%	20.5%
Long-term liabilities	24.0	12.6
Total liabilities	60.2%	33.1%
Stockholders' equity	39.8	66.9
Total liabilities & stockholders' equity	100.0%	100.0%

In the first example for Company A, reducing the operating data to component percentages helps the reader to see the major factors that brought about an increase in the rate of earnings per dollar of sales. In the second example, component percentages highlight the difference in the asset and capital structure of Companies A and B. Company A has a larger proportion of debt and a relatively larger amount of current assets; Company B is financed more heavily by use of stockholders' capital and has a relatively larger investment in plant assets.

When information is reduced to simple terms, there may be some loss of clarity or completeness, but there may be some gains. Component percentages emphasize relative size; they obscure differences in absolute amounts. For example, if Company A has managed to increase its net income from 6.2 to 8.6% of sales only by cutting sales volume in half, there is no hint of this in the common size income statements. Similarly, the common size balance sheets will not reveal, for example, the fact that Company A may be four times the size of Company B.

Changes over Time The analytical information that can be gleaned from the financial statements of only one year is limited. We have seen in previous chapters the difficulty of measuring income and financial position accurately. Furthermore, the company's experience in any given year may not be typical. Investigating performance during several periods is therefore a useful form of analysis.

Most corporate annual reports now include a 5-, 10-, or 15-year summary of important financial data. The selected figures below, for example, are taken from the annual report of International Corporation.[1] We can see at a glance that the sales, net income, and cash dividends of International Corporation are growing steadily.

	INTERNATIONAL CORPORATION *Sales, Net Income, and Dividends*				
	Year 5	Year 4	Year 3	Year 2	Year 1
Sales (millions)	$4,248	$3,573	$3,239	$2,863	$2,591
Net income (millions)	526	477	431	364	305
Net income per share (dollars)	9.66	9.03	8.20	6.96	5.84
Cash dividends per share (dollars)	4.30	4.00	3.17	2.27	1.60

There are a number of ways to reduce this five-year record of items to be analyzed to a form that aids analysis. In the schedule on page 1052 relating to sales and net income, the dollar increase each year over the previous year, the percentage increase over the previous year, and the *trend percentage* in relation to the first year in the series are shown for International Corporation.

Each of these computations points up the change in sales and net income over the five-year period in a slightly different way. If the analyst is primarily interested in absolute change, the dollar changes tell the story. The percentage of increase or decrease year by year expresses

---

[1] When financial data for a number of years are reported, common practice is to report the *most recent* data in the first column and the older data in succeeding columns to the right. We shall follow this practice in this chapter.

	INTERNATIONAL CORPORATION						
	Analysis of Changes over Five-year Period						
Year	Dollar increase over previous year (in millions of dollars)		Percentage increase over previous year		Trend percentage in relation to Year 1	
	Sales	Net income	Sales	Net income	Sales	Net income
1					100.0%	100.0%
2	$272	$59	10.5%	19.3%	110.5	119.3
3	376	67	13.1	18.4	125.0	141.3
4	334	46	10.3	10.7	137.9	156.4
5	675	49	18.9	10.3	163.9	172.5

growth in relation to the prior year's performance. Trend percentages (computed by dividing the figure for each year by the figure for the base year) reveal a total growth of 63.9% in sales volume and an increase of 72.5% in net income over a period of four years.

A great deal of importance has been placed in recent years on the **compound growth** rates in earnings. Those companies whose earnings increase at a rate substantially above the average rate for other companies are referred to as **growth companies.** The compound growth rate in net income for the International Corporation during the Years 2 through 5, for example, is the simple average of the percentage increases in net income over the previous year. Thus 19.3 + 18.4 + 10.7 + 10.3, or 58.7 ÷ 4 years, gives a compound growth rate in net income of approximately 14.7%. This figure can also be estimated from compound interest tables by first determining the increase in net income for a period of years (72.5% in four years for International Corporation) and then determining the interest rate that would result in a compound amount of 1 of 1.725 over the four-year period.[2]

Analytical objectives

The outcome of business decisions (to buy or sell a company's securities or to extend or refuse to extend credit, for example) naturally depends on future events. Financial statements are essentially a record of the past. Outsiders, therefore, study financial statements as evidence of past performance which may be useful in making predictions of future performance. The management of an enterprise is responsible for earning as large a return as possible on the resources invested in the business, consistent with the objectives of maintaining a sound

[2] Net income for Year 5 is approximately 173% of Year 1 net income, or 1.73 in terms of a decimal value. Compound interest tables show that $1 would accumulate to $1.69 in four years at 14%, or to $1.81 in four years at 16%. Since $1.73 is $\frac{4}{12}$ between $1.69 and $1.81, the interpolated compound growth rate would be 14% + $\frac{4}{12}$ of 2%, or approximately 14.7%.

financial condition, meeting social responsibilities, and conducting the business in accordance with high ethical standards. Insofar as the attainment of these objectives can be measured quantitatively—and quantitative information is usually only a part of the basis for any decision—financial statements provide useful information.

In looking at past performance and present position, the financial analyst seeks answers to two primary questions: (1) What is the company's earnings performance? and (2) is the company in sound financial condition? We can therefore examine the process of analysis within the framework of these two questions.

ANALYSIS OF EARNINGS PERFORMANCE

Unfortunately an outsider usually does not have access to many of the important details that lie behind reported net income. Most published income statements are highly condensed. The outsider usually must content himself with a general review of the relationship between revenue, total operating expenses, and net income. This usually requires a careful analysis of gross profit percentages and *operating expense ratios* (total operating expenses divided by net sales) over a period of years. Also, the outsider will look carefully at any items of nonoperating revenue and expense and extraordinary items in order to forecast the likely earning power of a company.

Net income and accounting practices

The point has been made throughout this text that the amount of net income reported in a given period can be materially affected by the accounting practices followed. These practices are selected by management; the independent auditor simply informs readers that the accounting practices used are "in conformity with generally accepted accounting principles (standards) applied on a basis consistent with that of the preceding year." Unfortunately, a wide variety of principles or standards is considered "generally accepted" and the analyst must first determine the accounting practices used and then evaluate the effect of such practices on reported net income. In other words, the analyst is concerned with the *quality of reported earnings.*

In recent years significant progress has been made in reducing areas of differences in financial reporting, and additional steps are contemplated by authoritative bodies. An encouraging sign is the inclusion in annual reports of a description of the accounting policies used in the preparation of financial statements.[3] The accounting for depreciation, inventories, leases, pension plans, unconsolidated subsidiaries, mergers and acquisitions, and income taxes, for example, are especially sig-

[3] *APB Opinion No. 22, "Disclosure of Accounting Policies,"* AICPA (New York: 1972).

nificant to the analyst. In addition, the notes accompanying financial statements provide useful information on these and other accounting and reporting matters.

Trend in earnings

The analysis of income performance should always cover several periods not only because of the difficulty of measuring income year by year, but also because it is important to know how a company performs in periods of both prosperity and adversity. Net income may be satisfactory in one year and shrink to nothing in the next because of unfavorable business conditions.

One of the first things an analyst looks for is the trend of revenue over a period of years. A rising trend of sales is usually a sign of an expanding company. Obviously the revenue trend is not the whole story, since a growth in sales volume is not always accompanied by a corresponding increase in net income. The ideal situation is to find a company maintaining a constant or increasing *rate* of net income on a rapidly growing sales volume.

The pattern of revenue and operating earnings throughout the business cycle is also an important factor. There is obviously greater risk in investing in or lending to a firm whose income varies widely with changes in business conditions, than in a company able to show **stability** of earnings throughout all phases of the business cycle. A firm that must cut back its operations severely during recessions inevitably suffers in terms of such factors as effective product planning and employee morale and may find it difficult to cover fixed expenses. Furthermore, earnings tend to sag faster than revenue because of the presence of fixed expenses. Investors are interested in identifying a **cyclical** company not only because the risk of investment is higher, but because the timing of their investment will depend on the company's performance in relation to cyclical trends. The shifts to **defensive stocks** (stocks of companies that perform well in all phases of the business cycle) when a recession is in the offing and to cyclical shares at the first sign of an upturn is a well-known investment strategy.

Return on investment

Businessmen invest capital with the objective of earning a satisfactory return. The rate that is earned depends on numerous factors, including the nature of competition and the risks inherent in the business. Management is often evaluated in terms of the rate it is able to earn on invested capital. Although outsiders cannot determine return on the investment for particular divisions or segments of a business, they can make some overall estimates of rate of return. This rate can serve as a valuable index in evaluating the relative standing of a particular company and the quality of its management.

The return on investment for any period is determined by dividing net income by average investment. The appropriate income figure to be used depends on the related concept of investment. This is illustrated below.

Appropriate income figure		*Concept of investment (in all cases an average for the period covered by the income figure)*
1 *Return on total assets:*		
Net income	÷	total assets
2 *Return on long-term capital:*		
Net income + interest on long-term debt	÷	total assets less current liabilities
3 Return on stockholders' equity:		
a Net income	÷	total stockholders' equity
b Net income applicable to common stock	÷	common stockholders' equity

In all cases net income should exclude any extraordinary items, and the investment would be computed as an average for the period. Computations 1 and 2 provide related measurements. Ratio 1 is a measure of the earnings (after income taxes and interest) that relate to the total resources under the control of the firm. It would be possible to add interest expense back to net income in order to arrive at an approximation of earnings before payment of interest to creditors but after income taxes. Some analysts prefer to compute return on total assets **before income taxes,** in which case a ratio of operating income to total assets is used. If total assets include some unproductive assets, bond sinking funds, or long-term investments, these assets and the related earnings generated by these assets may be excluded from rate of return computations.

Ratio 2 is a measure of return (after taxes) on long-term capital, reflecting the view that the portion of total assets financed by current liabilities should not be included in the investment base, since most of the cost of short-term financing is included in operating expenses (as a part of prices paid for goods and services) and is not stated as a separate item.

Ratio 3 is computed from the viewpoint of stockholders, and the alternatives (**3a** or **3b**) depend on whether the analyst is interested in the rate of return on total stockholders' equity or on common stockholders' equity.

The data for Barker Company at the top of page 1056 (given in millions of dollars) will be used to compute these returns on investment ratios.

Income statement data			Balance sheet data			
	Year 2	**Year 1**		**Year 2**	**Year 1**	**Year 0**
Sales	$130	$ 95	Current assets . .	$19	$20	$18
Other revenue . .	10	5				
Total revenue .	$140	$100	Less: Current			
			liabilities	6	10	9
Cost of goods			Working capital .	$13	$10	$ 9
sold	$ 95	$ 65				
Operating			Noncurrent assets	61	60	56
expenses . . .	26	20				
Interest expense .	1	1	Total	$74	$70	$65
Income tax						
expense	9	7	Long-term debt .	$19	$20	$21
Total expenses .	$131	$ 93	Preferred stock .	16	16	16
Net income . . .	$ 9	$ 7	Common stock-			
Preferred stock			holders' equity .	39	34	28
dividends . . .	1	1				
Available for			Total long-term			
common stock	$ 8	$ 6	capital	$74	$70	$65

The return on investment ratios described in the outline on page 1055 are computed below (all dollar figures are stated in millions):

Return on investment	Computation	
	Year 2	**Year 1**
1 Return on total assets	$\dfrac{\$9}{\frac{1}{2}(\$80 + \$80)} = \dfrac{\$9}{\$80} = 11.2\%$	$\dfrac{\$7}{\frac{1}{2}(\$80 + \$74)} = \dfrac{\$7}{\$77} = 9.1\%$
2 Return on long-term capital . . .	$\dfrac{\$9 + \$1}{\frac{1}{2}(\$74 + \$70)} = \dfrac{\$10}{\$72} = 13.9\%$	$\dfrac{\$7 + \$1}{\frac{1}{2}(\$70 + \$65)} = \dfrac{\$8}{\$67.5} = 11.9\%$
3 a Return on total stockholders' equity	$\dfrac{\$9}{\frac{1}{2}(\$55 + \$50)} = \dfrac{\$9}{\$52.5} = 17.1\%$	$\dfrac{\$7}{\frac{1}{2}(\$50 + \$44)} = \dfrac{\$7}{\$47} = 14.9\%$
b Return on common stockholders' equity	$\dfrac{\$8}{\frac{1}{2}(\$39 + \$34)} = \dfrac{\$8}{\$36.5} = 21.9\%$	$\dfrac{\$6}{\frac{1}{2}(\$34 + \$28)} = \dfrac{\$6}{\$31} = 19.4\%$

Interpreting Return on Investment All four measures of return on investment for the Barker Company show an improved performance in the second year. If we look at the underlying factors—the revenue generated per dollar of investment (or asset turnover rate) and the net income per dollar of revenue—we can obtain some additional insight:

	Year 2	Year 1
Revenue generated per dollar of assets:		
$\dfrac{\text{Total revenue}}{\text{Average investment (total assets)}}$	$\dfrac{\$140}{\$80} = \$1.75$	$\dfrac{\$100}{\$77} = \$1.30$
Net income per dollar of revenue:		
$\dfrac{\text{Net income}}{\text{Total revenue}}$	$\dfrac{\$9}{\$140} = 6.4\%$	$\dfrac{\$7}{\$100} = 7.0\%$

Although the firm earned a smaller margin of income per dollar of total revenue in the second year, it was able to improve its volume of revenue per dollar of investment from $1.30 to $1.75. This ratio may be referred to as the *asset turnover* rate and can be used to verify the rates of return on total assets as follows:

Year 2: $1.75 × 6.4% = 11.2 cent per dollar of assets, or 11.2%
Year 1: $1.30 × 7.0% = 9.1 cents per dollar of assets, or 9.1%

What we have done here is simply multiply the rate earned on revenue by the asset turnover rate in order to measure the earnings rate on assets. This concept is really a truism: If a profit of 3%, for example, can be earned on sales and $10 of sales is generated by each $1 of assets, then the rate earned on assets would be 10 × 3%, or 30%.

Trading on the Equity When a business unit borrows money for long-term purposes, it is said to be *trading on the equity.* The results from trading on the equity can be favorable or unfavorable to common stockholders. If the rate earned before interest and income taxes on total assets is greater than the interest rate paid for the use of money, the common stockholders will gain; if the interest rate is higher than the earnings rate on assets, then a loss arises from trading on the equity. Issuance of preferred stock produces similar results but is more "expensive" to the common stockholders because dividends on preferred stock are not deductible in computing taxable income.

The fact that the return on stockholders' equity for Barker Company is higher than the return on total assets is significant. The firm is successfully trading on the equity, that is, the total of interest on bonds and dividends on preferred stock is less than the earnings on capital raised through these *senior securities* (bonds payable and preferred stock). The company has about $20 million in long-term debt at an interest cost of about 5% before income taxes and $2\frac{1}{2}$% after income taxes, and it has $16 million in preferred stock paying dividends of approximately 6.3% ($1 ÷ $16). The company earned 11.2% after income taxes on its total assets during Year 2. Therefore, an average dollar furnished by issuance of senior securities earns considerably more than the fixed interest and dividends. This excess accrues to the common stockholders, resulting in a 21.9% rate earned on common stockholders' equity in Year 2 and 19.4% in Year 1.

Earnings and dividends per share

Since stockholders think in terms of the number of shares they own or plan to buy or sell, reducing corporate financial information to per-share terms puts it in a useful perspective for stockholders. Perhaps the most commonly used statistics relating to common stock are *earnings (or loss) per share* and dividends per share. These appear widely in financial press releases, prospectuses, proxy material, and reports to stockholders.

Comparative earnings per share data, supported by complete financial statements, can be useful in evaluating the performance of a company from the common stockholders' point of view. There is little doubt that earnings (or loss) per share is a highly significant summary figure, but it has some serious limitations and there are some dangers in focusing too much attention on this single index of performance.

The manner of computing and reporting of earnings per share has been a major concern not only of the accounting profession but also of the SEC and the major stock exchanges. The technical aspects of computing and reporting *primary* and *fully diluted* earnings per share are illustrated in Chapter 20.

Dividends on capital stock represent historical facts and should be reported at amounts actually paid, except in cases following stock splits or large stock dividends. In such cases, "the presentation of dividends per share should be in terms of the current equivalent number of shares outstanding at the time of the dividend, so that the earnings and dividends per share will be reported on a comparable basis. When dividends per share are presented on other than a historical basis, the basis of presentation should be disclosed."[4]

---

[4] *APB Opinion No. 9*, "Reporting the Results of Operations," AICPA (New York: 1966), p. 126.

Price-Earnings Ratio and Dividend Yield Investors in corporate securities are more interested in earnings and dividends in relation to the *market value* of their shares than in relation to the *book value* (see Chapter 20) of their stock interest, because market value measures the amount of money they forego at any given time by a decision to continue to hold the stock. To illustrate, suppose that John Adams owns one share of common stock in a company that currently earns $5 per share and pays a dividend of $2 per share. The book value of the stock is $40 per share and the current market price is $50. The fact that the company is earning a return of 12½% on stockholders' equity ($5 ÷ $40) is of secondary interest to Adams, since he gives up the use of $50 by the decision to own this share. Thus Adams views this investment as one producing an *earnings yield* of 10%($5 ÷ $50) and a *dividend yield* of only 4% ($2 ÷ $50). In investment circles the earnings yield is usually expressed in reverse as a *price-earnings ratio*[5] of 10 to 1 ($50 ÷ $5).

Intelligent investors watch carefully the relation between earnings, dividends, and the market prices of stock and seek to evaluate these relationships by analyzing the financial data available to them. The data below show these relationships for three companies.

	Company C	Company D	Company E
Earnings per share	$1.00	$2.50	$5.00
Dividends per share	$0.80	$1.50	$1.20
Market price per share during the year:			
High	$ 20	$ 52	$ 162
Low	$ 8	$ 36	$ 105
End	$ 12	$ 50	$ 150
Price-earnings ratio (year-end)	12–1	20–1	30–1
Dividend yield on market price at the end			
of the year	6.7%	3.0%	0.8%

This divergence in price-earnings and yield ratios (an even wider spread often exists among listed stocks) suggests that investors assess the risk and future prospects of these three investments in quite different terms. Company C, for example, may be a marginal producer in its industry with highly volatile earnings performance and low growth prospects. As a result, its stock sells at a low price-earnings ratio and

[5] The price-earnings ratios generally are determined using the primary earnings per share for the latest 12 months, excluding extraordinary items. Starting in October 1972, the price-earnings ratios for stocks traded on the New York and American Stock Exchanges have been reported in most daily newspapers, along with the annual price range, the daily high and low prices, the closing price, and the net price change from the previous day's closing price.

yields a fairly generous 6.7%. The stock of Company D sells at a much higher multiple of earnings and yields only 3% since a small proportion of current earnings is distributed to stockholders. Company E, on the other hand, appears to be a "growth company"; the price-earnings ratio for its stock is 30 to 1, yield is below 1%, and less than 25% of the current income is distributed to stockholders.

An investor who tries to determine whether the market price of a share of stock is reasonable must consider a variety of factors. All, however, relate to an estimate of the ultimate return on investment; this return will depend on the dividends received during the time the shares are held and the price obtained when the stock is sold, both of which are difficult to project with any degree of precision.

Earnings and Fixed Charges A company that finances its operations through long-term debt or preferred stock is committed to pay a fixed return to the holders of these securities. The commitment on long-term debt is clearly stronger than on preferred stock, since in the latter case the obligation is only that preferred dividends will be paid before any dividends on common are declared. A company that *passes* a preferred dividend has impaired its financial reputation to some degree, but a company that passes a bond interest payment is in serious financial trouble.

Bondholders and preferred stockholders have learned from experience that the relationships between earnings and dividend and fixed interest commitments are a good measure of the safety of their investment. The following information is used to illustrate two ratios commonly calculated to measure these relationships:

	Company F	Company G
Operating income	$600,000	$900,000
Less: Interest on long-term debt	200,000	100,000
Income before income tax expense	$400,000	$800,000
Less: Income tax expense	200,000	400,000
Net income	$200,000	$400,000
Less: Preferred dividends	50,000	200,000
Net income available to common stockholders	$150,000	$200,000

Times interest earned The times interest earned ratio may be computed in two ways as shown at the top of page 1061.

Since interest expense is deductible in arriving at taxable income, logic would seem to be on the side of method 1. Business managers and investors are strongly conditioned to an after-tax view of corporate

	Company F	Company G
Method 1: Times interest earned before income taxes:		
(a) *Operating income*	$600,000	$900,000
(b) *Interest charges*	200,000	100,000
Times interest earned (a ÷ b)	3 times	9 times
Method 2: Times interest earned after income taxes:		
Net income	$200,000	$400,000
(a) *Add back interest charges*	200,000	100,000
(b) *Income before interest charges*	$400,000	$500,000
Times interest earned (b ÷ a)	2 times	5 times

affairs, however, which may explain why method 2 is usually found in practice. The after-tax computation will always result in a more conservative figure for coverage of interest charges.

Times preferred dividends earned The computation of the number of times preferred dividends are earned may also be made in two ways, as illustrated below:

	Company F	Company G
Method 1: Net income to preferred dividends:		
(a) *Net income*	$200,000	$400,000
(b) *Preferred dividend requirement*	$ 50,000	$200,000
Times preferred dividends earned (a ÷ b)	4 times	2 times

These ratios make it appear that F Company's preferred dividends are better protected by earnings than its bond interest; yet bond interest obviously has a prior claim. To overcome this objection, the test of preferred dividend safety most often encountered is the number of times that *the combined interest charges and preferred dividends* are earned. The computations for these two companies appear at the top of page 1062.

"Times-earned" ratios are of interest not only to creditors and preferred stockholders but also to common stockholders. Holders of common stock know that a company that has to omit either interest or preferred dividends will suffer financial embarrassment at the very least; furthermore, they are concerned about a sufficiency of earnings to allow for common dividends. There is little mystery in interpreting times-earned ratios—the higher the ratio the more favorable for bondholders and preferred stockholders. The more difficult question is: How

	Company F	Company G
Method 2: Times interest charges and preferred		
dividends are earned:		
Interest charges	$200,000	$100,000
Preferred dividend requirement	50,000	200,000
(a) Total interest and dividend requirements	$250,000	$300,000
(b) Net income (after taxes) plus interest charges . .	400,000	500,000
Number of times interest charges and preferred		
dividends are earned (b ÷ a)	1.6 times	1.7 times

high should the ratios be to satisfy these two groups without being detrimental to the common stockholders? In general, the answer to this question will depend on the stability of past and potential earnings over the business cycle; if earnings are stable, lower times-earned ratios can be viewed as satisfactory.

In analyzing financial statements, the coverage of fixed charges should logically be expanded to include *all* fixed obligations of the reporting entity. A company must, for example, make regular payments on long-term leases, property taxes, and other relatively fixed commitments in addition to interest on long-term debt before dividends can be declared.[6] The ability of a business unit to generate sufficient revenue over variable expenses to cover fixed charges is one of the most important considerations to the analyst.

ANALYSIS OF FINANCIAL STRENGTH

A strong earnings record usually accompanies a strong financial position. Furthermore, an unsatisfactory financial position looks much less unfavorable in the face of a good earnings record; a company with proved earning power can usually work out its financial problems. Good earnings, however, is not the whole story. A company's ability to meet

[6] In computing the ratio of earnings to fixed charges, some companies have in the past deducted earnings on investments (interest and dividends earned) and gains on retirement of debt from the fixed charges. In *Accounting Series Release No. 119* (June 15, 1971), the Securities and Exchange Commission stated:

> The propriety of reducing fixed charges by amounts representing interest or investment income or gains on retirement of debt has been considered in the light of the purposes for which ratios of earnings to fixed charges are used and the Commission has determined that the reduction of fixed charges by the amount of either actual or imputed interest or investment income or debt retirement gains for the purpose of computing fixed charge ratios results in incorrect ratios and is therefore inappropriate. Accordingly, such reductions will no longer be deemed acceptable in registration statements or reports filed with the Commission.

its obligations, to weather adversity, to shift resources to meet changing conditions—in short, its financial strength, is an important factor to continuing survival and growth.

In seeking evidence of financial soundness, financial analysts look first at the relation between resources and obligations. They should ask questions such as: Will the company be able to meet its debts as they fall due? Has it the resources to meet current commitments and future demands for funds necessary to carry on the business successfully?

Ability to meet short-term obligations

A company's short-term financial strength is dependent on two primary factors: its working capital position and the speed with which it generates liquid assets.

The financial information for Company H shown on page 1064 will be used as a basis for discussion of these factors.

Working Capital Position The amount by which current assets exceed current liabilities is known as the *working capital* of a business. Changes in the amount of working capital from period to period are significant because working capital represents the margin of short-term debt-paying ability over short-term debt.

In addition to the dollar amount of working capital, two analytical indices of current position are often computed. The *current ratio* (current assets divided by current liabilities) helps put the amount of working capital in perspective by showing the relationship between current resources and short-term debt. The *quick ratio* (sometimes called the *acid-test ratio*) focuses on immediate liquidity. Inventories and short-term prepayments, the least liquid assets in the current asset category, are excluded from consideration in computing the quick ratio. Quick assets are defined as cash, marketable securities, and receivables, and the quick ratio is computed by dividing quick assets by current liabilities.

In terms of these three analytical measures, the current position of Company H is summarized at the bottom of page 1064.

Each of these three analytical measures contributes something to the whole picture. The company has maintained its working capital at about $500,000 during the three-year period. However, its relative short-term liquidity has worsened, as indicated by the steady decline in the current ratio from 2.1 to 1.4 and in the quick ratio from 1.0 to .5 during the three-year period. This is a picture of a company that may be heading into financial difficulty, unless these trends can be reversed. The growth of accounts payable from $170,000 to $680,000 during the last two years suggests that payments to creditors may be falling behind schedule. The analysis has thus brought to light a potential trouble spot in the firm's financial position. On the other hand, if the large increase in ac-

COMPANY H
Selected Financial Data
(in thousands of dollars)

	Year 3	Year 2	Year 1
Current assets:			
Cash	$ 50	$ 80	$ 60
Marketable securities	–0–	50	150
Receivables (net)	500	400	300
Inventory (fifo, cost)	1,100	700	500
Short-term prepayments	70	60	50
Total current assets	$1,720	$1,290	$1,060
Current liabilities:			
Notes payable	$ 120	$ 100	$ –0–
Accounts payable	680	330	170
Accrued liabilities	220	170	140
Current portion of long-term debt	180	200	200
Total current liabilities	$1,200	$ 800	$ 510
Net sales	$3,500	$3,000	$2,600
Cost of goods sold	(2,600)	(2,000)	(1,900)
Operating expenses	(600)	(500)	(400)
Interest on long-term debt	(48)	(49)	(50)
Income before income tax expense	$ 252	$ 451	$ 250
Income tax expense	122	231	125
Net income	$ 130	$ 220	$ 125

COMPANY H
Analysis of Current Position
(in thousands of dollars)

	Year 3	Year 2	Year 1
(a) Current assets	$1,720	$1,290	$1,060
(b) Current liabilities	1,200	800	510
Working capital (a – b)	$ 520	$ 490	$ 550
Current ratio (a ÷ b)	1.4	1.6	2.1
(c) Total quick assets (cash, marketable securities, and receivables)	$ 550	$ 530	$ 510
Quick ratio (c ÷ b)	.5	.7	1.0

counts payable is the result of large current expenditures for research and product development, or for inventories in anticipation of a sharp increase in sales, then the trend can be evaluated in a different light.

Need for Working Capital A business generates working capital through a series of events called the *operating cycle.* The operating cycle refers to the process of investing in inventories, converting these through sale into receivables, and transforming receivables by collection into cash, which is in turn used to pay current debts incurred for operating costs and to replace inventories. The average length of time necessary to complete this cycle is an important factor in determining a firm's working capital needs. A company with a very short operating cycle can manage comfortably on a relatively small amount of working capital and with relatively low quick and current ratios. A long operating cycle requires a larger margin of current assets and higher quick and current ratios unless the credit terms of suppliers can be extended accordingly. The average length of the operating cycle can be roughly estimated by adding the number of days' sales in average inventories to the average age of receivables.

Inventory turnover The total cost of all goods that have been moved out of inventories during the year is represented by the cost of goods sold figure on the income statement. Therefore the ratio of cost of goods sold to the average inventory during any period is a measure of the number of times that inventories turn over on the average and must be replaced. The higher this turnover ratio, the shorter the average time between investment in inventories and the sale transaction.

Average inventory should be determined by averaging monthly or quarterly inventory figures. This information is not usually available to external analysts, however, and therefore only an average of the inventory at the beginning and end of the year is ordinarily feasible. Because many companies adopt an accounting year that ends when inventories are at a minimum, inventory turnover computed in this manner may appear larger than it really is.

Dividing the annual cost of goods sold by average inventory produces a "times per year" turnover figure. Turnover may be expressed in days by dividing 365 by the number of turnovers per year.[7] An additional useful measure is the *number of days' sales in ending inventory,* computed by multiplying 365 days by the fraction of which the ending inventory is the numerator and cost of goods sold is the denominator. The three-year inventory analyses for Company H appear at the top of page 1066 (dollar figures are in thousands).

This computation shows that inventory turnover has slowed during the three-year period from a little over three months to about four

---

[7] A year is sometimes viewed as consisting of 300 business days in the computation of the number of days of sales in inventories or receivables.

	Year 3	Year 2	Year 1
(a) Cost of goods sold	$2,600	$2,000	$1,900
Inventory at beginning of year	$ 700	$ 500	$ 540*
Inventory at end of year . .	1,100	700	500
(b) Average inventory	$ 900	$ 600	$ 520
(c) Turnover per year (a ÷ b) . .	2.9 times	3.3 times	3.7 times
Number of days' sales in **average** inventory (365 ÷ c)	126 days	111 days	99 days
Number of days' sales in **ending** inventory	154 days	128 days	96 days

* Assumed

months, and that there is enough inventory on hand at the end of Year 3 to meet sales requirements at current levels for approximately five months (154 days).

For a manufacturing company, the overall inventory turnover can be estimated by dividing the cost of goods sold by the sum of the three inventories: materials, goods in process, and finished goods. A more precise computation would involve three separate turnover figures: (1) cost of goods sold divided by average finished goods inventory; (2) cost of goods manufactured divided by average goods in process inventory; and (3) materials used divided by average materials inventory.

It should be pointed out that the foregoing computations would be misleading if the replacement value of inventories were substantially higher than cost. In such cases, alternative measurements should be used to analyze the inventory position.

Receivables turnover The turnover of accounts receivable may be computed in a manner comparable to that just described for inventories. Unless a firm has a significant amount of cash sales, the total sales for any period represents the flow of claims into the receivable category. When the sales total is divided by the average balance of receivables during the period, the result is a rough indication of the average length of time necessary to convert receivables into cash. Ideally, only credit sales should be included in the sales figure, and an average monthly balance of **gross** receivables should be used. These refinements may not be possible in external analysis, however, and a less exact computation may serve the purpose of indicating favorable or unfavorable trends. The reasonableness of the ending balance in receivables may be evaluated by computing the **number of days' sales in receivables** at the end of the year. The receivables for Company H may be analyzed as follows (dollar figures are in thousands):

	Year 3	Year 2	Year 1
(a) Net sales	$3,500	$3,000	$2,600
Receivables at beginning of year	$ 400	$ 300	$ 280*
Receivables at end of year .	500	400	300
(b) Average receivables	$ 450	$ 350	$ 290
(c) Receivables turnover (a ÷ b)	7.8 times	8.6 times	9.0 times
Number of days' sales in **average** receivables (365 ÷ c)	47 days	42 days	41 days
Number of days' sales in **ending** receivables	52 days	49 days	42 days

* Assumed

It is evident that, barring a change in credit terms, collections have slowed down over the three-year period. The trend is obviously unfavorable; interpretation of the absolute figures depends on the credit terms and policies of the company.

Length of operating cycle By putting together the average days' sales in inventories and in receivables, we can obtain a rough estimate of the average length of the operating cycle for Company H as follows:

	Year 3	Year 2	Year 1
Average days to dispose of inventory	126	111	99
Average days to collect receivables	47	42	41
Average days in operating cycle	173	153	140

The operating cycle of this company has increased by more than a full month (33 days) from Year 1 to Year 3. If this has happened inadvertently, it may explain the unfavorable trend in the current and quick ratios. If the change is the result of deliberate company policy, it indicates the need for a greater amount of working capital to finance current operations.

Number of days' operations to cover working capital deficit When current liabilities exceed current assets, management may wish to estimate the length of time it would take to eliminate the working capital deficit from regular operations. For example, assume that the working capital for the Ross Company on March 31 shows a $20,000 deficit as shown at the top of page 1068.

Current assets	$ 60,000
Less: Current liabilities	80,000
Working capital deficit	$(20,000)

Assume further that the company's operations are relatively stable over a fiscal year and normally generate working capital as follows:

Net income for year	$ 75,000
Add: Depreciation and other expenses recognized during the year	
which do not require the use of working capital	45,000
Working capital normally provided by operations over 12-month period	$120,000

From the foregoing information management can determine that the working capital deficit will be covered in approximately two months, determined as follows:

$$\frac{\$20,00 \text{ (working capital deficit)}}{\$120,000 \text{ (annual working capital provided by operations)}} \times 365 \text{ days}$$

$$= 61 \text{ days}$$

Interpreting the analysis of current position

The following factors should be taken into account in interpreting the short-term position of a company as shown by the analytical procedures just described:

1 Creditors tend to adopt the view that the higher the current and quick ratios and the shorter the operating cycle, the better. From the viewpoint of company performance, there are upper limits. It is possible for a company to accumulate working capital in excess of the amount that can be profitably employed. Thus, excessive current and quick ratios are unfavorable indicators. Similarly, an unusually high rate of inventory turnover may indicate that a company is losing business by failing to maintain an adequate inventory to serve customers' needs. A rapid turnover of receivables may indicate overly severe credit policies that hold revenue below levels that could profitably be obtained by granting more liberal credit terms.

2 Because creditors and other outsiders place considerable emphasis on current position as evidence of short-run solvency, there is a temptation for managers to take steps just before statements are prepared to make current position appear better than it is. This process is called *window dressing.* By postponing purchases, allowing inventories to fall below normal levels, using all available cash to pay current liabilities, and pressing collections on accounts receivable, the current and quick ratios and inventory and re-

ceivable turnover ratios may be artificially improved. Decreases in receivable and inventory balances will raise turnover ratios. Any equal decrease in both current assets and current liabilities will improve a current ratio that is already greater than 1 to 1.

3 Even when no deliberate attempt has been made to present an artificially good picture, the current position shown on year-end statements is probably more favorable than at any other time of the year. This is particularly true when a company has adopted a **natural business year** that ends during an ebb in the seasonal swing of business activity. At times of peak activity receivables, inventories, and current liabilities tend to be at higher levels. There are, of course, many reasons why a natural business year is desirable, and accountants generally encourage companies to adopt such an accounting period. An analysis of current position based solely on year-end data will tend to overstate a company's average current position.

Analysis of capital structure

The way in which a firm has met its long-run financing needs is an important factor in assessing its financial strength. The important relationships in this area may be expressed, for analytical purposes, in several ways. One is to reduce the major elements of the equity side of the balance sheet to component percentages of total assets. Alternatively, we may concentrate on only the long-term sources of financing, known as the *capital structure* of a firm. The first approach is more widely used and is illustrated below:

Component percentages		*Debt and equity ratios*	
Total assets	100%	Debt ratio	28%
Sources of financing:		Equity ratio	72%
Current liabilities	10%	Debt to equity ratio (.28 ÷ .72)	39%
Long-term debt	18%		
Total debt	28%		
Preferred stock	9%		
Common stockholders' equity	63% 72%		
Total liabilities & stockholders' equity	100%		

Debt and Equity Ratios Analysts often condense the essence of the capital structure of a company into any one of three ratios. The *debt ratio* is the ratio of total debt to total assets; the *equity ratio* is the ratio of stockholders' equity to total assets; the *debt to equity ratio* is the ratio of total liabilities to stockholders' equity. Any one of these three ratios tells the essential story about the debt-equity relationship for any company, and the choice among them is a matter of personal preference.

Financial analysts compute other ratios to aid them in evaluating capital structure. For example, the ratio of total plant assets to stockholders' equity is sometimes used as a test of the adequacy of equity capital. If the investment in plant assets is high relative to stockholders' equity, this indicates that a company has borrowed heavily to invest in non-liquid assets, which may lead to difficulties should earnings not prove satisfactory.

Book value per share of stock, which was discussed in detail in Chapter 20, is a significant indicator of stockholders' investment in company assets. It should be recognized, however, that book value may have very little relationship either to the *intrinsic value* or to the current market price of stock.

Evaluating capital structure

Whatever ratios are used to establish capital structure relationships, the important question is the significance of the findings. What factors should be considered in evaluating the capital structure of a company?

Creditors' View   Creditors are primarily concerned with the safety of their capital. They view a relatively low debt ratio as a favorable factor because it indicates a substantial cushion of protection against a shrinkage in asset values. Since ultimate repayment of debt will come from either new borrowing or internal cash flow, all creditors are interested in long-run financial strength and a healthy earnings picture. The debt ratio and the times-interest-earned ratio are the prime indices of financial strength from the creditors' viewpoint.

As was pointed out in Chapter 16, the use of long-term leases as a method of financing has increased substantially in recent years. Frequently such leases are a substitute for other forms of long-term borrowing, and their existence should be carefully considered in evaluating capital structure.

Stockholders' View   Present or prospective stockholders are concerned with the company's ability to meet its long-term obligations, because failure to pay interest charges or meet maturities of debt is a serious matter affecting adversely both the credit standing of the company and the stockholders' interest. A very low debt ratio, or the absence of long-term debt, however, is not necessarily to the stockholders' advantage. To the extent that a company can earn a return in excess of the interest rate paid on long-term obligations, the stockholders' gain from the leverage factor inherent in a fixed commitment. However, this gain may be offset by the increased risk of bankruptcy and the subjective costs of the various protective covenants put into the debt contract by the lender, which may limit management's freedom of action.

It has been argued that the existence of long-term debt or other senior securities increases the risk borne by owners of the common stock and causes the stock to sell at a lower price-earnings ratio. In a well-managed and profitable firm, it is doubtful whether a reasonable amount of debt increases the common shareholders' risk sufficiently to be reflected in the price-earnings ratio. If the amount of long-term debt is excessive and earnings are not growing, it is likely that the advantage of increased trading on the equity will be offset by the dampening effect of the large debt on the price of common stock.

Capacity for additional investment and growth in earnings

A company is seldom able to maintain a stable position over a long period of time; it either changes and grows, or stagnates and dies. A healthy company must be able to finance the development of new products and customers as the old ones lose their profit potential, and to move in new directions as demand and technology change. An important element of financial strength is the ability to generate additional funds when they are needed.

In part this means the ability to borrow or to issue additional stock. A primary source of industrial growth in recent years, however, has been through the retention of earnings. Furthermore, because of the existence of expenses that are not a current drain on working capital, most businesses typically generate more working capital each period than the amount of net income (see Chapter 24). The amount of working capital provided by operations, less dividend and sinking fund requirements, offers a rough indicator of the internally generated funds available to expand the level of operations (build plant capacity, develop new products or markets, etc.) or to retire long-term debt.

Standards for comparison in analysis

When analysts have computed the significant dollar and percentage changes and ratios and has otherwise reduced the mass of financial data to digestible form, they need some criteria as a guide in evaluating these findings and in making decisions. Three possibilities are discussed in the following sections.

Past Record of the Company A comparison of analytical data over time (sometimes called *horizontal analysis,* in contrast to *vertical analysis* which deals with single-year financial statements) may reveal trends in performance and position that will aid in determining progress or lack of progress and may help in assessing future prospects. Many companies present trends in sales, earnings, and other data in graphic form. As a basis for forecasting, the projecting of past trends into the future has serious limitations, since changes may reverse direction at any time. However, knowing that the trend is favorable or unfavorable leads to further inquiry as to the underlying reasons.

Another limitation of horizontal analysis is that the past does not afford a basis for comparison with similarly situated companies. For example, if the sales of a company have increased 10% but industry sales have increased 50%, the 10% increase looks favorable but the company's sales performance in its industry is relatively poor.

Comparison with Competitors or Industry as a Whole Perhaps the best way to put a company's performance in perspective is to compare its position and operating results with those of similar firms. For example, a study by Dun & Bradstreet, Inc., of the financial statements of 52 drug manufacturers for a recent year showed the following:

	Current ratio	Net profits on net sales	Return on owners' investment	Total debt to owners' equity	Net sales to inventory (times)
Upper quartile . . .	3.5	11.3%	20.4%	35.8%	9.1
Median	2.6	6.8	15.4	43.5	6.3
Lower quartile . .	1.8	2.9	5.5	63.6	4.6

On the basis of this kind of information, an analyst examining the financial statements of a drug manufacturing firm could get some idea of the position of the firm in relation to others in the industry. Note that Dun & Bradstreet, Inc., computes the inventory activity by dividing net sales by the inventory figure. Although this is often done by financial analysts as a matter of convenience, this procedure does not give a turnover figure but simply relates the average level of inventory (at cost) to the sales volume for the year (at selling prices).

One of the difficulties in interfirm comparisons is that some companies that appear to be in the same industry are not in fact comparable. Industries are often difficult to define. Many companies have diversified their activities by moving into new fields or acquiring other companies whose business is not closely related, with the result that companies falling roughly within the same industry are no longer comparable in many respects. When such **diversified companies** report product line sales and net income figures, it is much easier to analyze their results in the major areas in which they operate.

Financial Reporting for Segments of a Business Enterprise In 1976 the FASB issued **Statement No. 14,** which established standards for disclosure of information about the reporting entity's operations in different industries, its foreign operations and export sales, and its major customers.[8] **FASB Statement No. 14** also required that a company operating

[8] *FASB Statement No. 14,* ''Financial Reporting for Segments of a Business Enterprise,'' FASB (Stamford: 1976), p. 1.

predominantly or exclusively in a single industry identify that industry. The information to be reported for each significant industry segment includes: revenue, profitability, identifiable assets, and other related disclosures such as depreciation and capital expenditures. A *significant industry segment* is one which: (1) includes 10% or more of the combined identifiable assets of the company; or (2) generates 10% or more of the company's revenue; or (3) generates 10% or more of the company's operating income or loss. The purpose of disclosing segment information is to assist users of financial statements in analyzing and understanding the company's past performance and future prospects.[9]

Comparison and Independent Statistical Measures It is often useful to relate certain financial indices for a firm to statistical measures. For example, comparing the trend of sales or net income with an *index of industrial production* may show whether a firm is growing more slowly or faster than the economy. Similarly, indices may be developed for sales and net income, for example, comparing the performance of a single company to the industry performance index during the same period. Price indices may be used to deflate sales figures to determine whether the growth in sales is a growth in physical volume or the result of price increases. It may also be possible to relate financial data to physical measures of production or output. For example, in analyzing railroads, such statistics as the average freight haul in miles per ton, or the average revenue per ton-mile, give a useful basis for comparing the operating performance of different railroads.

Inflation and analysis of financial statements

Financial statements prepared in terms of historical costs do not fully reflect the economic resources or the *real* income (in terms of purchasing power) of a business enterprise. Financial analysts should therefore attempt to evaluate the impact of inflation on the financial position and results of operations of the business they are evaluating. They should raise questions such as: How much of the income can be attributed to price increases? Are expenses (such as depreciation) understated in terms of current price levels? Is the company gaining or losing from inflation because of the composition of its assets and the amount of its liabilities? Financial statements adjusted for price-level changes are illustrated in Chapter 22.

Summary of ratios and other analytical measurements

The more widely used ratios and other measurements discussed in this chapter and their significance are summarized on pages 1074 and 1075.

The relevance of any of the foregoing measurements depends on the direction of its trend and on its relationship to some predetermined

[9] Ibid., p. 2.

Ratio or other measurement	Method of computation	Significance
1 Return on total assets	$$\frac{\textit{Net income} + \textit{interest expense}}{\textit{Average investment in assets}}$$	Measures the productivity of assets.
2 Return on common stockholders' equity	$$\frac{\textit{Net income} - \textit{preferred dividends}}{\textit{Average common stockholders' equity}}$$	Indicates the earning power on common stockholders' equity.
3 Earnings per share	$$\frac{\textit{Net income} - \textit{preferred dividends}}{\textit{Shares of common outstanding}}$$	Gives the amount of earnings applicable to a share of common stock.
4 Price-earnings ratio	$$\frac{\textit{Market price per share}}{\textit{Earnings per share}}$$	Indicates whether price of common stock is in line with earnings.
5 Dividend yield	$$\frac{\textit{Dividend per share}}{\textit{Market price per share}}$$	Shows the return to stockholders based on current price of stock.
6 Book value per share of common stock	$$\frac{\textit{Common stockholders' equity}}{\textit{Shares of common outstanding}}$$	Measures net assets, as reported in the accounts, applicable to each share of common stock.
7 Number of times interest earned (before income taxes)	$$\frac{\textit{Operating income}}{\textit{Annual interest expense}}$$	Measures the coverage of interest charges (particularly on long-term debt) before income taxes.

	Ratio or other measurement	Method of computation	Significance
8	Times preferred dividends earned	$\dfrac{\text{Net income}}{\text{Annual preferred dividends}}$	Shows the adequacy of current earnings to pay preferred dividends.
9	Current ratio	$\dfrac{\text{Current assets}}{\text{Current liabilities}}$	Measures short-run debt-paying ability.
10	Quick (acid test) ratio	$\dfrac{\text{Quick assets}}{\text{Current liabilities}}$	Measures short-term liquidity.
11	Inventory turnover	$\dfrac{\text{Cost of goods sold}}{\text{Average inventory}}$	Indicates management's ability to control the investment in inventory.
12	Receivables turnover	$\dfrac{\text{Net sales on credit}}{\text{Average receivables}}$	Indicates reasonableness of accounts receivable balance and effectiveness of collections.
13	Debt ratio	$\dfrac{\text{Total liabilities}}{\text{Total assets}}$	Shows the percentage of assets financed through borrowing and the extent of trading on the equity.
14	Equity ratio	$\dfrac{\text{Total stockholders' equity}}{\text{Total assets}}$	Shows the protection to creditors and the extent of trading on the equity.
15	Debt to equity ratio	$\dfrac{\text{Total debt}}{\text{Total stockholders' equity}}$	Indicates relationship between borrowed capital and capital invested by stockholders.

standard. The information available in financial statements can be of great value in appraising the financial position, in forecasting the earnings power, and in making other predictive judgments about a business entity. Relationships among reported data can be extremely informative. However, we must remember that financial statements have limitations and that intangible and qualitative factors may be far more important. For example, factors such as the following cannot be ignored by analysts in forecasting the likely earnings performance of a company: (1) Source of markets for the company's products or services; (2) growth potential for the company's products or services; (3) company's market share in its industry; (4) patent protection, if any, for major products; (5) sensitivity to economic fluctuations; and (6) effect of technological and environmental changes on the company's business.

Analysts should keep in mind that although the balance sheet is a statement of assets and claims against these assets, most assets are stated at historical cost and not all elements of value are included in the balance sheet (for example, good management, good credit standing, potential new products, internally developed goodwill, appreciation in the value of natural resources). Furthermore, the **quality of the reported assets** must be carefully evaluated. The income statement, on the other hand, is a product of matching historical costs with realized revenue and covers only a brief period of a company's life. In short, the income statement does not necessarily measure the **improvement in the company's economic wealth.** The dangers of attaching too much significance either to the balance sheet or to the income statement should be clearly recognized by those analyzing financial statements.

REVIEW QUESTIONS

1 Describe four sources from which an outsider might obtain financial information about a business.

2 Explain what is meant by the following terms:
    a Trend percentage   *d* Capital structure
    b Common size statements   *e* Growth companies
    c Trading on the equity   *f* Price-earnings ratio

3 a Discuss some inherent limitations of single-year financial statements for purposes of analysis and interpretation.
    b To what extent are these limitations overcome by the use of comparative statements?
    c In what possible ways can a 10-year summary of financial data be misleading?

4 Describe the effect of each of the transactions listed below on the indicated ratios. Will the ratio increase, decrease, or remain unchanged?

Transactions	Ratio
a Purchase of merchandise for cash	**a** Current ratio of 2 to 1
b Payment of accounts payable	**b** Quick ratio of .6 to 1
c Accounts receivable written off against Allowance for Doubtful Accounts	**c** Average age of accounts receivable of 60 days
d Declaration of cash dividend on preferred stock	**d** Equity ratio of 60%
e Distribution of a 10% stock dividend	**e** Loss per share of common stock, $1.20
f Conversion of long-term debt into common stock	**f** Return on total long-term capital
g Change from fifo to lifo during period of rising prices	**g** Inventory turnover

5 The following ratios have been suggested at one time or another by financial analysts. Briefly explain what each ratio indicates about a business and why you think it has or lacks significance.
   a Ratio of plant assets to long-term debt
   b Ratio of sales to working capital (working capital turnover)
   c Ratio of current liabilities to inventory
   d Ratio of total operating expenses to current liabilities
   e Ratio of plant assets to stockholders' equity
   f Ratio of long-term debt to working capital
   g Ratio of net sales to stockholders' equity
   h Ratio of net income to current assets

6 In analyzing the position and performance of a company it is necessary to have some standards or criteria for comparison. Suggest several standards which may be employed.

7 An estimate of inventory turnover is sometimes made by dividing net sales by average inventory. What is wrong with this method of computing inventory turnover?

8 Two companies have the same amount of working capital. The current debt-paying ability of one company is much weaker than the other. Explain how this could occur.

9 Explain how you would determine the ability of a given company to meet payments on long-term debt or to finance replacements of plant assets, assuming that you had available financial statements for the last five years.

10 If you were asked to choose three analytical computations (ratios, percentages, etc.) that would be of greatest use in appraising the financial statements of a company from the viewpoint of the following parties, which computations would you make, and why do you feel these are of prime importance?
   a Short-term creditor
   b Long-term creditor
   c Prospective purchaser of preferred stock
   d Prospective purchaser of common stock

11 In response to a request that its **profit margins on different products** be disclosed, the management of Panorama Products Company responded, "Public disclosure would cause us to suffer at the hands of our principal competitors, particularly in regard to one product which accounts for 90% of our sales." In what ways could the disclosure of product line information possibly be detrimental to Panorama Products Company?

12 The following comments are derived from an article in a financial journal:

> In seeking "textbook ratios" between current assets and current liabilities, some companies may be going overboard on building up cash, the vice president, finance, of an oil company stated. The official expressed the view that these ratios may not mean much any more.
>
> "In the old days, when these ratios were established, credit facilities weren't so readily available as they are today", the official stated. "There are elements of liquidity that don't show up on the balance sheet, such as a contractual line of bank credit, which may be just as solid as a savings account. But to some extent," the official concluded, "we're stuck with archaic ratios that the investment community likes to see."

Comment on the observations made by the oil company official.

13 In *FASB Statement No. 14,* "Financial Reporting for Segments of a Business Enterprise," the FASB established standards for disclosure of information about the reporting entity's operations in different industries, its foreign operations and export sales, and its major customers. Define a *significant industry segment* and indicate the type of information that should be reported for each such segment.

EXERCISES

Ex. 25-1 Kerrigan Company has the following capital structure (in millions): 5% bonds, $12.5; 6% preferred stock, $30.0; common stock (paid-in capital and retained earnings), $50.0. The average rate of return on long-term capital (after income taxes but before interest expense) is 8%. Compute the amount of earnings available for common stockholders.

Ex. 25-2 Seacrest Corporation reported earnings per share last year at $4.50 on 100,000 shares of stock outstanding. On April 1 of the current year, the company declared a 50% stock dividend and on October 1 issued 60,000 shares of stock for cash. Net income for the current year was $353,000. What is the amount of increase or decrease in earnings per share over last year?

Ex. 25-3 A partial list of trend and common size percentages for Munich Pie Company for Years 1 and 2 is shown below:

	Year 2	Year 1
Trend percentages:		
Sales (net)	120%	100%
Cost of goods sold	?	100
Gross profit on sales	?	100
Operating expenses and income taxes	?	100
Net income	?	100

Common size percentages:

Sales (net)	100%	100%
Cost of goods sold	?	?
Gross profit on sales	45%	?%
Operating expenses and income taxes	27.5	30
Net income	?%	10%

a Compute the missing trend and common size percentages.
b If the net income in Year 1 amounted to $10,000, compute the net income for Year 2.

Ex. 25-4 Information for Naples Tuna Company is presented below:

	Year 2	Year 1
Cash	$ 20,000	$ 30,000
Accounts receivable (net)	60,000	40,000
Inventories	45,000	35,000
Plant assets (net)	235,000	185,000
Total	$360,000	$290,000
Accounts payable	$ 50,000	$ 40,000
6% bonds payable	100,000	100,000
Capital stock, $5 par	130,000	100,000
Retained earnings	80,000	50,000
Total	$360,000	$290,000
Sales (all on account)	$180,000	$120,000
Cost of goods sold	100,000	70,000
Gross profit on sales	$ 80,000	$ 50,000
Operating expenses and income tax expense	50,000	30,000
Net income	$ 30,000	$ 20,000

Compute each of the following for Year 2:
a Quick (acid-test) ratio.
b Number of days' sales in accounts receivable at year-end. Assume a 365-day year.
c Inventory turnover.
d Book value per share of capital stock at year-end.
e Number of days' sales in inventories at year-end. Assume a 365-day year.

Ex. 25-5 The information on page 1080 (in thousands of dollars) for three companies is presented to you at the end of Year 10.

	Moe Company	Noe Company	Ohl Company
Total assets	$140,000	$140,000	$140,000
Current liabilities	$ 20,000	$ 50,000	$ 20,000
8% bonds payable, due in Year 15	40,000		
6% bonds payable, due in Year 20		10,000	
8% bonds payable, due in Year 22			80,000
Stockholders' equity	80,000	80,000	40,000
Total liabilities & stockholders'			
equity	$140,000	$140,000	$140,000
Net income	$ 14,000	$ 12,600	$ 9,800

Compute the following for each company:

a Number of times interest was earned (before income taxes). Assume income tax rate is 50%.

b Rate earned on ending stockholders' equity.

c Rate earned on total assets at end of year (before interest expense and income taxes of 50%).

Ex. 25-6 Following are financial statements of Cardinal Sign Company, a retail business. Dollar amounts are given in thousands of dollars:

CARDINAL SIGN COMPANY
Comparative Balance Sheets
December 31

Assets	Year 2	Year 1
Cash	$ 7,000	$ 4,000
Marketable securities	2,000	4,000
Accounts receivable (net)	13,000	9,000
Inventory	9,000	7,000
Buildings and equipment (net)	69,000	66,000
Total assets	$100,000	$90,000

Liabilities & Stockholders' Equity		
Current liabilities	$ 14,000	$16,000
Bonds payable, due in Year 15	24,000	20,000
Common stock, $10 par	30,000	30,000
Retained earnings	32,000	24,000
Total liabilities & stockholders' equity	$100,000	$90,000

Sales for Year 2 were $100 million and cost of goods sold amounted to $58 million. Other items from the income statement for Year 2 are: Interest expense, $2 million; income taxes, $10 million; and net income, $12 million.

Show how you would compute the following ratios (or measurements) for Year 2 by determining the appropriate dollar amounts (or other figures) to be used in computing each item. (You need not perform the division.)

Example: Debt ratio . . . . $38,000 ÷ $100,000
  a Current ratio
  b Quick (acid-test) ratio
  c Times interest earned (before income taxes)
  d Rate of gross profit on sales
  e Earnings per share

Ex. 25-7 The following common size income statements are available for Sigma Corporation for the two years ended December 31, Year 5, and Year 4:

	Year 5	Year 4
Sales	100%	100%
Cost of goods sold	55	70
Gross profit on sales	45%	30%
Operating expenses (including income tax expense)	20	18
Net income	25%	12%

The trend percentages for sales are as follows:

Year 5 . . . . 130%
Year 4 . . . . 100%

Compute the trend percentage for gross profit on sales for Year 5.

SHORT CASES FOR ANALYSIS AND DECISION

Case 25-1 Sudan Corporation needs additional capital for plant expansion. The board of directors is considering obtaining the funds by issuing additional short-term notes, long-term bonds, preferred stock, or common stock.

Instructions
  a What primary factors should the board of directors consider in selecting the best method of financing plant expansion?
  b One member of the board of directors suggests that the corporation should maximize trading on the equity, that is, using stockholders' equity as a basis for borrowing additional funds at a lower rate of interest than the expected earnings from the use of the borrowed funds.
    (1) Explain how trading on the equity affects earnings per share of common stock.
    (2) Explain how a change in income tax rates affects trading on the equity.
    (3) Under what circumstances should a corporation seek to trade on the equity to a substantial degree?
  c Two specific proposals under consideration by the board of directors are the issue of 7% subordinated income bonds of 7% cumulative, nonparticipating, nonvoting preferred stock, callable at par. In discussing the impact of the two alternatives on the debt to equity ratio, one member of the board of directors stated that the resulting debt to equity ratio would be the same under either alternative because the income bonds and preferred stock should be reported in the same balance sheet classification. What are the arguments (1) for and (2) against using the same balance sheet classification in reporting the subordinated income bonds and preferred stock?

Case 25-2 The information on the following page is extracted from reports to stockholders of three major corporations:

(1) Revenue has increased steadily for the past few years and last year rose 10% over that for the previous year to a record $1.6 billion. Earnings from operations rose 19% to $134.2 million, or $3.95 per common share after preferred dividends. Union's profits have grown steadily for the last five years. They have also exceeded industry growth. Our 19% increase compares with 12% for the gas industry and 9% for all industries. (Union Gas Company)

(2) Income reinvested in the business, which also is to the benefit of stockholders, was $130.1 million, or $2.40 per common share. (Steel Corporation)

(3) The information below relates to the Gulf Company:

	Year 3	Year 2	Year 1
Gross revenue (millions)	$133	$ 99	$70
Net income (millions)	$ 28	$ 18	$12
Working capital (millions)	$ 34	$ 52	$87
Current ratio	2 to 1	5 to 1	10 to 1
Property, plant, and equipment, net (millions)	$275	$145	$92

Instructions

a Do you think that the information regarding the company's growth compared to industry growth as presented by Union Gas Company is useful to stockholders? Are there any possibilities that such information can be misleading?

b Comment on the information taken from the annual report of Steel Corporation in view of the following additional facts for the latest year:

(1) Earnings amounted to $4.60 per share compared to an average of $6.59 per share 8 to 10 years ago.

(2) The rate earned on stockholders' equity amounted to less than 8%.

(3) The balance sheet included over $1.28 billion of marketable securities and over $268 million in cash.

c As a stockholder, would you be concerned over the decrease in the current ratio for the Gulf Company? Explain carefully.

Case 25-3 As the consultant to the president of Meadow Corporation, you are asked to compute some key ratios based on the figures appearing in the comparative financial statements. This information is to be used by the president to convince creditors that the corporation is solvent and to support the use of going-concern valuation procedures in the financial statements. The president wishes to save time by concentrating on only these key data.

The data requested and the computations taken from the financial statements follow:

	This Year	Last Year
Current ratio	2.5:1	2.0:1
Quick (acid-test) ratio	.7:1	1.2:1
Property, plant, and equipment to stockholders' equity ...	2.6:1	2.3:1
Sales to stockholders' equity	2.5:1	2.8:1
Net income	Up 30%	Down 10%
Earnings per common share	$3.12	$2.40
Book value per common share	Up 5%	Up 8%

Instructions

a The president asks that you prepare a list of brief comments stating how each of these items supports the solvency and going-concern potential of the business. These comments are to be used to support the presentation of data to creditors. You are to prepare the comments as requested, giving the implications and the limitations of each item separately and then the collective inference one may draw from them about the corporation's solvency and going-concern potential.

b Having done as the president requested in part **a**, prepare a brief listing of additional ratio-analysis-type data for the president which you think the creditors are going to ask for to supplement the data provided in part **a**. Explain why you think the additional data will be helpful to creditors in evaluating the solvency of Meadow Corporation.

c What warnings should you offer creditors about the limitations of using ratio analysis to evaluate the solvency and the going-concern valuations of assets?

Case 25-4 Betty Simpson, executive vice president of Donald Corporation, was having lunch with three students who were being considered for a position as her assistant. The vice president pointed out that quite a few of her clients were active in acquiring other companies and that "the person who will be hired should be able to make effective overall analyses of the financial strength and operating results of companies that are for sale." In order to get a better line on the business and financial acumen of the three students, she posed the following question to them:

> Suppose that I called one of you at 10 P.M. one evening and asked you to fly to Houston the next morning to investigate the operations and financial position of Agnew Corporation, which is for sale at a price of $5 million. I would like to have a preliminary report by phone before 5 P.M. on that same day and a final report within a week. Arrangements have been made for you to visit the corporate offices of Agnew Corporation. What approach would you take in preparing these reports?

The three students then proceeded to summarize their approach to this hypothetical assignment.

Instructions Assuming that you are one of the three students being considered for the position as assistant to the vice president, write a brief report summarizing the board areas you would evaluate and the approach you would take in preparing the preliminary and the final reports.

PROBLEMS

Group A

25A-1 You have been assigned by the acquisitions committee of a diversified company to examine a potential acquisition, Consumers Outlet, Inc. This company is a merchandiser which appears to be available because of the death of its founder and principal stockholder. Recent financial statements of Consumers Outlet, Inc., are shown on pages 1084 and 1085.

CONSUMERS OUTLET, INC.
Balance Sheet
January 31

Assets	Year 3	Year 2	Year 1
Cash	$ 130,000	$ 120,000	$ 100,000
Accounts receivable (net)	430,000	370,000	300,000
Inventory	400,000	400,000	200,000
Plant assets	900,000	800,000	700,000
Less: Accumulated depreciation	(325,000)	(250,000)	(200,000)
Total assets	$1,535,000	$1,440,000	$1,100,000

Liabilities & Stockholders' Equity

	Year 3	Year 2	Year 1
Accounts payable	$ 300,000	$ 260,000	$ 220,000
8% notes payable, due Jan. 31, Year 11 . .	280,000	280,000	–0–
Common stock, $25 par	690,000	690,000	690,000
Retained earnings	265,000	210,000	190,000
Total liabilities & stockholders' equity . .	$1,535,000	$1,440,000	$1,100,000

CONSUMERS OUTLET, INC.
Income Statement
For Years Ended January 31

	Year 3	Year 2
Sales	$3,000,000	$2,600,000
Cost of goods sold	$2,256,000	$2,002,000
Wages	350,000	271,000
Supplies	43,600	34,600
Depreciation	100,000	75,000
Interest expense	22,400	22,400
Loss on write-off of plant assets	75,000	105,000
Total deductions	$2,847,000	$2,510,000
Net income before income taxes	$ 153,000	$ 90,000
Income taxes	68,000	40,000
Net income	$ 85,000	$ 50,000
Earnings per share	$ 3.08	$ 1.81

Instructions
a Calculate the inventory turnover rate for Year 2 and Year 3.
b Calculate the current ratio for Year 3.
c Calculate a rate of return on average stockholders' equity for Year 3.
d Describe the cash flow for Year 3 by redrawing the statement of changes in financial position to explain the changes in cash position instead of working capital. Prepare a separate schedule to determine the cash provided from operations.
e Comment briefly on the operating results for Year 3.

CONSUMERS OUTLET, INC.
Statement of Changes in Financial Position (Working Capital Basis)
For Years Ended January 31

	Year 3	Year 2
Sources:		
Net income	$ 85,000	$ 50,000
Add: Depreciation	100,000	75,000
Loss write-off of plant assets	75,000	105,000
Notes payable	–0–	280,000
Total sources	$260,000	$510,000
Uses:		
Plant assets purchased	$200,000	$230,000
Dividends paid	30,000	30,000
Total uses	$230,000	$260,000
Increase in working capital	$ 30,000	$250,000

25A-2 Grande Company is considering extending credit to the Chico Company. It is estimated that sales to Chico Company would amount to $2,000,000 each year. Grande Company is a wholesaler that sells nationally. The Chico Company is a retail chain operation that has a number of stores in Florida. Grande Company has had a gross profit of approximately 60% in recent years and expects to have a similar gross profit on the Chico Company order. The Chico Company order is approximately 15% of Grande Company's present sales volume. Recent financial statements of Chico Company are presented below and on pages 1086 and 1087.

CHICO COMPANY
Balance Sheets
December 31
(000,000 omitted)

Assets	Year 10	Year 9	Year 8
Current assets:			
Cash	$ 1.6	$ 1.8	$ 2.6
Government securities (cost)	–0–	.2	.4
Accounts and notes receivable (net)	8.5	8.5	8.0
Inventories	2.8	3.2	2.8
Short-term prepayments	.6	.6	.7
Total current assets	$13.5	$14.3	$14.5
Property, plant and equipment (net)	5.9	5.4	4.3
Total assets	$19.4	$19.7	$18.8

Liabilities & Stockholders' Equity

Current liabilities:			
Notes payable	$ 4.2	$ 3.7	$ 3.2
Accounts payable	4.1	3.7	2.8
Accrued liabilities	1.0	1.1	.9
Total current liabilities	$ 9.3	$ 8.5	$ 6.9
Long-term debt, 8%	1.0 *	2.0	3.0
Total liabilities	$10.3	$10.5	$ 9.9
Stockholders' equity	9.1	9.2	8.9
Total liabilities & stockholders' equity	$19.4	$19.7	$18.8

* $1 million retired on Dec. 30, Year 10.

CHICO COMPANY
Income Statement
For the Years Ended December 31
(000,000 omitted)

	Year 10	Year 9	Year 8
Net sales	$24.9	$24.5	$24.2
Cost of goods sold	18.0	17.2	16.9
Gross profit on sales	$ 6.9	$ 7.3	$ 7.3
Selling expenses	$ 4.6	$ 4.4	$ 4.3
Administrative expenses	2.7	2.4	2.3
Total expenses	$ 7.3	$ 6.8	$ 6.6
Income (loss) before income taxes	$ (.4)	$ .5	$ .7
Income taxes (income tax credit)	(.2)	.2	.3
Net income (loss)	$ (.2)	$ .3	$ .4

CHICO COMPANY
Statements of Changes in Financial Position
For the Year Ended December 31
(000,000 omitted)

	Year 10	Year 9	Year 8
Sources of working capital:			
Net income (loss)	$(.2)	$ .3	$ .4
Add: Depreciation	.5	.5	.4
From operations	$ .3	$ .8	$ .8
Sale of building	–0–	–0–	.2
Sale of treasury stock	.1	.1	–0–
Total sources of working capital	$ .4	$ .9	$1.0

Uses of working capital:

Purchase of property, plant, and equipment	$ 1.0	$ 1.6	$ 1.2
Dividends	–0–	.1	.1
Retirement of long-term debt	1.0	1.0	–0–
Total uses of working capital	$ 2.0	$ 2.7	$ 1.3
Increase (decrease) in working capital	$ (1.6)	$ (1.8)	$ (.3)

Instructions
a Calculate for Year 10 the following ratios:
  (1) Rate of return on average total assets (before interest on long-term debt and income taxes)
  (2) Acid-test ratio
  (3) Rate of return on sales
  (4) Current ratio
  (5) Inventory turnover
b As part of the analysis to determine whether or not Grande Company should extend credit to Chico Company, assume that the ratios below were calculated from Chico Company's financial statements. For each ratio indicate whether it is a favorable, unfavorable, or neutral statistic in the decision to grant Chico Company credit. Briefly explain your choice for each ratio.

	Year 10	Year 9	Year 8
(1) Rate of return on total assets	(.87)%	1.12%	1.96%
(2) Rate of return on sales	(.69)%	.99%	1.69%
(3) Acid-test ratio	1.19 to 1	1.36 to 1	1.73 to 1
(4) Current ratio	1.67 to 1	1.92 to 1	2.39 to 1
(5) Inventory turnover (times)	4.52	4.32	4.41
(6) Equity relationships:			
Current liabilities	48.0%	43.0%	36.0%
Long-term liabilities	5.0	10.5	16.0
Stockholders' equity	47.0	46.5	48.0
Total	100.0%	100.0%	100.0%
(7) Asset relationships:			
Current assets	69.5%	72.5%	77.0%
Property, plant and equipment	30.5	27.5	23.0
Total	100.0%	100.0%	100.0%

c Would you grant credit to Chico Company? Support your answer with facts given in the problem.
d What additional information, if any, would you want before making a final decision?

25A-3 The comparative balance sheets for Feliz Corporation for Year 2 and Year 1 are given on page 1088.

FELIZ CORPORATION
Comparative Balance Sheets
December 31

Assets	Year 2	Year 1
Cash	$ 18,000	$ 12,000
Marketable securities (at cost, which is less than market value)	6,000	12,000
Accounts receivable	42,000	30,000
Less: Allowance for doubtful accounts	(12,000)	(6,000)
Inventory	27,000	21,000
Plant and equipment	270,000	261,000
Less: Accumulated depreciation	(69,000)	(60,000)
Total assets	$282,000	$270,000

Liabilities & Stockholders' Equity		
Accounts payable	$ 12,000	$ 15,000
Miscellaneous liabilities	9,000	3,000
8% long-term note payable, due in Year 12	60,000	60,000
Preferred stock	15,000	30,000
Common stock, $10 par	30,000	30,000
Paid in capital in excess of par	90,000	90,000
Retained earnings	66,000	42,000
Total liabilities & stockholders' equity	$282,000	$270,000

All sales were made on account and amounted to $450,000 in Year 2. Gross profit on sales was 40% of sales and net income was 10% of sales. Income taxes were 40% of income before income taxes.

Instructions Compute the following for Year 2:
a Return (before income taxes and interest) on total assets at end of Year 2
b Receivables turnover
c Inventory turnover
d Current ratio
e Quick ratio
f Times interest earned (before income taxes)

25A-4 Selected information taken from the financial statements for Jenson Corporation for the past four years is shown below:

	Year 10	Year 9	Year 8	Year 7
Net sales	$800,000	$642,000	$624,000	$580,000
Cost of goods sold	560,000	417,300	411,840	400,200
Gross profit on sales	240,000	224,700	212,160	179,800
Net income (after income taxes) . . .	56,000	25,680	30,000	34,500
Merchandise inventory (fifo basis),				
year-end	80,000	125,000	82,400	102,000
Accounts receivable, end of year . .	88,000	45,000	50,000	40,000
Industry sales index (Year 7 = 100) .	115	112	110	100

All sales are made on credit terms of 2/10, n/30. Use a 365-day year in your computations.

Instructions

a For each of the four years, compute the following and present in tabular form:
  (1) Gross profit as percentage of sales
  (2) Net income as percentage of sales
  (3) Expenses (including income taxes) as percentage of sales
  (4) Number of days' sales in ending inventory (nearest day)
  (5) Number of days' sales in ending accounts receivable (nearest day)
  (6) Index of company's sales to industry sales

b Briefly comment on the trend in each item (1) through (6) in part **a**.

25A-5 Comparative balance sheet, additional information, details of current assets and liabilities, and comparative income statements for Theresa Company for a two-year period are presented below and on page 1090 (all figures are rounded to the nearest thousand dollar):

THERESA COMPANY

Comparative Balance Sheet

December 31

(in thousands of dollars)

	Year 2	Year 1	Increase or (decrease)
Assets:			
Current assets	$2,340	$1,890	$450
Plant assets (net)	1,025	840	185
Total assets	$3,365	$2,730	$635
Liabilities & stockholders' equity:			
Current liabilities	$ 970	$ 900	$ 70
Long-term liabilities	400	500	(100)
Total liabilities	$1,370	$1,400	$ (30)
Capital stock, $20 par	$1,100	$ 800	$300
Paid-in capital in excess of par	342	100	242
Retained earnings	553	430	123
Total stockholders' equity	$1,995	$1,330	$665
Total liabilities & stockholders' equity	$3,365	$2,730	$635

Additional information

(1) Additional shares of capital stock were issued on January 2, Year 2.
(2) At the beginning of Year 1, inventories were $440,000 and net receivables were $620,000. Terms of sale are net 90 days.
(3) The market price of the capital stock was $22 per share at the end of Year 1 and $45 per share at the end of Year 2.
(4) Dividends paid on capital stock amounted to $50,000 in Year 1 and $88,000 in Year 2.

Instructions

a Make a comparative analysis of the working capital position of Theresa Company for the two years. Compute whatever ratios you feel are useful and write

THERESA COMPANY

Details of Current Assets and Liabilities

December 31

(in thousands of dollars)

	Year 2	Year 1	Increase or (decrease)
Current assets:			
Cash	$ 550	$ 440	$ 110
Receivables (net)	830	700	130
Inventory	750	500	250
Short-term prepayments	210	250	(40)
Total current assets	$2,340	$1,890	$ 450
Current liabilities:			
Accounts payable	$ 590	$ 690	$(100)
Accrued liabilities	380	210	170
Total current liabilities	$ 970	$ 900	$ 70

THERESA COMPANY

Comparative Income Statements

For Years Ended December 31

(in thousands of dollars)

	Year 2	Year 1	Percentage of net sales Year 2	Year 1
Net sales	$2,600	$2,300	100.0	100.0
Cost of goods sold	1,600	1,500	61.5	65.2
Gross profit on sales	$1,000	$ 800	38.5	34.8
Operating expenses	600	580	23.1	25.2
Operating income	$ 400	$ 220	15.4	9.6
Interest expense	20	25	.8	1.1
Income before income tax expense	$ 380	$ 195	14.6	8.5
Income tax expense	180	90	6.9	3.9
Net income	$ 200	$ 105	7.7	4.6

a brief statement of your conclusions as to favorable and unfavorable trends, from the viewpoint of a prospective short-term creditor. Assume there are 365 days in a year.

b Prepare an analysis of Theresa Company from the viewpoint of a prospective long-term investor in its capital stock. Compute any ratios you feel would be useful, and write a brief statement of your conclusions.

25A-6 The complete set of financial statements prepared by Outboard Corporation appears on pages 1091 and 1092.

OUTBOARD CORPORATION
Statement of Earnings and Retained Earnings
For Fiscal Year Ended August 31, Year 6

Sales		$3,500,000
Less: Returns and allowances		35,000
Net sales		$3,465,000
Less: Cost of goods sold		1,039,000
Gross profit on sales		$2,426,000
Less:		
Selling expenses	$1,000,000	
General and administrative expenses (Note 1)	1,079,000	2,079,000
Operating earnings		$ 347,000
Other revenue:		
Purchase discounts	$ 10,000	
Gain on increased value of investments in real estate . . .	100,000	
Gain on sale of treasury stock	200,000	
Correction of error in last year's statement	90,000	400,000
Ordinary earnings		$ 747,000
Add: Extraordinary item—gain on sale of plant assets		53,000
Earnings before income tax		$ 800,000
Less: Income tax expense		380,000
Net earnings		$ 420,000
Add: Beginning retained earnings		2,750,000
Subtotal		$3,170,000
Less:		
Dividends (12% stock dividend declared but not yet issued) $ 120,000		
Contingent liability (Note 4)	300,000	420,000
Ending unappropriated retained earnings		$2,750,000

Notes to financial statements
(1) Depreciation expense is included in general and administrative expenses. During the fiscal year, the company changed from the straight-line method of depreciation to the sum-of-the-years'-digits method.
(2) The company owns 40% of the outstanding stock of Gray, Inc. Because the ownership is less than 50%, consolidated financial statements with Gray, Inc., cannot be presented.
(3) As per federal income tax laws, goodwill is not amortized. The goodwill was acquired in Year 3.
(4) The amount due to Grant, Inc., is contingent upon the outcome of a lawsuit which is currently pending. The amount of loss, if any, is not expected to exceed $300,000.

Instructions Identify and explain the deficiencies in the presentation of Outboard's financial statements. There are **no** arithmetical errors in the statements. Organize your answer as follows:
a Deficiencies in the statement of earnings and retained earnings.
b Deficiencies in the statement of financial position.
c General comments.
  If an item appears on both financial statements, identify the deficiencies for each statement separately.

OUTBOARD CORPORATION
Statement of Financial Position
August 31, Year 6

Assets

Current assets:

Cash		$ 80,000
Accounts receivable, net		110,000
Inventory		130,000
Total current assets		$ 320,000

Other assets:

Land and building, net	$4,000,000	
Investments in real estate (current value)	1,508,000	
Investment in Gray, Inc., at cost (Note 2)	160,000	
Goodwill (Note 3)	250,000	
Discount on bonds payable	42,000	
Total other assets		5,960,000
Total assets		$6,280,000

Liabilities & Stockholders' Equity

Current liabilities:

Accounts payable		$ 140,000
Income taxes payable		320,000
Stock dividend payable		120,000
Total current liabilities		$ 580,000

Other liabilities:

Due to Grant, Inc. (Note 4)	$ 300,000	
Liability under employee pension plan	450,000	
Bonds payable (including portion due within one year)	1,000,000	
Deferred taxes	58,000	
Total other liabilities		1,808,000
Total liabilities		$2,388,000

Stockholders' equity:

Common stock	$1,000,000	
Paid-in capital in excess of par	142,000	
Unappropriated retained earnings	2,750,000	
Total stockholders' equity		3,892,000
Total liabilities & stockholders' equity		$6,280,000

Group B

25B-1 Antioch Corporation's management is concerned over the corporation's current financial position and return on investment. They request your assistance in analyzing their financial statements and furnish the following financial statements:

ANTIOCH CORPORATION

Statement of Working Capital Deficit

December 31, Year 2

Current liabilities		$223,050
Less current assets:		
Cash	$ 5,973	
Accounts receivable, net	70,952	
Inventory	113,125	190,050
Working capital deficit		$ 33,000

ANTIOCH CORPORATION

Income Statement

For Year Ended December 31, Year 2

Sales	$760,200
Cost of goods sold	452,500
Gross profit on sales	$307,700
Selling and general expenses, including $27,980 depreciation expense . . .	155,660
Income before income tax expense	$152,040
Income tax expense	76,020
Net income	$ 76,020

Assets other than current assets consisted of land, building, and equipment with a carrying value of $443,450 on December 31, Year 2.

Instructions Assuming that Antioch Corporation operates 365 days a year, compute the following (show your computations):
a Number of days' sales uncollected at December 31, Year 2.
b Inventory turnover. Assume that average inventory approximates the year-end balance.
c Number of days' operations to cover the working capital deficit.
d Rate of return on total assets as a product of asset turnover and the net income ratio (sometimes called profit margin).

25B-2 Selected statistics for San Pedro Sea Store for the most recent three years appear at the top of page 1094.

Instructions
a Prepare income statements in comparative form for the three years.
b Comment on the trend in sales volume, the gross profit percentage, and the net income percentage.
c Compute the accounts receivable turnover rates and comment on the trend in view of the changing credit terms. All sales are made on credit.

	Year 3	Year 2	Year 1
Gross profit percentage	36%	33⅓%	30%
Inventory turnover	20 times	25 times	14 times
Average inventory	$ 19,200	$18,000	$35,000
Average accounts receivable	$100,000	$84,375	$43,750
Income tax rate	40%	30%	20%
Net income as percentage of sales	12%	7%	6%
Maximum credit period allowed to customers . .	60 days	60 days	30 days

25B-3 The stock of Padre Company is listed on the New York Stock Exchange. The market price of its common stock was quoted at $18 per share at December 31, Year 5 and Year 4. Padre's balance sheet at December 31, Year 5 and Year 4 and statement of income and retained earnings for the years then ended are presented below:

PADRE COMPANY
Balance Sheet
(in thousands of dollars)

	December 31,	
Assets	**Year 5**	**Year 4**
Current assets:		
Cash	$ 3,500	$ 3,600
Marketable securities, at cost which approximates market . .	13,000	11,000
Accounts receivable, net of allowance for doubtful accounts .	105,000	95,000
Inventories, lower of cost or market	126,000	154,000
Short-term prepayments	2,500	2,400
Total current assets	$250,000	$266,000
Property, plant, and equipment, net of accumulated depreciation	311,000	308,000
Investments, at equity	2,000	3,000
Long-term receivables	14,000	16,000
Goodwill and patents, net of accumulated amortization	6,000	6,500
Other assets	7,000	8,500
Total assets	$590,000	$608,000

Liabilities & Stockholders' Equity

	Year 5	Year 4
Current liabilities:		
Notes payable	$ 5,000	$ 15,000
Accounts payable	38,000	48,000
Accrued liabilities	24,500	27,000
Income taxes payable	1,000	1,000
Payments due within one year on long-term debt	6,500	7,000
Total current liabilities	$ 75,000	$ 98,000

Long-term debt	169,000	180,000
Deferred income taxes	74,000	67,000
Other liabilities	9,000	8,000
Total liabilities	$327,000	$353,000

Stockholders' equity:

Common stock, $1 par; authorized 20,000,000 shares; issued		
and outstanding 10,000,000 shares	$ 10,000	$ 10,000
5% cumulative preferred stock, $100 par and liquidating value;		
authorized 50,000 shares; issued and outstanding 40,000		
shares	4,000	4,000
Additional paid-in capital	107,000	107,000
Retained earnings	142,000	134,000
Total stockholders' equity	$263,000	$255,000
Total liabilities & stockholders' equity	$590,000	$608,000

PADRE COMPANY
Statement of Income and Retained Earnings
(in thousands of dollars)

	Year ended December 31,	
	Year 5	Year 4
Net sales	$600,000	$500,000
Costs and expenses:		
Cost of goods sold	$490,000	$400,000
Selling, general, and administrative expenses	66,000	60,000
Other, net	7,000	6,000
Total costs and expenses	$563,000	$466,000
Income before income taxes	$ 37,000	$ 34,000
Income taxes	16,800	15,800
Net income	$ 20,200	$ 18,200
Retained earnings at beginning of period	134,000	126,000
Dividends on common stock	(12,000)	(10,000)
Dividends on preferred stock	(200)	(200)
Retained earnings at end of period	$142,000	$134,000

Instructions Based on the above information, compute items **a** through **h** for Year 5 (show supporting computations in good form):
a Current (working capital) ratio
b Quick (acid-test) ratio
c Number of days' sales in average receivables, assuming a business year consisting of 365 days and all sales on account
d Inventory turnover rate
e Book value per share of common stock
f Earnings per share on common stock

g Price-earnings ratio on common stock
h Dividend payout ratio

25B-4 The balance sheet, income statement, and related information for Felicity Music Company are shown below:

FELICITY MUSIC COMPANY
Balance Sheet
December 31, Year 1

Assets

Cash	$ 174,000
Accounts receivable	566,000
Inventories	320,000
Plant and equipment, net of accumulated depreciation	740,000
Patents	26,000
Other intangible assets	14,000
Total assets	$1,840,000

Liabilities & Stockholders' Equity

Accounts payable	$ 194,000
Income taxes payable	32,000
Miscellaneous accrued payables	38,000
4% bonds payable, due Year 18	300,000
Preferred stock, $100 par, 7% cumulative, nonparticipating, and callable at $110	200,000
Common stock, no-par value, 50,000 shares authorized, issued, and out-standing	400,000
Retained earnings	720,000
Treasury stock, 400 shares of preferred stock	(44,000)
Total liabilities & stockholders' equity	$1,840,000

FELICITY MUSIC COMPANY
Income Statement
For Year Ended December 31, Year 1

Net sales	$1,500,000
Cost of goods sold	900,000
Gross profit on sales	$ 600,000
Expenses (including bond interest expense)	498,000
Income before income tax expense	$ 102,000
Income tax expense	37,000
Net income	$ 65,000

Additional information There are no preferred dividends in arrears and the balances in the Accounts Receivable and Inventories accounts are unchanged from January 1, Year 1. There were no changes in the Bonds Payable, Preferred Stock, or Common Stock accounts during Year 1. All sales are made on credit.

Instructions From the information presented above, compute the following to the nearest decimal:

a Current ratio at December 31, Year 1.

b The number of times bond interest was earned during Year 1, using the theoretically preferable method.

c The number of times bond interest and preferred dividends were earned during Year 1, after income taxes but before interest expense.

d The number of days' sales in inventories at the end of Year 1. Use calendar days rather than working days.

e The average number of days in the operating cycle during Year 1.

f The book value per share of common stock at December 31, Year 1.

g The rate of return for Year 1, based on the year-end common stockholders' equity.

h The debt ratio, with debt defined as total liabilities, at December 31, Year 1.

i The equity ratio at December 31, Year 1.

25B-5 The capital structure of Grossmont Corporation at the end of the current year is as follows:

Long-term debt, 8%	$9,000,000
Capital stock, $25 par	6,000,000
Retained earnings	7,500,000

Grossmont Corporation reported earnings of $2 per share for the year, after income taxes of approximately 50% of before-tax net income. The common stock currently sells on the market at $80 per share.

The company is considering the need to raise $3.2 million of additional capital to finance a proposed plant expansion. Capital budgeting studies show that the additional plant should produce a return of 15%, or $480,000 per year before income taxes. Two proposals are being considered: (1) Issue additional 8% bonds at face value; (2) issue 40,000 shares of capital stock at the current market price of $80 per share.

At a board of directors meeting one of the directors commented: "The choice is obvious to me. With our stock selling at 40 times earnings, now is the time to take advantage of the stock market and issue additional shares." To this the controller replied, "You're wrong. Remember that Uncle Sam foots the bill for 50% of our bond interest, so bonds will cost us only 4% while we are earning a return of 15%. You can't beat that kind of margin."

Instructions

a Prepare an analysis which will demonstrate whether the director or the controller is correct, and state your own recommendations as to the choice of financing methods. (Ignore bond issue costs.)

b Would your answer in **(a)** be different if the issuance of additional bonds were expected to cause the price of the shares to fall to 30 times earnings after giving effect to the increase in earnings as a result of the plant expansion?

25B-6 Ratio analysis is often applied to test the reasonableness of the relationships among current financial data against those of prior financial data. Given prior financial relationships and a few key amounts, a CPA could prepare estimates of current financial data to test the reasonableness of data furnished by a client.

Seagram Sales Corporation has in recent prior years maintained the following relationships among the data on its financial statements:

(1) Gross profit rate on net sales	40%
(2) Net income rate on net sales	10%
(3) Rate of selling expenses to net sales	15%
(4) Accounts receivable turnover	8 per year

(5) Inventory turnover . . . . 6 per year

(6) Quick (acid-test) ratio . . . . 2 to 1

(7) Current ratio . . . . 3 to 1

(8) Quick-asset composition—8% cash, 32% marketable securities, 60% accounts receivable

(9) Asset turnover . . . . 2 per year

(10) Ratio of total assets to intangible assets . . . . 20 to 1

(11) Ratio of accumulated depreciation to cost of plant assets . . . . 1 to 3

(12) Ratio of accounts receivable to accounts payable . . . . 1.5 to 1

(13) Ratio of working capital to stockholders' equity . . . . 1 to 1.6

(14) Ratio of total debt to stockholders' equity . . . . 1 to 2

The corporation has a net income of $120,000 for Year 15, after income taxes at the rate of 50%, which resulted in earnings of $2.60 per share of common stock. Additional information includes the following:

(1) Capital stock authorized, issued (all in Year 2), and outstanding:
Common, $5 par, issued at 10% above par
Preferred, 6% cumulative, nonparticipating, $50 par, issued at 10% above par
(2) Market price per share of common stock at December 31, Year 15, $44¼.
(3) Preferred dividends paid in Year 15, $3,000.
(4) Times interest earned in Year 15, 33 times (after income taxes).
(5) The amounts of the following were the same at December 31, Year 15, as at January 1, Year 15; inventory, accounts receivable, 5% bonds payable—due Year 27, and total stockholders' equity.
(6) All purchases and sales were on account.

Instructions
a Prepare in good form the condensed (1) income statement and (2) balance sheet for the year ending December 31, Year 15, presenting the amounts you would expect to appear on Seagram's Sales Corporation's financial statements. Major captions appearing on the balance sheet are: Current Assets, Plant Assets, Intangible Assets, Current Liabilities, Long-term Liabilities, and Stockholders' Equity. In addition to the accounts given in the problem, you should include accounts for Short-term Prepayments, Accrued Liabilities, and Administrative Expenses. Supporting computations should be in good form.

b Compute the following for Year 15 (show your computations): (1) Rate of return on stockholders' equity, (2) price-earnings ratio for common stock, (3) dividends paid per share of common stock, and (4) dividends paid per share of preferred stock.

APPENDIX

COMPOUND INTEREST TABLES

Table 1 **Future Amount of \$1 at Compound Interest Due in *n* Periods:** $a_{\overline{n}|i} = (1 + i)^n$

n	½%	1%	1½%	2%	2½%	3%
1	1.005000	1.010000	1.015000	1.020000	1.025000	1.030000
2	1.010025	1.020100	1.030225	1.040400	1.050625	1.060900
3	1.015075	1.030301	1.045678	1.061208	1.076891	1.092727
4	1.020151	1.040604	1.061364	1.082432	1.103813	1.125509
5	1.025251	1.051010	1.077284	1.104081	1.131408	1.159274
6	1.030378	1.061520	1.093443	1.126162	1.159693	1.194052
7	1.035529	1.072135	1.109845	1.148686	1.188686	1.229874
8	1.040707	1.082857	1.126493	1.171659	1.218403	1.266770
9	1.045911	1.093685	1.143390	1.195093	1.248863	1.304773
10	1.051140	1.104622	1.160541	1.218994	1.280085	1.343916
11	1.056396	1.115668	1.177949	1.243374	1.312087	1.384234
12	1.061678	1.126825	1.195618	1.268242	1.344889	1.425761
13	1.066986	1.138093	1.213552	1.293607	1.378511	1.468534
14	1.072321	1.149474	1.231756	1.319479	1.412974	1.512590
15	1.077683	1.160969	1.250232	1.345868	1.448298	1.557967
16	1.083071	1.172579	1.268986	1.372786	1.484506	1.604706
17	1.088487	1.184304	1.288020	1.400241	1.521618	1.652848
18	1.093929	1.196147	1.307341	1.428246	1.559659	1.702433
19	1.099399	1.208109	1.326951	1.456811	1.598650	1.753506
20	1.104896	1.220190	1.346855	1.485947	1.638616	1.806111
21	1.110420	1.232392	1.367058	1.515666	1.679582	1.860295
22	1.115972	1.244716	1.387564	1.545980	1.721571	1.916103
23	1.121552	1.257163	1.408377	1.576899	1.764611	1.973587
24	1.127160	1.269735	1.429503	1.608437	1.808726	2.032794
25	1.132796	1.282432	1.450945	1.640606	1.853944	2.093778
26	1.138460	1.295256	1.472710	1.673418	1.900293	2.156591
27	1.144152	1.308209	1.494800	1.706886	1.947800	2.221289
28	1.149873	1.321291	1.517222	1.741024	1.996495	2.287928
29	1.155622	1.334504	1.539981	1.775845	2.046407	2.356566
30	1.161400	1.347849	1.563080	1.811362	2.097568	2.427262
31	1.167207	1.361327	1.586526	1.847589	2.150007	2.500080
32	1.173043	1.374941	1.610324	1.884541	2.203757	2.575083
33	1.178908	1.388690	1.634479	1.922231	2.258851	2.652335
34	1.184803	1.402577	1.658996	1.960676	2.315322	2.731905
35	1.190727	1.416603	1.683881	1.999890	2.373205	2.813862
36	1.196681	1.430769	1.709140	2.039887	2.432535	2.898278
37	1.202664	1.445076	1.734777	2.080685	2.493349	2.985227
38	1.208677	1.459527	1.760798	2.122299	2.555682	3.074783
39	1.214721	1.474123	1.787210	2.164745	2.619574	3.167027
40	1.220794	1.488864	1.814018	2.208040	2.685064	3.262038
41	1.226898	1.503752	1.841229	2.252200	2.752190	3.359899
42	1.233033	1.518790	1.868847	2.297244	2.820995	3.460696
43	1.239198	1.533978	1.896880	2.343189	2.891520	3.564517
44	1.245394	1.549318	1.925333	2.390053	2.963808	3.671452
45	1.251621	1.564811	1.954213	2.437854	3.037903	3.781596
46	1.257879	1.580459	1.983526	2.486611	3.113851	3.895044
47	1.264168	1.596263	2.013279	2.536344	3.191697	4.011895
48	1.270489	1.612226	2.043478	2.587070	3.271490	4.132252
49	1.276842	1.628348	2.074130	2.638812	3.353277	4.256219
50	1.283226	1.644632	2.105242	2.691588	3.437109	4.383906

TABLE 1 **1101**

Table 1   Future Amount of $1 (*continued*)

n	3½%	4%	4½%	5%	5½%	6%
1	1.035000	1.040000	1.045000	1.050000	1.055000	1.060000
2	1.071225	1.081600	1.092025	1.102500	1.113025	1.123600
3	1.108718	1.124864	1.141166	1.157625	1.174241	1.191016
4	1.147523	1.169859	1.192519	1.215506	1.238825	1.262477
5	1.187686	1.216653	1.246182	1.276282	1.306960	1.338226
6	1.229255	1.265319	1.302260	1.340096	1.378843	1.418519
7	1.272279	1.315932	1.360862	1.407100	1.454679	1.503630
8	1.316809	1.368569	1.422101	1.477455	1.534687	1.593848
9	1.362897	1.423312	1.486095	1.551328	1.619094	1.689479
10	1.410599	1.480244	1.552969	1.628895	1.708144	1.790848
11	1.459970	1.539454	1.622853	1.710339	1.802092	1.898299
12	1.511069	1.601032	1.695881	1.795856	1.901207	2.012196
13	1.563956	1.665074	1.772196	1.885649	2.005774	2.132928
14	1.618695	1.731676	1.851945	1.979932	2.116091	2.260904
15	1.675349	1.800944	1.935282	2.078928	2.232476	2.396558
16	1.733986	1.872981	2.022370	2.182875	2.355263	2.540352
17	1.794676	1.947901	2.113377	2.292018	2.484802	2.692773
18	1.857489	2.025817	2.208479	2.406619	2.621466	2.854339
19	1.922501	2.106849	2.307860	2.526950	2.765647	3.025600
20	1.989789	2.191123	2.411714	2.653298	2.917757	3.207135
21	2.059431	2.278768	2.520241	2.785963	3.078234	3.399564
22	2.131512	2.369919	2.633652	2.925261	3.247537	3.603537
23	2.206114	2.464716	2.752166	3.071524	3.426152	3.819750
24	2.283328	2.563304	2.876014	3.225100	3.614590	4.048935
25	2.363245	2.665836	3.005434	3.386355	3.813392	4.291871
26	2.445959	2.772470	3.140679	3.555673	4.023129	4.549383
27	2.531567	2.883369	3.282010	3.733456	4.244401	4.822346
28	2.620172	2.998703	3.429700	3.920129	4.477843	5.111687
29	2.711878	3.118651	3.584036	4.116136	4.724124	5.418388
30	2.806794	3.243398	3.745318	4.321942	4.983951	5.743491
31	2.905031	3.373133	3.913857	4.538039	5.258069	6.088101
32	3.006708	3.508059	4.089981	4.764941	5.547262	6.453387
33	3.111942	3.648381	4.274030	5.003189	5.852362	6.840590
34	3.220860	3.794316	4.466362	5.253348	6.174242	7.251025
35	3.333590	3.946089	4.667348	5.516015	6.513825	7.686087
36	3.450266	4.103933	4.877378	5.791816	6.872085	8.147252
37	3.571025	4.268090	5.096860	6.081407	7.250050	8.636087
38	3.696011	4.438813	5.326219	6.385477	7.648803	9.154252
39	3.825372	4.616366	5.565899	6.704751	8.069487	9.703507
40	3.959260	4.801021	5.816365	7.039989	8.513309	10.285718
41	4.097834	4.993061	6.078101	7.391988	8.981541	10.902861
42	4.241258	5.192784	6.351615	7.761588	9.475526	11.557033
43	4.389702	5.400495	6.637438	8.149667	9.996679	12.250455
44	4.543342	5.616515	6.936123	8.557150	10.546497	12.985482
45	4.702359	5.841176	7.248248	8.985008	11.126554	13.764611
46	4.866941	6.074823	7.574420	9.434258	11.738515	14.590487
47	5.037284	6.317816	7.915268	9.905971	12.384133	15.465917
48	5.213589	6.570528	8.271456	10.401270	13.065260	16.393872
49	5.396065	6.833349	8.643671	10.921333	13.783849	17.377504
50	5.584927	7.106683	9.032636	11.467400	14.541961	18.420154

Table 1 **Future Amount of $1** (*continued*)

n \ i	7%	8%	9%	10%	12%	15%
1	1.070000	1.080000	1.090000	1.100000	1.120000	1.150000
2	1.144900	1.166400	1.188100	1.210000	1.254400	1.322500
3	1.225043	1.259712	1.295029	1.331000	1.404928	1.520875
4	1.310796	1.360489	1.411582	1.464100	1.573519	1.749006
5	1.402552	1.469328	1.538624	1.610510	1.762342	2.011357
6	1.500730	1.586874	1.677100	1.771561	1.973823	2.313061
7	1.605781	1.713824	1.828039	1.948717	2.210681	2.660020
8	1.718186	1.850930	1.992563	2.143589	2.475963	3.059023
9	1.838459	1.999005	2.171893	2.357948	2.773079	3.517876
10	1.967151	2.158925	2.367364	2.593742	3.105848	4.045558
11	2.104852	2.331639	2.580426	2.853117	3.478550	4.652391
12	2.252192	2.518170	2.812665	3.138428	3.895976	5.350250
13	2.409845	2.719624	3.065805	3.452271	4.363493	6.152788
14	2.578534	2.937194	3.341727	3.797498	4.887112	7.075706
15	2.759032	3.172169	3.642482	4.177248	5.473566	8.137062
16	2.952164	3.425943	3.970306	4.594973	6.130394	9.357621
17	3.158815	3.700018	4.327633	5.054470	6.866041	10.761264
18	3.379932	3.996019	4.717120	5.559917	7.689966	12.375454
19	3.616528	4.315701	5.141661	6.115909	8.612762	14.231772
20	3.869684	4.660957	5.604411	6.727500	9.646293	16.366537
21	4.140562	5.033834	6.108808	7.400250	10.803848	18.821518
22	4.430402	5.436540	6.658600	8.140275	12.100310	21.644746
23	4.740530	5.871464	7.257874	8.954302	13.552347	24.891458
24	5.072367	6.341181	7.911083	9.849733	15.178629	28.625176
25	5.427433	6.848475	8.623081	10.834706	17.000064	32.918953
26	5.807353	7.396353	9.399158	11.918177	19.040072	37.856796
27	6.213868	7.988061	10.245082	13.109994	21.324881	43.535315
28	6.648838	8.627106	11.167140	14.420994	23.883866	50.065612
29	7.114257	9.317275	12.172182	15.863093	26.749930	57.575454
30	7.612255	10.062657	13.267678	17.449402	29.959922	66.211772
31	8.145113	10.867669	14.461770	19.194342	33.555113	76.143538
32	8.715271	11.737083	15.763329	21.113777	37.581726	87.565068
33	9.325340	12.676050	17.182028	23.225154	42.091533	100.699829
34	9.978114	13.690134	18.728411	25.547670	47.142517	115.804803
35	10.676581	14.785344	20.413968	28.102437	52.799620	133.175523
36	11.423942	15.968172	22.251225	30.912681	59.135574	153.151852
37	12.223618	17.245626	24.253835	34.003949	66.231843	176.124630
38	13.079271	18.625276	26.436680	37.404343	74.179664	202.543324
39	13.994820	20.115298	28.815982	41.144778	83.081224	232.924823
40	14.974458	21.724521	31.409420	45.259256	93.050970	267.863546
41	16.022670	23.462483	34.236268	49.785181	104.217087	308.043078
42	17.144257	25.339482	37.317532	54.763699	116.723137	354.249540
43	18.344355	27.366640	40.676110	60.240069	130.729914	407.386971
44	19.628460	29.555972	44.336960	66.264076	146.417503	468.495017
45	21.002452	31.920449	48.327286	72.890484	163.987604	538.769269
46	22.472623	34.474085	52.676742	80.179532	183.666116	619.584659
47	24.045707	37.232012	57.417649	88.197485	205.706050	712.522358
48	25.728907	40.210573	62.585237	97.017234	230.390776	819.400712
49	27.529930	43.427419	68.217908	106.718957	258.037669	942.310819
50	29.457025	46.901613	74.357520	117.390853	289.002190	1083.657442

TABLE 2 **1103**

Table 2 Present Value of \$1 at Compound Interest Due in *n* Periods: $p_{\overline{n}|i} = \dfrac{1}{(1 + i)^n}$

n \ i	1/2%	1%	1 1/2%	2%	2 1/2%	3%
1	0.995025	0.990099	0.985222	0.980392	0.975610	0.970874
2	0.990075	0.980296	0.970662	0.961169	0.951814	0.942596
3	0.985149	0.970590	0.956317	0.942322	0.928599	0.915142
4	0.980248	0.960980	0.942184	0.923845	0.905951	0.888487
5	0.975371	0.951466	0.928260	0.905731	0.883854	0.862609
6	0.970518	0.942045	0.914542	0.887971	0.862297	0.837484
7	0.965690	0.932718	0.901027	0.870560	0.841265	0.813092
8	0.960885	0.923483	0.887711	0.853490	0.820747	0.789409
9	0.956105	0.914340	0.874592	0.836755	0.800728	0.766417
10	0.951348	0.905287	0.861667	0.820348	0.781198	0.744094
11	0.946615	0.896324	0.848933	0.804263	0.762145	0.722421
12	0.941905	0.887449	0.836387	0.788493	0.743556	0.701380
13	0.937219	0.878663	0.824027	0.773033	0.725420	0.680951
14	0.932556	0.869963	0.811849	0.757875	0.707727	0.661118
15	0.927917	0.861349	0.799852	0.743015	0.690466	0.641862
16	0.923300	0.852821	0.788031	0.728446	0.673625	0.623167
17	0.918707	0.844377	0.776385	0.714163	0.657195	0.605016
18	0.914136	0.836017	0.764912	0.700159	0.641166	0.587395
19	0.909588	0.827740	0.753607	0.686431	0.625528	0.570286
20	0.905063	0.819544	0.742470	0.672971	0.610271	0.553676
21	0.900560	0.811430	0.731498	0.659776	0.595386	0.537549
22	0.896080	0.803396	0.720688	0.646839	0.580865	0.521893
23	0.891622	0.795442	0.710037	0.634156	0.566697	0.506692
24	0.887186	0.787566	0.699544	0.621721	0.552875	0.491934
25	0.882772	0.779768	0.689206	0.609531	0.539391	0.477606
26	0.878380	0.772048	0.679021	0.597579	0.526235	0.463695
27	0.874010	0.764404	0.668986	0.585862	0.513400	0.450189
28	0.869662	0.756836	0.659099	0.574375	0.500878	0.437077
29	0.865335	0.749342	0.649359	0.563112	0.488661	0.424346
30	0.861030	0.741923	0.639762	0.552071	0.476743	0.411987
31	0.856746	0.734577	0.630308	0.541246	0.465115	0.399987
32	0.852484	0.727304	0.620993	0.530633	0.453771	0.388337
33	0.848242	0.720103	0.611816	0.520229	0.442703	0.377026
34	0.844022	0.712973	0.602774	0.510028	0.431905	0.366045
35	0.839823	0.705914	0.593866	0.500028	0.421371	0.355383
36	0.835645	0.698925	0.585090	0.490223	0.411094	0.345032
37	0.831487	0.692005	0.576443	0.480611	0.401067	0.334983
38	0.827351	0.685153	0.567924	0.471187	0.391285	0.325226
39	0.823235	0.678370	0.559531	0.461948	0.381741	0.315754
40	0.819139	0.671653	0.551262	0.452890	0.372431	0.306557
41	0.815064	0.665003	0.543116	0.444010	0.363347	0.297628
42	0.811009	0.658419	0.535089	0.435304	0.354485	0.288959
43	0.806974	0.651900	0.527182	0.426769	0.345839	0.280543
44	0.802959	0.645445	0.519391	0.418401	0.337404	0.272372
45	0.798964	0.639055	0.511715	0.410197	0.329174	0.264439
46	0.794989	0.632728	0.504153	0.402154	0.321146	0.256737
47	0.791034	0.626463	0.496702	0.394268	0.313313	0.249259
48	0.787098	0.620260	0.489362	0.386538	0.305671	0.241999
49	0.783183	0.614119	0.482130	0.378958	0.298216	0.234950
50	0.779286	0.608039	0.475005	0.371528	0.290942	0.228107

Table 2 Present Value of $1 (*continued*)

n	3½%	4%	4½%	5%	5½%	6%
1	0.966184	0.961538	0.956938	0.952381	0.947867	0.943396
2	0.933511	0.924556	0.915730	0.907029	0.898452	0.889996
3	0.901943	0.888996	0.876297	0.863838	0.851614	0.839619
4	0.871442	0.854804	0.838561	0.822702	0.807217	0.792094
5	0.841973	0.821927	0.802451	0.783526	0.765134	0.747258
6	0.813501	0.790315	0.767896	0.746215	0.725246	0.704961
7	0.785991	0.759918	0.734828	0.710681	0.687437	0.665057
8	0.759412	0.730690	0.703185	0.676839	0.651599	0.627412
9	0.733731	0.702587	0.672904	0.644609	0.617629	0.591898
10	0.708919	0.675564	0.643928	0.613913	0.585431	0.558395
11	0.684946	0.649581	0.616199	0.584679	0.554911	0.526788
12	0.661783	0.624597	0.589664	0.556837	0.525982	0.496969
13	0.639404	0.600574	0.564272	0.530321	0.498561	0.468839
14	0.617782	0.577475	0.539973	0.505068	0.472569	0.442301
15	0.596891	0.555265	0.516720	0.481017	0.447933	0.417265
16	0.576706	0.533908	0.494469	0.458112	0.424581	0.393646
17	0.557204	0.513373	0.473176	0.436297	0.402447	0.371364
18	0.538361	0.493628	0.452800	0.415521	0.381466	0.350344
19	0.520156	0.474642	0.433302	0.395734	0.361579	0.330513
20	0.502566	0.456387	0.414643	0.376889	0.342729	0.311805
21	0.485571	0.438834	0.396787	0.358942	0.324862	0.294155
22	0.469151	0.421955	0.379701	0.341850	0.307926	0.277505
23	0.453286	0.405726	0.363350	0.325571	0.291873	0.261797
24	0.437957	0.390121	0.347703	0.310068	0.276657	0.246979
25	0.423147	0.375117	0.332731	0.295303	0.262234	0.232999
26	0.408838	0.360689	0.318402	0.281241	0.248563	0.219810
27	0.395012	0.346817	0.304691	0.267848	0.235605	0.207368
28	0.381654	0.333477	0.291571	0.255094	0.223322	0.195630
29	0.368748	0.320651	0.279015	0.242946	0.211679	0.184557
30	0.356278	0.308319	0.267000	0.231377	0.200644	0.174110
31	0.344230	0.296460	0.255502	0.220359	0.190184	0.164255
32	0.332590	0.285058	0.244500	0.209866	0.180269	0.154957
33	0.321343	0.274094	0.233971	0.199873	0.170871	0.146186
34	0.310476	0.263552	0.223896	0.190355	0.161963	0.137912
35	0.299977	0.253415	0.214254	0.181290	0.153520	0.130105
36	0.289833	0.243669	0.205028	0.172657	0.145516	0.122741
37	0.280032	0.234297	0.196199	0.164436	0.137930	0.115793
38	0.270562	0.225285	0.187750	0.156605	0.130739	0.109239
39	0.261413	0.216621	0.179665	0.149148	0.123924	0.103056
40	0.252572	0.208289	0.171929	0.142046	0.117463	0.097222
41	0.244031	0.200278	0.164525	0.135282	0.111339	0.091719
42	0.235779	0.192575	0.157440	0.128840	0.105535	0.086527
43	0.227806	0.185168	0.150661	0.122704	0.100033	0.081630
44	0.220102	0.178046	0.144173	0.116861	0.094818	0.077009
45	0.212659	0.171198	0.137964	0.111297	0.089875	0.072650
46	0.205468	0.164614	0.132023	0.105997	0.085190	0.068538
47	0.198520	0.158283	0.126338	0.100949	0.080748	0.064658
48	0.191806	0.152195	0.120898	0.096142	0.076539	0.060998
49	0.185320	0.146341	0.115692	0.091564	0.072549	0.057546
50	0.179053	0.140713	0.110710	0.087204	0.068767	0.054288

TABLE 2 **1105**

Table 2   Present Value of $1 (*continued*)

n \ i	7%	8%	9%	10%	12%	15%
1	0.934580	0.925926	0.917431	0.909091	0.892857	0.869565
2	0.873439	0.857339	0.841680	0.826446	0.797194	0.756144
3	0.816298	0.793832	0.772183	0.751315	0.711780	0.657516
4	0.762895	0.735030	0.708425	0.683013	0.635518	0.571753
5	0.712986	0.680583	0.649931	0.620921	0.567427	0.497177
6	0.666342	0.630170	0.596267	0.564474	0.506631	0.432328
7	0.622750	0.583490	0.547034	0.513158	0.452349	0.375937
8	0.582009	0.540269	0.501866	0.466507	0.403883	0.326902
9	0.543934	0.500249	0.460428	0.424098	0.360610	0.284262
10	0.508349	0.463193	0.422411	0.385543	0.321973	0.247185
11	0.475093	0.428883	0.387533	0.350494	0.287476	0.214943
12	0.444012	0.397114	0.355535	0.318631	0.256675	0.186907
13	0.414964	0.367698	0.326179	0.289664	0.229174	0.162528
14	0.387817	0.340461	0.299246	0.263331	0.204620	0.141329
15	0.362446	0.315242	0.274538	0.239392	0.182696	0.122894
16	0.338735	0.291890	0.251870	0.217629	0.163122	0.106865
17	0.316574	0.270269	0.231073	0.197845	0.145644	0.092926
18	0.295864	0.250249	0.211994	0.179859	0.130040	0.080805
19	0.276508	0.231712	0.194490	0.163508	0.116107	0.070265
20	0.258419	0.214548	0.178431	0.148644	0.103667	0.061100
21	0.241513	0.198656	0.163698	0.135131	0.092560	0.053131
22	0.225713	0.183941	0.150182	0.122846	0.082643	0.046201
23	0.210947	0.170315	0.137781	0.111678	0.073788	0.040174
24	0.197147	0.157699	0.126405	0.101526	0.065882	0.034934
25	0.184249	0.146018	0.115968	0.092296	0.058823	0.030378
26	0.172195	0.135202	0.106393	0.083905	0.052521	0.026415
27	0.160930	0.125187	0.097608	0.076278	0.046894	0.022970
28	0.150402	0.115914	0.089548	0.069343	0.041869	0.019974
29	0.140563	0.107328	0.082155	0.063039	0.037383	0.017369
30	0.131367	0.099377	0.075371	0.057309	0.033378	0.015103
31	0.122773	0.092016	0.069148	0.052099	0.029802	0.013133
32	0.114741	0.085200	0.063438	0.047362	0.026609	0.011420
33	0.107235	0.078889	0.058200	0.043057	0.023758	0.009931
34	0.100219	0.073045	0.053395	0.039143	0.021212	0.008635
35	0.093663	0.067635	0.048986	0.035584	0.018940	0.007509
36	0.087535	0.062625	0.044941	0.032349	0.016910	0.006529
37	0.081809	0.057986	0.041231	0.029408	0.015098	0.005678
38	0.076457	0.053690	0.037826	0.026735	0.013481	0.004937
39	0.071455	0.049713	0.034703	0.024304	0.012036	0.004293
40	0.066780	0.046031	0.031838	0.022095	0.010747	0.003733
41	0.062412	0.042621	0.029209	0.020086	0.009595	0.003246
42	0.058329	0.039464	0.026797	0.018260	0.008567	0.002823
43	0.054513	0.036541	0.024584	0.016600	0.007649	0.002455
44	0.050946	0.033834	0.022555	0.015091	0.006830	0.002134
45	0.047613	0.031328	0.020692	0.013719	0.006098	0.001856
46	0.044499	0.029007	0.018984	0.012472	0.005445	0.001614
47	0.041587	0.026859	0.017416	0.011338	0.004861	0.001403
48	0.038867	0.024869	0.015978	0.010307	0.004340	0.001220
49	0.036324	0.023027	0.014659	0.009370	0.003875	0.001061
50	0.033948	0.021321	0.013449	0.008519	0.003460	0.000923

Table 3 Future Amount of an Ordinary Annuity of $1 per Period: $A_{\overline{n}|i} = \dfrac{(1 + i)^n - 1}{i}$

n \ i	½%	1%	1½%	2%	2½%	3%
1	1.000000	1.000000	1.000000	1.000000	1.000000	1.000000
2	2.005000	2.010000	2.015000	2.020000	2.025000	2.030000
3	3.015025	3.030100	3.045225	3.060400	3.075625	3.090900
4	4.030100	4.060401	4.090903	4.121608	4.152516	4.183627
5	5.050251	5.101005	5.152267	5.204040	5.256329	5.309136
6	6.075502	6.152015	6.229551	6.308121	6.387737	6.468410
7	7.105879	7.213535	7.322994	7.434283	7.547430	7.662462
8	8.141409	8.285671	8.432839	8.582969	8.736116	8.892336
9	9.182116	9.368527	9.559332	9.754628	9.954519	10.159106
10	10.228026	10.462213	10.702722	10.949721	11.203382	11.463879
11	11.279167	11.566835	11.863262	12.168715	12.483466	12.807796
12	12.335562	12.682503	13.041211	13.412090	13.795553	14.192030
13	13.397240	13.809328	14.236830	14.680332	15.140442	15.617790
14	14.464226	14.947421	15.450382	15.973938	16.518953	17.086324
15	15.536548	16.096896	16.682138	17.293417	17.931927	18.598914
16	16.614230	17.257864	17.932370	18.639285	19.380225	20.156881
17	17.697301	18.430443	19.201355	20.012071	20.864730	21.761588
18	18.785788	19.614748	20.489376	21.412312	22.386349	23.414435
19	19.879717	20.810895	21.796716	22.840559	23.946007	25.116868
20	20.979115	22.019004	23.123667	24.297370	25.544658	26.870374
21	22.084011	23.239194	24.470522	25.783317	27.183274	28.676486
22	23.194431	24.471586	25.837580	27.298984	28.862856	30.536780
23	24.310403	25.716302	27.225144	28.844963	30.584427	32.452884
24	25.431955	26.973465	28.633521	30.421862	32.349038	34.426470
25	26.559115	28.243200	30.063024	32.030300	34.157764	36.459264
26	27.691911	29.525632	31.513969	33.670906	36.011708	38.553042
27	28.830370	30.820888	32.986679	35.344324	37.912001	40.709634
28	29.974522	32.129097	34.481479	37.051210	39.859801	42.930923
29	31.124395	33.450388	35.998701	38.792235	41.856296	45.218850
30	32.280017	34.784892	37.538681	40.568079	43.902703	47.575416
31	33.441417	36.132740	39.101762	42.379441	46.000271	50.002678
32	34.608624	37.494068	40.688288	44.227030	48.150278	52.502759
33	35.781667	38.869009	42.298612	46.111570	50.354034	55.077841
34	36.960575	40.257699	43.933092	48.033802	52.612885	57.730177
35	38.145378	41.660276	45.592088	49.994478	54.928207	60.462082
36	39.336105	43.076878	47.275969	51.994367	57.301413	63.275944
37	40.532785	44.507647	48.985109	54.034255	59.733948	66.174223
38	41.735449	45.952724	50.719885	56.114940	62.227297	69.159449
39	42.944127	47.412251	52.480684	58.237238	64.782979	72.234233
40	44.158847	48.886373	54.267894	60.401983	67.402554	75.401260
41	45.379642	50.375237	56.081912	62.610023	70.087617	78.663298
42	46.606540	51.878989	57.923141	64.862223	72.839808	82.023196
43	47.839572	53.397779	59.791988	67.159468	75.660803	85.483892
44	49.078770	54.931757	61.688868	69.502657	78.552323	89.048409
45	50.324164	56.481075	63.614201	71.892710	81.516131	92.719861
46	51.575785	58.045885	65.568414	74.330564	84.554034	96.501457
47	52.833664	59.626344	67.551940	76.817176	87.667885	100.396501
48	54.097832	61.222608	69.565219	79.353519	90.859582	104.408396
49	55.368321	62.834834	71.608698	81.940590	94.131072	108.540648
50	56.645163	64.463182	73.682828	84.579401	97.484349	112.796867

TABLE 3 **1107**

Table 3 Future Amount of an Ordinary Annuity of $1 (*continued*)

n \ i	3½%	4%	4½%	5%	5½%	6%
1	1.000000	1.000000	1.000000	1.000000	1.000000	1.000000
2	2.035000	2.040000	2.045000	2.050000	2.055000	2.060000
3	3.106225	3.121600	3.137025	3.152500	3.168025	3.183600
4	4.214943	4.246464	4.278191	4.310125	4.342266	4.374616
5	5.362466	5.416323	5.470710	5.525631	5.581091	5.637093
6	6.550152	6.632975	6.716892	6.801913	6.888051	6.975319
7	7.779408	7.898294	8.019152	8.142008	8.266894	8.393838
8	9.051687	9.214226	9.380014	9.549109	9.721573	9.897468
9	10.368496	10.582795	10.802114	11.026564	11.256260	11.491316
10	11.731393	12.006107	12.288209	12.577893	12.875354	13.180795
11	13.141992	13.486351	13.841179	14.206787	14.583498	14.971643
12	14.601962	15.025805	15.464032	15.917127	16.385591	16.869941
13	16.113030	16.626838	17.159913	17.712983	18.286798	18.882138
14	17.676986	18.291911	18.932109	19.598632	20.292572	21.015066
15	19.295681	20.023588	20.784054	21.578564	22.408664	23.275970
16	20.971030	21.824531	22.719337	23.657492	24.641140	25.672528
17	22.705016	23.697512	24.741707	25.840366	26.996403	28.212880
18	24.499691	25.645413	26.855084	28.132385	29.481205	30.905653
19	26.357181	27.671229	29.063562	30.539004	32.102671	33.759992
20	28.279682	29.778079	31.371423	33.065954	34.868318	36.785591
21	30.269471	31.969202	33.783137	35.719252	37.786076	39.992727
22	32.328902	34.247970	36.303378	38.505214	40.864310	43.392290
23	34.460414	36.617889	38.937030	41.430475	44.111847	46.995828
24	36.666528	39.082604	41.689196	44.501999	47.537998	50.815577
25	38.949857	41.645908	44.565210	47.727099	51.152588	54.864512
26	41.313102	44.311745	47.570645	51.113454	54.965981	59.156383
27	43.759060	47.084214	50.711324	54.669126	58.989109	63.705766
28	46.290627	49.967583	53.993333	58.402583	63.233510	68.528112
29	48.910799	52.966286	57.423033	62.322712	67.711354	73.629798
30	51.622677	56.084938	61.007070	66.438848	72.435478	79.058186
31	54.429471	59.328335	64.752388	70.760790	77.419429	84.801677
32	57.334502	62.701469	68.666245	75.298829	82.677498	90.889778
33	60.341210	66.209527	72.756226	80.063771	88.224760	97.343165
34	63.453152	69.857909	77.030256	85.066959	94.077122	104.183755
35	66.674013	73.652225	81.496618	90.320307	100.251364	111.434780
36	70.007603	77.598314	86.163966	95.836323	106.765189	119.120867
37	73.457869	81.702246	91.041344	101.628139	113.637274	127.268119
38	77.028895	85.970336	96.138205	107.709546	120.887324	135.904206
39	80.724906	90.409150	101.464424	114.095023	128.536127	145.058458
40	84.550278	95.025516	107.030323	120.799774	136.605614	154.761966
41	88.509537	99.826536	112.846688	127.839763	145.118923	165.047684
42	92.607371	104.819598	118.924789	135.231751	154.100464	175.950545
43	96.848629	110.012382	125.276404	142.993339	163.575989	187.507577
44	101.238331	115.412877	131.913842	151.143006	173.572669	199.758032
45	105.781673	121.029392	138.849965	159.700156	184.119165	212.743514
46	110.484031	126.870568	146.098214	168.685164	195.245719	226.508125
47	115.350973	132.945390	153.672633	178.119422	206.984234	241.098612
48	120.388257	139.263206	161.587902	188.025393	219.368367	256.564529
49	125.601846	145.833734	169.859357	198.426663	232.433627	272.958401
50	130.997910	152.667084	178.503028	209.347996	246.217476	290.335905

Table 3   **Future Amount of an Ordinary Annuity of $1** (*continued*)

n	7%	8%	9%	10%	12%	15%
1	1.000000	1.000000	1.000000	1.000000	1.000000	1.000000
2	2.070000	2.080000	2.090000	2.100000	2.120000	2.150000
3	3.214900	3.246400	3.278100	3.310000	3.374400	3.472500
4	4.439943	4.506112	4.573129	4.641000	4.779328	4.993375
5	5.750740	5.866601	5.984711	6.105100	6.352847	6.742381
6	7.153291	7.335929	7.523335	7.715610	8.115189	8.753738
7	8.654021	8.922803	9.200435	9.487171	10.089012	11.066799
8	10.259803	10.636628	11.028474	11.435888	12.299693	13.726819
9	11.977989	12.487558	13.021036	13.579477	14.775656	16.785842
10	13.816448	14.486562	15.192930	15.937425	17.548735	20.303718
11	15.783599	16.645487	17.560293	18.531167	20.654583	24.349276
12	17.888451	18.977126	20.140720	21.384284	24.133133	29.001667
13	20.140643	21.495297	22.953385	24.522712	28.029109	34.351917
14	22.550488	24.214920	26.019189	27.974983	32.392602	40.504705
15	25.129022	27.152114	29.360916	31.772482	37.279715	47.580411
16	27.888054	30.324283	33.003399	35.949730	42.753280	55.717472
17	30.840217	33.750226	36.973705	40.544703	48.883674	65.075093
18	33.999033	37.450244	41.301338	45.599173	55.749715	75.836357
19	37.378965	41.446263	46.018458	51.159090	63.439681	88.211811
20	40.995492	45.761964	51.160120	57.274999	72.052442	102.443583
21	44.865177	50.422921	56.764530	64.002499	81.698736	118.810120
22	49.005739	55.456755	62.873338	71.402749	92.502584	137.631638
23	53.436141	60.893296	69.531939	79.543024	104.602894	159.276384
24	58.176671	66.764759	76.789813	88.497327	118.155241	184.167841
25	63.249038	73.105940	84.700896	98.347059	133.333870	212.793017
26	68.676470	79.954415	93.323977	109.181765	150.333934	245.711970
27	74.483823	87.350768	102.723135	121.099942	169.374007	283.568766
28	80.697691	95.338830	112.968217	134.209936	190.698887	327.104080
29	87.346529	103.965936	124.135356	148.630930	214.582754	377.169693
30	94.460786	113.283211	136.307539	164.494023	241.332684	434.745146
31	102.073041	123.345868	149.575217	181.943425	271.292606	500.956918
32	110.218154	134.213537	164.036987	201.137767	304.847719	577.100456
33	118.933425	145.950620	179.800315	222.251544	342.429446	644.665525
34	128.258765	158.626670	196.982344	245.476699	384.520979	765.365353
35	138.236878	172.316804	215.710755	271.024368	431.663496	881.170156
36	148.913460	187.102148	236.124723	299.126805	484.463116	1014.345680
37	160.337402	203.070320	258.375948	330.039486	543.598690	1167.497532
38	172.561020	220.315945	282.629783	364.043434	609.830533	1343.622161
39	185.640292	238.941221	309.066463	401.447778	684.010197	1546.165485
40	199.635112	259.056519	337.882445	442.592556	767.091420	1779.090308
41	214.609570	280.781040	369.291865	487.851811	860.142391	2046.953854
42	230.632240	304.243523	403.528133	537.636992	964.359478	2354.996933
43	247.776497	329.583005	440.845665	592.400692	1081.082615	2709.246473
44	266.120851	356.949646	481.521775	652.640761	1211.812529	3116.633443
45	285.749311	386.505617	525.858734	718.904837	1358.230032	3585.128460
46	306.751763	418.426067	574.186021	791.795321	1522.217636	4123.897729
47	329.224386	452.900152	626.862762	871.974853	1705.883752	4743.482388
48	353.270093	490.132164	684.280411	960.172338	1911.589803	5466.004746
49	378.999000	530.342737	746.865648	1057.189572	2141.980579	6275.405458
50	406.528929	573.770156	815.083556	1163.908529	2400.018249	7217.716277

TABLE 4 **1109**

Table 4   Present Value of an Ordinary Annuity of \$1 per Period: $P_{\overline{n}|i} = \dfrac{1 - \dfrac{1}{(1 + i)^n}}{i}$

n \ i	1/2%	1%	1 1/2%	2%	2 1/2%	3%
1	0.995025	0.990099	0.985222	0.980392	0.975610	0.970874
2	1.985099	1.970395	1.955883	1.941561	1.927424	1.913470
3	2.970248	2.940985	2.912200	2.883883	2.856024	2.828611
4	3.950496	3.901966	3.854385	3.807729	3.761974	3.717098
5	4.925866	4.853431	4.782645	4.713460	4.645829	4.579707
6	5.896384	5.795476	5.697187	5.601431	5.508125	5.417191
7	6.862074	6.728195	6.598214	6.471991	6.349391	6.230283
8	7.822959	7.651678	7.485925	7.325481	7.170137	7.019692
9	8.779064	8.566018	8.360517	8.162237	7.970866	7.786109
10	9.730412	9.471305	9.222185	8.982585	8.752064	8.530203
11	10.677027	10.367628	10.071118	9.786848	9.514209	9.252624
12	11.618932	11.255077	10.907505	10.575341	10.257765	9.954004
13	12.556151	12.133740	11.731532	11.348374	10.983185	10.634955
14	13.488708	13.003703	12.543382	12.106249	11.690912	11.296073
15	14.416625	13.865053	13.343233	12.849264	12.381378	11.937935
16	15.339925	14.717874	14.131264	13.577709	13.055003	12.561102
17	16.258632	15.562251	14.907649	14.291872	13.712198	13.166118
18	17.172768	16.398269	15.672561	14.992031	14.353364	13.753513
19	18.082356	17.226009	16.426168	15.678462	14.978891	14.323799
20	18.987419	18.045553	17.168639	16.351433	15.589162	14.877475
21	19.887979	18.856983	17.900137	17.011209	16.184549	15.415024
22	20.784059	19.660379	18.620824	17.658048	16.765413	15.936917
23	21.675681	20.455821	19.330861	18.292204	17.332110	16.443608
24	22.562866	21.243387	20.030405	18.913926	17.884986	16.935542
25	23.445638	22.023156	20.719611	19.523456	18.424376	17.413148
26	24.324018	22.795204	21.398632	20.121036	18.950611	17.876842
27	25.198028	23.559608	22.067617	20.706898	19.464011	18.327031
28	26.067689	24.316443	22.726717	21.281272	19.964889	18.764108
29	26.933024	25.065785	23.376076	21.844385	20.453550	19.188455
30	27.794054	25.807708	24.015838	22.396456	20.930293	19.600441
31	28.650800	26.542285	24.646146	22.937702	21.395407	20.000428
32	29.503284	27.269589	25.267139	23.468335	21.849178	20.388766
33	30.351526	27.989693	25.878954	23.988564	22.291881	20.765792
34	31.195548	28.702666	26.481728	24.498592	22.723786	21.131837
35	32.035371	29.408580	27.075595	24.998619	23.145157	21.487220
36	32.871016	30.107505	27.660684	25.488842	23.556251	21.832253
37	33.702504	30.799510	28.237127	25.969453	23.957318	22.167235
38	34.529854	31.484663	28.805052	26.440641	24.348603	22.492462
39	35.353089	32.163033	29.364583	26.902589	24.730344	22.808215
40	36.172228	32.834686	29.915845	27.355479	25.102775	23.114772
41	36.987291	33.499689	30.458961	27.799489	25.466122	23.412400
42	37.798300	34.158108	30.994050	28.234794	25.820607	23.701359
43	38.605274	34.810008	31.521232	28.661562	26.166446	23.981902
44	39.408232	35.455454	32.040622	29.079963	26.503849	24.254274
45	40.207196	36.094508	32.552337	29.490160	26.833024	24.518713
46	41.002185	36.727236	33.056490	29.892314	27.154170	24.775449
47	41.793219	37.353699	33.553192	30.286582	27.467483	25.024708
48	42.580318	37.973959	34.042554	30.673120	27.773154	25.266707
49	43.363500	38.588079	34.524683	31.052078	28.071369	25.501657
50	44.142786	39.196118	34.999688	31.423606	28.362312	25.729764

Table 4 **Present Value of an Ordinary Annuity of $1** (*continued*)

n \ i	3½%	4%	4½%	5%	5½%	6%
1	0.966184	0.961538	0.956938	0.952381	0.947867	0.943396
2	1.899694	1.886095	1.872668	1.859410	1.846320	1.833393
3	2.801637	2.775091	2.748964	2.723248	2.697933	2.673012
4	3.673079	3.629895	3.587526	3.545951	3.505150	3.465106
5	4.515052	4.451822	4.389977	4.329477	4.270284	4.212364
6	5.328553	5.242137	5.157872	5.075692	4.995530	4.917324
7	6.114544	6.002055	5.892701	5.786373	5.682967	5.582381
8	6.873956	6.732745	6.595886	6.463213	6.334566	6.209794
9	7.607687	7.435332	7.268791	7.107822	6.952195	6.801692
10	8.316605	8.110896	7.912718	7.721735	7.537626	7.360087
11	9.001551	8.760477	8.528917	8.306414	8.092536	7.886875
12	9.663334	9.385074	9.118581	8.863252	8.618518	8.383844
13	10.302738	9.985648	9.682852	9.393573	9.117079	8.852683
14	10.920520	10.563123	10.222825	9.898641	9.589648	9.294984
15	11.517411	11.118387	10.739546	10.379658	10.037581	9.712249
16	12.094117	11.652296	11.234015	10.837770	10.462162	10.105895
17	12.651321	12.165669	11.707191	11.274066	10.864609	10.477260
18	13.189682	12.659297	12.159992	11.689587	11.246074	10.827603
19	13.709837	13.133939	12.593294	12.085321	11.607654	11.158116
20	14.212403	13.590326	13.007936	12.462210	11.950382	11.469921
21	14.697974	14.029160	13.404724	12.821153	12.275244	11.764077
22	15.167125	14.451115	13.784425	13.163003	12.583170	12.041582
23	15.620410	14.856842	14.147775	13.488574	12.875042	12.303379
24	16.058368	15.246963	14.495478	13.798642	13.151699	12.550358
25	16.481515	15.622080	14.828209	14.093945	13.413933	12.783356
26	16.890352	15.982769	15.146611	14.375185	13.662495	13.003166
27	17.285365	16.329586	15.451303	14.643034	13.898100	13.210534
28	17.667019	16.663063	15.742874	14.898127	14.121422	13.406164
29	18.035767	16.983715	16.021889	15.141074	14.333101	13.590721
30	18.392045	17.292033	16.288889	15.372451	14.533745	13.764831
31	18.736276	17.588494	16.544391	15.592811	14.723929	13.929086
32	19.068865	17.873552	16.788891	15.802677	14.904198	14.084043
33	19.390208	18.147646	17.022862	16.002549	15.075069	14.230230
34	19.700684	18.411198	17.246758	16.192904	15.237033	14.368141
35	20.000661	18.664613	17.461012	16.374194	15.390552	14.498246
36	20.290494	18.908282	17.666041	16.546852	15.536068	14.620987
37	20.570525	19.142579	17.862240	16.711287	15.673999	14.736780
38	20.841087	19.367864	18.049990	16.867893	15.804738	14.846019
39	21.102500	19.584485	18.229656	17.017041	15.928662	14.949075
40	21.355072	19.792774	18.401584	17.159086	16.046125	15.046297
41	21.599104	19.993052	18.566109	17.294368	16.157464	15.138016
42	21.834883	20.185627	18.723550	17.423208	16.262999	15.224543
43	22.062689	20.370795	18.874210	17.545912	16.363032	15.306173
44	22.282791	20.548841	19.018383	17.662773	16.457851	15.383182
45	22.495450	20.720040	19.156347	17.774070	16.547726	15.455832
46	22.700918	20.884654	19.288371	17.880067	16.632915	15.524370
47	22.899438	21.042936	19.414709	17.981016	16.713664	15.589028
48	23.091244	21.195131	19.535607	18.077158	16.790203	15.650027
49	23.276565	21.341472	19.651298	18.168722	16.862751	15.707572
50	23.455618	21.482185	19.762008	18.255925	16.931518	15.761861

TABLE 4 **1111**

Table 4 Present Value of an Ordinary Annuity of $1 (*continued*)

n \ i	7%	8%	9%	10%	12%	15%
1	0.934579	0.925926	0.917431	0.909091	0.892857	0.869565
2	1.808018	1.783265	1.759111	1.735537	1.690051	1.625709
3	2.624316	2.577097	2.531295	2.486852	2.401831	2.283225
4	3.387211	3.312127	3.239720	3.169865	3.037349	2.854978
5	4.100197	3.992710	3.889651	3.790787	3.604776	3.352155
6	4.766540	4.622880	4.485919	4.355261	4.111407	3.784483
7	5.389289	5.206370	5.032953	4.868419	4.563757	4.160420
8	5.971299	5.746639	5.534819	5.334926	4.967640	4.487322
9	6.515232	6.246888	5.995247	5.759024	5.328250	4.771584
10	7.023582	6.710081	6.417658	6.144567	5.650223	5.018769
11	7.498674	7.138964	6.805191	6.495061	5.937699	5.233712
12	7.942686	7.536078	7.160725	6.813692	6.194374	5.420619
13	8.357651	7.903776	7.486904	7.103356	6.423548	5.583147
14	8.745468	8.244237	7.786150	7.366687	6.628168	5.724476
15	9.107914	8.559479	8.060688	7.606080	6.810864	5.847370
16	9.446649	8.851369	8.312558	7.823709	6.973986	5.954235
17	9.763223	9.121638	8.543631	8.021553	7.119630	6.047161
18	10.059087	9.371887	8.755625	8.201412	7.249670	6.127966
19	10.335595	9.603599	8.950115	8.364920	7.365777	6.198231
20	10.594014	9.818147	9.128546	8.513564	7.469444	6.259331
21	10.835527	10.016803	9.292244	8.648694	7.562003	6.312462
22	11.061241	10.200744	9.442425	8.771540	7.644646	6.358663
23	11.272187	10.371059	9.580207	8.883218	7.718434	6.398837
24	11.469334	10.528758	9.706612	8.984744	7.784316	6.433771
25	11.653583	10.674776	9.822580	9.077040	7.843139	6.464149
26	11.825779	10.809978	9.928972	9.160945	7.895660	6.490564
27	11.986709	10.935165	10.026580	9.237223	7.942554	6.513534
28	12.137111	11.051078	10.116128	9.306567	7.984423	6.533508
29	12.277674	11.158406	10.198283	9.369606	8.021806	6.550877
30	12.409041	11.257783	10.273654	9.426914	8.055184	6.565980
31	12.531814	11.349799	10.342802	9.479013	8.084986	6.579113
32	12.646555	11.434999	10.406240	9.526376	8.111594	6.590533
33	12.753790	11.513888	10.464441	9.569432	8.135352	6.600463
34	12.854009	11.586934	10.517835	9.608575	8.156564	6.609099
35	12.947672	11.654568	10.566821	9.644159	8.175504	6.616607
36	13.035208	11.717193	10.611763	9.676508	8.192414	6.623137
37	13.117017	11.775179	10.652993	9.705917	8.207513	6.628815
38	13.193473	11.828869	10.690820	9.732651	8.220993	6.633752
39	13.264928	11.878582	10.725523	9.756956	8.233030	6.638045
40	13.331709	11.924613	10.757360	9.779051	8.243777	6.641778
41	13.394120	11.967235	10.786569	9.799137	8.253372	6.645025
42	13.452449	12.006699	10.813366	9.817397	8.261939	6.647848
43	13.506962	12.043240	10.837950	9.833998	8.269589	6.650302
44	13.557908	12.077074	10.860505	9.849089	8.276418	6.652437
45	13.605522	12.108402	10.881197	9.862808	8.282516	6.654293
46	13.650020	12.137409	10.900181	9.875280	8.287961	6.655907
47	13.691608	12.164267	10.917597	9.886618	8.292822	6.657310
48	13.730474	12.189136	10.933575	9.896926	8.297163	6.658531
49	13.766799	12.212163	10.948234	9.906296	8.301038	6.659592
50	13.800746	12.233485	10.961683	9.914814	8.304498	6.660515

INDEX